Finite Mathematics

Eleventh Edition

Northern Arizona University

Wiley Custom Learning Solutions

To order books or for customer service, please call 1(800)-CALL-WILEY (225-5945).

Printed in the United States of America.

ISBN 978-1-118-74066-8
Printed and bound by IPAK.

10 9 8 7 6 5 4 3 2 1

CUSTOM BRIEF CONTENTS

To the Student

How to Use this Book Effectively and Efficiently

As you begin this course in Finite Mathematics, you may feel overwhelmed by the number of topics covered. Don't worry! Your concerns are normal, and, with the help of your instructor and this text, you will be fine.

After teaching Finite Mathematics for over 30 years and dealing with the math-related questions of my four children, I know what you are going through. This text was written with you, the student, in mind, to help you master the basic concepts of Finite Mathematics.

The many learning aids featured in the text and displayed on the facing page, are there to make your study easier and more rewarding, helping you get the most from the time and effort you invest. If you attend class, work hard, and read and study this text, you will build the knowledge and skills you need to be successful. Here's how you can use this book to your benefit:

1. **Please, read the material assigned to you.** First, and most important, this book is meant to be read! You will find that the text has additional explanations and examples that will help you.
2. **Start your study of a section with *Preparing for this Section.*** Quickly, this list of concepts will show you what to expect from the section. Reviewing now will make the section easier to understand and will actually save you time and effort.
3. **Read the list of *Objectives.*** Provided at the beginning of each section, these will help you recognize the important ideas and skills developed in the section.
4. **Complete the *Now Work Problems.*** After a concept has been introduced and an example given, you will see Now Work Problem ##. Go to the exercises at the end of the section, work the problem cited, and check your answer in the back of the book. If you get it right, you can be confident in continuing on in the section. If you don't get it right, go back over the explanations and examples to see what you might have missed. Then rework the problem. Ask for help if you miss it again.

   If you follow these practices throughout the section, you will find that you have probably done many of your homework problems. In the exercises, every Now Work problem number is yellow with a pencil icon. All the odd-numbered problems have answers in the back of the book and worked-out solutions in the Student Solutions Manual. Be sure you have made an honest effort before looking at a worked-out solution.
5. **Use the *Chapter Review* feature.** This ensures familiarity with the definitions, formulas, and equations listed under Things To Know. If you are unsure of an item here, use the page reference to go back and review it. Go through the Objectives and be sure you can answer "Yes" to the question "I should be able to..." Review Exercises that relate to each objective are listed to help you.
6. **Lastly, do the problems in the *Review Exercises.*** Blue problem numbers indicate my suggestions for use in a practice test. Do some of the other problems in the review for more practice to prepare for your exam.

Please do not hesitate to contact me, through the publisher of this book, John Wiley and Sons, with any suggestions or comments that would improve this text. I look forward to hearing from you.

Best wishes,

Michael Sullivan

Use the Learning Tools!

Feature	Description
Chapter Opening and Project	Each chapter begins with a situational problem and ends with the related project.
OBJECTIVES	Each section begins with a list of objectives. The objective heading also appears in the text where each objective is covered. Use these as an outline of the important elements of the section.
PREPARING FOR THIS SECTION	Most sections begin with a list of key concepts to review, with page numbers. This gets you ready for the section.
NOW WORK THE 'ARE YOU PREPARED?' PROBLEMS	Special problems that support the PREPARING FOR THIS SECTION feature. Solve these problems to be sure you are ready for this section.
NOW WORK PROBLEMS	These follow most examples, and direct you to a related exercise. If you do this problem, you will have confidence in going on.
Step-by-Step, Annotated Examples	Examples contain detailed, intermediate steps. Many include additional annotations. Read and study with pencil and paper handy.
Graphing Calculator/ Spreadsheet Examples and Exercises	These *optional examples and problems* require the use of a graphing utility or a spreadsheet program such as Microsoft Excel, and are marked by a special icon and purple numbers.

Do Your Homework!

Problem Type	Description
'Are You Prepared?'	These assess your retention of the prerequisite material you'll need for the section. Answers are given at the end of the section exercises.
Concepts and Vocabulary	These short-answer questions, mainly fill-in-the-blank and true/false items, assess your understanding of key definitions and concepts in the current section.
Skill Building	Correlated to section examples, these problems provide straightforward practice.
Applications and Extensions	These problems allow you to apply your skills to real-world problems, and to explore concepts learned in this section.
Discussion and Writing	"Discussion and Writing" problems are indicated by green problem numbers. These support class discussion, verbalization of mathematical ideas, and writing and research projects.
NOW WORK PROBLEMS	Many examples refer you to a related homework problem at the end of the section. These related problems are marked by a [pencil icon] and yellow numbers.

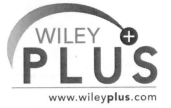

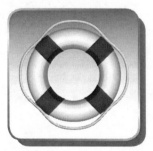

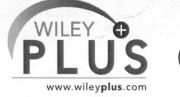

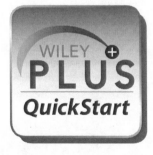

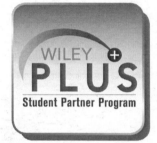

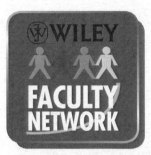

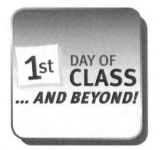

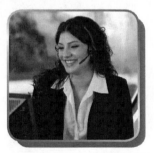

Finite Mathematics
An Applied Approach

Eleventh Edition

Finite Mathematics An Applied Approach

Michael Sullivan Chicago State University

JOHN WILEY & SONS, INC. WILEY

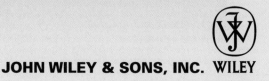

VICE PRESIDENT & PUBLISHER	Laurie Rosatone
ACQUISITIONS EDITOR	David Dietz
PROJECT EDITOR	Ellen Keohane
SENIOR EDITORIAL ASSISTANT	Pamela Lashbrook
MARKETING MANAGER	Jonathan Cotrell
MEDIA EDITOR	Melissa Edwards
PRODUCTION MANAGER	Dorothy Sinclair
PRODUCTION EDITOR	Sandra Dumas
DESIGN DIRECTOR	Harry Nolan
MEDIA ASSISTANT	Lisa Sabitini
PHOTO DEPARTMENT MANAGER	Hilary Newman
PHOTO EDITOR	Lisa Gee
PRODUCTION MANAGEMENT SERVICES	Robert and Carol Walters

This book was typeset in Minion at MPS Limited, a Macmillan Company and printed and bound by QuadGraphics, Inc. The cover was printed by QuadGraphics, Inc.

Founded in 1807, John Wiley & Sons, Inc. has been a valued source of knowledge and understanding for more than 200 years, helping people around the world meet their needs and fulfill their aspirations. Our company is built on a foundation of principles that include responsibility to the communities we serve and where we live and work. In 2008, we launched a Corporate Citizenship Initiative, a global effort to address the environmental, social, economic, and ethical challenges we face in our business. Among the issues we are addressing are carbon impact, paper specifications and procurement, ethical conduct within our business and among our vendors, and community and charitable support. For more information, please visit our website: www.wiley.com/go/citizenship.

The paper in this book was manufactured by a mill whose forest management programs include sustained yield harvesting of its timberlands. Sustained yield harvesting principles ensure that the number of trees cut each year does not exceed the amount of new growth.

This book is printed on acid-free paper.

ISBN 13 978-0470-45827-3

ISBN 13 978-0470-87639-8

Printed in the United States of America

10 9 8 7 6 5 4 3 2 1

To the Memory of My Parents
with Gratitude

And also to the Memory of Bob Walters,
My Production Manager for over 18 years,
A Dear Friend and an
Accomplished Professional

About the Author

Michael Sullivan

is Professor Emeritus in the Department of Mathematics and Computer Science at Chicago State University where he taught for 35 years before retiring. Dr. Sullivan is a member of the American Mathematical Society, the Mathematical Association of America, and the American Mathematical Association of Two Year Colleges. He is a past President of the Text and Academic Authors Association and represents that organization on the Authors Coalition of America. Mike has been writing textbooks since 1973, when this book was first published. Today he has 15 books in print, including three with John Wiley & Sons. He has four children: Kathleen, who teaches college mathematics; Michael, who teaches college mathematics; Dan, who is a director of sales for a college textbook publishing company; and Colleen, who teaches middle-school mathematics. Twelve grandchildren round out the family.

Other Books in this Series

Brief Calculus: An Applied Approach, 8th Edition, ISBN: 978-0-471-452-7

This accessible introduction to calculus is designed to demonstrate how calculus applies to various fields of study. The text is packed with real data and real-life applications to business, economics, and the social and life sciences. Applications using real data enhance student motivation. Many of these applications include source lines to show how mathematics is used in the real world.

Mathematics: An Applied Approach, 8th Edition, ISBN: 978-0-471-32784-4

This book combines the content of Finite Mathematics and Brief Calculus in a single textbook.

Preface to the Instructor

The Eleventh Edition

The Eleventh Edition of *Finite Mathematics* builds upon the solid foundation of previous editions. While the elements of previous editions that proved successful remain, many improvements have been made. Virtually every change is the result of thoughtful comments and suggestions from colleagues and students who have used previous editions. I am sincerely grateful for this feedback and have tried to incorporate changes that improve the flow and usability of the text, and demonstrate the use of mathematics in contemporary settings.

Features in the Eleventh Edition

Chapter Opening and Chapter Project

Each chapter begins with a situation that gives meaning to the mathematics, and ends with a related project.

A Look Back . . . A Look Forward

Each chapter contains a discussion of the relationship between what has been learned earlier and what is to be learned in the chapter.

Objectives

Each section begins with a list of learning objectives. The objectives also appear in the text as headings and are repeated in the Chapter Review alongside pertinent Examples and Review Exercises related to the objective.

Preparing for This Section

Most sections begin with a list of key concepts to review in preparation for the section. Page references are provided for easy access. Related "Are You Prepared?" problems are given at the beginning of the Exercise set to help students assess their understanding of these concepts. Answers to these problems are given at the end of the Exercise set.

Now Work Problems

Following most Examples, the student is directed to a related problem to assess understanding before going further in the text. The problem is colored yellow and has an icon to identify it.

Step-by-Step Examples

Examples provide detailed, step-by-step solutions, most with explanatory annotations.

Using Technology

These worked examples show students how to use a graphing calculator and/or Microsoft Excel to solve complex, computation-heavy problems (often these examples are first solved in the text using paper-and-pencil methods). Where appropriate, Using Technology examples show TI-84 Plus or Excel screens. Exercises that require use of a calculator or spreadsheet are indicated by icons and purple problem numbers.

Exercise Sets

The Exercise sets are divided into categories:

"Are You Prepared?" Problems

These relate to the review topics listed in PREPARING FOR THIS SECTION. For convenience, page references to the review material are included.

Concepts and Vocabulary

Easy true/false and fill-in-the-blank problems test vocabulary and important ideas found in the section.

Skill Building

These problems provide straightforward practice and are correlated to worked-out examples in the text.

Applications and Extensions

Applied problems that relate to real-world situations are given using a verbal description or a data set. Many of these are sourced using the most current data available. In some exercise sets, problems are given to challenge students to extend concepts into new areas.

Discussion and Writing

Indicated by exercise numbers colored green, these problems support class discussion collaborative learning, verbalization and writing of mathematical ideas. Some involve research projects.

New to the Eleventh Edition

- Where appropriate, new applied problems and examples have been added and ones that appeared dated or not-so-relevant have been deleted.
- All problems that contained time-sensitive information were updated to reflect the most current data available. Every effort was made to present problems in the light of current facts. This proved particularly challenging in some cases due to the extraordinary economic times we have been in.
- Every section was read and revised with clarity and efficiency of exposition in mind.

Organizational Changes to the Eleventh Edition

- Chapter 2, Systems of Linear Equations; Matrices, of the 10th edition has been divided into two distinct chapters: Chapter 2, Systems of Linear equations, and Chapter 3, Matrices. With this change, all the chapters in the book are roughly the same length, making test construction and classroom time easier to manage. In addition, these changes allow for more flexibility in choosing the content of a course.
- Chapters 6, 7, and 8 of the 10th edition have been consolidated into two chapters: Chapter 7, Probability, and Chapter 8, Additional Probability Topics. If you consult the Contents of the 11th edition, you will see the effect of this change. Now probability can be taught without the burden of handling the more difficult topic of permutations and combinations first. This change also allows for more flexibility in course construction, with the added benefit that the difficulty of the material proceeds more evenly than before.
- The section on the Binomial Theorem now appears in Appendix A.

Using the Eleventh Edition Effectively and Efficiently with Your Syllabus

To meet the varied needs of diverse syllabi, this book contains more than is likely to be covered in a Finite Mathematics course. As the chart below illustrates, *Finite Mathematics*, Eleventh Edition, has been organized with flexibility of use in mind. Even within a given chapter, certain sections can be treated as optional. See the detailed notes following the flow chart.

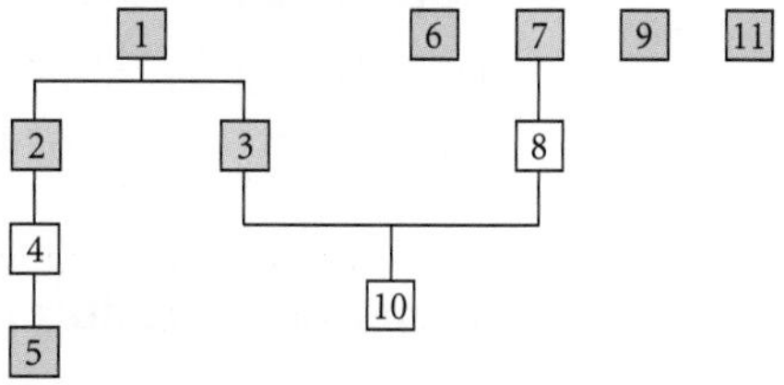

Chapter 1 Linear Equations

This chapter serves as the basis for Chapters 2, 3, and 4. It can be used as the starting point of a course. Sections 1.3 and 1.4 are optional.

Chapter 2 Systems of Linear Equations

This chapter discusses various methods for solving systems of linear equations.

Chapter 3 Matrices

This chapter provides an introduction to the algebra of matrices. Section 3.6 is optional.

Chapter 4 Linear Programming with Two Variables

This chapter discusses linear programming problems that can be solved geometrically.

Chapter 5 Linear Programming: Simplex Method

This chapter requires Sections 2.1 and 2.2 of Chapter 2 and Chapter 4. Appendix B, Using LINDO to Solve Linear Programming Problems, may be used to avoid the heavy computation that the simplex method requires.

Chapter 6 Finance

This chapter can be used as the starting point of a course. Section 6.5 is optional and provides an alternative approach to annuities and amortization.

Chapter 7 Probability

This chapter can be used as the starting point of a course.

Chapter 8 Additional Probability Topics

This chapter continues the study of probability, including the use of permutations and combinations.

Chapter 9 Statistics

While not absolutely necessary, coverage of Chapter 7 in advance may prove to be helpful.

Chapter 10 Markov Chains; Games

This chapter requires Sections 3.1 and 3.2 and Chapter 7. The topics covered here, Markov Chains (10.1–10.3) and Games (10.4–10.6) are independent of each other.

Chapter 11 Logic

This chapter can be used as the starting point of a course.

Appendix A: Review

This material serves as a just-in-time review of intermediate algebra topics. When applicable, its content is referenced in the text in the PREPARING FOR THIS SECTION feature.

Appendix B: Using LINDO to Solve Linear Programming Problems

This material presents an introduction to the software package LINDO, for solving linear programming problems.

Appendix C: Graphing Utilities

This appendix provides an overview of some common uses of a graphing calculator in finite mathematics.

The chapters from the Eighth Edition on Relations, Functions, and Induction (former Chapter 12) and Graphs and Trees (former Chapter 13) are available on the web at www.wiley.com/college/sullivan.

Acknowledgments

There are many colleagues I would like to thank for their input, encouragement, patience, and support in the development of the 11th edition. They have my deepest thanks and appreciation. I apologize for any omissions.

Contributors

- Michael Divinia and Jennifer Siegel, who worked on selected chapter openers and end-of-chapter projects.
- Jennifer Siegel, Mark McKibben, Beverly Fusfield, Gabrielle Andries and Jennifer Blue who wrote new applied problems and updated data sets and examples.
- Beverly Fusfield, who wrote the solutions manuals and developed the Computerized Test Bank.
- Mark McKibben, who checked the Computerized Test Bank.
- Jennifer Blue, who created the online videos.
- Celeste Hernandez, who checked the videos.
- Bill Ardis, who wrote the Graphing Calculator Manual.
- Gloria Langer, who worked on the PowerPoint Slides.

Accuracy Checkers

- Sandra Zirkes, Jada Hill, Celeste Hernandez and Gary Williams, who checked page proofs and answers.
- Ann Ostberg, who read page proofs and checked solutions

Reviewers of the Eleventh Edition

Alpona Banerjee, Evergreen Valley College
Bette Nelson, Alvin Community College
Catherine Remus, University of Tennessee, Knoxville
Glenn Hurlbert, Arizona State University
Ian Morrision, Fordham University
Issa A. Tall, Southern Illinois University, Carbondale
Lauren Fern, University of Montana
Mary Jane Sterling, Bradley University
Matthew Iklé, Adams State College
Maurice Geraghty, De Anza College
Peggy Hart, Doane College
Rama Rao, University of North Florida
Richard W. Coyne, Arizona State University
Sean Simpson, Westchester Community College
Shafiu Jibrin, Northern Arizona University
Thomas English, College of the Mainland
Thomas R. Schulte, California State University—Sacramento

Reviewers of Previous Editions

Barbara Allen, Delta, College • Portia Cornell, University of Redlands • Marilyn Creed, College of St. Benedict • Walter Czarnec, Framingham State • Michael Divinia, San Jose City College • Mark Dunster, San Diego State • Morteza Ebneshahrashoob, CSU Long Beach • Thomas English, College of the Mainland • K.L.D. Gunawardena, University of Wisconsin Oshkosh • Chungwu Ho, Evergreen Valley College • Eugene Hobbs, Oklahoma Baptist • Gary Hull, Frederick Community College • Joel Irish, University of Southern Maine • Murray Lieb, New Jersey Institute of Technology • Mark Littrell, Rio Hondo College • Janice Malouf, California State University Bakersfield • Sanford Miller, State University of New York Brockport • Jeff Mock, Diablo Valley College • Ian Morrison, Fordham University • Mehmet Orhon, University of New Hampshire • Judy Pretzer,

Delta College • Jorge Sarmiento, County College of Morris • Mohammad Sharifian, Compton County College • Joy St. John Johnson, Alabama A&M • James Stein, California State University Long Beach • Mary Jane Sterling, Bradley University • Jason Thrun, University of Wisconsin Platteville • Roy Tucker, Palo Alto College • Walter Denis Wallis, Southern Illinois University • Theodore Zarrabi, Boston College • Monte Zerger, Adams State College.

Recognition and thanks are due also to the following individuals at John Wiley for their valuable assistance in the preparation of this edition:

- Laurie Rosatone, for her confidence in this project
- David Dietz, for his support
- Ellen Keohane for her extraordinary ability to bring everything together
- Jonathan Cottrell, for his marketing skills
- Sandra Dumas, for overseeing production
- Bob and Carol Walters, for their organizational expertise in the production process

As this book went to press, Bob Walters passed away after a long and valiant struggle with lung disease. To say he will be missed is an understatement.

And to the entire Wiley sales force for their continued support and confidence. Finally, I welcome comments and suggestions for improving this text. Please do not hesitate to contact me through the publisher, John Wiley & Sons.

Sincerely,
Michael Sullivan

Supplements

Instructor Supplements

Instructor's Solutions Manual

Solutions to all the exercises in the text, matching the step-by-step methods used in worked examples in the textbook.

Instructor's PowerPoint Slides

Provided online, PowerPoint presentations include key figures, definitions, theorems, and procedures.

Companion Website

The companion website has many instructor and student resources in digital formats. It can be accessed at www.wiley.com/college/sullivan.

Computerized Test Bank

The Computerized Test Bank, created in Diploma software, is based on questions from the text and allows for varied question types. Using the Computerized Test Bank, professors can freely edit and/or create their own test questions. This software also has the ability to generate questions algorithmically and to create multiple versions of a test.

WileyPLUS

WileyPLUS is an innovative, research-based, online environment for effective teaching and learning.

What do students receive with *WileyPLUS*?

A Research-based Design. WileyPLUS provides an online environment that integrates relevant resources, including the entire digital textbook, in an easy-to-navigate framework that helps students study more effectively.

- **WileyPLUS** adds structure by organizing textbook content into smaller, more manageable "chunks."

- Related media, examples, and sample practice items reinforce the learning objectives.
- Innovative features such as calendars, visual progress tracking and self-evaluation tools improve time management and strengthen areas of weakness.

One-on-one Engagement. With *WileyPLUS* for *Finite Mathematics, Eleventh Edition* students receive 24/7 access to resources that promote positive learning outcomes. Students engage with related examples (in various media) and sample practice items, including:

- Videos
- Guided Online (GO) Tutorial problems
- Graphing Calculator Resource Manual
- Excel Data Files

Measurable Outcomes. Throughout each study session, students can assess their progress and gain immediate feedback. *WileyPLUS* provides precise reporting of strengths and weaknesses, as well as individualized quizzes, so that students are confident they are spending their time on the right things. With *WileyPLUS*, students always know the exact outcome of their efforts.

What do instructors receive with *WileyPLUS*?

WileyPLUS provides reliable, customizable resources that reinforce course goals inside and outside of the classroom as well as visibility into individual student progress. Pre-created materials and activities help instructors optimize their time:

Customizable Course Plan: *WileyPLUS* comes with a pre-created course plan designed by a subject matter expert uniquely for this course. Simple drag-and-drop tools make it easy to assign the course plan as-is or to modify it to reflect your course syllabus.

Pre-created Activity Types Include:

- Questions
- Readings and resources
- Presentation
- Print Tests
- Concept Mastery

Course Materials and Assessment Content:

- PowerPoint Slides
- Instructor's Solutions Manual
- Question Assignments: problems coded algorithmically with hints, links to text, whiteboard/show work feature and instructor-controlled problem solving help.
- Computerized Test Bank
- Printable Test Bank

Gradebook: *WileyPLUS* provides instant access to reports on trends in class performance, student use of course materials and progress towards learning objectives, helping inform decisions and drive classroom discussions.

Learn more at www.wileyplus.com.

Powered by proven technology and built on a foundation of cognitive research, *WileyPLUS* has enriched the education of millions of students, in over 20 countries around the world.

Applications Index

Business and Economics

Life and Physical Sciences

Social Sciences

Contents

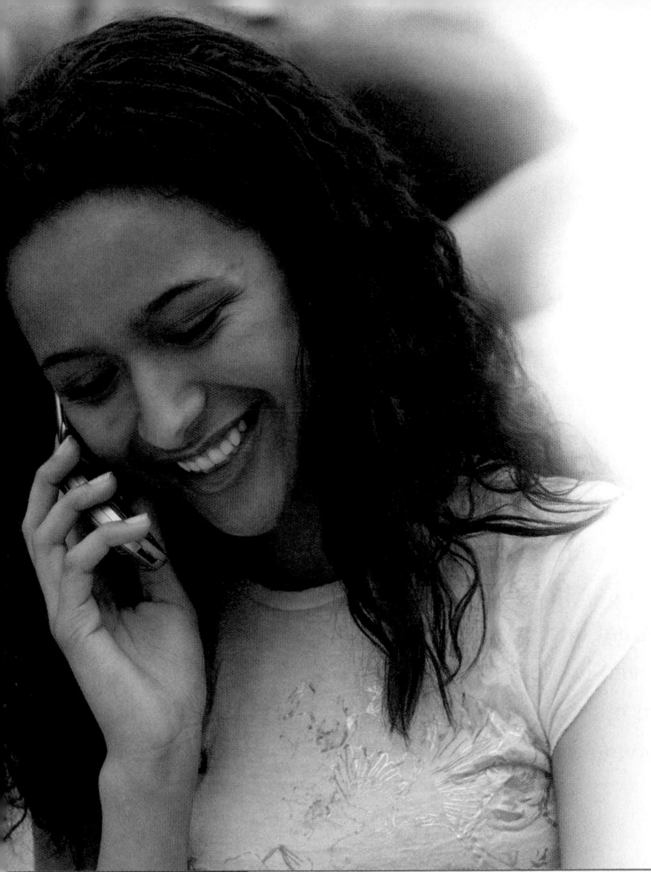

Linear Equations 1

You have been using a prepaid cell phone for a long while and have started to realize it is getting too expensive. To check out various cell phone plans to see which one is cheapest, you search online and are immediately overwhelmed by all of the choices. Is an unlimited talk time plan really the best way to go? Do you really need texting or Web capabilities? You are on a tight budget as a student and want to make the best choice possible so money will be left over each month for other expenses. The mathematics of this chapter provides the background for making the best decision to save the most money. The Chapter Project at the end of the chapter will help you choose the most economical plan to suit your needs.

OUTLINE

A Look Forward

In this chapter we make the connection between algebra and geometry through the rectangular coordinate system. The idea of using a system of rectangular coordinates dates back to ancient times, when such a system was used for surveying and city planning. Apollonius of Perga, in 200 B.C., used a form of rectangular coordinates in his work on conics, although this use does not stand out as clearly as it does in modern treatments. Sporadic use of rectangular coordinates continued until the 1600s. By that time, algebra had developed sufficiently so that René Descartes (1596–1650) and Pierre de Fermat (1601–1665) could take the crucial step, which was the use of rectangular coordinates to translate geometry problems into algebra problems, and vice versa. This step was important for two reasons. First, it allowed both geometers and algebraists to gain critical new insights into their subjects, which previously had been regarded as separate but now were seen to be connected in many important ways. Second, the insights gained made possible the development of calculus, which greatly enlarged the number of areas in which mathematics could be applied and made possible a much deeper understanding of these areas.

1.1 Lines

PREPARING FOR THIS SECTION *Before getting started, review the following:*

- Algebra Essentials (Appendix A, Section A.2, pp. A–16 to A–20 and A–24)

NOW WORK THE "ARE YOU PREPARED" PROBLEMS ON PAGE 16

OBJECTIVES
1. Graph linear equations (p. 3)
2. Graph a vertical line (p. 6)
3. Find the slope of a line and interpret it (p. 7)
4. Graph a line given a point on the line and the slope (p. 10)
5. Use the point–slope form of a line (p. 10)
6. Find the equation of a horizontal line (p. 11)
7. Find the equation of a line given two points (p. 12)
8. Use the slope–intercept form of a line (p. 12)
9. Solve applied problems involving linear equations (p. 14)

Rectangular Coordinates

We locate a point on the real number line by assigning it a single real number, called the *coordinate of the point*. For work in a two-dimensional plane, we locate points by using two numbers.

We begin with two real number lines located in the same plane: one horizontal and the other vertical. Call the horizontal line the **x-axis**, the vertical line the **y-axis**, and the point of intersection the **origin O**. Now assign coordinates to every point on these number lines as shown in Figure 1, using a convenient scale. We usually use the same scale on each axis. However, if the graph represents an application problem, scales appropriate to the application are used, which often results in different scales being used on each axis.

FIGURE 1

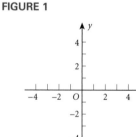

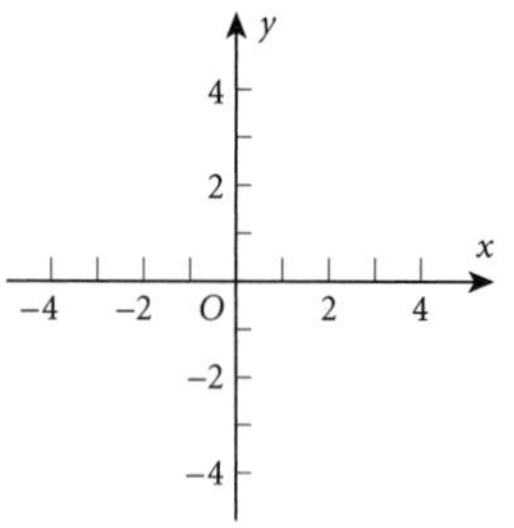

The origin O has a value of 0 on both the x-axis and the y-axis. We follow the usual convention that points on the x-axis to the right of O are associated with positive real numbers, and those to the left of O are associated with negative real numbers. Points on the y-axis above O are associated with positive real numbers, and those below O are associated with negative real numbers. In Figure 1, the x-axis and y-axis are labeled as x and y, respectively, and we have used an arrow at the end of each axis to denote the positive direction.

The coordinate system described here is called a **rectangular** or **Cartesian*** coordinate system. The plane formed by the x-axis and y-axis is sometimes called the **xy-plane**, and the x-axis and y-axis are referred to as the **coordinate axes.**

Any point P in the xy-plane can then be located by using an **ordered pair** (x, y) of real numbers. Let x denote the signed distance of P from the y-axis (*signed* in the sense that, if P is to the right of the y-axis, then $x > 0$, and if P is to the left of the y-axis, then $x < 0$), and let y denote the signed distance of P from the x-axis. The ordered pair (x, y), also called the **coordinates** of P, then gives us enough information to locate the point P in the plane.

* *Named after René Descartes (1596–1650), a French mathematician, philosopher, and theologian.*

For example, to locate the point whose coordinates are $(-3, 1)$, go 3 units along the x-axis to the left of O and then go straight up 1 unit. We **plot** this point by placing a dot at this location. See Figure 2, in which the points with coordinates $(-3, 1)$, $(-2, -3)$, $(3, -2)$, and $(3, 2)$ are plotted.

FIGURE 2

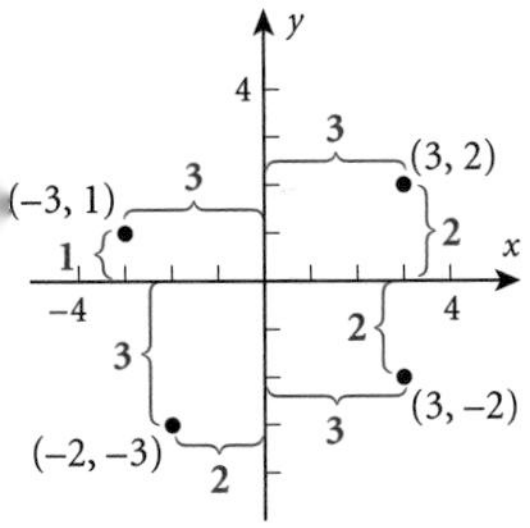

The origin has coordinates $(0, 0)$. Any point on the x-axis has coordinates of the form $(x, 0)$, and any point on the y-axis has coordinates of the form $(0, y)$.

If (x, y) are the coordinates of a point P, then x is called the **x-coordinate** of P, and y is the **y-coordinate** of P. We identify the point P by its coordinates (x, y) by writing $P = (x, y)$, referring to it as "the point (x, y)," rather than "the point whose coordinates are (x, y)."

The coordinate axes divide the xy-plane into four sections, called **quadrants**, as shown in Figure 3. In quadrant I, both the x-coordinate and the y-coordinate of all points are positive; in quadrant II, x is negative and y is positive; in quadrant III, both x and y are negative; and in quadrant IV, x is positive and y is negative. Points on the coordinate axes belong to no quadrant.

FIGURE 3

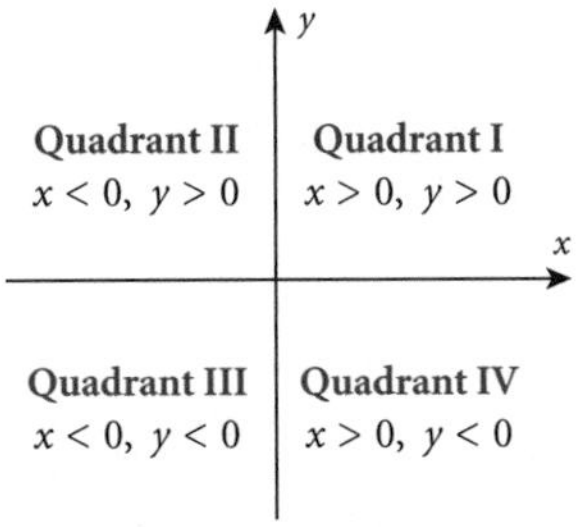

NOW WORK PROBLEM 9.

FIGURE 4

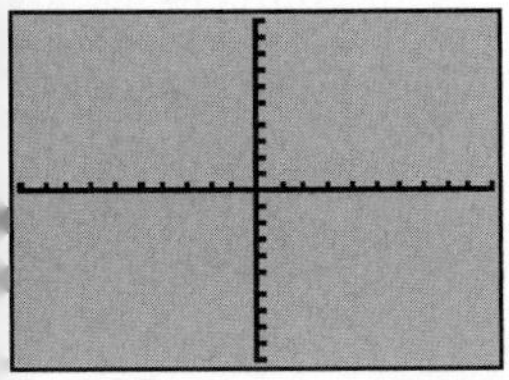

COMMENT On a graphing utility, you can set the scale on each axis. Once this has been done, you obtain the **viewing rectangle**. See Figure 4 for a typical viewing rectangle. You should now read Section C.1, The Viewing Rectangle, in Appendix C. ■

1 Graph Linear Equations

Definition A **linear equation in two variables** x and y is an equation equivalent to one of the form

$$Ax + By = C \qquad (1)$$

where A, B, C are real numbers and A and B are not both zero.

Examples of linear equations are

$3x - 5y - 6 = 0$ This equation can be written as

$3x - 5y = 6$ $A = 3, B = -5, C = 6$

$-3x = 2y - 1$ This equation can be written as

$-3x - 2y = -1$ $A = -3, B = -2, C = -1$

or as

$3x + 2y = 1$ $A = 3, B = 2, C = 1$

$y = \frac{3}{4}x - 5$ Here we can write

$-\frac{3}{4}x + y = -5$ $A = -\frac{3}{4}, B = 1, C = -5$

or

$3x - 4y = 20$ $A = 3, B = -4, C = 20$

$y = -5$ Here we can write

$0 \cdot x + y = -5$ $A = 0, B = 1, C = -5$

$x = 4$ Here we can write

$x + 0 \cdot y = 4$ $A = 1, B = 0, C = 4$

The **graph** of an equation is the set of all points (x, y) whose coordinates satisfy the equation. For example, $(0, 4)$ is a point on the graph of the equation $3x + 4y = 16$, because when we substitute 0 for x and 4 for y in the equation, we get

$$3 \cdot 0 + 4 \cdot 4 = 16 \quad 3x + 4y = 16, x = 0, y = 4$$

which is a true statement.

It can be shown that if A, B, and C are real numbers, with A and B not both zero, then the graph of the equation

$$Ax + By = C$$

is a **line**. This is the reason we call it a **linear equation.**

Conversely, any line is the graph of an equation of the form $Ax + By = C$.

Since any line can be written as an equation in the form $Ax + By = C$, we call this form the **general equation** of a line.

Given a linear equation, we can obtain its graph by plotting two points that satisfy its equation and connecting them with a line. Usually the easiest two points to use are the *intercepts*.

Definition

Intercepts

The points at which the graph of a linear equation crosses the axes are called **intercepts.** The ***x*-intercept** is the point at which the graph crosses the x-axis; the ***y*-intercept** is the point at which the graph crosses the y-axis.

FIGURE 5

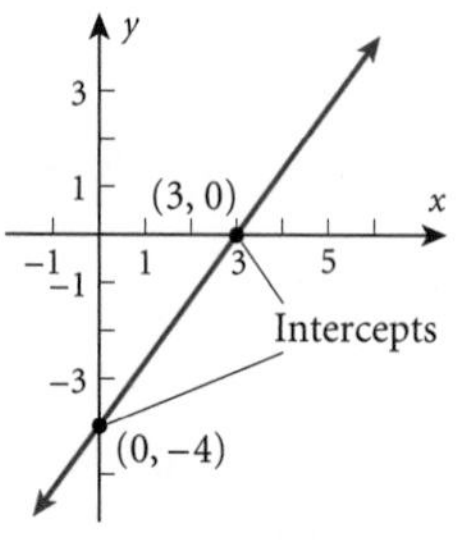

For example, the line shown in Figure 5 has the intercepts $(0, -4)$ and $(3, 0)$.

Steps for Finding the Intercepts of a Linear Equation

To find the intercepts of a linear equation $Ax + By = C$, where $A \neq 0$ or $B \neq 0$, follow these steps:

STEP 1 Let $y = 0$ and solve for x. This determines the x-intercept of the line.

STEP 2 Let $x = 0$ and solve for y. This determines the y-intercept of the line.

EXAMPLE 1 Finding the Intercepts of a Linear Equation

Find the intercepts of the equation $2x + 3y = 6$. Graph the equation.

SOLUTION

STEP 1 To find the x-intercept, we need to find the number x for which $y = 0$. We let $y = 0$ in the equation and proceed to solve for x:

$$\begin{aligned} 2x + 3y &= 6 \\ 2x + 3(0) &= 6 \quad y = 0 \\ 2x &= 6 \quad \text{Simplify.} \\ x &= 3 \quad \text{Solve for } x. \end{aligned}$$

The x-intercept is $(3, 0)$.

STEP 2 To find the y-intercept, we let $x = 0$ in the equation and solve for y:

$$\begin{aligned} 2x + 3y &= 6 \\ 2(0) + 3y &= 6 \quad x = 0 \\ 3y &= 6 \quad \text{Simplify.} \\ y &= 2 \quad \text{Solve for } y. \end{aligned}$$

The y-intercept is $(0, 2)$.

Since the equation is a linear equation, its graph is a line. We use the two intercepts $(3, 0)$ and $(0, 2)$ to graph it. See Figure 6. ■

FIGURE 6

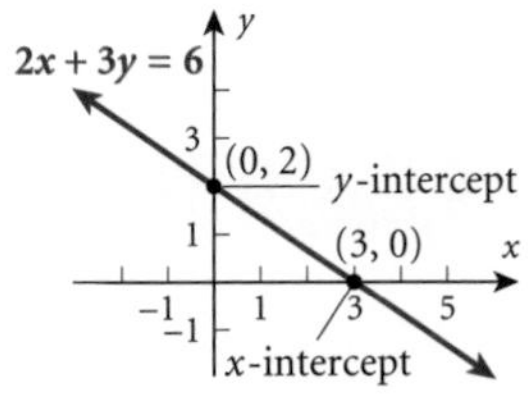

EXAMPLE 2 Graphing a Linear Equation

Graph the equation: $y = 2x + 5$

SOLUTION This equation can be written as

$$-2x + y = 5$$

This is a linear equation, so its graph is a line. The intercepts are $(0, 5)$ and $\left(-\frac{5}{2}, 0\right)$, which you should verify. To find a third point, arbitrarily let $x = 10$. Then $y = 2x + 5 = 2(10) + 5 = 25$, so $(10, 25)$ is a third point on the graph. See Figure 7.

x	y
0	5
$-\frac{5}{2}$	0
10	25

FIGURE 7

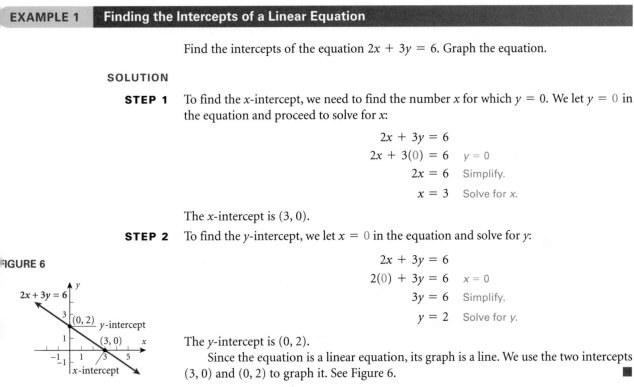

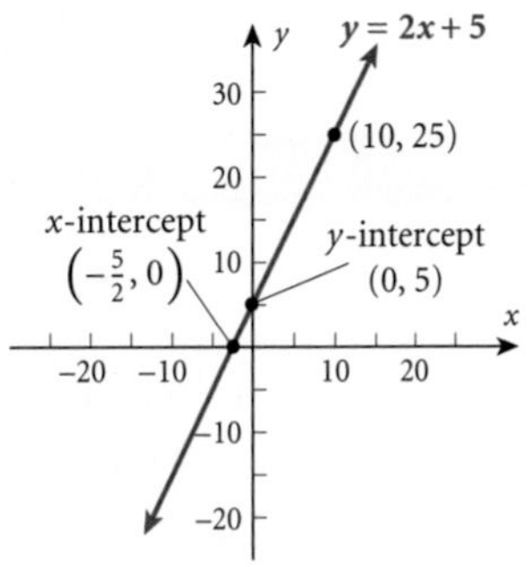

■

NOW WORK PROBLEM 13.

When a line passes through the origin, it has only one intercept. To graph such lines, we need to locate an additional point on the graph.

EXAMPLE 3 Graphing a Linear Equation

Graph the equation: $-x + 2y = 0$

FIGURE 8

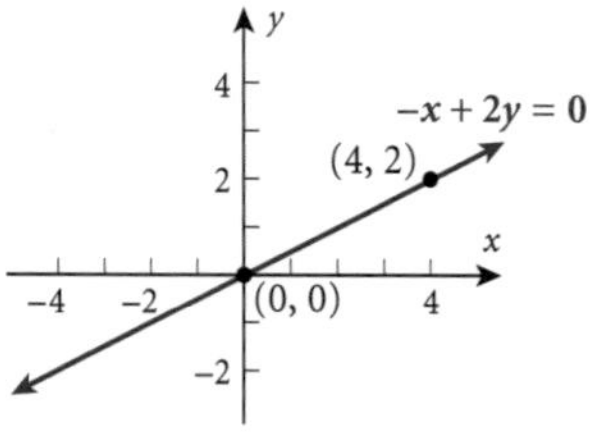

SOLUTION This is a linear equation, so its graph is a line. The only intercept is (0, 0). To locate another point on the graph, let $x = 4$. (This choice is arbitrary; any choice of x other than 0 could also be used.) Then

$$\begin{aligned} -4 + 2y &= 0 \quad -x + 2y = 0,\ x = 4 \\ 2y &= 4 \\ y &= 2 \end{aligned}$$

So, $y = 2$ when $x = 4$ and (4, 2) is a point on the graph. See Figure 8.

2 Graph a Vertical Line

EXAMPLE 4 Graphing a Vertical Line

FIGURE 9

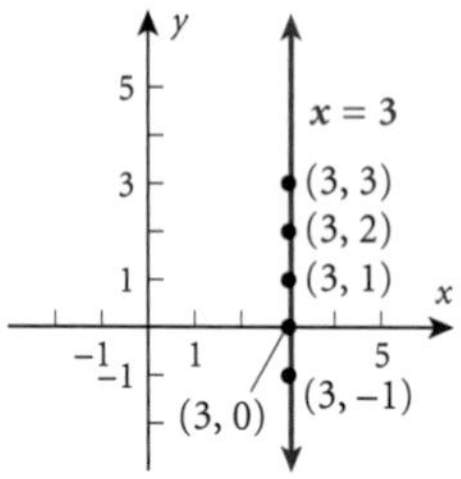

Graph the equation: $x = 3$

SOLUTION This is a linear equation $(1 \cdot x + 0 \cdot y = 3)$, so its graph is a line. Since $x = 3$, no matter what y-coordinate is used, the corresponding x-coordinate always equals 3. Consequently, the graph of the equation $x = 3$ is a *vertical* line with x-intercept (3, 0) as shown in Figure 9.

As suggested by Example 4, we have the following result:

Theorem

Equation of a Vertical Line

A vertical line is given by an equation of the form

$$x = a$$

where $(a, 0)$ is the x-intercept.

EXAMPLE 5 Finding the Equation of a Vertical Line

Find an equation for the vertical line containing the point $(-1, 6)$.

SOLUTION The x-coordinate of any point on a vertical line is always the same. Since $(-1, 6)$ is a point on the vertical line, its equation is $x = -1$.

NOW WORK PROBLEM 17(a).

3 Find the Slope of a Line and Interpret It

FIGURE 10

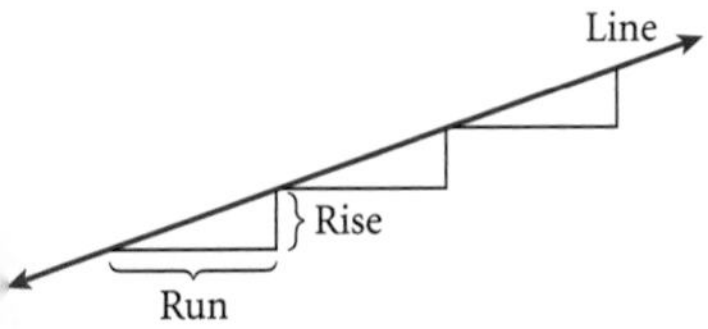

Consider the staircase illustrated in Figure 10. Each step contains exactly the same horizontal **run** and the same vertical **rise.** The ratio of the rise to the run, called the *slope*, is a numerical measure of the steepness of the staircase. For example, if the run is increased and the rise remains the same, the staircase becomes less steep. If the run is kept the same, but the rise is increased, the staircase becomes more steep. This important characteristic of a line is best defined using rectangular coordinates.

Definition

Slope of a Line

Let $P = (x_1, y_1)$ and $Q = (x_2, y_2)$ be two distinct points. If $x_1 \neq x_2$, the **slope** m of the nonvertical line containing P and Q is defined by the formula

$$m = \frac{y_2 - y_1}{x_2 - x_1} \qquad x_1 \neq x_2 \tag{2}$$

If $x_1 = x_2$, the slope m is undefined (since $x_1 = x_2$ results in division by 0) and the line is **vertical.**

If $y_1 = y_2$, the slope m is 0 and the line is **horizontal.**

Figure 11(a) provides an illustration of the slope of a nonvertical line; Figure 11(b) illustrates a vertical line.

FIGURE 11

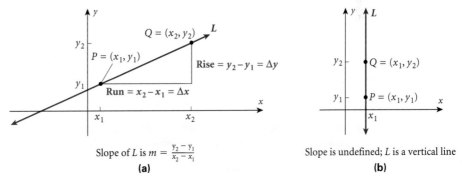

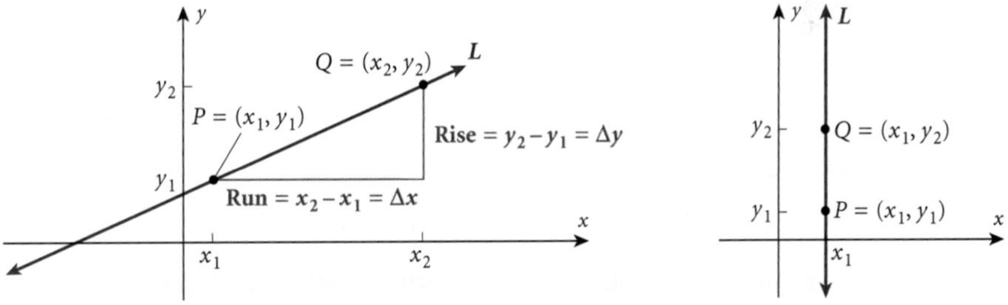

Slope of L is $m = \frac{y_2 - y_1}{x_2 - x_1}$
(a)

Slope is undefined; L is a vertical line
(b)

As Figure 11(a) illustrates, the slope m of a nonvertical line may be given as

$$m = \frac{y_2 - y_1}{x_2 - x_1} = \frac{\text{Rise}}{\text{Run}} = \frac{\text{Change in } y}{\text{Change in } x}$$

The change in y is usually denoted by Δy, read "delta y," and the change in x is denoted by Δx.

The slope m of a nonvertical line measures the amount y changes, Δy, as x changes from x_1 to x_2, Δx. This is called the **average rate of change of y with respect to x.** Then the slope m is

$$m = \frac{\Delta y}{\Delta x} = \text{Average rate of change of } y \text{ with respect to } x$$

EXAMPLE 6 Finding the Slope of a Line and Interpreting It

FIGURE 12

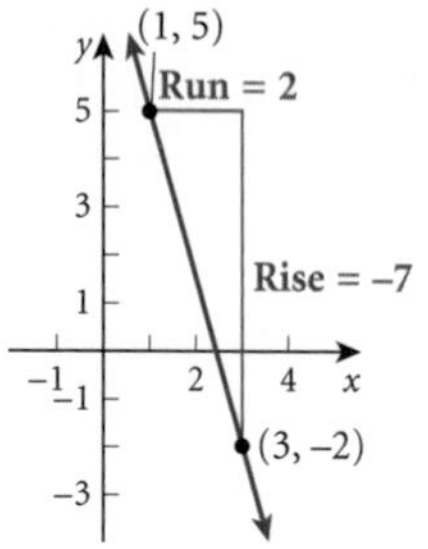

The slope m of the line containing the points $(1, 5)$ and $(3, -2)$ is

$$m = \frac{\Delta y}{\Delta x} = \frac{5-(-2)}{1-3} = \frac{7}{-2} = \frac{-7}{2} = -\frac{7}{2}$$

We interpret the slope to mean that for every 2-unit change in x, then y will change by -7 units. That is, if x increases by 2 units, then y decreases by 7 units. The average rate of change of y with respect to x is $-\frac{7}{2}$. See Figure 12.

NOW WORK PROBLEMS 23 AND 27.

Two comments about computing the slope of a nonvertical line may prove helpful:

1. Any two distinct points on the line can be used to compute the slope of the line. (See Figure 13 for justification.)
2. The slope of a line may be computed from $P = (x_1, y_1)$ to $Q = (x_2, y_2)$ or from Q to P because

$$\frac{y_2 - y_1}{x_2 - x_1} = \frac{y_1 - y_2}{x_1 - x_2}$$

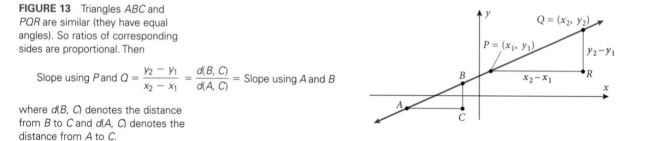

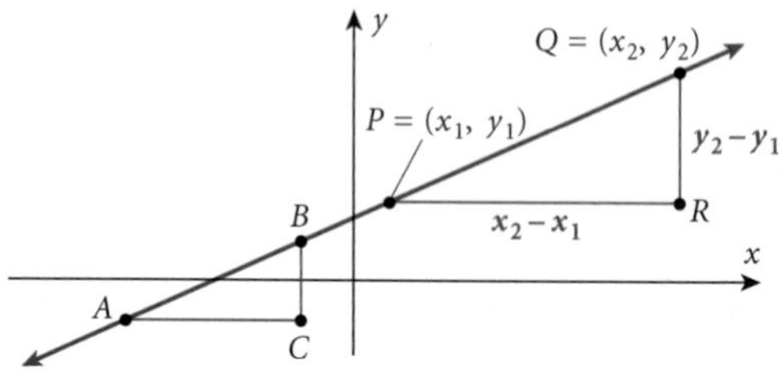

FIGURE 13 Triangles *ABC* and *PQR* are similar (they have equal angles). So ratios of corresponding sides are proportional. Then

$$\text{Slope using } P \text{ and } Q = \frac{y_2 - y_1}{x_2 - x_1} = \frac{d(B, C)}{d(A, C)} = \text{Slope using } A \text{ and } B$$

where $d(B, C)$ denotes the distance from B to C and $d(A, C)$ denotes the distance from A to C.

EXAMPLE 7 Finding the Slopes of Various Lines Containing the Same Point *P*

Compute the slopes of the lines L_1, L_2, L_3, and L_4 containing the following pairs of points. Graph all four lines on the same set of coordinate axes.

$$\begin{aligned} L_1&: \ P = (2, 3) \qquad Q_1 = (-1, -2) \\ L_2&: \ P = (2, 3) \qquad Q_2 = (3, -1) \\ L_3&: \ P = (2, 3) \qquad Q_3 = (5, 3) \\ L_4&: \ P = (2, 3) \qquad Q_4 = (2, 5) \end{aligned}$$

SOLUTION Let m_1, m_2, m_3, and m_4 denote the slopes of the lines L_1, L_2, L_3, and L_4, respectively.

FIGURE 14

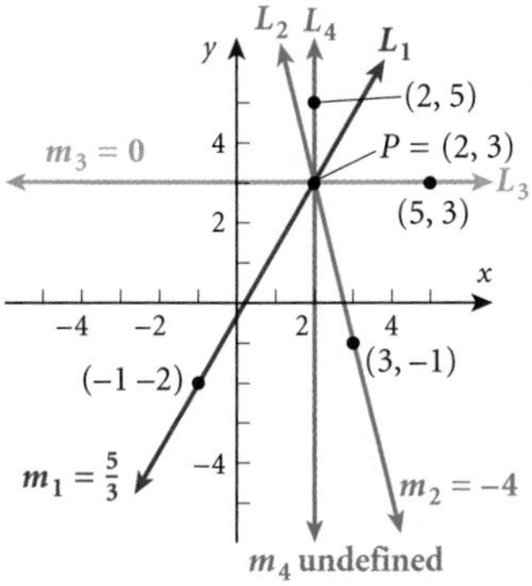

Then

$$m_1 = \frac{-2-3}{-1-2} = \frac{-5}{-3} = \frac{5}{3} \quad \text{A rise of 5 divided by a run of 3}$$

$$m_2 = \frac{-1-3}{3-2} = \frac{-4}{1} = -4 \quad \text{A rise of } -4 \text{ divided by a run of 1}$$

$$m_3 = \frac{3-3}{5-2} = \frac{0}{3} = 0 \quad \text{A rise of 0 divided by a run of 3}$$

m_4 is undefined — The x-coordinates of P and Q_4 are equal (both = 2).

The graphs of these lines are given in Figure 14. ■

As Figure 14 illustrates,

1. When the slope m of a line is positive, the line slants upward from left to right (L_1).
2. When the slope m is negative, the line slants downward from left to right (L_2).
3. When the slope m is 0, the line is horizontal (L_3).
4. When the slope m is undefined, the line is vertical (L_4).

COMMENT Now read Section C.3, Square Screens, in Appendix C. ■

SEEING THE CONCEPT On the same square screen, graph the following equations:

$Y_1 = 0$	Slope of line is 0.
$Y_2 = \frac{1}{4}x$	Slope of line is $\frac{1}{4}$.
$Y_3 = \frac{1}{2}x$	Slope of line is $\frac{1}{2}$.
$Y_4 = x$	Slope of line is 1.
$Y_5 = 2x$	Slope of line is 2.
$Y_6 = 6x$	Slope of line is 6.

See Figure 15. ■

FIGURE 15

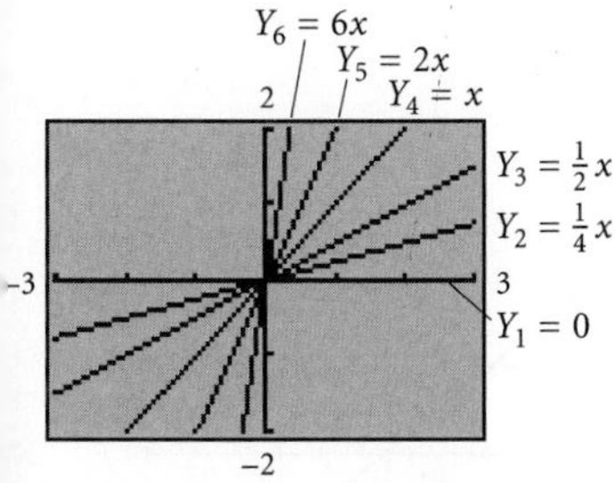

SEEING THE CONCEPT On the same square screen, graph the following equations:

$Y_1 = 0$	Slope of line is 0.
$Y_2 = -\frac{1}{4}x$	Slope of line is $-\frac{1}{4}$.
$Y_3 = -\frac{1}{2}x$	Slope of line is $-\frac{1}{2}$.
$Y_4 = -x$	Slope of line is −1.
$Y_5 = -2x$	Slope of line is −2.
$Y_6 = -6x$	Slope of line is −6.

See Figure 16. ■

FIGURE 16

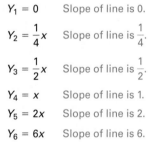

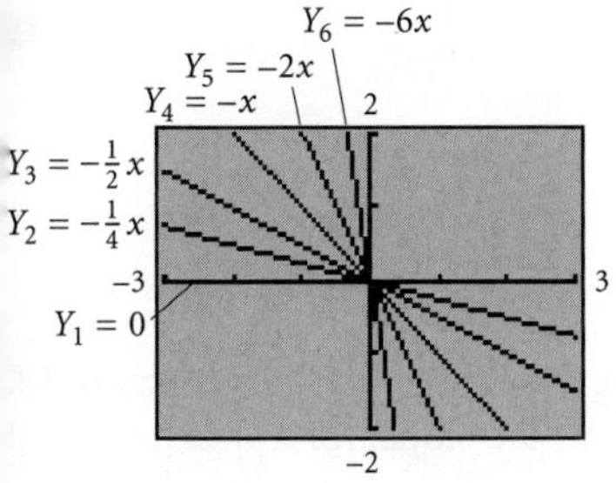

Figures 15 and 16 illustrate that the closer the line is to the vertical position, the greater the magnitude of the slope.

The next example illustrates how the slope of a line can be used to graph the line.

4 Graph a Line Given a Point on the Line and the Slope

EXAMPLE 8 Graphing a Line When Its Slope and a Point Are Given

Draw a graph of the line that contains the point (3, 2) and has a slope of

(a) $\frac{3}{4}$ **(b)** $-\frac{4}{5}$

SOLUTION **(a)** Slope $= \frac{\text{rise}}{\text{run}}$. The fact that the slope is $\frac{3}{4}$ means that for every horizontal movement (run) of 4 units to the right, there will be a vertical movement (rise) of 3 units. If we start at the given point (3, 2) and move 4 units to the right and 3 units up, we reach the point (7, 5). By drawing the line through this point and the point (3, 2), we have the graph. See Figure 17(a).

(b) The fact that the slope is $-\frac{4}{5} = \frac{-4}{5}$ means that for every horizontal movement of 5 units to the right, there will be a corresponding vertical movement of -4 units (a downward movement). If we start at the given point (3, 2) and move 5 units to the right and then 4 units down, we arrive at the point $(8, -2)$. By drawing the line through these points, we have the graph. See Figure 17(b).

Alternatively, we can set $-\frac{4}{5} = \frac{4}{-5}$ so that for every horizontal movement of -5 units (a movement to the left), there will be a corresponding vertical movement of 4 units (upward). This approach brings us to the point $(-2, 6)$, which is also on the graph shown in Figure 17(b).

FIGURE 17

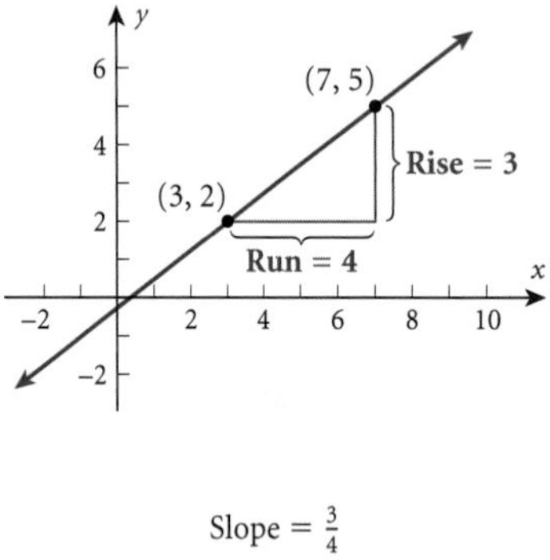

(a)

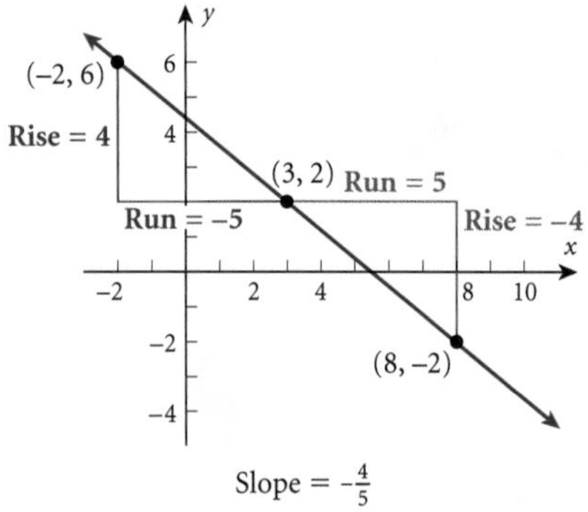

(b)

NOW WORK PROBLEM 35.

FIGURE 18

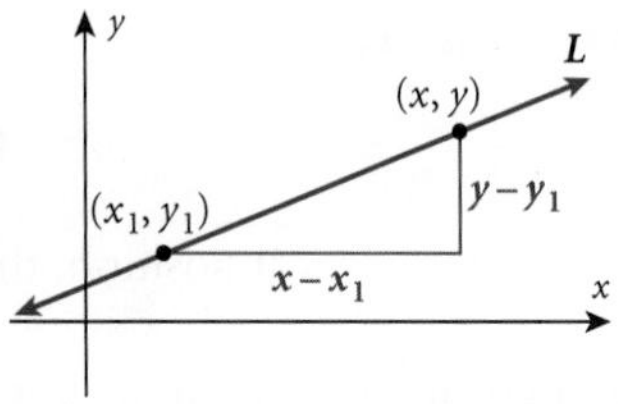

5 Use the Point–Slope Form of a Line

Let L be a nonvertical line with slope m and containing the point (x_1, y_1). See Figure 18. Since any two distinct points on L can be used to compute slope, for any other point (x, y) on L, we have

$$m = \frac{y - y_1}{x - x_1} \quad \text{or} \quad y - y_1 = m(x - x_1)$$

Theorem

Point–Slope Form of an Equation of a Line

An equation of a nonvertical line with slope m that contains the point (x_1, y_1) is

$$y - y_1 = m(x - x_1) \qquad (3)$$

EXAMPLE 9 Using the Point–Slope Form of a Line

FIGURE 19

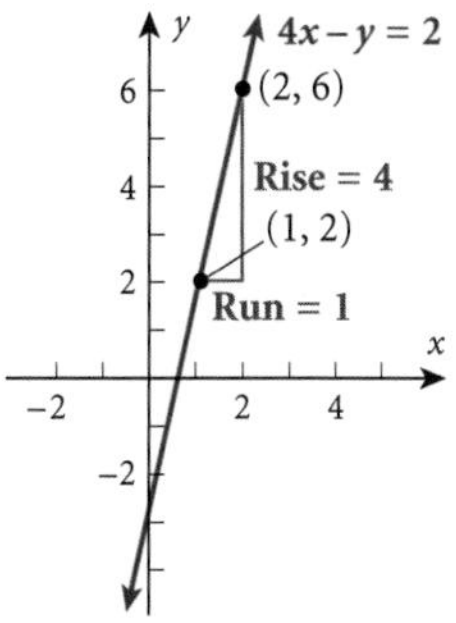

An equation of the line with slope 4 and containing the point (1, 2) can be found by using the point–slope form with $m = 4$, $x_1 = 1$, and $y_1 = 2$:

$$\begin{aligned} y - y_1 &= m(x - x_1) && \text{Point–slope form} \\ y - 2 &= 4(x - 1) && m = 4,\ x_1 = 1,\ y_1 = 2 \\ y - 2 &= 4x - 4 && \text{Simplify.} \\ 4x - y &= 2 && \text{General equation} \end{aligned}$$

See Figure 19. ■

NOW WORK PROBLEMS 17(c) AND 47.

6 Find the Equation of a Horizontal Line

EXAMPLE 10 Finding the Equation of a Horizontal Line

Find an equation of the horizontal line containing the point (3, 2). Graph the line.

FIGURE 20

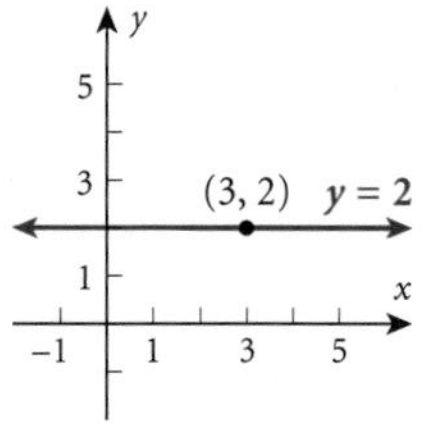

SOLUTION The slope of a horizontal line is 0. To get an equation, we use the point–slope form with $m = 0$, $x_1 = 3$, and $y_1 = 2$:

$$\begin{aligned} y - y_1 &= m(x - x_1) && \text{Point–slope form} \\ y - 2 &= 0 \cdot (x - 3) && m = 0,\ x_1 = 3,\ y_1 = 2 \\ y - 2 &= 0 \\ y &= 2 \end{aligned}$$

See Figure 20 for the graph. ■

As suggested by Example 10, we have the following result:

Theorem

Equation of a Horizontal Line

A horizontal line is given by an equation of the form

$$y = b$$

where $(0, b)$ is the y-intercept.

NOW WORK PROBLEM 17(b).

7 Find the Equation of a Line Given Two Points

EXAMPLE 11 Finding an Equation of a Line Given Two Points

Find an equation of the line containing the points (2, 3) and (−4, 5). Graph the line.

SOLUTION Since two points are given, we first compute the slope of the line:

$$m = \frac{5-3}{-4-2} = \frac{2}{-6} = \frac{1}{-3} = -\frac{1}{3}$$

We use the point (2, 3) and the fact that the slope $m = -\frac{1}{3}$ to get the point–slope form of the equation of the line:

$$y - 3 = -\frac{1}{3}(x - 2)$$

See Figure 21 for the graph.

FIGURE 21

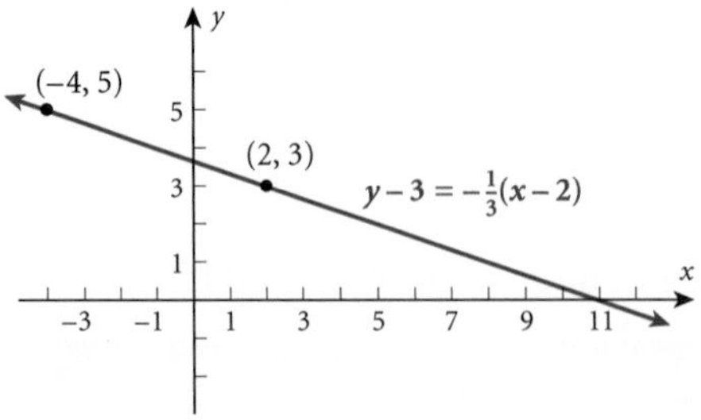

In the solution to Example 11 we could have used the point (−4, 5) instead of the point (2, 3). The equation that results, although it looks different, is equivalent to the equation we obtained in the example. (Try it for yourself.)

The general form of the equation of the line in Example 11 can be obtained by multiplying both sides of the point–slope equation by 3 and collecting terms:

$y - 3 = -\frac{1}{3}(x - 2)$	Point–slope equation
$3(y - 3) = 3\left(-\frac{1}{3}\right)(x - 2)$	Multiply by 3.
$3y - 9 = -1(x - 2)$	Simplify.
$3y - 9 = -x + 2$	Simplify.
$x + 3y = 11$	General equation

This is the general form of the equation of the line.

NOW WORK PROBLEM 51.

8 Use the Slope–Intercept Form of a Line

Another useful equation of a line is obtained when the slope m and y-intercept $(0, b)$ are known. In this case we know both the slope m of the line and a point $(0, b)$ on the line. Then we can use the point–slope form, Equation (3), to obtain the following equation:

$$y - y_1 = m(x - x_1) \quad \text{Point–slope form}$$
$$y - b = m(x - 0) \quad x_1 = 0,\ y_1 = b$$
$$y = mx + b \quad \text{Simplify and solve for } y.$$

Theorem

Slope–Intercept Form of an Equation of a Line

An equation of a line with slope m and y-intercept $(0, b)$ is

$$y = mx + b \tag{4}$$

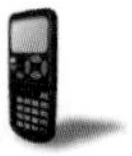

SEEING THE CONCEPT To see the role that the slope m plays in the equation $y = mx + b$, graph the following lines on the same square screen.

FIGURE 22

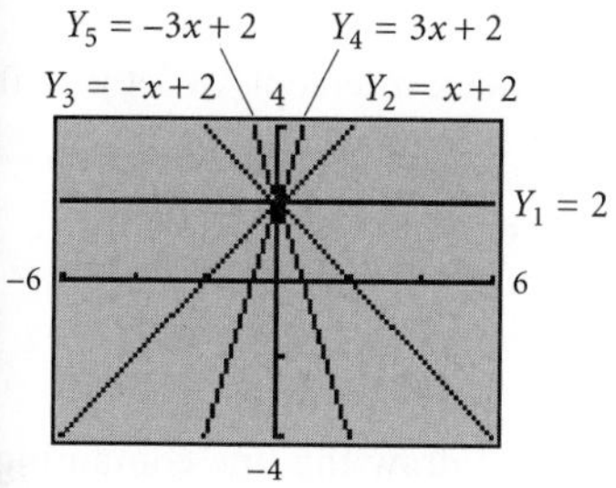

$$Y_1 = 2$$
$$Y_2 = x + 2$$
$$Y_3 = -x + 2$$
$$Y_4 = 3x + 2$$
$$Y_5 = -3x + 2$$

See Figure 22. What do you conclude about the lines $y = mx + 2$? ■

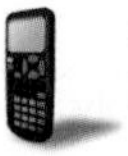

SEEING THE CONCEPT To see the role of b in the equation $y = mx + b$, graph the following lines on the same square screen.

FIGURE 23

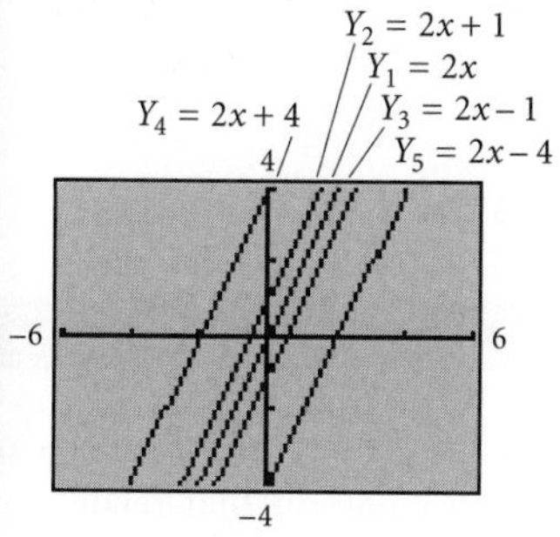

$$Y_1 = 2x$$
$$Y_2 = 2x + 1$$
$$Y_3 = 2x - 1$$
$$Y_4 = 2x + 4$$
$$Y_5 = 2x - 4$$

See Figure 23. What do you conclude about the lines $y = 2x + b$? ■

When an equation of a line is written in slope–intercept form, it is easy to find the slope m and y-intercept $(0, b)$ of the line. For example, suppose the equation of the line is

$$y = -2x + 3$$

Compare it to $y = mx + b$:

$$\begin{aligned} y &= -2x + 3 \\ &\quad\ \uparrow \quad\ \uparrow \\ y &= \ \ mx + b \end{aligned}$$

The slope of this line is -2 and its y-intercept is $(0, 3)$.

EXAMPLE 12 Finding the Slope and y-Intercept of a Line

Find the slope m and y-intercept $(0, b)$ of the line $2x + 4y = 8$. Graph the line.

SOLUTION To obtain the slope and y-intercept, we transform the equation into its slope–intercep form. To do this, we need to solve for y:

$$\begin{aligned} 2x + 4y &= 8 \\ 4y &= -2x + 8 \\ y &= -\frac{1}{2}x + 2 \end{aligned}$$

The coefficient of x, $-\frac{1}{2}$, is the slope, and the y-intercept is $(0, 2)$.

We can graph the line in either of two ways:

1. Use the fact that the y-intercept is $(0, 2)$ and the slope is $-\frac{1}{2}$. Then, starting at th point $(0, 2)$, go to the right 2 units and then down 1 unit to the point $(2, 1)$. Plot thes points and draw the line containing them. See Figure 24.
2. Locate the intercepts. The y-intercept is $(0, 2)$. To obtain the x-intercept, we let $y =$ (in the equation $2x + 4y = 8$ and solve for x. When $y = 0$, we have

$$\begin{aligned} 2x + 4 \cdot 0 &= 8 \qquad 2x + 4y = 8;\ y = 0 \\ 2x &= 8 \\ x &= 4 \end{aligned}$$

The intercepts are $(4, 0)$ and $(0, 2)$. Plot these points and draw the line containin them. Look again at Figure 24.

FIGURE 24

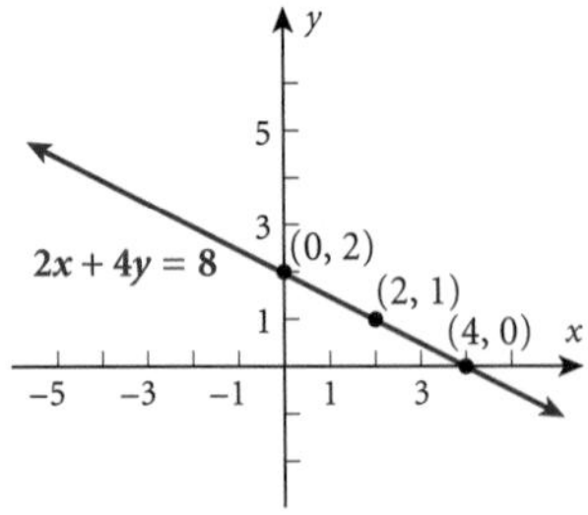

NOTE The second method, locating the intercepts, only produces one point when the lin passes through the origin. In this case some other point on the line must be found in order t graph the line. Refer back to Example 3.

NOW WORK PROBLEM 69.

9 Solve Applied Problems Involving Linear Equations

EXAMPLE 13 Daily Cost of Production

A factory that manufactures microwave ovens has daily fixed overhead expenses o $2000. Each microwave oven produced costs $100. Find an equation that relates th daily cost C to the number x of microwaves produced each day.

SOLUTION The fixed overhead expense of $2000 represents the fixed cost, the cost incurred no matte how many microwaves are produced. Since each microwave produced costs $100, th variable cost of producing x microwaves is $100x$. Then the total daily cost C of production i

$$C = 100x + 2000$$

The graph of this equation is given by the line in Figure 25. Notice that the fixed cos $2000 is represented by the y-intercept, while the $100 cost of producing eac microwave is the slope. Also notice that a different scale is used on each axis.

FIGURE 25

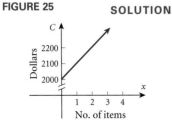

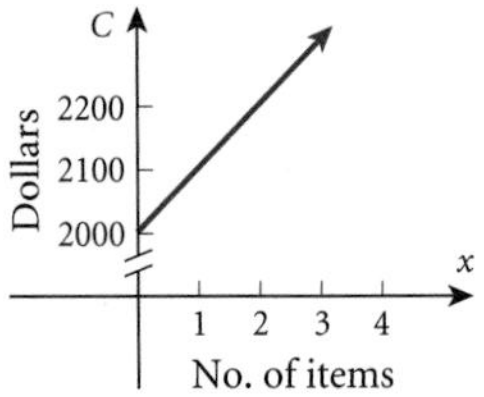

EXAMPLE 14 Predicting the Cost of a Home

In 2008 the cost of an average home in Chicago was \$251,364. In 2009 the cost was \$222,960.

(a) Assuming that the relationship between time and cost is linear, develop a formula for predicting the cost of an average home in 2010.

(b) Comment on whether you think this trend will continue.

Source: Sperling's Best Places; www.bestplaces.net

SOLUTION **(a)** We let x represent the year and y represent the cost. We seek a relationship between x and y. The assumption is that the equation relating x and y is linear. Two points on the graph of the linear equation relating x and y are

$$(2008,\ 251{,}364) \text{ and } (2009,\ 222{,}960)$$

The slope of this line is

$$\frac{222{,}960 - 251{,}364}{2009 - 2008} = -28{,}404$$

Using this fact and the point (2008, 251,364), the point–slope form of the equation of the line is

$$y - 251{,}364 = -28{,}404(x - 2008) \qquad y - y_1 = m(x - x_1)$$
$$y = 251{,}364 - 28{,}404(x - 2008)$$

For $x = 2010$ we predict the cost of an average home to be

$$\begin{aligned} y &= 251{,}364 - 28{,}404(x - 2008) \\ &= 251{,}364 - 28{,}404(2010 - 2008) \qquad x = 2010 \\ &= 251{,}364 - 56{,}808 \\ &= 194{,}556 \end{aligned}$$

We predict the average cost of a home in Chicago in 2010 to be \$194,556.

(b) This prediction of future cost is based on the assumption that annual changes in price remain the same. In this example, the assumption is that each year the cost of a house will go down \$28,404 (the slope of the line). If this assumption is not correct, the predicted cost may be incorrect. Also, it is not reasonable to expect home prices to decline for an extended length of time.

FIGURE 26

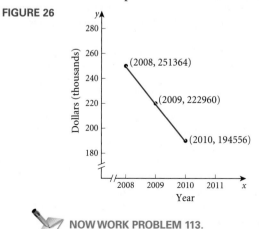

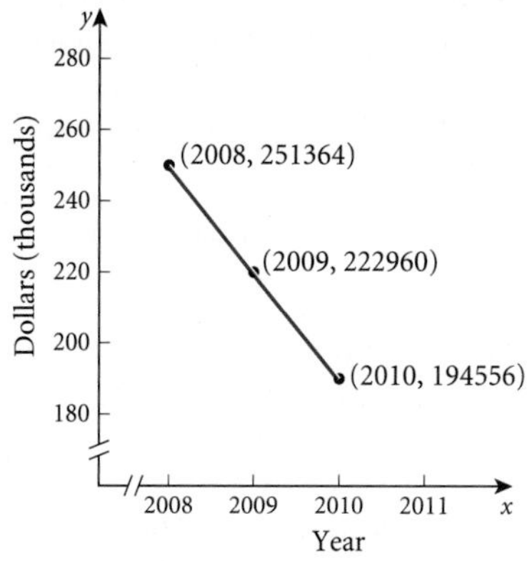

■

NOW WORK PROBLEM 113.

SUMMARY The graph of a linear equation, $Ax + By = C$, where A and B are not both zero, is a line. In this form it is referred to as the general equation of a line.

1. Given the general equation of a line, information can be found about the line:
   (a) Place the equation in slope–intercept form $y = mx + b$ to find the slope m and y-intercept $(0, b)$.
   (b) Let $x = 0$ and solve for y to find the y-intercept.
   (c) Let $y = 0$ and solve for x to find the x-intercept.
2. Given information about a line, an equation of the line can be found. The form of the equation to use depends on the given information. See the table below.

Given	Use	Equation
Point (x_1, y_1), slope m	Point–slope form	$y - y_1 = m(x - x_1)$
Two points (x_1, y_1), (x_2, y_2)	If $x_1 = x_2$, the line is vertical	$x = x_1$
	If $x_1 \neq x_2$, find the slope m: $m = \dfrac{y_2 - y_1}{x_2 - x_1}$ Then use the point–slope form	$y - y_1 = m(x - x_1)$
Slope m, y-intercept $(0, b)$	Slope–intercept form	$y = mx + b$

EXERCISE 1.1 Answers Begin on Page AN–1.

'Are You Prepared?' Problems Answers are given at the end of these exercises. If you get a wrong answer, read the pages listed in red.

1. ***True or False*** On the real number line, the coordinate of the origin is the number 0. (pp. A–16 to A–20)
2. Solve the equation: $2x + 6 = 10$ (p. A–24)

Concepts and Vocabulary

3. ***True or False*** To find the y-intercept of a linear equation, let $x = 0$ and solve for y.
4. The equation of a vertical line with x-intercept at $(-3, 0)$ is ______.
5. If the slope of a line is undefined, the line is ______.
6. The line $y = -4x + 6$ has slope ______ and y-intercept ______.
7. The point–slope form of the equation of a line with slope m containing the point (x_1, y_1) is ______.
8. If the graph of a line slants downward from left to right, its slope m is (positive, negative, zero).

Skill Building

9. Give the coordinates of each point in the following figure. Assume each coordinate is an integer.

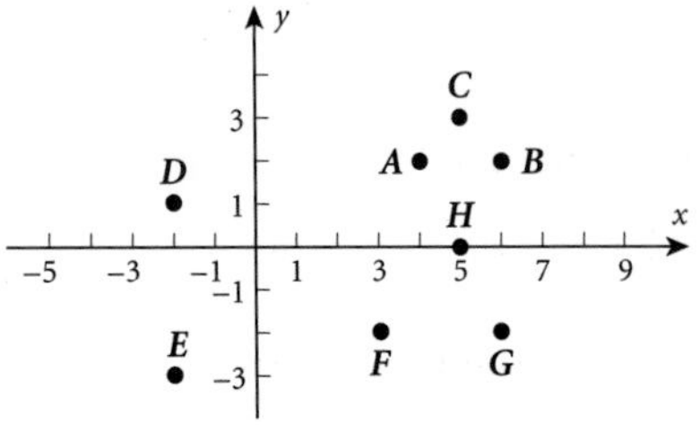

10. Plot each point in the xy-plane. Tell in which quadrant or on what coordinate axis each point lies.
    (a) $A = (-3, 2)$
    (b) $B = (6, 0)$
    (c) $C = (-2, -2)$
    (d) $D = (6, 5)$
    (e) $E = (0, -3)$
    (f) $F = (6, -3)$

11. Plot the points (2, 0), (2, −3), (2, 4), (2, 1), and (2, −1). Describe the collection of all points of the form (2, y), where y is a real number.

12. Plot the points (0, 3), (1, 3), (−2, 3), (5, 3), and (−4, 3). Describe the collection of all points of the form (x, 3), where x is a real number.

In Problems 13–16, use the given equation to fill in the missing values in each table. Use these points to graph the equation.

13. $y = 2x + 4$

x	0		2	−2	4	−4
y		0				

14. $y = -3x + 6$

x	0		2	−2	4	−4
y		0				

15. $2x - y = 6$

x	0		2	−2	4	−4
y		0				

16. $x + 2y = 8$

x	0		2	−2	4	−4
y		0				

In Problems 17–22 a point is given.

(a) *Find the equation of the vertical line containing the given point.*

(b) *Find the equation of the horizontal line containing the given point.*

(c) *Find the general equation of a line with slope 5 containing the given point.*

17. (2, −3) **18.** (5, 4) **19.** (−4, 1) **20.** (−6, −3) **21.** (0, 3) **22.** (−6, 0)

In Problems 23–26, find the slope of the line. Give an interpretation of the slope.

23.

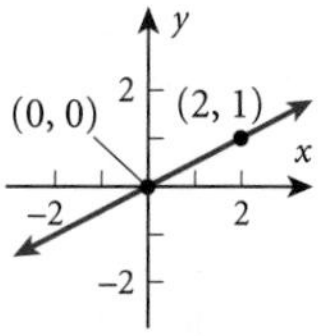

24.

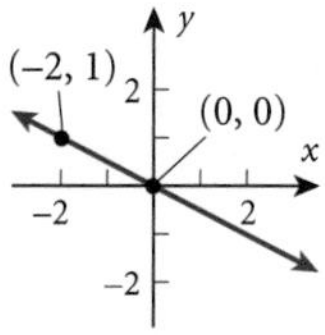

25.

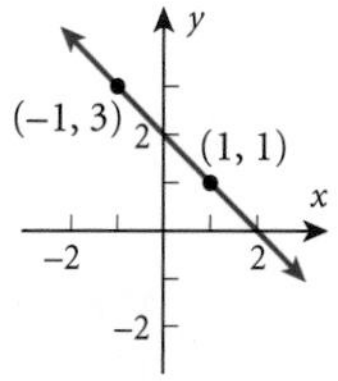

26.

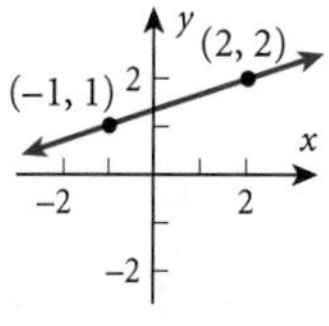

In Problems 27–34, plot each pair of points and find the slope of the line containing them. Interpret the slope and graph the line.

27. (2, 3); (1, 0) **28.** (1, 2); (3, 4) **29.** (−2, 3); (2, 1) **30.** (−1, 1); (2, 3)

31. (−3, −1); (2, −1) **32.** (4, 2); (−5, 2) **33.** (−1, 2); (−1, −2) **34.** (2, 0); (2, 2)

In Problems 35–42, graph the line containing the point P and having slope m.

35. $P = (1, 2)$; $m = 2$ **36.** $P = (2, 1)$; $m = 3$ **37.** $P = (2, 4)$; $m = -\frac{3}{4}$ **38.** $P = (1, 3)$; $m = -\frac{2}{3}$

39. $P = (-1, 3)$; $m = 0$ **40.** $P = (2, -4)$; $m = 0$ **41.** $P = (0, 3)$; slope undefined **42.** $P = (-2, 0)$; slope undefined

In Problems 43–64, find the general equation of each line; that is, write the equation in the form $Ax + By = C$.

43.

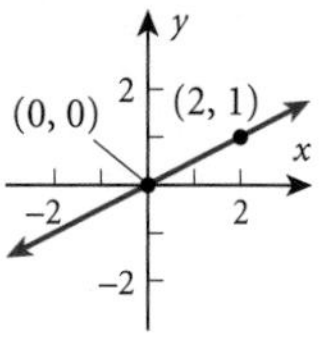

44.

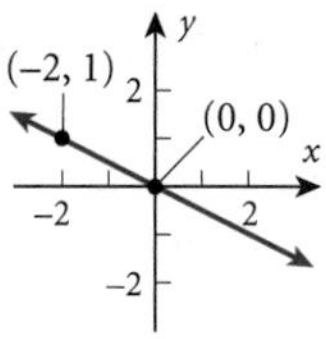

45.

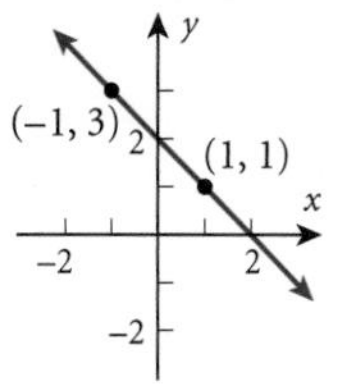

46.

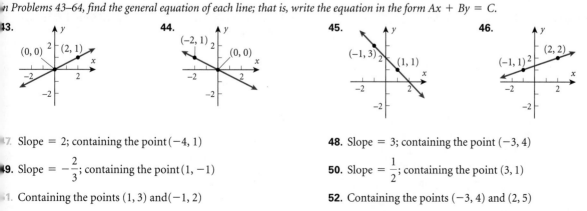

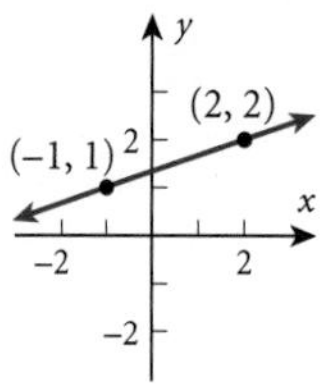

47. Slope = 2; containing the point (−4, 1)

48. Slope = 3; containing the point (−3, 4)

49. Slope $= -\frac{2}{3}$; containing the point (1, −1)

50. Slope $= \frac{1}{2}$; containing the point (3, 1)

51. Containing the points (1, 3) and (−1, 2)

52. Containing the points (−3, 4) and (2, 5)

53. Slope $= -2$; y-intercept $= (0, 3)$

54. Slope $= -3$; y-intercept $= (0, -2)$

55. Slope $= 3$; x-intercept $= (-4, 0)$

56. Slope $= -4$; x-intercept $= (2, 0)$

57. Slope $= \frac{4}{5}$; containing the point $(0, 0)$

58. Slope $= \frac{7}{3}$; containing the point $(0, 0)$

59. x-intercept $= (2, 0)$; y-intercept $= (0, -1)$

60. x-intercept $= (-4, 0)$; y-intercept $= (0, 4)$

61. Slope undefined; containing the point $(1, 4)$

62. Slope undefined; containing the point $(2, 1)$

63. Slope $= 0$; containing the point $(1, 4)$

64. Slope $= 0$; containing the point $(2, 1)$

In Problems 65–80, find the slope and y-intercept of each line. Graph the line.

65. $y = 2x + 3$

66. $y = -3x + 4$

67. $\frac{1}{2}y = x - 1$

68. $\frac{1}{3}x + y = 2$

69. $2x - 3y = 6$

70. $3x + 2y = 6$

71. $x + y = 1$

72. $x - y = 2$

73. $x = -4$

74. $y = -1$

75. $y = 5$

76. $x = 2$

77. $y - x = 0$

78. $x + y = 0$

79. $2y - 3x = 0$

80. $3x + 2y = 0$

In Problems 81–88, use a graphing utility to graph each linear equation. Be sure to use a viewing rectangle that shows the intercepts. Then locate each intercept rounded to two decimal places.

81. $1.2x + 0.8y = 2$

82. $-1.3x + 2.7y = 8$

83. $21x - 15y = 53$

84. $5x - 3y = 82$

85. $\frac{4}{17}x + \frac{6}{23}y = \frac{2}{3}$

86. $\frac{9}{14}x - \frac{3}{8}y = \frac{2}{7}$

87. $\pi x - \sqrt{3}y = \sqrt{6}$

88. $x + \pi y = \sqrt{15}$

In Problems 89–92, match each graph with the correct equation:

(a) $y = x$ (b) $y = 2x$ (c) $y = \frac{x}{2}$ (d) $y = 4x$

89.

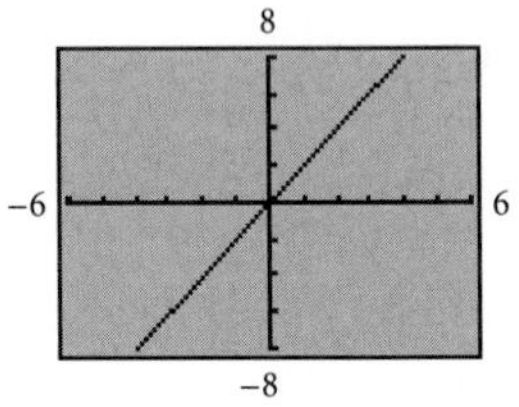

90.

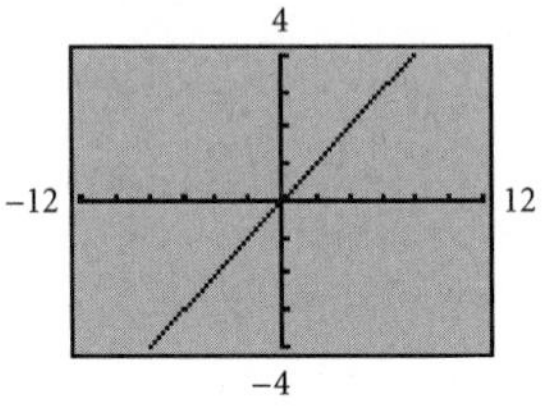

91.

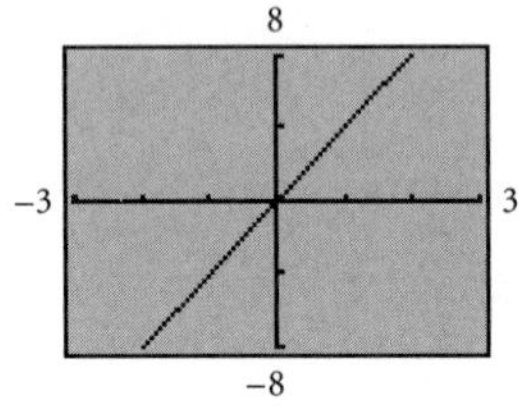

92.

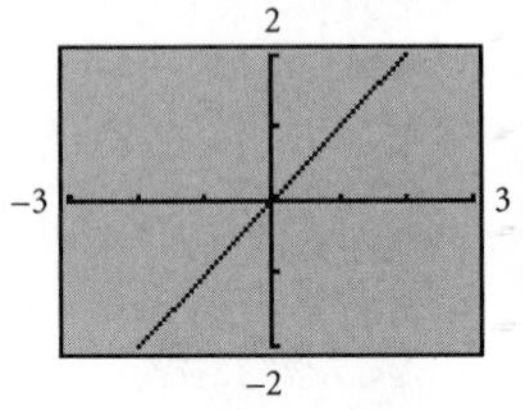

In Problems 93–96, write an equation of each line. Express your answer using either the general form or the slope-intercept form of the equation of a line, whichever you prefer.

93.

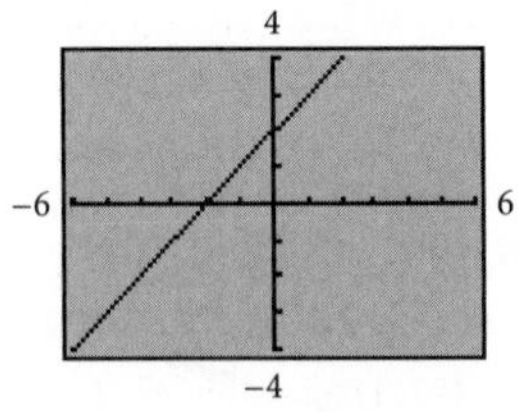

94.

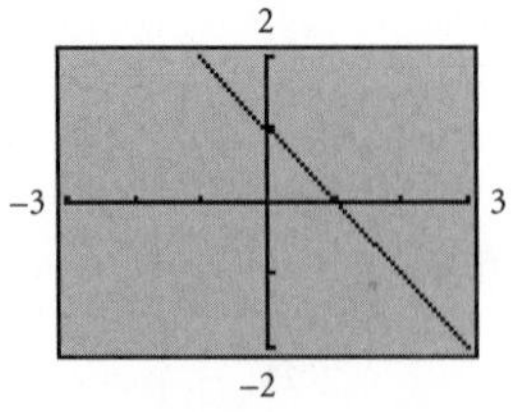

95.

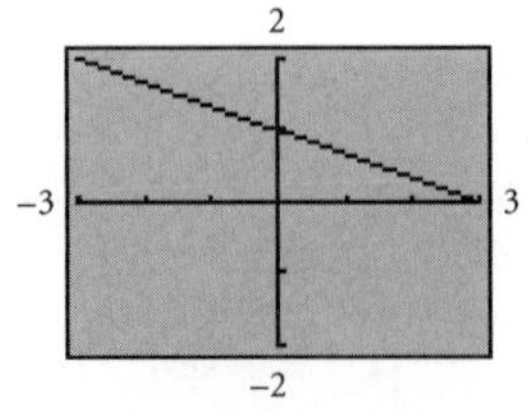

96.

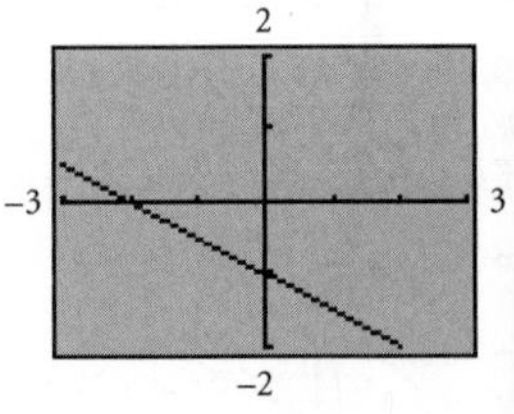

Applications

97. Cost of Operating a Car According to the American Automobile Association (AAA), the average annual cost of operating a standard-sized car, including gasoline, oil, tires, and maintenance decreased to \$0.54 per mile in 2009.

(a) Find a linear equation that relates the average cost C of operating a standard-sized car and the number x of miles it is driven.

(b) What is the annual cost if you drive 15,000 miles?

(c) Graph the linear equation for $0 \le x \le 50{,}000$.

(d) Write a practical sentence expressing how C changes for every unit increase in x.

Source: AAA.com

98. **Cost of Renting a Truck** In January 2010, the cost of renting a truck in Naples, FL, was \$224 per week plus a charge of \$0.52 per mile driven.

(a) Find a linear equation that relates the cost C for a weekly rental in which the truck is driven x miles.

(b) What is the rental cost if you drive 500 miles in a week?

(c) Graph the linear equation for $0 \leq x \leq 2000$.

(d) Write a practical sentence expressing how C changes for every unit increase in x.

(e) Write a practical sentence about the y-intercept.

Source: Budget, Tamiami Trail, Naples

99. **Electricity Rates in Illinois** Commonwealth Edison Company supplies electricity to residential customers for a monthly customer charge of \$8.23 plus 10.438 cents per kilowatt-hour for up to 400 kilowatt-hours.

(a) Find a linear equation that relates the monthly charge C, in dollars, to the number x of kilowatt-hours used in a month, $0 \leq x \leq 400$.

(b) Graph this equation.

(c) What is the monthly charge for using 100 kilowatt-hours?

(d) What is the monthly charge for using 300 kilowatt-hours?

(e) Write a practical sentence expressing how C changes for every unit change in x.

Source: Commonwealth Edison Company, January 2010.

100. **Electricity Rates in Florida** Florida Power & Light Company supplies electricity to residential customers for a monthly customer charge of \$5.69 plus 8.735 cents per kilowatt-hour for up to 1000 kilowatt-hours.

(a) Find a linear equation that relates the monthly charge C, in dollars, to the number x of kilowatt-hours used in a month, $0 \leq x \leq 1000$.

(b) Graph this equation.

(c) What is the monthly charge for using 200 kilowatt-hours?

(d) What is the monthly charge for using 500 kilowatt-hours?

(e) Write a practical sentence expressing how C changes for every unit change in x.

Source: Florida Power & Light Company, January 2010.

101. **Temperature Conversion** The relationship between Celsius (°C) and Fahrenheit (°F) degrees for measuring temperature is linear.

(a) Find a linear equation relating °C and °F if 0°C corresponds to 32°F and 100°C corresponds to 212°F.

(b) Use the equation to find the Celsius measure of 68°F.

102. **Temperature Conversion** The Kelvin (K) scale for measuring temperature is obtained by adding 273 to the Celsius temperature.

(a) Find a linear equation relating K and °C.

(b) Find a linear equation relating K and °F (see Problem 101).

103. **Water Preservation** At Harlan County Dam in Nebraska, the U.S. Bureau of Reclamation reports that the storage content of the reservoir increased from 315,000 acre-feet (102.7 billion gallons of water) on December 21, 2009 to 319,300 acre-feet (104.1 billion gallons of water) on January 20, 2010. Suppose that the rate of increase of water remains constant.

(a) Find a linear equation that relates the amount A of water, in billions of gallons, to the time t, in days. Use $t = 0$ for December 21, $t = 1$ for December 22, and so on.

(b) How much water was in the reservoir on December 31 ($t = 10$)?

(c) Interpret the slope.

(d) How much water is predicted to be in the reservoir on January 31, 2010 ($t = 41$)?

(e) The capacity of the dam is 814,111 acre-feet (265.5 billion gallons of water). If the outflow of water is not controlled, when will the reservior overflow and cause flooding?

(f) Comment on your answer to part (e).

Source: U.S. Bureau of Reclamation.

104. **Product Promotion** A cereal company finds that the number of people who will buy one of its products the first month it is introduced is linearly related to the amount of money it spends on advertising. If it spends \$4000 on advertising, 100,000 boxes of cereal will be sold, and if it spends \$6000, then 300,000 boxes will be sold.

(a) Find a linear equation describing the relation between the amount A spent on advertising and the number N of boxes sold.

(b) How much advertising is needed to sell 200,000 boxes of cereal?

(c) Write a practical sentence expressing how A changes for each unit increase in N.

105. **Predicting Sales** Suppose the sales of a company are given by

$$S = \$5000x + \$80{,}000$$

where x is measured in years and $x = 0$ corresponds to the year 2006.

(a) Find S when $x = 0$.

(b) Find S when $x = 3$.

(c) Find the predicted sales in 2012, assuming this trend continues.

(d) Find the predicted sales in 2015, assuming this trend continues.

106. **Disease Propagation** Research indicates that in a controlled environment, the number of diseased mice will increase linearly each day after one of the mice in the cage is infected with a particular type of disease-causing germ. There were 8 diseased mice 4 days after the first exposure and 14 diseased mice after 6 days. Write a linear equation that will give the number of diseased mice after any given number of days. If there were 40 mice in the cage, how long will it take until they are all infected?

107. **Wages of a Car Salesperson** In 2008, median earnings, including commissions, for car salespersons was \$21.43 per hour or \$857.31 per week. Dan receives \$400 per week for selling new and used cars. In addition, he receives 5% of the profit on any sales he generates.

(a) Find a linear equation that relates Dan's weekly salary S when he has sales that generate a profit of x dollars.

(b) If Dan has sales that generate a profit of \$4000, what are his weekly earnings?

(c) To equal the median earnings of a car salesperson, Dan would have to have sales that generate a profit of how many dollars?

Source: Bureau of Labor Statistics.

108. Oil Depletion The Alaskan oil fields, in operation since 1977, had an estimated reserve of 4.9 billion barrels in 1999. In 2009, the fields had an estimated reserve of 3.5 billion barrels. Assume the rate of depletion is constant.

(a) Find a linear equation that relates the amount A, in millions of barrels, of oil left in the fields at any time t, where t is the year.

(b) If the trend continues, when will the fields dry out?

(c) Write a practical sentence expressing how A changes for every unit change in t.

(d) The Jack Field, discovered in the Gulf of Mexico off the coast of Louisiana in 2006, is estimated to contain up to 15 billion barrels of oil. At the same rate of depletion, how long will this field last?

Source: Energy Information Administration

109. SAT Scores The average score on the mathematics portion of the SAT has been increasing over the past 10 years. In 1999 the average SAT mathematics score was 475, while in 2009 the average SAT mathematics score was 496. Assume the rate of increase is constant.

(a) Find a linear equation that relates the average SAT mathematics score S at any time t, where t is the year.

(b) If the trend continues, what will the average SAT mathematics score be in 2011?

Source: The College Board

110. Financial Statement In November 2005, SBC Communications acquired AT&T through a merger and formally adopted the AT&T name. After the merger, AT&T's net income increased from \$1.45 billion at the end of the first financial quarter in 2006 to \$1.81 billion at the end of the second financial quarter in 2006. Assume the rate of increase is constant.

(a) Find a linear equation that relates the net income I, in billions of dollars, and the time t. Use $t = 1$ for the first quarter of 2006, $t = 2$ for the second quarter of 2006, and so on.

(b) What is the projected net income for the fourth quarter?

(c) Write a practical sentence expressing how I changes for every unit change in t.

111. Percent of Population with Bachelor's Degrees In 1998 the percent of people over 25 years old who had a bachelor's degree or higher was 24.4%. By 2008, the percent of people over 25 with a bachelor's degree or higher was 29.4%. Assume the rate of increase is constant.

(a) Find a linear equation that relates the percent P of people over 25 with a bachelor's degree or higher at any time t, where t is the year.

(b) If the trend continues, estimate the percentage of people over 25 who will have a bachelor's degree or higher by 2011.

(c) Write a practical sentence expressing how P changes for every unit change in t.

Source: *Digest of Education Statistics*, 2008, National Center for Education Statistics.

112. College Degrees In 2000, 1,237,875 bachelor's degrees were conferred by colleges and universities in the United States. In 2007, 1,524,092 bachelor's degrees were awarded. Suppose we assume the relationship between time and degrees conferred is linear.

(a) Find a linear equation that relates the number N of bachelor's degrees awarded in the year t.

(b) If the trend continues, estimate the number of bachelor's degrees that are to be awarded in 2011.

(c) Write a practical sentence expressing how N changes for every unit change in t.

Source: *Digest of Education Statistics*, 2008. National Center for Education Statistics.

113. Predicting the Cost of a Home In 2008, the average cost of a home in Memphis was \$94,823. In 2009, the average cost was \$88,280.

(a) Assuming that the relationship between time and cost is linear, develop a formula for predicting the average cost of a home.

(b) What will be the average cost of a home in 2011?

Source: National Association of Realtors

114. Weight–Height Relation in the U.S. Army Assume the recommended weight w of females aged 17–20 years in the U.S. Army is linearly related to their height h. If an Army female who is 6[illegible] inches tall should weigh 139 pounds and an Army female who is 70 inches tall should weigh 151 pounds, find a linear equation that expresses recommended weight in terms of height.

115. Predicting Sales The total sales and other operating income for Chevron Corporation were \$214.091 billion in 2007 and \$264.908 billion in 2008.

(a) Assuming that the dollar amount of annual increase in total sales and other operating income will remain constant, find a linear equation expressing total sales and other operating income S for Chevron Corporation in terms of the time t in years.

(b) Use this equation to predict total sales and other operating income for Chevron Corporation in the year 2011.

Source: Chevron Corporation

116. Predicting Revenue The net revenue for Dell, Inc. for the fiscal year ending in 2009 was \$61.1 billion and its net revenue for the fiscal year ending in 2008 was \$61.13 billion.

(a) Assuming that the dollar amount of annual increase in net revenue will remain constant, find a linear equation expressing net revenue R for Dell, Inc. in terms of the time in years. Let $t = 0$ correspond to the fiscal year ending in 200[illegible]

(b) Use the equation found in part (a) to predict the net revenue for Dell, Inc. for the fiscal year ending in 2011.

Source: Dell, Inc.

117. Cost of Gasoline The average price of a gallon of regular gasoline in the United States on January 18, 2010 was \$2.739, and one year earlier, the average price of a gallon of regular gasoline was \$1.847. Suppose that the Smith family drives a 2010 GMC Yukon 1500 4WD, which has a fuel usage of 17 miles per gallon (city and highway combined).

(a) Find a linear equation that gives this family's annual fuel cost C as a function of the number x of miles driven in one year, using the price of a gallon of regular gasoline on January 18, 2010.

(b) Find a similar equation using the price of a gallon of regular gasoline one year earlier.

(c) Assuming the Smith family drives 15,000 miles annually, determine their annual fuel cost using the price of gasoline on January 18, 2010.

(d) Determine the Smith family's annual fuel cost using the price of gasoline one year earlier.

(e) What is the difference between these annual fuel costs?

Source: Energy Information Administration, United States Department of Energy and www.fueleconomy.gov

118. Cost of Gasoline Repeat parts (a)–(e) of Problem 117 for the Jones family who drive a 2010 Ford Fusion FWD that has a fuel usage of 39 miles per gallon (city and highway combined).

119. Credit and Debit Card Growth At the end of the first quarter of 2009, there were $N = 1147.5$ million credit and signature debit cards in force on the four major U.S. credit card networks and at the end of the first quarter of 2006, there were 954.7 million credit and signature debit cards in force. Let $t = 0$ correspond to the end of the first quarter of 2006.

(a) Find an equation of the line containing the points $(0, 954.7)$ and $(3, 1147.5)$.

(b) Give an interpretation of the slope of this line as an average rate of change.

(c) Use the equation of the line found in part (a) to estimate the number of credit and signature debit cards that will be in force on the four major U.S. credit card networks at the end of the first quarter of 2011.

(d) Use the equation of the line found in part (a) to estimate the year when the number of credit and signature debit cards that will be in force on the four major U.S. credit card networks will first exceed 1.5 billion cards.

Source: CardData

Discussion and Writing

120. Which of the following equations might have the graph shown? (More than one answer is possible.)

(a) $2x + 3y = 6$
(b) $-2x + 3y = 6$
(c) $3x - 4y = -12$
(d) $x - y = 1$
(e) $x - y = -1$
(f) $y = 3x - 5$
(g) $y = 2x + 3$
(h) $y = -3x + 3$

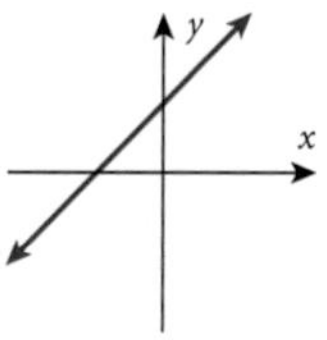

121. Which of the following equations might have the graph shown. (More than one answer is possible.)

(a) $2x + 3y = 6$
(b) $2x - 3y = 6$
(c) $3x + 4y = 12$
(d) $x - y = 1$
(e) $x - y = -1$
(f) $y = -2x + 1$
(g) $y = -\frac{1}{2}x + 10$
(h) $y = x + 4$

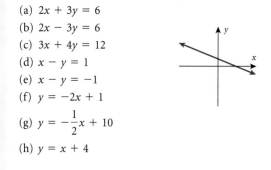

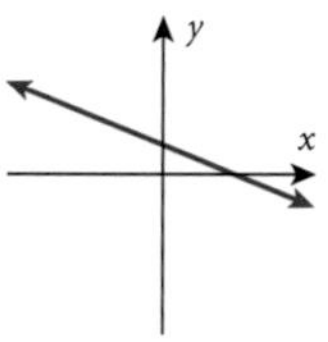

122. Which form of the equation of a line do you prefer to use? Justify your position with an example that shows that your choice is better than another. Have reasons.

123. Can every line be written in slope–intercept form? Explain.

124. Does every line have two distinct intercepts? Explain. Are there lines that have no intercepts? Explain.

125. What can you say about two lines that have equal slopes and equal y-intercepts?

126. What can you say about two lines with the same x-intercept and the same y-intercept? Assume that the x-intercept is not $(0, 0)$.

127. If two lines have the same slope, but different x-intercepts, can they have the same y-intercept?

128. If two lines have the same y-intercept, but different slopes, can they have the same x-intercept? What is the only way that this can happen?

129. Can a line have two distinct x-intercepts? Can a line have infinitely many x-intercepts?

130. Can a line have no x-intercept? Can a line have neither an x-intercept nor a y-intercept?

131. The accepted symbol used to denote the slope of a line is the letter m. Investigate the origin of this symbolism. Begin by consulting a French dictionary and looking up the French word *monter*. Write a brief essay on your findings.

'Are You Prepared?' Answers

1. True **2.** $\{2\}$

1.2 Pairs of Lines

Suppose we look at two lines in the same plane. See Figure 27. Then exactly one of th
following must hold:

1. They have no points in common, in which case the lines are **parallel**.
2. They have one point in common, in which case the lines **intersect**.
3. They have two points in common, in which case the lines are **coincident** or **identica**
and all the points on one of the lines are the same as the points on the other line.

FIGURE 27

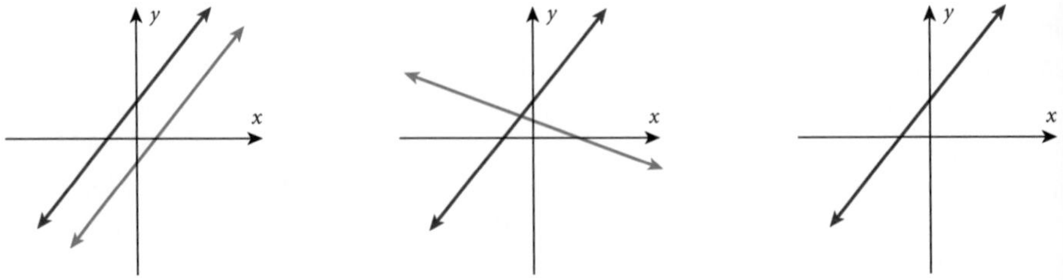

Parallel Lines: No points in common	Intersecting Lines: One point in common	Coincident Lines: All points on each line are the same
(a)	**(b)**	**(c)**

1 ## Show That Two Lines Are Coincident

Figure 28 illustrates vertical coincident lines and nonvertical coincident lines.

FIGURE 28

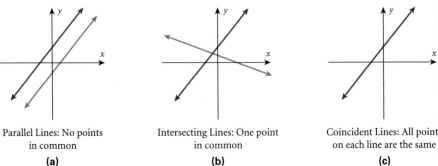

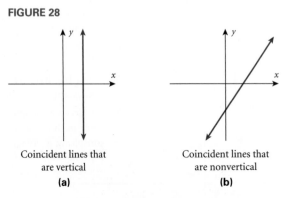

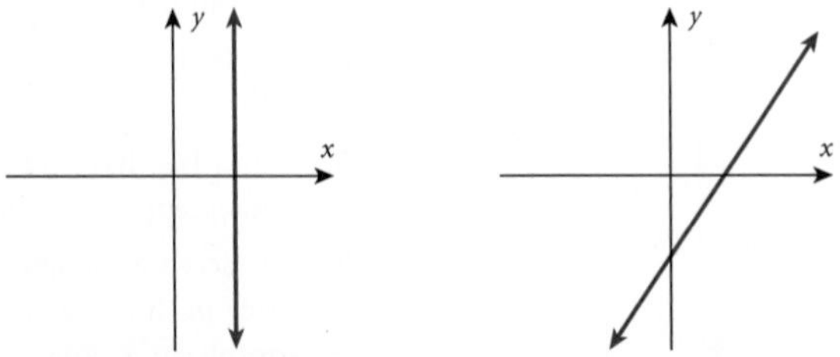

Coincident lines that are vertical	Coincident lines that are nonvertical
(a)	**(b)**

We are led to the following result.

Theorem

Coincident Lines

Coincident lines that are vertical have undefined slope and the same x-intercept. Coincident lines that are nonvertical have the same slope and the same intercepts.

To show that two nonvertical lines are coincident only requires that you show they have the same slope and the same y-intercept. Do you see why?

EXAMPLE 1 Showing That Two Lines Are Coincident

Show that the lines given by the following equations are coincident.

$$L:\ 2x - y = 5 \qquad M:\ -4x + 2y = -10$$

FIGURE 29

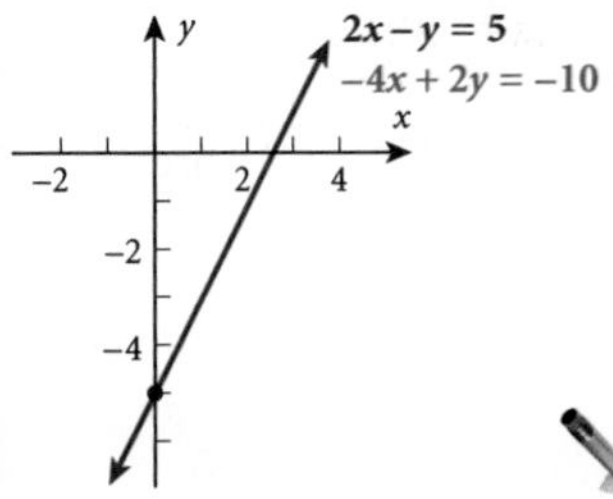

SOLUTION Write each equation in slope–intercept form:

$$\begin{aligned} L:\ 2x - y &= 5 \\ -y &= -2x + 5 \\ y &= 2x - 5 \end{aligned} \qquad \begin{aligned} M:\ -4x + 2y &= -10 \\ 2y &= 4x - 10 \\ y &= 2x - 5 \end{aligned}$$

The lines L and M have the same slope 2 and the same y-intercept $(0, -5)$ so they are coincident. See Figure 29. ■

NOW WORK PROBLEM 7.

2 Show That Two Lines Are Parallel

Look at the parallel lines in Figure 30.

FIGURE 30

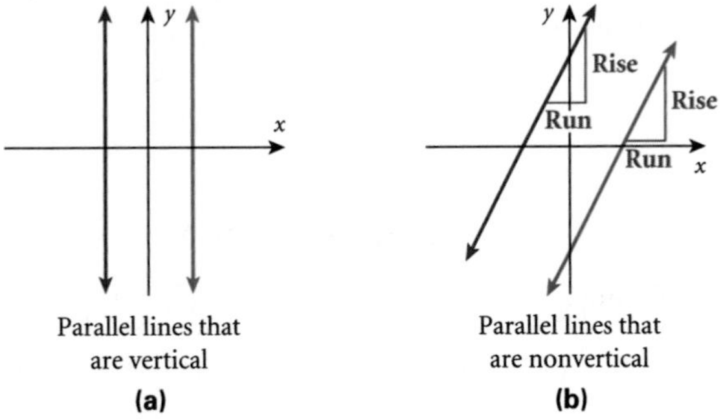

We see in Figure 30(a) that the two vertical parallel lines have different x-intercepts. For the two nonvertical parallel lines in Figure 30(b), equal runs result in equal rises. As a result, nonvertical parallel lines have the same slope. Since they also have no points in common, they will have different x- and y-intercepts.

Theorem

Parallel Lines

Parallel lines that are vertical have undefined slope and different x-intercepts. Parallel lines that are nonvertical have the same slope and different intercepts.

To show that two nonvertical lines are parallel only requires that you show they have the same slope and different y-intercepts. Do you see why?

EXAMPLE 2 Showing That Two Lines Are Parallel

Show that the lines given by the following equations below are parallel.

$$L: \quad 2x + 3y = 6 \qquad M: \quad 4x + 6y = 0$$

SOLUTION To see if these lines have equal slopes, write each equation in slope–intercept form:

$$\begin{array}{rclcrcl}
L: 2x + 3y &=& 6 & \qquad & M: 4x + 6y &=& 0 \\
3y &=& -2x + 6 & & 6y &=& -4x \\
y &=& -\frac{2}{3}x + 2 & & y &=& -\frac{2}{3}x \\
\text{Slope} &=& -\frac{2}{3} & & \text{Slope} &=& -\frac{2}{3} \\
y\text{-intercept} &=& (0, 2) & & y\text{-intercept} &=& (0, 0)
\end{array}$$

FIGURE 31

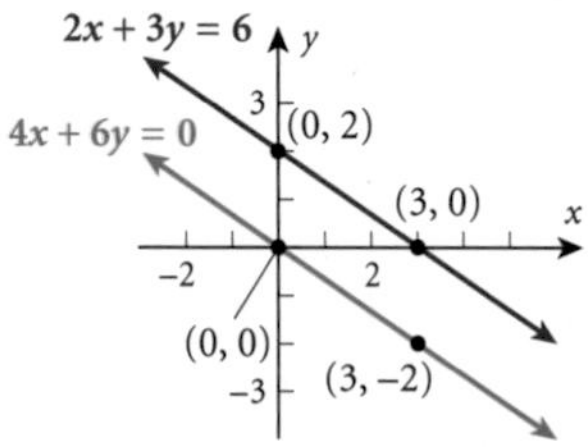

Since each has slope $-\frac{2}{3}$ but different y-intercepts, the lines are parallel. See Figure 31.

NOW WORK PROBLEM 3.

EXAMPLE 3 Finding the Equation of a Line Parallel to a Given Line

Given the line $x - 4y = 8$, find an equation for the line that contains the point (2, 1) and is parallel to the given line.

SOLUTION First find the slope of the line $x - 4y = 8$ by writing it in slope–intercept form $y = mx + b$:

$$\begin{aligned}
x - 4y &= 8 \\
-4y &= -x + 8 && \text{Proceed to solve for } y. \\
y &= \frac{1}{4}x - 2 && y = mx + b;\ m = \frac{1}{4};\ b = -2
\end{aligned}$$

The slope of the line is $\frac{1}{4}$.

We seek a line parallel to the given line that contains the point (2, 1). The slope of this line must be $\frac{1}{4}$. (Do you know why?) Using the point–slope form of the equation of a line, we have

$$\begin{aligned}
y - y_1 &= m(x - x_1) \\
y - 1 &= \frac{1}{4}(x - 2) && m = \frac{1}{4},\ x_1 = 2,\ y_1 = 1 \\
y - 1 &= \frac{1}{4}x - \frac{1}{2} \\
y &= \frac{1}{4}x + \frac{1}{2} && \text{Slope–intercept form} \\
x - 4y &= -2 && \text{General form}
\end{aligned}$$

Figure 32 illustrates the solution.

FIGURE 32

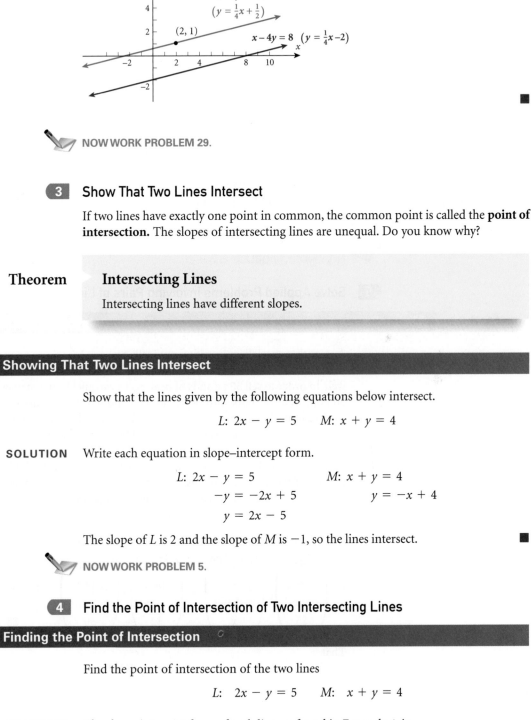

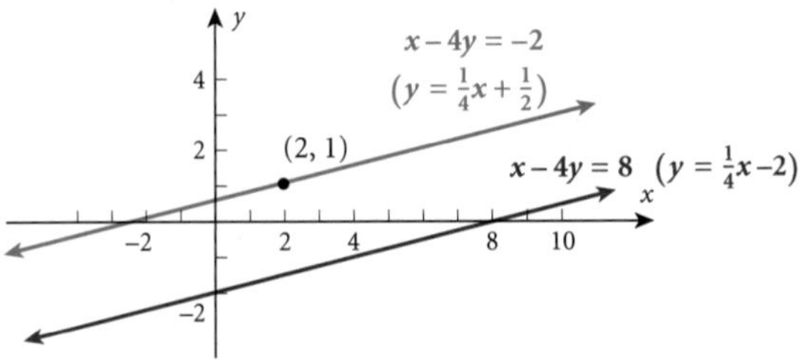

■

NOW WORK PROBLEM 29.

3 Show That Two Lines Intersect

If two lines have exactly one point in common, the common point is called the **point of intersection.** The slopes of intersecting lines are unequal. Do you know why?

Theorem **Intersecting Lines**

Intersecting lines have different slopes.

EXAMPLE 4 Showing That Two Lines Intersect

Show that the lines given by the following equations below intersect.

$$L: 2x - y = 5 \qquad M: x + y = 4$$

SOLUTION Write each equation in slope–intercept form.

$$\begin{aligned} L: 2x - y &= 5 \\ -y &= -2x + 5 \\ y &= 2x - 5 \end{aligned} \qquad \begin{aligned} M: x + y &= 4 \\ y &= -x + 4 \end{aligned}$$

The slope of L is 2 and the slope of M is -1, so the lines intersect. ■

NOW WORK PROBLEM 5.

4 Find the Point of Intersection of Two Intersecting Lines

EXAMPLE 5 Finding the Point of Intersection

Find the point of intersection of the two lines

$$L: \quad 2x - y = 5 \qquad M: \quad x + y = 4$$

SOLUTION The slope–intercept form of each line, as found in Example 4, is

$$L: \quad y = 2x - 5 \qquad M: \quad y = -x + 4$$

If (x_0, y_0) denotes the point of intersection, then (x_0, y_0) is a point on both L and M. A a result, we must have

$$y_0 = 2x_0 - 5 \quad \text{and} \quad y_0 = -x_0 + 4$$

Set these equal and solve for x_0.

FIGURE 33

$$2x_0 - 5 = -x_0 + 4$$
$$3x_0 = 9$$
$$x_0 = 3$$

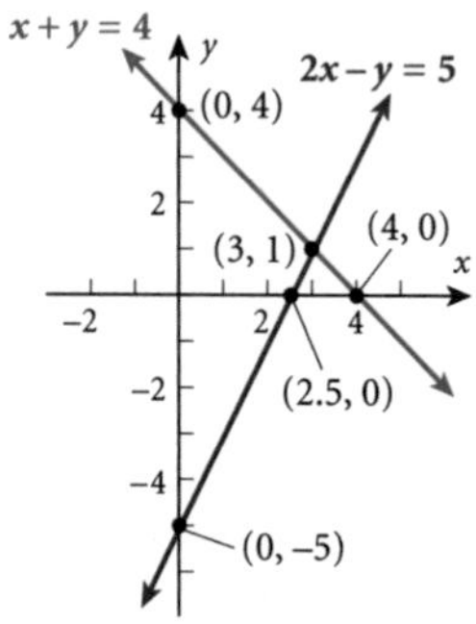

Substituting $x_0 = 3$ in $y_0 = 2x_0 - 5$ (or in $y_0 = -x_0 + 4$), we find

$$y_0 = 2x_0 - 5 = 2(3) - 5 = 1$$

The point of intersection of L and M is $(3, 1)$. See Figure 33.

✔ **CHECK:** To verify that the point $(3, 1)$ is on both L and M, we check to see if $x = 3$ $y = 1$ satisfies each equation.

$$L: \quad 2x - y = 2(3) - 1 = 6 - 1 = 5 \qquad M: \quad x + y = 3 + 1 = 4 \qquad ■$$

NOW WORK PROBLEM 15.

5 Solve Applied Problems Involving Pairs of Lines

EXAMPLE 6   **Mixing Peanuts**

A store that specializes in selling nuts sells cashews for $5 per pound and peanuts for $2 per pound. At the end of the month the manager finds that the peanuts are not selling well. In order to sell 30 pounds of peanuts more quickly, the manager decides to mix the 30 pounds of peanuts with some cashews and sell the mixture of peanuts and cashews for $3 a pound. How many pounds of cashews should be mixed with the peanuts so that the revenue remains the same as it would be selling the nuts separately?

SOLUTION   There are two unknowns: the number of pounds of cashews (call this x) and the number o pounds of the mixture (call this y). Since we know that the number of pounds of cashews plus 30 pounds of peanuts equals the number of pounds of the mixture, we can write

$$x + 30 = y \quad \text{or} \quad y = x + 30$$

Also, in order to keep revenue the same, we must have

$$\begin{pmatrix} \text{Price} \\ \text{per} \\ \text{pound} \\ \$5 \end{pmatrix} \cdot \begin{pmatrix} \text{Pounds} \\ \text{of} \\ \text{cashews} \\ x \end{pmatrix} + \begin{pmatrix} \text{Price} \\ \text{per} \\ \text{pound} \\ \$2 \end{pmatrix} \cdot \begin{pmatrix} \text{Pounds} \\ \text{of} \\ \text{peanuts} \\ 30 \end{pmatrix} = \begin{pmatrix} \text{Price} \\ \text{per} \\ \text{pound} \\ \$3 \end{pmatrix} \cdot \begin{pmatrix} \text{Pounds} \\ \text{of} \\ \text{mixture} \\ y \end{pmatrix}$$

That is,

$$5x + 2(30) = 3y$$

$$\frac{5}{3}x + 20 = y \qquad \text{Divide both sides by 3.}$$

We now have two equations

$$y = \frac{5}{3}x + 20 \qquad \text{and} \qquad y = x + 30$$

FIGURE 34

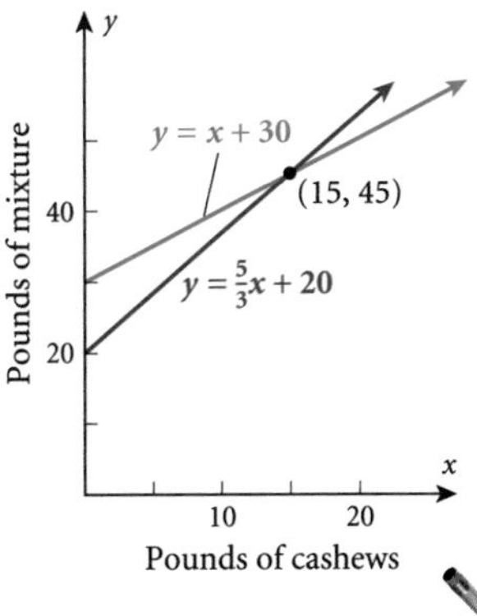

Since the number of pounds of the mixture, y, is the same in each case, we have

$$\frac{5}{3}x + 20 = x + 30$$

$$\frac{2}{3}x = 10$$

$$x = 15$$

The manager should mix 15 pounds of cashews with 30 pounds of peanuts. See Figure 34. Notice that the point of intersection (15, 45) represents the pounds of cashews (15) in the mixture (45 pounds). ■

NOW WORK PROBLEM 37.

EXAMPLE 7 Financial Planning

Kathleen has \$80,000 to invest and wants to earn \$2400 from it. She can invest in a safe, government-insured Certificate of Deposit, but it only pays 1% per year (\$800 per year.) To obtain a higher return, she agrees to invest some of her money in noninsured corporate bonds paying 6% per year. How much should be placed in each investment to achieve her goals?

SOLUTION To earn \$2400 on an \$80,000 investment requires a rate of interest of 3%. The question is how should Kathleen split her money between the two investments in order to realize her goal of earning a 3% rate of return on her money? We need two dollar amounts: the amount to invest in corporate bonds (call this x) and the amount to invest in the Certificate of Deposit (call this y). Since we know that the amount she invests in corporate bonds plus the amount she invests in the Certificate of Deposit equals \$80,000, we can write

$$x + y = \$80{,}000$$

Solving this for y, we get

$$y = \$80{,}000 - x$$

which is the amount that will be invested in the Certificate of Deposit. See Table 1.

TABLE 1

	Amount \$	Rate	Time yr	Interest \$
Bonds	x	6% = 0.06	1	$0.06x$
Certificate	$80{,}000 - x$	1% = 0.01	1	$0.01(80{,}000 - x)$
Total	80,000	3% = 0.03	1	$0.03(80{,}000) = 2400$

Since the total interest from the investments is equal to 0.03(\$80,000) = \$2400, the equation relating the interest earned on the accounts is given as

Interest earned on the bonds + Interest earned on the certificate = Total interest earned

$$0.06x + 0.01(80{,}000 - x) = 2400$$

(Note that the units are consistent: The unit is dollars on both sides of the equation. Now solve the equation for x, the amount invested in corporate bonds.

$$\begin{aligned} 0.06x + 800 - 0.01x &= 2400 \\ 0.05x + 800 &= 2400 \\ 0.05x &= 1600 \\ x &= 32{,}000 \end{aligned}$$

Kathleen should invest \$32,000 in corporate bonds and \$80,000 − \$32,000 = \$48,000 in the Certificate of Deposit.

NOW WORK PROBLEM 45.

SUMMARY

Pair of Lines	*Conclusion: The lines are*
Both vertical	(a) Coincident, if they have the same x-intercept (b) Parallel, if they have different x-intercepts
One vertical, one nonvertical	Intersecting
Neither vertical	Write the equation of each line in slope–intercept form: $y = m_1x + b_1, \quad y = m_2x + b_2$ (a) Coincident, if $m_1 = m_2, b_1 = b_2$ (b) Parallel, if $m_1 = m_2, b_1 \neq b_2$ (c) Intersecting, if $m_1 \neq m_2$

EXERCISE 1.2 Answers Begin on Page AN–3.

Concepts and Vocabulary

1. If two lines have no points in common, they are ______.

2. If two lines have different slopes, they will ______.

Skill Building

In Problems 3–14, determine whether the given pairs of lines are parallel, coincident, or intersecting.

3. L: $x + y = 10$; M: $3x + 3y = 6$

4. L: $x - y = 5$; M: $-2x + 2y = 8$

5. L: $2x + y = 4$; M: $2x - y = 8$

6. L: $2x + y = 8$; M: $2x - y = -4$

7. L: $-x + y = 2$; M: $2x - 2y = -4$

8. L: $x + y = -4$; M: $3x + 3y = -12$

9. L: $2x - 3y = -8$; M: $6x - 9y = -2$

10. L: $4x - 2y = -7$; M: $-2x + y = -2$

11. L: $3x - 4y = 1$; M: $x - 2y = -4$

12. L: $4x + 3y = 2$; M: $2x - y = -1$

13. L: $x = 3$; M: $y = -2$

14. L: $x = 4$; M: $x = -2$

In Problems 15–26, the given pairs of lines intersect. Find the point of intersection. Graph each pair of lines.

15. L: $x + y = 5$; M: $3x - y = 7$

16. L: $2x + y = 7$; M: $x - y = -4$

17. L: $x - y = 2$; M: $2x + y = 7$

18. L: $2x - y = -1$; M: $x + y = 4$

19. L: $4x + 2y = 4$; M: $4x - 2y = 4$

20. L: $4x - 2y = 8$; M: $6x + 3y = 0$

21. L: $3x - 4y = 2$; M: $x + 2y = 4$

22. L: $4x + 3y = 2$; M: $2x - y = 1$

23. L: $3x - 2y = -5$; M: $3x + y = -2$

24. L: $4x + y = 6$; M: $4x - 2y = 0$

25. L: $x = 4$; M: $y = -2$

26. L: $x = 0$; M: $y = 0$

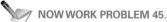

In Problems 27 and 28, find an equation for the line L. Express the answer using the general form or the slope–intercept form, whichever you prefer.

27.

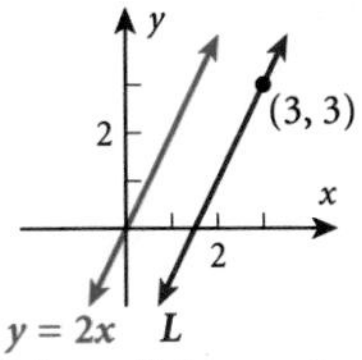

28.

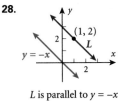

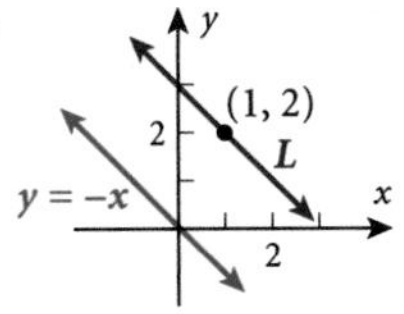

In Problems 29–34, find an equation for the line with the given properties. Express your answer using the general form or the slope–intercept form, whichever you prefer.

29. Parallel to the line $y = 4x$; containing the point $(-1, 2)$

30. Parallel to the line $y = -3x$; containing the point $(-1, 2)$

31. Parallel to the line $2x - y = -2$; containing the point $(0, 0)$

32. Parallel to the line $x - 2y = -5$; containing the point $(0, 0)$

33. Parallel to the line $x = 3$; containing the point $(4, 2)$

34. Parallel to the line $y = 3$; containing the point $(4, 2)$

35. Find the equation of the line containing the point $(-2, -5)$ and parallel to the line containing the points $(-2, 9)$ and $(3, -10)$.

36. Find the equation of the line containing the point $(-2, -5)$ and parallel to the line containing the points $(-4, 5)$ and $(2, -1)$.

Applications

37. **Mixing Candy** Sweet Delight Candies sells boxes of candy consisting of creams and caramels. Each box sells for \$8.00 and holds 50 pieces of candy (all pieces are the same size). If the caramels cost \$0.10 to produce and the creams cost \$0.20 to produce, how many caramels and creams should be in each box for no profit or loss? Would you increase or decrease the number of caramels in order to obtain a profit?

38. **Mixing Nuts** The manager of Nutt's Nuts regularly sells cashews for \$6.50 per pound, pecans for \$7.50 per pound, and peanuts for \$2.00 per pound. How many pounds of cashews and pecans should be mixed with 40 pounds of peanuts to obtain a mixture of 100 pounds that will sell for \$4.89 a pound so that the revenue is unchanged?

39. **Financial Planning** Mr. Nicholson has just retired and needs \$10,000 per year in supplementary income. He has \$150,000 to invest and can invest in AA bonds at 10% annual interest or in Savings and Loan Certificates at 5% interest per year. How much money should be invested in each so that he realizes exactly \$10,000 in extra income per year?

40. **Financial Planning** Mr. Nicholson finds after 2 years that because of inflation he now needs \$12,000 per year in supplementary income. How should he transfer his funds to achieve this amount? (Use the data from Problem 39.)

41. **Mixing Coffee** California Coffee Roasters sells Kona coffee for \$22.95 per pound and Colombian coffee for \$6.75 per pound. Suppose they offer a blend of those two coffees for a price of \$10.80 per pound. What amounts of Kona and Colombian coffees should be blended to obtain the desired mixture? *Hint:* Assume that the total weight of the blend is 100 pounds.

    Source: California Coffee Roasters.

42. **Livestock Feed** Both cornmeal and soybean meal are popular feed for livestock. The protein content of cornmeal is 22% and the protein content of soybean meal is 44%. A farmer wants a 300 pound mixture that is 30% protein. How much of each feed should he use to obtain the desired mixture? (Round answer to the nearest integer.)

43. **Mixing Acid** One solution is 15% acid and another is 5% acid. How many cubic centimeters of each should be mixed to obtain 100 cubic centimeters of a solution that is 8% acid?

44. **Financial Planning** A bank loaned \$10,000, some at an annual rate of 8% and some at an annual rate of 12%. If the income from these loans was \$1000, how much was loaned at 8%? How much at 12%?

45. **Investing in Gold** Suppose an investor purchased x ounces of gold in January 2006 at the prevailing price of \$549.86 per ounce and then sold this amount of gold in January 2010 for \$1112.30 per ounce.

    (a) Find an equation to express the realized gain, y, in terms of x.

    (b) Find the point of intersection of the graph of this equation with the graph of $y = 10{,}000$ to determine the number of ounces of gold (rounded to the nearest tenth) that would result in a gain of \$10,000.

    Source: The Financial Forecast Center

46. **Comparing Gasoline Costs** On January 21, 2010, the average price of a gallon of regular gasoline was \$2.775. The Environmental Protection Agency's fuel economy estimate for a 2010 Honda Civic Hybrid is 42 miles per gallon (city and highway combined), while the EPA's fuel economy estimate for a 2010 Ford Fusion Hybrid is 39 mpg (city and highway combined).

(a) Using the price of gasoline on January 21, 2010, find an equation to express the annual gasoline cost, y, in terms of the total annual miles driven, x, in a 2010 Honda Civic Hybrid.

(b) Find a similar equation for a 2010 Ford Fusion Hybrid.

(c) Graph each of these equations and find the point of intersection of these graphs with the graph of the line $x = 15{,}000$.

(d) Give an interpretation of the distance between these two points of intersection.

Source: US Energy Information Association and www.fueleconomy.gov

47. **HD Radio** On February 1, 2008, there were 1615 High Definition radio stations broadcasting a digital signal alongside their analog signal. On February 1, 2009, there were 1877 such stations. Assume the rate of increase is constant.

(a) Find an equation to express the number N of High Definition radio stations in terms of x, the number of days after February 1, 2008. Use 365 days in a year.

(b) Find the point of intersection of the graph of this equation with the graph of $y = 2000$ to predict the date on which the 2000th HD radio station began broadcasting.

Source: *This Week in Consumer Electronics*, March 9, 2009

Discussion and Writing

48. The figure below shows the graph of two parallel lines. Which of the following pairs of equations might have such a graph?

(a) $x - 2y = 3$
$x + 2y = 7$

(b) $x + y = 2$
$x + y = -1$

(c) $x - y = -2$
$x - y = 1$

(d) $x - y = -2$
$2x - 2y = -4$

(e) $x + 2y = 2$
$x + 2y = -1$

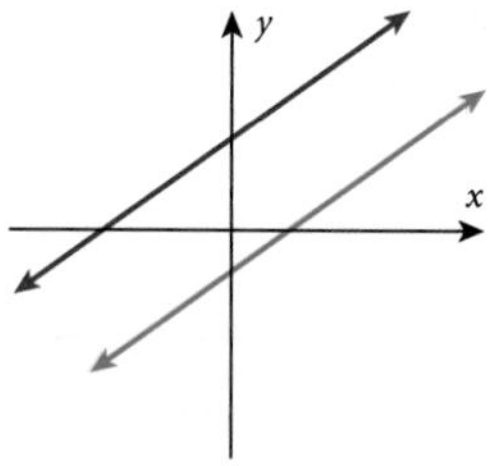

1.3 Applications in Business and Economics

OBJECTIVES
1 Solve problems involving the break-even point (p. 30)
2 Solve problems involving supply and demand equations (p. 33)

1 Solve Problems Involving the Break-Even Point

In many businesses the cost C of production and the number x of items produced can be expressed as a linear equation $C = mx + b$, where m represents the unit **variable cost** of producing each item and b is the **fixed cost**. Similarly, sometimes the revenue R obtained from sales and the number x of items produced can also be expressed as a linear equation of the form $R = px$, where p is the price charged for each unit sold. When the cost C of production exceeds the revenue R from the sales, the business is operating at a loss; when the revenue R exceeds the cost C, there is a profit; and when the revenue R and the cost C are equal, there is no profit or loss. The point at which $R = C$, that is, the point of intersection of the two lines, is usually referred to as the **break-even point**.

EXAMPLE 1 Finding the Break-Even Point

Sweet Delight Candies, Inc., has daily fixed costs from salaries, rent, and other operations of \$300. Each pound of candy produced costs \$1 and is sold for \$2.

(a) Find the cost C of production for x pounds of candy.

(b) Find the revenue R from selling x pounds of candy.

(c) What is the break-even point? That is, how many pounds of candy must be produced and sold daily to guarantee no loss and no profit?

(d) Graph C and R and label the break-even point.

SOLUTION **(a)** The cost C of production is the fixed cost of \$300 plus the variable cost of producing x pounds of candy at \$1 per pound. That is,

$$C = \$1 \cdot x + \$300 = x + 300$$

(b) The revenue R realized from the sale of x pounds of candy at the price of \$2 per pound is

$$R = \$2 \cdot x = 2x$$

FIGURE 35

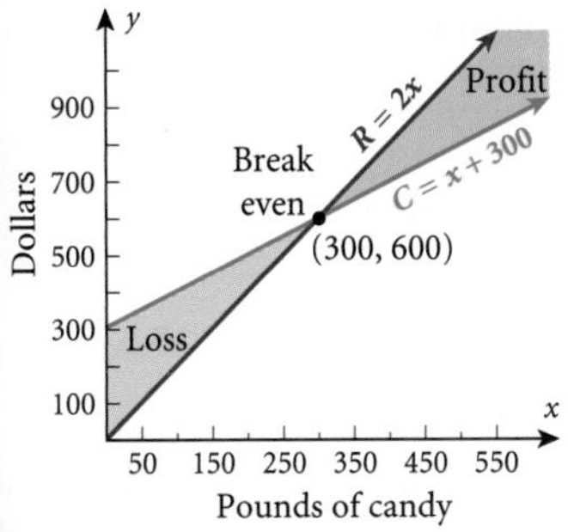

(c) The break-even point is the point where $R = C$.

$$R = C$$
$$2x = x + 300 \quad R = 2x,\ C = x + 300$$
$$x = 300 \quad \text{Solve for } x.$$

That is, 300 pounds of candy must be produced and sold daily to break even. The break-even point is (300, 600).

(d) Figure 35 shows the graphs of C and R and the break-even point. Notice that for $x > 300$, the revenue R always exceeds the cost C so that a profit results. Similarly, for $x < 300$, the cost exceeds the revenue, resulting in a loss. ■

NOW WORK PROBLEMS 3 AND 11.

EXAMPLE 2 Analyzing Break-Even Points

After negotiations with employees of Sweet Delight Candies and an increase in the price of sugar, the daily cost C of production for x pounds of candy changed to

$$C = \$1.05x + \$330$$

(a) If each pound of candy is sold for \$2.00, how many pounds must be produced and sold daily to make a profit?

(b) If the selling price is increased to \$2.25 per pound, what is the break-even point?

(c) If it is known that 325 pounds of candy can be produced and sold daily, what price should be charged per pound to guarantee no loss?

SOLUTION **(a)** If each pound is sold for \$2.00, the revenue R from sales is

$$R = \$2x$$

where x represents the number of pounds produced and sold daily. Set $R = C$ to find the break-even point.

$$R = C$$
$$2x = 1.05x + 330 \quad R = 2x,\ C = 1.05x + 330$$
$$0.95x = 330 \quad \text{Subtract } 1.05x \text{ from each side.}$$
$$x = \frac{330}{0.95} = 347.37 \quad \text{Solve for } x.$$

If 347 pounds or less of candy are produced and sold daily, a loss is incurred; if 348 pounds or more are sold daily, a profit results.

(b) If the selling price is increased to \$2.25 per pound, the revenue R from sales is

$$R = \$2.25x$$

The break-even point is the point where $R = C$.

$$\begin{aligned} R &= C \\ 2.25x &= 1.05x + 330 && R = 2.25x,\ C = 1.05x + 330 \\ 1.2x &= 330 \\ x &= \frac{330}{1.2} = 275 \end{aligned}$$

With the new selling price, the break-even point occurs when 275 pounds of candy are produced and sold daily.

(c) If we know that 325 pounds of candy will be produced and sold daily, the price per pound p needed to guarantee no loss (that is, to guarantee at worst a break-even point) is the solution of the equation

$$\begin{aligned} R &= C \\ xp &= 1.05x + 330 && R = xp,\ C = 1.05x + 330 \\ 325p &= (1.05)(325) + 330 && x = 325 \\ 325p &= 671.25 && \text{Simplify.} \\ p &= \$2.07 && \text{Solve for } p. \end{aligned}$$

The company should charge \$2.07 per pound to guarantee no loss, provided at least 325 pounds will be produced and sold daily. ■

EXAMPLE 3 Analyzing Break-Even Points

A producer sells items for \$0.30 each.

(a) Determine the revenue R from selling x items.

(b) If the cost for production is

$$C_1 = \$0.15x + \$105$$

where x is the number of items sold, find the break-even point.

(c) If the cost can be changed to

$$C_2 = \$0.12x + \$110$$

would it be advantageous?

(d) Graph R, C_1, and C_2 together.

SOLUTION **(a)** The revenue R from selling x items is

$$R = \$0.30x$$

(b) If the cost for production is $C_1 = \$0.15x + \$105$, then the break-even point is the point where $R = C_1$.

$$\begin{aligned} R &= C_1 \\ 0.3x &= 0.15x + 105 && R = 0.3x,\ C_1 = 0.15x + 105 \\ 0.15x &= 105 && \text{Simplify.} \\ x &= 700 && \text{Solve for } x. \end{aligned}$$

The break-even point occurs when 700 items are sold.

(c) If the revenue received remains at $R = \$0.3x$, but the cost for production changes to $C_2 = \$0.12x + \$110$, then the break-even point is the point where $R = C_2$.

$$R = C_2$$

$$0.3x = 0.12x + 110 \quad R = 0.3x,\ C_2 = 0.12x + 110$$

$$0.18x = 110 \quad \text{Simplify.}$$

$$x = 611.11 \quad \text{Solve for } x.$$

The break-even point for the cost in (a) was 700 items. Since the cost in (b) will require fewer items to be sold in order to break even, management should probably change over to the new cost.

(d) Figure 36 shows the graphs of R, C_1, and C_2.

FIGURE 36

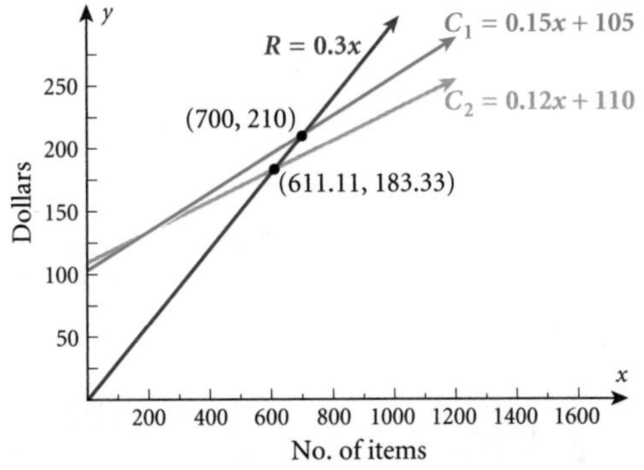

■

FIGURE 37

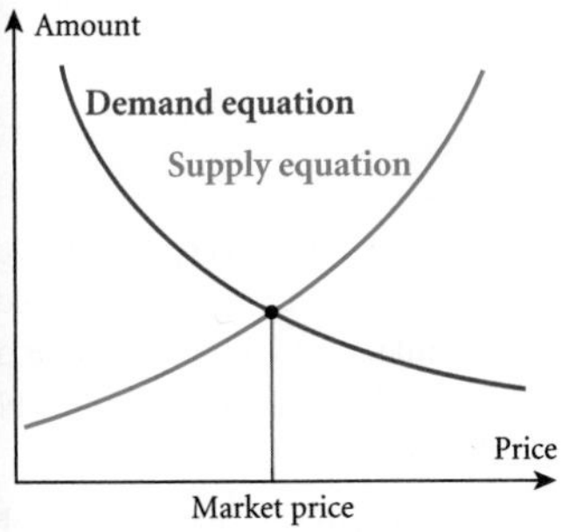

2 Solve Problems Involving Supply and Demand Equations

The **supply equation** in economics is used to specify the amount of a particular commodity that sellers are willing to offer in the market at various prices. The **demand equation** specifies the amount of a particular commodity that buyers are willing to purchase at various prices.

An increase in price p usually causes an increase in the supply S and a decrease in demand D. On the other hand, a decrease in price brings about a decrease in supply and an increase in demand. The **market price** is defined as the price at which supply and demand are equal (the point of intersection).

Figure 37 illustrates a typical supply/demand situation.

EXAMPLE 4 Supply and Demand

The supply and demand for flour have been estimated as being given by the equations

$$S = 0.8p + 0.5 \qquad D = -0.4p + 1.5$$

where p is measured in dollars and S and D are measured in pound units of flour. Find the market price and graph the supply and demand equations.

FIGURE 38

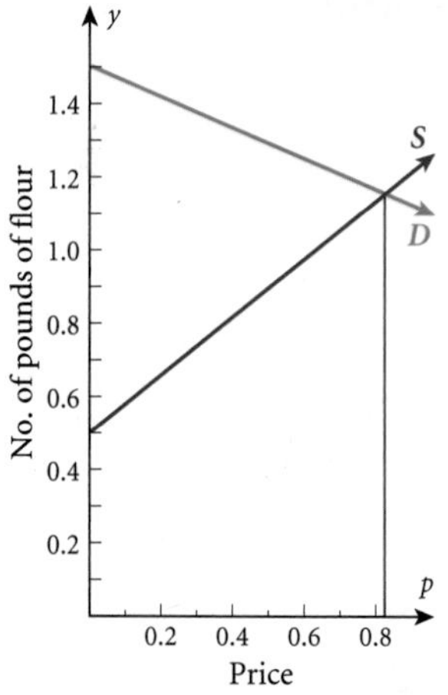

SOLUTION The market price p is the solution of the equation

$$S = D$$
$$0.8p + 0.5 = -0.4p + 1.5$$
$$1.2p = 1$$
$$p = 0.83$$

At a price of \$0.83 per pound, supply and demand for flour are equal. The graphs ar[e] shown in Figure 38.

NOW WORK PROBLEMS 9 AND 15.

EXERCISE 1.3 Answers Begin on Page AN–4.

Concepts and Vocabulary

1. ***True or False*** The break even point is the point of intersection of the revenue graph and the profit graph.

2. ***True or False*** An increase in price usually causes an increase i[n] supply and a decrease in demand.

Skill Building

In Problems 3–6, find the break-even point for the cost C of production and the revenue R. Graph each result. Indicate the break-even point an[d] where a profit results and where a loss results.

3. $C = \$10x + \$600 \quad R = \$30x$
4. $C = \$5x + \$200 \quad R = \$8x$
5. $C = \$0.20x + \$50 \quad R = \$0.30x$
6. $C = \$1800x + \$3000 \quad R = \$2500x$

In Problems 7–10, find the market price for each pair of supply and demand equations.

7. $S = p + 1 \quad D = 3 - p$
8. $S = 2p + 3 \quad D = 6 - p$
9. $S = 20p + 500 \quad D = 1000 - 30p$
10. $S = 40p + 300 \quad D = 1000 - 30p$

Applications

11. **Break-Even Point** A manufacturer produces game-day pennants at a cost of \$0.75 per item and sells them for \$1 per item. The daily operational overhead is \$300. What is the break-even point? Graph your result.

12. **Break-Even Point** If the manufacturer in Problem 11 is able to reduce the cost per item to \$0.65, but with a resultant increase to \$350 in operational overhead, is it advantageous to do so? Give reasons. Graph your result.

13. **Market Price of Sugar** The supply and demand equations for sugar have been estimated to be given by the equations

$$S = 0.7p + 0.4 \qquad D = -0.5p + 1.6$$

where p is the price in dollars per pound and S and D are in millions of pounds.

(a) Find the market price.

(b) What quantity of supply is demanded at this market price?

(c) Graph both the supply and demand equations.

(d) Interpret the point of intersection of the two lines.

14. **Supply and Demand** The market price for a certain produc[t] is \$5.00 per unit and occurs when 14,000 units are produced. At a price of \$1, no units are manufactured and, at a price o[f] \$19.00, no units will be purchased. Find the supply an[d] demand equations, assuming they are linear.

15. **Supply and Demand** For a certain commodity the suppl[y] equation is given by

$$S = 2p + 5$$

At a price of \$1, there is a demand for 19 units of th[e] commodity. If the demand equation is linear and the marke[t] price is \$3, find the demand equation.

16. **Supply and Demand** For a certain commodity the deman[d] equation is given by

$$D = -3p + 20$$

At a price of \$1, four units of the commodity are supplied. I[f] the supply equation is linear and the market price is \$4, fin[d] the supply equation.

17. DVD Club A DVD club offers four DVDs for $0.49 each plus shipping and handling and additional DVDs for $17.95 each plus shipping and handling. Shipping and handling is $2.31 per DVD. A discount retailer offers the same DVDs for $14.95 each plus 7% sales tax. What is the maximum number of DVDs that can be ordered from the club while keeping it a better deal than the discount retailer?

18. Broadcasting Profits The following table gives the operating expenses and revenues for radio and television broadcasting for the years 2004 and 2007.

		2004	2007
Radio	*Revenue (in billions)*	$13.817	$13.624
	Cost (in billions)	$9.920	$9.988
	Profit		

		2004	2007
Television	*Revenue (in billions)*	$35.599	$37.008
	Cost (in billions)	$28.312	$29.803
	Profit		

(a) Fill in the profit rows in each table.

(b) Find equations that relate the profit P_r for radio broadcasting and the profit P_t for television broadcasting in terms of the year t. Assume the relationships are linear.

(c) Using the equations from part (a), determine when the two media had the same profit.

Source: U.S. Census Bureau, 2010 *Statistical Abstract*

1.4 Scatter Diagrams; Linear Curve Fitting

OBJECTIVES
1 Draw and interpret scatter diagrams (p. 35)
2 Distinguish between linear and nonlinear relations (p. 36)
3 Use a graphing utility to find the line of best fit (p. 38)

1 Draw and Interpret Scatter Diagrams

A **relation** is a correspondence between two sets. If x and y are two elements in these sets and if a relation exists between x and y, then we say that x **corresponds to** y or that y **depends on** x and write $x \to y$. We may also write $x \to y$ as the ordered pair (x, y). Here, y is referred to as the **dependent** variable and x is called the **independent** variable.

Often we are interested in specifying the type of relation (such as an equation) that might exist between two variables. The first step in finding this relation is to plot the ordered pairs using rectangular coordinates. The resulting graph is called a **scatter diagram**.

EXAMPLE 1 Drawing a Scatter Diagram

The data listed in Table 2 represent the apparent temperature versus the relative humidity in a room whose actual temperature is 72° Fahrenheit.

TABLE 2

Relative Humidity (%), x	Apparent Temperature, y	(x, y)	Relative Humidity (%), x	Apparent Temperature, y	(x, y)
0	64	(0, 64)	60	72	(60, 72)
10	65	(10, 65)	70	73	(70, 73)
20	67	(20, 67)	80	74	(80, 74)
30	68	(30, 68)	90	75	(90, 75)
40	70	(40, 70)	100	76	(100, 76)
50	71	(50, 71)			

(a) Draw a scatter diagram by hand.

(b) Use a graphing utility to draw a scatter diagram.*

(c) Describe what happens to the apparent temperature as the relative humidity increases.

SOLUTION **(a)** To draw a scatter diagram by hand, we plot the ordered pairs listed in Table 2, with the relative humidity as the x-coordinate and the apparent temperature as the y-coordinate. See Figure 39(a). Notice that the points in a scatter diagram are not connected.

(b) Figure 39(b) shows the scatter diagram using a graphing utility.

FIGURE 39

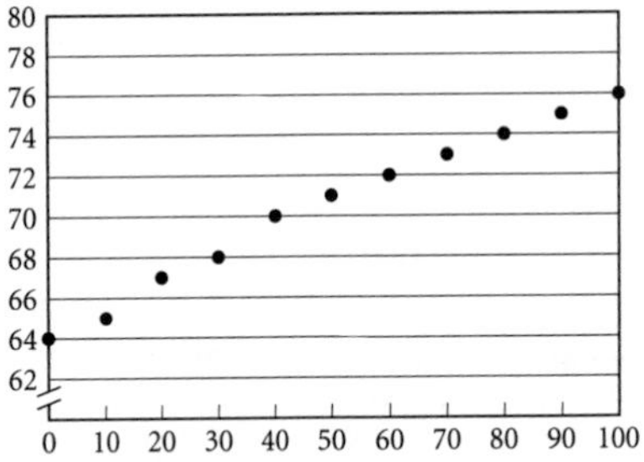

(a)

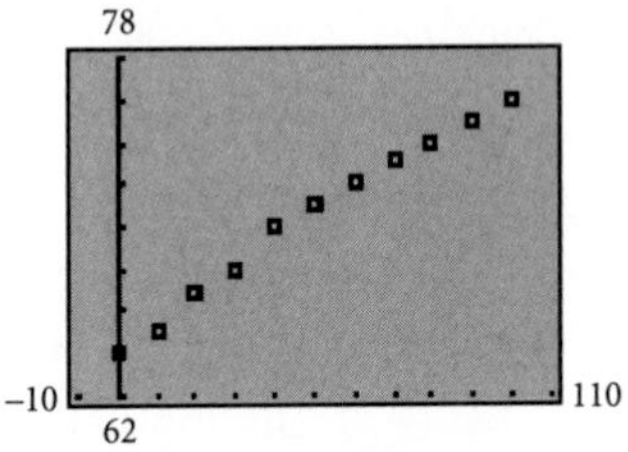

(b)

(c) We see from the scatter diagrams that, as the relative humidity increases, the apparent temperature increases. ■

NOW WORK PROBLEMS 9(a) and 9(d).

2 Distinguish Between Linear and Nonlinear Relations

Scatter diagrams are used to help us see the type of relation that may exist between two variables. In this text, we concentrate on distinguishing between linear and nonlinear relations. See Figure 40.

FIGURE 40

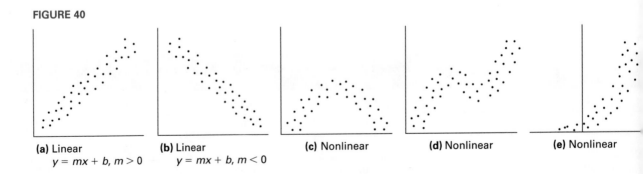

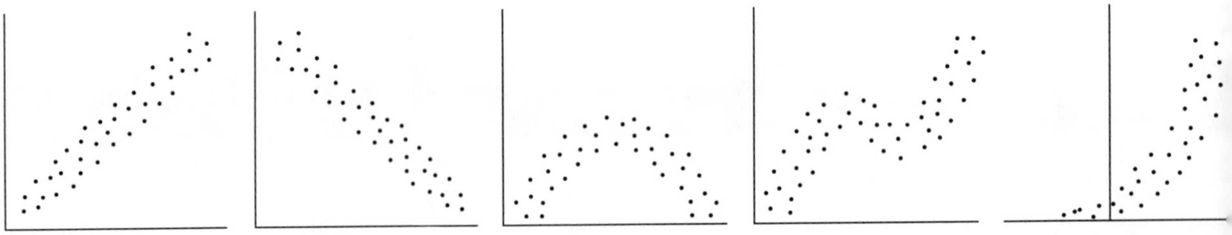

(a) Linear $y = mx + b,\ m > 0$

(b) Linear $y = mx + b,\ m < 0$

(c) Nonlinear

(d) Nonlinear

(e) Nonlinear

* *Consult your owner's manual for the proper keystrokes.*

EXAMPLE 2 **Distinguishing Between Linear and Nonlinear Relations**

Determine whether the relation between the two variables in Figure 41 is linear or nonlinear.

FIGURE 41

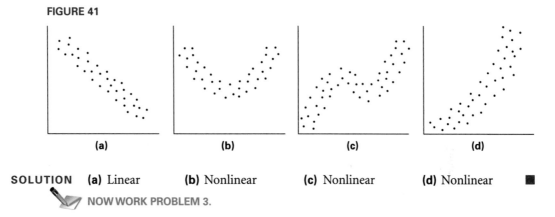

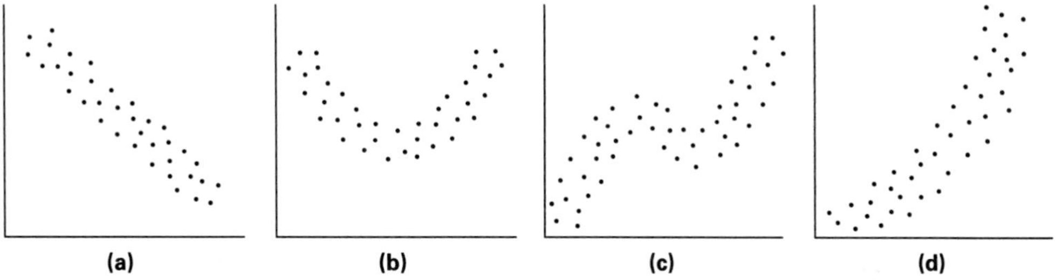

SOLUTION **(a)** Linear **(b)** Nonlinear **(c)** Nonlinear **(d)** Nonlinear ■

NOW WORK PROBLEM 3.

In this book we only study data whose scatter diagrams imply that a linear relation exists between the two variables.

Suppose that the scatter diagram of a set of data appears to be linearly related as in Figure 40(a) or (b). We might wish to find an equation of a line that relates the two variables. One way to obtain an equation for such data is to draw a line through two points on the scatter diagram and find the equation of the line.

EXAMPLE 3 **Find an Equation for Linearly Related Data**

Using the data in Table 2 from Example 1, select two points from the data and find an equation of the line containing the points.

(a) Graph the line on the scatter diagram obtained in Example 1(a).

(b) Graph the line on the scatter diagram obtained in Example 1(b).

SOLUTION Select two points, say (10, 65) and (70, 73). (You should select your own two points and complete the solution.) The slope of the line joining the points (10, 65) and (70, 73) is

$$m = \frac{73 - 65}{70 - 10} = \frac{8}{60} = \frac{2}{15}$$

The equation of the line with slope $\frac{2}{15}$ and passing through (10, 65) is found using the point–slope form with $m = \frac{2}{15}$, $x_1 = 10$, and $y_1 = 65$.

$$y - y_1 = m(x - x_1)$$

$$y - 65 = \frac{2}{15}(x - 10)$$

$$y = \frac{2}{15}x + \frac{191}{3}$$

(a) Figure 42(a) shows the scatter diagram with the graph of the line drawn by hand.

(b) Figure 42(b) shows the scatter diagram with the graph of the line using a graphing utility.

FIGURE 42

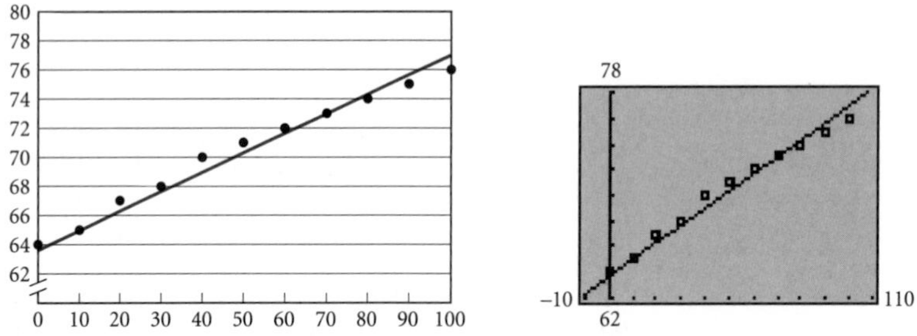

(a) (b)

NOW WORK PROBLEMS 9(b) and (c).

3 Use a Graphing Utility to Find the Line of Best Fit

The line obtained in Example 3 depends on the selection of points, which will vary from person to person. So the line that we found might be different from the line that you found. Although the line that we found in Example 3 appears to "fit" the data well, there may be a line that "fits better." Do you think your line fits the data better? Is there a line of *best fit*? As it turns out, there is a method for finding the line that best fits linearly related data (called the *line of best fit*).*

EXAMPLE 4 Finding the Line of Best Fit

Using the data in Table 2 from Example 1,

(a) Find the line of best fit using a graphing utility.

(b) Graph the line of best fit on the scatter diagram obtained in Example 1(b).

(c) Interpret the slope of the line of best fit.

(d) Use the line of best fit to predict the apparent temperature of a room whose actual temperature is 72°F and relative humidity is 45%.

SOLUTION **(a)** Graphing utilities contain built-in programs that find the line of best fit for a collection of points in a scatter diagram. (Look in your owner's manual under Linear Regression or Line of Best Fit for details on how to execute the program.) Upon executing the LINear REGression program on a TI-84 Plus, we obtain the results shown in Figure 43. The output the utility provides shows us the equation $y = ax + b$, where a is the slope of the line and $(0, b)$ is the y-intercept. The line of best fit that relates relative humidity to apparent temperature may be expressed as the line $y = 0.121x + 64.409$.

* *We show how this line of best fit is found algebraically in Chapter 2. Here we use a graphing utility to find the line of best fit.*

FIGURE 43

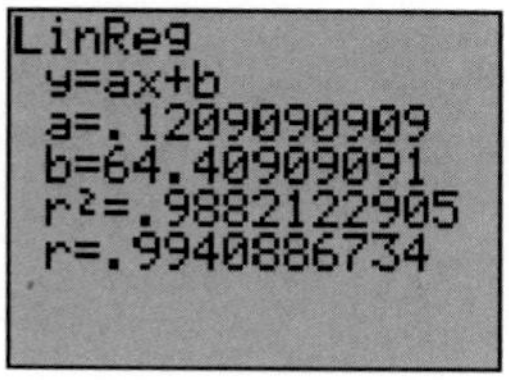

FIGURE 44

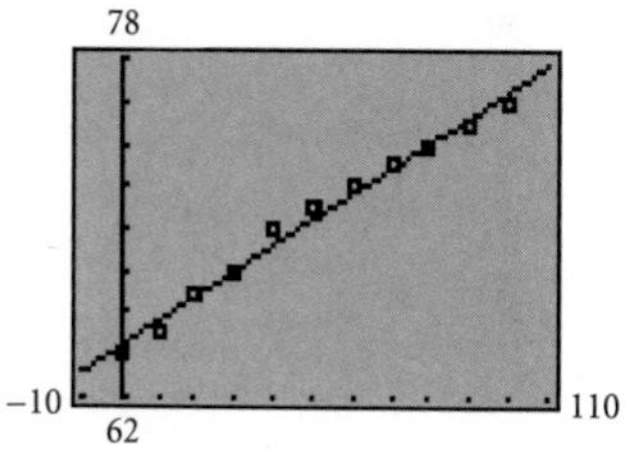

(b) Figure 44 shows the graph of the line of best fit, along with the scatter diagram.

(c) The slope of the line of best fit is 0.121, which means that, for every 1% increase in the relative humidity, apparent room temperature increases 0.121°F.

(d) Letting $x = 45$ in the equation of the line of best fit, we obtain $y = 0.121(45) + 64.409 \approx 70$°F, which is the apparent temperature in the room. ■

NOW WORK PROBLEMS 9(d), (e), AND (f).

Does the line of best fit appear to be a good fit? In other words, does the line appear to accurately describe the relation between temperature and relative humidity?

And just how "good" is this line of best fit? The answers are given by what is called the *correlation coefficient*. Look again at Figure 43. The last line of output is $r = 0.994$. This number, called the **correlation coefficient,** r, $-1 \le r \le 1$, is a measure of the strength of the *linear relation* that exists between two variables. The closer that $|r|$ is to 1, the more perfect the linear relationship is. If r is close to 0, there is little or no *linear* relationship between the variables. A negative value of r, $r < 0$, indicates that as x increases y decreases; a positive value of r, $r > 0$, indicates that as x increases y does also. The data given in Example 1, having a correlation coefficient of 0.994, are indicative of a strong linear relationship with positive slope.

EXERCISE 1.4 Answers Begin on Page AN–4.

Concepts and Vocabulary

1. ***True or False*** A scatter diagram is used to identify the type of relation that might exist between the independent variable and the dependent variable.

2. The mathematical measure of the goodness of fit of a line is called the _____ _____.

Skill Building

In Problems 3–8, examine the scatter diagram and determine whether the type of relation that may exist is linear or nonlinear.

3.

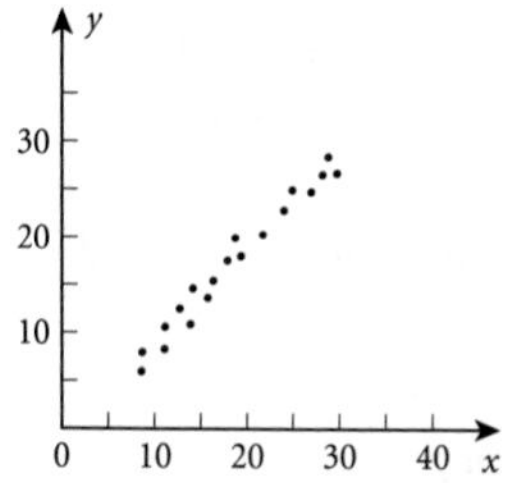

4.

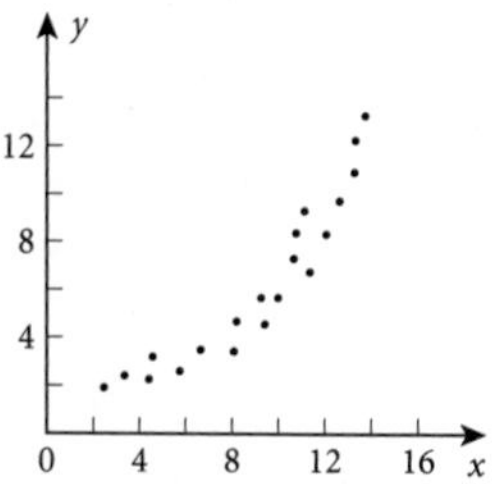

5.

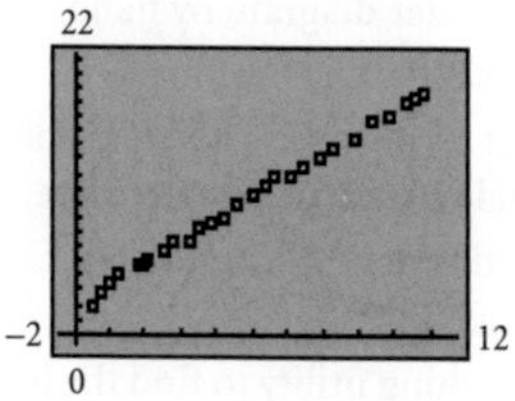

6. 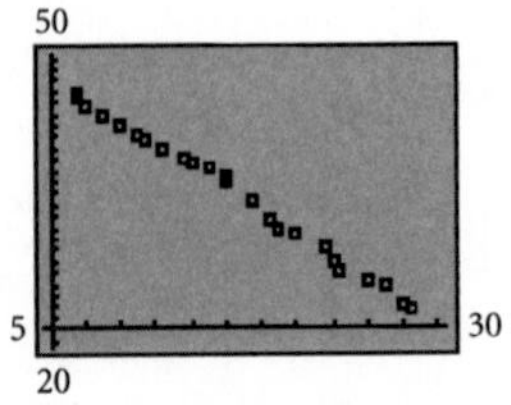

7. 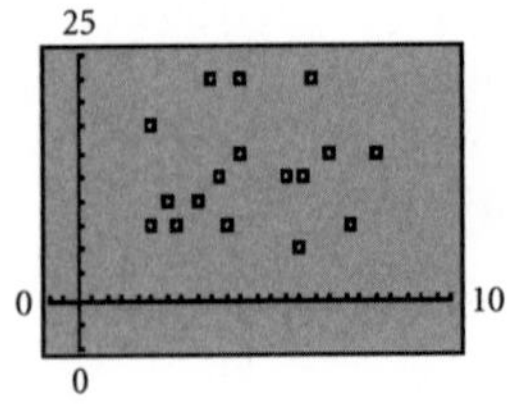

8. 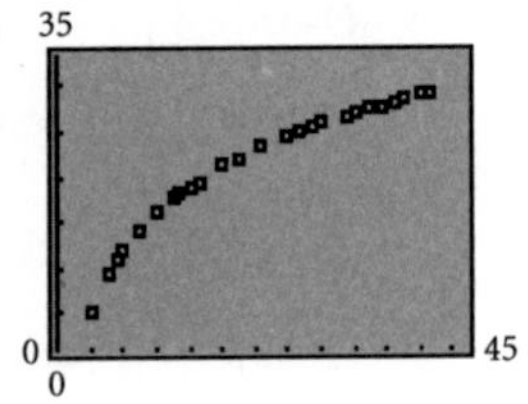

In Problems 9–16,
(a) *Draw a scatter diagram by hand.*
(b) *Select two points from the scatter diagram and find the equation of the line containing the points selected.**
(c) *Graph the line found in part (b) on the scatter diagram.*
(d) *Use a graphing utility to draw a scatter diagram.*
(e) *Use a graphing utility to find the line of best fit.*
(f) *Use a graphing utility to graph the line of best fit on the scatter diagram.*

9.

x	3	4	5	6	7	8	9
y	4	6	7	10	12	14	16

10.

x	3	5	7	9	11	13
y	0	2	3	6	9	11

11.

x	−2	−1	0	1	2
y	−4	0	1	4	5

12.

x	−2	−1	0	1	2
y	7	6	3	2	0

13.

x	20	30	40	50	60
y	100	95	91	83	70

14.

x	5	10	15	20	25
y	2	4	7	9	11

15.

x	−20	−17	−15	−14	−10
y	100	120	118	130	140

16.

x	−30	−27	−25	−20	−14
y	10	12	13	13	18

Applications

17. Consumption and Disposable Income An economist wishes to estimate a line that relates personal consumption expenditures C and disposable income I. Both C and I are in thousands of dollars. She interviews eight heads of households for families of size 3 and obtains the data below.

***I* (in thousands)**	20	20	18	27	36	37	45	50
***C* (in thousands)**	16	18	13	21	27	26	36	39

Let I represent the independent variable and C the dependent variable.

(a) Draw a scatter diagram by hand.
(b) Find a line that fits the data.*
(c) Interpret the slope. The slope of this line is called the **marginal propensity to consume.**
(d) Predict the consumption of a family whose disposable income is $42,000.
(e) Use a graphing utility to find the line of best fit to the data.

* *Answers will vary. We will use the first and last data points in the answer section.*

18. Marginal Propensity to Save The same economist as in Problem 17 wants to estimate a line that relates savings S and disposable income I. Let $S = I - C$ be the dependent variable and I the independent variable.

(a) Draw a scatter diagram by hand.
(b) Find a line that fits the data.
(c) Interpret the slope. The slope of this line is called the **marginal propensity to save.**
(d) Predict the savings of a family whose income is $42,000.
(e) Use a graphing utility to find the line of best fit.

19. Apparent Room Temperature The data on page 41 represent the apparent temperature versus the relative humidity in a room whose actual temperature is 65° F. Let h represent the independent variable and T the dependent variable.

(a) Use a graphing utility to draw a scatter diagram of the data.
(b) Use a graphing utility to find the line of best fit to the data.
(c) Graph the line of best fit on the scatter diagram drawn in part (a).
(d) Interpret the slope of the line of best fit.
(e) Determine the apparent temperature of a room whose actual temperature is 65°F if the relative humidity is 75%.

Relative Humidity, h(%)	Apparent Temperature, T (°F)
0	59
10	60
20	61
30	61
40	62
50	63
60	64
70	65
80	65
90	66
100	67

Source: National Oceanic and Atmospheric Administration

20. Apparent Room Temperature The data in the table represent the apparent temperature versus the relative humidity in a room whose actual temperature is 75°F. Let h represent the independent variable and let T be the dependent variable.

Relative Humidity, h(%)	Apparent Temperature, T (°F)
0	68
10	69
20	71
30	72
40	74
50	75
60	76
70	76
80	77
90	78
100	79

Source: National Oceanic and Atmospheric Administration

(a) Use a graphing utility to draw a scatter diagram of the data.

(b) Use a graphing utility to find the line of best fit to the data.

(c) Graph the line of best fit on the scatter diagram drawn in part (a).

(d) Interpret the slope of the line of best fit.

(e) Determine the apparent temperature of a room whose actual temperature is 75°F if the relative humidity is 75%.

21. The annual residential energy use in the United States from petroleum for the years 1997–2009 is given in the following table.

Year	Annual Residential Energy Use in the United States from Petroleum (in quadrillion btu)
1997	10.71
1998	10.28
1999	10.69
2000	11.24
2001	10.98
2002	11.25
2003	11.61
2004	11.43
2005	11.56
2006	10.8
2007	11.38
2008	11.48
2009	11.22

Source: U.S. Department of Energy, Energy Information Administration

Let E be the dependent variable representing annual energy use from petroleum and let t be the independent variable representing time. Let $t = 0$ correspond to the year 1995.

(a) Find the line of best fit for this data and then use this line to predict annual energy use from petroleum for the years 2015, 2030, and 2035.

(b) Compare your results with the following forecasts given by the U.S. Department of Energy. Can you explain any differences?

Year	Forecasted Annual Residential Energy Use in the United States from Petroleum (in quadrillion btu)
2015	11.07
2030	11.93
2035	12.12

CHAPTER 1 REVIEW OBJECTIVES

Section	Examples		You should be able to	Review Exercises
1.1	1, 2, 3	1	Graph linear equations (p. 3)	1–8
	4, 5	2	Graph a vertical line (p. 6)	12, 13
	6, 7	3	Find the slope of a line and interpret it (p. 7)	5–8(a), 46(b–e, g) 47(b–e), 48(c, d)
	8	4	Graph a line given a point on the line and the slope (p. 10)	5–8(a), 5–8(c), 9–11
	9	5	Use the point–slope form of a line (p. 10)	9–11, 14
	10	6	Find the equation of a horizontal line (p. 11)	11, 14
	11	7	Find the equation of a line given two points (p. 12)	5–8(b), 15–18
	12	8	Use the slope–intercept form of a line (p. 12)	21–26
	13, 14	9	Solve applied problems involving linear equations (p. 14)	45, 46
1.2	1	1	Show that two lines are coincident (p. 22)	28, 31
	2, 3	2	Show that two lines are parallel (p. 23)	19, 20, 27, 32
	4	3	Show that two lines intersect (p. 25)	29, 30
	5	4	Find the point of intersection of two intersecting lines (p. 25)	33–38
	6, 7	5	Solve applied problems involving pairs of lines (p. 26)	39, 40, 42
1.3	1, 2, 3	1	Solve problems involving the break even point (p. 30)	41
	4	2	Solve problems involving supply and demand equations (p. 33)	45
1.4	1	1	Draw and interpret scatter diagrams (p. 35)	43, 44, 46(a), 47(a), 48(a), 49(a)
	2	2	Distinguish between linear and nonlinear relations (p. 36)	43, 44, 48(b), 49(b)
	4	3	Use a graphing utility to find the line of best fit (p. 38)	46(f), 47(f), 48(e), 49

THINGS TO KNOW

Linear Equation, General Form (pp. 3 and 4) $Ax + By = C$ A, B not both zero

Vertical Line (p. 6) $x = a$ $(a, 0)$ is the x-intercept

Slope of a Line (p. 7) $m = \dfrac{y_2 - y_1}{x_2 - x_1}$ if $x_1 \neq x_2$; undefined if $x_1 = x_2$

Point–Slope Form of the Equation of a Line (p. 11) $y - y_1 = m(x - x_1)$
m is the slope of the line; (x_1, y_1) is a point on the line

Horizontal Line (p. 11) $y = b$ $(0, b)$ is the y-intercept

Slope–Intercept Form of the Equation of a Line (p. 13) $y = mx + b$
m is the slope of the line; $(0, b)$ is the y-intercept

Pair of Lines (pp. 22–25)	*Conclusion: The lines are*
Both vertical	(a) Coincident, if they have the same x-intercept (b) Parallel, if they have different x-intercepts
One vertical, one nonvertical	Intersecting
Neither vertical	Write the equation of each line in slope–intercept form: $y = m_1x + b_1, y = m_2x + b_2$ (a) Coincident, if $m_1 = m_2, b_1 = b_2$ (b) Parallel, if $m_1 = m_2, b_1 \neq b_2$ (c) Intersecting, if $m_1 \neq m_2$

REVIEW EXERCISES Answers to odd-numbered problems begin on page AN–6.

Blue problem numbers indicate the author's suggestions for use in a practice test.

In Problems 1–4, graph each equation.

1. $y = -2x + 3$
2. $y = 6x - 2$
3. $2y = 3x + 6$
4. $3y = 2x + 6$

In Problems 5–8, (a) find and interpret the slope of the line containing each pair of points; (b) find an equation for the line containing each pair of points. Write the equation using the general form or the slope–intercept form, whichever you prefer. (c) Graph each line.

5. $P = (1, 2) \quad Q = (-3, 4)$
6. $P = (-1, 3) \quad Q = (1, 1)$
7. $P = (-1, 5) \quad Q = (-2, 3)$
8. $P = (-2, 3) \quad Q = (0, 0)$

In Problems 9–20, find an equation of the line having the given characteristics. Write the equation using the general form or the slope–intercept form, whichever you prefer. Graph each line.

9. Slope $= -3$; containing the point $(2, -1)$
10. Slope $= 4$; containing the point $(-1, -3)$
11. Slope $= 0$; containing the point $(-3, 4)$
12. Slope undefined; containing the point $(-3, 4)$
13. Vertical; containing the point $(8, 5)$
14. Horizontal; containing the point $(5, 8)$
15. x-intercept $= (2, 0)$; containing the point $(4, -5)$
16. y-intercept $= (0, -2)$; containing the point $(5, -3)$
17. x-intercept $= (-3, 0)$; y-intercept $= (0, -4)$
18. Containing the points $(3, -4)$ and $(2, 1)$
19. Parallel to the line $2x + 3y = -4$; containing the point $(-5, 3)$
20. Parallel to the line $x + y = 2$; containing the point $(1, -3)$

In Problems 21–26, find the slope and y-intercept of each line. Graph each line.

21. $9x + 2y = 18$
22. $4x + 5y = 20$
23. $4x + 2y = 9$
24. $3x + 2y = 8$
25. $\frac{1}{2}x + \frac{1}{3}y = \frac{1}{6}$
26. $\frac{1}{4}x - \frac{1}{3}y = \frac{5}{12}$

In Problems 27–32, determine whether the two lines are parallel, coincident, or intersecting.

27. $3x - 4y = -12$, $6x - 8y = -9$
28. $2x + 3y = -5$, $4x + 6y = -10$
29. $x - y = -2$, $3x - 4y = -12$
30. $2x + 3y = 5$, $x + y = 2$
31. $4x + 6y = -12$, $2x + 3y = -6$
32. $-3x + y = 0$, $6x - 2y = -5$

In Problems 33–38, the given pair of lines intersect. Find the point of intersection. Graph the lines.

33. L: $x - y = 4$; M: $x + 2y = 7$
34. L: $x + y = 4$; M: $x - 2y = 1$
35. L: $x - y = -2$; M: $x + 2y = 7$
36. L: $2x + 4y = 4$; M: $2x - 4y = 8$
37. L: $2x - 4y = -8$; M: $3x + 6y = 0$
38. L: $3x + 4y = 2$; M: $x - 2y = 1$

39. **Financial Planning** Karen has just retired and finds she needs an additional \$10,000 per year to live on. Fortunately, she has a nest egg of \$90,000, which she can invest in somewhat risky B-rated bonds at 12% interest per year or in a well-known bank at 5% per year. How much money should she invest in each so that she realizes exactly \$10,000 in interest income each year?

40. **Mixing Acid** One solution is 20% HCl acid and another is 12% HCl acid. How many cubic centimeters of each solution should be mixed to obtain 100 cubic centimeters of a solution that is 15% HCl acid?

41. **Attendance at a Dance** A church group is planning a dance in the school auditorium to raise money for its school. The band they will hire charges \$500; the advertising costs are estimated at \$100; and food will be supplied at the rate of \$5 per person. The church group would like to clear at least \$900 after expenses.
    (a) Determine how many people need to attend the dance for the group to break even if tickets are sold at \$10 each.
    (b) Determine how many people need to attend in order to achieve the desired profit if tickets are sold for \$10 each.
    (c) Answer the above two questions if the tickets are sold for \$12 each.

42. Mixing Coffee A coffee manufacturer wants to market a new blend of coffee that will cost $6.00 per pound by mixing $5.00 per pound coffee and $7.50 per pound coffee. What amounts of the $5.00 per pound coffee and $7.50 per pound coffee should be blended to obtain the desired mixture?

[*Hint:* Assume the total weight of the desired blend is 100 pounds.]

In Problems 43 and 44, draw a scatter diagram for each set of data. Then determine whether the relation that may exist is linear or nonlinear.

43.

x	0	1	2	3	4	5	6
y	90	45	21	12	5	3	2

44.

x	3	5	7	9	11	13
y	74	70	67	58	55	51

45. Supply and Demand The supply and demand equations for corn are estimated to be

$$S = 0.8p + 0.2 \quad D = -0.4p + 1.8$$

where p is the price in dollars and S and D are in millions of bushels.

(a) Find the market price.

(b) What quantity is supplied at this price?

(c) Graph both S and D.

(d) Interpret the point of intersection.

46. Concentration of Carbon Monoxide in the Air The following data represent the average concentration of carbon monoxide in parts per million (ppm) in the air for 1992–2008.

Year	Concentration of Carbon Monoxide (ppm)
1992	5.47
1994	5.34
1996	4.44
1998	4.03
2000	3.51
2002	2.97
2004	2.57
2006	2.22
2008	1.88

Source: U.S. Environmental Protection Agency

(a) Treating the year as the x-coordinate and the average level of carbon monoxide as the y-coordinate, draw a scatter diagram of the data.

(b) What is the slope of the line joining the points $(1992, 5.47)$ and $(1998, 4.03)$?

(c) Interpret this slope.

(d) What is the slope of the line joining the points $(2000, 3.51)$ and $(2008, 2.57)$?

(e) Interpret this slope.

(f) Use a graphing utility to find the slope of the line of best fit for these data.

(g) Interpret this slope.

(h) How do you explain the differences among the three slopes obtained?

(i) What is the trend in the data? In other words, as time passes, what is happening to the average level of carbon monoxide in the air? Why do you think this is happening?

47. Housing Costs The following data represent the mean price of houses sold in the United States for 1998–2008.

Year	Price (Dollars)
1998	181,900
1999	195,600
2000	207,000
2001	213,200
2002	228,700
2003	246,300
2004	274,500
2005	297,000
2006	305,900
2007	313,600
2008	292,600

(a) Treating the year as the x-coordinate and the price of the houses as the y-coordinate, draw a scatter diagram of the data.

(b) What is the slope of the line joining the points $(1998, 181900)$ and $(2002, 228700)$?

(c) Interpret this slope.

(d) What is the slope of the line joining the points $(2002, 228700)$ and $(2008, 292600)$?

(e) Interpret this slope.

(f) Use a graphing utility to find the slope of the line of best fit for these data.

(g) Interpret this slope.

(h) How do you explain the differences among the three slopes obtained?

(i) What is the trend in the data? In other words, what is happening to the average price of a home in the United States? Why do you think this is happening?

Source: U.S. Census

48. Value of a Portfolio The following data represent the value of the Vanguard 500 Index Fund for 2003–2007.

Year	Value per Share
2003	102.67
2004	111.64
2005	114.92
2006	130.59
2007	135.15

(a) Treating the year as the x-coordinate and the value of the Vanguard 500 Index Fund as the y-coordinate, draw a scatter diagram of the data.

(b) Do the data appear to be linearly related?

(c) What is the slope of the line connecting $(2003, 102.67)$ and $(2007, 135.15)$?

(d) Interpret the slope.

(e) Use a graphing utility to find the line of best fit for these data.

(f) Assuming the line of best fit truly represents the trend in the data, predict the value of a share of Vanguard 500 Index Fund in the year 2008.

Source: The Vanguard Group, Inc.

49. Value of a Portfolio Investment ads typically contain statements such as "past performance is no guarantee of future performance." Vanguard's Web site shows the value of a share was \$83.09 in 2008 and \$102.67 in 2009.

(a) Add these data to the chart in Problem 48 and draw a revised scatter diagram representing the years 2003–2009.

(b) Do the data appear to be linearly related?

(c) What would you say about the prediction you made in Problem 48(f)?

(d) Statements like the one given in this problem are usually meant to warn investors that funds may not always do well. How does the statement apply in this problem?

50. Make up four problems that you might be asked to do given the two points $(-3, 4)$ and $(6, 1)$. Each problem should involve a different concept. Be sure that your directions are clearly stated.

51. Describe each of the following graphs in the xy-plane. Give justification.

(a) $x = 0$

(b) $y = 0$

(c) $x + y = 0$

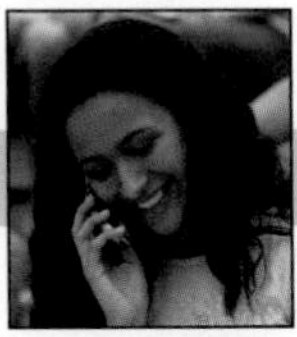

Chapter 1 Project

CHOOSING A CELLPHONE PLAN*

You have an important decision to make. You want to spend the least amount possible on your cell phone each month but still be able to talk to friends and family whenever you want. The plans found online have either unlimited minutes a month for a set price or they have a certain number of free minutes per month for a specific price and then a cost per minute if you exceed the allowable minutes. You decide to save money by not having texting or Web capabilities and will only compare plans for talk time. As it turns out, the equations involved are all linear, so the cell phone plans can be compared using techniques learned in this chapter.

You decide to compare two companies to start. Metro PCS offers unlimited minutes per month for a flat rate of \$60. This means that you can talk as much as you want and the bill will never change. Verizon offers a plan that costs \$39.99 per month for 450 free minutes and \$0.45 per each additional minute. Of course, if you talk less than 450 minutes a month, Verizon's plan is the better deal. However, if you talk more than 450 minutes a month, at some point Metro PCS becomes the better deal.

To analyze the situation, let x denote the number of minutes you talk on the cell phone per month.

All rates quoted have been taken from quotes in February 2010. There are other fees and taxes that are later added to each quote; these fees and taxes are ignored in our analysis.

1. Suppose M is the cost per month for the Metro PCS plan. Find a linear equation involving M and x to represent the amount you will have to pay.
2. Now let V be the cost per month for the Verizon plan. Find a linear equation involving V and x where $x \leq 450$. Also find a linear equation involving V and x where $x > 450$.
3. Graph the three linear equations found in part (1) and part (2) on the same set of coordinate axes. Be careful about the restrictions on x for the equations found in part (2).
4. Find the number of minutes at which Metro PCS becomes the cheaper plan each month by finding the point of intersection of two graphs. Label this point on your graph. Round to the nearest minute.
5. Explain how you can use the solution in part (4) to see which plan is more economical.
6. You are still not convinced that you have the best plan. You look up prices for T-Mobile plans and see that it will charge you \$49.99 a month for up to 650 minutes and \$0.50 for each additional minute. Let T be the cost per month for the T-Mobile plan. Find a linear equation that represents the cost if you talk less than 650 minutes a month and find a linear equation that represents the cost if you talk more than 650 minutes a month.
7. Graph the two equations from part (6) on the same graph you found in part (3).
8. It is now clear that if you talk less than 450 minutes a month, Verizon is the best plan to save money each month. Who has the cheapest plan if you talk 480 minutes a month?
9. For what range of minutes is Metro PCS or T-Mobile the cheapest?
10. If you only want to spend \$55 a month and want to use T-Mobile, how many minutes are you limited to per month over the allowable 650 minutes?
11. If Metro PCS charges \$10 a month extra to cover the cost of the phone for one year and Verizon's phone is free, how many minutes can you talk a month for the year you are paying the extra charge with Metro PCS where Verizon is the better deal?
12. Suppose a new job requires you to be on the phone between 2000 and 2400 minutes a month. You will need to do a lot of traveling and, unfortunately, the Metro PCS service does not have the nationwide coverage you will need. Discuss the suitability of the T-Mobile and Verizon cell phone plans for your new job.

Mathematical Questions from Professional Exams*

1. **CPA Exam** The Oliver Company plans to market a new product. Based on its market studies, Oliver estimates that it can sell 5500 units in 1992. The selling price will be \$2 per unit. Variable costs are estimated to be 40% of the selling price. Fixed costs are estimated to be \$6000. What is the break-even point?
   (a) 3750 units
   (b) 5000 units
   (c) 5500 units
   (d) 7500 units
2. **CPA Exam** The Breiden Company sells rodaks for \$6 per unit. Variable costs are \$2 per unit. Fixed costs are \$37,500. How many rodaks must be sold to realize a profit before income taxes of 15% of sales?
   (a) 9375 units
   (b) 9740 units
   (c) 11,029 units
   (d) 12,097 units
3. **CPA Exam** Given the following notations, what is the break-even sales level in units?

   SP = Selling price per unit

   FC = Total fixed cost

   VC = Variable cost per unit

   (a) $\dfrac{SP}{FC \div VC}$

   (b) $\dfrac{FC}{VC \div SP}$

   (c) $\dfrac{VC}{SP - FC}$

   (d) $\dfrac{FC}{SP - VC}$

4. **CPA Exam** At a break-even point of 400 units sold, the variable costs were \$400 and the fixed costs were \$200. What will the 401st unit sold contribute to profit before income taxes?
   (a) \$0
   (b) \$0.50
   (c) \$1.00
   (d) \$1.50
5. **CPA Exam** A graph is set up with "depreciation expense" on the vertical axis and "time" on the horizontal axis. Assuming linear relationships, how would the graphs for straight-line and sum-of-the-year's-digits depreciation, respectively, be drawn?
   (a) Vertically and sloping down to the right
   (b) Vertically and sloping up to the right
   (c) Horizontally and sloping down to the right
   (d) Horizontally and sloping up to the right

The following statement applies to Questions 6–8:
In analyzing the relationship of total factory overhead with changes in direct labor hours, the following relationship was found to exist: $Y = \$1000 + \$2X$.

6. **CPA Exam** The relationship as shown above is
   (a) Parabolic
   (b) Curvilinear
   (c) Linear
   (d) Probabilistic
   (e) None of the above
7. **CPA Exam** Y in the above equation is an estimate of
   (a) Total variable costs
   (b) Total factory overhead
   (c) Total fixed costs
   (d) Total direct labor hours
   (e) None of the above
8. **CPA Exam** The \$2 in the equation is an estimate of
   (a) Total fixed costs
   (b) Variable costs per direct labor hour
   (c) Total variable costs
   (d) Fixed costs per direct labor hour
   (e) None of the above

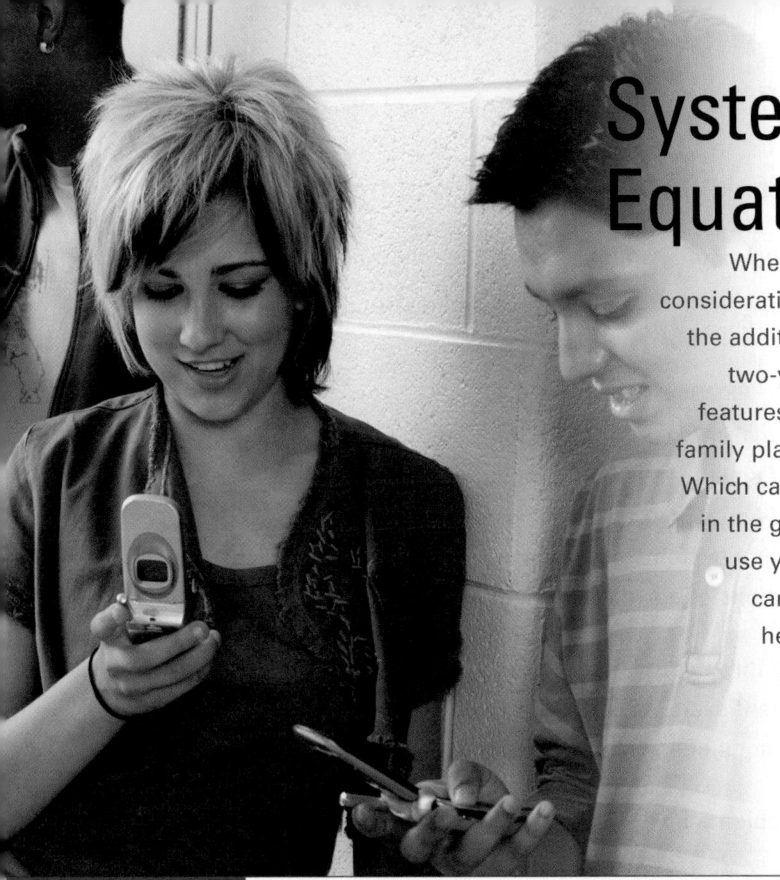

Systems of Linear Equations 2

When selecting a cell phone plan, a number of considerations will influence your decision. What are the additional costs for texting or Web access? Is a two-year service contract required? What extra features are needed, such as email capability or a family plan? Will you be making international calls? Which carrier offers the strongest cell phone signal in the geographical area where you will primarily use your phone? Some of these considerations can be quantified and included in a model to help compare cell phone plans. The Chapter Project at the end of this chapter develops such a model.

OUTLINE

A Look Back, A Look Forward

In Section 1.2 of Chapter 1, we discussed pairs of lines: coincident lines, parallel lines, and intersecting lines. Each line was given by a linear equation containing two variables. So a *pair* of lines is given by *two* linear equations containing two variables. We refer to this as a *system of two linear equations containing two variables.*

In this chapter we take up the problem of *solving* systems of linear equations containing two or more variables. As the section titles suggest, there are various ways to do this. The *method of substitution* for solving equations in several unknowns goes back to ancient times. The *method of elimination*, though it had existed for centuries, was put into systematic order by Karl Friedrich Gauss (1777–1855) and by Camille Jordan (1838–1922). This method led to the *matrix method* (Gauss–Jordan method) that is now used for solving large systems by computer.

2.1 Systems of Linear Equations: Substitution; Elimination

PREPARING FOR THIS SECTION *Before getting started, review the following:*

- Pairs of Lines (Section 1.2, pp. 22–26)
- Algebra Essentials (Appendix A, Section A.2, p. A–24)

NOW WORK THE 'ARE YOU PREPARED?' PROBLEMS ON PAGE 65

OBJECTIVES

1. Solve systems of equations by substitution (p. 53)
2. Solve systems of equations by elimination (p. 55)
3. Identify inconsistent systems of equations containing two variables (p. 57)
4. Express the solutions of a system of dependent equations containing two variables (p. 58)
5. Solve systems of three equations containing three variables (p. 59)
6. Identify inconsistent systems of equations containing three variables (p. 61)
7. Express the solutions of a system of dependent equations containing three variables (p. 62)
8. Solve applied problems involving systems of equations (p. 63)

EXAMPLE 1 Movie Theater Ticket Sales

A movie theater sells tickets for \$8.00 each, with seniors receiving a discount of \$2.00. One evening the theater took in \$3580 in revenue. If x represents the number of tickets sold at \$8.00 and y the number of tickets sold at the discounted price of \$6.00, write an equation that relates these variables.

SOLUTION Each nondiscounted ticket brings in \$8.00, so x tickets will bring in $8x$ dollars. Similarly, y discounted tickets bring in $6y$ dollars. Since the total brought in is \$3580, we must have

$$8x + 6y = 3580$$

■

This equation is an example of a **linear equation containing two variables.** Some other examples of linear equations are

$$2x + 3y = 2 \qquad 5x - 2y + 3z = 10 \qquad 8x_1 + 8x_2 - 2x_3 + 5x_4 = 0$$

2 variables 3 variables 4 variables

In general, an equation containing n variables is said to be **linear** if it can be written in the form

$$a_1x_1 + a_2x_2 + \cdots + a_nx_n = b$$

where $x_1, x_2, \ldots, x_n$ are n distinct variables,* $a_1, a_2, \ldots, a_n$, b are constants, and at least one of the a_i's is not 0.

* *The notation x_n is read as "x sub n." The number n is called a* ***subscript*** *and should not be confused with an exponent. We use subscripts to distinguish one variable from another when a large or undetermined number of variables is required.*

In Example 1, suppose that we also know that 525 tickets were sold that evening. Then we have another equation relating the variables x and y, namely,

$$x + y = 525$$

The two linear equations

$$\begin{aligned} 8x + 6y &= 3580 \\ x + y &= 525 \end{aligned}$$

form a *system* of linear equations.

In general, a **system of linear equations** is a collection of two or more linear equations, each containing one or more variables.

EXAMPLE 2 Examples of Systems of Linear Equations

(a) $\begin{cases} 2x + y = 5 & (1) \\ -4x + 6y = -2 & (2) \end{cases}$ Two equations containing two variables, x and y

(b) $\begin{cases} x + y + z = 6 & (1) \\ 3x - 2y + 4z = 9 & (2) \\ x - y - z = 0 & (3) \end{cases}$ Three equations containing three variables, x, y, and z

(c) $\begin{cases} x + y + z = 6 & (1) \\ x - y = 2 & (2) \end{cases}$ Two equations containing three variables, x, y, and z

(d) $\begin{cases} x + y + z = 6 & (1) \\ 2x + z = 4 & (2) \\ y + z = 2 & (3) \\ x = 4 & (4) \\ y = 2 & (5) \end{cases}$ Five equations containing three variables, x, y, and z

(e) $\begin{cases} x_1 - 2x_2 + x_3 - x_4 = 5 & (1) \\ 3x_1 + x_2 - x_3 - 5x_4 = 2 & (2) \end{cases}$ Two equations containing four variables, x_1, x_2, x_3, and x_4 ■

A brace, as shown above, to remind us that we are dealing with a system of linear equations. Notice that each equation in the system has been numbered for easy reference.

A **solution** of a system of linear equations consists of values of the variables that are solutions of each equation of the system. To **solve** a system of linear equations means to find all solutions of the system.

For example, $x = 2, y = 1$ is a solution of the system in Example 2(a) because

$$\begin{cases} 2x + y = 5 & (1) \\ -4x + 6y = -2 & (2) \end{cases} \qquad \begin{cases} 2(2) + 1 = 4 + 1 = 5 & (1) \\ -4(2) + 6(1) = -8 + 6 = -2 & (2) \end{cases}$$

Furthermore, $x = 2, y = 1$ is the only solution of this system. Do you know why? The lines represented by the equations have different slopes and so they intersect in a single point.

A solution of the system in Example 2(b) is $x = 3, y = 2, z = 1$, because

$$\begin{cases} x + y + z = 6 & (1) \\ 3x - 2y + 4z = 9 & (2) \\ x - y - z = 0 & (3) \end{cases} \qquad \begin{cases} 3 + 2 + 1 = 6 & (1) \\ 3(3) - 2(2) + 4(1) = 9 - 4 + 4 = 9 & (2) \\ 3 - 2 - 1 = 0 & (3) \end{cases}$$

Note that $x = 3, y = 3, z = 0$ is not a solution of the system in Example 2(b).

$$\begin{cases} x + y + z = 6 & (1) \\ 3x - 2y + 4z = 9 & (2) \\ x - y - z = 0 & (3) \end{cases} \qquad \begin{cases} 3 + 3 + 0 = 6 & (1) \\ 3(3) - 2(3) + 4(0) = 3 \neq 9 & (2) \\ 3 - 3 - 0 = 0 & (3) \end{cases}$$

Although these values satisfy Equations (1) and (3), they do not satisfy Equation (2). Any solution of the system must satisfy *each* equation of the system.

The system of equations given in Example 2(c) has multiple solutions. For example, $x=2$, $y=0$, $z=4$; $x=3$, $y=1$, $z=2$; $x=4$, $y=2$, $z=0$; $x=5$, $y=3$, $z=-2$ are each solutions, as you can verify. As it turns out, when a system of equations has multiple solutions, the number of solutions is infinite!

The system of equations given in Example 2(d) has no solution. Look at Equations (4) and (5), which tell us $x=4$ and $y=2$. Substitute these values into Equations (1) and (2). From Equation (1), we obtain $z=0$ and from Equation (2), we obtain $z=-4$. This contradiction means the system has no solution.

Definition

If a system of equations has at least one solution, it is said to be **consistent**; if it has no solution, it is said to be **inconsistent.** If a consistent system of equations has exactly one solution, the equations of the system are said to be **independent**; if it has an infinite number of solutions, the equations are called **dependent.**

NOW WORK PROBLEM 9.

Two Linear Equations Containing Two Variables

Based on the discussion in Section 1.2, we can view the problem of solving a system of two linear equations containing two variables as a geometry problem. Because the graph of each equation in such a system is a line, a system of two linear equations containing two variables represents a pair of lines. The lines either (1) are parallel or (2) are intersecting or (3) are coincident (that is, identical).

1. If the lines are parallel, then the system of equations has no solution, because the lines never intersect. The system is inconsistent.
2. If the lines intersect, then the system of equations has one solution, given by the point of intersection. The system is consistent and the equations are independent.
3. If the lines are coincident, then the system of equations has infinitely many solutions, represented by the totality of points on the line. The system is consistent and the equations are dependent.

Based on this, a system of equations is either

(I) Inconsistent with no solution

or

(II) Consistent with

(a) One solution (equations are independent)

or

(b) Infinitely many solutions (equations are dependent)

Figure 1 illustrates these conclusions.

FIGURE 1

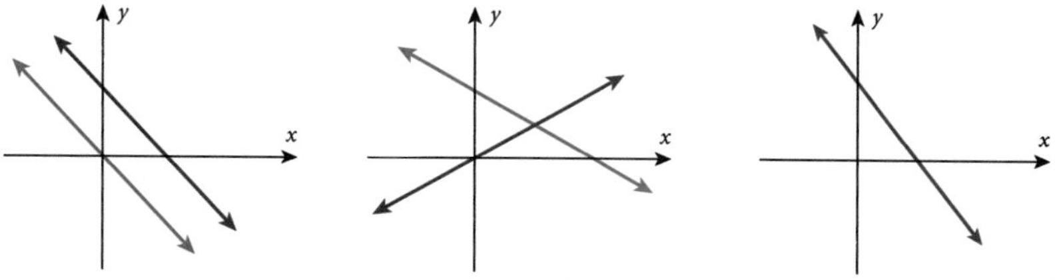

(a) Parallel lines; system has no solution and is inconsistent

(b) Intersecting lines; system has one solution and is consistent; the equations are independent

(c) Coincident lines; system has infinitely many solutions and is consistent; the equations are dependent

EXAMPLE 3 Graphing a System of Linear Equations

Graph the system: $\begin{cases} 2x + y = 5 & (1) \\ -4x + 6y = 12 & (2) \end{cases}$

SOLUTION Equation (1) is a line with x-intercept $\left(\frac{5}{2}, 0\right)$ and y-intercept $(0, 5)$. Equation (2) is a line with x-intercept $(-3, 0)$ and y-intercept $(0, 2)$.

Figure 2 shows their graphs. ■

FIGURE 2

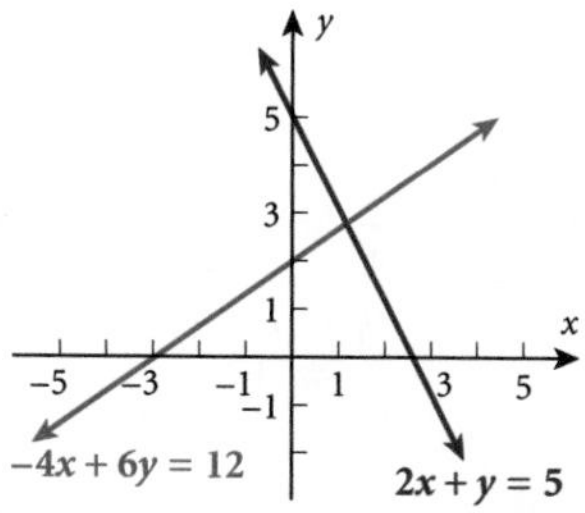

From the graph in Figure 2 we see that the lines intersect, so the system is consistent and the equations are independent. We can also use the graph as a means of approximating the solution. For this system the solution would appear to be close to the point $(1, 3)$. The actual solution, which you should verify, is $\left(\frac{9}{8}, \frac{11}{4}\right)$.

To obtain the exact solution, we use algebraic methods. The first algebraic method we take up is the *method of substitution.*

1 Solve Systems of Equations by Substitution

EXAMPLE 4 Solving a System of Equations Using Substitution

Solve: $\begin{cases} 2x + y = 5 & (1) \\ -4x + 6y = 12 & (2) \end{cases}$

SOLUTION Solve the first equation for y, obtaining

$$2x + y = 5 \qquad (1)$$
$$y = -2x + 5 \qquad \text{Subtract } 2x \text{ from each side}$$

Substitute this value of y in the second equation. This results in an equation containing one variable, which we can solve.

$$-4x + 6y = 12 \qquad (2)$$
$$-4x + 6(-2x + 5) = 12 \qquad \text{Substitute } y = -2x + 5 \text{ in } (2)$$
$$-4x - 12x + 30 = 12 \qquad \text{Remove parentheses.}$$
$$-16x = -18 \qquad \text{Combine like terms; subtract 30 from each side.}$$
$$x = \frac{-18}{-16} = \frac{9}{8} \qquad \text{Divide each side by } -16.$$

Once we know that $x = \dfrac{9}{8}$, we can find the value of y by **back-substitution**, that is, by substituting $\dfrac{9}{8}$ for x in one of the original equations.

Use the first equation.

$$2x + y = 5 \qquad\qquad\qquad (1)$$

$$2\left(\frac{9}{8}\right) + y = 5 \qquad\qquad \text{Substitute } x = \frac{9}{8} \text{ in (1).}$$

$$\frac{9}{4} + y = 5 \qquad\qquad\qquad \text{Simplify}$$

$$y = 5 - \frac{9}{4} \qquad\qquad \text{Subtract } \frac{9}{4} \text{ from each side.}$$

$$y = \frac{20}{4} - \frac{9}{4} = \frac{11}{4}$$

The solution of the system is $x = \dfrac{9}{8} = 1.125, y = \dfrac{11}{4} = 2.75$. We can also write the solution as the ordered pair $\left(\dfrac{9}{8}, \dfrac{11}{4}\right)$.

✔ **CHECK:**

$$\begin{cases} 2x + y = 5: & 2\left(\dfrac{9}{8}\right) + \dfrac{11}{4} = \dfrac{9}{4} + \dfrac{11}{4} = \dfrac{20}{4} = 5 \\[2ex] -4x + 6y = 12: & -4\left(\dfrac{9}{8}\right) + 6\left(\dfrac{11}{4}\right) = -\dfrac{9}{2} + \dfrac{33}{2} = \dfrac{24}{2} = 12 \end{cases}$$

FIGURE 3

$Y_1 = -2x + 5$

$Y_2 = \frac{2}{3}x + 2$

COMMENT We can also verify our algebraic solution in Example 4 using a graphing utility. First, we solve each equation for y. This is equivalent to writing each equation in slope–intercept form. Equation (1) in slope–intercept form is $Y_1 = -2x + 5$. Equation (2) in slope–intercept form is $Y_2 = \dfrac{2}{3}x + 2$. Figure 3 shows the graphs using a graphing utility. From the graph in Figure 3, we see that the lines intersect, so the system is consistent and the equations are independent. Using INTERSECT, we obtain the solution (1.125, 2.75), which is equivalent to $\left(\dfrac{9}{8}, \dfrac{11}{4}\right)$.

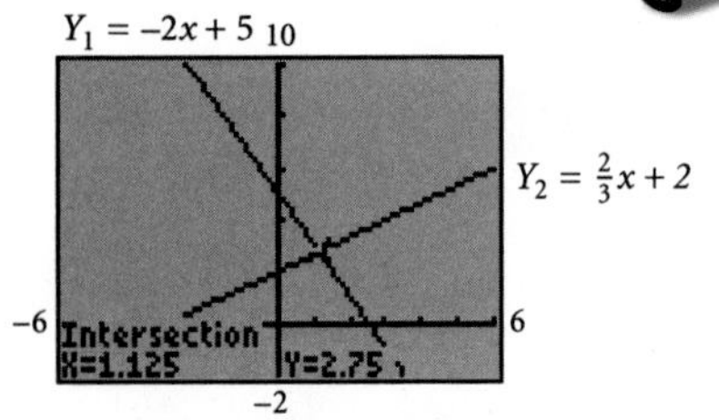

The method used to solve the system in Example 4 is called **substitution**.

Steps for Solving by Substitution

STEP 1 Pick one of the equations and solve for one of the variables in terms of the remaining variables.

STEP 2 Substitute the result in the remaining equations.

STEP 3 If one equation in one variable results, solve this equation. Otherwise, repeat Steps 1 and 2 until a single equation with one variable remains.

STEP 4 Find the values of the remaining variables by back-substitution.

STEP 5 Check the solution found.

EXAMPLE 5 **Solving a System of Equations Using Substitution**

Solve: $\begin{cases} 3x - 2y = 5 & (1) \\ 5x - y = 6 & (2) \end{cases}$

SOLUTION

STEP 1 After looking at the two equations, we conclude that it is easiest to solve for the variable y in Equation (2):

$$5x - y = 6 \quad (2)$$

$$5x - 6 = y \quad \text{Add } y \text{ and subtract 6 from each side.}$$

STEP 2 Substitute this result into Equation (1) and simplify:

$$3x - 2y = 5 \quad (2)$$

$$3x - 2(5x - 6) = 5 \quad y = 5x - 6$$

STEP 3

$$-7x + 12 = 5 \quad \text{Simplify.}$$

$$-7x = -7 \quad \text{Simplify.}$$

$$x = 1 \quad \text{Solve for } x.$$

STEP 4 Knowing $x = 1$, we can find y from the equation

$$y = 5x - 6 = 5(1) - 6 = -1 \quad x = 1$$

STEP 5 **CHECK:** $\begin{cases} 3(1) - 2(-1) = 3 + 2 = 5 \\ 5(1) - (-1) = 5 + 1 = 6 \end{cases}$

The solution of the system is $x = 1, y = -1$ or, using ordered pairs, $(1, -1)$. ■

NOW WORK PROBLEM 15 USING SUBSTITUTION.

2 Solve Systems of Equations by Elimination

A second method for solving a system of linear equations is the *method of elimination.* This method is usually preferred over substitution if substitution leads to fractions or if the system contains more than two variables. Elimination also provides the necessary motivation for solving systems using matrices, the subject of the next section.

The idea behind the method of elimination is to replace the original system of equations by an equivalent system so that adding two of the equations eliminates a variable. The rules for obtaining equivalent equations are the same as those studied earlier. However, we may also interchange any two equations of the system and/or replace any equation in the system by the sum (or difference) of that equation and a nonzero multiple of any other equation in the system.

Rules for Obtaining an Equivalent System of Equations

1. Interchange any two equations in the system.
2. Multiply (or divide) each side of an equation by the same nonzero constant.
3. Replace any equation in the system by the sum (or difference) of that equation and a nonzero multiple of any other equation in the system.

An example will give you the idea. As you work through the example, pay particular attention to the pattern being followed.

EXAMPLE 6 **Solving a System of Linear Equations Using Elimination**

Solve: $\begin{cases} 2x + 3y = 1 & (1) \\ -x + y = -3 & (2) \end{cases}$

SOLUTION Multiply each side of Equation (2) by 2 so that the coefficients of x in the two equations are opposites of one another. The result is the equivalent system

$$\begin{cases} 2x + 3y = 1 & (1) \\ -2x + 2y = -6 & (2) \end{cases}$$

Now replace Equation (2) of this system by the sum of the two equations, to obtain an equation containing just the variable y, which we can solve.

$$\begin{cases} 2x + 3y = 1 & (1) \\ \underline{-2x + 2y = -6} & (2) \end{cases}$$

$$5y = -5 \quad \text{Add (1) and (2).}$$

$$y = -1 \quad \text{Solve for } y.$$

Back-substitute this value for y in Equation (1) and simplify to get

$$2x + 3y = 1 \quad (1)$$

$$2x + 3(-1) = 1 \quad \text{Substitute } y = -1 \text{ in (1).}$$

$$2x = 4 \quad \text{Simplify.}$$

$$x = 2 \quad \text{Solve for } x.$$

The solution of the original system is $x = 2, y = -1$, or using ordered pairs, $(2, -1)$. We leave it to you to check the solution.

The procedure used in Example 6 is called the **method of elimination**. Notice the pattern of the solution. First, we eliminated the variable x from the second equation. Then we back-substituted; that is, we substituted the value found for y back into the first equation to find x.

Steps for Solving by Elimination

STEP 1 Select two equations from the system and replace them by two equivalent equations that, when added, eliminate at least one variable.

STEP 2 If there are additional equations in the original system, pair off each one with one of the equations selected in Step 1 and eliminate the same variable from them.

STEP 3 Continue Steps 1 and 2 on successive systems until one equation containing one variable remains.

STEP 4 Solve for this variable and back-substitute in previous equations until all the variables have been found.

STEP 5 Check the solution found.

NOW WORK PROBLEM 15 USING ELIMINATION.

Let's return to the movie theater example (Example 1).

EXAMPLE 7 **Movie Theater Ticket Sales**

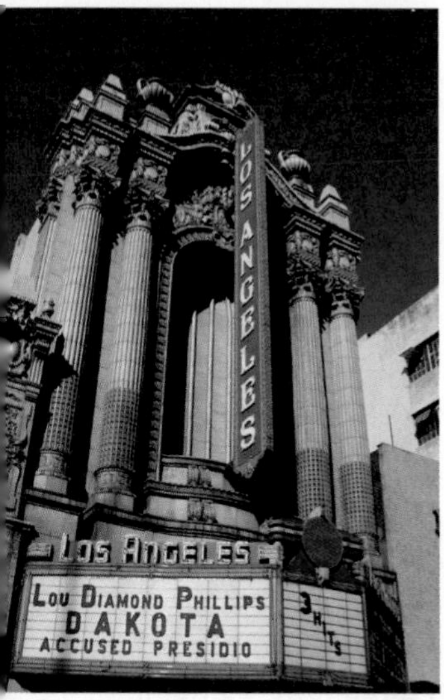

A movie theater sells tickets for \$8.00 each, with seniors receiving a discount of \$2.00. One evening the theater sold 525 tickets and took in \$3580 in revenue. How many of each type of ticket were sold?

SOLUTION If x represents the number of tickets sold at \$8.00 and y the number of tickets sold at the discounted price of \$6.00, then the given information results in the system of equations

$$\begin{cases} 8x + 6y = 3580 & (1) \\ x + y = 525 & (2) \end{cases}$$

Use elimination and multiply Equation (2) by -6; then add the equations.

$$\begin{aligned} &\begin{cases} 8x + 6y = 3580 \\ -6x - 6y = -3150 \end{cases} && \begin{matrix} (1) \\ (2) \end{matrix} \\ &2x = 430 && \text{Add (1) and (2).} \\ &x = 215 && \text{Solve for } x. \end{aligned}$$

Since $x + y = 525$, then $y = 525 - x = 525 - 215 = 310$. We conclude that 215 nondiscounted tickets and 310 senior discount tickets were sold. ■

NOW WORK PROBLEM 47.

3 Identify Inconsistent Systems of Equations Containing Two Variables

The previous examples dealt with consistent systems of equations that had one solution. The next two examples deal with two other possibilities that may occur, the first being a system that has no solution.

EXAMPLE 8 **An Inconsistent System of Linear Equations**

Solve: $\begin{cases} 2x + y = 5 & (1) \\ 4x + 2y = 8 & (2) \end{cases}$

SOLUTION We choose to use the method of substitution and solve Equation (1) for y.

$$\begin{aligned} 2x + y &= 5 && (1) \\ y &= -2x + 5 && \text{Substract } 2x \text{ from each side.} \end{aligned}$$

Now substitute $y = -2x + 5$ for y in Equation (2) and solve for x.

$$\begin{aligned} 4x + 2y &= 8 && (2) \\ 4x + 2(-2x + 5) &= 8 && \text{Substract } y = -2x + 5 \text{ in (2).} \\ 4x - 4x + 10 &= 8 && \text{Remove parentheses.} \\ 0 \cdot x &= -2 && \text{Subtract 10 from each side.} \end{aligned}$$

This equation has no solution. We conclude that the system itself has no solution and is therefore inconsistent. ■

Figure 4 illustrates the pair of lines whose equations form the system in Example 8. Notice that the graphs of the two equations are lines, each with slope -2; one line has y-intercept $(0, 5)$, the other has y-intercept $(0, 4)$. The lines are parallel and have no point of intersection. This geometric statement is equivalent to the algebraic statement that the system is inconsistent and has no solution.

FIGURE 4

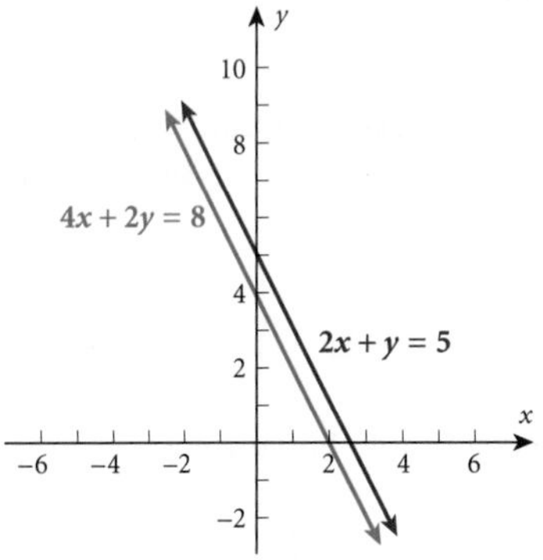

NOW WORK PROBLEM 19.

4 Express the Solutions of a System of Dependent Equations Containing Two Variables

EXAMPLE 9 Solving a System of Linear Equations with Infinitely Many Solutions

Solve: $\begin{cases} 2x + y = 4 & (1) \\ -6x - 3y = -12 & (2) \end{cases}$

SOLUTION Use the method of elimination:

$$\begin{cases} 2x + y = 4 & (1) \\ -6x - 3y = -12 & (2) \end{cases}$$

$$\begin{cases} 6x + 3y = 12 & (1) \\ -6x - 3y = -12 & (2) \end{cases}$$ Multiply each side of Equation (1) by 3.

$$\begin{cases} 6x + 3y = 12 & (1) \\ 0 = 0 & (2) \end{cases}$$ Replace Equation (2) by the sum of Equations (1) and (2).

The original system is equivalent to a system containing one equation, so the equations are dependent. This means that any values of x and y for which $6x + 3y = 12$ (or, equivalently, $2x + y = 4$) are solutions. For example, $x = 2, y = 0$; $x = 0, y = 4$; $x = -2$, $y = 8$; $x = 4, y = -4$; and so on, are solutions. There are, in fact, infinitely many values of x and y for which $2x + y = 4$, so the original system has infinitely many solutions. We will write the solutions of the original system either as

$$y = 4 - 2x$$

where x can be any real number, or as

$$x = 2 - \frac{1}{2}y$$

where y can be any real number.

Using ordered pairs, we write the solution as $\{(x, y) \mid y = -2x + 4,\ x \text{ any real number}\}$ or as $\left\{(x, y) \mid x = 2 - \frac{1}{2}y,\ y \text{ any real number}\right\}$. ■

FIGURE 5

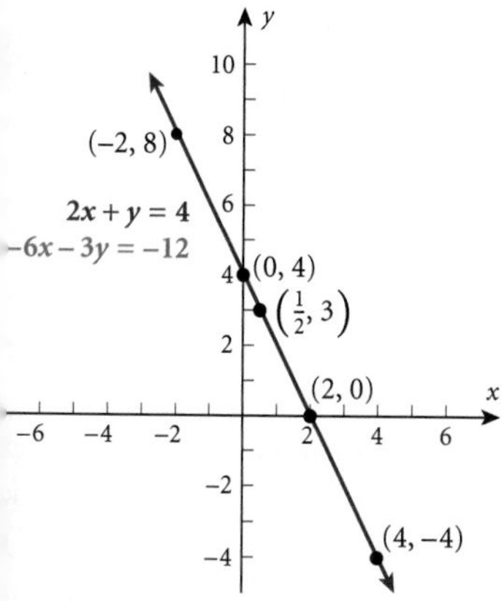

Figure 5 illustrates the situation presented in Example 9. Notice that the graphs of the two equations are lines, each with slope -2 and each with y-intercept $(0, 4)$. The lines are coincident. Notice also that Equation (2) in the original system is -3 times Equation (1), indicating that the two equations are dependent.

For the system in Example 9 we can find some of the infinite number of solutions by assigning values to x and then finding $y = 4 - 2x$. When we express the solution in this way, we call x a **parameter.**

If $x = 4$, then $y = -4$. This is the point $(4, -4)$ on the graph.

If $x = 0$, then $y = 4$. This is the point $(0, 4)$ on the graph.

If $x = \frac{1}{2}$, then $y = 3$. This is the point $\left(\frac{1}{2}, 3\right)$ on the graph.

Alternatively, if we express the solution in the form $x = 2 - \frac{1}{2}y$, then y is the parameter and we can assign values to y in order to find x.

If $y = -4$, then $x = 2 - \frac{1}{2}(-4) = 4$ This is the point $(4, -4)$ on the graph.

If $y = 0$, then $x = 2 - \frac{1}{2}(0) = 2$ This is the point $(2, 0)$ on the graph.

If $y = 8$, then $x = 2 - \frac{1}{2}(8) = -2$ This is the point $(-2, 8)$ on the graph.

NOW WORK PROBLEM 21.

5 Solve Systems of Three Equations Containing Three Variables

Just as with a system of two linear equations containing two variables, a system of three linear equations containing three variables has either (1) exactly one solution (a consistent system with independent equations), or (2) no solution (an inconsistent system), or (3) infinitely many solutions (a consistent system with dependent equations).

We can view the problem of solving a system of three linear equations containing three variables as a geometry problem. The graph of each equation in such a system is a plane in space. A system of three linear equations containing three variables represents three planes in space. Figure 6 illustrates some of the possibilities.

FIGURE 6

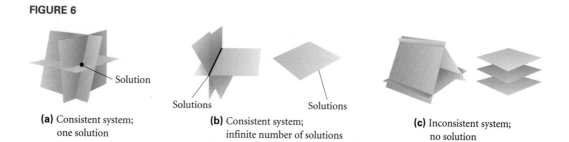

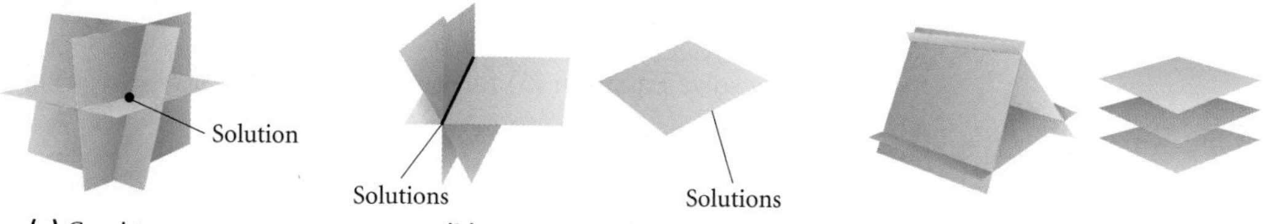

(a) Consistent system; one solution

(b) Consistent system; infinite number of solutions

(c) Inconsistent system; no solution

Typically, when solving a system of three linear equations containing three variables, we use the method of elimination. Recall that the idea behind the method of elimination is to form equivalent equations so that adding two of the equations eliminates a variable.

EXAMPLE 10 **Solving a System of Three Linear Equations with Three Variables Using Elimination**

Use the method of elimination to solve the system of equations.

$$\begin{cases} x + y - z = -1 & (1) \\ 4x - 3y + 2z = 16 & (2) \\ 2x - 2y - 3z = 5 & (3) \end{cases}$$

SOLUTION For a system of three equations, we attempt to eliminate one variable at a time, using pairs of equations, until an equation with a single variable remains. Our plan of attack on this system will be to use Equation (1) to eliminate the variable x from Equations (2) and (3). Alternatively, we could use Equation (1) to eliminate either y or z from Equations (2) and (3). Try one of these for yourself.

Begin by multiplying each side of Equation (1) by -4 and adding the result to Equation (2). (Do you see why? The coefficients of x are now opposites of each other.) Now multiply Equation (1) by -2 and add the result to Equation (3). Notice that these two procedures result in the removal of the x-variable from Equations (2) and (3).

$$\begin{array}{rl} x + y - z = -1 & \text{(1) Multiply by } -4. \\ 4x - 3y + 2z = 16 & \text{(2)} \end{array} \qquad \begin{array}{rl} -4x - 4y + 4z = 4 & \text{(1)} \\ 4x - 3y + 2z = 16 & \text{(2)} \\ \hline -7y + 6z = 20 & \text{Add.} \end{array}$$

$$\begin{array}{rl} x + y - z = -1 & \text{(1) Multiply by } -2. \\ 2x - 2y - 3z = 5 & \text{(3)} \end{array} \qquad \begin{array}{rl} -2x - 2y + 2z = 2 & \text{(1)} \\ 2x - 2y - 3z = 5 & \text{(3)} \\ \hline -4y - z = 7 & \text{Add.} \end{array}$$

$$\begin{cases} x + y - z = -1 & (1) \\ -7y + 6z = 20 & (2) \\ -4y - z = 7 & (3) \end{cases}$$

Now concentrate on Equations (2) and (3), treating them as a system of two equations containing two variables. It is easier to eliminate z. Multiply each side of Equation (3) by 6 and add Equations (2) and (3). The result is the new Equation (3).

$$\begin{array}{rl} -7y + 6z = 20 & \text{(2)} \\ -4y - z = 7 & \text{(3) Multiply by 6.} \end{array} \qquad \begin{array}{rl} -7y + 6z = 20 & \text{(2)} \\ -24y - 6z = 42 & \text{(3)} \\ \hline -31y = 62 & \text{Add.} \end{array} \qquad \begin{cases} x + y - z = -1 & (1) \\ -7y + 6z = 20 & (2) \\ -31y = 62 & (3) \end{cases}$$

Now solve Equation (3) for y by dividing both sides of the equation by -31.

$$\begin{cases} x + y - z = -1 & (1) \\ -7y + 6z = 20 & (2) \\ y = -2 & (3) \end{cases}$$

Back-substitute $y = -2$ in Equation (2) and solve for z.

$$\begin{aligned} -7y + 6z &= 20 && \text{(2)} \\ -7(-2) + 6z &= 20 && \text{Substitute } y = -2 \text{ in (2).} \\ 6z &= 6 && \text{Subtract 14 from each side.} \\ z &= 1 && \text{Divide each side by 6.} \end{aligned}$$

Finally, back-substitute $y = -2$ and $z = 1$ in Equation (1) and solve for x.

$$\begin{aligned} x + y - z &= -1 && \text{(1)} \\ x + (-2) - 1 &= -1 && \text{Substitute } y = -2 \text{ and } z = 1 \text{ in (1).} \\ x - 3 &= -1 && \text{Simplify.} \\ x &= 2 && \text{Add 3 to each side.} \end{aligned}$$

The solution of the original system is $x = 2$, $y = -2$, $z = 1$ or, using ordered triplets, $(2, -2, 1)$. You should verify this solution. ■

Look back over the solution given in Example 10. Note the pattern of removing one of the variables from two of the equations, followed by solving this system of two equations and two unknowns. Although which variables to remove is your choice, the methodology remains the same for all systems.

NOW WORK PROBLEM 31.

The previous example was a consistent system that had a unique solution. The next two examples deal with the two other possibilities that may occur.

6 Identify Inconsistent Systems of Equations Containing Three Variables

EXAMPLE 11 An Inconsistent System of Linear Equations

Solve: $\begin{cases} 2x + y - z = -2 & \text{(1)} \\ x + 2y - z = -9 & \text{(2)} \\ x - 4y + z = 1 & \text{(3)} \end{cases}$

SOLUTION Our plan of attack is the same as in Example 10. However, in this system, it seems easiest to eliminate the variable z first. Do you see why?

Add Equations (1) and (3). Add Equations (2) and (3).

$$\begin{aligned} 2x + y - z &= -2 && \text{(1)} \\ x - 4y + z &= -1 && \text{(3)} \\ \hline 3x - 3y &= -1 && \text{Add.} \end{aligned}$$

$$\begin{aligned} x + 2y - z &= -9 && \text{(2)} \\ x - 4y + z &= 1 && \text{(3)} \\ \hline 2x - 2y &= -8 && \text{Add.} \end{aligned}$$

$$\begin{cases} x - 4y + z = 1 & \text{(1)} \\ 3x - 3y = -1 & \text{(2)} \\ 2x - 2y = -8 & \text{(3)} \end{cases}$$

Now concentrate on Equations (2) and (3), treating them as a system of two equations containing two variables. Multiply each side of Equation (2) by $\frac{1}{3}$ and each side of Equation (3) by $\frac{1}{2}$.

$$\begin{array}{llll} 3x - 3y = -1 & \text{(2) Multiply by } \frac{1}{3}. & x - y = -\frac{1}{3} & (2) \\ 2x - 2y = -8 & \text{(3) Multiply by } \frac{1}{2}. & x - y = -4 & (3) \\ \hline & & -\frac{1}{3} = -4 & \end{array}$$

The contradiction tells us the system is inconsistent.

NOW WORK PROBLEM 33.

7 Express the Solutions of a System of Dependent Equations Containing Three Variables

EXAMPLE 12 Solving a System of Dependent Equations

Solve: $\begin{cases} x - 2y - z = 8 & (1) \\ 2x - 3y + z = 23 & (2) \\ 4x - 5y + 5z = 53 & (3) \end{cases}$

SOLUTION Multiply each side of Equation (1) by -2 and add the result to Equation (2). Also multiply each side of Equation (1) by -4 and add the result to Equation (3).

$$\begin{array}{llll} x - 2y - z = 8 & \text{(1) Multiply by } -2. & -2x + 4y + 2z = -16 & (1) \\ 2x - 3y + z = 23 & (2) & 2x - 3y + z = 23 & (2) \\ \hline & & y + 3z = 7 & \text{Add.} \end{array}$$

$$\begin{array}{llll} x - 2y - z = 8 & \text{(1) Multiply by } -4. & -4x + 8y + 4z = -32 & (1) \\ 4x - 5y + 5z = 53 & (3) & 4x - 5y + 5z = 53 & (2) \\ \hline & & 3y + 9z = 21 & \text{Add.} \end{array}$$

$$\begin{cases} x - 2y - z = 8 & (1) \\ y + 3z = 7 & (2) \\ 3y + 9z = 21 & (3) \end{cases}$$

Treat Equations (2) and (3) as a system of two equations containing two variables, and eliminate the y-variable by multiplying each side of Equation (2) by -3 and adding the result to Equation (3).

$$\begin{array}{llll} y + 3z = 7 & \text{Multiply by } -3. & -3y - 9z = -21 & \\ 3y + 9z = 21 & & 3y + 9z = 21 & \\ \hline & & 0 = 0 & \text{Add} \end{array}$$

$$\begin{cases} x - 2y - z = 8 & (1) \\ y + 3z = 7 & (2) \\ 0 = 0 & (3) \end{cases}$$

The original system is equivalent to a system containing two equations, so the original equations are dependent and the original system has infinitely many solutions. If we let represent any real number, then, solving Equation (2) for y, we determine that $y = -3z + 7$. Substitute this expression into Equation (1) to determine x in terms of z.

$$\begin{array}{rl} x - 2y - z = 8 & \text{(1)} \\ x - 2(-3z + 7) - z = 8 & \text{Substitute } y = -3z + 7 \text{ in (1).} \\ x + 6z - 14 - z = 8 & \text{Remove parentheses.} \\ x + 5z = 22 & \text{Combine like terms.} \\ x = -5z + 22 & \text{Solve for } x. \end{array}$$

Write the solution to the system as

$$\begin{cases} x = -5z + 22 \\ y = -3z + 7 \end{cases}$$

where z, the parameter, can be any real number.

To find specific solutions to the system, choose any value of z and use the equations $x = -5z + 22$ and $y = -3z + 7$ to determine x and y. For example, if $z = 0$, then $x = 22$ and $y = 7$, and if $z = 1$, then $x = 17$ and $y = 4$. ■

NOW WORK PROBLEM 35.

8 Solve Applied Problems Involving Systems of Equations

In economics, the **supply equation** is used to determine the amount of a product that a company is willing to make available for sale at a given price. The **demand equation** is the amount of a product that consumers are willing to purchase at a given price.

EXAMPLE 13 Supply and Demand Equations

Suppose that the quantity supplied S and the quantity demanded D of an mp3 player are given by the equations

$$S = 60p - 900 \qquad D = -15p + 2850$$

where p is the price, in dollars, of the mp3 player.

(a) The **equilibrium price** or **market price** of a product is the price at which quantity supplied equals quantity demanded. That is, the equilibrium price is the price for which $S = D$. Find the equilibrium price of the mp3 player.

(b) What is the **equilibrium quantity**, the amount demanded (or supplied) at the equilibrium price?

(c) Graph the supply equation and the demand equation. Label the equilibrium point.

(d) What happens when the price is less than the equilibrium price?

(e) What happens if the price exceeds the equilibrium price?

SOLUTION **(a)** To find the equilibrium price, solve the system of equations.

$$\begin{cases} S = 60p - 900 \\ D = -15p + 2850 \\ S = D \end{cases}$$

Using substitution, we are led to a single equation involving the price p.

$$\begin{aligned} 60p - 900 &= -15p + 2850 && S = 60p - 900;\ D = -15p + 2850;\ S = D \\ 60p &= -15p + 3750 && \text{Add 900 to each side.} \\ 75p &= 3750 && \text{Add } 15p \text{ to each side.} \\ p &= \$50 && \text{Divide each side by 75.} \end{aligned}$$

The equilibrium price is \$50 per mp3 player.

(b) To find the equilibrium quantity, we evaluate either S or D at $p = 50$.

$$S = 60(50) - 900 = 2100 \qquad S = 60p - 900;\ p = 50$$

The equilibrium quantity is 2100 mp3 players. At a price of \$50, the company will produce and sell 2100 mp3 players and have no shortages or excess inventory.

(c) Figure 7 shows the graphs of the supply and demand equations with the equilibriur point labeled.

(d) Look at Figure 7. If the price is less than $50, the demand is greater than the suppl which means the mp3 player would be hard to find.

(e) Look at Figure 7. If the price exceeds $50, supply is greater than demand, whic means there is excess inventory (unsold mp3 players).

FIGURE 7

$S = 60p - 900$

S, D

Quantity Supplied, Quantity Demanded

3000 (0, 2850)

Equilibrium point

2000 (50, 2100)

1000

$D = -15p + 2850$

(15, 0)

50   100 p

Price ($)

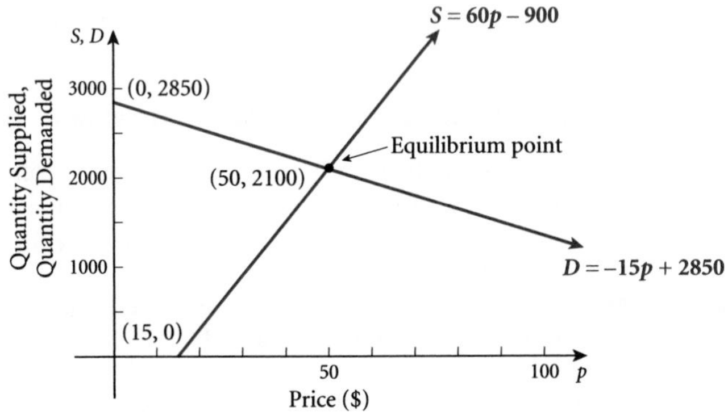

EXAMPLE 14   Financial Planning

Erica wants to invest long term the $30,000 she inherited from her great-aunt. Ove the next 10 years she hopes to have earnings averaging $2000 per year. Based on th yearly average return for 10 years ending December 31, 2009, her financial advisc recommended three funds: Franklin Total Return at 5%, Franklin Strategic Income ; 6%, and Franklin High Income at 7% that would allow Erica to achieve her goal whi providing diversification. Prepare a table showing the various ways Erica can achiev her goal.

Source: www.franklintempleton.com.

SOLUTION Begin by naming the variables: Let x be the amount invested in Total Return, y th amount invested in Strategic Incomes, and z the amount invested in High Income. The the average annual amount earned by each investment choice is expected to be

Total Return: $0.05x$ Strategic Income: $0.06y$ High Income: $0.07z$

Since Erica's goal is to average $2000 each year from these investments, we have th equation

$$0.05x + 0.06y + 0.07z = 2000$$

The total amount available to invest is $30,000, which leads to the equation

$$x + y + z = 30{,}000$$

These two equations form the system

$$\begin{cases} 0.05x + 0.06y + 0.07z = 2000 & (1) \\ x + y + z = 30{,}000 & (2) \end{cases}$$

Solve the system using elimination. We choose to eliminate z by multiplying Equation (2) by -0.07 and adding the equations.

$$\begin{cases} 0.05x + 0.06y + 0.07z = 2000 & (1) \\ -0.07x - 0.07y - 0.07z = -2100 & (2) \\ \hline -0.02x - 0.01y = -100 & \text{Add.} \end{cases}$$

Solve for y.

$$\begin{aligned} 0.01y &= -0.02x + 100 \\ y &= -2x + 10{,}000 && \text{Multiply by 100.} \end{aligned}$$

Back-substituting into the equation $x + y + z = 30{,}000$ and solving for z, we have

$$\begin{aligned} x + (-2x + 10{,}000) + z &= 30{,}000 && x + y + z = 30{,}000;\ y = -2x + 10{,}000 \\ -x + z &= 20{,}000 && \text{Simplify.} \\ z &= x + 20{,}000 && \text{Solve for } z. \end{aligned}$$

The solution of the system is

$$\begin{cases} y = -2x + 10{,}000 \\ z = x + 20{,}000 \end{cases}$$

where x is the parameter.

Now, the variable x must be nonnegative and cannot exceed \$5000, since any value of $x > 5000$ makes the variable y negative.

Set up a table as shown in Table 1.

TABLE 1

Total Return, x	Strategic Income, y	High Income, z	Amount Invested
0	10,000	20,000	30,000
1000	8000	21,000	30,000
2000	6000	22,000	30,000
3000	4000	23,000	30,000
4000	2000	24,000	30,000
5000	0	25,000	30,000

Table 1 shows six plans that Erica could follow to achieve her objective. ■

NOW WORK PROBLEM 65.

EXERCISE 2.1 Answers Begin on Page AN–9.

'Are You Prepared?' Problems Answers are given at the end of these exercises. If you get a wrong answer, read the pages listed in red.

1. ***True or False*** The lines $3x - 4y = 24$ and $3x - 4y = 12$ are parallel. (pp. 22–26)
2. Solve: $2x - 6 = 6 - 4x$ (p. A–24)
3. Find the point of intersection of the lines $y = 60x - 900$ and $y = -15x + 2850$. (pp. 22–26)
4. Solve for x if $2x + 3z = 6$. (p. A–24)

Concepts and Vocabulary

5. ***True or False*** A system of two linear equations containing two variables always has at least one solution.
6. A system of equations that has no solution is called ______.

Skill Building

In Problems 7–14, decide whether the values of the variables listed are solutions of the system of equations.

7. $\begin{cases} 2x - y = 5 \\ 5x + 2y = 8 \end{cases}$ $x = 2, y = -1$

8. $\begin{cases} 3x + 2y = 2 \\ x - 7y = -30 \end{cases}$ $x = 2, y = 4$

9. $\begin{cases} 3x + 4y = 4 \\ \frac{1}{2}x - 3y = -\frac{1}{2} \end{cases}$ $x = 2, y = \frac{1}{2}$

10. $\begin{cases} 2x + \frac{1}{2}y = 0 \\ 3x - 4y = -\frac{19}{2} \end{cases}$ $x = -\frac{1}{2}, y = 2$

11. $\begin{cases} 3x + 3y + 2z = 4 \\ x - y - z = 0 \\ 2y - 3z = -8 \end{cases}$ $x = 1, y = -1, z = 2$

12. $\begin{cases} 4x - z = 7 \\ 8x + 5y - z = 0 \\ -x - y + 5z = 6 \end{cases}$ $x = 2, y = -3, z = 1$

13. $\begin{cases} 3x + 3y + 2z = 4 \\ x - 3y + z = 10 \\ 5x - 2y - 3z = 8 \end{cases}$ $x = 2, y = -2, z = 2$

14. $\begin{cases} 4x - 5z = 6 \\ 5y - z = -17 \\ -x - 6y + 5z = 24 \end{cases}$ $x = 4, y = -3, z = 2$

In Problems 15–42, solve each system of equations. If the system has no solution, say that it is inconsistent.

15. $\begin{cases} 5x - y = 13 \\ 2x + 3y = 12 \end{cases}$

16. $\begin{cases} x + 3y = 5 \\ 2x - 3y = -8 \end{cases}$

17. $\begin{cases} 3x - 6y = 2 \\ 5x + 4y = 1 \end{cases}$

18. $\begin{cases} 2x + 4y = \frac{2}{3} \\ 3x - 5y = -10 \end{cases}$

19. $\begin{cases} 2x + y = 1 \\ 4x + 2y = 3 \end{cases}$

20. $\begin{cases} x - y = 5 \\ -3x + 3y = 2 \end{cases}$

21. $\begin{cases} x + 2y = 4 \\ 2x + 4y = 8 \end{cases}$

22. $\begin{cases} 3x - y = 7 \\ 9x - 3y = 21 \end{cases}$

23. $\begin{cases} 2x - 3y = -1 \\ 10x + y = 11 \end{cases}$

24 $\begin{cases} 3x - 2y = 0 \\ 5x + 10y = 4 \end{cases}$

25. $\begin{cases} 2x + 3y = 6 \\ x - y = \frac{1}{2} \end{cases}$

26. $\begin{cases} \frac{1}{2}x + y = -2 \\ x - 2y = 8 \end{cases}$

27. $\begin{cases} \frac{1}{2}x + \frac{1}{3}y = 3 \\ \frac{1}{4}x - \frac{2}{3}y = -1 \end{cases}$

28. $\begin{cases} \frac{1}{3}x - \frac{3}{2}y = -5 \\ \frac{3}{4}x + \frac{1}{3}y = 11 \end{cases}$

29. $\begin{cases} x - y = 6 \\ 2x - 3z = 16 \\ 2y + z = 4 \end{cases}$

30. $\begin{cases} 2x + y = -4 \\ -2y + 4z = 0 \\ 3x - 2z = -11 \end{cases}$

31. $\begin{cases} x - 2y + 3z = 7 \\ 2x + y + z = 4 \\ -3x + 2y - 2z = -10 \end{cases}$

32. $\begin{cases} 2x + y - 3z = -2 \\ -2x + 2y + z = -9 \\ 3x - 4y - 3z = 15 \end{cases}$

33. $\begin{cases} x - y - z = 1 \\ 2x + 3y + z = 2 \\ 3x + 2y = 0 \end{cases}$

34. $\begin{cases} 2x - 3y - z = 0 \\ -x + 2y + z = 5 \\ 3x - 4y - z = 1 \end{cases}$

35. $\begin{cases} x - y - z = 1 \\ -x + 2y - 3z = -4 \\ 3x - 2y - 7z = 0 \end{cases}$

36. $\begin{cases} 2x - 3y - z = 0 \\ 3x + 2y + 2z = 2 \\ x + 5y + 3z = 2 \end{cases}$

37. $\begin{cases} 2x - 2y + 3z = 6 \\ 4x - 3y + 2z = 0 \\ -2x + 3y - 7z = 1 \end{cases}$

38. $\begin{cases} 3x - 2y + 2z = 6 \\ 7x - 3y + 2z = -1 \\ 2x - 3y + 4z = 0 \end{cases}$

39. $\begin{cases} x + y - z = 6 \\ 3x - 2y + z = -5 \\ x + 3y - 2z = 14 \end{cases}$

40. $\begin{cases} x - y + z = -4 \\ 2x - 3y + 4z = -15 \\ 5x + y - 2z = 12 \end{cases}$

41. $\begin{cases} x + 2y - z = -3 \\ 2x - 4y + z = -7 \\ -2x + 2y - 3z = 4 \end{cases}$

42. $\begin{cases} x + 4y - 3z = -8 \\ 3x - y + 3z = 12 \\ x + y + 6z = 1 \end{cases}$

Applications

43. Dimensions of a Floor The perimeter of a rectangular floor is 90 feet. Find the dimensions of the floor if the length is twice the width.

44. Dimensions of a Field The length of fence required to enclose a rectangular field is 3000 meters. What are the dimensions of the field if the difference between its length and width i 50 meters?

45. Agriculture According to the Illinois Farm Business Management Association, in 2008 in the state of Illinois, the nonlan production cost for planting corn was \$512 per acre and th nonland cost for planting soybeans was $336 per acre. The average Illinois farm used 368 acres of land to raise corn and soybeans and budgeted $146,671 for planting these crops. If all the land and all the money budgeted is used, how many acres of each crop should be planted?

Source: Illinois Farm Business Management Association

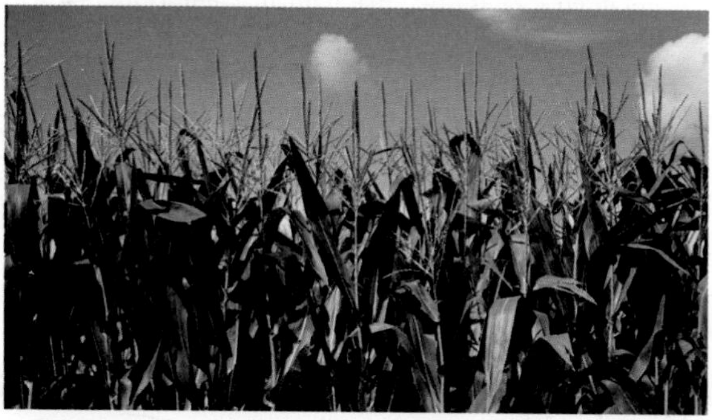

6. **Movie Theater Tickets** The Coral movie theater charges $9.00 for adults and $7.00 for senior citizens. On a day when 325 people paid an admission, the total receipts were $2495. How many who paid were adults? How many were seniors?

7. **Mixing Nuts** A store sells cashews for $5.00 per pound and peanuts for $1.50 per pound. The manager decides to mix 30 pounds of peanuts with some cashews and sell the mixture for $3.00 per pound. How many pounds of cashews should be mixed with the peanuts so that the mixture will produce the same revenue as would selling the nuts separately?

8. **Financial Planning** A recently retired couple needs $6000 per year to supplement their Social Security. They have $150,000 to invest to obtain this income. They have decided on two investment options: Corporate bonds yielding 6% per annum and a Bank Certificate yielding 3% per annum.

(a) How much should be invested in each to realize exactly $6000?

(b) If, after two years, the couple requires $7000 per year in income, how should they reallocate their investment to achieve the new amount?

9. **Cost of Food in Japan** In Osaka, Japan, the cost of three 1-liter cartons of whole milk and two 330-gram packages of tofu is 1002 yen. Three packages of tofu cost 8 yen more than two cartons of whole milk. What is the cost of a carton of whole milk? What is the cost for a package of tofu?

Source: www.tanutech.com/japan/jprice.html (July 2006)

0. **Cost of Fast Food** Four large cheeseburgers and two chocolate shakes cost a total of $7.90. Two shakes cost 15¢ more than one cheeseburger. What is the cost of a cheeseburger? What is the cost of a shake?

1. **Computing a Refund** The grocery store we use does not mark prices on its goods. My wife went to this store, bought three 1-pound packages of bacon and two cartons of eggs, and paid a total of $7.45. Not knowing that she went to the store, I also went to the same store, purchased two 1-pound packages of bacon and three cartons of eggs, and paid a total of $6.45. Now we want to return two 1-pound packages of bacon and two cartons of eggs. How much will be refunded?

52. **Blending Coffees** A coffee manufacturer wants to market a new blend of coffee that will cost $5 per pound by mixing $3.75-per-pound coffee and $8-per-pound coffee. What amounts of the $3.75-per-pound coffee and $8-per-pound coffee should be blended to obtain the desired mixture? [*Hint:* Assume the total weight of the desired blend is 100 pounds.]

53. **Pharmacy** A doctor's prescription calls for a daily intake of liquid containing 40 mg of vitamin C and 30 mg of vitamin D. Your pharmacy stocks two liquids that can be used: one contains 20% vitamin C and 30% vitamin D, the other 40% vitamin C and 20% vitamin D. How many milligrams of each liquid should be mixed to fill the prescription?

54. **Pharmacy** A doctor's prescription calls for the creation of pills that contain 12 units of vitamin B_{12} and 12 units of vitamin E. Your pharmacy stocks two powders that can be used to make these pills: one contains 20% vitamin B_{12} and 30% vitamin E, the other 40% vitamin B_{12} and 20% vitamin E. How many units of each powder should be mixed in each pill?

55. **Diet Preparation** A 600- to 700-pound yearling horse needs 33.0 grams of calcium and 21.0 grams of phosphorus per day for a healthy diet. A farmer provides a combination of rolled oats and molasses to provide those nutrients. Rolled oats provide 0.41 grams of calcium per pound and 1.95 grams of phosphorus per pound, while molasses provides 3.35 grams of calcium per pound and 0.36 grams of phosphorus per pound. How many pounds each of rolled oats and molasses should the farmer feed the yearling in order to meet the daily requirements?

Source: *Balancing Rations for Horses*, R. D. Setzler, Washington State University

56. **Restaurant Management** A restaurant manager wants to purchase 200 sets of dishes. One design costs $25 per set, while another costs $45 per set. If she only has $7400 to spend, how many of each design should be ordered?

57. **Theater Revenues** A Broadway theater has 500 seats, divided into orchestra, main, and balcony seating. Orchestra seats sell for $50, main seats for $35, and balcony seats for $25. If all the seats are sold, the gross revenue to the theater is $17,100. If all the main and balcony seats are sold, but only half the orchestra seats are sold, the gross revenue is $14,600. How many are there of each kind of seat?

58. **Theater Revenues** The Star movie theater charges $8.00 for adults, $4.50 for children, and $6.00 for senior citizens. One day the theater sold 405 tickets and collected $2320 in receipts. There were twice as many children's tickets sold as adult tickets. How many adults, children, and senior citizens went to the theater that day?

59. **Prices of Fast Food** One group of customers bought 8 deluxe hamburgers, 6 orders of large fries, and 6 large colas for $26.10.

A second group ordered 10 deluxe hamburgers, 6 large fries, and 8 large colas and paid \$31.60. Is there sufficient information to determine the price of each food item? If not, construct a table showing the various possibilities. Assume that the hamburgers cost between \$1.75 and \$2.25, the fries between \$0.75 and \$1.00. and the colas between \$0.60 and \$0.90.

60. **Prices of Fast Food** Use the information given in Problem 59. Suppose that a third group purchased 3 deluxe hamburgers, 2 large fries, and 4 large colas for \$10.95. Now is there sufficient information to determine the price of each food item? If so, determine each price.

61. **Supply and Demand** Suppose that the quantity supplied S and quantity demanded D of T-shirts at a concert are given by the following equations:

$$S = -200 + 50p$$
$$D = 1000 - 25p$$

where p is the price.

(a) Find the equilibrium price for T-shirts at this concert.
(b) What is the equilibrium quantity?
(c) Graph each equation and label the equilibrium point.
(d) What do you think will eventually happen to the price of T-shirts if quantity demanded is greater than quantity supplied?

62. **Supply and Demand** Suppose that the quantity supplied S and quantity demanded D of hot dogs at a baseball game are given by the following equations:

$$S = -2000 + 3000p$$
$$D = 10{,}000 - 1000p$$

where p is the price.

(a) Find the equilibrium price for hot dogs at the baseball game.
(b) What is the equilibrium quantity?
(c) Graph each equation and label the equilibrium point.
(d) What do you think will eventually happen to the price of hot dogs if quantity demanded is less than quantity supplied?

63. **IS-LM Model in Economics** In economics, the IS curve is a linear equation that represents all combinations of income Y and interest rates r that maintain an equilibrium in the market for goods in the economy. The LM curve is a linear equation that represents all combinations of income Y and interest rates r that maintain an equilibrium in the market for money in the economy. In an economy, suppose the equilibrium level of income (in millions of dollars) and interest rates satisfy the system of equations

$$\begin{cases} 0.06Y - 5000r = 240 \\ 0.06Y + 6000r = 900 \end{cases}$$

Find the equilibrium level of income and the interest rate.

64. **IS-LM Model in Economics** In economics, the IS curve is a linear equation that represents all combinations of income Y and interest rates r that maintain an equilibrium in the market for goods in the economy. The LM curve is a linear equation that represents all combinations of income Y and interest rates r that maintain an equilibrium in the market for money in the economy. In an economy, suppose the equilibrium level of income (in millions of dollars) and interest rates satisfy the system of equations

$$\begin{cases} 0.05Y - 1000r = 10 \\ 0.05Y + 800r = 100 \end{cases}$$

Find the equilibrium level of income and the interest rate.

65. **Financial Planning** Nathan wants to invest long term the \$70,000 profit he made on the sale of his house. Over 10 years he hopes to have earnings averaging \$5000 per year. Based on the yearly average return for 10 years ending December 31, 2009, his financial advisor recommended three funds: Mutual Shares at 4%, Franklin Strategic Income at 6%, and Franklin Small Cap Value at 8% that would allow Nathan to achieve his goal while providing diversification.

(a) Prepare a table showing the various ways Nathan can achieve his goal.
(b) What advice would you give him regarding the amount to invest and the choices available?

Source: Franklin Templeton

66. **Financial Planning** A married couple wants to invest \$60,000 long term to supplement their retirement income. They hope to have earnings averaging \$4000 per year. Based on the yearly average return for 10 years ending December 31, 2009, their financial advisor recommended three funds: Franklin Total Return at 5%, Franklin Strategic Income at 6%, and Franklin Small Cap Value at 8% that would allow them to achieve their goal while providing diversification.

(a) Prepare a table showing the various ways they can achieve their goal.
(b) After seeing the table, the couple asked that the amount invested in the Total Return Fund be twice that invested in the Small Cap Value Fund, how does that change the investment program?

Source: Franklin Templeton

Discussion and Writing

67. Make up three systems of two linear equations containing two variables, one that has no solution, one that has exactly one solution, and one that has infinitely many solutions. Give the three systems to a friend to solve and critique.

68. Write a brief paragraph outlining your strategy for solving a system of two linear equations containing two variables.

9. Do you prefer the method of substitution or the method of elimination for solving a system of two linear equations containing two variables? Give reasons.

70. Look at the table obtained in Example 14. What advice would you give this couple? Provide reasons.

'Are You Prepared?' Answers

1. True   **2.** $\{2\}$ **3.** $(50, 2100)$ **4.** $x = -\dfrac{3}{2}z + 3$

2.2 Systems of Linear Equations: Gaussian Elimination

OBJECTIVES   **1** Write the augmented matrix of a system of linear equations (p. 69)
   2 Write a system of linear equations from an augmented matrix (p. 71)
   3 Perform row operations on a matrix (p. 71)
   4 Solve a system of linear equations using Gaussian elimination (p. 73)
   5 Express the solution of a system with an infinite number of solutions (p. 78)
   6 Use Gaussian elimination to identify an inconsistent system (p. 81)
   7 Solve applied problems involving systems of equations (p. 81)

The systematic approach of the method of elimination for solving a system of linear equations provides another method of solution that involves a simplified notation using a *matrix*.

A **matrix** is defined as a rectangular array of numbers, enclosed by brackets. The numbers are referred to as the **entries** of the matrix. A matrix is further identified by naming its *rows* and *columns*. Some examples of matrices are

Column 1 Column 2

Row 1 $\begin{bmatrix} 8 & 0 \\ 1 & 3 \\ -2 & 4 \end{bmatrix}$
Row 2
Row 3

(a)

Column 1 Column 2 Column 3

Row 1 $\begin{bmatrix} 4 & 1 & -3 \\ 2 & 1 & 2 \end{bmatrix}$
Row 2

(b)

Column 1 Column 2

Row 1 $\begin{bmatrix} 4 & 3 \end{bmatrix}$

(c)

1 **Write the Augmented Matrix of a System of Linear Equations**

Consider the following systems of two linear equations containing two variables

$$\begin{cases} x + 4y = 14 \\ 3x - 2y = 0 \end{cases} \quad \text{and} \quad \begin{cases} u + 4v = 14 \\ 3u - 2v = 0 \end{cases}$$

We observe that, except for the symbols used to represent the variables, these two systems are identical. As a result, we can dispense altogether with the letters used to symbolize the variables, provided we have some means of keeping track of them. A matrix serves us well in this regard.

When a matrix is used to represent a system of linear equations, it is called the **augmented matrix** of the system. For example,

System of Equations

$$\begin{cases} x + 4y = 14 \quad (1) \\ 3x - 2y = 0 \quad (2) \end{cases}$$

Augmented Matrix

Row 1 [Equation (1)]
Row 2 [Equation (2)]

Column 1	Column 2	Column 3
x	y	right-hand side

$$\begin{bmatrix} 1 & 4 & \bigm| & 14 \\ 3 & -2 & \bigm| & 0 \end{bmatrix}$$

Here it is understood that column 1 contains the coefficients of the variable x, column 2 contains the coefficients of the variable y, and column 3 contains the numbers to the right of the equal sign. Each row of the matrix represents an equation of the system. Although not required, it has become customary to place a vertical bar in the matrix as a reminder of the equal sign.

In this book we shall follow the practice of using x and y to denote the variables for systems containing two variables. We will use x, y, and z for systems containing three variables; we will use subscripted variables (x_1, x_2, x_3, x_4, etc.) for systems containing four or more variables.

In writing the augmented matrix of a system, the variables of each equation must be on the left side of the equal sign and the constants on the right side. A variable that does not appear in an equation has a coefficient of 0.

EXAMPLE 1 Writing the Augmented Matrix of a System of Linear Equations

Write the augmented matrix of each system of equations.

(a) $$\begin{cases} 3x - 4y = -6 & (1) \\ 2x - 3y = -5 & (2) \end{cases}$$

(b) $$\begin{cases} 2x - y + z = 0 & (1) \\ x + z - 1 = 0 & (2) \\ x + 2y - 8 = 0 & (3) \end{cases}$$

(c) $$\begin{cases} 3x_1 - x_2 + x_3 + x_4 = 5 & (1) \\ 2x_1 + 6x_3 = 2 & (2) \end{cases}$$

SOLUTION **(a)** The augmented matrix is

$$\left[\begin{array}{cc|c} 3 & -4 & -6 \\ 2 & -3 & -5 \end{array}\right]$$

(b) Care must be taken that the system be written so that the coefficients of all variables are present (if any variable is missing, its coefficient is 0). Also, all constants must be to the right of the equal sign. We need to rearrange the given system as follows:

$$\begin{cases} 2x - y + z = 0 & (1) \\ x + z - 1 = 0 & (2) \\ x + 2y - 8 = 0 & (3) \end{cases}$$

$$\begin{cases} 2x - y + z = 0 & (1) \\ x + 0 \cdot y + z = 1 & (2) \\ x + 2y + 0 \cdot z = 8 & (3) \end{cases}$$

The augmented matrix is

$$\left[\begin{array}{ccc|c} 2 & -1 & 1 & 0 \\ 1 & 0 & 1 & 1 \\ 1 & 2 & 0 & 8 \end{array}\right]$$

(c) The augmented matrix is

$$\left[\begin{array}{cccc|c} 3 & -1 & 1 & 1 & 5 \\ 2 & 0 & 6 & 0 & 2 \end{array}\right]$$

■

NOW WORK PROBLEM 5.

2 Write a System of Linear Equations from an Augmented Matrix

EXAMPLE 2 Writing the System of Linear Equations from the Augmented Matrix

Write the system of linear equations corresponding to each augmented matrix.

(a) $\left[\begin{array}{cc|c} 5 & 2 & 13 \\ -3 & 1 & -10 \end{array}\right]$ **(b)** $\left[\begin{array}{ccc|c} 3 & -1 & -1 & 7 \\ 4 & 0 & 2 & 8 \\ 0 & 1 & 1 & 0 \end{array}\right]$

SOLUTION

(a) The matrix has two rows and so represents a system of two equations. The two columns to the left of the vertical bar indicate that the system has two variables. If x and y are used to denote these variables, the system of equations is

$$\begin{cases} 5x + 2y = 13 & (1) \\ -3x + y = -10 & (2) \end{cases}$$

(b) Since the augmented matrix has three rows, it represents a system of three equations. Since there are three columns to the left of the vertical bar, the system contains three variables. If x, y, and z are the three variables, the system of equations is

$$\begin{cases} 3x - y - z = 7 & (1) \\ 4x + 2z = 8 & (2) \\ y + z = 0 & (3) \end{cases}$$

■

3 Perform Row Operations on a Matrix

Row operations on a matrix are used to solve systems of equations when the system is written as an augmented matrix. There are three basic row operations.

Row Operations

1. Interchange any two rows.
2. Replace a row by a nonzero multiple of that row.
3. Replace a row by the sum of that row and a constant nonzero multiple of some other row.

These three row operations correspond to the three rules given earlier for obtaining an equivalent system of equations. When a row operation is performed on a matrix, the resulting matrix represents a system of equations equivalent to the system represented by the original matrix.

For example, consider the augmented matrix

$$\left[\begin{array}{rr|r} 1 & 2 & 3 \\ 4 & -1 & 2 \end{array}\right]$$

Suppose that we want to apply a row operation to this matrix that results in a matrix whose entry in row 2, column 1 is a 0. The row operation to use is

Multiply each entry in row 1 by -4 and add the result to the corresponding entry in row 2. (1

If we use R_2 to represent the new entries in row 2 and we use r_1 and r_2 to represent the original entries in rows 1 and 2, respectively, then we can represent the row operation in statement (1) by

$$R_2 = -4r_1 + r_2$$

Then

$$\left[\begin{array}{rr|r} 1 & 2 & 3 \\ 4 & -1 & 2 \end{array}\right] \xrightarrow[R_2 = -4r_1 + r_2]{} \left[\begin{array}{cc|c} 1 & 2 & 3 \\ -4(1) + 4 & -4(2) + (-1) & -4(3) + 2 \end{array}\right] = \left[\begin{array}{rr|r} 1 & 2 & 3 \\ 0 & -9 & -10 \end{array}\right]$$

As desired, we now have the entry 0 in row 2, column 1.

EXAMPLE 3 Applying a Row Operation to an Augmented Matrix

Apply the row operation $R_2 = -3r_1 + r_2$ to the augmented matrix

$$\left[\begin{array}{rr|r} 1 & -2 & 2 \\ 3 & -5 & 9 \end{array}\right]$$

SOLUTION The row operation $R_2 = -3r_1 + r_2$ tells us that the entries in row 2 are to be replaced by the entries obtained after multiplying each entry in row 1 by -3 and adding the result to the corresponding entry in row 2. Thus,

$$\left[\begin{array}{rr|r} 1 & -2 & 2 \\ 3 & -5 & 9 \end{array}\right] \xrightarrow[R_2 = -3r_1 + r_2]{} \left[\begin{array}{cc|c} 1 & -2 & 2 \\ -3(1) + 3 & (-3)(-2) + (-5) & -3(2) + 9 \end{array}\right] = \left[\begin{array}{rr|r} 1 & -2 & 2 \\ 0 & 1 & 3 \end{array}\right]$$

NOW WORK PROBLEM 17.

EXAMPLE 4 Finding a Particular Row Operation

Using the augmented matrix

$$\left[\begin{array}{rr|r} 1 & -2 & 2 \\ 0 & 1 & 3 \end{array}\right]$$

find a row operation that will result in this augmented matrix having a 0 in row 1, column 2.

SOLUTION We want a 0 in row 1, column 2. This result can be accomplished by multiplying row 2 by 2 and adding the result to row 1. That is, apply the row operation $R_1 = 2r_2 + r_1$.

$$\left[\begin{array}{rr|r} 1 & -2 & 2 \\ 0 & 1 & 3 \end{array}\right] \xrightarrow[R_1 = 2r_2 + r_1]{} \left[\begin{array}{cc|c} 2(0) + 1 & 2(1) + (-2) & 2(3) + 2 \\ 0 & 1 & 3 \end{array}\right] = \left[\begin{array}{rr|r} 1 & 0 & 8 \\ 0 & 1 & 3 \end{array}\right]$$

A word about the notation just introduced. A row operation such as $R_1 = 2r_2 + r_1$ changes the entries in row 1. Note also that for this type of row operation the entries in a given row are changed by multiplying the entries in some other row by an appropriate nonzero number and adding the results to the original entries of the row to be changed.

4 Solve a System of Linear Equations Using Gaussian Elimination

To solve a system of linear equations using matrices, we use row operations on the augmented matrix of the system to obtain a matrix that is in *row echelon form.*

Definition

A matrix is in **row echelon form** when

1. The entry in row 1, column 1 is a 1, and 0s appear below it.
2. The first nonzero entry in each row after the first row is a 1, 0s appear below it, and it appears to the right of the first nonzero entry in any row above.
3. Any rows that contain all 0s to the left of the vertical bar appear at the bottom.

For example, for a system of two linear equations containing two variables the augmented matrix is in row echelon form if it is in one of the forms

$$\underset{\text{(I)}}{\left[\begin{array}{cc|c} 1 & a & b \\ 0 & 0 & c \end{array}\right]} \quad \text{or} \quad \underset{\text{(II)}}{\left[\begin{array}{cc|c} 1 & a & b \\ 0 & 1 & c \end{array}\right]}$$

where a, b, and c are real numbers.

Look at the augmented matrix (I). The entry c in row 2 is either 0 or 1. If $c = 1$, then the system is inconsistent. (Do you see why? The second row gives rise to the equation $0x + 0y = 1$.) If $c = 0$, the system is consistent and has infinitely many solutions given by $x = b - ay$, where y is any real number.

Look at the augmented matrix (II). The second row represents the equation $y = c$. Then x can be found by back-substituting $y = c$ into the equation represented by the first row. The system is consistent and the solution is unique.

For a system of three equations containing three variables, the augmented matrix is in row echelon form if it is in one of the forms

$$\underset{\text{(I)}}{\left[\begin{array}{ccc|c} 1 & a & b & d \\ 0 & 1 & c & e \\ 0 & 0 & 1 & f \end{array}\right]} \quad \underset{\text{(II)}}{\left[\begin{array}{ccc|c} 1 & a & b & d \\ 0 & 1 & c & e \\ 0 & 0 & 0 & f \end{array}\right]} \quad \underset{\text{(III)}}{\left[\begin{array}{ccc|c} 1 & a & b & d \\ 0 & 0 & 1 & e \\ 0 & 0 & 0 & f \end{array}\right]} \quad \underset{\text{(IV)}}{\left[\begin{array}{ccc|c} 1 & a & b & d \\ 0 & 0 & 0 & e \\ 0 & 0 & 0 & f \end{array}\right]}$$

where a, b, c, d, e, and f are real numbers.

Look at the augmented matrix (1). We see that $z = f$ and that back-substitution using row 2 will get y and another back-substitution using row 1 will get x. The system is consistent and the solution is unique.

The remaining augmented matrices are consistent or inconsistent depending on the numbers a, b, c, d, e, and f. In practice, looking at the equations represented by the rows provides the necessary information.

The process of writing the augmented matrix of a system is called **Gaussian elimination.**

Two advantages of solving a system of equations by writing the augmented matrix in row echelon form are the following:

1. The process is algorithmic; that is, it consists of repetitive steps that can be programmed on a computer.
2. The process works on any system of linear equations, no matter how many equations or variables are present.

Let's see how Gaussian elimination is used to solve a system of linear equations. To see what is happening, we'll write the corresponding system of equations next to the matrix obtained after a row operation is performed.

EXAMPLE 5 Solving a System of Linear Equations Using Gaussian Elimination

Solve: $\begin{cases} 4x + 3y = 11 \\ x - 3y = -1 \end{cases}$

SOLUTION Write the augmented matrix that represents this system:

$$\left[\begin{array}{cc|c} 4 & 3 & 11 \\ 1 & -3 & -1 \end{array}\right] \qquad \begin{cases} 4x + 3y = 11 \\ x - 3y = -1 \end{cases}$$

The next step is to place a 1 in row 1, column 1. An interchange of rows 1 and 2 is the easiest way to do this.

$$\left[\begin{array}{cc|c} 4 & 3 & 11 \\ 1 & -3 & -1 \end{array}\right] \xrightarrow[R_2 = r_1]{R_1 = r_2} \left[\begin{array}{cc|c} 1 & -3 & -1 \\ 4 & 3 & 11 \end{array}\right] \qquad \begin{cases} x - 3y = -1 \\ 4x + 3y = 11 \end{cases}$$

Now we want a 0 under the entry 1 in column 1. (This eliminates the variable x from the second equation.) Use the row operation $R_2 = -4r_1 + r_2$.

$$\left[\begin{array}{cc|c} 1 & -3 & -1 \\ 4 & 3 & 11 \end{array}\right] \xrightarrow[R_2 = -4r_1 + r_2]{} \left[\begin{array}{cc|c} 1 & -3 & -1 \\ 0 & 15 & 15 \end{array}\right] \qquad \begin{cases} x - 3y = -1 \\ 15y = 15 \end{cases}$$

Now we want the entry 1 in row 2, column 2. (This makes it easy to solve for y.) Use $R_2 = \frac{1}{15}r_2$.

$$\left[\begin{array}{cc|c} 1 & -3 & -1 \\ 0 & 15 & 15 \end{array}\right] \xrightarrow[R_2 = \frac{1}{15}r_2]{} \left[\begin{array}{cc|c} 1 & -3 & -1 \\ 0 & 1 & 1 \end{array}\right] \qquad \begin{cases} x - 3y = -1 \\ y = 1 \end{cases}$$

This matrix is the row echelon form of the augmented matrix. The second row of the matrix on the right represents the equation $y = 1$. Using $y = 1$, back-substitute into the equation $x - 3y = -1$ (from the first row) to get

$$\begin{aligned} x - 3y &= -1 \\ x - 3(1) &= -1 \quad y = 1 \\ x &= 2 \end{aligned}$$

The solution of the system is $x = 2, y = 1$ or, using ordered pairs, (2, 1).

NOW WORK PROBLEM 39.

The steps used to solve the system of linear equations in Example 5 can be summarized as follows:

> ## Solving a System of Linear Equations Using Gaussian Elimination
>
> **STEP 1** Write the augmented matrix that represents the system.
>
> **STEP 2** Perform row operations that place the entry 1 in row 1, column 1.
>
> **STEP 3** Perform row operations that leave the entry 1 in row 1, column 1 unchanged, while causing 0s to appear below it in column 1.
>
> **STEP 4** Perform row operations that place the entry 1 in row 2, column 2, but leave the entries in column 1 unchanged. If it is impossible to place a 1 in row 2, column 2, then proceed to place a 1 in row 2, column 3. Once a 1 is in place, perform row operations to place 0s below it.
>
> **STEP 5** Now repeat Step 4, placing a 1 in the next row, but one column to the right, while leaving all entries in columns to the left unchanged. Continue until the bottom row or the vertical bar is reached. (If any rows are obtained that contain only 0's on the left side of the vertical bar, place such rows at the bottom of the matrix.)
>
> **STEP 6** The matrix that results is the row echelon form of the augmented matrix. Analyze the system of equations corresponding to it to solve the original system.

EXAMPLE 6   **Solving a System of Linear Equations Using Gaussian Elimination**

Solve: $\begin{cases} x - y + z = 8 & (1) \\ 2x + 3y - z = -2 & (2) \\ 3x - 2y - 9z = 9 & (3) \end{cases}$

SOLUTION

STEP 1   The augmented matrix of the system is

$$\begin{bmatrix} 1 & -1 & 1 & 8 \\ 2 & 3 & -1 & -2 \\ 3 & -2 & -9 & 9 \end{bmatrix}$$

STEP 2   Because the entry 1 is already present in row 1, column 1, we can go to Step 3.

STEP 3   Perform the row operations $R_2 = -2r_1 + r_2$ and $R_3 = -3r_1 + r_3$. Each of these leaves the entry 1 in row 1, column 1 unchanged, while causing 0s to appear under it.*

$$\begin{bmatrix} 1 & -1 & 1 & 8 \\ 2 & 3 & -1 & -2 \\ 3 & -2 & -9 & 9 \end{bmatrix} \xrightarrow[R_3 = -3r_1 + r_3]{R_2 = -2r_1 + r_2} \begin{bmatrix} 1 & -1 & 1 & 8 \\ 0 & 5 & -3 & -18 \\ 0 & 1 & -12 & -15 \end{bmatrix}$$

* You should convince yourself that doing both of these simultaneously is the same as doing the first followed by the second.

STEP 4 The easiest way to obtain the entry 1 in row 2, column 2 without altering column 1 is to interchange rows 2 and 3 (another way would be to multiply row 2 by $\frac{1}{5}$, but this introduces fractions).

$$\left[\begin{array}{rrr|r} 1 & -1 & 1 & 8 \\ 0 & 1 & -12 & -15 \\ 0 & 5 & -3 & -18 \end{array}\right]$$

To get a 0 under the 1 in row 2, column 2, perform the row operation $R_3 = -5r_2 + r_3$.

$$\left[\begin{array}{rrr|r} 1 & -1 & 1 & 8 \\ 0 & 1 & -12 & -15 \\ 0 & 5 & -3 & -18 \end{array}\right] \xrightarrow[R_3 = -5r_2 + r_3]{} \left[\begin{array}{rrr|r} 1 & -1 & 1 & 8 \\ 0 & 1 & -12 & -15 \\ 0 & 0 & 57 & 57 \end{array}\right]$$

STEP 5 Continuing, obtain a 1 in row 3, column 3 by using $R_3 = \frac{1}{57}r_3$.

$$\left[\begin{array}{rrr|r} 1 & -1 & 1 & 8 \\ 0 & 1 & -12 & -15 \\ 0 & 0 & 57 & 57 \end{array}\right] \xrightarrow[R_3 = \frac{1}{57}r_3]{} \left[\begin{array}{rrr|r} 1 & -1 & 1 & 8 \\ 0 & 1 & -12 & -15 \\ 0 & 0 & 1 & 1 \end{array}\right]$$

STEP 6 The matrix on the right is the row echelon form of the augmented matrix. The system of equations represented by the matrix in row echelon form is

$$\begin{cases} x - y + \quad z = \quad 8 & (1) \\ \quad\; y - 12z = -15 & (2) \\ \qquad\qquad z = \quad 1 & (3) \end{cases}$$

Using $z = 1$, back-substitute to get

$$\begin{cases} x - y + 1 = \quad 8 & (1) \\ \quad y - 12(1) = -15 & (2) \end{cases} \xrightarrow[\text{Simplify.}]{} \begin{cases} x - y = \quad 7 & (1) \\ \qquad y = -3 & (2) \end{cases}$$

So $y = -3$, and back-substituting into $x - y = 7$, we find that $x = 4$. The solution of the system is $x = 4$, $y = -3$, $z = 1$ or, using ordered triplets, $(4, -3, 1)$.

USING TECHNOLOGY

EXAMPLE 7 Solving a System of Linear Equations Using a Graphing Utility

Rework Example 6 using a graphing utility.

SOLUTION A graphing utility can be used to obtain the row echelon form of the augmented matrix. The augmented matrix of the system given in Example 6 is

$$\left[\begin{array}{rrr|r} 1 & -1 & 1 & 8 \\ 2 & 3 & -1 & -2 \\ 3 & -2 & -9 & 9 \end{array}\right]$$

Enter this matrix into a graphing utility and name it A. See Figure 8(a). Use the REF (Row Echelon Form) command on matrix A to obtain the results shown in Figure 8(b). Since the entire matrix does not fit on the screen, you will need to scroll right to see the rest of it. See Figure 8(c).

FIGURE 8

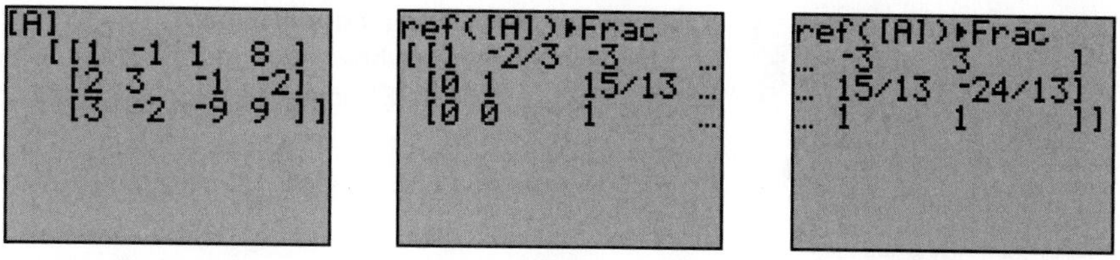

(a) (b) (c)

The system of equations represented by the matrix in row echelon form is

$$\begin{cases} x - \dfrac{2}{3}y - 3z = 3 & (1) \\ y + \dfrac{15}{13}z = -\dfrac{24}{13} & (2) \\ z = 1 & (3) \end{cases}$$

Using $z = 1$, back-substitute to get

$$\begin{cases} x - \dfrac{2}{3}y - 3(1) = 3 & (1) \\ y + \dfrac{15}{13}(1) = -\dfrac{24}{13} & (2) \end{cases} \xrightarrow{\text{Simplify.}} \begin{cases} x - \dfrac{2}{3}y = 6 & (1) \\ y = -\dfrac{39}{13} = -3 & (2) \end{cases}$$

Solve the second equation for y, to obtain $y = -3$. Back-substitute $y = -3$ into $x - \dfrac{2}{3}y = 6$, to find that $x = 4$. The solution of the system is $x = 4, y = -3, z = 1$ or, using ordered triplets, $(4, -3, 1)$. ■

Notice that the row echelon form of the augmented matrix using the graphing utility differs from the row echelon form in our algebraic solution, yet both matrices provide the same solution! This is because the two solutions used different row operations to obtain the row echelon form. In all likelihood, the two solutions parted ways in Step 4 of the algebraic solution, where we avoided introducing fractions by interchanging rows 2 and 3.

Sometimes it is advantageous to write a matrix in **reduced row echelon form**. In this form, row operations are used to obtain entries that are 0 above (as well as below) the leading 1 in a row. For example, the row echelon form obtained in the algebraic solution to Example 6 is

$$\left[\begin{array}{ccc|c} 1 & -1 & 1 & 8 \\ 0 & 1 & -12 & -15 \\ 0 & 0 & 1 & 1 \end{array}\right]$$

To write this matrix in reduced row echelon form, proceed as follows:

$$\left[\begin{array}{ccc|c} 1 & -1 & 1 & 8 \\ 0 & 1 & -12 & -15 \\ 0 & 0 & 1 & 1 \end{array}\right] \xrightarrow[R_1 = r_2 + r_1]{} \left[\begin{array}{ccc|c} 1 & 0 & -11 & -7 \\ 0 & 1 & -12 & -15 \\ 0 & 0 & 1 & 1 \end{array}\right] \xrightarrow[\substack{R_1 = 11r_3 + r_1 \\ R_2 = 12r_3 + r_2}]{} \left[\begin{array}{ccc|c} 1 & 0 & 0 & 4 \\ 0 & 1 & 0 & -3 \\ 0 & 0 & 1 & 1 \end{array}\right]$$

The matrix is now written in reduced row echelon form. The advantage of writing the matrix in this form is that the solution to the system, $x = 4, y = -3, z = 1$ is readily found without the need to back-substitute.

The process of writing the augmented matrix of a system of equations in reduced row echelon form is called **Gauss–Jordan elimination**.

FIGURE 9

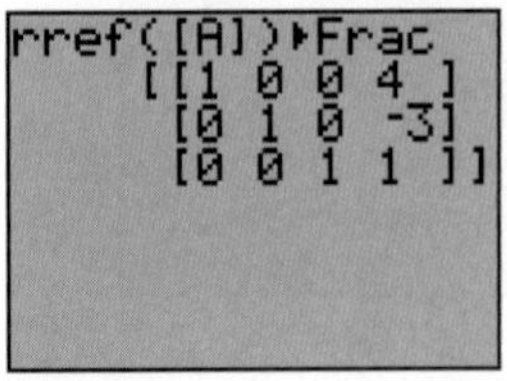

COMMENT Most graphing utilities also have the ability to put a matrix in reduced ro echelon form. Figure 9 shows the reduced row echelon form of the augmented matrix fro Example 7 using the RREF command on a TI-84 Plus graphing calculator.

NOW WORK PROBLEMS 45 AND 55.

5 Express the Solution of a System with an Infinite Number of Solutions

EXAMPLE 8 Solving a System of Linear Equations Using Gaussian Elimination (Infinitely Many Solutions)

Solve: $\begin{cases} 2x - 3y = 5 \\ 4x - 6y = 10 \end{cases}$

SOLUTION The augmented matrix representing this system is

$$\left[\begin{array}{cc|c} 2 & -3 & 5 \\ 4 & -6 & 10 \end{array}\right]$$

To place a 1 in row 1, column 1, use $R_1 = \frac{1}{2}r_1$:

$$\left[\begin{array}{cc|c} 2 & -3 & 5 \\ 4 & -6 & 10 \end{array}\right] \xrightarrow[R_1 = \frac{1}{2}r_1]{} \left[\begin{array}{cc|c} 1 & -\frac{3}{2} & \frac{5}{2} \\ 4 & -6 & 10 \end{array}\right]$$

To place a 0 in row 2, column 1, use $R_2 = -4r_1 + r_2$:

$$\left[\begin{array}{cc|c} 1 & -\frac{3}{2} & \frac{5}{2} \\ 4 & -6 & 10 \end{array}\right] \xrightarrow[R_2 = -4r_1 + r_2]{} \left[\begin{array}{cc|c} 1 & -\frac{3}{2} & \frac{5}{2} \\ 0 & 0 & 0 \end{array}\right]$$

The system of equations looks like

$$\begin{cases} x - \frac{3}{2}y = \frac{5}{2} \\ 0x + 0y = 0 \end{cases}$$

The second equation is true for any choice of x and y, so all numbers x and y that obe the first equation are solutions of the system. Since any point on the line $x - \frac{3}{2}y = \frac{5}{2}$ i a solution, there are an infinite number of solutions.

Using y as parameter, we can list some of these solutions by assigning values to y an then calculating x from the equation $x = \frac{3}{2}y + \frac{5}{2}$.

If $y = 0$, then $x = \frac{5}{2}$, so $x = \frac{5}{2}, y = 0$ is a solution.

If $y = 1$, then $x = 4$, so $x = 4, y = 1$ is a solution.

If $y = 5$, then $x = 10$, so $x = 10, y = 5$ is a solution.

If $y = -3$, then $x = -2$, so $x = -2, y = -3$ is a solution.

And so on.

We write the solution as

$$x = \frac{3}{2}y + \frac{5}{2}, \quad y \text{ is any real number}$$

or, using ordered pairs, as $\left\{(x, y) \middle| x = \frac{3}{2}y + \frac{5}{2}, y \text{ is any real number}\right\}$. ■

NOW WORK PROBLEM 41.

EXAMPLE 9 Solving a System of Linear Equations Using Gaussian Elimination (Infinitely Many Solutions)

$$\text{Solve: } \begin{cases} 6x - y - z = 4 & (1) \\ -12x + 2y + 2z = -8 & (2) \\ 5x + y - z = 3 & (3) \end{cases}$$

SOLUTION Start with the augmented matrix of the system. Then use row operations to obtain a 1 in row 1, column 1 and 0s in the remainder of column 1.

$$\left[\begin{array}{ccc|c} 6 & -1 & -1 & 4 \\ -12 & 2 & 2 & -8 \\ 5 & 1 & -1 & 3 \end{array}\right] \xrightarrow[R_1 = -r_3 + r_1]{} \left[\begin{array}{ccc|c} 1 & -2 & 0 & 1 \\ -12 & 2 & 2 & -8 \\ 5 & 1 & -1 & 3 \end{array}\right] \xrightarrow[\substack{R_2 = 12r_1 + r_2 \\ R_3 = -5r_1 + r_3}]{} \left[\begin{array}{ccc|c} 1 & -2 & 0 & 1 \\ 0 & -22 & 2 & 4 \\ 0 & 11 & -1 & -2 \end{array}\right]$$

Obtaining a 1 in row 2, column 2 without altering column 1 can be accomplished by $R_2 = -\frac{1}{22}r_2$, or by $R_3 = \frac{1}{11}r_3$ and interchanging rows 2 and 3, or by $R_2 = \frac{23}{11}r_3 + r_2$. We shall use the first of these.

$$\left[\begin{array}{ccc|c} 1 & -2 & 0 & 1 \\ 0 & -22 & 2 & 4 \\ 0 & 11 & -1 & -2 \end{array}\right] \xrightarrow[R_1 = -\frac{1}{22}r_2]{} \left[\begin{array}{ccc|c} 1 & -2 & 0 & 1 \\ 0 & 1 & -\frac{1}{11} & -\frac{2}{11} \\ 0 & 11 & -1 & -2 \end{array}\right] \xrightarrow[R_3 = -11r_2 + r_3]{} \left[\begin{array}{ccc|c} 1 & -2 & 0 & 1 \\ 0 & 1 & -\frac{1}{11} & -\frac{2}{11} \\ 0 & 0 & 0 & 0 \end{array}\right]$$

This matrix is in row echelon form. Because the bottom row consists entirely of 0s, the system actually consists of only two equations.

$$\begin{cases} x - 2y = 1 & (1) \\ y - \frac{1}{11}z = -\frac{2}{11} & (2) \end{cases}$$

From the second equation we get $y = \frac{1}{11}z - \frac{2}{11}$. Then back-substitute this solution for y into the first equation to get

$$x = 2y + 1 = 2\left(\frac{1}{11}z - \frac{2}{11}\right) + 1 = \frac{2}{11}z + \frac{7}{11}$$

The original system is equivalent to the system

$$\begin{cases} x = \dfrac{2}{11}z + \dfrac{7}{11} & (1) \\ y = \dfrac{1}{11}z - \dfrac{2}{11} & (2) \end{cases}$$

where z, the parameter, can be any real number.

Let's look at the situation. The original system of three equations is equivalent to a system containing two equations. This means that any values of x, y, z that satisfy both

$$x = \frac{2}{11}z + \frac{7}{11} \quad \text{and} \quad y = \frac{1}{11}z - \frac{2}{11}$$

will be solutions. For example, $z = 0, x = \frac{7}{11}, y = -\frac{2}{11}$; $z = 1, x = \frac{9}{11}, y = -\frac{1}{11}$; and $z = -1, x = \frac{5}{11}, y = -\frac{3}{11}$ are some of the solutions of the original system. There are, in fact, infinitely many values of x, y, and z for which the two equations are satisfied. That is, the original system has infinitely many solutions. We will write the solution of the original system as

$$\begin{cases} x = \dfrac{2}{11}z + \dfrac{7}{11} \\ y = \dfrac{1}{11}z - \dfrac{2}{11} \end{cases}$$

where z, the parameter, can be any real number.

We can also use Gauss–Jordan elimination to find the solution by writing the augmented matrix in reduced row echelon form. Starting with the row echelon form, we have

$$\left[\begin{array}{ccc|c} 1 & -2 & 0 & 1 \\ 0 & 1 & -\frac{1}{11} & -\frac{2}{11} \\ 0 & 0 & 0 & 0 \end{array}\right] \xrightarrow[R_1 = 2r_2 + r_1]{} \left[\begin{array}{ccc|c} 1 & 0 & -\frac{2}{11} & \frac{7}{11} \\ 0 & 1 & -\frac{1}{11} & -\frac{2}{11} \\ 0 & 0 & 0 & 0 \end{array}\right]$$

The matrix on the right is in reduced row echelon form. The corresponding system of equations is

$$\begin{cases} x - \dfrac{2}{11}z = \dfrac{7}{11} & (1) \\ y - \dfrac{1}{11}z = -\dfrac{2}{11} & (2) \end{cases}$$

or, equivalently,

$$\begin{cases} x = \dfrac{2}{11}z + \dfrac{7}{11} & (1) \\ y = \dfrac{1}{11}z - \dfrac{2}{11} & (2) \end{cases}$$

where z, the parameter, can be any real number.

NOW WORK PROBLEM 47.

6 Use Gaussian Elimination to Identify an Inconsistent System

EXAMPLE 10 Identifying an Inconsistent System of Linear Equations

Solve: $\begin{cases} x + y + z = 6 \\ 2x - y - z = 3 \\ x + 2y + 2z = 0 \end{cases}$

SOLUTION Proceed as follows, beginning with the augmented matrix.

$$\left[\begin{array}{rrr|r} 1 & 1 & 1 & 6 \\ 2 & -1 & -1 & 3 \\ 1 & 2 & 2 & 0 \end{array}\right] \xrightarrow[R_3 = -r_1 + r_3]{R_2 = -2r_1 + r_2} \left[\begin{array}{rrr|r} 1 & 1 & 1 & 6 \\ 0 & -3 & -3 & -9 \\ 0 & 1 & 1 & -6 \end{array}\right] \xrightarrow[\text{rows 2 and 3.}]{\text{Interchange}} \left[\begin{array}{rrr|r} 1 & 1 & 1 & 6 \\ 0 & 1 & 1 & -6 \\ 0 & -3 & -3 & -9 \end{array}\right] \xrightarrow[R_3 = 3r_2 + r_3]{} \left[\begin{array}{rrr|r} 1 & 1 & 1 & 6 \\ 0 & 1 & 1 & -6 \\ 0 & 0 & 0 & -27 \end{array}\right]$$

This matrix is in row echelon form. The bottom row is equivalent to the equation

$$0x + 0y + 0z = -27$$

which has no solution. The original system is inconsistent. ■

NOW WORK PROBLEM 27.

7 Solve Applied Problems Involving Systems of Equations

EXAMPLE 11 Calculating Production Output

FoodPerfect Corporation manufactures three models of the Perfect Foodprocessor. Each Model X processor requires 30 minutes of electrical assembly, 40 minutes of mechanical assembly, and 30 minutes of testing; each Model Y requires 20 minutes of electrical assembly, 50 minutes of mechanical assembly, and 30 minutes of testing; and each Model Z requires 30 minutes of electrical assembly, 30 minutes of mechanical assembly, and 20 minutes of testing. If 2500 minutes of electrical assembly, 3500 minutes of mechanical assembly, and 2400 minutes of testing are used in one day, how many of each model will be produced?

SOLUTION The table that follows summarizes the given information:

	Model			Time Used
	X	Y	Z	
Electrical Assembly	30	20	30	2500
Mechanical Assembly	40	50	30	3500
Testing	30	30	20	2400

Assign variables to represent the unknowns:

x = Number of Model X produced
y = Number of Model Y produced
z = Number of Model Z produced

Based on the table, we obtain the following system of equations:

$$\begin{cases} 30x + 20y + 30z = 2500 \\ 40x + 50y + 30z = 3500 \\ 30x + 30y + 20z = 2400 \end{cases} \xrightarrow[\text{equation by 10.}]{\text{Divide each}} \begin{cases} 3x + 2y + 3z = 250 & (1) \\ 4x + 5y + 3z = 350 & (2) \\ 3x + 3y + 2z = 240 & (3) \end{cases}$$

The augmented matrix of this system is

$$\left[\begin{array}{ccc|c} 3 & 2 & 3 & 250 \\ 4 & 5 & 3 & 350 \\ 3 & 3 & 2 & 240 \end{array}\right]$$

We could obtain a 1 in row 1, column 1 by using the row operation $R_1 = \frac{1}{3}r_1$, but the introduction of fractions is best avoided. Instead, use

$$R_2 = -1r_1 + r_2$$

to place a 1 in row 2, column 1. The result is

$$\left[\begin{array}{ccc|c} 3 & 2 & 3 & 250 \\ 4 & 5 & 3 & 350 \\ 3 & 3 & 2 & 240 \end{array}\right] \xrightarrow[R_3 = -r_1 + r_2]{} \left[\begin{array}{ccc|c} 3 & 2 & 3 & 250 \\ 1 & 3 & 0 & 100 \\ 3 & 3 & 2 & 240 \end{array}\right]$$

Next, interchange row 1 and row 2:

$$\left[\begin{array}{ccc|c} 3 & 2 & 3 & 250 \\ 1 & 3 & 0 & 100 \\ 3 & 3 & 2 & 240 \end{array}\right] \xrightarrow[\substack{R_1 = r_2 \\ R_2 = r_1}]{} \left[\begin{array}{ccc|c} 1 & 3 & 0 & 100 \\ 3 & 2 & 3 & 250 \\ 3 & 3 & 2 & 240 \end{array}\right]$$

Use $R_2 = -3r_1 + r_2$ and $R_3 = -3r_1 + r_3$ to obtain

$$\left[\begin{array}{ccc|c} 1 & 3 & 0 & 100 \\ 3 & 2 & 3 & 250 \\ 3 & 3 & 2 & 240 \end{array}\right] \xrightarrow[\substack{R_2 = -3r_1 + r_2 \\ R_3 = -3r_1 + r_3}]{} \left[\begin{array}{ccc|c} 1 & 3 & 0 & 100 \\ 0 & -7 & 3 & -50 \\ 0 & -6 & 2 & -60 \end{array}\right]$$

Use $R_2 = -1r_2$ followed by $R_2 = r_3 + r_2$:

$$\left[\begin{array}{ccc|c} 1 & 3 & 0 & 100 \\ 0 & -7 & 3 & -50 \\ 0 & -6 & 2 & -60 \end{array}\right] \xrightarrow[R_2 = -1r_2]{} \left[\begin{array}{ccc|c} 1 & 3 & 0 & 100 \\ 0 & 7 & -3 & 50 \\ 0 & -6 & 2 & -60 \end{array}\right] \xrightarrow[R_2 = r_3 + r_2]{} \left[\begin{array}{ccc|c} 1 & 3 & 0 & 100 \\ 0 & 1 & -1 & -10 \\ 0 & -6 & 2 & -60 \end{array}\right]$$

Next, use $R_3 = 6r_2 + r_3$ to obtain

$$\left[\begin{array}{ccc|c} 1 & 3 & 0 & 100 \\ 0 & 1 & -1 & -10 \\ 0 & -6 & 2 & -60 \end{array}\right] \xrightarrow[R_3 = 6r_2 + r_3]{} \left[\begin{array}{ccc|c} 1 & 3 & 0 & 100 \\ 0 & 1 & -1 & -10 \\ 0 & 0 & -4 & -120 \end{array}\right]$$

Next, use $R_3 = -\frac{1}{4}r_3$. The result is

$$\left[\begin{array}{ccc|c} 1 & 3 & 0 & 100 \\ 0 & 1 & -1 & -10 \\ 0 & 0 & -4 & -120 \end{array}\right] \xrightarrow[R_3 = -\frac{1}{4}r_3]{} \left[\begin{array}{ccc|c} 1 & 3 & 0 & 100 \\ 0 & 1 & -1 & -10 \\ 0 & 0 & 1 & 30 \end{array}\right]$$

The matrix is now in row echelon form. We find $z = 30$. From row 2, we have $y - z = -10$ so that $y = z - 10 = 30 - 10 = 20$. Finally, from row 1, we have $x + 3y = 100$ so $x = -3y + 100 = -60 + 100 = 40$. The solution of the system is $x = 40, y = 20, z = 30$. In one day 40 Model X, 20 Model Y, and 30 Model Z processors are produced. ■

NOW WORK PROBLEM 65.

EXAMPLE 12 Nutrition

A dietitian at Cook County Hospital wants a patient to have a meal that has 65 grams of protein, 95 grams of carbohydrates, and 905 milligrams of calcium. The hospital food service tells the dietitian that the dinner for today is chicken à la king, baked potatoes, and 2% milk. Each serving of chicken à la king has 30 grams of protein, 35 grams of carbohydrates, and 200 milligrams of calcium. Each serving of baked potatoes contains 4 grams of protein, 33 grams of carbohydrates, and 10 milligrams of calcium. Each glass of 2% milk contains 9 grams of protein, 13 grams of carbohydrates, and 300 milligrams of calcium. How many servings of each food should the dietitian provide for the patient?

SOLUTION Let c, p, and m represent the number of servings of chicken à la king, baked potatoes, and milk, respectively. The dietitian wants the patient to have 65 grams of protein. Each serving of chicken à la king has 30 grams of protein, so c servings will have $30c$ grams of protein. Each serving of baked potatoes contains 4 grams of protein, so p potatoes will have $4p$ grams of protein. Finally, each glass of milk has 9 grams of protein, so m glasses of milk will have $9m$ grams of protein. The same logic will result in equations for carbohydrates and calcium, and we have the following system of equations:

$$\begin{cases} 30c + 4p + 9m = 65 & \text{Protein equation} \\ 35c + 33p + 13m = 95 & \text{Carbohydrate equation} \\ 200c + 10p + 300m = 905 & \text{Calcium equation} \end{cases}$$

Begin with the augmented matrix and proceed as follows:

$$\left[\begin{array}{ccc|c} 30 & 4 & 9 & 65 \\ 35 & 33 & 13 & 95 \\ 200 & 10 & 300 & 905 \end{array}\right] \underset{R_1 = \left(\frac{1}{30}\right) r_1}{\rightarrow} \left[\begin{array}{ccc|c} 1 & \frac{2}{15} & \frac{3}{10} & \frac{13}{6} \\ 35 & 33 & 13 & 95 \\ 200 & 10 & 300 & 905 \end{array}\right] \underset{\substack{R_2 = -35r_1 + r_2 \\ R_3 = -200r_1 + r_3}}{\rightarrow} \left[\begin{array}{ccc|c} 1 & \frac{2}{15} & \frac{3}{10} & \frac{13}{6} \\ 0 & \frac{85}{3} & \frac{5}{2} & \frac{115}{6} \\ 0 & -\frac{50}{3} & 240 & \frac{1415}{3} \end{array}\right]$$

$$\underset{R_2 = \left(\frac{3}{85}\right) r_2}{\rightarrow} \left[\begin{array}{ccc|c} 1 & \frac{2}{15} & \frac{3}{10} & \frac{13}{6} \\ 0 & 1 & \frac{3}{34} & \frac{23}{34} \\ 0 & -\frac{50}{3} & 240 & \frac{1415}{3} \end{array}\right] \underset{R_3 = \left(\frac{50}{3}\right) r_2 + r_3}{\rightarrow} \left[\begin{array}{ccc|c} 1 & \frac{2}{15} & \frac{3}{10} & \frac{13}{6} \\ 0 & 1 & \frac{3}{34} & \frac{23}{34} \\ 0 & 0 & \frac{4105}{17} & \frac{8210}{17} \end{array}\right] \underset{R_3 = \left(\frac{17}{4105}\right) r_3}{\rightarrow} \left[\begin{array}{ccc|c} 1 & \frac{2}{15} & \frac{3}{10} & \frac{13}{6} \\ 0 & 1 & \frac{3}{34} & \frac{23}{34} \\ 0 & 0 & 1 & 2 \end{array}\right]$$

The matrix is now in echelon form. The final matrix represents the system

$$\begin{cases} c + \frac{2}{15}p + \frac{3}{10}m = \frac{13}{6} & (1) \\ p + \frac{3}{34}m = \frac{23}{34} & (2) \\ m = 2 & (3) \end{cases}$$

From (3), we determine that 2 glasses of milk should be served. Back-substitute $m = 2$ into Equation (2) to find that $p = \frac{1}{2}$, so $\frac{1}{2}$ of a baked potato should be served. Back-substitute these values into Equation (1) and find that $c = \frac{3}{2}$, so 1.5 servings of chicken à la king should be given to the patient to meet the dietary requirements. ■

EXERCISE 2.2 Answers Begin on Page AN–10.

Concepts and Vocabulary

1. An m by n rectangular array of numbers is called a(n) _____.

2. The matrix used to represent a system of linear equations is called a(n) _____ matrix.

3. ***True or False***: The augmented matrix of a system of two equations containing three variables has two rows and four columns.

4. ***True or False***: The matrix $\left[\begin{array}{cc|c} 1 & 3 & -2 \\ 0 & 1 & 5 \\ 0 & 0 & 0 \end{array}\right]$ is in row echelon form.

Skill Building

In Problems 5–16, write the augmented matrix of each system of equations.

5. $\begin{cases} 2x - 3y = 5 \\ x - y = 3 \end{cases}$

6. $\begin{cases} 4x + y = 5 \\ 2x + y = 5 \end{cases}$

7. $\begin{cases} 2x + y + 6 = 0 \\ 3x + y = -1 \end{cases}$

8. $\begin{cases} -3x - y = -3 \\ 4x - y + 2 = 0 \end{cases}$

9. $\begin{cases} 2x - y - z = 0 \\ x - y + z = 1 \\ 3x - y = 2 \end{cases}$

10. $\begin{cases} x + y + z = 3 \\ 2x + z = 0 \\ 3x - y - z = 1 \end{cases}$

11. $\begin{cases} 2x - 3y + z - 7 = 0 \\ x + y - z = 1 \\ 2x + 2y - 3z + 4 = 0 \end{cases}$

12. $\begin{cases} 5x - 3y + 6z + 1 = 0 \\ -x - y + z = 1 \\ 2x + 3y + 5 = 0 \end{cases}$

13. $\begin{cases} 4x_1 - x_2 + 2x_3 - x_4 = 4 \\ x_1 + x_2 + 6 = 0 \\ 2x_2 - x_3 + x_4 = 5 \end{cases}$

14. $\begin{cases} 3x_1 - 5x_2 + x_3 = 2 \\ x_1 - x_2 + x_3 = 6 \\ 2x_1 + x_3 + 4 = 0 \end{cases}$

15. $\begin{cases} x_1 - x_2 + x_3 - x_4 = 0 \\ 2x_1 + 3x_2 - x_3 + 4x_4 = 5 \end{cases}$

16. $\begin{cases} x_1 + x_2 + x_3 + x_4 = 4 \\ x_1 - 2x_2 + 3x_3 - 4x_4 = 5 \end{cases}$

In Problems 17–24, perform each row operation on the given augmented matrix.

17. $\left[\begin{array}{cc|c} 1 & -3 & -2 \\ 2 & -5 & 5 \end{array}\right]$ $R_2 = -2r_1 + r_2$

18. $\left[\begin{array}{cc|c} 1 & -3 & -3 \\ 2 & -5 & -4 \end{array}\right]$ $R_2 = -2r_1 + r_2$

19. $\left[\begin{array}{ccc|c} 1 & -3 & 4 & 3 \\ 2 & -5 & 6 & 6 \\ -3 & 3 & 4 & 6 \end{array}\right]$ (a) $R_2 = -2r_1 + r_2$ (b) $R_3 = 3r_1 + r_3$

20. $\left[\begin{array}{ccc|c} 1 & -3 & 3 & -5 \\ 2 & -5 & -3 & -5 \\ -3 & -2 & 4 & 6 \end{array}\right]$ (a) $R_2 = -2r_1 + r_2$ (b) $R_3 = 3r_1 + r_3$

21. $\left[\begin{array}{ccc|c} 1 & -3 & 2 & -6 \\ 2 & -5 & 3 & -4 \\ -3 & -6 & 2 & 6 \end{array}\right]$ (a) $R_2 = -2r_1 + r_2$ (b) $R_3 = 3r_1 + r_3$

22. $\left[\begin{array}{ccc|c} 1 & -3 & -4 & -6 \\ 2 & -5 & 6 & -6 \\ -3 & 1 & 4 & 6 \end{array}\right]$ (a) $R_2 = -2r_1 + r_2$ (b) $R_3 = 3r_1 + r_3$

23. $\left[\begin{array}{rrr|r} 1 & -3 & 1 & -2 \\ 2 & -5 & 6 & -2 \\ -3 & 1 & 4 & 6 \end{array}\right]$ (a) $R_2 = -2r_1 + r_2$ (b) $R_3 = 3r_1 + r_3$

24. $\left[\begin{array}{rrr|r} 1 & -3 & -1 & 2 \\ 2 & -5 & 2 & 6 \\ -3 & -6 & 4 & 6 \end{array}\right]$ (a) $R_2 = -2r_1 + r_2$ (b) $R_3 = 3r_1 + r_3$

In Problems 25–36, the row echelon form of a system of linear equations is given.
(a) Write the system of equations corresponding to the given matrix. Use x, y; or x, y, z; or x_1, x_2, x_3, x_4 as variables.
(b) Determine whether the system is consistent or inconsistent. If it is consistent, give the solution.

25. $\left[\begin{array}{rr|r} 1 & 2 & 5 \\ 0 & 1 & -1 \end{array}\right]$

26. $\left[\begin{array}{rr|r} 1 & -3 & -4 \\ 0 & 1 & 0 \end{array}\right]$

27. $\left[\begin{array}{rrr|r} 1 & 2 & 3 & 1 \\ 0 & 1 & 4 & 2 \\ 0 & 0 & 0 & 3 \end{array}\right]$

28. $\left[\begin{array}{rrr|r} 1 & 2 & -1 & 0 \\ 0 & 1 & -1 & 1 \\ 0 & 0 & 0 & 2 \end{array}\right]$

29. $\left[\begin{array}{rrr|r} 1 & 0 & 2 & -1 \\ 0 & 1 & -4 & -2 \\ 0 & 0 & 0 & 0 \end{array}\right]$

30. $\left[\begin{array}{rrr|r} 1 & 0 & 4 & 4 \\ 0 & 1 & 3 & 2 \\ 0 & 0 & 0 & 0 \end{array}\right]$

31. $\left[\begin{array}{rrrr|r} 1 & 2 & -1 & 1 & 1 \\ 0 & 1 & 4 & 1 & 2 \\ 0 & 0 & 1 & 2 & 3 \\ 0 & 0 & 0 & 1 & 4 \end{array}\right]$

32. $\left[\begin{array}{rrrr|r} 1 & 2 & 4 & 0 & 1 \\ 0 & 1 & -1 & 2 & 2 \\ 0 & 0 & 1 & 3 & 0 \\ 0 & 0 & 0 & 1 & -2 \end{array}\right]$

33. $\left[\begin{array}{rrrr|r} 1 & 2 & 0 & 4 & 2 \\ 0 & 1 & 1 & 3 & 3 \\ 0 & 0 & 1 & 0 & 0 \\ 0 & 0 & 0 & 0 & 0 \end{array}\right]$

34. $\left[\begin{array}{rrrr|r} 1 & 0 & 3 & 0 & 1 \\ 0 & 1 & 4 & 3 & 2 \\ 0 & 0 & 1 & 2 & 3 \\ 0 & 0 & 0 & 0 & 0 \end{array}\right]$

35. $\left[\begin{array}{rrrr|r} 1 & -2 & 0 & 1 & -2 \\ 0 & 1 & -3 & 2 & 2 \\ 0 & 0 & 1 & -1 & 0 \\ 0 & 0 & 0 & 0 & 0 \end{array}\right]$

36. $\left[\begin{array}{rrrr|r} 1 & 3 & 0 & 4 & 1 \\ 0 & 1 & 2 & -1 & 2 \\ 0 & 0 & 1 & 2 & 3 \\ 0 & 0 & 0 & 1 & 0 \end{array}\right]$

In Problems 37–54, solve each system of equations using Gaussian elimination or Gauss–Jordan elimination. If the system has no solution, say it is inconsistent.

37. $\begin{cases} 2x - 3y = 6 \\ 6x - 9y = 10 \end{cases}$

38. $\begin{cases} 3x + 9y = 4 \\ 2x + 6y = 1 \end{cases}$

39. $\begin{cases} 2x - 3y = 0 \\ 4x + 9y = 5 \end{cases}$

40. $\begin{cases} 3x - 4y = 3 \\ 6x + 2y = 1 \end{cases}$

41. $\begin{cases} 2x + 6y = 4 \\ 5x + 15y = 10 \end{cases}$

42. $\begin{cases} 3x + 5y = 5 \\ 6x + 10y = 10 \end{cases}$

43. $\begin{cases} x + y = 1 \\ 3x - 2y = \dfrac{4}{3} \end{cases}$

44. $\begin{cases} 4x - y = \dfrac{11}{4} \\ 3x + y = \dfrac{5}{2} \end{cases}$

45. $\begin{cases} 2x + y + z = 6 \\ x - y - z = -3 \\ 3x + y + 2z = 7 \end{cases}$

46. $\begin{cases} x + y + z = 5 \\ 2x - y + z = 2 \\ x + 2y - z = 3 \end{cases}$

47. $\begin{cases} 2x - 2y - z = 2 \\ 2x + 3y + z = 2 \\ 3x + 2y = 0 \end{cases}$

48. $\begin{cases} 2x - y - z = -5 \\ x + y + z = 2 \\ x + 2y + 2z = 5 \end{cases}$

49. $\begin{cases} 2x + y - z = 2 \\ x + 3y + 2z = 1 \\ x + y + z = 2 \end{cases}$

50. $\begin{cases} 2x + 2y + z = 6 \\ x - y - z = -2 \\ x - 2y - 2z = -5 \end{cases}$

51. $\begin{cases} x + y - z = 0 \\ 4x + 4y - 4z = -1 \\ 2x + y + z = 2 \end{cases}$

52. $\begin{cases} x + y - z = 0 \\ 4x + 2y - 4z = 0 \\ x + 2y + z = 0 \end{cases}$

53. $\begin{cases} 3x + y - z = \dfrac{2}{3} \\ 2x - y + z = 1 \\ 4x + 2y = \dfrac{8}{3} \end{cases}$

54. $\begin{cases} x - 3y = 1 \\ 2x - y + z = 1 \\ x + 2y + z = \dfrac{8}{3} \end{cases}$

In Problems 55–60, use a graphing utility to find the row echelon form (REF) and the reduced row echelon form (RREF) of the augmented matrix of each of the following systems. Solve each system. If the system has no solution, say it is inconsistent.

55. $\begin{cases} 2x - 2y + z = 2 \\ x - \dfrac{1}{2}y + 2z = 1 \\ 2x + \dfrac{1}{3}y - z = 0 \end{cases}$

56. $\begin{cases} x + y = -1 \\ x - z = 0 \\ y - z = 1 \end{cases}$

57. $\begin{cases} x + y + z = 4 \\ x - y - z = 0 \\ y - z = -4 \end{cases}$

58. $\begin{cases} 2x + y + z = 6 \\ x - y - z = -3 \\ 3x + y + 2z = 7 \end{cases}$

59. $\begin{cases} x_1 + x_2 + x_3 + x_4 = 20 \\ x_2 + x_3 + x_4 = 0 \\ x_3 + x_4 = 13 \\ x_2 - 2x_4 = -5 \end{cases}$

60. $\begin{cases} x_1 - 2x_2 + 3x_3 - 4x_4 = 40 \\ 4x_2 + 6x_4 = -10 \\ x_3 - x_4 = 12 \\ x_2 + 2x_4 = -10 \end{cases}$

Applications

61. Financial Planning Carla has \$120,000 to invest and wants to have an annual income of \$5000. As her financial consultant, you recommend that she invest in Treasury Bills that yield 2%, bank CDs that yield 4%, and corporate bonds that yield 6%. Being conservative, Carla wants the amount invested in corporate bonds to be half that invested in bank CDs. Find the amount she should place in each investment.

62. Financial Planning Kurt has \$20,000 to invest. As his financial planner, you recommend that he diversify into three mutual funds based on their average annual returns over the past 10 years ending December 31, 2009: Total Return at 5%, High Income at 7%, and Global Bond at 9%. Kurt wants to have an average annual return of \$1280 over the next 10 years. Since Kurt is worried that interest rates may go up resulting in bonds declining, he wants the amount invested in the Total Return Fund to be two times that invested in the Global Bond Fund. Find the amount in each investment.

63. Diet Preparation A hospital dietician is planning a meal consisting of three foods whose ingredients are summarized as follows:

	Chicken Breast (3-oz boneless, skinless)	Potato (1 average potato, 5.3 oz)	Spinach (1 cup, boiled & drained)
Grams of Protein	24	4	5
Grams of Carbohydrates	0	26	7
Grams of Fat	1.5	0	0.5

Determine the number of servings of each food needed to create a meal containing 38 grams of protein, 40 grams of carbohydrates, and 2.5 grams of fat.

Source: www.dietfacts.com

64. Ordering Cookies Sally's Girl Scout troop is selling cookies for the Christmas season. There are three different kinds of cookies in three different containers: *bags* that hold 1 dozen chocolate chip and 1 dozen oatmeal; *gift boxes* that hold 2 dozen chocolate chip, 1 dozen mint, and 1 dozen oatmeal; and *cookie tins* that hold 3 dozen mint and 2 dozen chocolate chip. Sally's mother is having a Christmas party and wants 6 dozen oatmeal; 10 dozen mint, and 14 dozen chocolate chip cookies. How can Sally fill her mother's order?

65. Production A juice company completes the preparation of its products by cleaning, filling, and labeling bottles. Each case of orange juice requires 10 minutes in the cleaning machine, 4 minutes in the filling machine, and 2 minutes in the labeling machine. For each case of tomato juice, the times are 12 minutes of cleaning, 4 minutes of filling, and 1 minute of labeling. Pineapple juice requires 9 minutes of cleaning, 6 minutes of filling, and 1 minute of labeling per case. If the company runs the cleaning machine for 398 minutes, the filling machine for 164 minutes, and the labeling machine for 58 minutes, how many cases of each type of juice are prepared?

66. Production The finishing stage of the manufacture of an automobile requires painting, drying, and polishing. The Rome Motor Company produces three types of cars: the Centurion, the Tribune, and the Senator. Each Centurion requires 8 hours for painting, 2 hours for drying, and 1 hour for polishing. A Tribune needs 10 hours for painting, 3 hours for drying, and 2 hours for polishing. It takes 16 hours of painting, 5 hours of drying, and 3 hours of polishing to prepare a Senator. If the company uses 240 hours for painting, 69 hours for drying, and 41 hours for polishing in a given month, how many of each type of car are produced?

67. Theater Seating The Fabulous Fox Theater in St. Louis, Missouri, offers several levels of seating, among them mezzanine, lower balcony, and middle balcony. One group of patrons buys 4 mezzanine tickets and 6 lower balcony tickets for \$558. Another group spends \$787 for 2 mezzanine tickets, 7 lower balcony tickets, and 8 middle balcony tickets. A third group purchases 3 lower balcony tickets and 12 middle balcony tickets for \$615. What is the individual price of a mezzanine ticket, a lower balcony ticket, and a middle balcony ticket?

Source: Fox Theater, St. Louis, Missouri. Based on seat pricing for the production of *MAMA MIA*, Feb., 2010.

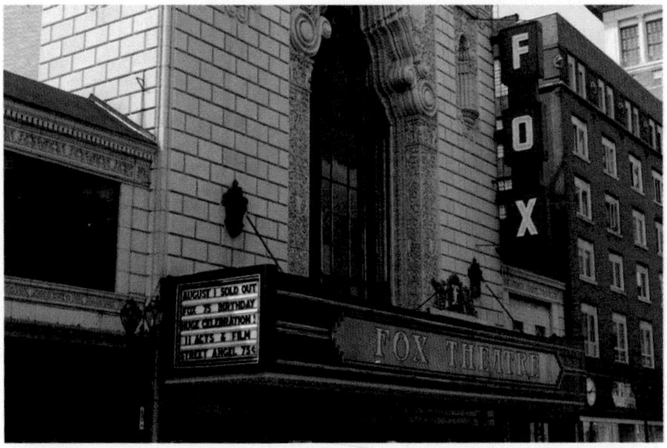

68. **Cost of Fast Food** One group of people purchased 10 hot dogs and 5 soft drinks at a cost of \$37.50. A second group bought 7 hot dogs and 4 soft drinks at a cost of \$27. What is the cost of a single hot dog? A single soft drink?

69. **Inventory Control** An art teacher finds that colored paper can be bought in three different packages. The first package has 20 sheets of white paper, 15 sheets of blue paper, and 1 sheet of red paper. The second package has 3 sheets of blue paper and 1 sheet of red paper. The last package has 40 sheets of white paper and 30 sheets of blue paper. If he needs 200 sheets of white paper, 180 sheets of blue paper, and 12 sheets of red paper, how many of each type of package should he order?

70. **Inventory Control** An interior decorator has ordered 12 cans of sunset paint, 35 cans of brown paint, and 18 cans of fuchsia paint. The paint store has special pair packs, containing 1 can each of sunset and fuchsia; darkening packs, containing 2 cans of sunset, 5 cans of brown, and 2 cans of fuchsia; and economy packs, containing 3 cans of sunset, 15 cans of brown, and 6 cans of fuchsia. How many of each type of pack should the paint store send to the interior decorator?

71. **Packaging** A recreation center wants to purchase compact discs (CDs) to be used in the center. There is no requirement as to the artists. The only requirement is that they purchase 40 rock CDs, 32 western CDs, and 14 blues CDs. There are three different shipping packages offered by the company. They are an *assorted* carton, containing 2 rock CDs, 4 western CDs, and 1 blues CD; a *mixed* carton containing 4 rock and 2 western CDs; and a *single* carton containing 2 blues CDs. What combination of these packages is needed to fill the center's order?

72. **Production** A luggage manufacturer produces three types of luggage: economy, standard, and deluxe. The company produces 1000 pieces of luggage at a cost of \$20, \$25, and \$30 for the economy, standard, and deluxe luggage, respectively. The manufacturer has a budget of \$20,700. Each economy luggage requires 6 hours of labor, each standard luggage requires 10 hours of labor, and each deluxe model requires 20 hours of labor. The manufacturer has a maximum of 6800 hours of labor available. If the manufacturer sells all the luggage, consumes the entire budget, and uses all the available labor, how many of each type of luggage should be produced?

73. **Mixing Nuts** Suppose that a store has three sizes of cans of nuts. The *large* size contains 2 pounds of peanuts and 1 pound of cashews. The *mammoth* size contains 1 pound of walnuts, 6 pounds of peanuts, and 2 pounds of cashews. The *giant* size contains 1 pound of walnuts, 4 pounds of peanuts, and 2 pounds of cashews. Suppose that the store receives an order for 5 pounds of walnuts, 26 pounds of peanuts, and 12 pounds of cashews. How can it fill this order with the given sizes of cans?

74. **Mixing Nuts** Suppose that the store in Problem 73 receives a new order for 6 pounds of walnuts, 34 pounds of peanuts, and 15 pounds of cashews. How can this order be filled with the given cans?

75. **Buying Stock** Karen has \$200,000 to invest. She will purchase chares in National City Bank preferred (NCC.B), IBM (IBM), and Express Scripts (ESRX). The table that follows shows the price she pays per share, the expected annual dividend, and the expected annual growth rate. Over the next 12 months, Karen wants these stocks to provide \$8000 in dividends with an average growth rate of 4%. How many shares of each stock should be purchased to achieve this goal?

	Price per Share	Expected Annual Dividend per Share	Expected Annual Growth Rate
NCC Pfd	25	2	0%
IBM	100	2	5%
Express Scripts	50	0	10%

Discussion and Writing

76. Write a brief paragraph or two that outlines your strategy for solving a system of linear equations using matrices.

77. When solving a system of linear equations using matrices, do you prefer to place the augmented matrix in row echelon form or in reduced row echelon form? Give reasons for your choice.

2.3 Systems of m Linear Equations Containing n Variables

OBJECTIVES

1. Analyze the reduced row echelon form of an augmented matrix (p. 89)
2. Solve a system of m linear equations containing n variables (p. 90)
3. Express the solution of a system with an infinite number of solutions (p. 92)
4. Solve applied problems involving systems of equations (p. 94)

Below is an example of a system of three linear equations containing four variables

$$\begin{cases} x_1 + 3x_2 + 5x_3 + x_4 = 2 \\ 2x_1 + 3x_2 + 4x_3 + 2x_4 = 1 \\ x_1 + 2x_2 + 3x_3 + x_4 = 1 \end{cases}$$

A general definition of a system of m linear equations containing n variables is given next.

Definition

System of m Linear Equations Containing n Variables

A **system of m linear equations containing n variables** $x_1, x_2, \ldots, x_n$ is of the form

$$\begin{cases} a_{11}x_1 + a_{12}x_2 + \cdots + a_{1n}x_n = b_1 & (1) \\ a_{21}x_1 + a_{22}x_2 + \cdots + a_{2n}x_n = b_2 & (2) \\ a_{31}x_1 + a_{32}x_2 + \cdots + a_{3n}x_n = b_3 & (3) \\ \quad \vdots \qquad\quad \vdots \qquad\qquad\quad \vdots \qquad\quad \vdots & \vdots \\ a_{i1}x_1 + a_{i2}x_2 + \cdots + a_{in}x_n = b_i & (i) \\ \quad \vdots \qquad\quad \vdots \qquad\qquad\quad \vdots \qquad\quad \vdots & \vdots \\ a_{m1}x_1 + a_{m2}x_2 + \cdots + a_{mn}x_n = b_m & (m) \end{cases}$$

where a_{ij} and b_i are real numbers, $i = 1, 2 \ldots, m, j = 1, 2, \ldots, n$.

A **solution** of a system of m linear equations containing n variables $x_1, x_2, \ldots, x_n$ is any ordered set $(x_1, x_2, \ldots, x_n)$ of real numbers for which *each* of the m linear equations of the system is satisfied.

Reduced Row Echelon Form

A system of m linear equations containing n variables will have either no solution, one solution, or infinitely many solutions. We can determine which of these possibilities occurs and, if solutions exist, find them, by performing row operations on the augmented matrix of the system until we arrive at the reduced row echelon form of the augmented matrix.

Let's review the conditions required for the reduced row echelon form:

Conditions for the Reduced Row Echelon Form of a Matrix

1. The first nonzero entry in each row is 1 and it has 0s above it and below it.
2. The leftmost 1 in any row is to the right of the leftmost 1 in the row above.
3. Any rows that contain all 0s to the left of the vertical bar appear at the bottom.

EXAMPLE 1 **Examples of Matrices That Are in Reduced Row Echelon Form**

(a) $\left[\begin{array}{ccc|c} 1 & 0 & -3 & 4 \\ 0 & 1 & -2 & 2 \end{array}\right]$ **(b)** $\left[\begin{array}{ccc|c} 1 & -2 & 0 & 1 \\ 0 & 0 & 1 & 3 \\ 0 & 0 & 0 & 5 \end{array}\right]$ **(c)** $\left[\begin{array}{cc|c} 1 & 0 & 3 \\ 0 & 1 & 4 \\ 0 & 0 & 0 \end{array}\right]$

EXAMPLE 2 **Examples of Matrices That Are Not in Reduced Row Echelon Form**

(a) $\left[\begin{array}{cc|c} 1 & 0 & 0 \\ 0 & 0 & 0 \\ 0 & 1 & 0 \end{array}\right]$ The second row contains all 0s and the third does not—this violates the rule that states that any rows with all 0s are at the bottom.

(b) $\left[\begin{array}{ccc|c} 1 & 0 & 2 & 4 \\ 0 & 2 & 4 & 3 \end{array}\right]$ The first nonzero entry in row 2 is not a 1.

(c) $\left[\begin{array}{cccc|c} 1 & 0 & 0 & 1 & 0 \\ 0 & 0 & 1 & 2 & 1 \\ 0 & 1 & 0 & 3 & 0 \end{array}\right]$ The leftmost 1 in the third row is not to the right of the leftmost 1 in the row above it. ■

NOW WORK PROBLEM 3.

1 Analyze the Reduced Row Echelon Form of an Augmented Matrix

EXAMPLE 3 **Analyzing the Reduced Row Echelon Form of an Augmented Matrix**

The matrix

$$\left[\begin{array}{ccc|c} 1 & 0 & 3 & 0 \\ 0 & 1 & 2 & 0 \\ 0 & 0 & 0 & 1 \\ 0 & 0 & 0 & 0 \end{array}\right]$$

is the reduced row echelon form of the augmented matrix of a system of four equations containing three variables. If the variables are x, y, z, the equation represented by the third row is

$$0 \cdot x + 0 \cdot y + 0 \cdot z = 1 \qquad \text{or} \qquad 0 = 1$$

Since $0 = 1$ is a contradiction, we conclude the system is inconsistent. ■

EXAMPLE 4 Analyzing the Reduced Row Echelon Form of an Augmented Matrix

The matrix

$$\left[\begin{array}{cccc|c} 1 & 0 & 0 & 2 & 5 \\ 0 & 1 & 0 & 1 & 2 \\ 0 & 0 & 1 & 3 & 4 \end{array}\right]$$

is the reduced row echelon form of a system of three equations containing four variables. If x_1, x_2, x_3, x_4 are the variables, the system of equations is

$$\begin{cases} x_1 + 2x_4 = 5 \\ x_2 + x_4 = 2 \\ x_3 + 3x_4 = 4 \end{cases} \quad \text{or} \quad \begin{cases} x_1 = -2x_4 + 5 \\ x_2 = -x_4 + 2 \\ x_3 = -3x_4 + 4 \end{cases}$$

The system has infinitely many solutions. In this form, the variable x_4 is the parameter. We assign values to the parameter x_4 from which the variables x_1, x_2, x_3 can be calculated. Some of the possibilities are

If $x_4 = 0$, then $x_1 = 5, x_2 = 2, x_3 = 4$.
If $x_4 = 1$, then $x_1 = 3, x_2 = 1, x_3 = 1$.
If $x_4 = 2$, then $x_1 = 1, x_2 = 0, x_3 = -2$.

And so on.

NOW WORK PROBLEM 9.

2 Solve a System of m Linear Equations Containing n Variables

EXAMPLE 5 Solving a System of Three Linear Equations Containing Two Variables

Solve: $\begin{cases} x - y = 2 \\ 2x - 3y = 2 \\ 3x - 5y = 2 \end{cases}$

SOLUTION The augmented matrix of this system is

$$\left[\begin{array}{cc|c} 1 & -1 & 2 \\ 2 & -3 & 2 \\ 3 & -5 & 2 \end{array}\right]$$

We will use Gauss–Jordan elimination to find the reduced row echelon form of the augmented matrix. The entry in row 1, column 1 is 1. Proceed to obtain a matrix in which all the remaining entries in column 1 are 0s by performing the row operations

$$R_2 = -2r_1 + r_2$$
$$R_3 = -3r_1 + r_3$$

The new matrix is

$$\left[\begin{array}{cc|c} 1 & -1 & 2 \\ 0 & -1 & -2 \\ 0 & -2 & -4 \end{array}\right]$$

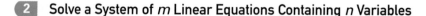

We want the entry in row 2, column 2 (now -1) to be 1. After using the row operation $R_2 = (-1)r_2$, we obtain

$$\left[\begin{array}{rr|r} 1 & -1 & 2 \\ 0 & 1 & 2 \\ 0 & -2 & -4 \end{array}\right]$$

Now we want the entry in row 1, column 2 and in row 3, column 2 to be 0. This can be accomplished by applying the row operations

$$R_1 = r_2 + r_1$$
$$R_3 = 2r_2 + r_3$$

The new matrix is

$$\left[\begin{array}{rr|r} 1 & 0 & 4 \\ 0 & 1 & 2 \\ 0 & 0 & 0 \end{array}\right]$$

This is the reduced row echelon form of the matrix. We conclude that the system has the solution $x = 4$, $y = 2$ or, using ordered pairs, $(4, 2)$. ■

COMMENT A graphing utility can be used to solve systems of *m* linear equations containing *n* variables. Check the solution to Example 5 using the RREF feature of your graphing utility. ■

EXAMPLE 6 Solving a System of Four Linear Equations Containing Three Variables

Solve: $\begin{cases} x - y + 2z = 2 \\ 2x - 3y + 2z = 1 \\ 3x - 5y + 2z = -3 \\ -4x + 12y + 8z = 10 \end{cases}$

SOLUTION We find the reduced row echelon form of the augmented matrix of this system, namely,

$$\left[\begin{array}{rrr|r} 1 & -1 & 2 & 2 \\ 2 & -3 & 2 & 1 \\ 3 & -5 & 2 & -3 \\ -4 & 12 & 8 & 10 \end{array}\right]$$

The entry 1 is already present in row 1, column 1. To obtain 0s elsewhere in column 1, use the row operations

$$R_2 = -2r_1 + r_2 \qquad R_3 = -3r_1 + r_3 \qquad R_4 = 4r_1 + r_4$$

The new matrix is

$$\left[\begin{array}{rrr|r} 1 & -1 & 2 & 2 \\ 0 & -1 & -2 & -3 \\ 0 & -2 & -4 & -9 \\ 0 & 8 & 16 & 18 \end{array}\right]$$

To obtain the entry 1 in row 2, column 2, use $R_2 = -r_2$, obtaining

$$\left[\begin{array}{rrr|r} 1 & -1 & 2 & 2 \\ 0 & 1 & 2 & 3 \\ 0 & -2 & -4 & -9 \\ 0 & 8 & 16 & 18 \end{array}\right]$$

To obtain 0s elsewhere in column 2, use

$$R_1 = r_2 + r_1 \qquad R_3 = 2r_2 + r_3 \qquad R_4 = -8r_2 + r_4$$

The new matrix is

$$\left[\begin{array}{rrr|r} 1 & 0 & 4 & 5 \\ 0 & 1 & 2 & 3 \\ 0 & 0 & 0 & -3 \\ 0 & 0 & 0 & -6 \end{array}\right]$$

We can stop here because the third row yields the equation

$$0 \cdot x + 0 \cdot y + 0 \cdot z = -3$$

We conclude the system is inconsistent. ■

NOW WORK PROBLEM 17.

3 Express the Solution of a System with an Infinite Number of Solutions

EXAMPLE 7 Solving a System of Two Linear Equations Containing Three Variables

Solve: $\begin{cases} x + y + z = 7 \\ x - y - 3z = 1 \end{cases}$

SOLUTION The augmented matrix of the system is

$$\left[\begin{array}{rrr|r} 1 & 1 & 1 & 7 \\ 1 & -1 & -3 & 1 \end{array}\right]$$

The reduced row echelon form (as you should verify) is

$$\left[\begin{array}{rrr|r} 1 & 0 & -1 & 4 \\ 0 & 1 & 2 & 3 \end{array}\right]$$

The system of equations represented by this matrix is

$$\begin{cases} x - z = 4 \\ y + 2z = 3 \end{cases} \quad \text{or} \quad \begin{cases} x = z + 4 \\ y = -2z + 3 \end{cases} \tag{1}$$

The system has infinitely many solutions. In the form (1), the variable z is the parameter. We can assign any value to z and use it to compute values of x and y.

✔ **CHECK:** Check the solution to Example 7 as follows:

$$x + y + z = (z + 4) + (-2z + 3) + z = 4 + 3 + z - 2z + z = 7$$
$$x - y - 3z = (z + 4) - (-2z + 3) - 3z = 4 - 3 + z + 2z - 3z = 1$$

The solution is verified. ■

The next example illustrates a system having an infinite number of solutions with two parameters.

EXAMPLE 8 Solving a System of Three Linear Equations Containing Four Variables

Solve: $\begin{cases} x_1 + x_2 + 2x_3 + 2x_4 = 2 \\ x_1 + x_3 + x_4 = 0 \\ x_2 + x_3 + x_4 = 2 \end{cases}$

SOLUTION The augmented matrix of the system is

$$\left[\begin{array}{cccc|c} 1 & 1 & 2 & 2 & 2 \\ 1 & 0 & 1 & 1 & 0 \\ 0 & 1 & 1 & 1 & 2 \end{array}\right]$$

The reduced row echelon form (as you should verify) is

$$\left[\begin{array}{cccc|c} 1 & 0 & 1 & 1 & 0 \\ 0 & 1 & 1 & 1 & 2 \\ 0 & 0 & 0 & 0 & 0 \end{array}\right]$$

The equations represented by this system are

$$\begin{cases} x_1 + x_3 + x_4 = 0 \\ x_2 + x_3 + x_4 = 2 \end{cases}$$

Rewrite this system in the form

$$\begin{cases} x_1 = -x_3 - x_4 \\ x_2 = -x_3 - x_4 + 2 \end{cases} \qquad \textbf{(2)}$$

The system has infinitely many solutions. In the form (2), the system has two parameters x_3 and x_4. Solutions are obtained by assigning the two parameters x_3 and x_4 arbitrary values. Some choices are shown in Table 2.

TABLE 2

x_3	x_4	x_1	x_2	(x_1, x_2, x_3, x_4)
0	0	0	2	(0, 2, 0, 0)
1	0	−1	1	(−1, 1, 1, 0)
0	2	−2	0	(−2, 0, 0, 2)

■

The variables used as parameters are not unique. We could have chosen x_1 and x_4 as parameters by rewriting the system of equations (2) in the following manner.

From the first equation

$$x_3 = -x_1 - x_4$$

replace the parameter x_3 in the second equation to produce

$$x_2 = 2 - x_3 - x_4 = 2 + x_1 + x_4 - x_4 = 2 + x_1$$

We then obtain the system

$$\begin{cases} x_2 = x_1 + 2 \\ x_3 = -x_1 - x_4 \end{cases}$$

showing the solution with x_1 and x_4 as parameters.

NOW WORK PROBLEM 23.

4 Solve Applied Problems Involving Systems of Equations

EXAMPLE 9 Financial Planning

A couple has \$60,000 to invest. They wish to earn an average of \$5000 per year on the investment over a 5 year period. Based on the yearly average return on mutual funds for 5 years ending December 31, 2009, they are considering the following funds: Franklin High Income at 5%, Royce 100K at 6%, TCW Small Capital Growth at 7%, and Franklin Natural Resources at 10%.

(a) As their financial advisor, prepare a table showing the various ways the couple can achieve their goal.

(b) Comment on the various possibilities and the overall plan.

SOLUTION Begin by naming the variables: Let x_1 be the amount invested in the High Income Fund, x_2 the amount invested in the Royce 100 K Fund, x_3 the amount invested in the Small Capital Growth Fund, and x_4 the amount in the Natural Resources Fund. Then the average annual amount earned by each investment choice would be

High Income: $0.05\,x_1$ Royce 100 K: $0.06\,x_2$ Small Capital Growth: $0.07\,x_3$ Natural Resources: $0.01\,x_4$

Since the couple requires \$5000 from these investments, we have the equation

$$0.05x_1 + 0.06x_2 + 0.07x_3 + 0.10x_4 = 5000$$

The total amount available to invest is \$60,000, which leads to the equation

$$x_1 + x_2 + x_3 + x_4 = 60{,}000$$

These two equations form the system

$$\begin{cases} 0.05x_1 + 0.06x_2 + 0.07x_3 + 0.10x_4 = 5000 & (1) \\ x_1 + x_2 + x_3 + x_4 = 60{,}000 & (2) \end{cases}$$

Write the augmented matrix of this system and proceed to row reduce.

$$\left[\begin{array}{cccc|c} 0.05 & 0.06 & 0.07 & 0.10 & 5000 \\ 1 & 1 & 1 & 1 & 60{,}000 \end{array}\right] \xrightarrow[\text{Interchange rows.}]{} \left[\begin{array}{cccc|c} 1 & 1 & 1 & 1 & 60{,}000 \\ 0.05 & 0.06 & 0.07 & 0.10 & 5000 \end{array}\right]$$

$$\xrightarrow[R_2 = -0.05r_1 + r_2]{} \left[\begin{array}{cccc|c} 1 & 1 & 1 & 1 & 60{,}000 \\ 0 & 0.01 & 0.02 & 0.05 & 2000 \end{array}\right]$$

$$\xrightarrow[R_2 = 100r_2]{} \left[\begin{array}{cccc|c} 1 & 1 & 1 & 1 & 60{,}000 \\ 0 & 1 & 2 & 5 & 200{,}000 \end{array}\right]$$

$$\xrightarrow[R_1 = -r_2 + r_1]{} \left[\begin{array}{cccc|c} 1 & 0 & -1 & -4 & -140{,}000 \\ 0 & 1 & 2 & 5 & 200{,}000 \end{array}\right]$$

This matrix is in reduced row echelon form. The solution of the system is

$$x_1 = x_3 + 4x_4 - 140{,}000$$

$$x_2 = -2x_3 - 5x_4 + 200{,}000$$

where x_3 and x_4 are parameters.

Now, each of the variables must be nonnegative and each must be less than or equal to 60,000. Set up the table shown in Table 3.

TABLE 3

High Income	Royce	Small Capital Growth	Franklin Natural Resources
20,000	0	0	40,000
0	25,000	0	35,000
12,000	10,000	0	38,000
17,000	0	5,000	38,000
6,000	16,000	2,000	36,000

Table 3 shows five plans that the couple could follow to achieve their financial goals.

(b) Of the five plans, the one that provides for some money to be invested in each of the four mutual funds is preferable as this gives more diversification to the investment. There are other plans that would also provide diversification across all four funds. A difficulty with the over all plan is that one fund, Franklin Natural Resources, must have more than half the money invested in it. The reason is that the expected yield in this fund is very high. The couple should probably set their required income level a little lower so that more diversification can be achieved in the investment. ■

NOW WORK PROBLEM 35.

SUMMARY

Steps for Solving a System of *m* Linear Equations Containing *n* Variables

STEP 1 Write the augmented matrix.

STEP 2 Find the reduced row echelon form of the augmented matrix.

STEP 3 Analyze this matrix to determine if the system has no solution, one solution, or infinitely many solutions.

EXERCISE 2.3 Answers Begin on Page AN–11.

Concepts and Vocabulary

1. ***True or False*** A system of three linear equations containing two variables is always inconsistent.

2. ***True or False*** A system of three linear equations containing four variables can have infinitely many solutions.

Skill Building

In Problems 3–8, tell whether the given matrix is in reduced row echelon form. If it is not, tell why.

3. $\left[\begin{array}{cc|c} 1 & 2 & 3 \\ 0 & 0 & 1 \\ 0 & 0 & 0 \end{array}\right]$

4. $\left[\begin{array}{cc|c} 1 & 2 & 3 \\ 0 & 0 & 0 \\ 0 & 0 & 0 \end{array}\right]$

5. $\left[\begin{array}{c|c} 0 & 1 \\ 1 & 0 \end{array}\right]$

6. $\left[\begin{array}{cc|c} 0 & 1 & 0 \\ 0 & 0 & 1 \\ 0 & 0 & 0 \end{array}\right]$

7. $\left[\begin{array}{cccc|c} 1 & 0 & 0 & 0 & 0 \\ 0 & 0 & 1 & 2 & 0 \\ 0 & 0 & 0 & 0 & 1 \\ 0 & 0 & 0 & 0 & 0 \end{array}\right]$

8. $\left[\begin{array}{cc|c} 1 & 0 & 1 \\ 0 & 1 & 2 \\ 0 & 0 & 0 \end{array}\right]$

In Problems 9–16, the reduced row echelon form of the augmented matrix of a system of linear equations is given. Tell whether the system h one solution, no solution, or infinitely many solutions. Write the solutions or, if there is no solution, say the system is inconsistent.

9. $\left[\begin{array}{ccc|c} 1 & 0 & -2 & 6 \\ 0 & 1 & 3 & 1 \end{array}\right]$

10. $\left[\begin{array}{cccc|c} 1 & 0 & 1 & -1 & 0 \\ 0 & 1 & 2 & 1 & 1 \\ 0 & 0 & 0 & 0 & 0 \end{array}\right]$

11. $\left[\begin{array}{ccc|c} 1 & 0 & 0 & -1 \\ 0 & 1 & 0 & 3 \\ 0 & 0 & 1 & 4 \\ 0 & 0 & 0 & 0 \end{array}\right]$

12. $\left[\begin{array}{cccc|c} 1 & 2 & 0 & 0 & -4 \\ 0 & 0 & 1 & 0 & -3 \\ 0 & 0 & 0 & 1 & 2 \\ 0 & 0 & 0 & 0 & 0 \end{array}\right]$

13. $\left[\begin{array}{ccc|c} 1 & 0 & -1 & 1 \\ 0 & 1 & 2 & 1 \end{array}\right]$

14. $\left[\begin{array}{cc|c} 1 & 0 & 1 \\ 0 & 1 & 1 \\ 0 & 0 & 0 \end{array}\right]$

15. $\left[\begin{array}{cccc|c} 1 & 0 & 0 & -1 & 4 \\ 0 & 1 & 2 & 3 & 0 \end{array}\right]$

16. $\left[\begin{array}{cccc|c} 1 & 0 & 2 & 4 & -1 \\ 0 & 1 & 3 & 5 & -2 \end{array}\right]$

In Problems 17–28, solve each system of equations by finding the reduced row echelon form of the augmented matrix. If there is no solution, sa the system is inconsistent.

17. $\begin{cases} 3x - 3y = 12 \\ 3x + 2y = -3 \\ 2x + y = 4 \end{cases}$

18. $\begin{cases} 6x + y = 8 \\ x - 3y = -5 \\ 2x + y = 2 \end{cases}$

19. $\begin{cases} 2x - 4y = 8 \\ x - 2y = 4 \\ -x + 2y = -4 \end{cases}$

20. $\begin{cases} 3x + y = 8 \\ 6x + 2y = 16 \\ -9x - 3y = -24 \end{cases}$

21. $\begin{cases} 2x + y + 3z = -1 \\ -x + y + 3z = 8 \end{cases}$

22. $\begin{cases} x + 2y + 3z = 5 \\ -2x + 6y + 4z = 0 \end{cases}$

23. $\begin{cases} x_1 + x_2 = 7 \\ x_2 - x_3 + x_4 = 5 \\ x_1 - x_2 + x_3 + x_4 = 6 \\ x_2 - x_4 = 10 \end{cases}$

24. $\begin{cases} x_1 + 2x_2 + 3x_3 - x_4 = 0 \\ 3x_1 - x_4 = 4 \\ x_2 - x_3 - x_4 = 2 \end{cases}$

25. $\begin{cases} 2x - 3y + 4z = 7 \\ x - 2y + 3z = 2 \end{cases}$

26. $\begin{cases} x - y + z = 5 \\ 2x - 2y + 2z = 8 \end{cases}$

27. $\begin{cases} x_1 + x_2 + x_3 + x_4 = 4 \\ 2x_1 - x_2 + x_3 = 0 \\ 3x_1 + 2x_2 + x_3 - x_4 = 6 \\ x_1 - 2x_2 - 2x_3 + 2x_4 = -1 \end{cases}$

28. $\begin{cases} x_1 + x_2 + x_3 + x_4 = 4 \\ -x_1 + 2x_2 + x_3 = 0 \\ 2x_1 + 3x_2 + x_3 - x_4 = 6 \\ -2x_1 + x_2 - 2x_3 + 2x_4 = -1 \end{cases}$

Applications

29. Pharmacy A doctor's prescription calls for a daily intake of a supplement containing 40 mg of vitamin C and 30 mg of vitamin D. Your pharmacy stocks three supplements that can be used: one contains 20% vitamin C and 30% vitamin D; a second, 40% vitamin C and 20% vitamin D; and a third, 30% vitamin C and 50% vitamin D. Create a table showing the possible combinations that could be used to fill the prescription.

30. Pharmacy A doctor's prescription calls for the creation of pills that contain 12 units of vitamin B_{12} and 12 units of vitamin E. Your pharmacy stocks three powders that can be used to make these pills: one contains 20% vitamin B_{12} and 30% vitamin E; a second, 40% vitamin B_{12} and 20% vitamin E; and a third, 30% vitamin B_{12} and 40% vitamin E. Create a table showing the possible combinations of each powder that could be mixed in each pill.

31. Weight Control To control his weight, Steven watches what he eats, paying particular attention to his intake of calories, carbohydrates, and fat. Each workweek (5 days) he consumes 700 calories, 20 grams of fat, and 100 grams of carbohydrates for lunch. He can choose from turkey bologna, bananas, low-fat cottage cheese, and low-fat chocolate milk. The nutritional information per serving for these items i provided in the table.

Food Item	Calories (kcal)	Fat (g)	Carbohydrates (g)
Turkey Bologna	184	13.20	4.85
Banana	92	0.48	23.43
Low-Fat Cottage Cheese	90	1.93	0.01
Low-Fat Chocolate Milk	72	2.00	10.40

Source: Nutri-facts.com

(a) Write a system of equations that describes Steven's intake of calories, carbohydrates, and fat. Be sure to name all variables.

(b) Solve the system by writing its augmented matrix in reduced row echelon form.

(c) Prepare a table showing various lunch options.

32. Making Ends Meet Newlyweds Nick and Dana each work two part-time jobs in order to make ends meet as they finish college. Nick's college schedule allows him to work a total of 30 hours per week both for a department store that pays him \$9.50 per hour and for a fast food restaurant that pays him \$8.50 per hour. Dana's college schedule allows her to work a total of 25 hours per week for a grocery store that pays her \$10.00 per hour and for a novelty shop that pays her \$8.00 per hour. The couple must earn \$500 per week in order to eat and pay bills.

(a) Write a system of equations that describes Nick and Dana's earnings opportunities. Be sure to name all variables.

(b) Solve the system by writing its augmented matrix in reduced row echelon form.

(c) Prepare a table showing various work options for Nick and Dana.

(d) What would you recommend to them?

33. Mutual Funds and College Tuition Bill and Colleen recently inherited \$50,000. They plan to invest the money in order to pay for their son Timmy's tuition. They anticipate they will need an average annual return of \$6000 in order to protect their capital and have enough to cover the tuition (based on the average 2010–2011 tuition for a 4-year public college). They will invest in four mutual funds with the following average annual returns over the 5-year period prior to December 31, 2009, rounded to the nearest whole percent: John Hancock Large Cap Equity Growth at 9%, T Rowe Price Emerging Markets at 13%, Templeton China World Fund at 14%, and TCW Small Cap Growth at 7%.

(a) Write a system of equations that describes Bill and Colleen's financial needs and restrictions. Be sure to name all variables.

(b) Solve the system by writing its augmented matrix in reduced row echelon form.

(c) Prepare a table showing various investment options.

(d) What investment advice would you give to Bill and Colleen?

Source: collegeboard.com

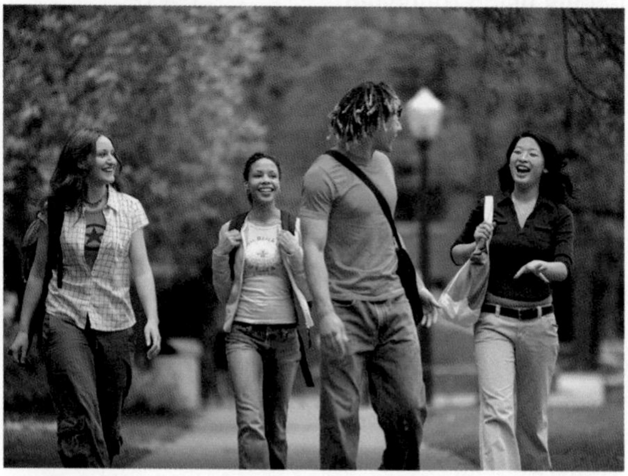

34. Mutual Funds and College Tuition Revisited Refer to Problem 33. Timmy is accepted into a university that charges \$9000 per year in tuition and fees. As a result, Bill and Colleen decide to alter their investment plan by not investing in the TCW Small Cap growth fund. Instead, they will invest in Latin America International Stock fund, which has an average annual return of 21% over the 5-year period ending December 31, 2009. The other mutual funds in which they invest remain the same.

(a) Write a system of equations that describes Bill and Colleen's financial needs and restrictions as modified by the higher tuition and fees and the change in investment strategy. Be sure to name all variables.

(b) Solve the system by writing its augmented matrix in reduced row echelon form.

(c) Prepare a table showing various investment options.

(d) What investment advice would you give to Bill and Colleen?

Sources: collegeboard.com, Franklin Templeton

35. **Investments** Three couples want to go into partnership to finance their own retail business in 2015. They wish to invest monies that would earn an average of \$2000 per annum for 5 years. As their financial consultant, you recommended they invest in certain mutual funds based on their performance over the past 5 years as a December 31, 2009: some money in the Franklin High Income fund that yielded 5%, some in Mutual Global Discovery that yielded 6%; some money in Templeton Global Bond that yielded 8%; and some money in Franklin International Small Cap Growth that yielded 12%. Prepare a table for each couple showing various ways that their goals can be achieved:

(a) If the first couple has \$20,000 to invest

(b) If the second couple has \$25,000 to invest

(c) If the third couple has \$30,000 to invest

(d) What advice would you give each couple? Give reasons.

36. Financial Planning A young couple has \$25,000 to invest. As their financial consultant, based on an average yearly return over a 5-year period ending on December 31, 2009, you recommend that they invest some money in Templeton Global Opportunity Trust that yielded 4%, some in the Franklin Mutual European Fund that yielded 6%; the John Hancock Large Cap Equity Growth Fund that yielded 9%; and Eastern European Equity A Fund that yielded 11%. Prepare a table showing various ways this couple can achieve the following goals:

(a) The couple wants \$1500 per year in income.

(b) The couple wants \$2000 per year in income.

(c) The couple wants \$2500 per year in income.

(d) What advice would you give this couple regarding the income that they require and the choices available? Give reasons.

37. Bacteria Control Three species of bacteria will be kept in one test tube and will feed on three resources. Each member of the first species consumes 3 units of the first resource and 1 unit of the third. Each bacterium of the second type consumes

1 unit of the first resource and 2 units each of the second and third. Each bacterium of the third type consumes 2 units of the first resource and 4 each of the second and third. If the test tube is supplied daily with 12,000 units of the first resource, 12,000 units of the second, and 14,000 units of the third, hc many of each species can coexist in equilibrium in the te tube so that all of the supplied resources are consume Prepare a table that shows some of the possibilities.

Discussion and Writing

38. Make up a system of three linear equations containing four variables that has infinitely many solutions. How many parameters will be in the solution to this system? Solve the system and create a table showing various solutions to the system of equations.

39. Make up a system of two linear equations containing fo variables that has infinitely many solutions. How many paramete will be in the solution to this system? Solve the system and crea a table showing various solutions to the system of equations.

CHAPTER 2 REVIEW OBJECTIVES

Section	Examples		You should be able to	Review Exercises
2.1	4, 5	1	Solve systems of equations by substitution (p. 53)	1–6
	6, 7	2	Solve systems of equations by elimination (p. 55)	1–6
	8	3	Identify inconsistent systems of equations containing two variables (p. 57)	4, 5
	9	4	Express the solutions of a system of dependent equations containing two variables (p. 58)	6
	10	5	Solve systems of three equations containing three variables (p. 59)	7–10
	11	6	Identify inconsistent systems of equations containing three variables (p. 61)	10
	12	7	Express the solutions of a system of dependent equations containing three variables (p. 62)	9
	13, 14	8	Solve applied problems involving system of equations (p. 63)	64, 37, 42
2.2	1	1	Write the augmented matrix of a system of linear equations (p. 69)	15–32
	2	2	Write the system from the augmented matrix (p. 71)	11–14
	3, 4	3	Perform row operations on a matrix (p. 71)	15–32
	5, 6	4	Solve a system of linear equations using Gaussian elimination (p. 73)	15–32
	8, 9	5	Express the solutions of a system with an infinite number of solutions (p. 78)	22
	10	6	Use the Gaussian elimination to identify an inconsistent system (p. 81)	21
	11, 12	7	Solve applied problems involving systems of equations (p. 81)	37, 42
2.3	3, 4	1	Analyze the reduced row echelon form of an augmented matrix (p. 89)	13–14, 33–36
	5, 6	2	Solve a system of m linear equations containing n variables (p. 90)	27–32
	7,8	3	Express the solution of a system with an infinite number of solutions (p. 92)	27–30
	9	4	Solve applied problems involving systems of equations (p. 94)	38–49

HINGS TO KNOW

ystems of Linear Equations (pp. 51–52)	Systems with a solution are consistent and either have a unique solution or have infinitely many solutions Systems with no solution are inconsistent
olving Systems of Linear Equations	Using substitution (pp. 53–55) Using elimination (pp. 55–56) Using Gaussian elimination (pp. 73–76) Using Gauss–Jordan elimination (p. 77)
Aatrix	Augmented matrix of a system of linear equations (p. 69) Row operations (p. 71)

REVIEW EXERCISES **Answers to odd-numbered problems begin on page AN-13.**

Blue problem numbers represent the author's suggestions for a Practice Test.

n Problems 1–10, solve each system of equations algebraically using the method of substitution or the method of elimination. If the system as no solution, say it is inconsistent.

1. $\begin{cases} 2x - y = 5 \\ 5x + 2y = 8 \end{cases}$

2. $\begin{cases} 2x + 3y = 2 \\ 7x - y = 3 \end{cases}$

3. $\begin{cases} x - 2y - 4 = 0 \\ 3x + 2y - 4 = 0 \end{cases}$

4. $\begin{cases} x - 3y + 4 = 0 \\ \frac{1}{2}x - \frac{3}{2}y + \frac{4}{3} = 0 \end{cases}$

5. $\begin{cases} 3x - 2y = 8 \\ x - \frac{2}{3}y = 12 \end{cases}$

6. $\begin{cases} 2x + 5y = 10 \\ 4x + 10y = 20 \end{cases}$

7. $\begin{cases} x + 2y - z = 6 \\ 2x - y + 3z = -13 \\ 3x - 2y + 3z = -16 \end{cases}$

8. $\begin{cases} x + 5y - z = 2 \\ 2x + y + z = 7 \\ x - y + 2z = 11 \end{cases}$

9. $\begin{cases} 2x - 4y + z = -15 \\ x + 2y - 4z = 27 \\ 5x - 6y - 2z = -3 \end{cases}$

10. $\begin{cases} x - 4y + 3z = 15 \\ -3x + y - 5z = -5 \\ -7x - 5y - 9z = 10 \end{cases}$

n Problems 11–14, write the system of equations corresponding to the given augmented matrix. In Problems 13–14, also write the solution.

11. $\left[\begin{array}{cc|c} 3 & 2 & 8 \\ 1 & 4 & -1 \end{array}\right]$

12. $\left[\begin{array}{ccc|c} 1 & 2 & 5 & -2 \\ 5 & 0 & -3 & 8 \\ 2 & -1 & 0 & 0 \end{array}\right]$

13. $\left[\begin{array}{ccc|c} 1 & 0 & 0 & 4 \\ 0 & 1 & 0 & 6 \\ 0 & 0 & 1 & -1 \end{array}\right]$

14. $\left[\begin{array}{ccc|c} 1 & 0 & 3 & 5 \\ 0 & 1 & 2 & 8 \end{array}\right]$

n Problems 15–32, use matrices to find the solution, if it exists, of each system of linear equations. If the system has infinitely nany solutions, write the solution using parameters and then list at least three solutions. If the system has no solution, ay it is inconsistent.

15. $\begin{cases} -5x + 2y = -2 \\ -3x + 3y = 4 \end{cases}$

16. $\begin{cases} -3x + 2y = 3 \\ -3x + 4y = 4 \end{cases}$

17. $\begin{cases} x + 2y + 5z = 6 \\ 3x + 7y + 12z = 23 \\ x + 4y = 25 \end{cases}$

18. $\begin{cases} x + 2y - z = -4 \\ 3x + 7y - z = -21 \\ x + 4y - 6z = -17 \end{cases}$

19. $\begin{cases} x + 2y + 7z = 2 \\ 3x + 7y + 18z = -1 \\ x + 4y + 2z = -13 \end{cases}$

20. $\begin{cases} x + 2y - 7z = -1 \\ 3x + 7y - 24z = 6 \\ x + 4y - 12z = 26 \end{cases}$

21. $\begin{cases} 2x - y + z = 1 \\ x + y - z = 2 \\ 3x - y + z = 0 \end{cases}$

22. $\begin{cases} 2x + 3y - z = 5 \\ x - y + z = 1 \\ 3x - 3y + 3z = 3 \end{cases}$

23. $\begin{cases} y - 2z = 6 \\ 3x + 2y - z = 2 \\ 4x + 3z = -1 \end{cases}$

24. $\begin{cases} 2x - y + 3z = 5 \\ x + 2z = 0 \\ 3x + 2y + z = -3 \end{cases}$

25. $\begin{cases} x - 3y = 5 \\ 3y + z = 0 \\ 2x - y + 2z = 2 \end{cases}$

26. $\begin{cases} x - z = 2 \\ 2x - y = 4 \\ x + y + z = 6 \end{cases}$

27. $\begin{cases} 3x + y - 2z = 3 \\ x - 2y + z = 4 \end{cases}$ **28.** $\begin{cases} 2x - y - 3z = 0 \\ x - 2y + z = 4 \end{cases}$ **29.** $\begin{cases} x + 2y - z = 5 \\ 2x - y + 2z = 0 \end{cases}$ **30.** $\begin{cases} x - y + 2z = 6 \\ 2x + 2y - z = -1 \end{cases}$

31. $\begin{cases} 2x - y = 6 \\ x - 2y = 0 \\ 3x - y = 6 \end{cases}$ **32.** $\begin{cases} x - 2y = 0 \\ 2x + y = 5 \\ x - 3y = 6 \end{cases}$

In Problems 33–36, analyze the solution, if any, of the system of equations having the given augmented matrix.

33. $\left[\begin{array}{ccc|c} 1 & 4 & 3 & 4 \\ 0 & 1 & 0 & -1 \\ 0 & 0 & 1 & 1 \end{array}\right]$ **34.** $\left[\begin{array}{ccc|c} 1 & 0 & -3 & 4 \\ 0 & 1 & 0 & 8 \\ 0 & 0 & 1 & 0 \end{array}\right]$ **35.** $\left[\begin{array}{cccc|c} 1 & 0 & 0 & 2 & 1 \\ 0 & 1 & 1 & 2 & 2 \\ 0 & 0 & 1 & 0 & 3 \end{array}\right]$ **36.** $\left[\begin{array}{cccc|c} 1 & 0 & 3 & 1 & 2 \\ 0 & 1 & 4 & 2 & 1 \end{array}\right]$

37. Mixture Sweet Delight Candies, Inc., sells boxes of candy consisting of creams and caramels. Each box sells for \$4 and holds 50 pieces of candy (all pieces are the same size). If the caramels cost \$0.05 to produce and the creams cost \$0.10 to produce, how many caramels and creams should be in each box for no profit and no loss? Would you increase or decrease the number of caramels in order to obtain a profit?

38. Cookie Orders A cookie company makes three kinds of cookies—oatmeal raisin, chocolate chip, and shortbread—packaged in small, medium, and large boxes. The small box contains 1 dozen oatmeal raisin and 1 dozen chocolate chip; the medium box has 2 dozen oatmeal raisin, 1 dozen chocolate chip, and 1 dozen shortbread; the large box contains 2 dozen oatmeal raisin, 2 dozen chocolate chip, and 3 dozen shortbread. If you require exactly 15 dozen oatmeal raisin, 10 dozen chocolate chip, and 11 dozen shortbread cookies, how many of each size box should you buy?

39. Mixture Problem A store sells almonds for \$6 per pound, cashews for \$5 per pound, and peanuts for \$2 per pound. One week the manager decides to prepare 100 16-ounce packages of nuts by mixing the peanuts, almonds, and cashews. Each package will be sold for \$4. The mixture is to produce the same revenue as selling the nuts separately. Prepare a table that shows some of the possible ways the manager can prepare the mixture.

40. Investments Three couples wish to invest monies that would earn an average of \$1800 per annum for a period of 5 years to finance their dream trip to Europe. As their financial consultant, you recommended they invest in certain mutual funds based on their performance over the past 5 years as of December 31, 2009: some money in Global Discovery at 6%, some money in Templeton Global Bond that yielded 8%, and some money in Franklin Natural Resource that yielded 10%. Prepare a table for each couple showing the various ways their goal can be achieved.

(a) If the first couple has \$20,000 to invest

(b) If the second couple has \$25,000 to invest

(c) If the third couple has \$30,000 to invest

Source: Franklin Templeton

41. Investments The Barkers want to retire in 10 years and buy a home in the Southwest. They have \$40,000 to invest over that period and plan to use their returns together with their initial investment and the profit on the sale of their existing home toward this purchase. As their financial consultant, you recommend they invest in mutual funds that had the following average returns per annum over the past 10 years as of December 31, 2009: some money in Franklin Strategic Income at 6%, some money in Franklin Small Cap Value that yielded 8%, and some money in Franklin Micro Cap Value that yielded 10%. Prepare a table showing the various ways this couple can achieve the following goals:

(a) They want \$2500 per year in income.

(b) They want \$3000 per year in income.

(c) They want \$3500 per year in income.

Source: Franklin Funds

42. Investments Kelly has \$20,000 to invest for a period of 10 years. As her financial planner, you recommend that she diversify into three Franklin Mutual Funds based on their average annual returns over the past 10 years ending December 31, 2009: Total Return at 5%, High Income at 7%, and Global Bond at 10%. Kelly wishes to earn an average of \$1390 per year in income. Also, Kelly wants her investment in Total Return to be \$3000 more than her investment in the Global Bond Fund. How much money should Kelly place in each investment?

Source: Franklin Funds

Chapter 2   Project

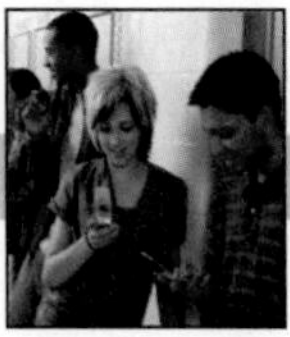

You decide to compare the basic charges for two cell phone plans that include texting and Web access. Here are the monthly costs for two plans.* Plan A includes a flat rate of $39.99 for 450 anytime minutes plus $.02 for each text message (sent or received) and $1.99 per megabyte of data usage (50 mobile Web pages will incur data usage charges for about .3 megabytes). For Plan A, additional minutes above 450 minutes cost $.45 per minute. Plan B includes a flat rate of $44.99 for 500 anytime minutes plus $.04 for each text message and $2.29 per megabyte of data usage. For Plan B, additional minutes above 500 minutes cost $.50 per minute.

The variables of the model are:

x: the number of anytime minutes used per month.

y: the number of text messages sent or received per month.

z: the number of megabytes of data usage per month.

A: the monthly cost for Plan A

B: the monthly cost for Plan B

1. Assume that $x \geq 450$ and express A as a linear expression involving x, y, and z.

2. Assume that $x \geq 500$ and express B as a linear expression involving x, y, and z.

3. Suppose that 600 anytime minutes were used for a given month. Find the values of y and z so that $A = B$. Let z be a parameter.

4. Suppose that 600 anytime minutes and 5 megabytes of data usage were billed for a given month. Let y_0 represent the number of text messages sent or received so that $A = B$ for that month. Find y_0. Determine which plan is less expensive for that month if $y > y_0$.

5. You estimate that you will send or receive about 350 text messages per month and use 8 megabytes of data per month. Assuming that $x \geq 500$, find the values of x for which $A \leq B$.

6. You decide that you will spend about $100 per month for your cell phone plan. Set $A = B = 100$ and find valid solutions for the resulting system of equations. Let z be a parameter. Note that solutions are valid only when $x \geq 500$, $y \geq 0$, and $z \geq 0$.

7. You estimate that you will use about 600 anytime minutes and require 3 megabytes of data usage in a given month. For what numbers of text messages would the cost of Plan B be less than or equal to the cost of Plan A for that month?

8. For what values of x will Plan A be less expensive than Plan B, if $y = z = 0$?

9. Suppose you learn of a third cell phone plan, Plan C, which includes unlimited text messaging and an unlimited data plan. The cost of Plan C is 59.99 for 500 anytime minutes. Each additional minute costs $.55 cents per minute. Let C represent the cost of Plan C. Find a linear expression for C in terms of the variables x, y, and z, assuming that $x \geq 500$.

10. If you expect to send or receive 450 text messages per month and use 10 megabytes of data per month, find the values of x for which $C \leq A$ and $C \leq B$, assuming that $x \geq 500$

11. If you expect to send or receive 800 text messages per month and do not expect to use your cell phone to access the Web, find the values of x for which $C \leq A$ and $C \leq B$, assuming $x \geq 500$. Then find the values of x for which $A \leq C$ and $A \leq B$, assuming that $x \geq 500$.

12. Suppose you expect to need between 600 and 1000 anytime minutes per month, an expect to send 400 text messages a month, and to have a data usage of about 8 megabytes per month. Determine which of the three plans (A, B, or C) would be the most economical.

Mathematical Questions from Professional Exams*

Use the following information to answer Problems 1–4:
Akron, Inc. owns 80% of the capital stock of Benson Company and 70% of the capital stock of Cashin, Inc. Benson Company owns 15% of the capital stock of Cashin, Inc. Cashin, Inc., in turn, owns 25% of the capital stock of Akron, Inc. These ownership interrelationships are illustrated in the diagram.

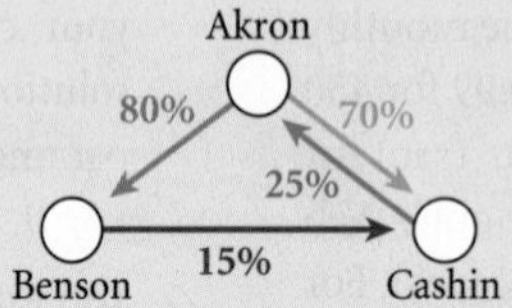

Net income before adjusting for interests in intercompany net income for each corporation follows:

Akron, Inc. $190,000
Benson Co. $170,000
Cashin, Inc. $230,000

Ignore all income tax considerations.

A_e = *Akron's consolidated net income; that is, its net income plus its share of the consolidated net income of Benson and Cashin*

B_e = *Benson's consolidated net income; that is, its net income plus its share of the consolidated net income of Cashin*

C_e = *Cashin's consolidated net income; that is, its net income plus its share of the consolidated net income of Akron*

1. **CPA Exam** The equation, in a set of simultaneous equations, which computes A_e is
   (a) $A_e = .75(190{,}000 + .8B_e + .7C_e)$
   (b) $A_e = 190{,}000 + .8B_e + .7C_e$
   (c) $A_e = .75(190{,}000) + .8(170{,}000) + .7(230{,}000)$
   (d) $A_e = .75(190{,}000) + .8B_e + .7C_e$

2. **CPA Exam** The equation, in a set of simultaneous equations, which computes B_e is
   (a) $B_e = 170{,}000 + .15C_e - .75A_e$
   (b) $B_e = 170{,}000 + .15C_e$
   (c) $B_e = .2(170{,}000) + .15(230{,}000)$
   (d) $B_e = .2(170{,}000) + .15C_e$

3. **CPA Exam** Cashin's minority interest in consolidated net income is
   (a) $.15(230{,}000)$
   (b) $230{,}000 + .25A_e$
   (c) $.15(230{,}000) + .25A_e$
   (d) $.15C_e$

4. **CPA Exam** Benson's minority interest in consolidated net income is
   (a) $34,316
   (b) $25,500
   (c) $45,755
   (d) $30,675

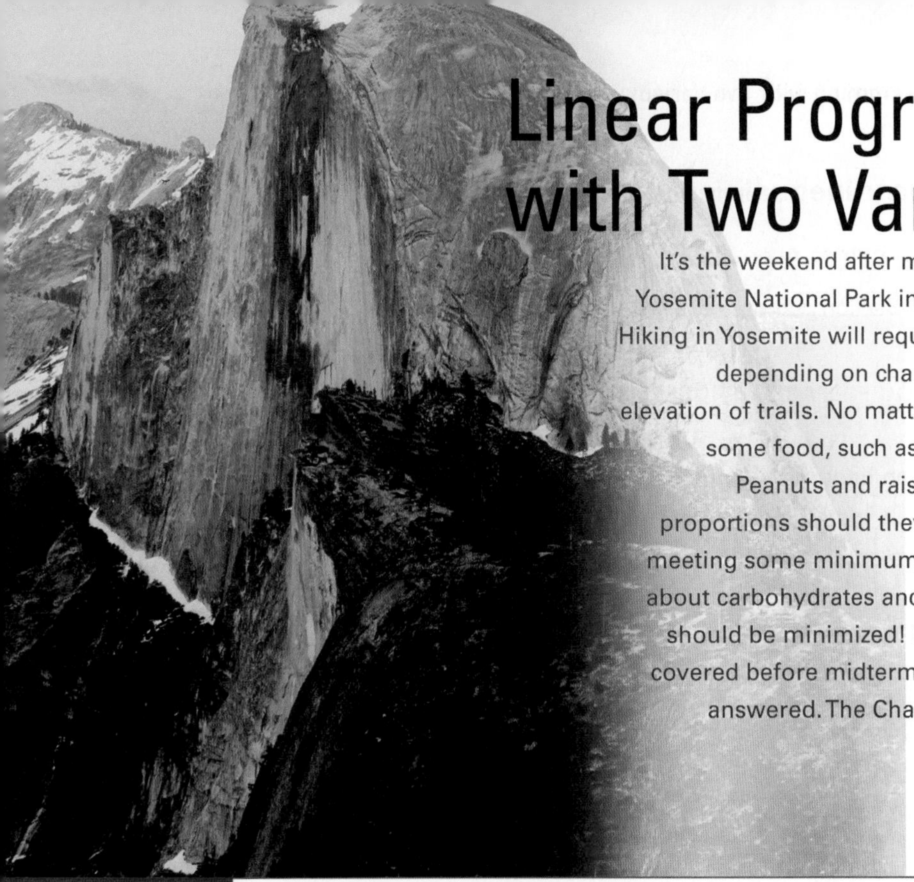

Linear Programming with Two Variables 4

It's the weekend after midterms, and a hiking trip to Yosemite National Park in California is on the agenda. Hiking in Yosemite will require some advance planning, depending on changes in weather, terrain, and elevation of trails. No matter where the hiking ends up, some food, such as a trail mix, will be required. Peanuts and raisins sound good. But in what proportions should they be mixed? And what about meeting some minimum calorie requirements? What about carbohydrates and protein? And, of course, fat should be minimized! Fortunately, this chapter was covered before midterms, so these questions can be answered. The Chapter Project at the end of the chapter will guide you.

A Look Back, A Look Forward

In Chapter 1, we discussed linear equations and applications that involve linear equations. In Chapter 2, we studied systems of linear equations. In this chapter, we discuss systems of linear inequalities and an important application involving linear equations and systems of linear inequalities: *linear programming*.

Whenever the analysis of a problem leads to minimizing or maximizing a linear expression in which the variables obey a collection of linear inequalities, a solution may be obtained using a linear programming model.

Historically, linear programming evolved out of the need to solve problems involving resource allocation by the U.S. Army during World War II. Among those who worked on such problems was George Dantzig, who later gave a general formulation of the linear programming problem and offered a method for solving it, called the *simplex method*. This method is discussed in Chapter 5.

In this chapter we study ways to solve linear programming problems that involve only two variables. As a result, we can use a geometric approach utilizing the graph of a system of linear inequalities to solve the problem.

4.1 Systems of Linear Inequalities

PREPARING FOR THIS SECTION *Before getting started, review the following:*

- Inequalities (Appendix A, Section A.2, pp. A–16 to A–18 and A–24 to A–25)
- Pairs of Lines (Section 1.2, pp. 22–26)
- Lines (Section 1.1, pp. 2–14)

NOW WORK THE 'ARE YOU PREPARED' PROBLEMS ON PAGE 187.

OBJECTIVES
1. Graph linear inequalities (p. 176)
2. Graph systems of linear inequalities (p. 179)
3. Solve applied problems involving systems of linear inequalities (p. 184)

Many applications contain language such as

"I only have at most \$50 to spend."

"No more than 40 hours of labor is available."

"Invest at least as much in stocks as in bonds."

To express statements such as these in mathematical terms requires an inequality. Fo example, if x is the amount to be invested in stocks and y is the amount to be invested i bonds, the statement "invest more in stocks than in bonds" can be expressed by th inequality $x > y$. This is an example of a *linear inequality in two variables x and y*.

Recall that a linear equation (linear equality) in two variables x and y is an equatio of the form

$$Ax + By = C \quad (1$$

where A, B, and C are real numbers and A and B are not both zero. If in Equation (1 we replace the equal sign by an inequality symbol, namely, one of the symbols $<$, $>$, $\leq$ or $\geq$, we obtain a **linear inequality in two variables** x and y.

For example, the expressions

$$3x + 2y \geq 4 \qquad 3x + 5y < -8 \qquad x - y > 0$$

are each linear inequalities in two variables. The first of these is called a **nonstri inequality** since the expression is satisfied when $3x + 2y = 4$, as well as whe $3x + 2y > 4$. The remaining two linear inequalities are **strict**.

1 Graph Linear Inequalities

The **graph of a linear inequality** in two variables x and y is the set of all points (x, y) fo which the inequality is satisfied.

EXAMPLE 1 Graphing a Linear Inequality

Graph the linear inequality: $2x + 3y \geq 6$

SOLUTION The linear inequality $2x + 3y \geq 6$ is equivalent to $2x + 3y > 6$ or $2x + 3y = 6$. So w begin by graphing the line $2x + 3y = 6$, noting that any point on this line will satisfy th inequality $2x + 3y \geq 6$. See Figure 1(a).

FIGURE 1

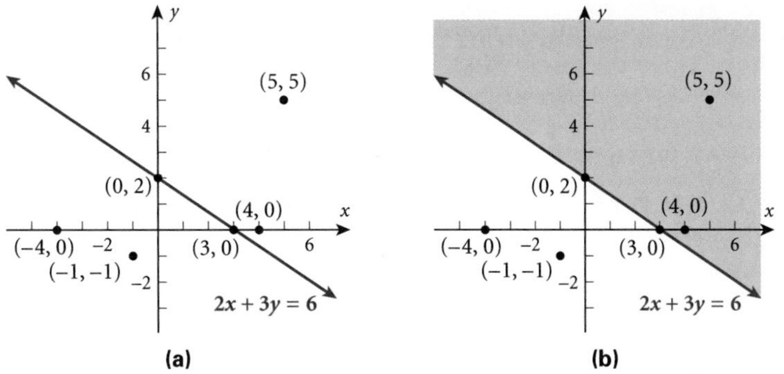

Now we test a few points, such as $(-1, -1)$, $(5, 5)$, $(4, 0)$, $(-4, 0)$, to see if they satisfy the inequality. We do this by substituting the coordinates of each point into the expression $2x + 3y$ and determining whether the result is ≥ 6 or < 6. Remember, we want $2x + 3y \geq 6$.

	$2x + 3y$	*Conclusion*
$(-1, -1)$:	$2(-1) + 3(-1) = -2 - 3 = -5 < 6$	Not part of the graph
$(5, 5)$:	$2(5) + 3(5) = 25 > 6$	Part of the graph
$(4, 0)$:	$2(4) + 3(0) = 8 > 6$	Part of the graph
$(-4, 0)$:	$2(-4) + 3(0) = -8 < 6$	Not part of the graph

Notice that the two points $(4, 0)$ and $(5, 5)$ that are part of the graph both lie on one side of the line $2x + 3y = 6$, while the points $(-4, 0)$ and $(-1, -1)$ that are not part of the graph lie on the other side. This is not an accident. The graph of the inequality consists of all points on the same side of the line as $(4, 0)$ and $(5, 5)$. The shaded region of Figure 1(b) illustrates the graph of the inequality. ■

The inequality in Example 1 is *nonstrict*, so the *corresponding line is part of the graph of the inequality*. If the inequality is *strict*, the *corresponding line is not part of the graph of the inequality*. We will indicate a strict inequality by using dashes to graph the line.

Steps for Graphing a Linear Inequality

STEP 1 Graph the corresponding linear equation, a line L. If the inequality is nonstrict, graph L using a solid line; if the inequality is strict, graph L using dashes.

STEP 2 Select a test point P not on the line L.

STEP 3 Substitute the coordinates of the test point P into the given inequality. If the coordinates of this point P satisfy the linear inequality, then all points on the same side of L as the point P satisfy the inequality. If the coordinates of the point P do not satisfy the linear inequality, then all points on the opposite side of L from P satisfy the inequality.

STEP 4 Shade (or strike) the region to be included.

EXAMPLE 2 Graphing a Linear Inequality

Graph the linear inequality: $2x - y < -4$

SOLUTION

STEP 1 The corresponding linear equation is the line

$$L: \quad 2x - y = -4$$

Since the inequality is strict, points on L are not part of the graph of the linear inequalit Graph L using a dashed line to indicate this fact. See Figure 2(a).

STEP 2 Select a point not on the line L to be tested, for example, (0, 0).

STEP 3 Test (0,0):

$$2x - y = 2(0) - 0 = 0 \qquad 2x - y < -4$$

Since 0 is not less than −4, the point (0, 0) does not satisfy the inequality. As a result, a points on the opposite side of L from (0, 0) satisfy the inequality.

STEP 4 The graph of $2x - y < -4$ is the shaded region of Figure 2(b).

FIGURE 2

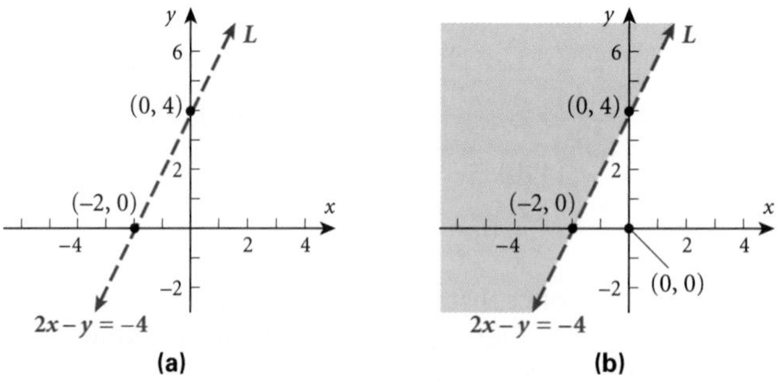

NOW WORK PROBLEM 15.

EXAMPLE 3 Graphing Linear Inequalities

Graph:

(a) $x \leq 3$ **(b)** $2x \leq y$

SOLUTION **(a)** The corresponding linear equation is $x = 3$, a vertical line. If we choose (0, 0) as th test point, we find that it satisfies the inequality $[0 \leq 3]$, so all points to the left o and on, the vertical line also satisfy the inequality. See Figure 3(a).

(b) The corresponding linear equation is $2x = y$. We choose the point (0, 2) as the te point. The point (0, 2) satisfies the inequality $[2(0) \leq 2]$, so all points on the sam side of the line as (0, 2) also satisfy the inequality. See Figure 3(b).

FIGURE 3

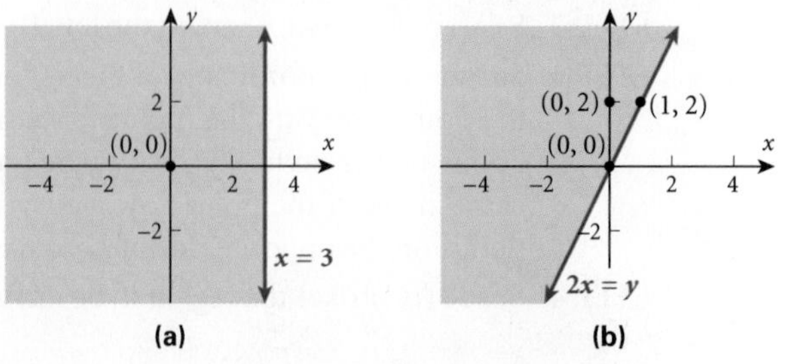

The set of points belonging to the graph of a linear inequality [for example, the shaded region in Figure 3(b)] is called a **half-plane**.

NOW WORK PROBLEM 13.

COMMENT A graphing utility can be used to obtain the graph of a linear inequality. See "Using a Graphing Utility to Graph Inequalities" in Appendix C, Section C.4, for a discussion. ■

2 Graph Systems of Linear Inequalities

Most applications that involve a linear inequality involve more than one linear inequality. For example, if x is the amount invested in stocks and y the amount invested in bonds, then both x and y must be nonnegative. If we also are told

"invest at least as much in stocks as in bonds"

"invest no more than \$5000 in bonds"

then we are led to the inequalities

$$x \geq y \qquad y \leq 5000 \qquad x \geq 0 \qquad y \geq 0$$

This is an example of *a system of linear inequalities.*

A **system of linear inequalities** is a collection of two or more linear inequalities. To **graph** a system of inequalities containing two variables x and y we locate all the points (x, y) whose coordinates satisfy *each* of the linear inequalities of the system.

EXAMPLE 4 Determining Whether a Point Belongs to the Graph of a System of Two Linear Inequalities

Determine which of the following points are part of the graph of the system of linear inequalities:

$$\begin{cases} 2x + y \leq 6 & (1) \\ x - y \geq 3 & (2) \end{cases}$$

(a) $P_1 = (6, 0)$ **(b)** $P_2 = (3, 5)$ **(c)** $P_3 = (0, 0)$ **(d)** $P_4 = (3, -2)$

SOLUTION We check to see if the given point satisfies each of the inequalities of the system.

(a) $P_1 = (6, 0)$

$$2x + y = 2(6) + 0 = 12 \qquad x - y = 6 - 0 = 6$$

$$2x + y \leq 6 \qquad x - y \geq 3$$

P_1 satisfies inequality (2) but not inequality (1), so P_1 is not part of the graph of the system.

(b) $P_2 = (3, 5)$

$$2x + y = 2(3) + 5 = 11 \qquad x - y = 3 - 5 = -2$$

$$2x + y \leq 6 \qquad x - y \geq 3$$

P_2 satisfies neither inequality (1) nor inequality (2), so P_2 is not part of the graph of the system.

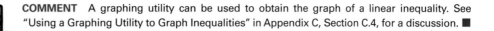

(c) $P_3 = (0, 0)$

$$2x + y = 2(0) + 0 = 0 \qquad x - y = 0 - 0 = 0$$
$$2x + y \le 6 \qquad x - y \ge 3$$

P_3 satisfies inequality (1) but not inequality (2), so P_3 is not part of the graph of the system.

(d) $P_4 = (3, -2)$

$$2x + y = 2(3) + (-2) = 4 \qquad x - y = 3 - (-2) = 5$$
$$2x + y \le 6 \qquad x - y \ge 3$$

P_4 satisfies both inequality (1) and inequality (2), so P_4 is part of the graph of the system.

NOW WORK PROBLEM 21.

Let's graph the information from Example 4. Figure 4(a) shows the graphs of the lines $2x + y = 6$ and $x - y = 3$ and the four points P_1, P_2, P_3, and P_4. Notice that because the two lines of the system intersect, the plane is divided into four regions. Since the graph of each linear inequality of the system is a half-plane, the graph of the system of linear inequalities is the intersection of these two half-planes. As a result, the region containing P_4 is the graph of the system. See Figure 4(b).

FIGURE 4

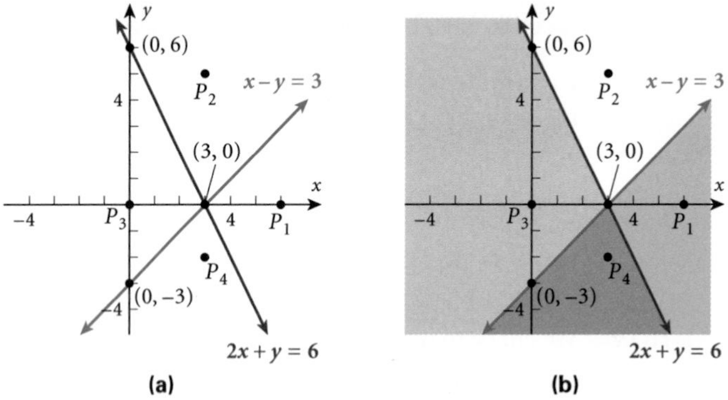

EXAMPLE 5 Graphing a System of Two Linear Inequalities

Graph the system: $\begin{cases} 2x - y \le -4 \\ x + y \ge -1 \end{cases}$

SOLUTION First graph each inequality separately. See Figures 5(a) and 5(b).

The solution of the system consists of all points common to these two half-planes. The region shaded gray in Figure 5(c) represents the solution of the system.

FIGURE 5

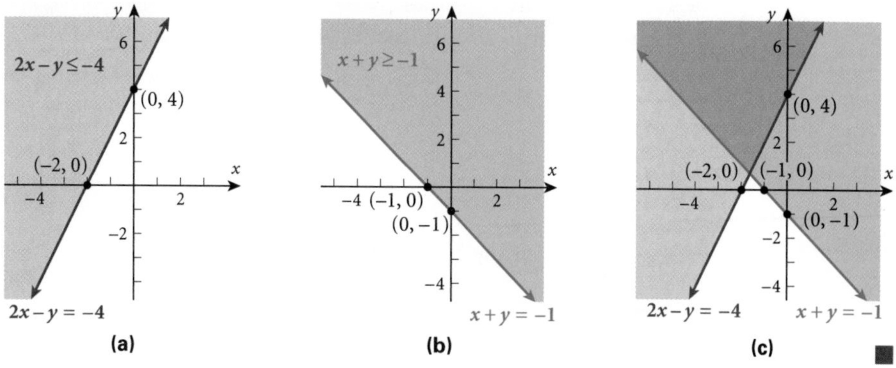

NOW WORK PROBLEMS 25 AND 33.

The lines in the system of linear inequalities given in Example 5 intersect. If the two lines of a system of two linear inequalities are parallel, the system of linear inequalities may or may not have a solution. Examples of such situations follow.

EXAMPLE 6 Graphing a System of Two Linear Inequalities

Graph the system: $\begin{cases} 2x - y \leq -4 \\ 2x - y \leq -2 \end{cases}$

SOLUTION First graph each inequality separately. See Figures 6(a) and 6(b). The region shaded gray in Figure 6(c) represents the solution of the system.

FIGURE 6

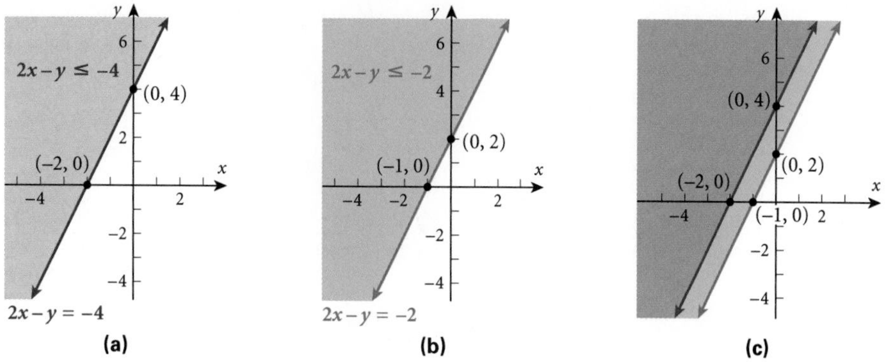

Notice that the solution of this system is the same as that of the single linear inequality $2x - y \leq -4$. ■

EXAMPLE 7 Graphing a System of Two Linear Inequalities

The solution of the system

$$\begin{cases} 2x - y \geq -4 \\ 2x - y \leq -2 \end{cases}$$

is the region shaded gray in Figure 7.

FIGURE 7

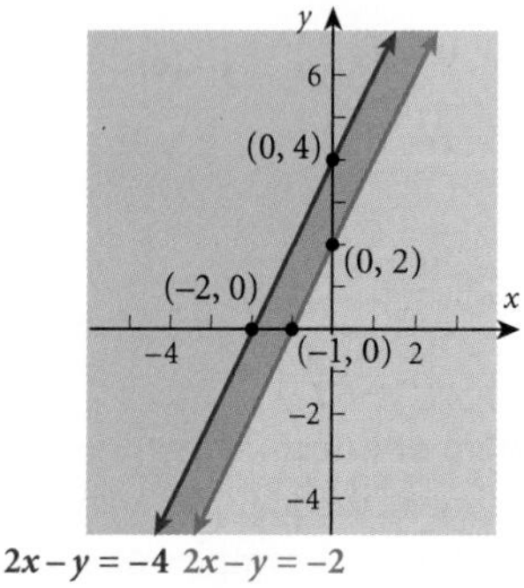

EXAMPLE 8 Graphing a System of Two Linear Inequalities

The system

$$\begin{cases} 2x - y \leq -4 \\ 2x - y \geq -2 \end{cases}$$

has no solution, as Figure 8 indicates (no gray region).

FIGURE 8

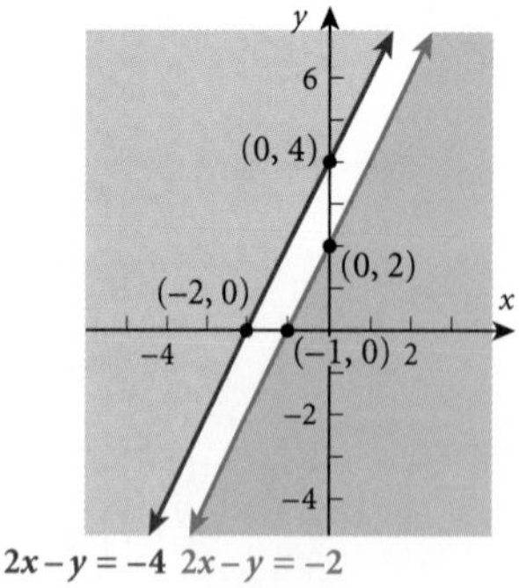

NOW WORK PROBLEM 37.

Until now, we have considered systems of only two linear inequalities. The nex example is of a system of four linear inequalities. As we shall see, the technique fo graphing such systems is the same as that used for graphing systems of two linea inequalities in two variables.

EXAMPLE 9 Graphing a System of Four Linear Inequalities

Graph the system:
$$\begin{cases} x + y \geq 2 \\ 2x + y \geq 3 \\ x \geq 0 \\ y \geq 0 \end{cases}$$

FIGURE 9

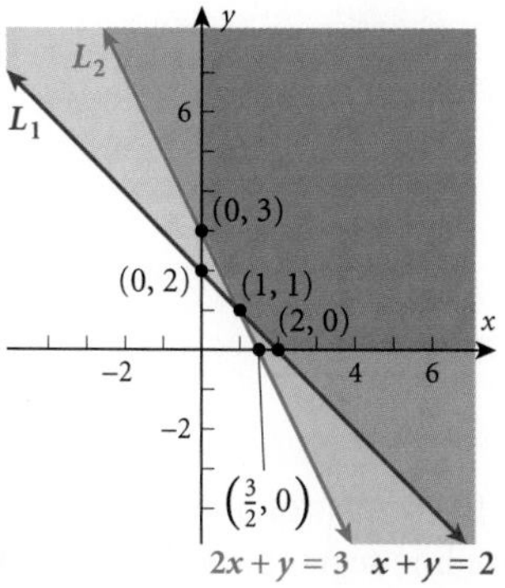

SOLUTION Again first graph the four lines:

$$L_1: \quad x + y = 2$$
$$L_2: \quad 2x + y = 3$$
$$L_3: \quad x = 0 \quad \text{(the } y\text{-axis)}$$
$$L_4: \quad y = 0 \quad \text{(the } x\text{-axis)}$$

The lines L_1 and L_2 intersect at the point $(1, 1)$, which you should verify. The inequalities $x \geq 0$ and $y \geq 0$ indicate that the graph of the system lies in quadrant I. The graph of the system consists of that part of the graphs of the inequalities $x + y \geq 2$ and $2x + y \geq 3$ that lie in quadrant I. See the dark blue region in Figure 9. ■

EXAMPLE 10 Graphing a System of Four Linear Inequalities

Graph the system:
$$\begin{cases} x + y \leq 2 \\ 2x + y \leq 3 \\ x \geq 0 \\ y \geq 0 \end{cases}$$

SOLUTION The lines associated with these linear inequalities are the same as those of the previous example. Again the inequalities $x \geq 0, y \geq 0$ indicate that the graph of the system lies in quadrant I. The graph of the system consists of the overlapping part of the graphs of the inequalities $x + y \leq 2$ and $2x + y \leq 3$ that lie in quadrant I. See Figure 10.

FIGURE 10

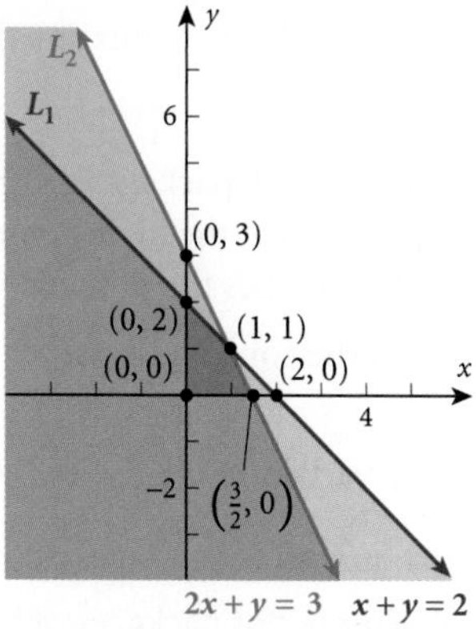

■

NOW WORK PROBLEM 39(a).

IN WORDS A set of points is bounded if it can be enclosed by a rectangle.

Some Terminology

Compare the graphs of the systems of linear inequalities given in Figures 9 and 10. The graph in Figure 9 is said to be **unbounded** in the sense that it extends infinitely far in some direction. The graph in Figure 10 is **bounded** in the sense that it can be enclosed by some rectangle of sufficiently large dimension. See Figure 11.

FIGURE 11

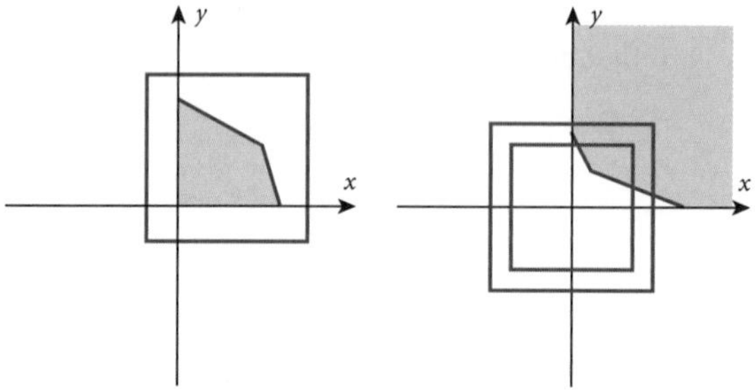

(a) Bounded graph **(b)** Unbounded graph

The boundary of each of the graphs in Figures 9 and 10 consists of line segments. In fact, the graph of any system of linear inequalities will have line segments as boundaries. The point of intersection of two line segments that form the boundary is called a **corner point*** of the graph. For example, the graph of the system given in Example 9 has the corner points (0, 3), (1, 1), and (2, 0). See Figure 9. The graph of the system given in Example 10 has the corner points (0, 2), (0, 0), $\left(\frac{3}{2}, 0\right)$, (1, 1). See Figure 10.

We shall soon see that the corner points of the graph of a system of linear inequalities play a major role in the procedure for solving linear programming problems.

NOW WORK PROBLEM 39(b).

3 Solve Applied Problems Involving Systems of Linear Inequalities

EXAMPLE 11 Analyzing a Mixture Problem

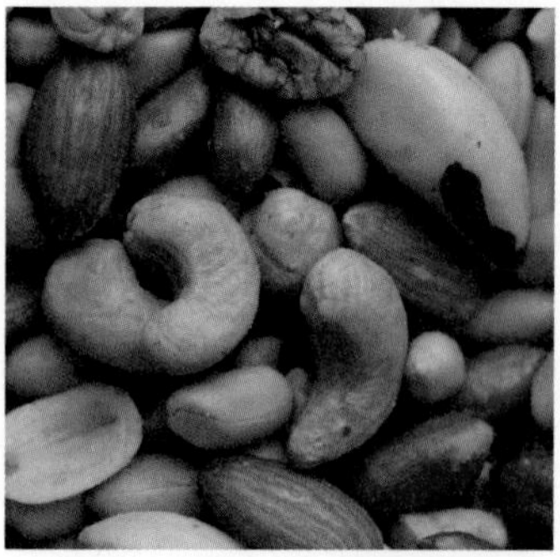

Nutt's Nuts has 75 pounds of cashews and 120 pounds of peanuts. These are to be mixed in 1-pound packages as follows: a low-grade mixture that contains 4 ounces of cashews and 12 ounces of peanuts and a high-grade mixture that contains 8 ounces of cashews and 8 ounces of peanuts.

(a) Use x to denote the number of packages of the low-grade mixture and use y to denote the number of packages of the high-grade mixture to be made. Write a system of linear inequalities that describes the possible number of each kind of package.

(b) Graph the system and list the corner points.

SOLUTION **(a)** We begin by naming the variables:

$$x = \text{Number of packages of low-grade mixture}$$
$$y = \text{Number of packages of high-grade mixture}$$

* *Some books use the term **vertex**.*

The only meaningful values for x and y are nonnegative values, so

$$x \geq 0 \qquad \text{and} \qquad y \geq 0$$

Next, note that there is a limit to the number of pounds of cashews and peanuts available. That is, the total number of pounds of cashews cannot exceed 75 pounds (1200 ounces), and the number of pounds of peanuts cannot exceed 120 pounds (1920 ounces). This means that

$$\begin{pmatrix}\text{Ounces of}\\ \text{cashews}\\ \text{required}\\ \text{for low-grade}\\ \text{mixture}\end{pmatrix}\begin{pmatrix}\text{Number of}\\ \text{packages of}\\ \text{low-grade}\\ \text{mixture}\end{pmatrix} + \begin{pmatrix}\text{Ounces of}\\ \text{cashews}\\ \text{required for}\\ \text{high-grade}\\ \text{mixture}\end{pmatrix}\begin{pmatrix}\text{Number of}\\ \text{packages}\\ \text{of high-}\\ \text{grade}\\ \text{mixture}\end{pmatrix} \begin{matrix}\text{cannot}\\ \text{exceed}\end{matrix}\ 1200$$

$$\begin{pmatrix}\text{Ounces of}\\ \text{peanuts}\\ \text{required}\\ \text{for low-grade}\\ \text{mixture}\end{pmatrix}\begin{pmatrix}\text{Number of}\\ \text{packages of}\\ \text{low-grade}\\ \text{mixture}\end{pmatrix} + \begin{pmatrix}\text{Ounces of}\\ \text{peanuts}\\ \text{for high-}\\ \text{grade}\\ \text{mixture}\end{pmatrix}\begin{pmatrix}\text{Number of}\\ \text{packages}\\ \text{of high-}\\ \text{grade}\\ \text{mixture}\end{pmatrix} \begin{matrix}\text{cannot}\\ \text{exceed}\end{matrix}\ 1920$$

In terms of the data given and the variables introduced, these statements can be written compactly as

$$4x + 8y \leq 1200$$
$$12x + 8y \leq 1920$$

The system of linear inequalities that gives the possible values of x and y is

$$\begin{cases} 4x + 8y \leq 1200 \\ 12x + 8y \leq 1920 \\ x \geq 0 \\ y \geq 0 \end{cases}$$

(b) The system of linear inequalities given above can be simplified to the equivalent form

$$\begin{cases} x + 2y \leq 300 & \text{Divide both sides by 4.} \\ 3x + 2y \leq 480 & \text{Divide both sides by 4.} \\ x \geq 0 \\ y \geq 0 \end{cases}$$

The graph of the system is given in Figure 12. Notice that the corner points of the graph are labeled. Three are easy to identify by inspection: (0, 0), (0, 150), and (160, 0).

The remaining one (90, 105) is found by solving the system of equations

$$\begin{cases} x + 2y = 300 \\ 3x + 2y = 480 \end{cases}$$

By subtracting the first equation from the second, we find $2x = 180$ or $x = 90$. Back-substituting in the first equation, we find $y = 105$.

FIGURE 12

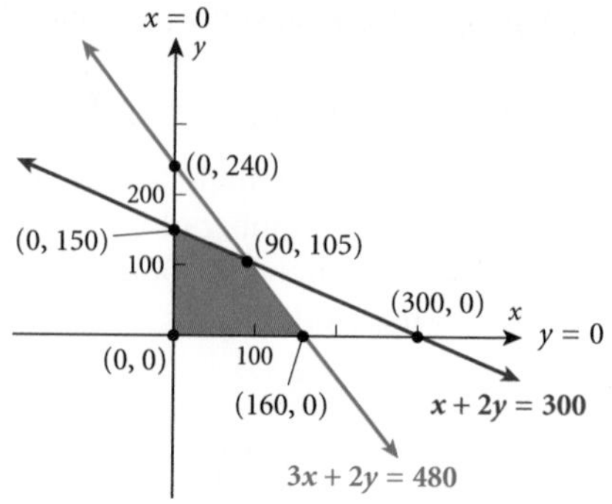

Any point in the dark blue region satisfies the conditions given in the problem. For example, the corner point (0, 150) represents the solution of having no low-grade mixture packages and 150 high-grade mixture packages. This solution uses 1200 ounces of cashews and 1200 ounces of peanuts.

NOW WORK PROBLEM 51.

EXAMPLE 12 Analyzing Investments

The Text and Academic Authors Association (TAA) plans to invest up to \$50,000 in the following two funds based on their average annual return for the past 5 years as of December 31, 2009: ICON Bond I at 4.35% and Frost Dividend Value Equity A at 5.25%. A minimum of \$10,000 is to go into the ICON Bond fund and a maximum of \$25,000 into the Frost Dividend fund. The governing board of TAA requires that the total average annual yield from these deposits be at least \$800.

(a) Let x represent the amount to be invested in the ICON Bond fund and let y represent the amount to be invested in the Frost Dividend fund. Write a system of inequalities representing possible amounts to be invested by TAA in these two funds.

(b) Graph the solution set for this system of inequalities and list its corner points.

(c) Interpret the meaning of each corner point.

Source: www.moneycentral.msn.com

SOLUTION **(a)** The variables x and y represent, respectively, the amount, in dollars, invested in the ICON Bond fund and the Frost Dividend fund. As a result, we must have

$$x \geq 0 \qquad y \geq 0$$

The statement "plans to deposit up to \$50,000" requires that

$$x + y \leq 50{,}000$$

The statement "a minimum of \$10,000 in the ICON Bond fund and a maximum of \$25,000 in the Frost Dividend fund" requires that

$$x \geq 10{,}000 \qquad y \leq 25{,}000$$

Finally, the statement "requires a total annual yield of at least \$800" means that the average yearly earnings from the ICON Bond fund ($0.0435x$) plus the average yearly earnings from the Frost Dividend fund ($0.0525y$) be at least \$800. That is,

$$0.0435x + 0.0525y \geq 800$$

Putting all this together, the possible amounts for x and y must obey the system of linear inequalities

$$\begin{cases} x \geq 0 \\ y \geq 0 \\ x + y \leq 50{,}000 \\ x \geq 10{,}000 \\ y \leq 25{,}000 \\ 0.0435x + 0.0525y \geq 800 \end{cases}$$

(b) The graph of the system is given in Figure 13. Every point (x, y) in the dark gray region will satisfy the conditions given.

(c) Each corner point represents an amount x and an amount y that satisfy the conditions given. For example, the corner point (10000, 25000) indicates that \$10,000 is invested in the ICON Bond fund and \$25,000 is invested in the Frost Dividend fund. The average yearly earnings for this scenario are $0.0435 \cdot 10000 + 0.0525 \cdot 25000 = \$1747.50$. See Table 1 for a listing of each corner point and the average yearly earnings.

FIGURE 13

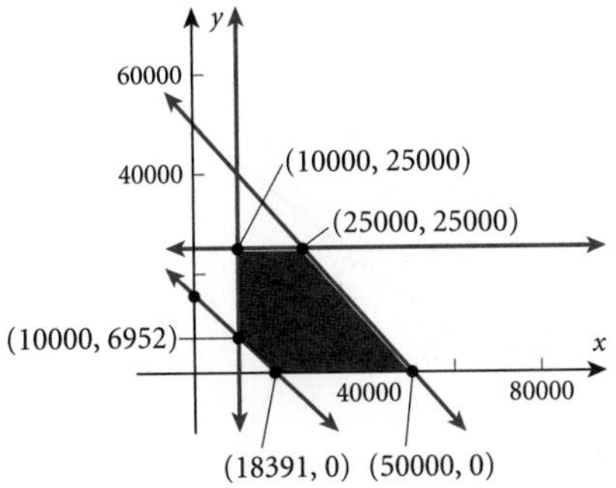

TABLE 1

Corner Point	Average Yearly Earnings
(18391, 0)	\$ 800
(50000, 0)	\$2175
(10000, 6952)	\$ 800
(10000, 25000)	\$1748
(25000, 25000)	\$2400

All values are rounded to the nearest dollar.

EXERCISE 4.1 Answers Begin on Page AN–19.

'Are You Prepared?' Problems Answers are given at the end of these exercises. If you get a wrong answer, read the pages listed in red.

1. ***True or False***
   (a) $-3 < -5$ (b) $-2 > -1$ (pp. A–16 to A–18)
2. The solution of the inequality $2x + 3 < 9$ is ________. (pp. A–24 to A–25)
3. Graph the line $2x + 3y = 6$. (pp. 2–14)
4. Find the point of intersection of the lines $3x + 2y = 480$ and $x + 2y = 300$. (pp. 22–26)
5. ***True or False*** The lines
   $$2x + y = 6 \quad \text{and} \quad y = 2x + 2$$
   are parallel. (pp. 22–26)

Concepts and Vocabulary

6. The graph of a linear inequality is called a(n) ________.
7. ***True or False*** Sometimes the graph of a system of linear inequalities will have no points.
8. ***True or False*** The graph of a system of linear inequalities is sometimes unbounded.

Skill Building

In Problems 9–20, graph each inequality.

9. $x \geq 0$

10. $y \geq 0$

11. $x < 4$

12. $y \leq 6$

13. $y \geq 1$

14. $x > 2$

15. $2x + y \leq 4$

16. $3x + 2y \geq 6$

17. $5x + y \geq 10$

18. $x + 2y > 4$

19. $x + 5y < 5$

20. $3x + y \leq 3$

21. Without graphing, determine which of the points $P_1 = (3, 8)$, $P_2 = (12, 9)$, $P_3 = (5, 1)$ are part of the graph of the following system:

$$\begin{cases} x + 3y \geq 0 \\ -3x + 2y \geq 0 \end{cases}$$

22. Without graphing, determine which of the poin $P_1 = (9, -5)$, $P_2 = (12, -4)$, $P_3 = (4, 1)$ are part of tl graph of the following system:

$$\begin{cases} x + 4y \leq 0 \\ 5x + 2y \geq 0 \end{cases}$$

23. Without graphing, determine which of the points $P_1 = (2, 3)$, $P_2 = (10, 10)$, $P_3 = (5, 1)$ are part of the graph of the following system:

$$\begin{cases} 3x + 2y \geq 0 \\ x + y \leq 15 \end{cases}$$

24. Without graphing, determine which of the poin $P_1 = (2, 6)$, $P_2 = (12, 4)$, $P_3 = (4, 2)$ are part of the graph o the following system:

$$\begin{cases} 2x - 5y \leq 0 \\ x + 3y \leq 15 \end{cases}$$

In Problems 25–32, determine which region a, b, c, or d represents the graph of the given system of linear inequalities. The regions a, b, c, and are nonoverlapping regions bounded by the indicated lines.

25. $\begin{cases} 5x - 4y \leq 8 \\ 2x + 5y \leq 23 \end{cases}$

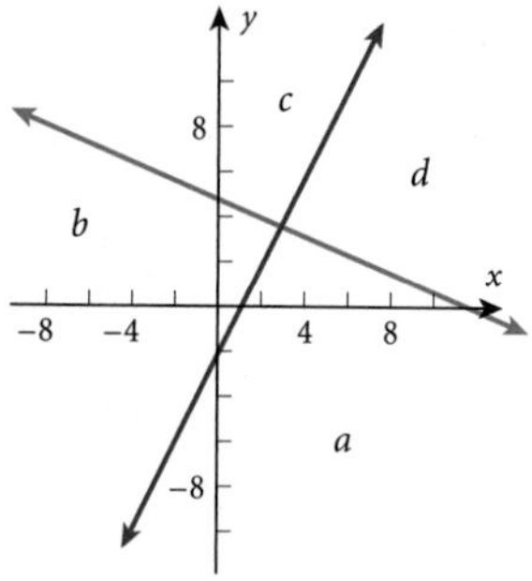

26. $\begin{cases} 4x - 5y \leq 0 \\ 4x + 2y \leq 28 \end{cases}$

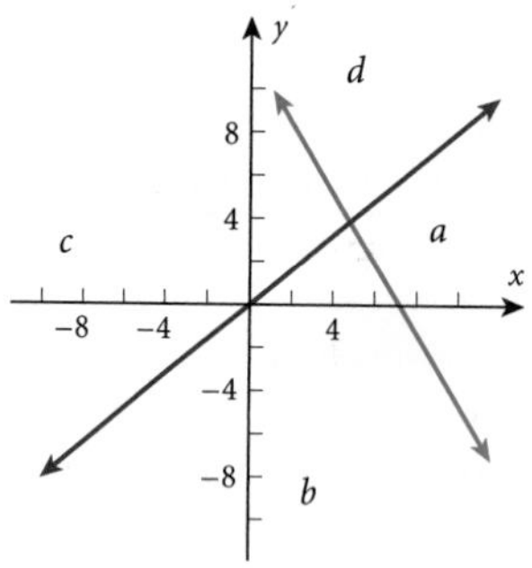

27. $\begin{cases} 2x - 3y \geq -3 \\ 2x + 3y \leq 16 \end{cases}$

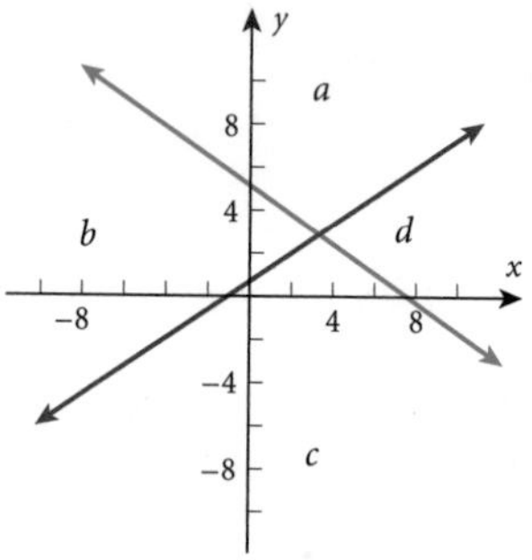

28. $\begin{cases} 6x - 5y \leq 5 \\ 2x + 4y \geq 30 \end{cases}$

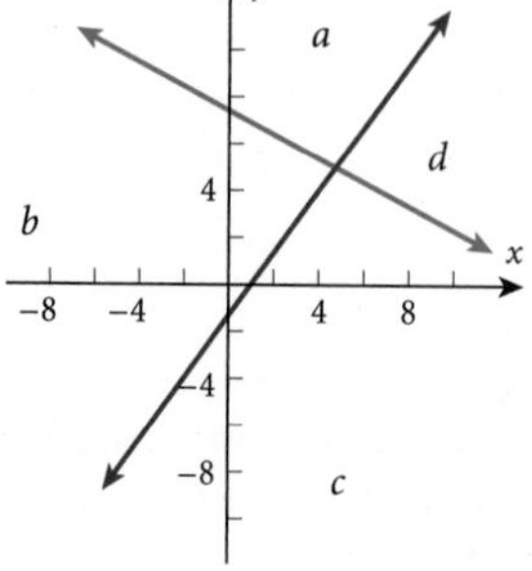

29. $\begin{cases} 5x - 3y \geq 3 \\ 2x + 6y \geq 30 \end{cases}$

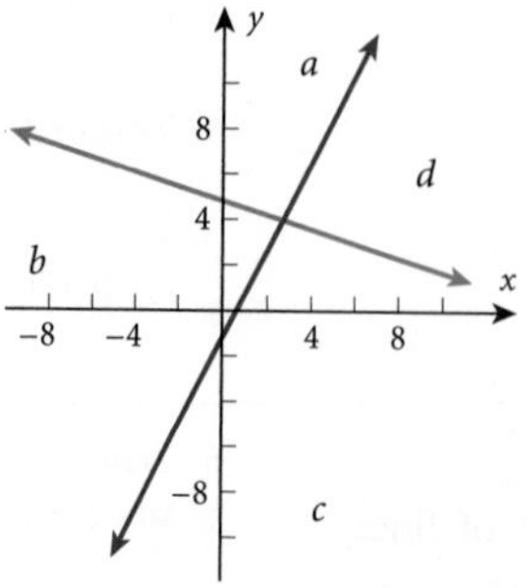

30. $\begin{cases} 5x - 5y \geq 10 \\ 6x + 4y \geq 48 \end{cases}$

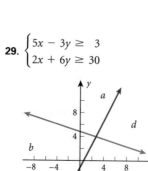

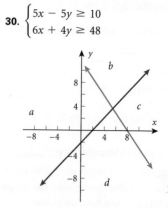

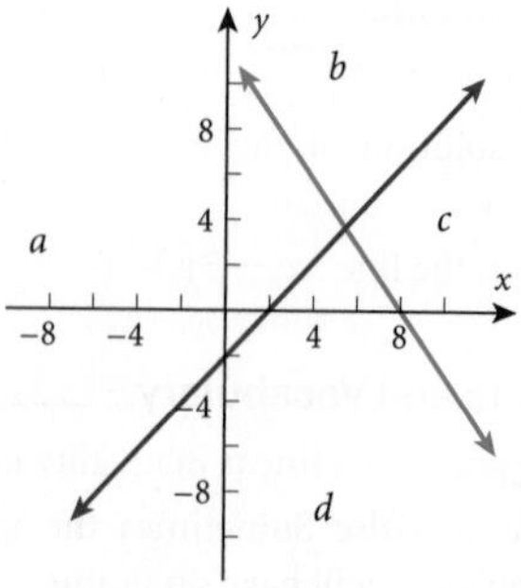

In Problems 31–38, graph each system of inequalities.

31. $\begin{cases} 2x + 3y \le 6 \\ x - y \ge 2 \end{cases}$

32. $\begin{cases} 3x - 2y \ge 6 \\ x + y \le 2 \end{cases}$

33. $\begin{cases} 4x - 3y \ge 12 \\ 4x + 3y \ge 12 \end{cases}$

34. $\begin{cases} 6x + 3y \le 6 \\ x - 3y \ge 1 \end{cases}$

35. $\begin{cases} 3x + 2y \le 6 \\ 3x + 2y \ge 0 \end{cases}$

36. $\begin{cases} x - 2y \le -4 \\ 2x - 4y \ge 0 \end{cases}$

37. $\begin{cases} 5x - 2y \le -10 \\ 10x - 4y \le 0 \end{cases}$

38. $\begin{cases} x + y \le 1 \\ x + y \le 2 \end{cases}$

In Problems 39–50, (a) graph each system of linear inequalities and (b) determine whether the graph is bounded or unbounded. List each corner point of the graph.

39. $\begin{cases} x + y \ge 2 \\ x \ge 0 \\ y \ge 0 \end{cases}$

40. $\begin{cases} 2x + 3y \le 6 \\ x \ge 0 \\ y \ge 0 \end{cases}$

41. $\begin{cases} x + y \ge 2 \\ 2x + 3y \le 6 \\ x \ge 0 \\ y \ge 0 \end{cases}$

42. $\begin{cases} x + y \ge 2 \\ 2x + 3y \le 12 \\ 3x + 2y \le 12 \\ x \ge 0 \\ y \ge 0 \end{cases}$

43. $\begin{cases} x + y \ge 2 \\ x + y \le 8 \\ 2x + y \le 10 \\ x \ge 0 \\ y \ge 0 \end{cases}$

44. $\begin{cases} x + y \ge 2 \\ x + y \le 8 \\ x + 2y \ge 1 \\ x \ge 0 \\ y \ge 0 \end{cases}$

45. $\begin{cases} x + y \ge 2 \\ 2x + 3y \le 12 \\ 3x + y \le 12 \\ x \ge 0 \\ y \ge 0 \end{cases}$

46. $\begin{cases} x + y \ge 2 \\ 2x + y \ge 3 \\ x \ge 0 \\ y \ge 0 \end{cases}$

47. $\begin{cases} x + 2y \ge 1 \\ y \le 4 \\ x \ge 0 \\ y \ge 0 \end{cases}$

48. $\begin{cases} x + 2y \ge 1 \\ x + 2y \le 10 \\ x + y \ge 2 \\ x + y \le 8 \\ x \ge 0 \\ y \ge 0 \end{cases}$

49. $\begin{cases} x + 2y \ge 2 \\ x + y \le 4 \\ 3x + y \le 3 \\ x \ge 0 \\ y \ge 0 \end{cases}$

50. $\begin{cases} 2x + y \ge 2 \\ 3x + 2y \le 6 \\ x + y \ge 2 \\ x \ge 0 \\ y \ge 0 \end{cases}$

Applications

51. **Mixture Problem** Nutt's Nuts has 60 pounds of almonds and 90 pounds of peanuts available. These are to be mixed in 1-pound packages as follows: a low-grade mixture that contains 4 ounces of almonds and 12 ounces of peanuts and a high-grade mixture that contains 8 ounces of almonds and 8 ounces of peanuts.
    (a) Use x to denote the number of packages of the low-grade mixture and use y to denote the number of packages of the high-grade mixture. Write a system of linear inequalities that describes the possible number of each kind of package.
    (b) Graph the system and list the corner points.

52. **Mixture Problem** Nutt's Nuts has 60 pounds of cashews and 90 pounds of peanuts available. These are to be mixed in 1-pound packages as follows: a low-grade mixture that contains 4 ounces of cashews and 12 ounces of peanuts and a high-grade mixture that contains 10 ounces of cashews and 6 ounces of peanuts.
    (a) Use x to denote the number of packages of the low-grade mixture and use y to denote the number of packages of the high-grade mixture. Write a system of linear inequalities that describes the possible number of each kind of package.
    (b) Graph the system and list the corner points.

53. **Manufacturing** Mike's Famous Toy Trucks company manufactures two kinds of toy trucks—a dumpster and a tanker. In the manufacturing process, each dumpster requires 3 hours of grinding and 4 hours of finishing, while each tanker requires 2 hours of grinding and 3 hours of finishing. The company has two grinders and three finishers, each of whom works at most 40 hours per week.
    (a) Using x to denote the number of dumpsters and y to denote the number of tankers, write a system of linear inequalities that describes the possible numbers of each truck that can be manufactured per week.
    (b) Graph the system and list its corner points.

54. **Manufacturing** Repeat Problem 53 if the company only has one grinder and two finishers available, each of whom works at most 40 hours per week.

55. **Financial Planning** The Harpers have up to \$25,000 to invest. As their financial advisor, you recommend they make the following investments in two funds based on their average yearly performance for the past 5 years ending December 31, 2009: at least \$15,000 in a Dividend Equity fund with an average yearly return of 6% and at most \$10,000 in a Global Bond fund with an average yearly return of 9%.
    (a) Using x to denote the amount of money invested in the Dividend Equity fund and y to denote the amount to be invested in the Global Bond fund, write a system of inequalities that describes this situation.

(b) Graph the system and list its corner points.

(c) Interpret the meaning of each corner point in relation to the investments it represents.

56. Financial Planning Use the information supplied in Problem 55, along with the fact that the couple will invest at least \$20,000, to answer parts (a), (b), and (c).

57. Nutrition A farmer prepares feed for livestock by combining two types of grain. Each unit of the first grain contains 1 unit of protein and 5 units of iron while each unit of the second grain contains 2 units of protein and 1 unit of iron. Each animal must receive at least 5 units of protein and 16 units of iron each day.

(a) Write a system of linear inequalities that describes the possible amounts of each grain the farmer needs to prepare. Be sure to name the variables.

(b) Graph the system and list the corner points.

58. Investment Strategy Kathleen wishes to invest up to a total of \$40,000 in class AA bonds and stocks. Furthermore, she believes that the amount invested in class AA bonds should be at most one-third of the amount invested in stocks.

(a) Write a system of linear inequalities that describes the possible amount of investments in each security. Be sure to name the variables.

(b) Graph the system and list the corner points.

59. Nutrition To maintain an adequate daily diet, nutritionists recommend the following: at least 85 g of carbohydrate, 70 g of fat, and 50 g of protein. An ounce of food A contains 5 g of carbohydrate, 3 g of fat, and 2 g of protein, while an ounce of food B contains 4 g of carbohydrate, 3 g of fat, and 3 g of protein.

(a) Write a system of linear inequalities that describes the possible quantities of each food. Be sure to name the variables.

(b) Graph the system and list the corner points.

60. Transportation A microwave company has two plants, one on the East Coast and one in the Midwest. It takes 25 hours (packing, transportation, and so on) to transport an order of microwaves from the eastern plant to its central warehouse and 20 hours from the Midwest plant to its central warehouse. It costs \$80 to transport an order from the eastern plant to the central warehouse and \$40 from the midwestern plant to its central warehouse. There are 1000 work-hours available for packing, transportation, and so on, and \$3000 for transportation cost.

(a) Write a system of linear inequalities that describes the transportation system. Be sure to name the variables.

(b) Graph the system and list the corner points.

61. Financial Planning In March 2010, a couple plans to invest \$30,000 in two funds based on their average yearly performance for the past 5 years ending December 31, 2009: ICON Bond fund with an average return of 4.35% and ING Mid Cap Opportunities with an average return of 5.05%. They wish to invest a minimum of \$3000 in the ICON Bond fund and a minimum of \$5000 in the ING Mid Cap Opportunities fund. They also want the total average annual yield from these funds to be at least \$500.

(a) Let x represent the amount to be invested in the ICON Bond fund and let y represent the amount to be invested in the ING Mid Cap Opportunities fund. Write a system of inequalities representing the possible amounts to be invested in these two funds.

(b) Graph the solution set for this system of inequalities and list its corner points.

(c) Interpret the meaning of each corner point.

Source: morningstar.com

62. Financial Planning The members of an investment club decide to deposit at least \$30,000 and up to \$100,000 in two funds based on their average annual returns for the past 5 years: the American Independent Stock I fund at 5% and the Multi Sector Bond Fixed Income fund at 4.75%. Also they decide that the amount invested in the American Independent Stock I fund should be at least \$8000 more than the amount invested in the Multi Sector Bond fund I.

(a) Let x represent the amount to be invested in the American Independent Stock I fund and let y represent the amount to be invested in the Multi Sector Bond Fixed Income fund. Write a system of inequalities representing the possible amounts to be invested in these two funds.

(b) Graph the solution set for this system of inequalities and list its corner points.

(c) Calculate the total annual yield from both accounts at each corner point of the solution set.

Source: morningstar.com

63. Mutual Funds The table lists two mutual funds: the John Hancock Large Cap Equity I fund and the T Rowe Price Latin America fund.

Fund	Average Annual Rate of Return for the Five-Year Period Ending 12-31-09
J Hancock Large Cap Equity	9.97%
T Rowe Price Latin America	23.65%

The manager of a pension fund is considering investing up to \$200,000 in these two mutual funds. She concludes that the amount invested in the T Rowe Price Latin America fund should be at least three times as much as the amount invested in the John Hancock Large Cap Equity fund and that a minimum of \$20,000 should be invested in the John Hancock Large Cap Equity fund.

(a) Let x represent the amount to be invested in the John Hancock Large Cap Equity fund and let y represent the amount to be invested in the T Rowe Price Latin America fund. Write a system of inequalities representing the possible amounts to be invested by this manager in these two funds.

(b) Graph the solution set for this system of inequalities and list its corner points.

(c) Calculate a projected annual return from both investments at each corner point of the solution set. Assume that the annual rate of return for each mutual fund will be equal to the average annual rate of return for the five-year period ending on 12-31-09.

Source: biz.yahoo.com

4. **Home Mortgages** On March 1, 2010, Fremont Bank offered no-closing-cost home mortgage at a 5.125% annual rate for 30-year fixed-rate loans and a 4.375% annual rate for 15-year fixed-rate loans. Suppose Fremont Bank is planning to allocate up to \$30 million for these two kinds of loans, with a minimum of \$5 million for each type of loan. Fremont Bank has also decided that the amount allocated to the 15-year loans should be no more than half the amount allocated to the 30-year loans.

(a) Let x represent the amount to be allocated to the 30-year fixed-rate loans, and let y represent the amount to be allocated to the 15-year fixed-rate loans. Write a system of inequalities representing possible amounts to be allocated to these two types of loans.

(b) Graph the solution set for this system of inequalities and list its corner points.

(c) For each corner point, calculate the total amount of interest received by Fremont Bank in the first month.

Source: Fremont Bank

iscussion and Writing

5. Make up a system of linear inequalities that has no solution.

6. Make up a system of linear inequalities that has a single point as a solution.

67. Draw a graph that is unbounded. How would you convince someone that it is, in fact, unbounded?

re You Prepared?' Answers

1. (a) False (b) False

2. $x < 3$

3.

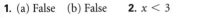

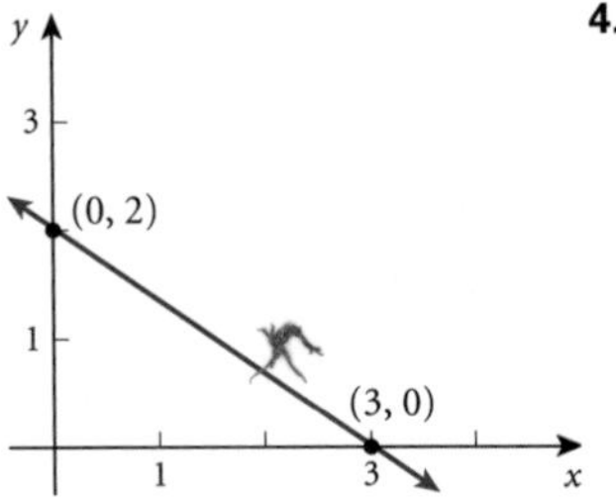

4. (90, 105)

5. False

4.2 A Geometric Approach to Linear Programming Problems with Two Variables*

OBJECTIVES
1. Identify a linear programming problem with two variables (p. 192)
2. Solve a linear programming problem with two variables (p. 193)

* *Because the word* programming *has come to be associated with the writing of computer code, many people have opted to change from the terminology* linear programming *to* linear optimization. *For now, we shall continue to use the historical and more familiar term* linear programming *in this chapter and the next chapter.*

1 Identify a Linear Programming Problem with Two Variables

To help see the characteristics of a linear programming problem, look again at Example 11 of the previous section.

> Nutt's Nuts has 75 pounds of cashews and 120 pounds of peanuts. These are to be mixed in 1-pound packages as follows: a low-grade mixture that contains 4 ounces of cashews and 12 ounces of peanuts and a high-grade mixture that contains 8 ounces of cashews and 8 ounces of peanuts.

Suppose that in addition to the information given above, we also know what the profit will be on each type of mixture. For example, suppose the profit is \$0.25 on each package of the low-grade mixture and is \$0.45 on each package of the high-grade mixture. The question of importance to the manager is "How many packages of each type of mixture should be prepared to maximize the profit?"

If P symbolizes the profit, x the number of packages of low-grade mixture, and y the number of high-grade packages, then the question can be restated as "What are the values of x and y so that the expression

$$P = \$0.25x + \$0.45y$$

is a maximum?"

This problem is typical of a **linear programming problem**. It requires that a certain linear expression, in this case the profit, be maximized. This linear expression is called the **objective function**. Furthermore, the problem requires that the maximum profit be achieved under certain restrictions or **constraints**, each of which are linear inequalities involving the variables. The linear programming problem may be restated as

Maximize

$$P = \$0.25x + \$0.45y \quad \text{Objective function}$$

subject to the conditions that

$$\begin{cases} x + 2y \le 300 & \text{Cashew constraint} \\ 3x + 2y \le 480 & \text{Peanut constraint} \\ x \ge 0 & \text{Nonnegativity constraint} \\ y \ge 0 & \text{Nonnegativity constraint} \end{cases}$$

In general, every linear programming problem has two components:

1. A linear objective function to be maximized or minimized.
2. A collection of linear inequalities that must be satisfied simultaneously.

Definition

Linear Programming Problem

A **linear programming problem** in two variables, x and y, consists of maximizing or minimizing an **objective function**

$$z = Ax + By$$

where A and B are given real numbers, not both zero, subject to certain conditions or **constraints** expressible as a system of linear inequalities in x and y. The points that satisfy all the constraints are called **feasible points**.

Let's look at this definition more closely. To maximize (or minimize) the quantity $z = Ax + By$ means to locate the points (x, y) that result in the largest (or smallest) value of z. But not all points (x, y) are eligible. Only the points that obey *all* the constraints are potential solutions. That is, only feasible points are eligible to be solutions.

2 Solve a Linear Programming Problem with Two Variables

In a linear programming problem we want to find the feasible point that maximizes (or minimizes) the objective function.

By a **solution to a linear programming problem** we mean a feasible point (x, y), together with the value of the objective function at that point, which maximizes (or minimizes) the objective function. If none of the feasible points maximizes (or minimizes) the objective function, or if there are no feasible points, then the linear programming problem has no solution.

EXAMPLE 1 Solving a Linear Programming Problem

Minimize

$$z = x + 2y$$

subject to the constraints

$$\begin{cases} x + y \geq 1 \\ x \geq 0 \\ y \geq 0 \end{cases}$$

SOLUTION The objective function to be minimized is $z = x + 2y$. The constraints are the linear inequalities

$$\begin{cases} x + y \geq 1 \\ x \geq 0 \\ y \geq 0 \end{cases}$$

FIGURE 14

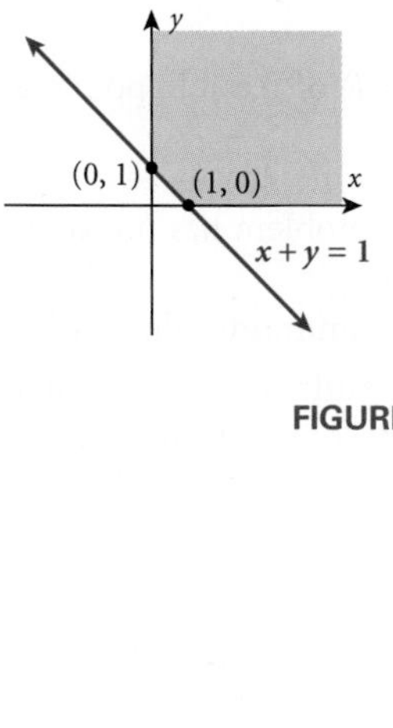

Begin by graphing the constraints. See Figure 14. The shaded portion illustrates the set of feasible points.

To see if there is a smallest z, graph $z = x + 2y$ for some choice of z, say, $z = 3$. See Figure 15. By moving the line $x + 2y = 3$ parallel to itself, we can observe what happens for different values of z. Since we want a minimum value for z, we try to move $z = x + 2y$ down as far as possible while keeping some part of the line within the set of feasible points. The "best" solution is obtained when the line just touches a corner point of the set of feasible points. If you refer to Figure 15, you will see that the best solution is $x = 1, y = 0$, which yields $z = 1$. There is no other feasible point for which z is smaller.

FIGURE 15

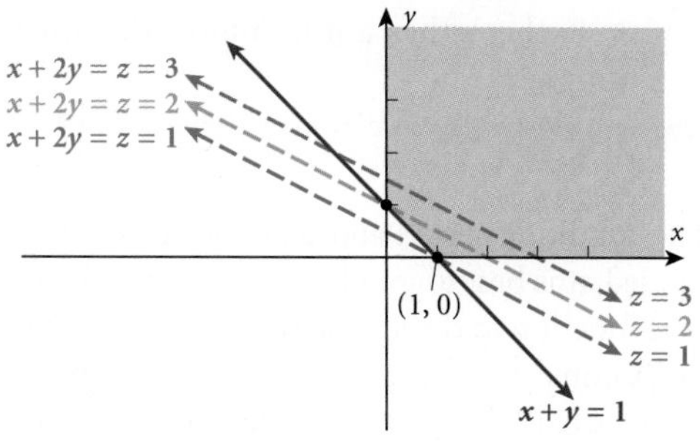

■

The next example illustrates a linear programming problem that has no solution.

EXAMPLE 2 A Linear Programming Without a Solution

Maximize

$$z = x + 2y$$

subject to the constraints

$$\begin{cases} x + y \geq 1 \\ x \geq 0 \\ y \geq 0 \end{cases}$$

FIGURE 16

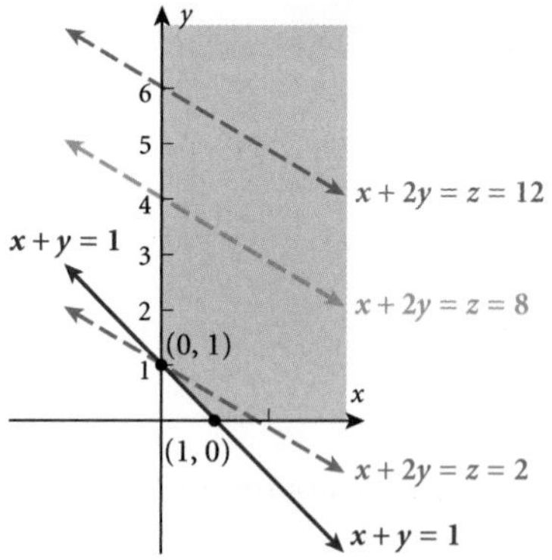

SOLUTION First, graph the constraints. See Figure 16. The shaded portion illustrates the set o feasible points. Notice that the graph is unbounded.

The graphs of the objective function $z = x + 2y$ for $z = 2$, $z = 8$, and $z = 12$ ar also shown in Figure 16. Observe that we continue to get larger values for z by movin the graph of the objective function upward. But there is no feasible point that will mak *z largest*. No matter how large a value is assigned to z, there is a feasible point that wi give a larger value. Since there is no feasible point that makes z largest, we conclude tha this linear programming problem has no solution. ■

Notice that the corresponding minimum problem—Minimize $z = x + 2y$ subject t the constraints given in Example 2—has a solution. The minimum value of z is $z =$ 1 obtained at the feasible point (1,0).

Examples 1 and 2 demonstrate that sometimes a linear programming problem ha a solution and sometimes it does not.

Theorem

Some Conditions Relating to the Solution of a Linear Programming Problem

Consider a linear programming problem with the set R of feasible points and objective function $z = Ax + By$.

1. If R is the empty set, then the linear programming problem has no solution and z has neither a maximum nor a minimum value.
2. If R is bounded, then z has both a maximum and a minimum value on R.
3. If R is unbounded, $A > 0$, $B > 0$, and the constraints include $x \geq 0$ and $y \geq 0$, then z has a minimum value on R but not a maximum value (see Example 2).

The conditions listed above are not exhaustive. When the set of feasible solutions i unbounded, it is best to graph the set of feasible solutions and some typical values of th objective function to determine whether a solution exists or not.

In Example 1 we found that the feasible point that minimizes z occurs at a corne point. In fact, if there are feasible points minimizing (or maximizing) the objectiv function, at least one will be at a corner point of the set of feasible points.

Theorem

Fundamental Theorem of Linear Programming with Two Variables

Consider a linear programming problem with the set R of feasible points and objective function $z = Ax + By$, where $x \geq 0, y \geq 0$. If a linear programming problem has a solution, it is located at a corner point of the set R of feasible points; if a linear programming problem has multiple solutions, at least one of them is located at a corner point of the set R of feasible points. In either case the corresponding value of the objective function is unique.

Since the objective function attains its maximum or minimum value at the corner points of the set of feasible points, we can outline a procedure for solving a linear programming problem provided that it has a solution.

Steps for Solving a Linear Programming Problem

If a linear programming problem has a solution, follow these steps to find it:

STEP 1 Write an expression for the quantity that is to be maximized or minimized (the objective function).

STEP 2 Determine all the constraints and graph the set of feasible points.

STEP 3 List the corner points of the set of feasible points.

STEP 4 Determine the value of the objective function at each corner point.

STEP 5 Select the maximum or minimum value of the objective function.

EXAMPLE 3 Solving a Linear Programming Problem

Maximize and minimize the objective function

$$z = x + 5y$$

subject to the constraints

$$\begin{cases} x + 4y \leq 12 \\ x \leq 8 \\ x + y \geq 2 \\ x \geq 0 \\ y \geq 0 \end{cases}$$

SOLUTION

STEP 1 The objective function is $z = x + 5y$.

STEP 2 The constraints consist of a system of five linear inequalities. Graph the system. See Figure 17. The shaded region illustrates the set of feasible points. Notice in Figure 17 that we have labeled each line from the system of linear inequalities. We have also labeled the corner points. Since the set of feasible points is bounded, we know th objective function has both a maximum and a minimum value in the region.

FIGURE 17

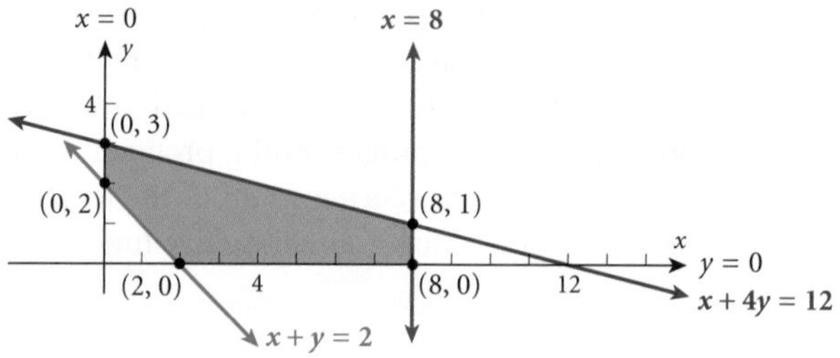

STEP 3 The corner points of the set of feasible points are

$$(0, 3) \qquad (8, 1) \qquad (8, 0) \qquad (2, 0) \qquad (0, 2)$$

STEP 4 Evaluate the objective function $z = x + 5y$ at each corner point. See Table 2.

TABLE 2

Corner Point (x, y)	Value of Objective Function $z = x + 5y$
(0, 3)	$z = 0 + 5(3) = 15$
(8, 1)	$z = 8 + 5(1) = 13$
(8, 0)	$z = 8 + 5(0) = 8$
(2, 0)	$z = 2 + 5(0) = 2$
(0, 2)	$z = 0 + 5(2) = 10$

STEP 5 The maximum value of z is 15, and it occurs at the point (0, 3). The minimum value o z is 2, and it occurs at the point (2, 0).

NOW WORK PROBLEMS 5 AND 21.

The Fundamental Theorem of Linear Programming indicates that it is possible for a feasible point that is not a corner point to minimize (or maximize) the objective function This occurs if the slope of the objective function is the same as the slope of one of th boundaries of the set of feasible points and if the two adjacent corner points are solutions Then all the points on the line segment joining the two corner points are also solutions. Th following example illustrates this situation.

EXAMPLE 4 Solving a Linear Programming Problem with Multiple Solutions

Minimize

$$z = x + 2y$$

subject to the constraints

$$\begin{cases} x + y \geq 1 \\ 2x + 4y \geq 3 \\ x \geq 0 \\ y \geq 0 \end{cases}$$

SOLUTION

STEP 1 The objective function is $z = x + 2y$.

STEP 2 The constraints consist of a system of four linear inequalities. The graph is given in Figure 18. Although the set of feasible points is unbounded, the linear programming problem will have a solution since condition 2 of the Criteria for the Existence of a Solution is satisfied. Check this for yourself.

FIGURE 18

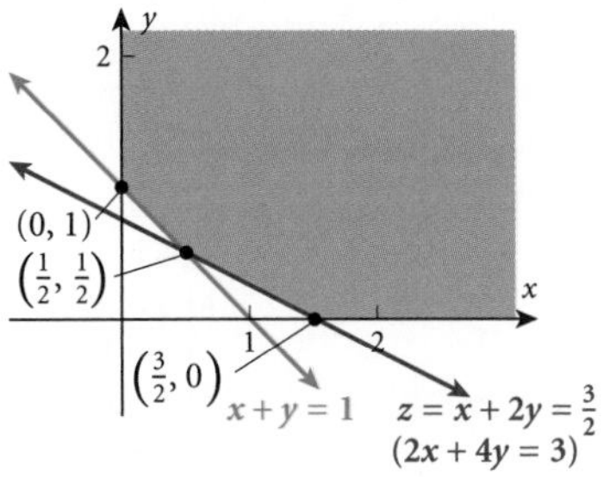

STEP 3 The corner points are $(0, 1)$, $\left(\frac{1}{2}, \frac{1}{2}\right)$, and $\left(\frac{3}{2}, 0\right)$.

STEP 4 At each corner point, the value of the objective function is:

$$(0, 1): \quad z = x + 2y = 0 + 2(1) = 2$$

$$\left(\frac{1}{2}, \frac{1}{2}\right): \quad z = x + 2y = \frac{1}{2} + 2\left(\frac{1}{2}\right) = 1.5$$

$$\left(\frac{3}{2}, 0\right): \quad z = x + 2y = \frac{3}{2} + 2(0) = 1.5$$

STEP 5 The minimum value is 1.5, obtained at the corner points $\left(\frac{1}{2}, \frac{1}{2}\right)$ and $\left(\frac{3}{2}, 0\right)$.

This linear program problem has multiple solutions. To see why, graph the objective equation $z = x + 2y$ for some choice of z and move it down. See Figure 19. We find that a minimum is reached when $z = \frac{3}{2}$. In fact, any point on the line $2x + 4y = 3$ between the adjacent corner points $\left(\frac{1}{2}, \frac{1}{2}\right)$ and $\left(\frac{3}{2}, 0\right)$ and including these corner points will minimize the objective function. Of course, the reason any feasible point on $2x + 4y = 3$ minimizes the objective equation $z = x + 2y$ is that these two lines each have slope $-\frac{1}{2}$.

FIGURE 19

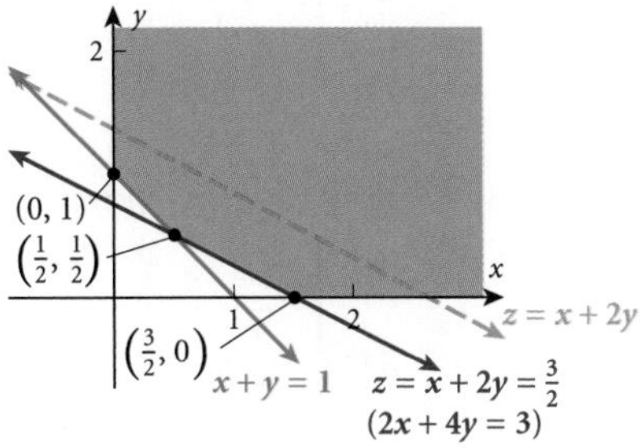

■

NOW WORK PROBLEM 33.

EXERCISE 4.2 Answers Begin on Page AN–21.

Concepts and Vocabulary

1. In a linear programming problem, the function to be maximized (or minimized) is called the _______ _________ .

2. In a linear programming problem, any point that satisfies the system of constraints is called a(n) _______ _______.

3. ***True or False*** Every linear programming problem has solution.

4. ***True or False*** Some linear programming problems hav multiple solutions.

Skill Building

In Problems 5–14, the figure on the right illustrates the graph of the set of feasible points of a linear programming problem. Find the maximum and minimum values of each objective function.

5. $z = 2x + 3y$

6. $z = 3x + 2y$

7. $z = x + y$

8. $z = 3x + 3y$

9. $z = x + 6y$

10. $z = 6x + y$

11. $z = 3x + 4y$

12. $z = 4x + 3y$

13. $z = 10x + y$

14. $z = x + 10y$

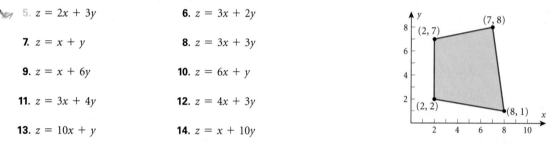

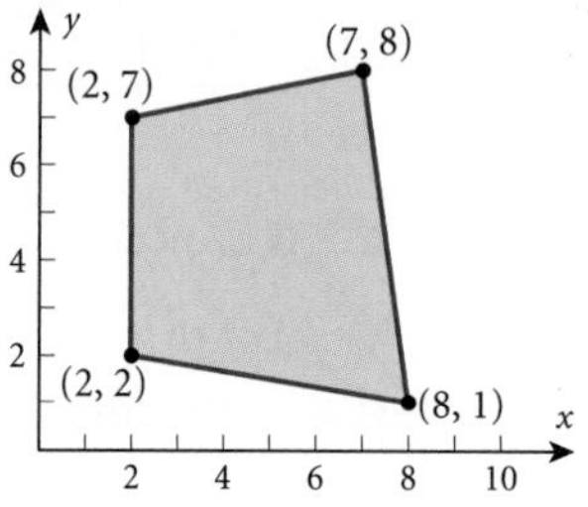

In Problems 15–20, list the corner points for each collection of constraints of a linear programming problem.

15. $\begin{cases} x \le 13 \\ 4x + 3y \ge 12 \\ x \ge 0 \\ y \ge 0 \end{cases}$

16. $\begin{cases} x \le 8 \\ 2x + 3y \ge 6 \\ x \ge 0 \\ y \ge 0 \end{cases}$

17. $\begin{cases} y \le 10 \\ x + y \le 15 \\ x \ge 0 \\ y \ge 0 \end{cases}$

18. $\begin{cases} y \le 8 \\ 2x + y \ge 10 \\ x \ge 0 \\ y \ge 0 \end{cases}$

19. $\begin{cases} x \le 10 \\ y \le 8 \\ 4x + 3y \ge 12 \\ x \ge 0 \\ y \ge 0 \end{cases}$

20. $\begin{cases} x \le 9 \\ y \le 12 \\ 2x + 3y \le 24 \\ x \ge 0 \\ y \ge 0 \end{cases}$

In Problems 21–28, maximize (if possible) the quantity $z = 5x + 7y$ *subject to the given constraints.*

21. $\begin{cases} x + y \le 2 \\ y \ge 1 \\ x \ge 0 \\ y \ge 0 \end{cases}$

22. $\begin{cases} 2x + 3y \le 6 \\ x \le 2 \\ x \ge 0 \\ y \ge 0 \end{cases}$

23. $\begin{cases} x + y \ge 2 \\ 2x + 3y \le 6 \\ x \ge 0 \\ y \ge 0 \end{cases}$

24. $\begin{cases} x + y \ge 2 \\ 2x + 3y \le 12 \\ 3x + 2y \le 12 \\ x \ge 0 \\ y \ge 0 \end{cases}$

25. $\begin{cases} x + y \ge 2 \\ x + y \le 8 \\ 2x + y \le 10 \\ x \ge 0 \\ y \ge 0 \end{cases}$

26. $\begin{cases} x + y \ge 2 \\ x + y \le 8 \\ x + 2y \ge 1 \\ x + 2y \le 10 \\ x \ge 0 \\ x \ge 0 \end{cases}$

27. $\begin{cases} x + y \le 10 \\ x \ge 6 \\ x \ge 0 \\ y \ge 0 \end{cases}$

28. $\begin{cases} x + y \le 8 \\ y \ge 2 \\ x \ge 0 \\ y \ge 0 \end{cases}$

In Problems 29–36, minimize (if possible) the quantity $z = 2x + 3y$ *subject to the given constraints.*

29. $\begin{cases} x + y \le 2 \\ y \le x \\ x \ge 0 \\ y \ge 0 \end{cases}$

30. $\begin{cases} 3x + y \le 3 \\ y \ge x \\ x \ge 0 \\ y \ge 0 \end{cases}$

31. $\begin{cases} x + y \ge 2 \\ x + 3y \le 12 \\ 3x + y \le 12 \\ x \ge 0 \\ y \ge 0 \end{cases}$

32. $\begin{cases} x + y \le 8 \\ 2x + 3y \ge 6 \\ x + y \ge 2 \\ x \ge 0 \\ y \ge 0 \end{cases}$

$$\begin{cases} x + y \geq 2 \\ x + y \leq 10 \\ 2x + 3y \leq 6 \\ x \geq 0 \\ y \geq 0 \end{cases}$$

34. $\begin{cases} 2y \leq x \\ x + 2y \leq 10 \\ x + 2y \geq 4 \\ x \geq 0 \\ y \geq 0 \end{cases}$

35. $\begin{cases} x + 2y \geq 1 \\ x + 2y \leq 10 \\ y \geq 2x \\ x + y \leq 8 \\ x \geq 0 \\ y \geq 0 \end{cases}$

36. $\begin{cases} 2x + y \geq 2 \\ x + y \leq 6 \\ 2x \geq y \\ x \geq 0 \\ y \geq 0 \end{cases}$

Problems 37–44, find the maximum and minimum values (if possible) of the given objective function subject to the constraints

$$\begin{cases} x + y \leq 10 \\ 2x + y \geq 10 \\ x + 2y \geq 10 \\ x \geq 0 \\ y \leq 0 \end{cases}$$

7. $z = x + y$

9. $z = 5x + 2y$

1. $z = 3x + 4y$

3. $z = 10x + y$

38. $z = 2x + 3y$

40. $z = x + 2y$

42. $z = 3x + 6y$

44. $z = x + 10y$

5. Find the maximum and minimum values of $z = 18x + 30y$ subject to the constraints $3x + 3y \geq 9$, $-x + 4y \leq 12$, and $4x - y \leq 12$, where $x \geq 0$ and $y \geq 0$.

6. Find the maximum and minimum values of $z = 20x + 16y$ subject to the constraints $4x + 3y \geq 12$, $-2x + 4y \leq 16$, and $6x - y \leq 18$, where $x \geq 0$ and $y \geq 0$.

47. Find the maximum and minimum values of $z = 7x + 6y$ subject to the constraints $2x + 3y \geq 6$, $-3x + 4y \leq 8$, and $5x - y \leq 15$, where $x \geq 0$ and $y \geq 0$.

48. Find the maximum and minimum values of $z = 6x + 3y$ subject to the constraints $2x + 2y \geq 4$, $-x + 5y \leq 10$, and $3x - 3y \leq 6$, where $x \geq 0$ and $y \geq 0$.

49. Maximize $z = -20x + 30y$ subject to the constraints $0 \leq x \leq 15$, $0 \leq y \leq 10$, $5x + 3y \geq 15$, and $-3x + 3y \leq 21$.

50. Maximize $z = -10x + 10y$ subject to the constraints $0 \leq x \leq 15$, $0 \leq y \leq 10$, $6x + y \geq 6$, and $-3x + y \leq 7$.

51. Maximize $z = -12x + 24y$ subject to the constraints $0 \leq x \leq 15$, $0 \leq y \leq 10$, $3x + 3y \geq 9$, and $-3x + 2y \leq 14$.

52. Maximize $z = -20x + 10y$ subject to the constraints $0 \leq x \leq 15$, $0 \leq y \leq 10$, $4x + 3y \geq 12$, and $-3x + y \leq 7$.

Discussion and Writing

3. Find conditions for a linear programming problem to have a solution (maximum, minimum, or both) if the set of feasible point is unbounded. Assume the constraints $x \geq 0$, $y \geq 0$ are not present. Further assume there are only two constraints whose corresponding equations intersect. Hint: Compare the slopes of the objection with the equations corresponding to the constraints.

4.3 Models Utilizing Linear Programming with Two Variables

OBJECTIVES   **1**   Solve applied problems using linear programming with two variables (p. 199)

1   Solve Applied Problems Using Linear Programming with Two Variables

Now let's solve the problem of the cashews and peanuts discussed at the start of the previous section.

EXAMPLE 1 Maximizing Profit

Nutt's Nuts has 75 pounds of cashews and 120 pounds of peanuts available. These a to be mixed in 1-pound packages as follows: a low-grade mixture that contains 4 ounc of cashews and 12 ounces of peanuts and a high-grade mixture that contains 8 ounc of cashews and 8 ounces of peanuts. The profit is \$0.25 on each package of th low-grade mixture and \$0.45 on each package of the high-grade mixture. How ma packages of each type of mixture should be prepared to maximize the profit?

SOLUTION Let x denote the number of packages of the low-grade mixture and y the number packages of the high-grade mixture. If P denotes the profit, then

$$P = 0.25x + 0.45y$$

STEP 1 We want to maximize P so $P = 0.25x + 0.45y$ is the objective function.

STEP 2 Look back at Example 11 of Section 4.1. The constraints consist of the system of line inequalities

$$\begin{cases} x + 2y \leq 300 & \text{The cashew constraint} \\ 3x + 2y \leq 480 & \text{The peanut constraint} \\ x \geq 0 & \text{The nonnegativity constraint} \\ y \geq 0 & \text{The nonnegativity constraint} \end{cases}$$

See Figure 20 for the graph of the set of feasible points. Notice that this set is bounded so the linear programming problem has a solution.

FIGURE 20

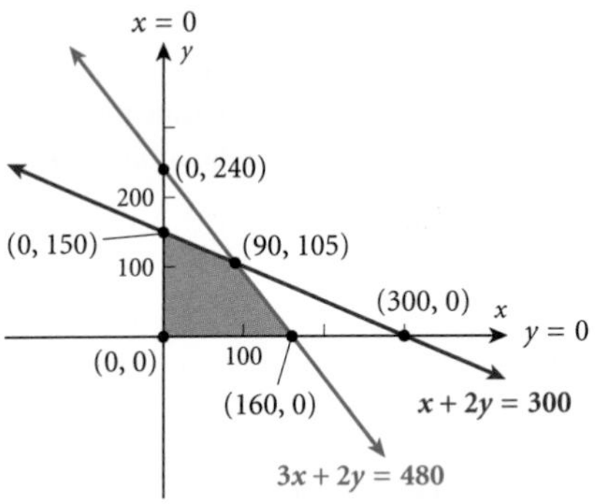

STEP 3 The corner points are (0, 0), (0, 150), (160, 0), and (90, 105).

STEP 4 In Table 3 we evaluate the objective function P at each corner point.

TABLE 3

Corner Point (x, y)	Value of Objective Function $P = (\$0.25)x + (\$0.45)y$
(0, 0)	$P = (0.25)(0) + (0.45)(0) = \$0$
(0, 150)	$P = (0.25)(0) + (0.45)(150) = \$67.50$
(160, 0)	$P = (0.25)(160) + (0.45)(0) = \$40.00$
(90, 105)	$P = (0.25)(90) + (0.45)(105) = \$69.75$

A maximum profit is obtained if 90 packages of low-grade mixture and 105 packages of high-grade mixture are made. The maximum profit obtainable under the conditions described is \$69.75. ■

NOW WORK PROBLEM 1.

EXAMPLE 2 Maximizing Profit

Mike's Famous Toy Trucks manufactures two kinds of toy trucks—a standard model and a deluxe model. In the manufacturing process each standard model requires 2 hours of grinding and 2 hours of finishing, and each deluxe model needs 2 hours of grinding and 4 hours of finishing. The company has two grinders and three finishers, each of whom works at most 40 hours per week. Each standard model toy truck brings a profit of \$3 and each deluxe model a profit of \$4. Assuming that every truck made will be sold, how many of each should be made to maximize profit?

SOLUTION First, name the variables:

$$x = \text{Number of standard models made}$$
$$y = \text{Number of deluxe models made}$$

The quantity to be maximized is the profit, which we denote by P. Since each standard models brings a profit of \$3 and each deluxe model a profit of \$4 we have

$$P = \$3x + \$4y$$

This is the objective function.

To manufacture one standard model requires 2 grinding hours and to make one deluxe model requires 2 grinding hours. The number of grinding hours needed to manufacture x standard and y deluxe models is

$$2x + 2y$$

But the total amount of grinding time available is only 80 hours per week. This means we have the constraint

$$2x + 2y \le 80 \quad \text{Grinding time constraint}$$

Similarly, for the finishing time we have the constraint

$$2x + 4y \le 120 \quad \text{Finishing time constraint}$$

By simplifying each of these constraints and adding the nonnegativity constraints $x \ge 0$ and $y \ge 0$, we can list all the constraints for this problem:

$$\begin{cases} x + y \le 40 & (1) \\ x + 2y \le 60 & (2) \\ x \ge 0 & (3) \\ y \ge 0 & (4) \end{cases}$$

Figure 21 illustrates the set of feasible points, which is bounded.

IGURE 21

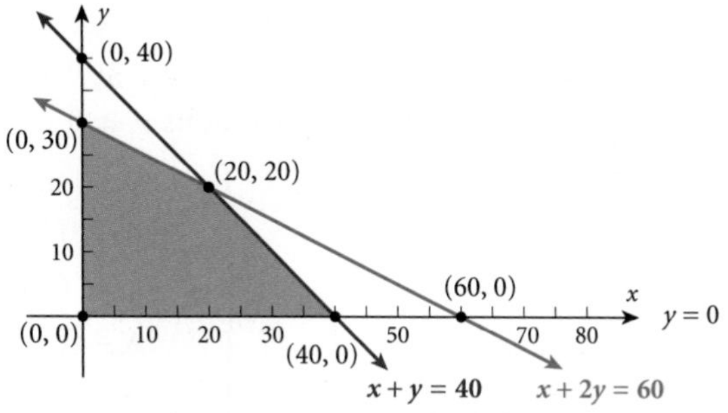

The corner points of the set of feasible points are

$$(0, 0) \qquad (0, 30) \qquad (40, 0) \qquad (20, 20)$$

Table 4 lists each corner point and the corresponding value of the objective equation:

TABLE 4

Corner Point (x, y)	Value of Objective Function $P = \$3x + \$4y$
$(0, 0)$	$P = 0$
$(0, 30)$	$P = \$120$
$(40, 0)$	$P = \$120$
$(20, 20)$	$P = 3(20) + 4(20) = \$140$

A maximum profit is obtained if 20 standard trucks and 20 deluxe trucks are manufac tured. The maximum profit is \$140.

EXAMPLE 3 Financial Planning

A couple has up to \$30,000 to invest in mutual funds. Their broker recommend investing in two funds based on their average annual return for the 5 years ending o December 31, 2009: the Templeton Global Bond fund yielding 8% and the Frankli International Small Cap Growth fund yielding 12%. After some consideration the coupl decides to invest at most \$12,000 in the Franklin International Small Cap Growth fun and at least \$6000 in the Templeton Global Bond fund. They also want the amoun invested in the Templeton Global Bond fund to exceed or equal the amount invested i the Franklin International Small Cap Growth fund. What should the broker recommen if the couple (quite naturally) wants to maximize the return on their investment?

Source: Franklin Templeton

SOLUTION First, name the variables:

x = Amount invested in the Global Bond fund

y = Amount invested in the Franklin International Small Cap Growth fund

The quantity to be maximized, the couple's return on investment, which we denote by P, i

$$P = 0.08x + 0.12y$$

This is the objective function.

The conditions specified by the problem are

Up to \$30,000 available to invest	$x + y \leq 30{,}00$
Invest at most \$12,000 in the Franklin International Small Cap growth fund	$y \leq 12{,}00$
Invest at least \$6000 in the Global Bond fund	$x \geq 6000$
Amount in the Global Bond fund must exceed or equal the amount in the Franklin International Small Cap growth fund	$x \geq y$

In addition, we must have the conditions $x \geq 0$ and $y \geq 0$. The total list of constraints i

$$\begin{cases} x + y \leq 30{,}000 & (1) \\ y \leq 12{,}000 & (2) \\ x \geq 6000 & (3) \\ x \geq y & (4) \\ x \geq 0 & (5) \\ y \geq 0 & (6) \end{cases}$$

Figure 22 illustrates the set of feasible points, which is bounded. The corner points of the set of feasible points are

(6000, 0)   (6000, 6000)   (12000, 12000)   (18000, 12000)   (30000, 0)

FIGURE 22

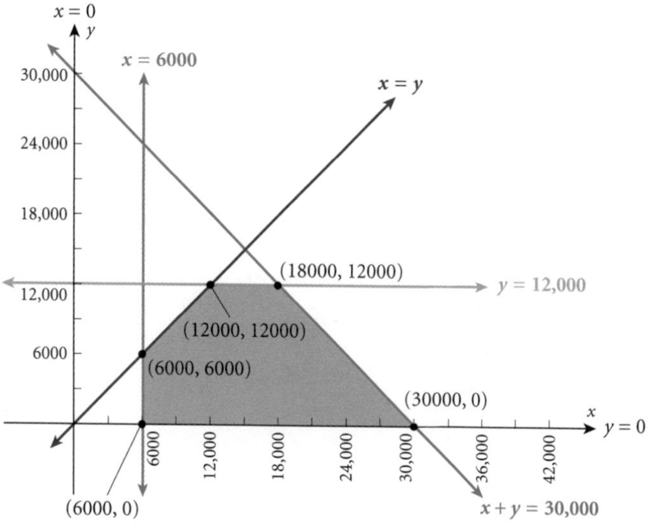

The corresponding return on investment at each corner point is

$$\begin{aligned}
(6000, 0)&: \quad P = 0.08(6000) + 0.12(0) = \$480\\
(6000, 6000)&: \quad P = 0.08(6000) + 0.12(6000) = 480 + 720 = \$1200\\
(12000, 12000)&: \quad P = 0.08(12{,}000) + 0.12(12{,}000) = 960 + 1440 = \$2400\\
(18000, 12000)&: \quad P = 0.08(18{,}000) + 0.12(12{,}000) = 1440 + 1440 = \$2880\\
(30000, 0)&: \quad P = 0.08(30{,}000) + 0.12(0) = \$2400
\end{aligned}$$

The maximum return on investment is \$2880, obtained by placing \$18,000 in the global Bond fund and \$12,000 in the Franklin International Small Cap growth fund. ■

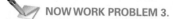

NOW WORK PROBLEM 3.

EXAMPLE 4 Manufacturing Vitamin Pills–Maximizing Profit

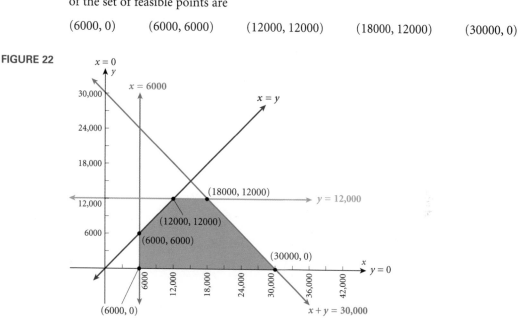

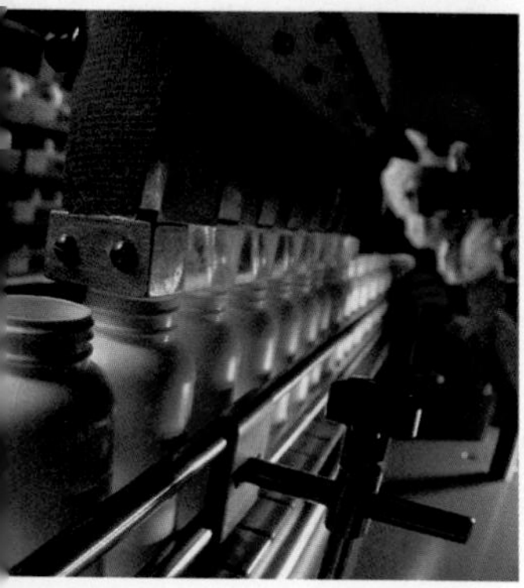

A pharmaceutical company makes two types of vitamins at its New Jersey plant—a high-potency, antioxidant vitamin and a vitamin enriched with added calcium. Each high-potency vitamin contains, among other things, 500 mg of vitamin C and 40 mg of calcium and generates a profit of \$0.10 per tablet. A calcium-enriched vitamin tablet contains 100 mg of vitamin C and 400 mg of calcium and generates a profit of \$0.05 per tablet. Each day the company has available 235 kg of vitamin C and 156 kg of calcium for use. Assuming all vitamins made are sold, how many of each type of vitamin should be manufactured to maximize profit?

Source: Centrum Vitamin Supplements.

SOLUTION First name the variables:

x = Number (in thousands) of high-potency vitamins to be produced

y = Number (in thousands) of calcium-enriched vitamins to be produced

We want to maximize the profit, P, which is given by:

$$P = 0.10x + 0.05y \quad \text{x and y in thousands}$$

Since 1 kg = 1,000,000 mg, the constraints, in mg, take the form

$$\begin{cases} 500x + 100y \leq 235{,}000 & \text{vitamin C constraint (in thousands of mg)} \\ 40x + 400y \leq 156{,}000 & \text{calcium constraint (in thousands of mg)} \\ x \geq 0 & \text{nonnegativity constraints (in thousands)} \\ y \geq 0 & \end{cases}$$

Figure 23 illustrates the set of feasible points, which is bounded. The corner points of the set of feasible points are

$$(0, 0) \qquad (0, 390) \qquad (400, 350) \qquad (470, 0)$$

FIGURE 23

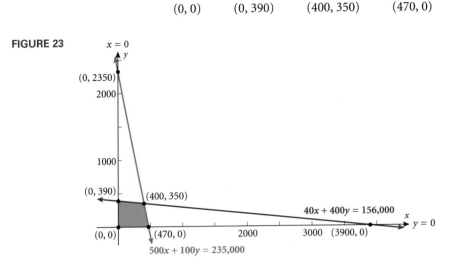

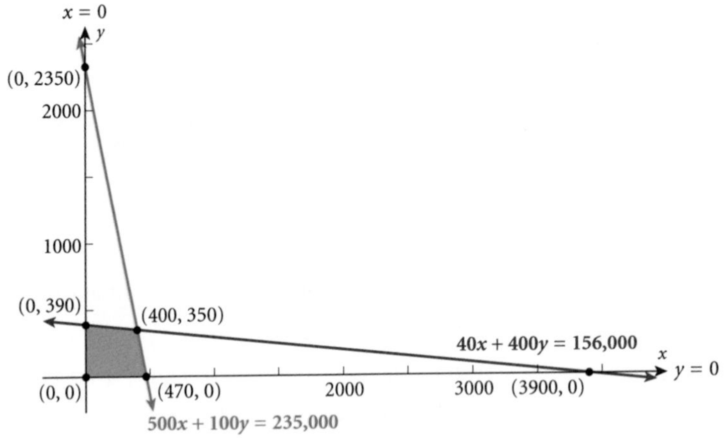

Since x and y are in thousands, the profit corresponding to each corner point is

$$\begin{aligned} (0, 0)&: \quad P = 0.10(0) + 0.05(0) = 0 = \$0 \\ (0, 390)&: \quad P = 0.10(0) + 0.05(390) = 19.5 \text{ thousand} = \$19{,}500 \\ (400, 350)&: \quad P = 0.10(400) + 0.05(350) = 57.5 \text{ thousand} = \$57{,}500 \\ (470, 0)&: \quad P = 0.10(470) + 0.05(0) = 47 \text{ thousand} = \$47{,}000 \end{aligned}$$

The maximum profit is \$57,500, obtained when 400,000 high-potency vitamins are produced (x = 400 thousand units) and 350,000 calcium-enriched vitamins are produced (y = 350 thousand units).

NOW WORK PROBLEM 5.

EXAMPLE 5 Minimizing Production Costs

A factory produces gasoline engines and diesel engines. Each week the factory is obligated to deliver at least 20 gasoline engines and at least 15 diesel engines. Due to physical limitations, however, the factory cannot make more than 60 gasoline engines nor more than 40 diesel engines in any given week. Finally, to prevent layoffs, a total of at least 50 engines must be produced.

(a) If gasoline engines cost \$450 each to produce and diesel engines cost \$550 each to produce, how many of each should be produced per week to minimize the cost?

(b) What is the excess capacity of the factory? That is, how many of each kind of engine is being produced in excess of the number that the factory is obligated to deliver?

SOLUTION **(a)** First name the variables:

$$x = \text{the number of gasoline engines produced}$$
$$y = \text{the number of diesel engines produced}$$

If C is the weekly cost of production in dollars, then

$$C = 450x + 550y$$

This is the objective function to be minimized.

The constraints are

$x \geq 20$	At least 20 gasoline engines produced per week
$y \geq 15$	At least 15 diesel engines produced per week
$x \leq 60$	No more than 60 gasoline engines produced
$y \leq 40$	No more than 40 diesel engines produced
$x + y \geq 50$	At least 50 engines produced
$x \geq 0, y \geq 0$	Nonnegativity constraints

Figure 24 shows the graph of the set of feasible points.

FIGURE 24

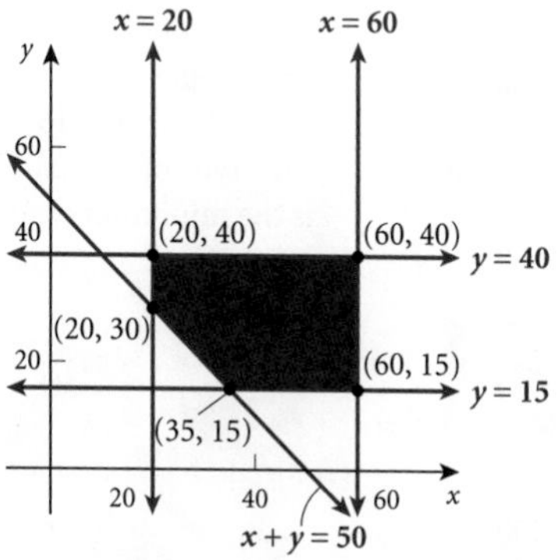

The corner points are (20, 30), (20, 40), (60, 40), (60, 15), and (35, 15). The cost C for each of these levels of production is

$$(20, 30)\text{:} \quad C = 450x + 550y = 450(20) + 550(30) = \$25{,}500$$
$$(20, 40)\text{:} \quad C = 450(20) + 550(40) = \$31{,}000$$
$$(60, 40)\text{:} \quad C = 450(60) + 550(40) = \$49{,}000$$
$$(60, 15)\text{:} \quad C = 450(60) + 550(15) = \$35{,}250$$
$$(35, 15)\text{:} \quad C = 450(35) + 550(15) = \$24{,}000$$

The minimum cost is \$24,000, obtained when 35 gasoline engines and 15 diesel engines are produced.

(b) The weekly obligation of the factory is to produce at least 20 gasoline engines and at least 15 diesel engines. The minimum cost of production produces an excess of 15 gasoline engines. ■

NOW WORK PROBLEM 7.

EXERCISE 4.3 Answers Begin on Page AN–21.

Applications

1. **Farm Management** A farmer has 70 acres of land available for planting either soybeans or wheat. The cost of preparing the soil, the workdays required, and the expected profit per acre planted for each type of crop are given in the following table:

	Soybeans	Wheat
Preparation cost per acre	\$60	\$30
Workdays required per acre	3	4
Profit per acre	\$180	\$100

The farmer cannot spend more than \$1800 in preparation costs nor use more than a total of 120 workdays.

(a) How many acres of each crop should be planted to maximize the profit?

(b) What is the maximum profit?

(c) What is the maximum profit if the farmer is willing to spend no more than \$2400 on preparation?

2. **Farm Management** A small farm in Illinois has 100 acres of land available on which to grow corn and soybeans. The following table shows the cultivation cost per acre, the labor cost per acre, and the expected profit per acre. The column on the right shows the amount of money available for each of these expenses. Find the number of acres of each crop that should be planted to maximize profit.

	Soybeans	Corn	Money Available
Cultivation cost per acre	\$40	\$60	\$1800
Labor cost per acre	\$60	\$60	\$2400
Profit per acre	\$200	\$250	

3. **Investment Strategy** An investment broker wants to invest up to \$20,000. She can invest in two mutual funds based on their yearly average return for the 5 years ending December 31, 2009: the Franklin Natural Resources fund yielding 10% and the Oppenheimer Developing Markets A fund yielding 15%. She wants to invest at least \$5000 in the Franklin Natural Resources fund and no more than \$8000 in the Oppenheimer Developing Markets A fund. How much should she invest in each type of fund to maximize her return?

4. **Investment Strategy** A financial consultant wishes to invest up to a total of \$30,000 in two types of securities, one that yields 10% per year and another that yields 8% per year. Furthermore, she believes that the amount invested in the first security should be at most one-third of the amount invested in the second security. What investment program should the consultant pursue in order to maximize income?

5. **Manufacturing Vitamin Pills** A pharmaceutical company has 300 kg of vitamin C and 220 kg of calcium available each day for the manufacture of high-potency, antioxidant vitamins ar vitamins enriched with added calcium. If each high-poten vitamin contains, among other things, 500 mg of vitamin C ar 40 mg of calcium and generates a profit of \$0.10 per table and each calcium-enriched vitamin tablet contains 100 mg vitamin C and 400 mg of calcium and generates a pro of \$0.05 per tablet, how many of each type of vitamin should manufactured to maximize profit?

Source: Centrum Vitamin Supplements

6. **Inventory** Blink Appliances has a sale on microwaves ar stoves. Each microwave requires 2 hours to unpack and set u and each stove requires 1 hour. The storeroom space is limite to 50 items. The budget of the store allows only 80 hours employee time for unpacking and setup. Microwaves sell f \$300 each, and stoves sell for \$200 each. How many of eac should the store order to maximize revenue?

7. **Banquet Seating** A banquet hall offers two types of tables f rent: 6-person rectangular tables at a cost of \$28 each ar 10-person round tables at a cost of \$52 each. Kathleen wou like to rent the hall for a wedding banquet and needs tables f 250 people. The room can have a maximum of 35 tables ar the hall only has 15 rectangular tables available. How many each type of table should be rented to minimize cost and wh is the minimum cost?

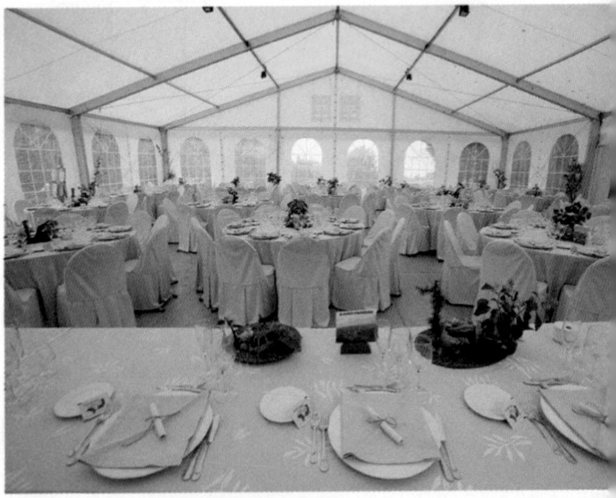

Source: facilities.princeton.edu

8. **Spring Break** The student activities department of a communi college plans to rent buses and vans for a spring-break tri Each bus has 40 regular seats and 1 handicapped seat; each v has 8 regular seats and 3 handicapped seats. The rental cost \$350 for each van and \$975 for each bus. If 320 regular and handicapped seats are required for the trip, how many vehic of each type should be rented to minimize cost?

Source: www.busrates.com

9. **Nutrition** As part of his weight-loss routine, Eric plans only eat 6-inch Turkey Breast and 6-inch Veggie Delit

sandwiches from Subway®. He wants at least 81 g of protein, 28 g of dietary fiber, and 300 g of carbohydrates, but wants to minimize his fat intake. How many of each sandwich should he eat in order to meet his requirements? What will his fat intake be?

Sandwich	Protein (g)	Fiber (g)	Carbohydrates (g)	Fat (g)
6″ Turkey Breast	18	4	46	4.5
6″ Veggie Delite®	9	4	44	3

Source: www.subway.com

0. **Rapid Prototype** A computer-aided drafting (CAD) instructor at a community college wants to use his rapid prototype machine to produce demo items for a seminar on engineering technology. He plans to bring two different types, a Golden Ruler and a Fibonacci Gauge. He will bring at least 20 of each. He has 45 cubic inches of filler and 95 cubic inches of material available to make the demos, but only has 86 hours of free time to run the machine. He is able to save time by running the demos in batches. Use the information in the table to determine how many of each demo item he needs to bring while minimizing total cost. What is his total cost?

Demo Type	Material (in^3/batch)	Filler (in^3/batch)	Batch Time (hrs)	Batch Size	Batch Cost ($)
Golden Ruler	10	3	7	8	22
Fibonacci Gauge	7.5	5	8.5	10	20

Source: Lewis & Clark Community College

1. **Manufacturing** A factory manufactures two products, each requiring the use of three machines. The first machine can be used at most 70 hours; the second machine at most 40 hours; and the third machine at most 90 hours. The first product requires 2 hours on machine 1, 1 hour on machine 2, and 1 hour on machine 3; the second product requires 1 hour each on machines 1 and 2, and 3 hours on machine 3. If the profit is \$40 per unit for the first product and \$60 per unit for the second product, how many units of each product should be manufactured to maximize profit?

2. **Dietary Requirements** A diet is to contain at least 400 units of vitamins, 500 units of minerals, and 1400 calories. Two foods are available: F_1, which costs \$0.05 per unit, and F_2, which costs \$0.03 per unit. A unit of food F_1 contains 2 units of vitamins, 1 unit of minerals, and 4 calories; a unit of food F_2 contains 1 unit of vitamins, 2 units of minerals, and 4 calories. Find the minimum cost for a diet that consists of a mixture of these two foods and also meets the minimal nutrition requirements.

3. **Dietary Requirements** A certain diet requires at least 60 units of carbohydrates, 45 units of protein, and 30 units of fat each day. Each ounce of Supplement A provides 5 units of carbohydrates, 3 units of protein, and 4 units of fat. Each ounce of Supplement B provides 2 units of carbohydrates, 2 units of protein, and 1 unit of fat. If Supplement A costs \$1.50 per ounce and Supplement B costs \$1.00 per ounce, how many ounces of each supplement should be taken daily to minimize the cost of the diet?

14. **Production Scheduling** In a factory, machine 1 produces 8-inch pliers at the rate of 60 units per hour and 6-inch pliers at the rate of 70 units per hour. Machine 2 produces 8-inch pliers at the rate of 40 units per hour and 6-inch pliers at the rate of 20 units per hour. It costs \$50 per hour to operate machine 1, and machine 2 costs \$30 per hour to operate. The production schedule requires that at least 240 units of 8-inch pliers and at least 140 units of 6-inch pliers be produced during each 10-hour day. Which combination of machines will cost the least money to operate?

15. **Home Mortgages** Fremont Bank offered no-closing-cost home mortgages at a 5.125% annual rate for 30-year fixed-rate loans and at a 4.375% annual rate for 15-year fixed-rate loans. Suppose that Fremont Bank is planning to allocate up to \$72 million for these two kinds of loans, with a minimum of \$15 million for each kind of loan. Also, Fremont Bank has decided that the amount allocated to the 30-year loans should be at most twice the amount allocated to the 15-year loans. How much should Fremont Bank allocate to each type of loan in order to maximize the total amount of interest that would be received in the first month of these loans? What is the total amount of interest that would be received in the first month, if the maximum solution is implemented?

    Source: Fremont Bank, March 2010

16. **Return on Investment** An investment broker is instructed by her client to invest \$20,000 in two funds based on their average annual returns for 5 years ending December 31, 2009: a Global Bond fund yielding 9% and the Yachtman fund yielding 7%. The client wants to invest at least \$8000 in the Yachtman fund and no more than \$12,000 in the Global Bond fund.

    (a) How much should the broker recommend that the client place in each investment to maximize income if the client insists that the amount invested in the Yachtman fund must equal or exceed the amount placed in the Global Bond fund?

    (b) How much should the broker recommend that the client place in each investment to maximize income if the client insists that the amount invested in the Yachtman fund must not exceed the amount placed in the Global Bond fund?

17. **Maximizing Profit on Ice Skates** A factory manufactures two kinds of ice skates: racing skates and figure skates. The racing skates require 6 work-hours in the fabrication department, whereas the figure skates require 4 work-hours there. The racing skates require 1 work-hour in the finishing department, whereas the figure skates require 2 work-hours there. The fabricating department has available at most 120 work-hours per day, and the finishing department has no more than 40 work-hours per day available. If the profit on each racing skate is \$10 and the profit on each figure skate is \$12, how many of each should be manufactured each day to maximize profit? (Assume that all skates made are sold.)

18. Maximizing Profit on Figurines A factory manufactures two kinds of ceramic figurines: a dancing girl and a mermaid. Each requires three processes: molding, painting, and glazing. The daily labor available for molding is no more than 90 work-hours, labor available for painting does not exceed 120 work-hours, and labor available for glazing is no more than 60 work-hours. The dancing girl requires 3 work-hours for molding, 6 work-hours for painting, and 2 work-hours for glazing. The mermaid requires 3 work-hours for molding, 4 work-hours for painting, and 3 work-hours for glazing. If the profit on each figurine is $25 for dancing girls and $30 for mermaids, how many of each should be produced each day to maximize profit? If management decides to produce the number of each figurine that maximizes profit, determine which of these processes has work-hours assigned to it that are not used.

19. Pollution Control A chemical plant produces two compounds A and B. For each compound A produced, 2 cubic feet of carbon monoxide and 6 cubic feet of sulfur dioxide are emitted into the atmosphere; to produce compound B, 4 cubic feet of carbon monoxide and 3 cubic feet of sulfur dioxide are emitted into the atmosphere. Government pollution standards permit the manufacturer to emit a maximum of 3000 cubic feet of carbon monoxide and 5400 cubic feet of sulfur dioxide per week. The manufacturer can sell all of the compounds that it produces and makes a profit of $1.50 per unit for compound A and $1.00 per unit for compound B. Determine the number of units of each compound to be produced each week to maximize profit without exceeding government standards.

20. Baby Food Servings Gerber Banana Plum Granola costs $0.89 per 5.5-oz serving; each serving contains 140 calories, 31 g of carbohydrates, and 0% of the recommended daily allowance of vitamin C. Gerber Mixed Fruit Carrot Juice costs $0.79 per 4-oz serving; each serving contains 60 calories, 13 g of carbohydrates, and 100% of the recommended daily allowance of vitamin C. Determine how many servings of each of the above foods would be needed to provide a child at least 160 calories, 40 g of carbohydrates, and 70% of the recommended daily allowance of vitamin C at minimum cost. Fractions of servings are permitted.

Source: Gerber Web site and Safeway Stores, Inc.

21. Production Scheduling A company produces two types of steel. Type 1 requires 2 hours of melting, 4 hours of cutting, and 10 hours of rolling per ton. Type 2 requires 5 hours of melting, 1 hour of cutting, and 5 hours of rolling per ton. Forty hours are available for melting, 20 for cutting, and 60 for rolling. Each ton of Type 1 produces $240 profit, and each ton of Type 2 yields $80 profit. Find the maximum profit and the production schedule that will produce this profit.

22. TV Advertising Nielsen TV ratings indicated that during the week of June 15–21, 2009, the news program *Dateline NBC* had an audience of 5.6 million viewers, while the news program *60 Minutes* on CBS had an audience of 8.3 million viewers. An advertiser has a budget of up to $1,000,000 to purchase 30-second commercial timeslots on these two news programs during the next three months. Suppose that each 30-second commercial timeslot on *Dateline NBC* costs $30,000 and ea 30-second commercial timeslot on *60 Minutes* costs $40,00 The advertiser wants to purchase at least eight 30-secor timeslots on each of the programs, *Dateline NBC* ar *60 Minutes*, but has stipulated that at least two-thirds of th 30-second timeslots that are purchased should be on *Dateli NBC*. How many 30-second timeslots should be purchased c each of these news programs to maximize the total number viewers? Assume that audience size will remain the san during the subsequent three months as it was during the we of June 15–21, 2009. How many viewers were there?

Source: for by the numbers.com

23. Diet Danny's Chicken Farm is a producer of frying chickens. order to produce the best fryers possible, the regular chicken fe is supplemented by four vitamins. The minimum amount of ea vitamin required per 100 ounces of feed is: vitamin 1, 50 uni vitamin 2, 100 units; vitamin 3, 60 units; vitamin 4, 180 uni Two supplements are available: supplement I costs $0.03 p ounce and contains 5 units of vitamin 1 per ounce, 25 units vitamin 2 per ounce, 10 units of vitamin 3 per ounce, and 35 un of vitamin 4 per ounce. Supplement II costs $0.04 per ounce a contains 25 units of vitamin 1 per ounce, 10 units of vitam 2 per ounce, 10 units of vitamin 3 per ounce, and 20 units vitamin 4 per ounce. How much of each supplement shou Danny buy to add to each 100 ounces of feed in order to minimi his cost but still have the desired vitamin amounts present?

24. Risk Management The table below shows the price per sha at the close of trading on March 1, 2010, the price to earnin ratio, and the dividend paid in the last quarter for Exx Mobil and Wells Fargo.

	Price per Share 3-1-10	Price to Earnings Ratio (P/E Ratio)	Last Quarterl Dividend per Share
Exxon Mobil Corporation	$65.40	16.51	$0.42
General Dynamics	$73.50	11.97	$0.38

A pension fund has decided to invest up to $800,000 purchase shares of stock in the above two companies. It wa the total dividends next quarter from these stocks to be at le $4500, but will not invest more than 60% of the $800,000 any one of these companies. When purchasing stock, this pe sion fund minimizes risk, which it calculates as follows:

Risk = (Amount invested in Stock A)(P/E Ratio for Stock
+ (Amount invested in Stock B)(P/E Ratio for Stock

How many shares of stock in each company should purchased to minimize risk? Assume dividends paid ne quarter are the same as in the previous quarters.

Source: moneycentral.msn.com

. **Financial Planning** In March 2010, a couple plans to invest \$45,000 in two funds based on their average yearly performance for the past 5 years ending December 31, 2009; ICON Bond fund with an average return of 4.35% and ING Mid Cap Opportunities with an average return of 5.05%. They wish to invest a minimum of \$10,000 in each of the accounts with a maximum investment of \$15,000 in the ICON Bond fund. They also decide that the amount invested in the ING Mid Cap Opportunities fund cannot exceed twice the amount deposited in the ICON Bond fund. How much should this couple invest in each fund in order to maximize their total annual yield?

. **Maximizing Rates of Return** The table lists two mutual funds: the John Hancock Large Cap Equity I fund and the T Rowe Price Latin America fund.

Fund	Rate of Return
Hancock Large Cap Equity I	9.97%
Rowe Price Latin America	23.65%

The manager of a pension fund plans to invest up to \$1,000,000 in these two mutual funds. He concludes that the amount invested in the John Hancock Large Cap Equity fund should be at least one fourth of the amount invested in the T Rowe Price Latin America fund and will invest a minimum of \$175,000 in the John Hancock Large Cap Equity fund. Also, not more than 70% of the total amount invested should be invested in any one of these funds. How much should be invested in each mutual fund to maximize the total projected annual return? Assume that the projected annual return for each mutual fund equals the average annual total rate of return during the 5-year period ending on December 31, 2009. What is the maximum total projected annual return?

Minimizing Travel Costs A national sales company is planning to conduct a weeklong sales meeting in San Francisco on August 14. On July 14, one month from that date, the lowest round trip airfare from New York City (NYC) to San Francisco is \$343 and the lowest round-trip airfare from Chicago to San Francisco is \$329. There are 28 sales representatives based in NYC and 22 sales representatives based in Chicago who could travel to San Francisco for this meeting. A total of at least 40 sales representatives from Chicago and NYC must attend this meeting with at least 12 from Chicago and at least 16 from NYC. How many sales representatives based in NYC and how many sales representatives based in Chicago should be sent to the San Francisco sales meeting, so as to minimize the total airfare? What is the minimum total airfare?

Source: Orbitz.com

28. **Maximizing Income** J. B. Rug Manufacturers has available 1200 square yards of wool and 1000 square yards of nylon for the manufacture of two grades of carpeting: high-grade, which sells for \$500 per roll, and low-grade, which sells for \$300 per roll. Twenty square yards of wool and 40 square yards of nylon are used in a roll of high-grade carpet, and 40 square yards of nylon are used in a roll of low-grade carpet. Forty work-hours are required to manufacture each roll of the high-grade carpet, and 20 work-hours are required for each roll of the low-grade carpet, at an average cost of \$6 per work-hour. A maximum of 800 work-hours are available. The cost of wool is \$5 per square yard and the cost of nylon is \$2 per square yard. How many rolls of each type of carpet should be manufactured to maximize income?
[*Hint:* Income = Revenue from sale − (Production cost for material + labor)]

29. The rug manufacturer in Problem 28 finds that maximum income occurs when no high-grade carpet is produced. If the price of the low-grade carpet is kept at \$300 per roll, in what price range should the high-grade carpet be sold so that income is maximized by selling some rolls of each type of carpet? Assume all other data remain the same.

scussion and Writing

. Refer to Example 5. What would you do to eliminate the excess capacity?

HAPTER 4 REVIEW OBJECTIVES

Section	Examples	You should be able to	Review Exercises
4.1	1, 2, 3	1 Graph linear inequalities (p. 176)	1–14
	4, 5, 6, 7, 8, 9, 10	2 Graph systems of linear inequalities (p. 179)	9–14
	11, 12	3 Solve applied problems involving systems of linear inequalities (p. 184)	34
4.2	1,2	1 Identify a linear programming problem with two variables (p. 192)	35–41
	1, 2, 3, 4	2 Solve a linear programming problem with two variables (p.193)	15–32
4.3	1, 2, 3, 4, 5	1 Solve applied problems using linear programming with two variables (p. 199)	33, 35–41

THINGS TO KNOW

Graphs of Inequalities (p. 176)
The graph of a strict inequality is represented by a dashed line and the half-plane satisfying the inequality.
The graph of a nonstrict inequality is represented by a solid line and the half-plane satisfying the inequality.

Graphs of Systems of Linear Inequalities (pp. 179–183)
The graph of a system of linear inequalities is the set of all points that satisfy each inequality in the system.
The graph is called bounded if some rectangle can be drawn around it.
The graph is called unbounded if it extends infinitely far in at least one direction.

Corner Point (p. 184)
A corner point is the intersection of two line segments that form the boundary of t graph of a system of linear inequalities.

Linear Programming (p. 192)
Maximize (or minimize) a linear objective function, $z = Ax + By$, subject to certa conditions, or constraints, expressible as linear inequalities in x and y. A feasible poi (x, y) is a point that satisfies the constraints of a linear programming problem.

Solution to a Linear Programming Problem (p. 193)
A solution to a linear programming problem is a feasible point that maximizes (or minimizes) the objective function together with the value of the objective function at that point.

Location of Solution (p. 195)
If a linear programming problem has a solution, it is located at a corner point of t graph of the feasible points.
If a linear programming problem has multiple solutions, at least one of them is locat at a corner point of the graph of the feasible points.
In either case, the corresponding value of the objective function is unique.

REVIEW EXERCISES **Answers begin on page AN–22.**

Blue problem numbers indicate the author's suggestions for use in a practice test.

In Problems 1–4, graph each linear inequality.

1. $x + 3y \le 0$ **2.** $4x + y \ge 0$ **3.** $5x + y > 10$ **4.** $2x + 3y < 6$

5. Without graphing, determine which of the points $P_1 = (4, -3)$, $P_2 = (2, -6)$, $P_3 = (8, -3)$ are part of the graph of the following system:

$$\begin{cases} x + 2y \le 8 \\ 2x - y \ge 4 \end{cases}$$

6. Without graphing, determine which of the poi $P_1 = (8, 6)$, $P_2 = (2, -5)$, $P_3 = (4, 1)$ are part of graph of the following system:

$$\begin{cases} 5x - y \ge 2 \\ x - 4y \le -2 \end{cases}$$

In Problems 7–8, determine which region—a, b, c, or d—represents the graph of the given system of linear inequalities.

7. $\begin{cases} 6x - 4y \le 12 \\ 3x + 2y \le 18 \end{cases}$

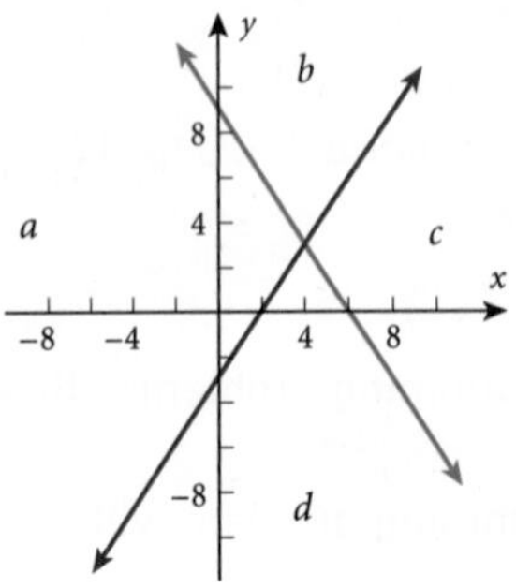

8. $\begin{cases} 6x - 5y \ge 5 \\ 6x + 6y \le 60 \end{cases}$

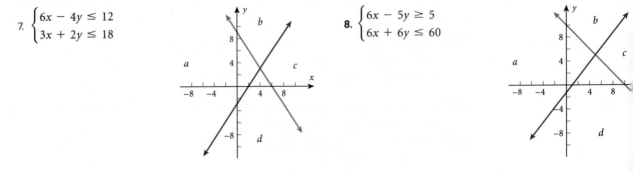

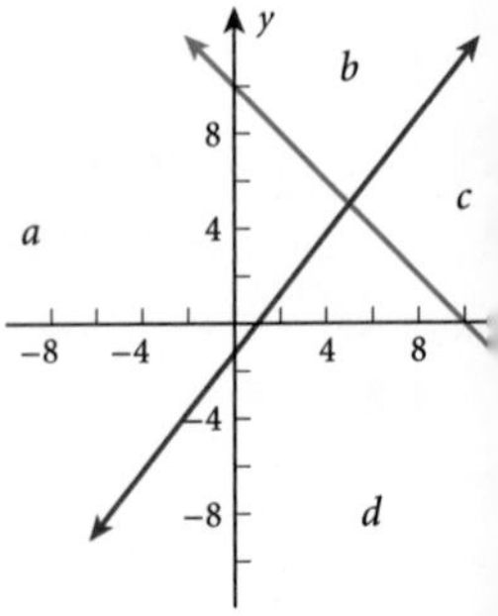

Problems 9–14, graph each system of linear inequalities. Locate the corner points and tell whether the graph is bounded or unbounded.

9. $\begin{cases} 3x + 2y \le 12 \\ x + y \ge 4 \\ x \ge 0 \\ y \ge 0 \end{cases}$

10. $\begin{cases} x + y \le 8 \\ 2x + y \ge 4 \\ x \ge 0 \\ y \ge 0 \end{cases}$

11. $\begin{cases} x + 2y \ge 4 \\ 3x + y \le 6 \\ x \ge 0 \\ y \ge 0 \end{cases}$

12. $\begin{cases} 2x + y \ge 4 \\ 3x + 2y \ge 6 \\ x \ge 0 \\ y \ge 0 \end{cases}$

13. $\begin{cases} 3x + 2y \ge 6 \\ 3x + 2y \le 12 \\ x + 2y \le 8 \\ x \ge 0 \\ y \ge 0 \end{cases}$

14. $\begin{cases} x + y \ge 8 \\ x + 2y \ge 10 \\ y \le 8 \\ x \ge 0 \\ y \ge 0 \end{cases}$

Problems 15–22, use the constraints below to solve each linear programming problem.

$$\begin{cases} x + 2y \le 40 \\ 2x + y \le 40 \\ x + y \ge 10 \\ x \ge 0 \\ y \ge 0 \end{cases}$$

15. Maximize $z = x + y$

16. Maximize $z = 2x + 3y$

17. Minimize $z = 5x + 2y$

18. Minimize $z = 3x + 2y$

19. Maximize $z = 2x + y$

20. Maximize $z = x + 2y$

21. Minimize $z = 2x + 5y$

22. Minimize $z = x + y$

Problems 23–26, maximize and minimize (if possible) the quantity $z = 15x + 20y$ subject to the given constraints.

23. $\begin{cases} x \le 5 \\ y \le 8 \\ 3x + 4y \ge 12 \\ x \ge 0 \\ y \ge 0 \end{cases}$

24. $\begin{cases} x + 2y \ge 4 \\ 3x + 2y \ge 6 \\ x \ge 0 \\ y \ge 0 \end{cases}$

25. $\begin{cases} 2x + 3y \le 22 \\ x \le 5 \\ y \le 6 \\ x \ge 0 \\ y \ge 0 \end{cases}$

26. $\begin{cases} x + 2y \le 20 \\ x + 10y \ge 36 \\ 5x + 2y \ge 36 \\ x \ge 0 \\ y \ge 0 \end{cases}$

Problems 27–32, solve each linear programming problem.

27. Maximize

$$z = 2x + 3y$$

subject to the constraints

$$\begin{cases} x \le 9 \\ y \le 8 \\ x + y \ge 3 \\ x \ge 0 \\ y \ge 0 \end{cases}$$

28. Maximize

$$z = 4x + y$$

subject to the constraints

$$\begin{cases} x \le 7 \\ y \le 8 \\ x + y \ge 2 \\ x \ge 0 \\ y \ge 0 \end{cases}$$

29. Maximize

$$z = x + 2y$$

subject to the constraints

$$\begin{cases} x + y \ge 1 \\ y \le 2x \\ x \le 8 \\ y \le 8 \\ x \ge 0 \\ y \ge 0 \end{cases}$$

30. Maximize

$$z = 3x + 4y$$

subject to the constraints

$$\begin{cases} x + 2y \ge 2 \\ 3x + 2y \le 12 \\ y \le 5 \\ x \ge 0 \\ y \ge 0 \end{cases}$$

31. Minimize

$$z = 3x + 2y$$

subject to the constraints

$$\begin{cases} x + 2y \ge 8 \\ 3x + y \ge 6 \\ x \le 8 \\ x \ge 0 \\ y \ge 0 \end{cases}$$

32. Minimize

$$z = 2x + 5y$$

subject to the constraints

$$\begin{cases} x \le 10 \\ y \le 12 \\ 2x + y \ge 10 \\ x - y \ge 0 \\ x \ge 0 \\ y \ge 0 \end{cases}$$

33. Blending Coffee Bill's Coffee House, a store that specializes in coffee, has available 75 pounds of pure Columbian coffee and 120 pounds of a house-brand coffee. These will be blended into 1 pound packages as follows: An economy blend that contains 4 ounces of pure Columbian coffee and 12 ounces of the house-brand coffee and a superior blend that contains 8 ounces of pure Columbian coffee and 8 ounces of the house-brand coffee.

(a) Using x to denote the number of packages of the economy blend and y to denote the number of packages of the superior blend, write a system of linear inequalities that describes the possible number of packages of each kind of blend.

(b) Graph the system and label the corner points.

(c) A profit of \$0.30 per package is made on the economy blend, whereas a profit of \$0.40 per package is made on the superior blend. How many packages of each mixture should be prepared to achieve a maximum profit? Assume that all packages prepared can be sold.

34. Manufacturing Trucks Mike's Toy Truck Company manufacturers two models of toy trucks, a standard model and a deluxe model. Each standard model requires 2 hours for painting and 3 hours for detail work; each deluxe model requires 3 hours for painting and 4 hours for detail work. Two painters and three detail workers are employed by the company, and each works 40 hours per week.

(a) Using x to denote the number of standard model trucks and y to denote the number of deluxe model trucks, write a system of linear inequalities that describes the possible number of each model of truck that can be manufactured in a week.

(b) Graph the system and label the corner points.

35. Maximizing Profit A ski manufacturer makes two types of skis: downhill and cross-country. Using the information given in the table below, how many of each type of ski should be made for a maximum profit to be achieved? What is the maximum profit?

	Downhill	Cross-Country	Maximum Time Available
Manufacturing Time per Ski	2 hours	1 hour	40 hours
Finishing Time per Ski	1 hour	1 hour	32 hours
Profit per Ski	\$70	\$50	

36. Production Scheduling A company sells two types of shoes. The first uses 2 units of leather and 2 units of synthetic material and yields a profit of \$8 per pair. The second ty[p] requires 5 units of leather and 1 unit of synthetic materi[al] and gives a profit of \$10 per pair. If there are 40 units [of] leather and 16 units of synthetic material available, ho[w] many pairs of each type of shoe should be manufactured [to] maximize profit? What is the maximum profit?

37. Baby Food Servings Gerber Banana Oatmeal and Pea[ch] costs \$0.79 per 4-oz serving; each serving contains 90 cal[o]ries, 19 g of carbohydrates, and 45% of the recommend[ed] daily allowance of vitamin C. Gerber Mixed Fruit Jui[ce] costs \$0.65 per 4-oz serving; each serving contains 60 cal[o]ries, 15 g of carbohydrates, and 100% of the recommend[ed] daily allowance of vitamin C. Determine how many servin[gs] of each of the above foods would be needed to provide [a] child with at least 130 calories, 30 g of carbohydrates, a[nd] 60% of the recommended daily allowance of vitamin C [at] minimum cost. Fractions of servings are permitted.

Source: Gerber Web site and Safeway Stores, Inc.

38. Maximizing Profit A company makes two explosives: lo[w] density and high density. Due to storage problems, [a] maximum of 100 pounds of low density and 150 pounds [of] high density explosives can be mixed and packaged ea[ch] week. One pound of low density takes 60 hours to mix a[nd] 70 hours to package; 1 pound of high density takes 40 hou[rs] to mix and 40 hours to package. The mixing department h[as] at most 7200 work-hours available each week, and packa[g]ing has at most 7800 work-hours available. If the profit f[or] 1 pound of low density is \$60 and for 1 pound of high densi[ty] is \$40, what is the maximum profit possible each week?

39. Manufacturing Vitamin Pills A pharmaceutical compa[ny] makes two types of vitamins at its New Jersey plant— [a] high-potency, antioxidant vitamin and a vitamin enrich[ed] with added calcium. Each high-potency vitamin contai[ns], among other things, 500 mg of vitamin C, 40 mg [of] calcium, and 100 mg of magnesium and generates a pro[fit] of \$0.10 per tablet. A calcium-enriched vitamin tab[let] contains 100 mg of vitamin C, 400 mg of calcium, and 40 m[g] of magnesium and generates a profit of \$0.05 per tabl[et]. Each day the company has available 300 kg of vitamin [C], 122 kg of calcium, and 65 kg of magnesium for use in t[he] production of the vitamins. How many of each type [of] vitamin should be manufactured to maximize profit?

Source: Centrum Vitamin Supplements.

40. Mixture A company makes two kinds of animal food, A a[nd] B, which contain two food supplements. It takes 2 pounds [of] the first supplement and one pound of the second to mak[e a] dozen cans of food A, and 4 pounds of the first suppleme[nt] and 5 pounds of the second to make a dozen cans of food [B]. On a certain day 80 pounds of the first suppleme[nt] and 70 pounds of the second are available. How ma[ny] cans of food A and food B should be made to maximize company profits, if the profit on a dozen cans of food A is \$3.00 and the profit on a dozen cans of food B is \$10.00?

. **Maximizing Yield** The purchase price paid on March 1, 2010, and the last quarterly dividend paid per share for stock in Boeing and Honeywell were as follows:

tock	Price per Share March 1, 2010	Last Quarterly Dividend per Share
oeing	\$64	0.42
oneywell	\$40	0.30

A mutual fund has decided to invest up to \$500,000 to purchase shares of stock in these two companies. It will purchase a minimum of 2000 shares of stock in each of the above companies but will not invest more than 60% of the total amount in any one of these companies. How many shares of stock in each company should be purchased to maximize the total projected dividend for the next quarter? Use the dividend for the last quarter as the projected dividend for the next quarter. What is the maximum total projected dividend?

Source: moneycentral.msn.com

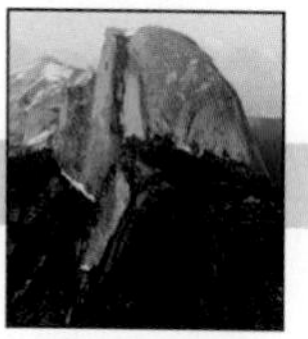

hapter 4 Project

LANCING NUTRIENTS

preparing a recipe, you must decide what ingredients and w much of each ingredient you will use. In these health-nscious days, you may also want to consider the amount of tain nutrients in your recipe. You may even be interested in nimizing some quantities (like calories or fat) or maximizing ers (like carbohydrates or protein). Linear programming hniques can help to do this.

For example, consider making a very simple trail mix from -roasted, unsalted peanuts and seedless raisins. Table 1 lists amounts of various dietary quantitites for these ingredients. e amounts are given per serving of the ingredient.

BLE 1 NUTRIENTS IN PEANUTS AND RAISINS

utrient	Peanuts Serving Size = 1 Cup	Raisins Serving Size = 1 Cup
alories (kcal)	850	440
rotein (g)	34.57	4.67
at(g)	72.50	0.67
arbohydrates (g)	31.40	114.74

urce: USDA National Nutrient Database for Standard erence. www.nal.gov/fnic/foodcomp.

Suppose that you want to make at most 6 cups of trail mix a day hike. You don't want either ingredient to dominate the xture, so you want the amount of raisins to be at least $\frac{1}{2}$ of the amount of peanuts and the amount of peanuts to be at least $\frac{1}{2}$ of the amount of raisins. You want the entire amount of trail mix you make to have fewer than 4000 calories, and you want to maximize the amount of carbohydrates in the mix.

1. Let x be the number of cups of peanuts you will use, let y be the number of cups of raisins you will use, and let c be the amount of carbohydrates in the mix. Find the objective function.
2. What constraints must be placed on the objective function?
3. Graph the set of feasible points for this problem.
4. Find the number of cups of peanuts and raisins that maximize the amount of carbohydrates in the mix.
5. How many grams of carbohydrates are in a cup of the final mix? How many calories?
6. Under all of the constraints given above, what recipe for trail mix will maximize the amount of protein in the mix? How many grams of protein are in a cup of this mix? How many calories?
7. Suppose you decide to eat at least 3 cups of the trail mix. Keeping the constraints given above, what recipe for trail mix will minimize the amount of fat in the mix?
8. How many grams of carbohydrates are in this mix?
9. How many grams of protein are in this mix?
10. Which of the three trail mixes would you use? Why?

Mathematical Questions from Professional Exams*

Use the following information to do Problems 1–3:

The Random Company manufactures two products, Zeta and Beta. Each product must pass through two processing operations. ▮ materials are introduced at the start of process 1. There are no work-in-process inventories. Random may produce either one prod▮ exclusively or various combinations of both products subject to the following constraints:

	Process No. 1	Process No. 2	Contribution Margin per Unit
Hours required to produce one unit of			
Zeta	1 hour	1 hour	$4.00
Beta	2 hours	3 hours	$5.25
Total capacity in hours per day	1000 hours	1275 hours	

A shortage of technical labor has limited Beta production to 400 units per day. There are no constraints on the production of Zeta ot▮ than the hour constraints in the above schedule. Assume that all relationships between capacity and production are linear, and that al▮ the above data and relationships are deterministic rather than probabilistic.

1. **CPA Exam** Given the objective to maximize total contribution margin, what is the production constraint for process 1?

   (a) Zeta + Beta ≤ 1000

   (b) Zeta + 2 Beta ≤ 1000

   (c) Zeta + Beta ≥ 1000

   (d) Zeta + 2 Beta ≥ 1000

2. **CPA Exam** Given the objective to maximize total contribution margin, what is the labor constraint for production of Beta?

   (a) Beta ≤ 400

   (b) Beta ≥ 400

   (c) Beta ≤ 425

   (d) Beta ≥ 425

3. **CPA Exam** What is the objective function of the data presented?

   (a) Zeta + 2 Beta = $9.25

   (b) ($4.00) Zeta + 3($5.25) Beta = Total contribution margin

   (c) ($4.00) Zeta + ($5.25) Beta = Total contribution margin

   (d) 2($4.00) Zeta + 3($5.25) Beta = Total contribution margin

4. **CPA Exam** Williamson Manufacturing intends to produce two products, X and Y. Product X requires 6 hours of time on machine 1 and 12 hours of time on machine 2. Product Y requires 4 hours of time on machine 1 and no time machine 2. Both machines are available for 24 hou▮ Assuming that the objective function of the total contributi▮ margin is $2X + $1Y, what product mix will produce ▮ maximum profit?

   (a) No units of product X and 6 units of product Y.

   (b) 1 unit of product X and 4 units of product Y.

   (c) 2 units of product X and 3 units of product Y.

   (d) 4 units of product X and no units of product Y.

5. **CPA Exam** Quepea Company manufactures two products ▮ and P, in a small building with limited capacity. The sell▮ price, cost data, and production time are given below:

	Product Q	Product ▮
Selling price per unit	$20	$17
Variable costs of producing and selling a unit	$12	$13
Hours to produce a unit	3	1

Based on this information, the profit maximizati▮ objective function for a linear programming soluti▮ may be stated as

   (a) Maximize $20Q + $17P.

   (b) Maximize $12Q + $13P.

   (c) Maximize $3Q + $1P.

   (d) Maximize $8Q + $4P.

6. **CPA Exam** Patsy, Inc., manufactures two products, X and Y. Each product must be processed in each of three departments: machining, assembling, and finishing. The hours needed to produce one unit of product per department and the maximum possible hours per department follow:

Department	Production Hours per Unit		Maximum Capacity in Hours
	X	Y	
Machining	2	1	420
Assembling	2	2	500
Finishing	2	3	600

Other restrictions follow:

$$X \geq 50 \quad Y \geq 50$$

The objective function is to maximize profits where profit = $\$4X + \$2Y$. Given the objective and constraints, what is the most profitable number of units of X and Y, respectively, to manufacture?

(a) 150 and 100

(b) 165 and 90

(c) 170 and 80

(d) 200 and 50

7. **CPA Exam** Milford Company manufactures two models, medium and large. The contribution margin expected is $12 for the medium model and $20 for the large model. The medium model is processed 2 hours in the machining department and 4 hours in the polishing department. The large model is processed 3 hours in the machining department and 6 hours in the polishing department. How would the formula for determining the maximization of total contribution margin be expressed?

(a) $5X + 10Y$

(b) $6X + 9Y$

(c) $12X + 20Y$

(d) $12X(2 + 4) + 20Y(3 + 6)$

8. **CPA Exam** Hale Company manufactures products A and B, each of which requires two processes, polishing and grinding. The contribution margin is $3 for product A and $4 for product B. The illustration shows the maximum number of units of each product that may be processed in the two departments.

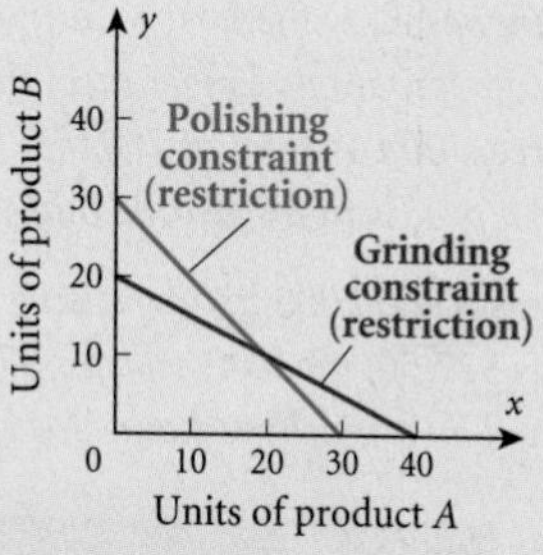

Considering the constraints (restrictions) on processing, which combination of products A and B maximizes the total contribution margin?

(a) 0 units of A and 20 units of B.

(b) 20 units of A and 10 units of B.

(c) 30 units of A and 0 units of B.

(d) 40 units of A and 0 units of B.

9. **CPA Exam** Johnson, Inc., manufactures product X and product Y, which are processed as follows:

	Machine A	Machine B
Product X	6 hours	4 hours
Product Y	9 hours	5 hours

The contribution margin is $12 for product X and $7 for product Y. The available time daily for processing the two products is 120 hours for machine A and 80 hours for machine B. How would the restriction (constraint) for machine B be expressed?

(a) $4X + 5Y$

(b) $4X + 5Y \leq 80$

(c) $6X + 9Y \leq 120$

(d) $12X + 7Y$

10. **CPA Exam** A small company makes only two products, with the following two production constraints representing two machines and their maximum availability:

$$2X + 3Y \leq 18$$
$$2X + Y \leq 10$$

where

$$X = \text{Units of the first product}$$
$$Y = \text{Units of the second product}$$

If the profit equation is $Z = \$4X + \$2Y$, the maximum possible profit is

(a) $20   (b) $21

(c) $18   (d) $24

(e) Some profit other than those given above

Questions 11–13 are based on the Jarten Company, which manufactures and sells two products. Demand for the two products has grow to such a level that Jarten can no longer meet the demand with its facilities. The company can work a total of 600,000 direct labor-hou annually using three shifts. A total of 200,000 hours of machine time is available annually. The company plans to use linear progran ming to determine a production schedule that will maximize its net return.

The company spends $2,000,000 in advertising and promotion and incurs $1,000,000 for general and administrative costs. The unit sa price for model A is $27.50; model B sells for $75.00 each. The unit manufacturing requirements and unit cost data are as shown belo Overhead is assigned on a machine-hour (MH) basis.

	Model A		Model B	
Raw material		$ 3		$ 7
Direct labor	1 DLH @ $8	8	1.5 DLH @ $8	12
Variable overhead	0.5 MH @ $12	6	2.0 MH @ $12	24
Fixed overhead	0.5 MH @ $4	2	2.0 MH @ $4	8
Cost		$19		$51

11. **CMA Exam** The objective function that would maximize Jarten's net income is

(a) $10.50A + 32.00B$

(b) $8.50A + 24.00B$

(c) $27.50A + 75.00B$

(d) $19.00A + 51.00B$

(e) $17.00A + 43.00B$

12. **CMA Exam** The constraint function for the direct labor is

(a) $1A + 1.5B \le 200{,}000$

(b) $8A + 12B \le 600{,}000$

(c) $8A + 12B \le 200{,}000$

(d) $1A + 1.5B \le 4{,}800{,}000$

(e) $1A + 1.5B \le 600{,}000$

13. **CMA Exam** The constraint function for the machine capacity is

(a) $6A + 24B \le 200{,}000$

(b) $(1/0.5)A + (1.5/2.0)B \le 800{,}000$

(c) $0.5A + 2B \le 200{,}000$

(d) $(0.5 + 0.5)A + (2 + 2)B \le 200{,}000$

(e) $(0.5 \times 1) + (1.5 \times 2.00) \le (200{,}000 \times 600{,}000)$

14. **CPA Exam** Boaz Company manufactures two model medium (X) and large (Y). The contribution margi expected is $24 for the medium model and $40 for th large model. The medium model is processed 2 hours i the machining department and 4 hours in the polishin department. The large model is processed 3 hours in th machining department and 6 hours in the polishin department. If total contribution margin is to be maxi mized, using linear programming, how would the objectiv function be expressed?

(a) $24X(2 + 4) + 40Y(3 + 6)$

(b) $24X + 40Y$

(c) $6X + 9Y$

(d) $5X + 10Y$

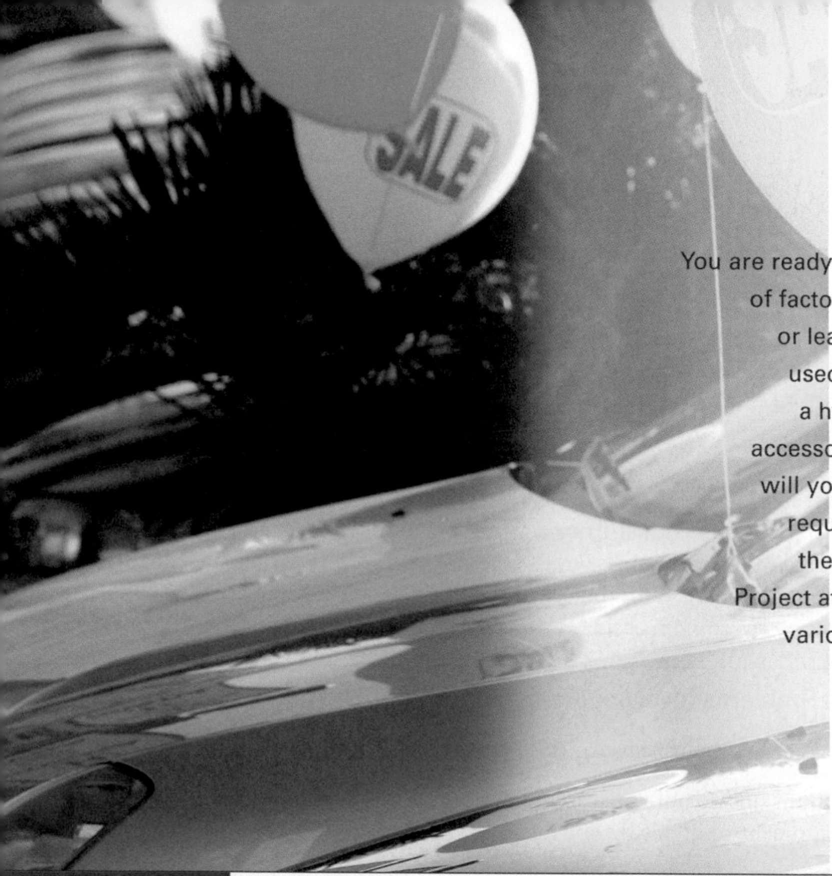

Finance 6

You are ready to get a car, but there are a number of factors to consider. Should you purchase or lease? Do you want a new car or will a used car do as well? Are you looking for a hybrid vehicle or an SUV? What extra accessories do you want or need? And how will you pay for the car? How much will be required for a down payment? What will the monthly payments be? The Chapter Project at the end of this chapter investigates various financing options for purchasing or leasing a car.

OUTLINE

A Look Back, A Look Forward

In earlier mathematics courses, you studied percents. In later courses, you studied exponential expressions and logarithmic expressions, which are reviewed in Appendix A, Section A.3. In this chapter we apply these topics to the field of finance, discussing simple interest, compound interest, simple annuities, sinking funds, and amortization.

6.1 Interest

OBJECTIVES
1. Solve problems involving percents (p. 294)
2. Solve problems involving simple interest (p. 295)
3. Solve problems involving discounted loans (p. 297)
4. Application: Pricing treasury bills* (p. 298)

Interest is money paid for the use of money. The total amount of money borrowec whether by an individual from a bank in the form of a loan or by a bank from a individual in the form of a savings account, is called the **principal**. The **rate of interes** is the amount charged for the use of the principal for a given length of time, usually o a yearly, or *per annum*, basis.

1 Solve Problems Involving Percents

Rates of interest are usually expressed as percents: 10% per annum, 14% per annum, $7\frac{1}{2}$% per annum, and so on. The word **percent** means "per hundred." The familiar symbol fo percent means to divide by one hundred. For example,

$$1\% = \frac{1}{100} = 0.01 \quad 12\% = \frac{12}{100} = 0.12 \quad 0.3\% = \frac{0.3}{100} = \frac{3}{1000} = 0.003$$

By reversing these ideas, decimals can be written as percents.

$$0.35 = \frac{35}{100} = 35\% \quad 1.25 = \frac{125}{100} = 125\% \quad 0.005 = \frac{5}{1000} = \frac{0.5}{100} = 0.5\% = \frac{1}{2}\%$$

NOW WORK PROBLEMS 5 AND 13.

EXAMPLE 1 Working with Percents

(a) Find 12% of 80. **(b)** What percent of 40 is 18?
(c) 8 is 15% of what number?

SOLUTION **(a)** The English word *of* translates to *multiply* when percents are involved. For exampl

$$12\% \text{ of } 80 = 12\% \text{ times } 80 = (0.12)\cdot(80) = 9.6$$

(b) Let x represent the unknown percent. Then

$$x\% \text{ of } 40 = 18 \qquad \text{What \% of 40 is 18?}$$

$$\frac{x}{100}\cdot 40 = 18 \qquad x\% = \frac{x}{100}$$

$$40x = 1800 \qquad \text{Multiply both sides by 100.}$$

$$x = \frac{1800}{40} \qquad \text{Divide both sides by 40.}$$

$$x = 45 \qquad \text{Simplify.}$$

So, 45% of 40 is 18.

* *Optional*

(c) Let x represent the number. Then

$$8 = 15\% \text{ of } x$$

$$8 = 0.15x \qquad 15\% = 0.15$$

$$x = \frac{8}{0.15} \qquad \text{Divide both sides by 0.15.}$$

$$x = 53.33 \qquad \text{Use a calculator.}$$

So, 8 is 15% of 53.33. ■

NOW WORK PROBLEMS 21, 27, AND 31.

EXAMPLE 2 Computing State Income Tax

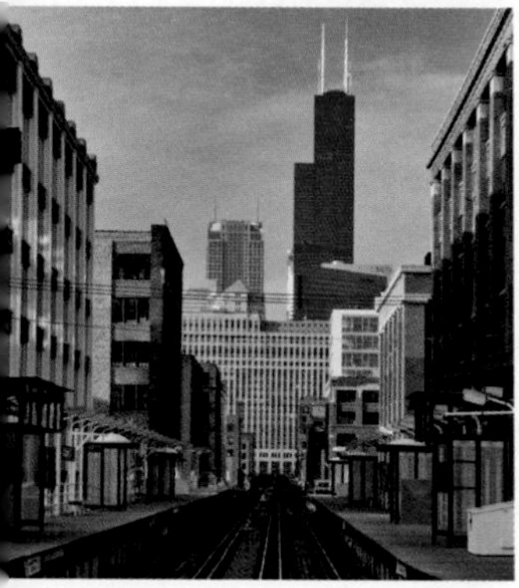

A resident of Illinois has base income, after adjustment for deductions, of \$18,000. The state income tax on this base income is 3%. What tax is due?

SOLUTION We need to find 3% of \$18,000. Convert 3% to its decimal equivalent and then multiply by \$18,000.

$$3\% \text{ of } \$18{,}000 = (0.03)(\$18{,}000) = \$540$$

The state income tax due is \$540.00. ■

2 Solve Problems Involving Simple Interest

Definition

Simple Interest

Simple interest is interest computed on the principal for the entire period it is borrowed.

Theorem

Simple Interest Formula

If a principal P is borrowed at a simple interest rate of $R\%$ per annum (where $R\%$ is expressed as the decimal $r = \frac{R}{100}$) for a period of t years, the interest I is

$$I = Prt \qquad (1)$$

Theorem The **amount** A owed at the end of t years is the sum of the principal P borrowed and the interest I charged. That is,

$$A = P + I = P + Prt = P(1 + rt) \qquad (2)$$

EXAMPLE 3 Computing Interest and the Amount Due on a Loan

A loan of \$250 is made for 9 months at a simple interest rate of 10% per annum. Wha is the interest charge? What amount is due after 9 months?

SOLUTION The actual period the money is borrowed for is 9 months, which is $\frac{9}{12} = \frac{3}{4}$ of a yea The interest charge is the product of the amount borrowed, \$250; the annual rate c interest, 10%, expressed as a decimal, 0.10; and the length of time in years, $\frac{3}{4}$. Us Formula (1) to find the interest charge I.

$$I = Prt$$

$$\text{Interest charge} = (\$250)(0.10)\left(\frac{3}{4}\right) = \$18.75$$

Using Formula (2), the amount A due after 9 months is

$$A = P + I = 250 + 18.75 = \$268.75$$

NOW WORK PROBLEM 35.

EXAMPLE 4 Computing the Rate of Interest on a Loan

A person borrows \$1000 for a period of 6 months. What simple interest rate is bein charged if the amount A that must be repaid after 6 months is \$1045?

SOLUTION The principal P is \$1000, the period is 6 months so $t = \frac{1}{2}$ year, and the amount A owe after 6 months is \$1045. We substitute the known values of A, P, and t in Formula (2 and then solve for r, the interest rate.

$$A = P + Prt \qquad \text{Formula (2)}$$

$$1045 = 1000 + 1000r\left(\frac{1}{2}\right) \qquad A = 1045;\ P = 1000;\ t = \frac{1}{2}$$

$$45 = 500r \qquad \text{Subtract 1000 from each side and simplif}$$

$$r = \frac{45}{500} = 0.09 \qquad \text{Solve for } r.$$

The per annum rate of interest is 9%.

NOW WORK PROBLEM 41.

EXAMPLE 5 Computing the Amount Due on a Loan

A company borrows $1,000,000 for 1 month at a simple interest rate of 9% per annum. How much must the company pay back at the end of 1 month?

SOLUTION The principal P is $1,000,000, the period t is 1 month $= \frac{1}{12}$ year, and the interest rate r is 0.09. The amount A that must be paid back is

$$\begin{aligned} A &= P(1 + rt) && \text{Formula (2)} \\ &= 1{,}000{,}000\left[1 + 0.09\left(\frac{1}{12}\right)\right] && P = 1{,}000{,}000;\ r = 0.09;\ t = \frac{1}{12} \\ &= 1{,}000{,}000(1.0075) \\ &= \$1{,}007{,}500 \end{aligned}$$

At the end of 1 month, the company must pay back $1,007,500. ■

3 Solve Problems Involving Discounted Loans

If a lender deducts the interest from the amount of the loan at the time the loan is made, the loan is said to be **discounted**. The interest deducted from the amount of the loan is the **discount**. The amount the borrower receives is called the **proceeds**.

Theorem **Discounted Loans**

Let r be the per annum rate of interest, t the time in years, and L the amount of the loan. Then the proceeds R is given by

$$R = L - Lrt = L(1 - rt) \qquad (3)$$

where Lrt is the discount, the interest deducted from the amount of the loan.

EXAMPLE 6 Computing the Proceeds of a Discounted Loan

A borrower signs a note for a discounted loan and agrees to pay the lender $1000 in 9 months at a 10% rate of interest. How much does this borrower receive?

SOLUTION The amount of the loan is $L = \$1000$. The rate of interest is $r = 10\% = 0.10$. The time is $t = 9$ months $= \frac{9}{12}$ year. The discount is

$$Lrt = \$1000(0.10)\left(\frac{9}{12}\right) = \$75$$

The discount is deducted from the loan amount of $1000, so that the proceeds, the amount the borrower receives, is

$$R = L - Lrt = 1000 - 75 = \$925$$ ■

NOW WORK PROBLEM 47.

EXAMPLE 7 **Computing the Simple Rate of Interest on a Discounted Loan**

What simple rate of interest is the borrower in Example 6 paying on the $925 that w borrowed for 9 months and paid back in the amount of $1000?

SOLUTION The principal P is $925, t is 9 months $= \frac{3}{4}$ of a year, and the amount A is $1000. If r the simple rate of interest, then, from Formula (2),

$$
\begin{aligned}
A &= P + Prt && \text{Formula (2)} \\
1000 &= 925 + 925r\left(\frac{3}{4}\right) && A = 1000;\ P = 925;\ t = \frac{3}{4} \\
75 &= 693.75r && \text{Simplify.} \\
r &= \frac{75}{693.75} = 0.108108 && \text{Solve for } r.
\end{aligned}
$$

The equivalent simple rate of interest for this loan is 10.81%.

EXAMPLE 8 **Finding the Amount of a Discounted Loan**

You wish to borrow $10,000 for 3 months. If the person you are borrowing from offe a discounted loan at 8%, how much must you repay at the end of 3 months?

SOLUTION The amount you receive, the proceeds, is $R =$ $10,000; the interest rate is $r = 0.08$; an the time t is 3 months $= \frac{1}{4}$ year. From Formula (3), the amount L you repay obeys th equation

$$
\begin{aligned}
R &= L(1 - rt) && \text{Formula (3)} \\
10{,}000 &= L\left[1 - 0.08\left(\frac{1}{4}\right)\right] && R = 10{,}000;\ r = 0.08;\ t = \frac{1}{4} \\
10{,}000 &= 0.98L && \text{Simplify.} \\
L &= \frac{10{,}000}{0.98} = \$10{,}204.08 && \text{Solve for } L.
\end{aligned}
$$

You will repay $10,204.08 for this loan.

NOW WORK PROBLEM 51.

4 Application: Pricing Treasury Bills

Treasury bills (T-bills) are short-term securities issued by the Federal Reserve. The bil do not specify a rate of interest. They are sold at public auction with financial institution making competitive bids. For example, a financial institution may bid $982,400 for 3-month $1 million treasury bill. At the end of 3 months the financial institutio receives $1 million, which includes the interest earned and the cost of the T-bill. Th bidding process is an example of a discounted loan.

EXAMPLE 9 **Bidding on Treasury Bills**

How much should a bank bid on a 6-month, $500,000 treasury bill if it wants a 0.25% discounted rate of interest? *

* *Based on actual rates as of March 2010.*

SOLUTION The maturity value, the amount to be repaid to the bank by the government, is $L = \$500{,}000$. The rate of interest is $r = 0.25\% = 0.0025$. The time is $t = 6 \text{ months} = \frac{1}{2}$ year. The proceeds R to the government are

$$\begin{aligned} R = L(1 - rt) &= \$500{,}000\left[1 - 0.0025\left(\frac{1}{2}\right)\right] \\ &= 500{,}000(0.99875) \\ &= 499{,}375 \end{aligned}$$

The bank should bid \$499,375 if it wants to earn 0.0025%. ■

NOW WORK PROBLEM 67.

EXERCISE 6.1 Answers Begin on Page AN–32.

Concepts and Vocabulary

1. If a principal P is borrowed at a simple interest rate r (expressed as a decimal) for a period of t years, the interest charge I is ________.

2. If a lender deducts the interest from the amount of the loan at the time the loan is made, the loan is said to be ________.

3. ***True or False*** For a simple interest loan with interest rate r (expressed as a decimal), the amount A due at the end of t years on a principal P borrowed is $P = A(1 + rt)$.

4. ***True or False*** For a discounted loan at a rate of interest r (expressed as a decimal), the discount is Lrt, where L is the amount of the loan and t is the time in years.

Skill Building

Problems 5–12, write each decimal as a percent.

5. 0.60 6. 0.40 7. 1.1 8. 1.2 9. 0.06 10. 0.07 11. 0.0025 12. 0.0015

Problems 13–20, write each percent as a decimal.

13. 25% 14. 15% 15. 100% 16. 300% 17. 6.5% 18. 4.3% 19. 0.05% 20. 0.012%

Problems 21–34, calculate the indicated quantity.

21. 15% of 1000
22. 20% of 500
23. 18% of 100
24. 10% of 50
25. 210% of 50
26. 135% of 1000
27. What percent of 80 is 4?
28. What percent of 60 is 5?
29. What percent of 5 is 8?
30. What percent of 25 is 45?
31. 20 is 8% of what number?
32. 25 is 12% of what number?
33. 50 is 15% of what number?
34. 40 is 18% of what number?

Problems 35–40, find the interest due on each loan.

35. \$1000 is borrowed for 3 months at 4% simple interest.
36. \$100 is borrowed for 6 months at 8% simple interest.
37. \$500 is borrowed for 9 months at 12% simple interest.
38. \$800 is borrowed for 8 months at 5% simple interest.
39. \$1000 is borrowed for 18 months at 10% simple interest.
40. \$100 is borrowed for 24 months at 12% simple interest.

Problems 41–46, find the simple interest rate for each loan.

41. \$1000 is borrowed; the amount owed after 6 months is \$1050.
42. \$500 is borrowed; the amount owed after 8 months is \$600.
43. \$300 is borrowed; the amount owed after 12 months is \$400.
44. \$600 is borrowed; the amount owed after 9 months is \$660.
45. \$900 is borrowed; the amount owed after 10 months is \$1000.
46. \$800 is borrowed; the amount owed after 3 months is \$900.

In Problems 47–50, find the proceeds for each discounted loan.

47. $1200 repaid in 6 months at 10%.

48. $500 repaid in 8 months at 9%.

49. $2000 repaid in 24 months at 8%.

50. $1500 repaid in 18 months at 10%.

In Problems 51–54, find the amount you must repay for each discounted loan. What is the equivalent simple interest rate for this loan?

51. The proceeds are $1200 for 6 months at 10%.

52. The proceeds are $500 for 8 months at 9%.

53. The proceeds are $2000 for 24 months at 8%.

54. The proceeds are $1500 for 18 months at 10%.

Applications

55. Buying a Stereo Madalyn wants to buy a $500 stereo set in 9 months. How much should she invest now at 3% simple interest to have the money then?

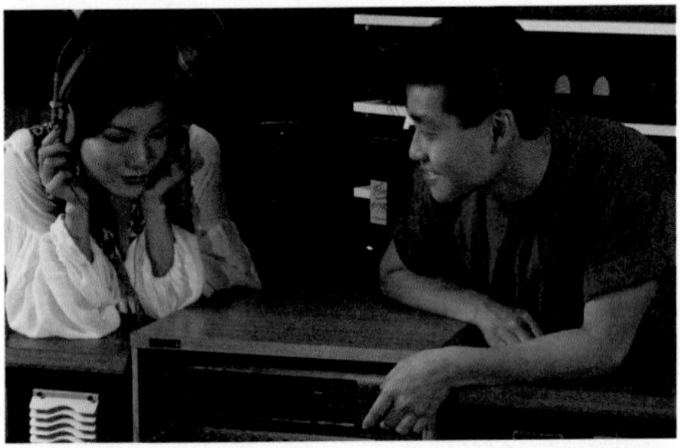

56. Interest on a Loan Mike borrows $10,000 for a period of 3 years at a simple interest rate of 10%. Determine the interest due on the loan.

57. Discounted Sheets A set of Egyptian cotton sheets has a list price of $130.00 but is on sale for $84.50. By what percent is the list price reduced?

58. Income Tax A resident of Missouri has base income, after exemptions and adjustments, of $24,000. The state income tax on this base income is $315 plus 6% of the excess over $9000. What tax is due?

Source: Missouri Department of Revenue

59. Home Equity Loan Sarah Jane needs to borrow $5000 to repair her roof. She can get a discounted loan from her bank at an 8.99% rate of interest for 18 months. What loan amount should be used so that she will receive the $5000 she needs?

60. Equipment Loan The owner of a restaurant needs to borrow $12,000 from a bank to buy some equipment. The bank will give the owner a discounted loan at an 11% rate of interest for 9 months. What loan amount should be used so that the owner will receive $12,000?

61. Payday Loan Jake's car needs repairs but he is short of ca A payday loan company charges a fee of $46.55 for a two-we loan of $250. This is equivalent to a discounted loan wi proceeds of $250 and a loan amount of $296.55. What p annum simple rate of interest is being charged?

Source: mycashnow.com

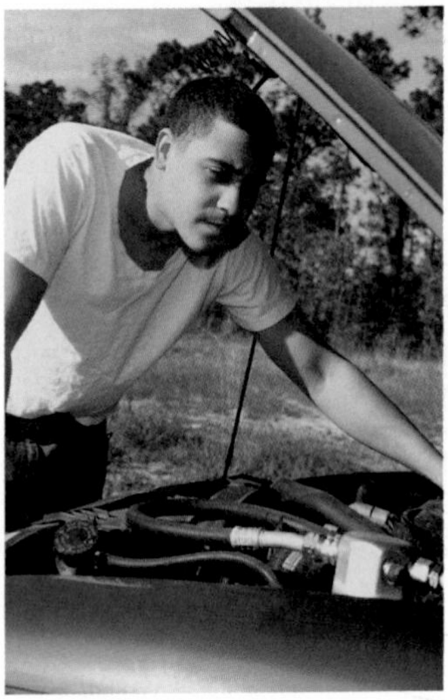

62. Home Equity Loan Fred's credit union offers a simple inter home equity loan that uses a daily rate. For such loa interest is computed using the following formula:

$$(\text{Loan balance}) \cdot (\text{daily rate}) \cdot (\text{days between payments})$$

If Fred borrows $15,000 at a daily periodic rate of 0.0001 and he pays the loan off in one single payment of $18,153.6 how long was the term of the loan?

Source: University Credit Union

63. Comparing Loans You need to borrow $1000 right now b can repay the loan in 6 months. Since you want to pay as lit interest as possible, which type of loan should you take: discounted loan at 9% per annum or a simple interest loan 10% per annum?

4. **Comparing Loans** You need to borrow $5000 right now but can repay the loan in 9 months. Since you want to pay as little interest as possible, which type of loan should you take: a discounted loan at 8% per annum or a simple interest loan at 8.5% per annum?

5. **Used Car Loan** In April 2010, the interest rate on 36-month used car loans was 5.74%. Suppose you have a contract to buy a used car for $8000.

(a) If a bank will lend you $8000 at a 5.74% simple rate of interest for 36 months, how much interest will be charged?

(b) What is the total amount of the loan?

(c) What is the monthly payment due?

Source: Nationwide Bank

oblems 66–70 involve treasury bills,

6. **Bidding on Treasury Bills** How much should a bank bid on a 6-month $3 million treasury bill to earn a 0.23% discounted rate of interest?

7. **Bidding on Treasury Bills** In May 2010, a bank bid $3,996,800 on a 3-month $4 million treasury bill. What was the discounted rate of interest?

68. **T-Bill Auctions** As the result of a treasury bill auction, 1-month T-bills were issued in April 2010, at a price of $999.87 per $1000 face value. How much interest would be received on the maturity date for an investment of $10,000? What is the per annum simple interest rate for this investment, rounded to the nearest thousandth of a percent?

Source: United States Treasury

69. **T-Bill Auction** As the result of a treasury bill auction, 3-month T-bills were issued in February 2009 at a price of $993.25 per $1000 face value. How much interest would be received on the maturity date for an investment of $100,000? What is the per annum simple interest rate for this investment, rounded to the nearest thousandth of a percent?

Source: United States Treasury

70. **T-Bill Auction** As the result of a treasury bill auction, 1-month T-bills were issued in January 2008 at a price of $997.48 per $1000 face value. How much interest would be received on the maturity date for an investment of $5,000? What is the per annum simple interest rate for this investment, rounded to the nearest thousandth of a percent?

Source: United States Treasury

iscussion and Writing

1. If a store marks up an item by 10% and later discounts it by 10%, is the new price the same as the original price? Give an example to support your answer.

2. If a stock drops in price by 10% and then improves its price by 10%, is the resulting price the same as the original price? Give an example to support your answer.

73. When a store gives a 40% discount off the selling price and then gives another 10% off, is that the same as a 50% discount? Give an example to support your answer.

74. Use the results of Problems 68–70 to discuss the trend in short-term interest rates. Compare that trend to current short-term rates and those of 6 months ago.

6.2 Compound Interest

PREPARING FOR THIS SECTION *Before getting started, review the following:*

- **Exponents and Logarithms (Appendix A, Section A.3, pp. A–28 to A–33)**

NOW WORK THE 'ARE YOU PREPARED?' PROBLEMS ON PAGE 311.

OBJECTIVES

1. Determine the future value of a lump sum of money (p. 302)
2. Find the effective rate of interest (p. 307)
3. Determine the present value of a lump sum of money (p. 308)
4. Determine the rate of interest required to double a lump sum of money (p. 310)
5. Determine the time required to double a lump sum of money (p. 310)

1 Determine the Future Value of a Lump Sum of Money

In working with problems involving interest, we use the term **payment period** as follow

Annually	Once per year
Semiannually	Twice per year
Quarterly	4 times per year
Monthly	12 times per year
Daily	365 times per year*

If the interest due at the end of each payment period is added to the principal, so th the interest computed for the next payment period is based on this new amount of t old principal plus interest, then the interest is said to have been **compounded.** That **compound interest** is interest paid on the initial principal and previously earned intere

EXAMPLE 1 Computing Compound Interest

A bank pays interest of 4% per annum compounded quarterly. If $200 is placed in savings account and the quarterly interest is left in the account, how much money is the account after 1 year?

SOLUTION At the end of the first quarter (3 months), the interest earned is found using the Simp Interest formula:

$$I = Prt = (\$200)(0.04)\left(\frac{1}{4}\right) = \$2.00$$

The new principal is $P + I = \$200 + \$2 = \$202$. The interest on this principal at t end of the second quarter is

$$I = (\$202)(0.04)\left(\frac{1}{4}\right) = \$2.02$$

The interest at the end of the third quarter on the principal of $\$202 + \$2.02 = \$204.02$

$$I = (\$204.02)(0.04)\left(\frac{1}{4}\right) = \$2.04$$

The interest at the end of the fourth quarter on the principal $\$204.02 + \$2.04 = \$206.06$ is

$$I = (\$206.06)(0.04)\left(\frac{1}{4}\right) = \$2.06$$

After 1 year, the total in the savings account is $\$206.06 + \$2.06 = \$208.12$.
These results are shown in Figure 1.

FIGURE 1

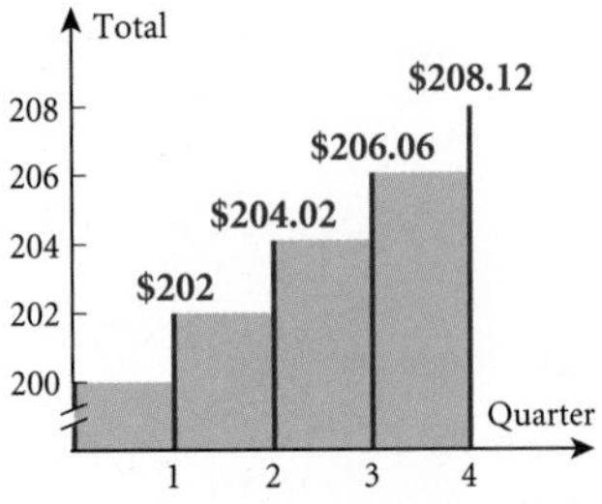

The pattern of the calculations performed in Example 1 leads to a general formu for compound interest. To fix our ideas, let P represent the principal to be invested a per annum interest rate r that is compounded n times per year, so the time of ea

* *Some banks use 360 times per year.*

compounding period is $\frac{1}{n}$ years. (For computing purposes, r is expressed as a decimal.)

The interest earned after each compounding period is given by the Simple Interest Formula, Formula (1) on page 295.

$$\text{Interest} = \text{principal} \times \text{rate} \times \text{time} = P \cdot r \cdot \frac{1}{n} = P \cdot \left(\frac{r}{n}\right)$$

The amount A after one compounding period is

$$A = P + P \cdot \left(\frac{r}{n}\right) = P \cdot \left(1 + \frac{r}{n}\right)$$

After two compounding periods, the amount A, based on the new principal $P \cdot \left(1 + \frac{r}{n}\right)$, is

$$A = \underbrace{P \cdot \left(1 + \frac{r}{n}\right)}_{\text{New principal}} + \underbrace{\left[P \cdot \left(1 + \frac{r}{n}\right)\right]\left(\frac{r}{n}\right)}_{\text{Interest on new principal}} \underset{\uparrow}{=} P \cdot \left(1 + \frac{r}{n}\right)\left(1 + \frac{r}{n}\right) = P \cdot \left(1 + \frac{r}{n}\right)^2$$

Factor out $P \cdot \left(1 + \frac{r}{n}\right)$.

After three compounding periods, the amount A is

$$A = P \cdot \left(1 + \frac{r}{n}\right)^2 + \left[P \cdot \left(1 + \frac{r}{n}\right)^2\right]\left(\frac{r}{n}\right) = P \cdot \left(1 + \frac{r}{n}\right)^2 \cdot \left(1 + \frac{r}{n}\right) = P \cdot \left(1 + \frac{r}{n}\right)^3$$

Continuing this way, after n compounding periods (1 year), the amount A is

$$A = P \cdot \left(1 + \frac{r}{n}\right)^n$$

Because t years will contain $n \cdot t$ compounding periods, after t years the amount A is

$$A = P \cdot \left(1 + \frac{r}{n}\right)^{nt}$$

Theorem

Compound Interest Formula

The amount A after t years due to a principal P invested at an annual interest rate r compounded n times per year is

$$A = P \cdot \left(1 + \frac{r}{n}\right)^{nt} \qquad (1)$$

EXPLORATION To see the effects of compounding interest monthly on an initial deposit of \$1, graph $Y_1 = \left(1 + \frac{r}{12}\right)^{12x}$ with $r = 0.06$ and $r = 0.12$ for $0 \le x \le 30$. What is the future value of \$1 in 30 years when the interest rate per annum is $r = 0.06$ (6%)? What is the future value of \$1 in 30 years when the interest rate per annum is $r = 0.12$ (12%)? Does doubling the interest rate double the future value?

For example, to rework Example 1, use $P = \$200$, $r = 0.04$, $n = 4$ (quarterly compounding), and $t = 1$ year to obtain

$$A = P \cdot \left(1 + \frac{r}{n}\right)^{nt} = 200\left(1 + \frac{0.04}{4}\right)^{4 \cdot 1} = \$208.12$$

In the Compound Interest Formula, the amount A is typically referred to as the **future value** of the account, while P is called the **present value.**

EXAMPLE 2 Working with the Compound Interest Formula

If \$1000 is borrowed at an annual rate of interest of 10% and no payments are made on this loan, what is the amount after 5 years if the compounding takes place

(a) Annually? **(b)** Monthly? **(c)** Daily?

How much interest is due in each case?

SOLUTION Use the Compound Interest Formula. The principal is $P = \$1000$, the annual rate of interest is $r = 0.10$, and $t = 5$ years.

(a) For annual compounding, $n = 1$. The amount A is

$$A = P\left(1 + \frac{r}{n}\right)^{nt} = (\$1000)(1 + 0.10)^5 = (\$1000)(1.61051) = \$1610.51$$

The interest due is

$$A - P = \$1610.51 - \$1000.00 = \$610.51$$

(b) For monthly compounding, $n = 12$. The amount A is

$$A = P\left(1 + \frac{r}{n}\right)^{nt} = (\$1000)\left(1 + \frac{0.10}{12}\right)^{60} = (\$1000)(1.64531) = \$1645.31$$

The interest due is

$$A - P = \$1645.31 - \$1000.00 = \$645.31$$

(c) For daily compounding, $n = 365$. The amount A is

$$A = P\left(1 + \frac{r}{n}\right)^{nt} = (\$1000)\left(1 + \frac{0.10}{365}\right)^{1825} = (\$1000)(1.64861) = \$1648.61$$

The interest due is

$$A - P = \$1648.61 - \$1000.00 = \$648.61$$

The results of Example 2 are summarized in Table 1.

TABLE 1

Per Annum Rate	Compounding Method	Interest Rate per Payment Period	Initial Principal	Amount after 5 Years	Interest Due
10%	Annual	0.10	\$1000	\$1610.51	\$610.51
10%	Monthly	$\frac{0.10}{12} = 0.00833$	\$1000	\$1645.31	\$645.31
10%	Daily	$\frac{0.10}{365} = 0.000274$	\$1000	\$1648.61	\$648.61

NOW WORK PROBLEM 9.

EXAMPLE 3 Comparing Investments Using Different Compounding Periods

Investing \$10,000 at an annual rate of 4% compounded annually, semiannually, quarterly, monthly, and daily will yield the following amounts after 1 year:

Annual compounding ($n = 1$):
$$A = P \cdot (1 + r) = (\$10{,}000)(1 + 0.04) = \$10{,}400.00$$

Semiannual compounding ($n = 2$):
$$A = P \cdot \left(1 + \frac{r}{2}\right)^2 = (\$10{,}000)\left(1 + \frac{0.04}{2}\right)^2 = \$10{,}404.00$$

Quarterly compounding ($n = 4$):
$$A = P \cdot \left(1 + \frac{r}{4}\right)^4 = (\$10{,}000)\left(1 + \frac{0.04}{4}\right)^4 = \$10{,}406.04$$

Monthly compounding ($n = 12$):
$$A = P \cdot \left(1 + \frac{r}{12}\right)^{12} = (\$10{,}000)\left(1 + \frac{0.04}{12}\right)^{12} = \$10{,}407.42$$

Daily compounding ($n = 365$):
$$A = P \cdot \left(1 + \frac{r}{365}\right)^{365} = (\$10{,}000)\left(1 + \frac{0.04}{365}\right)^{365} = \$10{,}408.08 \blacksquare$$

From Example 3, notice that the effect of compounding more frequently is that the amount after 1 year is higher: \$10,000 compounded 2 times a year at 4% results in \$10,404; \$10,000 compounded 12 times a year at 4% results in \$10,407.42; and \$10,000 compounded 365 times a year at 4% results in \$10,408.08. This leads to the following question: What would happen to the amount after 1 year if the number of times that the interest is compounded were increased without bound?

Let's find the answer. Suppose that P is the principal, r is the per annum interest rate, and n is the number of times that the interest is compounded each year. The amount after 1 year is

$$A = P \cdot \left(1 + \frac{r}{n}\right)^n$$

Rewrite this expression as follows:

$$A = P \cdot \left(1 + \frac{r}{n}\right)^n \underset{\frac{r}{n} = \frac{1}{\frac{n}{r}}}{\uparrow}= P \cdot \left(1 + \frac{1}{\frac{n}{r}}\right)^n \underset{n = \frac{n}{r} \cdot r}{\uparrow}= P \cdot \left[\left(1 + \frac{1}{\frac{n}{r}}\right)^{n/r}\right]^r \underset{h = \frac{n}{r}}{\uparrow}= P \cdot \left[\left(1 + \frac{1}{h}\right)^h\right]^r \qquad (2)$$

Now suppose that the number n of times that the interest is compounded per year g larger and larger. This is equivalent to $h = \frac{n}{r}$ getting larger and larger. Table 2 illustra what happens to the expression $\left(1 + \frac{1}{h}\right)^h$ as h takes on increasingly larger values; not it is getting closer to a particular number, which we designate as e.

TABLE 2

h	$\frac{1}{h}$	$1 + \frac{1}{h}$	$\left(1 + \frac{1}{h}\right)^h$
1	1	2	2
2	0.5	1.5	2.25
5	0.2	1.2	2.48832
10	0.1	1.1	2.59374246
100	0.01	1.01	2.704813829
1,000	0.001	1.001	2.716923932
10,000	0.0001	1.0001	2.718145927
100,000	0.00001	1.00001	2.718268237
1,000,000	0.000001	1.000001	2.718280469
1,000,000,000	10^{-9}	$1 + 10^{-9}$	2.718281827

Definition

The **number *e*** is defined as the number that the expression

$$\left(1 + \frac{1}{h}\right)^h \qquad (3)$$

approaches as h gets larger and larger.

Look again at Table 2. The bottom number in the right column is the numbe correct to nine decimal places and is the same as the entry given for e on your calcula (if expressed correctly to nine decimal places).* As it turns out, the number e is irrational number, so its decimal equivalent is a nonrepeating, nonterminating decima

Now return to Equation (2). As the number n of compounding periods increa without bound, then $h = \frac{n}{r}$ will also increase without bound, and the expression brackets on the far right of Equation (2) will equal the number e. The larger n gets, t closer $\left[\left(1 + \frac{1}{h}\right)^h\right]^r$ gets to e^r. In other words, no matter how frequent the compoundi the amount after 1 year has the definite ceiling Pe^r.

Definition

When interest at a per annum rate r is compounded on a principal P so that the amount after 1 year is Pe^r, we say the interest is **compounded continuously.**

* *Most calculators have the key* $\boxed{e^x}$ *or* $\boxed{\exp(x)}$*, which may be used to evaluate the expression* e^x *for a gi value of x. Consult your owner's manual.*

Theorem

Continuous Compounding

The amount A after t years due to a principal P invested at an annual interest rate r compounded continuously is

$$A = Pe^{rt} \tag{4}$$

EXAMPLE 4 **Using Continuous Compounding**

The amount A that results from investing a principal P of \$10,000 at an annual rate r of 4% compounded continuously for a time t of 1 year is

$$A = Pe^{rt} = \$10{,}000e^{0.04} = (\$10{,}000)(1.040811) = \$10{,}408.11$$ ■

NOW WORK PROBLEM 17.

2 Find the Effective Rate of Interest

The **effective rate of interest** is the equivalent annual simple rate of interest that would yield the same amount as compounding after 1 year.

For example, based on Example 4, a principal of \$10,000 will result in \$10,408.11 at a rate of 4% compounded continuously. To get this same amount using a simple rate of interest would require that interest of \$10,408.11 − \$10,000 = \$408.11 be earned on the principal. Since \$408.11 is 4.0811% of \$10,000, a simple rate of interest of 4.0811% is needed to equal 4% compounded continuously. The effective rate of interest of 4% compounded continuously is 4.0811%.

Based on the results of Examples 3 and 4, we find the following comparisons:

	Annual Rate	Effective Rate
Annual compounding	4%	4%
Semiannual compounding	4%	4.04%
Quarterly compounding	4%	4.0604%
Monthly compounding	4%	4.0742%
Daily compounding	4%	4.0808%
Continuous compounding	4%	4.0811%

EXAMPLE 5 **Computing the Effective Rate of Interest**

On January 1, 2010, \$2000 is placed in an Individual Retirement Account (IRA) that will pay interest of 3% per annum compounded continuously.

(a) What will the IRA be worth on January 1, 2030?

(b) What is the effective annual rate of interest?

SOLUTION **(a)** On January, 1, 2030, the initial principal of \$2000 will have earned interest of 3% compounded continuously for 20 years. The amount A after 20 years is

$$A = Pe^{rt} = \$2000e^{(0.03)(20)} = \$3644.24$$

(b) First, compute the interest earned on \$2000 at $r = 3\%$ compounded continuou after 1 year.

$$A = \$2000e^{0.03(1)} = \$2060.91$$

So the interest earned after 1 year is \$2060.91 − \$2000.00 = \$60.91. To find t effective rate of interest R, use the simple interest formula $I = PRt$, with $I = \$60.9$ $P = \$2000$, and $t = 1$.

$$\$60.91 = \$2000 \cdot R \cdot 1 \qquad I = PRt$$

$$R = \frac{\$60.91}{\$2000} = 0.0305 \qquad \text{Solve for } R.$$

The effective annual rate of interest R is 3.05%.

NOW WORK PROBLEM 33.

3 Determine the Present Value of a Lump Sum of Money

When people engaged in finance speak of the "time value of money," they are usua referring to the *present value* of money. The **present value** of A dollars to be received a future date is the principal that you would need to invest now so that it will grow to dollars in the specified time period. The present value of money to be received at a futu date is always less than the amount to be received, since the amount to be received will equ the present value (money invested now) *plus* the interest accrued over the time period.

We use the Compound Interest Formula to get a formula for present value. If P the present value of A dollars to be received after t years at a per annum interest rat compounded n times per year, then

$$A = P \cdot \left(1 + \frac{r}{n}\right)^{nt} \qquad \text{Compound Interest Formula}$$

To solve for P, divide both sides by $\left(1 + \frac{r}{n}\right)^{nt}$. The result is

$$\frac{A}{\left(1 + \frac{r}{n}\right)^{nt}} = P \quad \text{or} \quad P = A \cdot \left(1 + \frac{r}{n}\right)^{-nt}$$

Theorem

Present Value Formulas

The present value P of A dollars to be received after t years, assuming a per annum interest rate r compounded n times per year, is

$$P = A \cdot \left(1 + \frac{r}{n}\right)^{-nt} \tag{5}$$

If the interest is compounded continuously,

$$P = Ae^{-rt} \tag{6}$$

To prove (6), solve Formula (4) for P.

EXAMPLE 6 | **Computing the Present Value of $10,000**

How much money should be invested now at 4% per annum so that after 2 years the amount will be $10,000 when the interest is compounded

(a) Annually? **(b)** Monthly? **(c)** Daily? **(d)** Continuously?

SOLUTION In this problem we want to find the principal P needed now to get the amount $A = \$10,000$ after $t = 2$ years when the interest rate is $r = 0.04$. That is, we want to find the present value of $10,000.

(a) Since compounding is once per year, use Formula (5) with $n = 1$. The present value P of $10,000 is

$$P = A\left(1 + \frac{r}{n}\right)^{-nt} = 10,000(1 + 0.04)^{-2} = 10,000(0.924556) = \$9245.56$$

(b) Since compounding is 12 times per year, use Formula (5) with $n = 12$. The present value P of $10,000 is

$$P = A\left(1 + \frac{r}{n}\right)^{-nt} = 10,000\left(1 + \frac{0.04}{12}\right)^{-24} = 10,000(0.923239) = \$9232.39$$

(c) Since compounding is 365 times per year, use Formula (5) with $n = 365$. The present value P of $10,000 is

$$P = A\left(1 + \frac{r}{n}\right)^{-nt} = 10,000\left(1 + \frac{0.04}{365}\right)^{-730} = 10,000(0.923120) = \$9231.20$$

(d) Since compounding is continuous, use Formula (6).

$$P = Ae^{-rt} = 10,000e^{-0.04(2)} = 10,000(0.923116) = \$9231.16$$ ■

✎ NOW WORK PROBLEM 19.

EXAMPLE 7 | **Computing the Value of a Zero-coupon Bond**

A zero-coupon (noninterest-bearing) bond can be redeemed in 10 years for $1000. How much should you be willing to pay for it now if you want a return of

(a) 5% compounded monthly? **(b)** 4% compounded continuously?

SOLUTION **(a)** We seek the present value of $1000. Use Formula (5) with $A = \$1000$, $n = 12$, $r = 0.05$, and $t = 10$.

$$P = A \cdot \left(1 + \frac{r}{n}\right)^{-nt} = \$1000\left(1 + \frac{0.05}{12}\right)^{-12(10)} = \$607.16$$

For a return of 5% compounded monthly, you should pay $607.16 for the bond.

(b) Here use Formula (6) with $A = \$1000$, $r = 0.04$, and $t = 10$.

$$P = Ae^{-rt} = \$1000e^{-(0.04)(10)} = \$670.32$$

For a return of 4% compounded continuously, you should pay $670.32 for the bond. ■

✎ NOW WORK PROBLEM 85.

4 Determine the Rate of Interest Required to Double a Lump Sum of Money

EXAMPLE 8 Rate of Interest Required to Double an Investment

What annual rate of interest compounded annually should you seek if you want double your investment in 5 years?

SOLUTION If P is the principal and we want P to double, the amount A will be $2P$. Use t Compound Interest Formula (5) with $n = 1$ and $t = 5$ to find r.

$$A = P\cdot\left(1 + \frac{r}{n}\right)^{nt} \quad \text{Formula (5)}$$

$$2P = P\cdot(1 + r)^5 \quad A = 2P, n = 1, t = 5$$

$$2 = (1 + r)^5 \quad \text{Divide both sides by } P.$$

$$\sqrt[5]{2} = 1 + r \quad \text{Take the fifth root of each side}$$

$$r = \sqrt[5]{2} - 1 \approx 1.148698 - 1 = 0.148698 \quad \text{Solve for } r.$$

The annual rate of interest needed to double the principal in 5 years is 14.87%.

NOW WORK PROBLEM 37.

5 Determine the Time Required to Double a Lump Sum of Money

EXAMPLE 9 Time Required to Double an Investment

(a) How long will it take for an investment to double in value if it earns 5% compound annually?

(b) How long will it take for an investment to double in value if it earns 5% compound continuously?

SOLUTION **(a)** If P is the initial investment and we want P to double, the amount A we want will $2P$. Use the Compound Interest Formula (5) with $r = 0.05$, $n = 1$, and $A = 2P$.

$$A = P\left(1 + \frac{r}{n}\right)^{nt} \quad \text{Formula (5)}$$

$$2P = P(1 + 0.05)^t \quad A = 2P;\ n = 1;\ r = 0.05$$

$$2 = (1.05)^t \quad \text{Divide both sides by } P.$$

$$t = \log_{1.05} 2 \quad \text{Change to a logarithmic equatio}$$

$$t = \frac{\log 2}{\log 1.05} \approx 14.207 \quad \text{Apply the Change-of-Base Formu}$$

It will take about 14.2 years to double the investment at 5% compounded annually.

(b) If P is the initial investment and we want P to double, the amount A will be Use Formula (6) for continuously compounded interest with $r = 0.05$ and $A =$ Then

$$A = Pe^{rt} \quad \text{Formula (6)}$$

$$2P = Pe^{0.05t} \quad A = 2P, r = 0.05$$

$$2 = e^{0.05t} \quad \text{Divide both sides by } P.$$

$$0.05t = \ln 2 \qquad \text{Rewrite as a logarithmic equation.*}$$

$$t = \frac{\ln 2}{0.05} \approx 13.86 \qquad \text{Solve for } t.$$

It will take just under 14 years to double the investment at 5% compounded continuously. ■

NOW WORK PROBLEM 41.

* *When the base of a logarithm is the number e, that is, when $x = \log_e N$, it is customary to write the logarithm as $x = \ln N$. Most calculators have a key* [ln x] *for evaluating these logarithms.*

XERCISE 6.2 Answers Begin on Page AN–32.

re You Prepared?' Problems Answers are given at the end of these exercises. If you get a wrong answer, read the pages listed in red.

1. Evaluate: (a) $(1 + 0.05)^8$ (b) $\left(1 + \dfrac{0.08}{12}\right)^{-24}$ Round answers to 3 decimal places. (pp. A–28 to A–33)

2. Change the equation $y = \log_2 16$ to an exponential equation: ________ (pp. A–28 to A–33)

3. Change the equation $2 = (1.05)^t$ to a logarithmic equation: ________ (pp. A–28 to A–33)

4. Use the Change-of-Base Formula to evaluate $\log_{1.05} 2$: ________. Round your answer to 3 decimal places. (pp. A–28 to A–33)

oncepts and Vocabulary

5. ***True or False*** The more times in a year that interest is compounded, the more money there is after one year.

6. ***True or False*** If a rate of 9% interest is compounded monthly, the effective rate of interest is somewhat less than 9%.

7. When interest at a rate r is compounded on a principal P so that the amount after one year is Pe^r, the interest is said to be ________ ________.

8. The principal needed now to get \$1000 at a later date is called the ________ ________ of \$1000.

kill Building

Problems 9–18, find the amount that results from each investment.

9. \$100 invested at 4% compounded quarterly after a period of 2 years

10. \$50 invested at 6% compounded monthly after a period of 3 years

1. \$500 invested at 8% compounded quarterly after a period of $2\frac{1}{2}$ years

12. \$300 invested at 2% compounded monthly after a period of $1\frac{1}{2}$ years

3. \$600 invested at 5% compounded daily after a period of 3 years

14. \$700 invested at 6% compounded daily after a period of 2 years

5. \$10 invested at 2% compounded continuously after a period of 2 years

16. \$40 invested at 7% compounded continuously after a period of 3 years

7. \$100 invested at 3% compounded continuously after a period of $2\frac{1}{4}$ years

18. \$100 invested at 3% compounded continuously after a period of $3\frac{3}{4}$ years

Problems 19–28, find the principal needed now to get each amount; that is, find the present value.

9. To get \$100 after 2 years at 2% compounded monthly

20. To get \$75 after 3 years at 3% compounded quarterly

1. To get \$1000 after $2\frac{1}{2}$ years at 6% compounded daily

22. To get \$800 after $3\frac{1}{2}$ years at 2% compounded monthly

3. To get \$600 after 2 years at 4% compounded quarterly

24. To get \$300 after 4 years at 3% compounded daily

25. To get \$80 after $3\frac{1}{4}$ years at 2% compounded continuously

26. To get \$800 after $2\frac{1}{2}$ years at 3% compounded continuously

27. To get \$400 after 1 year at 4% compounded continuously

28. To get \$1000 after 1 year at 3% compounded continuously

In Problems 29–32, which of the two rates would yield the larger amount in 1 year? [Hint: Start with a principal of \$10,000 in each instance.]

29. 6% compounded quarterly or $6\frac{1}{4}$% compounded annually

30. 9% compounded quarterly or $9\frac{1}{4}$% compounded annually

31. 9% compounded monthly or 8.8% compounded daily

32. 8% compounded semiannually or 7.9% compounded dai

In Problems 33–36, find the effective rate of interest.

33. For 5% compounded quarterly
34. For 6% compounded monthly
35. For 5% compounded continuously
36. For 6% compounded continuously
37. What rate of interest compounded annually is required to double an investment in 3 years?
38. What rate of interest compounded annually is required to double an investment in 6 years?
39. What rate of interest compounded annually is required to triple an investment in 5 years?
40. What rate of interest compounded annually is required to triple an investment in 10 years?
41. (a) How long does it take for an investment to double in value if it is invested at 8% compounded monthly?
    (b) How long does it take if the interest is compounded continuously?
42. (a) How long does it take for an investment to triple in value if it is invested at 6% compounded monthly?
    (b) How long does it take if the interest is compounded continuously?
43. What rate of interest compounded quarterly will yield an effective interest rate of 7%?
44. What rate of interest compounded continuously will yield an effective interest rate of 6%?
45. If \$1000 is invested at 4% compounded
    (a) annually (b) monthly
    what is the amount A after 3 years? How much interest is earne
46. If \$2000 is invested at 5% compounded
    (a) annually (b) continuously
    what is the amount A after 5 years? How much interest earned?
47. If \$1000 is invested at 2% compounded quarterly, what is th amount A after
    (a) 2 years? (b) 3 years? (c) 4 years?
48. If \$2000 is invested at 4% compounded quarterly, what is th amount A after
    (a) 2 years? (b) 3 years? (c) 4 years?
49. If a bank pays 3% compounded semiannually, how muc should be deposited now to have \$5000
    (a) 4 years later? (b) 8 years later?
50. If a bank pays 2% compounded quarterly, how much shou be deposited now to have \$10,000
    (a) 5 years later? (b) 10 years later?
51. Mr. Nielsen wants to borrow \$1000 for 2 years. He is given th choice of (a) a simple interest loan at 12% or (b) a loan at 10% compounded monthly. Which loan results in less interest du
52. What principal is needed now to get \$1000 in 1 year at 3% compounded annually? How much should be invested to ge \$1000 in 2 years?

Applications and Extensions

53. **Time Required to Reach a Goal** If Tanisha has \$100 to invest at 3% per annum compounded monthly, how long will it be before she has \$150? If the compounding is continuous, how long will it be?
54. **Time Required to Reach a Goal** If Angela has \$100 to invest at 4% per annum compounded monthly, how long will it be before she has \$175? If the compounding is continuous, how long will it be?
55. **Time Required to Reach a Goal** How many years will it take for an initial investment of \$10,000 to grow to \$25,000? Assume a rate of interest of 6% compounded continuously.
56. **Time Required to Reach a Goal** How many years will it take for an initial investment of \$25,000 to grow to \$80,000? Assume a rate of interest of 5% compounded continuously.
57. **Price Appreciation of Homes** What will a \$90,000 house co 5 years from now if the price appreciation for homes over th period averages 3% compounded annually?
58. **Credit Card Interest** A department store charges 1.25% pe month on the unpaid balance for customers with charg accounts (interest is compounded monthly). A custome charges \$200 and does not pay her bill for 6 months. What the bill at that time?
59. **Saving for a Car** Jerome will be buying a used car for \$15,00 in 3 years. How much money should he ask his parents fo now so that, if he invests it at 5% compounded continuousl he will have enough to buy the car?
60. **Paying off a Loan** John will require \$3000 in 6 months to pa off a loan that has no prepayment privileges. If he has th

$3000 now, how much of it should he save in an account paying 3% compounded monthly so that in 6 months he will have exactly $3000 in the account?

1. **Return on a Stock** George is contemplating the purchase of 100 shares of a stock selling for $15 per share. The stock pays no dividends. The history of the stock indicates that it should grow at an annual rate of 15% per year. How much will the 100 shares of stock be worth in 5 years?

2. **Return on an Investment** A business purchased for $650,000 in 2008 is sold in 2011 for $850,000. What is the annual rate of return for this investment?

3. **Comparing Savings Plans** Jim places $1000 in a bank account that pays 5.6% compounded continuously. After 1 year, will he have enough money to buy a computer system that costs $1060? If another bank will pay Jim 5.9% compounded monthly, is this a better deal?

4. **Savings Plans** On January 1, Kim places $1000 in a certificate of deposit that pays 2.8% compounded continuously and matures in 3 months. Then Kim places the $1000 and the interest in a passbook account that pays 1.75% compounded monthly. How much does Kim have in the passbook account on May 1?

5. **Comparing IRA Investments** Will invests $2000 in his IRA in a bond trust that pays 5% interest compounded semiannually. His friend Henry invests $2000 in his IRA in a certificate of deposit that pays $4\frac{1}{2}$% compounded continuously. Who will have more money after 20 years, Will or Henry?

6. **Comparing Two Alternatives** Suppose that April has access to an investment that will pay 5% interest compounded continuously. Which is better: to be given $1000 now so that she can take advantage of this investment opportunity or to be given $1200 three years from now?

7. **Down Payment on a House** Tami and Todd will need $40,000 for a down payment on a house in 4 years. How much should they deposit in a savings account now so that they will be able to do this? The bank pays 3% compounded quarterly.

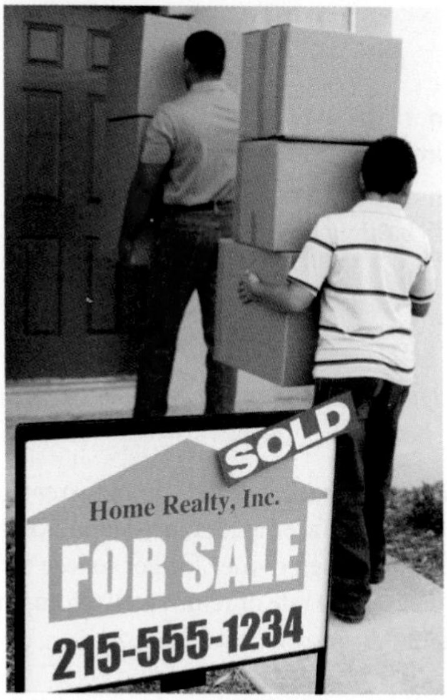

68. **Saving for College** A newborn child receives a $3000 gift toward a college education. How much will the $3000 be worth in 17 years if it is invested at 5% compounded quarterly?

69. **Gifting** A child's grandparents have opened a $6000 savings account for the child on the day of her birth. The account pays 3% compounded semiannually. The child will be allowed to withdraw the money when she reaches the age of 25. What will the account be worth at that time?

70. **Effective Rates of Interest** A bank advertises that it pays interest on saving accounts at the rate of 2.25% compounded daily.
    (a) Find the effective rate if the bank uses 360 days in determining the daily rate.
    (b) What is the effective rate if 365 days are used?

71. **Length of Investment** How many years will it take for an initial investment of $10,000 to grow to $25,000? Assume a rate of interest of 3% compounded daily.

72. **Length of Investment** How many years will it take for an initial investment of $25,000 to grow to $80,000? Assume a rate of interest of 4% compounded daily.

73. **Roth IRA** Jason and his wife put $4000 into a Roth IRA that pays 4% compounded annually. How much will the investment be worth after 30 years?

74. **Roth IRA** What annual rate of interest is required for an initial investment of $2000 in a Roth IRA to be worth $4500 in 20 years?

75. **College Savings** Tom and Anita have a new baby and want to start saving for college. The average tuition, fees, and room and board charges at a public four-year institution totaled $15,213 in 2008–2009. Assuming a 6% annual increase, this cost will rise to $43,423 when their child begins college in 2026. How much do they need to invest in 2010 at 8% per annum compounded continuously to afford 1 year at a public 4-year institution in 2026?
    Source: *Trends in College Pricing 2009*, College Board

76. **College Savings** The average tuition, fees, and room and board charges at a private four-year institution totaled $35,636 in 2008–2009. Assuming a 5% annual increase, this cost will rise to $85,762 for the academic year 2026–2027. For their newborn baby, how much will Tom and Anita need to invest in 2010 at 7% per annum compounded continuously to afford 1 year at a private 4-year institution in 2026 (to the nearest dollar)?
    Source: *Trends in College Pricing 2009*, College Board

77. **National Debt** The national debt was approximately $5.77 trillion on January 1, 2000, and approximately $12.31 trillion on January 1, 2010.
    (a) Find the annual rate of growth of the national debt in this 10-year period, assuming a constant annual rate of growth.
    (b) If this rate of growth continues, what would be the projected national debt on January 1, 2020?
    Source: U.S. Treasury

78. Cost of Energy The average U.S. household will spend \$2173 on energy use in the year 2010. This includes \$849 for heating, \$553 for appliances, \$302 for water heating, \$271 for cooling, and \$198 for lighting.

(a) Assuming a constant annual inflation rate of 2.3%, determine the projected amounts that the average U.S. household will spend on each of the forms of energy listed above in the year 2014.

(b) If energy costs increase at an annual rate of 4%, what will the average household spend on each form of energy in 2014?

Home Energy Cost
The average U.S. household will spend \$2173 on energy use in 2010. How it will be spent:

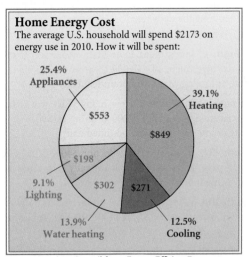

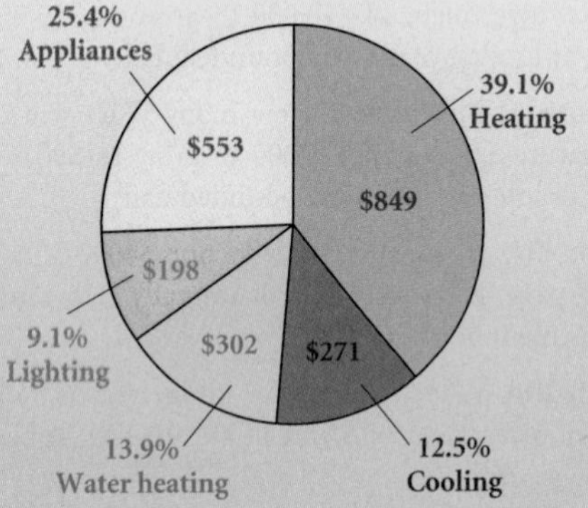

Source: American Council for an Energy-Efficient Economy

79. Analyzing Interest Rates on a Mortgage Colleen and Bill ha[ve] just purchased a house for \$650,000, with the seller holding [a] second mortgage of \$100,000. They promise to pay the sel[ler] \$100,000 plus all accrued interest 5 years from now. The sel[ler] offers them three interest options on the second mortgage:

(a) Simple interest at 6% per annum

(b) $5\frac{3}{4}$% interest compounded monthly

(c) $5\frac{1}{2}$% interest compounded continuously

Which option is best; that is, which results in the least inter[est] on the loan?

Inflation *Problems 80–84 require the following discussion.* ***Inflation*** *is a term used to describe the erosion of the purchasing power of mone[y]. For example, suppose the annual inflation rate is 3%. Then \$1000 worth of purchasing power now will have only \$970 worth of purchasi[ng] power in one year because 3% of the original \$1000* ($0.03 \times 1000 = 30$) *has been eroded due to inflation. In general, if the inflation averag[es] a rate of r over n years, the amount A that \$P will purchase after n years is*

$$A = P \cdot (1 - r)^n$$

where r is expressed as a decimal.

80. Inflation If the inflation rate averages 2%, how much will \$1000 purchase in 3 years?

81. Inflation If the amount that \$1000 will purchase is only \$950 after 2 years, what was the average inflation rate?

82. Inflation If the amount that \$1000 will purchase is only \$930 after 2 years, what was the average inflation rate?

83. Inflation If the average inflation rate is 2%, how long is until purchasing power is cut in half?

84. Inflation If the average inflation rate is 4%, how long is until purchasing power is cut in half?

Problems 85–88 involve zero-coupon bonds. A ***zero-coupon bond*** *is a bond that is sold now at a discount and will pay its face value at the tim[e] when it matures; no interest payments are made.*

85. Zero-Coupon Bonds A zero-coupon bond can be redeemed in 20 years for \$10,000. How much should you be willing to pay for it now if you want a return of:

(a) 5% compounded monthly?

(b) 5% compounded continuously?

86. Zero-Coupon Bonds A child's grandparents are considerin[g] buying a \$40,000 face value zero-coupon bond at birth so th[at] she will have enough money for her college education 17 yea[rs] later. If they want a rate of return of 4% compounded annuall[y], what should they pay for the bond?

7. **Zero-Coupon Bonds** How much should a \$10,000 face value zero-coupon bond, maturing in 10 years, be sold for now if its rate of return is to be 4% compounded annually?

8. **Zero-Coupon Bonds** If Pat pays \$12,485 for a \$25,000 face value zero-coupon bond that matures in 12 years, what is his annual rate of return?

9. **Time to Double or Triple an Investment** The formula

$$t = \frac{\ln m}{n \ln\left(1 + \frac{r}{n}\right)}$$

can be used to find the number of years t required to multiply an investment m times when r is the per annum interest rate compounded n times a year.

(a) How many years will it take to double the value of an IRA that compounds annually at the rate of 4%?

(b) How many years will it take to triple the value of a savings account that compounds quarterly at an annual rate of 3%?

(c) Give a derivation of this formula.

90. **Time to Reach an Investment Goal** The formula

$$t = \frac{\ln A - \ln P}{r}$$

can be used to find the number of years t required for an investment P to grow to a value A when compounded continuously at an annual rate r.

(a) How long will it take to increase an initial investment of \$1000 to \$8000 at an annual rate of 5%?

(b) What annual rate is required to increase the value of a \$2000 IRA to \$25,000 in 35 years?

(c) Give a derivation of this formula.

---

roblems 91–94 require the following discussion. The **Consumer Price Index (CPI)** *indicates the relative change in price over time for a fixed asket of goods and services. It is a cost of living index that helps measure the effect of inflation on the cost of goods and services. The CPI uses he base period 1982–1984 for comparison (the CPI for this period is 100). The CPI for January 2010 was 217.6. This means that \$100 in the eriod 1982–1984 had the same purchasing power as \$217.60 in January 2010. In general, if the rate of inflation averages a rate of r over n years, hen the CPI index after n years is*

$$\text{CPI} = \text{CPI}_0\left(1 + \frac{r}{100}\right)^n$$

here CPI_0 is the CPI index at the beginning of the n-year period.

ource: U.S. Bureau of Labor Statistics

1. **Consumer Price Index**

(a) The CPI was 169.3 in January 2000 and 217.6 in January 2010. Assuming that annual inflation remained constant for this time period, determine the average annual inflation rate.

(b) Using the inflation rate from part (a), in what year will the CPI reach 300?

2. **Consumer Price Index** If the January 2010 CPI was 217.6 and the average annual inflation rate is 2.3%, what will be the CPI in 5 years?

93. **Consumer Price Index** If the average annual inflation rate is 2.3%, how long will it take for the CPI index to double?

94. **Consumer Price Index** The base period for the CPI last changed in 1998. Under the previous weight and item structure, the CPI for 1995 was 456.5. If the average annual inflation rate was 5.57%, what year was used as the base period for the CPI?

iscussion and Writing

95. Explain in your own words what the term *compound interest* means. What does *continuous compounding* mean?

96. Explain in your own words the meaning of *present value*.

97. **Critical Thinking** You have just contracted to buy a house and will seek financing in the amount of \$100,000. You go to several banks. Bank 1 will lend you \$100,000 at the rate of 5.078% amortized over 30 years with a loan origination fee of 1.75%. Bank 2 will lend you \$100,000 at the rate of 4.310% amortized over 15 years with a loan origination fee of 1.5%. Bank 3 will lend you \$100,000 at the rate of 5.199% amortized over 30 years with no loan origination fee. Bank 4 will lend

you $100,000 at the rate of 4.840% amortized over 15 years with no loan origination fee. Which loan would you take? Why? Be sure to have sound reasons for your choice.

Use the information in the table to assist you. If the amount of the monthly payment does not matter to you, which loan would you take? Again, have sound reasons for your choice. Compare your final decision with others in the class. Discuss.

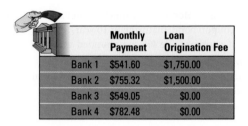

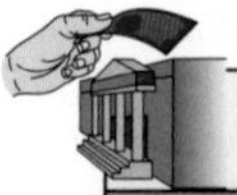

	Monthly Payment	Loan Origination Fee
Bank 1	$541.60	$1,750.00
Bank 2	$755.32	$1,500.00
Bank 3	$549.05	$0.00
Bank 4	$782.48	$0.00

'Are You Prepared?' Answers

1. (a) 1.477 (b) 0.853 **2.** $2^y = 16$ **3.** $t = \log_{1.05} 2$ **4.** 14.207

6.3 Annuities; Sinking Funds

PREPARING FOR THIS SECTION *Before getting started, review the following:*

- **Exponents and Logarithms (Appendix A, Section A.3, pp. A–28 to A–33)**

NOW WORK THE 'ARE YOU PREPARED?' PROBLEMS ON PAGE 326

OBJECTIVES
1. Solve problems involving annuities (p. 316)
2. Solve problems involving sinking funds (p. 320)

1 Solve Problems Involving Annuities

In the previous section we saw how to compute the future value of an investment whe a fixed amount of money is deposited in an account that pays interest compounde periodically. Often, however, people and financial institutions do not deposit money an then sit back and watch it grow. Rather, money is invested in small amounts at periodi intervals. Examples of such investments are annual life insurance premiums, monthl deposits in a bank, installment loan payments, and dollar averaging in the stock marke with 401(k) or 403(b) accounts.

An **annuity** is a sequence of equal periodic deposits. The periodic deposits can b annual, semiannual, quarterly, monthly, or any other fixed length of time. When th deposits are made at the same time the interest is credited, the annuity is termed **ordinar** We shall concern ourselves only with ordinary annuities in this book.

The **amount of an annuity** is the sum of all deposits made plus all interest accumulate

EXAMPLE 1 Finding the Amount of an Annuity

Find the amount of an annuity after 5 deposits if each deposit is equal to $100 and i made on an annual basis at an interest rate of 4% per annum compounded annually.

SOLUTION After 5 deposits the first $100 deposit will have accumulated interest compounde annually at 4% for 4 years. Using the Compound Interest Formula, the value A_1 of th first deposit of $100 after 4 years is

$$A_1 = \$100(1 + 0.04)^4 = \$100(1.16986) = \$116.99$$

The second deposit of \$100, made 1 year after the first deposit, will accumulate interest compounded at 4% for 3 years. Its value A_2 after 3 years is

GURE 2

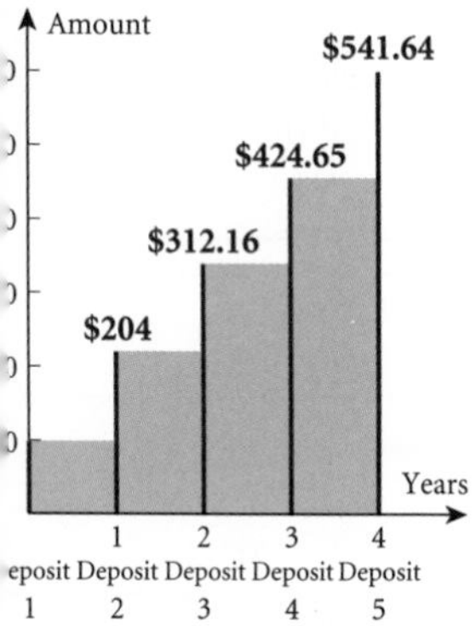

$$A_2 = \$100(1 + 0.04)^3 = \$100(1.12486) = \$112.49$$

Similarly, the third, fourth, and fifth deposits will have the values

$$A_3 = \$100(1 + 0.04)^2 = \$100(1.0816) = \$108.16$$
$$A_4 = \$100(1 + 0.04)^1 = \$100(1.04) = \$104.00$$
$$A_5 = \$100$$

The amount of the annuity after 5 deposits is

$$\begin{aligned} A_1 + A_2 + A_3 + A_4 + A_5 &= \$116.99 + \$112.49 + \$108.16 + \$104.00 + \$100.00 \\ &= \$541.64 \end{aligned}$$

Figure 2 illustrates the growth of the annuity described above. ■

Suppose the interest rate that an annuity earns is i per payment period (expressed as a decimal). For example, if an account pays 12% compounded monthly (12 times a year), then $i = \frac{0.12}{12} = 0.01$. If an account pays 8% compounded quarterly (4 times a year), then $i = \frac{0.08}{4} = 0.02$.

To develop a formula for the amount of an annuity, suppose that $\$P$ is deposited each payment period for n payment periods in an account that earns a rate of i per payment period. When the last deposit is made at the nth payment period, the first deposit of $\$P$ has earned interest compounded for $n - 1$ payment periods, the second deposit of $\$P$ has earned interest compounded for $n - 2$ payment periods, and so on. Table 3 shows the value of each deposit after n deposits have been made.

TABLE 3

Deposit	1	2	3	...	$n - 1$	n
Amount	$P \cdot (1 + i)^{n-1}$	$P \cdot (1 + i)^{n-2}$	$P \cdot (1 + i)^{n-3}$	...	$P \cdot (1 + i)$	P

The amount A of the annuity is the sum of the amounts shown in Table 3; that is,

$$\begin{aligned} A &= P \cdot (1 + i)^{n-1} + P \cdot (1 + i)^{n-2} + \cdots + P \cdot (1 + i) + P \\ &= P[1 + (1 + i) + \cdots + (1 + i)^{n-1}] \end{aligned}$$

The expression in brackets is the sum of a geometric sequence* with n terms and a common ratio of $(1 + i)$. As a result,

$$\begin{aligned} A &= P[1 + (1 + i) + \cdots + (1 + i)^{n-2} + (1 + i)^{n-1}] \\ &= P\frac{1 - (1 + i)^n}{1 - (1 + i)} = P\frac{1 - (1 + i)^n}{-i} = P\frac{(1 + i)^n - 1}{i} \end{aligned}$$

* *The sum of the first n terms of the geometric sequence with common ratio r is*

$$1 + r + r^2 + \cdots + r^{n-1} = \frac{1 - r^n}{1 - r}$$

See Appendix A, Section A.4, for a more detailed discussion.

We have established the following result:

Theorem

Amount of an Annuity

Suppose P is the deposit made at the end of each payment period for an annuity paying an interest rate of i per payment period. The amount A of the annuity after n deposits is

$$A = P \cdot \left[\frac{(1+i)^n - 1}{i}\right] \qquad (1)$$

WARNING Be careful using Formula (1). Remember that when the nth deposit is made, the first deposit has earned interest for $n - 1$ compounding periods. ■

EXAMPLE 2 Finding the Amount of an Annuity

Find the amount of an annuity after 5 deposits if a deposit of \$100 is made each year, 4% compounded annually. How much interest is earned?

SOLUTION The deposit is $P = \$100$. The number of deposits is $n = 5$ and the interest per payment period is $i = 0.04$. Using Formula (1), the amount A after 5 deposits is

$$A = P\left[\frac{(1+i)^n - 1}{i}\right] = 100\left[\frac{(1+0.04)^5 - 1}{0.04}\right] = \$100(5.416323) = \$541.63$$

The interest earned is the amount after 5 deposits less the 5 annual payments of \$100 each:

$$\text{Interest earned} = A - 500 = 541.63 - 500 = \$41.63$$

NOW WORK PROBLEM 5.

EXAMPLE 3 Finding the Amount of an Annuity

Mary decides to put aside \$100 every month in a credit union that pays 5% compounded monthly. After making 8 deposits, how much money does Mary have?

SOLUTION This is an annuity with $P = \$100$, $n = 8$ deposits, and interest $i = \frac{0.05}{12}$ per payment period. Using Formula (1), the amount A after 8 deposits is

$$A = P\left[\frac{(1+i)^n - 1}{i}\right] = 100\left[\frac{\left(1 + \frac{0.05}{12}\right)^8 - 1}{\frac{0.05}{12}}\right] = \$100(8.117644) = \$811.76$$

Mary has \$811.76 after making 8 deposits.

EXAMPLE 4   **Saving for College**

To save for her daughter's college education, Ms. Miranda decides to put $50 aside every month in a bank guaranteed-interest account paying 4% interest compounded monthly. She begins this savings program when her daughter is 3 years old. How much will she have saved by the time she makes the 180th deposit? How old is her daughter at this time?

SOLUTION   This is an annuity with $P = \$50$, $n = 180$ deposits, and $i = \dfrac{0.04}{12}$. The amount A saved is

$$A = P\left[\frac{(1 + i)^n - 1}{i}\right] = 50\left[\frac{\left(1 + \dfrac{0.04}{12}\right)^{180} - 1}{\dfrac{0.04}{12}}\right] = 50(246.090488) = \$12,304.52$$

Since there are 12 deposits per year, when the 180th deposit is made $\dfrac{180}{12} = 15$ years have passed and Ms. Miranda's daughter is 18 years old.   ■

 NOW WORK PROBLEM 25.

EXAMPLE 5   **Funding an IRA**

To save for retirement, Joe, at age 35, decides to place $2000 into an Individual Retirement Account (IRA) each year for the next 30 years. What will the value of the IRA be when Joe makes his 30th deposit? Assume that the rate of return of the IRA is 4% per annum compounded annually.

SOLUTION   This is an ordinary annuity with $n = 30$ annual deposits of $P = \$2000$. The rate of interest per payment period is $i = \dfrac{0.04}{1} = 0.04$. The amount A of the annuity after 30 deposits is

$$A = P\left[\frac{(1 + i)^n - 1}{i}\right] = 2000\left[\frac{(1 + 0.04)^{30} - 1}{0.04}\right] = 2000(56.084938) = \$112,169.88$$ ■

EXAMPLE 6   **Funding an IRA**

If Joe had begun his IRA at age 25, instead of 35, and made 40 deposits of $2000 each, what would his IRA be worth at age 65? Assume a rate of return of 4% per annum compounded annually.

SOLUTION   Now there are $n = 40$ deposits of $2000 per year. The amount A of this annuity is

$$A = P\left[\frac{(1 + i)^n - 1}{i}\right] = 2000\left[\frac{(1 + 0.04)^{40} - 1}{0.04}\right] = \$2000(95.025516) = \$190,051.03$$

Joe would have had $190,051.03 in his IRA when he is 65 if he had begun the IRA at age 25.   ■

 NOW WORK PROBLEM 25.

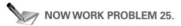

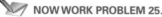

EXAMPLE 7 Finding the Time It Takes to Reach a Certain Savings Goal

How long does it take to save \$500,000 if you place \$500 per month in an accou
paying 6% compounded monthly?

SOLUTION This is an annuity in which the amount A is \$500,000, each deposit is $P = \$500$, and th interest is $i = \frac{0.06}{12}$ per payment period. We seek the number n of deposits needed reach \$500,000.

$$A = P\left[\frac{(1+i)^n - 1}{i}\right] \qquad \text{Formula (1)}$$

$$500{,}000 = 500\left[\frac{\left(1+\frac{0.06}{12}\right)^n - 1}{\frac{0.06}{12}}\right] \qquad A = 500{,}000;\ P = 500;\ i = \frac{0.06}{12}$$

$$5 = \left(1+\frac{0.06}{12}\right)^n - 1 \qquad \text{Simplify.}$$

$$6 = (1.005)^n \qquad \text{Simplify.}$$

$$n = \log_{1.005} 6 = \frac{\log 6}{\log 1.005} = 359.25 \text{ months}$$

Apply the definition of a logarithm. — Change-of-Base Formula — Payment period in months

It takes $359\frac{1}{4}$ months (almost 30 years) to save the \$500,000.

NOW WORK PROBLEM 39.

2 Solve Problems Involving Sinking Funds

A person with a debt may decide to accumulate sufficient funds to pay off the debt b agreeing to set aside enough money each month (or quarter, or year) so that when th debt becomes payable, the money set aside each month plus the interest earned wi equal the debt. The fund created by such a plan is called a **sinking fund.**

In working with sinking funds, we generally seek the deposit or payment require to reach a certain goal. In other words, we seek the payment P required to obtain th amount A in Formula (1).

EXAMPLE 8 Funding a Bond Obligation

The Board of Education received permission to issue \$4,000,000 in bonds to build a ne high school. The board is required to make payments every 6 months into a sinkin fund paying 4% compounded semiannually. At the end of 12 years the bond obligatio will be retired. What should each payment be?

SOLUTION This is an example of a sinking fund. The payment P required twice a year to accumulate \$4,000,000 in 12 years (24 payments at a rate of interest of $i = \frac{0.04}{2} = 0.02$ per payment period) obeys Formula (1).

$$A = P\left[\frac{(1+i)^n - 1}{i}\right] \quad \text{Formula (1)}$$

$$4{,}000{,}000 = P\left[\frac{(1+0.02)^{24} - 1}{0.02}\right] \quad A = 4{,}000{,}000;\ n = 24;\ i = 0.02$$

$$4{,}000{,}000 = P(30.421862) \quad \text{Simplify.}$$

$$P = \$131{,}484.39 \quad \text{Solve for } P.$$

The board will need to make a payment of \$131,484.39 every 6 months to redeem the bonds in 12 years. ■

NOW WORK PROBLEM 15.

EXAMPLE 9 Depletion Investment

A gold mine is expected to yield an annual net income of \$200,000 for the next 10 years, after which it will be worthless. An investor wants an annual return on his investment of 18%. If he can establish a sinking fund earning 5% annually, how much should he be willing to pay for the mine? Round the answer to the nearest dollar.

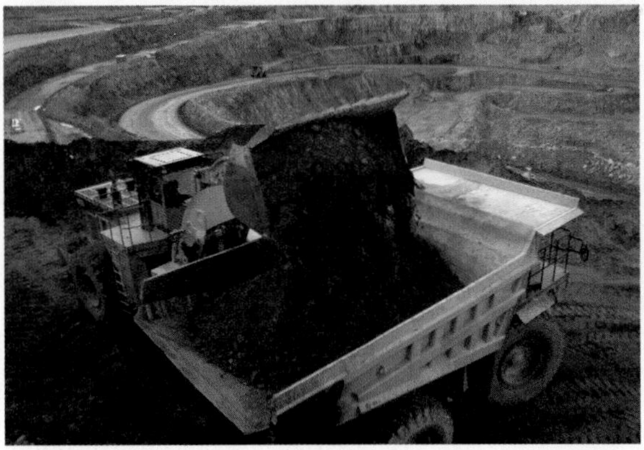

SOLUTION Let x denote the price to be paid for the mine. Then $0.18x$ represents an 18% annual Return On Investment (ROI).

The annual Sinking Fund Contribution (SFC) needed to recover the purchase price x in 10 years obeys Formula (1), where $A = x$, $n = 10$, $i = 0.05$, and $P = \text{SFC}$. Then

$$A = P\left[\frac{(1+i)^n - 1}{i}\right] \quad \text{Formula (1)}$$

$$x = \text{SFC}\left[\frac{(1+0.05)^{10} - 1}{0.05}\right] \quad A = x,\ n = 10,\ i = 0.05,\ P = \text{SFC}$$

$$x = \text{SFC}(12.57789254)$$

$$\text{SFC} = 0.079504575x \quad \text{Solve for SFC.}$$

The required annual Return On Investment (ROI) plus the annual Sinking Fun Contribution equals the annual net income of \$200,000.

$$\begin{pmatrix} \text{ROI} \\ \text{Annual return} \\ \text{on investment} \end{pmatrix} + \begin{pmatrix} \text{SFC} \\ \text{Annual sinking} \\ \text{fund contribution} \end{pmatrix} = \text{Annual income}$$

$$0.18x + 0.079504575x = \$200{,}000$$

$$0.259504575x = \$200{,}000$$

$$x = \$770{,}699$$

A purchase price of \$770,699 will achieve the investor's goals.

NOW WORK PROBLEM 33.

EXAMPLE 10 Funding Capital Improvements

A town needs \$1,000,000 for capital improvements. The town administration decide to finance the improvements with a 30-year bond that will pay 5% per annum interes twice a year. A sinking fund is to be set up 5 years in advance of the due date for th bonds to be paid off. The administration projects the sinking fund to have monthl payments and to earn 4% interest compounded monthly.

(a) What are the semiannual payments on the bond?

(b) What is the monthly payment required for the sinking fund?

(c) Construct a table that shows how the sinking fund grows over time.

SOLUTION **(a)** The amount borrowed is \$1,000,000 at 5% interest. The annual interest i (0.05) (1,000,000) = \$50,000, so the semiannual payments are \$25,000.

(b) The sinking fund payment is the value of P in Formula (1):

$$A = P\left[\frac{(1+i)^n - 1}{i}\right] \quad \text{Formula (1)}$$

Here $A = 1{,}000{,}000$, the amount to be accumulated, $n = 60$ (5 years of monthl payments), and $i = \frac{0.04}{12}$. The sinking fund payment P obeys

$$1{,}000{,}000 = P\left[\frac{\left(1+\frac{0.04}{12}\right)^{60} - 1}{\frac{0.04}{12}}\right]$$

$$1{,}000{,}000 = P(66.298978)$$

$$P = \$15{,}083.19$$

The monthly sinking fund payment is \$15,083.19.

(c) Table 4 shows the growth of the sinking fund over time. For example, the total in the account after payment number 12 is obtained by using Formula (1). Since the monthly payment of \$15,083.19 has been made for 12 months at 4% compounded monthly, the total amount in the account at this point in time is

$$\text{Total} = \$15{,}083.19\left[\frac{\left(1+\dfrac{0.04}{12}\right)^{12}-1}{\dfrac{0.04}{12}}\right] = \$15{,}083.19(12.222463) = \$184{,}353.73$$

TABLE 4

Payment Number	Sinking Fund Deposit, \$	Cumulative Deposits	Accumulated Interest, \$	Total, \$
1	15,083.19	15,083.19	0	15,083.19
12	15,083.19	180,998.28	3355.45	184,353.73
24	15,083.19	361,996.56	14,221.76	376,218.32
36	15,083.19	542,994.84	32,904.92	575,899.76
48	15,083.19	723,993.12	59,723.41	783,716.55
60	15,083.10	904,991.31	95,008.69	1,000,000.00

NOTE The deposit for payment number 60, the final payment, is \$15,083.10 because a deposit of \$15,083.19 results in a total of \$1,000,000.09. ■

NOW WORK PROBLEM 31.

USING TECHNOLOGY

EXAMPLE 11 Using Excel

Use Excel to solve Example 10, parts (b) and (c).

SOLUTION **(a)** Use the Payment Value function in Excel.

The syntax of the Payment Value function is

PMT(rate, nper, pv, fv, type)

rate is the interest rate per period.

nper is the total number of payments.

pv is the present value.

fv is the balance after the last payment is made.

type is the number 0 or 1 and indicates when payments are due. Use 0 for an ordinary annuity.

STEP 1 Set up the Excel spreadsheet as shown below:

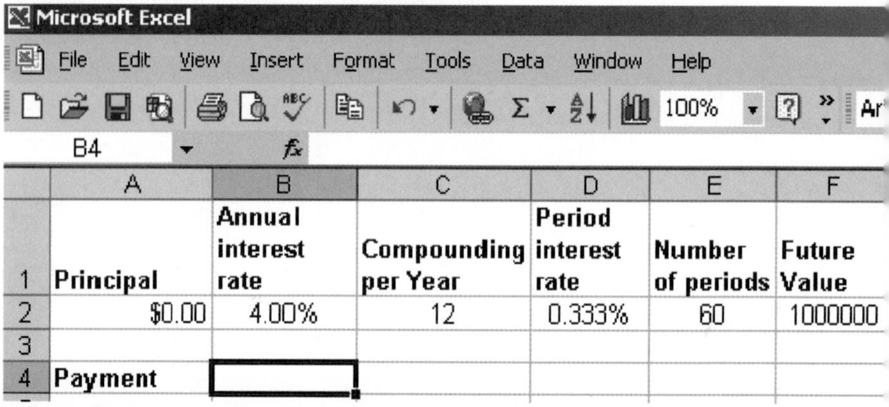

B4

	A	B	C	D	E	F
1	Principal	Annual interest rate	Compounding per Year	Period interest rate	Number of periods	Future Value
2	$0.00	4.00%	12	0.333%	60	1000000
3						
4	Payment					

STEP 2 Insert the Payment function in B4 as shown below in the *fx* bar.

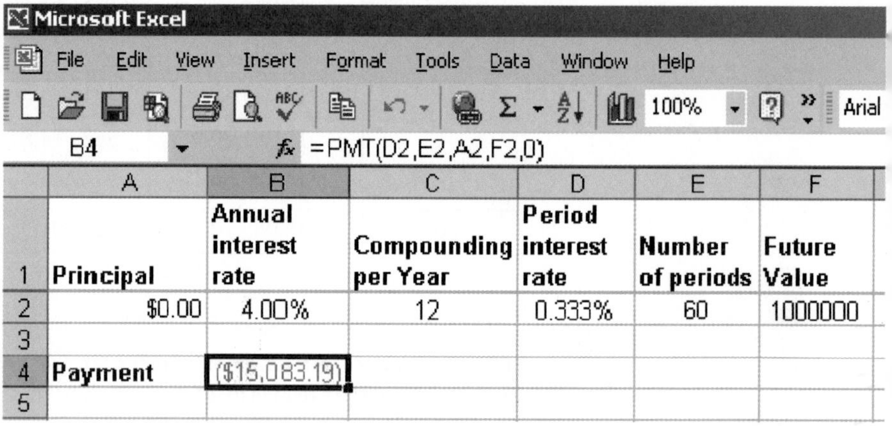

B4 =PMT(D2,E2,A2,F2,0)

	A	B	C	D	E	F
1	Principal	Annual interest rate	Compounding per Year	Period interest rate	Number of periods	Future Value
2	$0.00	4.00%	12	0.333%	60	1000000
3						
4	Payment	($15,083.19)				
5						

The administration has to deposit $15,083.19 each month into the sinking fund.

(b) Construct a table that shows how the sinking fund grows over time.

STEP 1 Set up the column headings in row 7.

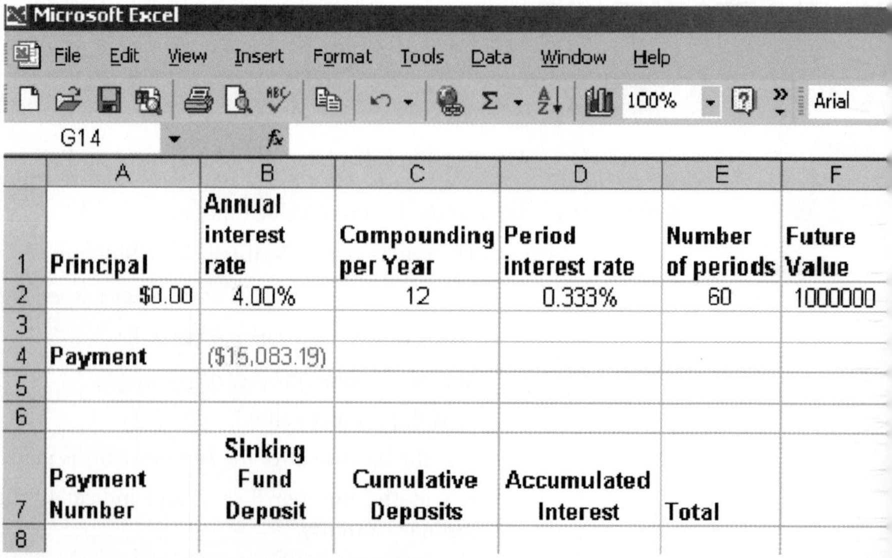

G14

	A	B	C	D	E	F
1	Principal	Annual interest rate	Compounding per Year	Period interest rate	Number of periods	Future Value
2	$0.00	4.00%	12	0.333%	60	1000000
3						
4	Payment	($15,083.19)				
5						
6						
7	Payment Number	Sinking Fund Deposit	Cumulative Deposits	Accumulated Interest	Total	
8						

STEP 2 Set up row 8.

- Payment number will be 1.
- Sinking fund deposit is \$15,083.19. This is stored in cell B4. \$15,083.19 is the deposit for each month; it must be positive and not change when the rest of the table is completed. Enter the formula = −1*B4 in B8.
- Cumulative deposits is number of payments times \$15,083.19. Enter the formula = A8*B8 in C8.
- The total is the future value of the sinking fund. The inputs are fixed except for the payment number, A8. Enter the formula = FV(D2,A8,B4,A2,0).
- Accumulated interest is found by subtracting the cumulative deposits from the total. Enter the formula = E8 − C8 into D8.

The formulas are given in the table below.

	Payment Number	Sinking Fund Deposit	Cumulative Deposits	Accumulated Interest	Total
7	Payment Number	Sinking Fund Deposit	Cumulative Deposits	Accumulated Interest	Total
8	1	=-1*B4	=A8*B8	=E8-C8	=FV(D2,A8,B4,A2,0)
9					

STEP 3 To complete the table, capture row 8 and drag down two rows. Change the payment number in A9 to 6 and A10 to 12. Highlight rows 9 and 10 and click and drag through row 18.

The completed table is given below.

1	Principal	Annual interest rate	Compounding per year	Period interest rate	Number of periods	Future value
2	\$0.00	4.00%	12	0.333%	60	1000000
3						
4	Payment		(\$15,083.19)			
5						
6						
7	Payment Number	Sinking Fund Deposit	Cumulative Deposits	Accumulated Interest	Total	
8	1	\$15,083.19	\$15,083.19	(\$0.00)	\$15,083.19	
9	12	\$15,083.19	\$180,998.28	\$3355.45	\$184,363.73	
10	24	\$15,083.19	\$361,996.56	\$14,221.76	\$376,218.32	
11	36	\$15,083.19	\$542,994.84	\$32,904.92	\$575,899.76	
12	48	\$15,083.19	\$723,993.12	\$59,723.41	\$783,716.55	
13	60	\$15,083.19	\$904,991.31	\$95,008.69	\$1,000,000.00	
14						
15						
16						
17						
18						
19						

■

NOW WORK PROBLEM 31 USING EXCEL.

EXERCISE 6.3 Answers Begin on Page AN–32.

'Are You Prepared?' Problems Answers are given at the end of these exercises. If you get a wrong answer, read the pages listed in red.

1. Evaluate: $(1 + 0.04)^4$. Round your answer to 5 decimal places. (pp. A–28 to A–33)

2. Evaluate: $\frac{(1 + 0.04)^{30} - 1}{0.04}$. Round your answer to 6 decim places. (pp. A–28 to A–33)

Concepts and Vocabulary

3. An ________ is a sequence of equal periodic deposits.

4. The sum of all the equal periodic deposits and the intere earned is called the ________ of the ________.

Skill Building

In Problems 5–14, find the amount of each annuity.

5. After 10 annual deposits of \$100 at 10% compounded annually

6. After 12 monthly deposits of \$200 at 5% compounde monthly

7. After 12 monthly deposits of \$400 at 2% compounded monthly

8. After 5 annual deposits of \$1000 at 3% compounded annual

9. After 36 monthly deposits of \$200 at 3% compounded monthly

10. After 40 semiannual deposits of \$2000 at 2% compounde semiannually

11. After 60 monthly deposits of \$100 at 4% compounded monthly

12. After 8 quarterly deposits of \$1000 at 4% compounde quarterly

13. After 10 annual deposits of \$9000 at 5% compounded annually

14. After 20 annual deposits of \$5000 at 4% compounde annually

In Problems 15–24, find the payment required for each sinking fund.

15. The amount required is \$10,000 after 5 years at 3% compounded monthly. What is the monthly payment?

16. The amount required is \$5000 after 180 days at 2% compounded daily. What is the daily payment?

17. The amount required is \$20,000 after $2\frac{1}{2}$ years at 2% compounded quarterly. What is the quarterly payment?

18. The amount required is \$50,000 after 10 years at 3% compounded semiannually. What is the semiannual paymen

19. The amount required is \$25,000 after 6 months at $5\frac{1}{2}\%$ compounded monthly. What is the monthly payment?

20. The amount required is \$100,000 after 25 years at $4\frac{1}{4}\%$ compounded annually. What is the annual payment?

21. The amount required is \$5000 after 2 years at 4% compounded monthly. What is the monthly payment?

22. The amount required is \$5000 after 2 years at 4% compounde semiannually. What is the semiannual payment?

23. The amount required is \$9000 after 4 years at 5% compounded annually. What is the annual payment?

24. The amount required is \$9000 after 2 years at 5% compounde quarterly. What is the quarterly payment?

Applications

25. **Market Value of a Mutual Fund** Al invests \$2500 a year in a mutual fund for 15 years. If the market value of the fund increases 5% per year, what will be the value of the fund after 15 deposits?

26. **Value of an Annuity** Todd and Tami pay \$300 every 3 months for 6 years into an ordinary annuity paying 4% compounded quarterly. What is the value of the annuity after 24 deposits?

27. **Saving for a Car** Sheila wants to invest an amount every 3 months so that she will have \$12,000 in 3 years to buy a new car. The account pays 2% compounded quarterly. How much should she deposit each quarter to have \$12,000 after 12 deposits?

28. **Saving for a House** In 4 years Colleen and Bill would like t have \$30,000 for a down payment on a house. How muc should they deposit each month into an account paying 4% compounded monthly to have \$30,000 after 48 deposits?

29. **Funding a Pension** Dan wishes to have \$350,000 in a pensio fund 20 years from now. How much should he deposit eac month into an account paying 5% compounded monthly t have \$350,000 after 240 deposits?

30. **Funding a Keogh Plan** Pat has a Keogh retirement plan (thi type of plan is tax-deferred until money is withdrawn). I deposits of \$7500 are made each year into an account payin 6% compounded annually, how much will be in the accoun after 25 years?

1. **Sinking Fund Payment** A company establishes a sinking fund to provide for the payment of a $100,000 debt maturing in 4 years. Contributions to the fund are to be made each year. Find the amount of each annual deposit if interest is 3% per annum. Prepare a table showing the annual growth of the sinking fund.

2. **Paying Off Bonds** A state has $5,000,000 worth of bonds that are due in 20 years. A sinking fund is established to pay off the debt. If the state can earn 6% annually on its money, what is the annual sinking fund deposit needed? Prepare a table showing the growth of the sinking fund every 5 years.

3. **Depletion Investment** An investor wants to know the amount she should pay for an oil well expected to yield an annual return of $30,000 for the next 30 years, after which the well will be dry. Find the amount she should pay to yield a 14% annual return if a sinking fund earns 5% annually. Round the answer to the nearest dollar.

4. **Time Needed for a Million Dollars** If you deposit $10,000 every year into an account paying 4% compounded annually, how long will it take to accumulate $1,000,000?

5. **Bond Payments** A city has issued bonds to finance a new library. The bonds have a total face value of $1,000,000 and are payable in 10 years. After 7 years, a sinking fund will be started to retire the bonds. If the interest rate on the fund is expected to be 4% compounded quarterly, what are the quarterly payments?

6. **Value of an IRA**
   (a) Tanya invested $2000 in an IRA each year for 10 years earning 4% compounded annually. At the end of 10 years she ceased the IRA payments, but continued to invest her accumulated amount at 5% compounded annually, for the next 30 years. What was the value of her IRA investment at the end of 10 years? What was the value of her investment at the end of the next 30 years?
   (b) Carol waited 10 years and started her IRA investment in the 11th year and invested $2000 per year for the next 30 years at 6% compounded annually. What was the value of her investment at the end of 30 years?
   (c) Who had more money at the end of the 40 year period?

37. **Managing a Condo** The Crown Colony Condo Association is required by law to set aside funds to replace its roof. The current cost to replace the roof is $100,000 and it will need to be replaced in 20 years. The cost of a roof is expected to increase at the rate of 3% per year. The Condo can invest in Treasuries yielding 4% paid semiannually.
   (a) What will the roof cost in 20 years?
   (b) If the Condo invests in the Treasuries, what semiannual payment is required to have the funds to replace the roof in 20 years?

38. **Managing a Condo** The Crown Colony Condo Association is required by law to set aside funds to replace its common-area carpet. The current cost to replace the carpet is $20,000 and it will need to be replaced in 6 years. The cost of carpet is expected to increase at the rate of 2% per year. The Condo can invest in Treasuries yielding 5% paid semiannually.
   (a) What will the carpet cost in 6 years?
   (b) If the Condo invests in the Treasuries, what semiannual payment is required to have the funds to replace the carpet in 6 years?

39. **Time to Save a Million Dollars** How many years will it take to save $1,000,000 if you place $600 per month in an account that earns 7% compounded monthly?

40. **Time to Save a Million Dollars** How many years will it take to save $1,000,000 if you place $1000 per month in an account that earns 3% compounded monthly?

41. **Saving for a Trip** Angie wants to plan a trip to Hawaii with her husband on their 20th wedding anniversary in two years. She anticipates that the all-inclusive trip will cost $9500 for both of them and wants to start saving. How much should she put into an account each month paying 2.75% compounded monthly to pay for the trip in two years?

   Source: Hawaii-aloha.com

42. **Saving for a Trip** Shane wants to plan a trip to Australia with his wife on her 30th birthday in three years. He anticipates that the all-inclusive trip will cost $7500 for both of them and wants to start saving. How much should he put into an account each month paying 3.25% compounded monthly to pay for the trip in three years?

   Source: www.seeanz.com

43. **Saving for Repairs** In May 2010, Bath Community Schools asked voters to approve the renewal of a building and site capital projects sinking fund. If the sinking fund is to generate $1 million over 5 years in an account that pays 5% compounded quarterly, how much should the school district deposit into the account each quarter?

   Source: Bath Community Schools Board of Education

44. **Planning for Growth** Based on trends in census data, a K–12 school district passed a 5-year tax levy that increases property tax by $0.20 per $1000 valuation. The district has approximately 40,000 homes with an average value of $145,000. The monies collected are placed in a building fund account paying 4.5% compounded annually. The tax revenue is deposited at the same time that interest is credited. What will be the value of the building fund at the end of the levy period?

45. **529 College Savings Plan** Pam and Tim decide to start saving money for their daughter's college education. They open a college savings plan (529) with a $400 initial investment and next month start to make monthly deposits of $100. If the account pays 6.00% compounded monthly, how much will the account be worth after 180 deposits of $100 each? Be sure to include the initial investment in the computation.

46. **529 College Savings Plan** Christine and Adam decide to start saving money for their son's college education. They open a college savings plan (529) with a $1000 initial investment and in 3 months start to make quarterly deposits of $700. If the account pays 4.75% compounded quarterly, how much will the account be worth after 64 deposits of

$700 each? Be sure to include the initial investment in the computation.

47. Lottery without Taxes Dan won $2.6 million in a state lottery and must decide between the lump sum payment of $1,326,000 or 26 annual payments of $100,000. Assuming he can invest all proceeds in a retirement plan that pays 8.5% compounded annually, how much will his winnings be worth after 25 years? Which option should he select?

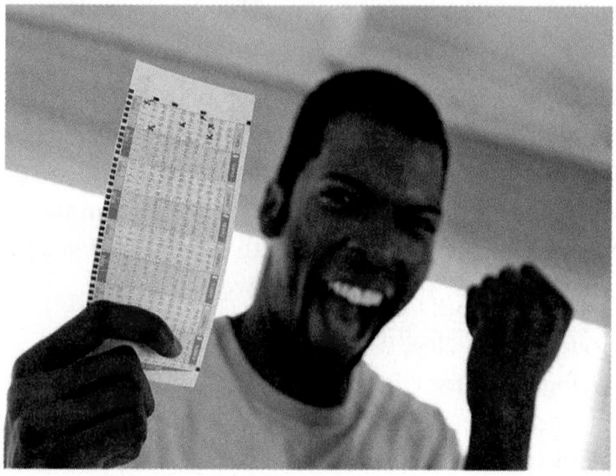

48. Lottery with Taxes Refer to Problem 47. Dan must pay federal taxes on his winnings. According to the 2010 federal tax schedule, he would pay a tax of $94,601 plus 35% of the amount over $349,700 if he takes the lump sum or a tax of $8,772.50 plus 25% of the amount over 63,700 if he takes the annual payments. Assuming the tax rates remain constant, determine how much his winnings will be worth after 25 years and which option Dan should select.

Source: www.illinoislottery.com; U.S. Department of the Treasury

49. Saving for a Car In January 2010, a new Honda Accord EX with manual transmission was listed at $23,830.

(a) Assuming a constant annual inflation rate of 3.23%, which was the annual percent increase in the U.S. Consumer Price Index for 2006, calculate a projection of what a new Honda Accord EX with manual transmission would cost in January 2014.

(b) If the sales tax where you plan to purchase this vehicle in January 2014 is 9.25%, what is the final cost of the Honda ?

(c) Beginning in January 2010, suppose that you make a monthly payment into a sinking fund that earns interest at a 2.75% annual rate, compounded monthly, in order to accumulate funds to purchase the new Honda in 4 years. What monthly payment will produce a balance in this sinking fund in January 2014 that equals the projected final cost of the 2014 Honda Accord EX?

Source: American Honda Motor Co., Inc.; and U.S. Department of Labor, Bureau of Labor Statistics

50. Saving for a Down Payment on a Home The median pri of an existing single-family detached home in Florida w $210,200 in March 2009 and increased to $218,200 in Marc 2010.

(a) What is the annual rate at which homes appreciated?

(b) If the median price of an existing single-family detache home in Florida continues to increase at the annual ra found in part (a), determine the projected median price an existing single-family detached home in Florida March 2014.

(c) Suppose you make monthly payments into a sinkin fund between March 2010 and March 2014 to generate down payment of 10% of this projected median pric Find the monthly payment required for this sinking fun assuming that this sinking fund earns 2.9%, compounde monthly.

Source: Florida Association of Realtors

51. Saving for College The average annual undergraduate colleg tuition and fees nationally for 2009–2010 for public 4-yea institutions totaled $7020. The College Board indicated that th inflation rate for tuition in 2009 was 6.5%.

(a) Assuming that this inflation rate is constant for the nex 17 years, determine the projected annual undergraduat college tuition and fees for public 4-year institutions fo 2023–2024, 2024–2025, 2025–2026, and 2026–2027.

(b) Determine a quarterly sinking fund payment, beginnin with the fourth quarter of 2012, so that at the end of 202 when the 45th payment is made, the sinking fund has value equal to the sum of the projected costs of each of th 4 years. Assume the sinking fund earns interest at a 4.2% annual rate, compounded quarterly.

Source: *Trends in College Pricing 2009*, College Board

52. Saving for College The average annual undergraduat college tuition and fees nationally for 2009–2010 for privat 4-year institutions totaled $26,273. The College Board indicate that the inflation rate for tuition in 2009 was 4.4%.

(a) Assuming that this inflation rate is constant for the nex 17 years, determine the projected annual undergraduat college tuition and fees for private 4-year institutions fo 2023–2024, 2024–2025, 2025–2026, and 2026–2027.

(b) Determine a quarterly sinking fund payment, beginning with the fourth quarter of 2012, so that at the end of 2023 when the 45th payment is made, the sinking fund has value equal to the sum of the projected costs of each of th 4 years. Assume the sinking fund earns interest at a 4.2% annual rate, compounded quarterly.

Source: *Trends in College Pricing 2009*, College Board

'Are You Prepared?' Answers

1. 1.16986 **2.** 56.084938

6.4 Present Value of an Annuity; Amortization

OBJECTIVES
1 Solve problems involving the present value of an annuity (p. 329)
2 Solve problems involving amortization (p. 332)
3 Application: Pricing corporate bonds* (p. 338)

1 Solve Problems Involving the Present Value of an Annuity

In Section 6.2 we defined present value (as it relates to the Compound Interest Formula) as the amount of money needed now to obtain an amount A in the future. A similar idea is used for periodic withdrawals.

Suppose you want to withdraw \$10,000 per year each year for the next 5 years from a retirement account that earns 5% compounded annually. How much money is required initially in this account for this to happen? In fact, the amount is the sum of the *present values* of each of the \$10,000 withdrawals. This leads to the following definition.

The **present value** of an annuity is the sum of the present values of the withdrawals. In other words, the present value of an annuity is the amount of money needed now so that if it is invested at a rate of i per payment period, n equal dollar amounts can be withdrawn without any money left over.

EXAMPLE 1 Finding the Present Value of an Annuity

Compute the amount of money required to pay out \$10,000 per year for 5 years at 5% compounded annually.

SOLUTION For the first \$10,000 withdrawal, the present value V_1 (the dollars needed now to withdraw \$10,000 in one year) is

$$V_1 = \$10{,}000(1 + 0.05)^{-1} = \$10{,}000(0.95238095) = \$9523.81$$

For the second \$10,000 withdrawal, the present value V_2 (the dollars needed now to withdraw \$10,000 in two years) is

$$V_2 = \$10{,}000(1 + 0.05)^{-2} = \$10{,}000(0.90702948) = \$9070.29$$

Similarly,

$$V_3 = \$10{,}000(1 + 0.05)^{-3} = \$10{,}000(0.8638376) = \$8638.38$$

$$V_4 = \$10{,}000(1 + 0.05)^{-4} = \$10{,}000(0.822702) = \$8227.02$$

$$V_5 = \$10{,}000(1 + 0.05)^{-5} = \$10{,}000(0.783526) = \$7835.26$$

The present value V for 5 withdrawals of \$10,000 each is

$$\begin{aligned} V &= V_1 + V_2 + V_3 + V_4 + V_5 \\ &= \$9523.81 + \$9070.29 + \$8638.38 + \$8227.02 + \$7835.26 \\ &= \$43{,}294.76 \end{aligned}$$

*Optional.

A person would need $43,294.76 now, invested at 5% per annum, in order to withdraw $10,000 per year for the next 5 years.

Table 5 summarizes the results obtained in Example 1. Table 6 lists the amount at the beginning of each year.

TABLE 5

Withdrawal	Present Value
1st	$\$10{,}000(1.05)^{-1} = \$9523.81$
2nd	$\$10{,}000(1.05)^{-2} = \$9070.29$
3rd	$\$10{,}000(1.05)^{-3} = \$8638.38$
4th	$\$10{,}000(1.05)^{-4} = \$8227.02$
5th	$\$10{,}000(1.05)^{-5} = \$7835.26$
Total	$43,294.76

TABLE 6

Year	Amount at the Beginning of the Year	Add Interest	Subtract Withdrawal
1	43,294.76	2164.74	10,000.00
2	35,459.50	1772.97	10,000.00
3	27,232.47	1361.62	10,000.00
4	18,594.09	929.70	10,000.00
5	9,523.79	476.21	10,000.00
6	0		

We seek a formula for the present value of an annuity. Suppose an annuity earns an interest rate of i per payment period and suppose we wish to make n withdrawals of $\$P$ at each payment period. The amount V_1 required for the first withdrawal (the present value of $\$P$) is

$$V_1 = P(1 + i)^{-1}$$

The amount V_2 required for the second withdrawal is

$$V_2 = P(1 + i)^{-2}$$

The amount V_n required for the nth withdrawal is

$$V_n = P(1 + i)^{-n}$$

The present value V of the annuity is the sum of the amounts $V_1, V_2, \ldots, V_n$

$$\begin{aligned} V = V_1 + \cdots + V_n &= P(1 + i)^{-1} + \cdots + P(1 + i)^{-n} \\ &= P(1 + i)^{-n}[1 + (1 + i) + \cdots + (1 + i)^{n-1}] \end{aligned}$$

The expression in brackets is the sum of the first n terms of a geometric sequence, whose ratio is $1 + i$. As a result,

$$V = P(1 + i)^{-n}\frac{1 - (1 + i)^n}{1 - (1 + i)} = P\frac{(1 + i)^{-n} - 1}{-i} = P\frac{1 - (1 + i)^{-n}}{i}$$

Theorem

Present Value of an Annuity

Suppose an annuity earns interest at the rate of i per payment period. If n withdrawals of $\$P$ are made at each payment period, the amount V required is

$$V = P \cdot \left[\frac{1 - (1 + i)^{-n}}{i}\right] \qquad (1)$$

Here V is called the **present value of the annuity.**

EXAMPLE 2 Getting By in College

A student requires \$200 each month for the next 10 months to cover miscellaneous expenses at school. A money market fund will pay her interest of 2% per annum compounded monthly. How much money should she ask for from her parents now so that she can withdraw \$200 each month for the next 10 months?

SOLUTION We seek the present value of an annuity. The monthly withdrawal is \$200, the interest rate is $i = \frac{0.02}{12}$ per month, and the number of withdrawals is $n = 10$. The money required for this is given by Formula (1):

$$V = P\left[\frac{1-(1+i)^{-n}}{i}\right] = \$200\left[\frac{1-\left(1+\frac{0.02}{12}\right)^{-10}}{\frac{0.02}{12}}\right] = \$200(9.90894) = \$1981.79$$

She should ask her parents for \$1981.79. ■

NOW WORK PROBLEM 1.

EXAMPLE 3 Determining the Cost of a Car

A man agrees to pay \$300 per month for 48 months to pay off a used car loan with no money down. If interest of 12% per annum is charged monthly, how much did the car originally cost? How much interest was paid?

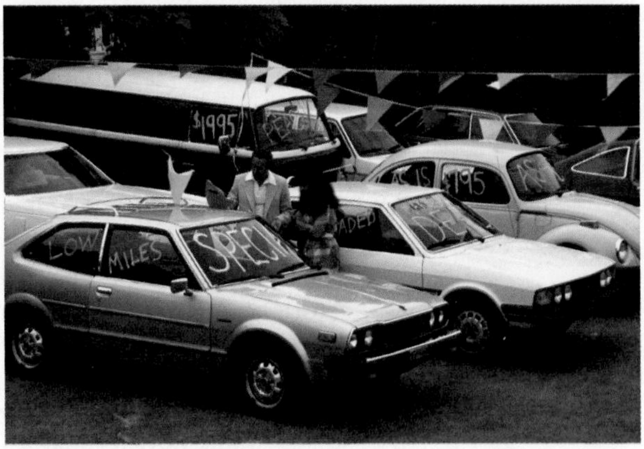

SOLUTION The cost of the car is the same as the present value V of an annuity of \$300 per month at 12% for 48 months. The original cost of the car is

$$V = P\left[\frac{1-(1+i)^{-n}}{i}\right] = 300\left[\frac{1-\left(1+\frac{0.12}{12}\right)^{-48}}{\frac{0.12}{12}}\right] = \$300(37.9739595) = \$11{,}392.19$$

The total payment is $(\$300)(48) = \$14{,}400$. The interest paid is

$$\$14{,}400 - \$11{,}392.19 = \$3007.81$$ ■

NOW WORK PROBLEM 15.

EXAMPLE 4 Lease or Purchase

A company may obtain a copying machine either by leasing it for 4 years (the useful life at an annual cost of $1000 or by purchasing the machine for $3000.

(a) Which alternative is preferable if the company can invest money at 5% per annum

(b) What if it can invest at 7% per annum?

SOLUTION **(a)** The company can invest money and receive 5% per annum. The cost of leasing th copying machine is $1000 each year for 4 years. The money needed now to mak these payments is the present value V of an annuity with $P = \$1000$, interes $i = 0.05$, and $n = 4$. Now

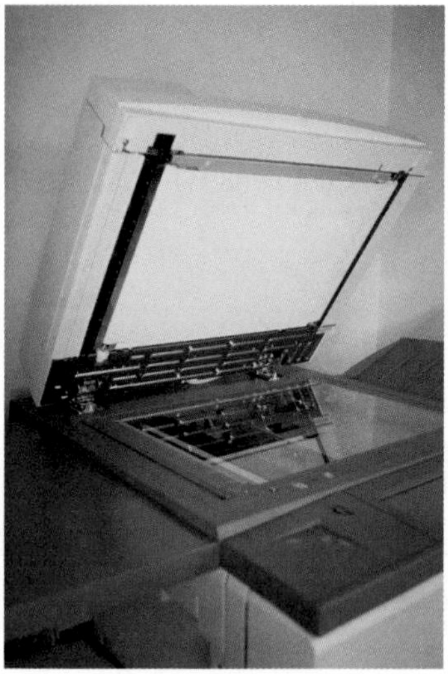

$$V = P\left[\frac{1-(1+i)^{-n}}{i}\right] = 1000\left[\frac{1-(1+0.05)^{-4}}{0.05}\right] = 1000(3.54595) = \$3545.9$$

The company would need $3545.95 now to lease the copier and can purchase it nov for $3000. It is better to purchase.

(b) The company can invest money and receive 7% per annum. The cost of leasing th copying machine is $1000 each year for 4 years. The money needed now to mak these payments is the present value V of an annuity with $P = \$1000$, interes $i = 0.07$, and $n = 4$. Now

$$V = P\left[\frac{1-(1+i)^{-n}}{i}\right] = 1000\left[\frac{1-(1+0.07)^{-4}}{0.07}\right] = 1000(3.38721) = \$3387.2$$

The company would need $3387.21 now to lease the copier. It is better to purchas for $3000 than to lease.

NOW WORK PROBLEM 45.

2 Solve Problems Involving Amortization

Look again at Example 3. What it also says is that if the man pays $300 per month fo 48 months with an interest of 12% compounded monthly, then the car is his. In othe words, he *amortized* the debt in 48 equal monthly payments. (The Latin word *mor* means "death." Paying off a loan is regarded as "killing" it.) A loan with a fixed rate o interest is said to be **amortized** if both principal and interest are paid by a sequenc of equal payments made over equal periods of time.

When a loan of V dollars is amortized at a rate of interest i per payment period ove n payment periods, the customary question is, "What is the payment P?" In other words in amortization problems, we want to find the payment P that, after n payment period at the rate of interest i per payment period, gives us a present value equal to the amoun of the loan. We need to find P in the formula

$$V = P\left[\frac{1-(1+i)^{-n}}{i}\right]$$

Solving for P, we find

$$P = V\left[\frac{1-(1+i)^{-n}}{i}\right]^{-1} = V\left[\frac{i}{1-(1+i)^{-n}}\right]$$

Theorem

Amortization

The payment P required to pay off a loan of V dollars borrowed for n payment periods at a rate of interest i per payment period is

$$P = V\left[\frac{i}{1-(1+i)^{-n}}\right] \tag{2}$$

EXAMPLE 5 Finding the Payment for an Amortized Loan

What monthly payment is necessary to pay off a loan of \$800 at 10% per annum

(a) In 2 years? **(b)** In 3 years? **(c)** What total amount is paid out for each loan?

SOLUTION **(a)** For the 2-year loan, $V = \$800$, $n = 24$, and $i = \frac{0.10}{12}$. The monthly payment P is

$$P = V\left[\frac{i}{1-(1+i)^{-n}}\right] = 800\left[\frac{\frac{0.10}{12}}{1-\left(1+\frac{0.10}{12}\right)^{-24}}\right] = \$800(0.04614493) = \$36.92$$

(b) For the 3-year loan, $V = \$800$, $n = 36$, and $i = \frac{0.10}{12}$. The monthly payment P is

$$P = V\left[\frac{i}{1-(1+i)^{-n}}\right] = 800\left[\frac{\frac{0.10}{12}}{1-\left(1+\frac{0.10}{12}\right)^{-36}}\right] = \$800(0.03226719) = \$25.81$$

(c) For the 2-year loan, the total amount paid out is $(36.92)(24) = \$886.08$; for the 3-year loan, the total amount paid out is $(\$25.81)(36) = \$929.16$. ■

NOW WORK PROBLEM 9.

EXAMPLE 6 Home Mortgage Payments

Mr. and Mrs. Corey have just purchased a \$300,000 house and have made a down payment of \$60,000. They can amortize the balance ($\$300,000 - \$60,000 = \$240,000$) at 6% for 30 years.

(a) What are the monthly payments?

(b) What is their total interest payment?

(c) After 20 years, what equity do they have in their house (that is, what is the sum of the down payment and the amount paid on the loan)?

SOLUTION **(a)** The monthly payment P needed to pay off the loan of \$240,000 at 6% for 30 years (360 months) is

$$P = V\left[\frac{i}{1-(1+i)^{-n}}\right] = \$240{,}000\left[\frac{\frac{0.06}{12}}{1-\left(1+\frac{0.06}{12}\right)^{-360}}\right] = \$240{,}000(0.0059955) = \$1438.92$$

(b) The total paid out for the loan is

$$(\$1438.92)(360) = \$518{,}011.20$$

The interest on this loan amounts to

$$\$518{,}011.20 - \$240{,}000 = \$278{,}011.20$$

(c) After 20 years (240 months) there remains 10 years (or 120 months) of payments. The present value of the loan is the present value of a monthly payment of \$1438.92 for 120 months at 6%, namely,

$$V = P\left[\frac{1-(1+i)^{-n}}{i}\right] = \$1438.92\left[\frac{1-\left(1+\frac{0.06}{12}\right)^{-120}}{\frac{0.06}{12}}\right]$$

$$= (\$1438.92)(90.073453) = \$129{,}608.49$$

The amount paid on the loan is

(Original loan amount) − (Present value) = \$240,000 − \$129,608.49 = \$110,391.51

The equity after 20 years is

(Down payment) + (Amount paid on loan) = \$60,000 + \$110,391.51 = \$170,391.51

NOTE This equity does not include any appreciation in the value of the house over the 20-year period.

Table 7 gives a partial schedule of payments for the loan in Example 5. It is interesting to observe how slowly the amount paid on the loan increases early in the payment schedule, with very little of the payment used to reduce principal, and how quickly the amount paid on the loan increases during the last 5 years.

TABLE 7

Payment Number	Monthly Payment	Principal	Interest	Amount Paid on Loan
1	\$1,438.92	\$ 238.92	\$1,200.00	\$ 238.92
60	\$1,438.92	\$ 320.67	\$1,118.26	\$ 16,669.54
120	\$1,438.92	\$ 432.53	\$1,006.39	\$ 39,154.26
180	\$1,438.92	\$ 583.42	\$ 855.50	\$ 69,482.77
240	\$1,438.92	\$ 786.94	\$ 651.98	\$110,391.39
300	\$1,438.92	\$1,061.47	\$ 377.45	\$165,570.99
360	\$1,438.92	\$1,431.76	\$ 7.16	\$240,000.00

NOW WORK PROBLEM 17.

USING TECHNOLOGY

EXAMPLE 7 **Using Excel**

Use Excel to solve Example 6, parts (a) and (c).

SOLUTION **(a)** Use the Excel function PMT to find the monthly payments. The function has the following syntax:

$$\text{PMT}(rate, nper, pv, fv, type)$$

rate is the interest rate per period.
nper is the total number of payment periods
pv is the initial deposit or present value
fv is the future value
type is the number 0 or 1: use 0 for an ordinary annuity

The values of the parameters of the PMT function are:

rate is $\frac{0.06}{12}$.
nper is $30*12 = 360$
pv is \$240,000
fv is 0
type is 0

The Excel spreadsheet is given below.

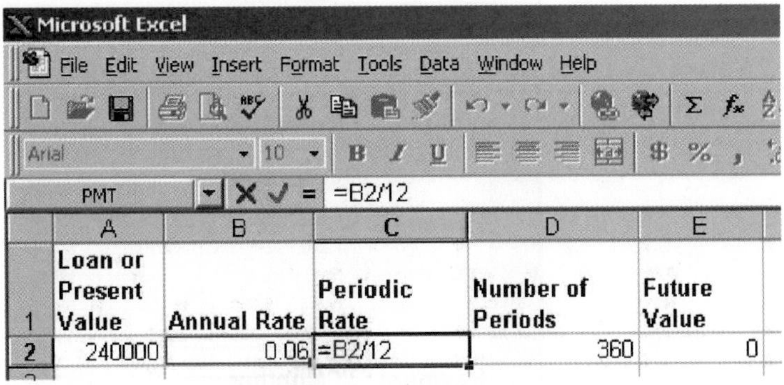

In cell B4 type $= \text{PMT}(C2, D2, A2, E2, 0)$

The final Excel spreadsheet for part (a) is given below.

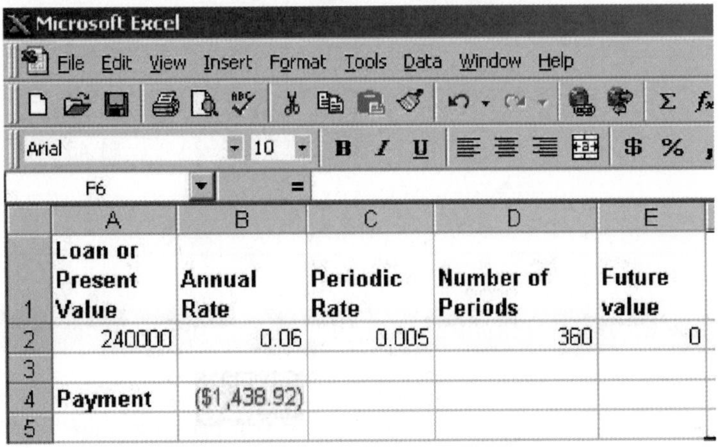

Mr. and Mrs. Corey's monthly payments are \$1438.92.

(c) To create an amortization table, use the Excel function PPMT to compute th monthly principal.

- Set up the table headings in row 7.
- In A8 enter 1 for payment number 1.
- In B8 enter the formula = −1*B4. (Recall the $ keeps the cell constant.)
- In C8 enter the formula = −1*PPMT(C2,A8,D2,A2,E2).
- In D8 enter the formula = B8 − C8.
- In E8 enter the formula = 240,000 + FV(C2, A8,B4,A2, 0).
- Highlight row 8, click and drag 2 rows (filling rows 9 and 10).
- Change A9 to 60 and A10 to 120.
- Highlight rows 9 and 10; click and drag the two rows to row 14 to get the re of the table.

The completed table is given below.

Microsoft Excel

	A	B	C	D	E
1	Loan or Present Value	Annual Rate	Periodic Rate	Number of Periods	Future Value
2	240000	0.06	0.005	360	0
3					
4	Payment	($1,438.92)			
5					
6					
7	Payment Number	Monthly Payment	Principal	Interest	Amount Paid on Loan
8	1	$1,438.92	$238.92	$1,200.00	$238.92
9	60	$1,438.92	$320.67	$1,118.26	$16,669.54
10	120	$1,438.92	$432.53	$1,006.39	$39,154.26
11	180	$1,438.92	$583.42	$855.50	$69,482.77
12	240	$1,438.92	$786.94	$651.98	$110,391.39
13	300	$1,438.92	$1,061.47	$377.45	$165,570.99
14	360	$1,438.92	$1,431.76	$7.16	$240,000.00

NOW WORK PROBLEM 17 USING EXCEL.

EXAMPLE 8 Determining the Amount of an Inheritance

When Mr. Nicholson died, he left an inheritance of $15,000 for his family to be paid t them over a 10-year period in equal amounts at the end of each year. If the $15,000 i invested at 4% per annum, what is the annual payout to the family?

SOLUTION This example asks what annual payment is needed at 4% for 10 years to disperse \$15,000. That is, we can think of the \$15,000 as a loan amortized at 4% for 10 years. The payment needed to pay off the loan is the yearly amount Mr. Nicholson's family will receive. The yearly payout P is

$$P = V\left[\frac{i}{1-(1+i)^{-n}}\right] = \$15{,}000\left[\frac{0.04}{1-(1+0.04)^{-10}}\right]$$

$$= \$15{,}000(0.1232909) = \$1849.36$$

■

EXAMPLE 9 Determining Retirement Income

Joan is 20 years away from retiring and starts saving \$100 a month in an account paying 6% compounded monthly. When she retires, she wishes to withdraw a fixed amount each month for 25 years. What will this fixed amount be?

SOLUTION After 20 years the amount A accumulated in her account is the amount of an annuity with $n = 240$ monthly payments of $P = \$100$ at an interest rate of $i = \frac{0.06}{12}$.

$$A = P\left[\frac{(1+i)^n - 1}{i}\right] = 100\left[\frac{\left(1+\frac{0.06}{12}\right)^{240} - 1}{\frac{0.06}{12}}\right]$$

$$= 100 \cdot (462.0408952) = \$46{,}204.09$$

The amount W she can withdraw each month for 25 years (300 months) at 6% compounded monthly is

$$W = 46{,}204.09\left[\frac{\frac{0.06}{12}}{1-\left(1+\frac{0.06}{12}\right)^{-300}}\right] = \$297.69$$

■

NOW WORK PROBLEM 23.

EXAMPLE 10 Capital Expenditure

A corporation is faced with a choice between two machines, both of which are designed to improve operations by saving on labor costs. Machine A costs \$8000 and will generate an annual labor savings of \$2000. Machine B costs \$6000 and will save \$1800 in labor annually. Machine A has a useful life of 7 years while machine B has a useful life of only 5 years. Assuming that the time value of money (the investment opportunity rate) of the corporation is 10% per annum, which machine is preferable? (Assume annual compounding and that the savings is realized at the end of each year.)

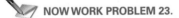

SOLUTION The company can invest money and receive 10% per annum. Machine A costs $80 and has a useful life of 7 years. The cost per year of Machine A is the annual payment required to amortize a loan of $8000 for 7 years at 10% per annum. We use Formula (with $V = 8000$, $i = 0.10$, and $n = 7$.

$$P = V\left[\frac{i}{1-(1+i)^{-n}}\right] = 8000\left[\frac{0.1}{1-(1+0.1)^{-7}}\right] = 8000(0.205405) = \$1643.24$$

The annual cost of Machine A to the company is $1643.24.

Similarly, Machine B, with a cost of $6000 and a useful life of 5 years, will cost t company each year an amount equal to the annual payment P required to amortize loan of $6000 for 5 years at 10% per annum. We use Formula (2) with $V = 600$ $i = 0.1$, and $n = 5$.

$$P = V\left[\frac{i}{1-(1+i)^{-n}}\right] = 6000\left[\frac{0.1}{1-(1+0.1)^{-5}}\right] = 6000(0.263797) = \$1582.78$$

The annual cost of Machine B is $1582.78.

Now we take into account the savings to the company in labor generated by eac machine. See Table 8.

TABLE 8

	A	B
Annual labor savings	$2000.00	$1800.00
Annual cost	$1643.24	$1582.78
Net savings	$ 356.76	$ 217.12

Machine A will generate more annual savings to the company than Machine Machine A is preferable to Machine B.

NOW WORK PROBLEM 47.

3 Application: Pricing Corporate Bonds

We begin with some definitions of terms related to corporate bonds.

Definition

Face Amount (Face Value or Par Value)

The **face amount** or **denomination** of a bond (normally $1000) is the amount paid to the bondholder at maturity. It is also the amount usually paid by the bondholder when the bond is originally issued.

Definition

Nominal Interest (Coupon Rate)

The **nominal interest** or **coupon rate** is the contractual interest paid on the bond.

Nominal interest is normally quoted as an annual percentage of the face amount. Nominal interest payments are conventionally made semiannually, so semiannual periods are used for compound interest calculations. For example, if a bond has a face amount of \$1000 and a coupon rate of 8%, then every 6 months the owner of the bond would receive $(\$1000)(0.08)\left(\frac{1}{2}\right) = \$40$.

But, because of market conditions, such as the current prime rate of interest, or the discount rate set by the Federal Reserve Board, or changes in the credit rating of the company issuing the bond, the price of a bond will fluctuate. When the bond price is higher than the face amount, it is trading at a **premium**; when it is lower, it is trading at a **discount**. For example, a bond with a face amount of \$1000 and a coupon rate of 8% may trade in the marketplace at a price of \$1100, which means the **true yield** is less than 8%.

To obtain the **true interest rate** of a bond, we view the bond as a combination of an annuity of semiannual interest payments plus a single future amount payable at maturity. The price of a bond is therefore the sum of the present value of the annuity of semiannual interest payments plus the present value of the single future payment at maturity. This present value is calculated by discounting at the true interest rate and assuming semiannual payment periods.

EXAMPLE 11 Pricing Bonds

A bond has a face amount of \$1000 and matures in 10 years. The nominal interest rate is 8.5%. What is the price of the bond to yield a true interest rate of 8%?

SOLUTION

STEP 1 Calculate the amount of each semiannual interest payment using the Simple Interest Formula:

$$(\$1000)\left(\frac{1}{2}\right)(0.085) = \$42.50$$

STEP 2 Calculate the present value of the annuity of semiannual payments:

Amount of each payment P from Step 1: \$ 42.50
Number n of payments (2×10 years): 20
True interest rate i per period
(half of stated true rate): 4%
Present value PV_1 of the annuity for V

$$PV_1 = P\left[\frac{1-(1+i)^{-n}}{i}\right] = (\$42.50)\left[\frac{1-(1+0.04)^{-20}}{0.04}\right] = \underline{\underline{\$\ 577.59}}$$

The present value PV_1 of the interest payments is \$577.59.

STEP 3 Calculate the present value of the amount payable at maturity:

Amount A payable at maturity: \$ 1000
Number n of semiannual compounding
periods before maturity: 20
True interest rate i per period: 4%
The present value PV_2 of the amount payable at maturity:

$$PV_2 = A(1+i)^{-n} = \$1000\,(1+0.04)^{-20} = \underline{\underline{\$\ 456.39}}$$

The present value PV_2 of the maturity value is \$456.39.

STEP 4 The price of the bond is the sum of the two present values:

Present value of the interest payments	$ 577.5
Present value of the maturity value	456.3
Price of bond (Add)	$1033.9

To yield 8%, the price of the bond should be $1033.98.

NOW WORK PROBLEM 49.

USING TECHNOLOGY

EXAMPLE 12 Using Excel

Use Excel to Solve Example 11.

SOLUTION

STEP 1 Calculate the amount of each semiannual interest payment:

$$(\$1000)(.5)(0.085) = \$42.50$$

STEP 2 Calculate the present value of the annuity of semiannual payments. Use the Excel functio PV(*rate, nper, pmt, fv, type*).

rate is the interest rate per period, 4%.
nper is the total number of payments, 20.
pmt is the payment made each period, $42.50.
fv is the future value of the annuity or loan, 0.
type is set to 0 for an ordinary annuity.

The result is given in the Excel spreadsheet below.

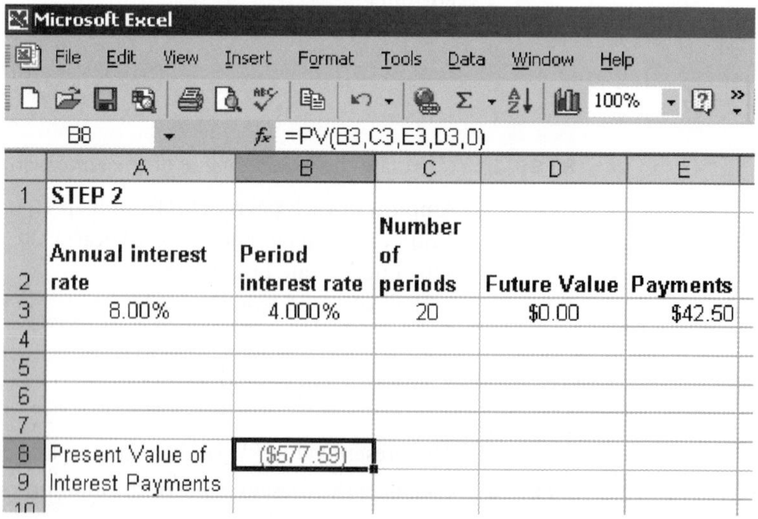
Microsoft Excel
File Edit View Insert Format Tools Data Window Help
100%
B8
=PV(B3,C3,E3,D3,0)
A B C D E
STEP 2
Annual interest rate
Period interest rate
Number of periods
Future Value
Payments
8.00%
4.000%
20
$0.00
$42.50
Present Value of Interest Payments
($577.59)

STEP 3 Calculate the present value of the amount payable at maturity. Use the Excel functio PV(*rate, nper, pmt, fv, type*).

rate is the interest rate per period, 4%.
nper is the total number of payments, 20.
pmt is the payment made each period, $0.00.
fv is the future value of the annuity or loan, 1000.
type is set to 0 for an ordinary annuity.

STEP 4 Determine the price of the bond. Add the two present values. The entire problem's Excel spreadsheet is given below.

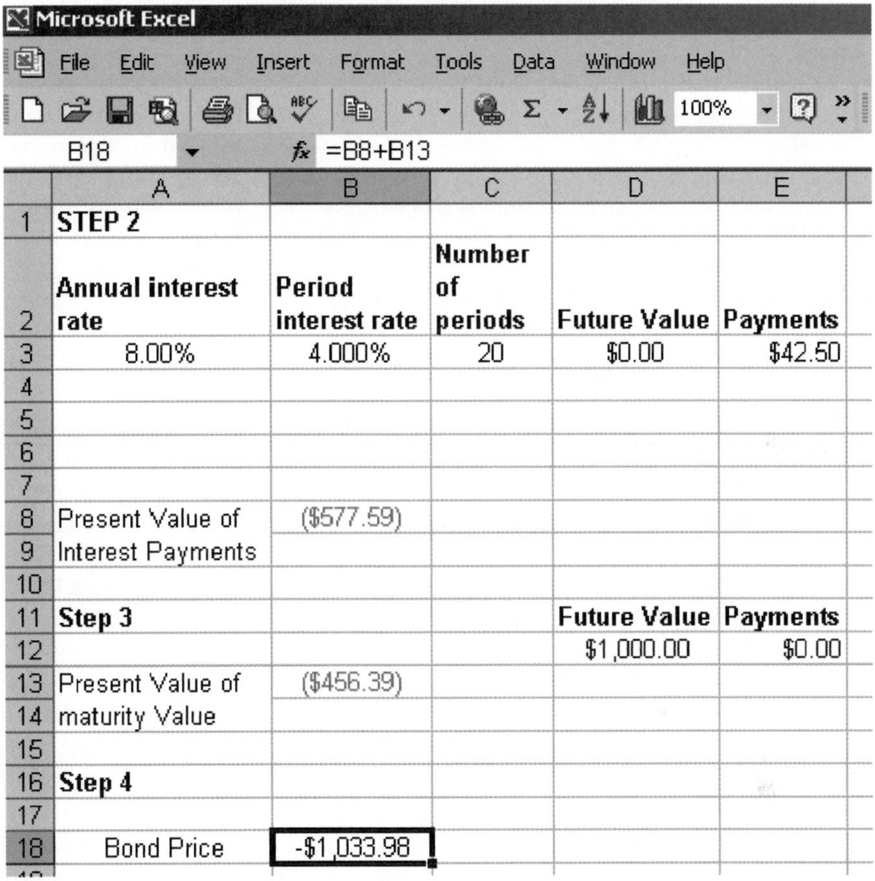

	A	B	C	D	E
1	**STEP 2**				
2	**Annual interest rate**	**Period interest rate**	**Number of periods**	**Future Value**	**Payments**
3	8.00%	4.000%	20	$0.00	$42.50
4					
5					
6					
7					
8	Present Value of	($577.59)			
9	Interest Payments				
10					
11	**Step 3**			**Future Value**	**Payments**
12				$1,000.00	$0.00
13	Present Value of	($456.39)			
14	maturity Value				
15					
16	**Step 4**				
17					
18	Bond Price	-$1,033.98			

NOW WORK PROBLEM 49 USING EXCEL.

EXERCISE 6.4 Answers Begin on Page AN–33.

kill Building

Problems 1–6, find the present value of each annuity.

1. The withdrawal is to be $500 per month for 36 months at 4% compounded monthly.
2. The withdrawal is to be $1000 per year for 3 years at 3% compounded annually.
3. The withdrawal is to be $100 per month for 9 months at 2% compounded monthly.
4. The withdrawal is to be $400 per month for 18 months at 5% compounded monthly.
5. The withdrawal is to be $10,000 per year for 20 years at 5% compounded annually.
6. The withdrawal is to be $2000 per month for 3 years at 4% compounded monthly.

In Problems 7–12, find the monthly payment of each loan.

7. A loan of $10,000 amortized over 48 months at 8%
8. A loan of $50,000 amortized over 120 months at 6%
9. A loan of $500,000 amortized over 360 months at 10%
10. A loan of $5,000 amortized over 36 months at 12%
11. A loan of $1,000,000 amortized over 360 months at 8%
12. A loan of $100,000 amortized over 60 months at 6%

Applications

13. **Loan Payments** What monthly payment is needed to pay off a loan of \$10,000 amortized at 12% compounded monthly for 2 years?

14. **Loan Payments** What monthly payment is needed to pay off a loan of \$500 amortized at 12% compounded monthly for 2 years?

15. **Retirement Planning** Mr. Doody, at age 65, can expect to live for 20 years. If he can invest at 5% per annum compounded monthly, how much does he need now to guarantee himself \$250 every month for the next 20 years?

16. **Retirement Planning** Sharon, at age 65, can expect to live for 25 years. If she can invest at 4% per annum compounded monthly, how much does she need now to guarantee herself \$300 every month for the next 25 years?

17. **Used Car Loan** In January 2011, the interest rate on 36-month used car loans was 7.4%. Suppose you have a contract to buy a used car for \$8000.
    (a) If a bank will lend you \$8000 amortized at 7.4% for 36 months, what is your monthly payment?
    (b) What is the total amount you pay?
    (c) What is the interest you pay?

18. **New Car Loan** In January 2011, the interest rate on 60-month new car loans was 6.93%. Suppose you have a contract to buy a new car for \$15,000.
    (a) If a bank will lend you \$15,000 amortized at 6.93% for 60 months, what is your monthly payment?
    (b) What is the total amount you pay?
    (c) What is the interest you pay?

19. **House Mortgage** A couple wishes to purchase a house for \$200,000 with a down payment of \$40,000. They can amortize the balance either at 8% for 20 years or at 9% for 25 years.
    (a) Which monthly payment is greater?
    (b) For which loan is the total interest paid greater?
    (c) After 10 years, which loan provides the greater equity?

20. **House Mortgage** A couple has decided to purchase a \$250,000 house using a down payment of \$20,000. They can amortize the balance at 6% for 25 years.
    (a) What is their monthly payment?
    (b) What is the total interest paid?
    (c) What is their equity after 5 years?
    (d) What is the equity after 20 years?

21. **Retirement Planning** John is 45 years old and wants to retire at 65. He wishes to make monthly deposits in an account paying 4% compounded monthly so when he retires he can withdraw \$300 a month for 30 years. How much should John deposit each month?

22. **Cost of a Lottery** The grand prize in an Illinois lottery is \$6,000,000, which will be paid out in 20 equal annual payments of \$300,000 each. Assume the first payment of \$300,000 is made, leaving the state with the obligation to pay o[illegible] \$5,700,000 in 19 equal yearly payments of \$300,000 each. H[illegible] much does the state need to deposit in an account paying 6[illegible] compounded annually to achieve this?

23. **College Expenses** Dan works during the summer to h[illegible] with expenses at school the following year. He is able [illegible] save \$100 each week for 12 weeks, and he invests it at [illegible] compounded weekly.
    (a) How much does he have after 12 weeks?
    (b) When school starts, Dan will begin to withdraw eq[illegible] amounts from this account each week. What is the m[illegible] Dan can withdraw each week for 34 weeks?

24. **Value of an IRA** A husband and wife contribute \$4000 p[illegible] year to an IRA paying 5% compounded annually for 20 yea[illegible]
    (a) What is the value of their IRA?
    (b) How much can they withdraw each year for 25 years at 5[illegible] compounded annually?

25. **Analyzing a Town House Purchase** Mike and Yola have ju[illegible] purchased a town house for \$200,000. They obtain financi[illegible] with the following terms: a 20% down payment and the ba[illegible]ance to be amortized over 30 years at 9%.
    (a) What is their down payment?
    (b) What is the loan amount?
    (c) How much is their monthly payment on the loan?
    (d) How much total interest do they pay over the life of the loa[illegible]
    (e) If they pay an additional \$100 each month toward t[illegible] loan, when will the loan be paid?
    (f) With the \$100 additional monthly payment, how mu[illegible] total interest is paid over the life of the loan?

26. **House Mortgage** Mr. Smith obtained a 25-year mortgage [illegible] a house. The monthly payments are \$2247.57 (principal a[illegible] interest) and are based on a 7% interest rate.
    (a) How much did Mr. Smith borrow?
    (b) How much interest will be paid?

27. **Car Payments** A car costs \$12,000. You put 20% down a[illegible] amortize the rest with equal monthly payments over a 3-ye[illegible] period at 15% to be compounded monthly. What will t[illegible] monthly payment be?

28. **Cost of Furniture** Jay pays \$320 per month for 36 months f[illegible] furniture, making no down payment.
    (a) If the interest charged is 0.5% per month on the unpa[illegible] balance, what was the original cost of the furniture?
    (b) How much interest did he pay?

29. **Paying for Restaurant Equipment** A restaurant owner bu[illegible] equipment costing \$20,000.
    (a) If the owner pays 10% down and amortizes the rest wi[illegible] equal monthly payments over 4 years at 12% compound[illegible] monthly, what will be the monthly payments?
    (b) How much interest is paid?

Refinancing a Mortgage A house that was bought 12 years ago for $150,000 is now worth $300,000. Originally, the house was purchased by paying 20% down with the rest financed through a 25-year mortgage at 6.5% interest. The owner (after making 144 equal monthly payments) is in need of cash, and would like to refinance the house. The finance company is willing to loan 80% of the new value of the house amortized over 25 years with the same interest rate. How much cash will the owner receive after paying the balance of the original loan?

1. **Comparing Mortgages** A home buyer is purchasing a $140,000 house. The down payment will be 20% of the price of the house, and the remainder will be financed by a 30-year mortgage at a rate of 6% interest compounded monthly. What will the monthly payment be? Compare the monthly payments and the total amounts of interest paid if a 15-year mortgage is chosen instead of a 30-year mortgage.

2. **Mortgage Payments** Mr. and Mrs. Hoch are interested in building a summer home that will cost $180,000. They intend to use the $60,000 equity in their present house as a down payment on the new one and will finance the rest with a 25-year mortgage at an interest rate of 5.1% compounded monthly. How large will their monthly payment be on the new house?

3. **IRA Withdrawals** How long will it take to exhaust an IRA of $100,000 if you withdraw $2000 every month? Assume a rate of interest of 5% compounded monthly.

4. **IRA Withdrawals** How long will it take to exhaust an IRA of $200,000 if you withdraw $3000 every month? Assume a rate of interest of 4% compounded monthly.

5. **Paying for College** In 2009–2010 the average total tuition, fees, and room and board charges for in-state students at public institutions was $15,213 or approximately $1690 per month for 9 months. Suppose Jeremy has a college fund that pays 4.8% compounded monthly. How much money must be in his college fund on August 1 in order to make 9 equal monthly withdrawals of $1690 beginning September 1 and leave a zero balance?

Source: *Trends in College Pricing 2009*, College Board

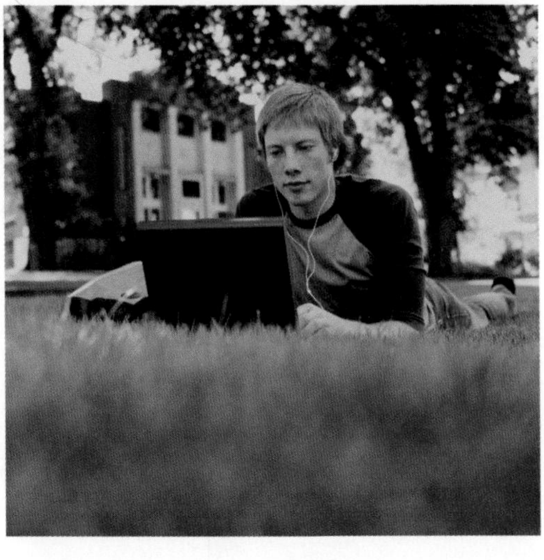

36. **First New Car** Nick recently graduated from college and began his first job. As a reward for these recent successes, he plans to purchase his first new car, a Ford Mustang GT. The base list price for a 2010 Ford Mustang GT Premium Coupe is $32,845. Since Nick is a first-time buyer, Ford will give him a $500 rebate. Nick will also receive $2500 for trading in his current car. Ford Credit will finance Nick's purchase for 6.9% annual interest compounded monthly for 72 months. What will Nick's monthly payment be?

Source: www.fordvehicles.com

37. **Research Endowment** A private foundation plans to fund a five-year $1,000,000 research project at a university. How much money must the foundation deposit into an account paying 7.8% annual interest compounded quarterly so that the university can make equal withdrawals at the end of each quarter totaling $1,000,000 over the five years?

38. **Scholarship Fund** An alumnus donates $100,000 to a university in order to fund a merit scholarship. The university invests the donation into an account paying 5.4% annual interest compounded annually. After one year the university will use this fund to award one scholarship per year for 20 years, at which time the fund is fully depleted. What will be the dollar amount of each scholarship?

39. **Refinancing a Home Loan** Suppose that a couple decides to refinance a 30-year home loan, after making monthly payments for 5 years. The original loan amount was $312,000 with an annual interest rate of 6.825%, compounded monthly. This couple accepts an offer from a California bank to refinance their loan with no closing costs. The new loan will be a 25-year loan and will have a lower interest rate, 6.125%, compounded monthly. With this refinancing, by how much will the monthly payments be reduced? Over the full term of the new loan, how much total interest will be saved?

40. **Refinancing a Home Loan** Suppose that a couple decides to refinance a 30-year home loan, after making monthly payments for 3 years. The original loan amount was $285,000 with an annual interest rate of 6.75%, compounded monthly. This couple accepts an offer from a California bank to refinance their loan with no closing costs. The new loan will be a 15-year loan but will have a lower interest rate, 5.5%, compounded monthly. With this refinancing, by how much will the monthly payments be increased? Over the full term of the new loan, how much total interest will be saved?

41. **Prepaying a Home Loan** After making minimum payments for 4 years on a 30-year home loan, a couple decides to pay an additional $150 per month toward the principal. The original loan amount was $235,000 with an annual interest rate of 6.125%, compounded monthly. By how many months (rounded to the nearest tenth) will the term of this loan be reduced with this additional monthly payment? Over the life of this loan, how much interest will be saved?

42. Adjustable Rate Mortgages A couple decides to accept an adjustable rate, 30-year mortgage, in which the interest rate is fixed for the first 5 years and then may be adjusted annually beginning with year 6. Suppose that this couple borrows $305,000 with the annual interest rate, compounded monthly, for the first 5 years set at 5.5%. Suppose that the interest rate is increased to 6.75% for the remaining term of the loan. Calculate the monthly payment during the first 5 years and after the first 5 years. Find the amount of interest that would be paid over the term of this loan.

43. Buying versus Leasing The state of Alaska negotiated multiple-award term contracts for the purchase and lease-purchase of copiers for state agencies. Among the options, a state office can lease a Xerox WC74289 copier for 36 months at $196.88 per month. The state office can also purchase the same copier outright for $5682. If the state office can invest money at 5.4% compounded monthly, which alternative is preferable?

Source: Contract No. W2010MFC0030 (www.doa.asaska.gov/pdf/4copiers)

44. Leasing Problem A corporation may obtain a machine either by leasing it for 5 years (the useful life) at an annual rent of $2000 or by purchasing the machine for $8100.

(a) If the corporation can borrow money at 10% per annum, which alternative is preferable?

(b) If the corporation can borrow money at 14% per annum, which alternative is preferable?

45. Leasing Decision A company can lease 10 trucks for 4 years (their useful life) for $50,000 a year, or it can purchase them for $175,000. If the company can earn 5% per annum on its money, which choice is preferable, leasing or purchasing?

46. Capital Expenditure Analysis In an effort to increase productivity, a corporation decides to purchase a new piece of equipment. Two models are available; both reduce labor costs. Model A costs $50,000, saves $12,000 per year in labor costs, and has a useful life of 10 years. Model B costs $42,000, saves $10,000 annually in labor costs, and has a useful life of 8 years. If the time value of money is 10% per annum, what piece of equipment provides a better investment?

47. Capital Expenditure Analysis Machine A costs $10,000 and has a useful life of 8 years, and machine B costs $8000 and has a useful life of 6 years. Suppose machine A generates an annual labor savings of $2000 while machine B generates an annu labor savings of $1800.

(a) Assuming the time value of money (investme opportunity rate) is 10% per annum, which machine preferable?

(b) If the time value of money is 14% per annum, whi machine is preferable?

Problems 48–53 involve pricing corporate bonds and Treasury not

48. Corporate Bonds A bond has a face amount of $1000 ar matures in 15 years. The nominal interest rate is 9%.

(a) What is the price of the bond that will yield an effecti interest rate of 8%?

(b) What is the price of the bond to yield an effective intere rate of 10%?

49. Corporate Bonds A bond has a face amount of $10,000 ar matures in 8 years. The nominal rate of interest on the bon is 6.25%. At what price would the bond yield a true rate interest of 6.5%?

50. Treasury Notes* Determine the selling price of a 10-ye Treasury note with a maturity value of $1000, a nomin interest rate of 3.500%, and a true interest rate of 3.548%.

Source: U.S. Treasury (This is an actual U.S. Treasury no issued on May 17, 2010.)

51. Treasury Notes* Determine the selling price of a 5-ye Treasury note, with a maturity value of $1000, a nomin interest rate of 2.125%, and a true interest rate of 2.130%.

Source: U.S. Treasury (This is an actual U.S. Treasury no issued on June 1, 2010.)

52. Treasury Notes* Determine the selling price of a 10-ye Treasury note with a maturity value of $1000, a nomin interest rate of 3.625%, and a true interest rate of 3.692%.

Source: U.S. Treasury (This is an actual U.S. Treasury no issued on February 16, 2010.)

53. Treasury Notes* Determine the selling price of a 5-ye Treasury note with a maturity value of $1000, a nomin interest rate of 2.625%, and a true interest rate of 2.665%.

Source: U.S. Treasury (This is an actual U.S. Treasury no issued on December 31, 2009.)

**Treasury notes pay interest semiannually.*

6.5 Annuities and Amortization Using Recursive Sequences

PREPARING FOR THIS SECTION *Before getting started, review the following:*

- Recursive Sequences (Appendix A, Section A.4, pp. A–34 to A–37)

NOW WORK THE 'ARE YOU PREPARED?' PROBLEMS ON PAGE 348.

OBJECTIVES
1. Use sequences and a graphing utility to solve annuity problems (p. 345)
2. Use sequences and a graphing utility to solve amortization problems (p. 347)

1 Use Sequences and a Graphing Utility to Solve Annuity Problems

In Section 6.2 we developed the Compound Interest Formula, which gives the future value when a fixed amount of money is deposited in an account that pays interest compounded periodically. Often, though, money is invested in equal amounts at periodic intervals. An **annuity** is a sequence of equal periodic deposits. The periodic deposits may be made annually, quarterly, monthly, or daily.

When deposits are made at the same time that the interest is credited, the annuity is called **ordinary**. We will only deal with ordinary annuities here. The **amount of an annuity** is the sum of all deposits made plus all interest paid.

Suppose that the initial amount deposited in an annuity is $\$M$, the periodic deposit is $\$P$, and the per annum rate of interest is r compounded N times per year.* The periodic deposit is made at the same time that the interest is credited, so N deposits are made per year. The amount A_n of the annuity after n deposits will equal the amount of the annuity after $n - 1$ deposits, A_{n-1}, plus the interest earned on this amount plus the periodic deposit P. That is,

$$\underset{\substack{\uparrow\\ \text{Amount after}\\ n \text{ deposits}}}{A_n} = \underset{\substack{\uparrow\\ \text{Amount in previous}\\ \text{period}}}{A_{n-1}} + \underset{\substack{\uparrow\\ \text{Interest}\\ \text{earned}}}{\frac{r}{N}A_{n-1}} + \underset{\substack{\uparrow\\ \text{Periodic}\\ \text{deposit}}}{P} = \left(1 + \frac{r}{N}\right)A_{n-1} + P$$

We have established the following result:

Theorem

Annuity Formula

If $A_0 = M$ represents the initial amount deposited in an annuity that earns a rate of r per annum compounded N times per year, and if P is the periodic deposit made at each payment period, then the amount A_n of the annuity after n deposits is given by the recursive sequence

$$A_0 = M, \qquad A_n = \left(1 + \frac{r}{N}\right)A_{n-1} + P, \qquad n \geq 1 \qquad (1)$$

**We use N to represent the number of times interest is compounded per annum instead of n, since n is the traditional symbol used with sequences to denote the term of the sequence.*

Formula (1) may be explained as follows: the money in the account initially, A_0, $M; the money in the account after $n-1$ payments, A_{n-1}, earns interest $\frac{r}{N}$ duri the nth period; so when the periodic payment of P dollars is added, the amount after payments, A_n, is obtained.

EXAMPLE 1 Saving for Spring Break

A trip to Cancun during spring break will cost $450 and full payment is due March To have the money, a student, on September 1, deposits $100 in a savings account th pays 4% per annum compounded monthly. Beginning October 1, on the first of ea month, the student deposits $50 in this account.

(a) Find a recursive sequence that explains how much is in the account aft n months.

(b) Use the TABLE feature to list the amounts of the annuity for the first 6 months.

(c) After the deposit on March 1 is made, is there enough in the account to pay for t Cancun trip?

(d) If the student deposits $60 each month, will there be enough for the trip?

SOLUTION **(a)** The initial amount deposited in the account is $A_0 = \$100$. The monthly deposit $P = \$50$, and the per annum rate of interest is $r = 0.04$ compounded $N = 12$ tim per year. The amount A_n in the account after n monthly deposits is given by t recursive sequence

$$A_0 = 100, \qquad A_n = \left(1 + \frac{r}{N}\right)A_{n-1} + P = \left(1 + \frac{0.04}{12}\right)A_{n-1} + 50$$

(b) In SEQuence mode on a TI-84 Plus, enter the sequence $\{A_n\}$ and create Table 8. C September 1 ($n = 0$), there is $100 in the account. After the first payment on October the value of the account is $150.33. After the second payment on November 1, t value of the account is $200.83. After the third payment on December 1, the value the account is $251.50, and so on.

(c) On March 1 ($n = 6$), there is only $404.53, not enough to pay for the trip Cancun.

(d) If the periodic deposit, P, is $60, then on March 1, there is $465.03 in the accour enough for the trip. See Table 9.

TABLE 8

n	u(n)
0	100
1	150.33
2	200.83
3	251.5
4	302.34
5	353.35
6	404.53

u(n)■(1+.04/12)...

TABLE 9

n	u(n)
0	100
1	160.33
2	220.87
3	281.6
4	342.54
5	403.68
6	465.03

u(n)■(1+.04/12)...

NOW WORK PROBLEM 7.

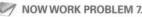

2 Use Sequences and a Graphing Utility to Solve Amortization Problems

Recursive sequences can also be used to compute information about loans. When equal periodic payments are made to pay off a loan, the loan is said to be **amortized**.

Theorem

Amortization Formula

If \$$B$ is borrowed at an interest rate of r per annum compounded monthly, the balance A_n due after n monthly payments of \$$P$ is given by the recursive sequence

$$A_0 = B, \qquad A_n = \left(1 + \frac{r}{12}\right)A_{n-1} - P, \qquad n \geq 1 \qquad (2)$$

Formula (2) may be explained as follows:

The initial loan balance is \$$B$. The balance due A_n after n payments will equal the balance due previously, A_{n-1}, plus the interest charged on that amount reduced by the periodic payment P.

EXAMPLE 2 Home Mortgage Payments

John and Wanda borrowed \$180,000 at 7% per annum compounded monthly for 30 years to purchase a home. Their monthly payment is determined to be \$1197.54.

(a) Find a recursive formula that represents their balance after each payment of \$1197.54 has been made.

(b) Determine their balance after the first payment is made.

(c) When will their balance be below \$170,000?

SOLUTION **(a)** We use Formula (2) with $A_0 = 180{,}000$, $r = 0.07$, and $P = \$1197.54$. Then

$$A_0 = 180{,}000 \qquad A_n = \left(1 + \frac{0.07}{12}\right)A_{n-1} - 1197.54$$

(b) In SEQuence mode on a TI-84 Plus, enter the sequence $\{A_n\}$ and create Table 10. After the first payment is made, the balance is $A_1 = \$179{,}852$.

(c) Scroll down until the balance is below \$170,000. See Table 11. After the 58th payment is made ($n = 58$), the balance is below \$170,000.

TABLE 10

n	u(n)
0	180000
1	179852
2	179704
3	179555
4	179405
5	179254
6	179102

u(n)■(1+.07/12)...

TABLE 11

n	u(n)
52	171067
53	170868
54	170667
55	170465
56	170262
57	170057
58	169852

u(n)■(1+.07/12)...

■

NOW WORK PROBLEM 3.

EXERCISE 6.5 Answers Begin on Page AN–33.

'Are You Prepared?' Problems Answers are given at the end of these exercises. If you get a wrong, answer, read the pages listed in red.

1. What is the 3rd term of the recursive sequence $s_1 = 2, s_{n+1} = 0.5\, s_n + 3$? (pp. A–34 to A–37)

2. Write a recursive sequence for the sequence $-2, 1, 4, 7, 10, \ldots$ (pp. A–34 to A–37)

Applications

3. **Credit Card Debt** John has a balance of \$3000 on his credit card that charges 1% interest per month on any unpaid balance. John can afford to pay \$100 toward the balance each month. His balance each month after making a \$100 payment is given by the recursively defined sequence

$$B_0 = \$3000, \quad B_n = 1.01B_{n-1} - 100$$

(a) Determine John's balance after making the first payment. That is, determine B_1.

(b) Using a graphing utility, determine when John's balance will be below \$2000. How many payments of \$100 have been made?

(c) Using a graphing utility, determine when John will pay off the balance. What is the total of all the payments?

(d) What was John's interest expense?

4. **Car Loans** Phil bought a car by taking out a loan for \$18,500 at 0.5% interest per month. Phil's normal monthly payment is \$434.47 per month, but he decides that he can afford to pay \$100 extra toward the balance each month. His balance each month is given by the recursively defined sequence

$$B_0 = \$18{,}500, \quad B_n = 1.005B_{n-1} - 534.47$$

(a) Determine Phil's balance after making the first payment. That is, determine B_1.

(b) Using a graphing utility, determine when Phil's balance will be below \$10,000. How many payments of \$534.47 have been made?

(c) Using a graphing utility, determine when Phil will pay off the balance. What is the total of all the payments?

(d) What was Phil's interest expense?

5. **Trout Population** A pond currently contains 2000 trout. A fish hatchery decides to add an additional 20 trout each month. In addition, it is known that the trout population is growing 3% per month. The size of the population after n months is given by the recursively defined sequence

$$p_0 = 2000, \quad p_n = 1.03p_{n-1} + 20$$

(a) How many trout are in the pond at the end of the second month? That is, what is p_2?

(b) Using a graphing utility, determine how long it will be before the trout population reaches 5000.

6. **Environmental Control** The Environmental Protection Agency (EPA) determines that Maple Lake has 250 tons of pollutants as a result of industrial waste and that 10% of the pollutants present are neutralized by solar oxidation every year. The EPA imposes new pollution control laws that result in 15 to[ns] of new pollutants entering the lake each year. The amount [of] pollutants in the lake at the end of each year is given by t[he] recursively defined sequence

$$p_0 = 250, \quad p_n = 0.9p_{n-1} + 15$$

(a) Determine the amount of pollutants in the lake at the e[nd] of the second year. That is, determine p_2.

(b) Using a graphing utility, provide pollutant amounts f[or] the next 20 years.

(c) What is the equilibrium level of pollution in Maple Lak[e]? That is, what is $\lim_{n\to\infty} p_n$?

7. **Roth IRA** On January 1, 2011, Bob decides to place \$500 at t[he] end of each quarter into a Roth Individual Retirement Accou[nt].

(a) Find a recursive formula that represents Bob's balance [at] the end of each quarter if the rate of return is assumed [to] be 8% per annum compounded quarterly.

(b) How long will it be before the value of the account excee[ds] \$100,000?

(c) What will be the value of the account in 25 years wh[en] Bob retires?

8. **Education IRA** On January 1, 2011, John's parents decide [to] place \$45 at the end of each month into an Education IRA.

(a) Find a recursive formula that represents the balance at t[he] end of each month if the rate of return is assumed to [be] 6% per annum compounded monthly.

(b) How long will it be before the value of the account excee[ds] \$4000?

(c) What will be the value of the account in 16 years wh[en] John goes to college?

9. **Home Loan** Bill and Laura borrowed \$150,000 at 6% p[er] annum compounded monthly for 30 years to purchase [a] home. Their monthly payment is determined to be \$899.[…]

(a) Find a recursive formula for their balance after ea[ch] monthly payment has been made.

(b) Determine Bill and Laura's balance after the first payme[nt].

(c) Using a graphing utility, create a table showing Bill a[nd] Laura's balance after each monthly payment.

(d) Using a graphing utility, determine when Bill and Laur[a's] balance will be below \$140,000.

(e) Using a graphing utility, determine when Bill and Lau[ra] will pay off the balance.

(f) Determine Bill and Laura's interest expense when the loan is paid.

(g) Suppose that Bill and Laura decide to pay an additional \$100 each month on their loan. Answer parts (a) to (f) under this scenario.

(h) Is it worthwhile for Bill and Laura to pay the additional \$100? Explain.

. Home Loan Jodi and Jeff borrowed \$120,000 at 6.5% per annum compounded monthly for 30 years to purchase a home. Their monthly payment is determined to be \$758.48.

(a) Find a recursive formula for their balance after each monthly payment has been made.

(b) Determine Jodi and Jeff's balance after the first payment.

(c) Using a graphing utility, create a table showing Jodi and Jeff's balance after each monthly payment.

(d) Using a graphing utility, determine when Jodi and Jeff's balance will be below \$100,000.

(e) Using a graphing utility, determine when Jodi and Jeff will pay off the balance.

(f) Determine Jodi and Jeff's interest expense when the loan is paid.

(g) Suppose that Jodi and Jeff decide to pay an additional \$100 each month on their loan. Answer parts (a) to (f) under this scenario.

(h) Is it worthwhile for Jodi and Jeff to pay the additional \$100? Explain.

re You Prepared?' Answers

. $s_3 = 5$ **2.** $s_1 = -2, \quad s_{n+1} = s_n + 3$

HAPTER 6 REVIEW OBJECTIVES

Section	Examples		You should be able to	Review Exercises
6.1	1, 2	1	Solve problems involving percents (p. 294)	1–11
	3–5	2	Solve problems involving simple interest (p. 295)	12, 13, 14, 19(a)
	6–9	3	Solve problems involving discounted loans (p. 297)	15, 16
6.2	1–4	1	Determine the future value of a lump sum of money (p. 302)	17, 18, 19(b), 44
	5	2	Find the effective rate of interest (p. 307)	24, 25, 41
	6, 7	3	Determine the present value of a lump sum of money (p. 308)	20, 21, 38, 42
	8	4	Determine the rate of interest required to double a lump sum of money (p. 310)	23
	9	5	Determine the time required to double a lump sum of money (p. 310)	22
6.3	1–7	1	Solve problems involving annuities (p. 316)	28, 36, 37, 43, 45
	8–11	2	Solve problems involving sinking funds (p. 320)	32, 33, 34, 40
6.4	1–4	1	Solve problems involving the present value of an annuity (p. 329)	26, 27, 35, 36, 43, 46, 48
	5–10	2	Solve problems involving amortization (p. 332)	29, 30, 31, 39, 47
6.5	1	1	Use sequences and a graphing utility to solve annuity problems (p. 345)	26, 27, 28, 34, 36, 37, 43, 45, 46
	2	2	Use sequences and a graphing utility to solve amortization problems (p. 347)	29, 30, 31, 39, 47

IMPORTANT FORMULAS

Simple Interest Formula (p. 295) $I = Prt$

Discounted Loans (p. 297) $R = L - Lrt$

Compound Interest Formula (pp. 303 and 307)

$$A = P\left(1 + \frac{r}{n}\right)^{nt}$$

$$A = Pe^{rt}$$

Amount of an Annuity (p. 318) $A = P\left[\frac{(1 + i)^n - 1}{i}\right]$

Present Value of an Annuity (p. 330) $V = P\left[\frac{1 - (1 + i)^{-n}}{i}\right.$

Amortization (p. 333) $P = V\left[\frac{i}{1 - (1 + i)^{-n}}\right]$

REVIEW EXERCISES **Answers to odd-numbered problems begin on page AN-34.**

Blue Problem numbers indicate the author's suggestions for a practice test.

In Problems 1–9, calculate the indicated quantity.

1. 3% of 500
2. 20% of 1200
3. 140% of 250
4. What percent of 200 is 40?
5. What percent of 350 is 75?
6. What percent of 50 is 125?
7. 12 is 15% of what number?
8. 25 is 6% of what number?
9. 11 is 0.5% of what number?

10. **Sales Tax** The sales tax in New York City is 8.875%. If the total charge for a DVD player (including tax) is \$162.75, what does the DVD player itself cost?

11. **Sales Tax** Indiana has a sales tax of 7%. Dan purchased gifts for his family worth \$330.00. How much sales tax will Dan have to pay on his purchase?

12. Find the interest I charged and amount A due, if \$400 is borrowed for 9 months at 12% simple interest.

13. Dan borrows \$500 at 9% per annum simple interest for 1 year and 2 months. What is the interest charged, and what is the amount due?

14. **Interest Due** Jim borrows \$14,000 for a period of 4 years at 6% simple interest. Determine the interest due on the loan.

15. **Loan Amount** Warren needs \$15,000 for a new machine for his auto repair shop. He obtains a 2-year discounted loan at 12% interest. How much must he repay to settle his debt?

16. **Treasury Bills** How much should a bank bid for a 15-month, \$5,000 Treasury bill in order to earn 2.5% simple interest?

17. Find the amount of an investment of \$100 after 2 years and 3 months at 3% compounded monthly.

18. Mike places \$200 in a savings account that pays 4% per annum compounded monthly. How much is in his account after 9 months?

19. **Choosing a Car Loan** A car dealer offers Mike the choice of two loans:
    (a) \$3000 for 3 years at 12% per annum simple interest
    (b) \$3000 for 3 years at 10% per annum compounded monthly
    Which loan costs Mike the least?

20. A mutual bond fund pays 9% per annum compounde monthly. How much should I invest now so that 2 yea from now I will have \$100 in the account?

21. **Saving for a Bicycle** Katy wants to buy a bicycle that cos \$75 and will purchase it in 6 months. How much shou she put in her savings account for this if she can get 3% p annum compounded monthly?

22. **Doubling Money** Marcia has \$220,000 saved for h retirement. How long will it take for the investment to doub in value if it earns 6% compounded semiannually?

23. **Doubling Money** What annual rate of interest will cause a investment to double in 12 years?

24. **Effective Rate of Interest** A bank advertises that it pa $3\frac{3}{4}$% interest compounded monthly. What is the effecti rate of interest?

25. **Effective Rate of Interest** What interest rate compounde quarterly has an effective interest rate of 6%?

26. **Saving for a Car** Mike decides he needs \$500 1 year fro now to buy a used car. If he can invest at 3% compounde monthly, how much should he save each month to bu the car?

27. **Saving for a House** Mr. and Mrs. Corey are newlywe and want to purchase a home, but they need a dow payment of \$40,000. If they want to buy their hom in 2 years, how much should they save each month in the savings account that pays 3% per annum compound monthly?

True Cost of a Car Mike has just purchased a used car and will make equal payments of \$50 per month for 18 months at 12% per annum charged monthly. How much did the car actually cost? Assume no down payment.

House Mortgage Mr. and Mrs. Ostedt have just purchased a \$400,000 home and made a 25% down payment. The balance can be amortized at 10% for 25 years.

(a) What are the monthly payments?

(b) How much interest will be paid?

(c) What is their equity after 5 years?

Inheritance Payouts An inheritance of \$25,000 is to be paid in equal amounts over a 5-year period at the end of each year. If the \$25,000 can be invested at 5% per annum, what is the annual payment?

House Mortgage A mortgage of \$125,000 is to be amortized at 9% per annum for 25 years. What are the monthly payments? What is the equity after 10 years?

Paying Off Construction Bonds A state has \$8,000,000 worth of construction bonds that are due in 25 years. What annual sinking fund deposit is needed if the state can earn 10% per annum on its money?

Depletion Problem How much should Mr. Graff pay for a gold mine expected to yield an annual return of \$20,000 and to have a life expectancy of 20 years, if he wants to have a 15% annual return on his investment and he can set up a sinking fund that earns 10% a year?

Depletion Problem An oil well is expected to yield an annual net return of \$25,000 for the next 15 years, after which it will run dry. An investor wants a return on his investment of 20%. He can establish a sinking fund earning 5% annually. How much should he pay for the oil well?

Retirement Income Mr. Doody, at age 70, is expected to live for 15 years. If he can invest at 4% per annum compounded monthly, how much does he need now to guarantee himself \$300 every month for the next 15 years?

Saving for the Future Hal deposited \$100 in an account paying 4% per annum compounded monthly for 25 years. At the end of the 25 years Hal retires. What is the largest amount he may withdraw monthly for the next 35 years?

Saving for College Mr. Jones wants to save for his son's college education. If he deposits \$500 every 6 months at 3% compounded semiannually, how much will he have on hand at the end of 8 years?

38. **Saving for the Future** How much money should be invested at 2% compounded quarterly in order to have \$20,000 in 6 years?

39. **Loan Payments** What monthly payment will amortize a loan of \$3000 borrowed at 12% compounded monthly for 2 years?

40. **Paying Off School Bonds** A school board issues bonds in the amount of \$20,000,000 to be retired in 25 years. After 20 years, how much must be paid each year into a sinking fund at 6% compounded annually to pay off the \$20,000,000?

41. What effective rate of interest corresponds to a rate of 9% compounded monthly?

42. If an amount was borrowed 5 years ago at 6% compounded quarterly, and \$6000 is owed now, what was the original amount borrowed?

43. **Trust Fund Payouts** John is the beneficiary of a trust fund set up for him by his grandparents. If the trust fund amounts to \$20,000 earning 8% compounded semiannually and he is to receive the money in equal semiannual installments for the next 15 years, how much will he receive each 6 months?

44. **IRA** Mike has \$4000 in his IRA. At 6% annual interest compounded monthly, how much will he have at the end of 20 years?

45. **Retirement Funds** An employee gets paid at the end of each month and \$60 is withheld from her paycheck for a retirement fund. The fund pays 1% per month (equivalent to 12% annually compounded monthly). What amount will be in the fund at the end of 30 months?

46. **Retirement Income** A man has \$50,000 invested at 6% compounded quarterly at the time he retires. If he wishes to withdraw money every 3 months for the next 7 years, what will be the size of his withdrawals?

47. **Buying a Car** A student borrowed \$4000 from a credit union toward purchasing a car. The interest rate on such a loan is 14% compounded quarterly, with payments due every quarter. The student wants to pay off the loan in 4 years. Find the quarterly payment.

48. **Leasing Decision** A firm can lease office furniture for 5 years (its useful life) for \$20,000 a year, or it can purchase the furniture for \$80,000. Which is a better choice if the firm can invest its money at 10% per annum?

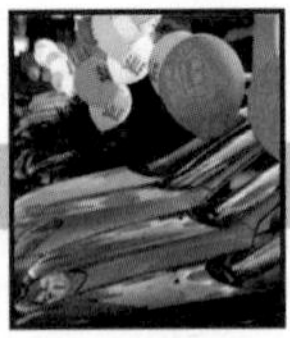

Chapter 6 Project

You've made a decision; you want to buy a new Toyota Prius. The cash purchase price of the vehicle you have selected is $23,700.

Here are some options the Toyota dealer has suggested.

1. **Option A** For this option a down payment of $3,000 is required with monthly payments at a 5% annual rate for 5 years. What is the monthly payment? What is the total amount of interest paid over the term of this loan?
2. **Option B** A bigger down payment will lower the monthly payments. With a down payment of $6,000, the dealer offers you a loan with monthly payments at a 4.8% annual rate for 6 years. What is the monthly payment? What is the total amount of interest paid over the term of this loan?
3. **Option C** Your bank offers a car loan with 20% down and monthly payments at a 5.5% annual rate for 7 years. What would be the principal amount for this loan? What would be the monthly payment for this loan? What would be the total amount of interest paid over the term of this loan?
4. Based on minimizing the total amount of interest paid, which option would you select? Which option would you select to minimize monthly payments?
5. One way to compare the three options is to compute the total present value of each option. To do this, we will use an annual rate of return of 8% per year, compounded monthly. For each of the above options, find the present value of the monthly payments and add this present value to the down payment for that option to find the total present value for that option. Which option minimizes total present value?
6. **Option D** A local credit union offers car loans that require a down payment of 15%, no monthly payments for 12 months, and then monthly payments for 5 years of $409. Find the total present value of Option D and compare to the total present values found in Problem 5. Hint: First find the present value, P_1, of the 5 years of payments, using an annual rate of return of 8%, compounded monthly. P_1 is the present value of the payments at the time when the payments begin (one year from purchase). Then find the principal P_0 that would generate P_1 in 1 year at an annual rate of 8%, compounded monthly. The total present value for Option D would be the down payment plus P_0.
7. **Option E** The Toyota dealer also offers a lease with purchase option for this Prius, which requires an initial payment of $1,500 and monthly lease payments for up to 4 years of $225. At any time within these 4 years you would have the option to purchase the Toyota Prius for a depreciated pric determined as follows: Each year the price of this Pri depreciates by an amount equal to 10% of the price in t previous year. *Hint:* Given an initial purchase price P, t depreciated price after 1 year would be $.9^*P$, the depreciat price after 2 years would be $.9^{2*}P$, and so on. Find t depreciated price after 3 years and after 4 years.
8. The total present value for Option E will be the initi payment, plus the present value of the lease payments, pl the present value of the depreciated price. Using an annu rate of return of 8%, compounded monthly, find (a) t total present value for Option E with purchase after 3 yea of leasing and (b) the total present value for Option E wi purchase after 4 years of leasing. In order to minimize to present value, should the purchase be made after 3 years leasing or after 4 years of leasing?
9. Compare Options, A, B, C, D, E (with purchase after 3 year and E (with purchase after 4 years). Which of these optio has the lowest total present value?
10. For Option E with purchase after 4 years, it would practical to set up a sinking fund to accumulate t amount needed to purchase the Prius after the 4-year leasi period. Determine the annual interest rate for Option with purchase after 4 years, as follows: Determine t required monthly payment into a sinking fund that ear interest at an annual rate of 8%, compounded month to accumulate the purchase price at the end of 4 years leasing. The monthly lease payment plus the monthly sinki fund payment provide a monthly payment that wou finance the purchase of the Prius after 4 years. These to monthly payments would pay off an amount equal to t purchase price minus the $1,500 initial payment for the lea agreement. Round this annual interest rate to the near hundredth of a percent. Also compute the total present val of Option E (with purchase after 4 years) by using t present value of the monthly sinking fund payments need to accumulate the purchase price in 4 years.
11. Use the method described in Problem 10 to compute t annual interest rate for Option E with purchase after 3 yea Also compute the total present value of Option E (wi purchase after 3 years) by using the present value of t monthly sinking fund payments needed to accumul the purchase price in 3 years.

Mathematical Questions from Professional Exams*

. **CPA Exam** Which of the following should be used to calculate the amount of the equal periodic payments that could be equivalent to an outlay of $3000 at the time of the last payment?

(a) Amount of 1

(b) Amount of an annuity of 1

(c) Present value of an annuity of 1

(d) Present value of 1

. **CPA Exam** A businessman wants to withdraw $3000 (including principal) from an investment fund at the end of each year for 5 years. How should he compute his required initial investment at the beginning of the first year if the fund earns 6% compounded annually?

(a) $3000 times the amount of an annuity of $1 at 6% at the end of each year for 5 years

(b) $3000 divided by the amount of an annuity of $1 at 6% at the end of each year for 5 years

(c) $3000 times the present value of an annuity of $1 at 6% at the end of each year for 5 years

(d) $3000 divided by the present value of an annuity of $1 at 6% at the end of each year for 5 years

. **CPA Exam** A businesswoman wants to invest a certain sum of money at the end of each year for 5 years. The investment will earn 6% compounded annually. At the end of 5 years, she will need a total of $30,000 accumulated. How should she compute the required annual investment?

(a) $30,000 times the amount of an annuity of $1 at 6% at the end of each year for 5 years

(b) $30,000 divided by the amount of an annuity of $1 at 6% at the end of each year for 5 years

(c) $30,000 times the present value of an annuity of $1 at 6% at the end of each year for 5 years

(d) $30,000 divided by the present value of an annuity of $1 at 6% at the end of each year for 5 years

ms 4–6 apply to the appropriate use of present value tables. ven below are the present value factors for $1.00 discounted 8% for 1 to 5 periods. Each of the following items is based on 5 interest compounded annually from day of deposit to day of thdrawal.

Periods	Present Value of $1 Discounted at 8% per Period
1	0.926
2	0.857
3	0.794
4	0.735
5	0.681

4. **CPA Exam** What amount should be deposited in a bank today to grow to $1000 3 years from today?

(a) $\dfrac{\$1000}{0.794}$

(b) $1000 × 0.926 × 3

(c) ($1000 × 0.926) + ($1000 × 0.857) + ($1000 × 0.794)

(d) $1000 × 0.794

5. **CPA Exam** What amount should an individual have in her bank account today before withdrawal if she needs $2000 each year for 4 years with the first withdrawal to be made today and each subsequent withdrawal at 1-year intervals? (She is to have exactly a zero balance in her bank account after the fourth withdrawal.)

(a) $2000 + ($2000 × 0.926) + ($2000 × 0.857) + ($2000 × 0.794)

(b) $\dfrac{\$2000}{0.735} \times 4$

(c) ($2000 × 0.926) + ($2000 × 0.857) + ($2000 × 0.794) + ($2000 × 0.735)

(d) $\dfrac{\$2000}{0.926} \times 4$

6. **CPA Exam** If an individual put $3000 in a savings account today, what amount of cash would be available 2 years from today?

(a) $3000 × 0.857 (b) $3000 × 0.857 × 2

(c) $\dfrac{\$3000}{0.857}$ (d) $\dfrac{\$3000}{0.926} \times 2$

Probability 7

Take a look at the back cover of your book. Do you see the bar code and the ISBN number? Have you ever wondered what all the numbers and hyphens mean? You know it identifies your book, but what else does it do? And what about the bar code on that bottle of water you just bought? You know, the UPC code. What do those numbers mean? Every product you buy, from food to drugs to clothing—just about everything—has a bar code that identifies the item purchased. How is this possible using just 12 digits? In this chapter we discuss counting techniques that, together with the Chapter Project, will explain these everyday codes.

OUTLINE

Look Back, A Look Forward

Chapters 1–5 we investigated applications of linear uations and inequalities. In Chapter 6 we introduced a new pic, *financial models*. In this chapter we begin yet another new topic, *probability*. As the Outline above shows, we begin by discussing *sets* and techniques for counting the *number of elements* in a set.

7.1 Sets

Set Notation

To treat a collection of distinct objects as a whole, we use the idea of a **set**. For examp[le]
the set of **digits** consists of the collection of numbers 0, 1, 2, 3, 4, 5, 6, 7, 8, and 9. If [we]
use the symbol D to denote the set of digits, then we can write

$$D = \{0, 1, 2, 3, 4, 5, 6, 7, 8, 9\}$$

In this notation the braces $\{ \}$ are used to enclose the objects, or **elements**, in the s[et.]
This method of denoting a set is called the **roster method**. A second way to denote a s[et]
is to use **set-builder notation**, where the set D of digits is written as

$$D = \{ \quad x \quad | \quad x \text{ is a digit}\}$$
↑↑ ↑   ↑   ↑   ↑

Read as "D is the set of all x such that x is a digit."

EXAMPLE 1   Examples of Set Notation

(a) $E = \{x | x \text{ is an even digit}\} = \{0, 2, 4, 6, 8\}$

(b) $O = \{x | x \text{ is an odd digit}\} = \{1, 3, 5, 7, 9\}$

EXAMPLE 2   Using Set Notation

(a) Let A denote the set that consists of all possible outcomes resulting from tossing a co[in]
two times and observing whether a head or tail occurs on each toss. If we let H den[ote]
heads and T denote tails, then the set A can be written as

$$A = \{HH, HT, TH, TT\}$$

where, for instance, TH means the first toss resulted in tails and the second to[ss]
resulted in heads.

(b) Let B denote the set consisting of all possible arrangements of the digits witho[ut]
repetition. Some typical elements of B are

1478906532   4875326019   3214569870

The number of elements in B is very large, so listing all of them is impractical. He[nce]
set-builder notation can be used to write

$$B = \{x | x \text{ is a ten-digit number in which no digit is repeated}\}$$

The elements of a set are never repeated. That is, we never write $\{3, 2, 2\}$; the correct listing is $\{3, 2\}$. Finally, the order in which the elements of a set are listed does not make any difference. The three sets

$$\{3, 2, 4\} \qquad \{2, 3, 4\} \qquad \{4, 3, 2\}$$

are different listings of the same set. The *elements* of a set distinguish the set—not the *order* in which the elements are written.

A set that has no elements is called the **empty set** or **null set** and is denoted by the symbol $\varnothing$.

1 Identify Relations between Pairs of Sets

We begin to develop an algebra for sets by defining what we mean by two sets being *equal.*

Definition

Equality of Sets

Let A and B be two sets. We say that A **is equal to** B, written as

$$A = B$$

if and only if A and B have the same elements. If A and B are not equal, we write

$$A \neq B$$

For example, $\{1, 2, 3\} = \{1, 3, 2\}$ and $\{1, 2\} \neq \{1, 2, 3\}$.

Two sets can also be compared using the ideas of *subset* and *proper subset.*

Definition

Subset

Let A and B be two sets. We say that A **is a subset of** B or that A **is contained in** B, written as

$$A \subseteq B$$

if and only if every element of A is also an element of B. If A is not a subset of B, we write

$$A \nsubseteq B$$

For example, $\{1, 2\} \subseteq \{1, 2, 3\}$ and $\{1, 2, 3, 4\} \nsubseteq \{1, 2\}$.

NOW WORK PROBLEMS 5 AND 7.

Subset can also be defined as follows: $A \subseteq B$ if and only if whenever x is an element of A, then x is an element of B for all x. This way of defining $A \subseteq B$ is useful for obtaining various laws that sets obey. For example, it follows that for any set A, $A \subseteq A$; that is, eve set is a subset of itself. Do you see why? Whenever x is in A, then x is in A!

The statement "A is a subset of B" is equivalent to saying "there are no eleme in set A that are not also elements in set B." In particular, suppose $A = \varnothing$. Since t empty set $\varnothing$ has no elements, there is no element of the set $\varnothing$ that is not also in That is,

$$\varnothing \subseteq B \qquad \text{for any set } B$$

Definition

Proper Subset

Let A and B be two sets. We say that A **is a proper subset of** B or that A **is properly contained in** B, written as

$$A \subset B$$

if and only if every element in the set A is also in the set B, but there is at least one element in set B that is *not* in set A. If A is *not* a proper subset of B, we write

$$A \not\subset B$$

For example, $\{1, 2\} \subset \{1, 2, 3, 4\}$, $\{1, 2, 3\} \not\subset \{1, 2\}$, and $\{1, 2\} \not\subset \{1, 2\}$. you see why? The set to the right of the $\subset$ symbol must have an element not found the set to the left of the $\subset$ symbol.

Notice that "A is a proper subset of B" means that there are *no* elements of A t are not also elements of B, but there is at least one element of B that is not in A. example, if B is any nonempty set, that is, any set having at least one element, then

$$\varnothing \subset B$$

Also, $A \not\subset A$; that is, a set is never a proper subset of itself.

The following example illustrates some uses of the three relationships, $=$, $\subseteq$, a $\subset$, just defined.

EXAMPLE 3 Identifying Relationships between Sets

Consider three sets A, B, and C given by

$$A = \{1, 2, 3\} \qquad B = \{1, 2, 3, 4, 5\} \qquad C = \{3, 2, 1\}$$

Some of the relationships between pairs of these sets are

(a) $A = C$ **(b)** $A \subseteq B$ **(c)** $A \subseteq C$ **(d)** $A \subset B$ **(e)** $C \subseteq A$ **(f)** $\varnothing \subseteq A$

Notice that if a set A is a subset of a set B, then either A is a proper subset of B or e A equals B. That is,

$$A \subseteq B \qquad \text{if and only if either} \qquad A \subset B \text{ or } A = B$$

Also, if A is a proper subset of B, we can infer that A is a subset of B, but A does not eq B. That is,

$$A \subset B \qquad \text{if and only if} \qquad A \subseteq B \text{ and } A \neq B$$

In applications the elements that may be considered are usually limited to some specific all-encompassing set, a *universal set*. For example, in discussing students eligible to graduate from Midwestern University, the discussion would be limited to students enrolled at the university.

Definition

Universal Set

The **universal set** U is defined as the set consisting of all elements under consideration.

If A is any set and if U is the universal set, then every element in A must be in U (since U consists of all elements under consideration). As a result,

$$A \subseteq U$$

for *any* set A.

GURE 1

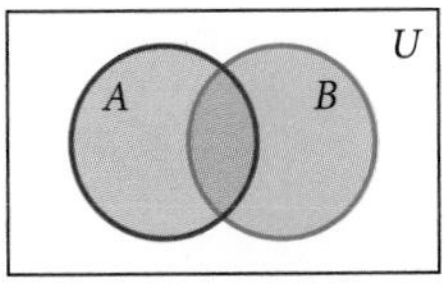

It is convenient to represent a set as the interior of a circle. Two or more sets may be depicted as circles enclosed in a rectangle, which represents the universal set. The circles may or may not overlap, depending on the situation. Such diagrams of sets are called **Venn diagrams.** See Figure 1.

2 Find the Union and Intersection of Two Sets

Continuing to develop an algebra of sets, we introduce two operations that may be performed on sets, *union* and *intersection*.

Definition

Union of Two Sets

Let A and B be any two sets. The **union** of A with B, written as

$$A \cup B$$

and read as "A union B" or as "A or B," is defined to be the set consisting of those elements either in A or in B or in both A and B. That is,

$$A \cup B = \{x | x \text{ is in } A \text{ or } x \text{ is in } B\}$$

GURE 2

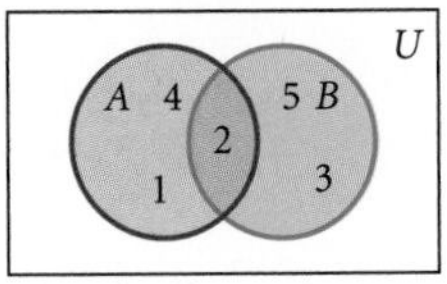

For example, if $A = \{1, 2, 4\}$ and $B = \{2, 3, 5\}$, then $A \cup B = \{1, 2, 3, 4, 5\}$. In the Venn diagram in Figure 2, the area with color corresponds to $A \cup B$.

Definition

Intersection of Two Sets

Let A and B be any two sets. The **intersection** of A with B, written as

$$A \cap B$$

and read as "A intersect B" or as "A and B," is defined as the set consisting of those elements that are in both A and B. That is,

$$A \cap B = \{x | x \text{ is in } A \text{ and } x \text{ is in } B\}$$

FIGURE 3

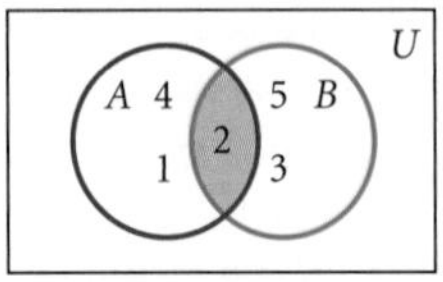

For example, if $A = \{1, 2, 4\}$ and $B = \{2, 3, 5\}$, then $A \cap B = \{2\}$.

In other words, to find the intersection of two sets A and B means to find the elemen *common to A and B.* In the Venn diagram in Figure 3 the region with color is $A \cap B$.

EXAMPLE 4 Finding the Union and Intersection of Two Sets

Use the sets

$$A = \{1, 3, 5\} \qquad B = \{3, 4, 5, 6\} \qquad C = \{6, 7\}$$

to find

(a) $A \cup B$ **(b)** $A \cap B$ **(c)** $A \cap C$

SOLUTION

(a) $A \cup B = \{1, 3, 5\} \cup \{3, 4, 5, 6\} = \{1, 3, 4, 5, 6\}$
(b) $A \cap B = \{1, 3, 5\} \cap \{3, 4, 5, 6\} = \{3, 5\}$
(c) $A \cap C = \{1, 3, 5\} \cap \{6, 7\} = \varnothing$

NOW WORK PROBLEMS 17 AND 19.

EXAMPLE 5 Interpreting the Intersection of Two Sets

Let T be the set of all taxpayers and let S be the set of all people over 65 years of ag Describe $T \cap S$.

SOLUTION $T \cap S$ is the set of all taxpayers who are also over 65 years of age.

Definition

Disjoint Sets

If two sets A and B have no elements in common, that is, if

$$A \cap B = \varnothing$$

then A and B are called **disjoint sets.**

FIGURE 4

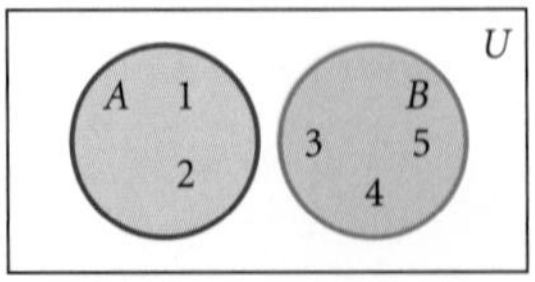

For example, if $A = \{1, 2\}$ and $B = \{3, 4, 5\}$, then $A \cap B = \varnothing$ so A and B a disjoint sets.

Two disjoint sets A and B are illustrated in the Venn diagram in Figure 4. Notice th the circles corresponding to A and B do not overlap.

EXAMPLE 6 Tossing a Die*

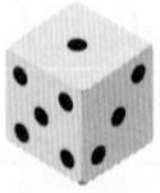

Suppose that a die is tossed. What is the universal set? Let A be the set of outcomes in whic an even number turns up; let B be the set of outcomes in which an odd number shows.

(a) Find A. **(b)** Find B. **(c)** Find $A \cap B$.

A **die (plural **dice**) is a cube with 1, 2, 3, 4, 5, or 6 dots showing on the six faces.*

SOLUTION Since only a 1, 2, 3, 4, 5, or 6 can result when a die is tossed, the universal set is $U = \{1, 2, 3, 4, 5, 6\}$. It follows that

(a) $A = \{2, 4, 6\}$

(b) $B = \{1, 3, 5\}$

(c) Notice that A and B have no elements in common. As a result, $A \cap B = \varnothing$ so the sets A and B are disjoint sets. ■

3 Find the Complement of a Set

Consider all the employees of a company as the universal set U. Let A be the subset of employees who smoke. Then all the nonsmokers will make up the subset of U that is called the *complement* of the set of smokers.

Definition

Complement of a Set

Let A be any set. The **complement** of A, written as*

$$\bar{A}$$

is defined as the set consisting of elements in the universal set U that are not in A. That is,

$$\bar{A} = \{x | x \text{ is not in } A\}$$

IGURE 5

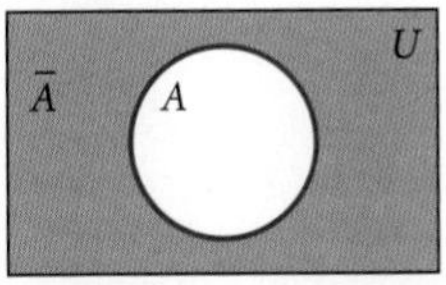

The region in color in Figure 5 illustrates the complement, $\bar{A}$. For any set A it follows that

$$A \cup \bar{A} = U \qquad A \cap \bar{A} = \varnothing \qquad \bar{\bar{A}} = A$$

EXAMPLE 7 Finding the Complement of a Set

Use the sets

$$U = \{a, b, c, d, e, f\} \qquad A = \{a, b, c\} \qquad B = \{a, c, f\}$$

to list the elements of the following sets:

(a) $\bar{A}$ **(b)** $\bar{B}$ **(c)** $\overline{A \cup B}$

(d) $\bar{A} \cap \bar{B}$ **(e)** $\overline{A \cap B}$ **(f)** $\bar{A} \cup \bar{B}$

SOLUTION **(a)** $\bar{A}$ consists of all the elements in U that are not in A:

$$\bar{A} = \{d, e, f\}$$

(b) Similarly,

$$\bar{B} = \{b, d, e\}$$

*Some books use A' or A^c for complement.

(c) To find $\overline{A \cup B}$, first list the elements in $A \cup B$:

$$A \cup B = \{a, b, c, f\}$$

The complement of the set $A \cup B$ is then

$$\overline{A \cup B} = \{d, e\}$$

(d) From parts (a) and (b) we find that

$$\overline{A} \cap \overline{B} = \{d, e, f\} \cap \{b, d, e\} = \{d, e\}$$

(e) As in part (c), first list the elements in $A \cap B$:

$$A \cap B = \{a, c\}$$

Then

$$\overline{A \cap B} = \{b, d, e, f\}$$

(f) From parts (a) and (b) we find that

$$\overline{A} \cup \overline{B} = \{d, e, f\} \cup \{b, d, e\} = \{b, d, e, f\}$$

NOW WORK PROBLEM 25.

4 Use Venn Diagrams

EXAMPLE 8 Using Venn Diagrams to Illustrate a Set

Use a Venn diagram to illustrate the set $(A \cup B) \cap C$.

SOLUTION First construct Figure 6(a). Then shade $A \cup B$ in green and C in yellow as shown i Figure 6(b). The region where the colors overlap is the set $(A \cup B) \cap C$.

FIGURE 6

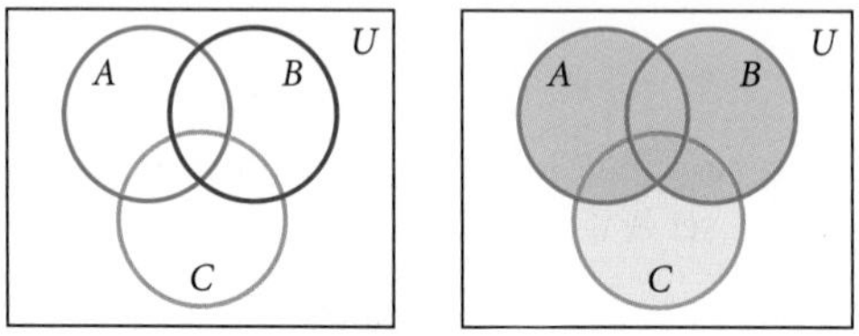

(a) (b)

EXAMPLE 9 Using a Venn Diagram to Illustrate the Equality of Two Sets

Use a Venn diagram to illustrate the following equality:

$$A \cup B = (A \cap \overline{B}) \cup (A \cap B) \cup (\overline{A} \cap B)$$

SOLUTION We begin with Figure 7. There $A \cap \overline{B}$ is the purple region. Now shade the region $A \cap \overline{B}$, $A \cap B$, and $\overline{A} \cap B$, as shown in Figure 8. The union of the three regions in Figure is the set $A \cup B$. See Figure 9.

FIGURE 7

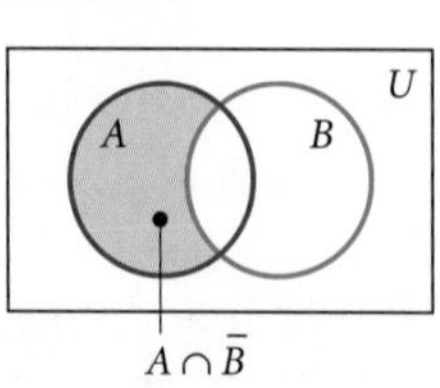

FIGURE 8

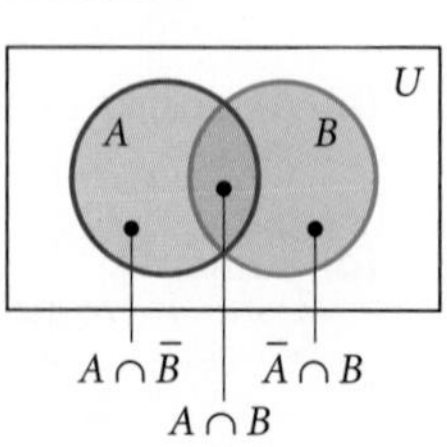

FIGURE 9

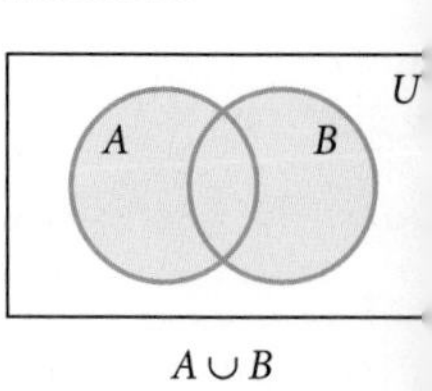

NOW WORK PROBLEMS 29 AND 35.

Look back at Example 7. The answers to parts (c) and (d) are the same, and the answers to parts (e) and (f) are the same. This is no coincidence. It is a consequence of two important properties involving intersections and unions of complements of sets, known as *De Morgan's properties*:

Theorem

De Morgan's Properties

Let A and B be any two sets. Then

$$\text{(a) } \overline{A \cup B} = \overline{A} \cap \overline{B} \qquad \text{(b) } \overline{A \cap B} = \overline{A} \cup \overline{B}$$

EXAMPLE 10 Using a Venn Diagram to Illustrate De Morgan's Properties

Use a Venn diagram to illustrate that $\overline{A \cup B} = \overline{A} \cap \overline{B}$.

SOLUTION First draw two diagrams, as shown in Figures 10(a) and 10(b).

FIGURE 10

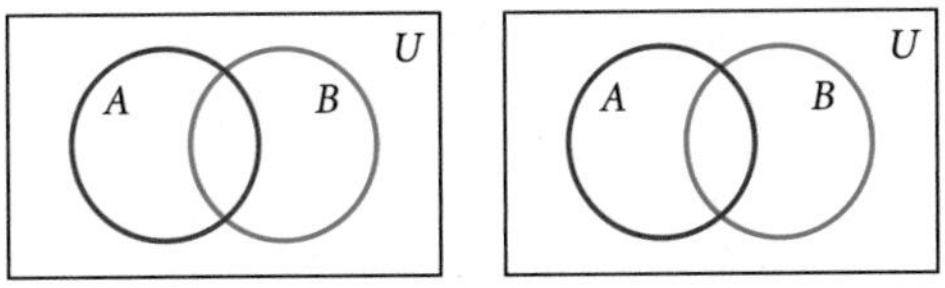

(a) (b)

Use the diagram on the left for $\overline{A \cup B}$ and the one on the right for $\overline{A} \cap \overline{B}$.
Figure 11 illustrates the completed Venn diagrams of these sets.

FIGURE 11

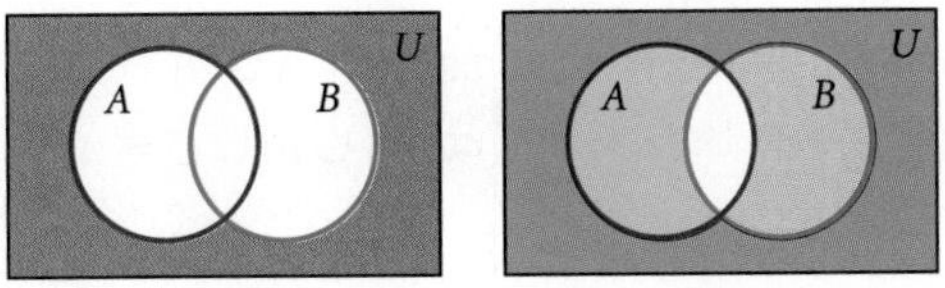

$\overline{A \cup B}$ (a) $\overline{A} \cap \overline{B}$ (b)

In Figure 11(a), $\overline{A \cup B}$ is represented by the region in color, and in Figure 11(b), $\overline{A} \cap \overline{B}$ is represented by the same region. This illustrates that the two sets $\overline{A \cup B}$ and $\overline{A} \cap \overline{B}$ are equal. ■

EXERCISE 7.1 Answers Begin on Page AN–35.

oncepts and Vocabulary

1. Insert $\subset$, $\subseteq$, or $=$ to make a true statement. More than one answer is possible. $\{1, 2, 3, 4\}$_____$\{1, 2, 3, 4\}$

2. Insert $\cup$ or $\cap$ to make a true statement. $\{1, 2, 3, 4\}$_____ $\{1, 3, 5, 7\} = \{1, 2, 3, 4, 5, 7\}$

3. Insert $\cup$ or $\cap$ to make a true statement. $\{1, 2, 3\}$_____ $\{2, 3, 4, 5\} = \{2, 3\}$

4. If $U = \{1, 2, 3, 4, 5\}$, then $\overline{\{1, 2\}} =$ _____.

Skill Building

In Problems 5–16, determine whether the given statement is true or false.

5. $\{1, 3, 2\} = \{2, 1, 3\}$
6. $\{2, 3\} \subseteq \{1, 2, 3\}$
7. $\{6, 7, 9\} \subseteq \{1, 6, 9\}$
8. $\{4, 8, 2\} = \{2, 4, 6, 8\}$
9. $\{6, 7, 9\} \subset \{1, 6, 9\}$
10. $\{4, 8, 2\} \subset \{2, 4, 6, 8\}$
11. $\{1, 2\} \cap \{2, 3, 4\} = \{2\}$
12. $\{2, 3\} \cap \{2, 3, 4\} = \{2, 3, 4\}$
13. $[\{4, 5\} \cap \{1, 2, 3, 4\}] \subseteq \{4\}$
14. $[\{1, 4\} \cup \{2, 3\}] \subseteq \{1, 2, 3, 4\}$
15. $\{1, 2, 3\} \cap \{3, 4, 5\} \subseteq \{3, 4, 5\}$
16. $\{1, 2, 3\} \cup \{3, 4, 5\} \subseteq \{3, 4, 5\}$

In Problems 17–24, write each expression as a single set.

17. $\{1, 2, 3\} \cap \{2, 3, 4, 5\}$
18. $\{0, 1, 3\} \cup \{2, 3, 4\}$
19. $\{1, 2, 3\} \cup \{2, 3, 4, 5\}$
20. $\{0, 1, 2\} \cap \{2, 3, 4\}$
21. $\{2, 4, 6, 8\} \cap \{1, 3, 5, 7\}$
22. $\{2, 4, 6\} \cup \{1, 3, 5\}$
23. $\{a, b, e\} \cup \{d, e, f, g\}$
24. $\{a, e, m\} \cup \{p, o, m\}$

25. If U = universal set = $\{0, 1, 2, 3, 4, 5, 6, 7, 8, 9\}$ and if $A = \{0, 1, 5, 7\}$, $B = \{2, 3, 5, 8\}$, $C = \{5, 6, 9\}$, find
 (a) $A \cup B$ (b) $B \cap C$
 (c) $A \cap B$ (d) $\overline{A \cap B}$
 (e) $\bar{A} \cap \bar{B}$ (f) $A \cup (B \cap A)$
 (g) $(C \cap A) \cap (\bar{A})$ (h) $(A \cap B) \cup (B \cap C)$

26. If U = universal set = $\{1, 2, 3, 4, 5\}$ and if $A = \{3, 5\}$, $B = \{1, 2, 3\}$, $C = \{2, 3, 4\}$, find
 (a) $\bar{A} \cap \bar{B}$ (b) $(A \cup B) \cap C$
 (c) $A \cup (B \cap C)$ (d) $(A \cup B) \cap (A \cup C)$
 (e) $\overline{A \cap C}$ (f) $\overline{A \cup B}$
 (g) $\bar{A} \cup \bar{B}$ (h) $(A \cap B) \cup C$

27. Let U = {All letters of the alphabet}, $A = \{b, c, d\}$, and $B = \{c, e, f, g\}$. List the elements of the sets:
 (a) $A \cup B$ (b) $A \cap B$
 (c) $\bar{A} \cap \bar{B}$ (d) $\bar{A} \cup \bar{B}$

28. Let $U = \{a, b, c, d, e, f\}$, $A = \{b, c\}$, and $B = \{c, d, e\}$. Li the elements of the sets:
 (a) $A \cup B$ (b) $A \cap B$
 (c) $\bar{A}$ (d) $\bar{B}$
 (e) $\overline{A \cap B}$ (f) $\overline{A \cup B}$

In Problems 29–36, use a Venn diagram to illustrate each set.

29. $\bar{A} \cap B$
30. $(\bar{A} \cap \bar{B}) \cup C$
31. $A \cap (A \cup B)$
32. $A \cup (A \cap B)$
33. $(A \cup B) \cap (A \cup C)$
34. $A \cup (B \cap C)$
35. $A = (A \cap B) \cup (A \cap \bar{B})$
36. $B = (A \cap B) \cup (\bar{A} \cap B)$

In Problems 37–40, use a Venn diagram to illustrate each property.

37. $A \cap (B \cup C) = (A \cap B) \cup (A \cap C)$ (Distributive property)
38. $A \cap (A \cup B) = A$ (Absorption property)
39. $\overline{A \cap B} = \bar{A} \cup \bar{B}$ (De Morgan's property)
40. $(A \cup B) \cup C = A \cup (B \cup C)$ (Associative property)

Applications

In Problems 41–46, describe each set in words.

$A = \{x | x$ is a customer of IBM$\}$
$B = \{x | x$ is a secretary employed by IBM$\}$
$C = \{x | x$ is a computer operator at IBM$\}$
$D = \{x | x$ is a stockholder of IBM$\}$
$E = \{x | x$ is a member of the Board of Directors of IBM$\}$

41. $A \cap E$
42. $B \cap D$
43. $A \cup D$
44. $C \cap E$
45. $\bar{A} \cap D$
46. $A \cup \bar{D}$

In Problems 47–52, describe each set in words.

U = {All college students}
M = {All male students}
S = {All students who smoke}
F = {All freshmen}

47. $M \cap S$
48. $M \cup S$
49. $\bar{M} \cup \bar{F}$
50. $\bar{M} \cap \bar{S}$
51. $F \cap S \cap M$
52. $F \cup S \cup M$

53. **U.S. Senate Judiciary Committee** The 111th U.S. Sena Committee on the Judiciary is composed of the following s of senators:

 J = {Leahy, Kohl, Feinstein, Feingold, Sessions, Hatc Grassley, Kyl, Schumer, Durbin, Cardin, Whitehous Klobuchar, Kaufman, Graham, Cornyn, Cobur Specter, Franken}.

 The Administrative Oversight subcommittee is composed the subset

 O = {Whitehouse, Feinstein, Feingold, Schumer, Cardi Kaufman, Franken, Sessions, Grassley, Kyl, Graham}.

 The Antitrust, Competition Policy, and Consumer Rights sul committee is composed of the subset

A = {Kohl, Schumer, Whitehouse, Klobuchar, Kaufman, Specter, Franken, Hatch, Grassley, Cornyn}.

(a) Find $O \cap A$ and explain what it represents.

(b) Find $\overline{O}$ and explain what it represents.

(c) Find $O \cup A$ and explain what it represents.

(d) Find $\overline{O \cup A}$ and explain what it represents.

Source: http://judiciary.senate.gov

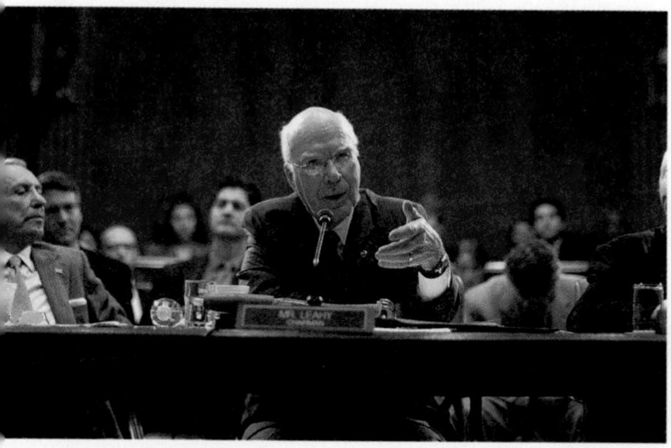

4. **10 Largest Companies** America's 10 largest corporations in 2009, according to *Fortune* magazine, are listed in the following set:

L = {Royal Dutch Shell, Exxon Mobil, Wal-Mart, BP, Chevron, Total, ConocoPhillips, ING Group, Sinopec, Toyota Motor}.

America's 10 most admired companies in 2009, also according to *Fortune* magazine, are listed in the following set:

A = {Apple, Google, Berkshire Hathaway, Johnson & Johnson, Amazon.com, Procter & Gamble, Toyota Motor, Goldman Sachs, Wal-Mart, Coca-Cola}.

(a) Find $L \cap A$ and explain what it represents.

(b) Find $L \cup A$ and explain what it represents.

Source: *Fortune* magazine

55. **Investments** A financial advisor maintains a database of clients and the stocks they own. A search of the database for clients who own stock in Intel Corp. (INTC) yields the following subset:

I = {Black, Bodden, Forbes, Gallaher, Murphy, Petevis, Russell, Smith, Stein, Sutton}.

Another search of the database for clients who own stock in Hewlett Packard (HPO) yields the subset

H = {Bodden, Brown, Earnest, Gallaher, Johnson, Randolph, Rhoades, Sutton}.

(a) Find $I \cup H$ and explain what it represents.

(b) Find $I \cap H$ and explain what it represents.

56. **Used Cars** A used car dealer maintains a database of customers and the vehicles they purchase. A search of the database for customers who purchased a minivan within the past year yields the subset

M = {Ahuja, Bachman, Crawford, Eilers, Martin, McKinney, Pogue, Sheets, Tripp, Yost}.

Another search of the database for clients who purchased a four-door sedan within the past year yields

S = {Arnold, Bachman, Carpenter, Godfrey, McKinney, Nicholson, Sheets, Simpson, Wyatt, Yost}.

(a) Find $M \cup S$ and explain what it represents.

(b) Find $M \cap S$ and explain what it represents.

57. List all the subsets of $\{a, b, c\}$.

58. List all the subsets of $\{a, b, c, d\}$.

iscussion and Writing

. Explain in your own words the concept of *subset*.

60. How would you explain to a fellow student the meaning of *union* and *intersection* of sets?

7.2 The Number of Elements in a Set

OBJECTIVES
1 Use the counting formula (p. 367)
2 Use Venn diagrams to analyze survey data (p. 367)

When we count objects, what we are actually doing is taking each object to be counted and matching each of these objects exactly once to the counting numbers 1, 2, 3, and so on, until no objects remain. Even before numbers had names and symbols assigned to them, this method of counting was used. Prehistoric peoples used rocks to determine how many cattle did not return from pasture. As each cow left, a rock was placed aside. As each cow returned, a rock was removed from the pile. If rocks remained after all the cows returned, it was then known that some cows were missing.

If A is any set, the notation $n(A)$ denotes the number of elements in A. For examp
for the set L of letters in the alphabet,

$$L = \{a, b, c, d, e, f, \dots, x, y, z\}$$

we have $n(L) = 26$.

Also, for the set

$$N = \{1, 2, 3, 4, 5\}$$

we have $n(N) = 5$.

The empty set $\varnothing$ has no elements, so

$$n(\varnothing) = 0$$

If the number of elements in a set is zero or a positive integer, we say that the set
finite. Otherwise, the set is said to be **infinite**. The area of mathematics that deals wi
the study of finite sets is called **finite mathematics**.

EXAMPLE 1 Analyzing Survey Data

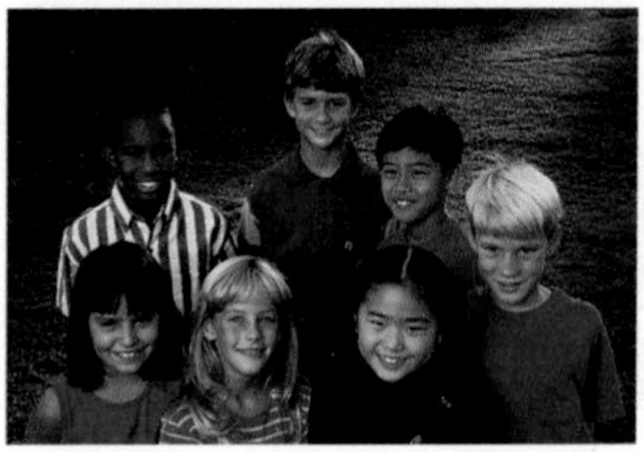

A survey of a group of children indicated there were 25 with brown eyes and 15 wi
black hair.

(a) If 10 children had both brown eyes and black hair, how many children interview
had either brown eyes or black hair?

(b) If 23 childen had neither brown eyes nor black hair, how many children in all we
interviewed?

SOLUTION Let A denote the set of children with brown eyes and B the set of children with bla
hair. Then the data given tell us

$$n(A) = 25 \qquad n(B) = 15$$

(a) Since 10 children had both brown eyes and black hair, we know that $n(A \cap B) = 1$
The number of children with either brown eyes or black hair is $n(A \cup B)$. B
$n(A \cup B)$ cannot be $n(A) + n(B)$, since those with both characteristics would th
be counted twice. To obtain $n(A \cup B)$, we need to subtract those with bo
characteristics from $n(A) + n(B)$ to avoid counting them twice. So,

$$n(A \cup B) = n(A) + n(B) - n(A \cap B) = 25 + 15 - 10 = 30$$

There are 30 children with either brown eyes or black hair.

(b) The sum of the number of children either in A or in B (30) and the number
children neither in A nor in B (23) is the total interviewed. The total number of childr
interviewed is

$$30 + 23 = 53$$

FIGURE 12

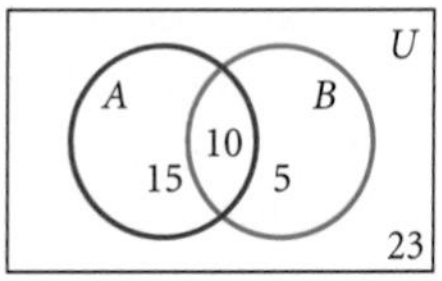

Figure 12 illustrates how a Venn diagram can be used to represent this situation.

In constructing Figure 12, since $n(A \cap B) = 10$, we begin by placing 10 in $A \cap$
Since $n(A) = 25$, A requires 15 more. Similarly, since $n(B) = 15$, B requires 5 mor
Now we can see that $n(A \cup B) = 15 + 10 + 5 = 30$. Since 23 are in neither A nor
we have $n(U) = 15 + 10 + 5 + 23 = 53$.

In Example 1 we discovered the following important relationship:

Theorem

Counting Formula

Let A and B be two finite sets. Then

$$n(A \cup B) = n(A) + n(B) - n(A \cap B) \qquad (1)$$

1 **Use the Counting Formula**

EXAMPLE 2   **Using the Counting Formula**

Let $A = \{a, b, c, d, e\}$, $B = \{a, e, g, u, w, z\}$. Find $n(A)$, $n(B)$, $n(A \cap B)$, and $n(A \cup B)$.

SOLUTION $n(A) = 5$ and $n(B) = 6$. To find $n(A \cap B)$, first find $A \cap B = \{a, e\}$. Then $n(A \cap B) = 2$. Since $A \cup B = \{a, b, c, d, e, g, u, w, z\}$, then $n(A \cup B) = 9$. This checks with the Counting Formula

$$n(A \cup B) = n(A) + n(B) - n(A \cap B) = 5 + 6 - 2 = 9 \qquad \blacksquare$$

NOW WORK PROBLEM 9.

2 **Use Venn Diagrams to Analyze Survey Data**

EXAMPLE 3   **Analyzing a Consumer Survey Using Venn Diagrams**

In a survey of 75 consumers, 12 indicated they were going to buy a new car, 18 said they were going to buy a new refrigerator, and 24 said they were going to buy a new stove. Of these, 6 were going to buy both a car and a refrigerator, 4 were going to buy a car and a stove, and 10 were going to buy a stove and refrigerator. One person indicated he was going to buy all three items.

(a) How many were going to buy none of these items?

(b) How many were going to buy only a car?

(c) How many were going to buy only a stove?

(d) How many were going to buy only a refrigerator?

(e) How many were going to buy a stove and refrigerator but not a car?

SOLUTION   Denote the sets of people buying cars, refrigerators, and stoves by C, R, and S, respectively. U will denote the universal set. Then we know from the data given that

$n(C) = 12$	12 buy cars.
$n(R) = 18$	18 buy refrigerators.
$n(S) = 24$	24 buy stoves.
$n(C \cap R) = 6$	6 buy both a car and a refrigerator.
$n(C \cap S) = 4$	4 buy both a car and a stove.
$n(S \cap R) = 10$	10 buy both a stove and a refrigerator.
$n(C \cap R \cap S) = 1$	1 buys all three.
$n(U) = 75$	75 consumers are surveyed.

Use the information above and put it into a Venn diagram using three interlocking circles labeled C, R, and S. Beginning with the fact that $n(C \cap R \cap S) = 1$, place a 1 in that set, as shown in Figure 13(a). Now we work our way out.

FIGURE 13

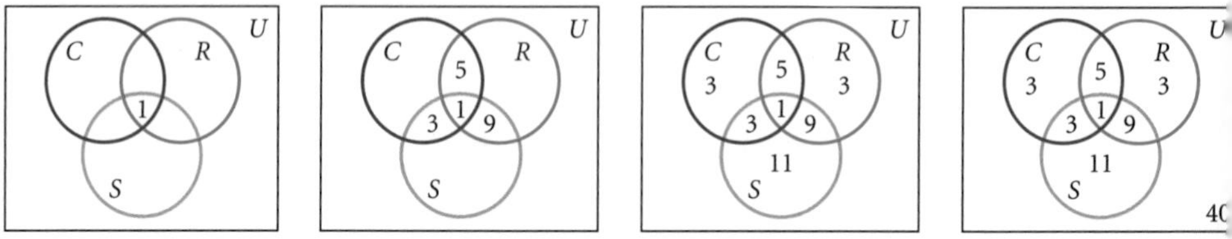

(a) (b) (c) (d)

Since $n(C \cap R) = 6$, $n(C \cap S) = 4$, and $n(S \cap R) = 10$, we place $6 - 1 = 5$ in the proper region (giving a total of 6 in the set $C \cap R$). Similarly, we place 3 and 9 in the proper regions for the sets $C \cap S$ and $S \cap R$. See Figure 13(b).

Now $n(C) = 12$, and 9 of these 12 are already accounted for, so 3 remain. Also $n(R) = 18$ with 15 accounted for so 3 remain, and $n(S) = 24$ with 13 accounted for so 11 remain. See Figure 13(c).

Finally, the number in $\overline{C \cup R \cup S}$ is the total of 75 less those accounted for in C, R and S, namely, $3 + 5 + 1 + 3 + 3 + 9 + 11 = 35$. That is,

$$n(\overline{C \cup R \cup S}) = 75 - 35 = 40$$

See Figure 13(d).

From this figure, we can conclude that

(a) 40 were going to buy none of the items;

(b) 3 were going to buy only a car;

(c) 11 were going to buy only a stove;

(d) 3 were going to buy only a refrigerator;

(e) 9 were going to buy a stove and refrigerator, not a car.

NOW WORK PROBLEM 19.

EXAMPLE 4 Analyzing Data

In a survey of 10,281 people, the following data were obtained:

Single: 3490	Single males:	1745	Single male over 18:	239
Male: 5822	Over 18 and male:	859		
Over 18: 4722	Over 18 and single:	1341		

The data are inconsistent. Why?

SOLUTION Denote the set of people who were single by S, male by M, and over 18 by H. Then we know that

$n(S) = 3490$	3490 are single.
$n(M) = 5822$	5822 are male.
$n(H) = 4722$	4722 are over 18.
$n(S \cap M) = 1745$	1745 are single and male.
$n(H \cap M) = 859$	859 are males over 18.
$n(H \cap S) = 1341$	1341 are single over 18.
$n(H \cap M \cap S) = 239$	239 are single, male, and over 18.
$n(U) = 10{,}281$	10,281 are surveryed.

GURE 14

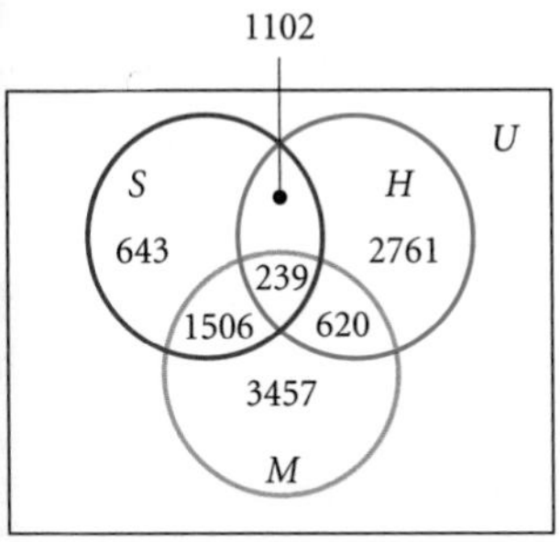

Construct the Venn diagram shown in Figure 14. Then

$$n(S \cup H \cup M) = 239 + 1102 + 620 + 1506 + 3457 + 643 + 2761 = 10{,}328$$

But this number exceeds the number of people surveyed, 10, 281. This means the data are inconsistent. ■

NOW WORK PROBLEM 27.

EXERCISE 7.2 Answers Begin on Page AN–35.

oncepts and Vocabulary

1. ***True or False*** If A and B are sets, then $n(A \cup B) = n(A) + n(B) + n(A \cap B)$.

2. $n(\{1, 2, 3, 4\}) =$ _____

kill Building

n Problems 3–8, use the sets $A = \{1, 2, 3, 4, 5, 6\}$ and $B = \{2, 4, 6, 8\}$ to find the number of elements in each set.

3. A
4. B
5. $A \cap B$
6. $A \cup B$
7. $(A \cap B) \cup A$
8. $(B \cap A) \cup B$

9. Find $n(A \cup B)$, given that $n(A) = 4$, $n(B) = 3$, and $n(A \cap B) = 2$.

0. Find $n(A \cup B)$, given that $n(A) = 14$, $n(B) = 11$, and $n(A \cap B) = 6$.

1. Find $n(A \cap B)$, given that $n(A) = 5$, $n(B) = 4$, and $n(A \cup B) = 7$.

2. Find $n(A \cap B)$, given that $n(A) = 8$, $n(B) = 9$, and $n(A \cup B) = 16$.

3. Find $n(A)$, given that $n(B) = 8$, $n(A \cap B) = 4$, and $n(A \cup B) = 14$.

4. Find $n(B)$, given that $n(A) = 10$, $n(A \cap B) = 5$, and $n(A \cup B) = 29$.

5. **Car Options** Motors, Inc., manufactured 325 cars with a GPS system, 216 with satellite radio, and 89 with both of these options. How many cars were manufactured if every car has at least one of these options?

16. **College Classes** Suppose that out of 1500 first-year students at a certain college, 350 are taking history, 300 are taking mathematics, and 270 are taking both history and mathematics. How many first-year students are taking history or mathematics?

In Problems 17–26, use the data in the figure to answer each question.

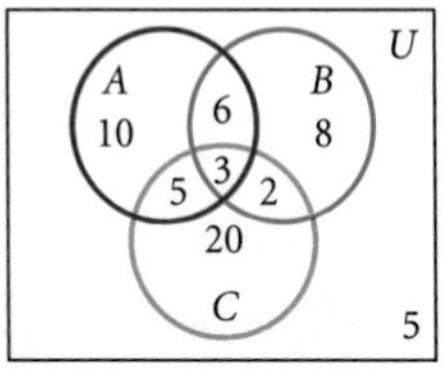

17. How many elements are in set A?
18. How many elements are in set B?
19. How many elements are in A or B?
20. How many elements are in B or C?

21. How many elements are in A but not B?

22. How many elements are in B but not C?

23. How many elements are in A or B or C?

24. How many elements are in neither A nor B nor C?

25. How many elements are in A and B and C?

26. How many elements are in U?

Applications

27. Single-Parent Households The table shows the number of single-parent households (in thousands) by marital status of the parent and geographic region in 2009.

	Northeast	Midwest	South	West
Maintained by Father				
Never married	99	132	174	105
Divorced	117	202	310	196
Separated	58	52	138	70
Widowed	19	18	33	20
Maintained by Mother				
Never married	854	1001	1782	790
Divorced	436	72	1279	684
Separated	355	301	833	459
Widowed	57	89	156	74

Source: U.S. Census Bureau, Current Population Survey, 2009 Annual Social and Economic Supplement

(a) How many households maintained by a mother are in the South?

(b) How many households in the Midwest are maintained by a divorced parent?

(c) How many households are maintained by a father who was never married or widowed?

28. The Venn diagram illustrates the number of seniors (S), female students (F), and students on the dean's list (D) at a small western college. Describe each number in terms of the sets S, F, or D.

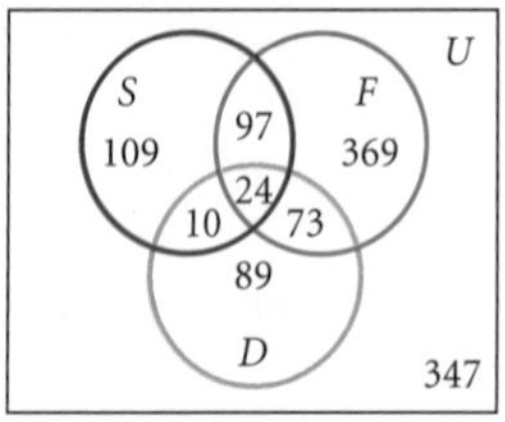

29. Civilian Employment The table shows seasonally adjusted employment figures (in thousands) by gender for U.S. civilians ages 20 years and older in March 2010.

	Male	Female
Employed	70,913	63,495
Unemployed	7882	5532
Not in Labor Force	27,403	44,947

Source: Bureau of Labor Statistics, March 2010

Find

(a) The number of U.S. civilians 20 years or older who a unemployed.

(b) The number of U.S. civilians 20 years or older who a unemployed or not in the labor force.

(c) The number of U.S. civilians 20 years or older who a female or employed.

(d) The number of U.S. civilians 20 years or older who a male but not in the labor force.

30. Military Personnel The table shows the number of active-du military personnel by branch of service, officer/enlisted statu and gender in 2008.

	Male	Female
Army		
Officer	74,000	13,500
Enlisted	392,000	59,700
Navy		
Officer	44,000	7700
Enlisted	235,000	41,400
Marine Corps		
Officer	19,000	1200
Enlisted	167,000	11,100
Air Force		
Officer	53,000	11,900
Enlisted	207,000	51,400

Source: www.census.gov/compendia/statab/cats/national security_veterans_affairs/military_personnel_and_expenditur .html. Table 498. Department of Defense Personnel: 1960 2008

Find

(a) The number of military personnel who are female Nav officers or female Marine Corps officers.

(b) The number of military personnel who are enlisted in th Army or Air Force.

(c) The number of military personnel who are female c enlisted.

(d) The number of military personnel who are neithe officers nor male.

. **Employment Analysis** In its January 1, 2010 Employment Analysis Summary, a community college provided the following table, which shows the number of layoffs by employment category, gender, and race (8/01/2004–7/31/2005).

Employment Category	White Male	White Female	Black Male	Black Female	Hispanic Male	Hispanic Female	Other Male	Other Female
Executive Managerial	5	3	1	1	0	0	1	0
Faculty	30	31	2	3	4	1	9	4
Professional Nonfaculty	54	76	5	5	2	6	3	10
Secretarial/Clerical	0	15	0	3	0	0	0	0
Technical/Paraprofessional	2	1	0	0	0	0	0	0
Qualified Crafts	8	2	0	0	1	0	1	0
Service/Maintenance	20	6	3	0	4	1	0	0

Find

(a) The number of layoffs who were executive managerial or faculty or professional nonfaculty.

(b) The number of layoffs who were female.

(c) The number of layoffs who were black female or faculty.

(d) The number of layoffs who were white male or executive managerial.

. **Industry Type and Location** Suppose 250 domestic CEOs were surveyed about their company's industry type and geographic location in the United States. The CEOs were allowed to choose only one industry type (manufacturing, communications, or finance) and one location (Northeast, Southeast, Midwest, or West). The results are given below.

	Northeast	Southeast	Midwest	West
Manufacturing	37	8	27	15
Communications	35	23	15	20
Finance	30	12	10	18

Find

(a) The number of CEOs whose response was not Southeast.

(b) The number of CEOs whose response was Communications or West.

(c) The number of CEOs whose response was Northeast but not Manufacturing.

(d) The number of CEOs whose response was Manufacturing or Communications or Midwest or West.

3. **Fitness Center** A fitness club is considering the purchase of additional exercise bikes and stair steppers for its cardiovascular room. Before deciding on its purchases, the club surveyed 250 of its members about the types of equipment they use regularly. The results follow:

170 use an exercise bike regularly
119 use a stair stepper regularly
67 use both regularly

(a) Draw a Venn diagram to illustrate this application.

(b) Of the 250 surveyed, how many members use an exercise bike or a stair stepper regularly?

(c) How many members use an exercise bike regularly but not a stair stepper?

(d) How many members use a stair stepper regularly but not an exercise bike?

(e) How many members use neither an exercise bike nor a stair stepper regularly?

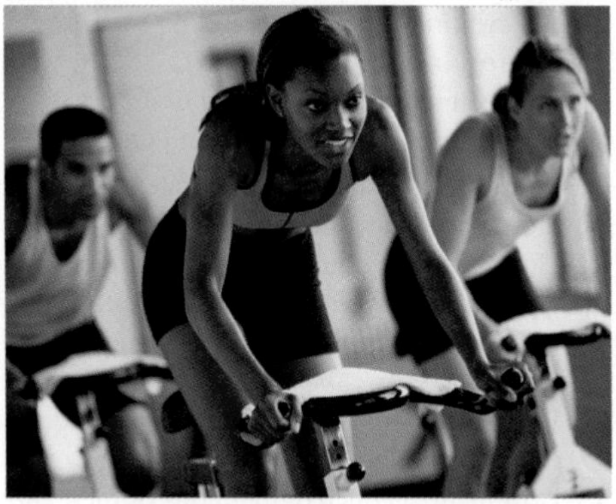

34. **Appetizers** A restaurant is considering an update to its list of appetizers by adding mozzarella sticks and onion rings to its menu. Before making the additions, the restaurant surveys 325 patrons about the appetizers they enjoy. The results follow:

218 enjoy mozzarella sticks
173 enjoy onion rings
126 enjoy both

(a) Draw a Venn diagram to illustrate this application.

(b) Of the 325 surveyed, how many patrons enjoy mozzarella sticks or onion rings?

(c) How many patrons enjoy mozzarella sticks but not onion rings?
(d) How many patrons enjoy onion rings but not mozzarella sticks?
(e) How many patrons enjoy neither mozzarella sticks nor onion rings?

35. Investments A financial advisor maintains a database on his 963 clients and their investments. A search of the database for clients who own stocks in the companies General Electric (GE), Ford Motor (F), and 3M (MMM) yields the following results:

142 clients own GE
123 clients own F
107 clients own MMM
31 clients own GE and F
25 clients own GE and MMM
19 clients own F and MMM
5 clients own all three

(a) Draw a Venn diagram to illustrate this situation.
(b) How many clients own only GE?
(c) How many clients own only F?
(d) How many clients own only MMM?
(e) How many clients own GE or MMM but not F?
(f) How many clients own GE and MMM but not F?
(g) How many clients own none of these three stocks?

36. Tax Returns One year, an accountant prepared individual income tax returns for 439 clients. For these individual tax returns, completion of the following schedules was required:

298 required schedule A (itemized deductions)
256 required schedule B (interest and ordinary dividends)
167 required schedule C (business income)
212 required schedules A and B
87 required schedules A and C
61 required schedules B and C
54 required schedules A, B, and C

(a) Draw a Venn diagram to illustrate this situation.
(b) How many individual tax returns required only schedule A?
(c) How many individual tax returns required only schedule B?
(d) How many individual tax returns required only schedule C?
(e) How many individual tax returns required schedules A or C but not B?
(f) How many individual tax returns required schedules A and C but not B?
(g) How many clients required none of these three schedules?

37. At a small midwestern college:

31 female seniors were on the dean's list
62 women were on the dean's list who were not seniors
45 male seniors were on the dean's list
87 female seniors were not on the dean's list
96 male seniors were not on the dean's list
275 women were not seniors and were not on the dean's list
89 men were on the dean's list who were not seniors
227 men were not seniors and were not on the dean's list

(a) How many were seniors?
(b) How many were women?
(c) How many were on the dean's list?
(d) How many were seniors on the dean's list?
(e) How many were female seniors?
(f) How many were women on the dean's list?
(g) How many were students at the college?

38. Survey Analysis In a survey of 75 business travelers, it wa found that of three daily newspaper, *New York Times, Wa Street Journal,* and *USA Today*

23 read New York *Times*
18 read *Wall Street Journal*
14 read *USA Today*
10 read *New York Times* and *Wall Street Journal*
9 read *New York Times* and *USA Today*
8 read *Wall Street Journal* and *USA Today*
5 read all three

(a) How many read none of these three magazines?
(b) How many read *New York Times* alone?
(c) How many read *Wall Street Journal* alone?
(d) How many read *USA Today?*
(e) How many read neither *New York Times* nor *Wall Stre Journal?*
(f) How many read *New York Times* or *Wall Street Journal* o both?

39. Car Sales Of the cars sold during the month of July, 90 ha heated seats, 100 had GPS, and 75 had satellite radio. Five cars ha all three of these extras. Twenty cars had none of these extra Twenty cars had only heated seats; 60 cars had only GPS; and 30 ca had only satellite radio. Ten cars had both GPS and satellite radi
(a) How many cars had both satellite radio and heated seat
(b) How many had both GPS and heated seats?
(c) How many had neither satellite radio nor GPS?
(d) How many cars were sold in July?
(e) How many had GPS or heated seats or both?

40. Incorrect Information A staff member at a large engineerin school was presenting data to show that the students the received a liberal education as well as a scientific one. "Look at ou record," she said. "Out of our senior class of 500 students, 281 a taking English, 196 are taking English and history, 87 are takin history and a foreign language, 143 are taking a foreign languag and English, and 36 are taking all of these." She was fired. Why

41. Blood Classification Blood is classified as being eithe Rh-positive or Rh-negative and according to type. If bloo contains an A antigen, it is type A; if it has a B antigen, it is type B if it has both A and B antigens, it is type AB; and if it has neithe antigen, it is type O. Use a Venn diagram to illustrate thes possibilities. How many different possibilities are there?

42. Survey Analysis A survey of 52 families from a suburb o Chicago indicated that there was a total of 241 children belo the age of 18. Of these, 109 were male; 132 were below the ag of 11; 143 had played Little League; 69 males were below th age of 11; 45 females under 11 had played Little League; and 3 males under 11 had played Little League.
(a) How many children over 11 and under 18 had playe Little League?
(b) How many females under 11 did not play Little League

3. **Survey Analysis** Of 100 personal computer users surveyed: 27 use HPs; 35 use Macs, 35 use Dell, 10 use both HPs and Macs, 10 use both HPs and Dell, 10 use both Macs and Dell, 3 use all three; and 30 use another computer brand. How many people exclusively use one of the three brands mentioned, that is, only HPs or only Macs or only Dell?

44. List all the subsets of $\{a, b, c\}$. How many are there?

45. List all the subsets of $\{a, b, c, d\}$. How many are there?

7.3 The Multiplication Principle

OBJECTIVES 1 Use the Multiplication Principle (p. 373)

1 Use the Multiplication Principle

EXAMPLE 1 Counting the Number of Possible Meals

The fixed-price dinner at Mabenka Restaurant provides the following choices:

Appetizer: soup or salad
Entree: baked chicken, broiled beef patty, baby beef liver, or roast beef au jus
Dessert: ice cream or cheesecake

How many different meals can be ordered?

SOLUTION Ordering such a meal requires three separate decisions:

Choose an Appetizer	Choose an Entree	Choose a Dessert
2 choices	4 choices	2 choices

Look at the **tree diagram** in Figure 15. We see that, for each choice of appetizer, there are 4 choices of entrees. And for each of these $2 \cdot 4 = 8$ choices, there are 2 choices for dessert. A total of

$$2 \cdot 4 \cdot 2 = 16$$

different meals can be ordered.

FIGURE 15

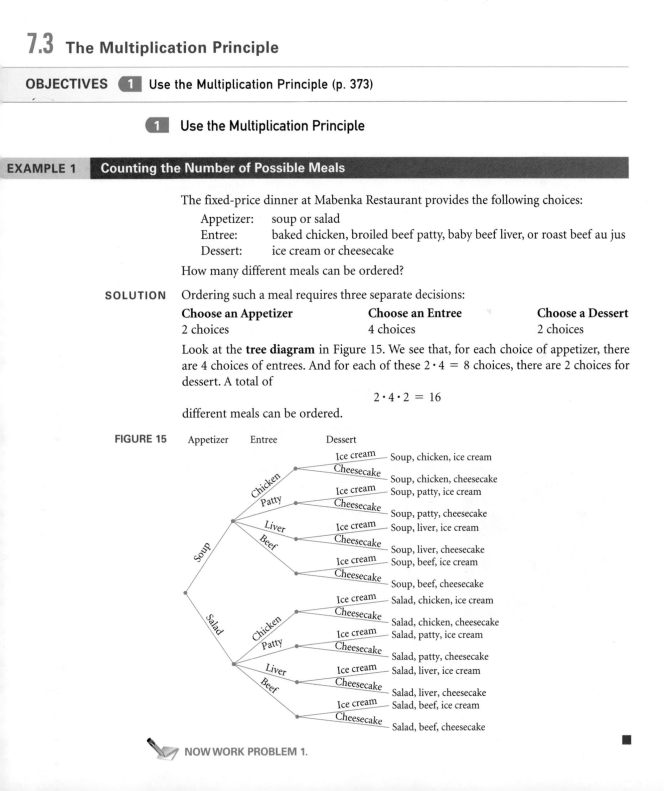

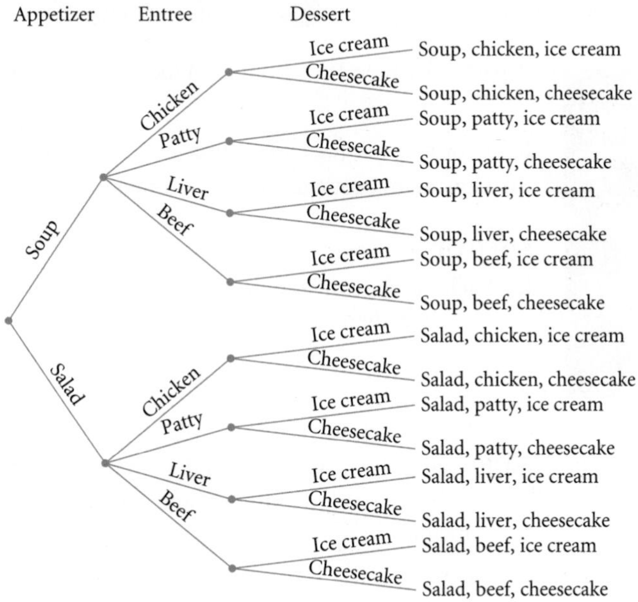

■

NOW WORK PROBLEM 1.

Example 1 demonstrates a general principle of counting.

Theorem

Multiplication Principle of Counting

If a task consists of a sequence of choices in which there are p selections for the first choice, q selections for the second choice, r selections for the third choice, and so on, then the task of making these selections can be done in

$$p \cdot q \cdot r \cdot \cdots$$

different ways.

EXAMPLE 2 Forming Codes

How many two-symbol code words can be formed if the first symbol is a letter (uppercase) and the second symbol is a digit?

SOLUTION It sometimes helps to begin by listing some of the possibilities. The code consists of a letter (uppercase) followed by a digit, so some possibilities are A1, A2, B3, X0, and so on. The task consists of making two selections. The first selection requires choosing an uppercase letter (26 choices) and the second task requires choosing a digit (10 choices). By the Multiplication Principle, there are

$$26 \cdot 10 = 260$$

different code words of the type described.

NOW WORK PROBLEM 3.

EXAMPLE 3 Combination Locks

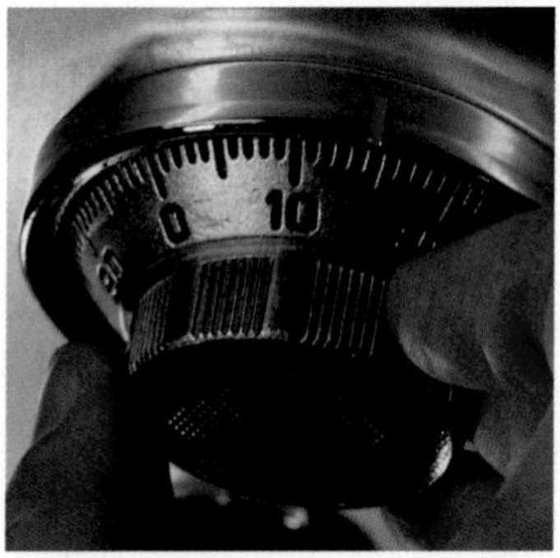

A particular type of combination lock has 100 numbers on it.

(a) How many sequences of three numbers can be formed to open the lock?

(b) How many sequences can be formed if no number is repeated?

SOLUTION

(a) Each of the three numbers can be chosen in 100 ways. By the Multiplication Principle, there are

$$100 \cdot 100 \cdot 100 = 1{,}000{,}000$$

different sequences.

(b) If no number can be repeated, then there are 100 choices for the first number, only 99 for the second number, and 98 for the third number. By the Multiplication Principle, there are

$$100 \cdot 99 \cdot 98 = 970{,}200$$

different sequences.

EXAMPLE 4 Counting the Number of Ways Four Offices Can Be Filled

In a city election there are four candidates for mayor, three candidates for vice-mayor, six candidates for treasurer, and two for secretary. In how many ways can these four offices be filled?

SOLUTION The task of filling an office can be divided into four choices:

Select a mayor	Select a vice-mayor	Select a treasurer	Select a secretary

Corresponding to each of the four possible mayors, there are three vice-mayors. These two offices can be filled in $4 \cdot 3 = 12$ different ways. Also, corresponding to each of these 12 possibilities, we have six different choices for treasurer—giving $12 \cdot 6 = 72$ different possibilities. Finally, to each of these 72 possibilities there correspond two choices for secretary. In all, these offices can be filled in $4 \cdot 3 \cdot 6 \cdot 2 = 144$ different ways. A partial illustration is given by the tree diagram in Figure 16.

FIGURE 16

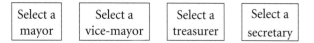

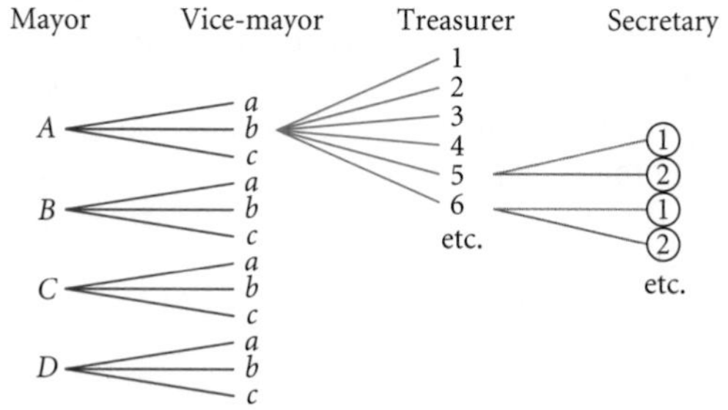

■

NOW WORK PROBLEM 11.

EXAMPLE 5 License Plates in South Carolina

Standard license plates in the state of South Carolina consist of three letters of the alphabet followed by three digits.

(a) The South Carolina system will allow how many possible license plates?

(b) Of these, how many will have all their digits distinct?

(c) How many will have distinct digits and distinct letters?

SOLUTION **(a)** There are six positions on the license plate to be filled, the first three by letters and the last three by digits. Each of the first three positions can be filled in any one of 26 ways, while each of the remaining three positions can each be filled in any of 10 ways. The total number of license plates, by the Multiplication Principle, is then

$$26 \cdot 26 \cdot 26 \cdot 10 \cdot 10 \cdot 10 = 17{,}576{,}000$$

(b) Here the tasks involved in filling the digit positions are slightly different. The first digit can be any one of 10, but the second digit can be only any one of 9 (we cannot duplicate the first digit); there are only 8 choices for the third digit (we cannot duplicate either the first or the second). By the Multiplication Principle, there are

$$26 \cdot 26 \cdot 26 \cdot 10 \cdot 9 \cdot 8 = 12{,}654{,}720$$

plates with no repeated digit.

(c) If the letters and digits are each to be distinct, then the total number of possib
license plates is

$$26 \cdot 25 \cdot 24 \cdot 10 \cdot 9 \cdot 8 = 11{,}232{,}000$$

NOW WORK PROBLEM 21.

EXERCISE 7.3 Answers Begin on Page AN–36.

Skill Building

1. **Shirts and Ties** A man has 5 shirts and 3 ties. How many different shirt and tie arrangements can he wear?

2. **Blouses and Skirts** A woman has 5 blouses and 8 skirts. How many different outfits can she wear?

3. **Four-Digit Numbers** How many four-digit numbers can be formed using the digits 0, 1, 2, 3, 4, 5, 6, 7, 8, and 9 if the first digit cannot be 0? Repeated digits are allowed.

4. **Five-Digit Numbers** How many five-digit numbers can be formed using the digits 0, 1, 2, 3, 4, 5, 6, 7, 8, and 9 if the first digit cannot be 0 or 1? Repeated digits are allowed.

5. There are 2 roads between towns A and B. There are 4 roads between towns B and C. How many different routes may one travel from town A to town C through town B?

6. REIT, Inc. wants to build a complex consisting of a factory, office building, and warehouse. If the building contractor has 3 different kinds of factories, 2 different office buildings, and 4 different warehouses, how many models must be built to show all possibilities to REIT, Inc.?

7. **Car Displays** Cars, Inc., has 3 different car models and 8 color schemes. If you are one of the dealers, how many cars must you display to show each possibility?

8. **Choosing an Outfit** A man has 3 pairs of shoes, 8 pairs of socks, 4 pairs of slacks, and 9 sweaters. How many outfits can he wear?

9. A house has 3 outside doors and 12 windows. In how man ways can a person enter the house through a window and ex through a door?

10. **License Plates** How many license plates consisting of 2 lette (uppercase) followed by 2 digits are possible?

11. **Lunch Selections** A restaurant offers 3 different salads, different main courses, 10 different desserts, and 4 differer drinks. How many different lunches—each consisting of salad, a main course, a dessert, and a drink—are possible?

12. **Arranging Books** Five different mathematics books are to b arranged on a student's desk. How many arrangements ar possible?

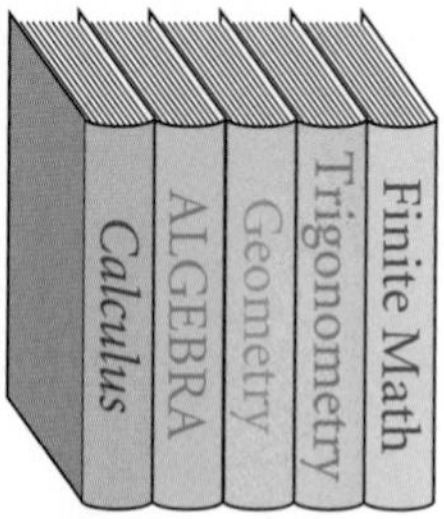

13. How many ways can 6 people be seated in a row of 6 seats?

14. **Codes** How many 4-letter code words are possible using th first 6 letters of the alphabet with no letters repeated? Hov many codes are there when letters are allowed to repeat?

Applications

In Problems 15–18, use the following discussion.

Students log on to the California Virtual Campus with a user name consisting of eight characters: four uppercase letters of the alphabet followed by four digits.

Source: California Virtual Campus.

15. **User Names** How many user names are theoretically possible for this system?

16. **User Names** How many user names have no repeated letters or digits?

17. **User Names** How many user names have no matching adjacent letters or digits?

18. **User Names** How many user names begin with A and end with 9?

19. **Baseball** In the World Series, the National League champion plays the American League champion. There are 16 teams in the National League and 14 teams in the American League How many different theoretical match-ups of two teams ar possible in the World Series?

Source: Major League Baseball, 2010

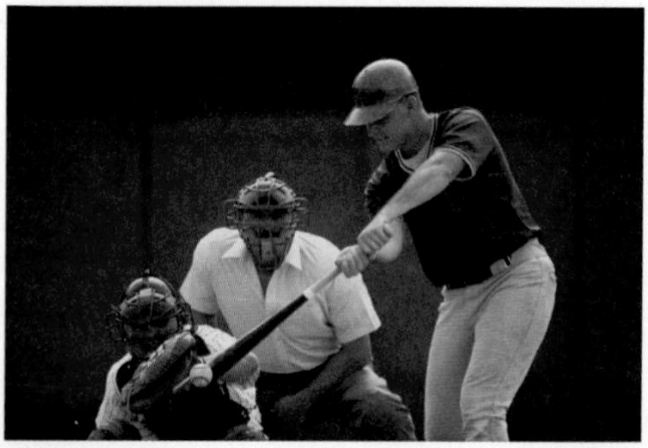

. **New Car Options** Marjorie is purchasing a new 2010 Honda Accord LX sedan and must choose her exterior accessories. There are four categories of accessories she may choose from (wheels, cargo handling, spoilers, and exterior protection) and she will only select one option from each category. If there are 3 types of wheels, 3 types of cargo handling, 2 types of spoilers, and 7 types of exterior protection, how many different accessory packages are possible?

Source: American Honda Motor Co.

1. **Car Insurance** Adam is purchasing car insurance for his new car and needs to decide on the protection for his vehicle. His insurance company offers coverage for comprehensive, collision, rental reimbursement, and towing/labor and Adam must select a level for each coverage. There are 9 levels of comprehensive, 9 levels for collision, 3 levels for rental reimbursement, and 2 levels for towing/labor. How many different types of vehicle coverage can Adam get?

2. **Car Insurance** Shawn is purchasing a used car for college and needs to obtain liability insurance. His insurance company offers 8 levels for bodily injury coverage and 6 levels for property damage coverage. If Shawn must carry both types of coverage, how many different liability policies does he have to choose from?

3. **Pharmaceutical Sales** A pharmaceutical sales rep will be responsible for 3 different products. He must select 1 pain reliever, 1 blood pressure medicine, and 1 antifungal medicine. If his company manufactures 5 types of pain relievers, 2 types of blood pressure medicine, and 3 types of antifungal medicine, how many different sales portfolios are possible?

4. **Pharmaceutical Sales** A pharmaceutical sales rep will be responsible for 4 different products. She must select 1 pain reliever, 1 antidepressant, 1 allergy medicine, and 1 high cholesterol medicine. If her company manufactures 7 types of pain relievers, 3 types of antidepressants, 6 types of allergy medicine, and 2 types of cholesterol medicine, how many different sales portfolios are possible?

25. **Ordering Pizza** After a night of studying for exams, David decides to order a pizza through the Domino's® Web site. He must choose among 4 different sizes, 2 different crusts, and 25 different toppings. How many different one-topping pizzas are possible?

Source: www.dominos.com

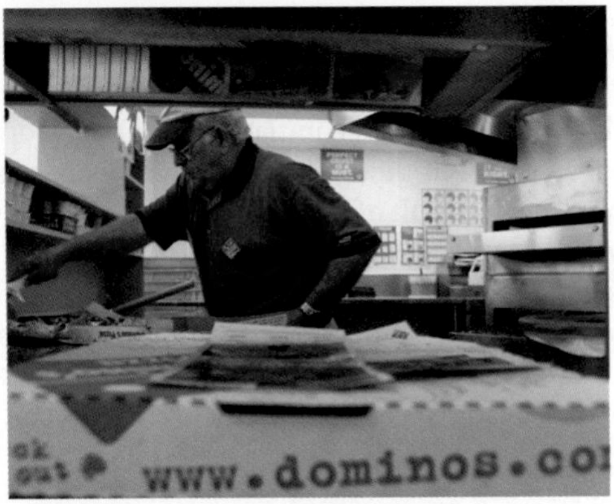

26. **Ordering Pizza** Betty and Dorothy plan to order pizza, soda, and a side item for dinner on movie night. They can choose from 9 specialty pizzas, 3 types of soda, and 11 side items. How many different meals are possible?

27. **Television Schedule** A television network had 19 comedy pilots to fill 3 remaining time slots in the Fall 2010 lineup: 9 P.M. Tuesday, 9:30 P.M. Tuesday, and 8 P.M. Thursday. How many different comedy lineups were possible?

28. **Television Schedule** A television network had 13 drama pilots to fill 5 remaining time slots in the Fall 2010 lineup: 10 P.M. Monday, 10 P.M. Wednesday, 10 P.M. Thursday, 9 P.M. Friday, 10 P.M. Sunday. How many different drama lineups were possible?

29. **Itineraries** A third-party auditor is hired by a fast-food chain to conduct audits at its 10 franchise stores. How many different ways can the audits be scheduled?

30. **Itineraries** The auditor in the previous problem must visit the store that is closest first and decides to visit the store that is furthest away last. If the remaining stores can be visited in any order, how many different ways can the audits be scheduled?

31. **Telephone Numbers** Find the number of 7-digit telephone numbers

    (a) With no repeated digits (lead 0 is allowed)

    (b) With no repeated digits (lead 0 not allowed)

    (c) With repeated digits allowed including a lead 0

32. **Ranking Candidates** How many ways are there to rank 7 candidates who apply for a job?

33. **Arranging Letters**

    (a) How many different ways are there to arrange the 7 letters in the word PROBLEM?

    (b) If we insist that the letter P comes first, how many ways are there?

    (c) If we insist that the letter P comes first and the letter M last, how many ways are there?

34. **Testing** On a math test there are 10 multiple-choice questions with 4 possible answers and 15 true–false questions. In how many possible ways can the 25 questions be answered?

35. **License Plate Possibilities** How many different license plate numbers can be made using 2 letters followed by 4 digits, if

    (a) Letters and digits may be repeated?

    (b) Letters may be repeated, but digits are not repeated?

    (c) Neither letters nor digits may be repeated?

36. **Security** A system has 7 switches, each of which may be either open or closed. The state of the system is described by indicating for each switch whether it is open or closed. How many different states of the system are there?

37. **Product Choice** An automobile manufacturer produces 3 different models. Models A and B can come in any of 3 body styles; model C can come in only 2 body styles. Each car also comes in either black or green. How many distinguishable car types are there?

38. Telephone Numbers How many 7-digit numbers can be formed if the first digit cannot be 0 or 9 and if the last digit is greater than or equal to 2 and less than or equal to 3? Repeated digits are allowed.

39. Home Choices A contractor constructs homes with 5 different choices of exterior finish, 3 different roof arrangements, and 4 different window designs. How many different types of homes can be built?

40. License Plate Possibilities A license plate consists of 1 letter, excluding O and I, followed by a 4-digit number that cannot have a 0 in the lead position. How many different plates are possible?

41. Bytes Using only the digits 0 and 1, how many different numbers consisting of 8 digits can be formed?

42. Stock Portfolios As a financial planner, you are asked to select one stock from each of the following groups: 8 DOW stocks, 15 NASDAQ stocks, and 4 global stocks. How many different portfolios are possible?

43. Combination Locks A combination lock has 50 numbers on it. To open it, you turn counterclockwise to a number, then rotate clockwise to a second number, and then counterclockwise to the third number. How many different lock combinations are there?

44. Opinion Polls An opinion poll is to be conducted amo college students. Eight multiple-choice questions, each wi 3 possible answers, will be asked. In how many different wa can a student complete the poll if exactly one response is give to each question?

45. Path Selection in a Maze The maze below is constructed s that a rat must pass through a series of one-way doors. Ho many different paths are there from start to finish?

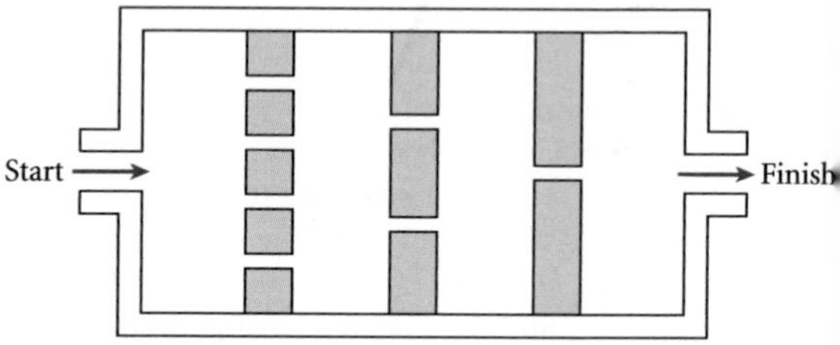

46. Codes How many 3-letter code words are possible using th first 10 letters of the alphabet if

(a) No letter can be repeated?

(b) Letters can be repeated?

(c) Adjacent letters cannot be the same?

7.4 Sample Spaces and the Assignment of Probabilities

OBJECTIVES

1. Find a sample space (p. 380)
2. Assign probabilities (p. 382)
3. Construct a probability model (p. 382)
4. Find probabilities involving equally likely outcomes (p. 383)

Introduction

Certain phenomena in the real world may be considered *chance phenomena*. These phenomena do not always produce the same observed outcome, and the outcome of any given observation of the phenomena may not be predictable. But they have a long-range behavior known as *statistical regularity*. Some examples of such cases, called *random events*, are given next.

- Tossing a fair coin gives a result that is either heads or tails. For any one throw, we cannot predict the result, although it is obvious that it is determined by definite causes (such as the initial velocity of the coin, the initial angle of the throw, and the surface on which the coin rests). Even though some of these causes can be controlled, we cannot predetermine the result of any particular toss. The result of tossing a coin is a *random event*.

  Although we cannot predict the result of any particular toss of the coin, if we perform a long sequence of tosses, we expect that the number of heads is approximately equal to the number of tails. That is, it seems *reasonable* to say that in any toss of this fair coin, heads or tails is *equally likely* to occur. As a result, we might *assign a probability* of $\frac{1}{2}$ for obtaining a head (or tail) on a particular toss.

- In throwing an ordinary die, we cannot predict the result with certainty. The result of throwing a die is a *random event*. We do know that one of the faces 1, 2, 3, 4, 5, or 6 will occur.

  The appearance of any particular face of the die is an *outcome*. If we perform a long series of tosses, any face is as *likely* to occur as any other, provided the die is fair. Here we might *assign a probability* of $\frac{1}{6}$ for obtaining a particular face.
- The sex of a newborn baby is either male or female. This, too, is an example of a *random event*.

  Our intuition tells us that a boy baby and a girl baby are *equally likely* to occur. If we follow this reasoning, we might *assign a probability* of $\frac{1}{2}$ to having a girl baby. However, if we consult the data about births in the United States found in Table 1, we see that it might be more accurate to assign a probability of 0.488 to having a girl baby.

TABLE 1

Year of Birth	Number of Births (in thousands) Boys b	Girls g	Total Number of Births (in thousands) $b+g$	Ratio of Births $\frac{b}{b+g}$	$\frac{g}{b+g}$
2006	2184	2081	4265	0.512	0.488
2005	2119	2019	4138	0.512	0.488
2004	2105	2007	4112	0.512	0.488
2003	2094	1996	4090	0.512	0.488
2002	2058	1964	4022	0.512	0.488
2001	2058	1968	4026	0.511	0.489
2000	2077	1982	4059	0.512	0.488
1999	2027	1933	3960	0.512	0.488
1998	2016	1925	3941	0.512	0.488
1997	1986	1895	3881	0.512	0.488
1996	1990	1901	3891	0.511	0.489
1995	1996	1903	3899	0.512	0.488
1994	2023	1930	3953	0.512	0.488
1993	2049	1951	4000	0.512	0.488
1992	2082	1983	4065	0.512	0.488
1991	2102	2009	4111	0.511	0.489
1990	2129	2029	4158	0.512	0.488

Source: National Center for Health Statistics

These examples demonstrate that in studying a sequence of random experiments it is not possible to forecast individual results. These are subject to irregular, random fluctuations that cannot be exactly predicted. However, if the number of observations is large—that is, if we deal with a *mass phenomenon*—some regularity appears. This leads to the study of probability.

Probability is concerned with experiments, real or conceptual, and their outcome In this study we try to formulate in a precise manner a mathematical model that close resembles the experiment in question. The first stage of development of such a math matical model is the building of a *probability model*. This model is then used to analy and predict outcomes of the experiment. The purpose of this section is to learn how probability model can be constructed.

1 Find a Sample Space

Definition

> A **sample space** of an experiment is the set of all possibilities that can occur as a result of the experiment. Each element of a sample space is called an **outcome.**

A sample space of an experiment plays the same role in probability as the univers set does in set theory. In this chapter we discuss only finite sample spaces, that is, samp spaces that have only a finite number of outcomes.

Notice in the definition we say *a* sample space, rather than *the* sample space, sinc an experiment can often be described in different ways.

EXAMPLE 1 Finding a Sample Space

Flip a coin. Find a sample space for this experiment.

SOLUTION The experiment consists of flipping a coin. The only possible outcomes are heads (H and tails (T). Therefore, a sample space for the experiment is the set $\{H, T\}$.

EXAMPLE 2 Finding a Sample Space

FIGURE 17

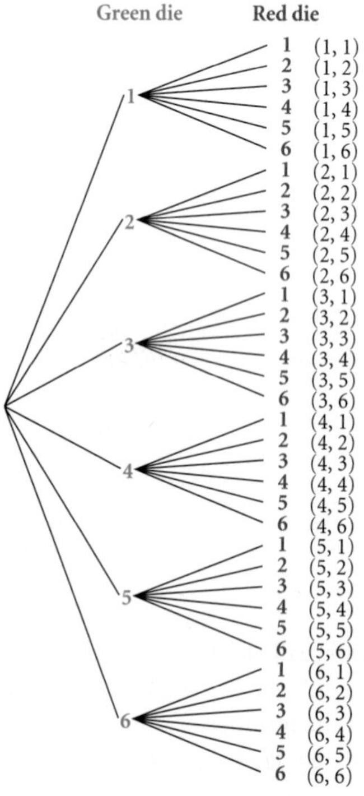

Consider an experiment in which two dice are rolled, one green and the other red. Th set of outcomes consists of all the different ways that the dice may come to rest. Find sample space for this experiment.

SOLUTION Since there are 6 possible ways for the green die to come up and 6 way for the red die to come up, the number of outcomes of rolling the two dice is $6 \cdot 6 = 36$

We use a tree diagram to obtain a list of the 36 outcomes. See Figure 17. Figure 1 gives a graphical representation of the 36 outcomes. The sample space consists of th 36 ordered pairs listed.

FIGURE 18

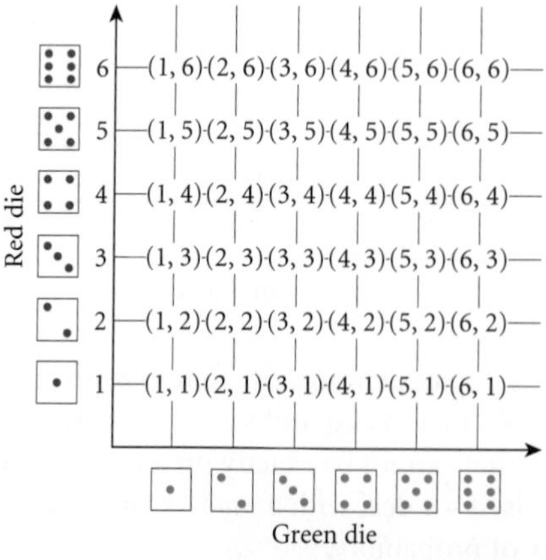

Other examples of experiments and their sample spaces are given below.

Experiment	Sample Space
(a) A spinner is marked from 1 to 8. An experiment consists of spinning the dial once.	$\{1, 2, 3, 4, 5, 6, 7, 8\}$
(b) An experiment consists of tossing two coins, a penny and a nickel, and observing whether the coins match (M) or do not match (D).	$\{M, D\}$
(c) An experiment consists of tossing a coin twice and observing the number of heads that appear.	$\{0, 1, 2\}$
(d) An experiment consists of tossing a coin twice and observing whether the coin falls heads (H) or tails (T) on each toss.	$\{HH, HT, TH, TT\}$
(e) An experiment consists of tossing three coins and observing whether the coins fall heads (H) or tails (T).	$\{HHH, HHT, HTH, HTT, THH, THT, TTH, TTT\}$

NOW WORK PROBLEM 7.

EXAMPLE 3 Finding a Sample Space

Describe a sample space for the experiment of selecting one family from the set of all possible three-child families.

SOLUTION One way of describing a sample space for this experiment is to list the number of girls in the family. The only possibilities are members of the set

$$\{0, 1, 2, 3\}$$

That is, a three-child family can have 0, 1, 2, or 3 girls. This sample space has four outcomes.

Another way of describing a sample space for this experiment is to denote B as "boy" and G as "girl." Then the sample space can be given as

$$\{BBB, BBG, BGB, BGG, GBB, GBG, GGB, GGG\}$$

where BBB means first child is a boy, second child is a boy, third child is a boy, and so on. This sample space has $2 \cdot 2 \cdot 2 = 8$ outcomes. See the tree diagram in Figure 19.

FIGURE 19

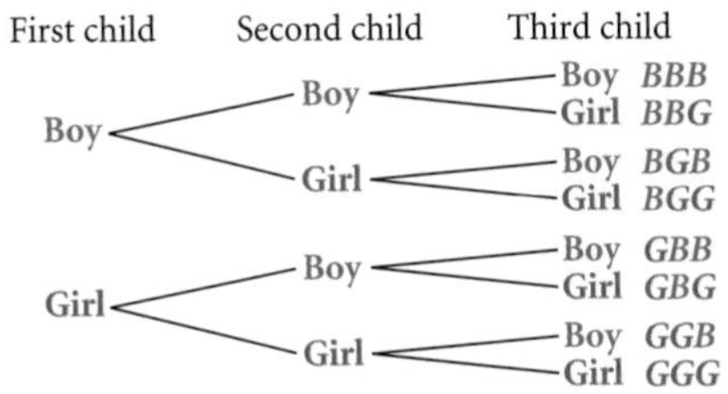
First child
Second child
Third child
Boy
Girl
Boy
Girl
Boy
Girl
Boy BBB
Girl BBG
Boy BGB
Girl BGG
Boy GBB
Girl GBG
Boy GGB
Girl GGG

■

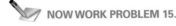

NOW WORK PROBLEM 15.

2 Assign Probabilities

Definition

Probability of an Outcome

Suppose the sample space S of an experiment has n outcomes given by

$$S = \{e_1, e_2, \ldots, e_n\}$$

To each outcome of S, we assign a real number, $P(e)$, called the **probability of the outcome** e, so that

$$P(e_1) \geq 0, P(e_2) \geq 0, \ldots, P(e_n) \geq 0 \qquad (1)$$

and

$$P(e_1) + P(e_2) + \cdots + P(e_n) = 1 \qquad (2)$$

Condition (1) states that each probability assignment must be nonnegative. Condition (2) states that the sum of all the probability assignments must equal one. Only assignments of probabilities satisfying both conditions (1) and (2) are valid.

EXAMPLE 4 Valid Probability Assignments

Let a die be thrown. A sample space S is then

$$S = \{1, 2, 3, 4, 5, 6\}$$

There are six outcomes in S: 1, 2, 3, 4, 5, 6.

One valid assignment of probabilities is

$$P(1) = \frac{1}{6} \qquad P(2) = \frac{1}{6} \qquad P(3) = \frac{1}{6} \qquad P(4) = \frac{1}{6} \qquad P(5) = \frac{1}{6} \qquad P(6) = \frac{1}{6}$$

This choice is consistent with the definition since the probability assigned to each outcome is nonnegative and their sum is 1. This assignment is made when the die is **fair**.

Another assignment that is valid is

$$P(1) = 0 \qquad P(2) = 0 \qquad P(3) = \frac{1}{3} \qquad P(4) = \frac{2}{3} \qquad P(5) = 0 \qquad P(6) = 0$$

This assignment, although unnatural, is made when the die is "loaded" in such a way that only a 3 or a 4 can occur and the 4 is twice as likely as the 3 to occur.

Many other assignments can also be made that are valid. ■

NOW WORK PROBLEM 23.

3 Construct a Probability Model

The sample space and the assignment of probabilities to each outcome of an experiment constitute a **probability model** for the experiment.

Constructing a Probability Model

To construct a probability model requires two steps:

STEP 1 Find a sample space. List all the possible outcomes of the experiment, or, if this is not easy to do, determine the number of outcomes of the experiment.

STEP 2 Assign to each outcome e a probability $P(e)$ so that

(a) $P(e) \geq 0$

(b) The sum of all the probabilities assigned to the outcomes equals 1.

Sometimes a probability model is referred to as a **stochastic model**.

EXAMPLE 5 Constructing a Probability Model

A coin is tossed. The coin is weighted so that heads (H) is 5 times more likely to occur than tails (T). Construct a probability model for this experiment.

SOLUTION

STEP 1 A sample space S for this experiment is

$$S = \{T, H\}$$

STEP 2 Let x denote the probability that tails occurs. Then

$$P(T) = x \quad \text{and} \quad P(H) = 5x \qquad \text{Heads is 5 times more likely than tails.}$$

Since the sum of all the probability assignments equals 1, we have

$$P(H) + P(T) = 5x + x = 1 \qquad \text{Sum of the probabilities equals 1.}$$

$$6x = 1 \qquad \text{Simplify.}$$

$$x = \frac{1}{6} \qquad \text{Solve for } x.$$

As a result, we assign the probabilities

$$P(T) = \frac{1}{6} \qquad P(H) = \frac{5}{6}$$

The above discussion constitutes the construction of a probability model for the experiment. ■

NOW WORK PROBLEM 49.

4 Find Probabilities Involving Equally Likely Outcomes

When the same probability is assigned to each outcome of a sample space, the outcomes are termed **equally likely outcomes**.

Equally likely outcomes often occur when items are selected randomly. For exampl in randomly selecting 1 person from a group of 10, the probability of selecting a particul individual is $\frac{1}{10}$. If a card is chosen randomly from a deck of 52 cards, the probability drawing a particular card is $\frac{1}{52}$. In general, if a sample space S has n equally like outcomes, the probability assigned to each outcome is $\frac{1}{n}$.

Definition

Event *E* in a Sample Space

Let a sample space S be given by

$$S = \{e_1, e_2, \ldots, e_n\}$$

An **event** E in S is any subset of S.

Theorem

Probability of an Event *E* in a Sample Space with Equally Likely Outcomes

If the sample space S of an experiment has n equally likely outcomes, and the event E in S contains m outcomes, then the probability of event E, written as $P(E)$, is

$$P(E) = \frac{\text{Number of outcomes in the event } E}{\text{Number of outcomes in } S} = \frac{m}{n} \tag{3}$$

To compute the probability of an event E in which the outcomes are equally likely, count the number of outcomes in E, and divide by the total number of outcomes in the sample space.

EXAMPLE 6 Finding Probabilities Involving Equally Likely Outcomes

If a person is chosen randomly from a group of 100 people, 60 females and 40 males, the probability of the event E, 'a male is chosen,' is:

$$P(E) = \frac{\text{Number of males}}{\text{Number of people}} = \frac{40}{100} = 0.4$$

EXAMPLE 7 Government Bonds

At the beginning of April 2010, the most recent issues of government bonds consisted of T-bills, bonds and notes, and Treasury inflation-protected securities (TIPS) bonds. See Table 2.

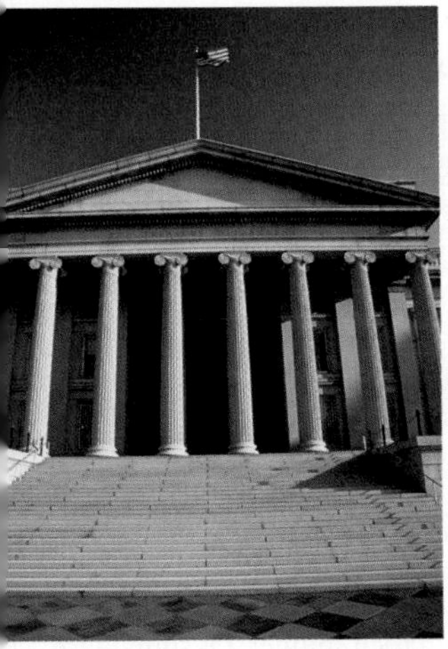

TABLE 2 GOVERNMENT BONDS

T-Bills	Bonds and Notes	Treasury Inflation-Protected Securities
13 week, 0.178% yield	3 year, 1.776% yield	4 year 6 month, 1.25% yield
26 week, 0.269% yield	5 year, 2.405% yield	9 year 9 month, 1.709% yield
	10 year, 3.692% yield	20 year, 1.43% yield
	30 year, 4.72% yield	30 year, 2.229% yield

Source: U.S. Treasury

(a) If a bond is picked at random, what is the probability it is a TIPS bond?
(b) If a bond is picked at random, what is the probability it is a 30-year bond?
(c) If a bond is picked at random, what is the probability its yield is more than 3%?
(d) If a bond is picked at random, what is the probability its maturity is 4 years or more?

SOLUTION **(a)** The sample space S consists of 10 government bonds. Since the selection of a bond is random, the outcomes in S are equally likely. If E is the event "Treasury inflation-protected securities," then

$$P(E) = \frac{\text{Number of Treasury inflation-protected securities bonds}}{\text{Number of government bonds}} = \frac{4}{10} = 0.4$$

(b) If F is the event "30-year bond," then $n(F) = 2$ and

$$P(F) = \frac{n(F)}{n(S)} = \frac{2}{10} = 0.2$$

(c) If G is the event "yield is more than 3%," then $n(G) = 2$ and

$$P(G) = \frac{n(G)}{n(S)} = \frac{2}{10} = 0.2$$

(d) If H is the event "maturity is 4 years or more," then $n(H) = 7$ and

$$P(H) = \frac{n(H)}{n(S)} = \frac{7}{10} = 0.7$$

■

NOW WORK PROBLEMS 27 AND 59.

EXERCISE 7.4 Answers Begin on Page AN–36.

oncepts and Vocabulary

1. ***True or False*** In assigning a probability $P(e)$ to an outcome e of a sample space S, $P(e)$ must be a positive number less than or equal to 1.

2. A box contains 3 red and 2 blue marbles. If a marble is chosen at random, the probability it is red is ________.

3. A ________ ________ of an experiment is the set of all possibilities that can result from performing the experiment.

4. ***True or False*** For a sample space $S = \{a, b, c\}$, a valid assignment of probabilities is $P(a) = 0.3$, $P(b) = 0.4$, $P(c) = 0.3$.

5. A(n) ________ is a subset of a sample space.

6. ***True or False*** In a sample space S with equally likely outcomes, the probability of an event E is $P(E) = n(S) - n(E)$.

Skill Building

In Problems 7–14, use the pictured spinners to list the outcomes of a sample space associated with each experiment.

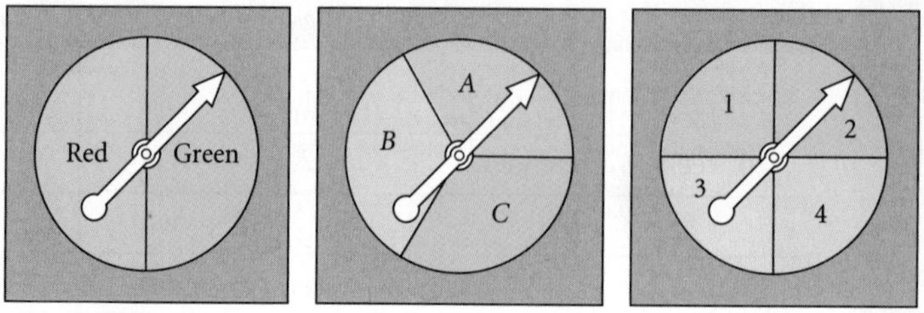

Spinner 1 Spinner 2 Spinner 3

7. First spinner 1 is spun and then spinner 2 is spun.
8. First spinner 2 is spun and then spinner 3 is spun.
9. Spinner 2 is spun twice.
10. Spinner 3 is spun twice.
11. Spinner 2 is spun twice and then spinner 3 is spun.
12. Spinner 3 is spun once and then spinner 2 is spun twice.
13. Spinners 1, 2, and 3 are each spun once in this order.
14. Spinners 3, 2, and 1 are each spun once in this order.

In Problems 15–22, find the number of outcomes of a sample space associated with each experiment.

15. Tossing a coin 4 times
16. Tossing a coin 5 times
17. Tossing 3 dice
18. Tossing 2 dice and then a coin
19. Selecting 2 cards in order (without replacement) from a regular deck of 52 cards*
20. Selecting 3 cards in order (without replacement) from regular deck of 52 cards
21. Picking two letters from the alphabet (Repetitions allowed; assume order is important.)
22. Picking two letters from the alphabet (No repetitions allowe assume order is important.)

In Problems 23–26, consider the experiment of tossing a coin twice. The table lists six possible assignments of probabilities for this experiment:

23. Which of the assignments of probabilities are valid?
24. Which of the assignments of probabilities should be used if the coin is known to be fair, that is, the outcomes are equally likely?
25. Which of the assignments of probabilities should be used if the coin is known to always come up tails?
26. Which of the assignments of probabilities should be used if tails is twice as likely as heads to occur?

	Sample Space			
	HH	*HT*	*TH*	*TT*
A	$\frac{1}{4}$	$\frac{1}{4}$	$\frac{1}{4}$	$\frac{1}{4}$
B	0	0	0	1
C	$\frac{3}{16}$	$\frac{5}{16}$	$\frac{5}{16}$	$\frac{3}{16}$
D	$\frac{1}{2}$	$\frac{1}{2}$	$-\frac{1}{2}$	$\frac{1}{2}$
E	$\frac{1}{8}$	$\frac{1}{4}$	$\frac{1}{4}$	$\frac{1}{8}$
F	$\frac{1}{9}$	$\frac{2}{9}$	$\frac{2}{9}$	$\frac{4}{9}$

A regular deck of cards has 52 cards. There are four suits of 13 cards each. The suits are called clubs (black), diamonds (red), hearts (red), and spades (black In each suit the 13 cards are labeled 2, 3, 4, 5, 6, 7, 8, 9, 10, J (jack), Q (queen), K (king), and A(ace), in order from lowest (2) to highest (A). Sometimes A considered to be 1.

ew Home Sales *The number of new home sales (in thousands) in the United States as of March 24, 2010, is given in the table below.*

	Northeast	Midwest	South	West
Feb–Mar 2009	47	94	402	143
April–Jun 2009	82	607	607	278
Jul–Sep 2009	114	179	623	302
Oct–Dec 2009	102	174	578	253
Jan–Feb 2010	67	91	299	170

Source: U.S. Census Bureau

ı Problems 63–70, use the information in the table above. Round your answers to three decimal places.

3. What is the probability a home selected at random was sold from Feb–Mar 2009?

4. What is the probability a home selected at random was sold in the South?

5. What is the probability a home selected at random was sold from Oct–Dec 2009?

6. What is the probability a home selected at random was sold in the Midwest?

7. What is the probability a home selected at random was sold in the West from Jul–Sep 2009?

8. What is the probability a home selected at random was sold in the South from Apr–Jun 2009?

9. What is the probability a home selected at random was sold in the Northeast from Jan–Feb 2010?

70. What is the probability a home selected at random was sold in the Midwest from Oct–Dec 2009?

71. Health Insurance Coverage The U.S. Census Bureau reported that 255,143,000 Americans were covered by health insurance in the year 2008 and 46,340,000 Americans were not covered by health insurance that year.

(a) What is the probability a randomly selected American in the year 2008 was covered by health insurance? Write the answer as a decimal rounded to three decimal places.

(b) What is the probability a randomly selected American in the year 2008 was not covered by health insurance?

Source: U.S. Census Bureau, Current Population Reports, *Income, Poverty, and Health Insurance Coverage in the United States: 2008*. Issued September 2009.

ometimes experiments are simulated using a random number function instead of actually performing the experiment. In Problems 72–77, use graphing utility to simulate each experiment.*

2. Tossing a Fair Coin Consider the experiment of tossing a fair coin. Simulate the experiment using a random number function, considering a toss to be tails (T) if the result is less than 0.5, and considering a toss to be heads (H) if the result is greater than or equal to 0.5. [*Note*: Most utilities repeat the action of the last entry if you simply press the ENTER, or EXE, key again.] Repeat the experiment 10 times. Using these 10 outcomes of the experiment you can estimate the probabilities $P(H)$ and $P(T)$ by the ratios

$$P(H) \approx \frac{\text{Number of times } H \text{ occurred}}{10}$$

$$P(T) \approx \frac{\text{Number of times } T \text{ occurred}}{10}$$

What are the actual probabilities? How close are the results of the experiment to the actual values?

73. Urn and Balls Consider the experiment of choosing a ball from an urn containing 18 red and 12 white balls. Simulate the experiment using a random number function, considering a selection to be a red ball (R) if the result is less than 0.6, and considering a toss to be a white ball (W) if the result is greater than or equal to 0.6. [*Note*: Most utilities repeat the action of the last entry if you simply press the ENTER, or EXE, key again.] Repeat the experiment 10 times. Using these 10 outcomes of the experiment you can estimate the probabilities $P(R)$ and $P(W)$ by the ratios

$$P(R) \approx \frac{\text{Number of times } R \text{ occurred}}{10}$$

$$P(W) \approx \frac{\text{Number of times } W \text{ occurred}}{10}$$

What are the actual probabilities? How close are the results of the experiment to the actual values?

** Most graphing utilities have a random number function (usually RAND or RND) for generating numbers between 0 and 1. Check your user's manual to see ıow to use this function.*

74. Tossing a Loaded Coin Consider the experiment of tossing a loaded coin in which heads is three times as likely as tails to occur. Simulate the experiment using a random number function, considering a toss to be tails (T) if the result is less than 0.25, and considering a toss to be heads (H) if the result is greater than or equal to 0.25. [*Note*: Most utilities repeat the action of the last entry if you simply press the ENTER, or EXE, key again.] Repeat the experiment 20 times. Using these 20 outcomes of the experiment you can estimate the probabilities $P(H)$ and $P(T)$ by the ratios

$$P(H) \approx \frac{\text{Number of times } H \text{ occurred}}{20}$$

$$P(T) \approx \frac{\text{Number of times } T \text{ occurred}}{20}$$

What are the actual probabilities? How close are the results of the experiment to the actual values?

75. Urn and Balls Consider the experiment of choosing a ball from an urn containing 15 red and 35 white balls. Simulate the experiment using a random number function, considering a selection to be a red ball (R) if the result is less than 0.3, and considering a toss to be a white ball (W) if the result is greater than or equal to 0.3. [*Note*: Most utilities repeat the action of the last entry if you simply press the ENTER, or EXE, key again.] Repeat the experiment 10 times. Using these 10 outcomes of the experiment you can estimate the probabilities $P(R)$ and $P(W)$ by the ratios

$$P(R) \approx \frac{\text{Number of times } R \text{ occurred}}{10}$$

$$P(W) \approx \frac{\text{Number of times } W \text{ occurred}}{10}$$

What are the actual probabilities? How close are the results of the experiment to the actual values?

76. Jar and Marbles Consider an experiment of choosing a marble from a jar containing 5 red, 2 yellow, and 8 white marbles. Simulate the experiment using a random number function on your calculator, considering a selection to be a red marble (R) if the result is less than or equal to 0.33, a yellow marble (Y) if the result is between 0.33 and 0.47, and a white marble (V if the result is greater than or equal to 0.47. [*Note*: Mo calculators repeat the action of the last entry if you simp press the ENTER, or EXE, key again.] Repeat the experime 10 times. Using these 10 outcomes of the experiment, you ca estimate the probabilities $P(R)$, $P(Y)$, and $P(W)$ by the rati

$$P(R) \approx \frac{\text{Number of times } R \text{ occurred}}{10}$$

$$P(Y) \approx \frac{\text{Number of times } Y \text{ occurred}}{10}$$

$$P(W) \approx \frac{\text{Number of times } W \text{ occurred}}{10}$$

What are the actual probabilities? How close are the results the experiment to the actual values?

77. Poker Game The probabilities in a game of poker that Adam Beatrice, or Cathy win are 0.22, 0.60, and 0.18, respectivel Simulate the game using a random number function on you calculator, considering that Adam won (A) if the result is le than or equal to 0.22, that Beatrice won (B) if the result between 0.22 and 0.82, and that Cathy won (C) if the result greater than or equal to 0.82. [*Note*: Most calculators repeat th action of the last entry if you simply press the ENTER, or EX key again.] Repeat the experiment 20 times; that is, simulate 2 games. Using these 20 outcomes of the experiment you ca estimate the probabilities $P(A)$, $P(B)$, and $P(C)$ by the ratic

$$P(A) \approx \frac{\text{Number of times } A \text{ won}}{20}$$

$$P(B) \approx \frac{\text{Number of times } B \text{ won}}{20}$$

$$P(C) \approx \frac{\text{Number of times } C \text{ won}}{20}$$

What are the actual values? How close are the results of th experiment to the actual values?

7.5 Properties of the Probability of an Event

In Section 7.4 we defined the probability of an event E in a sample space S with equally likely outcomes. We begin this section with a definition for the probability of an event E in a sample space S whose outcomes have been assigned valid probabilities, not necessarily all the same.

1 Find the Probability of an Event

Definition   **Event; Simple Event**

An **event** is any subset of a sample space. If an event has exactly one element, that is, if it consists of only one outcome, it is called a **simple event**.

For example, consider the experiment discussed in Example 3 of Section 7.4: selecting one family from the set of three-child families. A sample space S for this experiment is

$$S = \{BBB, BBG, BGB, BGG, GBB, GBG, GGB, GGG\}$$

where, for example, BGB means that the family selected had a boy as a first child, a girl as second child, and a boy as third child.

The event E that the family has two boys followed by a girl, $E = \{BBG\}$, consists of only one outcome and is a simple event.

The event F that the family consists of exactly two boys is

$$F = \{BBG, BGB, GBB\}$$

Notice that the event F is not a simple event but can be expressed as the union of the three simple events $\{BBG\}, \{BGB\}, \{GBB\}$. That is,

$$F = \{BBG\} \cup \{BGB\} \cup \{GBB\}$$

In fact, every event can be written as the union of simple events.

Since a sample space S is also an event, we can express a sample space S as the uni of simple events. If the sample space S consists of n outcomes,

$$S = \{e_1, e_2, \ldots, e_n\}$$

then

$$S = \{e_1\} \cup \{e_2\} \cup \cdots \cup \{e_n\}$$

Suppose valid probabilities have been assigned to each outcome of S. Let E be a event of S. Then either $E = \varnothing$ or E is a simple event or E is the union of two or mo simple events. We give the following definition for the probability of E.

Definition

Probability of an Event

If $E = \varnothing$, the event E is **impossible.** We define the **probability of $\varnothing$** as

$$P(\varnothing) = 0$$

If $E = \{e\}$ is a simple event, then $P(E) = P(e)$; that is, $P(E)$ equals the probability assigned to the outcome e.

$$P(E) = P(e)$$

If E is the union of r simple events $\{e_1\}, \{e_2\}, \ldots, \{e_r\}$, we define the **probability of E** to be the sum of the probabilities assigned to each simple event in E. That is,

$$P(E) = P(e_1) + P(e_2) + \cdots + P(e_r) \qquad (1)$$

If the sample space S is given by

$$S = \{e_1, e_2, \ldots, e_n\}$$

then the probability of S is

$$P(S) = P(e_1) + \cdots + P(e_n) = 1$$

That is, the probability of S, the sample space, is 1.

EXAMPLE 1 Finding the Probability of an Event

Each of the eight possible blood types is listed in Table 3 along with the percent of th U.S. population having that type. What is the probability that a randomly selecte person in the United States has a blood type that is Rh-negative?

SOLUTION The sample space S consists of the eight blood types, and the percents, when given a decimals, are the probability assignments for each element of the sample space. Fo example, the simple event "O positive" is assigned the probability 0.39.

Let E be the event that a randomly selected person in the United States has a bloo type that is Rh-negative. We seek $P(E)$. Since E is the union of the simple even {O negative}, {A negative}, {AB negative}, and {B negative}, we have

$$E = \{\text{O negative, A negative, AB negative, B negative}\}$$

ABLE 3

Blood Types
O Positive—39%
A Positive—31%
B Positive—9%
O Negative—9%
A Negative—6%
AB Positive—3%
B Negative—2%
AB Negative—1%

ource: AABB Facts
out Blood, 2010

The probabilities assigned each of these simple events are

$$P(\text{O negative}) = 0.09 \qquad P(\text{A negative}) = 0.06$$
$$P(\text{B negative}) = 0.02 \qquad P(\text{AB negative}) = 0.01$$

Then,

$$P(E) = P\{\text{O negative}\} + P\{\text{A negative}\} + P\{\text{AB negative}\} + P\{\text{B negative}\}$$
$$= 0.09 + 0.06 + 0.01 + 0.02 = 0.18$$

The probability is 0.18, or 18%, that a randomly selected person in the United States has Rh-negative blood. ■

NOW WORK PROBLEM 35.

2 Find the Probability of *E* or *F* When *E* and *F* Are Mutually Exclusive

Definition

Mutually Exclusive Events

Two or more events of a sample space *S* are said to be **mutually exclusive** if and only if they have no outcomes in common.

Since events are sets, two events *E* and *F* are mutually exclusive if they are disjoint, that is, if $E \cap F = \varnothing$.

Theorem

Probability of *E* or *F* If *E* and *F* Are Mutually Exclusive

Let *E* and *F* be two events of a sample space *S*. If *E* and *F* are mutually exclusive, that is, if $E \cap F = \varnothing$, then the probability of *E* or *F* is the sum of their probabilities. That is,

$$P(E \cup F) = P(E) + P(F) \quad \text{if } E \cap F = \varnothing \qquad (2)$$

This result follows since *E* and *F* can be written as a union of simple events in which no simple event of *E* appears in *F* and no simple event of *F* appears in *E*.

EXAMPLE 2 Finding the Probability of *E* or *F* When *E* and *F* Are Mutually Exclusive

Refer back to Table 3 on blood types in the United States. What is the probability a person chosen at random is type O or type A?

SOLUTION Define the events *E* and *F* as:

E: person selected is type O *F*: person selected is type A

Then

$$E = \{\text{O positive, O negative}\} \quad F = \{\text{A positive, A negative}\}$$

Now

$$P(E) = P(\text{O positive}) + P(\text{O negative}) = 0.39 + 0.09 = 0.48$$

$$P(F) = P(\text{A positive}) + P(\text{A negative}) = 0.31 + 0.06 = 0.37$$

Since $E \cap F = \varnothing$, the events E and F are mutually exclusive. Based on Formula (2), th probability of E or F, namely $P(E \cup F)$, is

$$P(E \cup F) = P(E) + P(F) = 0.48 + 0.37 = 0.85$$

So 85% of the U.S. population is either type O or type A.

NOW WORK PROBLEMS 15(a) AND 15(b).

3 Use the Additive Rule

The following result, called the *Additive Rule*, gives a formula for finding the probabilit of the union of two events whether they are mutually exclusive or not.

Theorem

Additive Rule

For any two events E and F of a sample space S, the probability of E or F is

$$P(E \cup F) = P(E) + P(F) - P(E \cap F) \qquad (3)$$

A proof of this result is outlined in Problem 63.

EXAMPLE 3 Using the Additive Rule

If $P(E) = 0.30$, $P(F) = 0.20$, and the probability of E or F is 0.40, what is the probabilit of E and F?

SOLUTION We are given $P(E) = 0.30$ and $P(F) = 0.20$. The probability of E or F i $P(E \cup F) = 0.40$. We seek the probability of E and F, namely, $P(E \cap F)$.

Use the Additive Rule, Formula (3).

$$P(E \cup F) = P(E) + P(F) - P(E \cap F)$$

$$0.40 = 0.30 + 0.20 - P(E \cap F) \qquad P(E \cup F) = 0.40,\ P(E) = 0.30,\ P(F) = 0.20$$

Solve for $P(E \cap F)$.

$$P(E \cap F) = 0.30 + 0.20 - 0.40 = 0.10$$

NOW WORK PROBLEM 5.

EXAMPLE 4 Using the Additive Rule

Refer back to Table 3 on blood types in the United States. What is the probability a person chosen at random is type O or Rh-negative?

SOLUTION Define the events E and F as

E: person selected is type O $\qquad$ F: person selected is Rh-negative

Then

$$E = \{\text{O positive, O negative}\}$$
$$F = \{\text{A negative, B negative, AB negative, O negative}\}$$
$$P(E) = P(\text{O positive}) + P(\text{O negative}) = 0.39 + 0.09 = 0.48$$
$$P(F) = P(\text{A negative}) + P(\text{B negative}) + P(\text{AB negative}) + P(\text{O negative})$$
$$= 0.06 + 0.02 + 0.01 + 0.09 = 0.18$$

Since $E \cap F = \{\text{O negative}\}$, then $P(E \cap F) = 0.09$. Using Formula (3), the probability of E or F, namely $P(E \cup F)$, is

$$P(E \cup F) = P(E) + P(F) - P(E \cap F) = 0.48 + 0.18 - 0.09 = 0.57$$

So 57% of the U.S. population is type O or Rh-negative. ■

4 Find the Probability of the Complement of an Event

Let E be an event of a sample space S. The complement of E is the event "Not E" in S.

Theorem

Probability of the Complement of an Event

Let E be an event of a sample space S. Then the probability that E does not occur is

$$P(\overline{E}) = 1 - P(E) \qquad \textbf{(4)}$$

where $\overline{E}$ is the complement of E.

Proof We know that

$$S = E \cup \overline{E} \qquad E \cap \overline{E} = \varnothing$$

Since E and $\overline{E}$ are mutually exclusive,

$$P(S) = P(E) + P(\overline{E})$$

Since $P(S) = 1$, it follows that

$$1 = P(E) + P(\overline{E}) \qquad P(S) = 1$$
$$P(\overline{E}) = 1 - P(E) \qquad \text{Solve for } P(\overline{E}).$$ ■

Formula (4) gives us a tool for finding the probability that an event does not occur if we know the probability that it does occur. The probability $P(\overline{E})$ that E does not occur is obtained by subtracting the probability $P(E)$ that E does occur from 1. We will see shortly that it is sometimes easier to find $P(E)$ by finding $P(\overline{E})$ and using Formula (4) than it is to proceed directly.

EXAMPLE 5 Using Formula (4)

A study of people over age 40 with an M.B.A. degree shows that it is reasonable to assig a probability of 0.756 that such a person will have annual earnings in excess of \$140,00 The probability that such a person will earn \$140,000 or less is then

$$1 - 0.756 = 0.244$$

NOW WORK PROBLEMS 15(c), 15(d), 15(e), AND 15(f).

5 Use a Venn Diagram to Find Probabilities

EXAMPLE 6 Using a Venn Diagram to Find Probabilities

Suppose E and F are two events for which

$$P(E) = 0.25 \quad P(F) = 0.45 \quad P(E \cap F) = 0.10$$

(a) Construct a Venn diagram to represent this situation.

(b) Find the probability of neither E nor F.

(c) Find the probability of E but not F.

SOLUTION **(a)** Begin with Figure 20(a) and the fact that $P(E \cap F) = 0.10$. Then, since $P(E) = 0.25$, insert $0.25 - 0.10 = 0.15$ in the remaining part of E. Similarly, inse $0.45 - 0.10 = 0.35$ in the remaining part of F. See Figure 20(b).

From Figure 20(b) we have

$$P(E \cup F) = 0.15 + 0.10 + 0.35 = 0.60$$

Alternatively use the Additive Rule. Then

$$P(E \cup F) = P(E) + P(F) - P(E \cap F) = 0.25 + 0.45 - 0.10 = 0.60$$

which checks.

Finally, since $P(S) = 1$, enter $1 - 0.60 = 0.40$ in the part outside the sets and F. See Figure 20(c).

FIGURE 20

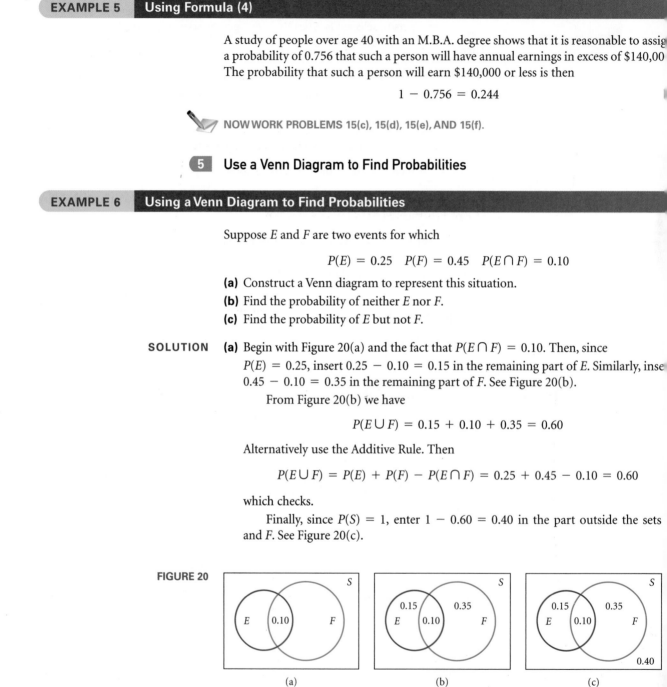

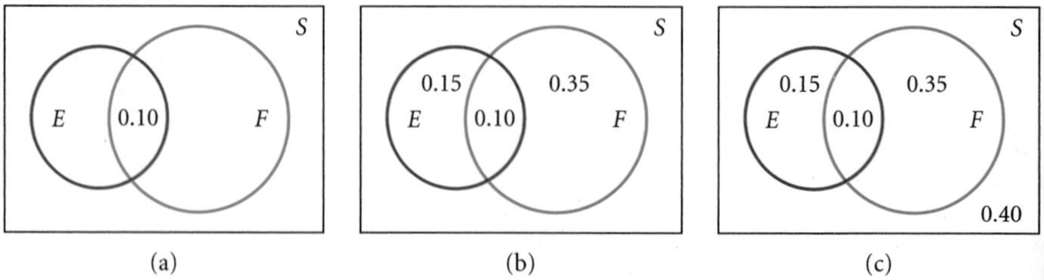

(b) From Figure 20(c), the probability of neither E nor F is 0.40.

(c) From Figure 20(c), the probability of E, but not F, is 0.15.

NOW WORK PROBLEM 13.

6 Use the Multiplication Principle to Find Probabilities

EXAMPLE 7 Finding Probabilities Using the Multiplication Principle

What is the probability that a four-digit telephone extension has one or more repeated digits? Assume no one digit is more likely than another to be used.

SOLUTION By the Multiplication Principle, there are $10^4 = 10{,}000$ distinct four-digit telephone extensions, so the number of outcomes in the sample space S is

$$n(S) = 10{,}000$$

We wish to find the probability that a four-digit telephone extension has one or more repeated digits. Define the event E as follows:

E: The extension has one or more repeated digits

Since it is difficult to count the outcomes of this event, we examine the complement of E to see if $\overline{E}$ is easier to count.

$\overline{E}$: No repeated digits in four-digit extension

We can find $n(\overline{E})$ by using the Multiplication Principle. The number of four-digit extensions that have *no* repeated digits is

$$n(\overline{E}) = 10 \cdot 9 \cdot 8 \cdot 7 = 5040$$

So,

$$P(\overline{E}) = \frac{n(\overline{E})}{n(S)} = \frac{5040}{10{,}000} = 0.504$$

The probability of one or more repeated digits is $P(E)$ and

$$P(E) = 1 - P(\overline{E}) = 1 - 0.504 = 0.496$$ ■

NOW WORK PROBLEM 53.

EXAMPLE 8 The Birthday Problem

An interesting problem, called the **birthday problem,** is to find the probability that in a group of r people there are at least two people who have the same birthday (the same month and day of the year). Assume a person is as likely to be born on one day as another.

SOLUTION First determine the number of outcomes in the sample space S. There are 365 possibilities for each person's birthday (we exclude February 29 for simplicity). Since there are r people in the group, there are 365^r possibilities for the birthdays. [For one person in the group, there are 365 days on which his or her birthday can fall; for two people, there are $(365)(365) = 365^2$ pairs of days; and, in general, using the Multiplication Principle, for r people there are 365^r possibilities.] That is,

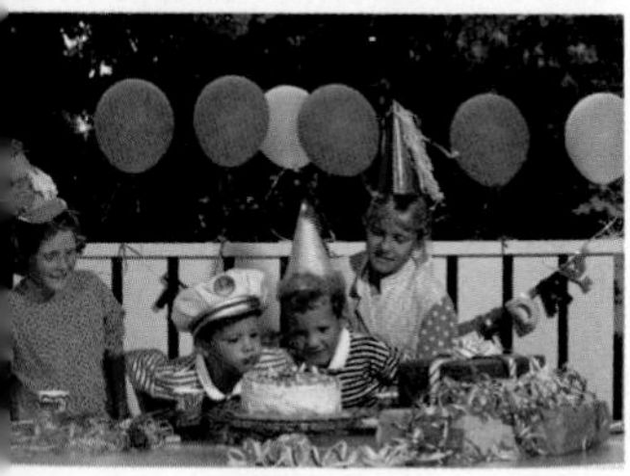

$$n(S) = 365^r$$

These outcomes are equally likely.

We wish to find the probability of the event E:

$$E\text{: At least two people have the same birthday}$$

It is difficult to count the elements in this set; it is much easier to count the elements the complement:

$$\overline{E}\text{: No two people have the same birthday}$$

We proceed to find $n(\overline{E})$ as follows:

Choose one person at random. There are 365 possibilities for his or her birthd Choose a second person. There are 364 possibilities for this birthday, if no two peop are to have the same birthday. Choose a third person. There are 363 possibilities left f this birthday. Finally, we arrive at the rth person. There are $365 - (r - 1)$ possibilit left for this birthday. By the Multiplication Principle, the total number of possibilities

$$n(\overline{E}) = 365 \cdot 364 \cdot 363 \cdot \cdots \cdot (365 - r + 1)$$

The probability of event $\overline{E}$ is

$$P(\overline{E}) = \frac{n(\overline{E})}{n(S)} = \frac{365 \cdot 364 \cdot 363 \cdot \cdots \cdot (365 - r + 1)}{365^r}$$

The probability that two or more people have the same birthday is then

$$P(E) = 1 - P(\overline{E})$$

For example, in a group of eight people, $r = 8$ and the probability that two or mc will have the same birthday is

$$\begin{aligned} P(E) &= 1 - \frac{365 \cdot 364 \cdot 363 \cdot 362 \cdot 361 \cdot 360 \cdot 359 \cdot 358}{365^8} \\ &= 1 - 0.93 \\ &= 0.07 \end{aligned}$$

Table 4 gives the probabilities for two or more people having the same birthd Notice that the probability is greater than $\frac{1}{2}$ for any group of 23 or more people.

TABLE 4

	Number of People															
	5	10	15	20	21	22	23	24	25	30	40	50	60	70	80	90
Probability That 2 or More Have Same Birthday	0.027	0.117	0.253	0.411	0.444	0.476	0.507	0.538	0.569	0.706	0.891	0.970	0.994	0.99916	0.99991	0.9999

NOW WORK PROBLEM 59.

7 Compute Odds

In many instances the probability of an event is expressed as *odds*—either *odds for* event or *odds against* an event.

Definition

If E is an event:

The **odds for** E are $\dfrac{P(E)}{P(\overline{E})}$ read as $P(E)$ to $P(\overline{E})$.

The **odds against** E are $\dfrac{P(\overline{E})}{P(E)}$ read as $P(\overline{E})$ to $P(E)$.

EXAMPLE 9 Computing Odds Given a Probability

Suppose the probability of the event

$$E\text{: It will rain}$$

is 0.3. Then $P(E) = 0.3$ and $P(\overline{E}) = 0.7$.

The odds for rain are

$$\frac{P(E)}{P(\overline{E})} = \frac{0.3}{0.7} = \frac{3}{7} \text{ read as 3 to 7}$$

The odds against rain are

$$\frac{P(\overline{E})}{P(E)} = \frac{0.7}{0.3} = \frac{7}{3} \text{ read as 7 to 3}$$

■

NOW WORK PROBLEM 23.

To obtain the probability of the event E when either the odds for E or the odds against E are known, use the following formulas:

Theorem

If the odds for E are a to b, then

$$P(E) = \frac{a}{a + b} \tag{5}$$

If the odds against E are a to b, then

$$P(E) = \frac{b}{a + b} \tag{6}$$

A proof of Equation (5) is outlined in Problem 64. You are asked to prove Equation (6) in Problem 66.

EXAMPLE 10 Computing a Probability from Odds

(a) The odds for a Republican victory in the next presidential election are 7 to 5. What is the probability that a Republican victory occurs?

(b) The odds against the Chicago Cubs winning the league pennant are 200 to 1. What is the probability that the Cubs win the pennant?

SOLUTION **(a)** The event E is "A Republican victory occurs." The odds for E are 7 to 5. Then

$$P(E) = \frac{7}{7+5} = \frac{7}{12} \approx 0.583$$

(b) The event F is "The Cubs win the pennant." The odds against F are 200 to 1. The

$$P(F) = \frac{1}{200+1} = \frac{1}{201} \approx 0.00498$$

NOW WORK PROBLEM 51.

EXERCISE 7.5 Answers Begin on Page AN–37.

Answers Begin on Page AN–37.

Concepts and Vocabulary

1. A(n) ________ is a subset of a sample space.
2. ***True or False*** If E and F are events, sometimes $P(E \cup F) = P(E) + P(F)$.
3. ***True or False*** If E is an event, then $P(E) = 1 + P(\bar{E})$.
4. ***True or False*** If the odds for an event E are 2 to 1, then $P(E) =$

Skill Building

In Problems 5–12, E and F are events of a sample space S.

5. $P(E) = 0.4, P(F) = 0.5, P(E \cap F) = 0.2$. Find $P(E \cup F)$.
6. $P(E) = 0.6, P(F) = 0.3, P(E \cap F) = 0.2$. Find $P(E \cup F)$.
7. $P(E) = 0.7, P(F) = 0.5, P(E \cup F) = 0.8$. Find $P(E \cap F)$.
8. $P(E) = 0.6, P(F) = 0.8, P(E \cup F) = 0.9$. Find $P(E \cap F)$.
9. $P(E) = 0.4, P(E \cap F) = 0.1, P(E \cup F) = 0.6$. Find $P(F)$.
10. $P(E \cap F) = 0.4, P(F) = 0.5, P(E \cup F) = 0.7$. Find $P(E)$.
11. $P(E) = 0.4$. Find $P(\bar{E})$.
12. $P(\bar{F}) = 0.5$. Find $P(F)$.
13. Let A and B be events of a sample space S and let $P(A) = 0.5$, $P(B) = 0.4$, and $P(A \cap B) = 0.2$. Find the probability of each of the following events:
    (a) A or B (b) A but not B
    (c) B but not A (d) Neither A nor B
14. Let A and B be events of a sample space S and l $P(A) = 0.7$, $P(B) = 0.4$, and $P(A \cap B) = 0.2$. Find the prob bility of each of the following events:
    (a) A or B (b) A but not B
    (c) B but not A (d) Neither A nor B
15. Let A and B be two mutually exclusive events of a sample spa S. If $P(A) = 0.6$ and $P(B) = 0.2$, find each of the followi probabilities:
    (a) $P(A \cap B)$ (b) $P(A \cup B)$ (c) $P(\overline{A \cup B})$
    (d) $P(\bar{B})$ (e) $P(\bar{A})$ (f) $P(\overline{A \cap B})$
16. Let A and B be two mutually exclusive events of a samp space. If $P(A) = 0.35$ and $P(B) = 0.60$, find each of t following probabilities:
    (a) $P(A \cap B)$ (b) $P(A \cup B)$ (c) $P(\overline{A \cup B})$
    (d) $P(\bar{B})$ (e) $P(\bar{A})$ (f) $P(\overline{A \cap B})$

In Problems 17–22, determine the probability of E for the given odds.

17. 3 to 1 for E
18. 4 to 1 against E
19. 7 to 5 against E
20. 2 to 9 for E
21. 1 to 1 for E (even)
22. 50 to 1 for E

In Problems 23–26, determine the odds for and against each event for the given probability.

23. $P(E) = 0.6$
24. $P(H) = \frac{1}{4}$
25. $P(F) = \frac{3}{4}$
26. $P(G) = 0.1$

Applications and Extensions

27. **Chicago Bears** The Chicago Bears football team has a probability of winning of 0.65 and of tying of 0.05. What is the probability of losing?

28. **Chicago Black Hawks** The Chicago Black Hawks hockey team has a probability of winning of 0.6 and a probability of losing of 0.25. What is the probability of a tie?

29. **Likelihood of Passing** Anne is taking courses in both mathematics and English. She estimates her probability of passing mathematics at 0.4 and English at 0.6, and she estimates her probability of passing at least one of them at 0.8. What is her probability of passing both courses?

30. **Dropping a Course** After midterm exams, Anne (see Problem 29) reassesses her probability of passing mathematics to 0.7. She feels her probability of passing at least one of these courses is still 0.8 but feels she has a probability of only 0.1 of passing both courses. If her probability of passing English is less than 0.4, she will drop English. Should Anne drop English?

31. **Car Repair** At the Milex tune-up and brake repair shop, the manager has found that a car will require a tune-up with a probability of 0.6, a brake job with a probability of 0.1, and both with a probability of 0.02.

(a) What is the probability that a car requires either a tune-up or a brake job?

(b) What is the probability that a car requires a tune-up but not a brake job?

(c) What is the probability that a car requires neither type of repair?

32. **Factory Shortages** A factory needs two raw materials, say, E and F. The probability of not having an adequate supply of material E is 0.06, whereas the probability of not having an adequate supply of material F is 0.04. A study shows that the probability of a shortage of both E and F is 0.02. What is the probability of the factory being short of either material E or F?

33. **TV Sets** In a survey of the number of TV sets in a house, the following probability table was constructed:

Number of TV sets	0	1	2	3	4 or more
Probability	0.05	0.24	0.33	0.21	0.17

Find the probability of a house having

(a) 1 or 2 TV sets

(b) 1 or more TV sets

(c) 3 or fewer TV sets

(d) 3 or more TV sets

(e) Fewer than 2 TV sets

(f) Not even 1 TV set

(g) 1, 2, or 3 TV sets

(h) 2 or more TV sets

34. **Supermarket Lines** Through observation it has been determined that the probability for a given number of people waiting in line at a particular checkout register of a supermarket is as shown in the table:

Number waiting in line	0	1	2	3	4 or more
Probability	0.10	0.15	0.20	0.24	0.31

Find the probability of

(a) At most 2 people in line

(b) At least 2 people in line

(c) At least 1 person in line

Problems 35–40 require the following discussion:

Blood Types *Each of the eight possible blood types is listed in the table below along with the percent of the U.S. population having that type.*

O Positive—39%	A Negative—6%
A Positive—31%	AB Positive—3%
B Positive—9%	B Negative—2%
O Negative—9%	AB Negative—1%

Source: AABB Facts about Blood, 2010

35. What is the probability a randomly selected person has a blood type that is Rh-positive?

36. What is the probability a randomly selected person has a blood type that is type O?

37. What is the probability a randomly selected person has a blood type that contains the A antigen? [*Hint*: AB blood contain both the A antigen and the B antigen.]

38. What is the probability a randomly selected person has a blood type that contains both the A and the B antigens?

39. What is the probability a randomly selected person has a blood type that is type O or Rh-positive?

40. What is the probability a randomly selected person has a blood type that is type AB or Rh-negative?

41. **Childbirth** In 2006, the probability a U.S. woman aged 15–44 years, who gave birth in the previous year, gave birth to her first child, was 0.457. What is the probability a U.S. woman aged 15–44 years who gave birth in the previous year had previously given birth?

Source: U.S. Census Bureau, *Fertility of American Women: June 2006*, Issued August 2008

42. **Tax Returns** As of October 31, 2008, 62% of tax refunds for the 2008 tax season were issued through direct deposit. If two refunds are selected at random, the probability that both were issued by direct deposit is 0.49. What is the probability at least one of the refunds is issued by direct deposit?

Source: Internal Revenue Service

43. Bridge Inventory In 2009, there were about 603,000 bridges in the United States, of which 150,000 were either deficient or obsolete. What are the odds that a randomly selected bridge in the United States is either deficient or obsolete?

Source: U.S. Federal Highway Administration

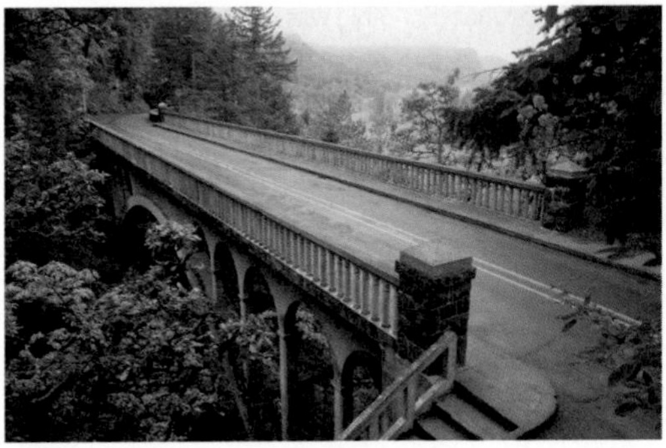

44. Trademarks In 2009, there were roughly 352,000 trademark applications filed in the United States. From these applications, about 320,000 trademarks were issued. What are the odds that a trademark application will result in a trademark being issued?

Source: U.S. Patent and Trademark Office, 2009

45. Apple iPhone Market Share According to the February 2010 Mobile Metrics Report issued by AdMob, the Apple iPhone accounted for 14.4% of the worldwide smart phone market. What is the probability that a smart phone owner chosen at random will not have an iPhone?

46. Family Cars A family owns two vehicles, a 12-year-old Geo Prizm and a 1-year-old Toyota Sienna. On any given morning, the probabilities that the vehicles will start are 0.98 and 0.84 for the Sienna and Prizm, respectively. If the probability at least one of the vehicles will start is 0.9968, what is the probability that they both start?

47. Patents The number and type of U.S. patents (in thousands) issued in 2009 are given in the table. What is the probability that a randomly selected patent issued in 2009 was either for a design or a botanical plant?

Type of Patent	Number Issued
Invention	165,212
Designs	23,915
Botanical plants	1096
Reissues	398

Source: U.S. Patent and Trademark Office, 2009

48. Small Business Loans The number of small business loans awarded to minority-owned businesses in 2007 is given in the table. What is the probability that a randomly selected small business loan awarded to a minority-owned business in 2007 was awarded to a Hispanic-American small business?

Minority Group	Number of Loans
African American	6,632
Asian American	13,455
Hispanic American	8,795
Native American	835

Source: U.S. Census Bureau, 2009

49. Mutual Funds A financial consultant estimates that there is 12% chance a mutual fund will outperform the market duri any given year. She also estimates that there is a 5% chan that the mutual fund will outperform the market for the ne two years. What is the probability that the mutual fund w outperform the market in at least one of the next two year

50. Airline Travel A poll asked respondents how many air tri they had taken on a commercial airliner in the past 12 month The results are given in the table below.

Number of air trips	0	1–2	3–4	5 or more
Percent of respondents	52	29	8	11

(a) What is the probability a respondent selected at rando did not travel by air in the last 12 months?

(b) What is the probability a respondent selected at rando made more than 2 air trips in the past 12 months?

(c) What is the probability a respondent selected at rando made fewer than 3 air trips in the past 12 months?

51. **Track** In a track contest the odds that A will win are 1 to 2, ar the odds that B will win are 2 to 3. Find the probability and th odds that A or B wins the race, assuming a tie is impossib

52. DUI It has been estimated that in 70% of the fatal acciden involving two cars, at least one of the drivers is drunk. If yo hear of a two-car fatal accident, what odds should you give friend for the event that at least one of the drivers was drun

53. What is the probability that a seven-digit phone number h one or more repeated digits?

54. What is the probability that a seven-digit phone numb contains the number 7?

55. Five letters, with repetition allowed, are selected from th alphabet. What is the probability that none is repeated?

56. Four letters, with repetition allowed, are selected from th alphabet. What is the probability that none of them is a vow (a, e, i, o, u)?

57. Picking Numbers If 30 students are asked to pick a numb between 1 and 60, what is the probability at least two w choose the same number?

58. Picking Numbers If 40 students are asked to pick a numb between 1 and 80, what is the probability at least two w choose the same number?

. **Birthday Problem** What is the probability that, in a group of 3 people, at least 2 were born in the same month (disregard day and year)?

. **Birthday Problem** What is the probability that, in a group of 6 people, at least 2 were born in the same month (disregard day and year)?

. **Birthday Problem** Find the probability 2 or more U.S. senators have the same birthday. (There are 100 senators.)

. **Birthday Problem** Find the probability 2 or more members of the House of Representatives have the same birthday. (There are 435 representatives.)

. Prove the Additive Rule, Formula (3) on page 394.

[*Hint*: From Example 9 in Section 7.1 (page 362) we have

$$E \cup F = (E \cap \bar{F}) \cup (E \cap F) \cup (\bar{E} \cap F)$$

Since $E \cap \bar{F}$, $E \cap F$, and $\bar{E} \cap F$ are pairwise disjoint, we can write

$$P(E \cup F) = P(E \cap \bar{F}) + P(E \cap F) + P(\bar{E} \cap F) \quad (1)$$

Write the sets E and F in the form

$$E = (E \cap F) \cup (E \cap \bar{F})$$
$$F = (E \cap F) \cup (\bar{E} \cap F)$$

Since $E \cap F$ and $E \cap \bar{F}$ are disjoint and $E \cap F$ and $\bar{E} \cap F$ are disjoint, we have

$$P(E) = P(E \cap F) + P(E \cap \bar{F})$$
$$P(F) = P(E \cap F) + P(\bar{E} \cap F) \quad (2)$$

Now combine (1) and (2).]

64. Prove Equation (5) on page 399.

[*Hint*: If the odds for E are a to b, then, by the definition of odds,

$$\frac{P(E)}{P(\bar{E})} = \frac{a}{b}$$

But $P(\bar{E}) = 1 - P(E)$. So

$$\frac{P(E)}{1 - P(E)} = \frac{a}{b}$$

Now solve for $P(E)$.]

65. Generalize the Additive Rule by showing the probability of the occurrence of at least one of the three events A, B, C is given by

$$P(A \cup B \cup C) = P(A) + P(B) + P(C)$$
$$-P(A \cap B) - P(A \cap C)$$
$$-P(B \cap C) + P(A \cap B \cap C)$$

66. Prove Equation (6) on page 399.

iscussion and Writing

. Thirty students are asked to pick a number between 1 and 60. Ask some friends what they think the probability is that at least 2 will choose the same number. Now find the probability using the birthday problem as a guide. Did your friends answer correctly? If not, write a paragraph to convince them of the correct answer.

7.6 Expected Value

OBJECTIVES **1** **Find the expected value (p. 405)**
2 **Solve applied problems involving expected value (p. 407)**

EXAMPLE 1 Examples of Expected Value

(a) Suppose that 1000 tickets are sold for a raffle that has the following prizes: one \$300 prize, two \$100 prizes, and one hundred \$1 prizes. Then, of the 1000 tickets, 1 ticket has a cash value of \$300, 2 are worth \$100, and 100 are worth \$1, while the remaining are worth \$0. The *expected value E* of a ticket is then

$$E = \frac{\$300 + (\$100 + \$100) + \overbrace{(\$1 + \$1 + \cdots + \$1)}^{100\text{ times}} + \overbrace{(\$0 + \$0 + \cdots + \$0)}^{897\text{ times}}}{1000}$$

$$= \$300 \cdot \frac{1}{1000} + \$100 \cdot \frac{2}{1000} + \$1 \cdot \frac{100}{1000} + \$0 \cdot \frac{897}{1000}$$

$$= \frac{\$600}{1000} = \$0.60$$

If the raffle is to be nonprofit to all, the charge for each ticket should be $0.60.

The situation above can also be viewed as follows: If we entered such a raffle ma times, $\frac{1}{1000}$ of the time we would win $300, $\frac{2}{1000}$ of the time we would win $100, a so on, with our winnings in the long run averaging $0.60 per ticket.

(b) Suppose that you are to receive $3.00 each time you obtain two heads when flippi a fair coin two times and $0 otherwise. Then the *expected value E* is

$$E = \$3.00 \cdot \frac{1}{4} + \$0 \cdot \frac{3}{4} = \$0.75$$

This means, if the game is to be fair, that you should be willing to pay $0.75 ea time you play the game.

(c) A game consists of flipping a fair coin. If a head shows, the player loses $1; but i tail shows, the player wins $2. That is, half the time the player loses $1 and the oth half the player wins $2. The *expected value E* of the game is

$$E = \$2 \cdot \frac{1}{2} + (-\$1) \cdot \frac{1}{2} = \$0.50$$

The player is expected to win an average of $0.50 on each play.

In each of the above examples, we arrive at the expected value E by multiplying t amount earned for a given outcome times the probability for that outcome to occur, a adding all the products.

Look back at Example 1(a). In the expression for the expected value in the raf problem, the term $\$300 \cdot \frac{1}{1000}$ is the product of the value $300 with its correspondi probability $\frac{1}{1000}$, namely, the probability of having a $300 ticket. Likewise, t probability of getting a $1 ticket is $\frac{100}{1000}$ and this produces the term $\$1 \cdot \frac{100}{1000}$ in t expression for the expected value, E. So the expression for E is obtained multiplying each ticket value by the probability of its occurrence and adding the resul

In Example 1(b), the term $\$3 \cdot \frac{1}{4}$ is the product of the value $3.00 with corresponding probability $\frac{1}{4}$, namely, the probability of obtaining HH. Likewise, t probability of getting HT, TH, and TT is $\frac{3}{4}$ with payoff $0, and this produces $\$0 \cdot \frac{3}{4}$ in t expression for the expected value.

Finally, in Example 1(c) the term $\$2 \cdot \frac{1}{2}$ is the product of the value $2.00 with corresponding probability $\frac{1}{2}$, namely, the probability of obtaining T. Likewise, t probability of getting H is $\frac{1}{2}$, with payoff −$1.

This leads to the following definition.

Definition

Expected Value

Let S be a sample space and let $A_1, A_2, \ldots, A_n$ be n events of S that form a **partition** of S. That is, the union of the n events is S and the n events are pair-wise disjoint:

$$A_1 \cup A_2 \cup \ldots \cup A_n = S \quad \text{and} \quad A_i \cap A_j = \emptyset,\ i \neq j,\ 1 \leq i \leq n,\ 1 \leq j \leq n$$

Let $p_1, p_2, \ldots, p_n$ be the probabilities, respectively, of the events $A_1, A_2, \ldots, A_n$. If each event $A_1, A_2, \ldots, A_n$ is assigned, respectively, the payoffs $m_1, m_2, \ldots, m_n$, the **expected value** E corresponding to these payoffs is

$$E = m_1 \cdot p_1 + m_2 \cdot p_2 + \cdots + m_n \cdot p_n \tag{1}$$

The term *expected value* should not be interpreted as a value that actually occurs in the experiment. In Example 1(a) there was no raffle ticket costing \$0.60. Rather, this number represents the average value of a raffle ticket.

In gambling, E is interpreted as the average winnings expected for the player in the long run. If E is positive, we say that the game is **favorable** to the player; if $E = 0$, we say the game is **fair;** and if E is negative, we say the game is **unfavorable** to the player.

When the payoff assigned to an outcome of an experiment is positive, it can be interpreted as a profit, winnings, gain, and so on. When it is negative, it represents losses, penalties, deficits, and so on.

1 Find the Expected Value

Steps for Finding the Expected Value

STEP 1 Partition a sample space S into n events $A_1, A_2, \ldots, A_n$.

STEP 2 Determine the probability $p_1, p_2, \ldots, p_n$ of each event $A_1, A_2, \ldots, A_n$. Since these events constitute a partition of S, it follows that

$$p_1 + p_2 + \cdots + p_n = 1.$$

STEP 3 Assign payoff values $m_1, m_2, \ldots, m_n$ to each event $A_1, A_2, \ldots, A_n$.

STEP 4 Calculate the expected value $E = m_1 \cdot p_1 + m_2 \cdot p_2 + \cdots + m_n \cdot p_n$.

EXAMPLE 2 Find the Expected Value

Consider the experiment of rolling a fair die. The player recovers an amount of dollars equal to the number of dots on the face that turns up, except when face 5 or 6 turns up, in which case the player will lose \$5 or \$6, respectively. What is the expected value of the game? Is the game fair?

SOLUTION

STEP 1   The sample space is $S = \{1, 2, 3, 4, 5, 6\}$. Each of these 6 outcomes constitutes an eve[nt] that forms a partition of S.

STEP 2   Since each outcome (event) is equally likely, the probability of each one is $\dfrac{1}{6}$.

STEP 3   Since the player wins $1 for the outcome 1, $2 for the outcome 2, $3 for a 3, and $4 fo[r] 4, and the player loses $5 for a 5 or equivalently wins $-$5 for a 5 and loses $6 for a 6 [or] equivalently wins $-$6 for a 6, we assign payoffs (the winnings of the player) as follow[s]:

Event	1	2	3	4	5	6
Payoff (winnings)	$1	$2	$3	$4	−$5	−$6

STEP 4   The expected value of the game is

$$E = \$1 \cdot \frac{1}{6} + \$2 \cdot \frac{1}{6} + \$3 \cdot \frac{1}{6} + \$4 \cdot \frac{1}{6} + (-\$5) \cdot \frac{1}{6} + (-\$6) \cdot \frac{1}{6}$$

$$= -\$\frac{1}{6} = -\$0.167$$

The player would expect to lose an average of 16.7 cents on each throw.

The game is not fair; it is unfavorable to the player.

NOW WORK PROBLEM 3.

EXAMPLE 3   **Find the Expected Value**

What is the expected number of heads in tossing a fair coin three times?

SOLUTION

STEP 1   The sample space is

$$S = \{HHH, HHT, HTH, HTT, THH, THT, TTH, TTT\}$$

Since we are interested in the number of heads and since a coin tossed three times w[ill] result in 0, 1, 2, or 3 heads, we partition S as follows:

$$A_1 = \{TTT\} \quad A_2 = \{HTT, THT, TTH\} \quad A_3 = \{HHT, HTH, THH\} \quad A_4 = \{HHH\}$$
$$\text{0 heads} \qquad\qquad \text{1 head} \qquad\qquad\qquad \text{2 heads} \qquad\qquad\qquad \text{3 head[s]}$$

STEP 2   The probability of each of these events is

$$P(A_1) = \frac{1}{8} \qquad P(A_2) = \frac{3}{8} \qquad P(A_3) = \frac{3}{8} \qquad P(A_4) = \frac{1}{8}$$

STEP 3   Since we are interested in the expected number of heads, we assign payoffs of 0, 1, 2, a[nd] 3, respectively, to A_1, A_2, A_3, and A_4.

STEP 4   The expected number of heads can now be found by multiplying each payoff by [the] corresponding probability and finding the sum of these values.

$$\text{Expected number of heads} = E = 0 \cdot \frac{1}{8} + 1 \cdot \frac{3}{8} + 2 \cdot \frac{3}{8} + 3 \cdot \frac{1}{8} = \frac{3}{2} = 1.5$$

On average, tossing a coin three times will result in 1.5 heads.

NOW WORK PROBLEM 13.

2 Solve Applied Problems Involving Expected Value

EXAMPLE 4 Bidding for Oil Wells

An oil company may bid for only one of two contracts for oil drilling in two different locations. If oil is discovered at location I, the profit to the company will be \$3,000,000. If no oil is found, the company's loss will be \$250,000. If oil is discovered at location II, the profit will be \$4,000,000. If no oil is found, the loss will be \$500,000. The probability of discovering oil at location I is 0.7, and at location II it is 0.6. Which field should the company bid on; that is, for which location is expected profit higher?

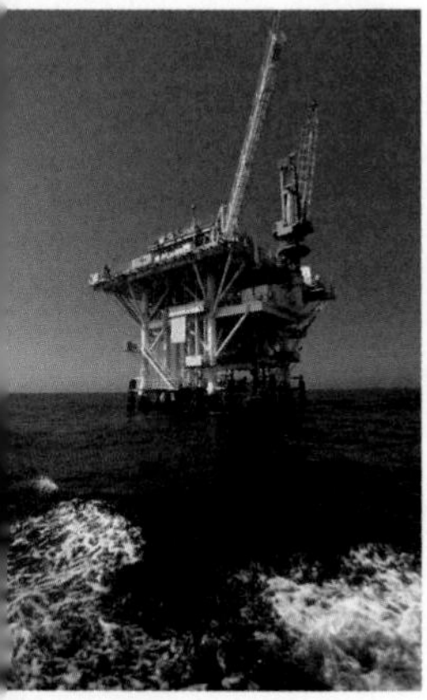

SOLUTION In the first location the company expects to discover oil 0.7 of the time at a profit of \$3,000,000. It would not discover oil 0.3 of the time at a loss of \$250,000. The expected profit E_{I} is therefore

$$E_{\text{I}} = (\$3{,}000{,}000)(0.7) + (-\$250{,}000)(0.3) = \$2{,}025{,}000$$

For the second location, the expected profit E_{II} is

$$E_{\text{II}} = (\$4{,}000{,}000)(0.6) + (-\$500{,}000)(0.4) = \$2{,}200{,}000$$

Since the expected profit for the second location exceeds that for the first, the oil company should bid on the second location. ■

NOW WORK PROBLEM 27.

EXAMPLE 5 Evaluating Insurance

Mr. Richmond is producing an outdoor concert. He estimates that he will make \$300,000 if it does not rain and make \$60,000 if it does rain. The weather bureau predicts that the chance of rain is 0.34 for the day of the concert.

(a) What are Mr. Richmond's expected earnings from the concert?

(b) An insurance company is willing to insure the concert for \$150,000 against rain for a premium of \$30,000. If he buys this policy, what are his expected earnings from the concert?

(c) Based on the expected earnings, should Mr. Richmond buy an insurance policy?

SOLUTION The sample space consists of two outcomes: R: Rain or N: No rain. The probability of rain is $P(R) = 0.34$; the probability of no rain is $P(N) = 0.66$.

(a) If it rains, the earnings are \$60,000; if there is no rain, the earnings are \$300,000. The expected earnings E are

$$\begin{aligned} E &= \$60{,}000 \cdot P(R) + \$300{,}000 \cdot P(N) \\ &= 60{,}000(0.34) + 300{,}000(0.66) \\ &= \$218{,}400 \end{aligned}$$

(b) With insurance, if it rains, the earnings are

$$\underbrace{\$150{,}000}_{\text{Insurance payout}} + \underbrace{\$60{,}000}_{\text{Concert profit}} - \underbrace{\$30{,}000}_{\text{Cost of insurance}} = \$180{,}000$$

With insurance, if it does not rain, the earnings are

$$\underset{\text{No insurance payout}}{\$0} + \underset{\text{Concert profit}}{\$300{,}000} - \underset{\text{Cost of insurance}}{\$30{,}000} = \$270{,}000$$

With insurance, the expected earnings E are

$$\begin{aligned} E &= \$180{,}000 \cdot P(R) + \$270{,}000 \cdot P(N) \\ &= 180{,}000(0.34) + 270{,}000(0.66) \\ &= \$239{,}400 \end{aligned}$$

(c) Since the expected earnings are higher with insurance, it would be better to obta the insurance.

NOW WORK PROBLEM 25.

EXAMPLE 6 Car Rentals

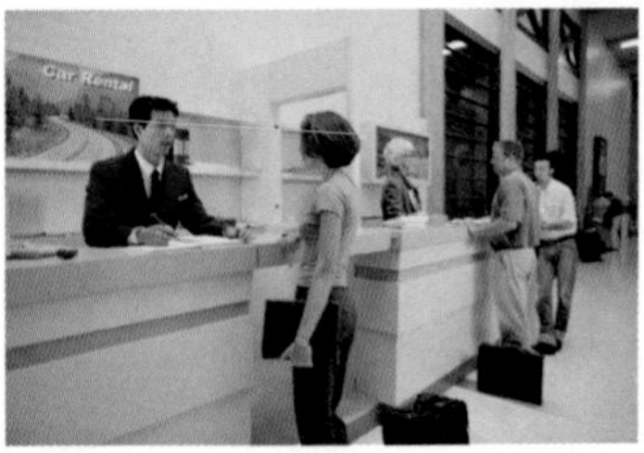

A national car rental agency rents luxury cars for $80 per day (gasoline is an addition expense to the customer). The daily cost per car (for example, lease costs and overhea is $15 per day. The daily profit depends on two factors: the demand for cars and t number of cars the company has available to rent. Previous rental records show th the daily demand for luxury cars is as given in Table 5:

TABLE 5

Number of Customers	8	9	10	11	12
Probability	0.10	0.10	0.30	0.30	0.20

Find the optimal number of cars the company should have available for rental. (This the number that yields the largest expected profit.)

SOLUTION We seek the expected profit for each possible number of cars. The largest expected pro will tell us how many cars to have on hand.

For example, if there are 10 cars available, the expected profit for 8, 9, or customers is found as follows:

For 8 customers, the revenue generated is $8(80) = \$640$ and the cost of the 10 ca is $10(15) = \$150$, for a profit of \$490. The probability of 8 customers is 0.1.

For 9 customers, the revenue generated is $9(80) = \$720$ and the cost of the 10 ca is \$150 for a profit of \$570. The probability of 9 customers is 0.1.

For 10 customers, the revenue generated is $10(80) = \$800$ and the cost the 10 cars is \$150 for a profit of \$650. The probability of 10 customers is 0.8, becau 10 cars are rented when 10, 11, or 12 customers show up.

The expected profit E is

$$E = \$490(0.1) + \$570(0.1) + \$650(0.8) = \$626$$

Table 6 lists the expected profit for 8 to 12 available cars. The optimal stock size 12 cars, since this number of cars maximizes expected profit.

TABLE 6

Number of Available Cars	8	9	10	11	12
Expected Profit	\$520	\$577	\$626	\$651	\$652

■

NOW WORK PROBLEM 23.

EXERCISE 7.6 Answers Begin on Page 37.

oncepts and Vocabulary

1. ***True or False*** Sometimes the expected value is a negative number.

2. If the expected value of a game is 0, the game is ________.

kill Building

3. For the data given below, compute the expected value.

Outcome	e_1	e_2	e_3	e_4
Probability	0.4	0.2	0.1	0.3
Payoff	2	3	−2	0

4. For the data below, compute the expected value.

Outcome	e_1	e_2	e_3	e_4
Probability	$\frac{1}{3}$	$\frac{1}{6}$	$\frac{1}{4}$	$\frac{1}{4}$
Payoff	1	0	4	−2

pplications and Extensions

5. **Weather and Attendance** Attendance at a football game in a certain city results in the following pattern. If it is extremely cold, the attendance will be 30,000; if it is cold, it will be 40,000; if it is moderate, 60,000; and if it is warm, 80,000. If the probabilities for extremely cold, cold, moderate, and warm are 0.08, 0.42, 0.42, and 0.08, respectively, how many fans are expected to attend the game?

6. **Analyzing a Game** A player rolls a fair die and receives a number of dollars equal to the number of dots appearing on the face of the die. What is the least the player should expect to pay in order to play the game?

7. **Analyzing a Game** Mary will win \$8 if she draws an ace from a set of 10 different cards from ace (1) to 10. How much should she pay for one draw?

8. **Analyzing a Game** Thirteen playing cards, ace through king, are placed randomly with faces down on a table. The prize for guessing correctly the face of any given card is \$1. What would be a fair price to pay for a guess?

9. **Analyzing a Game** David gets \$12 if he throws a double on a single throw of a pair of dice. How much should he pay for a throw?

10. **Analyzing a Game** You pay \$1 to toss 2 coins. If you toss 2 heads, you get \$2 (including your \$1); if you toss only 1 head, you get back your \$1; and if you toss no heads, you lose your \$1. Is this a fair game to play?

11. **Raffles** In a raffle 1000 tickets are being sold at \$1.00 each. The first prize is \$100, and there are 3 second prizes of \$50 each. By how much does the price of a ticket exceed its expected value?

12. **Raffles** In a raffle 1000 tickets are being sold at \$1.00 each. The first prize is \$100. There are 2 second prizes of \$50 each, and 5 third prizes of \$10 each. Jenny buys 1 ticket. How much more than the expected value of the ticket does she pay?

13. **Analyzing a Game** A fair coin is tossed 3 times, and a player wins \$3 if 3 tails occur, wins \$2 if 2 tails occur, and loses \$3 if no tails occur. If 1 tail occurs, no one wins.
    (a) What is the expected value of the game?
    (b) Is the game fair?
    (c) If the answer to part (b) is "No," how much should the player win or lose for a toss of exactly 1 tail to make the game fair?

14. **Analyzing a Game** Colleen bets \$1 on a 2-digit number. She wins \$75 if she draws her number from the set of all 2-digit numbers, {00, 01, 02, . . . , 99}; otherwise, she loses her \$1.
    (a) Is this game fair to the player?
    (b) How much is Colleen expected to lose in a game?

15. **Sports** Two teams have played each other 14 times. Team A won 9 games, and team B won 5 games. They will play again next week. Bob offers to bet \$6 on team A while you bet \$4 on team B. The winner gets the \$10. Is the bet fair to you in view of the past records of the two teams? Explain your answer.

16. **Department Store Sales** A department store wants to sell 11 purses that cost the store \$40 each and 32 purses that cost the store \$10 each. If all purses are wrapped in 43 identical boxes and if each customer picks a box randomly, find
    (a) Each customer's expectation.
    (b) The department store's expected profit if it charges \$15 for each box.

17. **Cards** Sarah draws a card from a deck of 52 cards. She receives 40¢ for a heart, 50¢ for an ace, and 90¢ for the ace of hearts. If the cost a draw is 15¢, should she play the game? Explain.

18. **Family Size** The following data give information about family size in the United States in 2009 for a household containing a husband a wife where the husband is in the 30–34 age bracket. A family is chosen at random. Find the expected number of children in the fami

Number of Children	0	1	2	3	4
Proportion of Families	19.9%	28.4%	30.7%	14.5%	6.5%

Source: U.S. Census Bureau

19. **Corporate Receipts** The following data give the number of tax returns (in thousands) filed in 2006 by S-corporations with to receipts under $1 million. Use the midpoint to find the expected receipts for a corporation with receipts of less than $1,000,000.

Size-class of Receipts	under $25,000	$25,000–$99,999	$100,000–$249,999	$250,000–$499,999	$500,000–$999,999
Midpoint	$12,500	$62,500	$175,000	$375,000	$750,000
Number of Returns	954,123	650,138	707,229	545,457	443,573

Source: Internal Revenue Service

20. **Number of Employees** The following data give the distribution of business establishments in 2006 by employment-size class f businesses with less than 1000 employees. Use the midpoint to find the expected number of employees for a business in this catego

Number of Employees	0 to 19	20 to 99	100 to 499	500 to 999
Midpoint	10	60	300	750
Probability	0.483	0.504	0.012	0.001

Source: U.S. Census Bureau, *County Business Patterns*

21. **Housing Sales** The following data give the number of new houses sold (in thousands) in the United States in 2009 for prices und $750,000. Use the midpoint to find the expected sale price of a new house.

Price	$0–$149,999	$150,000–$199,999	$200,000–$299,999	$300,000–$399,999	$400,000–$499,999	$500,000–$749,999
Midpoint	$75,000	$175,000	$250,000	$350,000	$450,000	$625,000
Number Sold	66	96	114	46	23	20

Source: U.S. Census Bureau

22. **Kentucky Derby** Of the 19 horses in the 2009 Kentucky Derby, the top two finishers (in order) were Mine That Bird and Pioneer of the Nile. On a $2 exacta bet (picking the top two horses in order), the house paid out $2074.80. That is, for every $2 bet, you either lost $2 or gained $2072.80. What was the house's expected earnings per $2 bet?

Source: www.thespread.com

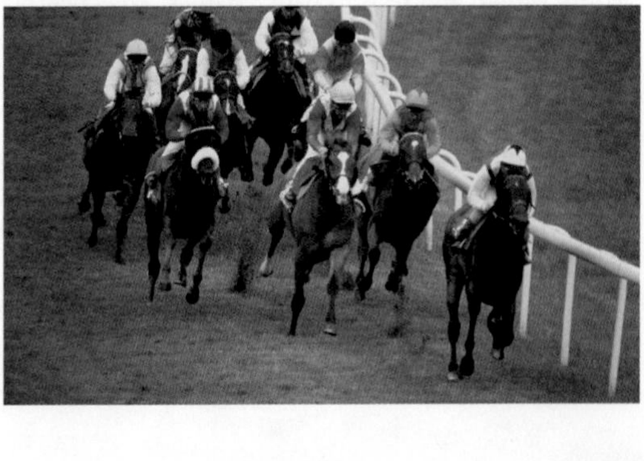

23. **Market Assessment** A truck rental agency has fixed costs $20 per truck per day and the revenue for each truck rented $90 per day. The daily demand is given in the table:

Number of Customers	7	8	9	10	11
Probability	0.10	0.20	0.40	0.20	0.1

(a) Find the expected number of customers.

(b) Determine the optimal number of trucks the compa should have on hand each day.

(c) What is the expected revenue in this case?

24. **Ski Rentals** Swen's Ski Rental rents skis, boots, and poles f $20 a day. The daily cost per set of skis is $6. It includ maintenance, storage, and overhead. Daily profits depend c daily demand for skis and the number of sets available. Sw knows that on a typical day the demand for skis is given the table.

Number of Customers	90	91	92	93	94	95	96	97
Probability	0.01	0.10	0.20	0.20	0.30	0.10	0.05	0.04

How many sets of skis should Swen have ready for rental to maximize his profit?

. **Life Insurance** A 20-year-old male purchases a 1-year life insurance policy worth \$250,000. The insurance company determines that he will survive the policy period with probability 0.9986.

(a) If the premium for the policy is \$450, what is the expected profit for the insurance company?

(b) At what value should the company set its premium so its expected profit will be \$250 per policy for 20-year-old males?

Source: National Center for Health Statistics

. **Life Insurance** A 20-year-old female purchases a 1-year life insurance policy worth \$250,000. The insurance company determines that she will survive the policy period with probability 0.9995.

(a) If the premium for the policy is \$300, what is the expected profit for the insurance company?

(b) At what value should the company set its premium so its expected profit will be \$250 per policy for 20-year-old females?

Source: National Center for Health Statistics

. **Site Selection** A company operating a chain of supermarkets plans to open a new store in 1 of 2 locations. It conducted a survey of the 2 locations and estimated that the first location will show an annual profit of \$15,000 if it is successful and a \$3000 loss otherwise. For the second location, the estimated annual profit is \$20,000 if successful and a \$6000 loss otherwise.

(a) If the probability of success at each location is $\frac{1}{2}$, what location should the management decide on in order to maximize its expected profit?

(b) If the probability of success at the first location is $\frac{2}{3}$ and at the second location is $\frac{1}{3}$, what location should be chosen?

28. Roulette In roulette there are 38 equally likely possibilities: the numbers 1–36, 0, and 00 (double zero). See the figure. What is the expected value for a gambler who bets \$1 on number 15 if she wins \$35 each time the number 15 turns up and loses \$1 if any other number turns up? If the gambler plays the number 15 for 200 consecutive times, what is the total expected gain?

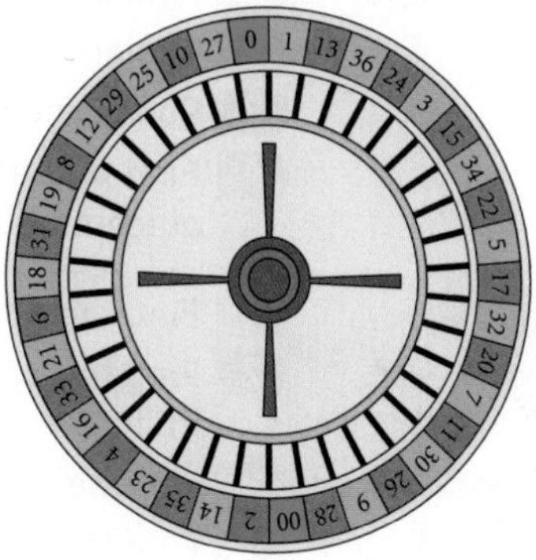

oblems 29 and 30 require the following information.

pected return *The* ***expected return E*** *for a portfolio is the weighted average of the individual expected returns. That is,* $E = \sum_{i=1}^{n} w_i E_i$, *where* *s the number of stocks in the portfolio,* w_i *is the weight or percent of investment for the ith stock, and* E_i *is the expected return for the ith stock.*

. **Diversifying Portfolios** An investor decides to create a portfolio that initially will contain two stocks: Wal-Mart and Viacom. He expects the Wal-Mart stock to have an annual return of 10% and the Viacom stock to have an annual return of 15%.

(a) If he invests equally in both stocks, what will be his expected annual return on the portfolio?

(b) How should he divide his investment in order to realize an annual return of 14% on his portfolio?

Source: money.cnn.com

. **Diversifying Portfolios** An investor decides to create a portfolio that initially will contain four stocks: Boeing, Apple Computers, Aetna, and Caterpillar. She expects the Boeing stock to have an annual return of 25%, the Apple Computers stock to have an annual return of 18%, the Aetna stock to have an annual return of 8%, and the Caterpillar stock to have an annual return of 10%.

(a) If she invests equally in all stocks, what will be her expected annual return on the portfolio?

(b) If she wants to keep half her investment evenly split between Apple Computer and Aetna, how should she divide the remaining half of her investment between the other two stocks in order to realize an annual return of 17.75% on her portfolio?

Source: money.cnn.com

iscussion and Writing

. Make up a game different than any given in the text that is favorable to the player.

. Look up the rules for a lottery and discuss the expected value of a ticket.

33. Refer to Example 8. As manager, would you have 11 or 12 luxury cars available to rent? Provide a rationale for your decision. Notice that the 12th car only generates \$1 more in profit than the 11 cars do.

CHAPTER 7 REVIEW OBJECTIVES

Section	Examples		You should be able to	Review Exercises
7.1	3	1	Identify relations between pairs of sets (p. 357)	1–16
	4, 5, 6	2	Find the union and intersection of two sets (p. 359)	3, 4, 6, 9, 11–13, 15–18 23–28, 37, 38
	7	3	Find the complement of a set (p. 361)	18 a, c–f, 24, 26, 28
	8, 9, 10	4	Use Venn diagrams (p. 362)	19–22
7.2	1, 2	1	Use the Counting Formula (p. 367)	29–34
	3, 4	2	Use Venn diagrams to analyze survey data (p. 367)	35, 36
7.3	1–5	1	Use the Multiplication Principle (p. 373)	63–66
7.4	1, 2, 3	1	Find a sample space (p. 380)	39–42
	4	2	Assign probabilities (p. 382)	43–46
	5	3	Construct a probability model (p. 382)	47a, 48a
	6, 7	4	Find probabilities involving equally likely outcomes (p. 383)	47b, 48b, 49, 50
7.5	1	1	Find the probability of an event (p. 391)	52, 53, 54, 55, 61, 62
	2	2	Find the probability of *E* or *F* when *E* and *F* are mutually exclusive (p. 393)	58, 59
	3, 4	3	Use the Additive Rule (p. 394)	51, 54b, 55b, 56b, 57a, 60
	5	4	Find the probability of the complement of an event (p. 395)	51b, 54a, 55a, 56a, 56c, 57b 57c, 58a, 58b, 59a, 59b
	6	5	Use a Venn diagram to find probabilities (p. 396)	56–59
	7, 8	6	Use the Multiplication Principle to find probabilities (p. 397)	67, 68
	9, 10	7	Compute odds (p. 398)	69–71
7.6	1, 2, 3	1	Find the expected value (p. 405)	72–78
	4, 5, 6	2	Solve applied problems involving expected value (p. 407)	72–78

THINGS TO KNOW

Set (p. 356)		Well-defined collection of distinct objects, called elements
Empty set (p. 357)	$\varnothing$	Set that has no elements
Equality (p. 357)	$A = B$	*A* and *B* have the same elements.
Subset (p. 357)	$A \subseteq B$	Each element of *A* is an element of *B*.
Proper subset (p. 358)	$A \subset B$	Each element of *A* is an element of *B*. but there is at least one element *B* not in *A*.
Universal set (p. 359)	U	Set consisting of all the elements that we wish to consider
Union (p. 359)	$A \cup B$	Set consisting of elements that belong to either *A* or *B*, or both
Intersection (p. 359)	$A \cap B$	Set consisting of elements that belong to both *A* and *B*
Complement (p. 361)	$\overline{A}$	Set consisting of elements of the universal set that are not in *A*

Finite set (p. 366)	The number of elements in the set is a nonnegative integer.
Infinite set (p. 366)	A set that is not finite
ounting Formula (p. 367)	$n(A \cup B) = n(A) + n(B) - n(A \cap B)$
ultiplication Principle (p. 374)	If a task consists of a sequence of choices in which there are p selections for the first choice, q selections for the second choice, and so on, then the task of making these selections can be done in $p \cdot q \cdot \cdots$ different ways.
robablility of an Event E with Equally Likely Outcomes (p. 384)	$P(E) = \dfrac{n(E)}{n(S)}$
utually Exclusive Events (p. 393)	If E and F are mutually exclusive events, $P(E \cup F) = P(E) + P(F)$.
dditive Rule (p. 394)	For any two events E and F, $P(E \cup F) = P(E) + P(F) - P(E \cap F)$.
robability of the Complement of an Event (p. 395)	$P(\overline{E}) = 1 - P(E)$
dds for E Are a to b (p. 399)	$P(E) = \dfrac{a}{a+b}$

EVIEW EXERCISES

Answers to odd-numbered problems begin on page AN-38.

ue problem numbers indicate the author's suggestions for a practice test.

Problems 1–16, replace the blank by any of the symbol(s) $\subset$, $\subseteq$, $=$ that result in a true statement. If none result in a true statement, rite "None of these." More than one answer may be possible.

1. $\varnothing$ __ $\{0\}$
2. $\{0\}$ __ $\{1, 0, 3\}$
3. $[\{5, 6\} \cap \{2, 6\}]$ __ $\{8\}$
4. $\{3\}$ __ $[\{2, 3\} \cup \{3, 4\}]$
5. $\{8, 9\}$ __ $\{9, 10, 11\}$
6. $\{1\}$ __ $[\{1, 3, 5\} \cup \{3, 4\}]$
7. $\{5\}$ __ $\{0, 5\}$
8. $\varnothing$ __ $\{1, 2, 3\}$
9. $\varnothing$ __ $[\{1, 2\} \cap \{3, 4, 5\}]$
10. $\{2, 3\}$ __ $\{3, 4\}$
11. $\{1, 2\}$ __ $[\{1\} \cup \{2\}]$
12. $\{5\}$ __ $[\{1\} \cup \{2, 3\}]$
13. $[\{4, 5\} \cap \{5, 6\}]$ __ $\{4, 5\}$
14. $\{6, 8\}$ __ $\{8, 9, 10\}$
15. $[\{6, 7, 8\} \cap \{6\}]$ __ $\{6\}$
16. $\{4\}$ __ $[\{6, 8\} \cap \{4, 8\}]$

17. For the sets

$$A = \{1, 3, 5, 6, 8\} \quad B = \{2, 3, 6, 7\} \quad C = \{6, 8, 9\}$$

find

(a) $(A \cap B) \cup C$ (b) $(A \cap B) \cap C$
(c) $(A \cup B) \cap B$ (d) $B \cup \varnothing$
(e) $A \cap \varnothing$ (f) $(A \cup B) \cup C$

18. For the sets U = universal set = $\{1, 2, 3, 4, 5, 6, 7\}$ and

$$A = \{1, 3, 5, 6\} \quad B = \{2, 3, 6, 7\} \quad C = \{4, 6, 7\}$$

find:

(a) $\overline{A \cap B}$ (b) $(B \cap C) \cap A$
(c) $\overline{B} \cup \overline{A}$ (d) $C \cup \overline{C}$
(e) $\overline{\overline{B}}$ (f) $A \cap \overline{B}$

19. Use a Venn diagram to illustrate the following sets:

(a) $A \cup \overline{B}$ (b) $(A \cap B) \cup \overline{B}$
(c) $B \cap \overline{A}$ (d) $(A \cup B) \cap C$
(e) $(A \cap B) \cap C$ (f) $\overline{(\overline{B} \cup C)}$

20. Use a Venn diagram to illustrate the following properties:

(a) $(A \cap B) \cap C = A \cap (B \cap C)$
(b) $\overline{A \cap B} = \overline{A} \cup \overline{B}$
(c) $A \cup (B \cap C) = (A \cup B) \cap (A \cup C)$
(d) $\overline{\overline{A}} = A$

21. Draw a Venn diagram that illustrates $A \cap B = \varnothing$.
22. Draw a Venn diagram that illustrates $A \subset B$.

In Problems 23–28, use

U = Universal set = $\{x | x$ is a state in the United States$\}$
$A = \{a | a$ is a state whose name begins with the letter $A\}$
$V = \{v | v$ is a state whose name ends with a vowel$\}$
$E = \{e | e$ is a state that lies east of the Mississippi River$\}$

to describe each set in words.

23. $A \cup V$
24. $A \cap \overline{V}$
25. $V \cap E$
26. $\overline{E}$
27. $(A \cup V) \cap E$
28. $\overline{A \cup V}$
29. If A and B are sets and if $n(A) = 24$, $n(A \cup B) = 33$, and $n(B) = 12$, find $n(A \cap B)$.

30. If $n(A) = 10, n(B) = 8,$ and $n(A \cap B) = 2,$ find $n(A \cup B)$.

31. (a) If $n(A \cap B) = 0, n(A) = 3,$ and $n(B) = 17,$ find $n(A \cup B)$.

(b) What can you conclude about the sets A and B?

32. (a) If $n(A) = 14, n(B) = 8,$ and $n(A \cap B) = 8,$ find $n(A \cup B)$.

(b) What can you conclude about the relation between A and B?

33. Suppose a die is tossed. Let A denote that the outcome is an even number; let B denote that the outcome is a number less than or equal to 3. How many elements are in $A \cap B$? How many elements are in $A \cup B$?

34. Suppose a die is tossed. Let A denote the outcome is an even number; let B denote the outcome is divisible by 3. How many elements are in $A \cap B$? How many elements are in $A \cup B$?

35. Car Options During June, Colleen's Motors sold 75 cars with heated seats, 95 with GPS, and 100 with a sunroof. Twenty cars had all three options. 10 cars had none of these options, and 10 cars were sold that had only heated seats. In addition, 50 cars had both a sunroof and a GPS, and 60 cars had both a sunroof and heated seats.

(a) How many cars were sold in June?

(b) How many cars had only a GPS?

36. Student Survey In a survey of 125 college students, it was found that of three newspapers, the *Wall Street Journal, New York Times,* and *Chicago Tribune:*

60 read the *Chicago Tribune*
40 read the *New York Times*
15 read the *Wall Street Journal*
25 read the *Chicago Tribune* and *New York Times*
8 read the *New York Times* and *Wall Street Journal*
3 read the *Chicago Tribune* and *Wall Street Journal*
1 read all three

(a) How many read none of these papers?

(b) How many read only the *Chicago Tribune*?

(c) How many read neither the *Chicago Tribune* nor the *New York Times*?

37. If U = universal set = $\{1, 2, 3, 4, 5\}$ and $B = \{1, 4, 5\}$, find all sets A for which $A \cap B = \{1\}$.

38. If U = universal set = $\{1, 2, 3, 4, 5\}$ and $B = \{1, 4, 5\}$, find all sets A for which $A \cup B = \{1, 2, 4, 5\}$.

39. Tossing a Coin A coin is tossed 5 times. We are interested in the number of heads that show. List the outcomes of the sample space.

40. Rolling a Die A die is rolled 10 times. We are interested the number of times an even number shows. List t outcomes of the sample space.

41. Two-Child Families A survey of families with 2 children made, and the gender of the children is recorded. Descri the sample space and draw a tree diagram of this experimer

42. The spinner pictured is spun 3 times. Each time the color noted. List the outcomes of the sample space. Draw a tr diagram of the experiment.

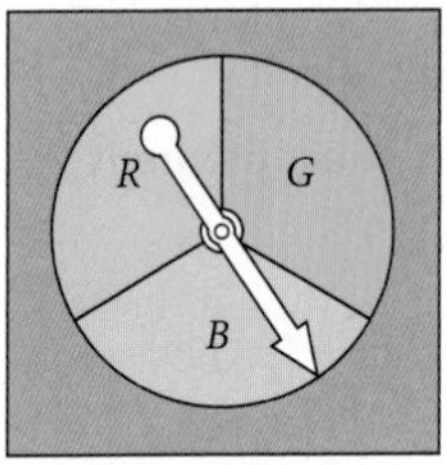

43. Jars and Coins A jar has 15 coins: 4 pennies, 5 dimes, an 6 quarters. A coin is selected from the jar. Assign val probabilities to the outcomes of this experiment.

44. Choosing a Ball A bag has 12 golf balls, 5 of which a cracked. A golf ball is chosen from the bag at randon Assign valid probabilities to this experiment.

45. Tossing a Weighted Die A die is weighted so that 2 and appear twice as often as 1, 3, 4, and 6. The die is tosse Assign valid probabilities to this experiment.

46. Tossing an Unfair Coin A coin is not fair. When tosse heads shows up 4 times more often than tails. Assign vali probabilities to this experiment.

47. Four-Child Families Families with 4 children were surveye

(a) Construct a probability model describing the possib number of girls in the family. (Assume the probabili a child is a girl is 0.5.)

(b) Find the probability that

(i) No children are girls.
(ii) Exactly 2 children are girls.
(iii) At least one boy and one girl.
(iv) At least one child is a boy.

48. Tossing a Fair Coin A fair coin is tossed three times.

(a) Construct a probability model corresponding to th experiment.

(b) Find the probabilities of the following events:

(i) The first toss is tails.
(ii) The first toss is heads.
(iii) Either the first toss is tails or the third toss is head
(iv) At least one of the tosses is heads.
(v) There are at least 2 tails.
(vi) No tosses are heads.

9. **Selecting Marbles** A jar contains 3 white marbles, 2 yellow marbles, 4 red marbles, and 5 blue marbles. Two marbles are picked at random. What is the probability that

(a) Both are blue?

(b) Exactly 1 is blue?

(c) At least 1 is blue?

0. **Drawing Cards** Two cards are drawn from a 52-card deck. What is the probability that

(a) 1 card is black and 1 card is red?

(b) Both cards are the same color?

(c) Both cards are red?

1. Let A and B be events with $P(A) = 0.3$, $P(B) = 0.5$, and $P(A \cap B) = 0.2$. Find the probability that

(a) A or B happens.

(b) A does not happen.

(c) Neither A nor B happens.

(d) Either A does not happen or B does not happen.

2. **Loaded Die** A loaded die is rolled 400 times, and the following outcomes are recorded:

Face	1	2	3	4	5	6
No. Times Showing	32	45	84	74	92	73

Estimate the probability of rolling a

(a) 3 (b) 5 (c) 6

3. **Tossing an Unfair Coin** An unfair coin is tossed 300 times and outcomes are recorded

Outcomes	H	T
No. Times Occurring	243	57

Estimate the probability of tossing a

(a) head (b) tail

4. A survey of a group of criminals shows that 65% came from low-income families, 40% from broken homes, and 30% came from low-income families and broken homes. Define

E: Criminal came from low-income family

F: Criminal came from broken home

A criminal is selected at random.

(a) Find the probability that the criminal is not from a low-income family.

(b) Find the probability that the criminal comes from a broken home or a low-income family.

(c) Are E and F mutually exclusive?

55. **Working Students** A survey of a group of 18- to 22-year-olds revealed that 63% were college students, 50% held jobs, and 35% did both. Define

E: The respondent is a college student.

F: The respondent has a job.

A respondent is selected at random.

(a) Find the probability that the respondent does not have a job.

(b) Find the probability that the respondent is a student or holds a job.

(c) Are E and F mutually exclusive?

56. If E and F are events with $P(E \cup F) = \frac{5}{8}$, $P(E \cap F) = \frac{1}{3}$, and $P(E) = \frac{1}{2}$, find

(a) $P(\overline{E})$ (b) $P(F)$ (c) $P(\overline{F})$

57. If $P(E) = 0.2$, $P(F) = 0.6$, and $P(E \cap F) = 0.1$, find

(a) $P(E \cup F)$ (b) $P(\overline{E})$ (c) $P(\overline{E \cap F})$

58. If E and F represent mutually exclusive events, $P(E) = 0.30$, and $P(F) = 0.45$, find each of the probabilities:

(a) $P(\overline{E})$ (b) $P(\overline{F})$ (c) $P(E \cap F)$

(d) $P(E \cup F)$ (e) $P(\overline{E \cap F})$ (f) $P(\overline{E \cup F})$

(g) $P(\overline{E} \cup \overline{F})$ (h) $P(\overline{E} \cap \overline{F})$

59. If $P(E) = 0.25$, $P(F) = 0.3$, and $P(E \cup F) = 0.55$, find each of the probabilities:

(a) $P(\overline{E})$ (b) $P(\overline{F})$ (c) $P(E \cap F)$

(d) $P(\overline{E \cap F})$ (e) $P(\overline{E} \cap \overline{F})$ (f) $P(\overline{E} \cup \overline{F})$

60. **Choosing a Card** A card is drawn from a 52-card deck. Define

E: The card is red.

F: The card is a face card (J, Q, or K).

Find the probability that it is either red or a face card.

61. Consider the experiment of spinning the spinner shown in the figure 3 times. (Assume the spinner cannot fall on a line.)

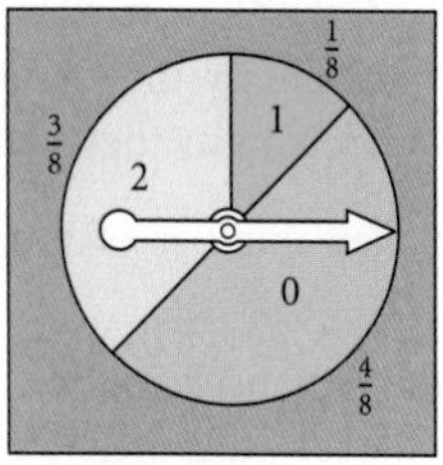

(a) Are all outcomes equally likely?

(b) If not, which of the outcomes has the highest probability?

(c) Let F be the event, "Each digit will occur exactly once." Find $P(F)$.

62. M&M Candies A bowl contains 22 M&M candies; 4 are red, 6 are green, and 12 are blue. A piece of candy is chosen, and its color is noted.

(a) Is each color equally likely to be picked?

(b) Which outcome has the highest probability of occurring?

(c) Suppose you took 3 pieces of candy without looking. Define the event

E: Each color is represented.

What is $P(E)$?

63. How many house styles are possible if a contractor offers 3 choices of roof designs, 4 choices of window designs, and 6 choices of brick?

64. In a cafeteria the $6.95 lunch menu lets you choose 1 salad, 1 entree, 1 dessert, and 1 beverage. If today's menu features 3 different salads, 5 different entrees, 6 different desserts, and 10 different beverages, how many distinct meals could one order?

65. How many different answers are possible in a true-false test consisting of 10 questions?

66. License Plate Numbers An automobile license number contains 1 or 2 letters followed by a 4-digit number. Compute the maximum number of different licenses.

67. Birthday Problem Fifteen people are in a room. Each is asked the day of the month (e.g., 1–31) he or she was born. What is the probability each person was born on a different day of the month?

68. Birthday Problem There are 5 people in the Smith family. What is the probability at least 2 of them have birthdays in the same month?

69. Gender of Children A family chosen at random has 4 children. What are the odds that all four are boys?

70. Bears Win! A bettor is willing to give 7 to 6 odds that the Bears will win the NFL title. What is the probability of the Bears winning?

71. Football Pool You want to enter a football pool. The daily paper states the odds the Giants will win Sunday's game are 5:3. What is the probability the Giants will win Sunday's game? What is the probability they will lose?

72. What is the expected number of girls in families having exactly 3 children?

73. Evaluating a Game Frank pays $0.70 to play a certain game. He draws 2 balls (together) from a bag containing 2 red balls and 4 green balls. He receives $1 for each red ball that he draws. Has he paid too much? By how much?

74. Playing the Lottery In a lottery 1000 tickets are sold at $0.25 each. There are 3 cash prizes: $100, $50, and $30. Alice buys 8 tickets.

(a) What would have been a fair price for a ticket?

(b) How much extra did Alice pay?

75. Evaluating a Game The figure shows a spinning game f which a person pays $0.30 to purchase an opportunity spin the dial. The numbers in the figure indicate the amou of payoff and its corresponding probability in parenthes Find the expected value of this game. Is the game fair?

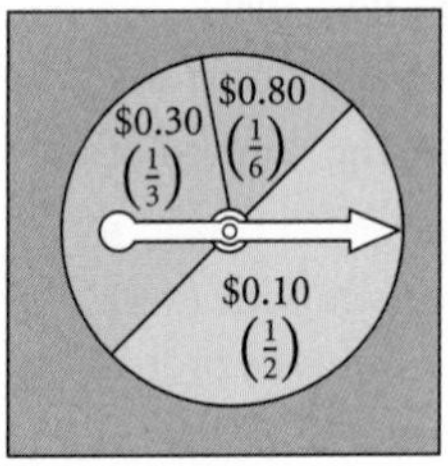

76. Evaluating a Game Consider the 3 boxes in the figure. Th game is played in 2 stages. The first stage is to choose a ba from box A. If the result is a ball marked I, then we go to bo I and select a ball from there. If the ball is marked II, the we select a ball from box II. The number drawn on th second stage is the gain. Find the expected value of this gam

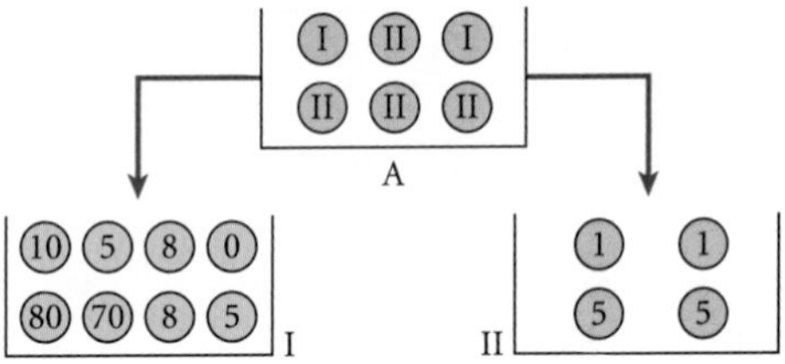

77. European Roulette A European roulette wheel has only 3 compartments, 18 red, 18 black, and 1 green. A player wi be paid $2 (including his $1 bet) if he picks correctly th color of the compartment in which the ball finally rest Otherwise, he loses $1. Is the game fair to the player?

78. Insuring against Weather The profits from an outdo sporting event are affected by inclement weather. Th promoter of the event expects it to net a profit of $750,000 the weather is dry but only $20,000 if the weather is wet. Th historical probability of rain is 5% for the day of the even

(a) What is the expected profit from the event?

(b) The promoter can buy $500,000 weather insurance fo a premium of $50,000. Based on expected profit, woul it be wise to buy insurance? Explain your reasoning.

(c) Suppose the chance of rain is 20% and the insuran costs $70,000. Based on the new information, what the expected profit from the event?

(d) Based on expected profit, would it be wise to bu insurance? Explain your reasoning.

Chapter 7 Project

ENTIFICATION NUMBERS: HOW MANY ARE ENOUGH?

you look carefully around you, you will see batches of numbers id letters on almost everything: on products in every store, 1 books, and certainly on the credit cards in your wallet. Even ough they may contain letters of the alphabet, these numbers e called **identification numbers**. They serve to identify the oduct, the book, or the person who owns the credit card.

Producing identification numbers is a lot more difficult an just deciding to print numbers on products or books. very system of identification numbers has a plan that tells actly how to assign those numbers. These plans must nfront several issues. First, there must be enough numbers r all of the things that you expect to number. Since giving the me identification number to different items would defeat the urpose of having an identification number, it is important at the plan have a way to give a unique number to each item. is also necessary to be able to check for errors in the entification number. This check helps to prevent misidentifying ems. As a result, most identification number plans include a umber, called a **check digit**, for this purpose. We consider two examples of identification numbers that you have probably already seen many times.

The Universal Product Code The Universal Product Code, or UPC, appears on just about every item you buy from a major store. It is designed to help the store track inventory and to make price changes easier. Figure 1 shows three examples. The first is from a box of Bigelow tea, the second is from a box of Xerox toner cartridges, and the third is from the front page of a newspaper.

There are two parts to the code: a bar code and a UPC number. Notice that the UPC number has 12 digits. The first 6 digits identify the producer and the next 5 digits identify the exact product. The final digit is the check digit.

Of the 6 digits identifying the producer, the first digit is particularly important. This digit, which appears at the far left of the code and is called the **number system character**, tells the type of product. Table 1 lists the number system characters currently in use. The numbers 1, 8, and 9 have been reserved for future use. The 5 digits that identify the product can be any digits whatsoever. Once the first 11 digits are known, the check digit is calculated from them.

FIGURE 1 Universal Product Codes

0 72310 00192 3

0 95205 60881 6 UPC

7 68663 30909 9

TABLE 1 UPC NUMBER SYSTEM CHARACTERS

0	Standard UPC number (for any type of product)
2	Random-weight items (produce, meats, etc.)
3	Pharmaceuticals
4	In-store marketing (gift cards, store-specific coupons)
5	Manufacturer's coupons
6	Standard UPC number (for any type of product)
7	Standard UPC number (for any type of product)

1. Under the current system, how many different producer numbers are possible?
2. If all digits were allowed for the number system character, how many more producer numbers would be created?
3. How many possible correct UPC codes are there? Assume all possible producer numbers are allowed.

The International Standard Book Number The International Standard Book Number, or ISBN, is used to identify works published anywhere in the world. The number is used to tra[…] and identify books quickly. Table 2 shows some examples.

TABLE 2 ISBN'S FOR VARIOUS BOOKS

The Last Song by Nicholas Sparks	978-0-446-54755-0
Cien Años de Soledad by Gabriel Garcia Marquez	978-84-204-7183-9
Probability and Statistics for Computer Science by James Johnson	978-0-470-38342-1
The Very Hungry Caterpillar by Eric Carle	978-0-399-22690-8
Les Trois Mousquetaires by Alexandre Dumas	978-2-266-19604-8
Le Véritable Amour by Jacqueline Harpman	978-2-930311-10-4
Solstices by Ananda Devi	978-99903-23-34-4
A Dictionary of Modern Legal Usage by Bryan Garner	978-0-19-514236-5
Finite Mathematics, 10th Edition, by Michael Sullivan	978-0-470-12863-3
Finite Mathematics, 11th Edition, by Michael Sullivan	978-0-470-45827-1

The 13-digit ISBN is a numerical code unique to books but aligns with number identification systems used globally for most consumer products. The first block of numbers designates the type of product or industry. That is, 978 indicates book publishing.

Notice that each ISBN has 13 digits, which are divided into 5 blocks with 4 hyphens. The first block always has 3 digits, 978. The final block always contains just 1 digit: the check digit. The other four blocks can contain anywhere from 1 to 7 numbers, but the total number of digits in the four blocks must always be 12. Only digits are used for these groups; no letters are allowed.

The second block tells the language or country in which the book was published. Books from English-speaking areas are assigned the numbers 0 or 1, those from French-speaking areas are assigned 2, those from German-speaking areas are assigned 3, and so on. Since a smaller country will likely produce fewer books, these countries get longer country codes. For example, the code for Spain is 84, and the code for Mauritius (an island nation in the Indian Ocean) is 99903. The third block identifies the publisher. For example, John Wiley and Sons has publisher number 470, so we see that this company published *Probability and Statistics for Computer Science* as well as this book. The fourth block identifies the individual book. Notice that the number of digits in this block limits the number of different titles a publisher can publish without needing to g[…] another publisher number. Thus Ancrage Press, whic[…] published *Le Véritable Amour,* only has two digits (or 100 title[…] for its use. Publishers that produce large numbers of titles a[…] given shorter publisher numbers to accommodate more title[…]

4. How many different titles may John Wiley and So[…] publish using the publisher number 470?
5. How many different titles may be published in Mauritiu[…] [*Hint:* In this case, four digits define the publisher and t[…] title. First consider how many different four-digit bloc[…] are possible. Then consider how many different ways […] hyphen may be inserted into the four-digit block.]
6. How many correct ISBN codes are possible for a book fro[…] the English-speaking area?
7. In practice, the number of correct ISBN codes is limited […] restrictions on both the format of the country code and t[…] format of the publisher number. For the English-speakir[…] area, the publisher number must be in the following range[…] 00–19, 200–699, 7000–8499, 85000–89999, 900000–94999[…] and 9500000–9999999. With these restrictions on t[…] publisher number, how many correct ISBN codes are possib[…] for a book from the English-speaking area?
8. Research the use of a check digit in the ISBN. Write a bri[…] report on what you find.

Mathematical Questions from Professional Exams*

1. **CPA Exam** The Stat Company wants more information on the demand for its products. The following data are relevant:

Units Demanded	Probability of Unit Demand	Total Cost of Units Demanded
0	0.10	$0
1	0.15	1.00
2	0.20	2.00
3	0.40	3.00
4	0.10	4.00
5	0.05	5.00

What is the total expected value or payoff with perfect information?

(a) $2.40 (b) $7.40 (c) $9.00 (d) $9.15

2. **CPA Exam** Your client wants your advice on which of 2 alternatives he should choose. One alternative is to sell an investment now for $10,000. Another alternative is to hold the investment 3 days, after which he can sell it for a certain selling price based on the following probabilities:

Selling Price	Probability
$ 5,000	0.4
$ 8,000	0.2
$12,000	0.3
$30,000	0.1

Using probability theory, which of the following is the most reasonable statement?

(a) Hold the investment 3 days because the expected value of holding exceeds the current selling price.

(b) Hold the investment 3 days because of the chance of getting $30,000 for it.

(c) Sell the investment now because the current selling price exceeds the expected value of holding.

(d) Sell the investment now because there is a 60% chance that the selling price will fall in 3 days.

3. **CPA Exam** The ARC Radio Company is trying to decide whether to introduce as a new product a wrist "radiowatch" designed for shortwave reception of exact time as broadcast by the National Bureau of Standards. The "radiowatch" would be priced at $60, which is exactly twice the variable cost per unit to manufacture and sell it. The incremental fixed costs necessitated by introducing this new product would amount to $240,000 per year. Subjective estimates of the probable demand for the product are shown in the following probability distribution:

Annual Demand	6,000	8,000	10,000	12,000	14,000	16,000
Probability	0.2	0.2	0.2	0.2	0.1	0.1

The expected value of demand for the new product is

(a) 11,000 units (b) 10,200 units (c) 9000 units
(d) 10,600 units (e) 9800 units

4. **CPA Exam** In planning its budget for the coming year, King Company prepared the following payoff probability distribution describing the relative likelihood of monthly sales volume levels and related contribution margins for product A:

Monthly Sales Volume	Contribution Margin	Probability
4,000	$ 80,000	0.20
6,000	120,000	0.25
8,000	160,000	0.30
10,000	200,000	0.15
12,000	240,000	0.10

What is the expected value of the monthly contribution margin for product A?

(a) $140,000 (b) $148,000
(c) $160,000 (d) $180,000

5. **CPA Exam** A decision tree has been formulated for the possible outcomes of introducing a new product line. Branches related to alternative 1 reflect the possible payoffs from introducing the product without an advertising campaign. The branches for alternative 2 reflect the possible payoffs with an advertising campaign costing $40,000.

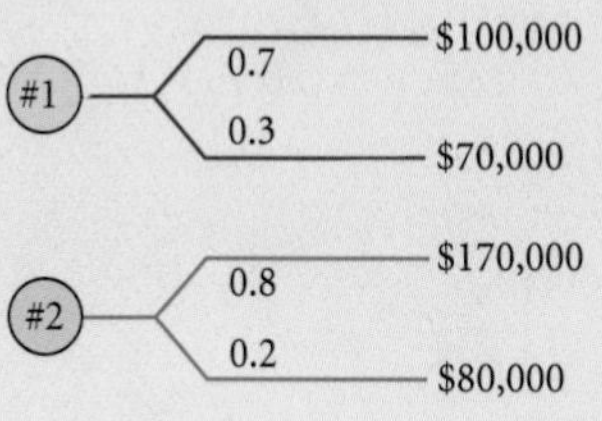

The expected values of alternatives 1 and 2, respectively, are

(a) #1: $(0.7 \times \$100{,}000) + (0.3 \times \$70{,}000)$
#2: $(0.8 \times \$170{,}000) + (0.2 \times \$80{,}000)$

(b) #1: $(0.7 \times \$100{,}000) + (0.3 \times \$70{,}000)$
#2: $(0.8 \times \$130{,}000) + (0.2 \times \$40{,}000)$

(c) #1: $(0.7 \times \$100{,}000) + (0.3 \times \$70{,}000)$
#2: $(0.8 \times \$170{,}000) + (0.2 \times \$80{,}000) - \$40{,}000$

(d) #1: $(0.7 \times \$100{,}000) + (0.3 \times \$70{,}000) - \$40{,}000$
#2: $(0.8 \times \$170{,}000) + (0.2 \times \$80{,}000) - \$40{,}000$

6. **CPA Exam** A battery manufacturer warrants its automobile batteries to perform satisfactorily for as long as the owner keeps the car. Auto industry data show that only 20% of car buyers retain their cars for 3 years or more. Historical data suggest the following:

Number of Years Owned	Probability of Battery Failure	Battery Exchange Costs	Percentage of Failed Batteries Returned
Less than 3 years	0.4	$50	75%
3 years or more	0.6	$20	50%

If 50,000 batteries were sold this year, what is the estimate warranty cost?

(a) $375,000 (b) $435,000

(c) $500,000 (d) $660,000

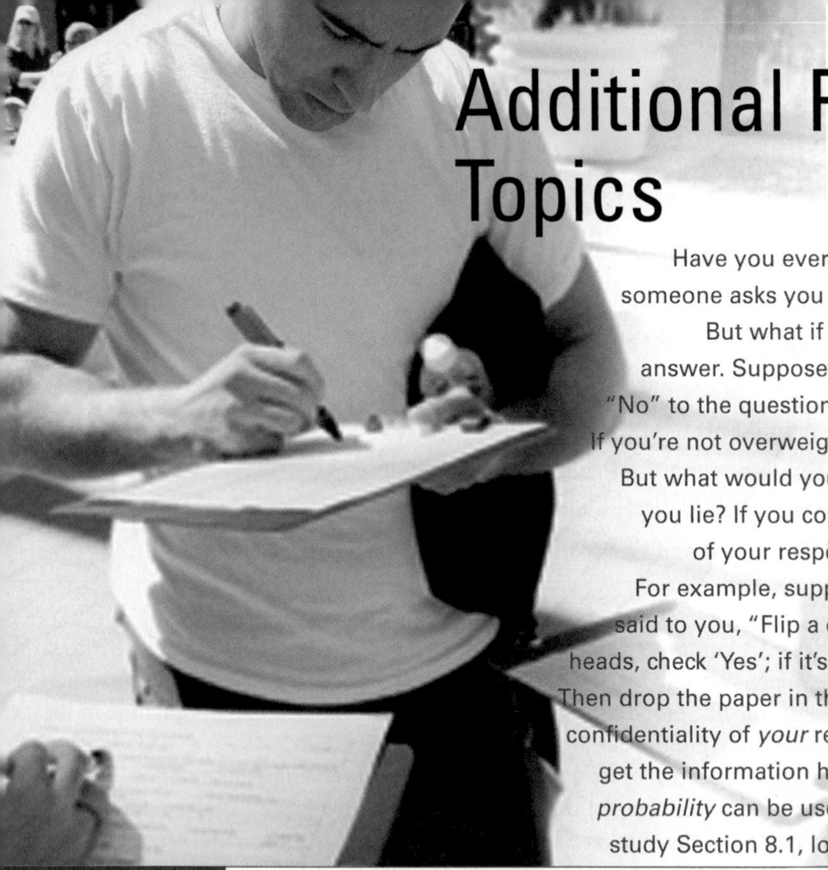

Additional Probability Topics 8

Have you ever participated in a survey? You know, someone asks you a question and you give an answer. But what if the question is one you'd rather not answer. Suppose you were asked to answer "Yes" or "No" to the question "Do you feel you are overweight?" If you're not overweight, you'd probably answer honestly. But what would you do if you *were* overweight? Would you lie? If you could be assured of the confidentiality of your response, would that make a difference? For example, suppose the person asking the question said to you, "Flip a coin and don't tell me the face. If it's heads, check 'Yes'; if it's tails, answer the question honestly. Then drop the paper in the box." This process guarantees the confidentiality of *your* response. But how does the surveyor get the information he wants? As it turns out, *conditional probability* can be used to complete the survey. After you study Section 8.1, look at the Chapter Project for details.

OUTLINE

A Look Back, A Look Forward

In Chapter 7 we developed the Multiplication Principle as a counting tool and used it to find probabilities. In this chapter we continue our study of probability with the notions of *conditional probability* and *independent events*. These lead to *Bayes' Theorem*, a formula used in many applications. Then we develop additional counting techniques, *permutations and combinations*, that lead us to the *binomial probability model*, which is also used in many applications.

8.1 Conditional Probability

PREPARING FOR THIS SECTION *Before getting started, review the following:*

- Properties of the Probability of an Event (Section 7.5, pp. 391–400)

NOW WORK THE 'ARE YOU PREPARED'? PROBLEMS ON PAGE 429.

OBJECTIVES
1. Find a conditional probability (p. 423)
2. Find probabilities using the Product Rule (p. 425)
3. Find probabilities using a tree diagram (p. 426)
4. Find conditional probabilities from a data table (p. 428)

Whenever we compute the probability of an event, we do it relative to the entire sampl space. When we ask for the probability $P(E)$ of the event E, this probability $P(E$ represents the likelihood that a chance experiment will produce an outcome in the set relative to the sample space S.

However, sometimes we want to compute the probability of an event E of a sampl space relative to another event F of the same sample space. That is, if we have *pric* information that the outcome must be in a set F, this information should be used t reappraise the likelihood that the outcome will also be in E. Called *conditional probabilit* this reappraised probability is denoted by $P(E|F)$, and is read as the *probability of E given F* It represents the answer to the question, "How probable is E, given that F has occurred?"

EXAMPLE 1 Example of Conditional Probability

FIGURE 1

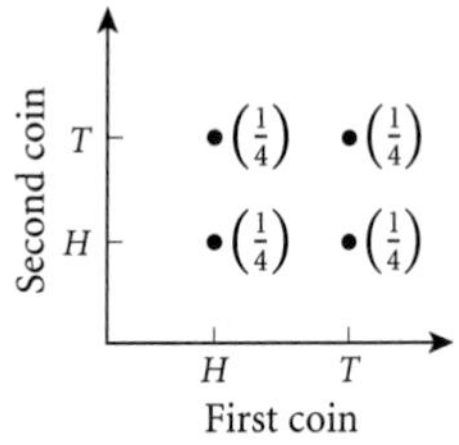

Consider the experiment of flipping two fair coins. A sample space S is

$$S = \{HH, HT, TH, TT\}$$

Figure 1 illustrates the sample space and the probability of each outcome.

Suppose the experiment is performed by another person and we have no knowledg of the result, but we are informed that at least one tail was tossed. This information mean the outcome HH could not have occurred. But the remaining outcomes HT, TH, TT ar still possible. How does this alter the probabilities of the remaining outcomes?

FIGURE 2

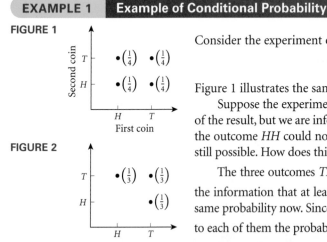

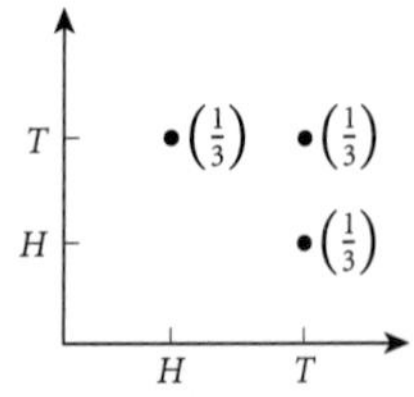

The three outcomes TH, HT, TT were each assigned the probability $\frac{1}{4}$ *before* we kne the information that at least one tail occurred, so it is not reasonable to assign them th same probability now. Since only three equally likely outcomes are now possible, we assig to each of them the probability $\frac{1}{3}$. See Figure 2.

EXAMPLE 2 Example of Conditional Probability

Suppose a population of 1000 people includes 70 accountants and 520 females. There are 40 females who are accountants. A person is chosen at random, and we are told the person i female. Since there are 520 females, 40 of whom are accountants, the probabilit the person is an accountant, given that the person is female, is $\frac{40}{520}$. That is, the *conditiona probability* of the event E (accountant) assuming the event F (the person chosen i female) is $\frac{40}{520} = \frac{1}{13}$.

We use the symbol $P(E|F)$, read "the probability of E given F," to denote conditional probability. For Example 2, if E is the event "A person chosen at random is an accountant" and F is the event "A person chosen at random is female," we would write

$$P(E|F) = \frac{40}{520} = \frac{1}{13}$$

GURE 3

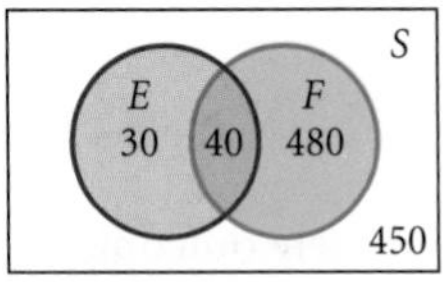

Figure 3 illustrates a Venn diagram for Example 2. Notice that the quotient of the number of entries in E and F, 40, with the number that are in F, 520, is $P(E|F)$. That is,

$$P(E|F) = \frac{40}{520} = \frac{n(E \cap F)}{n(F)}$$

Since

$$P(E|F) = \frac{n(E \cap F)}{n(F)} = \frac{\frac{n(E \cap F)}{n(S)}}{\frac{n(F)}{n(S)}} = \frac{P(E \cap F)}{P(F)}$$

we define conditional probability as follows:

Definition

Conditional Probability

Let E and F be events of a sample space S and suppose $P(F) > 0$. The **conditional probability of the event E, assuming the event F,** denoted by $P(E|F)$, is defined as

$$P(E|F) = \frac{P(E \cap F)}{P(F)} \quad \textbf{(1)}$$

1 Find a Conditional Probability

EXAMPLE 3 Finding a Conditional Probability

Consider the experiment of selecting one family from the set of three-child families. A sample space S for this experiment is

$$S = \{BBB, BBG, BGB, BGG, GBB, GBG, GGB, GGG\}$$

We assume that each outcome is equally likely, so that each outcome is assigned a probability of $\frac{1}{8}$. Let E be the event, "The family has exactly two boys" and let F be the event "The first child is a boy." What is the probability that the family has exactly two boys, given that the first child is a boy?

SOLUTION We want to find $P(E|F)$. The events E and F are

$$E = \{BBG, BGB, GBB\} \qquad F = \{BBB, BBG, BGB, BGG\}$$

Since $E \cap F = \{BBG, BGB\}$, we have

$$P(E \cap F) = \frac{2}{8} = \frac{1}{4} \qquad P(F) = \frac{4}{8} = \frac{1}{2}$$

Now use Formula (1) to get

$$P(E|F) = \frac{P(E \cap F)}{P(F)} = \frac{\frac{1}{4}}{\frac{1}{2}} = \frac{1}{2}$$

In a three-child family, the probability the family exactly has two boys, given that the fir child is a boy, is $\frac{1}{2}$.

FIGURE 4

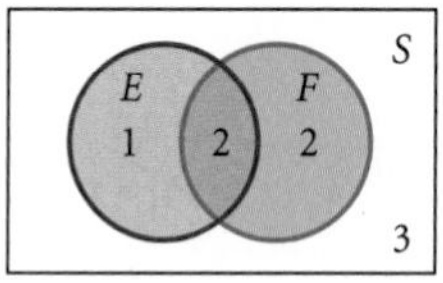

Since the sample space S of Example 3 consists of equally likely outcomes, we ca also compute $P(E|F)$ using the Venn diagram in Figure 4. Then

$$P(E|F) = \frac{n(E \cap F)}{n(F)} = \frac{2}{4} = \frac{1}{2}$$

Let's analyze the situation in Example 3 more carefully. Look again at Figure 4. Th event E is "the family has exactly 2 boys." We have computed the probability of event E knowing event F has occurred. This means we are computing a probability relative to *new sample space F*. That is, F is treated as the universal set and we should consider onl the part of E that is included in F, namely, $E \cap F$. So if E is any subset of the sample spac S, then $P(E|F)$ provides the reappraisal of the likelihood that an outcome of th experiment will be in the set E if we have prior information that it must be in the set F

NOW WORK PROBLEM 7.

EXAMPLE 4 Finding Probabilities

Suppose E and F are events of a sample space S for which

$$P(E) = 0.7 \qquad P(F) = 0.8 \qquad P(E \cap F) = 0.6$$

Find

(a) $P(E \cup F)$ **(b)** $P(E|F)$ **(c)** $P(F|E)$ **(d)** $P(\overline{E}|\overline{F})$

SOLUTION **(a)** To find $P(E \cup F)$, we use the Additive Rule.

$$P(E \cup F) = P(E) + P(F) - P(E \cap F) = 0.7 + 0.8 - 0.6 = 0.9$$

(b) To find the conditional probability $P(E|F)$, we use Formula (1).

$$P(E|F) = \frac{P(E \cap F)}{P(F)} = \frac{0.6}{0.8} = 0.75$$

(c) To find the conditional probability $P(F|E)$, we use a variation of Formula (1) replacing E by F and F by E. The result is

$$P(F|E) = \frac{P(F \cap E)}{P(E)} = \frac{0.6}{0.7} = 0.857$$

(d) To find the conditional probability $P(\overline{E}|\overline{F})$, we use a variation of Formula (1), replacing E by $\overline{E}$ and F by $\overline{F}$. The result is

$$P(\overline{E}|\overline{F}) = \frac{P(\overline{E} \cap \overline{F})}{P(\overline{F})}$$

Since $\overline{E} \cap \overline{F} = \overline{E \cup F}$ (De Morgan's property), we have

$$P(\overline{E}|\overline{F}) = \frac{P(\overline{E \cup F})}{P(\overline{F})} = \frac{1 - P(E \cup F)}{1 - P(F)} = \frac{1 - 0.9}{1 - 0.8} = \frac{0.1}{0.2} = 0.50$$

↑ Use the probability of a complement.

■

NOW WORK PROBLEMS 27 AND 29.

2 Find Probabilities Using the Product Rule

In Formula (1), multiply both sides of the equation by $P(F)$.

$$P(E|F) = \frac{P(E \cap F)}{P(F)} \quad \text{Formula (1)}$$

$$P(F) \cdot P(E|F) = P(E \cap F) \quad \text{Multiply by } P(F).$$

This formula is referred to as the **Product Rule:**

Theorem

Product Rule

For two events E and F, the probability of the event E and F, namely, $P(E \cap F)$, is given by

$$P(E \cap F) = P(F) \cdot P(E|F) \qquad (2)$$

EXAMPLE 5 Finding Probabilities Using the Product Rule

Two cards are drawn in order (without replacement) from a regular deck of 52 cards. What is the probability that the first card is a diamond and the second is red?

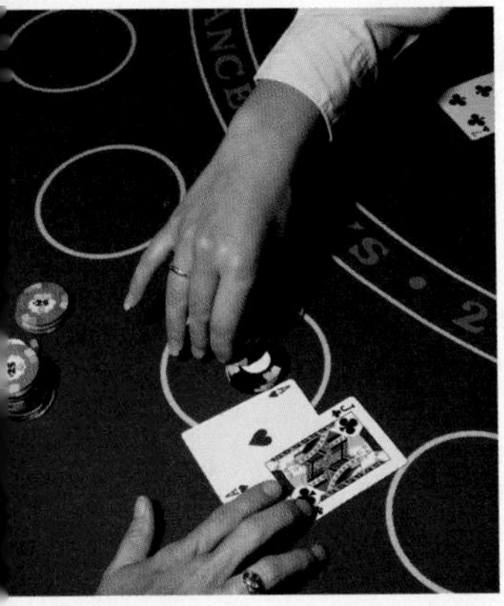

SOLUTION Define the events

E: The first card is a diamond

F: The second card is red

We seek the probability of E and F, namely, $P(E \cap F)$.

Since there are 52 cards in the deck, of which 13 are diamonds, it follows that

$$P(E) = \frac{13}{52} = \frac{1}{4}$$

If E occurred, it means that there are only 51 cards left in the deck, of which 25 are red, so

$$P(F|E) = \frac{25}{51}$$

By the Product Rule,

$$P(E \cap F) = P(F \cap E) = P(E) \cdot P(F|E) = \frac{1}{4} \cdot \frac{25}{51} = \frac{25}{204}$$

3 Find Probabilities Using a Tree Diagram

A tree diagram is helpful for problems like that of Example 5. See Figure 5.

FIGURE 5

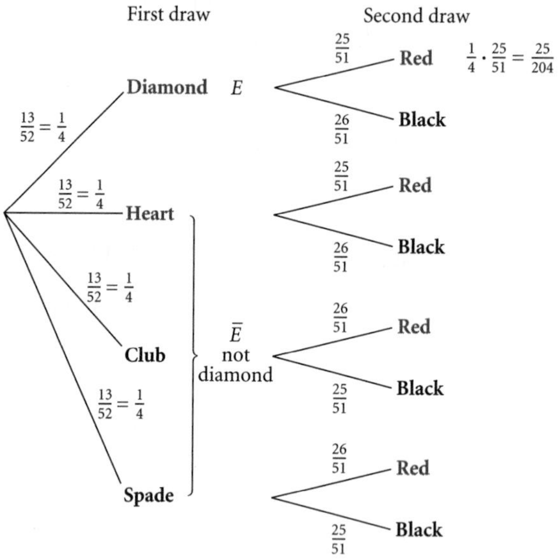

The branch leading to E: "Diamond" has probability $\frac{13}{52} = \frac{1}{4}$; the branch leading t "Heart" also has probability $\frac{13}{52} = \frac{1}{4}$; and the branch leading to "Club" (or "Spade") h probability $\frac{13}{52} = \frac{1}{4}$. These must add up to 1 since no other possibilities (branches) are pos sible. The branch from "Diamond" to "Red" is the conditional probability of drawing a re card on the second draw after a diamond on the first draw, $P(\text{Red}|\text{Diamond})$, which is $\frac{25}{51}$ The branch from "Diamond" to "Black" is the conditional probability $P(\text{Black}|\text{Diamond}$ which is $\frac{26}{51}$ (26 black cards and 51 total cards remain after a diamond on the first draw The remaining entries are obtained similarly. Notice that the probability the first card i a diamond and the second is red corresponds to tracing the top branch of the tree. Th Product Rule then tells us to multiply the branch probabilities.

A further advantage of using a tree diagram is that it enables us to easily answe other questions about the experiment. For example, based on Figure 5, we see that

(a) Probability the first card is a heart and the second is black equals $\frac{1}{4} \cdot \frac{26}{51} = \frac{13}{102}$

(b) Probability the first card is a club and the second is red equals $\frac{1}{4} \cdot \frac{26}{51} = \frac{13}{102}$

(c) Probability the first card is a spade and the second is black equals $\frac{1}{4} \cdot \frac{25}{51} = \frac{25}{204}$

NOW WORK PROBLEM 35.

EXAMPLE 6 **Using a Tree Diagram and the Product Rule**

From a box containing four white, three yellow, and one green ball, two balls are drawn one at a time without replacing the first ball before the second is drawn. Use a tree diagram to find the probability that one white and one yellow ball are drawn.

SOLUTION To fix our ideas, define the events

W: White ball drawn Y: Yellow ball drawn G: Green ball drawn

The tree diagram for this experiment is given in Figure 6.

FIGURE 6

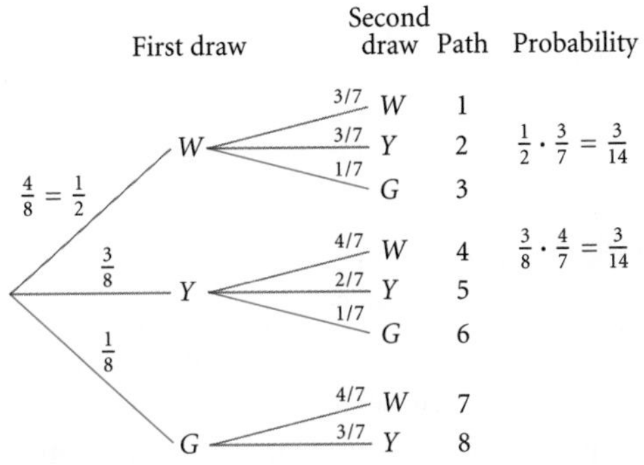

The event of drawing one white ball and one yellow ball can occur in two ways: drawing a white ball first and then a yellow ball (path 2 of the tree diagram in Figure 6), or drawing a yellow ball first and then a white ball (path 4).

Consider path 2. Since four of the eight balls are white, on the first draw we have

$$P(W) = P(W \text{ on 1st}) = \frac{4}{8} = \frac{1}{2}$$

Since one white ball has been removed, leaving seven balls in the box, of which three are yellow, on the second draw we have

$$P(Y|W) = P(Y \text{ on 2nd}|W \text{ on 1st}) = \frac{3}{7}$$

For path 2 we have

$$P(W) \cdot P(Y|W) = P(W \text{ on 1st}) \cdot P(Y \text{ on 2nd}|W \text{ on 1st}) = \frac{1}{2} \cdot \frac{3}{7} = \frac{3}{14}$$

Similarly, for path 4 we have

$$P(Y) \cdot P(W|Y) = P(Y \text{ on 1st}) \cdot P(W \text{ on 2nd}|Y \text{ on 1st}) = \frac{3}{8} \cdot \frac{4}{7} = \frac{3}{14}$$

Since the two events are mutually exclusive, the probability of drawing one white ball and one yellow ball is the sum of these two probabilities:

$$\frac{3}{14} + \frac{3}{14} = \frac{6}{14} = \frac{3}{7}$$ ■

NOW WORK PROBLEM 37.

EXAMPLE 7 Using a Tree Diagram to Find Conditional Probabilities

Motors, Inc., has two plants to manufacture cars. Plant I manufactures 80% of the cars an plant II manufactures 20%. At plant I, 85 out of every 100 cars are rated standard quali or better. At plant II, only 65 out of every 100 cars are rated standard quality or better.

(a) What is the probability that a customer obtains a standard quality car if he buys a ca from Motors, Inc.?

(b) What is the probability that the car came from plant I if it is known that the car is standard quality?

SOLUTION Begin with the tree diagram in Figure 7.

FIGURE 7

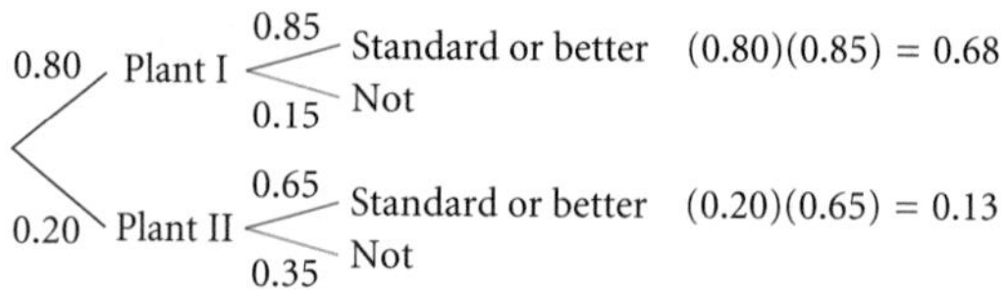

Define the following events:

I: Car came from plant I II: Car came from plant II

A: Car is of standard quality

(a) There are two ways a standard car can be obtained: either it is standard and cam from plant I, or else it is standard and came from plant II. By the Product Rule,

$$P(A \cap \text{I}) = P(\text{I}) \cdot P(A|\text{I}) = (0.8)(0.85) = 0.68$$
$$P(A \cap \text{II}) = P(\text{II}) \cdot P(A|\text{II}) = (0.2)(0.65) = 0.13$$

Since $A \cap \text{I}$ and $A \cap \text{II}$ are mutually exclusive, we have

$$P(A) = P(A \cap \text{I}) + P(A \cap \text{II}) = 0.68 + 0.13 = 0.81$$

(b) To compute $P(\text{I}|A)$, use the definition of conditional probability.

$$P(\text{I}|A) = \frac{P(\text{I} \cap A)}{P(A)} = \frac{0.68}{0.81} = 0.8395$$

NOW WORK PROBLEM 73.

4 Find Conditional Probabilities from a Data Table

EXAMPLE 8 Finding Conditional Probabilities from a Data Table

On April 30, 2010, the market breadth for stocks traded consisted of the data shown i Table 1. What is the probability an issue selected at random advanced given it is High Yield

TABLE 1 MARKET BREADTH

	All Issues	Investment Grade	High Yield	Conver-tible
Advances	2958	2062	732	164
Declines	2194	1563	533	98
Unchanged	201	91	107	3
52 Week High	391	200	147	44
52 Week Low	32	23	9	0

SOLUTION Define the events A and H as

A: Issue advanced $\qquad$ H: Issue is high yield

We seek the probability of A given H, that is, $P(A|H)$. Now by Formula (1)

$$P(A|H) = \frac{P(A \cap H)}{P(H)}$$

To use this formula, we need to find $P(A \cap H)$ and $P(H)$. Since the selection is random, we count the elements in the sample space S, the event $A \cap H$, and the event H.

The total number of issues in the sample space S is $n(S) = 2958 + 2194 + 201 = 5353$. Of these, the number of issues that advanced and are high yield is $n(A \cap H) = 732$ and the number of issues that are high yield is $n(H) = 732 + 533 + 107 = 1372$. Then

$$P(A \cap H) = \frac{n(A \cap H)}{n(S)} = \frac{732}{5353} = 0.137$$

$$P(H) = \frac{n(H)}{n(S)} = \frac{1372}{5353} = 0.256$$

$$P(A|H) = \frac{P(A \cap H)}{P(H)} = \frac{0.137}{0.256} = 0.535$$

The probability an issue selected at random advanced given it is high yield is 0.535. ■

NOW WORK PROBLEM 77.

EXERCISE 8.1 Answers Begin on Page AN–39.

'Are You Prepared?' Problems Answers are given at the end of these exercises. If you get a wrong answer, read the pages listed in red.

1. Two cards are drawn in order (without replacement) from a regular deck of 52 cards. What is the probability the first card is a diamond? (pp. 391–400)
2. If E and F are events of a sample space for which $P(E) = 0.7$, $P(F) = 0.8$, find $P(E \cap F) = 0.6$, find $P(E \cup F)$. (pp. 391–400)

Concepts and Vocabulary

3. ***True or False*** The conditional probability of the event E given the event F is denoted by $P(F|E)$.
4. If E and F are two events and $P(F) > 0$, then $P(E|F) =$ ____.

Skill Building

In Problems 5–12, use the Venn diagram below to find each probability.

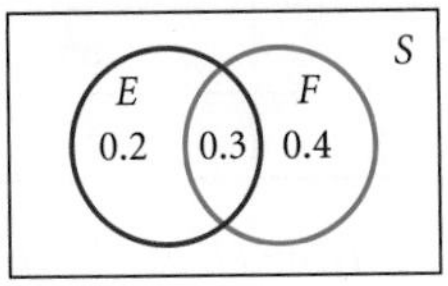

5. $P(E)$ 6. $P(F)$ 7. $P(E|F)$ 8. $P(F|E)$
9. $P(E \cap F)$ 10. $P(E \cup F)$ 11. $P(\overline{E})$ 12. $P(\overline{F})$
13. If E and F are events with $P(E) = 0.2$, $P(F) = 0.4$, and $P(E \cap F) = 0.1$, find the probability of E given F. Also find $P(F|E)$.
14. If E and F are events with $P(E) = 0.5$, $P(F) = 0.6$, and $P(E \cap F) = 0.3$, find the probability of E given F. Also find $P(F|E)$.
15. If E and F are events with $P(E \cap F) = 0.2$ and $P(E|F) = 0.4$, find $P(F)$.
16. If E and F are events with $P(E \cap F) = 0.2$ and $P(E|F) = 0.6$, find $P(F)$.
17. If E and F are events with $P(F) = \frac{5}{13}$ and $P(E|F) = \frac{4}{5}$, find $P(E \cap F)$.
18. If E and F are events with $P(F) = 0.38$ and $P(E|F) = 0.46$, find $P(E \cap F)$.
19. If E and F are events with $P(E \cap F) = \frac{1}{3}$, $P(E|F) = \frac{1}{2}$, and $P(F|E) = \frac{2}{3}$, find
    (a) $P(E)$ (b) $P(F)$
20. If E and F are events with $P(E \cap F) = 0.1$, $P(E|F) = 0.25$, and $P(F|E) = 0.125$, find
    (a) $P(E)$ (b) $P(F)$

In Problems 21–26, find each probability by referring to the following tree diagram:

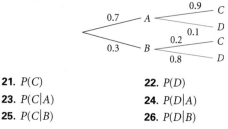

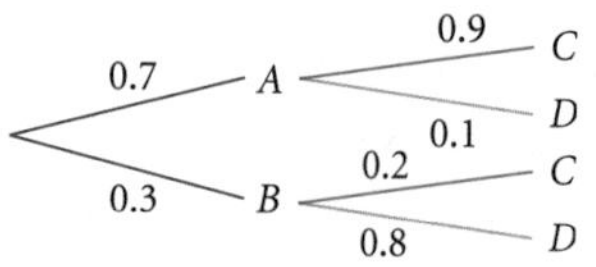

21. $P(C)$ **22.** $P(D)$

23. $P(C|A)$ **24.** $P(D|A)$

25. $P(C|B)$ **26.** $P(D|B)$

In Problems 27–32, E and F are events in a sample space S for whi

$$P(E) = 0.5 \qquad P(F) = 0.4 \qquad P(E \cup F) = 0.8$$

Find each probability.

27. $P(E \cap F)$ **28.** $P(E|F)$

29. $P(F|E)$ **30.** $P(\overline{E}|F)$

31. $P(E|\overline{F})$ **32.** $P(\overline{E}|\overline{F})$

Applications and Extensions

33. Three-Child Families

(a) For a 3-child family, find the probability of exactly 2 girls, given that the first child is a girl.

(b) For a 3-child family, find the probability of exactly 1 girl, given that the first child is a boy.

34. Family Size In a small town it is known that 20% of the families have no children, 30% have 1 child, 20% have 2 children, 16% have 3 children, 8% have 4 children, and 6% have 5 or more children. Find the probability that a family has more than 2 children if it is known that it has at least 1 child.

35. Drawing Cards Two cards are drawn in order (without replacement) from a regular deck of 52 cards.

(a) What is the probability that the first card is a heart and the second is red?

(b) What is the probability that the first card is red and the second is a heart?

36. Drawing Cards Two cards are drawn in order from a regular deck of 52 cards without replacement.

(a) What is the probability that the second card is a queen?

(b) What is the probability that both cards are queens?

37. Selecting Balls From a box containing 3 white, 2 green, and 1 yellow ball, 2 balls are drawn one at a time without replacing the first ball before the second is drawn. Find the probability that 1 white and 1 yellow ball are drawn.

38. Selecting Marbles A box contains 2 red, 4 green, 1 black, and 8 yellow marbles. If 2 marbles are selected in order without replacement, what is the probability that one is red and one is green?

39. Cards A card is drawn at random from a regular deck of 52 cards. What is the probability that

(a) The card is a red ace?

(b) The card is a red ace if it is known an ace was picked?

(c) The card is a red ace if it is known a red card was picked?

40. Cards A card is drawn at random from a regular deck of 52 cards. What is the probability that

(a) The card is a black jack?

(b) The card is a black jack if it is known a jack was picked?

(c) The card is a black jack if it is known a black card was picked?

In Problems 41–52, use the table to obtain probabilities for events i a sample space S.

	E	F	G	Totals
H	0.10	0.06	0.08	0.24
I	0.30	0.14	0.32	0.76
Totals	0.40	0.20	0.40	1.00

For Problems 41–48, read each probability directly from the table:

41. $P(E)$ **42.** $P(G)$ **43.** $P(H)$

44. $P(I)$ **45.** $P(E \cap H)$ **46.** $P(E \cap I)$

47. $P(G \cap H)$ **48.** $P(G \cap I)$

For Problems 49–52, use Formula (1) to find each conditiona probability.

49. $P(E|H)$ **50.** $P(E|I)$ **51.** $P(G|H)$ **52.** $P(G|I$

Surveys *In Problems 53–60, use the table below, which shows th result of a survey conducted by a deodorant producer.*

	Like the Deodorant	Did Not Like the Deodorant	No Opinion
Group I	180	60	20
Group II	110	85	12
Group III	55	65	7

Define the events E, F, G, H, and K as follows:

E: *Customer likes the deodorant*
F: *Customer does not like the deodorant*
G: *Customer is from group I*
H: *Customer is from group II*
K: *Customer is from group III*

Find each conditional probability and state in words the meaning o each one.

53. $P(E|G)$ **54.** $P(G|E)$ **55.** $P(H|E)$ **56.** $P(K|E)$

57. $P(F|G)$ **58.** $P(G|F)$ **59.** $P(H|F)$ **60.** $P(K|F)$

oting Preferences *In Problems 61–66, use the information that llows. A recent poll of residents in a certain community revealed the llowing information about voting preferences:*

	Democrat	Republican	Independent
Male	50	40	30
Female	60	30	25

vents M, F, D, R, and I are defined as follows:

M: Resident is male.
F: Resident is female.
D: Resident is a Democrat.
R: Resident is a Republican.
I: Resident is an Independent.

ind each conditional probability and state in words the meaning of ach one.

1. $P(F|I)$ **62.** $P(R|F)$ **63.** $P(M|D)$

4. $P(D|M)$ **65.** $P(M|R \cup I)$ **66.** $P(I|M)$

7. Graduate Profiles The following table summarizes the graduating class of a midwestern university:

	Arts and Sciences A	Education E	Business B	Total
Male, M	342	424	682	1448
Female, F	324	102	144	570
Total	666	526	826	2018

A student is selected at random from the graduating class. Find the probability that the student

(a) is male.
(b) is receiving an arts and sciences degree.
(c) is a female receiving a business degree.
(d) is a female, given that the student is receiving an education degree.
(e) is receiving an arts and sciences degree, given that the student is a male.
(f) is a female, given that the student is receiving an arts and sciences degree or an education degree.
(g) is not receiving a business degree and is male.
(h) is female, given that an education degree is not received.

68. Beer Preferences The following data are the result of a survey conducted by a marketing company to determine beer preferences.

	Do Not Drink Beer N	Prefer Light Beer L	Prefer Regular Beer R	Total
Female, F	224	420	622	1266
Male, M	196	512	484	1192
Total	420	932	1106	2458

A respondent is selected at random. Find the probability that

(a) the respondent does not drink beer.
(b) the respondent is a female.
(c) the respondent is a female who prefers regular beer.
(d) the respondent prefers regular beer, given that the respondent is male.
(e) the respondent is male, given that the respondent prefers regular beer.
(f) the respondent is female, given that the respondent prefers regular beer or does not drink beer.

Blood Types *In Problems 69–72, use the information given below. Round your answers to three decimal places.*

Blood Types
O Positive—39%
A Positive—31%
B Positive—9%
O Negative—9%
A Negative—6%
AB Positive—3%
B Negative—2%
AB Negative—1%

Source: www.aabb.org/blood, April 2010

69. What is the probability a randomly selected person has a blood type that is type B given that the person is Rh-positive?

70. What is the probability a randomly selected person has a blood type that is type AB given that the person is Rh-negative?

71. What is the probability a randomly selected person has a blood type that is Rh-positive given that the person is type O?

72. What is the probability a randomly selected person has a blood type that is Rh-negative given that the person is type A?

73. Marketing A marketing firm randomly sends a mass promotional mailing to 20% of the households in a new market area. From experience the firm knows that the probability of response to a mailing is 0.07. What is the probability that a household receives the mailing and responds?

74. Maintaining Stock The store manager knows from experience that the probability the store runs out of Raspberry Lemonade Gatorade when it is on sale is 0.90. The probability the Gatorade is on sale is 0.24. What is the probability Gatorade is on sale and the store runs out of stock?

75. Internet Sales A September 2010 marketing survey of Internet purchases resulted in the probabilities in the table.

Age	Purchase Value $0–$99.99	$100–$499.99	≥$500.00
<30	0.20	0.07	0.18
30–50	0.12	0.21	0.10
>50	0.06	0.04	0.02

(a) What is the probability a purchase was made by a person younger than 30 years of age?

(b) If a purchase was $500.00 or more, what is the probability that it was made by a person over 50 years old?

(c) Given that the purchase was between $100 and $499.99, what is the probability it was made by a consumer between the ages of 30 and 50?

76. Multiple Jobs According to the U.S. Bureau of Labor Statistics, there is a 5.84% chance that a randomly selected employed individual has more than one job. There is also a 52.6% probability that a randomly selected employed individual is male, given that he has more than one job.

(a) What is the probability that a randomly selected employed individual is male and has more than one job?

(b) Would it be unusual to randomly select such an individual?

Market Breadth April 30, 2010 *In Problems 77–80, use the table below. Round your answers to three decimal places.*

	All Issues	Investment Grade	High Yield	Conv
Advances	2958	2062	732	164
Declines	2194	1563	533	98
Unchanged	201	91	107	3
52 Week High	391	200	147	44
52 Week Low	32	23	9	0

77. What is the probability an issue selected at random declined given it is high yield?

78. What is the probability an issue selected at random is high yield given it advanced?

79. What is the probability an issue selected at random made a 52-week high given it is investment grade?

80. What is the probability an issue selected at random is investment grade given it made a 52-week high?

81. Health Insurance Coverage The following data represent the numbers, in thousands, of persons with and without health insurance coverage by age in the year 2008.

	Age <18	18–44	45–64	≥65
Health Insurance	74,403	110,676	77,237	36,790
No Health Insurance	8,149	26,037	10,784	686

Source: *Income, Poverty and Health Insurance Coverage in the United States, 2008,* U.S. Census Bureau

(a) What is the probability that a randomly selected individual who is less than 18 years old has no health insurance?

(b) What is the probability that a randomly selected individual who has no health insurance is less than 18 years old?

(c) What is the probability that a randomly selected individual who has health insurance is less than 18 years old?

82. Private vs Public Schools Of the first-year students in a certain college, it is known that 40% attended private secondary schools and 60% attended public schools. The registrar reports that 30% of all students who attended private school maintain an A average in their first year at college and that 24% of all first-year students had an A average. At the end of the year, one student is chosen at random from the class. If the student has an A average, what is the conditional probability that the student attended a private school? [*Hint*: Use a tree diagram.]

Problems 83–84 require the following discussion.

Craps *In a popular dice game, the player rolls a pair of fair dice. If the total number of spots is 7 or 11, the player wins. If the total number of spots is 2, 3, or 12, the player loses. If the player rolls any other total, the total rolled becomes the player's "point" and the player continues to roll the pair of dice. To win the game after establishing the player's "point," the player must re-roll a total equal to the "point" that has been established before rolling a total of 7. The player loses at this stage if a total of 7 is rolled while attempting to re-roll the player's "point."*

Source: The International Bone Rollers Guild, Games with Ordinary Dice, from *According to Hoyle*, by Richard L. Frey.

83. Let E be the event that the player rolls a total of 8 on the first roll. (Therefore, the player's "point" is 8.) Let W be the event that the player wins the game. Find $P(W|E)$.

84. Let E be the event that the player rolls a total of 5 on the first roll. (Therefore, the player's "point" is 5.) Let W be the event that the player wins the game. Find $P(W|E)$.

85. Job Applications "Temp Help" uses a preemployment test to screen applicants for the job of programmer. The test is passed by 70% of the applicants. Among those who pass the test, 85% complete training successfully. In an experiment a random sample of applicants who do not pass the test is also employed. Training is successfully completed by only 40% of this group. If no preemployment test is used, what percentage of applicants would you expect to complete the training successfully?

6. Cigarette Smoking in the U.S. The American Heart Association reported that, for people 18 years of age or older in the United States, an estimated 24.8 million men (23.1%) and 21.1 million women (18.3%) are cigarette smokers. Find the probability that a randomly selected person 18 years of age or older in the United States is a cigarette smoker. Write the answer as a decimal, rounded to the nearest thousandth. Assume one half the population is male.

Source: American Heart Association, January 30, 2008.

7. Cigarette Smoking in Britain The British government reported that, in Great Britain in the year 2008, of the 19.498 million men 16 years of age or older, 22% smoked cigarettes; of the 22.435 million women 16 years of age or older, 21% smoked cigarettes. Find the probability that a randomly selected person 16 years of age or older in Great Britain in the year 2008 was a cigarette smoker. Write the answer as a decimal, rounded to the nearest thousandth. Assume one half the population is male.

Source: Living in Britain—2008 General Lifestyle Survey, Social Survey Division of the Office for National Statistics, Great Britain 2008.

8. Voting In a rural area in the north, registered Republicans outnumber registered Democrats by 3 to 1. In a recent election all Democrats voted for the Democratic candidate and enough Republicans also voted for the Democratic candidate so that the Democrat won by a ratio of 5 to 4.

(a) If a voter is selected at random, what is the probability he or she is Republican?

(b) What is the probability a voter is Republican, if it is known that he or she voted for the Democratic candidate?

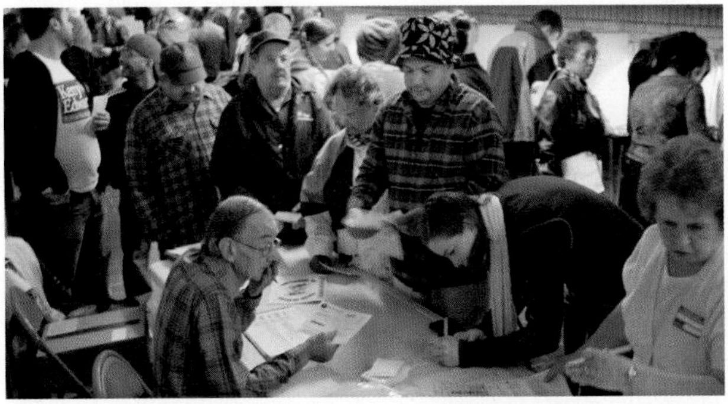

89. If E and F are two events with $P(E) > 0$ and $P(F) > 0$, show that

$$P(F) \cdot P(E|F) = P(E) \cdot P(F|E)$$

90. Show that $P(E|E) = 1$ when $P(E) \neq 0$.

91. Show that $P(E|F) + P(\overline{E}|F) = 1$.

92. If S is the sample space, show that $P(E|S) = P(E)$.

93. If $P(E) > 0$ and $P(E|F) = P(E)$, show that $P(F|E) = P(F)$.

'Are You Prepared?' Answers

1. $\frac{1}{4}$ **2.** 0.9

8.2 Independent Events

OBJECTIVES

1. Show two events are independent (p. 435)
2. Find $P(E \cap F)$ for independent events E and F (p. 437)
3. Find probabilities for several independent events (p. 438)
4. Model: Optimal testing size for components (p. 439)

EXAMPLE 1 Example of Independent Events

Consider a group of 36 students. Define the events E and F as

E: Student has blue eyes F: Student is female

With regard to these two characteristics, suppose it is found that the 36 students are distributed as shown in Table 2. What is $P(E|F)$?

TABLE 2

	Blue Eyes E	Not Blue Eyes $\overline{E}$	Total
Female, F	12	12	24
Male, $\overline{F}$	6	6	12
Total	18	18	36

SOLUTION If we choose a student at random, the following probabilities can be obtained from th table:

$$P(E) = \frac{18}{36} = \frac{1}{2} \qquad P(F) = \frac{24}{36} = \frac{2}{3}$$

$$P(E \cap F) = \frac{12}{36} = \frac{1}{3}$$

Then we find that

$$P(E|F) = \frac{P(E \cap F)}{P(F)} = \frac{\frac{1}{3}}{\frac{2}{3}} = \frac{1}{2} = P(E)$$

The probability of E given F equals the probability of E. This situation can b described by saying that the information that the event F has occurred does not affec the probability of the event E. If this is the case, we say that *E is independent of F.*

Definition

E is Independent of F

Let E and F be two events of a sample space S with $P(F) > 0$. **The event E is independent of the event F** if and only if

$$P(E|F) = P(E)$$

Theorem

Let E, F be events for which $P(E) > 0$ and $P(F) > 0$. If E is independent of F, then F is independent of E.

A proof is outlined in Problem 45.

This result forms the basis for the following definition.

Definition

Independent Events

If two events have positive probabilities and if either event is independent of the other, the events are called **independent events**.

The following result will be used frequently. A proof is outlined in Problem 44.

Theorem

Criterion for Independent Events

Two events E and F of a sample space S are independent events if and only if

$$P(E \cap F) = P(E) \cdot P(F) \qquad \textbf{(1)}$$

Theorem

The Criterion for Independent Events actually consists of two statements:

1. If $P(E \cap F) = P(E) \cdot P(F)$ for two events E and F, then the events E and F are independent.
2. If two events E and F are independent, then $P(E \cap F) = P(E) \cdot P(F)$.

Use statement 1 to show that two events are independent.
Use statement 2 when we know or are told two events are independent.

1 Show Two Events Are Independent

EXAMPLE 2 Showing Two Events Are Independent

Suppose $P(E) = \frac{1}{4}$, $P(F) = \frac{2}{3}$, and $P(E \cap F) = \frac{1}{6}$. Show that E and F are independent events.

SOLUTION We see if Equation (1) holds.

$$P(E) \cdot P(F) = \frac{1}{4} \cdot \frac{2}{3} = \frac{1}{6}$$

$$P(E \cap F) = \frac{1}{6}$$

Since Equation (1) holds, by the Criterion for Independence, E and F are independent events. ■

NOW WORK PROBLEM 7.

EXAMPLE 3 Showing Two Events Are Independent

Suppose a red die and a green die are thrown. Let event E be "Throw a 5 with the re[d] die," and let event F be "Throw a 6 with the green die." Show that E and F a[re] independent events.

SOLUTION In this experiment the events E and F are

$$E = \{(5, 1), (5, 2), (5, 3), (5, 4), (5, 5), (5, 6)\}$$
$$F = \{(1, 6), (2, 6), (3, 6), (4, 6), (5, 6), (6, 6)\}$$

Since the sample space has 36 outcomes that are equally likely, we have

$$P(E) = \frac{6}{36} = \frac{1}{6} \qquad P(F) = \frac{6}{36} = \frac{1}{6}$$

Also, the event E and F is

$$E \cap F = \{(5, 6)\}$$

so that

$$P(E \cap F) = \frac{1}{36}$$

Since $P(E) \cdot P(F) = \frac{1}{6} \cdot \frac{1}{6} = \frac{1}{36} = P(E \cap F)$, E and F are independent events.

EXAMPLE 4 Testing for Independent Events

In a T-maze a mouse may run to the right, R, or to the left, L. Suppose its behavior i[n] making such "choices" is random so that R and L are equally likely outcomes. A mous[e] is put through the T-maze three times. Define events E, G, and H as

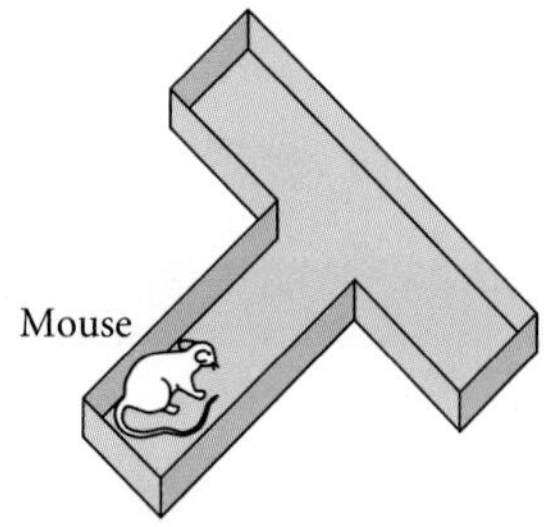

E: Run to the right 2 or more consecutive times

G: Run to the left on first trial

H: Run to the right on second trial

(a) Show that E and G are not independent.

(b) Show that G and H are independent.

SOLUTION A sample space S for this experiment is

$$S = \{LLL, LLR, LRL, LRR, RLL, RLR, RRL, RRR\}$$

where, for example, LLR means run to the left the first and second time and run to th[e] right the third time. S has eight outcomes, and the outcomes are equally likely.

(a) The events E and G are

$$E = \{RRL, LRR, RRR\}$$
$$G = \{LLL, LLR, LRL, LRR\}$$

Then

$$P(E) = \frac{n(E)}{n(S)} = \frac{3}{8} \qquad P(G) = \frac{n(G)}{n(S)} = \frac{4}{8} = \frac{1}{2}$$

Also, the event E and G is

$$E \cap G = \{LRR\}$$

so

$$P(E \cap G) = \frac{1}{8}$$

Since $P(E) \cdot P(G) = \frac{3}{8} \cdot \frac{1}{2} = \frac{3}{16}$, we find that $P(E \cap G) \neq P(E) \cdot P(G)$. The events E and G are not independent.

(b) The event H is

$$H = \{RRL, RRR, LRL, LRR\}$$

so

$$P(H) = \frac{1}{2}$$

The event G and H and its probability are

$$G \cap H = \{LRL, LRR\} \qquad P(G \cap H) = \frac{1}{4}$$

Since $P(G) \cdot P(H) = \frac{1}{2} \cdot \frac{1}{2} = \frac{1}{4}$, $P(G \cap H) = P(G) \cdot P(H)$. The events G and H are independent. ■

Example 4 illustrates that the question of whether two events are independent can be answered simply by determining whether Equation (1) is satisfied. Although we may often suspect two events E and F as being independent, our intuition must be checked by computing $P(E)$, $P(F)$, and $P(E \cap F)$ and determining whether $P(E \cap F) = P(E) \cdot P(F)$.

NOW WORK PROBLEM 27.

2 Find $P(E \cap F)$ for Independent Events E and F

VARNING The two events E and F nust be independent in order to use quation (1) to find $P(E \cap F)$. ■

If E and F are two independent events and $P(E)$ and $P(F)$ are known, then we can use Equation (1) to find $P(E \cap F)$, the probability of the event E and F.

EXAMPLE 5 Finding $P(E \cap F)$ for Independent Events E and F

Suppose E and F are independent events with $P(E) = 0.4$ and $P(F) = 0.3$. Find $P(E \cap F)$.

SOLUTION Since E and F are independent, we can use Equation (1) to find $P(E \cap F)$.

$$\begin{aligned} P(E \cap F) &= P(E) \cdot P(F) \qquad \text{Equation (1)} \\ &= (0.4) \cdot (0.3) \\ &= 0.12 \end{aligned}$$

■

NOW WORK PROBLEM 3.

For some probability models, an assumption of independence is made.

EXAMPLE 6 Planting Seeds

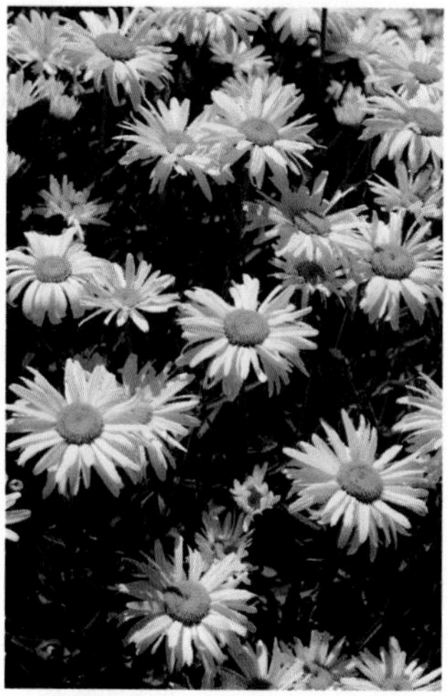

In a group of seeds, $\frac{1}{4}$ of which should produce white flowers, the best germination th can be obtained is 75%. If one seed is planted, what is the probability that it will gro into a white flower? Assume that germination and the production of a white flower a independent events.

SOLUTION Let G and W be the events

W: The seed will produce a white flower

G: The plant will grow

Then

$$P(W) = \frac{1}{4} \quad P(G) = 0.75 = \frac{3}{4}$$

Since G and W are independent events, the probability that the plant grows and i flower is white, namely, $P(W \cap G)$, is

$$P(W \cap G) = P(W) \cdot P(G) = \frac{1}{4} \cdot \frac{3}{4} = \frac{3}{16}$$

A white flower will grow 3 out of 16 times.

NOW WORK PROBLEM 21.

There is a danger that mutually exclusive events and independent events may b confused. A source of this confusion is the common expression, "Events ar independent if they have nothing to do with each other." This expression provides description of independence when applied to everyday events; but when it is applied t sets, it suggests nonoverlapping. Nonoverlapping sets are mutually exclusive but i general are not independent.

3 Find Probabilities for Several Independent Events

The concept of independent events can be applied to more than two events:

Independent Events

A set $\{E_1, E_2, \ldots, E_n\}$ of n events is called **independent** if the occurrence of one or more of them does not change the probability of any of the others. It can be shown that, for such events,

$$P(E_1 \cap E_2 \cap \cdots \cap E_n) = P(E_1) \cdot P(E_2) \cdot \cdots \cdot P(E_n) \qquad (2)$$

EXAMPLE 7 Finding Probabilities of Independent Events

A new skin cream can cure skin infection 90% of the time. If five randomly selected people with skin infections use this cream, what is the probability that

(a) All five are cured?

(b) All five still have the infection?

Assume that the choice of a person and the elimination of the infection are independent.

SOLUTION **(a)** Let

E_1: First person does not have the infection
E_2: Second person does not have the infection
E_3: Third person does not have the infection
E_4: Fourth person does not have the infection
E_5: Fifth person does not have the infection

Then

$$P(E_1) = 0.9 \quad P(E_2) = 0.9 \quad P(E_3) = 0.9 \quad P(E_4) = 0.9 \quad P(E_5) = 0.9$$

Since the events E_1, E_2, E_3, E_4, E_5, are independent, we have

$$\begin{aligned} P(\text{all 5 are cured}) &= P(E_1 \cap E_2 \cap E_3 \cap E_4 \cap E_5) \\ &= P(E_1) \cdot P(E_2) \cdot P(E_3) \cdot P(E_4) \cdot P(E_5) \\ &= (0.9)^5 \\ &= 0.59 \end{aligned}$$

The probability all five are cured is 0.59.

(b) Let

$\overline{E}_i$: ith person has the infection, $i = 1, 2, 3, 4, 5$

Then

$$\begin{aligned} P(\overline{E}_i) &= 1 - 0.9 = 0.1 \\ P(\text{all 5 are infected}) &= P(\overline{E}_1 \cap \overline{E}_2 \cap \overline{E}_3 \cap \overline{E}_4 \cap \overline{E}_5) \\ &= P(\overline{E}_1) \cdot P(\overline{E}_2) \cdot P(\overline{E}_3) \cdot P(\overline{E}_4) \cdot P(\overline{E}_5) \\ &= (0.1)^5 \\ &= 0.00001 \end{aligned}$$

The probability none is cured is 0.00001. ■

4 Model: Optimal Testing Size for Components

IGURE 8

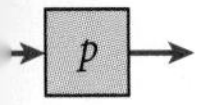

A factory produces electronic components, and each component must be tested. If the component is good, it will allow the passage of current; if the component is defective, it will block the passage of current. Let p denote the probability that a component is good. See Figure 8. If we test each component, the number of tests required equals the number of components. If the number of components is large, this will increase the production cost of the electronic components since one test is required per component.

IGURE 9

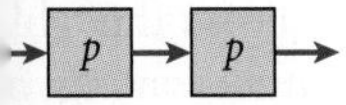

To reduce the number of tests, a quality control engineer proposes, instead, a new testing procedure: Connect the components pairwise in series, as shown in Figure 9.

If the current passes two components in series, then both components are good and only one test is required. Now, each component has probability p of being good. Further, the events "the first component is good" and "the second component is good" a independent. By the Product Rule, the probability both components are good is $p \cdot p = p$

If the current does not pass, the components must be tested separately. In this ca three tests are required. The probability that three tests are needed is $1 - p^2$ (1 min probability both are good). The expected number of tests for a pair of components is

$$E = 1 \cdot p^2 + 3 \cdot (1 - p^2) = p^2 + 3 - 3p^2 = 3 - 2p^2$$

The number of tests saved for a pair is

$$2 - (3 - 2p^2) = 2p^2 - 1$$

The number of tests saved per component is

$$\frac{2p^2 - 1}{2} = p^2 - \frac{1}{2} \text{ tests saved per component}$$

The greater the probability p that the component is good, the greater the saving. Fo example, if p is almost 1, we have a saving of almost $1 - \frac{1}{2}$ or $\frac{1}{2}$, which is 50% of th original number of tests needed. Of course, if p is small, say, less than 0.7, we do not sa anything since $(0.7)^2 - \frac{1}{2}$ is less than 0, so the extra tests provide no benefit.

If the reliability of the components manufactured is very high, it might even b advisable to test larger groups. Suppose three components are connected in series. Se Figure 10.

FIGURE 10

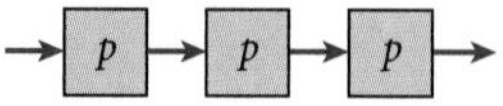

Individual testing requires three tests. For group testing we have

1 test needed with probability p^3
4 tests needed with probability $1 - p^3$

The expected number of tests is

$$E = 1 \cdot p^3 + 4 \cdot (1 - p^3) = 4 - 3p^3 \text{ tests}$$

The number of tests saved per component is

$$\frac{\text{number of tests saved}}{\text{number of components}} = \frac{3 - (4 - 3p^3)}{3} = \frac{3p^3 - 1}{3} = p^3 - \frac{1}{3}$$

If the components are arranged in groups of four connected in series, then th number of tests saved per component is

$$p^4 - \frac{1}{4}$$

In general, for groups of n, the number of tests saved per component is

$$p^n - \frac{1}{n}$$

Notice from the above formula that as n, the group size, gets very large, th number of tests saved per component gets very, very small.

Table 3 shows the expected tests saved per component for $p = 0.9$. From the tab we see that the optimal group size is four, resulting in a substantial saving o approximately 41%.

TABLE 3

Group Size	Expected Tests Saved per Component $p = 0.9$	Percent Saving
2	$p^2 - \frac{1}{2} = 0.81 - 0.50 = 0.31$	31
3	$p^3 - \frac{1}{3} = 0.729 - 0.333 = 0.396$	39.6
4	$p^4 - \frac{1}{4} = 0.6561 - 0.25 = 0.4061$	40.61
5	$p^5 - \frac{1}{5} = 0.59049 - 0.2 = 0.39049$	39.05
6	$p^6 - \frac{1}{6} = 0.531 - 0.167 = 0.364$	36.4
7	$p^7 - \frac{1}{7} = 0.478 - 0.143 = 0.335$	33.5
8	$p^8 - \frac{1}{8} = 0.430 - 0.125 = 0.305$	30.5

NOW WORK PROBLEM 35.

EXERCISE 8.2 Answers Begin on Page AN–39.

Concepts and Vocabulary

1. ***True or False*** If E and F are mutually exclusive, then they are also independent.

2. If E and F are two independent events, then $P(E \cap F) =$ ____.

Skill Building

3. If E and F are independent events and if $P(E) = 0.4$ and $P(F) = 0.6$, find $P(E \cap F)$.

4. If E and F are independent events and if $P(E) = 0.6$ and $P(E \cap F) = 0.2$, find $P(F)$.

5. If E and F are independent events, find $P(F)$ if $P(E) = 0.2$ and $P(E \cup F) = 0.3$.

6. If E and F are independent events, find $P(E)$ if $P(F) = 0.3$ and $P(E \cup F) = 0.6$.

7. Suppose E and F are two events such that $P(E) = \frac{4}{21}$, $P(F) = \frac{7}{12}$, and $P(E \cap F) = \frac{2}{9}$. Are E and F independent?

8. If E and F are two events such that $P(E) = 0.25$, $P(F) = 0.36$, and $P(E \cap F) = 0.09$, are E and F independent?

9. If E and F are two independent events with $P(E) = 0.2$, and $P(F) = 0.4$, find
(a) $P(E|F)$ (b) $P(F|E)$ (c) $P(E \cap F)$ (d) $P(E \cup F)$

10. If E and F are independent events with $P(E) = 0.3$ and $P(F) = 0.5$, find
(a) $P(E|F)$ (b) $P(F|E)$ (c) $P(E \cap F)$ (d) $P(E \cup F)$

11. If E, F, and G are three independent events with $P(E) = \frac{2}{3}$, $P(F) = \frac{3}{7}$, and $P(G) = \frac{2}{21}$, find $P(E \cap F \cap G)$.

12. If E_1, E_2, E_3, and E_4 are four independent events with $P(E_1) = 0.6$, $P(E_2) = 0.3$, $P(E_3) = 0.5$, and $P(E_4) = 0.4$, find $P(E_1 \cap E_2 \cap E_3 \cap E_4)$.

13. If $P(E) = 0.3$, $P(F) = 0.2$, and $P(E \cup F) = 0.4$, what is $P(E|F)$? Are E and F independent?

14. If $P(E) = 0.4$, $P(F) = 0.6$, and $P(E \cup F) = 0.7$, what is $P(E|F)$? Are E and F independent?

Applications and Extensions

15. **T-maze** In a T-maze a mouse may turn to the right (R) and receive a mild shock, or to the left (L) and get a piece of cheese. Its behavior in making such "choices" is studied by psychologists. Suppose a mouse runs a T-maze 3 times. List the set of all possible outcomes and assign valid probabilities to each outcome under the assumption that the first two times the maze is run the mouse chooses equally between left and right, but on the third run, the mouse is twice as likely to choose cheese.

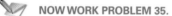

Assume the mouse has no memory so the trials are independent. Find the probability of each of the events listed.

(a) E: Run to the right exactly 2 consecutive times.
(b) F: Never run to the right.
(c) G: Run to the left on the first trial.
(d) H: Run to the right on the second trial.

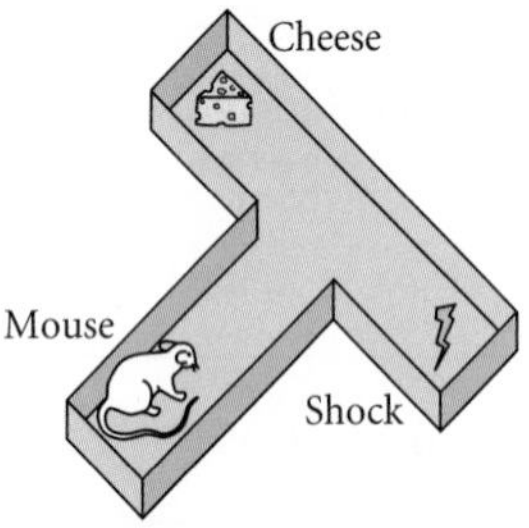

16. Drawing Cards A first card is drawn at random from a regular deck of 52 cards and is then put back into the deck. A second card is drawn. What is the probability that

(a) The first card is a club?
(b) The second card is a heart, given that the first is a club?
(c) The first card is a club and the second is a heart?
(d) The first card is an ace?
(e) The second card is a king, given that the first card is an ace?
(f) The first card is an ace and the second is a king?

17. Selecting Marbles A box has 10 marbles in it, 6 red and 4 white. Suppose we draw a marble from the box, replace it, and then draw another. Find the probability that

(a) Both marbles are red.
(b) Just one of the two marbles is red.

18. Survey In a survey of 100 people, categorized as drinkers or nondrinkers, with or without a liver ailment, the following data were obtained:

	Liver Ailment F	No Liver Ailment $\overline{F}$
Drinkers, E	52	18
Nondrinkers, $\overline{E}$	8	22

(a) Are the events E and F independent?
(b) Are the events $\overline{E}$ and $\overline{F}$ independent?
(c) Are the events E and $\overline{F}$ independent?

19. Cardiovascular Disease Records show that a child of parents with heart disease has a probability of $\frac{3}{4}$ of inheriting the disease. Assuming independence, what is the probability that, for a couple with heart disease that have two children:

(a) Both children have heart disease.
(b) Neither child has heart disease.
(c) Exactly one child has heart disease.

20. Sex of Newborns The probability of a newborn baby being a girl is 0.49. Assuming that the sex of one baby is independent of the sex of all other babies—that is, the events are independent—what is the probability that all four babies born in a certain hospital on one day are girls?

21. Germination In a group of seeds, $\frac{1}{3}$ of which should produce violets, the best germination that can be obtained is 60%. If one seed is planted, what is the probability that it will grow into a violet? Assume independence.

22. Insurance By examining the past driving records of 840 randomly selected drivers over a period of 1 year, the following data were obtained.

	Under 25 U	Over 25 $\overline{U}$	Totals
Accident, A	40	5	45
No Accident, $\overline{A}$	285	510	795
Totals	325	515	840

(a) What is the probability of a driver having an accident given that the person is under 25?
(b) What is the probability of a driver having an accident given that the person is over 25?
(c) Are events U and A independent?
(d) Are events U and $\overline{A}$ independent?
(e) Are events $\overline{U}$ and A independent?
(f) Are events $\overline{U}$ and $\overline{A}$ independent?

23. Quality Control Efraim Furniture Manufacturing Company hires two people who work independently to identify defects in workmanship.

(a) If the probability an inspector misses a defective piece is 0.20, what is the probability both inspectors pass a defective piece of furniture?
(b) How many inspectors should be hired to ensure the probability of failing to identify a defective piece is less than 0.01?

24. AARP Life Insurance Underwriters for AARP sell life insurance to anyone 55 years of age. They know that the probability a 55-year-old male will live to age 56 is 0.992225, and they make life insurance rates accordingly.

(a) What is the probability that 10 randomly chosen 55-year-old males all live to age 56?
(b) What is the probability that at least one of the ten 55-year-old males dies within the next year?

25. Stock Selection As a stockbroker, you recommend two stocks to a client. Each stock has a 60% probability of increasing over the next year. Assuming that the performance of the two stocks are independent of each other, what is the probability that both stocks will increase in value over the next year? What is the probability that at least one stock will not increase in value?

26. Earnings and a Bachelor's Degree According to the U.S. Census Bureau, the probability that a randomly selected individual in the United States earns more than $75,000 per year is 18.4%. The probability a randomly selected individual in the United States earns more than $75,000 given that the individual has earned a bachelor's degree is 35%. Are the events "earn more than $75,000 per year" and "earned a bachelor's degree" independent?

Health Insurance The contingency table representing the numbers, in thousands, of persons with and without health insurance coverage by age in the year 2007 is as follows:

	Age			
	<18	18–44	45–64	≥65
Health Insurance	74,403	110,676	77,237	36,790
No Health Insurance	8,149	26,037	10,784	686

Source: *Income, Poverty and Health Insurance Coverage in the United States, 2008,* U.S. Census Bureau

(a) Determine $P(<18 \text{ years old})$ and $P(<18 \text{ years old} \mid \text{no health insurance})$.

(b) Are the events "<18 years old" and "no health insurance" independent?

. **Women in Business** The data below represent the number of women-owned businesses (in thousands) in the United States during 2002.

Type of Business	With Paid Employees	Without Paid Employees	Total
Construction	52	150	202
Manufacturing	40	70	110
Trade	188	878	1066
Other	533	3694	4227
Total	813	4792	5605

Source: U.S. Census Bureau

(a) What is the probability that a woman-owned business is in trade, given that the business has paid employees?

(b) What is the probability that a woman-owned business has no paid employees, given that the business is in construction?

(c) Are the events "Manufacturing" and "With Paid Employees" independent?

. **Pumping Station** A pumping station at a hydroelectric plant operates two identical pumps. Each pump has a probability of failure of 0.05, and the probability that both pumps fail is 0.0025.

(a) Are failures in the two pumps mutually exclusive? Explain.

(b) What is the probability that at least one of the pumps fails?

(c) Are failures in the two pumps independent?

30. Ambulatory Care The following table represents the number of ambulatory care visits (in millions) to various locations in 2006 by gender.

Gender	Physician Office	Outpatient Dept.	Emergency Room	Total
Male	368.5	40.2	54.2	462.9
Female	533.1	61.4	64.9	659.4
Total	901.6	102.1	119.1	1122.8

Source: U.S. National Center for Health Statistics

(a) What is the probability that an ambulatory visit will be to an emergency room, given that the patient is female?

(b) What is the probability that the patient is male, given that the ambulatory visit is to a physician's office?

(c) Are the events "Male" and "Physician Office" independent?

31. Property Crime In a survey of 500 property crimes, the following data were obtained:

Residence	Burglary	Vehicle Theft	Theft	Total
Urban	44	14	162	220
Suburban	30	10	106	146
Rural	26	4	104	134
Total	100	28	372	500

(a) What is the probability of being burglarized, given the residence is suburban?

(b) What is the probability that the residence is rural, given that there has been a vehicle theft?

(c) Are the events "Rural" and "Vehicle Theft" independent?

(d) Are the events "Urban" and "Burglary" independent?

32. Voting Patterns The following data show the number of voters in a sample of 1000 from a large city, categorized by religion and their voting preference.

	Democrat D	Republican R	Independent I	Totals
Catholic, C	160	150	90	400
Protestant, P	220	220	60	500
Jewish, J	20	30	50	100
Totals	400	400	200	1000

(a) Find the probability a person is a Democrat.

(b) Find the probability a person is a Catholic.

(c) Find the probability a person is Catholic, knowing the person is a Democrat.

(d) Are the events R and D independent?

(e) Are the events P and R independent?

33. Election A candidate for office believes that $\frac{2}{3}$ of registered voters in her district will vote for her in the next election. If two registered voters are independently selected at random, what is the probability that

(a) Both of them will vote for her in the next election?

(b) Neither will vote for her in the next election?

(c) Exactly one of them will vote for her in the next election?

34. Keys Selection A woman has 10 keys but only 1 fits her door. She tries them successively (without replacement). Find the probability that a key fits in exactly 5 tries.

35. **Testing Components**

(a) Create a table like Table 3 if the probability a component is good is 0.8. Find the optimal group size. What is the percent saving for the optimal group size?

(b) Create a table like Table 3 if the probability a component is good is 0.95. Find the optimal group size. What is the percent saving for the optimal group size?

(c) Create a table like Table 3 if the probability a component is good is 0.99. Find the optimal group size. What is the percent saving for the optimal group size?

36. Testing Components Compute the expected number of tests saved per component if on the first test the current does not pass through 2 components in series, but on the second test the current does pass through 1 of them. A third test is not made (since the other component is obviously defective).

37. Allergy Testing A person's blood needs to be tested for an allergic reaction to 20 known allergens. The tests can either be done individually, resulting in 20 tests, or they can be done by combining 20 allergens and testing the blood. In the second method, if the test is negative then one test suffices for the 20 allergens, but if it is positive then each allergen is tested separately, resulting in 20 + 1 tests for 20 allergens. Assume the probability p that the test is positive is the same for each allergen and that each allergen is independent.

(a) What is the probability that a test is positive using the second method?

(b) What is the expected number of tests needed if the second method is utilized?

(c) What is the number of tests saved per individual when the second method is used?

38. Chevalier de Mere's Problem Which of the following random events do you think is more likely to occur?

(a) To obtain a 1 on at least one die in a simultaneous throw of four fair dice

(b) To obtain at least one pair of 1s in a series of 24 throws of a pair of fair dice

[*Hint*: Part (a):

$$P(\text{No 1s are obtained}) = \frac{5^4}{6^4} = \frac{625}{1296} = 0.4823$$

Part (b): The probability of not obtaining a double 1 on any given toss is $\frac{35}{36}$. So

$$P(\text{no double 1s are obtained}) = \left(\frac{35}{36}\right)^{24} = 0.509]$$

39. Show that whenever two events are both independent and mutually exclusive, then at least one of them is impossible.

40. Let E be any event. If F is an impossible event, show that E and F are independent.

41. Show that if E and F are independent events, so are $\overline{E}$ and $\overline{F}$. [*Hint*: Use De Morgan's properties.]

42. Show that if E and F are independent events and $P(E) \neq 0, P(F) \neq 0$, then E and F are not mutually exclusive.

43. Suppose $P(E) > 0, P(F) > 0$ and E is independent of F. Show that F is independent of E.

[*Hint.* First we note that

$$P(F) \cdot P(E|F) = P(F) \cdot \frac{P(E \cap F)}{P(F)} = P(E \cap F)$$

and

$$P(E) \cdot P(F|E) = P(E) \cdot \frac{P(F \cap E)}{P(E)} = P(E \cap F)$$

Then $P(F) \cdot P(E|F) = P(E) \cdot P(F|E)$. Now use the fact that E is independent of F, that is, $P(E|F) = P(E)$, to show that F is independent of E, that is, $P(F|E) = P(F)$.]

44. Prove Formula (1) on page 435.

[*Hint*: If E and F are independent events, then

$$P(E|F) = \frac{P(E \cap F)}{P(F)} \quad \text{and} \quad P(E|F) = P(E)$$

Now show that $P(E \cap F) = P(E) \cdot P(F)$.

Conversely, suppose $P(E \cap F) = P(E) \cdot P(F)$. Use the fact that

$$P(E|F) = \frac{P(E \cap F)}{P(F)}$$

to show that $P(E|F) = P(E)$.]

Discussion and Writing

45. Give examples of two events that are

(a) Independent but not mutually exclusive

(b) Not independent but mutually exclusive

(c) Not independent and not mutually exclusive

8.3 Bayes' Theorem

PREPARING FOR THIS SECTION *Before getting started, review the following:*

- Sets (Section 6.1, pp. 356–363)

NOW WORK THE 'ARE YOU PREPARED' PROBLEMS ON PAGE 453.

OBJECTIVES
1. Solve probability problems: sample space partitioned into two sets (p. 446)
2. Solve probability problems: sample space partitioned into three sets (p. 447)
3. Use Bayes' Theorem to solve probability problems (p. 450)
4. Find a *priori* and a *posteriori* probabilities (p. 451)

In this section we consider experiments with sample spaces that are divided or partitioned into two (or more) mutually exclusive events. This study involves a further application of conditional probabilities and leads us to the famous *Bayes' Theorem*, named after Thomas Bayes, who first published it in 1763.

EXAMPLE 1 Introduction to Bayes' Theorem

Given two urns, suppose urn I contains four black and seven white balls. Urn II contains three black, one white, and four yellow balls. We select an urn at random and then draw a ball. What is the probability that a black ball is chosen?

SOLUTION Let U_I and U_{II} stand for the events "Urn I is selected" and "Urn II is selected," respectively. Similarly, let B, W, Y stand for the event that "a black," "a white," or "a yellow" ball is chosen, respectively. Since the urn is selected at random and there are two of them, we have

$$P(U_I) = \frac{1}{2} \qquad P(U_{II}) = \frac{1}{2}$$

If urn I is selected, the probability a black ball is chosen is $\frac{4}{11}$ and the probability a white ball is chosen is $\frac{7}{11}$.

If urn II is selected, the probability a black ball is chosen is $\frac{3}{8}$, the probability a white ball is chosen is $\frac{1}{8}$, and the probability a yellow ball is chosen is $\frac{4}{8}$.

We seek the probability a black ball is chosen; that is, we seek $P(B)$.

SOLUTION A **Using a Tree Diagram**
Construct the tree diagram shown in Figure 11.

FIGURE 11

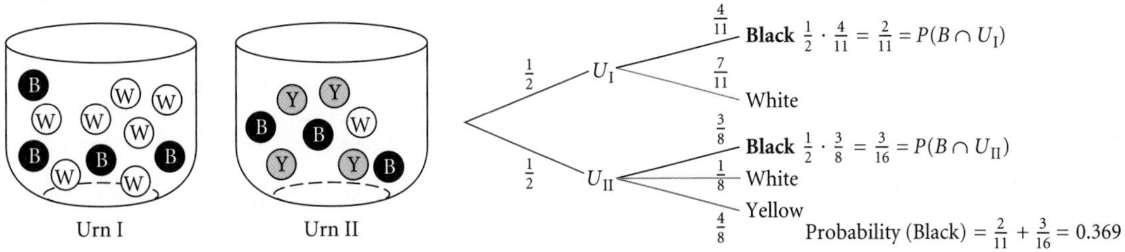

Then the probability a black ball is chosen is

$$P(B) = \frac{2}{11} + \frac{3}{16} = \frac{65}{176} = 0.369$$

SOLUTION B **Using Conditional Probability**

We know that

$$P(U_{\mathrm{I}}) = P(U_{\mathrm{II}}) = \frac{1}{2}$$

$$P(B|U_{\mathrm{I}}) = \frac{4}{11} \qquad P(B|U_{\mathrm{II}}) = \frac{3}{8}$$

The event B can be written as

$$B = (B \cap U_{\mathrm{I}}) \cup (B \cap U_{\mathrm{II}})$$

Since $B \cap U_{\mathrm{I}}$ and $B \cap U_{\mathrm{II}}$ are mutually exclusive, we add their probabilities. Then

$$P(B) = P(B \cap U_{\mathrm{I}}) + P(B \cap U_{\mathrm{II}})$$ (

Using the Product Rule, we have

$$P(B \cap U_{\mathrm{I}}) = P(U_{\mathrm{I}}) \cdot P(B|U_{\mathrm{I}}) \qquad P(B \cap U_{\mathrm{II}}) = P(U_{\mathrm{II}}) \cdot P(B|U_{\mathrm{II}})$$ (

Combining (1) and (2), we have

$$P(B) = P(U_{\mathrm{I}}) \cdot P(B|U_{\mathrm{I}}) + P(U_{\mathrm{II}}) \cdot P(B|U_{\mathrm{II}})$$
$$= \frac{1}{2} \cdot \frac{4}{11} + \frac{1}{2} \cdot \frac{3}{8} = \frac{2}{11} + \frac{3}{16} = 0.369$$

1 Solve Probability Problems: Sample Space Partitioned into Two Sets

FIGURE 12

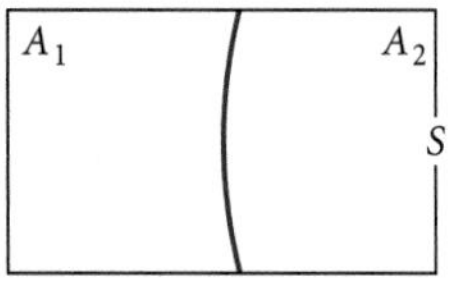

(a)

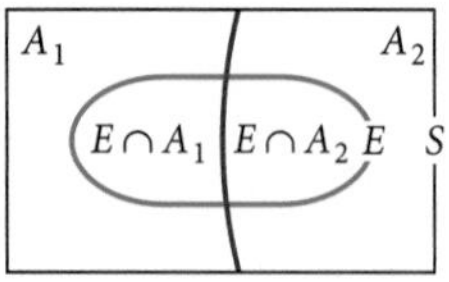

(b)

The preceding discussion leads to the following generalization.

Suppose A_1 and A_2 are two nonempty, mutually exclusive events of a sample space and the union of A_1 and A_2 is S; that is, suppose

$$A_1 \neq \varnothing \qquad A_2 \neq \varnothing \qquad A_1 \cap A_2 = \varnothing \qquad S = A_1 \cup A_2$$

See Figure 12(a). The events A_1 and A_2 form a **partition** of S.

Now if E is any event in S, then E can be written in the form

$$E = (E \cap A_1) \cup (E \cap A_2)$$

See Figure 12(b).

The sets $E \cap A_1$ and $E \cap A_2$ are disjoint since

$$(E \cap A_1) \cap (E \cap A_2) = (E \cap E) \cap (A_1 \cap A_2) = E \cap \varnothing = \varnothing$$

Using the Product Rule, the probability of E is

$$P(E) = P(E \cap A_1) + P(E \cap A_2)$$
$$= P(A_1) \cdot P(E|A_1) + P(A_2) \cdot P(E|A_2) \qquad (3)$$

Formula (3) is used to find the probability of an event E of a sample space when th sample space is partitioned into two sets A_1 and A_2.

Figure 13 shows a tree diagram depicting Formula (3). You may find it easier to remember Formula (3) by constructing Figure 13.

FIGURE 13

$$P(E) = P(A_1) \cdot P(E|A_1) + P(A_2) \cdot P(E|A_2)$$

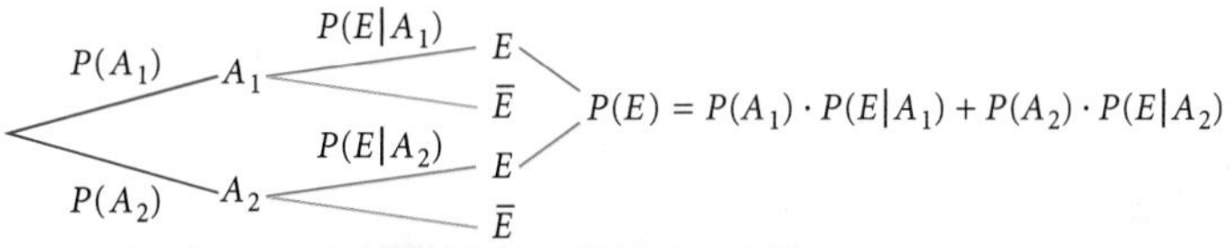

EXAMPLE 2   Admissions Tests for Medical School

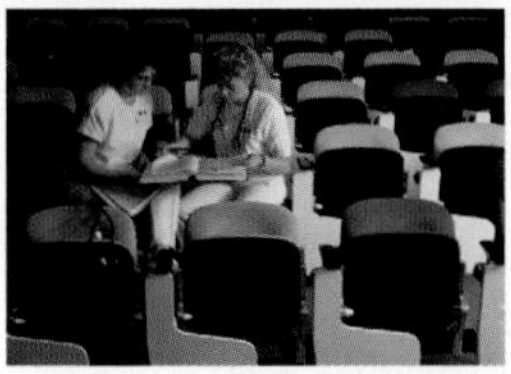

Of the applicants to a medical school, 80% are eligible to enter and 20% are not. To aid in the selection process, an admissions test is administered that is designed so that an eligible candidate will pass 90% of the time, while an ineligible candidate will pass only 30% of the time. What is the probability that an applicant will pass the admissions test?

SOLUTION A   **Using a Tree Diagram**
Figure 14 provides a tree diagram solution.

FIGURE 14

```
                    0.9   Pass   (0.8)(0.9) = 0.72
        0.8   Eligible
                    0.1   Fail

                    0.3   Pass   (0.2)(0.3) = 0.06
        0.2   Ineligible
                    0.7   Fail
```

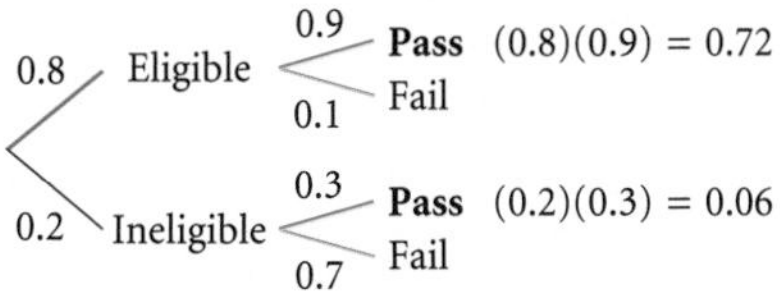

Probability of passing = 0.72 + 0.06 = 0.78

SOLUTION B   **Using Conditional Probability**
The sample space S consists of the applicants for admission, and S can be partitioned into the following two events:

A_1:   Eligible applicant A_2:   Ineligible applicant

These two events are mutually exclusive, and their union is S. See Figure 15.
The event E is

E: Applicant passes admissions test

FIGURE 15

A_1 : Eligible A_2 : Ineligible

E : pass admission test S

Now

$$P(A_1) = 0.8 \qquad\qquad P(A_2) = 0.2$$
$$P(E|A_1) = 0.9 \qquad\qquad P(E|A_2) = 0.3$$

Using Formula (3), we have

$$P(E) = P(A_1) \cdot P(E|A_1) + P(A_2) \cdot P(E|A_2) = (0.8)(0.9) + (0.2)(0.3) = 0.78$$

The probability that an applicant will pass the admissions test is 0.78.   ■

 NOW WORK PROBLEM 19.

2 Solve Probability Problems: Sample Space Partitioned into Three Sets

If a sample space S is partitioned into three sets A_1, A_2, and A_3 so that

$$S = A_1 \cup A_2 \cup A_3$$
$$A_1 \cap A_2 = \varnothing \qquad A_2 \cap A_3 = \varnothing \qquad A_1 \cap A_3 = \varnothing$$
$$A_1 \neq \varnothing \qquad A_2 \neq \varnothing \qquad A_3 \neq \varnothing$$

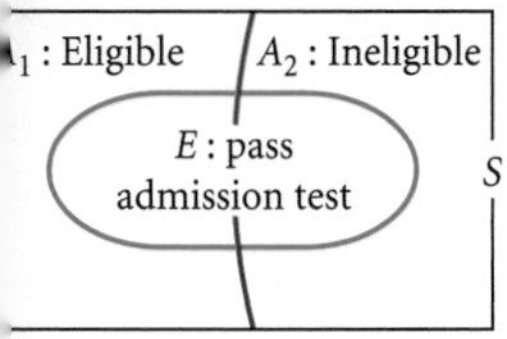

then any event E in S can be written as

$$E = (E \cap A_1) \cup (E \cap A_2) \cup (E \cap A_3)$$

See Figure 16.

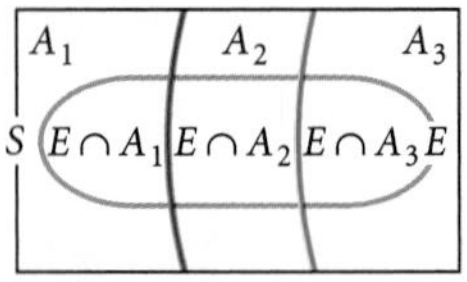

Since $E \cap A_1$, $E \cap A_2$, and $E \cap A_3$ are mutually exclusive events, the probability event E is

FIGURE 16

A_1	A_2	A_3
S	$(E \cap A_1)(E \cap A_2)(E \cap A_3)$ E	

$$P(E) = P(E \cap A_1) + P(E \cap A_2) + P(E \cap A_3)$$
$$= P(A_1) \cdot P(E|A_1) + P(A_2) \cdot P(E|A_2) + P(A_3) \cdot P(E|A_3) \tag{4}$$

Formula (4) is used to find the probability of an event E of a sample space when the sample space is partitioned into three sets A_1, A_2, and A_3.

See Figure 17 for a tree diagram depicting Formula (4). Again, you may find easier to remember Formula (4) by constructing Figure 17.

FIGURE 17

$$P(E) = P(A_1) \cdot P(E|A_1) + P(A_2) \cdot P(E|A_2) + P(A_3) \cdot P(E|A_3)$$

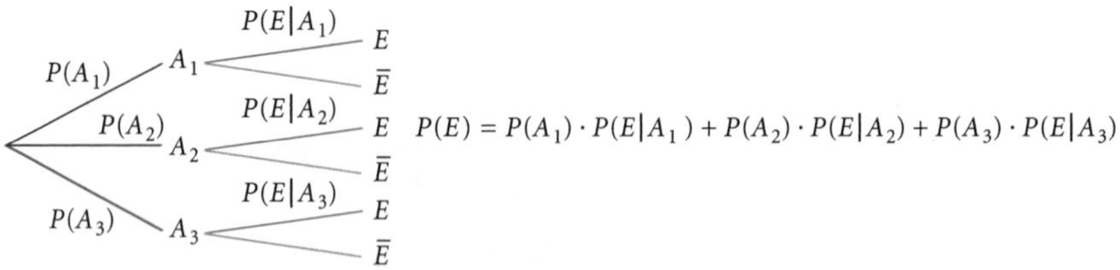

EXAMPLE 3   Quality Control

Three machines, I, II, and III, manufacture 0.4, 0.5, and 0.1 of the total production in a plant respectively. The percentage of defective items produced by I, II, and III is 2%, 4%, and 1%, respectively. For an item chosen at random, what is the probability that it is defective?

SOLUTION   **Using a Tree Diagram**

Figure 18 gives a tree diagram solution.

FIGURE 18

```
            0.02
0.4 / Machine 1 ——— Defective      (0.4)(0.02) = 0.008
         0.98 ——— Nondefective
            0.04
0.5 / Machine 2 ——— Defective      (0.5)(0.04) = 0.020
         0.96 ——— Nondefective
            0.01
0.1 \ Machine 3 ——— Defective      (0.1)(0.01) = 0.001
         0.99 ——— Nondefective
```

Probability for defective $= 0.008 + 0.020 + 0.001 = 0.029$

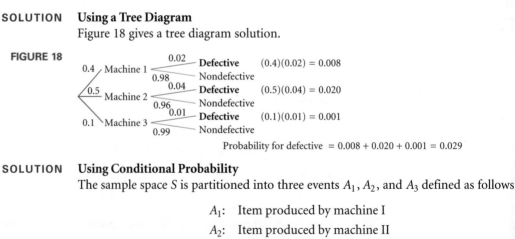

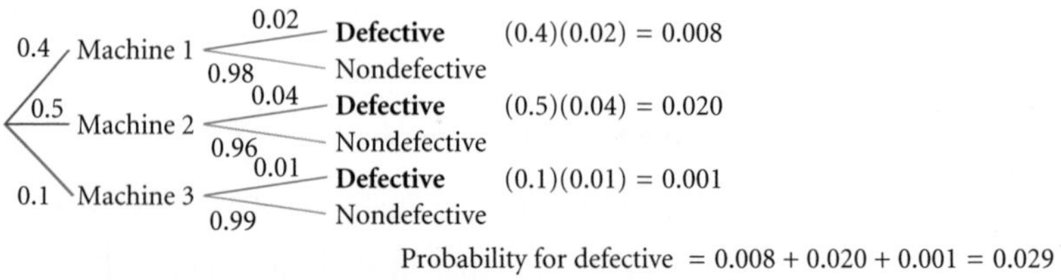

SOLUTION   **Using Conditional Probability**

The sample space S is partitioned into three events A_1, A_2, and A_3 defined as follows

A_1: Item produced by machine I

A_2: Item produced by machine II

A_3: Item produced by machine III

The events A_1, A_2, and A_3 are mutually exclusive and their union is S. Define the event E in S to be

E: Item is defective

Now

$$P(A_1) = 0.4 \qquad P(A_2) = 0.5 \qquad P(A_3) = 0.1$$
$$P(E|A_1) = 0.02 \qquad P(E|A_2) = 0.04 \qquad P(E|A_3) = 0.01$$

Using Formula (4), we find

$$P(E) = (0.4)(0.02) + (0.5)(0.04) + (0.1)(0.01)$$
$$= 0.008 + 0.020 + 0.001 = 0.029 \qquad \blacksquare$$

NOW WORK PROBLEMS 11 AND 21.

To generalize Formulas (3) and (4) to a sample space S partitioned into n subsets, we require the following definition:

Definition

Partition

A sample space S is **partitioned** into n subsets $A_1, A_2 \ldots, A_n$, provided:

(a) Each subset is nonempty.

(b) The intersection of any two of the subsets is empty.

(c) $A_1 \cup A_2 \cup \cdots \cup A_n = S$

Let S be a sample space and let $A_1, A_2, A_3, \ldots, A_n$ be n events that form a partition of the set S. If E is any event in S, then

$$E = (E \cap A_1) \cup (E \cap A_2) \cup \cdots \cup (E \cap A_n)$$

Since $E \cap A_1, E \cap A_2, \ldots, E \cap A_n$ are mutually exclusive events, we have

$$P(E) = P(E \cap A_1) + P(E \cap A_2) + \cdots + P(E \cap A_n) \tag{5}$$

In (5) replace $P(E \cap A_1), P(E \cap A_2), \ldots, P(E \cap A_n)$ using the Product Rule. Then we obtain the formula

$$P(E) = P(A_1) \cdot P(E|A_1) + P(A_2) \cdot P(E|A_2) + \cdots + P(A_n) \cdot P(E|A_n) \tag{6}$$

EXAMPLE 4 | **Admissions Tests for Medical School**

Return to Example 2. Of the applicants to a medical school, 80% are eligible to enter and 20% are not. To aid in the selection process, an admissions test is administered that is designed so that an eligible candidate will pass 90% of the time, while an ineligible candidate will pass only 30% of the time. If an applicant passes the admissions test, what is the probability he or she is eligible?

SOLUTION We follow the solution to Example 2 using conditional probability. The sample space S is partitioned into the two events:

$$A_1: \quad \text{Eligible applicant} \qquad A_2: \quad \text{Ineligible applicant}$$

The event E is

$$E: \quad \text{Applicant passes the admissions test}$$

The probability we seek is $P(A_1|E)$.

Using the definition of conditional probability and the Product Rule,

$$P(A_1|E) = \frac{P(A_1 \cap E)}{P(E)} = \frac{P(A_1) \cdot P(E|A_1)}{P(E)} \quad (7)$$

Using the results obtained in Example 2, namely, $P(A_1) = 0.8$, $P(E|A_1) = 0.9$, and $P(E) = 0.78$, we have

$$P(A_1|E) = \frac{P(A_1) \cdot P(E|A_1)}{P(E)} = \frac{(0.8)(0.9)}{0.78} = \frac{0.72}{0.78} = 0.923$$

The admissions test is a reasonably effective device. If an applicant passes the admission test, the probability is over 0.92 that the applicant is eligible for admission. In other words, less than 8% of the students passing the test are ineligible.

NOW WORK PROBLEM 23.

3 Use Bayes' Theorem to Solve Probability Problems

Equation (7) is a special case of Bayes' Theorem when the sample space is partitioned into two sets A_1 and A_2. The general formula is given below.

Bayes' Theorem

Let S be a sample space partitioned into n events, $A_1, \ldots, A_n$. Let E be any event of S for which $P(E) > 0$. The probability of the event A_j $(j = 1, 2, \ldots, n)$, given the event E, is

$$P(A_j|E) = \frac{P(A_j) \cdot P(E|A_j)}{P(E)} = \frac{P(A_j) \cdot P(E|A_j)}{P(A_1) \cdot P(E|A_1) + P(A_2) \cdot P(E|A_2) + \cdots + P(A_n) \cdot P(E|A_n)} \quad (8)$$

The proof is left as an exercise (see Problem 54).

EXAMPLE 5 Quality Control: Source of Defective Cars

Motors, Inc. has three plants. Plant I produces 35% of the car output, plant II produces 20%, and plant III produces the remaining 45%. One percent of the output of plant I is defective, as is 1.8% of the output of plant II, and 2% of the output of plant III. The annual total output of Motors, Inc., is 1,000,000 cars. A car is chosen at random from the annual output and it is found to be defective.

(a) What is the probability the defective car came from plant I?

(b) What is the probability the defective car came from plant II?

(c) What is the probability the defective car came from plant III?

SOLUTION Define the following events:

E: Car is defective
A_1: Car produced by plant I
A_2: Car produced by plant II
A_3: Car produced by plant III

The probabilities we seek are

(a) $P(A_1|E)$: the probability a car was produced by plant I, given that it was defective.
(b) $P(A_2|E)$: the probability a car was produced by plant II, given that it was defective.
(c) $P(A_3|E)$: the probability a car was produced by plant III, given that it was defective.

From information given in the problem we know the following probabilities:

$$\begin{aligned} P(A_1) &= 0.35 \qquad & P(E|A_1) &= 0.010 \\ P(A_2) &= 0.20 \qquad & P(E|A_2) &= 0.018 \\ P(A_3) &= 0.45 \qquad & P(E|A_3) &= 0.020 \end{aligned} \tag{9}$$

Now use Bayes' Theorem to find $P(A_1|E)$, $P(A_2|E)$, and $P(A_3|E)$. To apply Formula (8), begin by finding the denominator $P(E)$.

$$\begin{aligned} P(E) &= P(A_1)P(E|A_1) + P(A_2)P(E|A_2) + P(A_3)P(E|A_3) \\ &= (0.35)(0.01) + (0.20)(0.018) + (0.45)(0.02) = 0.0161 \end{aligned}$$

and

(a) $$P(A_1|E) = \frac{P(A_1) \cdot P(E|A_1)}{P(E)} = \frac{(0.35)(0.01)}{0.0161} = 0.217$$

(b) $$P(A_2|E) = \frac{P(A_2) \cdot P(E|A_2)}{P(E)} = \frac{(0.2)(0.018)}{0.0161} = 0.224$$

(c) $$P(A_3|E) = \frac{P(A_3) \cdot P(E|A_3)}{P(E)} = \frac{(0.45)(0.02)}{0.0161} = 0.559 \tag{10}$$

Given that a defective car is chosen, the probability it came from plant A_1 is 0.217, from plant A_2 is 0.224, and from plant A_3 is 0.559. ■

NOW WORK PROBLEM 29.

4 Find *A Priori* and *A Posteriori* Probabilities

In Bayes' Theorem the probabilities $P(A_j)$ are referred to as *a priori* probabilities, while the $P(A_j|E)$ are called *a posteriori* probabilities. We use Example 5 to explain the reason for this terminology. Knowing nothing else about a car, the probability that it was produced by plant I is given by $P(A_1)$, so $P(A_1)$ can be regarded as a "before the fact," or *a priori*, probability. With the additional information that the car is defective, we reassess the likelihood of whether it came from plant I and compute $P(A_1|E)$. Then $P(A_1|E)$ can be viewed as an "after the fact," or *a posteriori*, probability.

Note that $P(A_1) = 0.35$, while $P(A_1|E) = 0.217$. So the knowledge that a car is defective decreases the chance that it came from plant I.

EXAMPLE 6 Testing for Cancer

The residents of a community are examined for cancer. The examination results are classified as positive (+) if a malignancy is suspected, and as negative (−) if there are no indications of a malignancy. If a person has cancer, the probability of a positive result from the examination is 0.98. If a person does not have cancer, the probability o positive result is 0.15. If 5% of the community has cancer, what is the probability o person not having cancer if the examination is positive?

SOLUTION Define the following events:

A_1: Person has cancer
A_2: Person does not have cancer
E: Examination is positive

We want to know the probability of a person not having cancer if it is known t the examination is positive; that is, we wish to find $P(A_2|E)$.

We are given the probabilities:

$$P(A_1) = 0.05 \qquad P(A_2) = 0.95$$
$$P(E|A_1) = 0.98 \qquad P(E|A_2) = 0.15$$

Using Bayes' Theorem, Formula (8), we get

$$P(A_2|E) = \frac{P(A_2)\cdot P(E|A_2)}{P(A_1)\cdot P(E|A_1) + P(A_2)\cdot P(E|A_2)}$$
$$= \frac{(0.95)(0.15)}{(0.05)(0.98) + (0.95)(0.15)} = 0.744$$

So, even if the examination is positive, the person examined is more likely (74.4 not to have cancer than to have cancer. The reason the test is designed this way is tha is better for a healthy person to be examined more thoroughly than for someone w cancer to go undetected. Simply stated, the test is useful because of the high probabi (98%) that a person with cancer will not go undetected.

EXAMPLE 7 Car Repair Diagnosis

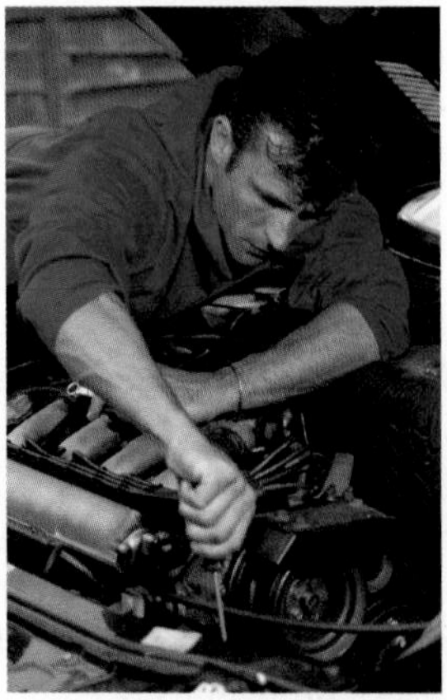

The manager of a car repair shop knows from past experience that when a cal received from a person whose car will not start, the probabilities for various troub (assuming no two can occur simultaneously) are as given in Table 4.

TABLE 4

Event	Trouble	Probability
A_1	Flooded	0.3
A_2	Battery cable loose	0.2
A_3	Points bad	0.1
A_4	Out of gas	0.3
A_5	Something else	0.1

The manager also knows that if the person will hold the gas pedal down and try to st the car, the probability that it will start (E) is

$$P(E|A_1) = 0.9 \quad P(E|A_2) = 0 \quad P(E|A_3) = 0.2 \quad P(E|A_4) = 0 \quad P(E|A_5) = 0.$$

(a) If a person has called and is instructed to "hold the pedal down . . . ," what is probability that the car will start?

(b) If the car does start after holding the pedal down, what is the probability that the was flooded?

SOLUTION **(a)** We first find $P(E)$. Using Formula (6) for $n = 5$ (the sample space is partitioned into five sets), we have

$$P(E) = P(A_1) \cdot P(E|A_1) + P(A_2) \cdot P(E|A_2) + P(A_3) \cdot P(E|A_3)$$
$$+ P(A_4) \cdot P(E|A_4) + P(A_5) \cdot P(E|A_5)$$
$$= (0.3)(0.9) + (0.2)(0) + (0.1)(0.2) + (0.3)(0) + (0.1)(0.2)$$
$$= 0.27 + 0.02 + 0.02 = 0.31$$

See Figure 19 for the tree diagram.

FIGURE 19

Probability of starting = 0.31

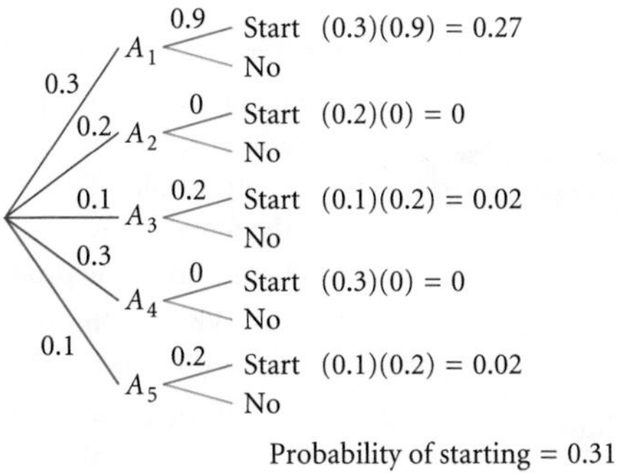

(b) We seek the probability $P(A_1|E)$. To find the *a posteriori* probability $P(A_1|E)$, use Bayes' Theorem, Formula (8).

$$P(A_1|E) = \frac{P(A_1) \cdot P(E|A_1)}{P(E)} = \frac{(0.3)(0.9)}{0.31} = 0.87$$

The probability that the car was flooded, after it is known that holding down the pedal started the car, is 0.87. ∎

✎ NOW WORK PROBLEM 35.

EXERCISE 8.3 Answers Begin on Page AN–41.

'Are You Prepared?' Problem Answer is given at the end of these exercises. If you get a wrong answer, read the pages listed in red.

1. If A and B are two disjoint sets, then $A \cap B = $ _____. (p. 356–363)

Concepts and Vocabulary

2. If A_1 and A_2 are two nonempty, mutually exclusive events in a sample space S for which $A_1 \cup A_2 = S$, then A_1 and A_2 form a _____ of S.

3. **True or False** If A_1 and A_2 form a partition of a sample space S and if E is an event in S, then $P(E) = P(A_1) \cdot P(E|A_1) + P(A_2) \cdot P(E|A_2)$.

4. **True or False** If A_1 and A_2 form a partition of a sample space S and if E is an event in S, then $P(A_1|E) = \dfrac{P(A_2) \cdot P(E|A_2)}{P(E)}$.

Skill Building

In Problems 5–18, find the indicated probabilities by referring to the tree diagram below.

```
        0.6   Ē
   0.3 A
        0.4   E
0.6  B  0.8   Ē
        0.2   E
   0.1 C 0.3   Ē
        0.7   E
```

5. $P(E|A)$
6. $P(\bar{E}|A)$
7. $P(E|B)$
8. $P(\bar{E}|B)$
9. $P(E|C)$
10. $P(\bar{E}|C)$
11. $P(E)$
12. $P(\bar{E})$
13. $P(A|E)$
14. $P(B|\bar{E})$
15. $P(C|E)$
16. $P(A|\bar{E})$
17. $P(B|E)$
18. $P(C|\bar{E})$

19. Events A_1 and A_2 form a partition of a sample space S with $P(A_1) = 0.4$ and $P(A_2) = 0.6$. If E is an event in S with $P(E|A_1) = 0.03$ and $P(E|A_2) = 0.02$, compute $P(E)$.

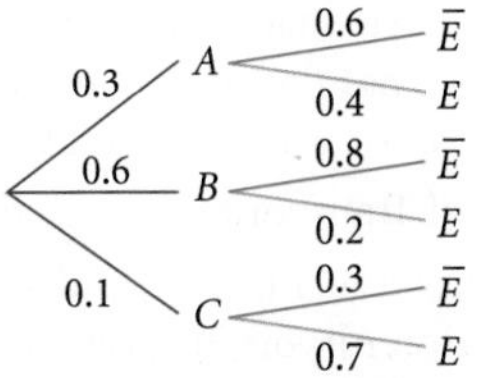

20. Events A_1 and A_2 form a partition of a sample space S with $P(A_1) = 0.3$ and $P(A_2) = 0.7$. If E is an event in S with $P(E|A_1) = 0.04$ and $P(E|A_2) = 0.01$, compute $P(E)$.

21. Events A_1, A_2, and A_3 form a partition of a sample space S with $P(A_1) = 0.6, P(A_2) = 0.2$, and $P(A_3) = 0.2$. If E is an event in S with $P(E|A_1) = 0.01, P(E|A_2) = 0.03$, and $P(E|A_3) = 0.02$, compute $P(E)$.

22. Events A_1, A_2, and A_3 form a partition of a sample space S with $P(A_1) = 0.3, P(A_2) = 0.2$, and $P(A_3) = 0.5$. If E is an event in S with $P(E|A_1) = 0.01, P(E|A_2) = 0.02$, a $P(E|A_3) = 0.02$, compute $P(E)$.

23. Use the information in Problem 19 to find $P(A_1|E)$ and $P(A_2|$

24. Use the information in Problem 20 to find $P(A_1|E)$ and $P(A_2|$

25. Use the information in Problem 21 to find $P(A_1|E), P(A_2|$ and $P(A_3|E)$.

26. Use the information in Problem 22 to find $P(A_1|E), P(A_2|$ and $P(A_3|E)$.

Applications and Extensions

27. Three jars contain colored balls as follows:

Jar	Red, R	White, W	Blue, B
I	5	6	5
II	3	4	9
III	7	5	4

One jar is chosen at random and a ball is withdrawn.

(a) What is the probability the ball is red?

(b) What is the probability the ball is white?

(c) What is the probability the ball is blue?

(d) If the ball is red, what is the probability it came from Jar I?

(e) If the ball is blue, what is the probability it came from Jar II?

(f) If the ball is white, what is the probability it came from Jar III?

28. Car Production Cars are being produced by two factories, but factory I produces twice as many cars as factory II in a given time. Factory I is known to produce 2% defectives and factory II produces 1% defectives. A car is examined and found to be defective.

(a) What is the probability the car is defective if it came from factory I?

(b) What is the probability the car is defective if it came from factory II?

(c) What is the probability the car came from factory I if it is defective?

(c) What is the probability the car came from factory II if it is defective?

29. Color Blindness According to the 2000 U.S. Census, 50.9% of the U.S. population is female. NBC news reported that 1 out of 12 males, but only 1 out of 250 females is color-blind. Given that a person randomly chosen from the U.S. population is color-blind, what is the probability that the person is a male?

Source: U.S. Census Bureau.

30. Hospital Bills A hospital billing department knows that the probability patients 60 or older pay the balance of their bill after one billing is 80%, while for a person under the age of 60 the probability is 45%. Seventy percent of the hospital's patients are 60 years or older.

(a) What is the probability the balance is paid after one billing?

(b) The balance of the bill is not paid after one billing. What is the probability the patient was 60 years or older?

31. Advertising Castaway Cruise lines mails a promotio advertisement to 10,000 potential customers, 6500 males a 3500 females. Of the mailing, 80% of the males and 40% the females have cruised on Castaway before. A customer w has received the promotion calls and books a cruise.

(a) What is the probability the customer has never sai with Castaway?

(b) If the customer has never cruised with Castaway, wha the probability he is male?

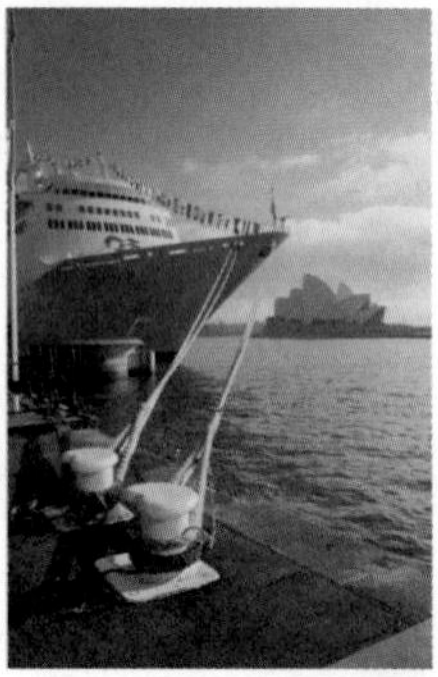

32. Market Research From past experience Kave Jewelers kn that 80% of their customers in the month before Christn are male. Market research shows that 75% of adult males a 30% of adult females watch professional football. So K buys advertising spots during Sunday football games. An ad walks into a Kave Jewelers on December 15.

(a) What is the probability the person has seen an ad?

(b) If a customer who shops at Kave has seen an ad, wha the probability the customer is female?

(c) If a customer has not seen an ad, what is the probabi the customer is male?

33. On-Time Performance You are meeting a friend at Fort My Airport. According to the Bureau of Transportation Statistics 2009 flights into Fort Myers were on time 81.3% of the time, Southwest had a better record and is on time 84.5% of the ti You cannot remember what airline she is taking but you kn that in the past she has flown on Southwest 70% of the ti The plane is late. What is the probability she is on Southw

Source: Bureau of Transportation Statistics (www.bts.gov)

34. Air Travel Liz flies regularly from Midway Airport in Chic to Hartsfield-Jackson Airport in Atlanta using AirTran Airw 75% of the time and Delta Airlines 25% of the time. In 2

AirTran's on-time percentage for this flight was 73.3%. Delta's on-time percentage for this flight was 71.3%. If a randomly selected flight arrives on time, what is the probability Liz is on a Delta Airlines flight?

Source: Bureau of Transportation Statistics

5. **Customer Surveys** Juan Morales is a restauranteur who owns three authentic Mexican restaurants in the towns of Riverside, Springfield, and Centerville. To receive customer feedback, Juan provides postage-paid survey cards at each establishments which can be completed by patrons and mailed directly to him. By keeping records on the returned surveys, Juan has learned that 40% are from patrons of the Riverside restaurant, 25% are from patrons of the Springfield restaurant, and 35% are from patrons of the Centerville restaurant. Juan has also learned that the percent of surveys returned with negative feedback are 8%, 12%, and 9% for the three restaurants, respectively.

(a) If Juan receives a survey in the mail, what is the probability that it will give negative feedback?

(b) If Juan receives a survey with negative feedback, what is the probability it is from a patron of the Riverside restaurant?

(c) If Juan receives a survey with negative feedback, what is the probability it is from a patron of the Springfield restaurant?

6. **Female Unemployment** Based on information from the Bureau of Labor Statistics, of women in the civilian labor force, 51.8% are married, 28.2% have never been married, 12.8% are divorced, 4.1% are separated, and 3.1% are widowed. Of the married women, 3.6% are unemployed; of the never-married women, 8.5% are unemployed; of the divorced women, 5.2% are unemployed; of the separated women, 8.3% are unemployed; of the widowed women, 5.7% are unemployed.

(a) What is the probability a randomly selected woman from the civilian labor force is unemployed?

(b) If an unemployed woman is selected, what is the probability she is married?

(c) If an unemployed woman is selected, what is the probability she never married?

(d) If an unemployed woman is selected, what is the probability she is divorced?

(e) If an unemployed woman is selected, what is the probability she is separated?

(f) If an unemployed woman is selected, what is the probability she is widowed?

Source: Bureau of Labor Statistics, Employment Status by marital status and sex, 2008

7. **Individual Tax Audits** In 2008, the audit risk for the average individual filing a federal income tax return was about 1 in 100. For individuals with an adjusted gross income of $1 million or higher, the audit risk was about 1 in 16. About 1 in 250 individuals filing federal income tax returns have adjusted gross incomes of $1 million or higher. If an individual income tax return has been chosen to be audited, find the probability that the individual's adjusted gross income is $1 million or higher.

Source: Internal Revenue Service

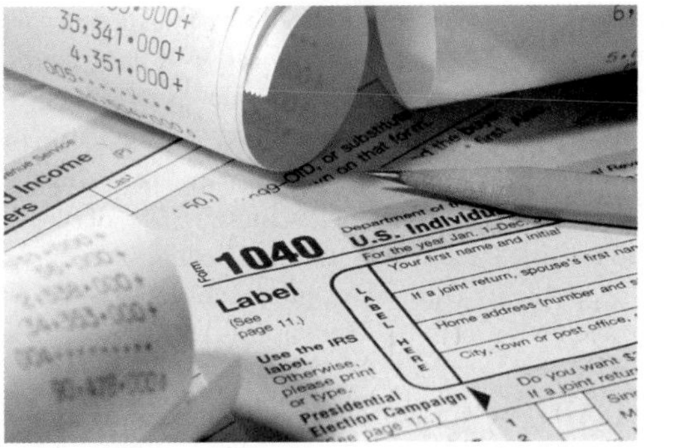

38. **Promotional Coupon** An office supply store desires to increase sales of its store brand toner cartridges over its sales of less profitable name brand cartridges. To do so, it mass mails a sales flyer to its entire database of current customers. Each flyer contains a personalized coupon for $30 off the purchase of any store brand toner cartridge. Of its current customers, 24% have previously purchased store brand cartridges. From past experience, store management knows that about 46% of customers who have made a previous purchase of an item will redeem a coupon for that item. Management also knows that about 15% of personalized coupons are redeemed.

(a) If a redeemed coupon is selected at random, what is the probability that it was used by a customer who had previously purchased a store brand cartridge?

(b) If a customer who has not previously purchased a store brand toner cartridge is randomly selected, what is the probability that he or she will redeem the personalized promotional coupon?

39. **Occupations** Based on data from the Bureau of Labor Statistics, 36.3% of employed persons in the United States have occupations classified as management, professional, and related; 16.8% have occupations classified as service; 24.5% have occupations classified as sales and office; 10.2% have occupations classified as natural resources, construction, and maintenance; 12.2% have occupations classified as production, transportation, and material moving. Women hold 50.8% of the management, professional, and related occupations, 57.2% of the service occupations, 63.2% of the sales and office occupations, 4.2% of the natural resources, construction, and maintenance occupations, 22.4% of the production, transportation, and material moving occupations.

(a) What percentage of employed persons in the United States are women?

(b) If an employed woman is selected, what is the probability her occupation is classified as management, professional, and related?

(c) If an employed woman is selected, what is the probability her occupation is classified as service?

(d) If an employed woman is selected, what is the probability her occupation is classified as sales and office?

Source: Bureau of Labor Statistics, Employed persons by detailed occupation, sex, race, and Hispanic or Latino ethnicity, 2008

40. Medical Diagnosis In a certain small town, 16% of the population developed lung cancer. If 45% of the population are smokers, and 85% of those developing lung cancer are smokers, what is the probability that a smoker in this population will develop lung cancer?

41. Voting Pattern In Cook County, 55% of the registered voters are Democrats, 30% are Republicans, and 15% are Independents. During a recent election, 35% of the Democrats voted, 65% of the Republicans voted, and 75% of the Independents voted.

(a) What is the probability that someone who voted is a Democrat?

(b) What is the probability someone who voted is a Republican?

(c) What is the probability someone who voted is Independent?

42. Quality Control A computer manufacturer has three assembly plants. Records show that 2% of the computers shipped from plant A turn out to be defective, as compared to 3% of those that come from plant B and 4% of those that come from plant C. In all, 30% of the manufacturer's total production comes from plant A, 50% from plant B, and 20% from plant C. If a customer finds that his computer is defective, what is the probability it came from plant B?

43. Oil Drilling An oil well is to be drilled in a certain location. The soil there is either rock (probability 0.53), clay (probability 0.21), or sand. If it is rock, a geological test gives a positive result with 35% accuracy; if it is clay, this test gives a positive result with 48% accuracy; and if it is sand, the test gives a positive result with 75% accuracy. The test is positive.

(a) What is the probability that the soil is rock?

(b) What is the probability that the soil is clay?

(c) What is the probability that the soil is sand?

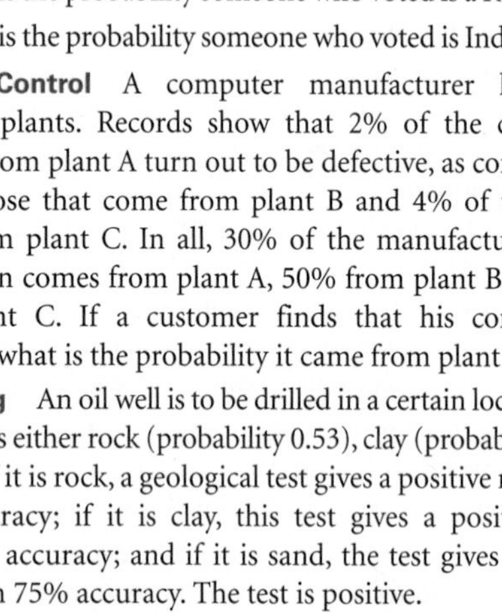

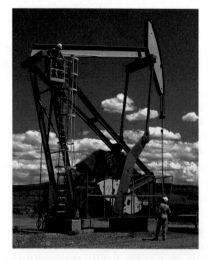

44. Oil Drilling A geologist is using seismographs to test for oil. It is found that if oil is present, the test gives a positive result 95% of the time, and if oil is not present, the test gives a positive result 2% of the time. Oil is actually present in 1% of the cases tested. If the test shows positive, what is the probability that oil is present?

45. Political Polls In conducting a political poll, a pollster divid the United States into four sections: Northeast (N), containi 40% of the population; South (S), containing 10% of t population; Midwest (M), containing 25% of the populatio and West (W), containing 25% of the population. From the p it is found that in the next election 40% of the people in t Northeast say they will vote for Republicans, in the South 56 will vote Republican, in the Midwest 48% will vote Republica and in the West 52% will vote Republican.

(a) What is the probability that a person chosen at rando will vote Republican?

(b) Assuming a person votes Republican, what is t probability that he or she is from the Northeast?

46. TB Screening Suppose that if a person with tuberculosis given a TB screening, the probability that his or her conditi will be detected is 0.90. If a person without tuberculosis given a TB screening, the probability that he or she will diagnosed incorrectly as having tuberculosis is 0.3. Suppos further, that 11% of the adult residents of a certain city ha tuberculosis. If one of these adults is diagnosed as havi tuberculosis based on the screening, what is the probabili that he or she actually has tuberculosis? Interpret your resu

47. Detective Columbo An absent-minded nurse is to gi Mr. Brown a pill each day. The probability that the nur forgets to administer the pill is $\frac{2}{3}$. If he receives the pill, t probability that Mr. Brown will die is $\frac{1}{3}$. If he does not get h pill, the probability that he will die is $\frac{3}{4}$. Mr. Brown died. Wh is the probability that the nurse forgot to give Mr. Brow the pill?

48. Marketing To introduce a new beer, a company conducted survey. It divided the United States into four regions: easter northern, southern, and western. The company estimates th 35% of the potential customers for the beer are in the easte region, 30% are in the northern region, 20% are in the southe region, and 15% are in the western region. The survey indica that 50% of the potential customers in the eastern region, 40% the potential customers in the northern region, 36% of t potential customers in the southern region, and 42% of those the western region will buy the beer. If a potential custom chosen at random indicates that he or she will buy the beer, wh is the probability that the customer is from the southern regio

49. Car Insurance and Age Insurers know that young drive between the ages of 16 and 24 have 2.6 times more acciden than older drivers and that 13% of all drivers are between t ages of 16 and 24. In 2007, the probability an adult w involved in an accident was 0.024 and resulted in 5,811,0 reported crashes.

(a) If an accident is reported what is the probability it involv a young driver?

(b) Twenty percent of a company's insureds are you drivers. A claim is made. What is the probability t driver was 25 or older?

Source: www.nhta.gov, www.iii.org

Medical Test A scientist designed a medical test for a certain disease. Among 100 patients who have the disease, the test will show the presence of the disease in 97 cases out of 100, and will fail to show the presence of the disease in the remaining 3 cases out of 100. Among those who do not have the disease, the test will erroneously show the presence of the disease in 4 cases out of 100, and will show that there is no disease in the remaining 96 cases out of 100.

(a) What is the probability that a patient who tested positive on this test actually has the disease, if it is estimated that 20% of the population has the disease?

(b) What is the probability that a patient who tested positive on this test actually has the disease, if it is estimated that 4% of the population has the disease?

(c) What is the probability that a patient who took the test twice and tested positive both times actually has the disease, if it is estimated that 4% of the population has the disease?

Testing for HIV An article in the *New York Times* some time ago reported that college students are beginning to routinely ask to be tested for the AIDS virus. The standard test for the HIV virus is the Elias test, which tests for the presence of HIV antibodies. It is estimated that this test has a 99.8% sensitivity and a 99.8% specificity. A 99.8% sensitivity means that, in a large-scale screening test, for every 1000 people tested who have the virus we can expect 998 people to test positive and 2 to have a false negative test. A 99.8% specificity means that, in a large-scale screening test, for every 1000 people tested who do not have the virus we can expect 998 people to have a negative test and 2 to have a false positive test.

(a) The *New York Times* article remarks that it is estimated that about 2 in every 1000 college students have the HIV virus. Assume that a large group of randomly chosen college students, say 100,000, are tested by the Elias test. If a student tests positive, what is the chance that this student has the HIV virus?

(b) What would this probability be for a population at high risk, where 5% of the population has the HIV virus?

(c) Suppose Jack tested positive on an Elias test. Another Elias test* is performed and the results are positive again. Assuming that the tests are independent, what is the probability that Jack has the HIV virus?

52. Test for Tuberculosis A faster and simpler diagnostic test for the presence of tuberculosis bacilli, called "FASTPlaqueTB," was evaluated in Cape Town, South Africa, and found to have the following reliability. For those subjects known to have the tuberculosis bacilli, the FASTPlaqueTB test was positive 70% of the time. For those subjects known not to have the tuberculosis bacilli, the FASTPlaqueTB test was negative 99% of the time. Statistics indicate that about 14.2% of the people in Cape Town have the tuberculosis bacilli.

(a) What is the probability that a randomly selected person from Cape Town will have a positive FASTPlaqueTB test result?

(b) What is the probability that a person who tests positive actually has tuberculosis bacilli?

53. Show that $P(E|F) = 1$ if F is a subset of E and $P(F) \neq 0$.

54. Prove Bayes' Theorem, Formula (8).

* *Actually, in practice, if a person tests positive on an Elias test, then two more Elias tests are carried out. If either is positive, then one more confirmatory test, called the Western blot test, is carried out. If this is positive, the person is assumed to have the HIV virus.*

e You Prepared?' Answer

∅

8.4 Permutations

PREPARING FOR THIS SECTION *Before getting started, review the following:*

- The Multiplication Principle (Section 7.3, pp. 373–376)

NOW WORK THE "ARE YOU PREPARED" PROBLEMS ON PAGE 463.

OBJECTIVES
1 Evaluate factorials (p. 458)
2 Solve counting problems involving permutations [distinct, with repetition] (p. 459)
3 Solve counting problems involving permutations [distinct, without repetition] (p. 460)

In the next two sections we use the Multiplication Principle to discuss two general types of counting problems, called *permutations* and *combinations*. These concepts arise often in applications, especially in probability. Before discussing permutations, we introduce a useful shorthand notation—the *factorial symbol*.

Definition

Factorial

The symbol $n!$, read as "***n factorial***," is defined as

$$
\begin{aligned}
0! &= 1\\
1! &= 1\\
2! &= 2\cdot 1 = 2\\
3! &= 3\cdot 2\cdot 1 = 6\\
4! &= 4\cdot 3\cdot 2\cdot 1 = 24
\end{aligned}
$$

and, in general, for $n \geq 1$ an integer,

$$n! = n\cdot(n-1)\cdot(n-2)\cdot \cdots \cdot 3\cdot 2\cdot 1 \qquad (1)$$

1 Evaluate Factorials

To compute $n!$, find the product of all consecutive integers from n down to 1, inclusi or from 1 up to n, inclusive. Remember that, by definition, $0! = 1$.

Look at Equation (1). It follows that

$$n! = n(n-1)! \qquad (2)$$

Formula (2) can be useful for evaluating expressions containing factorials.

EXAMPLE 1 Evaluating Expressions Containing Factorials

(a) $5! = 5\cdot 4\cdot 3\cdot 2\cdot 1 = 120$

(b) $\dfrac{5!}{4!} = \dfrac{5\cdot 4!}{4!} = 5$

(c) $\dfrac{52!}{5!47!} = \dfrac{52\cdot 51\cdot 50\cdot 49\cdot 48\cdot 47!}{5\cdot 4\cdot 3\cdot 2\cdot 1\cdot 47!} = 2{,}598{,}960$

(d) $\dfrac{7!}{(7-5)!5!} = \dfrac{7!}{2!5!} = \dfrac{7\cdot 6\cdot 5!}{2!5!} = \dfrac{7\cdot 6}{2} = 21$

(e) $\dfrac{50\cdot 49\cdot 48\cdot 47\cdot 46}{50!} = \dfrac{50\cdot 49\cdot 48\cdot 47\cdot 46}{50\cdot 49\cdot 48\cdot 47\cdot 46\cdot 45!} = \dfrac{1}{45!}$

NOW WORK PROBLEM 7.

Factorials grow very quickly. Compare the following:

$$
\begin{aligned}
5! &= 120\\
10! &= 3{,}628{,}800\\
15! &= 1{,}307{,}674{,}368{,}000
\end{aligned}
$$

In fact, if your calculator has a factorial key, you will find that $69! = 1.71\cdot 10^{98}$, while produces an error message—indicating you have exceeded the range of the calculat

Because of this, it is important to "cancel out" factorials whenever possible so that "out of range" errors may be avoided. For example, to calculate $\frac{100!}{95!}$, we write

$$\frac{100!}{95!} = \frac{100 \cdot 99 \cdot 98 \cdot 97 \cdot 96 \cdot \cancel{95!}}{\cancel{95!}} = 9.03 \cdot 10^9$$

Permutations

Definition

A **permutation** is an ordered arrangement of r objects chosen from n objects.

We discuss three types of permutations:

1. The n objects are distinct (different), and repetition is allowed in the selection of r of them. [Distinct, with repetition]
2. The n objects are distinct (different), and repetition is not allowed in the selection of r of them, where $r \leq n$. [Distinct, without repetition]
3. The n objects are not distinct, and we use all of them in the arrangement. [Not distinct]

We take up the first two types here and deal with the third type in the next section.

2 Solve Counting Problems Involving Permutations [Distinct, with Repetition]

EXAMPLE 2 Counting Airport Codes [Permutation: Distinct, with Repetition]

The International Airline Transportation Association (IATA) assigns three-letter codes to represent airport locations. For example, the airport code for Ft. Lauderdale, Florida, is FLL. Notice that repetition is allowed in forming this code. How many airport codes are possible?

SOLUTION We are choosing 3 letters from 26 letters and arranging them in order. In the ordered arrangement a letter may be repeated. This is an example of a permutation with repetition in which 3 objects are chosen from 26 distinct objects.

The task of counting the number of such arrangements consists of making three selections. Each selection requires choosing a letter of the alphabet (26 choices). By the Multiplication Principle, there are

$$26 \cdot 26 \cdot 26 = 17{,}576$$

different airport codes. ■

The solution given to Example 2 can be generalized.

Theorem

Permutations: Distinct Objects, with Repetition

The number of ordered arrangements of r objects chosen from n objects, in which the n objects are distinct and repetition is allowed, is n^r.

NOW WORK PROBLEM 31.

3 Solve Counting Problems Involving Permutations [Distinct, without Repetition]

EXAMPLE 3 Forming Codes [Permutation: Distinct, without Repetition]

Suppose that we wish to establish a three-letter code using any of the 26 upperca letters of the alphabet, but we require that no letter be used more than once. How ma different three-letter codes are there?

SOLUTION Some of the possibilities are: ABC, ABD, ABZ, ACB, CBA, and so on. The task consists making three selections. The first selection requires choosing from 26 letters. Because letter can be used more than once, the second selection requires choosing fro 25 letters. The third selection requires choosing from 24 letters. (Do you see why?) the Multiplication Principle, there are

$$26 \cdot 25 \cdot 24 = 15{,}600$$

different three-letter codes with no letter repeated.

For this second type of permutation, we introduce the following notation:

> The notation $\boldsymbol{P(n, r)}$ represents the number of ordered arrangements of r objects chosen from n distinct objects, where $r \leq n$ and repetition is not allowed.

For example, the question posed in Example 3 asks for the number of ways that the letters of the alphabet can be arranged in order using three nonrepeated letters. The answe

$$P(26, 3) = 26 \cdot 25 \cdot 24 = 15{,}600$$

EXAMPLE 4 Lining Up People

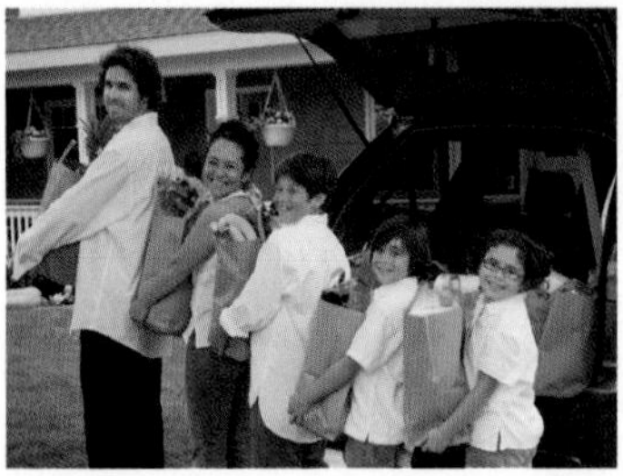

In how many ways can 5 people be lined up?

SOLUTION The 5 people are distinct. Once a person is in line, that person will not repeated elsewhere in the line; and, in lining up people, order is important. We have permutation of 5 objects taken 5 at a time. We can line up 5 people in

$$P(5, 5) = \underbrace{5 \cdot 4 \cdot 3 \cdot 2 \cdot 1}_{\text{5 factors}} = 120 \text{ ways}$$

NOW WORK PROBLEM 33.

To arrive at a formula for $P(n, r)$, we note that the task of obtaining an order arrangement of n objects in which only $r \leq n$ of them are used, without repeati any of them, requires making r selections. For the first selection, there are n choices; the second selection, there are $n - 1$ choices; for the third selection, there are $n -$ choices; . . . ; for the rth selection, there are $n - (r - 1)$ choices. By the Multiplicati Principle, we have

$$\begin{aligned} P(n, r) &= \overset{\text{1st}}{n} \cdot \overset{\text{2nd}}{(n-1)} \cdot \overset{\text{3rd}}{(n-2)} \cdot \cdots \cdot \overset{r\text{th}}{[n-(r-1)]} \\ &= n \cdot (n-1) \cdot (n-2) \cdot \cdots \cdot (n-r+1) \end{aligned}$$

This formula for $P(n, r)$ can be compactly written using factorial notation.

$$P(n, r) = n \cdot (n-1) \cdot (n-2) \cdot \cdots \cdot (n-r+1)$$
$$= n \cdot (n-1) \cdot (n-2) \cdot \cdots \cdot (n-r+1) \cdot \frac{(n-r) \cdot \cdots \cdot 3 \cdot 2 \cdot 1}{(n-r) \cdot \cdots \cdot 3 \cdot 2 \cdot 1} = \frac{n!}{(n-r)!}$$

Theorem

Number of Permutations of *r* Objects Chosen from *n* Distinct Objects without Repetition

The number of arrangements of n objects using $r \le n$ of them, in which

1. the n objects are distinct,
2. once an object is used it cannot be repeated, and
3. order is important,

is given by the formula

$$P(n, r) = \frac{n!}{(n-r)!} \qquad (3)$$

EXAMPLE 5 Computing Permutations

Evaluate:

(a) $P(7, 3)$ **(b)** $P(6, 1)$ **(c)** $P(52, 5)$

SOLUTION We shall work parts (a) and (b) in two ways.

(a)
$$P(7, 3) = \underbrace{7 \cdot 6 \cdot 5}_{\text{3 factors}} = 210$$

or

$$P(7, 3) = \frac{7!}{(7-3)!} = \frac{7!}{4!} = \frac{7 \cdot 6 \cdot 5 \cdot \cancel{4!}}{\cancel{4!}} = 210$$

(b)
$$P(6, 1) = \underbrace{6}_{\text{1 factor}}$$

or

$$P(6, 1) = \frac{6!}{(6-1)!} = \frac{6!}{5!} = \frac{6 \cdot \cancel{5!}}{\cancel{5!}} = 6$$

GURE 20

(c) Figure 20 shows the solution using a TI-84 Plus graphing calculator:

$$P(52, 5) = 311{,}875{,}200$$ ■

NOW WORK PROBLEM 17.

Here is a short list of problems with their solutions given in $P(n, r)$ notation. Notice in each problem that the objects are distinct, no object is repeated, and order is important.

Problem	Solution
Find the number of ways of choosing five people from a group of 10 and arranging them in a line.	$P(10, 5)$
Find the number of six-letter "words" that can be formed with no letter repeated.	$P(26, 6)$
Find the number of seven-digit telephone numbers, with no repeated digit (allow 0 for a first digit).	$P(10, 7)$
Find the number of ways of arranging eight people in a line.	$P(8, 8)$

NOW WORK PROBLEM 25.

EXAMPLE 6 The Birthday Problem

All we know about Shannon, Patrick, and Ryan is that they have different birthdays. we listed all the possible ways this could occur, how many would there be? Assume th there are 365 days in a year.

SOLUTION This is an example of a permutation in which 3 birthdays are selected from a possib 365 days, and no birthday may repeat itself. The number of ways that this can occur

$$P(365, 3) = \frac{365!}{(365 - 3)!} = \frac{365 \cdot 364 \cdot 363 \cdot \cancel{362!}}{\cancel{362!}} = 365 \cdot 364 \cdot 363 = 48{,}228{,}180$$

There are 48,228,180 ways in a group of three people that each can have a differe birthday.

NOW WORK PROBLEM 49.

EXAMPLE 7 Answering Test Questions

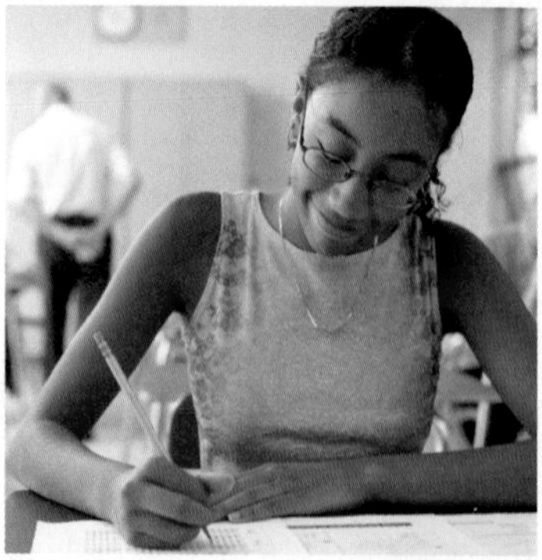

A student has six questions on an examination and is allowed to answer the questio in any order. In how many different orders could the student answer these questions?

SOLUTION We seek the number of ordered arrangements of the six questions usir all six of them. The number is given by

$$P(6, 6) = \frac{6!}{(6 - 6)!} = \frac{6!}{0!} = \frac{6!}{1} = 720$$

Example 7 leads us to formulate the next result.

Theorem The number of permutations (arrangements) of n distinct objects using all n of them is given by

$$\boldsymbol{P(n, n) = n!}$$

For example, in a class of n students, there are $n!$ ways of positioning all the students in a line.

EXAMPLE 8 Arranging Books on a Shelf

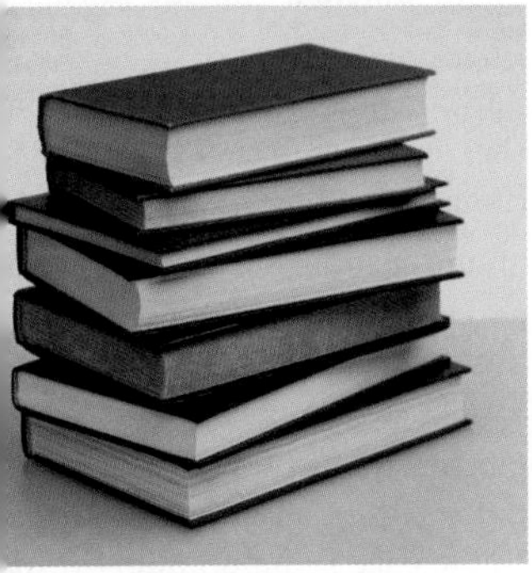

You own eight mathematics books and six computer science books and wish to fill seven positions on a shelf. If the first four positions are to be occupied by math books and the last three by computer science books, in how many ways can this be done?

SOLUTION We think of the problem as consisting of two tasks. Task 1 is to fill the first four positions with four of the eight mathematics books. This can be done in $P(8, 4)$ ways. Task 2 is to fill the remaining three positions with three of six computer books. This can be done in $P(6, 3)$ ways. By the Multiplication Principle, the seven positions can be filled in

$$P(8, 4) \cdot P(6, 3) = \frac{8!}{4!} \cdot \frac{6!}{3!} = 8 \cdot 7 \cdot 6 \cdot 5 \cdot 6 \cdot 5 \cdot 4 = 201{,}600$$

different ways. ■

NOW WORK PROBLEM 39.

XERCISE 8.4 Answers Begin on Page AN–41.

'e You Prepared?' Problems Answers are given at the end of these exercises. If you get a wrong answer, read the pages listed in red.

How many different 4-digit numbers can be formed from the set {0, 1, 2, 3, 4, 5, 6, 7, 8, 9} if no digit is to be repeated? (p. 373–376)

2. If a coin is tossed 5 times, how many different sequences of heads and tails are possible? (p. 373–376)

ncepts and Vocabulary

$0! =$ ____; $3! =$ ____

4. $P(n, r) =$ ____

True or False The number of ordered arrangements of r objects chosen from n objects, in which the n objects are distinct and repetition is allowed, is r^n.

6. ***True or False*** $P(n, n) = n$

ill Building

Problems 7–24, evaluate each expression.

$\frac{5!}{2!}$ **8.** $\frac{8!}{2!}$ **9.** $\frac{10!}{8!}$ **10.** $\frac{11!}{9!}$ **11.** $\frac{9!}{8!}$ **12.** $\frac{10!}{9!}$ **13.** $\frac{8!}{2!6!}$ **14.** $\frac{9!}{3!6!}$

. $P(7, 2)$ **16.** $P(8, 1)$ **17.** $P(8, 7)$ **18.** $P(6, 6)$ **19.** $P(6, 0)$

. $P(6, 4)$ **21.** $\frac{8!}{(8-3)!3!}$ **22.** $\frac{9!}{(9-5)!5!}$ **23.** $\frac{6!}{(6-6)!6!}$ **24.** $\frac{7!}{(0-0)!7!}$

25. List all the ordered arrangements of 5 objects a, b, c, d, and e, choosing 3 at a time without repetition. What is $P(5, 3)$?

27. List all the ordered arrangements of 4 objects 1, 2, 3, and 4, choosing 3 at a time without repetition. What is $P(4, 3)$?

26. List all the ordered arrangements of 5 objects a, b, c, d, an choosing 2 at a time without repetition. What is $P(5, 2)$?

28. List all the ordered arrangements of 6 objects 1, 2, 3, 4, 5, 6, choosing 2 at a time without repetition. What is $P(6, 2)$?

Applications

29. **Forming Codes** How many two-letter codes can be formed using the letters A, B, C, and D? Repeated letters are allowed.

30. **Forming Codes** How many two-letter codes can be formed using the letters A, B, C, D, and E? Repeated letters are allowed.

31. **Forming Numbers** How many three-digit numbers can be formed using the digits 0 and 1? Repeated digits are allowed.

32. **Forming Numbers** How many three-digit numbers can be formed using the digits 0, 1, 2, 3, 4, 5, 6, 7, 8, and 9? Repeated digits are allowed.

33. **Lining Up People** In how many ways can 4 people be lined up?

34. **Stacking Boxes** In how many ways can 5 different boxes be stacked?

35. **Forming Codes** How many different three-letter codes are there if only the letters A, B, C, D, and E can be used and no letter can be used more than once?

36. **Forming Codes** How many different four-letter codes are there if only the letters A, B, C, D, E, and F can be used and no letter can be used more than once?

37. **Seating Arrangements** How many ways are there to seat 5 people in 8 chairs?

38. **Seating Arrangements** How many ways are there to seat 4 people in a 6-passenger automobile?

39. **Stocks on the NYSE** Companies whose stocks are listed on the New York Stock Exchange (NYSE) have their company name represented by either 1, 2, or 3 letters (repetition of letters is allowed). What is the maximum number of companies that can be listed on the NYSE?

40. **Stocks on the NASDAQ** Companies whose stocks are listed on the NASDAQ stock exchange have their company name represented by either 4 or 5 letters (repetition of letters is allowed). What is the maximum number of companies that can be listed on the NASDAQ?

41. **New Printers** An accounting firm is upgrading the network printers in each of its three branch offices and will select from among 7 different models, though each office may have different printers. How many ways can the firm purchase three printers for the offices?

42. **New Copiers** The college of arts and sciences at a university decides to replace the copiers in each of its 6 departments. If the dean can select from 4 different models and each department can have a different type of copier, how many ways can the dean purchase the new copiers?

43. **Television Schedule** A television network has four 30-minute time slots for comedies and has 14 shows to choose from for the fall lineup. How many different comedy lineups possible?

44. **Television Schedule** A television network has eight 60-min time slots for dramas and has 15 shows to choose from for fall lineup. How many different drama lineups are possible?

45. **Promotion Schedule** A radio station has six promotio time slots available during a weekend and 11 businesses wish to have the station broadcast from their location. How ma different promotional schedules are possible?

46. **Comic Strips** A newspaper must select 9 daily comic str from a list of 17 final candidates. If the strips are the same s and shape and position on the page is important, how ma different layouts are possible for the comics page?

47. **Accounting Audits** A chief accounting officer must cond audits at each of the company's 21 facilities located in differ states. If she can only visit 8 facilities each month, how ma different travel itineraries are possible the first month?

48. **Call Letters** In the United States, all new radio stations west the Mississippi River use four call letters, but the call letters m begin with "K." How many different sets of call letters possible west of the Mississippi River if repeated letters allowed? How many are allowed if repeated letters are not allow

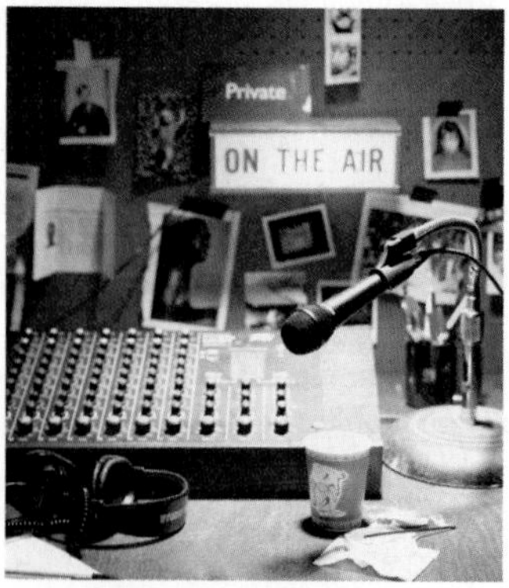

49. **Birthday Problem** In how many ways can 2 people each ha different birthdays? Assume that there are 365 days in a ye

50. **Birthday Problem** In how many ways can 5 people each ha different birthdays? Assume that there are 365 days in a ye

51. **Arranging Letters**

(a) How many different ways are there to arrange the 6 lett in the word SUNDAY?

(b) If we insist that the letter S come first, how many ways there?

(c) If we insist that the letter S come first and the letter Y last, how many ways are there?

2. **Arranging Books** There are 5 different French books and 5 different Spanish books. How many ways are there to arrange them on a shelf if

(a) Books of the same language must be grouped together, French on the left, Spanish on the right?

(b) French and Spanish books must alternate in the grouping, beginning with a French book?

3. **Distributing Books** In how many ways can 8 different books be distributed to 12 children if no child gets more than one book?

4. **Networks** A computer must assign each of 4 outputs to one of 8 different printers. In how many ways can it do this provided no printer gets more than one output?

55. **Lottery Tickets** From 1500 lottery tickets that are sold, 3 tickets are to be selected for first, second, and third prizes. How many possible outcomes are there?

56. **Personnel Assignment** A salesperson is needed in each of 7 different sales territories. If 10 equally qualified persons apply for the jobs, in how many ways can the jobs be filled?

57. **Choosing Officers** A club has 15 members. In how many ways can 4 officers consisting of a president, vice-president, secretary, and treasurer be chosen?

58. **Psychology Testing** In an ESP experiment a person is asked to select and arrange 3 cards from a set of 6 cards labeled A, B, C, D, E, and F. Without seeing the cards, a second person is asked to give the arrangement. Determine the number of possible responses by the second person if he simply guesses.

iscussion and Writing

). Create a problem different from any found in the text that requires a permutation to solve. Give it to a friend to solve and critique.

re You Prepared?' Answers

1. $10 \cdot 9 \cdot 8 \cdot 7 = 5040$ 2. $2^5 = 32$

8.5 Combinations

OBJECTIVES
1. Solve counting problems involving combinations (p. 466)
2. Solve counting problems involving permutations [*n* objects, not all distinct] (p. 469)
3. Find probabilities using counting techniques (p. 471)

Permutations focus on the order in which objects are arranged. However, in many cases, order is not important. For example, in a draw poker hand, the order in which you receive the cards is not relevant—all that matters is what cards are received. That is, with poker hands, we are concerned only with what *combination* of cards we have—not the particular order of the cards.

The following examples illustrate the distinction between selections in which order is important and those for which order is not important.

EXAMPLE 1 Arranging Letters

From the four letters a, b, c, d, choose two without repeating any letter

(a) If order is important **(b)** If order is not important

SOLUTION **(a)** If order is important, there are $P(4, 2) = 4 \cdot 3 = 12$ possible selections, namely,

ab *ac* *ad* *ba* *bc* *bd* *ca* *cb* *cd* *da* *db* *dc*

See Figure 21.

(b) If order is not important, only 6 of the 12 selections found in part (a) are listed, namely,

ab *ac* *ad* *bc* *bd* *cd* ■

GURE 21

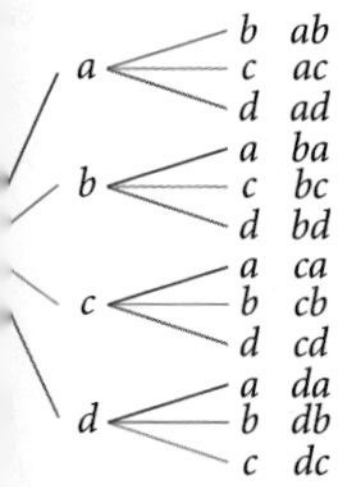

$P(4, 2) = 12$

Notice that the number of ordered selections, 12, is $2! = 2$ times the number of unordered selections, 6. The reason is that each unordered selection consists of tw letters that allow for 2! rearrangements. For example, the selection *ab* in the unorder list gives rise to *ab* and *ba* in the ordered list.

EXAMPLE 2 Arranging Letters

FIGURE 22

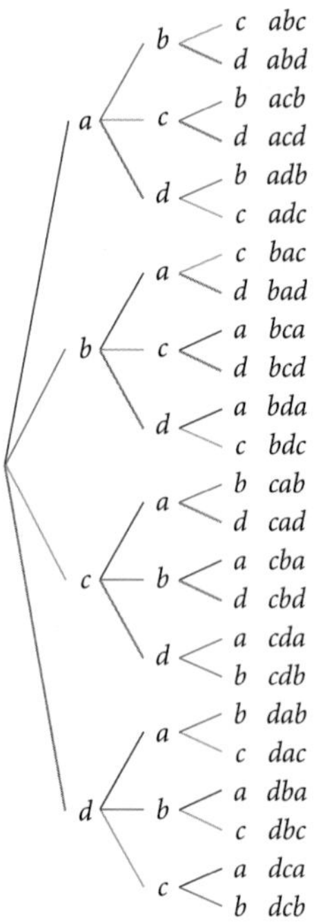

$P(4, 3) = 24$

From the four letters *a*, *b*, *c*, *d*, choose three without repeating any letter

(a) If order is important **(b)** If order is not important

SOLUTION

(a) If order is important, there are $P(4, 3) = 4 \cdot 3 \cdot 2 = 24$ possible selections, name

abc *abd* *acb* *acd* *adb* *adc* *bac* *bad* *bca* *bcd* *bda* *ba*

cab *cad* *cba* *cbd* *cda* *cdb* *dab* *dac* *dba* *dbc* *dca* *dc*

See Figure 22.

(b) If order is not important, only 4 of the 24 selections found in part (a) are liste namely,

abc *abd* *acd* *bcd*

Notice that the number of ordered selections, 24, is $3! = 6$ times the number of unordered selections, 4. The reason is that each unordered selection consists of thr letters that allow for 3! rearrangements. For example, the selection *abc* in the unordere list gives rise to *abc*, *acb*, *bac*, *bca*, *cab*, *cba* in the ordered list.

Unordered selections are called *combinations.*

1 Solve Counting Problems Involving Combinations

Definition

A **combination** is an arrangement, without regard to order, of *r* objects selected from *n* distinct objects without repetition, where $r \le n$. The notation $C(n, r)$ represents the number of combinations of *n* distinct objects using *r* of them.

$C(n, r)$ is also referred to as the number of **combinations of *n* objects taken *r* at time.**

To obtain a formula for $C(n, r)$, we first observe that each unordered selection of *r* objects will give rise to *r*! ordered selections. That is, the number of ordered selection $P(n, r)$, is *r*! times the number of unordered selections, $C(n, r)$:

$$P(n, r) = r!C(n, r)$$

If we solve this equation for $C(n, r)$, we find

$$C(n, r) = \frac{P(n, r)}{r!} = \frac{n!}{(n - r)!r!}$$

We have proved the following result:

Theorem

Number of Combinations of *n* Distinct Objects Taken *r* at a Time

The number of arrangements of n objects using $r \leq n$ of them, in which

1. the n objects are distinct,
2. once an object is used, it cannot be repeated, and
3. order is not important,

is given by the formula

$$C(n, r) = \frac{n!}{(n - r)!r!} \qquad (1)$$

EXAMPLE 3 Evaluating $C(n, r)$

Use Formula (1) to find the value of each expression.

(a) $C(3, 1)$ **(b)** $C(6, 3)$ **(c)** $C(n, n)$ **(d)** $C(n, 0)$ **(e)** $C(52, 5)$

SOLUTION **(a)** $C(3, 1) = \frac{3!}{(3-1)!1!} = \frac{3!}{2!1!} = \frac{3 \cdot \cancel{2} \cdot 1}{\cancel{2} \cdot 1 \cdot 1} = 3$

(b) $C(6, 3) = \frac{6!}{(6-3)!3!} = \frac{6 \cdot 5 \cdot 4 \cdot \cancel{3!}}{3! \cdot \cancel{3!}} = \frac{\cancel{6} \cdot 5 \cdot 4}{\cancel{6}} = 20$

FIGURE 23

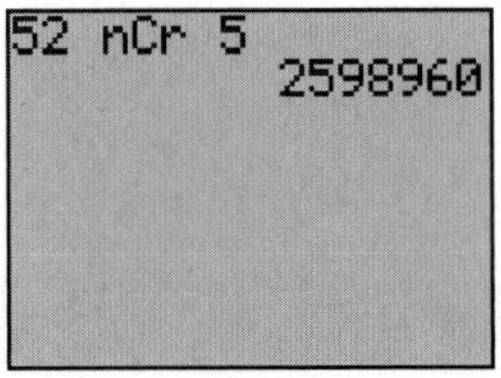

(c) $C(n, n) = \frac{n!}{(n-n)!n!} = \frac{\cancel{n!}}{0!\cancel{n!}} = \frac{1}{1} = 1$

(d) $C(n, 0) = \frac{n!}{(n-0)!0!} = \frac{\cancel{n!}}{\cancel{n!}0!} = \frac{1}{1} = 1$

(e) Figure 23 shows the solution using a TI-84 Plus graphing calculator:

$$C(52, 5) = 2{,}598{,}960$$

■

NOW WORK PROBLEM 5.

EXAMPLE 4 Forming Committees

From 5 faculty members, a committee of 2 is to be formed. In how many ways can this be done?

SOLUTION The formation of committees is an example of a combination. The 5 faculty members are all different. The members of the committee are distinct. Order is not important. (On committees it is membership, not the order of selection, that is important.) For the situation described, we can form

$$C(n, r) = C(5, 2) = \frac{5!}{3!2!} = 10 \qquad n = 5, r = 2$$

different committees. ■

Here are some other problems that are examples of combinations. The solutions a given in $C(n, r)$ notation.

Problem	Solution
Find the number of ways of selecting 4 people from a group of 6	$C(6, 4)$
Find the number of committees of 6 that can be formed from the U.S. Senate (100 members)	$C(100, 6)$
Find the number of ways of selecting 5 courses from a catalog containing 200	$C(200, 5)$

NOW WORK PROBLEM 13.

EXAMPLE 5 Playing Cards

From a deck of 52 cards a hand of 5 cards is dealt. How many different hands are possib

SOLUTION Such a hand is an unordered selection of 5 cards from a deck of 52. So the number different hands is

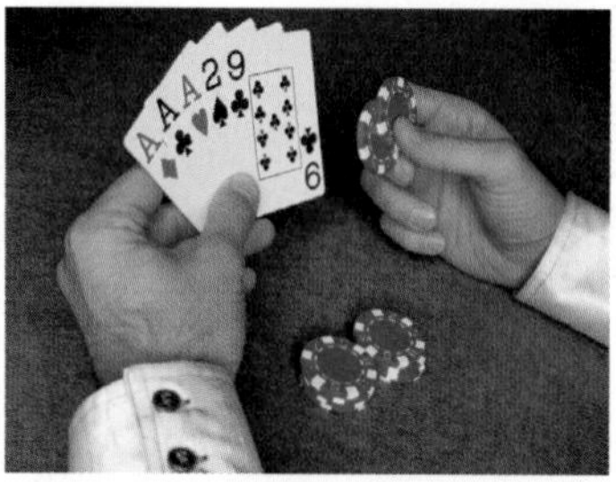

$$C(52, 5) = \frac{52!}{47!5!} = \frac{52 \cdot 51 \cdot 50 \cdot 49 \cdot 48 \cdot \cancel{47!}}{5 \cdot 4 \cdot 3 \cdot 2 \cdot 1 \cdot \cancel{47!}} = 2{,}598{,}960$$

EXAMPLE 6 Six-Bit Strings

A bit is a 0 or a 1. A six-bit string is a sequence of length six consisting of 0's and 1 How many six-bit strings contain

(a) Exactly one 1? **(b)** Exactly two 1's?

SOLUTION **(a)** To form a six-bit string having one 1, we only need to specify where the single 1 located (the other positions are 0s). The location for the 1 can be chosen in

$$C(6, 1) = 6 \text{ ways}$$

(b) Here, we must choose two of the six positions to contain 1's. There are

$$C(6, 2) = 15 \text{ strings}$$

with exactly two 1's and four 0's.

NOW WORK PROBLEM 23.

EXAMPLE 7 Forming Committees

In how many ways can a committee consisting of 2 faculty members and 3 students be formed if 6 faculty members and 10 students are eligible to serve on the committee?

SOLUTION The problem can be separated into two parts: the number of ways that the faculty members can be chosen, $C(6, 2)$, and the number of ways that the student members can be chosen, $C(10, 3)$. By the Multiplication Principle, the committee can be formed in

$$C(6, 2) \cdot C(10, 3) = \frac{6!}{4!2!} \cdot \frac{10!}{7!3!} = \frac{6 \cdot 5 \cdot \cancel{4!}}{\cancel{4!}2!} \cdot \frac{10 \cdot 9 \cdot 8 \cdot \cancel{7!}}{\cancel{7!}3!}$$

$$= \frac{30}{2} \cdot \frac{720}{6} = 1800$$

different ways. ■

NOW WORK PROBLEM 29.

EXAMPLE 8 Forming Committees

From 6 women and 4 men a committee of 3 is to be formed. The committee must include at least 2 women. In how many ways can this be done?

SOLUTION A committee of 3 that includes at least 2 women will contain either exactly 2 women and 1 man, or exactly 3 women and 0 men. Since no committee can contain exactly 2 women and simultaneously exactly 3 women, once we have counted the number of ways a committee with exactly 2 women and the number of ways a committee with exactly 3 women can be formed, their sum will give the number of ways exactly 2 women or exactly 3 women can be on the committee. [Refer to the Counting Formula (1) on page 367, noting that the sets are disjoint.]

Following the solution to Example 7, a committee of exactly 2 women and 1 man can be formed from 6 women, 4 men in $C(6, 2) \cdot C(4, 1)$ ways, while a committee of exactly 3 women, 0 men can be formed in $C(6, 3) \cdot C(4, 0)$ ways. A committee of 3 consisting of at least 2 women can be formed in

$$C(6, 2) \cdot C(4, 1) + C(6, 3) \cdot C(4, 0) = \frac{6!}{4!2!} \cdot \frac{4!}{3!1!} + \frac{6!}{3!3!} \cdot \frac{4!}{4!0!}$$

$$= 15 \cdot 4 + 20 \cdot 1 = 60 + 20 = 80 \text{ ways}$$ ■

2 Solve Counting Problems Involving Permutations [*n* objects, not all distinct]

Our previous discussion of permutations required that the objects we were arranging be distinct. We now examine what happens when some of the objects are the same.

EXAMPLE 9 Forming Different Words

How many different three-letter words (real or imaginary) can be formed from the letters in the word

(a) MAD? **(b)** DAD?

SOLUTION **(a)** The three distinct letters in MAD can be rearranged in

$$P(3, 3) = 3! = 6 \text{ ways}$$

They are MAD, MDA, AMD, ADM, DAM, DMA.

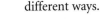

(b) Straightforward listing shows that there are only three ways of rearranging t[ ] letters in the word DAD:

DAD, DDA, and ADD

The word DAD in Example 9 contains 2 Ds, and it is this duplication that results [ ] fewer rearrangements for DAD than for MAD. In the next example we describe a way [ ] dealing with the problem of duplication.

EXAMPLE 10   **Forming Different Words**

How many different "words" can be formed using all the letters of the six-letter word[ ]

M A M M A L ?

SOLUTION   Any such word will have 6 letters formed from 3 Ms, 2 As, and 1 L. To form a word, thir[ ] of six blank positions that will have to be filled by the above letters.

$\overline{1}\ \overline{2}\ \overline{3}\ \overline{4}\ \overline{5}\ \overline{6}$

We separate the construction of a word into three tasks.

Task 1 Choose the positions for the 3 M's.

Task 2 Choose the positions for the 2 A's.

Task 3 Choose the position for the L.

Doing this sequence of tasks will result in a word and, conversely, every rearrangeme[ ] of MAMMAL will be obtained from this sequence of tasks.

Task 1 can be done in $C(6, 3)$ ways. There are now three positions left for the 2 A[ ] so Task 2 can be done in $C(3, 2)$ ways. Five blanks have been filled, so that the L must [ ] in the remaining blank. That is, Task 3 can be done in $C(1, 1)$ way. The Multiplicatio[ ] Principle says that the number of rearrangements is

$$C(6, 3) \cdot C(3, 2) \cdot C(1, 1) = \frac{6!}{3!3!} \cdot \frac{3!}{1!2!} \cdot \frac{1!}{0!1!}$$

$$= \frac{6!}{3!2!1!}$$

The form of the answer in Example 10 is suggestive of a general result. Had th[ ] letters in MAMMAL been distinct, there would have been $P(6, 6) = 6!$ rearrangemen[ ] possible. This is the numerator of the answer. The presence of 3 M's, 2 A's, and 1 [ ] reduces the number of different words as shown in the denominator above. Th[ ] reasoning can be used to derive the following general result.

Theorem   **Permutation Involving n Objects That Are Not Distinct**

The number of permutations of n objects, of which n_1 are of one kind, n_2 are of a second kind, ..., and n_k are of a kth kind, is given by

$$\frac{n!}{n_1! \cdot n_2! \cdots \cdots n_k!} \tag{2}$$

where $n_1 + n_2 + \cdots + n_k = n$.

EXAMPLE 11 Arranging Flags

How many different vertical arrangements are possible for 10 flags if 2 are white, 3 are red, and 5 are blue?

SOLUTION Here we want the different arrangements of 10 objects, which are not all distinct. Using Formula (2), we have

$$\frac{10!}{2!3!5!} = \frac{10 \cdot 9 \cdot 8 \cdot 7 \cdot \cancel{6} \cdot \cancel{5!}}{2 \cdot \cancel{3} \cdot \cancel{2} \cdot \cancel{5!}} = 2520$$

different arrangements. ■

NOW WORK PROBLEM 27.

3 Find Probabilities Using Counting Techniques

EXAMPLE 12 Finding Probabilities Using Counting Techniques

From a box containing four white, three yellow, and one green ball, two balls are selected one at a time without replacing the first before the second is selected. Find the probability that one white and one yellow ball are selected.

SOLUTION The experiment consists of selecting 2 balls from 8 balls: 4 white, 3 yellow, 1 green. The number of ways that 2 balls can be selected from 8 balls without replacement is $C(8, 2) = 28$. The number of elements in the sample S is $n(S) = 28$.

Define the events E and F as

E: A white ball is selected

F: A yellow ball is selected

We seek the probability of E and F, that is, $P(E \cap F)$.

The number of ways a white ball can be selected is $C(4, 1) = 4$ and the number of ways a yellow ball can be selected is $C(3, 1) = 3$. By the Multiplication Principle, the number of ways a white and yellow ball can be selected is

$$C(4, 1) \cdot C(3, 1) = 4 \cdot 3 = 12$$

That is, $n(E \cap F) = 12$. Since the outcomes are equally likely, the probability of selecting a white ball and a yellow ball is

$$P(E \cap F) = \frac{n(E \cap F)}{n(S)} = \frac{C(4, 1) \cdot C(3, 1)}{C(8, 2)} = \frac{12}{28} = \frac{3}{7}$$ ■

Compare the solution given here to Example 12 with the solution given to Example 6 on page 427. Which solution do you prefer?

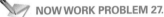

EXAMPLE 13 Finding Probabilities Using Counting Techniques

A box contains 12 lightbulbs, of which 5 are defective. All bulbs look alike and have equal probability of being chosen. Three lightbulbs are selected and placed in a box.

(a) What is the probability that all 3 are defective?

(b) What is the probability that exactly 2 are defective?

(c) What is the probability that at least 2 are defective?

SOLUTION The number of elements in the sample space S is equal to the number of combinations of 12 lightbulbs taken 3 at a time, namely,

$$C(12, 3) = \frac{12!}{3!\,9!} = 220$$

So, $n(S) = 220$.

(a) Define E as the event, "3 bulbs are defective." Then E can occur in $C(5, 3)$ ways, that is, the number of ways in which 3 defective bulbs can be chosen from 5 defective ones. So, $n(E) = C(5, 3)$. The probability $P(E)$ is

$$P(E) = \frac{n(E)}{n(S)} = \frac{C(5, 3)}{C(12, 3)} = \frac{\frac{5!}{3!\,2!}}{220} = \frac{10}{220} = 0.045$$

(b) Define F as the event, "2 bulbs are defective." To obtain 2 defective bulbs when 3 are chosen requires that we select 2 defective bulbs from the 5 available defective ones and 1 good bulb from the 7 good ones. By the Multiplication Principle, this can be done in the following number of ways:

$$n(F) = C(5, 2) \cdot C(7, 1) = \frac{5!}{2!\,3!} \cdot \frac{7!}{1!\,6!} = 10 \cdot 7 = 70$$

$C(5, 2)$: Number of ways to select 2 defectives from 5 defectives

$C(7, 1)$: Number of ways to select 1 good bulb from 7 good ones

The probability of selecting exactly 2 defective bulbs is therefore

$$P(F) = P(\text{exactly 2 defectives}) = \frac{n(F)}{n(S)} = \frac{C(5, 2) \cdot C(7, 1)}{C(12, 3)} = \frac{70}{220} = 0.318$$

(c) Define G as the event, "At least 2 are defective." The event G is equivalent to asking for the probability of selecting either exactly 2 or exactly 3 defective bulbs. Since these events are mutually exclusive, the sum of their probabilities will give the probability of G. Using the results found in parts (a) and (b), we find

$$P(G) = P(\text{Exactly 2 defectives}) + P(\text{Exactly 3 defectives})$$
$$= P(F) + P(E) = 0.318 + 0.045 = 0.363$$

NOW WORK PROBLEM 49.

EXAMPLE 14 Dogs of the Dow

"Dogs of the Dow" is a stock-picking strategy devoted to selecting the highest dividend-yielding stocks of the 30 blue chip stocks that make up the Dow Jones Industrial Average. The table below shows the top 10 stocks listed on the "Dogs of the Dow" Web site on December 31, 2009.

Company The Dow stocks ranked by yield on 12/31/2009	Yield on 12/31/2009
AT&T	5.85
Verizon	5.73
DuPont	4.87
Kraft	4.27
Merck	4.16
Chevron	3.53
McDonald's	3.52
Pfizer	3.52
Home Depot	3.11
Boeing	3.10

Source: www.dogsofthedow.com

(a) If two of these stocks are randomly selected, what is the probability both have yields above 4.25%?

(b) If three of these stocks are randomly selected, what is the probability at least one of them will have a yield above 4.25%?

SOLUTION **(a)** We are selecting 2 of the 10 stocks, so the number of elements in the sample space S is equal to the number of combinations of 10 stocks taken 2 at a time, namely,

$$C(10, 2) = \frac{10!}{2!\,8!} = 45$$

So, $n(S) = 45$.

Define E as the event "both stocks have yields above 4.25%." Of the stocks listed, 4 have yields above 4.25%, so E can occur in $C(4, 2) = \frac{4!}{2!\,2!} = 6$ ways. So, $n(E) = 6$.

The probability $P(E)$ is

$$P(E) = \frac{n(E)}{n(s)} = \frac{C(4, 2)}{C(10, 2)} = \frac{6}{45} = 0.133$$

(b) This time, 3 of the 10 stocks are being selected, so the number of elements in the sample space S is equal to the number of combinations of 10 stocks taken 3 at a time, namely,

$$C(10, 3) = \frac{10!}{3!\,7!} = 120$$

So, $n(S) = 120$.

Define F as the event "at least one of the three stocks has a yield above 4.25%." Event F is equivalent to "exactly one with yield above 4.25%" or "exactly two with yields above 4.25%" or "exactly three with yields above 4.25%." Since these a mutually exclusive, we have

$$P(F) = P(\text{exactly 1 above 4.25\%}) + P(\text{exactly 2 above 4.25\%}) + P(\text{exactly 3 above 4.25\%})$$

Selecting exactly one stock with a yield above 4.25% means we simultaneous select exactly two stocks with yields below 4.25%. Since there are 4 stocks in the li with yields above 4.25% and 6 stocks with yields below 4.25%, we can do th $C(4, 1) \cdot C(6, 2) = 60$ ways. Likewise, we can select exactly two stocks with yiel above 4.25% in $C(4, 2) \cdot C(6, 1) = 36$ ways, and we can select exactly three stoc with yields above 4.25% in $C(4, 3) \cdot C(6, 0) = 4$ ways. So, the desired probability

$$P(F) = \frac{C(4, 1) \cdot C(6, 2)}{C(10, 3)} + \frac{C(4, 2) \cdot C(6, 1)}{C(10, 3)} + \frac{C(4, 3) \cdot C(6, 0)}{C(10, 3)}$$

$$= \frac{60}{120} + \frac{36}{120} + \frac{4}{120} = \frac{100}{120} = 0.833$$

NOTE We could have solved Example 14(b) alternatively by using the complement of F. The $\overline{F}$ is the event "none of the three stocks have yield above 4.25%." The event $\overline{F}$ can occur i $C(4, 0) \cdot C(6, 3) = 20$ ways, and

$$P(\overline{F}) = \frac{C(4, 0) \cdot C(6, 3)}{C(10, 3)} = \frac{20}{120} = 0.167$$

So,

$$P(F) = 1 - P(\overline{F}) = 1 - 0.167 = 0.833$$

NOW WORK PROBLEM 41.

EXAMPLE 15 Quality Control

A laboratory contains 10 electron microscopes, of which 2 are defective. If al microscopes are equally likely to be chosen and if 4 are chosen, what is the expecte number of defective microscopes?

SOLUTION The sample of 4 microscopes can contain 0, 1, or 2 defective microscopes. Th probability p_0 that none in the sample is defective is

$$p_0 = \frac{C(2, 0) \cdot C(8, 4)}{C(10, 4)} = \frac{1}{3}$$

Similarly, the probabilities p_1 and p_2 for 1 and 2 defective microscopes are

$$p_1 = \frac{C(2, 1) \cdot C(8, 3)}{C(10, 4)} = \frac{8}{15} \quad \text{and} \quad p_2 = \frac{C(2, 2) \cdot C(8, 2)}{C(10, 4)} = \frac{2}{15}$$

Since we are interested in determining the expected number of defectiv microscopes, we assign a payoff of 0 to the outcome "0 defectives are selected," a payof of 1 to the outcome "1 defective is chosen," and a payoff of 2 to the outcome "2 defective are chosen." The expected value E is then

$$E = 0 \cdot p_0 + 1 \cdot p_1 + 2 \cdot p_2 = \frac{8}{15} + \frac{4}{15} = \frac{4}{5}$$

Of course, we cannot have $\frac{4}{5}$ of a defective microscope. However, we can interpret this to mean that in the long run, such a sample will average just under 1 defective microscope.

Observe that $\dfrac{4}{5}$ is a reasonable answer for the expected number of defective microscopes since $\dfrac{1}{5}$ of the microscopes in the laboratory are defective and a random sample consisting of 4 of these microscopes is selected.

The Pascal Triangle

Sometimes the notation $\dbinom{n}{r}$, read as "from n choose r," is used in place of the combination notation $C(n, r)$.

Suppose that we arrange the values of $\dbinom{n}{r}$ in a triangular display, as shown next and in Figure 24.

FIGURE 24 Pascal triangle

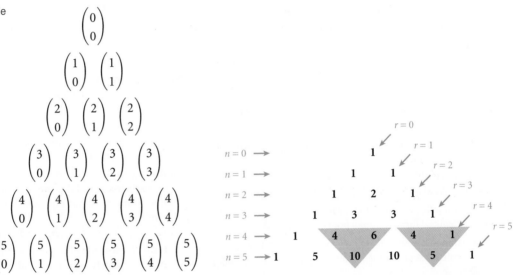

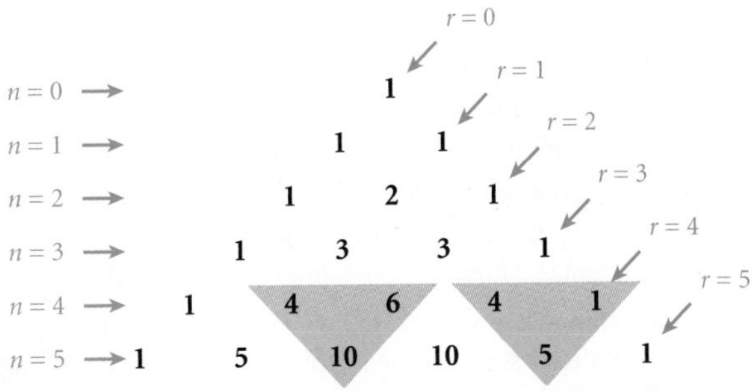

This display is called the **Pascal triangle**, named after Blaise Pascal (1623–1662), a French mathematician.

The Pascal triangle has 1's down the sides. To get any other entry, add the two nearest entries in the row above it. The shaded triangles in Figure 24 illustrate this feature of the Pascal triangle. Based on this feature, the row corresponding to $n = 6$ is found as follows:

$$n = 5 \rightarrow \quad 1 \quad 5 \quad 10 \quad 10 \quad 5 \quad 1$$
$$n = 6 \rightarrow \quad 1 \quad 6 \quad 15 \quad 20 \quad 15 \quad 6 \quad 1$$

Although the Pascal triangle provides an interesting and organized display of the values of $\dbinom{n}{r}$, in practice it is not all that helpful. For example, if you wanted to know the value of $\dbinom{12}{5}$, you would need to produce 13 rows of the triangle before seeing the answer. It is much faster to use the fact that

$$\binom{n}{r} = C(n, r) = \frac{n!}{(n - r)!\,r!}$$

The numbers $C(n, r) = \binom{n}{r}$ are also called **binomial coefficients.** To learn why, read 'Th Binomial Theorem' in Section A.5 of Appendix A.

EXERCISE 8.5 Answers Begin on Page AN–41.

Concepts and Vocabulary

1. A _______ is an arrangement, without regard to order, of r objects chosen from n distinct objects without repetition, where $r \le n$.

2. The number of combinations of 5 objects taken 2 at a time $C(5, 2) =$ ____.

3. ***True or False*** If $r \le n$, then $P(n, r) = n!C(n, r)$.

4. ***True or False*** Some permutations involve n objects that are n distinct.

Skill Building

In Problems 5–12, find the value of each expression.

5. $C(6, 4)$
6. $C(5, 4)$
7. $C(7, 2)$
8. $C(8, 7)$
9. $C(5, 1)$
10. $C(8, 1)$
11. $C(8, 6)$
12. $C(8, 4)$

13. List all the combinations of 5 objects a, b, c, d, and e taken 3 at a time. What is $C(5, 3)$?

14. List all the combinations of 5 objects a, b, c, d, and e taken 2 at a time. What is $C(5, 2)$?

15. List all the combinations of 4 objects 1, 2, 3, and 4 taken 3 at a time. What is $C(4, 3)$?

16. List all the combinations of 6 objects 1, 2, 3, 4, 5, and 6 taken 3 at a time. What is $C(6, 3)$?

17. Establishing Committees In how many ways can a committee of 4 students be formed from a pool of 7 students?

18. Establishing Committees In how many ways can a committee of 3 professors be formed from a department having 8 professors?

19. Tenure Selection A math department is allowed to tenure 4 of 17 eligible teachers. In how many ways can the selection for tenure be made?

20. Bridge Hands How many different hands are possible in a bridge game? (A bridge hand consists of 13 cards dealt from a deck of 52 cards.)

21. Forming a Committee There are 20 students in the Math Club. In how many ways can a subcommittee of 3 members be formed?

22. Relay Teams How many different relay teams of 4 persons can be chosen from a group of 10 runners?

23. **Eight-Bit Strings** How many eight-bit strings contain exactly three 1's?

24. Eight-Bit Strings How many eight-bit strings contain exactly two 1's?

25. Forming Words How many different 9-letter words (real or imaginary) can be formed from the letters in the word ECONOMICS?

26. Forming Words How many different 11-letter words (real o imaginary) can be formed from the letters in the wor MATHEMATICS?

27. **Arranging Lights** How many different ways can 3 re 4 yellow, and 5 blue bulbs be arranged in a string of Christm tree lights with 12 sockets?

28. Arranging Trees In how many ways can 3 apple tree 4 peach trees, and 2 plum trees be arranged along a fenc line if one does not distinguish between trees of the sam kind?

29. **Forming a Committee** A student dance committee is to b formed consisting of 2 boys and 3 girls. If the membership i to be chosen from 4 boys and 8 girls, how many differen committees are possible?

30. Forming a Committee The student relations committee of college consists of 2 administrators, 3 faculty members, and students. Four administrators, 8 faculty members, an 20 students are eligible to serve. How many different committee are possible?

31. Forming Teams In how many ways can 12 children be place on 3 distinct teams of 3, 5, and 4 members?

32. Forming Committees A group of 9 people is going to b formed into committees of 4, 3, and 2 people. How man committees can be formed if

(a) A person can serve on any number of committees?

(b) No person can serve on more than one committee?

33. Powerball Powerball is a lottery played in 29 states Washington, D.C., and the U.S. Virgin Islands. A ticket consist of five distinct numbers selected from 1 to 55 and a sixt "Powerball" number selected from 1 to 42. The order of th first five numbers is unimportant. The Powerball can be th same as one of the first five numbers because it is drawn fron a separate number pool from the first five numbers. How many distinct Powerball tickets are possible?

Source: www.powerball.com

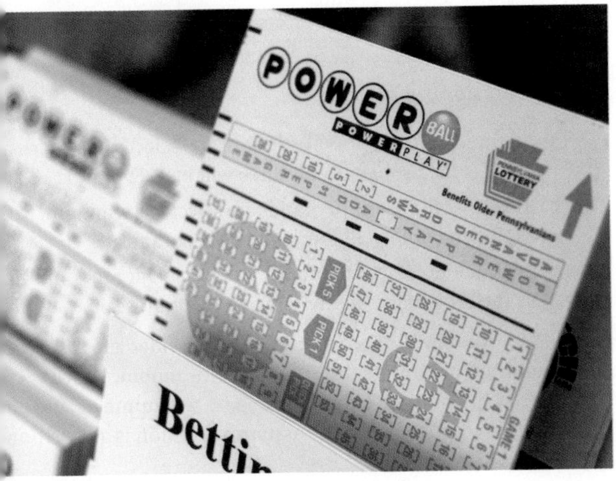

34. **Mega Millions** Mega Millions is a lottery played in 12 states. A ticket consists of five distinct numbers between 1 and 56 and one "Mega Ball" number between 1 and 46. The order of the first five numbers is unimportant. The Mega Ball number can be the same as one of the first five numbers because it is drawn from a separate number pool from the first five numbers. How many distinct Mega Millions tickets are possible?

Source: www.megamillions.com

35. **Contract Negotiations** A college has 90 full-time faculty members. Of these, 25 are in the Math and Science Division, 23 are in the Allied Health Division, 15 are in the Liberal Arts Division, 8 are in the Business Division, and 19 are in the Computer and Technology Division. For contract negotiations, a 7-member team will be formed by selecting one member from each division, plus 2 "at large" members who may be selected from any of the remaining faculty. How many negotiating teams are possible?

36. **Company Drawing** A company employs 80 people. At the annual company picnic, the company randomly draws the names of 5 employees for prizes. The prize list consists of the following: two fully paid trips for two to Jamaica, three \$1500 cash prizes. The remaining 75 employees get \$100 each. Assuming no employee receives more than one prize, how many different ways can the prizes be distributed among the employees?

37. **Auditing** To audit the 58 accounts payable of a small firm, the auditor randomly selects a sample of 8 account balances for review. How many samples are possible?

38. **Auditing** Refer to Problem 37. Suppose that 5 of the 58 accounts contain errors.

(a) How many samples (of the 8 account balances) are possible that contain exactly 1 error?

(b) Exactly 2 errors?

(c) Exactly 3 errors?

(d) Exactly 4 errors?

(e) Exactly 5 errors?

(f) How many samples are possible that contain at least one error?

(g) How many samples are possible that contain no errors?

39. **Forming Committees** The U.S. Senate has 100 members. Suppose it is desired to place each senator on exactly 1 of 7 possible committees. The first committee has 22 members, the second has 13, the third has 10, the fourth has 5, the fifth has 16, and the sixth and seventh have 17 apiece. In how many ways can these committees be formed?

40. **Hockey** There are 15 teams in the Eastern Conference of the National Hockey League for the 2009–2010 season, divided into 3 divisions of 5 teams each. Eight of these teams will participate in the playoffs. The division winner from each division goes to the playoffs; in addition, the next 5 ranked teams in the conference, based on regular season records, will participate in the playoffs. How many different collections of eight teams from the Eastern Conference could go to the playoffs?

Source: National Hockey League.

41. **Dogs of the Dow** Refer to Example 14 on page 473. The table below shows the top 10 dividend yielding stocks along with their prices that were listed on the "Dog of the Dow" Web site on December 31, 2009.

Company The Dow stocks ranked by yield on 12/31/2009	Price on 12/31/2009	%Yield on 12/31/2009
AT&T	28.03	5.85
Verizon	33.13	5.73
DuPont	33.67	4.87
Kraft	27.18	4.27
Merck	36.54	4.16
Chevron	76.99	3.53
McDonald's	62.44	3.52
Pfizer	18.19	3.52
Home Depot	28.93	3.11
Boeing	54.13	3.1

Source: www.dogsofthedow.com

(a) If two of these stocks are randomly selected, what is the probability both have prices above \$50?

(b) If two of these stocks are randomly selected, what is the probability neither will have prices above \$50?

(c) If two of these stocks are randomly selected, what is the probability at least one will have a price above \$50?

42. Dogs of the Dow Refer to Problem 41.

(a) If three of these stocks are randomly selected, what is the probability all three will have prices below $50?

(b) If three of these stocks are randomly selected, what is the probability exactly two will have prices below $50?

(c) If three of these stocks are randomly selected, what is the probability at least two will have prices below $50?

43. Puppies of the Dow Refer to Problem 41. The "Puppies of the Dow" are the five lowest-priced stocks in the Dogs of the Dow list.

(a) List the five Puppies of the Dow.

(b) If two of these "puppies" are randomly selected, what is the probability both will have yields above 4%?

(c) If two of these "puppies" are randomly selected, what is the probability exactly one will have a yield above 4%?

(d) If two of these "puppies" are randomly selected, what is the probability neither will have a yield above 4%?

(e) If two of these "puppies" are randomly selected, what is the probability at least one will have a yield above 4%?

44. Puppies of the Dow Refer to Problems 41 and 43.

(a) If five stocks from the Dogs of the Dow list are randomly selected, what is the probability all five will be Puppies of the Dow?

(b) If five stocks from the Dogs of the Dow list are randomly selected, what is the probability exactly three will be Puppies of the Dow?

(c) If five stocks from the Dogs of the Dow list are randomly selected, what is the probability at least two will be Puppies of the Dow?

45. Auditing For an internal audit of the 35 accounts payable of a small firm, the auditor randomly selects a sample of 5 account balances for review. Suppose 3 of the 35 accounts contain errors.

(a) What is the probability the auditor will not select any accounts with errors?

(b) What is the probability the auditor will select exactly one account with errors?

(c) What is the probability the auditor will select at least two accounts with errors?

46. Top Global Brands Each year, *BusinessWeek* publishes an annual ranking of the best global brands by brand value. The table below identifies the top 10 global brands for 2009.

2009 Rank	Name	Country
1	Coca-Cola	U.S.
2	IBM	U.S.
3	Microsoft	U.S.
4	GE	U.S.
5	Nokia	Finland
6	McDonald's	U.S.
7	Google	U.S.
8	Toyota	Japan
9	Intel	U.S.
10	Disney	U.S.

Source: *BusinessWeek*

(a) If three of these top 10 brands are selected at random, what is the probability all three will be U.S. brands?

(b) If four of these top 10 brands are selected at random, what is the probability all four will be U.S. brands?

(c) If five of these top 10 brands are selected at random, what is the probability all five will be U.S. brands?

47. Cell Phone SIM Codes A cell phone provider assigns a code to each of its SIM (subscriber identity module) cards. The codes start with one letter followed by five numbers and end with two additional letters. (Assume repetition is allowed, and order is important.)

(a) How many different cell phone codes are there?

(b) What is the probability a code selected at random ends in AA?

(c) What is the probability a code selected at random begins with A and ends with A?

(d) What is the probability a code selected at random has no repeated letter and no repeated number?

(e) What is the probability a code selected at random has no repeated letter and all five numbers are the same?

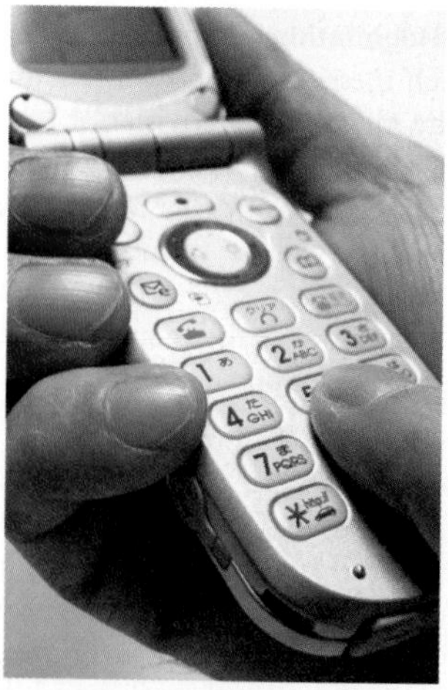

48. Pin Numbers A student loan administrator distributes pin numbers to its debtors. Each pin consists of two letters followed by three numbers. (Assume repetition is allowed, and order is important.)

(a) How many different pin numbers are there?

(b) What is the probability a pin number selected at random ends in 000?

(c) What is the probability a pin number selected at random begins with AA?

(d) What is the probability a pin number selected at random begins with A and ends with 00?

(e) What is the probability a pin number selected at random has a repeated letter and different numbers?

9. **Defective Refrigerator** Through a mix-up on the production line, 6 defective refrigerators were shipped out with 44 good ones. If 5 are selected at random, what is the probability that all 5 are defective? What is the probability that at least 2 of them are defective?

0. **Defective Transformers** In a shipment of 50 transformers, 10 are known to be defective. If 30 transformers are picked at random, what is the probability that all 30 are nondefective? Assume that all transformers look alike and have an equal probability of being chosen.

1. **Favorable Extentions** The employees of a company have four-digit extensions. Extensions ending in 00 are considered favorable because they are easy to remember. Suppose extensions are given out randomly and digits can be repeated.

(a) What is the probability of having a favorable extension?

(b) What is the probability of having a favorable extension if the first digit cannot be 0?

2. **Winning a Pool** Each week eight persons contribute $10.00 to a pool. Every Friday one name is drawn out of a hat containing the eight names and the winner receives the $80.00.

(a) What is the probability that the same person wins three weeks in a row?

(b) What is the probability that a particular person does not win in 5 weeks?

(c) What is the probability that 5 different people win in each of the next 5 weeks?

3. **Forming Committees** There are 59 Democrats and 41 Republicans in the U.S. Senate. A committee of seven senators is to be formed by selecting members of the Senate randomly.

(a) What is the probability the committee is composed of all Democrats?

(b) What is the probability the committee is composed of all Republicans?

(c) What is the probability the committee is composed of 4 Democrats and 3 Republicans?

54. **Quality Control** A shipment of 120 computer cases that contains 5 defective cases was sent to an assembly plant. The quality control manager at the assembly plant randomly selects 5 cases and inspects them. What is the probability exactly one case is defective?

55. **Quality Control** The purchasing director of a bank has just received a shipment of 100 printers. She has been told that the shipment includes 5 defective printers. She randomly selects two printers and tests them. If both printers work the purchasing director accepts the shipment. What is the probability the shipment is rejected?

56. **United States Senate as of January 2010** Use the information in the table to answer the questions.

	Democrats	Republicans	Independents
Terms expire in January 2011	16	18	0
Terms expire in January 2013	21	10	2
Terms expire in January 2015	20	13	0

Source: www.senate.gov

(a) Suppose that a member of the U.S. Senate was randomly selected. Given that the term of that senator will expire in January 2013, what is the probability that this senator is a Democrat?

(b) Suppose that three members of the U.S. Senate were randomly selected. Given that the term of each of these senators will expire in January 2013 or in January 2015, what is the probability that all three of these senators were Republicans?

(c) Suppose that two members of the U.S. Senate were randomly selected. Given that one of these senators is a Democrat and the other is a Republican, what is the probability that the term of each of these senators will expire in January 2011?

(d) Suppose that a committee of five U.S. senators was randomly selected. Given that the term of each of these senators will expire before 2014, what is the probability that at least three of the senators on this committee were Democrats?

57. **Stud Poker** Five cards are dealt at random from a regular deck of 52 playing cards. Find the probability that

(a) All are hearts.

(b) Exactly 4 are spades.

(c) Exactly 2 are clubs.

58. **Bridge** In a game of bridge find the probability that a hand of 13 cards consists of 5 spades, 4 hearts, 3 diamonds, and 1 club.

59. **Poker Hands** Find the probability of obtaining each of the following poker hands:

(a) Royal flush (10, J, Q, K, A all of the same suit)

(b) Straight flush (5 cards in sequence in a single suit, but not a royal flush)

(c) Four of a kind (4 cards of the same face value)

(d) Full house (one pair and one triple of the same face values)

(e) Flush (5 nonconsecutive cards each of the same suit)

(f) Straight (5 consecutive cards, not all of the same suit)

60. **Elevator Problem** An elevator starts with 5 passengers and stops at 8 floors. Find the probability that no 2 passengers leave at the same floor. Assume that all arrangements of discharging the passengers have the same probability.

8.6 The Binomial Probability Model

OBJECTIVES

1. Find binomial probabilities (p.482)
2. Solve applied problems involving the binomial probability model (p. 484)
3. Find the expected value in a Bernoulli trial (p. 487)
4. Model: error-correcting codes for the digital transmission of data (p. 489)

Bernoulli Trials

In this section we study experiments that use a probability model called the *binomi* *probability model.* The model was first studied by J. Bernoulli about 1700, and for th reason the model is sometimes referred to as a *Bernoulli trial.*

The **binomial probability model** is a sequence of trials, each of which consists c the repetition of a single experiment. We assume the outcome of one experiment doe not affect the outcome of any other one; that is, we assume the trials to be independen Furthermore, we assume that there are only two possible outcomes for each trial an label them A, for *success*, and F, for *failure.*

We denote the probability of success by $p = P(A)$; $p = P(A)$ remains the sam from trial to trial. In addition, since there are only two outcomes in each trial, th probability of failure, denoted by q, must be $1 - p$, so

$$q = 1 - p = P(F)$$

Notice that $p + q = 1$.

Any random experiment for which the binomial probability model is appropriat is called a *Bernoulli trial.*

Definition

Bernoulli Trial

Random experiments are called **Bernoulli trials** if

(a) The same experiment is repeated two or more times.

(b) There are only two possible outcomes, success and failure, on each trial.

(c) The repeated trials are independent.

(d) The probability of each outcome remains the same for each trial.

Many real-world situations have the characteristics of the binomial probability model. Here are some examples.

- In repeatedly running a subject through a T-maze, we may label a turn to the left by A and a turn to the right by F. The assumption of independence on each trial is equivalent to presuming the subject has no memory.
- In opinion polls one person's response is independent of any other person's response, and we may designate the answer "Yes" by an A and any other answer ("No" or "Don't know") by an F.
- In testing TVs, we have a sequence of independent trials (each test of a particular TV is a trial), and we label a nondefective TV with an A and a defective one with an F.

- In determining whether 9 out of 12 persons will recover from a tropical disease, we assume that each of the 12 persons has the same chance of recovery from the disease and that their recoveries are independent (they are not treated by the same doctor or in the same hospital). We may designate "recovery" by A and "nonrecovery" by F.

EXAMPLE 1   **Tossing a Coin Three Times**

Discuss the experiment of tossing a coin three times.

SOLUTION   We define a success as heads (H) and a failure as tails (T). The coin may be fair or loaded, so we let p be the probability of heads and q be the probability of tails.

The sample space for this experiment is

$$\{HHH,\quad HHT,\quad HTH,\quad HTT,\quad THH,\quad THT,\quad TTH,\quad TTT\}$$

As before, HHT means that the first two tosses are heads and the third is tails. The tree diagram in Figure 25 lists all the possible outcomes and their respective probabilities.

FIGURE 25

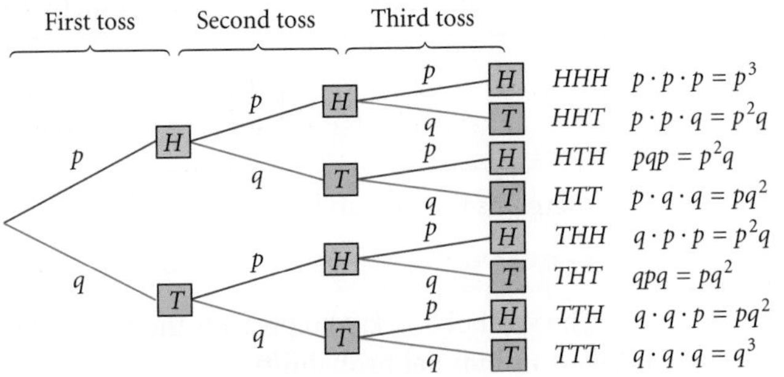

In a binomial probability problem we are usually interested in the probability of an exact number of successes (or in the probability of at least a certain number of successes).

For example, suppose we are interested in the probability of obtaining exactly two heads in the experiment of tossing a coin three times. The event "exactly two heads" consists of the outcomes

$$HHT, HTH, THH$$

The outcome HHT has probability $ppq = p^2q$ since the two heads each have probability p and the tail has probability q. In the same way, the other two outcomes, HTH and THH, in which there are two heads and one tail, also have probabilities p^2q. Therefore, the probability that exactly two heads appear is equal to the sum of the probabilities of the three outcomes and so is given by $3p^2q$.

The outcome HHH, in which all three tosses are heads, has a probability $ppp = p^3$. In a similar way we can compute the remaining probabilities:

$$P(\text{Exactly 1 head}) = 3pq^2 \qquad P(\text{No heads}) = q^3 \qquad\blacksquare$$

1 Find Binomial Probabilities

When considering repeated trials in excess of three, it would be extremely tedious t solve the problem using a tree diagram. This is why we seek a general formula.

Suppose the probability of a success in a Bernoulli trial is p and suppose we wish t find the probability of exactly k successes in n repeated trials. One possible outcome i

$$\underbrace{AAA\cdots A}_{k \text{ successes}} \cdot \underbrace{FF\cdots F}_{n-k \text{ failures}} \qquad (1$$

where k successes come first, followed by $n - k$ failures. The probability of this outcome

$$\underbrace{ppp\cdots p}_{k \text{ factors}} \cdot \underbrace{qq\cdots q}_{n-k \text{ factors}} = p^k q^{n-k}$$

The k successes could also be obtained by rearranging the letters A and F in Displa (1) above. Then the number of such sequences must equal the number of ways o choosing k successes in n trials—namely, $C(n, k) = \binom{n}{k} = \dfrac{n!}{k!(n-k)!}$.* If we multipl this number by the probability of obtaining any one such sequence, we arrive at th following general result:

Theorem

Formula for $b(n, k; p)$

In a Bernoulli trial the probability of exactly k successes in n trials is given by

$$b(n, k; p) = \binom{n}{k} p^k q^{n-k} = \frac{n!}{k!\,(n-k)!} p^k q^{n-k} \qquad (2)$$

where p is the probability of success and $q = 1 - p$ is the probability of failure.

The symbol $b(n, k; p)$ represents the probability of exactly k successes in n trials and is called a **binomial probability**.

NOW WORK PROBLEM 7.

EXAMPLE 2 Example of a Bernoulli Trial; Finding a Binomial Probability

A common example of a Bernoulli trial is the experiment of tossing a fair coin.

1. There are exactly two possible mutually exclusive outcomes on each trial or toss (heads or tails).
2. The probability of a particular outcome (say, heads) remains constant from trial to trial (toss to toss).
3. The outcome on any trial (toss) is independent of the outcome on any other trial (toss).

Find the probability of obtaining exactly one tail in six tosses of a fair coin.

* *Recall that the notation* $\binom{n}{k}$*, read as "from n choose k," can be used in place of the combination notation C(n, k).*

SOLUTION Let T denote the outcome "Tail shows" (success) and let H denote the outcome "Head shows" (failure). Using Formula (2), in which $k = 1$ (one success), $n = 6$ (the number of trials), and $p = \frac{1}{2} = P(T)$ (the probability of success using a fair coin), we obtain

$$P(\text{Exactly 1 success}) = b\left(6, 1; \frac{1}{2}\right) = \binom{6}{1}\left(\frac{1}{2}\right)^1\left(\frac{1}{2}\right)^{6-1} = \frac{6}{64} = 0.0938$$ ■

NOW WORK PROBLEM 21.

COMMENT: A graphing utility can be used to compute binomial probabilities. Figure 26 shows $b(6, 1; 0.5)$ using a TI-84 Plus calculator. Check your manual. Notice that for this calculator $b(6, 1; 0.5)$ is entered as $b(6, 0.5, 1)$.

FIGURE 26

■

USING TECHNOLOGY

EXAMPLE 3 Using Excel

Use Excel to solve Example 2. Make a table to find the probabilities of getting exactly 0, 1, 2, 3, 4, 5, or 6 tails.

SOLUTION

STEP 1 Use the Excel function BINOMDIST (). The function is found under the category *Statistical.*

STEP 2 The syntax for the function is

BINOMDIST (*# of successes, # of trials, probability of success, cumulative*)

Cumulative is a logical variable. Set *cumulative* equal to FALSE to find the probability.

STEP 3 Set up the Excel spreadsheet.

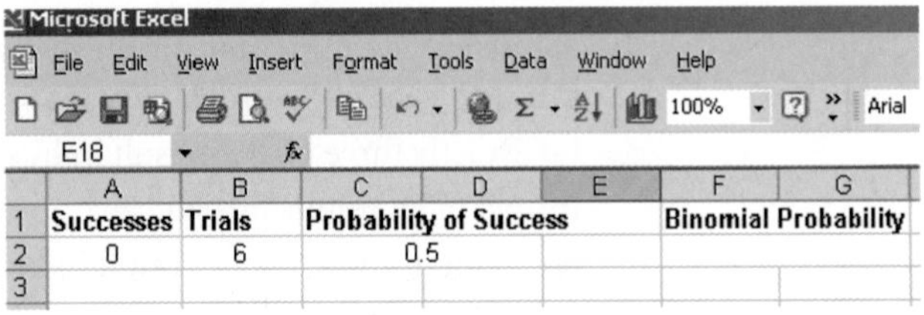

STEP 4 Enter the function in F2. Keep the number of trials and the probability of succes constant by using $.

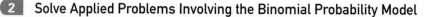

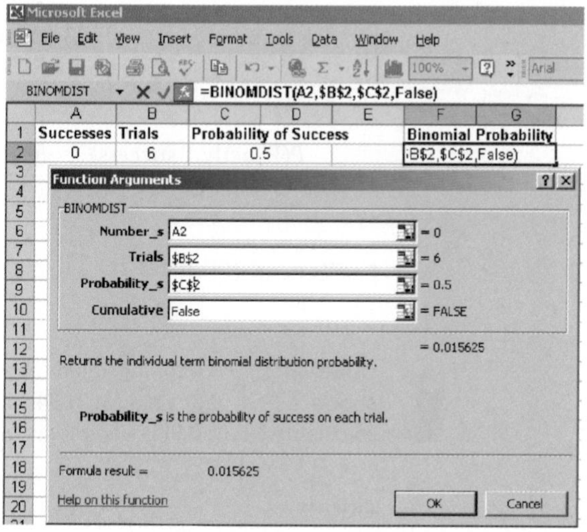

STEP 5 The probability of getting zero tails when tossing a coin 6 times is given below.

Successes	Trials	Probability of Success	Binomial Probability
0	6	0.5	0.015625

STEP 6 To find the probability of getting exactly 1, 2, 3, 4, 5, or 6 tails, highlight row 2 and clic and drag to row 8.

Successes	Trials	Probability of Success	Binomial Probability
0	6	0.5	0.015625
1	6	0.5	0.09375
2	6	0.5	0.234375
3	6	0.5	0.3125
4	6	0.5	0.234375
5	6	0.5	0.09375
6	6	0.5	0.015625

NOW WORK PROBLEM 21 USING EXCEL.

2 Solve Applied Problems Involving the Binomial Probability Model

EXAMPLE 4 Baseball

A pitcher gives up a hit on the average of once every five pitches. If nine pitches are thrown, what is the probability that

(a) Exactly three pitches result in hits?

(b) No pitch results in a hit?

(c) Eight or more pitches result in hits?

(d) No more than seven pitches result in hits?

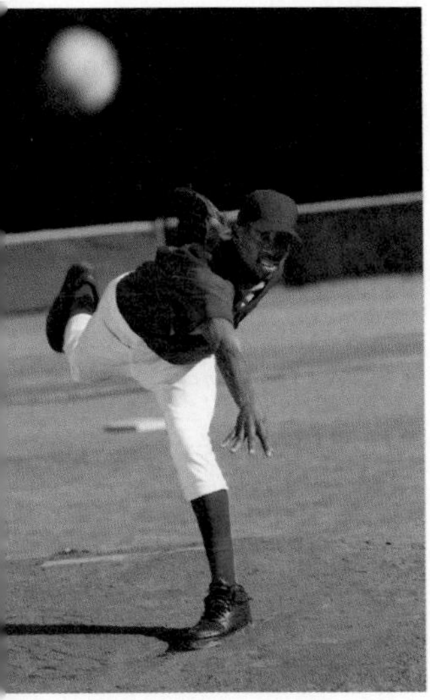

SOLUTION In this example $p = P(\text{Success}) = P(\text{Allowing a hit}) = \dfrac{1}{5} = 0.2$. The number of trials is the number of pitches, so $n = 9$. Finally, k is the number of pitches that result in hits.

(a) If exactly three pitches result in hits, then $k = 3$. Using $n = 9, p = 0.2$, and $q = 1 - p = 0.8$, we find

$$P(\text{Exactly 3 hits}) = b(9, 3; 0.2) = \binom{9}{3}(0.2)^3(0.8)^6 = 0.1762$$

(b) If none of the nine pitches resulted in a hit, $k = 0$.

$$P(\text{Exactly 0 hits}) = b(9, 0; 0.2) = \binom{9}{0}(0.2)^0(0.8)^9 = 0.1342$$

(c) Nine pitches are thrown, so the event "eight or more pitches result in hits" is equivalent to the events: "exactly 8 result in hits" or "exactly 9 result in hits." Since these events are mutually exclusive, we have

$$P(\text{At least 8 hits}) = P(\text{Exactly 8 hits}) + P(\text{Exactly 9 hits})$$

$$= b(9, 8; 0.2) + b(9, 9; 0.2) = 0.0000189$$

(d) "No more than seven pitches result in hits" means 0, 1, 2, 3, 4, 5, 6, or 7 pitches result in a hit. We could add $b(9, 0; 0.2)$, $b(9, 1; 0.2)$, and so on, but it is easier to use the formula $P(E) = 1 - P(\overline{E})$. The complement of "No more than 7" is "at least 8." We use the result of part (c) to find:

$$P(\text{No more than 7 hits}) = 1 - P(\text{At least 8 hits})$$

$$= 1 - [b(9, 8; 0.2) + b(9, 9; 0.2)] = 0.999981 \quad \blacksquare$$

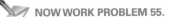

NOW WORK PROBLEM 55.

COMMENT: A graphing utility can be used to compute cumulative probabilities. Figure 27 shows the probability of 0 through 7 successes in 9 trials where the probability of success is 0.2 using a TI-84 Plus. This is the same result obtained in Example 4(d).

FIGURE 27

```
binomcdf(9,.2,7)
          .999981056
```

EXAMPLE 5 **Quality Control**

A machine produces lightbulbs to meet certain specifications, and 80% of the bulbs produced meet these specifications. A sample of six bulbs is taken from the machine's production and placed in a box. What is the probability that at least three of them fail to meet the specifications?

SOLUTION In this example the number of trials is $n = 6$. We are looking for the probability of the event

$$E\text{: At least 3 fail to meet specifications}$$

Since the experiment consists of choosing 6 bulbs, the event E is the union of th mutually exclusive events: "Exactly 3 fail," "Exactly 4 fail," "Exactly 5 fail," and "Exactly fail." We use Formula (2) with $n = 6$ and $k = 3, 4, 5$, and 6. Since the probability of bulb failing to meet specifications is 0.20, we have

$$\begin{aligned} P(\text{Exactly 3 fail}) &= b(6, 3; 0.20) = 0.0819 \\ P(\text{Exactly 4 fail}) &= b(6, 4; 0.20) = 0.0154 \\ P(\text{Exactly 5 fail}) &= b(6, 5; 0.20) = 0.0015 \\ P(\text{Exactly 6 fail}) &= b(6, 6; 0.20) = 0.0001 \end{aligned}$$

Then,

$$P(\text{At least 3 fail}) = P(E) = 0.0819 + 0.0154 + 0.0015 + 0.0001 = 0.0989$$

Another way of getting this answer is to compute the probability of th complementary event

$$\overline{E}\text{: Fewer than 3 fail}$$

Then

$$\begin{aligned} P(\overline{E}) &= P(\text{Exactly 2 fail}) + P(\text{Exactly 1 fail}) + P(\text{Exactly 0 fail}) \\ &= b(6, 2; 0.20) + b(6, 1; 0.20) + b(6, 0; 0.20) \\ &= 0.2458 + 0.3932 + 0.2621 = 0.9011 \end{aligned}$$

Then,

$$P(\text{At least 3 fail}) = 1 - P(\overline{E}) = 1 - 0.9011 = 0.0989$$

as before.

NOW WORK PROBLEM 37.

EXAMPLE 6 Product Testing

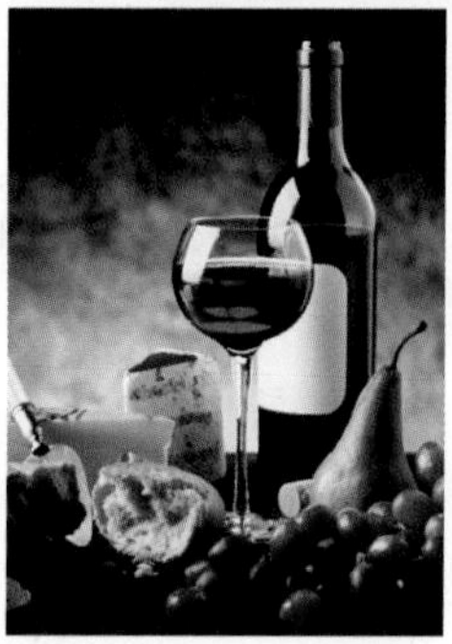

A man claims to be able to distinguish between two kinds of wine with 90% accurac and presents his claim to an agency interested in promoting the consumption of one c the two kinds of wine. The following experiment is conducted to check his claim. Th claimant is to taste the two types of wine and distinguish between them. This is to b done nine times with a 3-minute break after each taste. It is agreed that if the claiman is correct at least six out of the nine times, he will be hired.

(a) What is the probability the claimant will pass if he is guessing?

(b) What is the probability the claimant will pass if his claim of being able to distinguis the wines with 90% accuracy is correct?

SOLUTION This situation can be modeled as a binomial probability model with $n = 9$ trials A success is defined as a correct identification.

(a) If the claimant is guessing, the probability of success is $\frac{1}{2}$. To be hired, the claiman must have at least 6 successes. The probability of this happening is

$$\begin{aligned} b\left(9, 6; \frac{1}{2}\right) + b\left(9, 7; \frac{1}{2}\right) + b\left(9, 8; \frac{1}{2}\right) + b\left(9, 9; \frac{1}{2}\right) &= 0.1641 + 0.0703 + 0.0176 + 0.002 \\ &= 0.2540 \end{aligned}$$

There is a likelihood of 0.254 (just over 25%) that he will pass if he is just guessing.

(b) If the claim is correct, the probability of success is 0.9. The probability of at least 6 successes in this instance is

$$b(9, 6; 0.90) + b(9, 7; 0.90) + b(9, 8; 0.90) + b(9, 9; 0.90) = 0.0446 + 0.1722 + 0.3874 + 0.3874$$
$$= 0.9916$$

If the claim is correct, the probability of success exceeds 99%. ■

Notice that the test in Example 6 is fair to the claimant since it practically assures him the position if his claim is true. However, the company may not like the test because 25% of the time a person who guesses will pass the test.

NOW WORK PROBLEM 61.

EXAMPLE 7 **Testing a Serum or Vaccine**

Suppose that the normal rate of infection of a certain disease in cattle is 25%. To test a newly discovered serum, healthy animals are injected with the serum. How can we evaluate the result of the experiment?

SOLUTION In a probability experiment, an event with a probability less than 0.05 is considered unusual. So we can evaluate the effects of the serum by determining how many treated animals contract the disease. Then we calculate the probability that number of cattle would have been infected if they had not been vaccinated. If the probability is less than 0.05 we conclude the serum is effective.

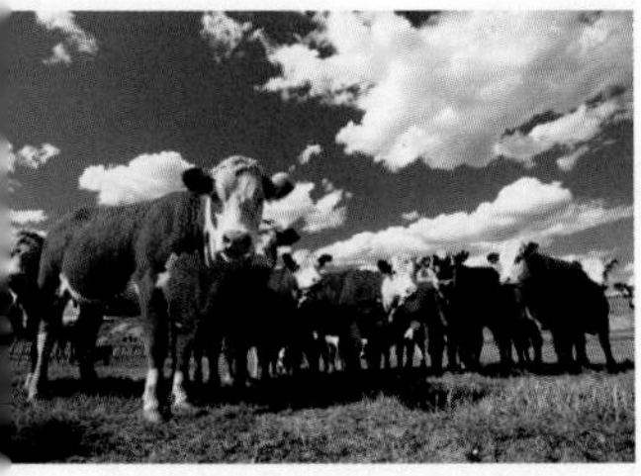

In this example, n is the number of cattle vaccinated; k is the number of cattle that are infected; and $p = 0.25$ is the probability an untreated cow is infected.

For example, if we vaccinate 10 cattle and none of them are infected, we compute $b(10, 0; 0.25) = 0.056$. This is a small probability, indicating that the serum may have had an effect, but it is not conclusive.

However, if we enlarge the sample and vaccinate 20 animals, the probability that less than 2 become infected is

$$b(20, 0; 0.25) + b(20, 1; 0.25) = 0.0032 + 0.0211 = 0.0243.$$

Since this is less than 0.05, we conclude the serum is effective. ■

3 Find the Expected Value in a Bernoulli Trial

In 100 tosses of a coin, what is the expected number of heads? If a student guesses at random on a true–false exam with 50 questions, what is the expected grade? These are specific instances of the following more general question:

In n trials of a Bernoulli process, what is the expected number of successes?

In a Bernoulli trial, let p denote the probability of success on any individual trial. If $n = 1$ (one trial), then the expected number of successes is

$$E = 1 \cdot p + 0 \cdot (1 - p) = p$$

If $n = 2$ (two trials), then either 0, 1, or 2 successes can occur. The expected number E of successes is

$$E = 2 \cdot p^2 + 1 \cdot 2p(1 - p) + 0 \cdot (1 - p)^2 = 2p$$

If $n = 3$ (three trials), then either 0, 1, 2, or 3 successes can occur. The expected number E of successes is

$$\begin{aligned} E &= 3 \cdot p^3 + 2 \cdot 3p^2(1 - p) + 1 \cdot 3p(1 - p)^2 + 0 \cdot (1 - p)^3 \\ &= 3p^3 + 6p^2 - 6p^3 + 3p - 6p^2 + 3p^3 \\ &= 3p \end{aligned}$$

This pattern leads to the following result:

Theorem

Expected Value for Bernoulli Trials

In a Bernoulli process with n trials the expected number of successes is

$$E = np$$

where p is the probability of success on any single trial.

The intuitive idea behind the result is fairly simple. Thinking of probabilities as percentages, if success results p percent of the time, then out of n attempts, p percent of them, namely, np, should be successful.

EXAMPLE 8 Expected Value in a Bernoulli Trial

In flipping a fair coin five times, what is the expected number of tails?

SOLUTION The six events 0 tails, 1 tail, 2 tails, 3 tails, 4 tails, 5 tails are events that constitute a partition of the sample space. The respective probability of each of these events is

$$\binom{5}{0}\left(\frac{1}{2}\right)^5 \quad \binom{5}{1}\left(\frac{1}{2}\right)^5 \quad \binom{5}{2}\left(\frac{1}{2}\right)^5 \quad \binom{5}{3}\left(\frac{1}{2}\right)^5 \quad \binom{5}{4}\left(\frac{1}{2}\right)^5 \quad \binom{5}{5}\left(\frac{1}{2}\right)^5$$

If we assign the payoffs 0, 1, 2, 3, 4, 5 respectively to each event, then the expected number of tails is

$$\begin{aligned} E = 0 \cdot \binom{5}{0}\left(\frac{1}{2}\right)^5 + 1 \cdot \binom{5}{1}\left(\frac{1}{2}\right)^5 + 2 \cdot \binom{5}{2}\left(\frac{1}{2}\right)^5 \\ + 3 \cdot \binom{5}{3}\left(\frac{1}{2}\right)^5 + 4 \cdot \binom{5}{4}\left(\frac{1}{2}\right)^5 + 5 \cdot \binom{5}{5}\left(\frac{1}{2}\right)^5 = \frac{5}{2} \end{aligned}$$

Using the result $E = np$ is much easier. For $n = 5$ and $p = \frac{1}{2}$, we obtain $E = (5)\left(\frac{1}{2}\right) = \frac{5}{2}$.

NOW WORK PROBLEM 65.

EXAMPLE 9 Expected Value in a Bernoulli Trial

A multiple-choice test contains 100 questions, each with four choices. If a person guesses, what is the expected number of correct answers?

SOLUTION This is an example of a Bernoulli trial. The probability for success (a correct answer) when guessing is $p = \frac{1}{4}$. Since there are $n = 100$ questions, the expected number of correct answers is

$$E = np = (100)\left(\frac{1}{4}\right) = 25$$

■

NOW WORK PROBLEM 71.

4 Model: Error-Correcting Codes for the Digital Transmission of Data

Electronically transmitted data, whether from computer to computer or from a satellite to a ground station, are normally in the form of strings of 0s and 1s—that is, in binary form. Bursts of noise or faults in relays, for example, may at times garble the transmission and produce errors so that the message received is not the same as the one originally sent. For example,

001	$\mapsto$	101
Message sent	Noisy channel	Message received

is a transmission where the message received is in error since the initial 0 has been changed to a 1.

A naive way of trying to protect against such error would be to repeat the message. So instead of transmitting 001, we would send 001001. Then, were the same error to creep in as it did before, the received message would be

101001

The receiver would certainly know an error had occurred since the last half of the message is not a duplicate of the first half. But the receiver would have no way of recovering the original message since there is no way to know where the error happened. That is, the receiver would not be able to distinguish between the two messages

001001 and 101101

There are more sophisticated ways of coding binary data with redundancy that not only allow the detection of errors but simultaneously locate and correct them so that the original message can be recovered. These are referred to as *error-correcting codes* and are commonly used in computer-implemented transmissions.

One such code is the (7, 4) Hamming code named after Richard Hamming, a former researcher at AT&T Laboratories. It is a code of length seven, meaning that an individual message is a string consisting of seven items, each of which is either a 0 or 1. (The 4 refers to the fact that the first four elements in the string can be freely chosen by the sender, while the remaining three are determined by a fixed rule and constitute the redundancy that gives the code its error-correction capability.) The (7, 4) Hamming code is capable of locating and correcting a single error. That is, if during transmission a 1 has been changed to a 0 or vice versa in one of the seven locations, the Hamming code is capable of detecting and correcting this. While we will not explain how or why the Hammi code works, we will analyze the benefit obtained by its use.

By an error we mean that an individual 1 has been changed to a 0 or that a 0 h been changed to a 1. We assume that the probability q of an error happening remai constant during transmission. Then $p = 1 - q$ is the probability that an individu symbol remains unchanged. In practice, values of q are close to 0 and values of p clo to 1 since we would usually be using a reliable channel. See Figure 28.

FIGURE 28

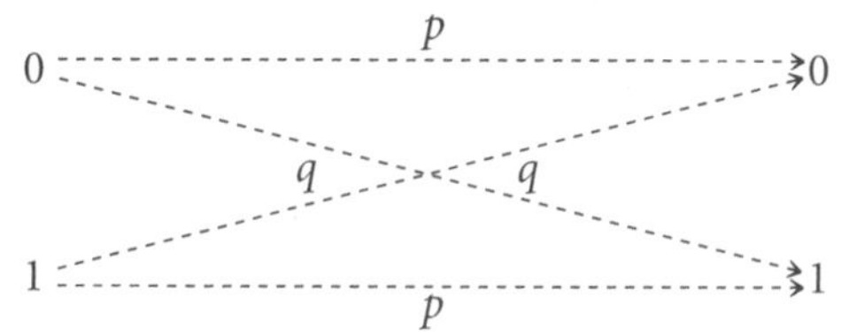

We also assume that errors occur randomly and independently. This means we ca think of the transmission of a binary string of length seven as a Bernoulli trial.

EXAMPLE 10 Analyzing a Message of Length 7

A message consisting of 7 symbols is transmitted. The probability p a symbol remai unchanged by the transmission is $p = 0.98$.

(a) What is the probability the message is received without any alteration?

(b) If a Hamming code is employed, the message will be received without alteratic even if one symbol is changed. What is the probability the message is receive correctly using a Hamming code?

SOLUTION **(a)** Since p is the probability of no alteration of a single symbol and the message consis of 7 symbols, the probability the message is received without any changes is

$$b(7, 7; p) = p^7 = (0.98)^7 = 0.8681$$

The message is received without error almost 87% of the time.

(b) Using a Hamming code, the message is received correctly even if one symbol changed. The probability the message is received without any change now is

$$b(7, 7; p) + b(7, 6; p) = p^7 + 7p^6q = (0.98)^7 + 7(0.98)^6(0.02) = 0.9921$$

Using the Hamming code, the probability the message is received without error h improved to over 99%.

There are codes in use that correct more than a single error. One such code, know by the initials of its originators as a BCH code, is a code of length 15 (messages a binary strings of length 15) that corrects up to two errors. Sending a message of lengt 15 with no error-correcting code results in a probability of $b(15, 15; p) = p^{15}$ of th correct message being received. Using the BCH code that can correct two or fewe errors, the probability that a message will be correctly received becomes

$$\underbrace{b(15, 15; p)}_{\text{No errors}} + \underbrace{b(15, 14; p)}_{\text{1 error}} + \underbrace{b(15, 13; p)}_{\text{2 errors}}$$

EXAMPLE 11 Analyzing a Message of Length 15

A message consisting of 15 symbols is transmitted. The probability p a symbol remains unchanged by the transmission is $p = 0.98$.

(a) What is the probability the message is received without any alteration?

(b) If a BCH code is employed, the message will be received without alteration even if one or two symbols are changed. What is the probability the message is received correctly using a BCH code?

SOLUTION **(a)** Since p is the probability of no alteration of a single symbol and the message consists of 15 symbols, the probability the message is received without any changes is

$$b(15, 15; p) = p^{15} = (0.98)^{15} = 0.7386$$

The message is received without error almost 74% of the time.

(b) Using a BCH code, the message is received correctly even if one or two symbols are changed. The probability the message is received without any change now is

$$\begin{aligned} b(15, 15; p) + b(15, 14; p) + b(15, 13; p) &= p^{15} + 15p^{14}q + 105p^{13}q^2 \\ &= (0.98)^{15} + 15(0.98)^{14}(0.02) + 105(0.98)^{13}(0.02)^2 \\ &= 0.9970 \end{aligned}$$

Using the BCH code, the probability the message is received without error has improved to over 99%. ■

Codes that can correct a high number of errors are clearly very desirable. Yet a basic result in the theory of codes states that as the error-correcting capability of a code increases, so, of necessity, must its length. But lengthier codes require more time for transmission and are clumsier to use. Here, speed and correctness are at odds.

EXERCISE 8.6 Answers Begin on Page AN–42.

Concepts and Vocabulary

1. ***True or False*** In a Bernoulli trial, the same experiment is repeated two or more times, but the probability of a particular outcome varies from trial to trial.
2. ***True or False*** In a Bernoulli trial, the same experiment is repeated two or more times and the repeated trials are independent.
3. In a Bernoulli trial, the probability of exactly k successes in n trials is $b(n, k; p)=$________, where p is the probability of success and $q = 1 - p$ is the probability of failure.
4. In a binomial probability model, the probability of exactly 3 successes in 7 trials with the probability of success being 0.3 is written as b (______, ______; ______).
5. ***True or False*** In a Bernoulli trial, the probability of at least 5 successes in 6 trials is $b(6, 5; p) + b(6, 6; p)$, where p is the probability of success and $q = 1 - p$ is the probability of failure.
6. In a Bernoulli process with n trials, the expected number of successes is $E=$_____, where p is the probability of success.

Skill Building

In Problems 7–20, use Formula (2), page 482, to compute each binomial probability.

7. $b(7, 4; 0.20)$ 8. $b(8, 5; 0.30)$ 9. $b(15, 8; 0.80)$ 10. $b(8, 5; 0.70)$ 11. $b\left(15, 10; \frac{1}{2}\right)$ 12. $b(12, 6; 0.90)$

13. $b(15, 3; 0.3) + b(15, 2; 0.3) + b(15, 1; 0.3) + b(15, 0; 0.3)$ 14. $b(8, 6; 0.4) + b(8, 7; 0.4) + b(8, 8; 0.4)$

15. $n = 3,\ k = 2,\ p = \frac{1}{3}$ 16. $n = 3,\ k = 1,\ p = \frac{1}{3}$ 17. $n = 3,\ k = 0,\ p = \frac{1}{6}$

18. $n = 3,\ k = 3,\ p = \frac{1}{6}$ 19. $n = 5,\ k = 3,\ p = \frac{2}{3}$ 20. $n = 5,\ k = 0,\ p = \frac{2}{3}$

21. Find the probability of obtaining exactly 6 successes in 10 trials when the probability of success is 0.3.
22. Find the probability of obtaining exactly 5 successes in 9 trials when the probability of success is 0.2.
23. Find the probability of obtaining exactly 9 successes in 12 trials when the probability of success is 0.8.
24. Find the probability of obtaining exactly 8 successes in 15 trials when the probability of success is 0.75.
25. Find the probability of obtaining at least 5 successes in 8 trials when the probability of success is 0.30.
26. Find the probability of obtaining at most 3 successes in 7 trials when the probability of success is 0.20.

In Problems 27–32, a fair coin is tossed 8 times.

27. What is the probability of obtaining exactly 1 head?
28. What is the probability of obtaining exactly 2 heads?
29. What is the probability of obtaining at least 5 tails?
30. What is the probability of obtaining at most 2 tails?
31. What is the probability of obtaining exactly 2 heads if it is known that at least 1 head appeared?
32. What is the probability of obtaining exactly 3 heads if it is known that at least 1 head appeared?

33. In five rolls of two fair dice, what is the probability of obtaining a sum of 7 exactly twice?
34. In seven rolls of two fair dice, what is the probability of obtaining a sum of 11 exactly three times?
35. An experiment is performed 4 times, with 2 possible outcomes, F (failure) and A (success), with probabilities $\frac{1}{4}$ and $\frac{3}{4}$, respectively.
    (a) Draw a tree diagram for the experiment.
    (b) Find the probability of exactly 2 successes and 2 failures using the tree diagram.
    (c) Verify your answer to part (b) using Formula (2).
36. An experiment is performed 3 times, with 2 possible outcomes, F (failure) and A (success), with probabilities $\frac{1}{3}$ and $\frac{2}{3}$, respectively.
    (a) Draw a tree diagram for the experiment.
    (b) Find the probability of 1 success and 2 failures using the tree diagram.
    (c) Verify your answer to part (b) using Formula (2).

Applications

37. **Quality Control** Suppose that 5% of the items produced by a factory are defective. If 8 items are chosen at random, what is the probability
    (a) Exactly 1 is defective? (b) Exactly 2 are defective?
    (c) At least 1 is defective? (d) Fewer than 3 are defective?
38. **Opinion Poll** Suppose that 60% of the voters intend to vote for a conservative candidate. What is the probability a survey polling 8 people reveals that 3 or fewer intend to vote for a conservative candidate?
39. **Family Structure** What is the probability in a family with exactly 6 children:
    (a) 3 are boys?
    (b) At least 5 are boys?
    (c) At least 2, but less than 4, are girls?
40. **Family Structure** What is the probability in a family of 7 children:
    (a) 4 are girls?
    (b) At least 2 are girls?
    (c) At least 2 and not more than 4 are girls?
41. **Guessing on a True–False Exam** In a 20-item true–false examination, a student guesses on each question.
    (a) What is the probability the student will obtain all correct answers?
    (b) If 12 correct answers constitute a passing grade, what is the probability the student will pass?
    (c) What are the odds in favor of passing?
42. **True–False Tests**
    (a) In a 15-item true–false examination, what is the probability that a student who guesses on each question will get at least 10 correct answers?
    (b) If another student has 0.8 probability of correctly answering each question, what is the probability that the student will answer at least 12 questions correctly?

3. Cheating on Taxes *Money* magazine reported that 12% of people admit they think it is acceptable to cheat on their taxes. Suppose 15 people are randomly selected.

(a) What is the probability that at least five admit they think it is acceptable to cheat on taxes?

(b) What is the probability that fewer than three admit they think it is acceptable to cheat on taxes?

(c) What is the probability that none admit they think it is acceptable to cheat on taxes?

Source: Rosato, Donna. *Money Magazine*. Feb. 23, 2007

4. Individual Tax Audits In 2009, the IRS audited about 1% of all individual income tax returns. Suppose that 10 individual income tax returns from 2009 are randomly selected.

(a) What is the probability that none was audited?

(b) What is the probability that exactly one was audited?

(c) What is the probability that more than one was audited?

Source: Internal Revenue Service

5. Filing Tax Returns The IRS estimates that 10% of all individual income tax returns filed each year are submitted on the last day of filing. Suppose that eight individual income tax returns are randomly selected.

(a) What is the probability that exactly two were submitted on the last day of filing?

(b) What is the probability that exactly five were submitted on the last day of filing?

(c) What is the probability that none were submitted on the last day of filing?

Source: American Society for Quality. *The Quarterly Quality Report*, Mar. 2007 (www.asq.org)

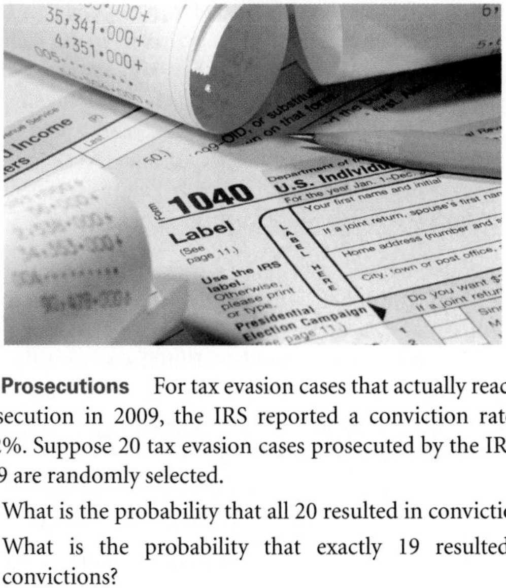

6. IRS Prosecutions For tax evasion cases that actually reached prosecution in 2009, the IRS reported a conviction rate of 87.2%. Suppose 20 tax evasion cases prosecuted by the IRS in 2009 are randomly selected.

(a) What is the probability that all 20 resulted in convictions?

(b) What is the probability that exactly 19 resulted in convictions?

(c) What is the probability that at least 18 resulted in convictions?

Source: Internal Revenue Service

47. Worker Satisfaction A study by the Society for Human Resource Management, an international association of human resource professionals, found that 80% of workers liked their jobs. Suppose 10 workers are randomly selected.

(a) What is the probability that all ten like their jobs?

(b) What is the probability that exactly nine like their jobs?

(c) What is the probability that no more than seven like their jobs?

Source: Society for Human Resource Management, June 27, 2005

48. Worker Satisfaction A Sperion® Workplace Snapshot survey conducted by Harris Interactive® found that 32% of workers listen to music while working, a practice believed to increase job satisfaction and productivity. Suppose 6 workers are selected at random.

(a) What is the probability that exactly three listen to music while working?

(b) What is the probability that more than four listen to music while working?

(c) What is the probability that two or fewer listen to music while working?

Source: Spherion Press Release, Sept. 18, 2006 (www.spherion.com)

49. Clipping Coupons According to the Promotion Marketing Association, 77% of all Americans use coupons, saving more than $3 billion each year on purchases. Suppose 18 Americans are randomly selected.

(a) What is the probability that exactly 14 use coupons?

(b) What is the probability that at least 14 use coupons?

(c) What is the probability that at least 16 use coupons?

Source: Glanton, Dahleen. "Coupon clippers clean up." *Chicago Tribune*. May 8, 2005 (www.chicagotribune.com)

50. Volunteerism According to the Bureau of Labor Statistics, 26.8% of the U.S. population did volunteer work during the twelve months prior to September 2009. Suppose 14 people from the U.S. population are randomly selected.

(a) What is the probability that exactly six had volunteered?

(b) What is the probability that fewer than six had volunteered?

(c) What is the probability that more than six had volunteered?

Source: Bureau of Labor Statistics. "Volunteering in the United States, 2009." Jan. 26, 2010

51. Insurance Fraud The National Insurance Crime Bureau estimates that 15% of auto theft claims involve fraud. Suppose 12 auto theft claims are randomly selected.

(a) Determine the probability none of the claims involve fraud.

(b) Determine the probability six claims involve fraud.

(c) Determine the probability at least one of the claims involve fraud.

Source: www.statefarm.com citing the National Insurance Crime Bureau

52. Auto Loan Approval Bev is a loan officer at a privately owned bank. From years of experience, Bev knows that 84% of auto loan applications are approvable. Bev has recently received 15 auto loan applications that she must examine.

(a) What is the probability that all 15 applications are approvable?

(b) What is the probability that at least one application must be rejected?

(c) What is the probability that fewer than 10 of the applications are approvable?

53. Air Passenger No-Shows The airline industry reports that 12% of ticketed passengers fail to show up on time for the scheduled flight. A scheduled flight of a small jet with 44 seats is sold out.

(a) Determine the probability two passengers will be no-shows.

(b) Determine the probability none of the passengers will be no-shows.

(c) Determine the probability at least two of the passengers will be no-shows.

Source: De Lollis, Barbara, "Airlines give fliers fewer chances to do the bump," *USA Today*, Dec. 19, 2005 (www.usatoday.com)

54. Airline Bumps To counter the cost of passenger no-shows, airlines frequently overbook flights. If the number of passengers that show up for a flight is greater than the number of seats available, then some passengers must be bumped from that flight (usually voluntarily through incentives). A *USA Today* analysis of government statistics showed that airlines bump about 12 of every 10,000 passengers. Suppose a shuttle from an airport parking lot is carrying 18 independent air passengers.

(a) Determine the probability that none of them will be bumped from their flight.

(b) Determine the probability that exactly one of them will be bumped from their flight.

(c) Determine the probability that more than one of them will be bumped from their flights.

Source: De Lollis, Barbara, "Airlines give fliers fewer chances to do the bump," *USA Today*, Dec. 19, 2005 (www.usatoday.com)

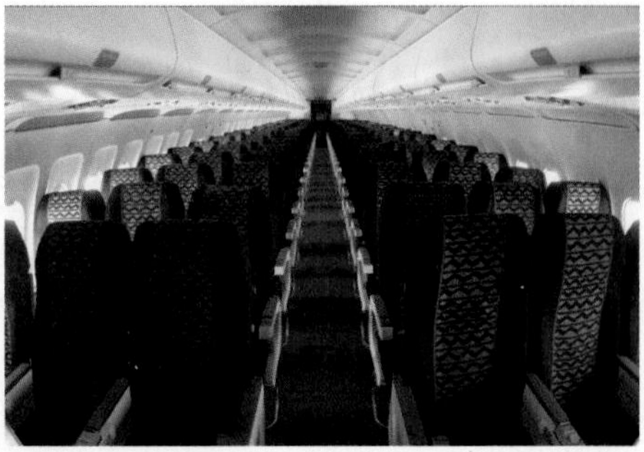

55. **Batting Averages** A baseball player has a 0.250 battin average.

(a) What is the probability that the player will have at least hits in 4 times at bat?

(b) What is the probability of at least 1 hit in 4 times at ba

56. Target Shooting If the probability of hitting a target $\frac{2}{3}$ and 10 shots are fired independently, what is the probabilit of the target being hit at least twice?

57. Opinion Poll Mr. Austin and Ms. Moran are running fo public office. A survey conducted just before the day of electio indicates that 60% of the voters prefer Mr. Austin and 40% prefer Ms. Moran. If 8 people are chosen at random and aske their preference, find the probability that all 8 people will expre a preference for Ms. Moran.

58. Screening Employees To screen prospective employees, company gives a 10-question multiple-choice test. Eac question has 4 possible answers, of which 1 is correct. The chanc of answering the questions correctly by just guessing is $\frac{1}{4}$ o 25%. Find the probability of answering, by chance:

(a) Exactly 3 questions correctly.

(b) No questions correctly.

(c) At least 8 questions correctly.

(d) No more than 7 questions correctly.

59. Heart Attack Approximately 23% of North America unexpected deaths are due to heart attacks. What is th probability that 4 of the next 10 unexpected deaths reporte in a certain community will be due to heart attacks?

60. Support for the President A Fox News/Opinion Dynami Poll conducted with 900 registered voters in the United State on April 20–21, 2010, found that 46% approved of the jo Barack Obama was doing as president. Assuming that this po reflects national opinion, if 30 voters were randomly selecte what is the probability at least 10, but less than 15, woul approve of the job Barack Obama is doing as president?

Source: Fox News Opinion/Dynamics Poll

61. **Product Testing** A supposed coffee connoisseur claims sh can distinguish between a cup of instant coffee and a cup o drip coffee 80% of the time. You give her 6 cups of coffee an tell her that you will grant her claim if she correctly identifie at least 5 of the 6 cups.

(a) What are her chances of having her claim granted if she in fact only guessing?

(b) What are her chances of having her claim rejected when i fact she really does have the ability she claims?

62. Opinion Poll Opinion polls based on small samples ofte yield misleading results. Suppose 65% of the people in a ci are opposed to a bond issue and the others favor it. If 7 peopl are asked for their opinion, what is the probability that majority of them will favor the bond issue?

3. **The Aging Population** The 2008 United States Census showed that 12.3% of the United States population was 65 years of age or older. Suppose that in the year 2008, 10 people were randomly selected from the United States population.

(a) What is the probability that exactly four of these people would be 65 years of age or older?
(b) What is the probability that none of these people would be 65 years of age or older?
(c) What is the probability that at most five of these people would be 65 years of age or older?

Source: United States Census Bureau

4. **Age Distribution** The 2008 United States Census showed that 87.7% of the U.S. population was younger than 65 years old. Suppose that in the year 2008, 10 people were randomly selected from the U.S. population.

(a) What is the probability that exactly 8 of these people would be younger than 65?
(b) What is the probability that all of these people would be younger than 65?
(c) What is the probability that at most five of these people would be 65 years of age or older?

Source: United States Census Bureau, 2008

. **Tossing a Die** Find the number of times the face 5 is expected to occur in a sequence of 2000 throws of a fair die.

6. **Tossing a Coin** What is the expected number of tails that will turn up if a fair coin is tossed 582 times?

7. **Quality Control** A certain kind of lightbulb has been found to have a 0.02 probability of being defective. A shop owner receives 500 lightbulbs of this kind. How many of these bulbs are expected to be defective?

8. **Pass/Fail** A student enrolled in a math course has a 0.9 probability of passing the course. In a class of 20 students, how many would you expect to fail the math course?

9. **Healthcare Costs** In a December 2009 Gallup poll, 14% of adults in the United States indicated that healthcare costs were the most important financial problem facing their family. For a random sample of 20 adults, what is the expected number that would say healthcare costs were the most important financial problem facing their family?

Source: The Gallup Organization

70. **Emergency Savings** A report by CNN in February 2007 stated that only 40% of adult Americans have separate savings for an emergency. For a random sample of 120 adult Americans, what is the expected number that will have separate savings for an emergency?

Source: www.cnn.com

71. **Drug Reaction** A doctor has found that the probability that a patient who is given a certain drug will have unfavorable reactions to the drug is 0.002. If a group of 500 patients is going to be given the drug, how many of them does the doctor expect to have unfavorable reactions?

72. **True–False Test** A true–false test consisting of 30 questions is scored by subtracting the number of wrong answers from the number of right ones. Find the expected number of correct answers of a student who just guesses on each question. What will the expected test score be?

73. **Hamming Code** There is a Hamming code of length 15 that corrects a single error. Assuming $p = 0.98$, find the probability that a message transmitted using this code will be correctly received.

74. **Golay Code** There is a binary code of length 23 (called the Golay code) that can correct up to 3 errors. With $p = 0.98$, find the probability that a message transmitted using the Golay code will be correctly received.

75. **BCH Code** There is a binary code of length 31 [called the binary $(31, 31, p)$ BCH code] used for some pagers that can correct up to two errors. If the probability that an individual character is transmitted correctly is 0.97, find the probability that a message transmitted using this code will be correctly received.

Source: www.eccpage.com

metimes experiments are simulated using a random number function instead of actually performing the experiment. Problems 76–79, use a graphing utility to simulate each experiment.*

6. **Tossing a Fair Coin** Consider the experiment of tossing a coin 4 times and counting the number of heads occurring in these 4 tosses. Simulate the experiment using a random number function on your calculator, considering a toss to be tails (T) if the result is less than 0.5, and considering a toss to be heads (H) if the result is greater than or equal to 0.5. Record the number of heads in 4 tosses. [*Note*: Most calculators repeat the action of the last entry if you simply press the ENTER, or EXE, key again.] Repeat the experiment 10 times, obtaining a sequence of 10 numbers. Using these 10 numbers you can estimate the probability of k heads, $P(k)$, for each $k = 0, 1, 2, 3, 4$, by the ratio

$$\frac{\text{Number of times } k \text{ appears in your sequence}}{10}$$

Enter your estimates in the table on the next page. Calculate the actual probabilities using the binomial probability formula, and enter these numbers in the table. How close are your numbers to the actual values?

ost graphing utilities have a random number function (usually RAND or RND) for generating numbers between 0 and 1. Check your user's manual to see w to use this function on your graphing calculator.

k	Your Estimate of $P(k)$	Actual Value of $P(k)$
0		
1		
2		
3		
4		

77. **Tossing a Loaded Coin** Consider the experiment of tossing a loaded coin 4 times and counting the number of heads occurring in these 4 tosses. Simulate the experiment using a random number function on your calculator, considering a toss to be tails (T) if the result is less than 0.80, and considering a toss to be heads (H) if the result is greater than or equal to 0.80. Record the number of heads in 4 tosses. Repeat the experiment 10 times, obtaining a sequence of 10 numbers. Using these 10 numbers you can estimate the probability of k heads, $P(k)$, for each $k = 0, 1, 2, 3, 4$, by the ratio

$$\frac{\text{Number of times } k \text{ appears in your sequence}}{10}$$

Enter your estimates in a table. Calculate the actual probabilities using the binomial probability formula, and enter these numbers in your table. How close are your numbers to the actual values?

k	Your Estimate of $P(k)$	Actual Value of $P(k)$
0		
1		
2		
3		
4		

78. **Tossing a Fair Coin** Consider the experiment of tossing fair coin 8 times and counting the number of heads occurri in these 8 tosses. Simulate the experiment using a rando number function on your calculator, considering a toss to b tails (T) if the result is less than 0.50, and considering a toss be heads (H) if the result is greater than or equal to 0.5 Record the number of heads in 8 tosses. Repeat the exper ment 10 times, obtaining a sequence of 10 numbers. Usir these 10 numbers you can estimate the probability of 3 head $P(3)$, by the ratio

$$\frac{\text{Number of times 3 appears in your sequence}}{10}$$

Calculate the actual probability using the binomi probability formula. How close is your estimate to the actu value?

79. **Tossing a Loaded Coin** Consider the experiment of tossi a loaded coin 8 times and counting the number of hea occurring in these 8 tosses. Simulate the experiment usi a random number function on your calculator, considering toss to be tails (T) if the result is less than 0.80, and consideri a toss to be heads (H) if the result is greater than or equal 0.80. Record the number of heads in 8 tosses. Repeat th experiment 10 times, obtaining a sequence of 10 number Using these 10 numbers you can estimate the probability 3 heads, $P(3)$, by the ratio

$$\frac{\text{Number of times 3 appears in your sequence}}{10}$$

Calculate the actual probability using the binomi probability formula. How close is your estimate to th actual value?

CHAPTER 8 REVIEW OBJECTIVES

Section	Examples	You should be able to	Review Exercises
8.1	1, 2, 3, 4	1 Find a conditional probability (p. 423)	1–4, 13–18, 58a, 58b, 59c, 60c, 66
	5	2 Find probabilities using the Product Rule (p. 425)	5–6, 19–24, 59a, 60a, 62
	6, 7	3 Find probabilities using a tree diagram (p. 426)	59, 60
	8	4 Find conditional probabilities from a data table (p. 428)	61a, 61b

8.2	1, 2, 3, 4	1	Show two events are independent (p. 435)	57, 61c, 61d, 62f
	5, 6	2	Find $P(E \cap F)$ for independent events E and F (p. 437)	63, 64
	7	3	Find probabilities for several independent events (p. 438)	65
8.3	2	1	Solve probability problems: sample space partitioned into two sets (p. 446)	9–12
	3, 4	2	Solve probability problems: sample space partitioned into three sets (p. 447)	25–32
	5	3	Use Bayes' Theorem to solve probability problems (p. 450)	9–12, 25–32
	6, 7	4	Find *a priori* and *a posteriori* probabilities (p. 451)	71, 72
8.4	1	1	Evaluate factorials (p. 458)	33–38
	2	2	Solve counting problems involving permutations [distinct,with repetition] (p. 459)	46a, 52
	3, 4, 6, 7, 8	3	Solve counting problems involving permutations [distinct, without repetition] (p. 460)	40–42, 43a, 44a, 46b, 47, 48
8.5	1, 2, 3, 4, 5, 6, 7, 8	1	Solve counting problems involving combinations (p. 466)	39, 43b, 44b, 45, 46c, 49, 50, 51
	9, 10, 11	2	Solve counting problems involving permutations [n objects, not all distinct] (p. 469)	53, 54, 55, 56
	12, 13, 14, 15	3	Find the probabilities using counting techniques (p. 471)	67–70
8.6	1, 2, 3	1	Find binomial probabilities (p. 482)	73, 74
	4, 5, 6, 7	2	Solve applied problems involving the binomial probabilities model (p. 484)	73, 74
	8, 9	3	Find the expected value in a Bernoulli trial (p. 487)	75

HINGS TO KNOW

onditional Probability (p. 423) $P(E|F) = \dfrac{P(E \cap F)}{P(F)}, P(F) \neq 0$

oduct Rule (p. 425) $P(E \cap F) = P(F) \cdot P(E|F)$

is independent of *F* (p. 434) $P(E|F) = P(E)$

riterion for Independent Events (p. 435) E, F are independent if and only if $P(E \cap F) = P(E) \cdot P(F)$

obability of an Event *E* in Partitioned Sample Space (p. 449)

$$P(E) = P(A_1) \cdot P(E|A_1) + P(A_2) \cdot P(E|A_2) + P(A_3) \cdot P(E|A_3) + \cdots + P(A_n) \cdot P(E|A_n)$$

Bayes' Theorem (p. 450) $P(A_j|E) = \dfrac{P(A_j) \cdot P(E|A_j)}{P(E)}$

Factorial (p. 458) $0! = 1 \quad n! = n(n-1) \cdots (3)(2)(1)$ The product of the first n positive integers.

Permutation (p. 459) An ordered arrangement of r objects chosen from n objec

Distinct, with Repetition (p. 459) n^r The n objects are distinct (different) and repetition is lowed in the selection of r of them.

Distinct, without Repetition (p. 461) $P(n, r) = n(n-1) \cdot \cdots \cdot [n-(r-1)] = \dfrac{n!}{(n-r)!}$ The n objects are distinct (different) and repetition is r allowed in the selection of r of them, where $r \leq$

Combination (pp. 466–467) $C(n, r) = \dfrac{P(n, r)}{r!} = \dbinom{n}{r} = \dfrac{n!}{(n-r)!r!}$ An arrangement, without regard to order, of r objects selec from n distinct objects without repetition, where $r \leq n$.

***n* Objects, Not Distinct** (p. 470) $\dfrac{n!}{n_1!n_2! \cdots n_k!}$ The number of permutations of n objects of which n_1 are one kind, n_2 are of a second kind, ..., and n_k are of a kind, where $n = n_1 + n_2 + \cdots + n_k$.

Binomial Probability Formula (p. 482) $b(n, k; p) = \dbinom{n}{k} p^k q^{n-k}, q = 1 - p$

Expected Value for Bernoulli Trials (p. 488) $E = np$

REVIEW EXERCISES **Answers to odd-numbered problems begin on page AN–43.**

Blue Problem numbers indicate the author's suggestions for a practice test.

In Problems 1–12, use the tree diagram below to find the indicated probability:

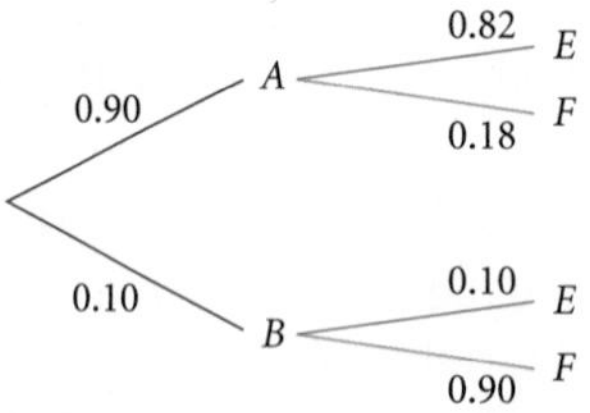

1. $P(E|A)$
2. $P(F|A)$
3. $P(E|B)$
4. $P(F|B)$
5. $P(A \cap E)$
6. $P(A \cap$
7. $P(B \cap E)$
8. $P(B \cap F)$
9. $P(A|E)$
10. $P(A|F)$
11. $P(B|E)$
12. $P(B|F)$

In Problems 13–32, use the tree diagram below to find the indicated probability:

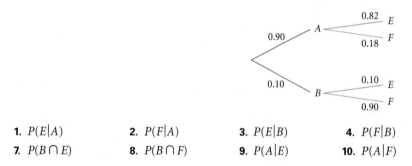

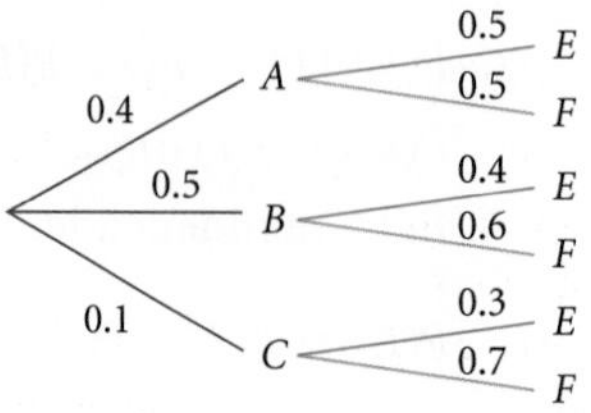

3. $P(E|A)$ 14. $P(F|A)$ 15. $P(E|B)$ 16. $P(F|B)$ 17. $P(E|C)$ 18. $P(F|C)$ 19. $P(A \cap E)$
0. $P(A \cap F)$ 21. $P(B \cap E)$ 22. $P(B \cap F)$ 23. $P(C \cap E)$ 24. $P(C \cap F)$ 25. $P(E)$ 26. $P(F)$
7. $P(A|E)$ 28. $P(A|F)$ 29. $P(B|E)$ 30. $P(B|F)$ 31. $P(C|E)$ 32. $P(C|F)$

Problems 33–38, evaluate each expression.

3. $0!$ 34. $(8 - 3)!$ 35. $\frac{7!}{4!}$ 36. $\frac{10!}{2!8!}$ 37. $\frac{12!}{11!}$ 38. $\frac{6!}{(6-3)!\,3!}$

9. In how many different ways can a committee of 3 people be formed from a group of 5 people?
0. In how many different ways can 4 people line up?
1. In how many different ways can 3 books be placed on a shelf?
2. In how many different ways can 3 people be seated in 4 chairs?
3. You are to set up a code of 3-digit words using the digits 1, 2, 3, 4, 5, 6 without using any digit more than once in the same word.
   (a) What is the maximum number of words in such a language?
   (b) If the words 124, 142, etc., designate the same word, how many different words are possible?
4. You are to set up a code of 2-digit words using the digits 1, 2, 3, 4 without using any digit more than once.
   (a) What is the maximum number of words in such a language?
   (b) If all words of the form *ab* and *ba* are the same, how many words are possible?
5. **Forming Committees** There are 7 boys and 6 girls willing to serve on a committee. How many 7-member committees are possible if a committee is to contain:
   (a) 3 boys and 4 girls?
   (b) At least one member of each sex?
6. **Choosing Double-Dip Cones** Juan's Ice Cream Parlor offers 31 different flavors to choose from and specializes in double-dip cones.
   (a) How many different cones are there to choose from if you may select the same flavor for each dip?
   (b) How many different cones are there to choose from if you cannot repeat any flavor? Assume that a cone with vanilla on top of chocolate is different from a cone with chocolate on top of vanilla.
   (c) How many different cones are there if you consider any cone having chocolate on top and vanilla on the bottom the same as having vanilla on top and chocolate on the bottom?
7. **Arranging Books** A person has 4 history, 5 English, and 6 mathematics books. How many ways can the books be arranged on a shelf if books on the same subject must be together?

48. **Choosing Names** A newborn child can be given 1, 2, or 3 names. In how many ways can a child be named if we can choose from 100 names?
49. **Forming Committees** In how many ways can a committee of 8 boys and 5 girls be formed if there are 10 boys and 11 girls eligible to serve on the committee?
50. **Football Teams** A football squad has 7 linemen, 11 linebackers, and 9 safeties. How many different teams composed of 5 linemen, 3 linebackers, and 3 safeties can be formed?
51. There are 5 rotten plums in a crate of 25 plums. How many samples of 4 of the 25 plums contain
    (a) Only good plums?
    (b) Three good plums and 1 rotten plum?
    (c) One or more rotten plums?
52. An admissions test given by a university contains 10 true–false questions. Eight or more of the questions must be answered correctly in order to be admitted.
    (a) How many different ways can the answer sheet be filled out?
    (b) How many different ways can the answer sheet be filled out so that 8 or more questions are answered correctly?
53. How many 6-letter words (real or imaginary) can be made from the word FINITE?
54. How many 7-letter words (real or imaginary) can be made from the word MESSAGE?
55. **Arranging Books** Jessica has 10 books to arrange on a shelf. How many different arrangements are possible if she has 3 identical copies of *Harry Potter and the Sorcerer's Stone* and 2 identical copies of *Finite Mathematics*?
56. **Arranging Pennants** Mike has 9 pennants to arrange on a pole. How many different arrangements are possible if 4 pennants are blue, 2 are yellow, and 3 are green?
57. **Rolling a Loaded Die** A die is loaded so that when it is rolled an outcome of 6 is 3 times more likely to occur than any other number. The die is rolled twice. Define

    E: A 3 appears on the first roll.

    F: A 6 appears on the second roll.

    Show that the events *E* and *F* are independent.

58. The records of Midwestern University show that in one semester, 38% of the students failed mathematics, 27% of the students failed physics, and 9% of the students failed mathematics and physics. A student is selected at random.

(a) If a student failed physics, what is the probability that he or she failed mathematics?

(b) If a student failed mathematics, what is the probability that he or she failed physics?

(c) What is the probability that he or she failed mathematics or physics?

59. In a certain population of people, 25% are blue-eyed and 75% are brown-eyed. Also, 10% of the blue-eyed people are left-handed and 5% of the brown-eyed people are left-handed.

(a) What is the probability that a person chosen at random is blue-eyed and left-handed?

(b) What is the probability that a person chosen at random is left-handed?

(c) What is the probability that a person is blue-eyed, given that the person is left-handed?

60. College Majors At a local college 55% of the students are female and 45% are male. Also 40% of the female students are education majors, and 15% of the males are education majors.

(a) What is the probability a student selected at random is male and an education major?

(b) What is the probability a student selected is an education major?

(c) What is the probability a student is female given the person is an education major?

61. Score Distribution Two forms of a standardized math exam were given to 100 students. The following are the results.

Score	Form A	Form B	Total
Over 80%	8	12	20
Under 80%	32	48	80
Total	40	60	100

(a) What is the probability that a student who scored over 80% took form A?

(b) What is the probability that a student who took form A scored over 80%?

(c) Show that the events "scored over 80%" and "took form A" are independent.

(d) Are the events "scored over 80%" and "took form independent?

62. ACT Scores The following data compare ACT scores students with their performance in the classroom [bas on a maximum 4.0 grade point average (GPA)].

GPA	Below 21	22–27	Above 28	Total
3.6–4.0	8	56	104	168
3.0–3.5	47	70	30	147
Below 3	47	34	4	85
Total	102	160	138	400

A graduating student is selected at random. Find t probability that

(a) The student scored above 28.

(b) The student's GPA is 3.6–4.0.

(c) The student scored above 28 with GPA of 3.6–4.0.

(d) The student's ACT score was in the 22–27 range.

(e) The student had a 3.0–3.5 GPA.

(f) Show that "ACT above 28" and "GPA below 3" are n independent.

63. E and F are independent events. Find $P(E|F)$ if $P(F) = 0$ and $P(E \cap F) = 0.2$.

64. E and F are independent events. Find $P(E)$ $P(E \cup F) = 0.6$ and $P(F) = 0.1$.

65. Shooting Free Throws A basketball player hits 70% of h free throws. Assuming independence on successive throw what is the probability of

(a) Missing the first throw and then getting 3 in a row?

(b) Making 10 free throws in a row?

66. Majoring in Business At the College at Old Westbury, 20 of the students are business majors and the rest major something else. Although 70% of the business majors ta Finite Mathematics, only 10% of the other majors ta Finite Mathematics. A student is chosen at random. She taking Finite Mathematics. What is the probability she is business major?

67. Three envelopes are addressed for 3 secret letters written invisible ink. A secretary randomly places each of the lette in an envelope and mails them. What is the probability th at least 1 person receives the correct letter?

68. Jones lives at O (see the figure). He owns 5 gas statio located 4 blocks away (dots). Each afternoon he checks one of his gas stations. He starts at O. At each intersecti he flips a fair coin. If it shows heads, he will head nor (N); otherwise, he will head toward the east (E). What the probability that he will end up at gas station G before coming to one of the other stations?

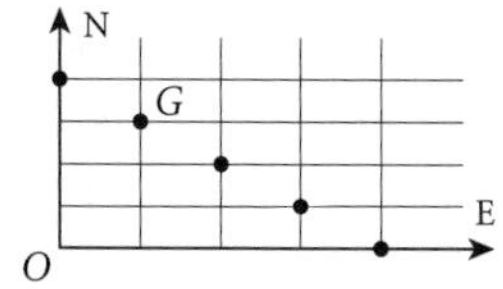

. **Defective Machine** The calibration of a filling machine broke, causing it to underfill 10 jars of jam. The jars were accidentally mixed in with 62 properly filled jars. All the jars look the same. Four jars are chosen from the batch and weighed. What is the probability

(a) All 4 jars are underweight?

(b) Exactly 2 jars are underweight?

(c) At most 1 jar is underweight?

. **Broken Calculators** Three broken calculators were inadvertently packed in a case of 12 calculators. Two were chosen from the case.

(a) What is the probability both are broken?

(b) What is the probability neither is broken?

(c) What is the probability at least 1 is broken?

. **Quality Control** In a factory three machines, A_1, A_2, and A_3, produce 55%, 30%, and 15% of total production, respectively. The percentage of defective output of these machines is 1%, 2%, and 3%, respectively. An item is chosen at random and it is defective.

(a) What is the probability that it came from machine A_1?

(b) From A_2?

(c) From A_3?

72. **Test for Cancer** A lung cancer test has been found to have the following reliability. The test detects 85% of the people who have cancer and does not detect 15% of these people. Among the noncancerous group it detects 92% of the people not having cancer, whereas 8% of this group are detected erroneously as having lung cancer. Statistics show that about 1.8% of the population has lung cancer. Suppose an individual is given the test for lung cancer and it detects the disease. What is the probability that the person actually has lung cancer?

73. **Advertising** Management believes that 1 out of 5 people watching a television advertisement about their new product will purchase the product. Five people who watched the advertisement are picked at random.

(a) What is the probability none of these people will purchase the product?

(b) What is the probability exactly 3 will purchase the product?

74. **Baseball** Suppose that the probability of a player hitting a home run is $\frac{1}{20}$. In 5 tries what is the probability that the player hits at least 1 home run?

75. **Tossing Coins** What is the expected number of heads when a coin is tossed 7 times?

76. **Recovery Rate** The recovery rate from a flu is 0.9. If 4 people have this flu, what is the probability that

(a) All will recover? (b) Exactly 2 will recover?

(c) At least 2 will recover?

Assume independence.

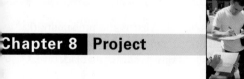

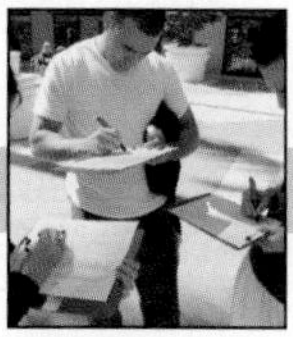

Chapter 8 Project

SKING SENSITIVE QUESTIONS USING CONDITIONAL PROBABILITY

your journalism class, a group project places you in charge determining what proportion of the students at your school e overweight. You decide to conduct a survey of a sample of e student body, and (of course) you will need to ask the rvey respondents the question "Are you overweight?" There a problem in being so direct, however. Even though the rvey is anonymous, some respondents might not want to swer this question truthfully. They might be afraid that you uld somehow figure out who they were by their responses, or ey just might not care to share that information with you. u could call a question such as "Are you overweight?" **sensitive question.** Nevertheless, you want to estimate the proportion of overweight students at your school. How can you get an idea of that proportion without driving some of your respondents to lie? It turns out that conditional probability provides a way to handle this problem.

Consider conducting the survey in the following manner: Before answering the sensitive question, the respondent flips a coin. We assume that it is a fair coin; that is, heads appears with probability $\frac{1}{2}$. If the flip is tails, the respondent is instructed to answer "Yes" to the sensitive question; if the flip is heads, the respondent is instructed to answer the question truthfully. Since no one except the respondent has any idea whether the flip was a head or a tail, no one except the respondent knows whether a "Yes" response means "the coin came up tails" or "I am overweight." In this way, the respondent might be more inclined to answer the question truthfully if required to do so.

Define the events:

E: The respondent answer "Yes"

H: The flip is a head

T: The flip is a tail

After you tabulate the results to your survey, you will know $P(E)$, the proportion of your respondents that answered "Yes."

1. Why are you interested in finding $P(E|H)$?
2. Find an equation for $P(E)$ that involves $P(E|H)$ and $P(E|T)$.
3. Explain why $P(E|T) = 1$; then solve the equation found in part 2 for $P(E|H)$.
4. If 82 of 100 respondents answered "Yes," what is your best estimate for the proportion of overweight students at your school?

Suppose that you want to get a bit more information: You want respondents to check one of the three boxes labeled "underweight," "less than 20 pounds overweight," or "more than 20 pounds overweight." Once again, use a coin-flipping strategy. If the flip is tails, the respondent is instructed to check the "more than 20 pounds overweight" box; if the flip is heads, the respondent is instructed to answer the question truthfull

Define the events:

A: The respondent answers "underweight."

B: The respondent answers "less than 20 pounds overweight."

C: The respondent answers "more than 20 pounds overweight."

H: The flip is heads.

T: The flip is tails.

5. Express $P(A|H)$ as an equation.
6. Express $P(B|H)$ as an equation.
7. Express $P(C|H)$ as an equation.

Suppose you survey 300 students and get the followi results:

Number checking "Underweight" 3

Number checking "Less than 20 pounds overweight" 5

Number checking "More than 20 pounds overweight" 22

8. What is your best estimate for the proportion of studen at your school who are underweight, less than 20 poun overweight, and more than 20 pounds overweight?
9. Write a one-page report that summarizes your findin and the methodology you used.

Mathematical Questions from Professional Exams

1. **Actuary Exam—Part II** If P and Q are events having positive probability in the same sample space S such that $P \cap Q = \varnothing$, then all of the following pairs are independent EXCEPT
   (a) $\varnothing$ and P (b) P and Q
   (c) P and S (d) P and $P \cap Q$
   (e) $\varnothing$ and the complement of P

2. **Actuary Exam—Part II** A box contains 12 varieties of candy and exactly 2 pieces of each variety. If 12 pieces of candy are selected at random, what is the probability that a given variety is represented?
   (a) $\dfrac{2^{12}}{(12!)^2}$ (b) $\dfrac{2^{12}}{24!}$ (c) $\dfrac{2^{12}}{\binom{24}{12}}$
   (d) $\dfrac{11}{46}$ (e) $\dfrac{35}{46}$

3. **Actuary Exam—Part II** What is the probability that a card hand drawn at random and without replaceme from a regular deck consists entirely of black cards?
   (a) $\dfrac{1}{17}$ (b) $\dfrac{2}{17}$ (c) $\dfrac{1}{8}$
   (d) $\dfrac{3}{17}$ (e) $\dfrac{4}{17}$

4. **Actuary Exam—Part II** Events S and T are independe with $\Pr(S) < \Pr(T)$, $\Pr(S \cap T) = \dfrac{6}{25}$, and $\Pr(S|T)$ - $\Pr(T|S) = 1$. What is $\Pr(S)$?
   (a) $\dfrac{1}{25}$ (b) $\dfrac{1}{5}$ (c) $\dfrac{5}{25}$
   (d) $\dfrac{2}{5}$ (e) $\dfrac{3}{5}$

5. **Actuary Exam—Part II** What is the least number of independent times that an unbiased die must be thrown to make the probability that all throws do not give the same result greater than .999?

(a) 3 (b) 4 (c) 5

(d) 6 (e) 7

6. **Actuary Exam—Part II** In a group of 20,000 men and 10,000 women, 6% of the men and 3% of the women have a certain affliction. What is the probability that an afflicted member of the group is a man?

(a) $\frac{3}{5}$ (b) $\frac{2}{3}$ (c) $\frac{3}{4}$

(d) $\frac{4}{5}$ (e) $\frac{8}{9}$

7. **Actuary Exam—Part II** An unbiased die is thrown 2 independent times. Given that the first throw resulted in an even number, what is the probability that the sum obtained is 8?

(a) $\frac{5}{36}$ (b) $\frac{1}{6}$ (c) $\frac{4}{21}$

(d) $\frac{7}{36}$ (e) $\frac{1}{3}$

8. **Actuary Exam—Part II** If the events S and T have equal probability and are independent with $\Pr(S \cap T) = p > 0$, then $\Pr(S) =$

(a) $\sqrt{p}$ (b) p^2 (c) $\frac{P}{2}$

(d) p (e) $2p$

9. **Actuary Exam—Part II** The probability that both S and T occur, the probability that S occurs and T does not, and the probability that T occurs and S does not are all equal to p. What is the probability that either S or T occurs?

(a) p (b) $2p$ (c) $3p$

(d) $3p^2$ (e) p^3

10. **Actuary Exam—Part II** What is the probability that a bridge hand contains 1 card of each denomination (i.e., 1 ace, 1 king, 1 queen, . . . , 1 three, 1 two)?

(a) $\frac{13!}{13^{13}}$ (b) $\frac{4^{13}}{\binom{52}{13}}$ (c) $\frac{\binom{52}{4}}{\binom{52}{13}}$

(d) $\left(\frac{1}{13}\right)^{13}$ (e) $\frac{13^4}{\binom{52}{13}}$

11. **Actuary Exam—Part II** What is the probability that 10 independent tosses of an unbiased coin result in no fewer than 1 head and no more than 9 heads?

(a) $\left(\frac{1}{2}\right)^9$ (b) $1 - 11\left(\frac{1}{2}\right)^9$ (c) $1 - 11\left(\frac{1}{2}\right)^{10}$

(d) $1 - \left(\frac{1}{2}\right)^9$ (e) $1 - \left(\frac{1}{2}\right)^{10}$

Statistics 9

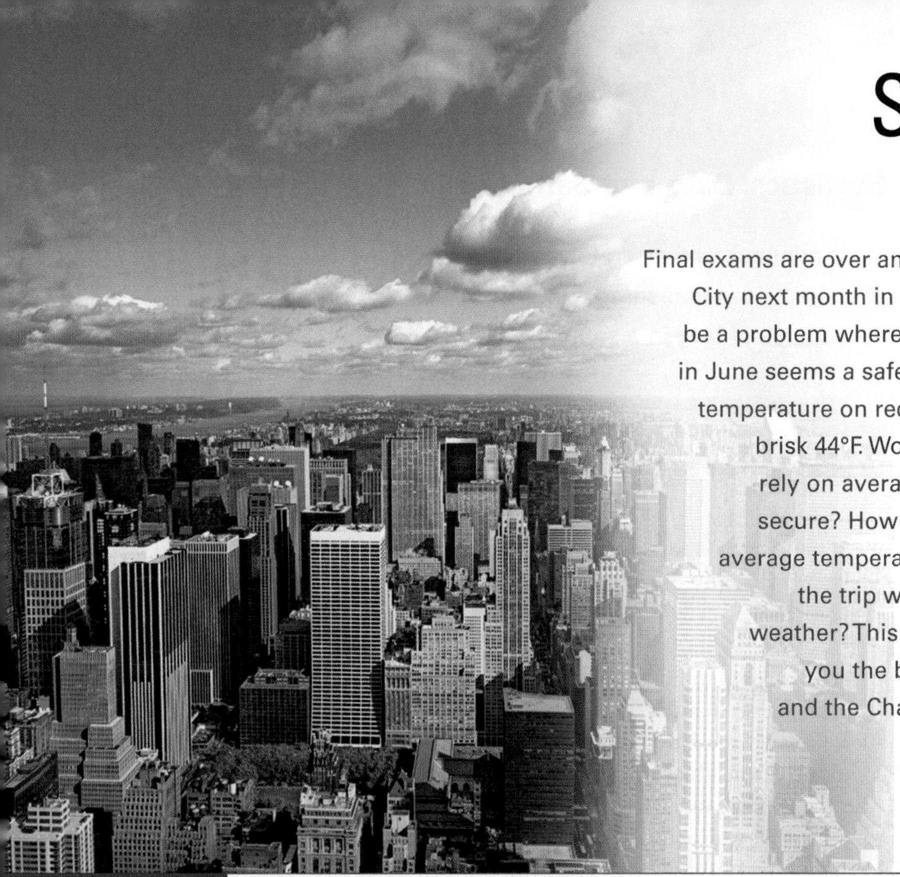

Final exams are over and a weekend trip to New York City next month in June is the plan. Weather can be a problem wherever one travels, but New York in June seems a safe choice. But is it? The highest temperature on record is 101°F and the lowest a brisk 44°F. Wow, what a difference! Can we rely on average temperatures to feel more secure? How do we use information about average temperatures to assess the likelihood the trip will not be affected by extreme weather? This chapter on statistics will give you the background to do an analysis, and the Chapter 9 Project will guide you. Have a great trip!

OUTLINE

A Look Back, A Look Forward

This chapter, like many of the chapters in this book, can be covered right away, but a better sense of the subject is obtained if probability from Chapter 7 is studied first. Rectangular coordinates, studied earlier in Chapter 1, are also used here.

This chapter provides only an introduction to statistics, an area of mathematics that is as rich and as varied as algebra and geometry. When you finish this chapter, you will have been exposed to many of the concepts studied in more detail in a full course, giving you a head start. If you don't intend to take a full course in statistics, then this chapter will give you an overview of the terminology and applications studied in statistics.

9.1 Introduction to Statistics: Data and Sampling

OBJECTIVES
1. Identify continuous and discrete variables (p. 506)
2. Obtain a simple random sample (p. 507)
3. Identify sources of bias in a sample (p. 507)

We have all heard of *statistics*, but do we really know what statistics is?

Definition

Statistics is the science of collecting, arranging, analyzing, and interpreting information to draw conclusions or answer questions.

By making observations, statisticians collect **data** in the form of measurements or count A measurable characteristic is called a **variable**. Variables fall into two general group If a variable measures an attribute or a trait of the individual being studied, it is **qualitative variable.** Eye color and favorite type of music are examples of qualitativ variables. Other variables provide numerical measures of the individual. These are calle **quantitative variables.** If a quantitative variable can assume any real value betwee certain limits, it is called a **continuous variable.** A quantitative variable is called **discrete variable** if it can assume only a finite set of values or as many values as there a whole numbers. Examples of continuous variables are weight, height, length, and tim Examples of discrete variables are the number of votes a candidate gets in an election an the number of new cars sold by a dealership.

1 Identify Continuous and Discrete Variables

It is important to be able to identify whether a variable is continuous or discrete becaus it determines the kind of statistical analysis that can be used.

EXAMPLE 1 Identifying Continuous and Discrete Variables

State the variable in the following experiments and determine whether it is continuou or discrete.

(a) Record the number of months in 2007 that a salesperson signs more than 10 ne accounts.

(b) Measure the length of time a smoker can blow into a tube before taking a breath.

(c) Count the number of defective parts produced by a certain machine in an hour.

SOLUTION

(a) The variable is the number of months. It is discrete because it can have only th values 0, 1, 2, 3, 4, 5, 6, 7, 8, 9, 10, 11, and 12.

(b) The variable is time. It is continuous because it can take on any value within certai limits, say from 0 to 90 seconds.

(c) The variable is the number of defective parts. It is discrete; it is a whole number. ■

NOW WORK PROBLEMS 5 AND 7.

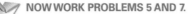

The set of observations made of the variable in an experiment is called **data**. In collecting data it is often impossible or impractical to observe an entire group, called the **population**. So instead of examining the entire population, often a small segment, called a **sample**, is chosen to be observed. It would be difficult, for example, to question all cigarette smokers in order to study the effects of smoking. Therefore, a sample of smokers is usually selected.

The method of selecting the sample is important if we want the results to be reliable. It is essential that the individuals in the sample have characteristics similar to those of the population they are intended to represent.

2 Obtain a Simple Random Sample

There are several ways to select a representative sample. The simplest and most reliable method of sampling is called *simple random sampling*. In a **simple random sample**, every member of the population has an equal probability of being selected into the sample.

EXAMPLE 2 Obtaining a Simple Random Sample

Janet is the president of the Marketing Society. She wants to know the opinion of the members concerning a proposed guest speaker. There are 150 members in the club, and rather than ask each one's opinion, Janet decides to ask a simple random sample of 10 members. How should Janet choose the sample?

SOLUTION Janet needs to choose 10 members of the Marketing Society, and she wants every member of the society to have an equal opportunity to be chosen. She writes each member's name on a separate sheet of paper and puts the papers in a box. She mixes the papers and selects 10 sheets. She asks the 10 members whose names she chose their opinions. ■

NOW WORK PROBLEM 17.

A more efficient way to select a simple random sample would be to assign a number to each member of the population. Then a random number generator or a list of random numbers can be used to identify the members that will make up the simple random sample.

COMMENT: Graphing utilities have random generators built into them. Check your user's manual to learn how to generate random numbers on your graphing utility. ■

3 Identify Sources of Bias in a Sample

If the sample is not chosen in a way that every member of the population has an equal probability of being selected, a **biased sample** could result. Bias occurs when a segment of the population is either overrepresented or underrepresented in the sample. The data collected from a biased sample often do not reflect the population accurately. For example, if we want to study the relationship between smoking cigarettes and lung cancer, we cannot choose a sample of smokers who all live in the same location. The individuals chosen might have characteristics peculiar to their environment that give a false impression with respect to all smokers.

EXAMPLE 3 Identify Sources of Bias in a Sample

Janet decides that it is too difficult to obtain a simple random sample of the membe of the Marketing Society, so she asks 10 freshmen from her Introduction to Marketin class their opinions about the proposed speaker. Identify a possible source of bias i this sample.

SOLUTION Janet polled only freshmen. As a result, sophomore, junior, and senior members of th Marketing Society were underrepresented in the sample. If the speaker had appeal to particular level of student, the results would not represent the opinion of the population. ■

NOW WORK PROBLEM 23.

When a sample is representative of a population, important conclusions about th population can often be inferred from analysis of the data collected. The phase of statistic dealing with conditions under which such inference is valid is called **inductive statistic** or **inferential statistics.** Since such inference cannot be absolutely certain, the language o probability is often used in stating conclusions. When a meteorologist makes a weathe forecast, weather data collected over a large region are studied; based on the study, th forecast is given in terms of probabilities. A typical forecast might be, "There is a 20% chance of rain tomorrow."

EXERCISE 9.1 Answers Begin on Page AN–44.

Concepts and Vocabulary

1. A measurable characteristic is called a(n) _____.

2. In a(n) _____ _____ _____ every member of the population has an equal probability of being selected.

3. ***True or False*** A discrete variable can assume any real valu between certain limits.

4. If, in a sample, a segment of the population is overrepresente or underrepresented, the sample is _____.

Skill Building

In Problems 5–16, identify the variable in each experiment and determine whether it is continuous or discrete.

5. A statistician observes the number of heads that occur when a coin is tossed 1000 times.

6. A statistician counts the number of red pieces of candy in each of 100 one-ounce bags of M&Ms.

7. The Environmental Protection Agency (EPA) determines the average gas mileage for each of 500 randomly chosen Honda Accords.

8. A General Electric (GE) quality control team measures how long it takes each of 500 lightbulbs to burn out.

9. A statistician measures the time a person who arrives at a neighborhood McDonald's between noon and 1:00 P.M. waits in line.

10. A pharmaceutical firm measures the time it takes for a drug to take effect.

11. A marketing analyst surveys 500 people and asks the numb of airplane flights they took in the last 12 months.

12. A sales manager counts the number of calls made in a da before a sale is made.

13. An urban planner counts the number of people who cross particular intersection between 1:00 P.M. and 3:00 P.M.

14. A carpet manufacturer counts the number of missed stitch in a 100-yard roll of carpeting.

15. A quality control team measures how long a phone battery las

16. A psychologist observes how many times a subject blin when being told a scary story.

In Problems 17–22, list some possible ways to choose random samples for each study.

17. A study to determine public opinion about a certain television program.

18. A study to determine favorite brands of cereal.

19. A study of the opinions of people toward Medicare.

20. A study to determine opinions about an election of a U.S president.

21. A study of the number of savings accounts per family in th United States.

22. A national study of the monthly budget for a family of fou

iscussion and Writing

3. The following is an example of a biased sample: In a study of political party preferences, poorly dressed interviewers obtained a significantly greater proportion of answers favoring Democratic party candidates in their samples than did their well-dressed and wealthier-looking counterparts. Give two more examples of biased samples.

4. In a study of the number of savings accounts per family, a sample of accounts totaling less than $10,000 was taken and, from the owners of these accounts, information about the total number of accounts owned by all family members was obtained. Criticize this sample.

25. It is customary for news reporters to sample the opinions of a few people to find out how the population at large feels about the events of the day. A reporter questions people on a downtown street corner. Is there anything wrong with such an approach?

26. In 1936 the *Literary Digest* conducted a poll to predict the presidential election. Based on its poll, it predicted the election of Landon over Roosevelt. In the actual election, Roosevelt won. The sample was taken by drawing the mailing list from telephone directories and lists of car owners. What was wrong with the sample?

9.2 Representing Qualitative Data Graphically: Bar Graphs; Pie Charts

OBJECTIVES

1 Construct a bar graph from data (p. 509)
2 Construct a pie chart from data (p. 510)
3 Analyze a graph (p. 513)

In this section we discuss qualitative data. The data as collected are called **raw data**. Raw data are often organized to make them more useful. The organization of data involves the presentation of the collected measurements or counts in a form suitable for determining logical conclusions. Usually tables or graphs are used to represent the collected data. There are two popular methods for graphically displaying qualitative data: **bar graphs** and **pie charts**. Both are used when the data can be separated into categories. A bar graph will show the number or the percent of data that is in each category, while a pie chart will show only the percent of data in each category.

1 Construct a Bar Graph from Data

EXAMPLE 1 Constructing a Bar Graph from Data

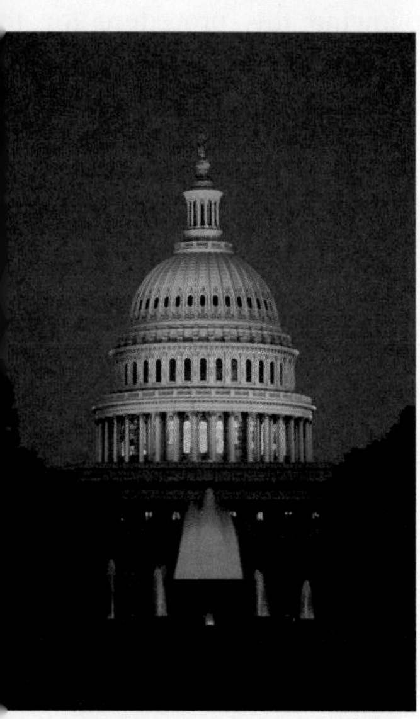

For the fiscal year 2009 (October 2008–September 2009), the federal government spent a total of $3.5176 trillion. The breakdown of expenditures (in billions of dollars) is given in Table 1. Construct a bar graph of the data.

TABLE 1

Social Security, Medicare, and other retirement	$1168.7
National defense, veterans, and foreign affairs	$794.0
Net interest (interest on the public debt)	$186.9
Physical, human, and community development	$553.3
Social programs	$741.2
Law enforcement and general government	$73.5
TOTAL	$3517.6

Source: U.S. Treasury Department.

SOLUTION A horizontal axis is used to indicate each category of spending and a vertical axis is used to represent the amount spent in each category. For each category of spending we draw rectangles of equal width whose heights represent the amount spent in the category. The rectangles will not touch each other. See Figure 1.

FIGURE 1

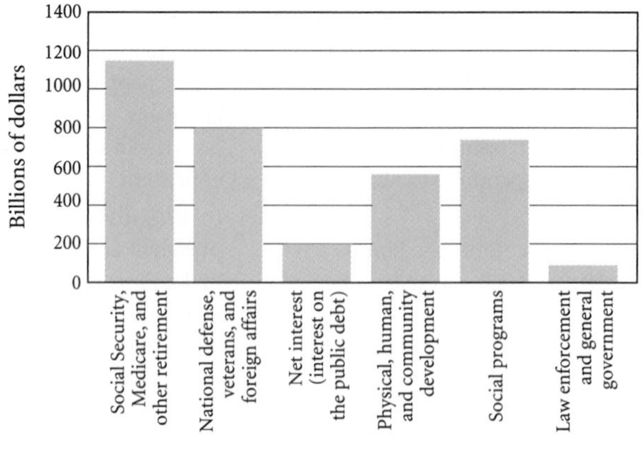

NOW WORK PROBLEM 5(a)–(c).

2 Construct a Pie Chart from Data

EXAMPLE 2 Constructing a Pie Chart from Data

Use the data given in Table 1 to construct a pie chart.

SOLUTION To construct a pie chart, a circle is divided into sectors, one sector for each categor of data. The size of each sector is proportional to the total amount spent. Sinc Social Security, Medicare, and other retirement is \$1168.7 billion and tot spending is \$3.5176 trillion = \$3517.6 billion, the percent of data in this category $\frac{1168.7}{3517.6} \approx 0.33 = 33\%$. Therefore, Social Security, Medicare, and other retirement wi make up 33% of the pie chart. Since a circle has 360°, the degree measure of the sector fo this category of spending is $0.33(360°) \approx 120°$. Following this procedure for th remaining categories of spending, we obtain Table 2.

TABLE 2

Category	Spending (in billions)	Percent of Total Spending	Degree Measure of Sector*
Social Security, Medicare, and other retirement	\$1168.7	33%	120°
National defense, veterans, and foreign affairs	\$794.0	23%	81°
Net interest (interest on the public debt)	\$186.9	5%	19°
Physical, human, and community development	\$553.3	16%	57°
Social programs	\$741.2	21%	76°
Law enforcement and general government	\$73.5	2%	8°
TOTAL	\$3517.6		

**The data in column 4 do not add up to 360° due to rounding.*

To construct a pie chart by hand, use a protractor to approximate the angles for each sector. See Figure 2.

FIGURE 2

Government Spending 2009

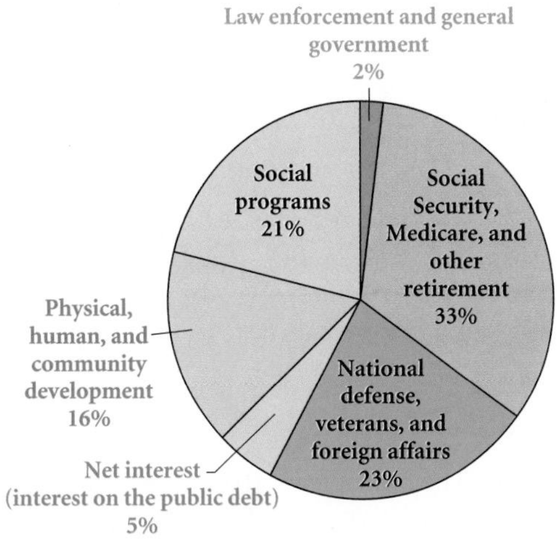

■

NOW WORK PROBLEM 7.

USING TECHNOLOGY

EXAMPLE 3 Using Excel to Construct a Pie Chart

Use Excel to construct a pie chart for the data in Table 1.

SOLUTION

STEP 1 Enter the data into Excel, highlight it, and under Insert select the Chart Wizard.

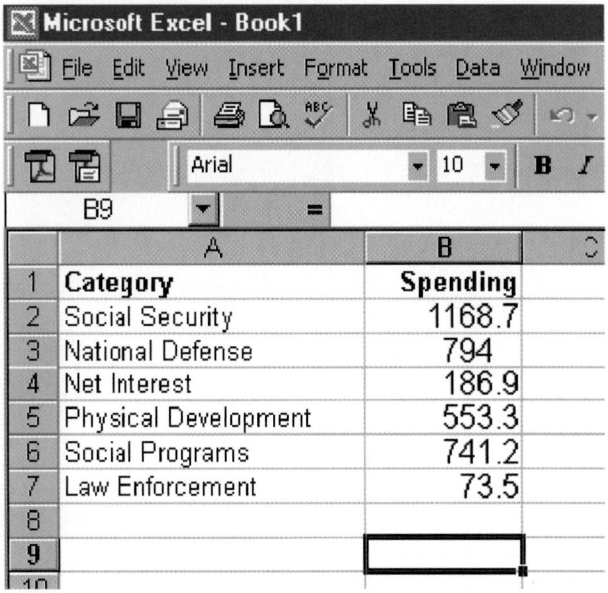

	A	B
1	**Category**	**Spending**
2	Social Security	1168.7
3	National Defense	794
4	Net Interest	186.9
5	Physical Development	553.3
6	Social Programs	741.2
7	Law Enforcement	73.5
8		
9		

STEP 2 For the chart type, select Pie.

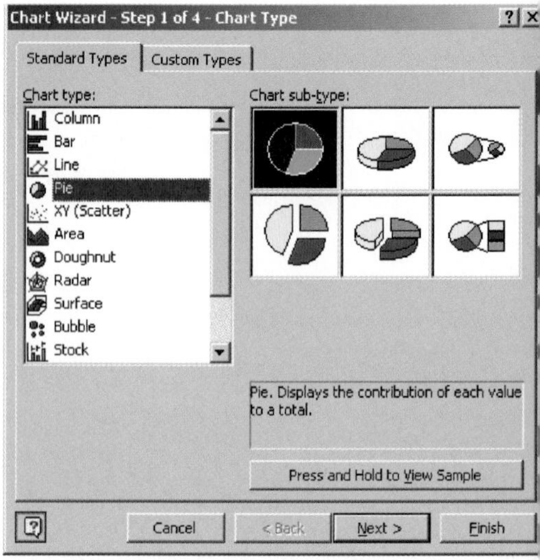

STEP 3 Click Next. The basic pie chart will appear. Click Next again. This screen provides the options for the pie chart. Click on Legend. Turn the legend off by clicking in the box Show Legend. Then highlight the Data Label tab.

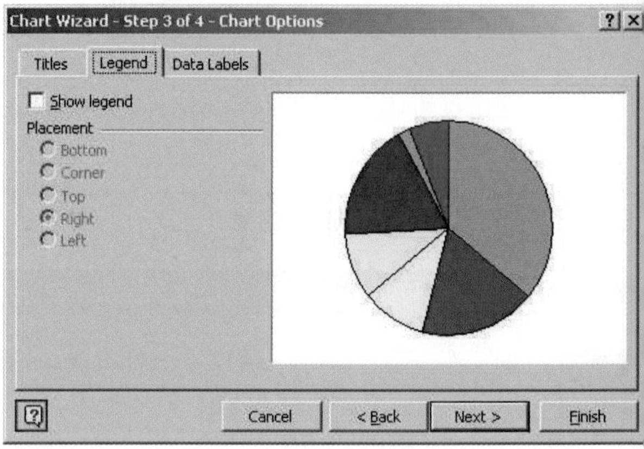

STEP 4 Click on Category name and Percentage.

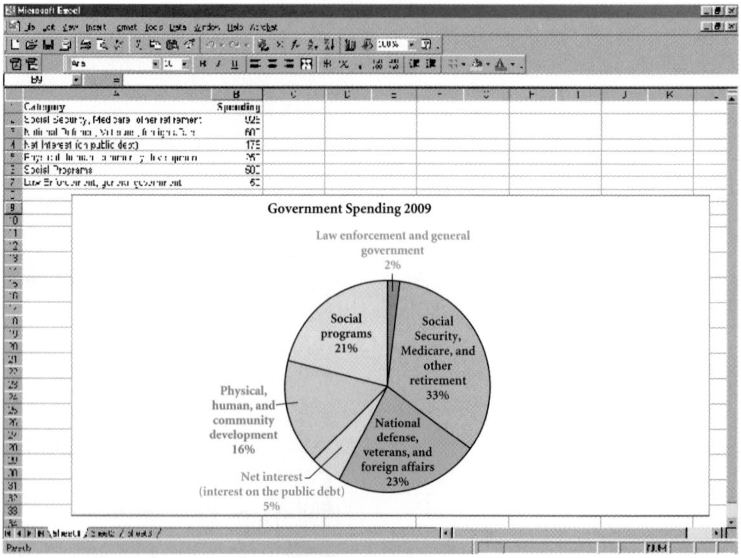

NOW WORK PROBLEM 7(b) USING EXCEL.

3 Analyze a Graph

One reason for graphing data by drawing bar graphs or pie charts is to quickly determine certain information about the data. The decision of which graph to use sometimes depends on preference but other times depends on the amount of data available. Bar graphs can be used whenever the data can be divided into categories, regardless if all categories are considered. However, pie charts can be created only if all possible categories of the variable under consideration are represented. Pie charts are most useful when comparing parts to the whole, whereas bar graphs are more useful for comparing the categories to each other but not to the whole.

EXAMPLE 4 Analyzing a Pie Chart

The pie chart in Figure 3 represents the sources of revenue for the United States federal government in its fiscal year 2009. Answer the questions below using the pie chart. Total revenue for the fiscal year 2009 was $2.103 trillion.

FIGURE 3

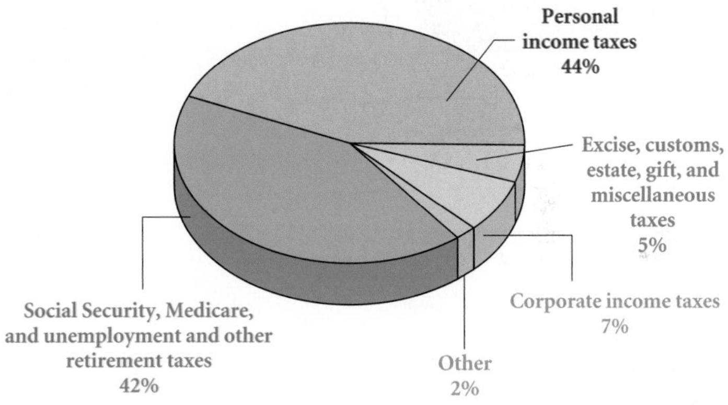

Source: U.S. Treasury Department.

(a) What is the largest source of revenue for the federal govenment? What is the amount?

(b) What is the smallest source of revenue for the federal government? What is the amount?

(c) How much revenue does the government collect from Social Security, Medicare, etc.?

SOLUTION **(a)** The largest source of revenue for the federal government is personal income taxes. The government collects

$$(0.44)(2.103 \text{ trillion}) = \$0.925 \text{ trillion} = \$925 \text{ billion}$$

from this source.

(b) The smallest source of revenue for the federal government is other sources. The government collects

$$(0.02)(2.103 \text{ trillion}) = 0.042 \text{ trillion} = \$42 \text{ billion}$$

from this source.

(c) The revenue collected from Social Security, Medicare, etc. is

$$(0.42)(2.103 \text{ trillion}) = (0.883 \text{ trillion}) = \$883 \text{ billion}$$

NOW WORK PROBLEM 15.

EXERCISE 9.2 Answers Begin an Page AN–44.

Concepts and Vocabulary

1. Two popular ways to display data that can be separated into categories are in _____ and _____.

2. ***True or False*** In a bar graph the width of the rectangle depends on the size of the category.

3. ***True or False*** In a pie chart a circle is divided into equa sectors, one for each category represented by the data.

4. ***True or False*** A bar graph can be used any time there ar categorical data, but a pie chart can be used only if all th categories under consideration are represented.

Skill Building

5. Family Income The data below represent median family income (in dollars) by region of the country in 2007.

Region	Median Family Income
Northeast	$51,624
Midwest	$48,014
South	$45,464
West	$56,291

Source: U.S. Bureau of the Census.

(a) Draw a bar graph of the data.
(b) Which region has the highest median income?
(c) Which region has the lowest median income?
(d) Discuss the use of a pie chart to represent this situation.

6. Family Income The data below represent the median family income (in dollars) by region of the country in 2005.

Region	Median Family Income
Northeast	$62,133
Midwest	$57,453
South	$51,352
West	$57,985

Source: U.S. Bureau of the Census.

(a) Draw a bar graph of the data.
(b) Which region has the highest median income?
(c) Which region has the lowest median income?
(d) Compare the results to those from Problem 5. Which region had the largest decrease in median income between 2005 and 2007?
(e) Discuss the use of a pie chart to represent this situation.

7. Population Distribution The data below represent th number of families (in thousands) by region of the countr in 2008.

Region	Number of Families
Northeast	54,123
Midwest	53,885
South	91,951
West	57,945

Source: U.S. Bureau of the Census.

(a) Draw a bar graph of the data.
(b) Draw a pie chart of the data.
(c) Which chart seems to summarize the data better? Why
(d) Which region has the most families?
(e) Which region has the fewest families?

8. Family Size The data below represent the number (in thou sands) of families by size of the family in 2008.

Family Size	Number of Families
2 people	35,797
3 people	17,431
4 people	14,972
5 people	6,952
6 people	2,382
7 or more	1,340

Source: U.S. Bureau of the Census.

(a) Draw a bar graph of the data.

(b) Draw a pie chart of the data.

(c) Which chart seems to summarize the data better? Why?

(d) What is the most common size of a family in the United States?

(e) What percent of families have 5 or more members?

(f) If you were a marketing consultant planning to market a product to families, what size families would you target? Why?

9. **Household Income** The data that follow represent the median income (in dollars) of families by type of household in 2007.

Family Household	Median Income
Married-couple families	$72,589
Female householder—no spouse	$30,296
Male householder—no spouse	$44,358

Source: U.S. Bureau of the Census.

(a) Draw a bar graph of the data.

(b) Which household type has the highest median income?

(c) Which household type has the lowest median income?

(d) Why do you think that there is such a large discrepancy?

10. **Household Income** The data that follow represent the median income (in dollars) of families by type of household in 2005.

Family Household	Median Income
Married-couple families	$66,067
Female householder—no spouse	$30,650
Male householder—no spouse	$46,756

Source: U.S. Census Bureau 2006, Current Population Survey.

(a) Draw a bar graph of the data.

(b) Which household type has the highest median income?

(c) Which household type has the lowest median income?

(d) Why do you think that there is such a large discrepancy?

(e) Comparing the data here with that in Problem 9, which group had the largest increase in median income from 2005 to 2007?

11. **Causes of Death** The data in the following table represent the causes of death for Americans in 2006.

Cause of Death	Number
Heart disease	631,636
Cancer	559,888
Cerebrovascular diseases	137,119
Respiratory diseases	124,583
Accidents	121,599
Diabetes mellitus	72,449
Alzheimer's disease	72,432
Influenza and pneumonia	56,326
Kidney failure	45,344
Septicemia	34,234
Suicide	33,300
All other causes	537,354

Source: *National Vital Statistics Reports*, Vol. 57, No. 14, April 12, 2009.

(a) Draw a bar graph of the data.

(b) Is it appropriate to draw a pie chart? Justify your answer.

(c) What was the leading cause of death among Americans in 2006?

12. **Automobile Costs** The following data represent the total amount spent (in billions of dollars) in the United States on automobiles and their maintenance in 2008.

Category	Expenditures
New motor vehicles	$184.5
Net purchases of used motor vehicles	$105.4
Motor vehicle parts and accessories	$52.4
Motor vehicle fuels, lubricants, and fluids	$386.4
Motor vehicle maintenance and repair	$158.5
Other motor vehicle services	$63

Source: U.S. Bureau of Economic Analysis.

(a) Draw a bar graph of the data.

(b) Draw a pie chart of the data.

(c) Which graph seems to summarize the data better?

(d) What is the largest expense?

(e) What portion of the expenditures is spent on maintenance and repair?

Applications

13. On-Time Performance The bar graph below represents the overall percentage of reported flight operations arriving on time in May 2010

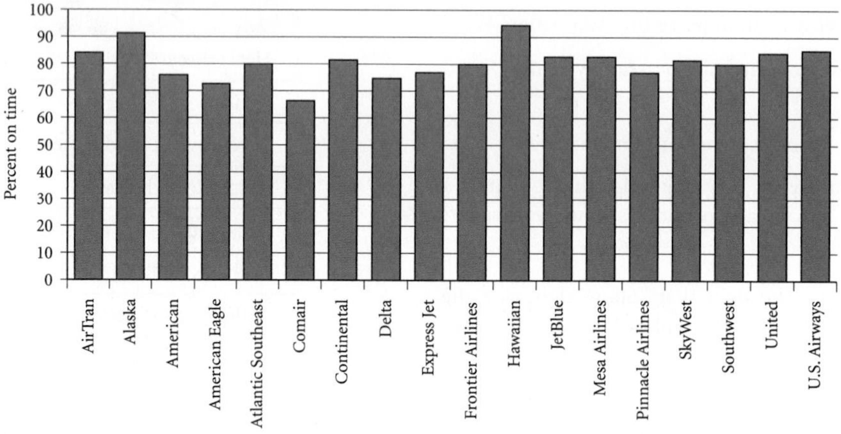

Source: Bureau of Transportation Statistics.

(a) Which airline has the highest percentage of on-time flights?

(b) Which airline has the lowest percentage of on-time flights?

(c) Estimate the percentage of United Airlines' flights that are on time.

14. Income Required for a Loan The bar graph that follows shows the minimum annual income required for a $150,000 loan using fixed-loan interest rates available on July 11, 2010. Taxes and insurance are assumed to be $300 monthly.

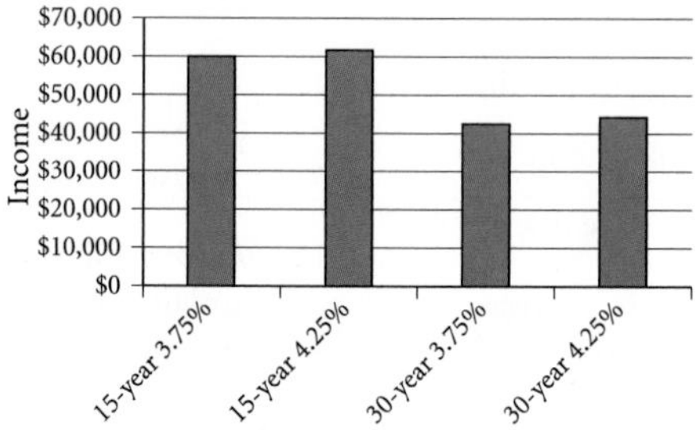

Source: www.interest.com.

(a) Which loan requires the most annual income? (b) Which loan requires the least annual income?

(c) Estimate the minimum annual income required for the loan types found in part (a) and part (b).

15. **Consumer Price Index** The Consumer Price Index (CPI) is an index that measures inflation. It is calculated by obtaining the price of a market basket of goods each month. The market basket, along with the percentages of each product (relative importance), for May 2010 is given in the following pie chart:

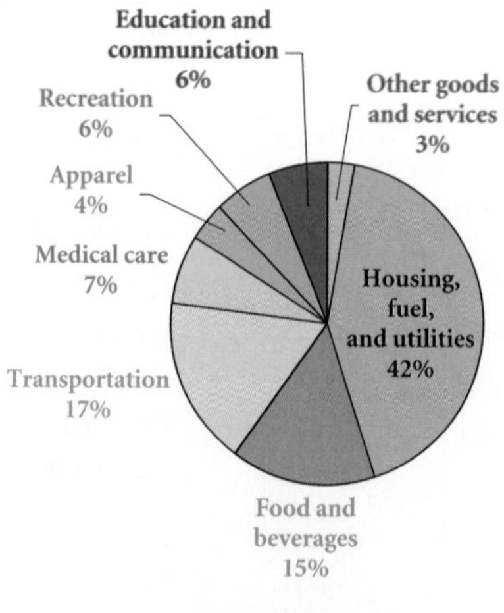

Source: Bureau of Labor Statistics.

(a) What is the largest component of the CPI?

(b) What is the smallest component of the CPI?

(c) Senior citizens spend about 17.2% of their cash incomes on medical care. Why do you think they feel the CPI weight for medical care is too low?

Source: Liqun Liu, Andrew J. Rettenmaier, and Zijun Wang. *The Rising Burden of Health Spending on Seniors.* National Center for Policy Analysis, Study No. 297, Feb. 2007.

16. **Asset Allocation** According to financial planners, an individual's investment mix should change over a person's lifetime. The longer an individual's time horizon, the more the individual should invest in stocks. Jim has 40 years to retirement, has a preference for growth, and can withstand significant fluctuation in market value, so his financial planner suggests that his retirement portfolio be diversified according to the asset mix provided in the pie chart.

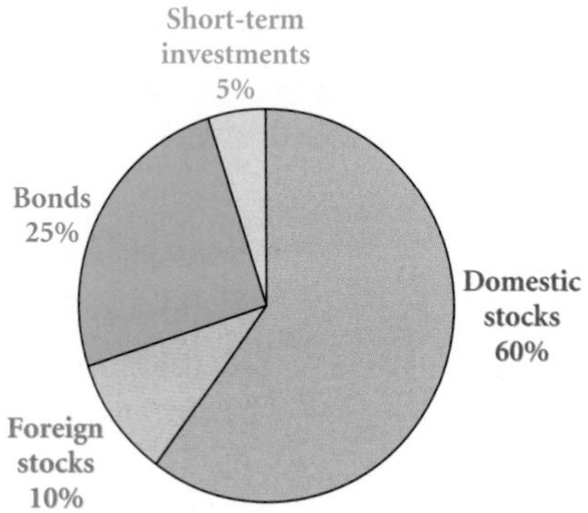

Source: Fidelity Investments

(a) How much should Jim invest in stocks?

(b) How much should Jim invest in bonds?

(c) The return on bonds over long periods of time is less than that of stocks. Explain why you think the financial planner recommended what she did for bonds.

9.3 Organizing and Displaying Quantitative Data

PREPARING FOR THIS SECTION *Before getting started, review the following:*

- Rectangular Coordinates (Section 1.1, pp. 2–3)

NOW WORK THE 'ARE YOU PREPARED?' PROBLEMS ON PAGE 528.

OBJECTIVES

1. Form a frequency table (p. 518)
2. Construct a line chart (p. 519)
3. Group data into class intervals (p. 519)
4. Build a histogram (p. 522)
5. Draw a frequency polygon (p. 526)
6. Draw an ogive (p. 527)
7. Identify the shape of a distribution (p. 528)

Often studies result in data represented by a large collection of numbers. If the data are to be interpreted, they must be organized. In this section we discuss the organization of quantitative data. One way to organize such data is by using a *frequency table.*

1 Form a Frequency Table

EXAMPLE 1 Forming a Frequency Table

Table 3 lists the weights of a random sample of 71 children selected from a group of 10,000.

(a) List the data from smallest to highest in a table.

(b) Form a frequency table of the data.

TABLE 3 WEIGHTS OF 71 STUDENTS, IN POUNDS

69	71	71	55	52	55	58	58	58	62	67	94
82	94	95	89	89	104	93	93	58	62	67	62
94	85	92	75	75	79	75	82	94	105	115	104
105	109	94	92	89	85	85	89	95	92	105	71
72	72	79	79	85	72	79	119	89	72	72	69
79	79	69	93	85	93	79	85	85	69	79	

SOLUTION **(a)** Certain information available from the sample becomes more evident once the data are ordered according to some scheme. If the 71 measurements are written from smallest to highest, we obtain Table 4.

TABLE 4

52	55	55	58	58	58	58	62	62	62	67	67
69	69	69	69	71	71	71	72	72	72	72	72
75	75	75	79	79	79	79	79	79	79	79	82
82	85	85	85	85	85	85	85	89	89	89	89
89	92	92	92	93	93	93	93	94	94	94	94
94	95	95	104	104	105	105	105	109	115	119	

(b) Once Table 4 has been constructed, it becomes easy to present the data in a **frequency table**. This is done as follows: Each weight that occurs is listed once. Tally marks are used to record each occurrence of a weight. Then the **frequency** f with which each weight occurs is recorded. See Table 5.

TABLE 5

Weight	Tally	Frequency, f	Weight	Tally	Frequency, f
52	/	1	85	𝍸 //	7
55	//	2	89	𝍸	5
58	////	4	92	///	3
62	///	3	93	////	4
67	//	2	94	𝍸	5
69	////	4	95	//	2
71	///	3	104	//	2
72	𝍸	5	105	///	3
75	///	3	109	/	1
79	𝍸 ///	8	115	/	1
82	//	2	119	/	1

■

NOW WORK PROBLEM 5(a).

2 Construct a Line Chart

EXAMPLE 2 Constructing a Line Chart

Use Table 5 to construct a line chart for the data given in Table 3.

SOLUTION A **line chart** is obtained using rectangular coordinates. The vertical axis (y-axis) denotes the frequency f and the horizontal axis (x-axis) denotes the weight data. Points are plotted according to the information in Table 5 and a vertical line is drawn from each point to the horizontal axis. See Figure 4.

FIGURE 4

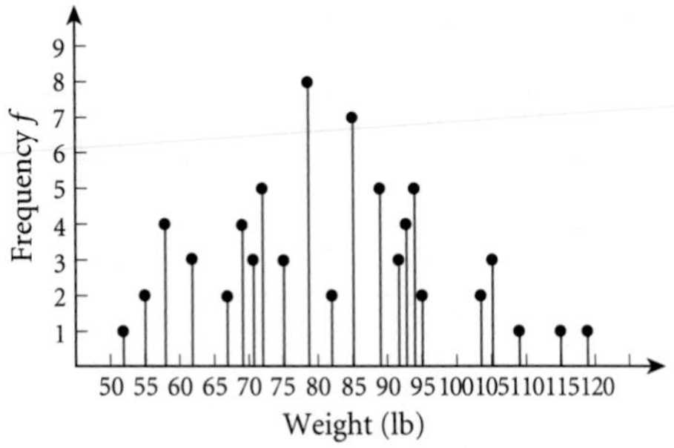

■

NOW WORK PROBLEM 5(b).

3 Group Data into Class Intervals

When data are collected and few repeated entries are obtained, the data are usually easier to organize by grouping them and constructing a *histogram*.

Table 6 lists the monthly electric bills, in dollars, of a sample of 71 residential customers, beginning with the smallest bill.

TABLE 6 MONTHLY ELECTRIC BILLS (IN DOLLARS)

52.30	55.61	55.71	58.01	58.41	58.51	58.91	62.33	62.50	62.71
67.13	67.23	69.51	69.67	69.80	69.82	71.34	71.65	71.83	72.15
72.22	72.41	72.59	72.67	75.11	75.71	75.82	79.03	79.06	79.09
79.15	79.28	79.32	79.51	79.62	82.32	82.61	85.09	85.13	85.25
85.31	85.41	85.51	85.58	89.21	89.32	89.49	89.61	89.78	92.41
92.63	92.89	93.05	93.19	93.28	93.91	94.17	94.28	94.31	94.52
94.71	95.32	95.51	104.31	104.71	105.21	105.37	105.71	109.34	115.71
119.38									

The first step in grouping data is to calculate the *range.*

Definition

The **range** of a set of numbers is the difference between the largest and the smallest number in the set. That is

$$\text{Range} = \text{Largest value} - \text{Smallest value}$$

For the data in Table 6 the range is

$$\text{Range} = 119.38 - 52.30 = 67.08$$

To group these data, we divide the range into intervals of equal size, called **class intervals.** Table 7 shows the data using 14 class intervals, each of size $5, beginning with the interval 50–54.99.

TABLE 7

	Class Interval	Tally	Frequency
1	50–54.99	/	1
2	55–59.99	~~////~~ /	6
3	60–64.99	///	3
4	65–69.99	~~////~~ /	6
5	70–74.99	~~////~~ ///	8
6	75–79.99	~~////~~ ~~////~~ /	11
7	80–84.99	//	2
8	85–89.99	~~////~~ ~~////~~ //	12
9	90–94.99	~~////~~ ~~////~~ //	12
10	95–99.99	//	2
11	100–104.99	//	2
12	105–109.99	////	4
13	110–114.99		0
14	115–119.99	//	2

Example 3 below shows how to group the data of Table 6 into class intervals of size \$10.

EXAMPLE 3 Grouping Data into Class Intervals

For the monthly electric bills listed in Table 6, group the data into class intervals each of size \$10.

SOLUTION First we determine the first class interval. Since the smallest bill is \$52.30 and we want a class interval of size \$10, we choose \$50 to \$59.99 as the first interval. The intervals will be from \$50.00 to \$59.99, from \$60.00 to \$69.99, up to the interval \$110 to \$119.99. We can stop here since the largest bill, \$119.38, is in this interval. Table 8 shows the result of using class intervals of size \$10.

TABLE 8

	Class Interval	Tally	Frequency
1	50–59.99	𝍸 //	7
2	60–69.99	𝍸 ////	9
3	70–79.99	𝍸 𝍸 𝍸 ////	19
4	80–89.99	𝍸 𝍸 ////	14
5	90–99.99	𝍸 𝍸 ////	14
6	100–109.99	𝍸 /	6
7	110–119.99	//	2

■

NOW WORK PROBLEM 5(c).

We use Tables 7 and 8 to introduce some vocabulary.

The class intervals shown in Tables 7 and 8 each begin at 50 and end at 119.99, so as to include all the data from Table 6. The first number in a class interval is called the **lower class limit**; the second number is called the **upper class limit**. We choose these limits so that each item in Table 6 can be assigned to one and only one class interval. The **midpoint** of a class interval is found by adding two consective lower class limits and dividing the sum by 2. The **class width** is the difference between consecutive lower class limits.

When the data are represented in the form of Table 7 (or Table 8), they are said to be **grouped data**. Notice that once raw data are converted to grouped data, it is impossible to retrieve or recover the original data. The best we can do is to choose the midpoint of each class interval as a representative for each class. In Table 8, for example, the actual electric bills of \$104.31, \$104.71, \$105.21, \$105.37, \$105.71, and \$109.34 are viewed as being represented by the midpoint of the class interval from 100 to 109.99, namely,

$$\frac{100 + 110}{2} = 105$$

Next we present the grouped data of Table 8 in a graph called a **histogram**.

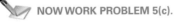

4 Build a Histogram

EXAMPLE 4 Building a Histogram

Build a histogram for the grouped data of Table 8.

SOLUTION To build a histogram for the data in Table 8, we construct a set of adjoining rectangle having as base the size of the class interval and as height the frequency of occurrence o data in that particular interval. The center of the base is the midpoint of each class interval. Figure 5 shows the histogram for the data in Table 8.

FIGURE 5

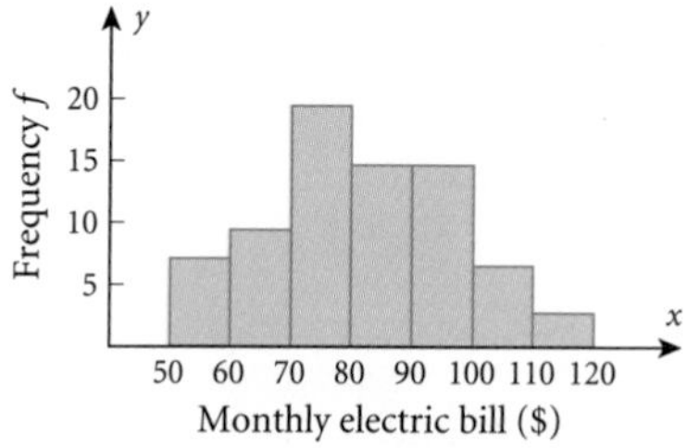

NOW WORK PROBLEM 5(d).

USING TECHNOLOGY

EXAMPLE 5 Using Excel

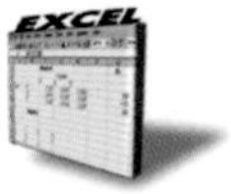

Use Excel to work Examples 3 and 4.

SOLUTION

STEP 1 Enter the data given in Table 6 in column B. [This is the tedious part. Usually the data will be entered electronically.]

In column D, enter the maximum value of the class intervals of the frequency table. These are called the **Bin values** in Excel.

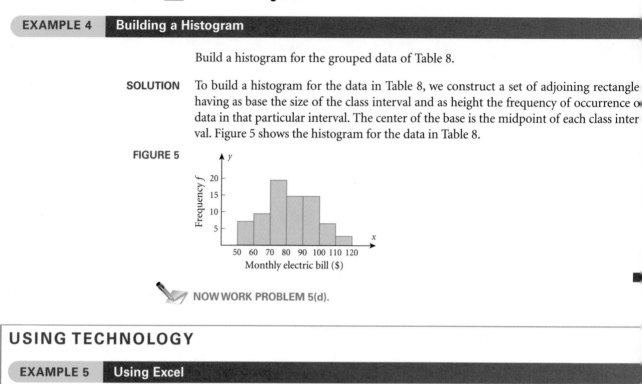

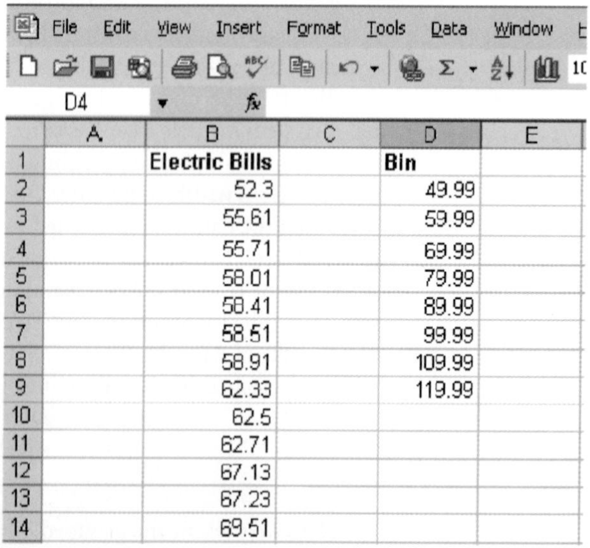

	A	B	C	D	E
1		Electric Bills		Bin	
2		52.3		49.99	
3		55.61		59.99	
4		55.71		69.99	
5		58.01		79.99	
6		58.41		89.99	
7		58.51		99.99	
8		58.91		109.99	
9		62.33		119.99	
10		62.5			
11		62.71			
12		67.13			
13		67.23			
14		69.51			

STEP 2 Click on Tools and then Data Analysis. (If Data Analysis isn't available, click on Add-ins.)

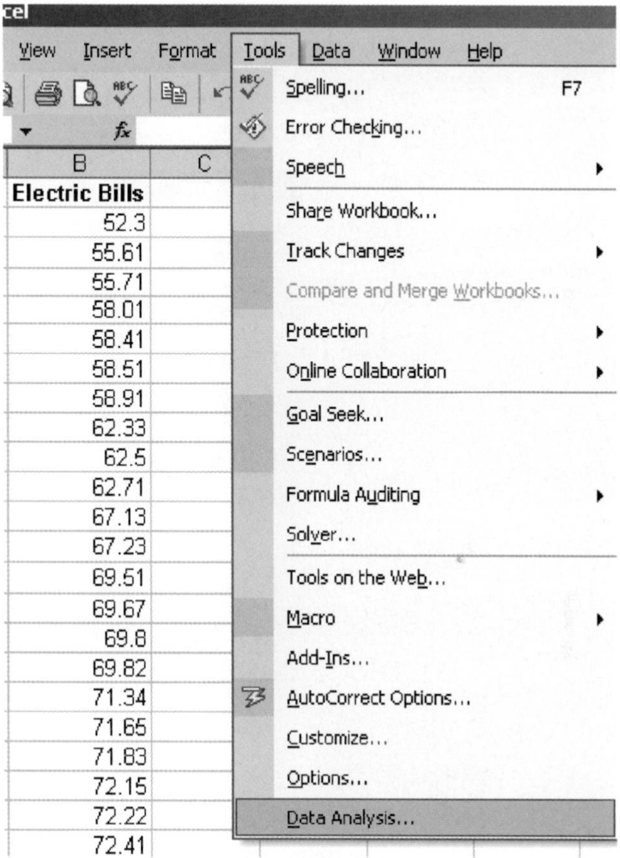

STEP 3 Highlight Histogram and click on OK.

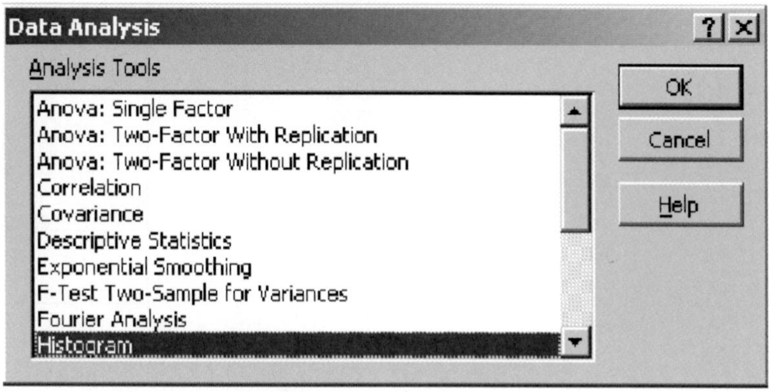

STEP 4 **Input Range** is the cells containing the data.
Bin Range is the cells containing the class intervals.
Output Range is the upper left cell where the frequency table will go.
New Worksheet Ply is the name of the histogram.
Cumulative Percentage gives the percentage of the data less than or equal to the bin value
Chart Output gives the histogram.
To enter the data, click and drag on the appropriate cells.

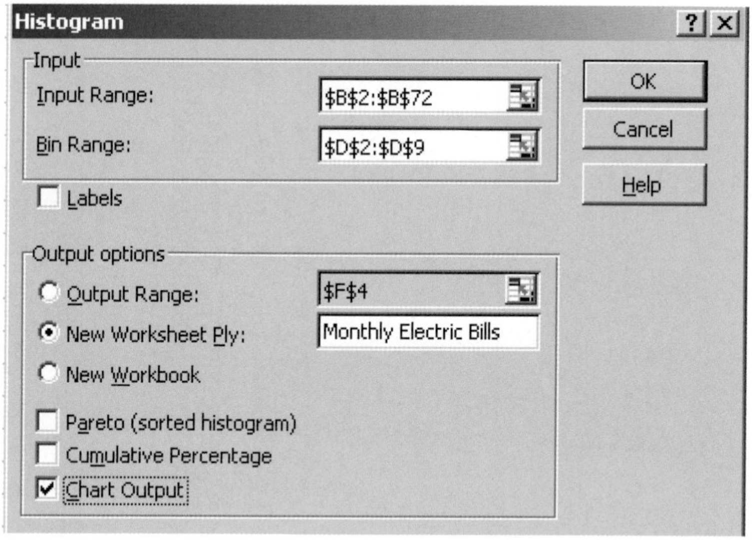

The frequency table and histogram are produced after clicking on OK.

Bin	*Frequency*
49.99	0
59.99	7
69.99	9
79.99	19
89.99	14
99.99	14
109.99	6
119.99	2
More	0

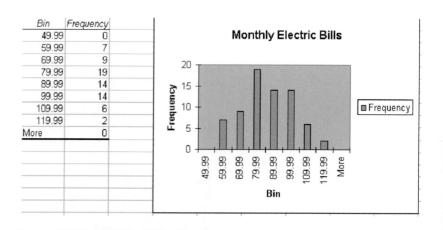

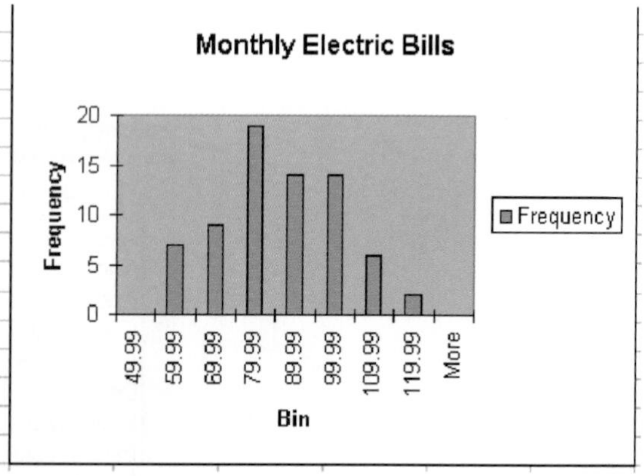

STEP 5 To eliminate the spaces between the bars, double click on one of the bars to get the screen below.

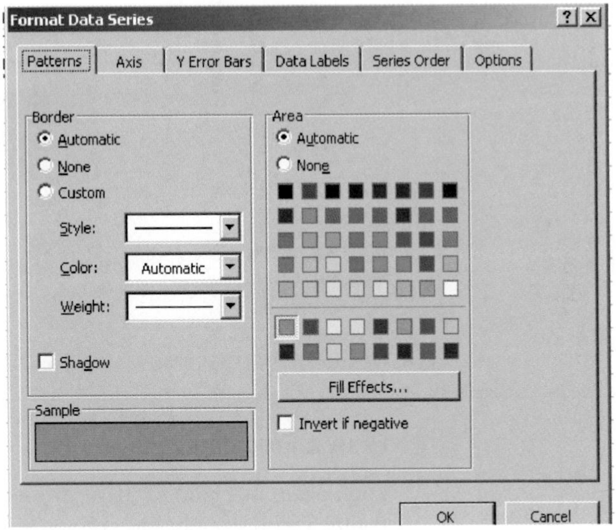

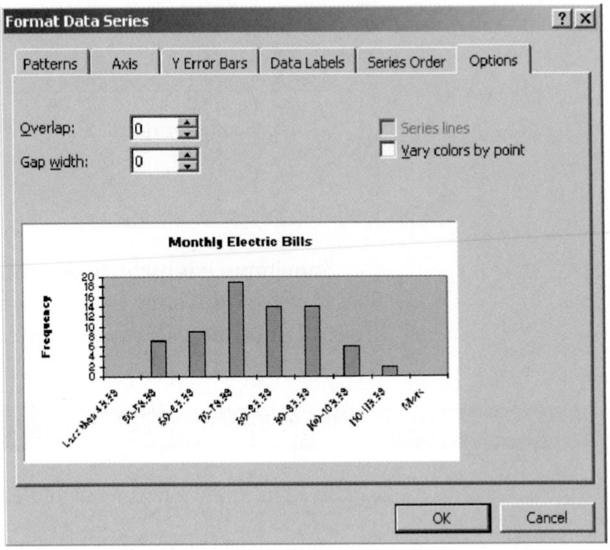

Select the Options tab and make the gap zero.
The final histogram is given next.

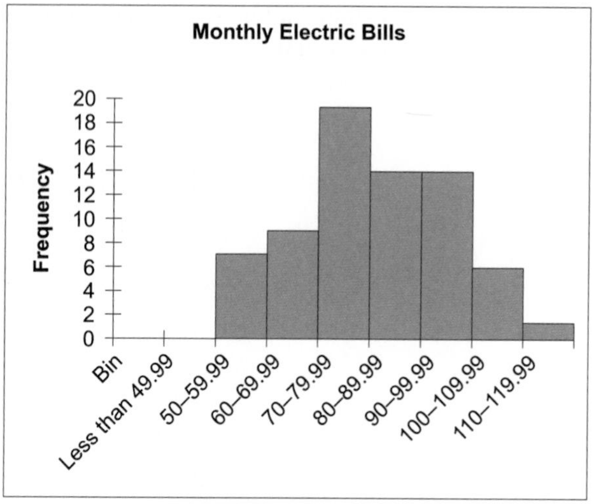

NOW WORK PROBLEMS 5(a), (b), (c), AND (d) USING EXCEL.

5 Draw a Frequency Polygon

Look again at Figure 5. If we connect the midpoints of the tops of the rectangles in Figure 5 with straight line segments, we obtain a line graph called a **frequency polygon.** Figure 6 shows the frequency polygon for the histogram obtained in Example 4.

FIGURE 6

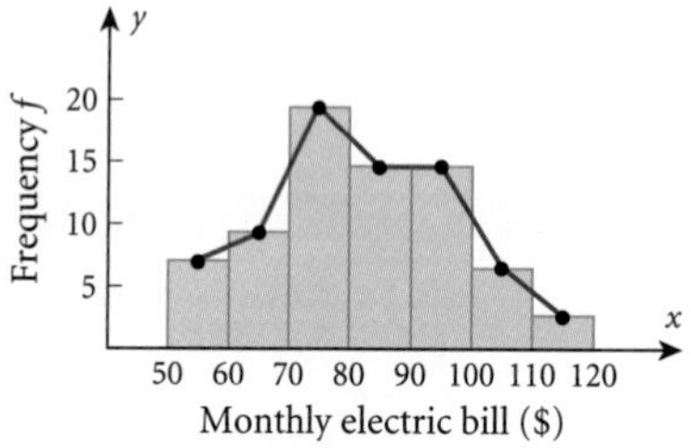

NOW WORK PROBLEM 5(e).

Sometimes it is useful to determine how many data points fall below a certain value. This is called *calculating cumulative frequencies,* and it is done by adding the frequencies from all class intervals less than or equal to the class interval being considered.

EXAMPLE 6 Creating a Cumulative Frequency Table

Create a cumulative frequency table for the data in Table 8.

SOLUTION We compute the cumulative frequency by determining the frequency of measurements at or below a given point. For the data in Table 8 we start in the lowest class interval ($50–$59.99) and note that there are 7 bills in this interval. So we put 7 in the column labeled *cf* (cumulative frequency) of Table 9 in the row for $50–$59.99. Next we add the number of bills in the second class interval ($60–$69.99), 9, to the cumulative total from the first interval 7 + 9 = 16, and place 16 in column *cf* of the second interval. We then continue with the third interval, adding 19 to 16, and place the sum, 35, in the *cf* column of the third interval, and so on. The last entry in the *cf* column should equal the total number of bills in the sample. The numbers in the *cf* column are called the **cumulative frequencies.**

TABLE 9

Class Interval	*f*	*cf*
50–59.99	7	7
60–69.99	9	16
70–79.99	19	35
80–89.99	14	49
90–99.99	14	63
100–109.99	6	69
110–119.99	2	71

NOW WORK PROBLEM 5(f).

6 Draw an Ogive

The graph in which the horizontal axis represents class intervals and the vertical axis represents cumulative frequencies is called an **ogive** (pronounced "Oh jive").

EXAMPLE 7 Draw an Ogive

Use the cumulative frequency table in Table 9 to draw an ogive.

SOLUTION Draw two axes and put the class intervals on the horizontal axis and the cumulative frequencies on the vertical axis. Plot 0 at the lower class limit of the smallest interval and then plot each cumulative frequency at the upper class limit of each class interval. Finally connect the points with straight line segments. See Figure 7.

FIGURE 7

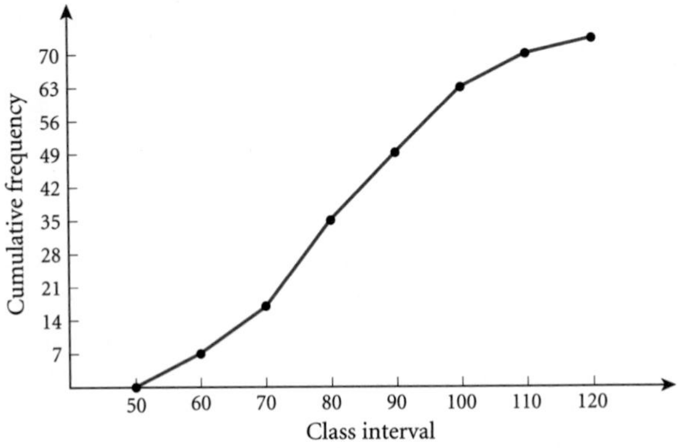

■

NOW WORK PROBLEM 5(g).

7 Identify the Shape of a Distribution

One advantage of using histograms to display data is that they show the shape o distribution. While many shapes are possible, two shapes are of particular intere When the data in the frequency table are evenly spaced around a central point, distribution is called **symmetric.**

Symmetric distributions are either bell shaped or uniform. Common examples symmetric distributions include IQ scores (bell shaped) and the outcomes when a f die is repeatedly tossed (uniform). Histograms depicting symmetric distributions shown in Figures 8(a) and (b).

FIGURE 8

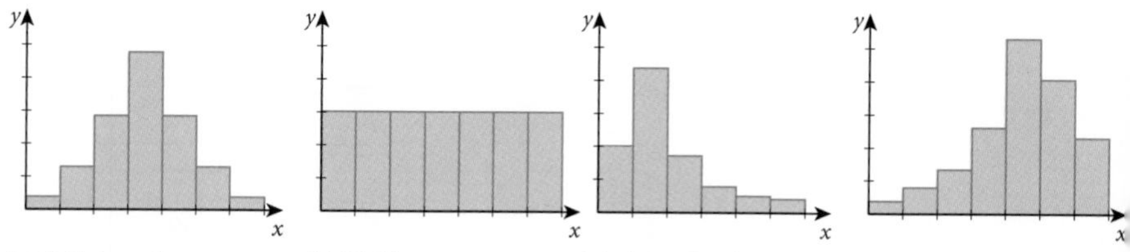

(a) Bell shaped (b) Uniform (c) Skewed right (d) Skewed left

Skewed distributions have most outcomes clustered at one end of the distributi with fewer values at the other end. When the sparse data are to the right of the cluster data, the distribution is called **skewed right**. A histogram of the distribution will have tail on the right. See Figure 8(c). A good example of a skewed right distribution is annu income. Most individuals have incomes clustered around \$46,000, but a few individua such as some CEOs and entertainers, have much greater incomes.

When the sparse data are to the left of the clusterd data, the distribution is call **skewed left** and a histogram of the distribution will have a longer tail on the left, as Figure 8(d). An example of a skewed left distribution is age of death in the United State

EXERCISE 9.3 Answers Begin on Page AN–45.

'Are You Prepared?' Problem Answers are given at the end of these exercises. If you get a wrong answer, read the pages listed in red.

1. List the quadrant in which each point is located. (pp. 2–3)
(a) $(-3, 4)$ (b) $(1, 5)$

Concepts and Vocabulary

2. ***True or False*** If data are skewed right, then the histogram has a long tail at the right end of the graph.

3. When grouping data, the range is divided into _____ _____ of equal size.

4. The graph of a cumulative frequency distribution is called a _____.

Skill Building

5. The following scores were made on a 60-item test:

25	30	34	37	41	42	46	49	53
26	31	34	37	41	42	46	50	53
28	31	35	37	41	43	47	51	54
29	32	36	38	41	44	48	52	54
30	33	36	39	41	44	48	52	55
30	33	37	40	42	45	48	52	

(a) Set up a frequency table for the above data.
(b) Draw a line chart for the data.
(c) Group the data into class intervals of size 2, beginnin with the interval 24–25.9.
(d) Build the histogram for the data.
(e) Draw the frequency polygon for this histogram.
(f) Find the cumulative frequencies.
(g) Draw the ogive.

6. Use the test scores given in Problem 5.
   (a) Group the data into class intervals of size 5, beginning with the interval 24–28.9.
   (b) Build the histogram for the data.
   (c) Draw the frequency polygon for the histogram.
   (d) Find the cumulative frequencies.
   (e) Draw the ogive.

7. Use Table 5 (p. 519) in the text.
   (a) Group the data into class intervals of size 5 beginning with the interval 50–54.9.
   (b) Build the histogram for the data.
   (c) Draw the frequency polygon for this histogram.
   (d) Find the cumulative frequencies.
   (e) Draw the ogive.

8. Use Table 5 (p. 519) in the text.
   (a) Group the data into class intervals of size 10, beginning with the interval 50–59.9. How many class intervals now exist?
   (b) Build the histogram for the data.
   (c) Draw the frequency polygon for this histogram.
   (d) Find the cumulative frequencies.
   (e) Draw the ogive.
   (f) Discuss the advantages/disadvantages of using a class interval size of 10 compared to a smaller interval size such as 5.

In Problems 9 and 10, identify the shape of the distribution as uniform, bell shaped, skewed right, or skewed left.

9.

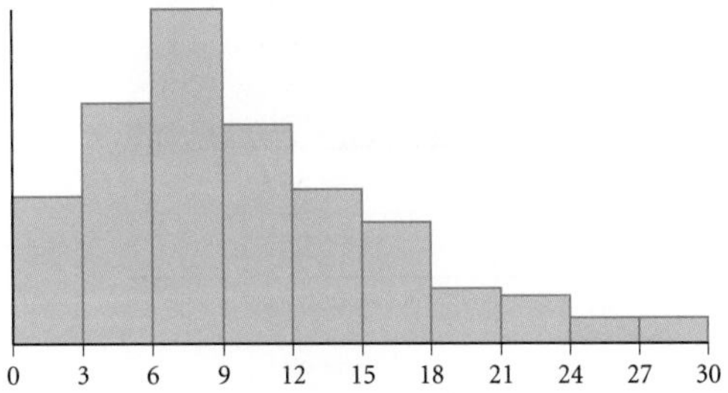

10.

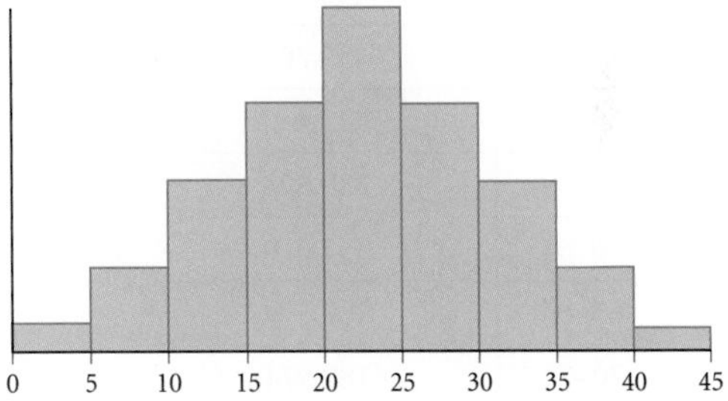

Applications

11. Licensed Drivers in Florida The histogram that follows gives the number of licensed drivers between the ages of 20 and 84 in the state of Florida in 2008.

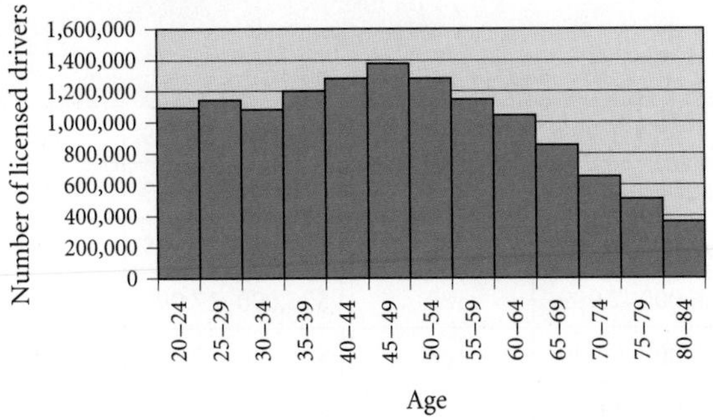

Source: Federal Highway Administration, Highway Statistics 2008.

(a) Determine the number of class intervals.
(b) What is the lower class limit of the first class interval? What is the upper class limit of the first class interval?
(c) Determine the class width.
(d) Approximately how many licensed drivers are 70 to 84 years old?
(e) Which class interval has the most licensed drivers?
(f) Which class interval has the fewest licensed drivers?
(g) Describe the shape of the distribution.
(h) Draw a frequency polygon for the given data.

12. IQ Scores The histogram below represents the IQ scores of students enrolled in College Algebra at a local university.

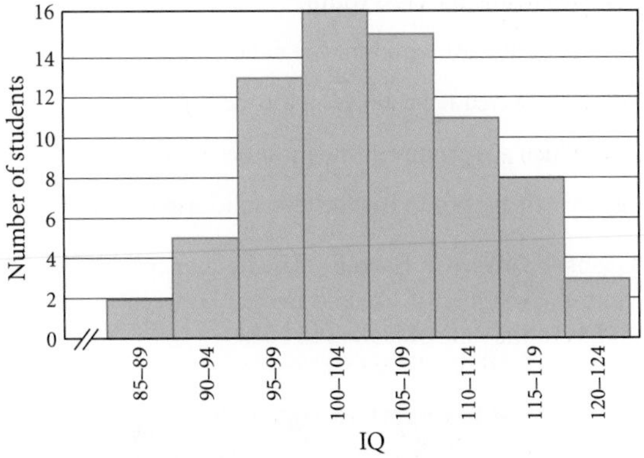

(a) Determine the number of class intervals.
(b) What is the lower class limit of the first class interval? What is the upper class limit of the first class interval?
(c) Determine the class width.
(d) How many students have an IQ between 100 and 104?
(e) How many students have an IQ above 110?
(f) How many students are enrolled in College Algebra?
(g) Describe the shape of the distribution.
(h) Draw a frequency polygon for the given data.

13. Licensed Drivers in Tennessee The frequency table below provides the number of licensed drivers between the ages of 20 and 84 in the state of Tennessee in 2008.

Age	Number of Licensed Drivers
20–24	348,587
25–29	372,032
30–34	365,111
35–39	404,931
40–44	406,831
45–49	435,706
50–54	422,420
55–59	380,898
60–64	331,010
65–69	250,679
70–74	182,974
75–79	133,888
80–84	91,318

Source: Federal Highway Administration, Highway Statistics 2008.

(a) Determine the number of class intervals.

(b) What is the lower class limit of the first class interval? What is the upper class limit of the first class interval?

(c) Determine the class width.

(d) Build the histogram for the data.

(e) Draw a frequency polygon for the data.

(f) Which age group has the most licensed drivers?

(g) Which age group has the fewest licensed drivers?

14. Licensed Drivers in Hawaii The frequency table below provides the number of licensed drivers between the ages of 20 and 84 in the state of Hawaii in 2008.

Age	Number of Licensed Drivers
20–24	73,199
25–29	85,097
30–34	78,820
35–39	83,318
40–44	83,966
45–49	89,520
50–54	88,939
55–59	82,912
60–64	67,048
65–69	43,570
70–74	30,668
75–79	24,088
80–84	16,195

Source: Federal Highway Administration, Highway Statistics 2008.

(a) Determine the number of class intervals.

(b) What is the lower class limit of the first class interva What is the upper class limit of the first class interval?

(c) Determine the class width.

(d) Build the histogram for the data.

(e) Draw a frequency polygon of the data.

(f) Which age group has the most licensed drivers?

(g) Which age group has the fewest licensed drivers?

15. Undergraduate Tuition The data below represent the cost undergraduate tuition and fees at all four-year public an private nonprofit colleges in the United States for 2006–200

Tuition (Dollars)	Number of 4-Year Colleges	Tuition (Dollars)	Number of 4-Year Colleges
$0–1,999	19	$20,000–21,999	117
$2,000–3,999	132	$22,000–23,999	100
$4,000–5,999	308	$24,000–25,999	83
$6,000–7,999	180	$26,000–27,999	53
$8,000–9,999	106	$28,000–29,999	45
$10,000–11,999	99	$30,000–31,999	36
$12,000–13,999	89	$32,000–33,999	46
$14,000–15,999	98	$34,000–35,999	32
$16,000–17,999	125	$36,000–37,999	6
$18,000–19,999	116		

Source: *Chronicle of Higher Education, Tuition and Fees,* 2006–2007

(a) Determine the number of class intervals.

(b) What is the lower class limit of the first class interval What is the upper class limit of the first class interval?

(c) Determine the class width.

(d) Build the histogram for the data.

(e) Draw a frequency polygon of the data.

(f) What range of tuition occurs most frequently?

. **Hourly Earnings** The following table gives the average hourly earnings of production workers in manufacturing in 2008 for 20 states.

State	Hourly Earnings	State	Hourly Earnings	State	Hourly Earnings
AK	17.31	AL	15.68	AR	14.17
CA	16.79	CT	21.42	DE	17.24
HI	18.93	IL	16.44	IN	18.47
KY	17.38	MA	20.33	ME	19.72
MI	22.11	NH	17.31	OH	19.37
PA	15.77	RI	13.94	TN	14.69
VT	16.51	WI	17.94		

Source: Northeast-Midwest Institute.

(a) Group the data into 5 class intervals of equal width beginning with the interval 13.00–14.99.

(b) Build the histogram for these data.

(c) Draw the frequency polygon for this histogram.

7. **Birth Rates** The following data give the 2007 birth rates per 1000 people for 20 states.

State	Birth Rate	State	Birth Rate	State	Birth Rate
AL	14	AZ	16.2	AK	16.2
CA	15.5	CT	11.9	DE	14.1
FL	13.1	GA	15.9	IL	14.1
KS	15.1	LA	15.4	MI	12.4
NV	16.1	NJ	13.4	OR	13.2
PA	12.1	SC	14.3	TN	14.1
VA	14.1	WI	13		

Source: *National Vital Statistics Reports*, Vol. 57, No. 12, March 2009.

(a) Group the data into 8 class intervals of equal width beginning with the interval 11.9–12.4.

(b) Build the histogram for these data.

(c) Draw the frequency polygon for this histogram.

18. **Birth Rates** The following data give the 2007 birth rates per 1000 women for women between the ages of 15 and 44 years old.

Age	Birth Rate
15–19	42.5
20–24	106.4
25–29	117.5
30–34	99.9
35–39	47.5
40–44	9.5

Source: *National Vital Statistics Reports*, Vol. 57, No. 12, March 18, 2009.

(a) Determine the number of class intervals.

(b) What is the lower class limit of the first class interval? What is the upper class limit of the first class interval?

(c) Determine the class width.

(d) Build the histogram for the data.

(e) Draw a frequency polygon of the data.

(e) What age group has the highest birth rate?

19. **HIV Death Rates** The following data give the 2007 death rates (number of deaths per 100,000 people) from HIV-related illnesses for 20 states.

State	Death Rate	State	Death Rate	State	Death Rate
AL	4.0	AZ	1.7	CA	3.0
CT	4.0	FL	8.4	HI	1.6
IL	2.4	IA	3.3	KY	1.3
MD	7.8	MI	1.9	MO	2.2
NV	3.1	NJ	5.7	NY	7.0
NC	4.2	OR	1.4	VA	3.0
WA	1.7	WI	0.9		

Source: *National Vital Statistics Reports*, Vol. 57, No. 12, March 18, 2009.

(a) Group the data into 5 class intervals of equal width beginning with the interval 0–1.9.

(b) Build the histogram for these data.

(c) Draw the frequency polygon for this histogram.

20. Cancer Death Rates The following data give the 2007 death rates (number of deaths per 100,000 people) attributed to cancer for 20 states.

State	Death Rate	State	Death Rate	State	Death Rate
AL	216.6	AZ	159.9	CA	150.5
CT	194.9	FL	219.6	HI	172.5
IL	187.6	IA	213.4	KY	228.5
MD	181.2	MI	199.4	MO	210.6
NV	168.8	NJ	196.8	NY	183.9
NC	192.9	OR	197.3	VA	181.6
WA	178.8	WI	195.7		

Source: *National Vital Statistics Reports*, Vol. 57, No. 1 March 18, 2009.

(a) Group the data into 4 class intervals of equal widt beginning with the interval 150–169.9.

(b) Build the histogram for these data.

(c) Draw the frequency polygon for this histogram.

'Are You Prepared?' Answers

1. (a) II (b) I

9.4 Measures of Central Tendency

OBJECTIVES
1. Find the mean of a set of data (p. 533)
2. Find the mean for grouped data (p. 534)
3. Find the median of a set of data (p. 535)
4. Find the median for grouped data (p. 535)
5. Identify the mode of a set of data (p. 538)

The idea of taking an *average* is familiar to practically everyone. Often we hear peopl talk about average salary, average height, average grade, and so on. The idea of averag is so commonly used it should not surprise you to learn that several kinds of average are used in statistics.

Averages are called *measures of central tendency* because they estimate the "center of the data collected. The three most common measures of central tendency are th *(arithmetic) mean, median,* and *mode.* Of these, the mean is the one most often used.

Definition

Arithmetic Mean

The **arithmetic mean**, or **mean**, of a set of n real numbers $x_1, x_2, \ldots x_n$ is defined as the number

$$\bar{x} = \frac{x_1 + x_2 + \cdots + x_n}{n} \tag{1}$$

where n is the number of items in the set.

1 Find the Mean of a Set of Data

EXAMPLE 1 Finding the Mean of a Set of Data

Professor Murphy tested 8 students in her Finite Mathematics class. The scores on the test were 100, 94, 85, 79, 70, 69, 65, and 62. What is the mean score?

SOLUTION To compute the mean $\bar{x}$, add up the 8 scores and divide by 8.

$$\bar{x} = \frac{100 + 94 + 85 + 79 + 70 + 69 + 65 + 62}{8} = \frac{624}{8} = 78$$ ■

NOW WORK PROBLEM 7(a).

An interesting fact about the mean is that the sum of deviations of each item from the mean is zero. In Example 1 the deviation of each score from the mean $\bar{x} = 78$ is $(100 - 78), (94 - 78), (85 - 78), (79 - 78), (70 - 78), (69 - 78), (65 - 78)$, and $(62 - 78)$. Table 10 lists each score, the mean, and the deviation from the mean. If we add the deviations from the mean, we obtain a sum of zero.

TABLE 10

Score	Mean	Deviation from Mean
62	78	−16
65	78	−13
69	78	−9
70	78	−8
79	78	1
85	78	7
94	78	16
100	78	22
		Sum of Deviations: 0

For any set of data the following result is true:

Theorem For any set of data, the sum of the deviations from the mean is zero.

2 Find the Mean for Grouped Data

EXAMPLE 2 Finding the Mean for Grouped Data

Find the mean for the grouped data given in Table 8 (repeated in the first two colum of Table 11 below).

SOLUTION Follow the steps below.

STEP 1 Find the midpoint (m_i) of each of the class intervals and enter the result in column 3 Table 11. For example, the midpoint of the class interval 80–89.99 is

$$\frac{80 + 90}{2} = 85$$

STEP 2 Multiply the entry m_i in column 3 by the frequency f_i for that class interval and enter t product in column 4, which is labeled $f_i m_i$.

STEP 3 Add the entries in column 4; sum of $f_i m_i = 5775$.

TABLE 11

Class Interval	f_i	m_i	$f_i m_i$
50–59.99	7	55	385
60–69.99	9	65	585
70–79.99	19	75	1425
80–89.99	14	85	1190
90–99.99	14	95	1330
100–109.99	6	105	630
110–119.99	2	115	230
	$n = 71$		$5775 =$ Sum of $f_i m_i$

STEP 4 The mean $\bar{x}$ is then computed by dividing the sum of $f_i m_i$ by the number n of entries. That i

$$\bar{x} = \frac{5775}{71} = 81.34$$

Definition

Arithmetic Mean for Grouped Data

For grouped data, the mean $\bar{x}$ is given as

$$\bar{x} = \frac{\Sigma f_i m_i}{n} \tag{2}$$

where

Σ denotes the sum of the entries $f_i m_i$

f_i = number of entries in the ith class interval

m_i = midpoint of ith class interval

n = number of items

When data are grouped, the original data are lost due to grouping. As a result, the mean obtained by using Formula (2) is only an approximation to the actual mean. The reason for this is that using Formula (2) amounts to computing the **weighted average** midpoint of the class intervals (weighted by the frequency of items in that interval).

COMMENT: Graphing utilities can be used to find measures of central tendency for both grouped and ungrouped data. Figure 9 illustrates the calculation of the mean for the grouped data in Example 2 on a TI-84 Plus. The midpoint for each interval was entered into L_1 and the frequency into L_2. Then one-variable statistics were computed using L_1 and L_2. The mean is $\bar{x} = 81.34$ (rounded to two decimal places). Consult your user's manual for the commands needed to compute measures of central tendency on your graphing utility.

FIGURE 9

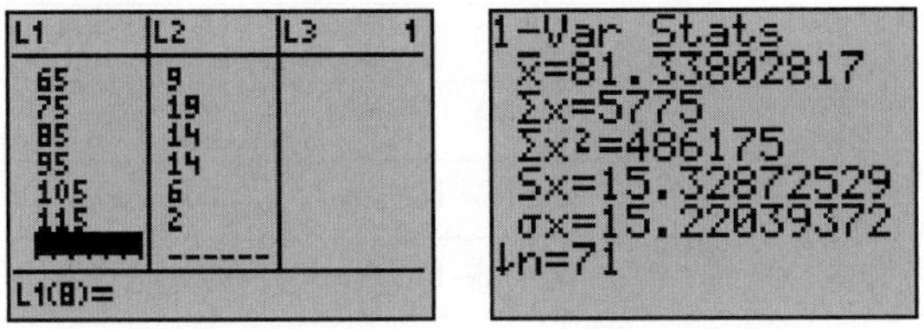

■

NOW WORK PROBLEM 19(a).

3 Find the Median of a Set of Data

Definition

Median

The **median** of a set of real numbers arranged in order of magnitude is the middle value if the number of items is odd, and it is the mean of the two middle values if the number of items is even.

EXAMPLE 3 Finding the Median of a Set of Data

(a) The set of data $\underbrace{2, 2, 3, 4}_{\text{4 items}}, 5, \underbrace{7, 7, 7, 11}_{\text{4 items}}$ has median 5.

(b) The set of data $\underbrace{2, 2, 3, 3}_{\text{4 items}}, 4, 5, \underbrace{7, 7, 7, 11}_{\text{4 items}}$ has median 4.5 since

$$\frac{4 + 5}{2} = 4.5$$

■

NOW WORK PROBLEM 7(b).

4 Find the Median for Grouped Data

Finding the median for grouped data requires more work. As with the mean, the median for grouped data only approximates the actual median that would have been obtained prior to grouping the data.

EXAMPLE 4 Finding the Median for Grouped Data

Find the median for the grouped data in Table 12 (based on Table 8, p. 521.)

TABLE 12

	Class Interval	Tally	Frequency
1	50–59.99	~~////~~ //	7
2	60–69.99	~~////~~ ////	9
3	70–79.99	~~////~~ ~~////~~ ~~////~~ ////	19
4	80–89.99	~~////~~ ~~////~~ ////	14
5	90–99.99	~~////~~ ~~////~~ ////	14
6	100–109.99	~~////~~ /	6
7	110–119.99	//	2

SOLUTION Follow the steps below.

STEP 1 Find the interval containing the median.

The median is the middle value when the 71 items are in ascending order. So tl median in this sample is the 36th entry. We start counting the tallies, beginning with th class interval 50–59.99, until we come as close as we can to 36. This brings us to the cla interval 70–79.99, since through this interval there are 35 data items. The median w lie in the next class interval, 80–89.99.

STEP 2 In the interval containing the median, count the number p of items remaining to reac the median.

Since we have accounted for 35 data items, there is $36 - 35 = 1$ item left, so $p =$

STEP 3 If f is the frequency for the interval containing the median and i is the class width, the the interpolation factor is

$$\text{interpolation factor} = \frac{p}{f} \cdot i$$

For the grouped data in Table 12, we have $p = 1, f = 14$, and $i = 10$, so

$$\text{interpolation factor} = \frac{P}{f} \cdot i = \frac{1}{14} \cdot (10) = 0.71 \qquad p = 1,\ f = 14,\ i = 10$$

STEP 4 The median M is

$$M = \begin{bmatrix} \text{lower limit of interval} \\ \text{containing the median} \end{bmatrix} + [\text{interpolation factor}]$$

For the grouped data in Table 12, the median M is

$$M = 80 + 0.71 = 80.71$$

Definition

Median for Grouped Data

The median M for grouped data is approximated by

$$M = \begin{bmatrix} \text{lower limit of interval} \\ \text{containing the median} \end{bmatrix} + \left[\frac{p}{f} \cdot i \right] \qquad (3)$$

where

p = number required to reach the median from the lower limit of the interval containing the median

f = frequency in this interval

i = class width

NOW WORK PROBLEM 19(b).

As with the mean, the median of a set of grouped data is an approximation to the actual median. For Example 4, if we go back to the original data listed in Table 6, we obtain the true median $M = 82.32$.

The median of a set of data or grouped data is sometimes called the **fiftieth percentile** and is denoted by Q_{50} to indicate that 50% of the data are less than or equal to it. Similarly, we can define Q_{25}, or the first quartile, as the point that separates the lowest 25% of the data from the upper 75%, and Q_{75}, or the third quartile, as the point that separates the lower 75% of the data from the upper 25% of the data.

USING TECHNOLOGY

EXAMPLE 5 Using Excel to Find the Mean and the Median

Use Excel to find the mean and the median of the data given in Table 6. (Refer to Example 5 Using Excel on page 522).

SOLUTION Excel has the statistical functions Average( ) and Median( ).

STEP 1 Click on the Insert function on the tool bar.

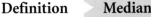

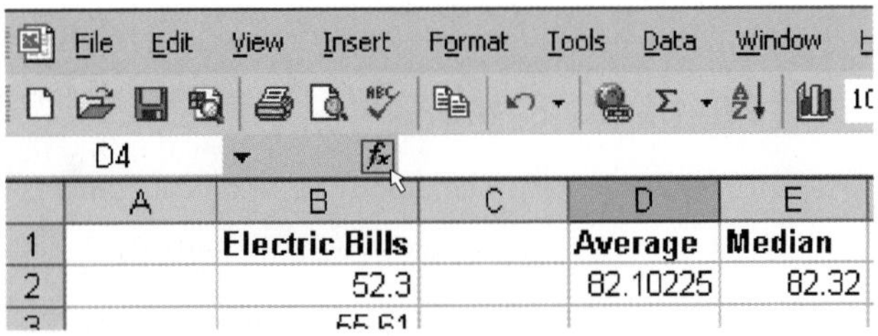

STEP 2 Select Statistical in the Category drop-down menu. Then highlight Average and click O
After STEPS 3 and 4, find the median by highlighting Median and clicking OK.

Insert Function	? ✕
Search for a function:	
Type a brief description of what you want to do and then click Go	Go
Or select a category: Statistical	▼
Select a function:	
AVEDEV	
AVERAGE	
AVERAGEA	
BETADIST	
BETAINV	
BINOMDIST	
CHIDIST	

AVERAGE(number1,number2,...)
Returns the average (arithmetic mean) of its arguments, which can be numbers or names, arrays, or references that contain numbers.

Help on this function | OK | Cancel |

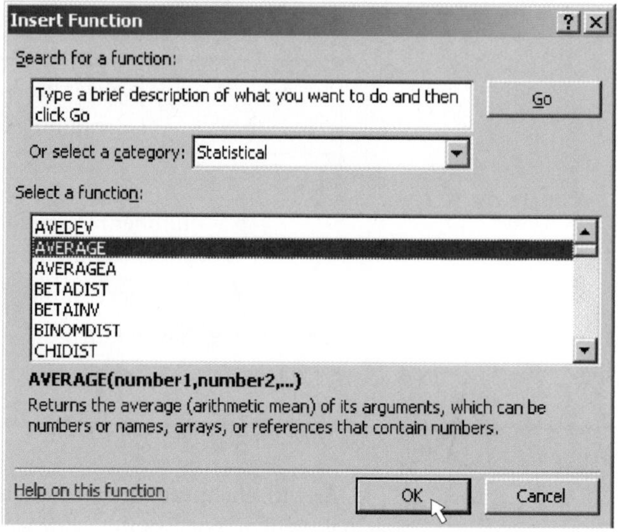

STEP 3 There are two ways to insert the cells that are used to find the average and the media.
  (a) Highlight the cells.
     or
  (b) Type the location of the first cell followed by a colon and the location of the last ce

Average	Median
=AVERAGE(B2:B72)	=MEDIAN(B2:B72)

STEP 4 The average and median are given below.

File	Edit	View	Insert	Format	Tools	Data	Window	

D4   fx

	A	B	C	D	E
1		Electric Bills		Average	Median
2		52.3		82.10225	82.32
3		55.61			

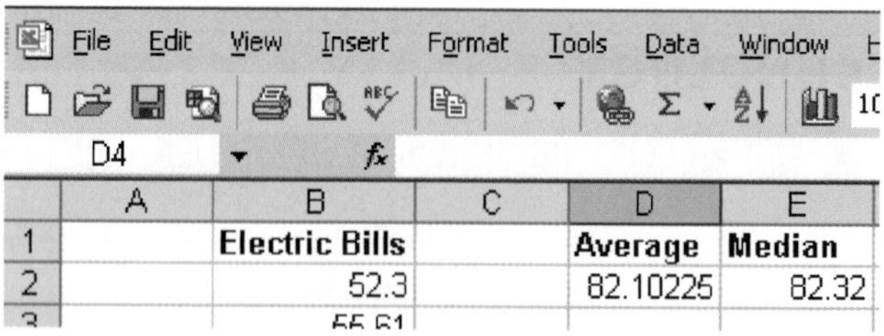

NOW WORK PROBLEMS 7(a) AND 7(b) USING EXCEL.

5   **Identify the Mode of a Set of Data**

A third commonly used measure of central tendency is called the *mode*.

Definition   **Mode**

The **mode** of a set of real numbers is the value that occurs with the greatest frequency.

The mode does not necessarily exist, and if it does, it is not always unique.

EXAMPLE 6 **Set of Data with No Mode**

The set of data 2, 3, 4, 5, 7, 15 has no mode, since each data value occurs only once. ■

EXAMPLE 7 **A Bimodal Set of Data**

The set of data 2, 2, 2, 3, 3, 7, 7, 7, 11, 15 has two modes, 2 and 7, since both 2 and 7 occur three times. This data set is called **bimodal**. ■

NOW WORK PROBLEM 7(c).

Sample Mean and Population Mean

Depending on the nature of the data, there are two types of means: the *sample mean* and the *population mean*.

Definition

Sample Mean

If the data used in computing the mean form a sample $x_1, x_2, x_3, \ldots x_n$, of n items taken from the population of N items, $n < N$, the **sample mean $\bar{x}$** is defined as the number

$$\bar{x} = \frac{x_1 + x_2 + x_3 + \cdots + x_n}{n} \tag{4}$$

Definition

Population Mean

If the data used in computing the mean are from the entire population $x_1, x_2, x_3, \ldots x_N$, of N items, the **population mean μ** (the Greek letter pronounced "mew") is defined as

$$\mu = \frac{x_1 + x_2 + x_3 + \cdots + x_N}{N} \tag{5}$$

Notice that Formula (4) and Formula (5) for the calculation of the mean are identical: In both cases the items are summed and the result is divided by the number of items. The distinction between a sample mean $\bar{x}$ and a population mean μ, namely, whether a sample of the population is used or whether the entire population is used, will be made clear in the next section.

EXERCISE 9.4 Answers Begin on Page AN–49.

Concepts and Vocabulary

1. Three common measures of central tendency are _____, _____, and _____.

2. ***True or False*** The mean found from grouped data only approximates the true mean.

3. ***True or False*** Some data have more than one mode.

4. When a set of data has two modes, it is called ______.

5. The symbol used to denote the population mean is ______, and the symbol used to denote the sample mean is ______.

6. ***True or False*** Before computing the mean, the data must put in numerical order.

Skill Building

In Problems 7–14, find (a) the mean, (b) the median, and (c) the mode (if it exists) of each set of data.

7. 21, 25, 43, 36

8. 16, 18, 24, 30

9. 55, 55, 80, 92, 70

10. 90, 80, 82, 82, 70

11. 65, 82, 82, 95, 70

12. 62, 71, 83, 90, 75

13. 48, 65, 80, 92, 80, 75

14. 95, 90, 91, 82, 80, 80

Applications

15. **Baseball Players** During 2010 spring training, the ages of the 40 men on the New York Yankees roster were:

33	24	27	24	35	28	37	38	40	25
29	33	24	38	27	36	24	34	26	30
25	26	29	29	33	27	29	27	24	23
25	24	25	25	25	27	23	23	23	26

Source: Major League Baseball.

(a) Find the mean age of the players.

(b) Find the median age of the players.

(c) Identify the modal age of the players if one exists.

16. **Baseball Players** During 2010 spring training, the ages of the 40 men on the Atlanta Braves roster were:

26	23	34	24	35	37	24	31	25	40
25	38	26	33	30	27	33	24	28	38
26	26	25	32	32	20	28	27	25	26
23	25	26	25	22	26	28	22	23	26

Source: Major League Baseball.

(a) Find the mean age of the players.

(b) Find the median age of the players.

(c) Identify the modal age of the players if one exists.

17. **Investments** If an investor purchased 50 shares of IBM stock at $85 per share, 90 shares at $105 per share, 120 shares at $110 per share, and another 75 shares at $130 per share, what is the mean cost per share?

18. **Revenue** If a farmer sells 120 bushels of corn at $4 per bushel, 80 bushels at $4.10 per bushel, 150 bushels at $3.90 per bushel, and 120 bushels at $4.20 per bushel, what is the mean income per bushel?

19. **Mother's Age** The following data give the number of births the United States in 2007 by the age of the mother for wom aged 15 to 45. (The numbers of births are given in thousand

Age of Mother	No. of Births
15–19	445
20–24	1082
25–29	1208
30–34	962
35–39	499
40–44	105

Source: *National Vital Statistics Reports*, March 2009.

(a) Find the mean age of a woman who gave birth in 20

(b) Find the median age of a woman who gave birth in 20

20. **Multiple Births** The following data give the number multiple births (two or more children) in the United States the year 2007 of mothers aged 15–45.

Age of Mother	No. of Births
15–19	7,201
20–24	25,115
25–29	37,270
30–34	40,444
35–39	25,860
40–44	6,202

Source: *National Vital Statistics Reports*, March 2009.

(a) Find the mean age of a mother whose pregnancy result in multiple births in 2007.

(b) Find the median age of a mother whose pregnan resulted in multiple births in 2007.

Licensed Drivers in Tennessee Refer to the data provided in Problem 13, Exercise 9.3. Find

(a) The mean age of a licensed driver in Tennessee.

(b) The median age of a licensed driver.

Licensed Drivers in Hawaii Refer to the data provided in Problem 14, Exercise 9.3. Find

(a) The mean age of a licensed driver in Hawaii.

(b) The median age of a licensed driver.

Undergraduate Tuition 2006–2007 Refer to the data provided in Problem 15, Exercise 9.3. Find the mean tuition at a four-year college in 2006–2007.

Birth Rates Refer to the data provided in Problem 18, Exercise 9.3. Find the mean age.

Faculty Salary The annual salaries of five faculty members in the mathematics department at a large university are \$34,000, \$35,000, \$36,000, \$36,500, and \$65,000.

(a) Compute the mean and the median.

(b) Which measure describes the situation more realistically?

(c) If you were among the four lower-paid members, which measure would you use to describe the situation? What if you were the one making \$65,000?

26. Administrative Professionals The distribution of the annual earnings of 3072 administrative professionals in 2008 by the International Association of Administrative Professionals is summarized in the table below. Find (a) the mean salary and (b) the median salary.

Annual Earnings. \$	Number
15,000–24,999	224
25,000–34,999	864
35,000–44,999	1120
45,000–54,999	640
55,000–64,999	224

9.5 Measures of Dispersion

OBJECTIVES

1. Find the standard deviation of sample data (p. 543)
2. Find the standard deviation for grouped data (p. 546)
3. Use the Empirical Rule to describe a bell-shaped distribution (p. 547)
4. Use Chebychev's theorem (p. 549)

EXAMPLE 1 Comparing Mean and Median for a Set of Sample Data

Find the mean and median for each of the following sets of sample data:

$$S_1: \quad 4, 6, 8, 10, 12, 14, 16$$
$$S_2: \quad 6, 7, 9, 10, 11, 13, 14$$

SOLUTION For S_1, the mean $\bar{x}_1$ and median M_1 are

$$\bar{x}_1 = \frac{4 + 6 + 8 + 10 + 12 + 14 + 16}{7} = \frac{70}{7} = 10 \qquad M_1 = 10$$

For S_2, the mean $\bar{x}_2$ and median M_2 are

$$\bar{x}_2 = \frac{6 + 7 + 9 + 10 + 11 + 13 + 14}{7} = \frac{70}{7} = 10 \qquad M_2 = 10$$

Notice that each set of scores has the same mean and the same median. Now look Figure 10. Do you see that the data in S_1 seem to be more spread out from the mean than those in S_2?

FIGURE 10

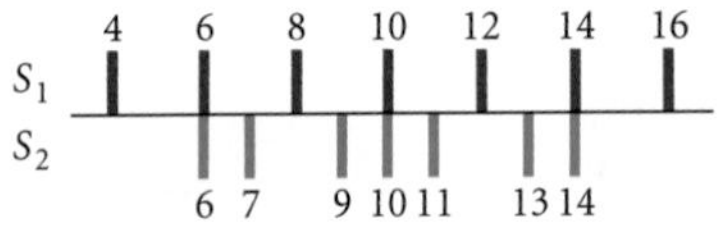

We seek a way to measure the extent to which scores are spread out. Such measu are called *measures of dispersion.*

Range

The simplest measure of dispersion is the **range,** which we have already defined as t difference between the largest value and the smallest value. For the sets S_1 and S_2 Example 1, we compute the range of S_1 to be $R_1 = 16 - 4 = 12$ and the range of S_2 be $R_2 = 14 - 6 = 8$. We conclude that the range is easy to find but that it depends only two data items so it is affected by extreme values in the data set, and it tells us no ing about how the rest of the data are spread out.

Variance

Another measure of dispersion, the **variance**, uses all the data values. The variance i measure of deviation from the mean. Recall that the sum of the deviations from the me adds up to zero, so just using deviations from the mean will not be of much use. Si some of the deviations are positive and some are negative, by squaring the deviations a finding their arithmetic mean, we obtain a positive number called the *variance.* Like t population mean and sample mean, we distinguish between the *population variance* a the *sample variance.*

Definition

Population Variance

If the data used are the entire population $x_1, x_2, x_3, \ldots x_N$, the **population variance σ^2**, the Greek letter sigma squared, is defined as

$$\sigma^2 = \frac{(x_1 - \mu)^2 + (x_2 - \mu)^2 + \cdots + (x_N - \mu)^2}{N} \qquad (1)$$

where

$$\mu = \frac{x_1 + x_2 + x_3 + \cdots + x_N}{N}$$

is the population mean and N is the number of items in the population.

Definition

Sample Variance

If the data used are a sample $x_1, x_2, x_3, \ldots x_n$ of the population, the **sample variance** s^2 is defined as

$$s^2 = \frac{(x_1 - \bar{x})^2 + (x_2 - \bar{x})^2 + \cdots + (x_n - \bar{x})^2}{n - 1} \tag{2}$$

where

$$\bar{x} = \frac{x_1 + x_2 + x_3 + \cdots + x_n}{n}$$

is the sample mean and n is the number of items in the sample.

Notice that we divide by $n - 1$ in the formula for the sample variance [Formula (2)]. The reason for this is that statisticians have found that when using the sample variance to estimate the population variance, a better agreement is obtained by dividing by $n - 1$.

EXAMPLE 2 Finding the Sample Variance for a Set of Sample Data

Calculate the sample variance for sets S_1 and S_2 of Example 1.

SOLUTION For $S_1, \bar{x} = 10$ and $n = 7$, so that

$$s_1^2 = \frac{(4-10)^2 + (6-10)^2 + (8-10)^2 + (10-10)^2 + (12-10)^2 + (14-10)^2 + (16-10)^2}{7-1} = 18.67$$

For $S_2, \bar{x} = 10$ and $n = 7$, so that

$$s_2^2 = \frac{(6-10)^2 + (7-10)^2 + (9-10)^2 + (10-10)^2 + (11-10)^2 + (13-10)^2 + (14-10)^2}{7-1} = 8.67$$

Since the sample variance for set S_1 is larger than the sample variance for set S_2, we conclude that the data in set S_1 are more widely dispersed than the data in set S_2, confirming what we saw in Figure 10. ■

1 Find the Standard Deviation of Sample Data

In computing the variance, we square the deviations from the mean. This means, for example, that if our data represent dollars, then the variance has the units "dollars squared." To remedy this, we use the square root of the variance, called the *standard deviation.*

Definition

Standard Deviation of Sample Data*

The **standard deviation** of a set $x_1, x_2 \ldots, x_n$ of n data items taken from the population is defined as

$$s = \sqrt{\frac{(x_1 - \bar{x})^2 + (x_2 - \bar{x})^2 + \cdots + (x_n - \bar{x})^2}{n - 1}} = \sqrt{\frac{\Sigma(x_i - \bar{x})^2}{n - 1}} \qquad (3)$$

where $\bar{x}$ is the sample mean and Σ means to add up all the deviations squared.

For the sample data in Example 1 the standard deviation for S_1 is

$$s_1 = \sqrt{\frac{36 + 16 + 4 + 0 + 4 + 16 + 36}{7 - 1}} = \sqrt{\frac{112}{6}} = \sqrt{18.67} = 4.32$$

and the standard deviation for S_2 is

$$s_2 = \sqrt{\frac{16 + 9 + 1 + 0 + 1 + 9 + 16}{7 - 1}} = \sqrt{\frac{52}{6}} = \sqrt{8.67} = 2.94$$

Again, the fact that the standard deviation of the set S_2 is less than the standard deviati of the set S_1 indicates that the data of S_2 are more clustered around the mean than tho of S_1.

EXAMPLE 3 Finding the Standard Deviation of Sample Data

Find the standard deviation for the sample data

100, 90, 90, 85, 80, 75, 75, 75, 70, 70, 65, 65, 60, 40, 40, 40

SOLUTION The sample mean is

$$\bar{x} = \frac{100 + 2 \cdot 90 + 85 + 80 + 3 \cdot 75 + 2 \cdot 70 + 2 \cdot 65 + 60 + 3 \cdot 40}{16} = 70$$

The deviations from the mean and their squares are computed in Table 13 on page 54 Based on Formula (3), the standard deviation is

$$s = \sqrt{\frac{4950}{15}} = 18.17$$

NOW WORK PROBLEM 7.

* *The* ***standard deviation*** σ ***for population data*** *is defined as*

$$\sigma = \sqrt{\frac{(x_1 - \mu)^2 + (x_2 - \mu)^2 + \cdots + (x_N - \mu)^2}{N}} = \sqrt{\frac{\Sigma(x_i - \mu)^2}{N}} \qquad (4)$$

where μ is the population mean and $x_1, x_2, x_3, \ldots, x_N$ is the population.

EXAMPLE 4 Finding the Standard Deviation of Sample Data

Find the standard deviation of the sample data

80, 80, 80, 80, 75, 75, 75, 75, 70, 70, 65, 65, 60, 60, 55, 55

SOLUTION Here the mean is $\bar{x} = 70$ for the 16 scores. Table 14 below gives the deviations from the mean and their squares. The standard deviation is

$$s = \sqrt{\frac{1200}{15}} = 8.94$$

■

These two examples show that although the samples have the same mean, 70, and the same sample size, 16, the data in Example 3 deviate further from the mean than do the data in Example 4.

In general, a relatively small standard deviation indicates that the measures tend to cluster close to the mean, and a relatively large standard deviation shows that the measures are widely scattered from the mean.

LE 13

cores, x	Deviation from the Mean, $x - \bar{x}$	Deviation Squared, $(x - \bar{x})^2$
40	−30	900
40	−30	900
40	−30	900
60	−10	100
65	−5	25
65	−5	25
70	0	0
70	0	0
75	5	25
75	5	25
75	5	25
80	10	100
85	15	225
90	20	400
90	20	400
100	30	900
an $\bar{x} = 70$	Sum = 0	Sum = 4950
$n = 16$		

TABLE 14

Scores, x	Deviation from the Mean, $x - \bar{x}$	Deviation Squared, $(x - \bar{x})^2$
55	−15	225
55	−15	225
60	−10	100
60	−10	100
65	−5	25
65	−5	25
70	0	0
70	0	0
75	5	25
75	5	25
75	5	25
75	5	25
80	10	100
80	10	100
80	10	100
80	10	100
Mean $\bar{x} = 70$	Sum = 0	Sum = 1200
$n = 16$		

2 Find the Standard Deviation for Grouped Data

To find the standard deviation for grouped data, we use the formula

$$s = \sqrt{\frac{(m_1 - \bar{x})^2 \cdot f_1 + (m_2 - \bar{x})^2 \cdot f_2 + \cdots + (m_k - \bar{x})^2 \cdot f_k}{n - 1}} = \sqrt{\frac{\Sigma[(m_i - \bar{x})^2 \cdot f_i]}{n - 1}} \qquad (5)$$

where $m_1, m_2, \ldots, m_k$ are the class midpoints; $f_1, f_2, \ldots, f_k$ are the respective frequencies of each class interval; n is the number of data items, that is, $n = f_1 + f_2 + \cdots + f_k$; and $\bar{x}$ is the sample mean.

EXAMPLE 5 Finding Standard Deviation for Grouped Data

Find the standard deviation for the grouped data given in Table 8, page 521, a repeated below in Table 15.

TABLE 15

	Class Interval	Frequency
1	50–59.99	7
2	60–69.99	9
3	70–79.99	19
4	80–89.99	14
5	90–99.99	14
6	100–109.99	6
7	110–119.99	2

SOLUTION We have already found (see Example 2, p. 534) that the mean for this grouped data is

$$\bar{x} = 81.34$$

The class midpoints are 55, 65, 75, 85, 95, 105, and 115. The deviations of the mean fro the class midpoints, their squares, and the products of the squares by the respecti frequencies are listed in Table 16.

TABLE 16

Class Midpoint	f_i	$m_i - \bar{x}$	$(m_i - \bar{x})^2$	$(m_i - \bar{x})^2 \cdot f_i$
55	7	−26.34	693.80	4856.6
65	9	−16.34	267.00	2403.0
75	19	−6.34	40.20	763.8
85	14	3.66	13.40	187.6
95	14	13.66	186.60	2612.4
105	6	23.66	559.80	3358.8
115	2	33.66	1133.00	2266.0
Sum	71			16,448.2

Using Formula (5), the standard deviation is

$$s = \sqrt{\frac{16{,}448.2}{70}} = 15.33$$

■

NOW WORK PROBLEM 13.

A little computation shows that the sum of the deviations of the approximate mean from the class midpoints is not exactly zero. This is due to the fact that we are using an approximation to the mean. Remember, we cannot compute the exact mean for grouped data.

SING TECHNOLOGY

EXAMPLE 6 Using Excel to Find Standard Deviation

Use Excel to find the standard deviation of the grouped data given in Table 15.

SOLUTION

File Edit View Insert Format Tools Data Window Help

G2 =SQRT(F9/70)

	A	B	C	D	E	F	G	H
1	*f*	*m*	*f* · *m*	*m* -*x* (bar)	(*m* -*x* (bar))^2	(*m* -*x* (bar))^2 (f)	Standard	Deviation
2	7	55	385	-26.34	693.80	4856.57	15.33	
3	9	65	585	-16.34	267.00	2402.96		
4	19	75	1425	-6.34	40.20	763.72		
5	14	85	1190	3.66	13.40	187.54		
6	14	95	1330	13.66	186.60	2612.34		
7	6	105	630	23.66	559.80	3358.77		
8	2	115	230	33.66	1133.00	2265.99		
9	71		5775			16447.89		

■

COMMENT: Finding standard deviations by hand is extremely tedious. We have just seen that Excel calculates the standard deviation quickly and accurately. Graphing utilities are also designed to compute the standard deviation of a set of data points. Figure 11 illustrates the standard deviation of the grouped data from Table 15 on a TI-84 Plus. Here the class midpoints are put in L_1 and the class frequencies are put in L_2, as in Figure 11(a). The standard deviation is given by *Sx*, seen in Figure 11(b). Note that the population standard deviation is also calculated and is given by σx. Consult your user's manual to find the method of calculating standard deviations on your graphing utility.

FIGURE 11

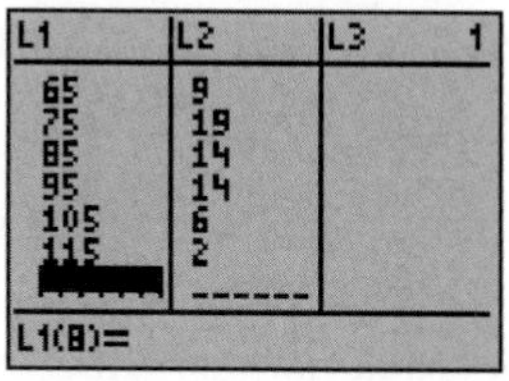

(a)

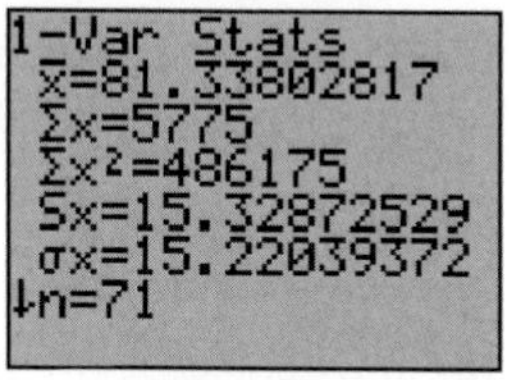

(b)

■

3 Use the Empirical Rule to Describe a Bell-Shaped Distribution

If the data being analyzed have a distribution that is bell shaped, the **Empirical Rule** describes the percentage of outcomes that are within *k* standard deviations of the mean.

Theorem **The Empirical Rule**

If a distribution is bell shaped, then

- Approximately 68% of the data are within one standard deviation of the mean.
- Approximately 95% of the data are within two standard deviations of the mean.
- Approximately 99.7% of the data are within three standard deviations of the mean.

The Empirical Rule can be used for both sample data and population da provided that the distribution is roughly bell shaped. See Figure 12.

FIGURE 12

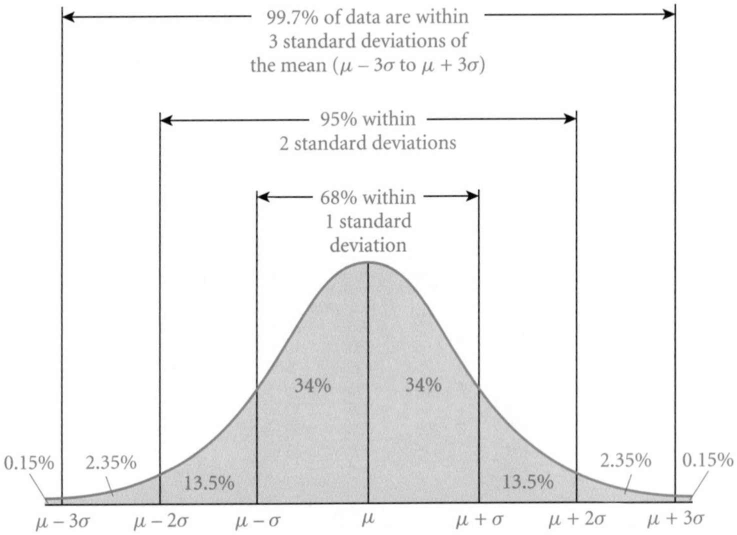

EXAMPLE 7 Using the Empirical Rule

The histogram of the data in Table 8 is approximately bell shaped. Refer to Figure (p. 522).

(a) According to the Empirical Rule, what percentage of electric bills should be with two standard deviations of the mean?

(b) Using the Empirical Rule, determine the percentage of electric bills that are betwe $50.68 and $112.00.

(c) Using the raw data in Table 6 (p. 520), calculate the exact percentage of electric bi that are between $50.68 and $112.00.

SOLUTION **(a)** According to the Empirical Rule, approximately 95% of the electric bills should within two standard deviations of the mean.

(b) Since $50.68 is two standard deviations below the mean and $112.00 is two standa deviations above the mean, the Empirical Rule states that approximately 95% of t bills are between $50.68 and $112.00.

(c) Using Table 6 (p. 520), we find that 69 (97%) of the customers surveyed had electr bills between $50.68 and $112.00. This is close to the percentage predicted by t Empirical Rule.

NOW WORK PROBLEM 27.

4 Use Chebychev's Theorem

Suppose we are analyzing an experiment with numerical outcomes and that the experiment has population mean μ and population standard deviation σ. We wish to estimate the probability that a randomly chosen outcome lies within k units of the mean.

Chebychev's Theorem*

For any distribution of numbers with population mean μ and population standard deviation σ, the probability that a randomly chosen outcome lies between $\mu - k$ and $\mu + k$ is at least $1 - \frac{\sigma^2}{k^2}$.

EXAMPLE 8 Using Chebychev's Theorem

Suppose that an experiment with numerical outcomes has population mean 4 and population standard deviation 1. Use Chebychev's theorem to estimate the probability that an outcome lies between 2 and 6.

SOLUTION Here, $\mu = 4, \sigma = 1$. Since we wish to estimate the probability that an outcome lies between 2 and 6, the value of k is $k = 6 - \mu = 6 - 4 = 2$ (or $k = \mu - 2 = 4 - 2 = 2$). Then by Chebychev's theorem, the desired probability is at least

$$1 - \frac{\sigma^2}{k^2} = 1 - \frac{1}{2^2} = 1 - \frac{1}{4} = 0.75$$

That is, we expect at least 75% of the outcomes of this experiment to lie between 2 and 6. ■

NOW WORK PROBLEM 31.

EXAMPLE 9 Using Chebychev's Theorem

An office supply company sells boxes containing 100 paper clips. Because of the packaging procedure, not every box contains exactly 100 clips. From previous data it is known that the average number of clips in a box is indeed 100 and the standard deviation is 2.8. If the company ships 10,000 boxes, estimate the number of boxes having between 94 and 106 clips, inclusive.

SOLUTION Our experiment involves counting the number of clips in the box. For this experiment we have $\mu = 100$ and $\sigma = 2.8$. Therefore, by Chebychev's theorem the fraction of boxes having between $100 - 6 = 94$ and $100 + 6 = 106$ clips ($k = 6$) should be at least

$$1 - \frac{(2.8)^2}{6^2} = 1 - 0.22 = 0.78$$

That is, we expect at least 78% of 10,000 boxes, or about 7800 boxes, to have between 94 and 106 clips. ■

* *Named after the nineteenth-century Russian mathematician P. L. Chebychev.*

The importance of Chebychev's theorem stems from the fact that it applies to a data—only the population mean and population standard deviation must be know However, the estimate is a crude one. Other results (such as the *normal distribution* gi later) produce more accurate estimates about the probability of falling within k units the mean.

EXERCISE 9.5 Answers Begin on Page AN–49.

Concepts and Vocabulary

1. The range, variance, and standard deviation measure the _____ of the distribution.
2. ***True or False*** A disadvantage of using the range to measure dispersion is that it only uses the two extreme data points.
3. The Empirical Rule states that if the distribution of the data is bell shaped, about _____ percent of the outcomes will be within one standard deviation of the mean.
4. When calculating the sample standard deviation for n ite we divide by _____.
5. ***True or False*** The standard deviation is preferred to variance because the units are squared.
6. ***True or False*** Chebychev's theorem is used to estimate probability that an outcome is within k standard deviation the mean.

Skill Building

In Problems 7–12, compute the standard deviation for each set of sample data.

7. 4, 5, 9, 9, 10, 14, 25
8. 6, 8, 10, 10, 11, 12, 18
9. 62, 58, 70, 70
10. 55, 65, 80, 80, 90
11. 85, 75, 62, 78, 100
12. 92, 82, 75, 75, 82

In Problems 13 and 14, calculate the mean and the standard deviation of the sample data below.

13.

Class	Frequency
10–16	1
17–23	3
24–30	10
31–37	12
38–44	5
45–51	2

14.

Class	Frequency
0–3	2
4–7	5
8–11	8
12–15	6
16–19	3

Applications

15. **Lightbulb Life** A sample of 6 lightbulbs was chosen and their lifetimes measured. The bulbs lasted 968, 893, 769, 845, 922, and 915 hours. Calculate the mean and the standard deviation of the lifetimes of the lightbulbs.

16. **Aptitude Scores** A sample of 25 applicants for admission to Midwestern University had the following scores on the quantitative part of an aptitude test:

591	570	425	472	555
490	415	479	517	570
606	614	542	607	441
502	506	603	488	460
550	551	420	590	482

Find the mean and standard deviation of these scores.

17. **Baseball Players** During 2010 spring training, the ages the 40 men on the New York Yankees roster were

33	24	27	24	35	28	37	38	40	25
29	33	24	38	27	36	24	34	26	30
25	26	29	29	33	27	29	27	24	23
25	24	25	25	25	27	23	23	23	26

Source: Major League Baseball.

(a) Find the range of the players' ages.

(b) Find the standard deviation, assuming sample data.

(c) Find the standard deviation, assuming population d

(d) Decide whether the data are sample or populati Give reasons.

18. **Baseball Players** During 2010 spring training, the ages of the 40 men on the Atlanta Braves roster were

26	23	34	24	35	37	24	31	25	40
25	38	26	33	30	27	33	24	28	38
26	26	25	32	32	20	28	27	25	26
23	25	26	25	22	26	28	22	23	26

Source: Major League Baseball.

(a) Find the range of the players' ages.
(b) Find the standard deviation, assuming sample data.
(c) Find the standard deviation, assuming population data.
(d) Decide whether the data are sample or population. Give reasons.

19. **Mother's Age** The following data give the number of births in the United States in 2007 by the age of the mother for women under the age of 45. (The numbers of births are given in thousands.)

Age of Mother	No. of Births
10–14	6
15–19	445
20–24	1082
25–29	1208
30–34	962
35–39	499
40–44	105

Source: *National Vital Statistics Reports*, 2009.

(a) Are these sample data or population data? Justify your reasoning.
(b) Find the standard deviation of the mothers' ages.

20. **Charge Accounts** A department store takes a sample of its customer charge accounts and finds the following:

Outstanding Balance ($)	Number of Accounts
0–49	15
50–99	41
100–149	80
150–199	60
200–249	8

Find the mean and the standard deviation of the outstanding balances.

21. **Earthquakes** The data below list the number of earthquakes recorded worldwide during 2009 that measured below 8 on the Richter scale.

Magnitude	Earthquakes
0–0.9	21
1.0–1.9	26
2.0–2.9	3009
3.0–3.9	2899
4.0–4.9	6908
5.0–5.9	1776
6.0–6.9	142
7.0–7.9	16

Source: National Earthquake Information Center.

(a) Are these sample data or population data?
(b) Find the mean magnitude of the earthquakes worldwide in 2009.
(c) Find the standard deviation of the magnitude of the earthquakes recorded in 2009.

22. **Earthquakes** The data below list the number of earthquakes recorded in the United States in 2009 that measured below 8 on the Richter scale.

Magnitude	Earthquakes
0–0.9	17
1.0–1.9	26
2.0–2.9	2374
3.0–3.9	1491
4.0–4.9	293
5.0–5.9	55
6.0–6.9	4
7.0–7.9	0

Source: National Earthquake Information Center.

(a) Are these sample data or population data?
(b) Find the mean magnitude of the earthquakes in the United States in 2009.
(c) Find the standard deviation of the magnitude of the earthquakes recorded in the United States in 2009.

23. **Licensed Drivers in Tennessee** Refer to the data in Problem 13, Exercise 9.3.

(a) Find the standard deviation assuming sample data.
(b) Find the standard deviation assuming population data.
(c) Decide whether the data are sample or population. Give reasons.

24. Licensed Drivers in Hawaii Refer to the data provided in Problem 14, Exercise 9.3.

(a) Find the standard deviation assuming sample data.

(b) Find the standard deviation assuming population data.

(c) Decide whether the data are sample or population. Give reasons.

25. Undergraduate Tuition 2006–2007 Refer to the data provided in Problem 15, Exercise 9.3.

(a) Are these data from a population or from a sample? Justify your answer.

(b) Find the standard deviation of tuition.

26. Birth Rates Refer to the data provided in Problem 18, Exercise 9.3.

(a) Are these data from a population or from a sample? Justify your answer.

(b) Find the standard deviation.

27. The Empirical Rule One measure of intelligence is the Stanford-Binet Intelligence Quotient (IQ). IQ scores have a bell-shaped distribution with a mean of 100 and a standard deviation of 15.

(a) What percentage of persons have an IQ score between 70 and 130?

(b) What percentage of persons have an IQ score less than 70 or greater than 130?

(c) What percentage of persons have an IQ score greater than 130?

28. The Empirical Rule SAT Math scores have a bell-shaped distribution with a mean of 515 and a standard deviation of 116.

Source: College Board, 2008.

(a) What percentage of SAT scores are between 399 and 631?

(b) What percentage of SAT scores are less than 399 or greater than 631?

(c) What percentage of SAT scores are greater than 747?

29. The Empirical Rule The weight, in grams, of the pair of kidneys in adult males between the ages of 40 and 49 have a bell-shaped distribution with a mean of 325 grams and a standard deviation of 30 grams.

(a) About 95% of kidneys will be between what weights?

(b) What percentage of kidneys weigh between 235 grams and 415 grams?

(c) What percentage of kidneys weigh less than 235 grams or more than 415 grams?

(d) What percentage of kidneys weigh between 295 grams and 385 grams?

30. The Empirical Rule The distribution of the length of bolts has a bell shape with a mean of 4 inches and a standard deviation of 0.007 inch.

(a) About 68% of bolts manufactured will be between what lengths?

(b) What percentage of bolts will be between 3.986 inches and 4.014 inches?

(c) If the company discards any bolts less than 3.986 inch[es] or greater than 4.014 inches, what percentage of bol[ts] manufactured will be discarded?

(d) What percentage of bolts manufactured will be betwee[n] 4.007 inches and 4.021 inches?

31. Chebychev's Theorem Suppose that an experiment wi[th] numerical outcomes has mean 25 and standard deviation 3. U[se] Chebychev's theorem to tell what percentage of outcomes lie

(a) Between 19 and 31.

(b) Between 20 and 30.

(c) Between 16 and 34.

(d) Less than 19 or more than 31.

(e) Less than 16 or more than 34.

32. Cost of Meat A survey reveals that the mean price for [a] pound of beef is \$3.20 with a standard deviation of \$0.40. U[se] Chebychev's theorem to determine the probability that [a] randomly selected pound of beef costs

(a) Between \$2.80 and \$3.60.

(b) Between \$2.50 and \$3.90.

(c) Between \$2.20 and \$4.20.

(d) Between \$2.40 and \$4.00.

(e) Less than \$2.40 or more than \$4.00.

33. Quality Control A watch company determines that each b[ox] of 500 watches has an average of 6 defective watches wi[th] standard deviation 2. Suppose that 1000 boxes are produce[d]. Use Chebychev's theorem to estimate the number of box[es] having between 0 and 12 defective watches.

34. Sales The average sale at a department store is \$51.25, wi[th] a standard deviation of \$8.50. Find the smallest interval su[ch] that by Chebychev's theorem at least 90% of the store's sal[es] fall within it.

35. Annual Births The table gives the number of live births [in] the United States for 2001 through 2006.

Year	Births
2006	4,265,555
2005	4,138,349
2004	4,112,052
2003	4,089,950
2002	4,021,726
2001	4,025,933

Source: *National Vital Statistics Reports*, 2009.

(a) Are these population or sample data? Justify your reasonin[g].

(b) Calculate the mean number of births over the six-ye[ar] period.

(c) Calculate the standard deviation of births over the six-ye[ar] period.

(d) Are the mean and the standard deviations you calculate[d] exact or are they approximations? Explain your reasonin[g].

(e) Do the number of births differ greatly over the six-year period? Justify your reasoning.

6. Fishing The number of salmon caught in each of two rivers over the past 15 years is as follows:

River I Number Caught	Years	River II Number Caught	Years
500–1499	4	750–1249	2
1500–2499	8	1350–1799	3
2500–3499	2	1800–2249	4
3500–4499	1	2250–2699	4
		2700–3149	2

(a) Are these population or sample data?

(b) Find the mean and the standard deviation of the number of fish caught in each river.

(c) Are the mean and the standard deviation calculated in part (b) approximate or exact? Explain.

(d) Using the statistics you calculated, discuss which river should be preferred for fishing.

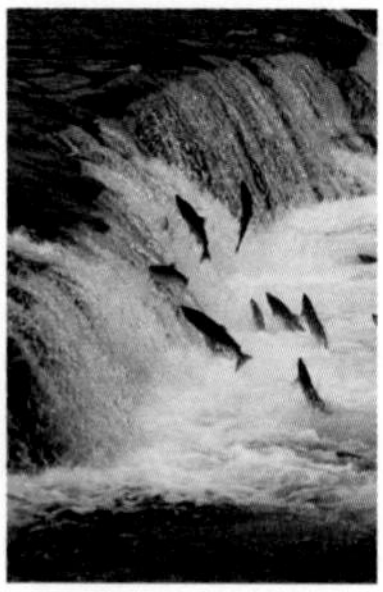

9.6 The Normal Distribution

PREPARING FOR THIS SECTION *Before getting started, review the following:*

- The Binomial Probability Model (Section 8.6, pp. 480–491)

NOW WORK THE 'ARE YOU PREPARED?' PROBLEMS ON PAGE 562.

OBJECTIVES
1. Find a Z-score (p. 556)
2. Use the standard normal curve (p. 557)
3. Approximate a binomial distribution by the standard normal distribution (p. 560)

Frequency polygons or frequency distributions can assume almost any shape or form, depending on the data. However, the data obtained from many experiments often follow a common pattern. For example, heights of adults, weights of adults, and test scores all lead to data that have the same kind of frequency distribution. This distribution is referred to as the **normal distribution** or the **Gaussian distribution.** Because it occurs so often in practical situations, it is generally regarded as the most important distribution, and much statistical theory is based on it. The graph of the normal distribution, called the **normal curve**, is the bell-shaped curve shown in Figure 13.

FIGURE 13

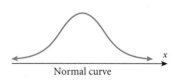

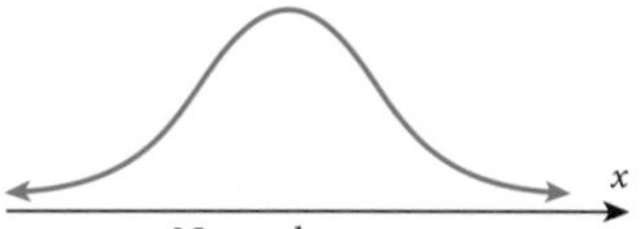

Normal curve

We list some properties of the normal distribution next.

Properties of the Normal Distribution

1. Graphs of normally distributed data are bell shaped and are symmetric with respect to a vertical line at the mean μ. See Figure 14.
2. The mean, median, and mode of a normal distribution are equal.
3. The area enclosed by the normal curve and the x-axis is always equal to 1 square unit. The shaded region in Figure 14 has an area of 1 square unit.
4. The probability that an outcome of a normally distributed experiment is between a and b equals the area under the associated normal curve from $x = a$ to $x = b$. See the shaded region in Figure 15.
5. The standard deviation of a normal distribution plays a major role in describing the area under the normal curve. As shown in Figure 16, the standard deviation is related to the area under the normal curve as follows:
   (a) About 68.27% of the total area under the curve is within 1 standard deviation of the mean (from $\mu - \sigma$ to $\mu + \sigma$).
   (b) About 95.45% of the total area under the curve is within 2 standard deviations of the mean (from $\mu - 2\sigma$ to $\mu + 2\sigma$).
   (c) About 99.73% of the total area under the curve is within 3 standard deviations of the mean (from $\mu - 3\sigma$ to $\mu + 3\sigma$).

FIGURE 14

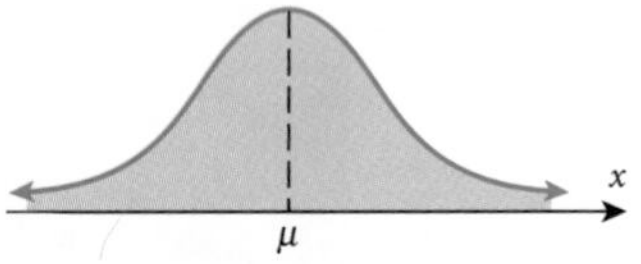

FIGURE 15

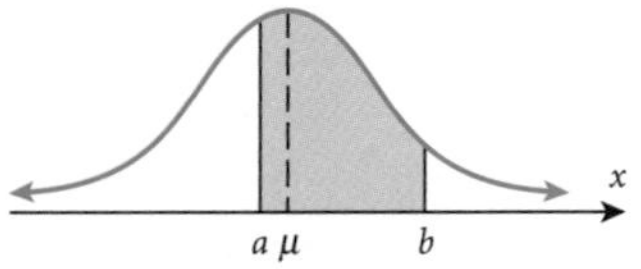

Probability between a and b = area of the shaded region

Notice that Property 5 is essentially the Empirical Rule we discussed in Section 9.5. It is also worth noting that, in theory, the normal curve will never touch the x-axis but will extend to infinity in either direction.

FIGURE 16

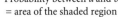

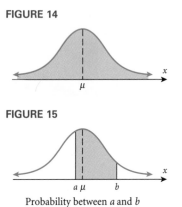

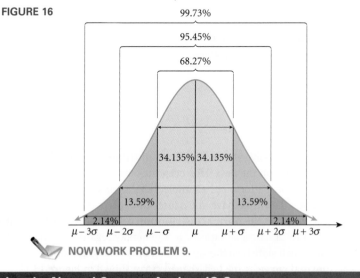

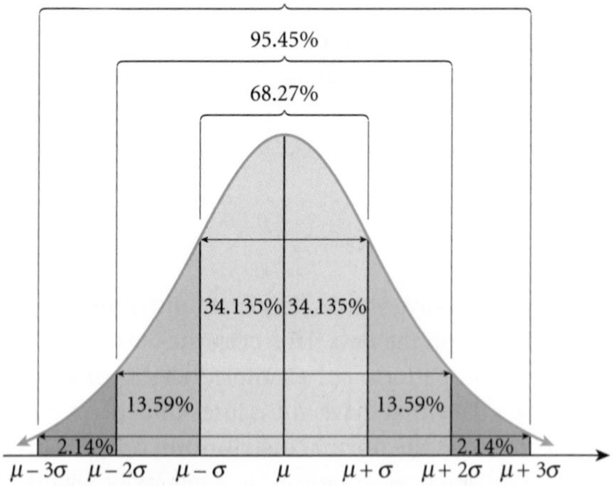

NOW WORK PROBLEM 9.

EXAMPLE 1 Using the Normal Curve to Analyze IQ Scores

At Jefferson High School the average IQ score of the 1200 students is 100, with standard deviation of 15. The IQ scores have a normal distribution.

(a) How many students have an IQ between 85 and 115?
(b) How many students have an IQ between 70 and 130?
(c) How many students have an IQ between 55 and 145?
(d) How many students have an IQ under 55 or over 145?
(e) How many students have an IQ over 145?

SOLUTION Figure 17 shows a normal distribution with mean = 100 and standard deviation = 15.

FIGURE 17

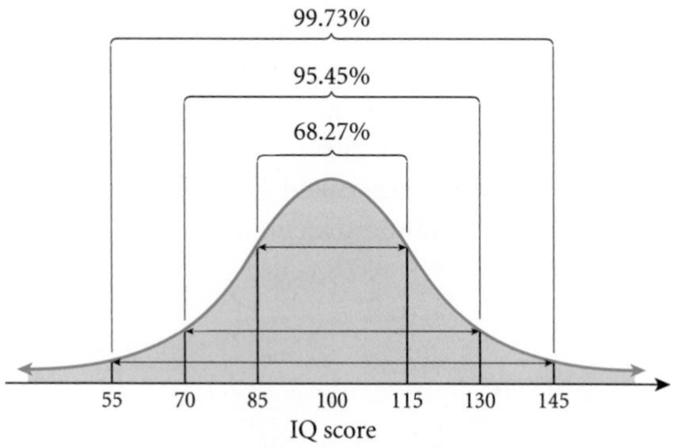

(a) The IQ scores have a normal distribution and the mean is 100. Since the standard deviation σ is 15, then 1σ on either side of the mean is from 85 to 115. By Property 5(a) we know that 68.27% of 1200, or

$$(0.6827)(1200) = 819 \text{ students}$$

have IQs between 85 and 115.

(b) The scores from 70 to 130 extend 2σ $(= 30)$ on either side of the mean. By Property 5(b) we know that 95.45% of 1200, or

$$(0.9545)(1200) = 1145 \text{ students}$$

have IQs between 70 and 130.

(c) The scores from 55 to 145 extend 3σ $(= 45)$ on either side of the mean. By Property 5(c) we know that 99.73% of 1200, or

$$(0.9973)(1200) = 1197 \text{ students}$$

have IQs between 55 and 145.

(d) There are three students $(1200 - 1197)$ who have scores that are not between 55 and 145.

(e) One or two students have IQs above 145. ■

NOW WORK PROBLEM 29.

A normal distribution is completely determined by the mean μ and the standard deviation σ. Normal distributions of data with different means or different standard deviations give rise to different normal curves.

Figure 18 indicates how the normal curve changes when the standard deviation changes. Each normal curve has the same mean 0.

As the standard deviation increases, the normal curve spreads out [Figure 18(c)], indicating a greater likelihood for the outcomes to be far from the mean. A compressed curve [Figure 18(a)] indicates that the outcomes are more likely to be close to the mean.

FIGURE 18

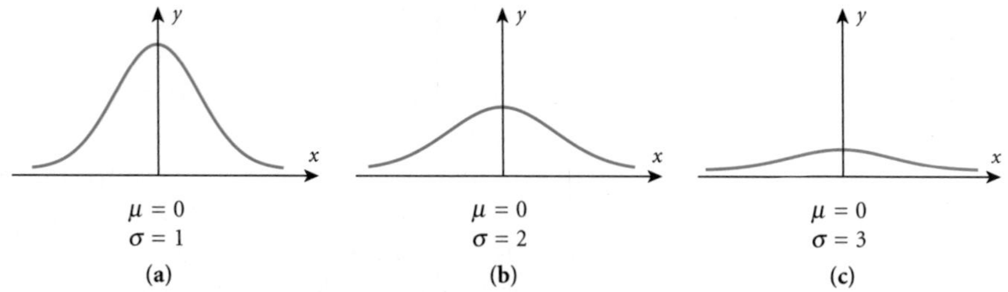

Standard Normal Curve

It would be a hopeless task to attempt to tabulate areas under a normal curve for ever conceivable value of μ and σ. Fortunately, we are able to transform all the observa tions to one table—the table corresponding to the so-called **standard normal curv** which is the normal curve for which $\mu = 0$ and $\sigma = 1$. This is accomplished b introducing new data, called *Z-scores*. A *Z*-score transforms any normal value with mean μ and a standard deviation σ to a normal value with mean 0 and standar deviation 1.

Definition

Z-Score

If data are normally distributed, then the **Z-score** of a value x is defined by

$$Z = \frac{\text{Difference between } x \text{ and } \mu}{\text{Standard deviation}} = \frac{x - \mu}{\sigma} \tag{1}$$

where

x = original data point

μ = mean of the original data

σ = standard deviation of the original data

The transformed data obtained using Equation (1) will always have a *zero mean* an a *standard deviation of one*. Such data are said to be expressed in **standard units** o **standard scores.**

A *Z*-score can be interpreted as the number of standard deviations that the origin score is away from its mean. So, by expressing data in terms of standard units, it become possible to make a comparison of distributions.

1 Find a *Z*-score

EXAMPLE 2 Finding *Z*-Scores

On a test, 80 is the mean and 7 is the standard deviation. What is the *Z*-score of a score o

(a) 88? **(b)** 62?

Interpret your results. Graph the normal curve.

SOLUTION **(a)** Here, 88 is the original score. Using Equation (1) with $x = 88$, $\mu = 80$, $\sigma = 7$, we ge

$$Z = \frac{x - \mu}{\sigma} = \frac{88 - 80}{7} = \frac{8}{7} = 1.1429$$

(b) Here, 62 is the original score. Using Equation (1) with $x = 62$, $\mu = 80$, and $\sigma = 7$ we get

$$Z = \frac{62 - 80}{7} = \frac{-18}{7} = -2.5714$$

The *Z*-score of 1.1429 tells us that the original score of 88 is 1.1429 standar deviations *above* the mean. The *Z*-score of -2.5714 tells us that the original score c 62 is 2.5714 standard deviations *below* the mean. A negative *Z*-score always mean that the score is below the mean. See Figure 19 for a graph of the normal curve.

FIGURE 19

$x = 80 + 1.1429\sigma$

$x = 80 - 2.5714\sigma$

59 62	66	73	80	87 88	94	101
$\mu - 3\sigma$	$\mu - 2\sigma$	$\mu - 1\sigma$	μ	$\mu + 1\sigma$	$\mu + 2\sigma$	$\mu + 3\sigma$

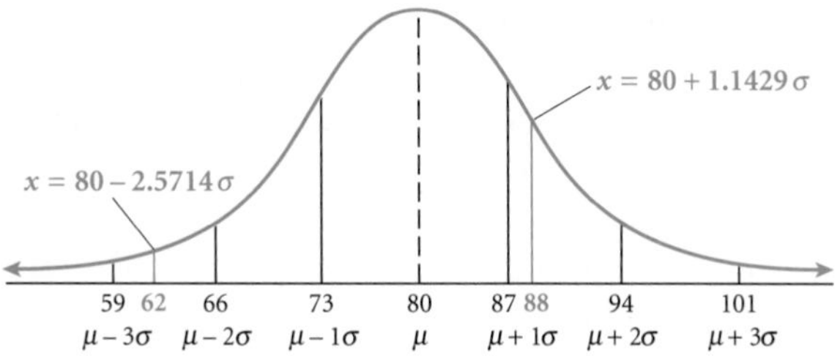

 NOW WORK PROBLEM 13.

2   **Use the Standard Normal Curve**

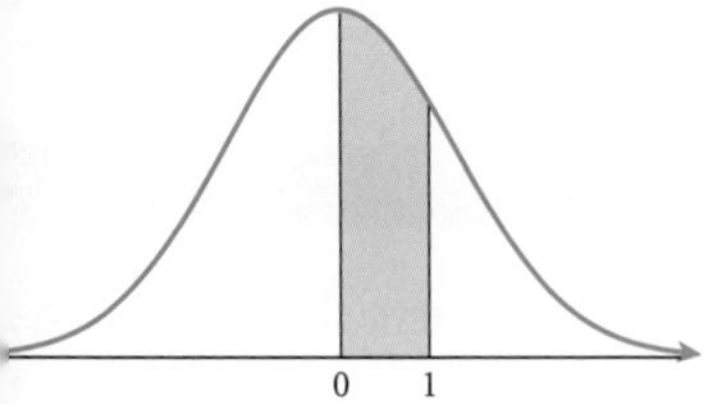

The normal curve in Figure 20 with mean $\mu = 0$ and standard deviation $\sigma = 1$ is the standard normal curve. For this curve the areas between $Z = -1$ and 1, $Z = -2$ and 2, $Z = -3$ and 3 are equal, respectively, to 68.27%, 95.45%, and 99.73% of the total area under the curve, which is 1. To find the areas cut off between other points, we proceed as follows:

The area under portions of the standard normal curve can be calculated by hand by using the standard normal curve table, which is printed on the inside back cover of this text. The table gives the area under the curve between the mean $\mu = 0$ and select positive Z-scores. Areas between $\mu = 0$ and negative values of Z are obtained using symmetry. Since a normal distribution is symmetric about its mean, the area under the standard normal curve to the right of $\mu = 0$ equals the area under the curve to the left of $\mu = 0$; each area equals $\dfrac{1}{2}$.

Given a Z-score rounded to two decimal points, the area between 0 and absolute value of $|Z|$ is found by locating the standard score truncated to one decimal place in the left column of the table and then by moving across the row to the entry under the second decimal place. This value represents the area between 0 and Z.

FIGURE 20

0   1

EXAMPLE 3   **Using the Standard Normal Curve**

(a) Find the area included between 0 and 0.6 on a standard normal curve. Refer to the shaded area in Figure 21(a).

(b) Find the area included between 0.6 and 1.86 on a standard normal curve. Refer to the shaded area in Figure 21(b).

FIGURE 21

0 0.6	0 0.6 1.86
(a)	(b)

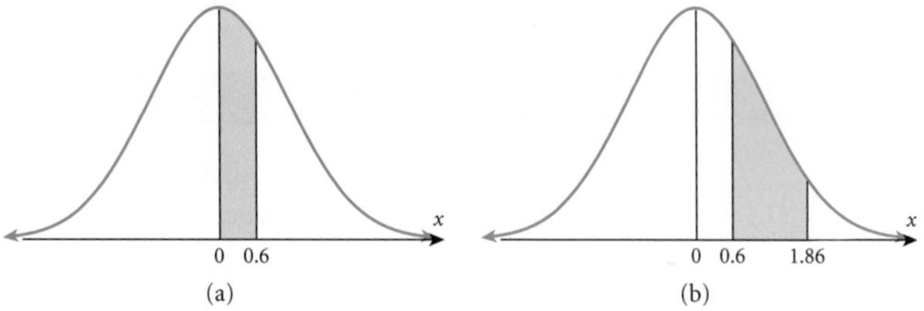

SOLUTION   Use the standard normal curve table, which is printed on the inside back cover.

(a) To find the area between 0 and 0.6, we find $Z = 0.6$ in the table. Corresponding $Z = 0.6$ is the value 0.2257, which is the area under the curve between the mean and 0.6. In other words, 22.57% of the area under the standard normal curve will between 0 and 0.6.

(b) We begin by checking the table to find the area of the curve cut off between the mean and a point equivalent to a standard score of 0.6. This value is 0.2257, as found in part (a). Next, we continue down the table in the left-hand column un we come to a standard score of 1.8. By looking across the row to the column below 0.06, we find that 0.4686 of the area is included between the mean and 1.8 The area under the curve between the points 0.6 and 1.86 is the difference between the two areas, $0.4686 - 0.2257$, which is 0.2429. We can then state that approximate 24.29% of the area under the curve falls between 0.6 and 1.86, or that *the probability a score falling between these two values is about 0.2429.*

NOW WORK PROBLEM 15.

EXAMPLE 4   Using the Standard Normal Curve

We want to determine the area under the standard normal curve that falls betwee a standard score of -0.39 and one of 1.86.

SOLUTION   See Figure 22.

FIGURE 22

$-0.39\ \ 0\ \ 0.39\quad 1.86$

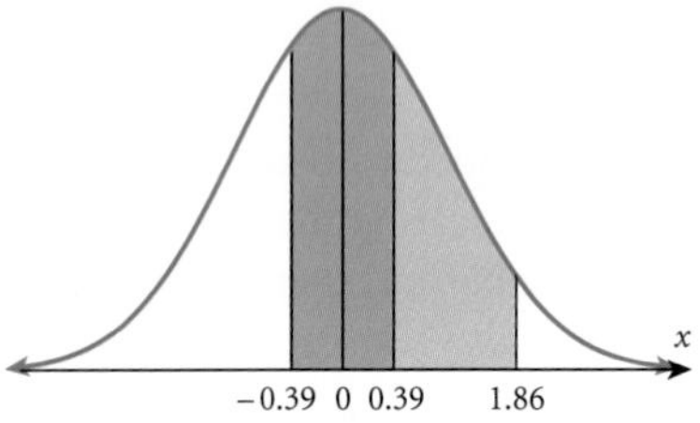

There are no values for negative standard scores in the standard normal curve tabl Because of the symmetry of normal curves, standard scores equal in absolute value, gi equal areas when taken from the mean. From the table we find that a standard score f 0.39 cuts off an area of 0.1517 between it and the mean. A standard score of 1.8 includes 0.4686 of the area of the curve between it and the mean. The area include between -0.39 and 1.86 is then equal to the sum of these two areas, $0.1517 + 0.468$ which is 0.6203. Approximately 62.03% of the area is between -0.39 and 1.86. In oth words, the probability of a score falling between these two values is about 0.6203.

EXAMPLE 5   Using the Standard Normal Curve

The scores on a test are normally distributed with a mean of 78 and a standar deviation of 7. What is the probability that a test chosen at random has a score betwee 80 and 90?

SOLUTION   To find the probability of obtaining a score between 80 and 90 on the test, we need find the area under a normal curve from $x_1 = 80$ to $x_2 = 90$.

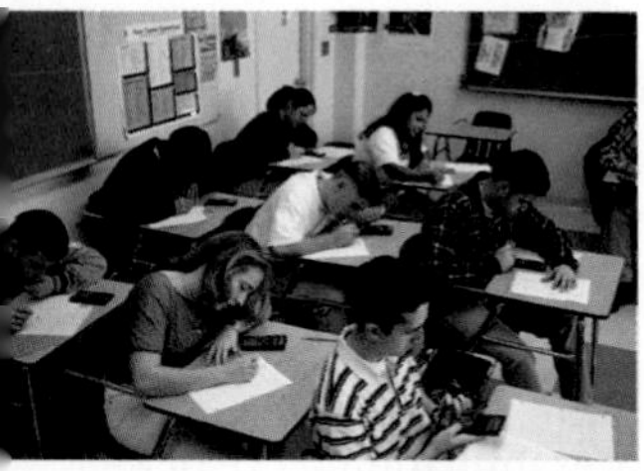

We begin by finding the Z-scores Z_1 of $x_1 = 80$ and Z_2 of $x_2 = 90$.

$$Z_1 = \frac{x_1 - \mu}{\sigma} = \frac{80 - 78}{7} = 0.29$$

$$Z_2 = \frac{x_2 - \mu}{\sigma} = \frac{90 - 78}{7} = 1.71$$

From the standard normal curve table, the area A_1 from the mean to Z_1 and the area A_2 from the mean to Z_2 are $A_1 = 0.1141$ and $A_2 = 0.4564$.

See Figure 23. The area between Z_1 and Z_2 is the difference between A_2 and A_1.

$$A_2 - A_1 = 0.4564 - 0.1141 = 0.3423$$

So, the probability of obtaining a test score between 80 and 90 is 0.3423, or 34.23%.

FIGURE 23

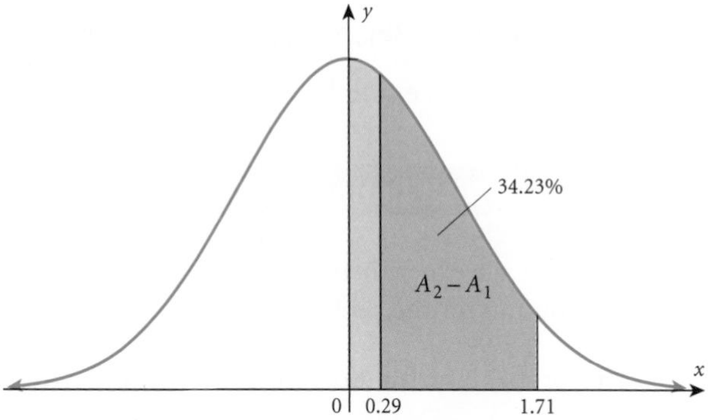

COMMENT: A graphing utility can be used to find the area under a portion of a normal curve. The graphing utility uses the actual distribution mean and standard deviation and computes the area beneath the normal curve over the interval of interest all in one step. See Figure 24. The information needed for computing the solution is $x_1 = 80$, $x_2 = 90$, $\mu = 78$, and $\sigma = 7$. The result, normalcdf(80, 90, 78, 7) = 0.344 indicates that for a normal curve with mean 78 and standard deviation 7, 34.4% of the area beneath the curve is between $x_1 = 80$, and $x_2 = 90$, so the probability of obtaining a test score between 80 and 90 on the test is 0.344 or 34.4%. The two answers vary due to rounding.   ■

FIGURE 24

```
normalcdf(80,90,
8,7)
        .3443104453
```

An advantage of transforming data points to Z-scores is that it allows us to compare scores that are on different scales. That is, using Z-scores we can compare a variable x_1 from a normal distribution with mean μ_1 and standard deviation σ_1 to a variable x_2 from a different normal distribution that has a mean μ_2 and standard deviation σ_2. This is illustrated in the next example.

EXAMPLE 6   Comparing Exam Scores

A student receives a grade of 82 on a final examination in biology for which the mean is 73 and the standard deviation is 9. In his final examination in sociology, for which the mean grade is 81 and the standard deviation is 15, he receives an 89. In which examination is his relative standing higher?

SOLUTION In their present forms these distributions are not comparable since they have differe[nt] means and, more important, different standard deviations. In order to compare t[he] data, we transform the data to standard scores. For the biology test data the Z-score f[or] the student's examination score of 82 is

$$Z = \frac{82 - 73}{9} = \frac{9}{9} = 1$$

For the sociology test data, the Z-score for the student's examination score of 89 is

$$Z = \frac{89 - 81}{15} = \frac{8}{15} = 0.533$$

This means the student's score in the biology exam is 1 standard deviation above t[he] mean, while his score in the sociology exam is 0.533 standard deviation above the mea[n]. So the student's **relative standing** is higher in biology.

NOW WORK PROBLEM 37.

3 Approximate a Binomial Distribution by the Standard Normal Distribution

We start with an example.

EXAMPLE 7 Finding the Frequency Distribution for a Binomial Probability

Consider an experiment in which a fair coin is tossed 10 times. Find the frequen[cy] distribution for the probability of tossing a head. Graph the frequency distribution.

SOLUTION The probability for obtaining exactly k heads is given by a binomial distributio[n] $b\left(10, k; \frac{1}{2}\right)$. The distribution is given in Table 17. If we graph this frequency distributio[n] we obtain the line chart shown in Figure 25. When we connect the tops of the lines [of] the line chart, we obtain a curve that approximates a *normal curve,* as shown.

TABLE 17

No. Heads	Probability of $b\left(10, k; \frac{1}{2}\right)$
0	0.0010
1	0.0098
2	0.0439
3	0.1172
4	0.2051
5	0.2461
6	0.2051
7	0.1172
8	0.0439
9	0.0098
10	0.0010

FIGURE 25

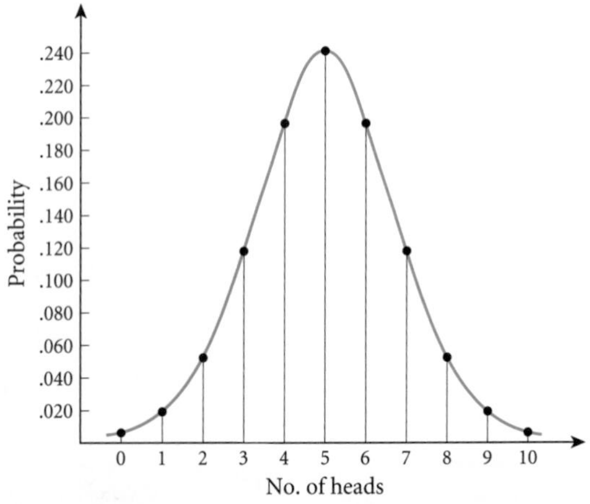

This particular distribution for $n = 10$ and $p = \frac{1}{2}$ is a result of the choice of n and [p]. As a matter of fact, the line chart for any binomial probability $b(n, k; p)$ will give a[n] approximation to a normal curve provided n is large or p is close to $\frac{1}{2}$.

Probabilities associated with binomial experiments are readily obtainable from the formula $b(n, k; p)$ when n is small. If n is large, we can compute the binomial probabilities by an approximating procedure using a normal curve. It turns out that the normal distribution provides a very good approximation to the binomial distribution when the product $n \cdot p \cdot (1 - p) \geq 10$.

The mean μ for the binomial distribution is given by $\mu = np$ (see Expected Value for Bernoulli Trials on page 488). It can be shown that the standard deviation is $\sigma = \sqrt{npq}$, where $q = 1 - p$.

EXAMPLE 8 Quality Control

A company manufactures 60,000 pencils each day. Quality control studies have shown that, on the average, 4% of the pencils are defective. A random sample of 500 pencils is selected from each day's production and tested. What is the probability that in the sample there are

(a) At least 12 and no more than 24 defective pencils?

(b) 32 or more defective pencils?

SOLUTION **(a)** Since $n = 500$ is very large, it is appropriate to use a normal curve approximation for the binomial distribution. With $n = 500$, $p = 0.04$, and $q = 1 - p = 0.96$, we have

$$\mu = np = 500(0.04) = 20 \qquad \sigma = \sqrt{npq} = \sqrt{500(0.04)(0.96)} = 4.38$$

To find the approximate probability that the number of defective pencils in a sample is at least 12 and no more than 24, we find the area under a normal curve from $x = 11.5$ to $x = 24.5$.

We subtract 0.5 from the lower limit and add 0.5 to the upper limit because we are using a continuous distribution to approximate discrete variables. Whenever we approximate a binomial probability using the normal distribution we enlarge the interval by 0.5 on each end. This is called **correcting for continuity**. See Figure 26.

FIGURE 26

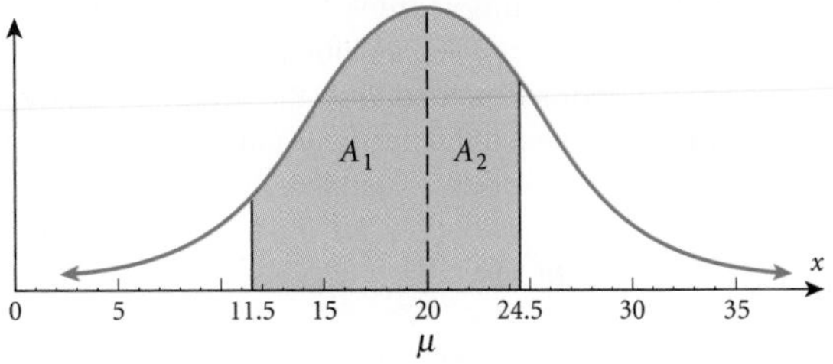

Areas A_1 and A_2 are found by converting to Z-scores and using the standard normal curve table.

$$x = 11.5: \quad Z_1 = \frac{x - \mu}{\sigma} = \frac{11.5 - 20}{4.38} = -1.94 \qquad A_1 = 0.4738$$

$$x = 24.5: \quad Z_2 = \frac{x - \mu}{\sigma} = \frac{24.5 - 20}{4.38} = 1.03 \qquad A_2 = 0.3485$$

$$\text{Total area} = A_1 + A_2 = 0.4738 + 0.3485 = 0.8223$$

The approximate probability of the number of defective pencils in the sample being at least 12 and no more than 24 is 0.8223.

(b) Remember, to correct for continuity, we subtract 0.5 from the lower limit of 32 an use 31.5. We want to find the area A_2 to the right of 31.5, as indicated in Figure 2. We know that the area to the right of the mean is 0.5, and if we subtract the area A from 0.5, we will obtain A_2.

First, we find the area A_1:

$$Z = \frac{x - \mu}{\sigma} = \frac{31.5 - 20}{4.38} = 2.63 \qquad A_1 = 0.4957$$

Then

$$A_2 = 0.5 - A_1 = 0.5 - 0.4957 = 0.0043$$

The approximate probability of finding 32 or more defective pencils in the sampl is 0.0043.

FIGURE 27

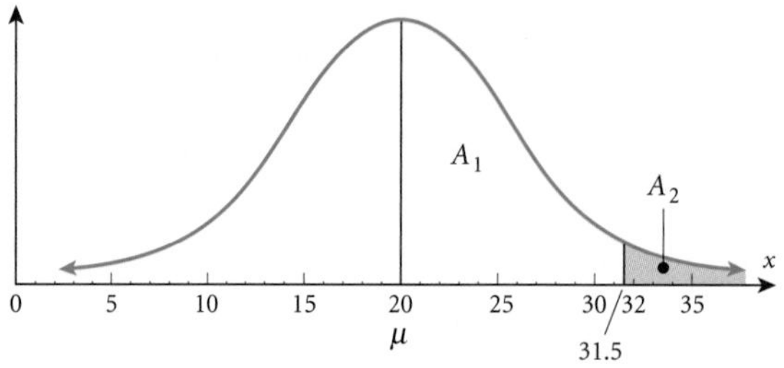

NOW WORK PROBLEM 43.

FIGURE 28

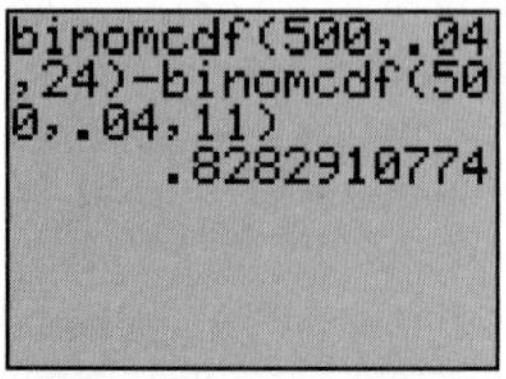

FIGURE 29

COMMENT: Graphing utilities can calculate exact values for the binomial distribution even the number of Bernoulli trials, n, is large. This makes the normal approximation less importar than it had been in the past. Check the user's manual for your graphing utility to learn how t compute the cumulative binomial distribution. Then redo Example 8 with exact values, an compare the exact solutions to the approximations obtained in Example 8.

The results of Example 8, using a TI-84 Plus graphing calculator, are shown in Figures 2 and 29. When calculating the probability that the number of defective pencils is betwee 12 and 24, we find the difference between the probability that the number of defective penci is less than or equal to 24 and the probability that the number of defective pencils is less tha or equal to 11. See Figure 28.

To find the probability that there are at least 32 defective pencils, we use one minus th probability of the complement. That is, we calculate one minus the probability there are 3 or fewer defective pencils, as illustrated in Figure 29.

The solutions obtained with the graphing utility differ from the normal approximation in Example 8 because the approximation uses the continuous variables of a normal distribu tion in place of the discrete variables of the binomial distribution.

EXERCISE 9.6 Answers Begin on Page AN–49.

'Are You Prepared?' Problems Answers are given at the end of these exercises. If you get a wrong answer, read the pages listed in red.

1. ***True or False*** In a binomial probability model, each trial has only two possible outcomes. (p. 480)
2. Find the probability of obtaining 1, 2, or 3 successes in 5 trials of a binomial experiment if the probability of success is 0.2. (p. 482)
3. ***True or False*** In a binomial probability model, with n trial where the probability of success is p, the expected number E o successes is $E = np$. (p. 488)

Concepts and Vocabulary

4. The graph of a normal probability distribution is symmetric about the _____.
5. To standardize a normal random variable, we find a _____.
6. A standard normal distribution always has a mean of _____ and a standard deviation of _____.
7. If the area under the standard normal curve between and Z is 0.4, what is the area under the curve between − and 0?
8. ***True or False*** A Z-score can be interpreted as the number o standard deviations the original score is from its mean.

Skill Building

Problems 9–12, for each normal curve determine μ and σ by inspection.

9. 34.135%

10. 34.135%

80 90 100 110 120

6 7 8 9 10

11. 68.27%

16 17 18 19 20

12. 68.27%

1.6 1.8 2.0 2.2 2.4

13. Given a normal distribution with a mean of 13.1 and a standard deviation of 9.3, find the Z-score equivalent of the following scores in this distribution:

(a) $x = 7$ (b) $x = 9$ (c) $x = 13$

(d) $x = 29$ (e) $x = 37$ (f) $x = 41$

14. Given a normal distribution with a mean of 15.2 and a standard deviation of 5.1, find the Z-score equivalent of the following scores in this distribution:

(a) $x = 8$ (b) $x = 9$ (c) $x = 16$

(d) $x = 22$ (e) $x = 23$ (f) $x = 25$

15. Given the following Z-scores on a standard normal distribution, find the area under the standard normal curve between each score and the mean.

(a) $Z = 0.89$ (b) $Z = 1.10$ (c) $Z = 3.06$

(d) $Z = -1.22$ (e) $Z = 2.30$ (f) $Z = -0.75$

16. Given the following Z-scores on a standard normal distribution, find the area under the standard normal curve between each score and the mean.

(a) $Z = 1.85$ (b) $Z = 1.15$ (c) $Z = -1.60$

(d) $Z = 2.50$ (e) $Z = -2.31$ (f) $Z = 0.25$

In Problems 17–20, use the standard normal curve table to find the area of each shaded region under the standard normal curve.

17.

−0.5

18.

1 2

19.

−1.2 1.5

20.

−0.5 0 0.5

In Problems 21–26, suppose a binomial experiment consists of 750 trials and the probability of success for each trial is 0.4. Then

$$\mu = np = 300 \quad \text{and} \quad \sigma = \sqrt{npq} = \sqrt{(750)(0.4)(0.6)} = 13.4$$

approximate the probability of obtaining the number of successes indicated by using a normal curve.

21. 285–315   **22.** 280–320   **23.** 300 or more   **24.** 300 or less   **25.** 325 or more   **26.** 275 or less

Applications

27. Assigning Grades An instructor assigns grades in an examination according to the following procedure:

A   if the score exceeds $\mu + 1.6\sigma$

B   if the score is between $\mu + 0.6\sigma$ and $\mu + 1.6\sigma$

C   if the score is between $\mu - 0.3\sigma$ and $\mu + 0.6\sigma$

D   if the score is between $\mu - 1.4\sigma$ and $\mu - 0.3\sigma$

F   if the score is below $\mu - 1.4\sigma$

What percent of the class receives each grade, assuming that the scores are normally distributed?

28. Assigning Grades Professor Morgan uses a normal distribution to assign grades in his Finite Mathematics class. He assigns an A to students scoring more than 2 standard deviations above the mean and an F to students scoring more than two standard deviations below the mean. He assigns a B to students who score between 1.2 and 2 standard deviations above the mean and a D to students who score between 1.6 and 2 standard deviations below the mean. All other students get a C. What percent of the class receives each grade assuming the scores are normally distributed?

29. Women's Heights The average height of 2000 women in a random sample is 64 inches. The standard deviation is 2 inches. The heights have a normal distribution.

(a) How many women in the sample are between 62 and 66 inches tall?

(b) How many women in the sample are between 60 and 68 inches tall?

(c) How many women in the sample are between 58 and 70 inches tall?

(d) How many women in the sample are more than 70 inches tall?

(e) How many women in the sample are shorter than 58 inches?

30. Weight of Corn Flakes in a Box Corn flakes come in a box that says it holds a mean weight of 16 ounces of cereal. The standard deviation is 0.1 ounce. Suppose that the manufacturer packages 600,000 boxes with weights that have a normal distribution.

(a) How many boxes weigh between 15.9 and 16.1 ounces?

(b) How many boxes weigh between 15.8 and 16.2 ounces?

(c) How many boxes weigh between 15.7 and 16.3 ounces?

(d) How many boxes weigh under 15.7 or over 16.3 ounces?

(e) How many boxes weigh under 15.7 ounces?

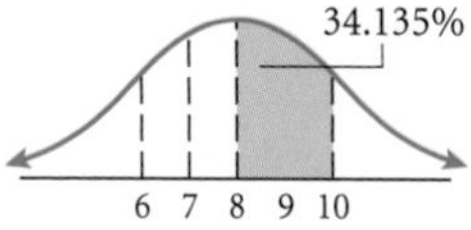

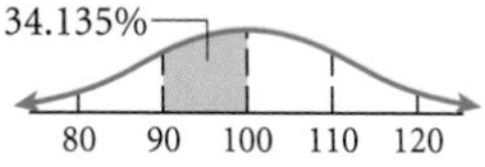

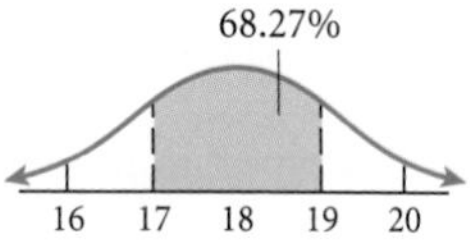

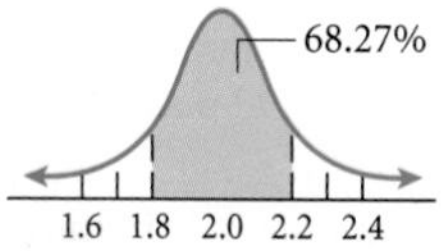

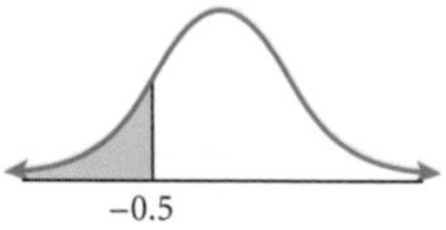

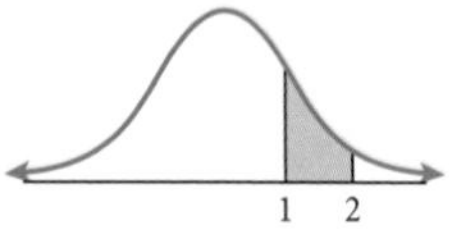

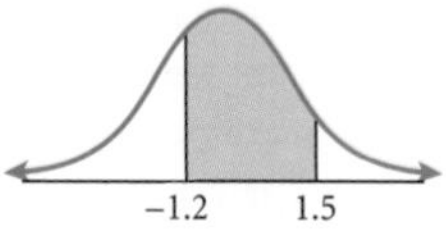

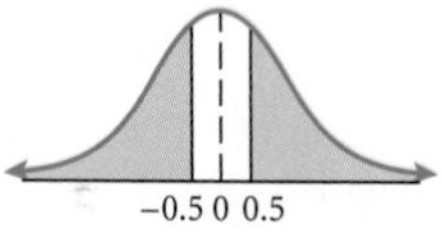

31. Student Weights The weight of 100 college students closely follows a normal distribution with a mean of 130 pounds and a standard deviation of 5.2 pounds.

(a) How many of these students would you expect to weigh at least 142 pounds?

(b) What range of weights would you expect to include the middle 70% of the students in this group?

32. Time to Do Taxes The Internal Revenue Service claims it takes an average of 3.7 hours to complete a 1040 tax form. Assuming the time to complete the form is normally distributed with a standard deviation of 30 minutes:

(a) What percent of people would you expect to complete the form in less than 5 hours?

(b) What time interval would you expect to include the middle 50% of the tax filers?

33. Life Expectancy of Clothing If the average life of a certain make of clothing is 40 months with a standard deviation of 7 months, what percentage of these clothes can be expected to last from 28 months to 42 months? Assume that clothing lifetime follows a normal distribution.

34. Life Expectancy of Shoes Records show that the average life expectancy of a pair of shoes is 2.2 years with a standard deviation of 1.7 years. A manufacturer guarantees that shoes lasting less than a year are replaced free. For every 1000 pairs sold, how many pairs should the manufacturer expect to replace free? Assume a normal distribution.

35. Movie Theater Attendance The attendance over a weekly period of time at a movie theater is normally distributed with a mean of 10,000 and a standard deviation of 1000 persons. Find

(a) The number in the lowest 70% of the attendance figures.

(b) The percent of attendance figures that falls between 8500 and 11,000 persons.

(c) The percent of attendance figures that differs from the mean by 1500 persons or more.

36. Test Scores Scores on an aptitude test are normally distributed with a mean of 980 and a standard deviation of 110. If 10,000 students take the test,

(a) How many would you expect to score between 900 and 1200?

(b) How many would you expect to score above 1400?

(c) How many would you expect to score below 750?

37. Comparing Test Scores Colleen, Mary, and Kathleen are vying for a position as editor. Colleen, who is tested with group I, gets a score of 76 on her test; Mary, who is tested with group II, gets a score of 89; and Kathleen, who is tested with group III, gets a score of 21. If the average score for group I is 82, for group II is 93, and for group III is 24, and if the standard deviation for each group is 7, 2, and 9, respectively, which person has the highest relative standing?

38. In Mathematics 135 the average final grade is 75.0 and the standard deviation is 10.0. The professor's grade distribution shows that 15 students with grades from 68.0 to 82.0 received Cs. Assuming the grades follow a normal distribution, how many students are in Mathematics 135?

39. (a) Draw the line chart and frequency curve for the probability of a head in an experiment in which a biased coin is tossed 15 times and the probability that a head occurs is 0.3. [*Hint:* Find $b(15, k; 0.30)$ for $k = 0, 1, \ldots, 15$.]

(b) Discuss the shape of the curve.

(c) What are the mean and the standard deviation of the distribution?

40. Follow the same directions as in Problem 39 for an experiment in which a biased coin is tossed 25 times and the probability that a head appears is $\frac{3}{4}$.

In Problems 41–44, use a normal approximation to the binomial distribution.

41. Lifetime Batting Averages A baseball player has a lifetime batting average of 0.250. In a season, this player comes to bat 300 times.

(a) What is the probability that at least 80 and no more than 90 hits occur?

(b) What is the probability that 85 or more hits occur?

42. Hitting a Target A skeet shooter has a long-established probability of hitting a target of 0.75. In a particular session, 200 attempts are made.

(a) What is the probability that at least 135 and no more than 160 are successful?

(b) What is the probability that 160 or more are successful?

43. Quality Control A company manufactures 100,000 packages of jelly beans each week. On average, 3% of the packages do not seal properly. A random sample of 500 packages is selected at the end of the week. What is the probability that in this sample at least 10 are not properly sealed?

44. Quality Control A company manufactures 200,000 pairs of pantyhose per week. On average 4% of the pairs are defective. A random sample of 300 pairs are selected each week. What is the probability that more than 5 pairs in the sample are defective?

45. Graph the standard normal curve using a graphing utility. For what value of x does the function assume its maximum? The equation is given by

$$y = \frac{1}{\sqrt{2\pi}} e^{-(1/2)x^2}$$

46. Graph the normal curve with $\mu = 10$ and $\sigma = 2$ using a graphing utility. For what value of x does the function assume its maximum? The equation is given by

$$y = \frac{1}{2\sqrt{2\pi}} e^{-(1/8)(x-10)^2}$$

47. Quality Control Refer to Problem 43. Use a graphing utility to compute the exact probability that the sample contains at least 10 bags of improperly sealed jelly beans.

48. Quality Control Refer to Problem 44. Use a graphing utility to compute the exact probability that the sample contains at least 5 pairs that are defective?

Discussion and Writing

49. **Quality Control** Refer to Problem 43. Suppose that each week a random sample of 500 packages of jelly beans is selected and every week there are at least 25 improperly sealed bags of jelly beans. What would you conclude about the statistics given in Problem 43?

50. **Quality Control** Refer to Problem 44. Suppose that each week a random sample of 300 pairs of pantyhose is selected and every week there are at least 20 defective pairs in the sample. What would you conclude about the statistics given in Problem 44?

'Are You Prepared?' Answers

1. True **2.** $P(1, 2, \text{or } 3 \text{ successes}) = 0.6656$ **3.** True

CHAPTER 9 REVIEW OBJECTIVES

Section	Examples		You should be able to	Review Exercises
9.1	1	1	Identify continuous and discrete variables (p. 506)	1–6
	2	2	Obtain a simple random sample (p. 507)	7, 8
	3	3	Identify sources of bias in a sample (p. 507)	9, 10
9.2	1	1	Construct a bar graph from (p. 509)	11a–14a
	2, 3	2	Construct a pie chart data (p. 510)	11b–14b
	3	3	Analyze a graph (p. 513)	15–18
9.3	1	1	Form a frequency table (p. 518)	19a, 21a, 23a, 24a
	2	2	Construct a line chart (p. 519)	19b, 21b, 23b, 24b
	3, 5	3	Group data into class intervals (p. 519)	19c, 20a, 21c, 22a, 23c, 24c
	4, 5	4	Build a histogram (p. 522)	19c, 20b, 21d, 22b, 23d, 24d, 25a, 26a
	6	5	Draw a frequency polygon (p. 526)	19d, 20e, 21e, 22c, 23e, 24e, 25b, 26b
	7	6	Draw an ogive (p. 527)	19g, 20e, 21h, 22e, 23h, 24h
		7	Identify the shape of a distribution (p. 528)	19e, 21f, 23f, 24f
9.4	1, 5	1	Find the mean of a set of data (p. 533)	27a–32a, 33b, 34b
	2	2	Find the mean for grouped data (p. 534)	35a, 36a
	3, 5	3	Find the median of a set of data (p. 535)	27b–32b
	4	4	Find the median for grouped data (p. 535)	35b, 36b
	6, 7	5	Identify the mode of a set of data (p. 538)	27c–32c
9.5	3, 4	1	Find the standard deviation of sample data (p. 543)	27e–32e, 33c, 34c
	5, 6	2	Find the standard deviation for grouped data (p. 546)	35c, 36c
	7	3	Use the Empirical Rule to describe a bell-shaped distribution (p. 547)	37, 38
	8, 9	4	Use Chebychev's theorem (p. 549)	39–42
9.6	2	1	Find a Z-score (p. 556)	43–48
	3, 4, 5, 6	2	Use the standard normal curve (p. 557)	49–60
	7, 8	3	Approximate a binomial distribution by the standard normal distribution (p. 560)	61–64

IMPORTANT FORMULAS

Mean for Sample Data (p. 532 and p. 539) $\bar{x} = \dfrac{x_1 + x_2 + \cdots + x_n}{n}$

Mean for Population Data (p. 539) $\mu = \dfrac{x_1 + x_2 + \cdots + x_N}{N}$

Mean for Grouped Data (p. 534) $\bar{x} = \dfrac{\Sigma f_i m_i}{n}$

Standard Deviation of Sample Data (p. 544) $s = \sqrt{\dfrac{(x_1 - \bar{x})^2 + (x_2 - \bar{x})^2 + \cdots + (x_n - \bar{x})^2}{n - 1}} = \sqrt{\dfrac{\Sigma (x_i - \bar{x})^2}{n - 1}}$

Standard Deviation for Population Data (p. 544) $\sigma = \sqrt{\dfrac{(x_1 - \mu)^2 + (x_2 - \mu)^2 + \cdots + (x_N - \mu)^2}{N}} = \sqrt{\dfrac{\Sigma (x_i - \mu)^2}{N}}$

Standard Deviation for Grouped Data (p. 546) $s = \sqrt{\dfrac{(m_1 - \bar{x})^2 \cdot f_1 + (m_2 - \bar{x})^2 \cdot f_2 + \cdots + (m_k - \bar{x})^2 \cdot f_k}{n - 1}}$

$$= \sqrt{\dfrac{\Sigma [(m_i - \bar{x})^2 \cdot f_i]}{n - 1}}$$

***Z*-Score** (p. 556) $Z = \dfrac{x - \mu}{\sigma}$

REVIEW EXERCISES **Answers to odd-numbered problems begin on page AN–50.**

Blue problem numbers represent the author's suggestions for a Practice Test.

In Problems 1–6, determine the variable in the experiment and state whether it is continuous or discrete.

1. A municipal hospital epidemiologist measures the circumference of each newborn baby's head.

2. An immigration officer asks each alien how long he or she expects to stay in the country.

3. A pollster counts how many people are in favor of a new law.

4. A statistician counts the number of hits a major league baseball player gets in a season.

5. A quality control manager lists the number of defective products manufactured each day.

6. A human resources clerk records the days an employee calls in sick.

7. **Opinion Poll** The student activities president wants to poll students for their opinions regarding a band to play on campus. Describe how she can choose a simple random sample of 100 students to poll.

8. Retirement Plans An employee benefits officer wants to poll employees of a bank regarding their retirement plans. How can he choose a simple random sample of 50 employees?

9. Opinion Poll An urban planner wants to poll the citizens of East Norwich regarding their opinions about a proposed road construction project that would interfere with rush hour traffic for the next 18 months. He asks 200 people as they leave the neighborhood supermarket between 10:00 A.M. and 3:00 P.M. on Thursday. What is wrong with the urban planner's sample?

10. Theater Attendance A researcher wants to determine how often the citizens of Muttontown attend the theater. She interviews 50 people at the local senior citizens' center. What is wrong with this researcher's sample?

11. The following data show how office workers in Chicago get to work:

Means of Transportation	Percentage
Ride alone	64
Carpool	5
Ride bus	30
Other	1

(a) Construct a bar graph of the data.

(b) Construct a pie chart of the data.

(c) Which of the graphs seems more informative to you? Why?

12. Getting to Work According to the 2000 census, Americans traveled to work in the following ways. The numbers are given in thousands.

Means of Transportation	Number
Drove	112,904
Used public transportation	6,030
Walked	3,721
Other	1,540

(a) Construct a bar graph of the data.
(b) Construct a pie chart of the data.
(c) Which of the graphs seems more informative to you? Why?

13. To study their attitudes toward a new product, 1000 people were interviewed. Their response is given in the following table:

Attitude	No. of Responses
Do not like	420
Like	360
Like very much	220

(a) Construct a bar graph of the data.
(b) Construct a pie chart of the data.
(c) Which of the graphs seems more informative to you? Why?

14. Vacation Travel An Internet travel agency surveyed 1000 of its clients to determine their mode of transportation for their last vacation. The agency found that 635 people drove, 280 flew, and 85 cruised to their destination.
(a) Construct a bar graph of the data.
(b) Construct a pie chart of the data.
(c) Which of the graphs seems more informative to you? Why?

15. College Enrollment The pie chart represents the race or ethnicity of students enrolled in four-year colleges in the United States in the fall of 2007. A total of 9,160,973 students were enrolled.

Enrollment in Four-Year Colleges by Race/Ethnicity, 2007

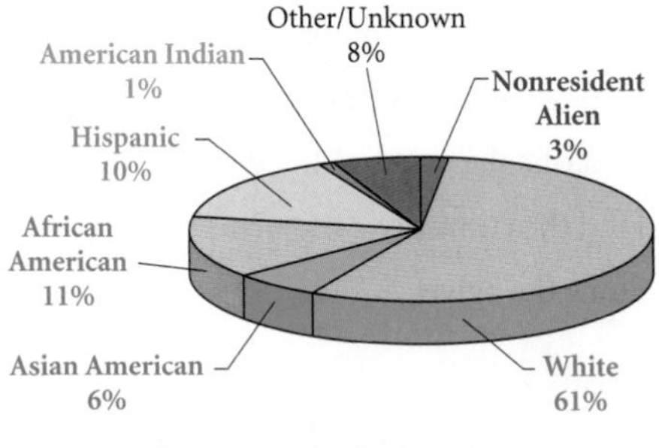

Source: National Science Foundation, Division of Science Resources Statistics.

(a) What group made up the smallest percentage of four-year college enrollment?
(b) If Asian Americans represent roughly 4% of the total population in the United States, were they underrepresented or overrepresented in four-year colleges in 2007?
(c) Approximately how many Hispanics were enrolled in four-year colleges in 2007?

16. Home Runs In 2001 Barry Bonds hit 73 home runs, breaking Mark McGwire's major league record. The bar graph shows where he hit each home run ball.

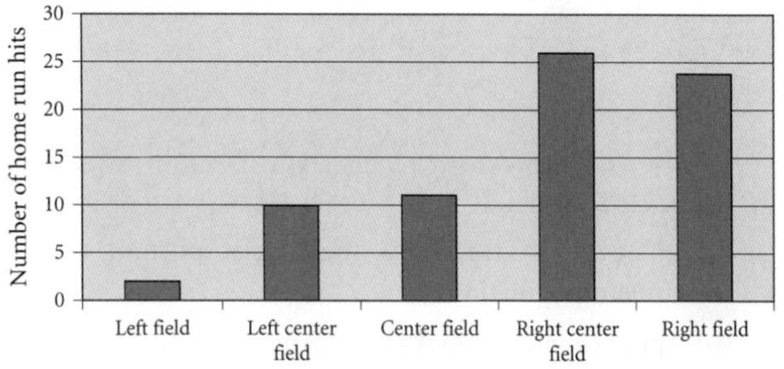

(a) In what direction were the fewest of his home runs hit?
(b) What percent of the home runs were hit to left center field?
(c) Where were almost 25% of the home runs hit?
(d) If you were a fielding coach for the opposing team and Barry Bonds was at bat, what advice would you give to your outfielders?

17. Educational Attainment The bar graph depicts the highest level of education attained by people in the United States in 2009.

Educational Attainment

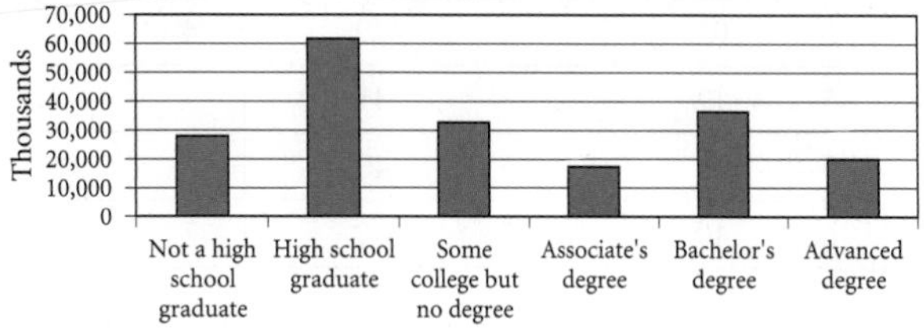

Source: U.S. Census Bureau.

(a) What is the highest level of education that most Americans have obtained?
(b) How many Americans have at least a bachelor's degree?
(c) How many people in the United States do not have a high school diploma?
(d) How many people have gone to college but do not have a bachelor's degree?

18. College Enrollment The pie chart represents the race or ethnicity of students enrolled in two-year colleges in the United States in the fall of 2007. A total of 6,638,938 students were enrolled.

Enrollment in Two-Year Colleges by Race/Ethnicity, 2007

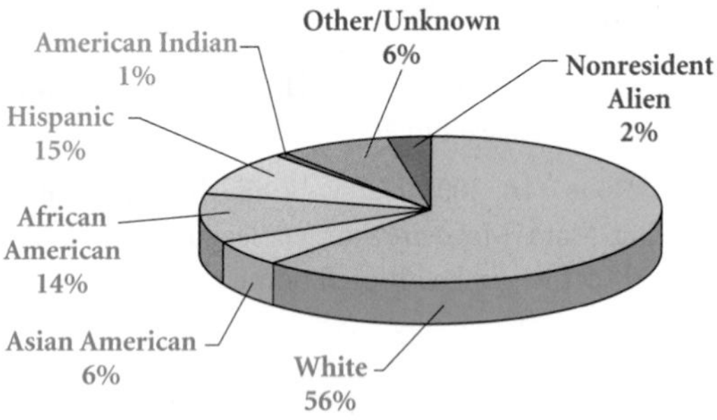

Source: National Science Foundation, Division of Science Resources Statistics.

(a) What group represents the largest portion of the student population?

(b) Approximately how many American Indians were enrolled in a two-year college in 2007?

(c) Approximately how many African Americans were enrolled in two-year colleges in 2007?

19. Test Scores The following scores were made on a mat exam:

80	90	82	21	100	55	80	62	78	52
21	73	80	44	72	63	91	85	33	66
78	42	87	90	90	70	48	75	83	77
63	85	69	80	41	87	66	52	71	60
74	70	73	95	89	41	92	68	100	72

(a) Set up a frequency table for the above data. What is th range?

(b) Draw a line chart for the data.

(c) Build a histogram for the data using a class interval o size 10 beginning with the interval 20.0–29.9.

(d) Draw a frequency polygon on the histogram.

(e) Describe the shape of the distribution.

(f) Find the cumulative frequencies.

(g) Draw the ogive.

20. Test Scores Use the data from Problem 19:

(a) Group the data into class intervals of size 5, startin with the interval 20.0–24.9.

(b) Build a histogram for the data using a class interval o size 5.

(c) Draw a frequency polygon on the histogram.

(d) Find the cumulative frequencies.

(e) Draw the ogive.

---

21. Track Championship At the high school track championships, 42 boys participated in the 1600-meter race. Their time (rounded to the nearest second) were

4 min	30 sec	4 min	12 sec	4 min	46 sec	4 min	15 sec	4 min	46 sec	4 min	40 sec
4	30	4	22	4	39	4	56	4	50	5	01
5	08	5	12	5	20	5	20	5	31	5	18
5	06	4	40	4	52	4	36	5	02	5	06
5	12	5	31	5	37	5	40	5	55	5	43
5	48	5	40	6	01	6	32	6	12	6	10
6	40	6	02	7	05	7	15	6	30	5	20

(a) Set up a frequency table for the above data. What is the range?

(b) Draw a line chart for the data.

(c) Group the data into class intervals of size 30 seconds, starting with the interval 4 minutes 0 seconds–4 minutes 29 seconds.

(d) Build the histogram for the data.

(e) Draw a frequency polygon on the histogram.

(f) Describe the shape of the distribution.

(g) Find the cumulative frequencies.

(h) Draw the ogive.

22. **Track Championship** Use the data in Problem 21.

(a) Group the data into class intervals of size 1 minute, starting with the interval 4 minutes 0 seconds–4 minutes 59 seconds.

(b) Build the histogram for the data.

(c) Draw a frequency polygon on the histogram.

(d) Find the cumulative frequencies.

(e) Draw the ogive.

23. **Baseball Players** During 2010 spring training, the ages of the 40 men on the New York Yankees roster were

33	24	27	24	35	28	37	38	40	25
29	33	24	38	27	36	24	34	26	30
25	26	29	29	33	27	29	27	24	23
25	24	25	25	25	27	23	23	23	26

Source: Major League Baseball.

(a) Make a frequency table of the players' ages.

(b) Construct a line chart of the data.

(c) Group the data into class intervals of size 5, beginning with the interval 20.0–24.9. How many class intervals are there?

(d) Build the histogram for the data.

(e) Draw the frequency polygon on the histogram.

(f) Describe the shape of the distribution.

(g) Find the cumulative frequencies.

(h) Draw the ogive.

24. **Baseball Players** During 2010 spring training, the ages of the 40 men on the Atlanta Braves roster were

26	23	34	24	35	37	24	31	25	40
25	38	26	33	30	27	33	24	28	38
26	26	25	32	32	20	28	27	25	26
23	25	26	25	22	26	28	22	23	26

Source: Major League Baseball.

(a) Make a frequency table of the players' ages.

(b) Construct a line chart of the data.

(c) Group the data into class intervals of size 5, beginning with the interval 20.0–24.9. How many class intervals are there?

(d) Build the histogram for the data.

(e) Draw the frequency polygon on the histogram.

(f) Describe the shape of the distribution.

(g) Find the cumulative frequencies.

(h) Draw the ogive.

25. **Tax Returns** The following table gives the number of individual tax returns (in millions) with an adjusted gross income under $50,000 for the 2007 tax year.

Adjusted Gross Income, $	Number of Returns
0–9,999	3.75
10,000–19,999	13.2
20,000–29,999	15.5
30,000–39,999	12.5
40,000–49,999	9.2

Source: IRS, Statistics of Income Division.

(a) Graph the data using a histogram.

(b) Draw a frequency polygon on the histogram.

26. **Tax Returns** The following table gives the number of individual tax returns (in millions) with an adjusted gross income under $50,000 for the 2006 tax year.

Adjusted Gross Income, $	Number of Returns
0–9,999	3.8
10,000–19,999	13.2
20,000–29,999	15.4
30,000–39,999	12.1
40,000–49,999	8.7

Source: IRS, Statistics of Income Division.

(a) Graph the data using a histogram.

(b) Draw a frequency polygon on the histogram.

(c) Compare the data to the previous problem. Comment on any similarities or differences.

In Problems 27–32, find (a) the mean, (b) the median, (c) the mode, if it exists, (d) the range, and (e) the standard deviation of each sample of data.

27. 12, 10, 8, 2, 0, 4, 10, 5, 4, 8, 0

28. 195, 5, 2, 2, 2, 2, 1, 0

29. 2, 5, 5, 7, 7, 7, 9, 9, 11, 100

30. −5, 2, 3, 8, −6, 9, 11, 10, −2, 8, −4, 0

31. 5, 7, 7, 9, 10, 11, 1, 6, 2, 12

32. 12, 10, 8, 10, 6, 10, 14

33. In seven different rounds of golf, Joe scores 74, 72, 76, 81, 77, 76, and 73.

(a) Do you think these are sample data or population data? Explain your answer.

(b) What is Joe's mean golf score?

(c) Find the standard deviation of Joe's golf scores.

34. The 10 fish caught on Tuesday weighed 16.2 pounds, 15 pounds, 12.3 pounds, 20 pounds, 8 pounds, 6.5 pounds, 8 pounds, 10.8 pounds, 12 pounds, and 9 pounds.

(a) Do you think these are sample data or population data? Explain your answer.

(b) What is the mean weight of the fish?

(c) Find the standard deviation of the fishes' weights.

35. Population Distribution The U.S. Census Bureau gives information about the age distribution of persons living in the United States. The following data give the estimated number (in thousands) of females for various ages in 2009.

Age	Population	Age	Population
0–4	10,412	50–54	11,083
5–9	10,073	55–59	9,770
10–14	9,751	60–64	8,234
15–19	10,486	65–69	6,273
20–24	10,446	70–74	4,925
25–29	10,562	75–79	4,176
30–34	9,780	80–84	3,524
35–39	10,185	85–89	2,395
40–44	10,487	90–94	1,077
45–49	11,535	95–99	319
		100–104	55

Source: U.S. Census Bureau.

(a) Approximate the mean age of a female in 2009.

(b) Approximate the median age of a female in 2009.

(c) Approximate the standard deviation of the age of the females.

36. Population Distribution The U.S. Census Bureau gives information about the age distribution of persons living in the United States. The following data give the estimated number (in thousands) of males for various ages in 2009.

Age	Population	Age	Population
0–4	10,887	50–54	10,677
5–9	10,535	55–59	9,204
10–14	10,222	60–64	7,576
15–19	11,051	65–69	5,511
20–24	11,093	70–74	4,082
25–29	11,115	75–79	3,149
30–34	10,107	80–84	2,298
35–39	10,353	85–89	1,266
40–44	10,504	90–94	424
45–49	11,295	95–99	82
		100–104	87

Source: U.S. Census Bureau.

(a) Approximate the mean age of a male in 2009.

(b) Approximate the median age of a male in 2009.

(c) Approximate the standard deviation of the age of the males.

37. The Empirical Rule A random sample of 200 lightbulbs has a mean life of 600 hours and a standard deviation of 53 hours.

(a) A histogram of the data indicates the sample data follow a bell-shaped distribution. According to the Empirical Rule, 99.7% of lightbulbs have lifetimes between _____ and _____ hours.

(b) Assuming the data are bell shaped, determine the percentage of lightbulbs that will have a life between 494 and 706 hours.

(c) Assuming the data are bell shaped, what percentage of lightbulbs will last between 547 and 706 hours?

(d) If the company that manufactures the lightbulbs guarantees to replace any bulb that does not last at least 441 hours, what percentage of lightbulbs can the firm expect to have to replace, according to the Empirical Rule?

38. **The Empirical Rule** In a random sample of 250 toner cartridges, the mean number of pages a toner cartridge can print is 4302 and the standard deviation is 340.

(a) Suppose a histogram of the data indicates that the sample data follow a bell-shaped distribution. According to the Empirical Rule, 99.7% of toner cartridges will print between _____ and _____ pages.

(b) Assuming that the distribution of the data is bell shaped, determine the percentage of toner cartridges whose print total is between 3622 and 4982 pages.

(c) If the company that manufactures the toner cartridges guarantees to replace any cartridge that does not print at least 3622 pages, what percent of cartridges can the firm expect to be responsible for replacing, according to the Empirical Rule?

In Problems 39–42, use Chebychev's theorem to find the probability.

39. **Jelly Jars** A machine fills jars with 12 ounces of jam. The machine is not exact and jars have a standard deviation of 0.05 ounce. In a lot of 1000 jars, how many jars would you expect to have between 11.9 and 12.1 ounces of jam?

40. **Machining** A die cast stamps out metal washers with a mean outer diameter of 2.5 cm and a variance of 0.01 cm^2. In a shipment of 10,000 washers, how many would you expect to have an outer diameter between 2.3 and 2.7 cm?

41. **Sacks of Potatoes** Potatoes are packed in 10-pound bags. Each bag has a mean weight of 10 pounds with a standard deviation of 0.25 pound. What is the probability that a bag picked at random weighs less than 9.5 pounds or more than 10.5 pounds?

42. **Shrimp by the Pound** Shrimp are priced by size; the larger the shrimp, the more expensive the cost. Jumbo shrimp have 9 shrimp to the pound with a standard deviation of 0.75 shrimp. What is the probability that a pound of jumbo shrimp contains fewer than 8 or more than 10 shrimp?

In Problems 43–48, compute the Z-score for the data point x, using the given population mean and standard deviation.

43. $\mu = 10, \sigma = 3, x = 8$

44. $\mu = 14, \sigma = 3, x = 20$

45. $\mu = 1, \sigma = 5, x = 8$

46. $\mu = 140, \sigma = 15, x = 125$

47. $\mu = 55, \sigma = 3, x = 60$

48. $\mu = 32, \sigma = 13, x = 10$

In Problems 49–52, calculate the area under the normal curve.

49. Between $Z = -2.75$ and $Z = -1.35$

50. Between $Z = 1.2$ and $Z = 1.75$

51. Between $Z = -0.75$ and $Z = 2.1$

52. Between $Z = -1.5$ and $Z = 0.34$

53. A normal distribution has a mean of 25 and a standard deviation of 5.

(a) What proportion of the scores will fall between 20 and 30?

(b) What proportion of the scores will lie above 35?

54. A set of 600 scores is normally distributed. How many scores would you expect to find

(a) Between $\pm 1\sigma$ of the mean?

(b) Between 1σ and 3σ above the mean?

(c) Between $\pm \frac{2}{3}\sigma$ of the mean?

55. **Average Life of a Dog** The average life expectancy of a dog is 14 years, with a standard deviation of about 1.25 years. Assuming that the life spans of dogs are normally distributed, approximately how many dogs will die before reaching the age of 10 years, 4 months?

56. **Life of a Battery** The average life span of a phone battery is 20 months with a standard deviation of 1.5 months. Assuming the battery life is normally distributed, what is the probability that a battery chosen at random will last more than 24 months?

57. **Comparing Test Scores** Bob got an 89 on the final exam in mathematics and a 79 on the sociology exam. In the mathematics class the average grade was 79 with a standard deviation of 5, and in the sociology class the average grade was 72 with a standard deviation of 3.5. Assuming that the grades in both subjects were normally distributed, in which class did Bob rank higher?

58. **Comparing Test Scores** Marty took 3 tests in science this semester. His grades were 58, 79, and 83. If the mean score and standard deviation of the tests were 50 and 7, 73 and 4, and 75 and 8, respectively, on which test did Marty have the highest standing?

59. Suppose it is known that the number of items produced each week in a factory has a mean of 40. If the variance of a week's production is known to equal 25, then what can be said about the probability that this week's production will be between 30 and 50?

60. From past experience a teacher knows that the test scores of students taking an examination have a mean of 75 and a variance of 25. What can be said about the probability that a student chosen at random will score between 65 and 85?

In Problems 61–64 use the normal approximation to the binomial distribution.

61. **Blood Tests** A blood test for an antigen gives a positive result with a probability of 0.7. In testing 200 blood samples, what is the probability of obtaining more than 160 positive results?

62. **Color-blindness** The probability a male is color-blind is 0.30. In a sample of 1000 males, what is the probability that fewer than 200 are color-blind?

63. **Toll Gates** An automatic gate malfunctions, failing to open, with a probability 0.05. What is the probability that in 500 operations, the gate fails to work between 20 and 30 times?

64. **Licensing Tests** A professional licensing test has a 60% pass rate. What is the probability that, in a group of 200 randomly selected test takers, between 110 and 125 pass the test?

Chapter 9 Project

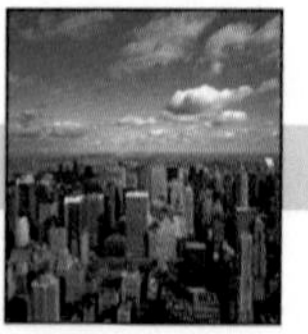

"AVERAGE" WEATHER

The daily weather forecast that appears in a local newspaper or on television often contains information regarding the average high and low temperatures, air quality, and other information. This information helps a reader or viewer to make a comparison between historical and actual temperatures, rainfall, humidity level, pollen, air pollutants, and so on. These figures are the result of the application of statistics to a large collection of data. In this example, we compare the actual weather to the reported averages.

Part of what makes travel comfortable and enjoyable is good weather. Suppose that you want to visit New York City, which is notorious for extreme weather. To avoid the cold of winter and the extreme heat of summer, you decide to visit in June. According to *USA Today*, the average high temperature is 80°F, the average low temperature is 63°F, and the average rainfall is 3.6 inches. The highest temperature recorded was 101°F and the lowest temperature recorded was 44°F. However, you are curious about the deviation from these averages and discover the data shown in Table 1 for June 2009.

ABLE 1 DATA FOR JUNE 2009

Day	High of (°F)	Low of (°F)	Precip. (in)	Day	High of (°F)	Low of (°F)	Precip. (in)
1	71	53	0	16	70	55	0
2	80	60	0.1	17	68	60	0.38
3	72	54	1	18	65	61	1.92
4	68	56	0.06	19	77	63	0
5	60	55	0.88	20	71	63	0.51
6	76	60	0	21	78	64	0.22
7	82	66	0	22	75	66	0
8	75	60	1.15	23	80	65	0.17
9	71	59	0.7	24	76	64	0.13
10	67	59	0.09	25	79	67	0
11	67	59	0.68	26	83	63	0.73
12	80	67	0.01	27	81	64	0.02
13	73	61	0.15	28	82	65	0
14	73	57	0.24	29	81	67	0
15	72	56	0.26	30	84	65	0.66

Source: National Weather Service.

We shall investigate how June 2009 compared to an average month.

1. Calculate the mean high temperature, the mean low temperature, and the total rainfall.
2. The *mean temperature* for the month is defined as the mean of the daily temperatures (the midpoint of the high and low temperatures). What is the mean temperature for this month?
3. Show that we can calculate the mean monthly temperature by calculating the mean of the mean high temperature and the mean low temperature.
4. What are the median high and the median low temperatures for the month? How do they compare with the corresponding mean temperatures? Interpret the differences.
5. Is there a modal high temperature? If so, what is it? Is there a modal low temperature? If so, what is it?
6. Compare the mean, median, and modal high temperatures. Do the same for the low temperatures. What do you conclude?
7. Calculate the standard deviation of the high and low temperatures. A normal distribution is symmetric around its mean, so the mean, the median, and the mode are all equal. What kind of errors might one expect if one were to use the normal distribution to estimate the probability of obtaining a low temperature between 60°F and 65°F on a day in June based on the 2009 data? [*Hint*: Try a geometric argument. That is, use a graph.]
8. Make a frequency table for the daily high temperatures and one for the daily low temperatures. Then group each set of data into class intervals of equal degree width. Use 51°–55°F as the first interval.
9. Build a histogram for each set of grouped data and draw a frequency polygon on each histogram.
10. Examine the histograms and determine the modes of the high and low temperature frequency distributions. If the earlier calculations indicated that the month was close to the average, what do the modes tell you?
11. Find the approximate mean high temperature for June 2009 and the approximate standard deviation using the grouped data. Are they good approximations of the actual mean high temperature and its standard deviation? Explain your reasoning.
12. Repeat Problem 11 for the grouped low temperatures.

Mathematical Questions from Professional Exams*

1. **Actuary Exam—Part II** Under the hypothesis that a pair of dice are fair, the probability is approximately 0.95 that the number of 7s appearing in 180 throws of the dice will lie within $30 \pm K$. What is the value of K?

   (a) 2 (b) 4 (c) 6 (d) 8 (e) 10

2. **Actuary Exam—Part II** If X is normally distributed with mean μ and variance μ^2 and if $P(-4 < X < 8) = 0.9974$, then $\mu =$

   (a) 1 (b) 2 (c) 4 (d) 6 (e) 8

3. **Actuary Exam—Part II** A manufacturer makes golf bal[l] whose weights average 1.62 ounces, with a standar[d] deviation of 0.05 ounce. What is the probability that th[e] weight of a group of 100 balls will lie in the interva[l] 162 ± 0.5 ounces?

   (a) 0.18 (b) 0.34 (c) 0.68 (d) 0.84 (e) 0.96

Answers to Odd-Numbered Problems

CHAPTER 1 Linear Equations

Exercise 1.1 (p. 16)

3. True **4.** $x = -3$ **5.** Vertical **6.** $m = -4$; y-intercept: $(0, 6)$ **7.** $y - y_1 = m(x - x_1)$ **8.** negative

9. $A = (4, 2)$; $B = (6, 2)$; $C = (5, 3)$; $D = (-2, 1)$; $E = (-2, -3)$; $F = (3, -2)$; $G = (6, -2)$; $H = (5, 0)$

11. The set of points of the form $(2, y)$, where y is a real number, is a vertical line passing through $(2, 0)$ on the x-axis.

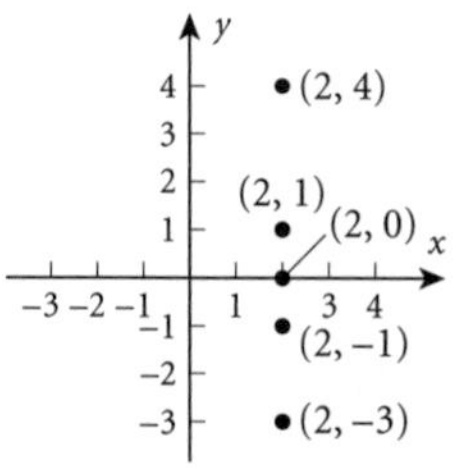

13.

x	0	−2	2	−2	4	−4
y	4	0	8	0	12	−4

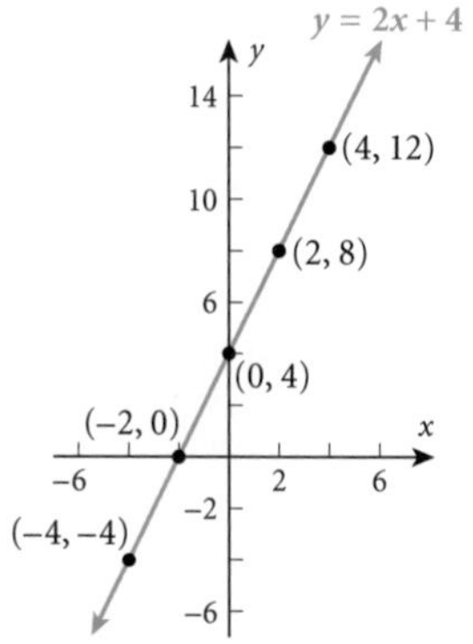

15.

x	0	3	2	−2	4	−4
y	−6	0	−2	−10	2	−14

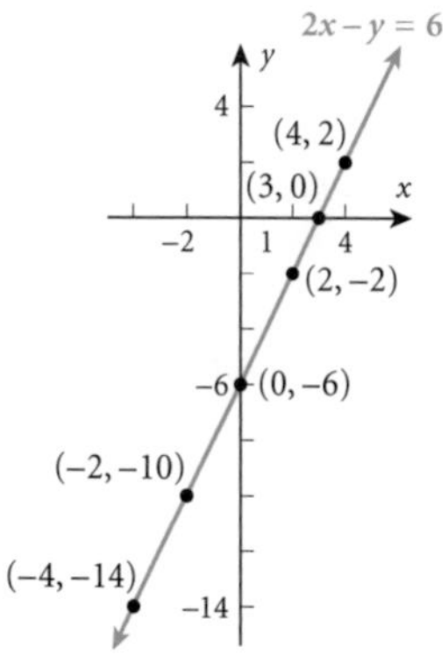

17. **(a)** Vertical line: $x = 2$
(b) Horizontal line: $y = -3$
(c) $5x - y = 13$

19. **(a)** Vertical line: $x = -4$
(b) Horizontal line: $y = 1$
(c) $5x - y = -21$

21. **(a)** vertical line: $x = 0$
(b) horizontal line: $y = 3$
(c) $5x - y = -3$

23. $m = \frac{1}{2}$ A slope of $\frac{1}{2}$ means that for every 2 unit change in x, y changes 1 unit.

25. $m = -1$ A slope of -1 means that for every 1 unit change in x, y changes by (-1) unit.

27. $m = 3$ A slope of 3 means that for every 1 unit change in x, y will change 3 units.

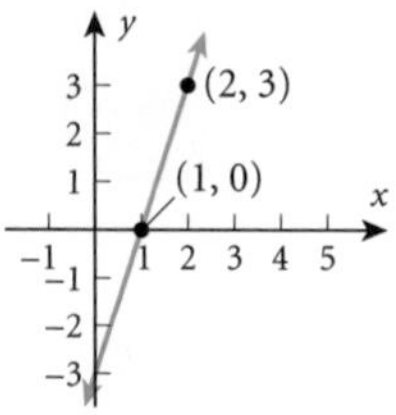

29. $m = -\frac{1}{2}$ A slope of $-\frac{1}{2}$ means that for every 2 unit change in x, y will change (-1) unit.

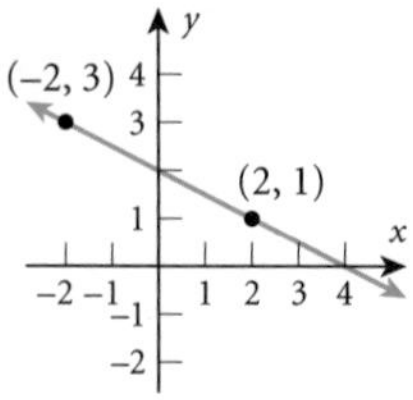

31. $m = 0$ A slope of 0 means that regardless how x changes, y remains constant.

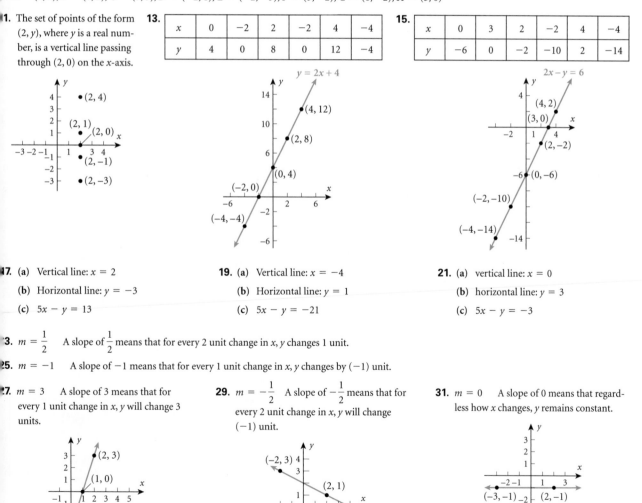

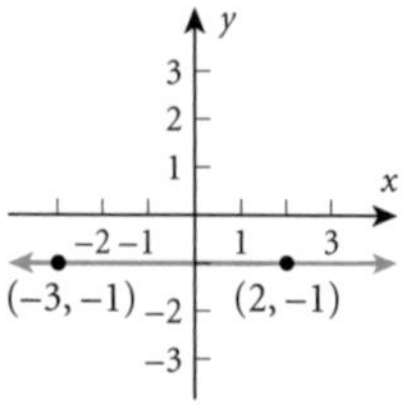

33. The slope is not defined.

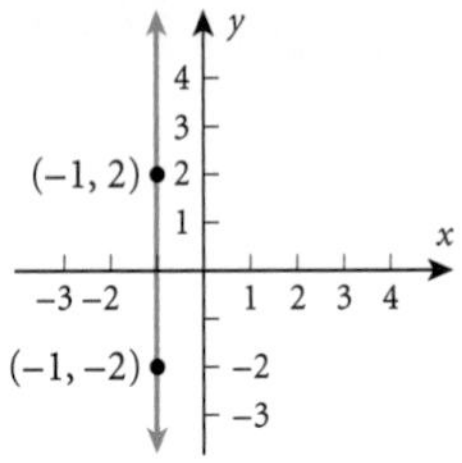

35.

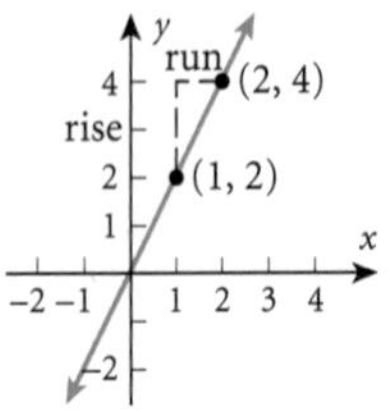

37.

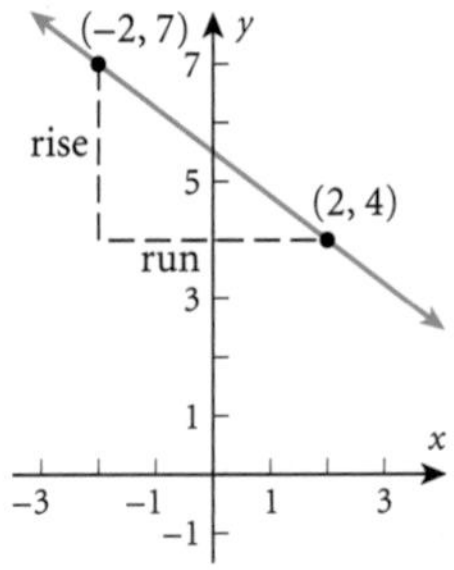

39.

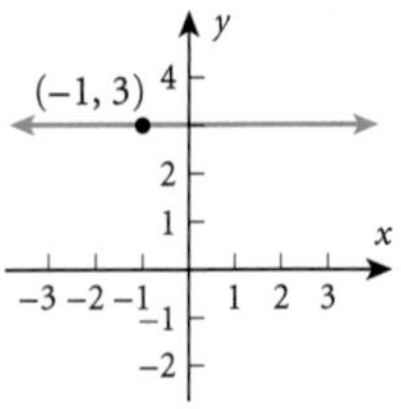

41.

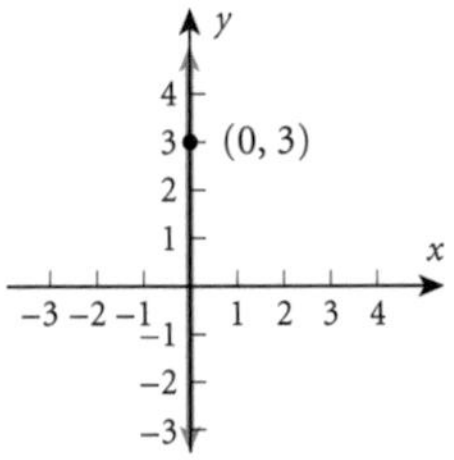

43. $x - 2y = 0$ **45.** $x + y = 2$ **47.** $2x - y = -9$ **49.** $2x + 3y = -1$ **51.** $x - 2y = -5$ **53.** $2x + y = 3$

55. $3x - y = -12$ **57.** $4x - 5y = 0$ **59.** $x - 2y = 2$ **61.** $x = 1$ **63.** $y = 4$

65. slope: $m = 2$;
y-intercept: $(0, 3)$

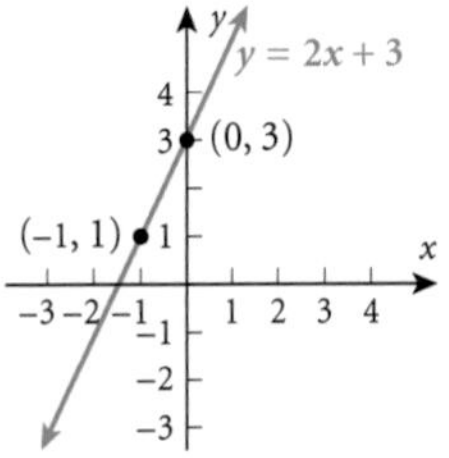

67. slope: $m = 2$;
y-intercept: $(0, -2)$

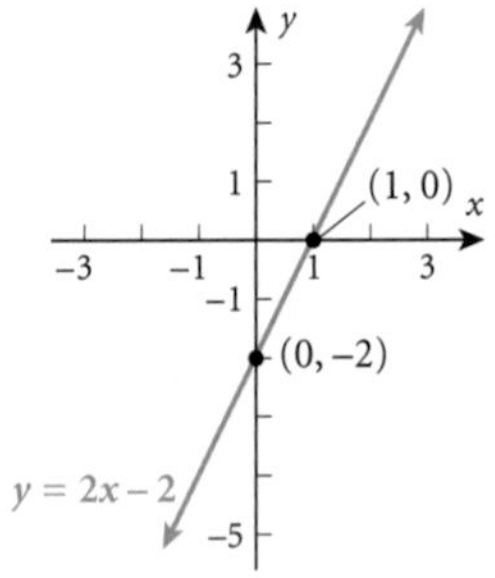

69. slope: $m = \dfrac{2}{3}$;
y-intercept: $(0, -2)$

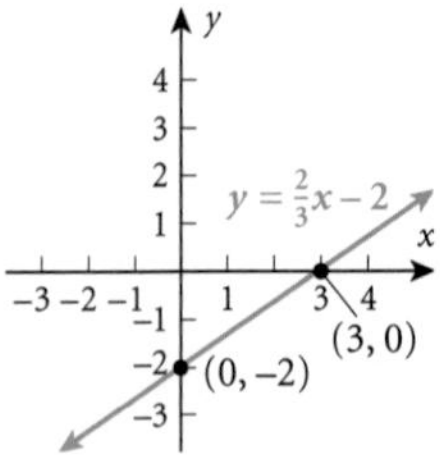

71. slope: $m = -1$; y-intercept:
$(0, 1)$

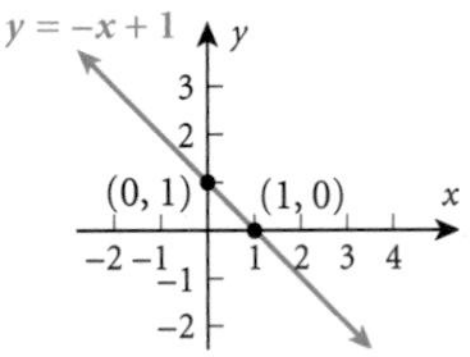

73. Slope is not defined; there is
no y-intercept.

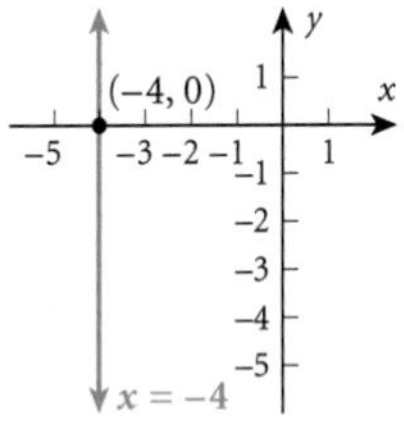

75. slope: $m = 0$; y-intercept:
$(0, 5)$

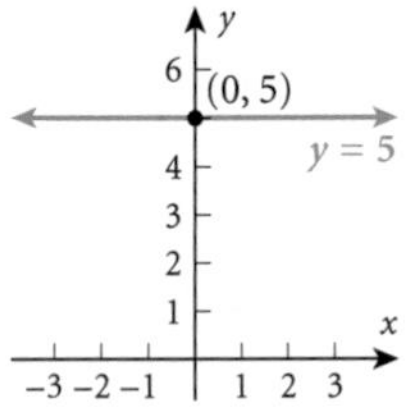

77. slope: $m = 1$; y-intercept: $(0, 0)$

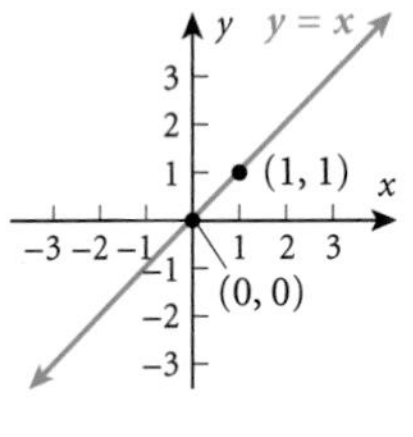

79. slope: $m = \dfrac{3}{2}$; y-intercept:
$(0, 0)$

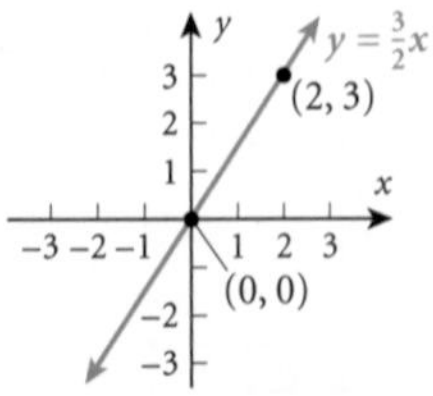

81. Window:
X min = -10; X max = 10
Y min = -10; Y max = 10

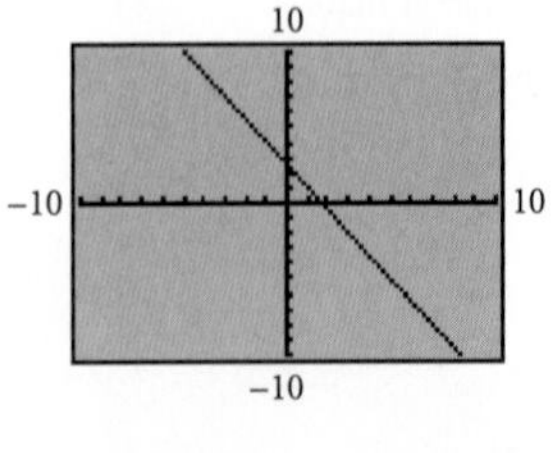

x-intercept: $(1.67, 0)$;
y-intercept: $(0, 2.50)$

83. Window:
X min = -10; X max = 10
Y min = -10; Y max = 10

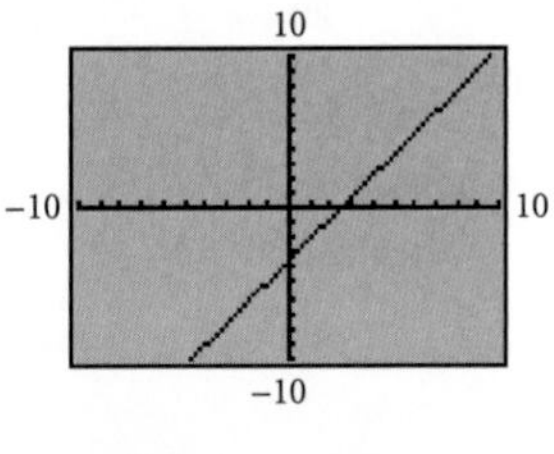

x-intercept: $(2.52, 0)$;
y-intercept: $(0, -3.53)$

85. Window:
X min = -10; X max = 10
Y min = -10; Y max = 10

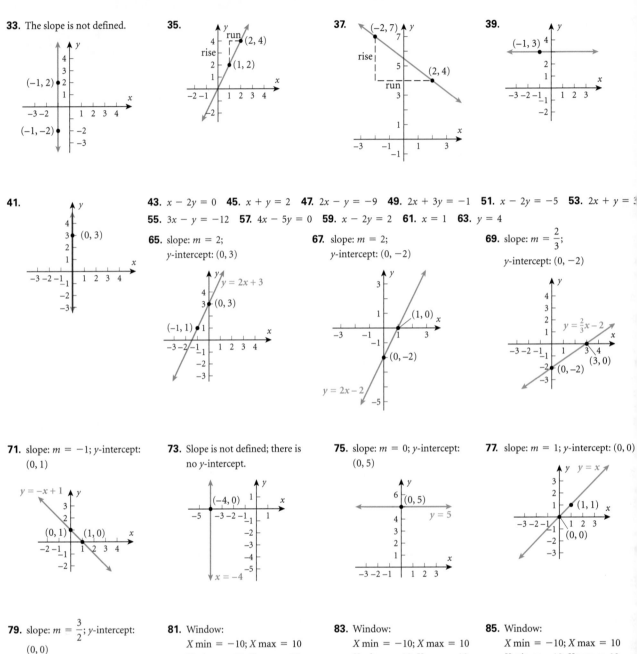

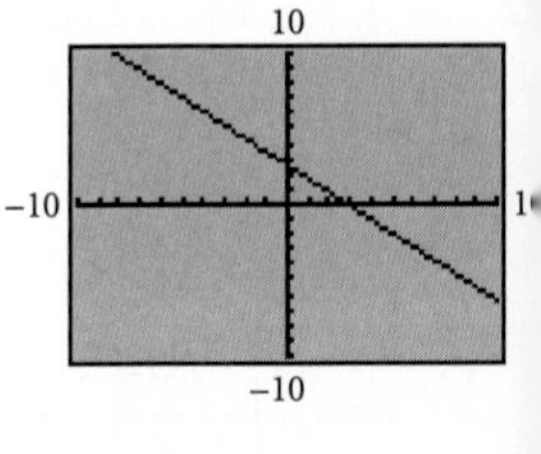

x-intercept: $(2.83, 0)$;
y-intercept: $(0, 2.56)$

7. Window:
$X\min = -10; X\max = 10;$
$Y\min = -10; Y\max = 10$

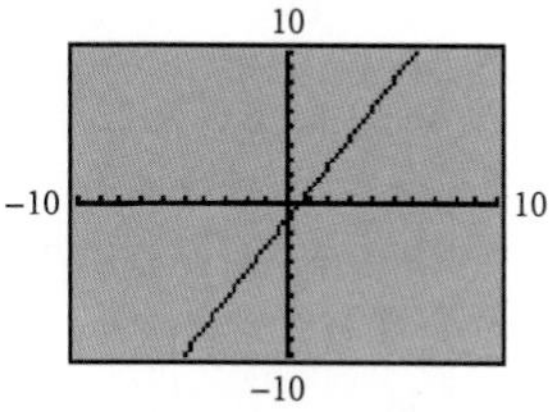

x-intercept: (0.78, 0);
y-intercept: (0, −1.41)

89. (b) **91.** (d) **93.** $y = x + 2$ or $x - y = -2$ **95.** $y = -\frac{1}{3}x + 1$ or $x + 3y = 3$

97. (a) $C = 0.54x$
(b) $C = \$8100$
(c)

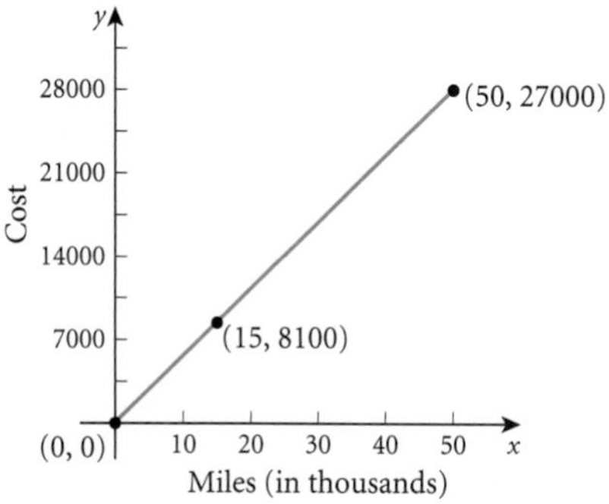

(d) The slope represents the additional cost of driving a standard-sized car another mile.

99. (a) $C = 0.10438x + 8.23, 0 \le x \le 400$
(b)

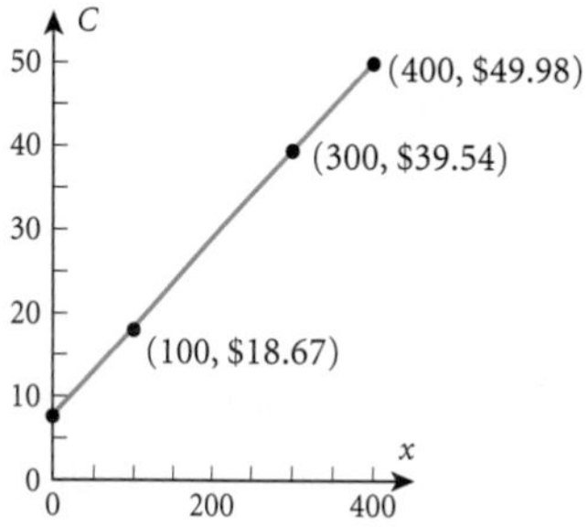

(c) The monthly charge for using 100 KWH is \$18.67.
(d) The monthly charge for using 300 KWH is \$39.54.
(e) For every extra KWH used (up to 400 KWH), the electric bill increases by 10.438 cents.

1. (a) $C = \frac{5}{9}(F - 32)$ (b) $C = 20°$ **103.** (a) $A = 0.0467t + 102.7$ (b) There were 103.167 billion gallons in the reservoir on December 31.) The slope indicates that the reservoir gains 0.0467 million gallons of water per day. (d) On January 31, 2010 we predict 104.6147 billion gallons of ater in the reservoir. (e) The reservoir will be full after 3586 days. **105.** (a) \$80,000.00 (b) \$95,000.00 (c) In 2012 sales are predicted to be 10,000.00. (d) In 2015 sales are predicted to be \$125,000.00. **107.** (a) $S = 0.05x + 400$ (b) Dan earns \$600.00. (c) Dan must generate a ofit of \$9146.20 to make the median earnings. **109.** (a) $S = 2.1(t - 1999) + 475$ (b) In 2011 the average mathematics SAT score is predicted to 500. **111.** (a) $P = .5(t - 1998) + 24.4$ (b) If the trend continues, in 2011 about 30.9% of people over 25 years of age will have a bachelor's degree higher. (c) The slope is the annual average increase in the percent of people over 25 years of age who hold bachelor's degrees or higher. 3. (a) $C = -6543(t - 2008) + 94823$ (b) \$75,194 **115.** (a) $S = 50.817(t - 2007) + 214.091$ (b) The predicted total sales and erating income of Chevron Corporation is predicted to be \$417.359 billion in 2011. **117.** (a) $C = \frac{2.739}{17}x$ (b) $C = \frac{1.847}{17}x$ (c) The Smiths spend 2417 on gasoline at the 2010 price. (d) The Smiths spend \$1630 on gasoline at the 2009 price. (e) They spend \$787 more at the 2010 price than at e 2009 price. **119.** (a) $N = 64.3t + 954.7$ (b) The slope indicates that the number of credit and debit cards in force is increasing at an average rate 64.3 million cards per year. (c) There will be an estimated 1.276 billion credit and debit cards in force at the end of the first quarter of 2011. (d) In 14 will be an estimated 1.5 billion credit and debit cards in force. **121.** (a), (c), (f), (g) **123.** Vertical lines cannot be written in slope–intercept rm. **125.** Two lines with equal slopes and equal y-intercepts have the same graphs. **127.** If two lines have the same slope but different x-intercepts, ey cannot have the same y-intercepts. **129.** yes; yes (the line $y = 0$). **130.** yes; no

xercise 1.2 (p. 28)

parallel **2.** intersect **3.** parallel **5.** intersecting **7.** coincident **9.** parallel **11.** intersecting **13.** intersecting **15.** (3, 2)

7. (3, 1)

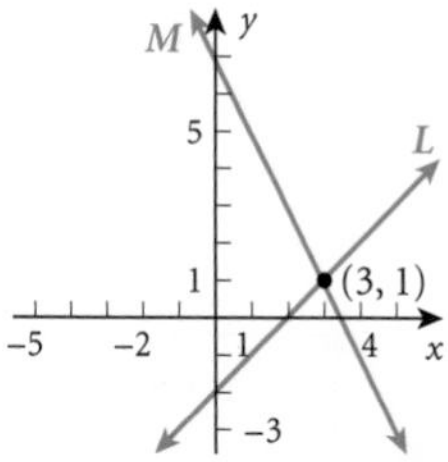

19. (1, 0)

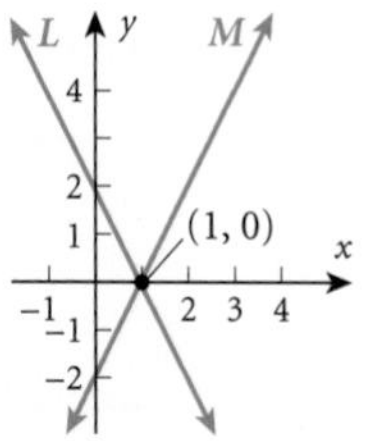

21. (2, 1)

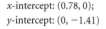

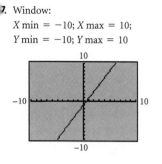

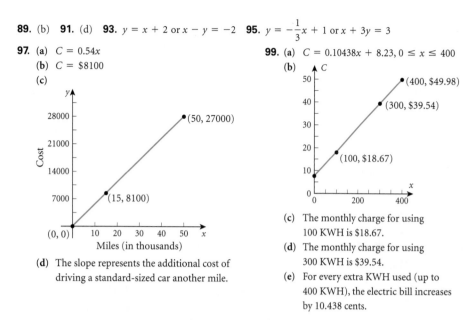

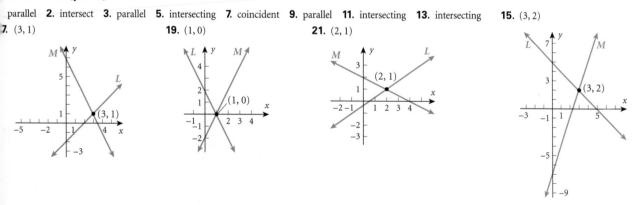

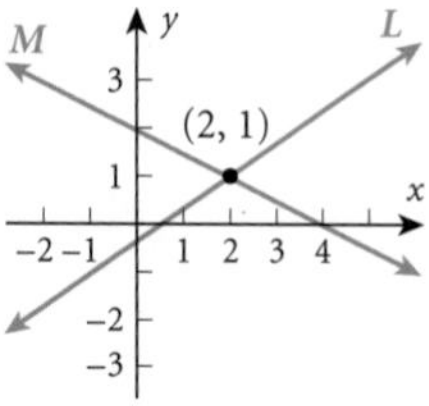

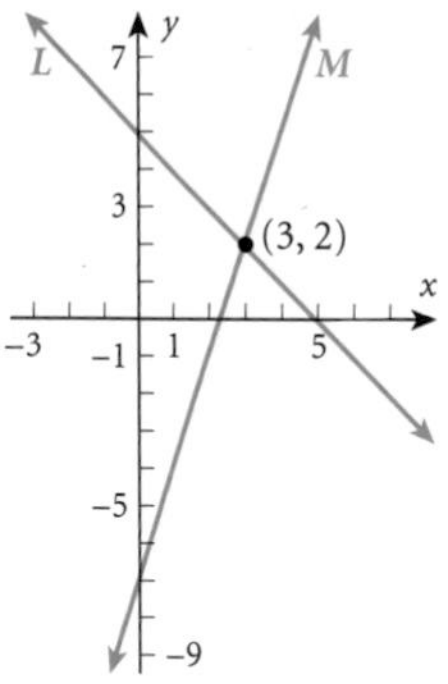

23. $(-1, 1)$

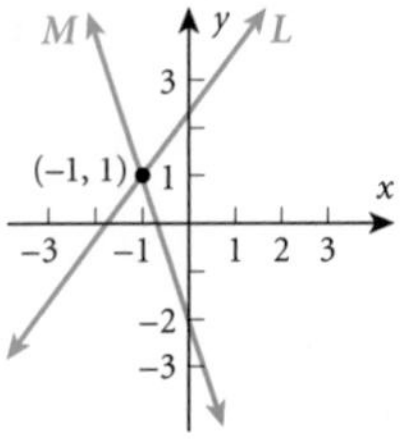

25. $(4, -2)$

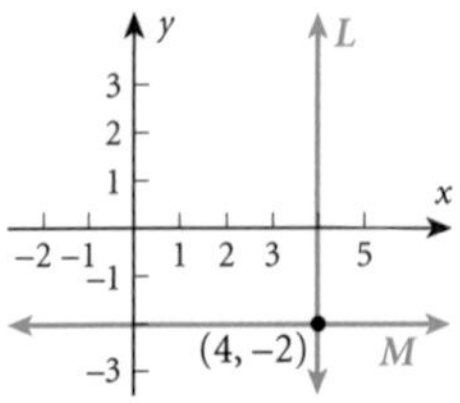

27. $y = 2x - 3$ or $2x - y = 3$ **29.** $y = 4x + 6$ or $4x - y = -6$ **31.** $y = 2x$ or $2x - y = 0$ **33.** $x = 4$

35. $y = -\frac{19}{5}x - \frac{63}{5}$ or $19x + 5y = -63$

37. To break even, put 20 caramels and 30 creams into each box; increase the number of caramels to obtain a profit. **39.** Mr. Nicholson should invest \$50,000 in AA Bonds and \$100,000 in Savings and Loan Certificates. **41.** Mix 25 pounds of Kona coffee with 75 pounds of Colombian coffee to obtain a blend worth \$10.80 per pound.

43. Mix 30 cubic centimeters of the 15% solution with 70 cubic centimeters of the 5% solution to obtain a solution that is 8% acid.

45. **(a)** $y = 562.44x$ **(b)** A purchase of 17.8 ounces of gold would have resulted in a gain of \$10,000.00. **47.** **(a)** $N = \frac{262}{365}x + 1615$ **(b)** $x = 536.450$; the 2000th station is predicted to have aired on July 22, 2009.

Exercise 1.3 (p. 34)

1. False **2.** True

3. The break-even point is $x = 30$.

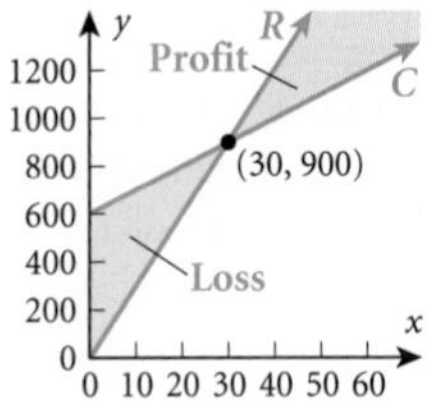

5. The break-even point is $x = 500$.

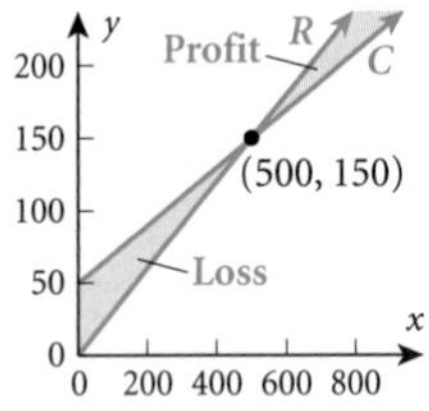

7. The market price is \$1.00.

9. The market price is \$10.00.

11. The break-even point occurs when $x = 1200$ game-day pennants are produced and sold.

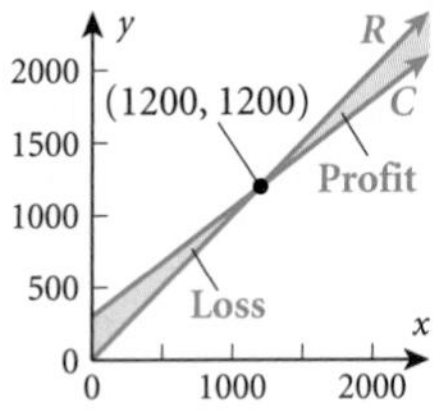

13. **(a)** Market price: \$1.00
(b) Supply demanded at market price: 1.1 million pounds

(c)

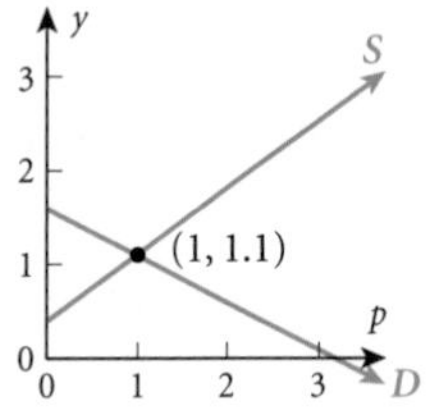

(d) The point of intersection is called market equilibrium. It is the price where supply produced equals the amount demanded.

15. $D = -4p + 23$

17. At most 16 DVDs can be ordered from the club to keep the price lower than that of the discount retailer.

Exercise 1.4 (p. 39)

1. True **2.** Correlation coefficient **3.** A relation exists, and it appears to be linear. **5.** A relation exists, and it appears to be linear. **7.** No relation exists.

9. **(a)**

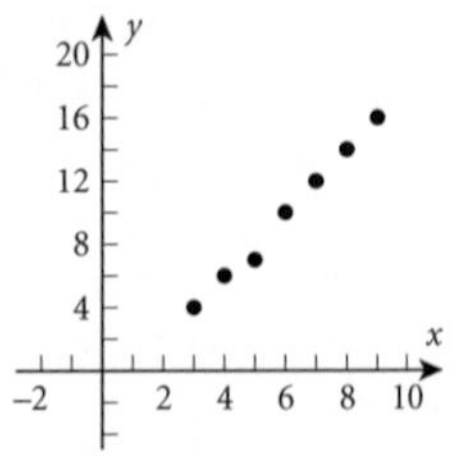

(b) $y = 2x - 2$

(c)

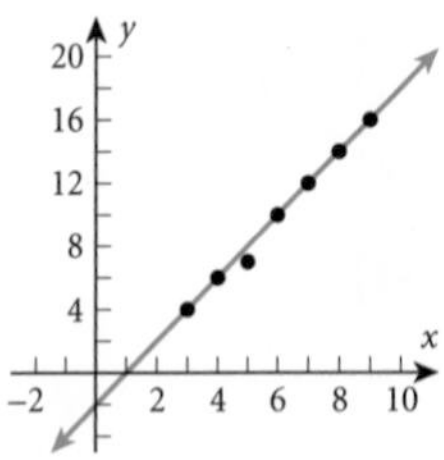

(d)

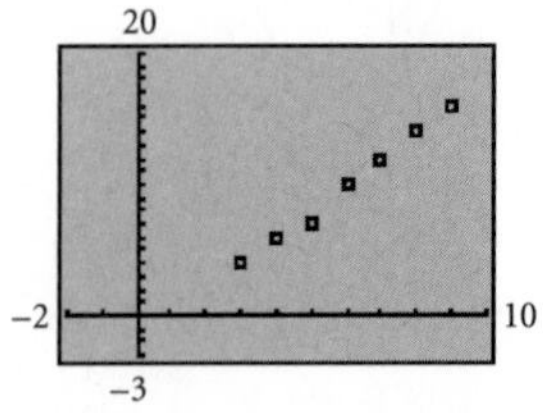

(e) Using the LinReg program, the line of best fit is: $y = 2.0357x - 2.3571$.

(f)

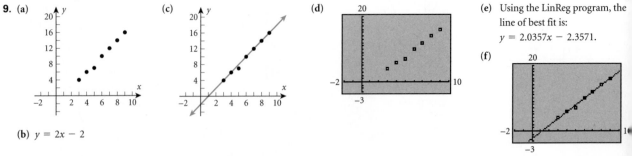

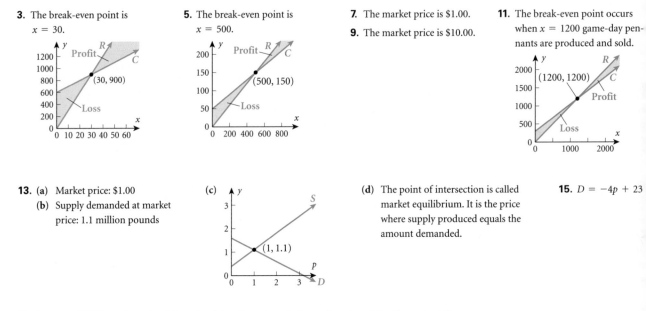

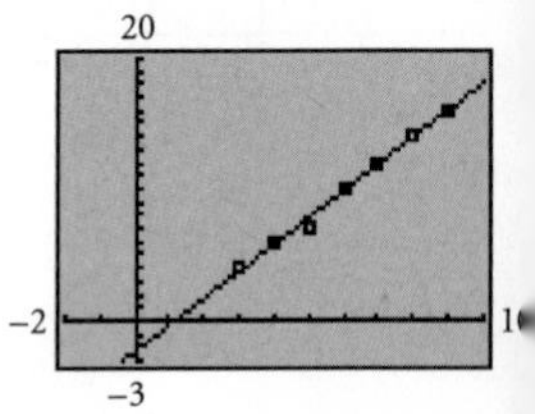

1. **(a)**

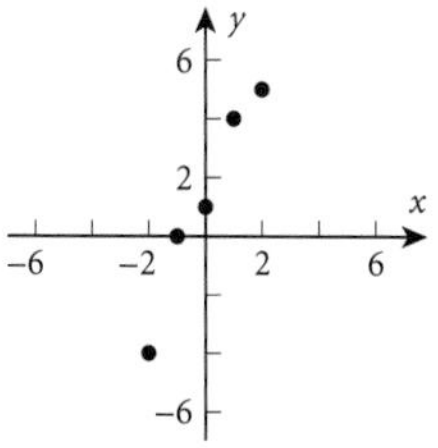

(c)

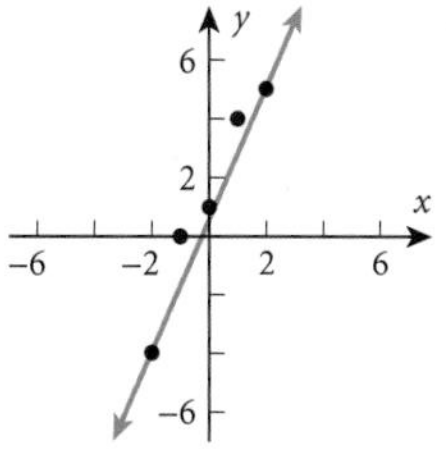

(d)

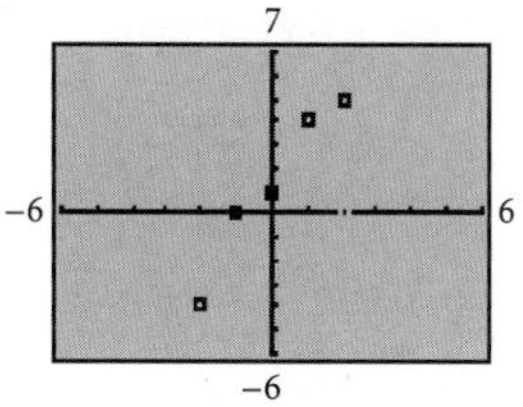

(e) Using the LinReg program, the line of best fit is: $y = 2.2x + 1.2$.

(f)

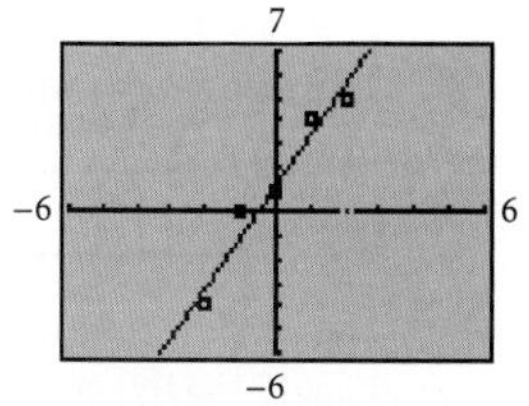

(b) $y = \frac{9}{4}x + \frac{1}{2}$

3. **(a)**

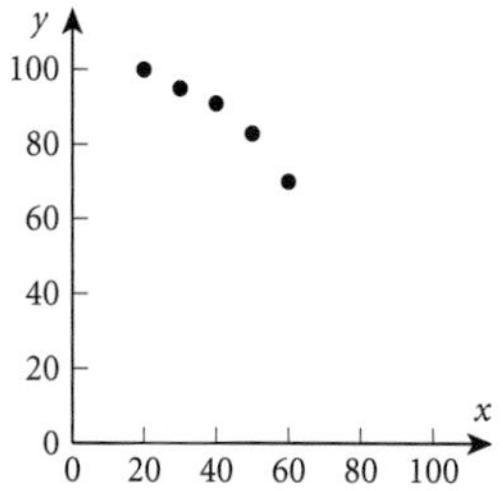

(c)

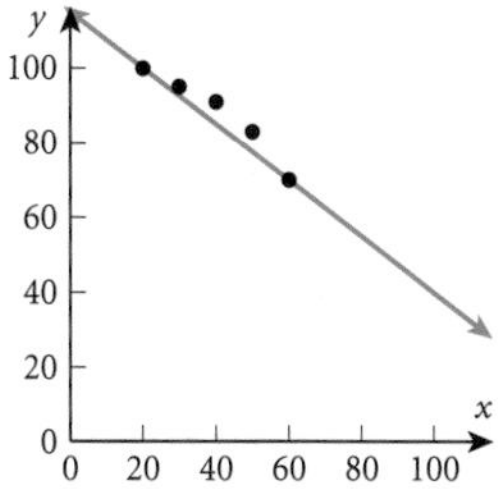

(d)

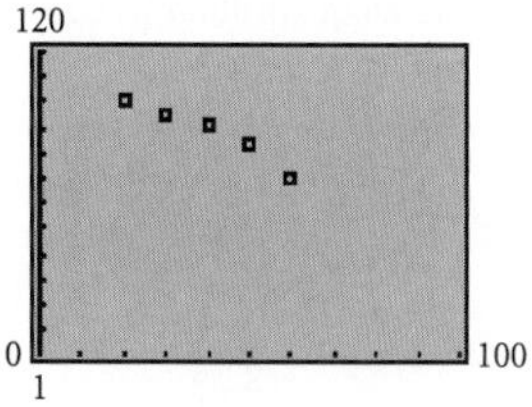

(e) Using the LinReg function, the line of best fit is: $y = -0.72x + 116.6$.

(f)

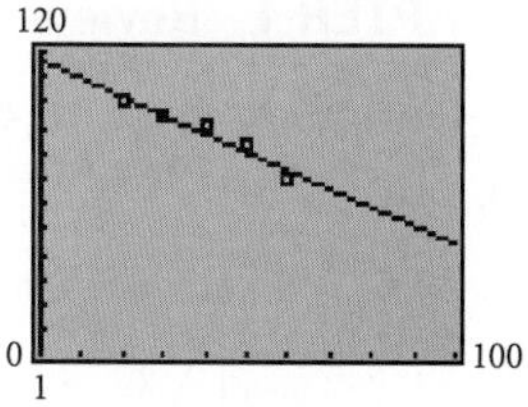

(b) $y = -\frac{3}{4}x + 115$

5. **(a)**

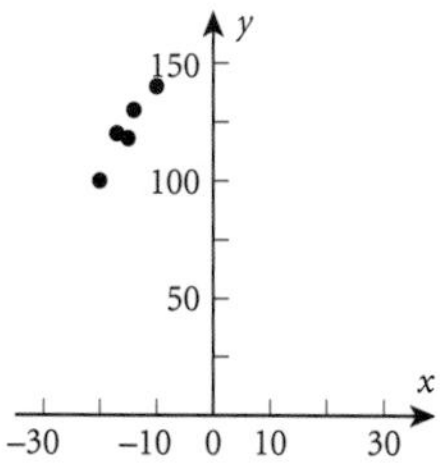

(c)

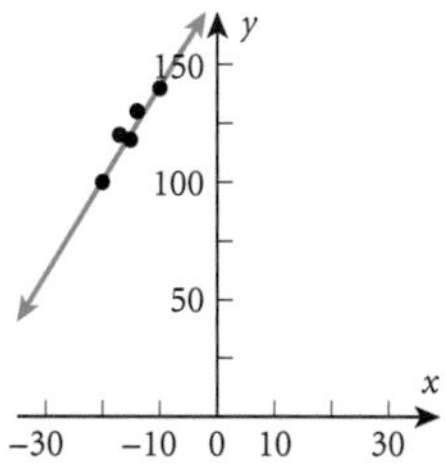

(d)

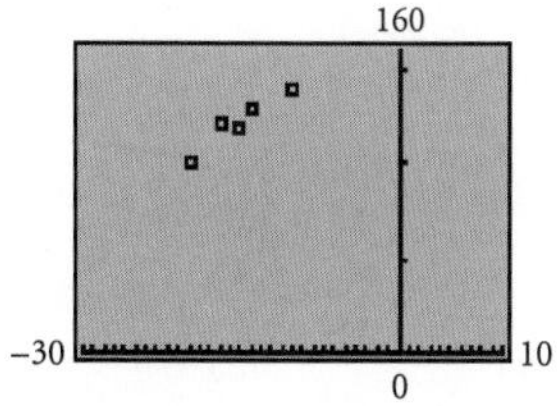

(e) Using the LinReg function, the line of best fit is: $y = 3.86131x + 180.29197$.

(f)

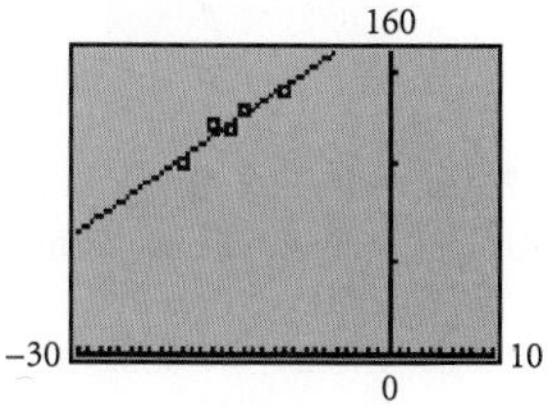

(b) $y = 4x + 180$

7. **(a)**

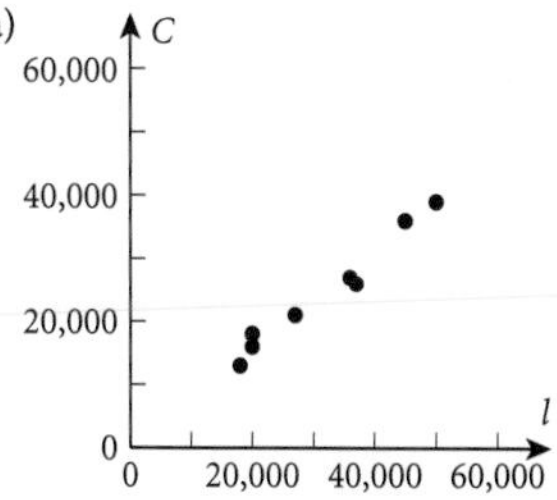

(b) $C = \frac{23}{30}I + \frac{2}{3}$

(c) The slope of this line indicates that a family will spend \$23 of every extra \$30 of disposable income.

(d) A family with a disposable income of \$42,000 is predicted to consume \$32,200 worth of goods.

(e) Using the LinReg function on the graphing utility, the line of best fit is: $y = 0.75489x + 0.62663$.

9. **(a)**

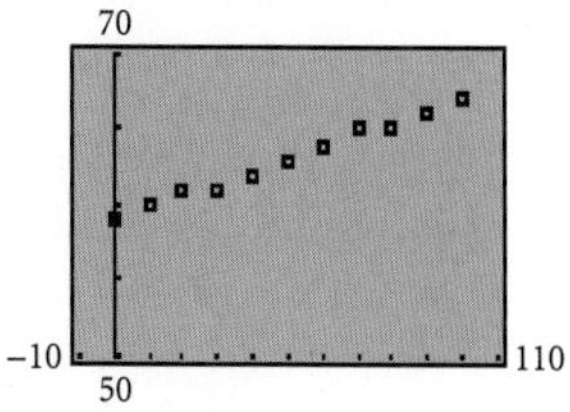

(b) Using the LinReg function, the line of best fit is: $y = 0.07818x + 59.0909$.

(c)

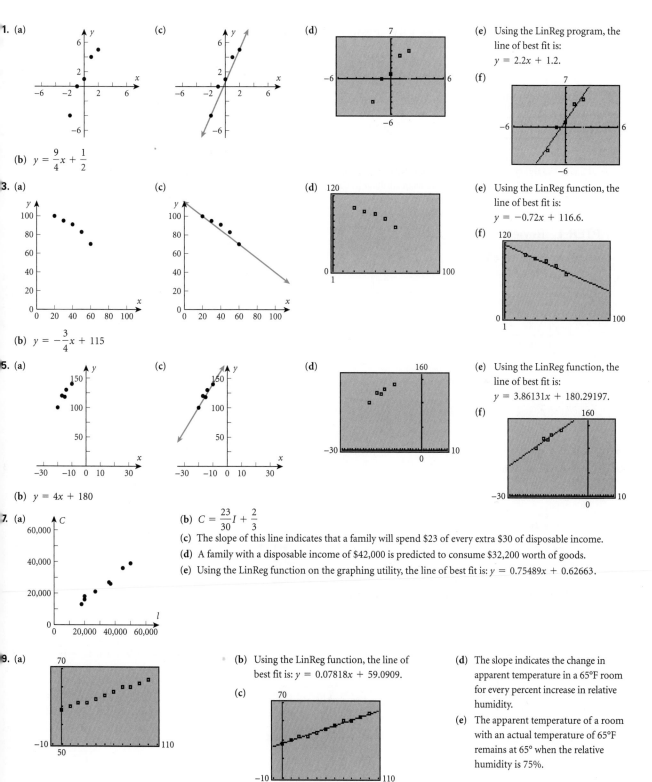

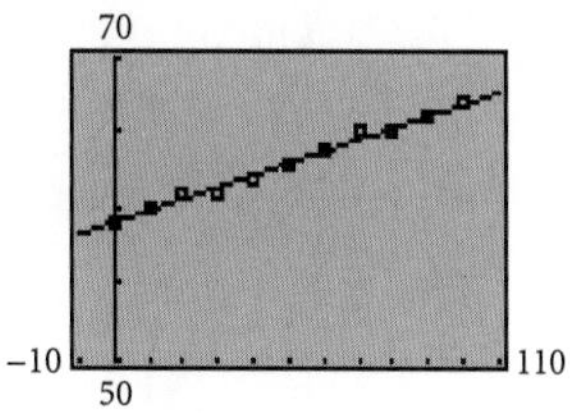

(d) The slope indicates the change in apparent temperature in a 65°F room for every percent increase in relative humidity.

(e) The apparent temperature of a room with an actual temperature of 65°F remains at 65° when the relative humidity is 75%.

21. (a) Using the LinReg function, the line of best fit is $y = 0.0651t + 10.6049$.

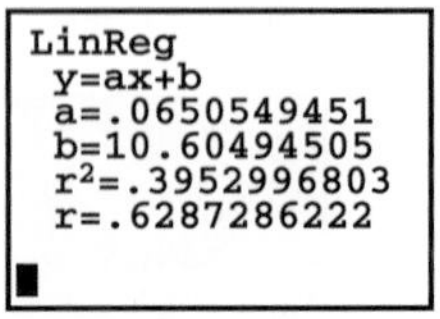

The predicted energy use in 2015, $t = 20$, is $y = 0.0651(20) + 10.6049 \approx 11.91$ quadrillion BTU. The predicted energy use in 2030, $t = 35$, is $y = 0.0651(35) + 10.6049 \approx 12.88$ quadrillion BTU.

(b) When we graph the scatterplot and the line of best fit, we see t the points are not strictly linear. Therefore, estimates based on line of the best fit are approximations. The line of best fit m differ depending on which points are chosen. The U.S. Dept. Energy may have used more or less data points to make its pred tions. They also may not have used a linear model.

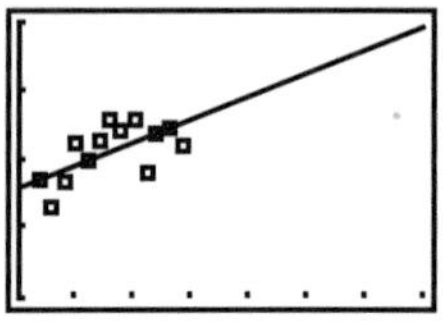

CHAPTER 1 Review

Review Exercises (p. 43)

1.

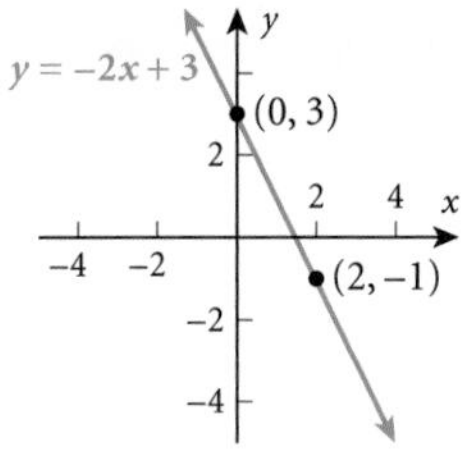

3.

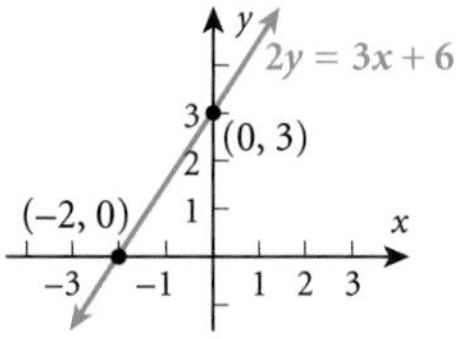

5. (a) $m = -\frac{1}{2}$; A slope $= -\frac{1}{2}$ means tha for every 2 units x moves to the right moves down 1 unit.

(b) $y = -\frac{1}{2}x + \frac{5}{2}$ or $x + 2y = 5$

(c)

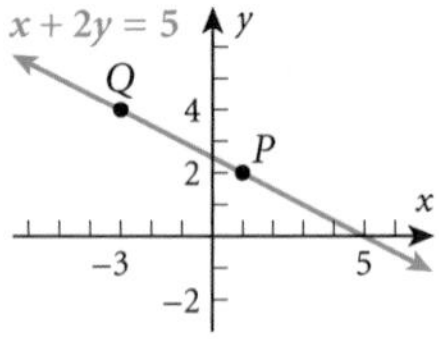

7. (a) $m = 2$; A slope $= 2$ means that for every 1 unit change in x, y increases 2 units.

(b) $y = 2x + 7$ or $2x - y = -7$

(c)

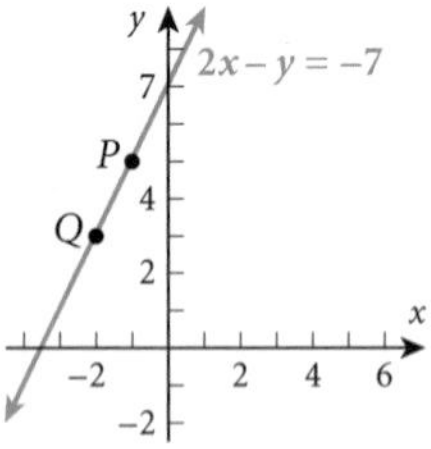

9. $y = -3x + 5$ or $3x + y = 5$

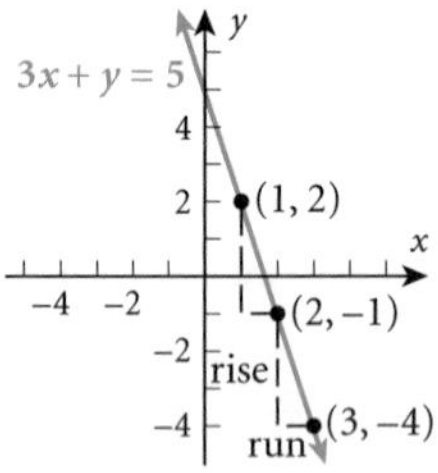

11. $y = 4$

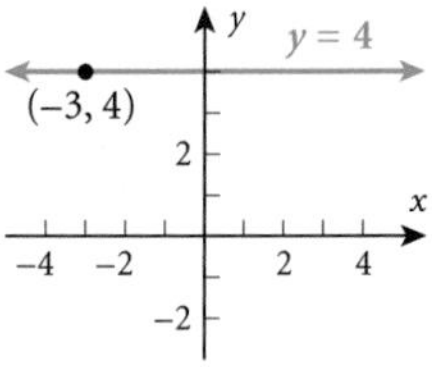

13. $x = 8$

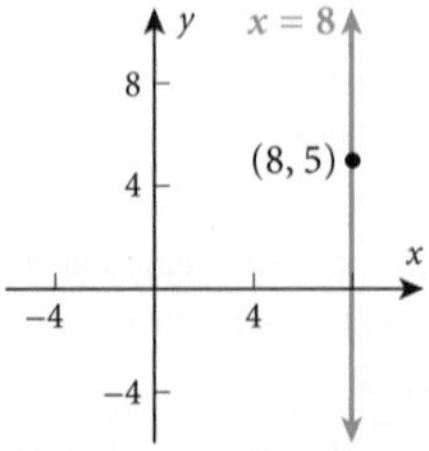

15. $y = -\frac{5}{2}x + 5$ or $5x + 2y = 10$

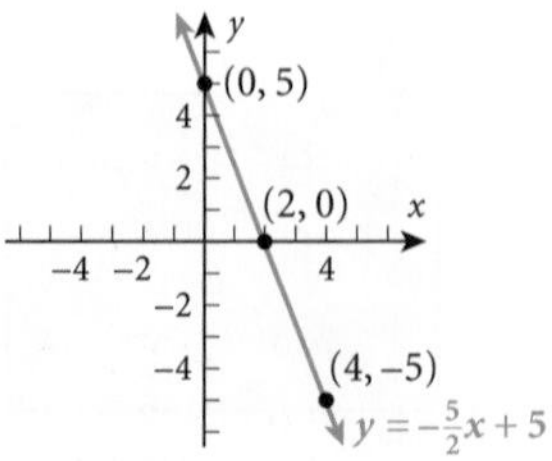

17. $y = -\frac{4}{3}x - 4$ or $4x + 3y = -12$

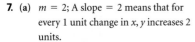

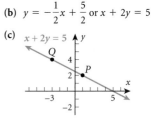

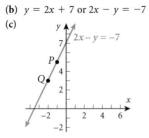

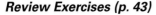

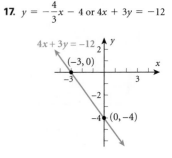

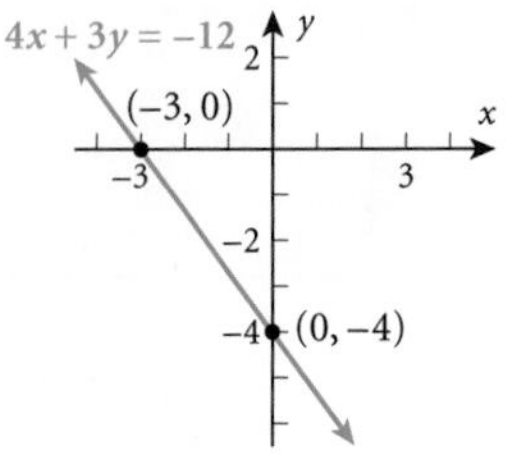

9. $y = -\frac{2}{3}x - \frac{1}{3}$ or $2x + 3y = -1$

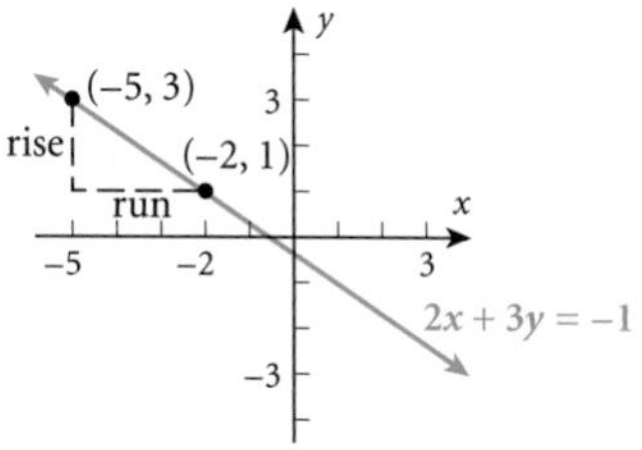

21. $m = -\frac{9}{2}$, y-intercept $(0, 9)$

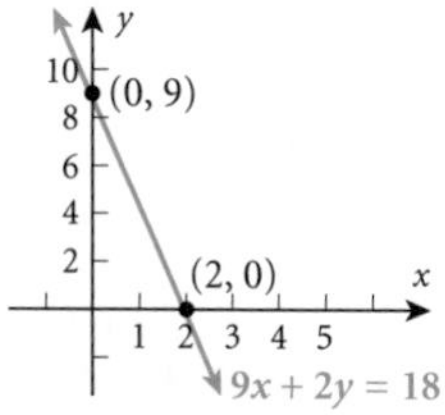

23. $m = -2$, y-intercept: $\left(0, \frac{9}{2}\right)$

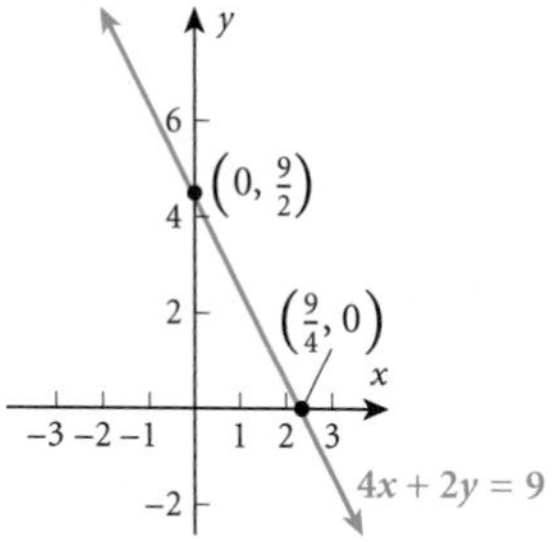

5. $m = -\frac{3}{2}$, y-intercept: $\left(0, \frac{1}{2}\right)$

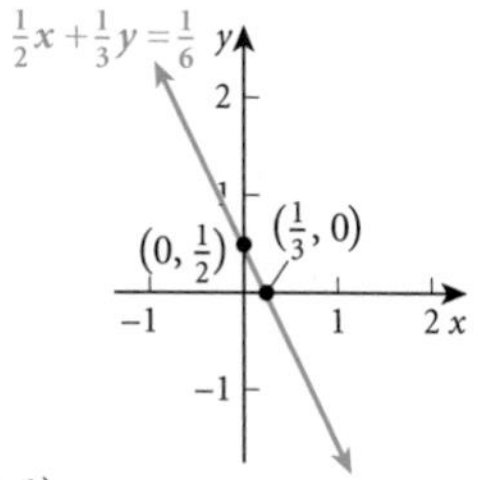

27. parallel **29.** intersecting **31.** coincident

33. $(5, 1)$

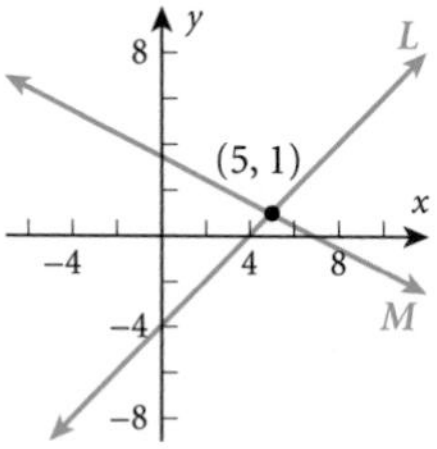

35. $(1, 3)$

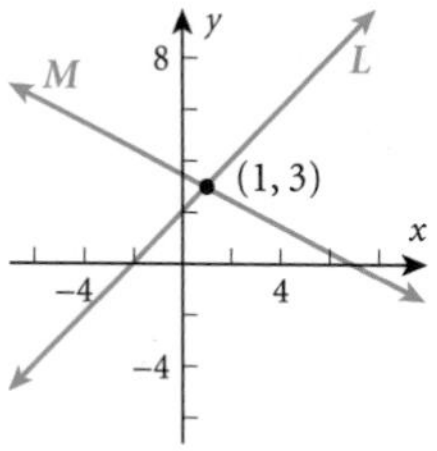

7. $(-2, 1)$

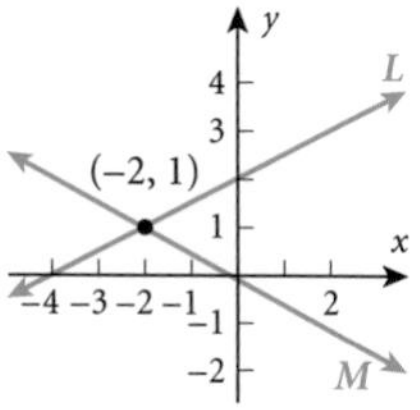

39. Invest \$78,571.43 in B-rated bonds and \$11,428.57 in the well-known bank.

41. **(a)** 120 people need to attend for the group to break even.
(b) 300 people need to attend to achieve the \$900 profit.
(c) If tickets are sold for \$12.00 each, 86 people must attend to break even, and 215 people must attend to achieve a profit of \$900.

43. Relation does not appear to be linear.

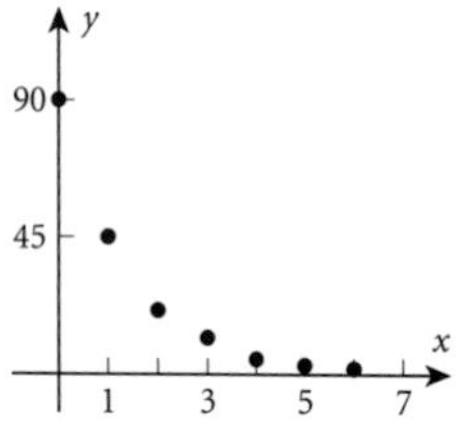

5. **(a)** The market price for corn is \$1.33.
(b) 1.264 million bushels will be supplied at the market price.
(c)

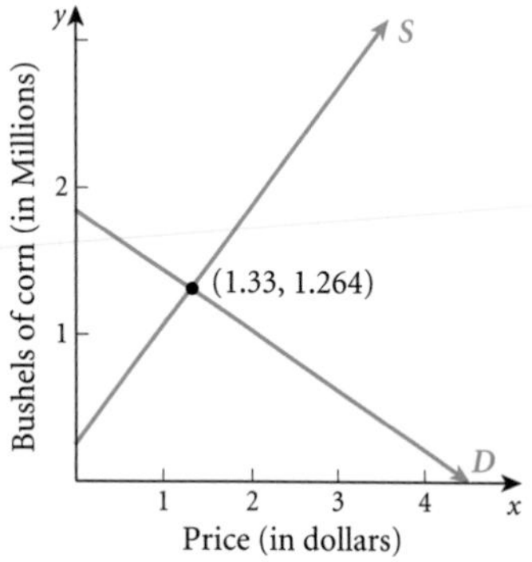

(d) At a price of \$1.33 per bushel the supply and the demand for corn are equal.

7. **(a)**

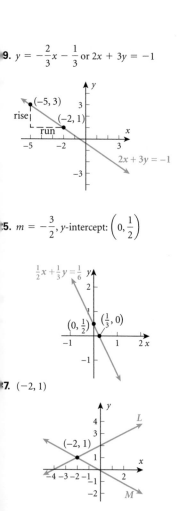

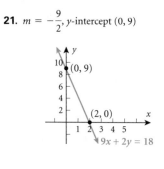

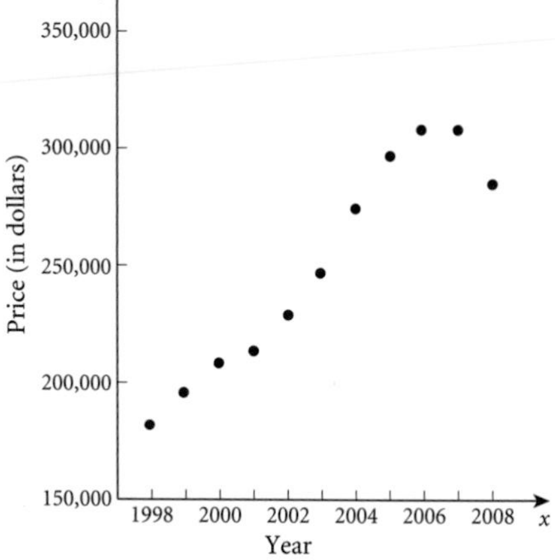

(b) The slope is 11,700.
(c) The mean price of houses sold in the United States increased by an average of \$11,700 per year from 1998 through 2002.
(d) The slope is 10,650.
(e) The mean price of houses sold in the United States increased by an average of \$10,650 per year from 2002 through 2008.
(f) The slope of the line of best fit is 13,960.
(g) The mean price of houses sold in the United States increased by an average of \$13,960 per year from 1998 through 2008.
(h) The average annual increase in mean price of houses sold in the United States is not constant. The slope depends on the points used to calculate it.
(i) The average price of houses sold in the United States is starting to decline.

49. **(a)**

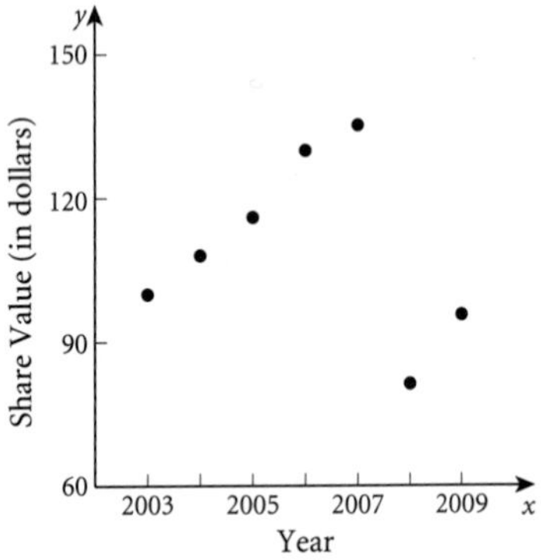

(b) The data do not appear to be linearly related.

51. **(a)** The graph of $x = 0$ is the y-axis. It is a vertical line; the slope is not defined.

(b) The graph of $y = 0$ is the x-axis. It is a horizontal line and has a slope of zero.

(c) The graph of $x + y = 0$ is a decreasing line with a slope of -1 and a y-intercept of $(0, 0)$. It passes through the origin.

Mathematical Questions from Professional Exams

1. b **2.** d **3.** d **4.** b

5. c **6.** c **7.** b **8.** b

CHAPTER 2 Systems of Linear Equations

xercise 2.1 (p. 65)

False **6.** Inconsistent **7.** Yes **9.** No **11.** Yes **13.** Yes

. The solution of the system is $x = 3$ and $y = 2$ or $(3, 2)$. **17.** The solution of the system is $x = \frac{1}{3}$ and $y = -\frac{1}{6}$ or $\left(\frac{1}{3}, -\frac{1}{6}\right)$.

. The system is inconsistent.

. The solutions of the system are $y = -\frac{1}{2}x + 2$ where x is any real number, or as $x = -2y + 4$ where y is any real number or, using ordered pairs, $x, y) | x = -2y + 4$, y any real number$\}$ or $\{(x, y) | y = -\frac{1}{2}x + 2$, x any real number$\}$. **23.** The solution of the system is $x = 1$ and $y = 1$ or $(1, 1)$.

. The solution of the system is $x = \frac{3}{2}$ and $y = 1$ or $\left(\frac{3}{2}, 1\right)$. **27.** The solution of the system is $x = 4$ and $y = 3$ or $(4, 3)$.

. The solution of the system is $x = 8$, $y = 2$, and $z = 0$ or $(8, 2, 0)$.

. The solution of the system is $x = 2$, $y = -1$, and $z = 1$ or $(2, -1, 1)$. **33.** The system is inconsistent. **35.** The solutions of the system are $x = 5z - 2$, $y = 4z - 3$ where z is any real number. **37.** The system is inconsistent. **39.** The solution of the system is $x = 1$, $y = 3$, and $z = -2$ or $(1, 3, -2)$.

. The solution of the system is $x = -3$, $y = \frac{1}{2}$, and $z = 1$ or $\left(-3, \frac{1}{2}, 1\right)$. **43.** The dimensions of the floor are 30 ft × 15 ft.

. They should plant 130.8 acres of corn and 237.2 acres of soybeans. **47.** 22.5 pounds of cashews should be mixed with the peanuts. **49.** A package tofu costs 156 yen and a carton of milk costs 230 yen. **51.** The amount of the refund should be \$5.56. **53.** 50 mg of the first liquid (20% vitamin C d 30% vitamin D) should be mixed with 75 mg of the second liquid. **55.** Use 9.16 pounds of rolled oats and 8.73 pounds of molasses.

. The theater has 100 orchestra seats, 210 main seats, and 190 balcony seats.

. There is not sufficient information to determine the price of each food item. Possible prices include:

Price of a Hamburger	Price of Fries	Price of Cola
\$2.15	\$0.88	\$0.60
\$2.00	\$0.93	\$0.75
\$1.95	\$0.95	\$0.80
\$1.85	\$0.98	\$0.90

61. **(a)** The equilibrium price is \$16.00.

(b) The equilibrium quantity is 600 T-shirts.

(c)

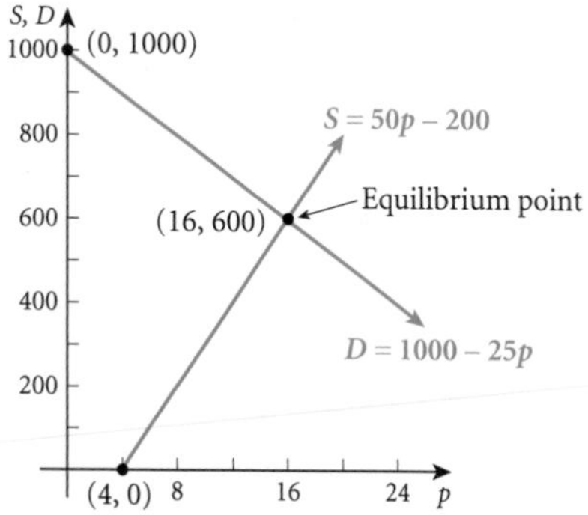

(d) If the quantity demanded is greater than the quantity supplied the price of the T-shirts will increase.

. For this IS-LM model the equilibrium level of income Y is

$$\$9000 \text{ million} = \$9{,}000{,}000{,}000$$

and the equilibrium level of interest rate is 0.06 or 6%.

65. **(a)**

Mutual Shares, x	Strategic Income, y	Small Cap Value, z
0	\$30,000	\$40,000
\$5,000	\$20,000	\$45,000
\$10,000	\$10,000	\$50,000
\$15,000	0	\$55,000

(b) Answers will vary.

Exercise 2.2 (p. 84)

1. matrix **2.** augmented **3.** True **4.** True **5.** $\left[\begin{array}{rr|r} 2 & -3 & 5 \\ 1 & -1 & 3 \end{array}\right]$ **7.** $\left[\begin{array}{rr|r} 2 & 1 & -6 \\ 3 & 1 & -1 \end{array}\right]$ **9.** $\left[\begin{array}{rrr|r} 2 & -1 & -1 & 0 \\ 1 & -1 & 1 & 1 \\ 3 & -1 & 0 & 2 \end{array}\right]$ **11.** $\left[\begin{array}{rrr|r} 2 & -3 & 1 & 7 \\ 1 & 1 & -1 & 1 \\ 2 & 2 & -3 & -4 \end{array}\right]$

13. $\left[\begin{array}{rrrr|r} 4 & -1 & 2 & -1 & 4 \\ 1 & 1 & 0 & 0 & -6 \\ 0 & 2 & -1 & 1 & 5 \end{array}\right]$ **15.** $\left[\begin{array}{rrrr|r} 1 & -1 & 1 & -1 & 0 \\ 2 & 3 & -1 & 4 & 5 \end{array}\right]$ **17.** $\left[\begin{array}{rr|r} 1 & -3 & -2 \\ 0 & 1 & 9 \end{array}\right]$ **19.** **(a)** $\left[\begin{array}{rrr|r} 1 & -3 & 4 & 3 \\ 0 & 1 & -2 & 0 \\ -3 & 3 & 4 & 6 \end{array}\right]$ **(b)** $\left[\begin{array}{rrr|r} 1 & -3 & 4 & 3 \\ 2 & -5 & 6 & 6 \\ 0 & -6 & 16 & 15 \end{array}\right]$

21. **(a)** $\left[\begin{array}{rrr|r} 1 & -3 & 2 & -6 \\ 0 & 1 & -1 & 8 \\ -3 & -6 & 2 & 6 \end{array}\right]$ **(b)** $\left[\begin{array}{rrr|r} 1 & -3 & 2 & -6 \\ 2 & -5 & 3 & -4 \\ 0 & -15 & 8 & -12 \end{array}\right]$ **23.** **(a)** $\left[\begin{array}{rrr|r} 1 & -3 & 1 & -2 \\ 0 & 1 & 4 & 2 \\ -3 & 1 & 4 & 6 \end{array}\right]$ **(b)** $\left[\begin{array}{rrr|r} 1 & -3 & 1 & -2 \\ 2 & -5 & 6 & -2 \\ 0 & -8 & 7 & 0 \end{array}\right]$

25. **(a)** $\begin{cases} x + 2y = 5 \\ y = -1 \end{cases}$ **(b)** The system is consistent and the solution is $x = 7$ and $y = -1$ or $(7, -1)$.

27. **(a)** $\begin{cases} x + 2y + 3z = 1 \\ y + 4z = 2 \\ 0 = 3 \end{cases}$ **(b)** The system is inconsistent. **29.** **(a)** $\begin{cases} x + 2z = -1 \\ y - 4z = -2 \\ 0 = 0 \end{cases}$ **(b)** The system is consistent and has an infinite number of solutions. The solutions are $x = -2z - 1$, $y = 4z - 2$, where z is any real number.

31. **(a)** $\begin{cases} x_1 + 2x_2 - x_3 + x_4 = 1 \\ x_2 + 4x_3 + x_4 = 2 \\ x_3 + 2x_4 = 3 \\ x_4 = 4 \end{cases}$ **(b)** The system is consistent. The solutions are $x_1 = -44$, $x_2 = 18$, $x_3 = -5$, $x_4 = 4$ or $(-44, 18, -5, 4)$.

33. **(a)** $\begin{cases} x_1 + 2x_2 + 4x_4 = 2 \\ x_2 + x_3 + 3x_4 = 3 \\ x_3 = 0 \\ 0 = 0 \end{cases}$ **(b)** The system is consistent. The solutions are $x_1 = 2x_4 - 4$, $x_2 = -3x_4 + 3$, $x_3 = 0$ where x_4 is any real number.

35. **(a)** $\begin{cases} x_1 - 2x_2 + x_4 = -2 \\ x_2 - 3x_3 + 2x_4 = 2 \\ x_3 - x_4 = 0 \end{cases}$ **(b)** The system is consistent. The solutions are $x_1 = x_4 + 2$, $x_2 = x_4 + 2$, $x_3 = x_4$, where x_4 is any real number.

37. The system is inconsistent. **39.** The solution of the system is $x = \frac{1}{2}$ and $y = \frac{1}{3}$ or $\left(\frac{1}{2}, \frac{1}{3}\right)$.

41. The solutions of the system are $y = -\frac{1}{3}x + \frac{2}{3}$ where x is any real number, or $x = -3y + 2$ where y is any real number, or written as ordered pairs, $\left\{(x, y) \mid y = -\frac{1}{3}x + \frac{2}{3}, x \text{ any real number}\right\}$ or $\{(x, y) \mid x = -3y + 2, y \text{ any real number}\}$. **43.** The solution of the system is $x = \frac{2}{3}, y = \frac{1}{3}$ or $\left(\frac{2}{3}, \frac{1}{3}\right)$.

45. The solution of the system is $x = 1, y = 4, z = 0$ or $(1, 4, 0)$. **47.** The solution of the system is $x = \frac{8}{5}, y = -\frac{12}{5}, z = 6$ or $\left(\frac{8}{5}, -\frac{12}{5}, 6\right)$.

49. The solution of the system is $x = 2, y = -1, z = 1$, or $(2, -1, 1)$.

51. The system is inconsistent. **53.** The solution of the system is $x = \frac{1}{3}, y = \frac{2}{3}, z = 1$ or $\left(\frac{1}{3}, \frac{2}{3}, 1\right)$.

55. Row echelon form (REF):

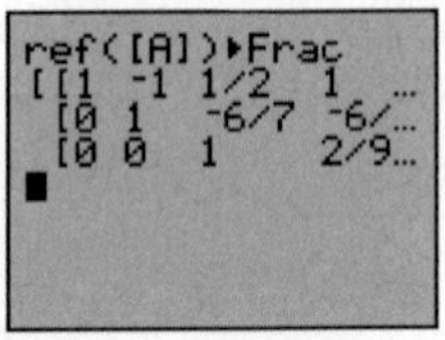

Reduced row echelon form (RREF):

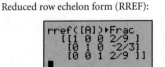

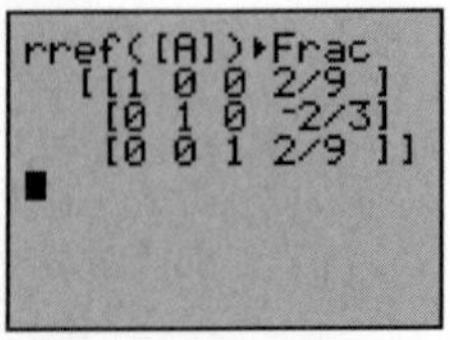

The solution of the system is $x = \frac{2}{9}, y = -\frac{2}{3}, z = \frac{2}{9}$ or $\left(\frac{2}{9}, -\frac{2}{3}, \frac{2}{9}\right)$

7. Row echelon form (REF):

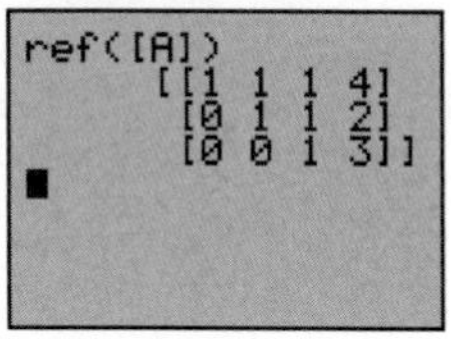

Reduced row echelon form (RREF):

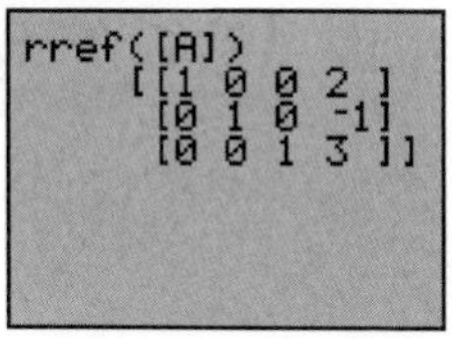

The solution of the system is $x = 2, y = -1, z = 3$ or $(2, -1, 3)$.

9. Row echelon form (REF):

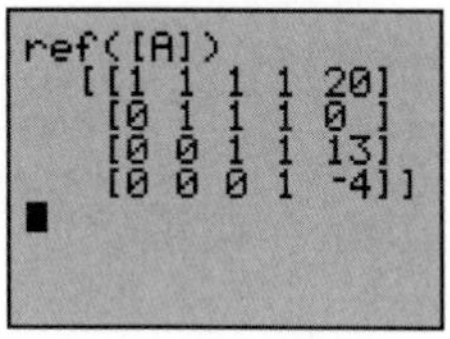

Reduced row echelon form (RREF):

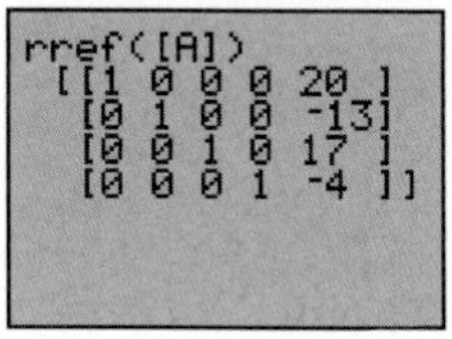

The solution of the system is $x_1 = 20, x_2 = -13, x_3 = 17, x_4 = -4$ or $(20, -13, 17, -4)$.

1. Carla should invest \$22,500 in treasury bills, \$65,000 in bank CDs, d \$32,500 in corporate bonds.

3. The meal should consist of 1 serving of chicken, 1 serving of tatoes, and 2 servings of spinach.

5. 20 cases of orange juice, 12 cases of tomato juice, and 6 cases of neapple juice are prepared.

7. A mezzanine ticket costs \$66; a lower balcony seat costs \$49; a middle lcony seat costs \$39.

69. The teacher should order 2 of the first package (20 white, 15 blue, 1 red), 10 of the second package (3 blue, 1 red), and 4 of the third package.

71. The recreation center should purchase 4 assorted cartons, 8 mixed cartons, and 5 single cartons.

73. To fill the order use 2 large cans, 1 mammoth can, and 4 giant cans.

75. Karen should buy 3200 shares of NCC.B, 800 shares of IBM, and 800 shares of ESRX.

xercise 2.3 (p. 95)

False **2.** True **3.** Yes **5.** No, the leftmost 1 in the 2nd row is not to the right of the leftmost 1 in the 1st row. **7.** Yes

Infinitely many solutions. $\begin{cases} x = 2z + 6 \\ y = -3z + 1 \end{cases}$, where z is the parameter. **11.** One solution, $x = -1, y = 3$, and $z = 4$.

3. Infinitely many solutions, $\begin{cases} x = z + 1 \\ y = -2z + 1 \end{cases}$, where z is the parameter. **15.** Infinitely many solutions, $\begin{cases} x_1 = x_4 + 4 \\ x_2 = -2x_3 - 3x_4 \end{cases}$, where x_3 and x_4 are e parameters. **17.** $\left[\begin{array}{cc|c} 1 & 0 & 0 \\ 0 & 1 & 0 \\ 0 & 0 & 1 \end{array}\right]$ The system is inconsistent. **19.** $\left[\begin{array}{cc|c} 1 & -2 & 4 \\ 0 & 0 & 0 \\ 0 & 0 & 0 \end{array}\right]$ The solutions of the system are $x = 2y + 4$, where y is the parameter.

1. $\left[\begin{array}{ccc|c} 1 & 0 & 0 & -3 \\ 0 & 1 & 3 & 5 \end{array}\right]$ The solutions of the system are $\begin{cases} x = -3 \\ y = -3z + 5 \end{cases}$, where z is the parameter.

3. $\left[\begin{array}{cccc|c} 1 & 0 & 0 & 0 & -17 \\ 0 & 1 & 0 & 0 & 24 \\ 0 & 0 & 1 & 0 & 33 \\ 0 & 0 & 0 & 1 & 14 \end{array}\right]$ The solution of the stem is $x_1 = -17, x_2 = 24, x_3 = 33$, and $x_4 = 14$.

5. $\left[\begin{array}{ccc|c} 1 & 0 & -1 & 8 \\ 0 & 1 & -2 & 3 \end{array}\right]$ The solutions are $\begin{cases} x = z + 8 \\ y = 2z + 3 \end{cases}$, here z is the parameter.

7. $\left[\begin{array}{cccc|c} 1 & 0 & 0 & 0 & 1 \\ 0 & 1 & 0 & 0 & 2 \\ 0 & 0 & 1 & 0 & 0 \\ 0 & 0 & 0 & 1 & 1 \end{array}\right]$

The solution of the system is $x_1 = 1, x_2 = 2, x_3 = 0$, and $x_4 = 1$.

29.

mg of 1st Supplement	mg of 2nd Supplement	mg of 3rd Supplement
50	75	0
41.25	75.625	5
32.5	76.25	10
23.75	76.875	15
15	77.5	20
0	78.571	28.57

31. **(a)** Let x_1 be the servings of turkey bologna, x_2 be the servings of bananas, x_3 be the servings of low-fat cottage cheese, and x_4 be the servings of chocolate milk that Steven eats.

$$\begin{cases} 184x_1 + 92x_2 + 90x_3 + 72x_4 = 700 \\ 13.2x_1 + 0.48x_2 + 1.93x_3 + 2x_4 = 20 \\ 4.85x_1 + 23.43x_2 + 0.01x_3 + 10.4x_4 = 100 \end{cases}$$

(b) $\left[\begin{array}{cccc|c} 1 & 0 & 0 & 0.117 & 1.188 \\ 0 & 1 & 0 & 0.420 & 4.022 \\ 0 & 0 & 1 & 0.132 & 1.238 \end{array}\right]$; $\begin{cases} x_1 = -0.117x_4 + 1.188 \\ x_2 = -0.420x_4 + 4.022 \\ x_3 = -0.132x_4 + 1.238 \end{cases}$

where x_4 is the parameter

(c)

Steven's Lunch Choices—Number of Servings			
Turkey Bologna	Bananas	Cottage Cheese	Chocolate Milk
1.2	4.0	1.2	0
1.1	3.6	1.1	1
1.0	3.2	1.0	2
0.8	2.8	0.8	3
0.7	2.3	0.7	4
0.6	1.9	0.6	5
0.5	1.5	0.4	6
0.4	1.1	0.3	7
0.3	0.7	0.2	8
0.1	0.2	0.1	9

33. **(a)** Let x_1 be the amount invested in John Hancock Large Cap Equity Growth fund, x_2 be the amount invested in T Rowe Price Emerging Markets fund, x_3 be the amount invested in Templeton China World fund, and x_4 be the amount invested in TCW Small Cap growth fund.

$$\begin{cases} x_1 + x_2 + x_3 + x_4 = 50{,}000 \\ 0.09x_1 + 0.13x_2 + 0.14x_3 + 0.07x_4 = 6{,}000 \end{cases}$$

(b) $\left[\begin{array}{cccc|c} 1 & 0 & -0.25 & 1.5 & 12{,}500 \\ 0 & 1 & 1.25 & -0.5 & 37{,}500 \end{array}\right]$

$$\begin{cases} x_1 = 0.25x_3 - 1.5x_4 + 12{,}500 \\ x_2 = -1.25x_3 + 0.5x_4 + 37{,}500 \end{cases}$$

where x_3 and x_4 are parameters

(c)

Amount Invested			
John Hancock Large Cap	Emerging Markets	Templeton China	Small Cap Growth
\$12,500	\$37,500	\$0	\$0
\$15,000	\$25,000	\$10,000	\$0
\$17,500	\$12,500	\$20,000	\$0
\$20,000	\$0	\$30,000	\$0
\$5000	\$40,000	\$0	\$5000
\$5000	\$5000	\$30,000	\$10,000

35. **(a)** Possible investment strategies for a couple with \$20,000.00 to invest.

Amount Invested			
High Income	Global Discovery	Global Bond	Small Cap Growth
\$0	\$0	\$10,000	\$10,000
\$0	\$6667	\$0	\$13,333
\$5714	\$0	\$0	\$14,286

(b) Possible investment strategies for a couple with \$25,000.00 to invest.

Amount Invested			
High Income	Global Discovery	Global Bond	Small Cap Growth
\$0	\$0	\$25,000	\$0
\$10,000	\$5000	\$0	\$10,000
\$13,333	\$0	\$1667	\$10,000

(c) Possible investment strategies for a couple with \$30,000.00 to invest.

Amount Invested			
High Income	Global Discovery	Global Bond	Small Cap Growth
\$0	\$26,667	\$0	\$3333
\$0	\$20,000	\$10,000	\$0
\$22,857	\$0	\$0	\$7143
\$13,333	\$0	\$16,667	\$0

37.

Bacteria 1	Bacteria 2	Bacteria 3
2000	6000	0
2000	4000	1000
2000	2000	2000
2000	0	3000

eview Exercises (p. 99)

$x = 2, y = -1$ or $(2, -1)$ **3.** $x = 2, y = -1$ or $(2, -1)$ **5.** No solution, the system is inconsistent. **7.** $x = -1, y = 2, z = -3$ or $(-1, 2, -3)$

$\begin{cases} x = \frac{7}{4}z + \frac{39}{4} \\ y = \frac{9}{8}z + \frac{69}{8} \end{cases}$ **11.** $\begin{cases} 3x + 2y = 8 \\ x + 4y = -1 \end{cases}$ **13.** $x = 4, y = 6, z = -1$ or $(4, 6, -1)$ **15.** $x = \frac{14}{9}, y = \frac{26}{9}$ or $\left(\frac{14}{9}, \frac{26}{9}\right)$

7. $x = -103, y = 32, z = 9$ or $(-103, 32, 9)$ **19.** $x = 29, y = -10, z = -1$ or $(29, -10, -1)$ **21.** No solution, the system is inconsistent.

3. $x = 9, y = -\frac{56}{3}, z = -\frac{37}{3}$ or $\left(9, -\frac{56}{3}, -\frac{37}{3}\right)$ **25.** $x = 29, y = 8, z = -24$ or $(29, 8, -24)$

7. $\begin{cases} x = \frac{3}{7}z + \frac{10}{7} \\ y = \frac{5}{7}z - \frac{9}{7} \end{cases}$ where z is a parameter. Answers will vary. Three possible solutions are $x = \frac{10}{7}, y = -\frac{9}{7}$, when $z = 0$; $x = \frac{13}{7}, y = -\frac{4}{7}$, when $z = 1$;

d $x = 1, y = -2$, when $z = -1$. **29.** $\begin{cases} x = -0.6z + 1 \\ y = 0.8z + 2 \end{cases}$ Answers will vary. Three solutions are: $x = 1, y = 2$, when $z = 0$; $x = 0.4, y = 2.8$, when $z = 1$;

$= 1.6, y = 1.2$, when $z = -1$; **31.** No solution, the system is inconsistent. **33.** One solution, $x = 5, y = -1$, and $z = 1$; or $(5, -1, 1)$

5. Infinitely many solutions, $\begin{cases} x_1 = -2x_4 + 1 \\ x_2 = -2x_4 - 1 \\ x_3 = 3 \end{cases}$ where x_4 is a parameter.

7. Each box should contain 20 caramels and 30 creams. o obtain a profit, increase the number of caramels in each ox (decreasing the number of creams).

39.

Almonds	Cashews	Peanuts
5	60	35
20	40	40
35	20	45
50	0	50

1. **(a)** To attain \$2500 per year in income:

Strategic Income	Small Cap Value	Micro Cap Value
\$35,000	\$5000	\$0
\$35,500	\$4000	\$500
\$36,000	\$3000	\$1000
\$36,500	\$2000	\$1500
\$37,000	\$1000	\$2000
\$37,500	\$0	\$2500

(b) To attain \$3000 per year in income:

Strategic Income	Small Cap Value	Micro Cap Value
\$10,000	\$30,000	\$0
\$13,000	\$24,000	\$3000
\$16,000	\$18,000	\$6000
\$19,000	\$12,000	\$9000
\$22,000	\$6000	\$12,000
\$25,000	\$0	\$15,000

(c) To attain \$3500 per year in income:

Strategic Income	Small Cap Value	Micro Cap Value
\$0	\$25,000	\$15,000
\$2500	\$20,000	\$17,500
\$5000	\$15,000	\$20,000
\$7500	\$10,000	\$22,500
\$10,000	\$5000	\$25,000
\$12,500	\$0	\$27,500

athematical Questions from Professional Exams

b **2.** b **3.** d **4.** c

CHAPTER 3 Matrices

Exercise 3.1 (p. 117)

3. 2×3 **4.** True **5.** True **6.** False **7.** 2×2, a square matrix **9.** 3×2 **11.** 3×2 **13.** 2×1, a column matrix **15.** False; the dimensions must be the same for two matrices to be equal. **17.** True **19.** True **21.** True **23.** True **25.** False; the dimensions must be the same for two matrices to be equal.

27. $\begin{bmatrix} 1 & 1 \\ 6 & 7 \end{bmatrix}$ **29.** $\begin{bmatrix} 6 & 18 & 0 \\ 12 & -6 & 3 \end{bmatrix}$ **31.** $\begin{bmatrix} 2 & 4 & -8 \\ 1 & -4 & -1 \end{bmatrix}$ **33.** $\begin{bmatrix} 13a & 54 \\ -2b & -7 \\ -2c & -6 \end{bmatrix}$ **35.** $\begin{bmatrix} 1 & -1 & 4 \\ -5 & 1 & -1 \end{bmatrix}$ **37.** $\begin{bmatrix} 13 & -6 & -7 \\ -6 & 1 & -7 \end{bmatrix}$ **39.** $\begin{bmatrix} 9 & -5 & -6 \\ 1 & 1 & -3 \end{bmatrix}$

41. $\begin{bmatrix} -2 & -17 & 32 \\ 28 & 14 & 23 \end{bmatrix}$ **43.** $A + B = \begin{bmatrix} 3 & -5 & 4 \\ 5 & 3 & 3 \end{bmatrix} = B + A$ **45.** $A + (-A) = \begin{bmatrix} 0 & 0 & 0 \\ 0 & 0 & 0 \end{bmatrix} = 0$ **47.** $2B + 3B = \begin{bmatrix} 5 & -10 & 0 \\ 25 & 5 & 10 \end{bmatrix} = 5B$

49. $x = -4$ and $z = 4$ **51.** $x = 5$ and $y = 1$ **53.** $x = 4$, $y = -6$, and $z = 6$

55.

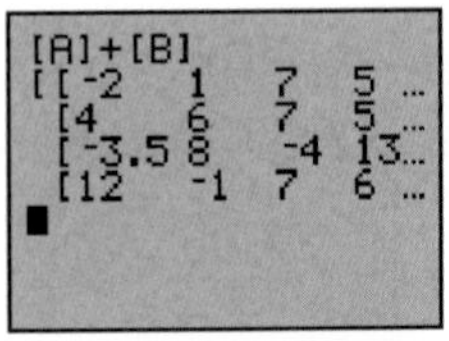
[A]+[B]
[[-2 1 7 5 ...
[4 6 7 5...
[-3.5 8 -4 13...
[12 -1 7 6 ...

57.

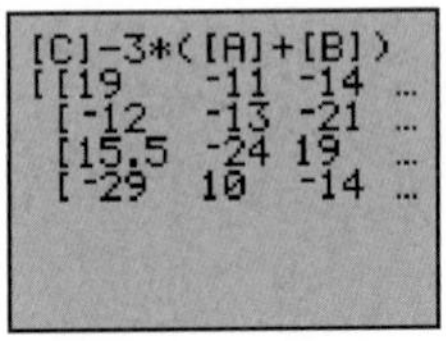
[C]-3*([A]+[B])
[[19 -11 -14 ...
[-12 -13 -21 ...
[15.5 -24 19 ...
[-29 10 -14 ...

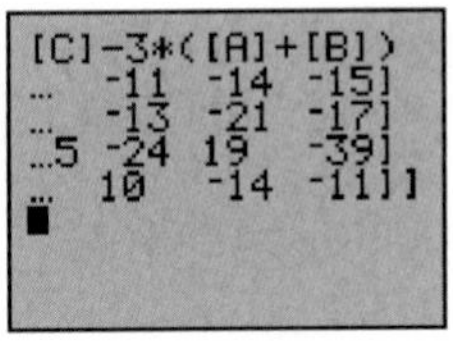
[C]-3*([A]+[B])
... -11 -14 -15]
... -13 -21 -17]
...5 -24 19 -39]
... 10 -14 -11]]

59.

	Democrats	Republicans	Independents
Under $25,000	351	271	73
Over $25,000	203	215	55

61.

	LAS	ENG	EDUC
Male	250	225	80
Female	250	75	120

63. (a)

	Assoc.	Bach.	Master	Doctor
M	275,000	633,000	275,000	27,600
F	460,000	949,000	418,000	27,300

(b) The rows represent the distribution of the projected postsecondary degrees for each gender. Row 1 represents the degrees projected to be earned by males, and row 2 represents the projections for females. The columns represent the distribution of the projected number of each postsecondary degree by gender. Column 1 represents associate degrees, column 2 bachelor's degrees, column 3 master's degrees, and column 4 doctoral degrees.

(c)

	M	F
Assoc.	275,000	460,000
Bachelor	633,000	949,000
Master	275,000	418,000
Doctorate	27,600	27,300

(d) The rows of this matrix represent the numbers of various postsecondary degrees, associate, bachelor, master, and doctoral, respectively, projected to be earned distributed between the two genders: male (column 1) and female (column 2). Column 1 represents the numbers of the various degrees projected to be earned by males and column 2 represents the numbers of the various degrees projected to be earned by females.

65.

	Local	State	Federal
Male	685,790	1,307,706	187,996
Female	99,766	101,460	13,284

67. (a) January Sales

	Sub	Int	SUV
City	350	225	80
Suburban	375	200	75

February Sales

	Sub	Int	SUV
City	300	175	40
Suburban	325	150	50

(b) Combined January/February Sales

	Sub	Int	SUV
City	650	400	120
Suburban	700	350	125

(c) January Sales

	City	Suburban
Sub	350	375
Int	225	200
SUV	80	75

February Sales

	City	Suburban
Sub	300	325
Int	175	150
SUV	40	50

(d) Combined January/February Sales

	City	Suburban
Sub	650	700
Int	400	350
SUV	120	125

69. (a) Doctoral degrees earned by gender:

2008

	Soc Sc	Hum	Educ
M	3121	2256	2163
F	4387	2465	4414

2007

	Soc Sc	Hum	Educ
M	2979	2588	2103
F	4214	2518	4340

(b) Doctoral degrees earned over 2 years by gender:

	Soc Sc	Hum	Educ
M	6100	4844	4266
F	8601	4983	8754

(c) Difference in the numbers of doctoral degrees awarded from 2007 to 2008:

	Soc Sc	Hum	Educ
M	142	−332	60
F	173	−53	74

71. $A = [0.74 \quad 0.77 \quad 0.70]$

Exercise 3.2 (p. 131)

3. 3×7 **4.** True **5.** True **6.** False **7.** $[14]$ **9.** $[4]$ **11.** $[18 \quad -8]$ **13.** $\begin{bmatrix} 4 & 2 \\ 2 & 8 \end{bmatrix}$ **15.** $[4 \quad 6]$ **17.** $\begin{bmatrix} 4 & -14 \\ 12 & -32 \end{bmatrix}$ **19.** $\begin{bmatrix} 4 & 2 \\ 2 & 8 \\ 9 & 8 \end{bmatrix}$

21. $\begin{bmatrix} 9 & 1 \\ 5 & 4 \\ 11 & 7 \end{bmatrix}$ **23.** BA is defined and is a 3×4 matrix. **25.** AB is not defined. **27.** $(BA)C$ is not defined. **29.** $BA + A$ is defined and is a 3×4 matrix. **31.** $CB - A$ is not defined. **33.** $\begin{bmatrix} -1 & 10 & -1 \\ -4 & 16 & -8 \end{bmatrix}$ **35.** $\begin{bmatrix} 11 & 5 \\ 13 & -9 \end{bmatrix}$ **37.** $\begin{bmatrix} 6 & 10 \\ 8 & 2 \\ -4 & 5 \end{bmatrix}$ **39.** $\begin{bmatrix} 3 & -1 \\ 4 & 2 \end{bmatrix}$ **41.** $\begin{bmatrix} 8 & 4 & 22 \\ 4 & 32 & 16 \end{bmatrix}$

43. $\begin{bmatrix} -14 & 7 \\ -20 & -6 \end{bmatrix}$ **45.** $\begin{bmatrix} 10 & 30 & 37 \\ 15 & 16 & 50 \\ -6 & 20 & -8 \end{bmatrix}$ **47.** $D(CB) = \begin{bmatrix} -6 & 42 & -9 \\ 1 & 20 & 6 \\ -7 & 4 & -18 \end{bmatrix} = (DC)B$ **49.** $AB = \begin{bmatrix} 5 & -2 \\ 6 & 4 \end{bmatrix} \neq \begin{bmatrix} 7 & -3 \\ 6 & 2 \end{bmatrix} = BA$

51. $\begin{bmatrix} 0.5 & 16 & -30 & 25 \\ 21 & 14 & 28 & 64 \\ 19.5 & 8 & -23 & 33 \\ -9.5 & 45 & -9 & 83 \end{bmatrix}$ **53.** $\begin{bmatrix} 31.5 & 251 & -31.5 & 143 \\ 861 & 350 & 791 & 420 \\ 369.5 & 115 & 206.5 & 215 \\ 412.5 & 882 & 451.5 & 491 \end{bmatrix}$ **55.** $\begin{bmatrix} 66 & 74 & 94 & 38 \\ 71 & 13 & 106 & 28 \\ 165 & 124.5 & 79 & 52 \\ 158 & -3 & 152 & 46 \end{bmatrix}$ **57.** $\begin{bmatrix} -5 & 23 & -102 & 44 \\ -108 & -56 & -70 & 122 \\ 108 & -152 & -67 & 36 \\ -346 & 279 & -249 & 187 \end{bmatrix}$

59. **(a)** Matrix A represents the price at the close of the trading on July 7, 2009, of a share of Chevron Corporation, Conoco Phillips, and Exxon Mobil Corporation, respectively. A is 1×3. **(b)** $AB = [37{,}899.50 \quad 44{,}595.60 \quad 27{,}623.30]$; matrix AB represents the amount each of the three persons spent on the three stocks on July 7, 2009, at their closing price. **(c)** $BC = \begin{bmatrix} 690 \\ 540 \\ 680 \end{bmatrix}$; matrix BC represents the total number shares of Chevron Corporation, Conoco Phillips, and Exxon Mobil Corporation, respectively, purchased by the three persons at the close of trading on July 7, 2009.

61. **(a)**

	Credit Hours JJC	Credit Hours CSU
$A =$ John	12	4
Marsha	8	8

	Cost per Credit
$B =$ JJC	103
CSU	249

(b) A is 2×2 **(c)** B is 2×1 **(d)** $AB = \begin{bmatrix} 2232 \\ 2816 \end{bmatrix}$

(e) AB is 2×1. The rows are John and Marsha; the column is cost of tuition. **(f)** The entries in AB are the total amounts (in dollars) that each student spends on tuition.

63. **(a)**

$A =$	GE	TM	JNJ
Oct. 2008	22	73	64
April 2009	11	78	53
Oct. 2009	17	79	61

$B =$	Bill	Dan
GE	50	40
TM	30	60
JNJ	20	30

(b) A is 3×3 **(c)** B is 3×2 **(d)** $AB = \begin{bmatrix} 4570 & 7180 \\ 3950 & 6710 \\ 4440 & 7250 \end{bmatrix}$

(e) AB is 3×2; The rows are the dates and the columns are Bill and Dan. **(f)** The entries are the total value of the three stocks Dan and Bill own in October 2008, April 2009, and October 2009. **65.** Lee spent \$372 and Chan spent \$257. **67.** $x = 1$ or $x = \frac{1}{2}$ **69.** $a = d$ and $b = -c$

71. $A^2 = \begin{bmatrix} a & 1-a \\ 1+a & -a \end{bmatrix} \cdot \begin{bmatrix} a & 1-a \\ 1+a & -a \end{bmatrix} = \begin{bmatrix} 1 & 0 \\ 0 & 1 \end{bmatrix}$ **73.** $AB = \begin{bmatrix} ac - bd & ad + bc \\ -bc - ad & -bd + ac \end{bmatrix} = \begin{bmatrix} ca - db & cb + da \\ -da - cb & -db + ca \end{bmatrix} = BA$

75. $A^2 = \begin{bmatrix} 7 & 2 \\ -4 & -1 \end{bmatrix} A^3 = \begin{bmatrix} 17 & 5 \\ -10 & -3 \end{bmatrix} A^4 = \begin{bmatrix} 41 & 12 \\ -24 & -7 \end{bmatrix}$ **77.** $A^2 = \begin{bmatrix} \frac{3}{8} & \frac{5}{8} \\ \frac{5}{16} & \frac{11}{16} \end{bmatrix} A^3 = \begin{bmatrix} \frac{11}{32} & \frac{21}{32} \\ \frac{21}{64} & \frac{43}{64} \end{bmatrix} A^4 = \begin{bmatrix} \frac{43}{128} & \frac{85}{128} \\ \frac{85}{256} & \frac{171}{256} \end{bmatrix}$

79. Answers will vary, but as n gets larger A^n becomes approximately equal to $\begin{bmatrix} \frac{1}{3} & \frac{2}{3} \\ \frac{1}{3} & \frac{2}{3} \end{bmatrix}$.

81.

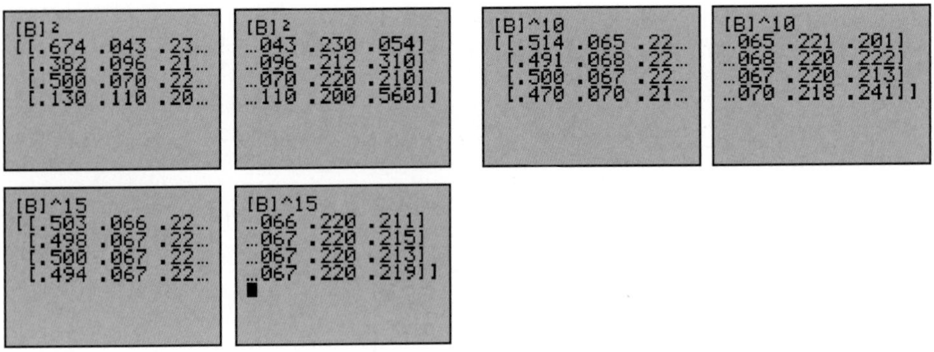

Exercise 3.3 (p. 148)

3. inverse **4.** False **5.** $\begin{bmatrix} 1 & 2 \\ 2 & 3 \end{bmatrix}\begin{bmatrix} -3 & 2 \\ 2 & -1 \end{bmatrix} = \begin{bmatrix} 1 & 0 \\ 0 & 1 \end{bmatrix}$ **7.** $\begin{bmatrix} -1 & -2 \\ 3 & 4 \end{bmatrix}\begin{bmatrix} 2 & 1 \\ -\frac{3}{2} & -\frac{1}{2} \end{bmatrix} = \begin{bmatrix} 1 & 0 \\ 0 & 1 \end{bmatrix}$ **9.** $\begin{bmatrix} 1 & 2 & 3 \\ 2 & 3 & 4 \\ 1 & 2 & 1 \end{bmatrix}\begin{bmatrix} -\frac{5}{2} & 2 & -\frac{1}{2} \\ 1 & -1 & 1 \\ \frac{1}{2} & 0 & -\frac{1}{2} \end{bmatrix} = \begin{bmatrix} 1 & 0 & 0 \\ 0 & 1 & 0 \\ 0 & 0 & 1 \end{bmatrix}$

11. $\begin{bmatrix} 5 & -7 \\ -2 & 3 \end{bmatrix}$ **13.** $\begin{bmatrix} 4 & -1 \\ 3 & -1 \end{bmatrix}$ **15.** $\begin{bmatrix} \frac{3}{2} & -\frac{1}{2} \\ -2 & 1 \end{bmatrix}$ **17.** $\begin{bmatrix} 0 & 0 & 1 \\ 0 & 1 & 0 \\ 1 & 0 & 0 \end{bmatrix}$ **19.** $\begin{bmatrix} \frac{4}{9} & \frac{1}{9} & \frac{1}{9} \\ \frac{4}{3} & -\frac{2}{3} & \frac{1}{3} \\ \frac{7}{9} & -\frac{5}{9} & \frac{4}{9} \end{bmatrix}$ **21.** $\begin{bmatrix} 1 & -1 & 2 \\ -1 & 2 & -3 \\ -1 & 1 & -1 \end{bmatrix}$ **23.** $\begin{bmatrix} 2 & -1 & -1 & -2 \\ -1 & 1 & 1 & 2 \\ -2 & 1 & 2 & 3 \\ -1 & 1 & 1 & 1 \end{bmatrix}$

25. $\left[\begin{array}{cc|cc} 4 & 6 & 1 & 0 \\ 2 & 3 & 0 & 1 \end{array}\right] \Rightarrow \left[\begin{array}{cc|cc} 1 & \frac{3}{2} & \frac{1}{4} & 0 \\ 0 & 0 & -\frac{1}{2} & 1 \end{array}\right]$ **27.** $\left[\begin{array}{cc|cc} -8 & 4 & 1 & 0 \\ -4 & 2 & 0 & 1 \end{array}\right] \Rightarrow \left[\begin{array}{cc|cc} 1 & -\frac{1}{2} & -\frac{1}{8} & 0 \\ 0 & 0 & -\frac{1}{2} & 1 \end{array}\right]$ **29.** $\left[\begin{array}{ccc|ccc} 1 & 1 & 1 & 1 & 0 & 0 \\ 3 & -4 & 2 & 0 & 1 & 0 \\ 0 & 0 & 0 & 0 & 0 & 1 \end{array}\right]$ **31.** $\begin{bmatrix} 2 & -1 \\ -1 & 1 \end{bmatrix}$

33. Inverse does not exist. **35.** $A^{-1} = \begin{bmatrix} \frac{1}{5} & \frac{2}{5} \\ \frac{2}{5} & -\frac{1}{5} \end{bmatrix}$; $B^{-1} = \begin{bmatrix} -\frac{1}{5} & \frac{3}{5} \\ \frac{2}{5} & -\frac{1}{5} \end{bmatrix}$; $A^{-1} - B^{-1} = \begin{bmatrix} \frac{2}{5} & -\frac{1}{5} \\ 0 & 0 \end{bmatrix}$ **37.** $\begin{bmatrix} 42 & -18 & -5 \\ -9 & 4 & 1 \\ -7 & 3 & 1 \end{bmatrix}\begin{bmatrix} 2 \\ 1 \\ 3 \end{bmatrix} = \begin{bmatrix} 51 \\ -11 \\ -8 \end{bmatrix}$

39. $x = 36, y = -14$ or $(36, -14)$ **41.** $x = 2, y = 1$ or $(2, 1)$ **43.** $x = 88, y = -36$ or $(88, -36)$

45. $x = \frac{14}{9}, y = \frac{26}{3}, z = \frac{65}{9}$ or $\left(\frac{14}{9}, \frac{26}{3}, \frac{65}{9}\right)$ **47.** $x = \frac{20}{3}, y = 24, z = \frac{56}{3}$ or $\left(\frac{20}{3}, 24, \frac{56}{3}\right)$ **49.** $x = -\frac{14}{9}, y = \frac{10}{3}, z = \frac{16}{9}$ or $\left(-\frac{14}{9}, \frac{10}{3}, \frac{16}{9}\right)$

51. $\begin{bmatrix} 0.00545 & 0.0509 & -0.0066 \\ 0.01036 & -0.0186 & 0.0095 \\ -0.0193 & 0.0116 & 0.0344 \end{bmatrix}$ **53.** $\begin{bmatrix} 0.0249 & -0.0360 & -0.0057 & 0.0059 \\ -0.0171 & 0.0521 & 0.0292 & -0.0305 \\ 0.0206 & 0.0081 & -0.0421 & 0.0005 \\ -0.0175 & 0.0570 & 0.0657 & 0.0619 \end{bmatrix}$

55. $\begin{bmatrix} \frac{1}{4} & -\frac{1}{16} & -\frac{9}{32} & \frac{5}{16} & \frac{3}{32} \\ -\frac{3}{2} & \frac{1}{8} & \frac{49}{16} & -\frac{21}{8} & \frac{5}{16} \\ \frac{7}{4} & -\frac{3}{16} & -\frac{91}{32} & \frac{47}{16} & -\frac{23}{32} \\ -\frac{1}{2} & \frac{3}{8} & \frac{11}{16} & -\frac{7}{8} & \frac{7}{16} \\ -\frac{5}{4} & \frac{5}{16} & \frac{77}{32} & -\frac{41}{16} & \frac{17}{32} \end{bmatrix}$

57. $x = 4.567, y = -6.444, z = -24.075$ **59.** $x = -1.187, y = 2.457, z = 8.265$ **61.** **(a)** Invest \$2291.21 in the mid cap fund and \$708.79 in the bond fund for a 5% rate of return. **(b)** Invest \$1467.03 in the mid cap fund and \$1532.97 in the bond fund for an $5\frac{1}{2}$% rate of return. **(c)** Invest \$642.86 in the mid cap fund and \$2357.14 in the bond fund for a 6% rate of return. **63.** **(a)** Invest \$4132.54 in the small cap growth fund, \$3132.54 in the large cap value fund, and \$734.92 in the international fund for a 4% rate of return. **(b)** Invest \$3736.89 in the small cap growth fund, \$2736.89 in the large cap value fund, and \$1526.22 in the international fund for a 4.5% rate of return. **(c)** Invest \$3341.25 in the small cap growth fund, \$2341.25 in the large cap value fund, and \$2317.50 in the international fund for a 5% rate of return.

65. **(a)** When profit is \$300,000, the president's bonus is \$20,512.82, the CFO's bonus is \$12,820.51, and the vice president's bonus is \$10,256.41. **(b)** When profit is \$500,000, the president's bonus is \$34,188.03 the CFO's bonus is \$21,367.52, and the vice president's bonus is \$17,094.01. **(c)** When profit is \$750,000, the president's bonus is \$51,282.05, the CFO's bonus is \$32,051.28, and the vice president's bonus is \$25,641.03. **67.** Do you have a dish? **69.** 9 40 −17 22 171 −24 9 85 −7 5 130 9 20 175 −20 8 59 −10 9 46 −17 12 117 −9 21 211 −16 **71.** **(a)** 9 93 −5 7 81 −5 14 149 −8 15 94 −21 19 96 −33 25 230 −24 **(b)** 23 169 −27 21 111 −36 20 93 −35 14 147 −8 **(c)** 12 141 −4 19 139 −23 3 126 15 2 53 5 14 179 −2

73. **(a)** The encrypted ID is $E = \begin{bmatrix} 3 & 3 & 11 \\ 9 & 15 & 10 \\ 7 & 7 & 15 \\ 4 & 13 & 6 \end{bmatrix}$ or written out: 3 3 11 9 15 10 7 7 15 4 13 6. **(b)** The original ID is $D = \begin{bmatrix} 4 & 6 & 8 \\ 0 & 2 & 4 \\ 9 & 6 & 1 \\ 8 & 9 & 5 \end{bmatrix}$ or written out: 4 6 8 0 2 4 9 6 1 8 9 5. **75.** $\begin{bmatrix} -3 & 2 \\ 2 & -1 \end{bmatrix}$ **77.** $\begin{bmatrix} 2 & 1 \\ -\frac{3}{2} & -\frac{1}{2} \end{bmatrix}$

Exercise 3.4: Application in Economics (p. 159)

1. A's wages = C's wages = \$30,000; B's wages = \$22,500 **3.** A's wages = \$12,000; B's wages = \$22,000; C's wages = \$30,000 **5.** $X = \begin{bmatrix} 203.28 \\ 166.98 \\ 137.85 \end{bmatrix}$ **7.** Farmer's wages = \$20,000; Builder's wages = \$18,000; Tailor's wages = \$12,000; Rancher's wages = \$25,000 **9.** $X = \begin{bmatrix} 160 \\ 75.385 \end{bmatrix}$ **11.** If \$27,000 is allotted to the financial planner, then the physician earns \$19,500 and the attorney earns \$16,500.

Exercise 3.4: Application in Accounting (p. 163)

1.

Department	Total Costs Dollars	Direct Costs. Dollars	Indirect Costs for Services from Departments Dollars	
			S_1	S_2
S_1	3109.09	2000	345.45	763.64
S_2	2290.91	1000	1036.36	254.55
P_1	3354.54	2500	345.45	509.09
P_2	2790.91	1500	1036.36	254.55
P_3	3854.54	3000	345.45	509.09
Totals	15,399.99	10,000	3109.07	2290.92

Total of the service charges allocated to P_1, P_2, and P_3: \$2999.99
Sum of the direct costs of the service departments, S_1, and S_2: \$3000

3.

Department	Total Costs (in Dollars)	Direct Cost (in Dollars)	Indirect Costs for Services (in Dollars)	
S_1	1745.45	800	349.09	596.36
S_2	5963.64	4000	174.55	1789.09
P_1	2445.45	1500	349.09	596.36
P_2	2216.37	500	523.64	1192.73
P_3	3338.18	1200	349.09	1789.09
Totals	15,709.09	8000	1745.46	5963.63

Total of the service charges allocated to P_1, P_2, and P_3: \$4800
Sum of the direct costs of the service departments, S_1, and S_2: \$4800

Exercise 3.4: Application in Statistics (p. 168)

1. $\begin{bmatrix} 4 & 3 \\ 1 & 1 \\ 2 & 0 \end{bmatrix}$ **3.** $\begin{bmatrix} 1 & 0 & 1 \\ 11 & 12 & 4 \end{bmatrix}$ **5.** $[8 \quad 6 \quad 3]$ **7.** **(a)** Not symmetric **(b)** Symmetric **(c)** Not symmetric Yes, for two matrices to be equal, they must have the same dimensions. **9.** **(a)** $y = \frac{54}{35}x + \frac{27}{5}$ **(b)** 17,743 units will be supplied. **11.** $y = 1.498x + 36.135$ **13.** $N = 0.93t + 6.75$; 22.56 million persons are predicted to have diagnosed diabetes in the year 2011.

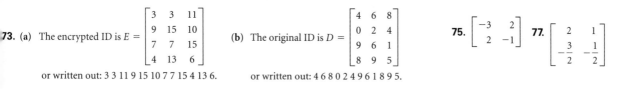

Review Exercises (p. 170)

1. $\begin{bmatrix} 4 & -4 \\ 3 & 9 \\ 4 & 0 \end{bmatrix}$ The dimension is 3 × 2. **3.** $\begin{bmatrix} 6 & 0 \\ 12 & 24 \\ -6 & 12 \end{bmatrix}$ The dimension is 3 × 2. **5.** $\begin{bmatrix} 4 & -3 & 0 \\ 12 & -2 & -8 \\ -2 & 5 & -4 \end{bmatrix}$ The dimension is 3 × 3.

7. $\begin{bmatrix} 8 & -13 & 8 \\ 9 & 2 & -10 \\ 18 & -17 & 4 \end{bmatrix}$ The dimension is 3 × 3. **9.** $\begin{bmatrix} 12 & -16 & 8 \\ 21 & 0 & -18 \\ 16 & -12 & 0 \end{bmatrix}$ The dimension is 3 × 3. **11.** $\begin{bmatrix} 9 & -8 \\ 8 & 22 \\ 7 & 2 \end{bmatrix}$ The dimension is 3 × 2.

13. $\begin{bmatrix} 3 & -4 \\ 1 & 5 \\ 5 & -2 \end{bmatrix} = C$. The dimension is 3 × 2. **15.** $\begin{bmatrix} 12 & -16 & 8 \\ 21 & 0 & -18 \\ 16 & -12 & 0 \end{bmatrix}$ The dimension is 3 × 3. **17.** $\begin{bmatrix} \frac{1}{3} & 0 \\ \frac{2}{3} & 1 \end{bmatrix}$

19. Inverse does not exist. **21.** $\begin{bmatrix} \frac{1}{16} & \frac{1}{32} & \frac{1}{4} \\ \frac{3}{16} & \frac{3}{32} & -\frac{1}{4} \\ -\frac{3}{16} & \frac{13}{32} & \frac{1}{4} \end{bmatrix}$ **23.** $AB = BA$ when $x = w$ and $y = -z$.

25. (a) Coded with matrix A: 79 82 29 50 41 58 70 52 83 90 29 30 29 34 Coded with matrix B: 111 42 8 93 92 92 76 82 76 70 68 32 52 14 4
(b) Coded with matrix A: 98 100 60 60 64 72 49 50 44 32 94 92 60 60 Coded with matrix B: 158 78 60 115 74 88 92 52 56 142 48 88 77 32 4
(c) Message: I forgot my pin.

27. (a) $A =$ Price [28.50 19.50 13.30] (columns: Microsoft, Intel, Dell) (b) $B =$

	Juanita	Debbie	Dawn
Microsoft	20	15	10
Intel	30	25	20
Dell	10	20	25

(c) $AB = [1288.00 \quad 1181.00 \quad 1007.50]$. The entries of matrix AB represent the cost of Juanita's, Debbie's, and Dawn's purchases, respectively, in dollars.

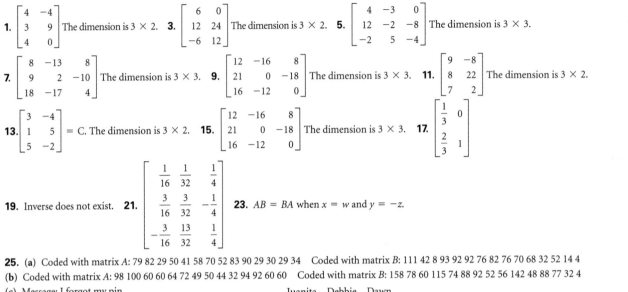

CHAPTER 4 Linear Programming with Two Variables

Exercise 4.1 (p. 187)

6. half-plane **7.** True **8.** True

9.
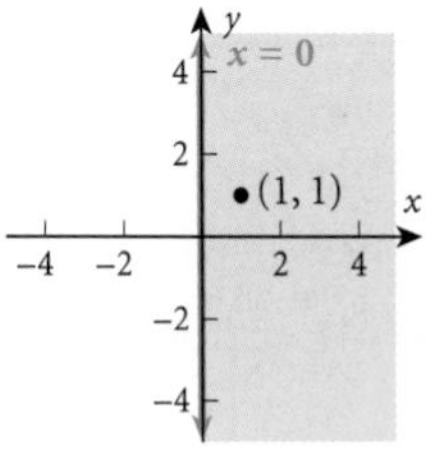

11.
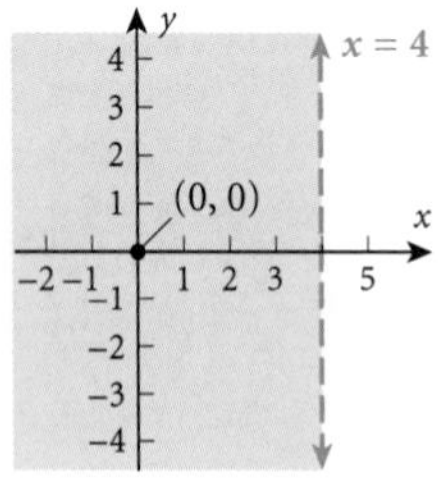

13.
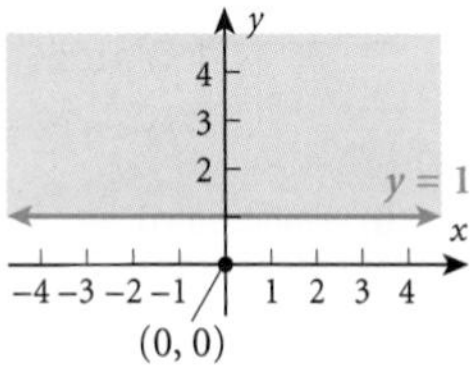

15.
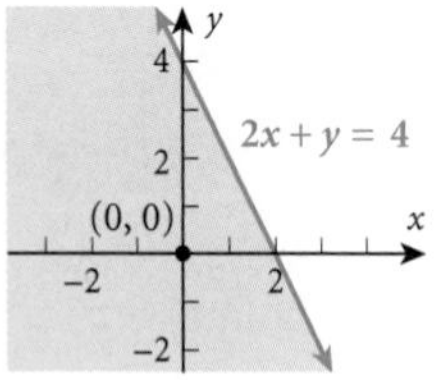

17.
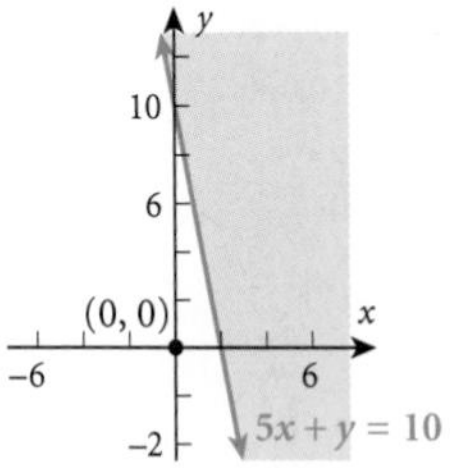

19.
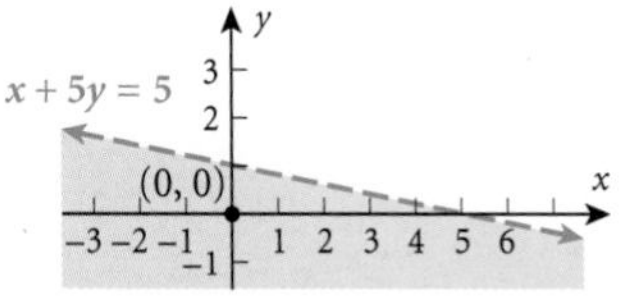

21. P_1 is part of the graph of the system, P_2 and P_3 are not.

23. P_1 and P_3 are part of the graph of the system, P_2 is not.

25. b **27.** c **29.** d

31.
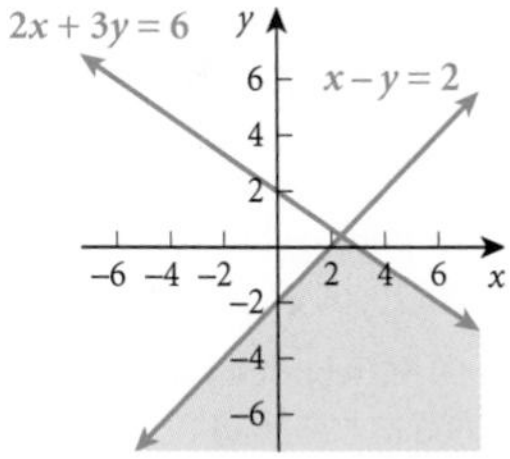

33.
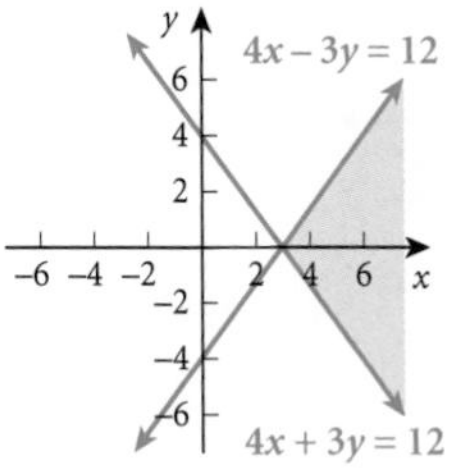

35.
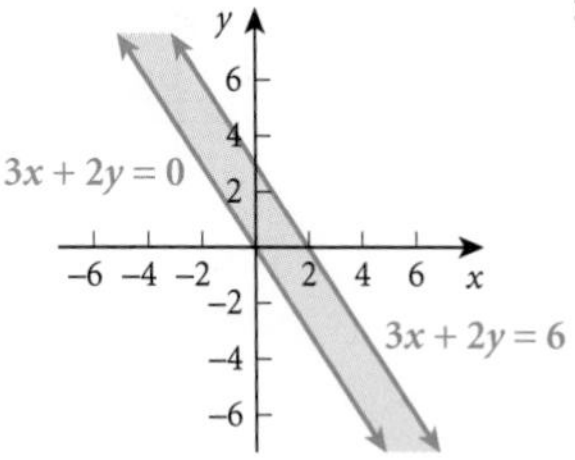

37.
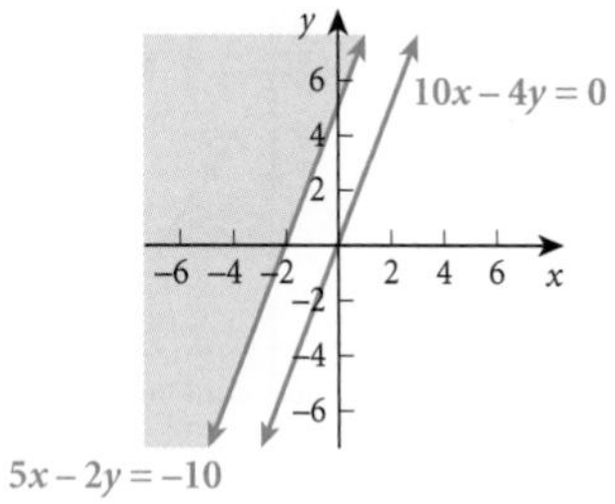

39. (a)
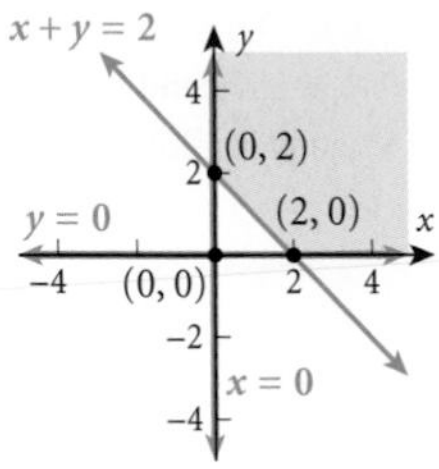

(b) Unbounded.
Corner points: (2, 0), (0, 2).

41. (a)
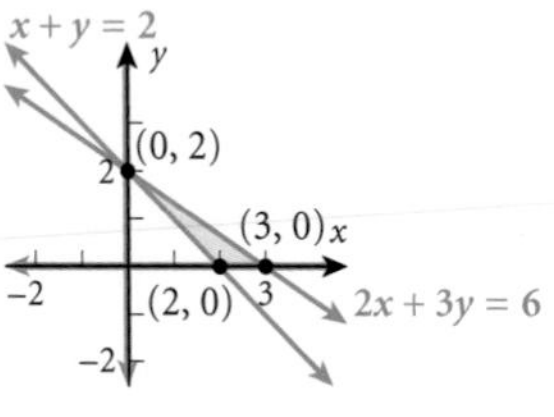

(b) Bounded.
Corner points: (2, 0), (3, 0), (0, 2).

43. (a)
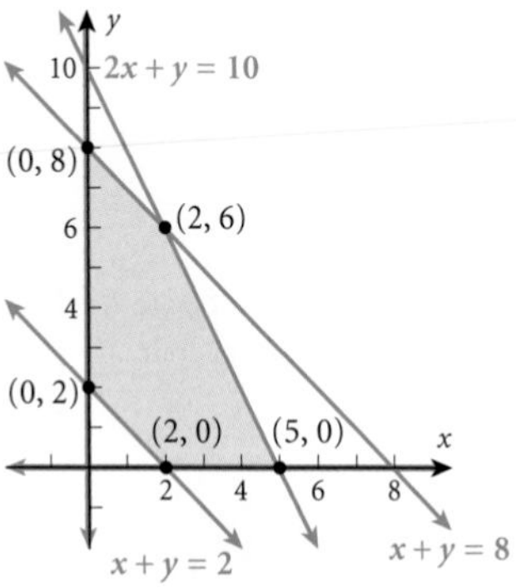

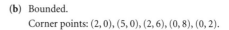

(b) Bounded.
Corner points: (2, 0), (5, 0), (2, 6), (0, 8), (0, 2).

45. (a)

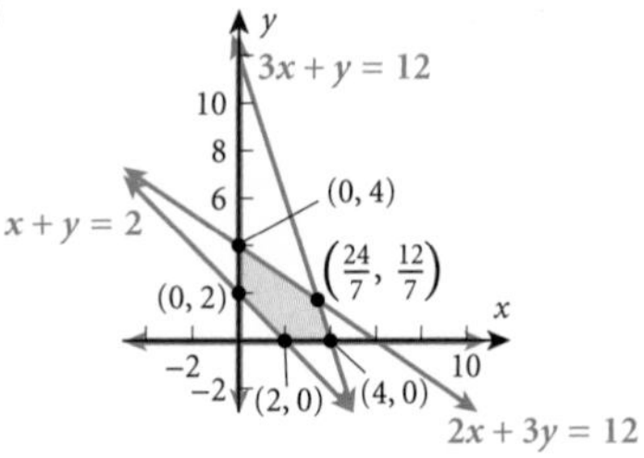

$3x + y = 12$
$x + y = 2$
$(0, 4)$
$\left(\frac{24}{7}, \frac{12}{7}\right)$
$(0, 2)$
$(2, 0)$ $(4, 0)$
$2x + 3y = 12$

(b) Bounded.

Corner points: $(2, 0)$, $(4, 0)$, $\left(\frac{24}{7}, \frac{12}{7}\right)$, $(0, 4)$, $(0, 2)$.

47. (a)

$(0, 4)$ $y = 4$
$\left(0, \frac{1}{2}\right)$
$(1, 0)$
$x + 2y = 1$

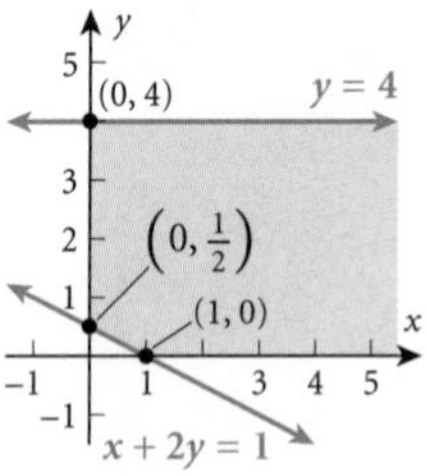

(b) Unbounded.

Corner points: $(1, 0)$, $\left(0, \frac{1}{2}\right)$, $(0, 4)$.

49. (a)

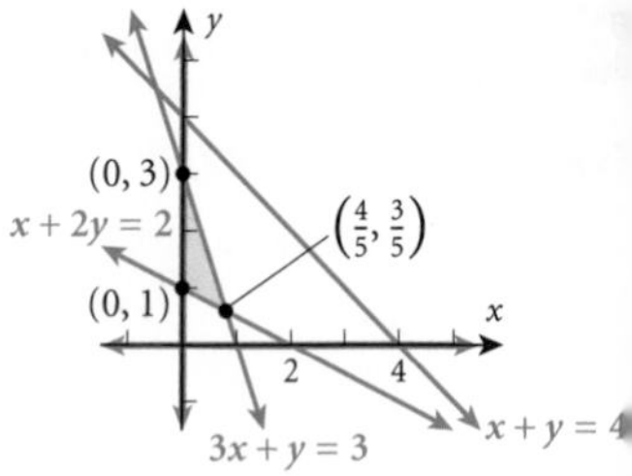

$(0, 3)$
$x + 2y = 2$ $\left(\frac{4}{5}, \frac{3}{5}\right)$
$(0, 1)$
$3x + y = 3$ $x + y = 4$

(b) Bounded.

Corner points: $\left(\frac{4}{5}, \frac{3}{5}\right)$, $(0, 3)$, $(0, 1)$.

51. (a)
$$\begin{cases} \dfrac{1}{4}x + \dfrac{1}{2}y \le 60 \\ \dfrac{3}{4}x + \dfrac{1}{2}y \le 90 \\ x \ge 0 \\ y \ge 0 \end{cases}$$

(b)

$x = 0$
$\frac{3}{4}x + \frac{1}{2}y = 90$
180
$(0, 120)$ $(60, 90)$
$\frac{1}{4}x + \frac{1}{2}y = 60$
$(0, 0)$ $(120, 0)$ 240 $y = 0$

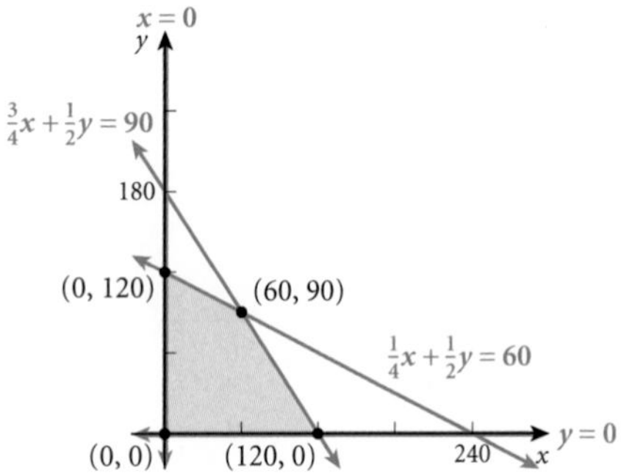

Corner points are $(0, 0)$, $(120, 0)$, $(60, 90)$, $(0, 120)$.

53. (a)
$$\begin{cases} 3x + 2y \le 80 \\ 4x + 3y \le 120 \\ y \ge 0 \\ x \ge 0 \end{cases}$$

(b)

$(0, 40)$
$\left(\frac{80}{3}, 0\right)$
$(0, 0)$ 10 20
$3x + 2y = 80$ $4x + 3y = 120$

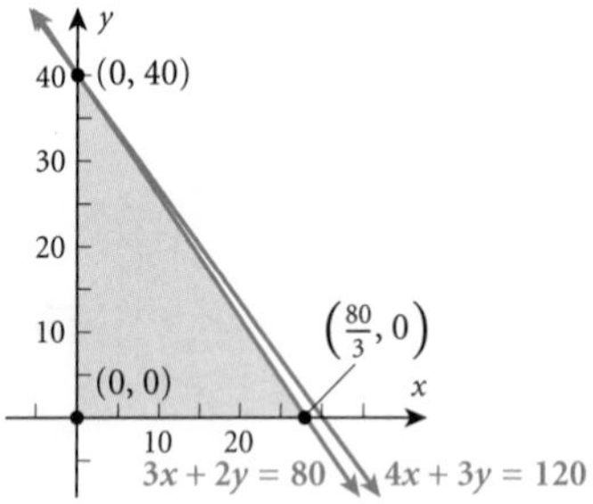

Corner points: $(0, 0)$, $\left(\frac{80}{3}, 0\right)$, $(0, 40)$.

55. (a)
$$\begin{cases} x + y \le 25{,}000 \\ x \ge 15{,}000 \\ y \le 10{,}000 \\ y \ge 0 \\ x \ge 0 \end{cases}$$

(b) $x + y = 25{,}000$

$x = 15{,}000$
$20{,}000$ $(15000, 10000)$
$y = 10{,}000$
$5{,}000$
$(15000, 0)$ $(25000, 0)$

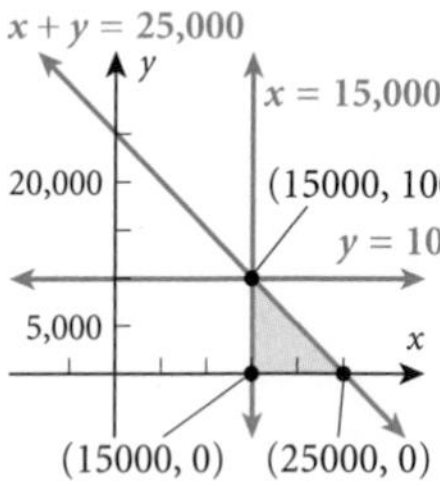

Corner points: $(15000, 0)$, $(25000, 0)$, $(15000, 10000)$.

(c) $(15000, 0)$ represents investing $15,000 in Dividend Equity fund. $(25000, 0)$ represents investing $25,000 in Dividend Equity fund. $(15000, 10000)$ represents investing $15,000 in Dividend Equity fund and $10,000 in Global Bond fund.

57. (a) x = number of units of grain 1
y = number of units of grain 2
$$\begin{cases} x + 2y \ge 5 \\ 5x + y \ge 16 \\ x \ge 0 \\ y \ge 0 \end{cases}$$

(b)

$(0, 16)$
$(3, 1)$
$(5, 0)$
$5x + y = 16$ $x + 2y = 5$

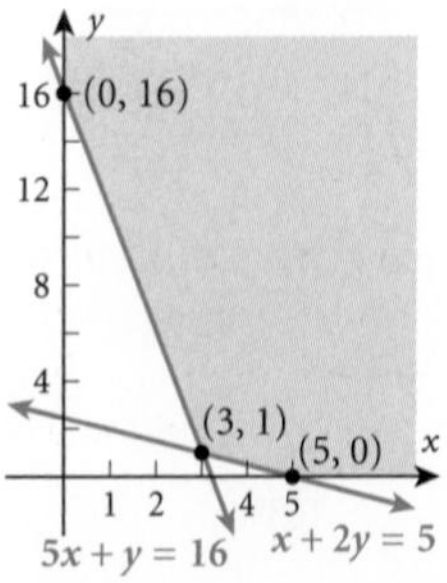

Corner points: $(0, 16)$, $(3, 1)$, $(5, 0)$.

59. (a) x = number of oz. of food A
y = number of oz. of food B
$$\begin{cases} 5x + 4y \ge 85 \\ 3x + 3y \ge 70 \\ 2x + 3y \ge 50 \\ x \ge 0 \\ y \ge 0 \end{cases}$$

(b) $3x + 3y = 70$

$\left(0, \frac{70}{3}\right)$
20
$\left(20, \frac{10}{3}\right)$
10
$(25, 0)$
5 10 15
$5x + 4y = 85$ $2x + 3y = 50$

Corner points: $\left(0, \frac{70}{3}\right)$, $\left(20, \frac{10}{3}\right)$, $(25, 0)$.

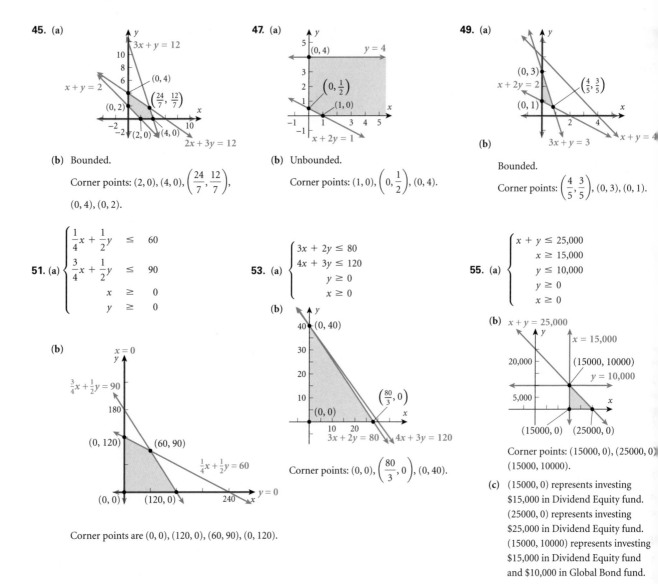

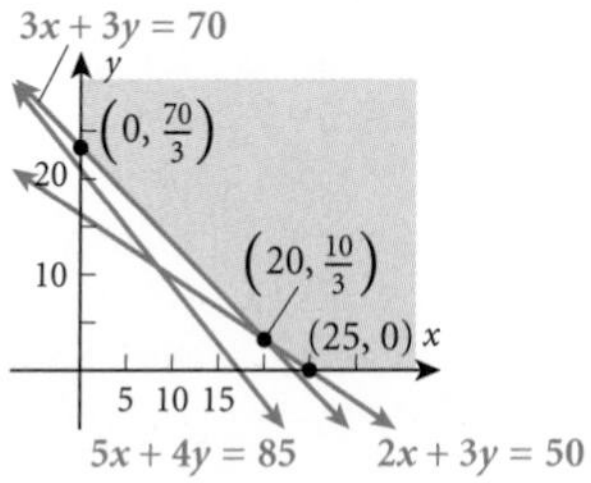

61. (a) $\begin{cases} x + y \leq 30{,}000 \\ 0.0435x + 0.0505y \geq 500 \\ x \geq 3{,}000 \\ y \geq 5{,}000 \end{cases}$

(b)

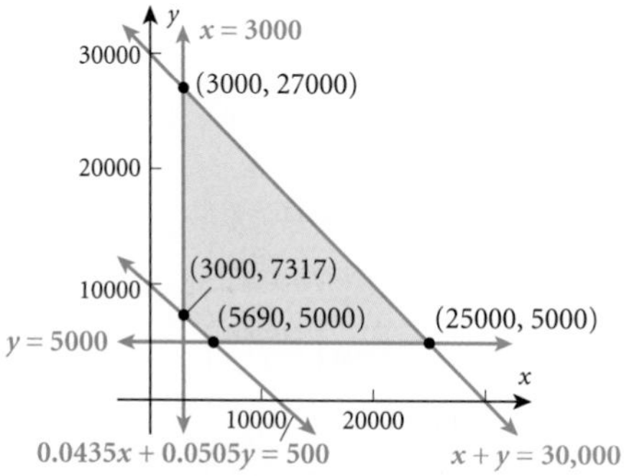

Corner points: (5690, 5000), (25000, 5000), (3000, 7317), (3000, 27000).

(c) Each corner point represents an amount x deposited in the ICON bond fund and an amount y deposited in ING Mid Cap Opportunities fund that satisfy the conditions given.

63. (a) $\begin{cases} x + y \leq 200{,}000 \\ 3x - y \leq 0 \\ x \geq 20{,}000 \end{cases}$

(b)

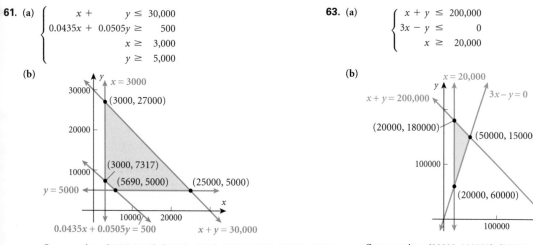

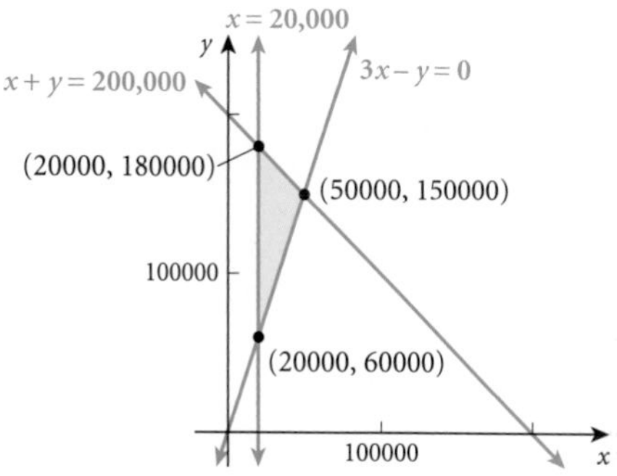

Corner points: (20000, 180000), (20000, 60000), (50000, 150000).

(c) Projected annual return at (20000, 180000) is $44,564, at (20000, 60000) is $16,184, and at (50000, 150000) is $40,460.

Exercise 4.2 (p. 198)

1. Objective function **2.** Feasible point **3.** False **4.** True **5.** Maximum of 38 at $(7, 8)$. Minimum of 10 at $(2, 2)$. **7.** Maximum of 15 at $(7, 8)$. Minimum of 4 at $(2, 2)$. **9.** Maximum of 55 at $(7, 8)$. Minimum of 14 at any point on the line segment between $(2, 2)$ and $(8, 1)$. **11.** Maximum of 53 at $(7, 8)$. Minimum of 14 at $(2, 2)$. **13.** Maximum of 81 at $(8, 1)$. Minimum of 22 at $(2, 2)$. **15.** Corner points: $(0, 4)$, $(3, 0)$, $(13, 0)$. **17.** Corner points: $(0, 0)$, $(15, 0)$, $(5, 10)$, $(0, 10)$. **19.** Corner points: $(3, 0)$, $(10, 0)$, $(10, 8)$, $(0, 8)$, $(0, 4)$. **21.** Maximum of 14 at $(0, 2)$. **23.** Maximum of 15 at $(3, 0)$. **25.** Maximum of 56 at $(0, 8)$. **27.** Maximum of 58 at $(6, 4)$. **29.** Minimum of 0 at $(0, 0)$. **31.** Minimum of 4 at $(2, 0)$. **33.** Minimum of 4 at $(2, 0)$. **35.** Minimum of $\frac{3}{2}$ at $\left(0, \frac{1}{2}\right)$. **37.** Maximum of 10 at any point on the line $x + y = 10$ between $(0, 10)$ and $(10, 0)$. Minimum of $\frac{20}{3}$ at $\left(\frac{10}{3}, \frac{10}{3}\right)$. **39.** Maximum of 50 at $(10, 0)$. Minimum of 20 at $(0, 10)$. **41.** Maximum of 40 at $(0, 10)$. Minimum of $\frac{70}{3}$ at $\left(\frac{10}{3}, \frac{10}{3}\right)$. **43.** Maximum of 100 at $(10, 0)$. Minimum of 10 at $(0, 10)$. **45.** Maximum of 192 at $(4, 4)$. Minimum of 54 at $(3, 0)$. **47.** Maximum of 58 at $(4, 5)$. Minimum of 12 at $(0, 2)$. **49.** Maximum of 240 at $(3, 10)$. **51.** Maximum of 216 at $(2, 10)$.

Exercise 4.3 (p. 206)

1. (a) 24 acres of soy beans and 12 acres of wheat should be planted to maximize profit.
(b) Maximum profit is $5520.00.
(c) Maximum profit is $7200.00 if preparation constraint is raised to $2400.00.

3. She should invest $12,000 in the Natural Resources fund and $8000 in the Developing Markets funds for a maximum return of $2400.
5. Manufacture 500,000 of each vitamin for a maximum profit of $75,000.
7. Kathleen should rent 15 rectangular tables and 16 round tables for a minimum cost of $1252.00.

9. Eric should eat 2 turkey breast sandwiches and 5 Veggie Delite® sandwiches to meet his dietary requirements and minimize his fat intake at 24 grams.
11. The factory should manufacture 15 of the first product and 25 of the second product, maximizing the profit at $2100.00. **13.** The minimum cost is $22.50. It can be attained using 7.5 oz of Supplement A and 11.25 oz of Supplement B or using 15 oz of Supplement A and no Supplement B. Other solutions are on the line segment joining (7.5, 11.25) and (15, 0). **15.** Fremont Bank should allocate $24 million to 15-year mortgages and $48 million to 30-year mortgages to maximize the month's interest income at $292,500. **17.** The factory should manufacture 10 pairs of racing skates and 15 pairs of figure skates to obtain a maximum profit of $280.00. **19.** The chemical plant should produce 700 units of compound A and 400 units of compound B to obtain a maximum profit of $1450.00 while remaining below government pollution standards. **21.** The maximum profit of $1280.00 is made when 4 tons of Type 1 steel and 4 tons of Type 2 steel are produced. **23.** The minimum cost is $0.19 when Danny adds 5 ounces of Supplement I and 1 ounce of Supplement II to every 100 ounces of feed.
25. The couple should deposit $15,000 in the ICON Bond fund and $30,000 in the ING Mid Cap fund. Their average annual interest income will be $2167.50.
27. Eighteen sales representatives from New York City and 22 from Chicago should be sent to the meeting to minimize the total airfare. The minimum airfare is $13,412.00. **29.** If high-grade carpet is priced between $520 and $620 per roll, some of each type of carpet will be manufactured to maximize income.

Review Exercises (p. 210)

1.

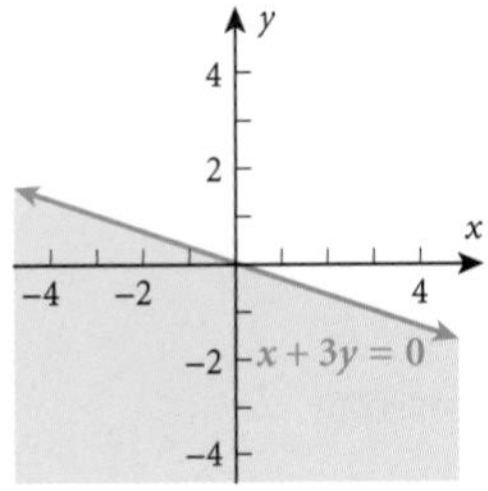

3.

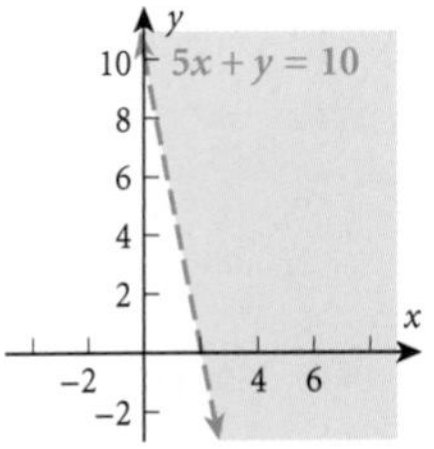

5. All 3 points P_1, P_2, and P_3 are part of the graph of the system. **7.** a

9. Bounded.

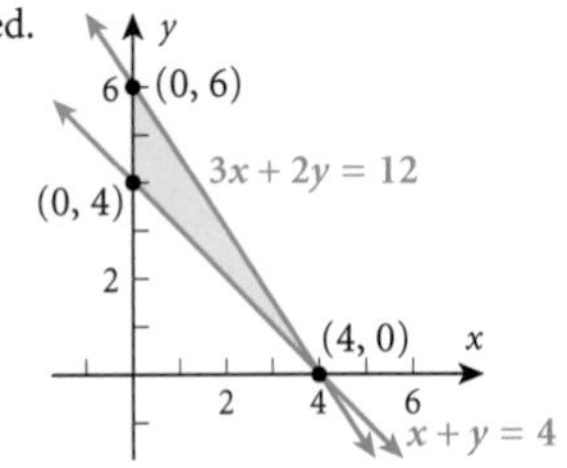

Corner points: (4, 0), (0, 4), (0, 6).

11. Bounded.

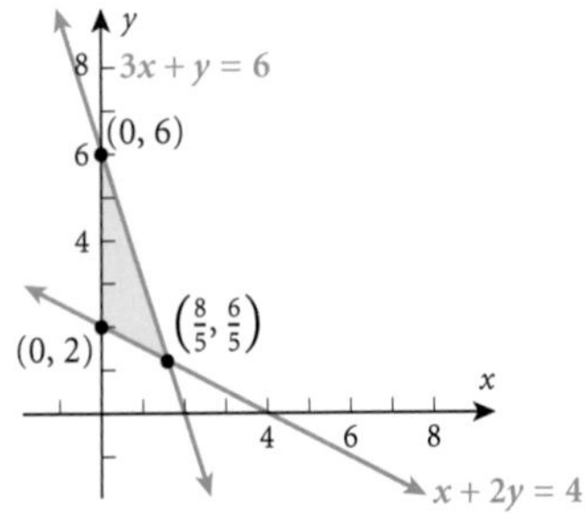

Corner points: (0, 2) $\left(\frac{8}{5}, \frac{6}{5}\right)$, (0, 6).

13. Bounded.

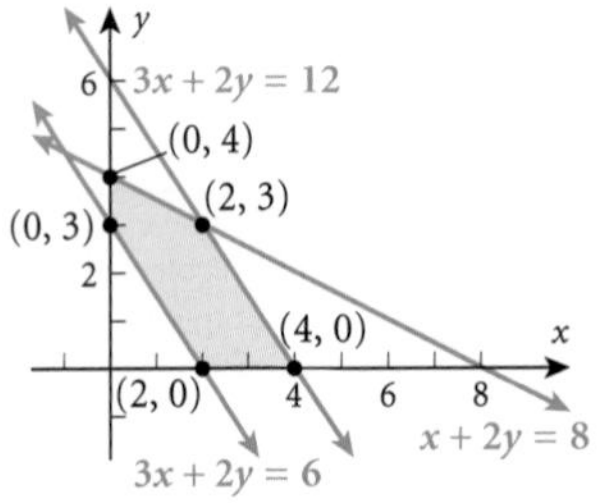

Corner points: (2, 0), (4, 0), (2, 3), (0, 3), (0, 4).

15. Maximum of $\frac{80}{3}$ at $\left(\frac{40}{3}, \frac{40}{3}\right)$.

17. Minimum of 20 at (0, 10).

19. Maximum of 40 at (20, 0), $\left(\frac{40}{3}, \frac{40}{3}\right)$, and at any point on the line segment $2x + y = 40$ connecting them.

21. Minimum of 20 at (10, 0).

23. Maximum of 235 at (5, 8). Minimum of 60 at (4, 0), (0, 3) and at all points on the line segment $3x + 4y = 12$, connecting them.

25. Maximum of 155 at (5, 4). Minimum of 0 at (0, 0).

27. Maximum of 42 at (9, 8). **29.** Maximum of 24 at (8, 8).

31. Minimum of $\frac{48}{5}$ at $\left(\frac{4}{5}, \frac{18}{5}\right)$.

33. (a) $\begin{cases} \frac{1}{4}x + \frac{1}{2}y \le 75 \\ \frac{3}{4}x + \frac{1}{2}y \le 120 \\ x \ge 0 \\ y \ge 0 \end{cases}$

(b)

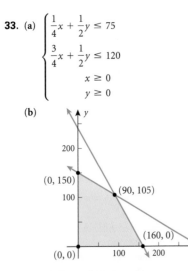

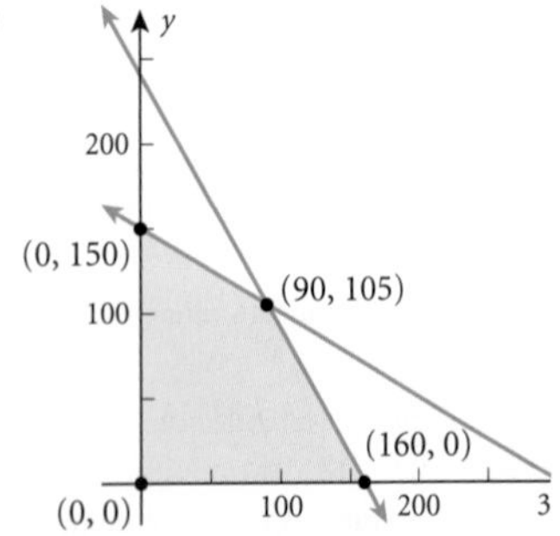

(c) Bill should prepare 90 packages of economy blend and 105 packages of superior blend to obtain a maximum profit of $69.00.

35. Produce 8 pairs of downhill skis and 24 pairs of cross-country skis for a maximum profit of $1760.

37. Give the child 1.58 servings of Gerber Banana Oatmeal and Peach and no Gerber Mixed Fruit Juice for a minimum cost of $1.25.

39. Manufacture 550,000 high-potency vitamins and 250,000 thousand calcium-enriched vitamins for a maximum profit of $67,500.

41. To maximize the projected dividend, the fund should purchase 3125 shares of Boeing and 7500 shares of Honeywell. The projected dividend is $3562.50.

Mathematical Questions from Professional Exams

1. b **2.** a **3.** c **4.** c **5.** d **6.** c **7.** c **8.** b **9.** b **10.** a **11.** b **12.** e **13.** c **14.** b

CHAPTER 5 Linear Programming: Simplex Method

Exercise 5.1 (p. 232)

3. True **4.** Slack variables **5.** False **6.** True **7.** Standard **9.** Nonstandard **11.** Nonstandard **13.** Nonstandard **15.** Standard **17.** Cannot be modified **19.** Cannot be modified

21. Can be modified. The constraints become

$$x_1 - x_2 - x_3 \le 6$$
$$-2x_1 + 3x_2 \le 12$$
$$x_3 \le 2$$
$$x_1 \ge 0, x_2 \ge 0, x_3 \ge 0$$

23.

$$\begin{aligned} P - 2x_1 - x_2 - 3x_3 &= 0 \\ 5x_1 + 2x_2 + x_3 + s_1 &= 20 \\ 6x_1 - x_2 + 4x_3 + s_2 &= 24 \\ x_1 + x_2 + 4x_3 + s_3 &= 16 \end{aligned}$$
$$x_1 \ge 0 \quad x_2 \ge 0 \quad x_3 \ge 0 \quad s_1 \ge 0 \quad s_2 \ge 0 \quad s_3 \ge 0$$

The initial simplex tableau is

BV	P	x_1	x_2	x_3	s_1	s_2	s_3	RHS
s_1	0	5	2	1	1	0	0	20
s_2	0	6	−1	4	0	1	0	24
s_3	0	1	1	4	0	0	1	16
P	1	−2	−1	−3	0	0	0	0

25.

$$\begin{aligned} P - 3x_1 - 5x_2 &= 0 \\ 2.2x_1 - 1.8x_2 + s_1 &= 5 \\ 0.8x_1 + 1.2x_2 + s_2 &= 2.5 \\ x_1 + x_2 + s_3 &= 0.1 \end{aligned}$$
$$x_1 \ge 0, x_2 \ge 0, s_1 \ge 0, s_2 \ge 0, s_3 \ge 0$$

The initial simplex tableau is

BV	P	x_1	x_2	s_1	s_2	s_3	RHS
s_1	0	2.2	−1.8	1	0	0	5
s_2	0	0.8	1.2	0	1	0	2.5
s_3	0	1	1	0	0	1	0.1
P	1	−3	−5	0	0	0	0

27.

$$\begin{aligned} P - 2x_1 - 3x_2 - x_3 &= 0 \\ x_1 + x_2 + x_3 + s_1 &= 50 \\ 3x_1 + 2x_2 + x_3 + s_2 &= 10 \end{aligned}$$
$$x_1 \ge 0, x_2 \ge 0, x_3 \ge 0, s_1 \ge 0, s_2 \ge 0$$

The initial simplex tableau is

BV	P	x_1	x_2	x_3	s_1	s_2	RHS
s_1	0	1	1	1	1	0	50
s_2	0	3	2	1	0	1	10
P	1	−2	−3	−1	0	0	0

29.

$$\begin{aligned} P - 3x_1 - 4x_2 - 2x_3 &= 0 \\ 3x_1 + x_2 + 4x_3 + s_1 &= 5 \\ x_1 - x_2 + s_2 &= 5 \\ 2x_1 - x_2 + x_3 + s_3 &= 6 \end{aligned}$$
$$x_1 \ge 0, x_2 \ge 0, x_3 \ge 0, s_1 \ge 0, s_2 \ge 0, s_3 \ge 0$$

The initial tableau is

BV	P	x_1	x_2	x_3	s_1	s_2	s_3	RHS
s_1	0	3	1	4	1	0	0	5
s_2	0	1	−1	0	0	1	0	5
s_3	0	2	−1	1	0	0	1	6
P	1	−3	−4	−2	0	0	0	0

31. Maximize $P = x_1 + 2x_2 + 5x_3$
subject to the constraints

$$x_1 - 2x_2 - 3x_3 \le 10$$
$$-3x_1 - x_2 + x_3 \le 12$$
$$x_1 \ge 0, x_2 \ge 0\ x_3 \ge 0$$

System with slack variables:

$$\begin{aligned} P - x_1 - 2x_2 - 5x_3 &= 0 \\ x_1 - 2x_2 - 3x_3 + s_1 &= 10 \\ -3x_1 - x_2 + x_3 + s_2 &= 12 \end{aligned}$$
$$x_1 \ge 0, x_2 \ge 0, x_3 \ge 0, s_1 \ge 0, s_2 \ge 0$$

Initial tableau:

BV	P	x_1	x_2	x_3	s_1	s_2	RHS
s_1	0	1	−2	−3	1	0	10
s_2	0	−3	−1	1	0	1	12
P	1	−1	−2	−5	0	0	0

33. Maximize $P = 2x_1 + 3x_2 + x_3 + 6x_4$
subject to the constraints

$$\begin{aligned} -x_1 + x_2 + 2x_3 + x_4 &\le 10 \\ -x_1 + x_2 - x_3 + x_4 &\le 8 \\ x_1 + x_2 + x_3 + x_4 &\le 9 \\ x_1 \ge 0, x_2 \ge 0, x_3 \ge 0, x_4 &\ge 0 \end{aligned}$$

System with slack variables:

$$\begin{aligned} P - 2x_1 - 3x_2 - x_3 - 6x_4 &= 0 \\ -x_1 + x_2 + 2x_3 + x_4 + s_1 &= 10 \\ -x_1 + x_2 - x_3 + x_4 + s_2 &= 8 \\ x_1 + x_2 + x_3 + x_4 + s_3 &= 9 \end{aligned}$$

$$x_1 \ge 0, x_2 \ge 0, x_3 \ge 0, x_4 \ge 0, s_1 \ge 0, s_2 \ge 0, s_3 \ge 0$$

Initial tableau:

BV	P	x_1	x_2	x_3	x_4	s_1	s_2	s_3	RHS
s_1	0	−1	1	2	1	1	0	0	10
s_2	0	−1	1	−1	1	0	1	0	8
s_3	0	1	1	1	1	0	0	1	9
P	1	−2	−3	−1	−6	0	0	0	0

35. **(a)** Tableau after the pivot:

BV	P	x_1	x_2	s_1	s_2	RHS
s_1	0	0	$\frac{4}{3}$	1	$-\frac{1}{3}$	140
x_1	0	1	$\frac{2}{3}$	0	$\frac{1}{3}$	160
P	1	0	$-\frac{4}{3}$	0	$\frac{1}{3}$	160

(b) Corresponding system of equations:

$$\begin{aligned} s_1 &= -\frac{4}{3}x_2 + \frac{1}{3}s_2 + 140 \\ x_1 &= -\frac{2}{3}x_2 - \frac{1}{3}s_2 + 160 \\ P &= \frac{4}{3}x_2 - \frac{1}{3}s_2 + 160 \end{aligned}$$

(c) Current values: $P = 160$; $s_1 = 140$; $x_1 = 160$

37. **(a)** Tableau after pivot:

BV	P	x_1	x_2	x_3	s_1	s_2	s_3	RHS
s_1	0	0	$\frac{4}{3}$	$\frac{8}{3}$	1	0	$-\frac{1}{3}$	18
s_2	0	0	$-\frac{7}{3}$	$-\frac{5}{3}$	0	1	$-\frac{2}{3}$	20
x_1	0	1	$\frac{2}{3}$	$\frac{4}{3}$	0	0	$\frac{1}{3}$	6
P	1	0	$-\frac{4}{3}$	$-\frac{5}{3}$	0	0	$\frac{1}{3}$	6

(b) Corresponding system of equations:

$$\begin{aligned} s_1 &= -\frac{4}{3}x_2 - \frac{8}{3}x_3 + \frac{1}{3}s_3 + 18 \\ s_2 &= \frac{7}{3}x_2 + \frac{5}{3}x_3 + \frac{2}{3}s_3 + 20 \\ x_1 &= -\frac{2}{3}x_2 - \frac{4}{3}x_3 - \frac{1}{3}s_3 + 6 \\ P &= \frac{4}{3}x_2 + \frac{5}{3}x_3 - \frac{1}{3}s_3 + 6 \end{aligned}$$

(c) Current values:
$P = 6$; $s_1 = 18$; $s_2 = 20$; $x_1 = 6$

39. **(a)** Tableau after pivot:

BV	P	x_1	x_2	x_3	x_4	s_1	s_2	s_3	s_4	RHS
s_1	0	0	0	1	$\frac{3}{2}$	1	$\frac{3}{2}$	0	0	56
x_1	0	1	0	0	$\frac{1}{2}$	0	$\frac{1}{2}$	0	0	12
s_3	0	0	−3	1	0	0	0	1	0	28
s_4	0	0	−3	0	1	0	0	0	1	24
P	1	0	−2	−3	$-\frac{7}{2}$	0	$\frac{1}{2}$	0	0	12

(b) Corresponding system of equations:

$$\begin{aligned} s_1 &= -x_3 - \frac{3}{2}x_4 - \frac{3}{2}s_2 + 56 \\ x_1 &= -\frac{1}{2}x_4 - \frac{1}{2}s_2 + 12 \\ s_3 &= 3x_2 - x_3 + 28 \\ s_4 &= 3x_2 - x_4 + 24 \\ P &= 2x_2 + 3x_3 + \frac{7}{2}x_4 - \frac{1}{2}s_2 + 12 \end{aligned}$$

(c) Current values:
$P = 12$; $s_1 = 56$; $x_1 = 12$; $s_3 = 28$; $s_4 = 24$

41. **(a)** P is the profit, x_1 is the number of sleeping dolls, x_2 is the number of talking dolls, and x_3 is the number of walking dolls.

(b) Maximize

$P = 6x_1 + 6x_2 + 8x_3$
subject to the constraints

$$\begin{aligned} x_1 + x_2 + x_3 &\le 60 \\ 6x_1 + 7.5x_2 + 9x_3 &\le 405 \end{aligned}$$

$$x_1 \ge 0 \quad x_2 \ge 0 \quad x_3 \ge 0$$

(c) System with slack variables added:

$$\begin{aligned} x_1 + x_2 + x_3 + s_1 &= 60 \\ 6x_1 + 7.5x_2 + 9x_3 + s_2 &= 405 \\ P - 6x_1 - 6x_2 - 8x_3 &= 0 \end{aligned}$$

$$x_1 \ge 0 \quad x_2 \ge 0 \quad x_3 \ge 0 \quad s_1 \ge 0 \quad s_2 \ge 0$$

(d) Initial tableau:

BV	P	x_1	x_2	x_3	s_1	s_2	RHS
s_1	0	1	1	1	1	0	60
s_2	0	6	7.5	9	0	1	405
P	1	−6	−6	−8	0	0	0

3. (a) P is the daily profit, x_1 is the number of shirts produced, x_2 is the number of jackets produced, and x_3 is the number of pairs of pants produced each day.

(b) Maximize

$$P = 19x_1 + 34x_2 + 15x_3$$

subject to the constraints

$$10x_1 + 20x_2 + 20x_3 \le 500$$
$$20x_1 + 40x_2 + 30x_3 \le 900$$
$$x_1 + x_2 + x_3 \le 30$$
$$x_1 \ge 0 \quad x_2 \ge 0 \quad x_3 \ge 0$$

(c) System with slack variables added:

$$10x_1 + 20x_2 + 20x_3 + s_1 = 500$$
$$20x_1 + 40x_2 + 30x_3 + s_2 = 900$$
$$x_1 + x_2 + x_3 + s_3 = 30$$
$$P - 19x_1 - 34x_2 - 15x_3 = 0$$
$$x_1 \ge 0 \quad x_2 \ge 0 \quad x_3 \ge 0 \quad s_1 \ge 0 \quad s_2 \ge 0 \quad s_3 \ge 0$$

(d) Initial tableau:

BV	P	x_1	x_2	x_3	s_1	s_2	s_3	RHS
s_1	0	10	20	20	1	0	0	500
s_2	0	20	40	30	0	1	0	900
s_3	0	1	1	1	0	0	1	30
P	1	−19	−34	−15	0	0	0	0

5. (a) P is the return on her investments; x_1 is the amount invested in the money market, x_2 is the amount invested in the mutual fund, and x_3 is the amount invested in the CD.

(b) Maximize

$$P = 0.0105x_1 + 0.05x_2 + 0.0166x_3$$

Subject to the constraints

$$x_1 + x_2 + x_3 \le 25{,}000$$
$$x_2 + x_3 \le 10{,}000$$
$$-x_1 + x_3 \le 1{,}500$$
$$x_1 \ge 0 \quad x_2 \ge 0 \quad x_3 \ge 0$$

(c) System with slack variables added:

$$x_1 + x_2 + x_3 + s_1 = 25{,}000$$
$$x_2 + x_3 + s_2 = 10{,}000$$
$$-x_1 + x_3 + s_3 = 1{,}500$$
$$P - 0.0105x_1 - 0.05x_2 - 0.0166x_3 = 0$$
$$x_1 \ge 0 \quad x_2 \ge 0 \quad x_3 \ge 0 \quad s_1 \ge 0 \quad s_2 \ge 0 \quad s_3 \ge 0$$

(d) Initial tableau:

BV	P	x_1	x_2	x_3	s_1	s_2	s_3	RHS
s_1	0	1	1	1	1	0	0	25,000
s_2	0	0	1	1	0	1	0	10,000
s_3	0	−1	0	1	0	0	1	1,500
P	1	−0.0105	−0.05	−0.0166	0	0	0	0

Exercise 5.2 (p. 252)

1. False **2.** True **3.** False **4.** Column **5.** (b); the pivot element is 1 in row s_1, column x_1 **7.** (a); the solution is $P = \frac{256}{7}, x_1 = \frac{32}{7}, x_2 = 0$ **9.** (c) **11.** (b); the pivot element is 1 in row x_1, column s_1 **13.** The maximum is $P = \frac{204}{7} = 29\frac{1}{7}$ when $x_1 = \frac{24}{7}, x_2 = \frac{12}{7}$. **15.** The maximum is $P = 8$ when $x_1 = \frac{2}{3}, x_2 = \frac{2}{3}$. **17.** The maximum is $P = 6$ when $x_1 = 2, x_2 = 0$. **19.** There is no maximum for P; the feasible region is unbounded. **21.** The maximum is $P = 30$ when $x_1 = 0, x_2 = 0, x_3 = 10$. **23.** The maximum is $P = 42$ when $x_1 = 1, x_2 = 10, x_3 = 0, x_4 = 0$. **25.** The maximum is $P = 40$ when $x_1 = 20, x_2 = 0, x_3 = 0$. **27.** The maximum is $P = 50$ when $x_1 = 0, x_2 = 15, x_3 = 5, x_4 = 0$.

29. (a) Let P be the daily profit, x_1 be the number of pairs of Jean I produced daily, x_2 be the number of pairs of Jean II produced daily, and x_3 be the number of pairs of Jean III produced daily.

Maximize

$$P = 4x_1 + 4.5x_2 + 6x_3$$

subject to the constraints

$$8x_1 + 12x_2 + 18x_3 \le 5200$$
$$12x_1 + 18x_2 + 24x_3 \le 6000$$
$$4x_1 + 8x_2 + 12x_3 \le 2200$$
$$x_1 \ge 0 \quad x_2 \ge 0 \quad x_3 \ge 0$$

(b) Maximum $P = 2000$, when $x_1 = 500, x_2 = 0, x_3 = 0, s_1 = 1200, s_2 = 0$, and $s_3 = 200$

(c) A maximum daily profit of \$2000 is made when 500 pairs of Jean I are produced and neither Jean II nor Jean III is produced.

31. (a) Let P be the weekly profit, x_1 be the number of rolls of birthday wrapping paper sold per week, x_2 be the number of rolls of holiday wrapping paper sold weekly, and x_3 be the number of rolls of wedding wrapping paper sold per week.
Maximize
$P = x_1 + x_2 + 2x_3$
subject to the constraints

$$\begin{aligned} 3x_1 + 5x_2 + 4x_3 &\le 500 \\ 10x_1 + 15x_2 + 12x_3 &\le 1800 \\ \frac{1}{2}x_1 \qquad + x_3 &\le 75 \\ x_1 \ge 0 \quad x_2 \ge 0 \quad x_3 &\ge 0 \end{aligned}$$

(b) Maximum $P = 190$, when $x_1 = 0, x_2 = 40, x_3 = 75, s_1 = 0, s_2 = 300,$ and $s_3 = 0$

(c) The lacrosse team makes a maximum profit of \$190 a week when constrained as in the problem by selling no rolls of birthday wrapping paper, 40 rolls of holiday wrapping paper, and 75 rolls of wedding wrapping paper.

33. (a) Let P denote the revenue, x_1 denote the number of Can I nuts packaged, x_2 denote the number of Can II nuts packaged, and x_3 denote the number of Can III nuts packaged.
Maximize $P = 28x_1 + 24x_2 + 21x_3$
subject to the constraints

$$\begin{aligned} 3x_1 + 4x_2 + 5x_3 &\le 500 \\ x_1 + \frac{1}{2}x_2 \qquad &\le 100 \\ x_1 + \frac{1}{2}x_2 \qquad &\le 50 \\ x_1 \ge 0 \quad x_2 \ge 0 \quad x_3 &\ge 0 \end{aligned}$$

(b) Maximum $P = 2870$, when $x_1 = 50, x_2 = 0, x_3 = 70, s_1 = 0, s_2 = 50,$ and $s_3 = 0$

(c) Revenue is maximized at \$2870.00 when 50 packages of Can I nuts, 70 packages of Can III nuts, and no packages of Can II nuts are produced.

35. (a) The store should order 45 sleeping dolls, 15 walking dolls, and no talking dolls to maximize profit.

(b) The maximum profit is \$390.00.

37. (a) Steven should produce 15 shirts, 15 jackets, and no pants to maximize his profit.

(b) The maximum profit is \$795.00.

39. (a) Let P denote the company's revenue and let x_1, x_2, and x_3 represent the number of gallons of regular, premium, and super premium gasoline, respectively, to be refined. The company wants to refine amounts that will maximize its revenue subject to its available resources.

Maximize

$P = 2.80x_1 + 2.97x_2 + 3.08x_3$

subject to the constraints

$$\begin{aligned} 0.6x_1 + 0.7x_2 + 0.8x_3 &\le 140{,}000 \\ 0.4x_1 + 0.3x_2 + 0.2x_3 &\le 120{,}000 \\ x_1 + x_2 + x_3 &\le 225{,}000 \\ x_1 \ge 0 \quad x_2 \ge 0 \quad x_3 &\ge 0 \end{aligned}$$

(b) The maximum is $P = 638{,}500$, obtained when $x_1 = 175{,}000$, $x_2 = 50{,}000$, and $x_3 = 0$.

(c) To achieve a maximize revenue of \$638,500, the company should refine 175,000 gallons of regular gasoline, 50,000 gallons of premium gasoline, and no super premium gasoline.

41. (a) Let P be the total yield, x_1 be the amount invested in stocks, x_2 be the amount invested in corporate bonds, and x_3 be the amount invested in municipal bonds.

Maximize

$P = 0.08x_1 + 0.05x_2 + 0.03x_3$

subject to the constraints

$$\begin{aligned} x_1 + x_2 + x_3 &\le 90{,}000 \\ x_1 \qquad\qquad &\le 45{,}000 \\ x_2 - x_3 &\le 18{,}000 \\ x_1 \ge 0 \quad x_2 \ge 0 \quad & x_3 \ge 0 \end{aligned}$$

(b) The maximum is $P = 5580$, obtained when $x_1 = 45{,}000$, $x_2 = 31{,}500$, and $x_3 = 13{,}500$.

(c) The financial consultant can maximize her client's investment income while maintaining her investment strategy by investing $45,000 in stocks, $31,500 in corporate bonds, and $13,500 in municipal bonds. The maximum return will be $5580.

43. (a) Let P denote the profit, x_1 denote the number of acres of soybeans planted, x_2 denote the number of acres of corn planted, and x_3 denote the number of acres of wheat planted.

Maximize:

$P = 70x_1 + 90x_2 + 50x_3$

subject to the constraints

$$\begin{aligned} x_1 + x_2 + x_3 &\le 200 \\ 40x_1 + 50x_2 + 30x_3 &\le 18{,}000 \\ 20x_1 + 30x_2 + 15x_3 &\le 4{,}200 \\ x_1 \ge 0 \quad x_2 \ge 0 \quad & x_3 \ge 0 \end{aligned}$$

(b) Maximum $P = 14{,}400$, when $x_1 = 180$, $x_2 = 20$, $x_3 = 0$, $s_1 = 0$, $s_2 = 9800$, and $s_3 = 0$

(c) The farmer realizes a maximum profit of $14,400 when planting 180 acres of soybeans, 20 acres of corn, and no wheat.

45. (a) Let P denote the profit, x_1 denote the number of televisions shipped from Chicago, x_2 denote the number shipped from New York, and x_3 denote the number shipped from Denver.

Maximize:

$P = 70x_1 + 80x_2 + 40x_3$

subject to the constraints

$$\begin{aligned} x_1 + x_2 + x_3 &\le 400 \\ 50x_1 + 40x_2 + 80x_3 &\le 20{,}000 \\ 6x_1 + 8x_2 + 4x_3 &\le 3{,}000 \\ x_1 \ge 0 \quad x_2 \ge 0 \quad & x_3 \ge 0 \end{aligned}$$

(b) The Maximum $P = 31{,}000$, obtained when $x_1 = 100$, $x_2 = 300$, $x_3 = 0$.

(c) The manufacturer will obtain a maximum profit of $31,000 if it ships 100 televisions from Chicago, 300 televisions from New York, and none from Denver.

47. (a) Kami should invest $15,000 in the money market, $10,000 in the mutual fund, and nothing in the CD. (b) The maximum return on Kami's investments is $657.50.

Exercise 5.3 (p. 266)

3. True **4.** $\begin{bmatrix} 8 & 1 & -2 \\ 6 & 4 & 2 \end{bmatrix}$ **5.** True **6.** $\ge$ **7.** Duality principle **8.** False **9.** Standard form **11.** Not in standard form **13.** Not in standard form

15. Maximize

$$P = 2y_1 + 6y_2$$

subject to the constraints

$$\begin{aligned} y_1 + 2y_2 &\le 2 \\ y_1 + 3y_2 &\le 3 \\ y_1 \ge 0 \quad y_2 &\ge 0 \end{aligned}$$

17. Maximize

$$P = 5y_1 + 4y_2$$

subject to the constraints

$$\begin{aligned} y_1 + 2y_2 &\le 3 \\ y_1 + y_2 &\le 1 \\ y_1 \qquad &\le 1 \\ y_1 \ge 0 \quad y_2 &\ge 0 \end{aligned}$$

19. Maximize

$$P = 60y_1 + 90y_2$$

subject to the constraint

$$\begin{aligned} y_1 + 3y_2 &\le 3 \\ y_1 + 2y_2 &\le 4 \\ y_1 + y_2 &\le 1 \\ 2y_1 + 2y_2 &\le 2 \\ y_1 \ge 0 \quad y_2 &\ge 0 \end{aligned}$$

21. The minimum is $C = 6$ when $x_1 = 0, x_2 = 2$. **23.** The minimum is $C = 12$ when $x_1 = 0, x_2 = 4$.

25. The minimum is $C = \frac{21}{5}$ when $x_1 = \frac{8}{5}, x_2 = 0, x_3 = \frac{13}{5}$. **27.** The minimum is $C = 5$ when $x_1 = 1, x_2 = 1, x_3 = 0, x_4 = 0$.

29. Minimize the cost by assigning 7 employees to work on Friday, 15 to work on Saturday, and 8 to work on Sunday. The minimum cost is $4150. No one is scheduled to work a Friday–Sunday schedule.

31. (a) Let C be the cost of the order; let x_1 be the number of Lunch #1 ordered, x_2 the number of Lunch #2 ordered, and x_3 the number of Lunch #3 ordered.
Minimize

$$C = 6.2x_1 + 7.4x_2 + 9.1x_3$$

subject to the constraints

$$\begin{aligned} x_1 \qquad\qquad &\ge 4 \\ x_1 + x_2 + x_3 &\ge 9 \\ x_1 \qquad + x_3 &\ge 6 \\ x_2 + x_3 &\ge 5 \\ x_1 \ge 0 \quad x_2 \ge 0 \quad x_3 &\ge 0 \end{aligned}$$

(b) Minimum $C = 65.2$ when $x_1 = 4, x_2 = 3$, and $x_3 = 2$.

(c) Mrs. Mintz spends the least amount, $65.20, when she orders 4 of Lunch #1, 3 of Lunch #2, and 2 of Lunch #3.

33. (a) Let C be the cost of the supplements, x_1 be the number of pill P needed, and x_2 the number of pill Q needed.
Minimize

$$C = 3x_1 + 4x_2$$

subject to the constraints

$$\begin{aligned} 5x_1 + 10x_2 &\ge 50 \\ 2x_1 + x_2 &\ge 8 \\ x_1 \ge 0 \quad x_2 &\ge 0 \end{aligned}$$

(b) Minimum $C = 22$; when $x_1 = 2$ and $x_2 = 4$

(c) Mr. Jones minimizes his cost at $0.22 when he adds 2 P pills and 4 Q pills to his diet.

35. Katy should mix 1 kilogram of dried peaches and 1 kilogram of dried pears to meet her requirements and to minimize the sodium content. The minimum sodium content is 230 milligrams.

Exercise 5.4 (p. 281)

1. False **2.** $-z$ **3.** True **4.** False **5.** The maximum is $P = 44$ when $x_1 = 4, x_2 = 8$. **7.** The maximum is $P = 27$ when $x_1 = 9, x_2 = 0, x_3 = 0$.

9. The maximum is $P = 7$ when $x_1 = 1, x_2 = 2$. **11.** $x_1 = 0, x_2 = 0, x_3 = \frac{20}{3}, z = \frac{20}{3}$

13. (a) Minimize

$$C = 400x_1 + 100x_2 + 200x_3 + 200x_4$$

subject to the constraints

$$\begin{aligned} x_1 + x_2 \qquad\qquad &\le 600 \\ x_3 + x_4 &\le 400 \\ x_1 \qquad + x_3 \qquad &\ge 500 \\ x_2 \qquad + x_4 &\ge 300 \\ x_1 \ge 0 \quad x_2 \ge 0 \quad x_3 \ge 0 \quad x_4 &\ge 0 \end{aligned}$$

(b) Minimum $C = 150{,}000$ when $x_1 = 100, x_2 = 300, x_3 = 400, x_4 = 0$

(c) Private Motors minimizes shipping charges at $150,000 by shipping 100 engines from M1 to A1, 300 engines from M1 to A2, 400 engines from M2 to A1, and no engines from M2 to A2.

15. (a) Let C denote the total shipping cost, and x_1 the number of GPS systems shipped from W_1 to D_1; x_2 the number shipped from W_1 to D_2; x_3 the number shipped from W_2 to D_1; and x_4 the number shipped from W_2 to D_2.

The manufacturer wants to fill the orders at the lowest possible cost.

Minimize

$C = 8x_1 + 12x_2 + 13x_3 + 7x_4$

subject to the constraints

$$\begin{aligned} x_1 \quad + x_3 \quad &= 20 \\ x_2 \quad + x_4 &= 30 \\ x_1 + x_2 \quad &\le 40 \\ x_3 + x_4 &\le 15 \end{aligned}$$

$x_1 \ge 0 \quad x_2 \ge 0 \quad x_3 \ge 0 \quad x_4 \ge 0$

(b) Minimum is $C = 445$ when $x_1 = 20, x_2 = 15, x_3 = 0, x_4 = 15$.

(c) The GPS systems manufacturer minimizes shipping costs at $445 by shipping 20 GPS systems from warehouse W_1 to dealer D_1, shipping 15 GPS systems from W_1 to D_2, and 15 GPS systems from W_2 to D_2.

17. (a) Let x_1 represent the amount spent on newspaper advertising, and x_2 represent the amount spent on radio advertising. C is the total cost of advertising.

Minimize

$C = x_1 + x_2$

subject to the constraints

$50x_1 + 70x_2 \ge 100{,}000$

$40x_1 + 20x_2 \ge 120{,}000$

$x_1 \ge 0 \quad x_2 \ge 0$

(b) Minimum is $C = 3000$ when $x_1 = 3000$ and $x_2 = 0$

(c) The appliance store will spend the least on advertising, $3000, and reach the intended audience, if it spends all $3000 on newspaper advertising and nothing on radio advertising.

19. She should use 25 cups of corn, 50 cups of peas, 25 cups of green beans, and 100 cups of sliced carrots to minimize the calories. The minimum number of calories per serving is 45.

21. Purchase 615.0 shares of Duke Energy, 434.9 shares of H. J. Heinz, 534.5 shares of General Electric, and 432.2 shares of Ferrellgas Partners.

The minimum average price/earnings ratio is

$$\frac{45345.21}{2016.6} = 22.49$$

The annual yield for this optimal investment strategy is 2398.14.

Review Exercises (p. 284)

1. In standard form **3.** In standard form **5.** Not in standard form **7.** Not in standard form

9.

BV	P	x_1	x_2	x_3	s_1	s_2	s_3	RHS
s_1	0	2	5	1	1	0	0	100
s_2	0	1	3	1	0	1	0	80
s_3	0	2	3	3	0	0	1	120
P	1	−2	−1	−3	0	0	0	0

11.

BV	P	x_1	x_2	s_1	s_2	s_3	RHS
s_1	0	1	5	1	0	0	200
s_2	0	5	3	0	1	0	450
s_3	0	1	1	0	0	1	120
P	1	−6	−3	0	0	0	0

13.

BV	P	x_1	x_2	x_3	x_4	s_1	s_2	RHS
s_1	0	1	3	1	2	1	0	20
s_2	0	4	1	1	6	0	1	80
P	1	−1	−2	−1	−4	0	0	0

15. (a) The pivot element 2 is found in row s_2, column x_2. The new tableau after pivoting is

BV	P	x_1	x_2	s_1	s_2	RHS
x_1	0	1	0	−4	$-\frac{5}{2}$	15
x_2	0	0	1	1	$\frac{1}{2}$	5
P	1	0	0	1	$\frac{7}{2}$	125

(b) The resulting system of equations is

$$x_1 = 15 + 4s_1 + \frac{5}{2}s_2$$

$$x_2 = 5 - s_1 - \frac{1}{2}s_2$$

$$P = 125 - s_1 - \frac{7}{2}s_2$$

(c) The new tableau is the final tableau. The solution is maximum $P = 125$ when $x_1 = 15$ and $x_2 = 5$.

17. (a) The pivot element 1 is found in row s_1, column x_1. The new tableau after pivoting is

BV	P	x_1	x_2	x_3	s_1	s_2	RHS
x_1	0	1	1	−1	1	0	10
s_2	0	0	1	1	0	1	4
P	1	0	1	−5	2	0	20

(b) The resulting system of equations is

$$x_1 = 10 - x_2 + x_3 - s_1$$
$$s_2 = 4 - x_2 - x_3$$
$$P = 20 - x_2 + 5x_3 - 2s_1$$

(c) The problem requires additional pivoting. The new pivot element 1 is found in row s_2, column x_3.

19. (a) The pivot element 0.5 is found in row s_1, column x_1. The tableau after pivoting is

BV	P	x_1	x_2	s_1	s_2	RHS
x_1	0	1	1	2	0	2
s_2	0	0	0.5	−2	1	1
P	1	0	0.5	5	0	5

(b) The resulting system of equations is

$$x_1 = 2 - x_2 - 2s_1$$
$$s_2 = 1 - 0.5x_2 + 2s_1$$
$$P = 5 - 0.5x_2 - 5s_1$$

(c) The new tableau is the final tableau. The maximum is $P = 5$ when $x_1 = 2$ and $x_2 = 0$.

21. (a) The pivot element 1 is found in row s_3, column x_1. The tableau after pivoting is

BV	P	x_1	x_2	x_3	s_1	s_2	s_3	RHS
s_1	0	0	0	4	1	−6	1	10
x_2	0	0	1	8	0	−4	1	8
x_1	0	1	0	3	0	−5	1	3
P	1	0	0	13	0	−15	3	14

(b) The resulting system of equations is

$$s_1 = 10 - 4x_3 + 6s_2 - s_3$$
$$x_2 = 8 - 8x_3 + 4s_2 - s_3$$
$$x_1 = 3 - 3x_3 + 5s_2 - s_3$$
$$P = 14 - 13x_3 + 15s_2 - 3s_3$$

(c) No solution exists since in the pivot column (s_2) all 3 entries are negative.

23. The maximum is $P = 22{,}500$ when $x_1 = 0, x_2 = 100, x_3 = 50$. **25.** The maximum is $P = 352$ when $x_1 = 0, x_2 = \frac{6}{5}, x_3 = \frac{28}{5}$. **27.** In standard form **29.** Not in standard form, constraints are not written as greater than or equal to inequalities **31.** Not in standard form, constraints are not written as greater than or equal to inequalities

33. Maximize $P = 8y_1 + 2y_2$

subject to the constraints

$$2y_1 + y_2 \le 2$$
$$2y_1 - y_2 \le 1$$
$$y_1 \ge 0 \quad y_2 \ge 0$$

35. Maximize $P = 100y_1 + 50y_2$

subject to the constraints

$$y_1 + 2y_2 \le 5$$
$$y_1 + y_2 \le 4$$
$$y_1 \le 2$$
$$y_1 \ge 0 \quad y_2 \ge 0$$

37. Minimum is $C = 7$ when $x_1 = 3, x_2 = 1$ **39.** Minimum is $C = 275$ when $x_1 = 25, x_2 = 0, x_3 = 75$ **41.** Maximum is $P = 20$ when $x_1 = 0, x_2 = 4$ **43.** Minimum is $C = 6$ when $x_1 = 3, x_2 = 0$ **45.** Maximum is $P = 12{,}250$ when $x_1 = 0, x_2 = 5, x_3 = 25$

47. (a) Let P denote the profit, and let x_1 represent the number of cocktail tables and x_2 the number of end tables made each day.

Sanding, staining, and varnishing times, given in hours, have been changed to minutes.

Maximize

$$P = 20x_1 + 15x_2$$

subject to the constraints

$$4x_1 + 8x_2 \le 360$$
$$4x_1 + 10x_2 \le 360$$
$$8x_1 + 4x_2 \le 360$$
$$x_1 \ge 0 \qquad x_2 \ge 0 \qquad x_3 \ge 0$$

(b) Maximum $P = \frac{2025}{2} = 1012.5$,

obtained when $x_1 = \frac{135}{4} = 33.75$,

and $x_2 = \frac{45}{2} = 22.5$.

(c) The furniture maker can obtain a maximum profit of \$1012.50 while maintaining the time constraints if 33.75 cocktail tables and 22.5 end tables are manufactured each day. That is, profit is maximized by producing 135 cocktail tables and 90 end tables over a four-day period. The maximum profit for the four days is \$4050.

49. **(a)** C denotes cost of a pound of meat, x_1 denotes the amount of beef in the pound, and x_2 denotes the amount of pork in the pound.
Minimize
$C = 1.89x_1 + 1.29x_2$
subject to the constraints

$$x_1 + x_2 = 1$$
$$0.75x_1 + 0.60x_2 \geq 0.70$$
$$x_1 \geq 0 \quad x_2 \geq 0$$

(b) Minimum $C = 1.69$ when $x_1 = \frac{2}{3}$ and $x_2 = \frac{1}{3}$

(c) The minimum cost of the meat loaf is $1.69 per pound when the butcher mixes $\frac{2}{3}$ pound of ground beef with $\frac{1}{3}$ pound of ground pork.

Mathematical Questions from Professional Exams (p. 290)

1. c **2.** d **3.** c **4.** a **5.** b **6.** a **7.** c **8.** d **9.** d **10.** a **11.** d

CHAPTER 6 Finance

Exercise 6.1 (p. 299)

1. Prt **2.** Discounted **3.** False **4.** True **5.** 60% **7.** 110% **9.** 6% **11.** 0.25% **13.** 0.25 **15.** 1.00 **17.** 0.065 **19.** 0.0005 **21.** 150 **23.** 18 **25.** 105 **27.** 5% **29.** 160% **31.** 250 **33.** $\frac{1000}{3} \approx 333.33$ **35.** \$10 **37.** \$45 **39.** \$150 **41.** 10% **43.** 33.3% **45.** 13.3% **47.** \$1140 **49.** \$1680 **51.** \$1263.16; 10.53% **53.** \$2380.95; 9.52% **55.** \$489.00 **57.** The list price is reduced by 35%. **59.** She should get a loan of \$5779.34. **61.** This is a 408.13% rate of interest. **63.** Take the discounted loan at 9% per annum. **65.** **(a)** The interest charged is \$1377.60. **(b)** \$9377.60 is the total loan. **(c)** The monthly payment is \$260.49. **67.** 0.0032 = 0.32% **69.** \$675 in interest was received. The annual simple interest rate is 0.027 = 2.7%. **71.** No **73.** No

Exercise 6.2 (p. 311)

5. True **6.** False **7.** Compounded continuously **8.** Present value **9.** \$108.29 **11.** \$609.50 **13.** \$697.09 **15.** \$10.41 **17.** \$106.98 **19.** \$96.08 **21.** \$860.72 **23.** \$554.09 **25.** \$74.97 **27.** \$384.32 **29.** $6\frac{1}{4}$% compounded annually yields more in a year than 6% compounded quarterly. **31.** 9% compounded monthly yields more in a year than 8.8% compound daily. **33.** Effective rate of interest is 5.095%. **35.** Effective rate of interest is 5.127%. **37.** To double an investment in 3 years requires an interest rate of 25.99%. **39.** To triple an investment in 5 years requires an interest rate of 24.573%. **41.** **(a)** It will take 8.69 years to double money invested at 8% compounded monthly. **(b)** It will take 8.66 years to double money invested at 8% compounded continuously. **43.** 6.823% compounded quarterly has an effective rate of 7%. **45.** **(a)** After 3 years, A = \$1124.86; \$124.86 interest has been earned. **(b)** After 3 years, A = \$1127.27; \$127.27 interest has been earned. **47.** **(a)** A = \$1040.77 after 2 years. **(b)** A = \$1061.68 after 3 years. **(c)** A = \$1083.07 after 4 years. **49.** **(a)** Deposit \$4438.56 to have \$5000 in 4 years. **(b)** Deposit \$3940.16 to have \$5000 in 8 years. **51.** The loan at 10% compounded monthly results in less interest due. **53.** At 3% compounded monthly, it will take 13.53 years for \$100 to grow to \$150. At 3% compounded continuously, it will take 13.52 years to reach \$150. **55.** It takes 15.27 years for \$10,000 to grow to \$25,000 at 6% compounded continuously. **57.** The house will appreciate to \$104,335 in 5 years. **59.** Jerome should ask his parents for \$12,910.62. **61.** George's stock should be worth \$3017.04. **63.** Jim will not have enough money; he will be \$2.40 short. The second investment is a better deal. **65.** At the end of 20 years, Will will have \$450.92 more than Harry. **67.** They should deposit \$35,492.71 into the savings account. **69.** The account will be worth \$12,631.45 on the child's 25th birthday. **71.** It takes 30.54 years for \$10,000 to grow to \$25,000 at 3% compounded daily. **73.** After 30 years, the IRA will be worth \$12,973.59. **75.** Tom and Anita should invest \$10,288.11 to have the money needed in 18 years. **77.** **(a)** 7.87% **(b)** 26.26 trillion dollars. **79.** Option (a) is best with interest of \$30,000. **81.** If \$1000 purchases \$950 after 2 years, the inflation rate is 2.5%. **83.** At 2% annual inflation rate, money's value is halved in 34.3 years. **85.** **(a)** Pay \$3686.45 if the interest rate is 5% compounded monthly. **(b)** Pay \$3678.79 if the interest rate is 5% compounded continuously. **87.** The bond should be sold for \$6755.64 for an interest rate of 4% per annum. **89.** **(a)** At 4% annual interest, it takes 17.7 years to double an investment. **(b)** At 3% annual interest, it takes 36.8 years to triple an investment. **(c)** $mP = P\left(1+\frac{r}{n}\right)^{nt}$ $\quad m = \left(1+\frac{r}{n}\right)^{nt}$ $\quad \ln m = nt \cdot \ln\left(1+\frac{r}{n}\right)$ $\quad \frac{\ln m}{n \cdot \ln\left(1+\frac{r}{n}\right)} = t$

91. **(a)** Average annual inflation was 2.54%. **(b)** In 2022 the CPI will reach 300. **93.** It will take 30.5 years.

Exercise 6.3 (p. 326)

3. Annuity **4.** Amount; annuity **5.** \$1593.74 **7.** \$4844.25 **9.** \$7524.11 **11.** \$6629.90 **13.** \$113,201.03 **15.** \$154.69 per month **17.** \$1955.41 per quarter **19.** \$4119.18 per month **21.** \$200.46 per month **23.** \$2088.11 per year **25.** \$53,946.41 **27.** \$972.80 **29.** \$851.51 per month **31.** \$23,902.70 per year

Payment \$	Sinking Fund Deposit \$	Cumulative Deposits	Accumulated Interest	Total \$
1	23,902.70	23,902.70	0	23,902.70
2	23,902.70	47,805.40	717.081	48,522.48
3	23,902.70	71,708.10	2172.76	73,880.88
4	23,902.70	95,610.80	4389.18	99,999.98

33. The investor should pay $193,484 for the well. **35.** $78,848.79 per quarter **37.** **(a)** $180,611.12 **(b)** $2990.15 semiannually **39.** It will take about 34 years to accumulate. **41.** Angie should deposit $385.50 monthly. **43.** The school district should deposit $44,320.39 per quarter **45.** The account will be worth $30,068.42. **47.** After 25 years, the lump sum will be worth $10,192,646.88; the annual payments will be worth $8,635,455.48. Dan should select the lump sum payment. **49.** **(a)** The projected price of the Honda is $27,061.24. **(b)** The projected price including tax is $29,564.40. **(c)** Monthly payments of $583.37 are needed in the sinking fund. **51.** **(a)** The projected tuition and fees are as follows:

Year	2023–2024	2024–2025	2025–2026	2026–2027	Total
Projected Tuition and Fees	$16,952.42	$18,054.32	$19,227.85	$20,477.67	$74,712.26

(b) To pay for the projected four years of college, a quarterly payment of $1307.35 should be made.

Exercise 6.4 (p. 341)

1. $16,935.38 **3.** $892.55 **5.** $124,622.10 **7.** $P = \$244.13$ **9.** $P = \$4387.86$ **11.** $P = \$7337.65$ **13.** $470.73 per month **15.** $37,881.33 **17.** **(a)** $248.48 monthly **(b)** Total payment is $8945.28. **(c)** Interest is $945.28. **19.** **(a)** The monthly payment for the 9% loan is $1342.71 and the monthly payment for the 8% loan is $1338.30. The monthly payment for the 9% loan is larger. **(b)** The total interest paid is larger for the 9% loan, $242,813 compared to $161,192. **(c)** After 10 years the equity from the 8% loan is larger, $89,695.33 compared to $67,617.64. **21.** John should deposit $171.33 per month. **23.** **(a)** After 12 weeks, Dan has $1201.27. **(b)** Dan can withdraw $35.45 per week for 34 weeks. **25.** **(a)** $40,000 is the down payment **(b)** $160,000 is the amount of loan **(c)** $1287.40 per month **(d)** $303,464 is the total interest on the loan **(e)** 22 years, 4 months to pay off the loan **(f)** $211,823.20 total interest with payments of $1387.40 per month. **27.** $332.79 per month **29.** **(a)** $474.01 per month **(b)** interest paid: $4752.48 **31.** 30 year: monthly payment—$671.50; total interest—$129,740; 15 year: monthly payment—$945.12; total interest—$58,121.60 **33.** In about 4 years and 8 months the IRA will be depleted. **35.** Jeremy needs $14,910.21 in his college fund on August 1. **37.** The foundation must invest $821,530.33 to meet the project's goal. **39.** Monthly payments are reduced by $128.07. They will pay $38,361 less in interest. **41.** 61.9 months; $50,870.77 in interest is saved by prepaying the loan. **43.** The present value of the money, $6529.84, is more than the purchase price, so purchasing is preferable. **45.** The present value of the money, $177,297.53, is greater than the purchase price, so purchasing is preferable. **47.** **(a)** If the time value of money is 10%, then Machine A is preferable. **(b)** If the time value of money is 14%, then Machine A is still preferable. **49.** A price of $9845.95 will yield a true interest of 6.5%. **51.** The bond sold for $999.76. **53.** The bond sold for $998.14.

Exercise 6.5 (p. 348)

3. **(a)** After 1 payment, the balance is $2930. **(b)** After 14 payments the balance is less than $2000. **(c)** John pays off the balance on the 36th payment. **(d)** He pays a total of $584.62 in interest. **5.** **(a)** 2162 trout are in the pond after 2 months. **(b)** In the 26th month the population reaches 5000 trout. **7.** **(a)** $A_0 = 500, A_n = 1.02A_{n-1} + 500.$ **(b)** After 81 quarters, there is more than $100,000 in the IRA. **(c)** $159,738 in 25 years.

9. **(a)** $A_0 = 150{,}000, A_n = \left(1 + \frac{0.06}{12}\right)A_{n-1} - 899.33.$ **(b)** $149,850.67 remains after the 1st payment.

(c)

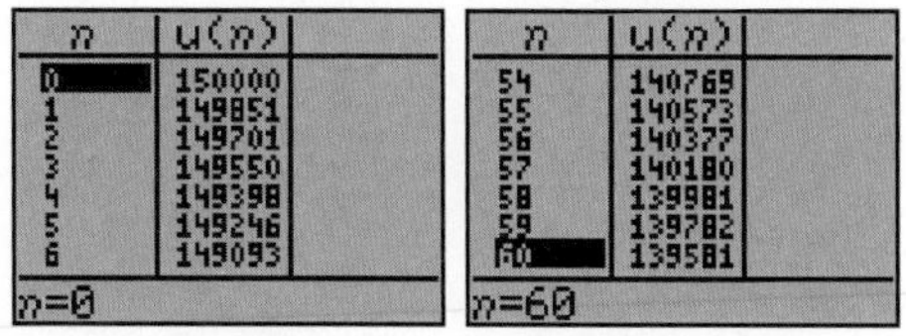

(d) After 4 years and 10 months (58 payments) the balance is below $140,000.

(e) With the 360th payment (30 years) the loan is paid.

(f) A total of $173,754.57 in interest was paid.

(g) **a.** $A_0 = 150{,}000, A_n = \left(1 + \frac{0.06}{12}\right)A_{n-1} - 999.33$ **b.** After the 1st payment, $149,750.67 is owed

c.

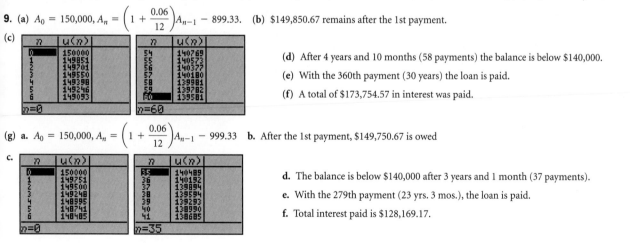

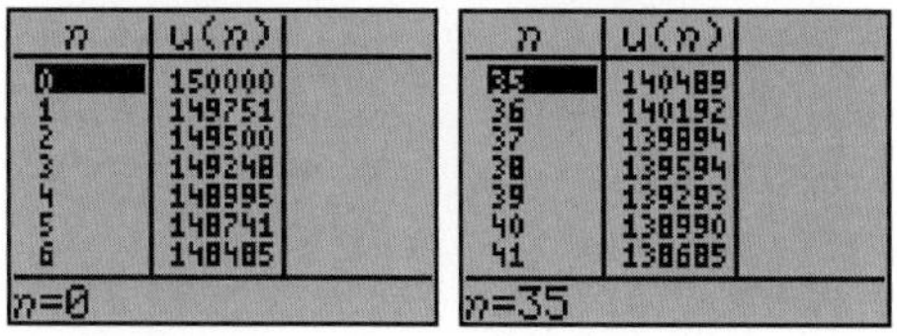

d. The balance is below $140,000 after 3 years and 1 month (37 payments).

e. With the 279th payment (23 yrs. 3 mos.), the loan is paid.

f. Total interest paid is $128,169.17.

Review Exercises (p. 350)

1. 15 **3.** 350 **5.** $21\frac{3}{7}\%$ **7.** 80 **9.** 2200 **11.** Dan paid \$23.10 in sales tax. **13.** \$52.50 interest is charged. Dan must repay \$552.50. **15.** Warren must pay \$19,736.84 to settle his debt. **17.** \$106.97 **19.** The 10% per annum compounded monthly loan will cost Mike less. **21.** Katy should deposit \$73.88. **23.** 5.95% **25.** 5.87% compounded quarterly has an effective rate of 6%. **27.** The Coreys should save \$1619.25 per month. **29.** **(a)** The Ostedts' monthly payments are \$2726.10. **(b)** They will pay \$517,830 in interest. **(c)** After 5 years, their equity is \$117,508.93. **31.** The monthly payments are \$1,049.00. The equity after 10 years is \$21,576 plus any down payment. **33.** Mr. Graff should pay \$119,432 for the mine. **35.** Mr. Doody needs \$40,557.64 to meet his goals. **37.** Mr. Jones will have saved \$8966.18. **39.** The monthly payments are \$141.22. **41.** The effective rate of interest is 9.38%. **43.** John will receive \$1156.60 every 6 months for 15 years. **45.** After 30 months there will be \$2087.09 in the fund. **47.** The student's quarterly payment is \$330.74.

Mathematical Questions from Professional Exams (p. 353)

1. b **2.** c **3.** b **4.** b **5.** d **6.** a **7.** c

CHAPTER 7 Probability

Exercise 7.1 (p. 363)

1. $\subseteq, =$ **2.** $\cup$ **3.** $\cap$ **4.** $\{3, 4, 5\}$ **5.** True **7.** False **9.** False **11.** True **13.** True **15.** True **17.** $\{2, 3\}$ **19.** $\{1, 2, 3, 4, 5\}$ **21.** $\varnothing$ **23.** $\{a, b, d, e, f, g\}$ **25. (a)** $\{0, 1, 2, 3, 5, 7, 8\}$ **(b)** $\{5\}$ **(c)** $\{5\}$ **(d)** $\{0, 1, 2, 3, 4, 6, 7, 8, 9\}$ **(e)** $\{4, 6, 9\}$ **(f)** $\{0, 1, 5, 7\} = A$ **(g)** $\varnothing$ **(h)** $\{5\}$ **27. (a)** $\{b, c, d, e, f, g\}$ **(b)** $\{c\}$ **(c)** $\{a, h, i, j, k, l, m, n, o, p, q, r, s, t, u, v, w, x, y, z\}$ **(d)** $\{a, b, d, e, f, g, h, i, j, k, l, m, n, o, p, q, r, s, t, u, v, w, x, y, z\}$

29.

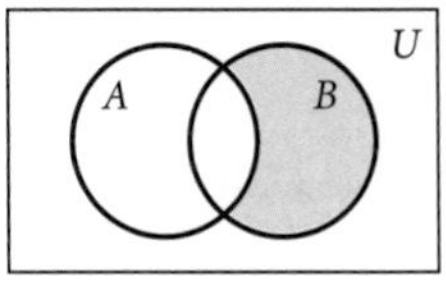

$\bar{A} \cap B$

31.

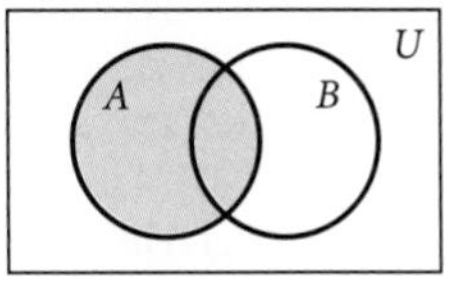

$A \cap (A \cup B)$

33.

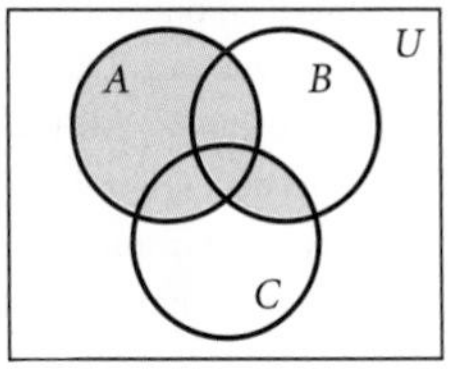

$(A \cup B) \cap (A \cup C)$

35.

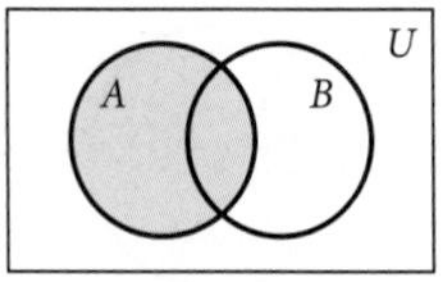

$A = (A \cap B) \cup (A \cap \bar{B})$

37.

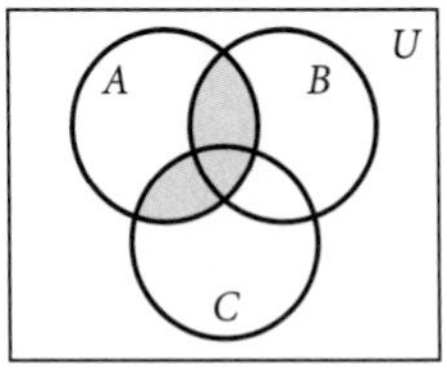

$A \cap (B \cup C) = (A \cap B) \cup (A \cap C)$

39.

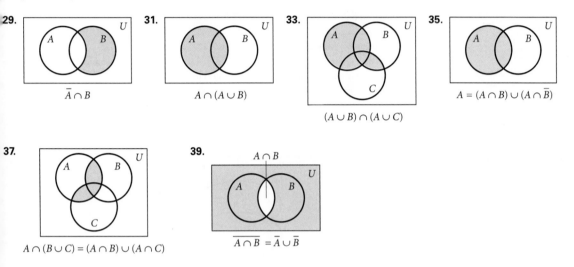

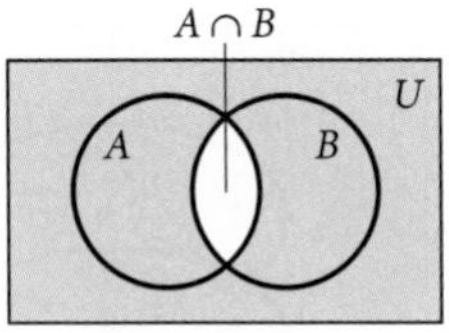

$\overline{A \cap B} = \bar{A} \cup \bar{B}$

41. $A \cap E$ is the set of members of the board of directors of IBM who are also customers of IBM. **43.** $A \cup D$ is the set of customers of IBM or stockholders of IBM. **45.** $\bar{A} \cap D$ is the set of all persons who are not customers of IBM and own IBM stock. **47.** $M \cap S$ is the set of all male students who smoke. **49.** $\bar{M} \cup \bar{F}$ is the set of sophomores, juniors, and seniors together with all the female students. **51.** $F \cap S \cap M$ is the set of male freshmen who smoke. **53. (a)** $O \cap A =$ {Whitehouse, Schumer, Kaufman, Franken, Grassley}. This set represents the members of the Judiciary Committee who are on both the Administrative Oversight subcommittee and the Antitrust, Competition Policy, and Consumer Rights subcommittee. **(b)** $\bar{O} =$ {Leahy, Kohl, Hatch, Durbin, Klobuchar, Cornyn, Coburn, Specter}. This set represents the members of the Judiciary Committee who are not members of the Administrative Oversight subcommittee. **(c)** $O \cup A =$ {Whitehouse, Feinstein, Feingold, Schumer, Cardin, Kaufman, Franken, Sessions, Grassley, Kyl, Graham, Kohl, Klobuchar, Specter, Hatch, Cornyn}. This set represents the members of the Judiciary Committee who are on either the Administrative Oversight subcommittee or the Antitrust, Competition Policy, and Consumer Rights subcommittee. **(d)** $\overline{O \cup A} =$ {Leahy, Coburn, Durbin}. This set represents the members of the Judiciary Committee who are on neither the Administrative Oversight subcommittee nor the Antitrust, Competition Policy, and Consumer Rights subcommittee. **55. (a)** $I \cup H =$ {Black, Bodden, Brown, Earnest, Forbes, Gallaher, Johnson, Murphy, Petevis, Randolph, Rhoades, Russell, Smith, Stein, Sutton}. This set represents the clients who own either Intel stock or Hewlett-Packard stock. **(b)** $I \cap H =$ {Bodden, Gallaher, Sutton}. This set represents the clients who own both Intel stock and Hewlett-Packard stock. **57.** The subsets of $\{a, b, c\}$ are $\varnothing$, $\{a\}$, $\{b\}$, $\{c\}$, $\{a, b\}$, $\{a, c\}$, $\{b, c\}$, $\{a, b, c\}$.

Exercise 7.2 (p. 369)

1. False **2.** 4 **3.** $n(A) = 6$ **5.** $n(A \cap B) = 3$ **7.** $n[(A \cap B) \cup A] = 6$ **9.** $n(A \cup B) = 5$ **11.** $n(A \cap B) = 2$ **13.** $n(A) = 10$ **15.** 452 cars were manufactured. **17.** $n(A) = 24$ **19.** $n(A \cup B) = 34$ **21.** $n(A \cap \bar{B}) = 15$ **23.** $n(A \cup B \cup C) = 54$ **25.** $n(A \cap B \cap C) = 3$ **27. (a)** 4,050,000 households are maintained by a mother in the South. **(b)** 274,000 households in the Midwest are maintained by a divorced parent. **(c)** 600,000 households are maintained by a father who was never married or widowed. **29. (a)** 13,414,000 U.S. civilians 20 years or older were unemployed. **(b)** 85,764,000 U.S. civilians 20 years or older were unemployed or not in the labor force. **(c)** 184,887,000 U.S. civilians 20 years or older were female or employed. **(d)** 27,403,000 U.S. civilians 20 years or older were male and not in the labor force. **31. (a)** 256 layoffs were executive managerial, faculty, or professional nonfaculty. **(b)** 168 layoffs were female. **(c)** 93 layoffs were black female or faculty. **(d)** 125 layoffs were white male or executive managerial.

33. (a)

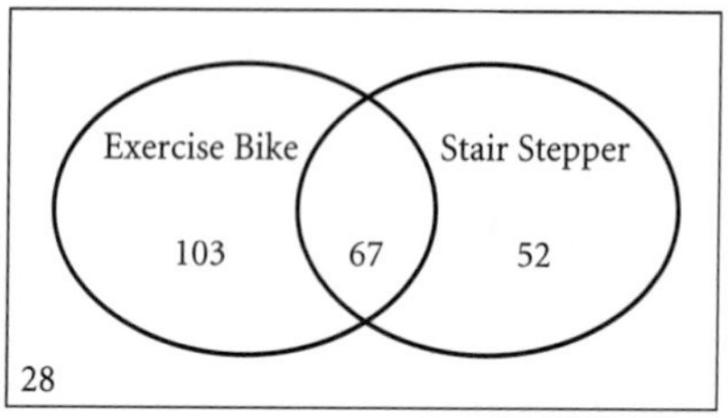

(b) 222 members surveyed use an exercise bike or stair stepper regularly.
(c) 103 members surveyed regularly use an exercise bike but not a stair stepper.
(d) 52 members surveyed regularly use a stair stepper but not an exercise bike.
(e) 28 members surveyed use neither an exercise bike nor a stair stepper regularly.

35. (a)

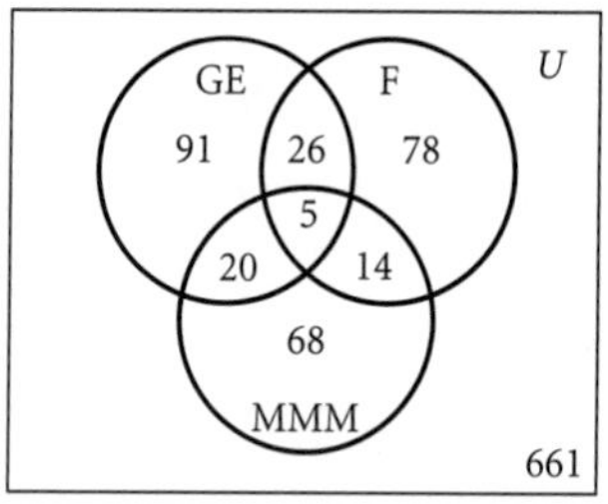

(b) 91 clients own only GE.
(c) 78 clients own only F.
(d) 68 clients own only MMM.
(e) 179 clients own GE or MMM, but not F.
(f) 20 clients own GE and MMM, but not F.
(g) 661 clients own none of the three stocks.

37. (a) 259 were seniors.
(b) 455 were women.
(c) 227 were on the dean's list.
(d) 76 seniors were on the dean's list.
(e) 118 seniors were female.
(f) 93 women were on the dean's list.
(g) 912 students were in the college.

39. (a) 40 cars had satellite radio and heated seats.
(b) 35 cars had GPS and heated seats.
(c) 40 cars had neither satellite radio nor GPS.
(d) 205 cars were sold in July.
(e) 155 cars were sold with GPS or heated seats or both.

41.

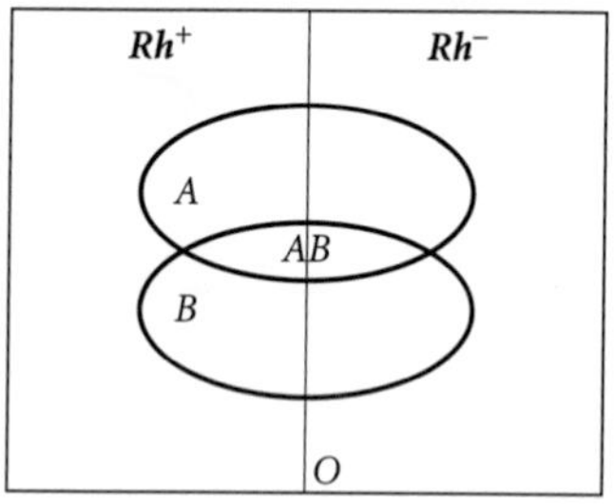

There are 8 different blood types.

43. 46 use only one of the three brands.
45. $\varnothing, \{a\}, \{b\}, \{c\}, \{d\}, \{a, b\}, \{a, c\}, \{a, d\}, \{b, c\}, \{b, d\}, \{c, d\}, \{a, b, c\}, \{a, b, d\}, \{a, c, d\}\ \{b, c, d\}, \{a, b, c, d\}$. There are 16 subsets of $\{a, b, c, d\}$.

Exercise 7.3 (p. 376)

1. There are 15 shirt and tie combinations. **3.** 9000 four-digit numbers are possible. **5.** There are 8 routes from A to C through B. **7.** Display 24 cars. **9.** There are 36 ways to enter through a window and exit through a door. **11.** 960 lunches are possible. **13.** The people can sit 720 ways. **15.** $26^4 \cdot 10^4 = 4{,}569{,}760{,}000$ user names are possible. **17.** There are $26 \cdot 25^3 \cdot 10 \cdot 9^3 = 2{,}961{,}562{,}500$ user names with no adjacent repeats. **19.** Theoretically there are 224 possible match-ups. **21.** Adam can get 486 different types of coverage. **23.** There are 30 different sales portfolios to choose from. **25.** There are 200 different one-topping pizzas. **27.** There were 5814 possible lineups. **29.** The audits can be scheduled 3,628,800 ways. **31.** (a) There are 604,800 telephone numbers without repeated digits. (b) There are 544,320 telephone numbers without repeated digits that do not begin with zero. (c) There are 10^7 telephone numbers without restrictions. **33.** (a) There are 5040 ways to arrange P, R, O, B, L, E, M. (b) There are 720 ways to arrange R, O, B, L, E, M. (c) There are 120 ways to arrange R, O, B, L, E. **35.** (a) 6,760,000 different license plates are possible. (b) 3,407,040 license plates without repeated digits can be made. (c) 3,276,000 license plates with no repeated letters or digits can be made. **37.** 16 distinguishable car types are produced. **39.** 60 types of homes can be built. **41.** 256 different numbers can be formed. **43.** 125,000 different lock combinations are possible. **45.** There are 8 different paths through the maze.

Exercise 7.4 (p. 385)

1. False **2.** 0.6 **3.** sample space **4.** True **5.** event **6.** False **7.** A sample space is $\{RA, RB, RC, GA, GB, GC\}$ where R = Red and G = Green. **9.** A sample space is $\{AA, AB, AC, BA, BB, BC, CA, CB, CC\}$. **11.** A sample space is $\{AA1, AB1, AC1, BA1, BB1, BC1, CA1, CB1, CC1, AA2, AB2, AC2, BA2, BB2, BC2, CA2, CB2, CC2, AA3, AB3, AC3, BA3, BB3, BC3, CA3, CB3, CC3, AA4, AB4, AC4, BA4, BB4, BC4, CA4, CB4, CC4\}$. **13.** A sample space is $\{RA1, RB1, RC1, GA1, GB1, GC1, RA2, RB2, RC2, GA2, GB2, GC2, RA3, RB3, RC3, GA3, GB3, GC3, RA4, RB4, RC4, GA4, GB4, GC4\}$ where R = Red and G = Green. **15.** 16 **17.** 216 **19.** 2652 **21.** 676 **23.** Valid assignments are A, B, C, F. **25.** Assignment B should be used.

27. If W is the event a white ball is picked, then $P(W) = \frac{3}{23}$. **29.** If G is the event a green ball is picked, then $P(G) = \frac{7}{23}$. **31.** If E is the event a white ball or a red ball is picked, then $P(E) = \frac{8}{23}$. **33.** If H is the event a white ball or a blue ball is picked, then $P(H) = \frac{11}{23}$. **35.** If E is the event the ace of hearts is drawn, $P(E) = \frac{1}{52}$. **37.** If S is the event a spade is drawn, then $P(S) = \frac{1}{4}$.

39. If F is the event a picture card is drawn, then $P(F) = \frac{3}{13}$. **41.** If E is the event a card with a number less than 6 is drawn, then $P(E) = \frac{5}{13}$. **43.** If A is the event the card is not an ace, then $P(A) = \frac{12}{13}$. **45.** $S = \{MD, MR, MO, FD, FR, FO\}$, where M (male), F (female), D (dry), R (regular), and O (oily). There are 6 outcomes in the sample space.

47. (a)

e_i	e_1	e_2	e_3	e_4	e_5	e_6	e_7	e_8	e_9	e_{10}	e_{11}	e_{12}	e_{13}	e_{14}	e_{15}	e_{16}
S	GGGG	GGGB	GGBG	GBGG	BGGG	GGBB	GBBG	BBGG	GBGB	BGGB	BGBG	GBBB	BGBB	BBGB	BBBG	BBBB
$P(e_i)$	$\frac{1}{16}$	$\frac{1}{16}$	$\frac{1}{16}$	$\frac{1}{16}$	$\frac{1}{16}$	$\frac{1}{16}$	$\frac{1}{16}$	$\frac{1}{16}$	$\frac{1}{16}$	$\frac{1}{16}$	$\frac{1}{16}$	$\frac{1}{16}$	$\frac{1}{16}$	$\frac{1}{16}$	$\frac{1}{16}$	$\frac{1}{16}$

(b) (i) $P(\text{1st two children are girls}) = \frac{1}{4}$ (ii) $P(\text{all children are boys}) = \frac{1}{16}$ (iii) $P(\text{at least one girl}) = \frac{15}{16}$ (iv) $P(\text{1st and last children are girls}) = \frac{1}{4}$

49.

Income Level	Probability
<\$25,000	$P(<\$25{,}000) \approx 0.247$
\$25,000–\$49,999	$P(\$25{,}000\text{–}\$49{,}999) \approx 0.249$
\$50,000–\$74,999	$P(\$50{,}000\text{–}\$74{,}999) \approx 0.179$
\$75,000–\$99,999	$P(\$75{,}000\text{–}\$99{,}999) \approx 0.119$
≥\$100,000	$P(\geq\$100{,}000) \approx 0.205$

51. $P(\$50{,}000\text{–}\$90{,}999) \approx 0.298$

53. $P(<\$50{,}000) \approx 0.496$

55. $P(\text{MasterCard}) \approx 0.352$

57. $P(\text{American Express or Discover}) \approx 0.179$

59. $P(\text{Price} > \$50.00) = \frac{7}{15}$

61. $P(\$40.00 \leq \text{Price} \leq \$50.00) = \frac{1}{15}$ **63.** 0.132 **65.** 0.212 **67.** 0.058 **69.** 0.013 **71.** (a) $P(\text{American has health insurance}) = 0.846$ (b) $P(\text{American has no health insurance}) = 0.154$ **73.** $P(R) = 0.6$, $P(W) = 0.4$, answers will vary but the results should be fairly close to the actual probabilities. **75.** $P(R) = 0.3$, $P(W) = 0.7$, answers will vary but the results should be fairly close to the actual probabilities. **77.** $P(A) = 0.22$, $P(B) = 0.60$, $P(C) = 0.18$, answers will vary but the results should be fairly close to the actual probabilities.

Exercise 7.5 (p. 400)

1. event **2.** True **3.** False **4.** False **5.** $P(E \cup F) = 0.7$ **7.** $P(E \cap F) = 0.4$ **9.** $P(F) = 0.3$ **11.** $P(\overline{E}) = 0.6$ **13.** (a) $P(A \cup B) = 0.7$ (b) $P(A \cap \overline{B}) = 0.3$ (c) $P(B \cap \overline{A}) = 0.2$ (d) $P(\overline{A \cup B}) = 0.3$ **15.** (a) $P(A \cap B) = 0$ (b) $P(A \cup B) = 0.8$ (c) $P(\overline{A \cup B}) = 0.2$ (d) $P(\overline{B}) = 0.8$ (e) $P(\overline{A}) = 0.4$ (f) $P(\overline{A \cap B}) = 1$ **17.** $P(E) = \frac{3}{4}$ **19.** $P(E) = \frac{5}{12}$ **21.** $P(E) = \frac{1}{2}$ **23.** The odds for E: 3 to 2; the odds against E: 2 to 3 **25.** The odds for F: 3 to 1; The odds against F: 1 to 3 **27.** Define E: The Bears win; F: The Bears tie. $P(\overline{E \cup F}) = 0.30$ **29.** Define M: Anne passes mathematics; E: Anne passes English. $P(M \cap E) = 0.2$ **31.** Define T: Car needs a tune-up; B: Car needs a brake job. (a) $P(T \cup B) = 0.68$ (b) $P(T \cap \overline{B}) = 0.58$ (c) $P(\overline{T \cup B}) = 0.32$ **33.** (a) $P(1 \text{ or } 2) = 0.57$ (b) $P(1 \text{ or more}) = 0.95$ (c) $P(0, 1, 2 \text{ or } 3) = 0.83$ (d) $P(3 \text{ or more}) = 0.38$ (e) $P(0 \text{ or } 1) = 0.29$ (f) $P(0) = 0.05$ (g) $P(1, 2 \text{ or } 3) = 0.78$ (h) $P(2 \text{ or more}) = 0.71$ **35.** Define E: A person selected at random has Rh-positive blood. $P(E) = 0.82$ **37.** Define E: A person selected at random has blood that contains the A antigen. $P(E) = 0.41$ **39.** Define E: A person selected at random is type O; F: a person selected at random is Rh-positive. $P(E \cup F) = 0.91$. **41.** If E is the event a woman aged 15–44 who gave birth in 2006 had her first child, then $P(\overline{E}) = 0.543$. **43.** Odds for a randomly selected bridge being deficient or obsolete are 150 to 453. **45.** The probability a smart phone owner chosen at random will not have an iPhone is 0.856. **47.** If D is the event the patent was for design and B the event it was for botanical plants, then $P(D \cup B) = 0.129$. **49.** If E is the event a fund outperforms the market in year one and F the event it outperforms the market in year two, then $P(E \cup F) = 0.19$. **51.** $P(A \cup B) = \frac{11}{15}$; the odds for A or B winning are 11 to 4. **53.** Probability of a repeated digit is 0.940. **55.** Probability of no repeated letters is 0.0055. **57.** The probability at least two students choose the same number is almost 1. **59.** The probability at least 2 of 3 people are born in the same month is 0.236. **61.** The probability at least 2 senators have the same birthday is almost 1.

Exercise 7.6 (p. 409)

1. True **2.** fair **3.** $E = 1.2$ **5.** $E = 50{,}800$ fans **7.** Mary should pay 80 cents per game. **9.** Dave should pay \$2 to play. **11.** The price exceeds the expected value by \$0.75. **13.** (a) $E = \$0.75$ (b) No, the game is not fair. (c) To make the game fair, a player should lose \$2.00 if 1 tail is thrown. **15.** It is not fair to you; your expected loss is \$0.43. **17.** The expected loss is 1.2 cents, so Sarah should not play.

19. The expected receipts of the chosen corporation are \$216,194. **21.** The expected sale price of a new house is \$244,384. **23.** **(a)** The truck rental agency expects 9 customers per day. **(b)** To maximize expected profit the agency should have 10 trucks on hand each day. **(c)** The expected profit if 10 trucks are available is \$601. **25.** **(a)** The insurance company can expect a profit of \$100. **(b)** The company should set the premium at \$600.

27. **(a)** Management should choose the second location to maximize expected profit. **(b)** Management should choose the first location to maximize expected profit. **29.** **(a)** The investor's expected return is 12.50%. **(b)** To realize a return of 14%, the investor's portfolio should be split with 20% Wal-Mart stock and 80% Viacom stock.

Review Exercises (p. 413)

1. $\subset, \subseteq$ **3.** none of these **5.** none of these **7.** $\subset, \subseteq$ **9.** $\subseteq, =$ **11.** $\subseteq, =$ **13.** $\subset, \subseteq$ **15.** $\subseteq, =$
17. **(a)** $\{3, 6, 8, 9\}$ **(b)** $\{6\}$ **(c)** B **(d)** B **(e)** $\varnothing$ **(f)** $\{1, 2, 3, 5, 6, 7, 8, 9\}$

19. **(a)**

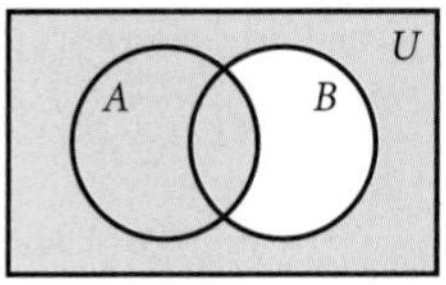

$A \cup \bar{B}$

(b)

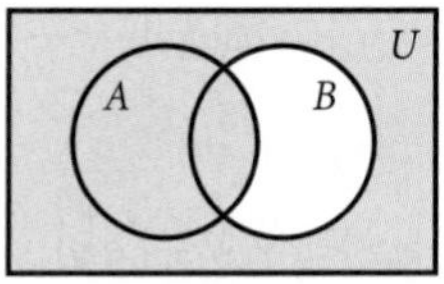

$(A \cap B) \cup \bar{B}$

(c)

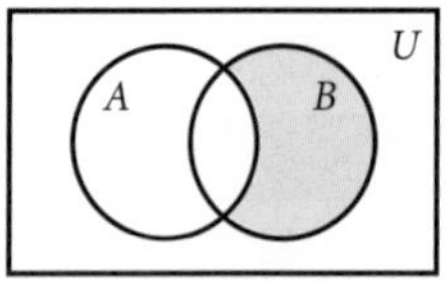

$B \cap \bar{A}$

(d)

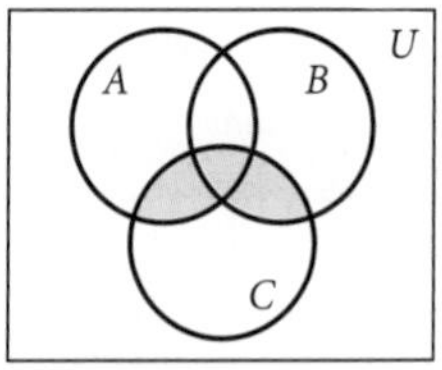

$(A \cup B) \cap C$

(e)

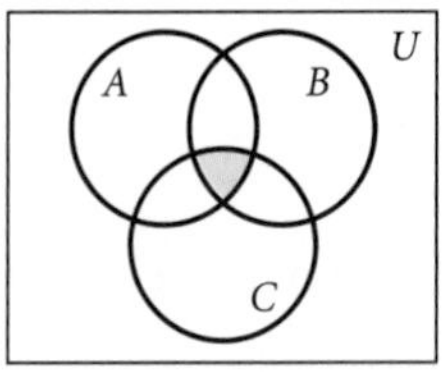

$(A \cap B) \cap (C)$

(f)

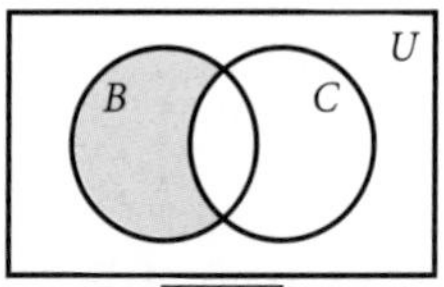

$(\overline{\bar{B} \cup C})$

21.

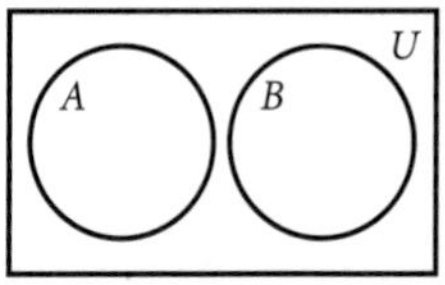

23. The set of all states whose names begin with *A* or end with a vowel. **25.** The set of all states whose names end with a vowel and lie east of the Mississippi River. **27.** The set of all states whose names start with an *A* or end with a vowel and that lie east of the Mississippi River.

29. $n(A \cap B) = 3$ **31.** **(a)** $n(A \cup B) = 20$ **(b)** *A* and *B* are disjoint. **33.** $n(A \cap B) = 1$; $n(A \cup B) = 5$ **35.** **(a)** 165 cars were sold in June. **(b)** 40 cars had only a GPS. **37.** $\{1\}, \{1, 2\}, \{1, 3\}, \{1, 2, 3\}$

39. $S = \{0, 1, 2, 3, 4, 5\}$ **41.** The outcomes for each child are boy (B) and girl (G). The sample space is {BB, BG, GB, GG}.

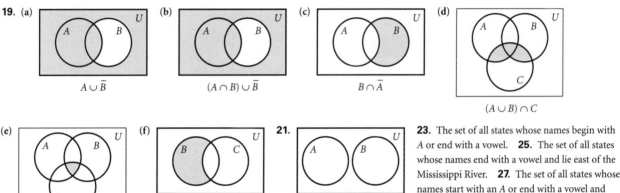

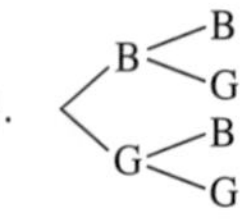

43. $P(\text{penny}) = \frac{4}{15}$, $P(\text{dime}) = \frac{1}{3}$, $P(\text{quarter}) = \frac{2}{5}$ **45.** $P(1) = \frac{1}{8}$, $P(2) = \frac{1}{4}$, $P(3) = \frac{1}{8}$, $P(4) = \frac{1}{8}$, $P(5) = \frac{1}{4}$, $P(6) = \frac{1}{8}$

47. **(a)**

Numbers of Girls	0	1	2	3	4
Probability	$\frac{1}{16}$	$\frac{1}{4}$	$\frac{3}{8}$	$\frac{1}{4}$	$\frac{1}{16}$

(b) (i) $P(0) = \frac{1}{16}$ (ii) $P(2) = \frac{3}{8}$ (iii) $P(\text{at least 1 boy and 1 girl}) = \frac{7}{8}$ (iv) $1 - P(4) = \frac{15}{16}$

49. **(a)** Probability both are blue is $\frac{10}{91}$. **(b)** Probability exactly 1 is blue is $\frac{45}{91}$. **(c)** Probability at least 1 is blue is $\frac{55}{91}$.

51. **(a)** $P(A \cup B) = 0.6$ **(b)** $P(\bar{A}) = 0.7$ **(c)** $P(\overline{A \cup B}) = 0.4$ **(d)** $P(\bar{A} \cup \bar{B}) = 0.8$ **53.** **(a)** $P(H) = \frac{243}{300} = 0.81$ **(b)** $P(T) = \frac{57}{300} = 0.19$
55. **(a)** $P(\bar{F}) = 0.50$ **(b)** $P(E \cup F) = 0.78$ **(c)** *E* and *F* are not mutually exclusive because $P(E \cap F) \neq 0$.

57. **(a)** $P(E \cup F) = 0.7$ **(b)** $P(\bar{E}) = 0.8$ **(c)** $P(\overline{E \cap F}) = 0.9$ **59.** **(a)** $P(\bar{E}) = 0.75$ **(b)** $P(\bar{F}) = 0.7$ **(c)** $P(E \cap F) = 0$ **(d)** $P(\overline{E \cap F}) = 1$ **(e)** $P(\bar{E} \cap \bar{F}) = 0.45$ **(f)** $P(\bar{E} \cup \bar{F}) = 1$ **61.** **(a)** No. **(b)** Outcome 0,0,0 has the highest probability. **(c)** $P(F) = \frac{9}{64}$

63. There are 72 different styles. **65.** There are 1024 different ways to answer. **67.** Probability all are born on different days is 0.017.

69. The odds of having 4 boys in a 4-child family are 1 to 15. **71.** The probability the Giants win Sunday's game is $\frac{5}{8}$. The probability the Giants lose Sunday's game is $\frac{3}{8}$. **73.** Frank has paid $3\frac{1}{3}$ cents too much for the game. **75.** The expected value of the game is $28\frac{1}{3}$ cents. The game is not fair.
77. The game is not fair to the player; he expects to lose almost 3 cents on a play.

Mathematical Questions From Professional Exams

1. a **2.** a **3.** b **4.** b **5.** b or c **6.** d

CHAPTER 8 Additional Probability Topics

:xercise 8.1 (p. 429)

False **4.** $P(E|F) = \dfrac{P(E \cap F)}{P(F)}$ **5.** $P(E) = 0.5$ **7.** $P(E|F) = 0.429$ **9.** $P(E \cap F) = 0.3$ **11.** $P(\bar{E}) = 0.5$ **13.** $P(E|F) = 0.25, P(F|E) = 0.5$ **5.** $P(F) = 0.5$ **17.** $P(E \cap F) = \dfrac{4}{13}$ **19.** **(a)** $P(E) = \dfrac{1}{2}$ **(b)** $P(F) = \dfrac{2}{3}$ **21.** $P(C) = 0.69$ **23.** $P(C|A) = 0.9$ **25.** $P(C|B) = 0.2$ **7.** $P(E \cap F) = 0.1$ **29.** $P(F|E) = 0.2$ **31.** $P(E|\bar{F}) = 0.667$ **33.** **(a)** Probability exactly 2 girls, given 1st child is a girl is $\dfrac{1}{2}$. **(b)** Probability exactly girl, given 1st child is a boy is $\dfrac{1}{2}$. **35.** **(a)** Probability of drawing a heart and then red is $\dfrac{25}{204}$. **(b)** Probability of drawing red and then a heart is $\dfrac{25}{204}$. **7.** Probability of drawing 1 white and 1 yellow ball is $\dfrac{1}{5}$. **39.** **(a)** Probability of drawing a red ace is $\dfrac{1}{26}$. **(b)** Probability of drawing a red ace given an ce was drawn is $\dfrac{1}{2}$. **(c)** Probability of drawing a red ace given a red card was drawn is $\dfrac{1}{13}$. **41.** $P(E) = 0.40$ **43.** $P(H) = 0.24$ **45.** $P(E \cap H) = 0.10$ **7.** $P(G \cap H) = 0.08$ **49.** $P(E|H) = \dfrac{10}{24} \approx 0.417$ **51.** $P(G|H) = \dfrac{1}{3} \approx 0.333$ **53.** $P(E|G) = \dfrac{9}{13} \approx 0.692$; the probability the customer likes the leodorant given he/she is in group I is $\dfrac{9}{13}$. **55.** $P(H|E) = \dfrac{22}{69} \approx 0.319$; the probability the customer is from group II given he/she likes the leodorant is approximately 0.319. **57.** $P(F|G) = \dfrac{3}{13} \approx 0.231$; the probability the customer does not like the deodorant given he/she is in group I is pproximately 0.231. **59.** $P(H|F) = \dfrac{17}{42} \approx 0.405$; the probability the customer is from group II given he/she does not like the deodorant is pproximately 0.405. **61.** $P(F|I) = \dfrac{5}{11} \approx 0.455$; the probability the resident is female given he/she is an Independent is approximately 0.455. **3.** $P(M|D) = \dfrac{5}{11} \approx 0.455$; the probability the resident is male given he/she is a Democrat is approximately 0.455. **65.** $P(M|R \cup I) = \dfrac{70}{125} = 0.56$; The probability the resident is male given he/she is either a Republican or Independent is 0.56. **67.** **(a)** $P(M) = \dfrac{724}{1009}$ **(b)** $P(A) = \dfrac{333}{1009}$ **c)** $P(F \cap B) = \dfrac{72}{1009}$ **(d)** $P(F|E) = \dfrac{51}{263}$ **(e)** $P(A|M) = \dfrac{171}{724}$ **(f)** $P(F|A \cup E) = \dfrac{213}{596}$ **(g)** $P(M \cap \bar{B}) = \dfrac{383}{1009}$ **(h)** $P(F|\bar{E}) = \dfrac{117}{373}$ **69.** $P(B|Rh+) = \dfrac{9}{82} \approx 0.110$ **71.** $P(Rh+|O) = \dfrac{39}{48} \approx 0.813$ **73.** $P(\text{receives mailing and responds}) = 0.014$ **75.** **(a)** 45% of the purchases were made by persons under 30 years of age. **(b)** The probability a purchase of at least \$500 was made by someone older than 50 is 0.067. **(c)** There is 0.65625 probability that a purchase between \$100 and \$499.99 was made by a person between the ages of 30 and 50. **77.** The probability he issue declined given it is high yield is 0.388. **79.** The probability an issue is at a 52-week high given it is investment grade is 0.054. **81.** **(a)** $P(\text{no health insurance}|{<}18 \text{ years old}) = 0.099$ **(b)** $P(\text{individual} <18 \text{ years old}|\text{no health insurance}) = 0.178$ **(c)** $P(\text{individual} <18 \text{ years old}|\text{has health insurance}) = 0.249$ **83.** $P(W|E) = \dfrac{5}{11}$ **85.** $P(\text{a person completes training}) = 0.715$ **87.** $P(\text{person smokes}|\text{over 16 years of age}) = 0.215$

Exercise 8.2 (p. 441)

1. False **2.** $P(E) \cdot P(F)$ **3.** $P(E \cap F) = 0.24$ **5.** $P(F) = 0.125$ **7.** No, $P(E \cap F) = \dfrac{2}{9} \neq \dfrac{1}{9} = P(E)P(F)$. **9.** **(a)** $P(E|F) = 0.2$ **(b)** $P(F|E) = 0.4$ **(c)** $P(E \cap F) = 0.08$ **(d)** $P(E \cup F) = 0.52$ **11.** $P(E \cap F \cap G) = \dfrac{4}{147}$ **13.** $P(E|F) = 0.5$ No, $P(E \cap F) = 0.1 \neq 0.06 = P(E)P(F)$ **15.** $P(RRR) = \dfrac{1}{12}, P(RRL) = \dfrac{2}{12}, P(RLR) = \dfrac{1}{12}, P(LRR) = \dfrac{1}{12}, P(RLL) = \dfrac{2}{12}, P(LRL) = \dfrac{2}{12}, P(LLR) = \dfrac{1}{12}, P(LLL) = \dfrac{2}{12}$ **(a)** $P(E) = \dfrac{1}{4}$ **(b)** $P(F) = \dfrac{1}{6}$ **(c)** $P(G) = \dfrac{1}{2}$ **(d)** $P(H) = \dfrac{1}{2}$ **17.** **(a)** Probability both are red is $\dfrac{9}{25}$. **(b)** Probability one is red is $\dfrac{12}{25}$. **19.** **(a)** Probability both children have heart disease is $\dfrac{9}{16}$. **(b)** Probability neither child is diseased is $\dfrac{1}{16}$. **(c)** Probability exactly 1 has disease is $\dfrac{3}{8}$. **21.** $P(\text{seed produces a violet}) = 0.20$ **23.** **(a)** $P(\text{both inspectors miss a defect}) = 0.04$ **(b)** Three inspectors should be hired to ensure the probability of failing to identify the defect is less than 0.01. **25.** $P(\text{both stocks increase}) = 0.36$; $P(\text{at least one stock does not increase}) = 0.64$ **27.** **(a)** $P({<}18 \text{ years old}) = 0.239$; $P({<}18 \text{ years old}|\text{no health insurance}) = 0.178$ **(b)** The events are not independent since $P({<}18 \text{ years old}) \neq P({<}18 \text{ years old}|\text{no health insurance})$. **29.** **(a)** The failures in the two pumps are not mutually exclusive; there is 0.25% chance they both fail. **(b)** $P(\text{at least 1 pump fails}) = 0.0975$ **(c)** Failures are independent because $P(\text{both fail}) = 0.0025 = P(\text{one fails}) \cdot P(\text{second fails})$

31. **(a)** $P(\text{burglary}|\text{suburban}) = 0.205$ **(b)** $P(\text{rural}|\text{vehicle theft}) = 0.143$ **(c)** The events "rural" and "vehicle theft" are not independent since $P(R) \cdot P(VT) = 0.015 \neq P(R \cap VT) = 0.008$. **(d)** The events "urban" and "burglary" are independent since $P(U) \cdot P(B) = 0.088 = P(U \cap B)$.

33. **(a)** Probability both vote for the candidate is $\frac{4}{9}$. **(b)** Probability neither votes for the candidate is $\frac{1}{9}$. **(c)** Probability one votes for the candidate is $\frac{4}{9}$.

35. **(a)** $p = 0.8$

Group Size	Expected Tests Saved per Component $p = 0.8$	Percent Saving
2	$p^2 - \frac{1}{2} = 0.64 - 0.50 = 0.14$	14.0
3	$p^3 - \frac{1}{3} = 0.512 - 0.333 = 0.179$	17.9
4	$p^4 - \frac{1}{4} = 0.410 - 0.25 = 0.160$	16.0
5	$p^5 - \frac{1}{5} = 0.328 - 0.2 = 0.128$	12.8
6	$p^6 - \frac{1}{6} = 0.262 - 0.167 = 0.095$	9.5
7	$p^7 - \frac{1}{7} = 0.210 - 0.143 = 0.067$	6.7
8	$p^8 - \frac{1}{8} = 0.168 - 0.125 = 0.043$	4.3

The optimal group size is 3. Its percent saving is 17.9%.

(b) $p = 0.95$

Group Size	Expected Tests Saved per Component $p = 0.95$	Percent Saving
2	$p^2 - \frac{1}{2} = 0.903 - 0.50 = 0.403$	40.3
3	$p^3 - \frac{1}{3} = 0.857 - 0.333 = 0.524$	52.4
4	$p^4 - \frac{1}{4} = 0.815 - 0.25 = 0.565$	56.5
5	$p^5 - \frac{1}{5} = 0.774 - 0.2 = 0.574$	57.4
6	$p^6 - \frac{1}{6} = 0.735 - 0.167 = 0.568$	56.8
7	$p^7 - \frac{1}{7} = 0.698 - 0.143 = 0.555$	55.5
8	$p^8 - \frac{1}{8} = 0.663 - 0.125 = 0.538$	53.8

The optimal group size is 5. Its percent saving is 57.4%.

(c) $p = 0.99$

Group Size	Expected Tests Saved per Component $p = 0.99$	Percent Saving
2	$p^2 - \frac{1}{2} = 0.4801$	48.01
3	$p^3 - \frac{1}{3} = 0.6370$	63.70
4	$p^4 - \frac{1}{4} = 0.7106$	71.06
5	$p^5 - \frac{1}{5} = 0.7510$	75.10
6	$p^6 - \frac{1}{6} = 0.7748$	77.48
7	$p^7 - \frac{1}{7} = 0.7892$	78.92

Group Size	Expected Tests Saved per Component $p = 0.99$	Percent Saving
8	$p^8 - \frac{1}{8} = 0.7977$	79.77
9	$p^9 - \frac{1}{9} = 0.8024$	80.24
10	$p^{10} - \frac{1}{10} = 0.80438$	80.438
11	$p^{11} - \frac{1}{11} = 0.80443$	80.443
12	$p^{12} - \frac{1}{12} = 0.80305$	80.305
13	$p^{13} - \frac{1}{13} = 0.80060$	80.060

The optimal group size is 11. Its percent saving is 80.443.

37. **(a)** The probability pooled test is positive is $1 - (1 - p)^{20}$.

(b) The expected number of tests needed is $21 - 20(1 - p)^{20}$.

(c) The pooled method saves $20(1 - p)^{20} - 1$ tests per individual.

Exercise 8.3 (p. 453)

1. Partition **3.** True **4.** False **5.** $P(E|A) = 0.4$ **7.** $P(E|B) = 0.2$ **9.** $P(E|C) = 0.7$ **11.** $P(E) = 0.31$ **13.** $P(A|E) = \frac{12}{31}$ **15.** $P(C|E) = \frac{7}{31}$ **17.** $P(B|E) = \frac{12}{31}$ **19.** $P(E) = 0.024$ **21.** $P(E) = 0.016$ **23.** $P(A_1|E) = 0.5; P(A_2|E) = 0.5$ **25.** $P(A_1|E) = 0.375; P(A_2|E) = 0.375; P(A_3|E) = 0.25$ **27.** (a) $P(\text{Red}) = \frac{5}{16}$ (b) $P(\text{White}) = \frac{5}{16}$ (c) $P(\text{Blue}) = \frac{3}{8}$ (d) $P(\text{Jar I}|\text{Red}) = \frac{1}{3}$ (e) $P(\text{Jar II}|\text{Blue}) = \frac{1}{2}$ (f) $P(\text{Jar III}|\text{White}) = \frac{1}{3}$ **29.** $P(\text{male}|\text{color blind}) = 0.953$ **31.** (a) The probability is 0.34 that the customer had never cruised on *Castaway*. (b) The probability is 0.38 that the person was male given the caller had never cruised on *Castaway*. **33.** Since the plane is late, there is a 0.659 probability she is on Southwest. **35.** (a) There is a 0.0935 probability that the survey has negative feedback. (b) If the survey contains negative feedback, there is a 0.342 probability it is from the Riverside restaurant. (c) If the survey contains negative feedback, there is a 0.321 probability it is from the Springfield restaurant. **37.** If the tax return is audited, the probability is 0.025 that the filer made more than $1,000,000. **39.** (a) 46.7% of employed persons in the United States are women. (b) $P(\text{management, professional, and related}|\text{woman}) = 0.395$ (c) $P(\text{service}|\text{woman}) = 0.206$ (d) $P(\text{sales and office}|\text{woman}) = 0.332$ **41.** (a) $P(\text{Democrat}|\text{voted}) = 0.385$; (b) $P(\text{Republican}|\text{voted}) = 0.39$ (c) $P(\text{Independent}|\text{voted}) = 0.225$ **43.** (a) $P(\text{Rock}|\text{positive}) = 0.385$; (b) $P(\text{Clay}|\text{positive}) = 0.209$; (c) $P(\text{Sand}|\text{positive}) = 0.405$ **45.** (a) $P(\text{Republican}) = 0.466$; (b) $P(\text{Northeast}|\text{Republican}) = 0.343$ **47.** The probability the nurse forgot is $\frac{9}{11}$. **49.** (a) The probability the accident involved a young driver is 0.28. (b) The probability the driver was 25 or older is 0.72. **51.** (a) Given a student tests positive, the probability of having HIV is 0.5. (b) In a high risk population, if the test is positive the probability of having HIV is 0.963. (c) If Jack tests positive twice, then he has a 0.996 probability of having the HIV virus. **53.** If $P(F) \neq 0$ and F is a subset of E, then $E \cap F = F$ and $P(E \cap F) = P(F) \neq 0$. So $P(E|F) = \frac{P(E \cap F)}{P(F)} = \frac{P(F)}{P(F)} = 1.$

Exercise 8.4 (p. 463)

3. 1; 6 **4.** $\frac{n!}{(n-r)!}$ **5.** False **6.** False **7.** 60 **9.** 90 **11.** 9 **13.** 28 **15.** 42 **17.** 40,320 **19.** 1 **21.** 56 **23.** 1

25. The ordered arrangements of length 3 formed from the letters *a*, *b*, *c*, *d*, and *e* are:

abc, abd, abe, acb, acd, ace, adb, adc, ade, aeb, aec, aed,
bac, bad, bae, bca, bcd, bce, bda, bdc, bde, bea, bec, bed,
cab, cad, cae, cba, cbd, cbe, cda, cdb, cde, cea, ceb, ced,
dab, dac, dae, dba, dbc, dbe, dca, dcb, dce, dea, deb, dec,
eab, eac, ead, eba, ebc, ebd, eca, ecb, ecd, eda, edb, edc

$P(5, 3) = 60$

27. 123, 124, 132, 134, 142, 143, 213, 214, 231, 234, 241, 243, 312, 314, 321, 324, 341, 342, 412, 413, 421, 423, 431, 432; $P(4, 3) = 24$ **29.** 16 two-letter codes **31.** 8 three-digit numbers **33.** 24 ways **35.** 60 three-letter codes **37.** There are 6720 ways to seat 5 people in 8 chairs. **39.** 18,278 companies can be on the NYSE. **41.** There are $7^3 = 343$ different ways to purchase printers. **43.** $P(14, 4) = 24{,}024$ different comedy lineups are possible. **45.** $P(11, 6) = 332{,}640$ different promotion schedules are possible.

47. $P(21, 8) = 8{,}204{,}716{,}800$ different itineraries are possible. **49.** There are 132,860 ways 2 people can have different birthdays. **51.** (a) There are 720 arrangements of letters S, U, N, D, A, Y (b) There are 120 arrangements if S comes first. (c) There are 24 arrangements if S must come first and Y last. **53.** There are 19,958,400 ways the books can be distributed **55.** There are 3,368,253,000 ways to win. **57.** There are 32,760 ways officers can be chosen.

Exercise 8.5 (p. 476)

1. combination **2.** 10 **3.** False **4.** True **5.** 15 **7.** 21 **9.** 5 **11.** 28 **13.** *abc, abd, abe, acd, ace, ade, bcd, bce, bde, cde*; $C(5, 3) = 10$ **15.** 123, 124, 134, 234; $C(4, 3) = 4$ **17.** 35 ways **19.** 2380 ways **21.** 1140 ways **23.** 56 8-bit strings have exactly three 1s. **25.** 90,720 different 9 letter words. **27.** 27,720 ways **29.** 336 different committees **31.** 27,720 ways **33.** There are 146,107,962 different Powerball tickets. **35.** There can be 4,680,270,000 different negotiating teams. **37.** The auditor can choose 1,916,797,311 different samples. **39.** There are $\frac{100!}{22! \cdot 13! \cdot 10! \cdot 5! \cdot 16! \cdot 17! \cdot 17!} = 1.157 \times 10^{76}$ ways **41.** (a) $\frac{1}{15}$ (b) $\frac{7}{15}$ (c) $\frac{8}{15}$ **43.** (a) AT&T, Verizon, Kraft, Pfizer, Home Depot (b) $\frac{3}{10}$ (c) $\frac{3}{5}$ (d) $\frac{1}{10}$ (e) $\frac{9}{10}$ **45.** (a) $P(\text{no account with errors is selected}) = 0.620$ (b) $P(\text{one account with errors is selected}) = 0.332$ (c) $P(\text{at least two accounts with errors are selected}) = 0.048$ **47.** (a) There are 1,757,600,000 different phone codes. (b) $P(\text{code ends in AA}) = 0.00148$ (c) $P(\text{code begins and ends in A}) = 0.00148$ (d) $P(\text{code has no repeats}) = 0.268$ (e) $P(\text{code has no repeated letters, but all the same number}) = 0.0000888$ **49.** $P(\text{all 5 refrigerators are defective}) = 2.83 \times 10^{-6}$; $P(\text{at least two refrigerators are defective}) = 0.103$ **51.** (a) $P(\text{favorable extension}) = \frac{1}{100}$ (b) $P(\text{favorable extension if first digit cannot be 0}) = \frac{9}{1000}$ **53.** (a) $P(\text{committee is all Democrat}) = 0.0213$ (b) $P(\text{committee is all Republican}) = 0.0014$ (c) $P(\text{committee has 4 Democrats and 3 Republicans}) = 0.3031$ **55.** $P(\text{shipment rejected}) = 0.098$ **57.** (a) $P(\text{all hearts}) = 0.0005$ (b) $P(\text{exactly 4 spades}) = 0.0107$ (c) $P(\text{2 are clubs}) = 0.274$ **59.** (a) $P(\text{royal flush}) = 1.539 \times 10^{-6}$ (b) $P(\text{straight flush}) = 1.385 \times 10^{-5}$ (c) $P(\text{4 of a kind}) = 2.401 \times 10^{-4}$ (d) $P(\text{full house}) = 0.0014$ (e) $P(\text{flush}) = 0.0020$ (f) $P(\text{straight}) = 0.0039$

Exercise 8.6 (p. 491)

1. False **2.** True **3.** $\binom{n}{k}p^kq^{n-k} = \dfrac{n!}{k!(n-k)!}p^kq^{n-k}$ **4.** $b(7, 3; 0.3)$ **5.** True **6.** np **7.** $b(7, 4; 0.20) = 0.0287$ **9.** $b(15, 8; 0.80) = 0.0138$ **11.** $b\left(15, 10; \frac{1}{2}\right) = \dfrac{3003}{32{,}768} = 0.0916$ **13.** 0.2969 **15.** $b\left(3, 2; \frac{1}{3}\right) = \frac{2}{9}$ **17.** $b\left(3, 0; \frac{1}{6}\right) = \frac{125}{216} \approx 0.5787$ **19.** $b\left(5, 3; \frac{2}{3}\right) = \frac{80}{243} \approx 0.3292$ **21.** $b(10, 6; 0.3) = 0.0368$ **23.** $b(12, 9; 0.8) = 0.2362$ **25.** $P(\text{at least 5 successes}) = 0.0580$ **27.** $b\left(8, 1; \frac{1}{2}\right) = \frac{1}{32}$ **29.** $P(\text{at least 5 tails}) = \frac{93}{256} \approx 0.3633$ **31.** $P(2\text{ H} \mid \text{at least 1 H occurs}) = \frac{28}{255} \approx 0.1098$ **33.** $b\left(5, 2; \frac{1}{6}\right) = \frac{625}{3888} \approx 0.1608$ **35.** **(a)**

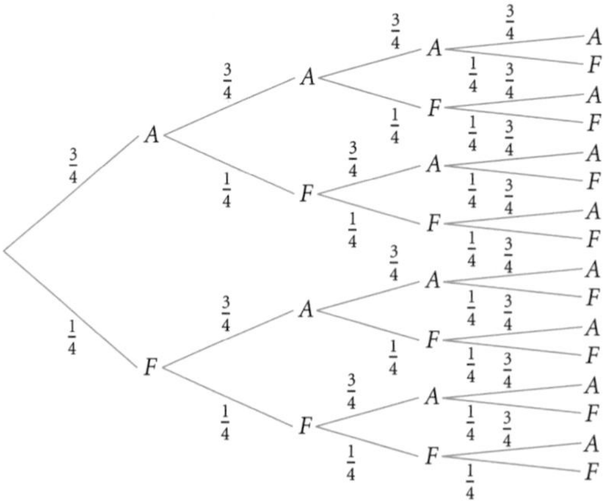

(b) $P(\text{Exactly 2 successes}) = \frac{54}{256}$ **(c)** $b\left(4, 2; \frac{1}{4}\right) = \frac{54}{256}$ **37.** **(a)** $b(8, 1; 0.05) = 0.2793$ **(b)** $b(8, 2; 0.05) = 0.0515$ **(c)** $1 - b(8, 0; 0.05) = 0.3366$ **(d)** $P(\text{Fewer than 3 defective}) = 0.9942$ **39.** **(a)** $b(6, 3; 0.5) = \frac{5}{16} = 0.3125$; **(b)** $b(6, 5; 0.5) + b(6, 6; 0.5) = \frac{7}{64} \approx 0.1094$ **(c)** $b(6, 2; 0.5) + b(6, 3; 0.5) = \frac{35}{64} \approx 0.5469$ **41.** **(a)** Probability of getting all answers correct is $b\left(20, 20; \frac{1}{2}\right) = \left(\frac{1}{2}\right)^{20} = 9.537 \times 10^{-7}$. **(b)** Probability of passing or the probability of getting at least 12 correct is 0.2517. **(c)** The odds in favor of passing are about 1 to 3. **43.** **(a)** Probability that at least 5 of those surveyed think it is acceptable to cheat is 0.0265. **(b)** Probability fewer than 3 people surveyed think it is acceptable to cheat is 0.7346. **(c)** Probability that no one thinks it is acceptable to cheat is $b(15, 0; 0.12) = 0.1470$. **45.** **(a)** Probability two of the returns were filed on April 15 is $b(8, 2; 0.10) = 0.1488$. **(b)** Probability five of the returns were filed on April 15 is $b(8, 5; 0.10) = 0.0004$. **(c)** Probability that none of the returns were filed on April 15 is $b(8, 0; 0.10) = 0.4305$. **47.** **(a)** Probability that all like their jobs is $b(10, 10; 0.8) = 0.107$. **(b)** Probability that 9 persons liked their jobs is $b(10, 9; 0.8) = 0.2684$. **(c)** Probability that no more than 7 persons liked their jobs is 0.3222. **49.** **(a)** Probability that exactly 14 of those selected use coupons is $b(18, 14; 0.77) = 0.2205$. **(b)** Probability that at least 14 of those selected use coupons is 0.5988. **(c)** Probability that at least 16 of those selected use coupons is 0.1813. **51.** **(a)** Probability none of the 12 claims involves fraud is 0.1422. **(b)** Probability six of the 12 claims involve fraud is 0.004. **(c)** Probability at least one of the 12 claims involve fraud is 0.8578. **53.** **(a)** Probability two passengers of the 44 do not show is 0.0635. **(b)** Probability all 44 passengers show up is 0.0036. **(c)** Probability at least two passengers of the 44 do not show is 0.9748. **55.** **(a)** Probability the player has at least two hits in four times at bat is 0.2617. **(b)** Probability the player has at least one hit in four times at bat is 0.6836. **57.** $b(8, 8; 0.40) = (0.40)^8 = 0.0007$ **59.** $b(10, 4; 0.23) = 0.1225$ **61.** **(a)** $P(\text{At least 5 correct}) = \frac{7}{64} \approx 0.1094$ **(b)** $P(\text{fewer than 5 correct}) = 0.3446$ **63.** **(a)** $b(10, 4; 0.123) = 0.0219$ **(b)** $b(10, 0; 0.123) = 0.2692$ **(c)** $P(\text{At most 5 are over 65}) = 0.9995$ **65.** $E = \frac{2000}{6} = 333\frac{1}{3}$ times **67.** $E = 10$ lightbulbs. **69.** The expected number of adults surveyed who would say that health care costs are paramount is $E = np = 3$. **71.** $E = 1$ person would be expected to have an unfavorable reaction. **73.** The probability the message is correctly received is 0.9647. **75.** The probability the code is correctly received is 0.9349.

77.

k	Actual Value of $P(k)$
0	0.4096
1	0.4096
2	0.1536
3	0.0256
4	0.0016

79.

k Number of Heads	0	1	2	3	4	5	6	7	8
Actual Value of $P(k)$	0.1678	0.3355	0.2936	0.1468	0.0459	0.0092	0.0011	0.0001	0.0000

Review Exercises (p. 498)

1. $P(E|A) = 0.82$ **3.** $P(E|B) = 0.10$ **5.** $P(B \cap E) = 0.738$ **7.** $P(B \cap E) = 0.01$ **9.** $P(A|E) = 0.9866$ **11.** $P(B|E) = 0.0134$ **13.** $P(E|A) = 0.5$ **15.** $P(E|B) = 0.4$ **17.** $P(E|C) = 0.3$ **19.** $P(A \cap E) = 0.2$ **21.** $P(B \cap E) = 0.2$ **23.** $P(C \cap E) = 0.03$ **25.** $P(E) = 0.43$ **27.** $P(A|E) = 0.4651$ **29.** $P(B|E) = 0.4651$ **31.** $P(C|E) = 0.0698$ **33.** 1 **35.** 210 **37.** 12 **39.** There are 10 ways to form the committee. **41.** There are 6 ways to place the books. **43.** **(a)** There are 120 words. **(b)** There are 20 words if order is not important. **45.** **(a)** There are 525 different committees. **(b)** There are 1715 different committees. **47.** There are 12,441,600 ways. **49.** There are 20,790 different committees. **51.** **(a)** There are 4845 samples that will contain only good plums. **(b)** There are 5700 samples that will contain 3 good plums and 1 rotten plum. **(c)** There are 7805 samples that will contain one or more rotten plums. **53.** 360 words can be made. **55.** There are 302,400 ways she can arrange the books. **57.** $E = \{(3, 1), (3, 2), (3, 3), (3, 4), (3, 5), (3, 6)\}$ $F = \{(1, 6), (2, 6), (3, 6), (4, 6), (5, 6), (6, 6)\}$ $E \cap F = \{(3, 6)\}$; $P(E) = \frac{1}{8}$; $P(F) = \frac{3}{8}$; $P(E \cap F) = \frac{3}{64} = P(E) \cdot P(F)$ so E and F are independent. **59.** Define E: A person has blue eyes, F: A person has brown eyes, G: A person is left handed. **(a)** $P(E \cap G) = 0.025$ **(b)** $P(G) = 0.0625$ **(c)** $P(E|G) = 0.4$ **61.** Define E: scored over 80% and F: took form A **(a)** $P(F|E) = \frac{2}{5}$ **(b)** $P(E|F) = \frac{1}{5}$ **(c)** Yes, because $P(E \cap F) = 0.08 = P(E)P(F)$. **(d)** Yes, because $P(E \cap \bar{F}) = 0.12 = P(E)P(\bar{F})$. **63.** $P(E|F) = 0.5$ **65.** **(a)** Probability (misses the 1st and gets the next 3) = 0.1029. **(b)** Probability (makes 10 in a row) = 0.0282. **67.** Probability at least one matched is $\frac{2}{3}$. **69.** **(a)** Probability all are underweight is 0.0002. **(b)** Probability 2 are underweight is 0.083. **(c)** Probability at most 1 is underweight is 0.910. **71.** **(a)** The probability is 0.3438 that the defective part came from machine A_1. **(b)** The probability is 0.375 that the defective part came from machine A_2. **(c)** The probability is 0.2813 that the defective part came from machine A_3. **73.** **(a)** $b(5, 0; 0.20) = 0.3277$ **(b)** $b(5, 3; 0.20) = 0.0512$ **75.** One would expect $E = np = \frac{7}{2} = 3.5$ heads when tossing a coin 7 times.

Mathematical Questions from Professional Exams (p. 502)

1. b **2.** e **3.** b **4.** d **5.** b **6.** d **7.** b **8.** a **9.** c **10.** b **11.** d

CHAPTER 9 Statistics

Exercise 9.1 (p. 508)

1. Variable **2.** simple random sample **3.** False **4.** biased **5.** Number of heads; discrete **7.** Average gas mileage; continuous **9.** Time a person waits in line; continuous **11.** Number of airplane flights; discrete **13.** Number of people; discrete **15.** Life of a phone battery; continuous **17, 19, 21.** Answers will vary. All answers should include a method to choose a sample in which each member of the population has an equal chance of being selected. **23.** Answers will vary. **25.** Answers will vary.

Exercise 9.2 (p. 514)

1. bar graphs; pie charts **2.** False **3.** False **4.** True

5. (a)

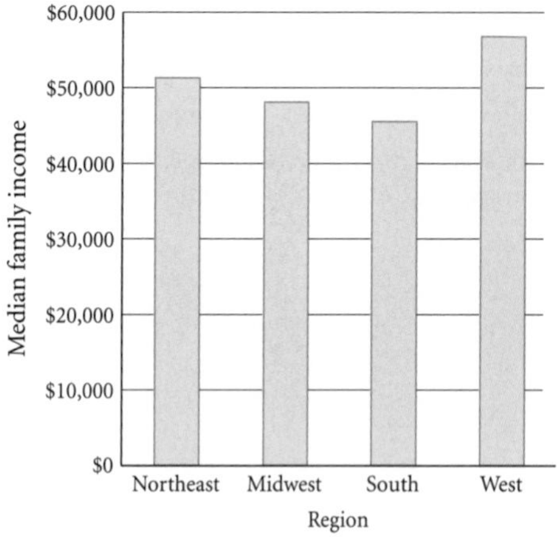

(b) West has the highest median income.

(c) South has the lowest median income.

(d) Answers will vary. All discussions should conclude that pie charts are inappropriate.

7. (a)

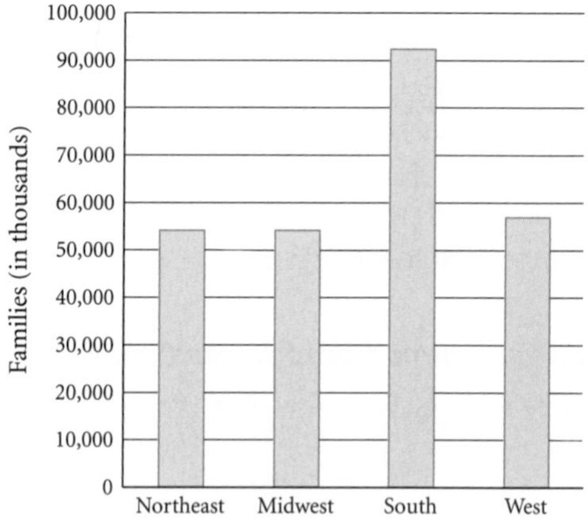

(b)

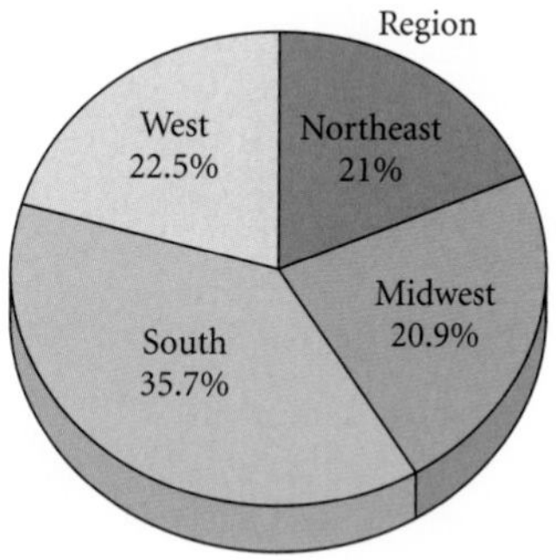

(d) The South has the most families.

(e) The Midwest has the fewest families.

9. (a)

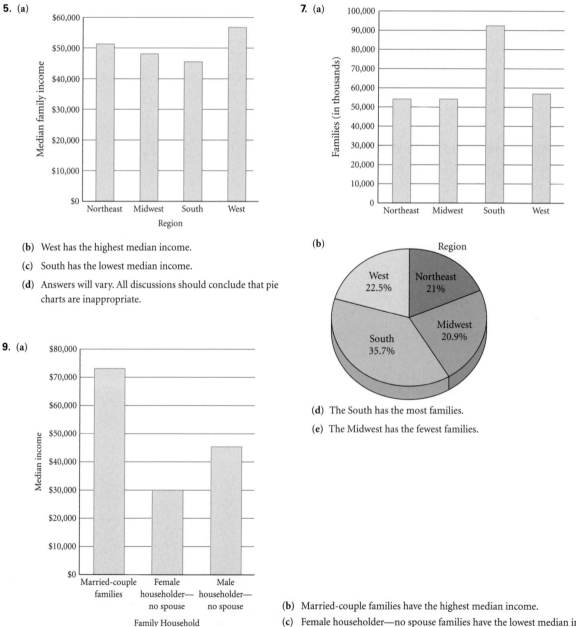

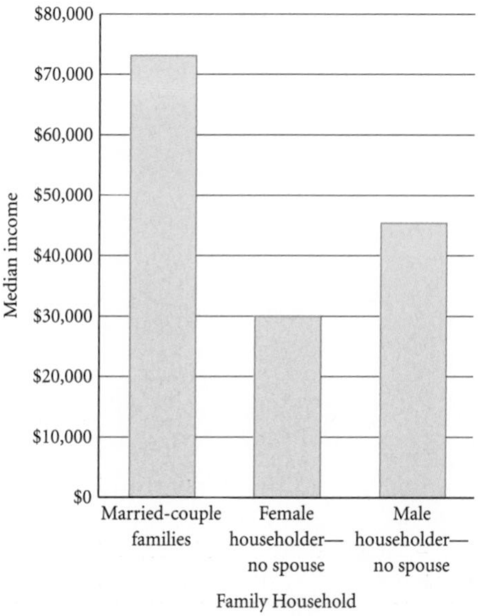

(b) Married-couple families have the highest median income.

(c) Female householder—no spouse families have the lowest median income.

1. (a)

Causes of Death

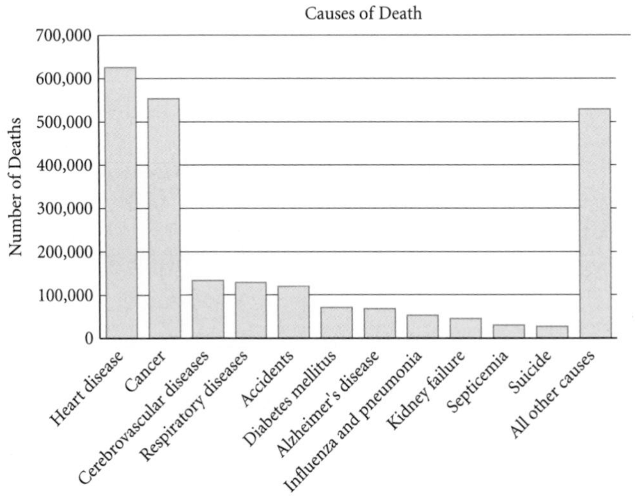

(b) Pie chart is appropriate since all categories are represented.
(c) Heart disease was the leading cause of death in 2006.

Exercise 9.3 (p. 528)

1. True   **3.** Class Intervals   **4.** Ogive

5. (a)

Score	Frequency	Score	Frequency
25	1	41	5
26	1	42	3
28	1	43	1
29	1	44	2
30	3	45	1
31	2	46	2
32	1	47	1
33	2	48	3
34	2	49	1
35	1	50	1
36	2	51	1
37	4	52	3
38	1	53	2
39	1	54	2
40	1	55	1

(b)

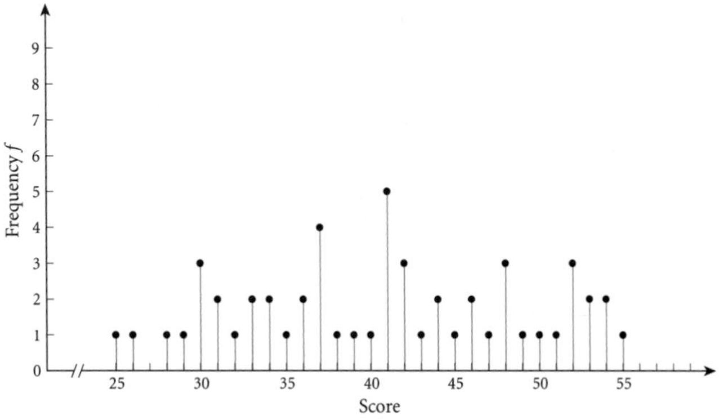

(c)

Class	Frequency	Class	Frequency	Class	Frequency	Class	Frequency
24–25.9	1	32–33.9	3	40–41.9	6	48–49.9	4
26–27.9	1	34–35.9	3	42–43.9	4	50–51.9	2
28–29.9	2	36–37.9	6	44–45.9	3	52–53.9	5
30–31.9	5	38–39.9	2	46–47.9	3	54–55.9	3

13. (a) Hawaiian Air had the highest percentage of on-time flights.   **(b)** Comair had the lowest percentage of on-time flights.   **(c)** About 85% of United Airlines' flights were on time.

15. (a) Housing, fuel, and utilities are the largest component of the CPI, making up 42% of the CPI.   **(b)** Other goods and services form the smallest component of the CPI. This sector comprises 3% of the CPI.

(d)

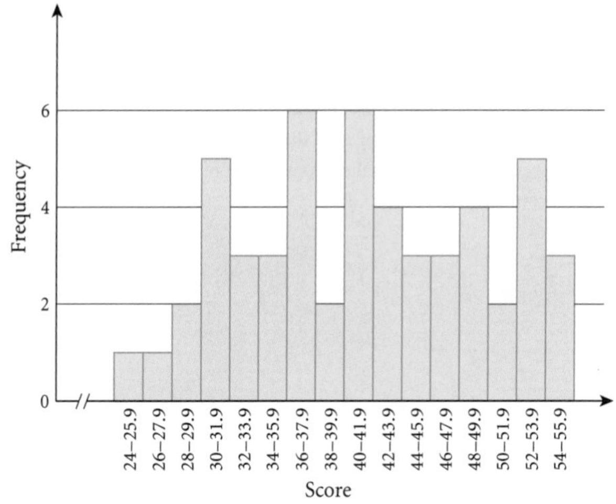

(e)

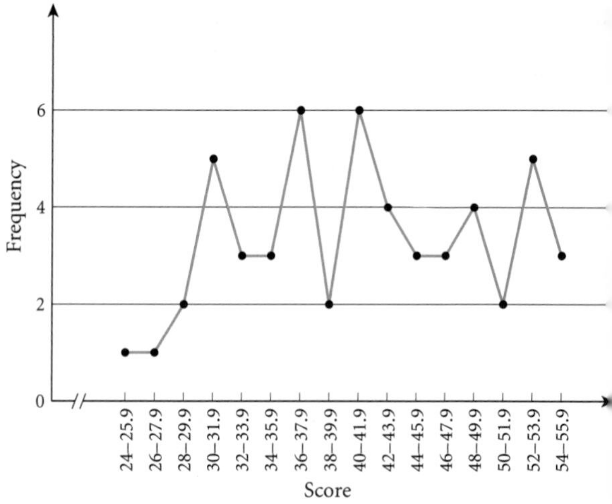

(f)

Class	Cumulative Frequency	Class	Cumulative Frequency
24–25.9	1	40–41.9	29
26–27.9	2	42–43.9	33
28–29.9	4	44–45.9	36
30–31.9	9	46–47.9	39
32–33.9	12	48–49.9	43
34–35.9	15	50–51.9	45
36–37.9	21	52–53.9	50
38–39.9	23	54–55.9	53

(g)

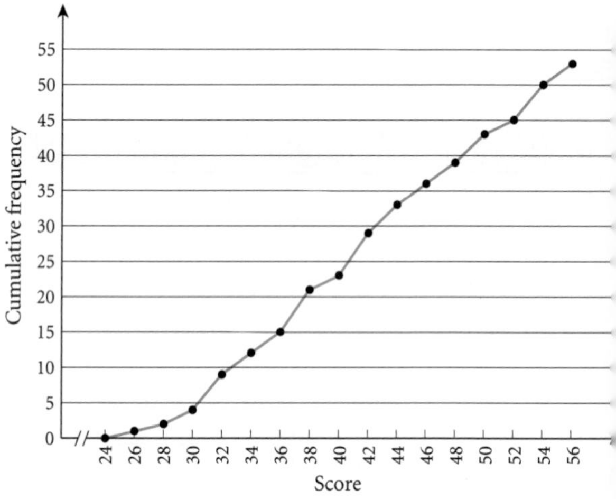

7. (a)

Class	Frequency	Class	Frequency	Class	Frequency	Class	Frequency
50–54.9	1	70–74.9	8	90–94.9	12	110–114.9	0
55–59.9	6	75–79.9	11	95–99.9	2	115–119.9	2
60–64.9	3	80–84.9	2	100–104.9	2		
65–69.9	6	85–89.9	12	105–109.9	4		

(b)

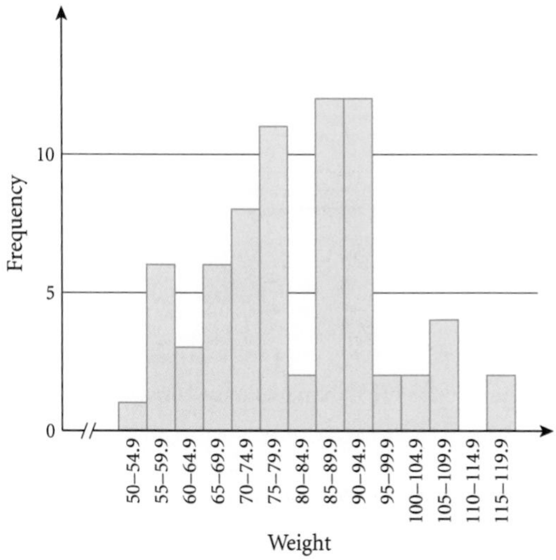

(c)

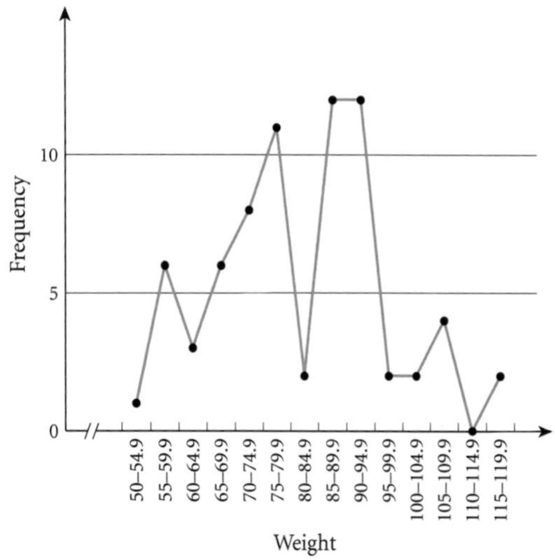

(d)

Class	Cumulative Frequency	Class	Cumulative Frequency	Class	Cumulative Frequency	Class	Cumulative Frequency
50–54.9	1	70–74.9	24	90–94.9	61	110–114.9	69
55–59.9	7	75–79.9	35	95–99.9	63	115–119.9	71
60–64.9	10	80–84.9	37	100–104.9	65		
65–69.9	16	85–89.9	49	105–109.9	69		

(e)

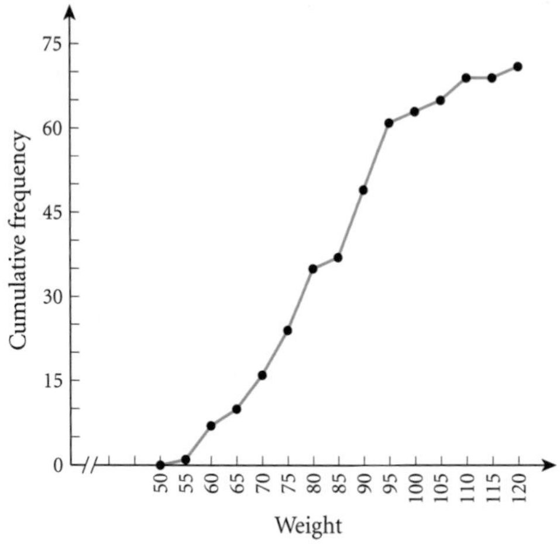

9. Skewed right **11.** **(a)** There are 13 class intervals. **(b)** The lower class limit of the 1st class interval is 20 years; the upper class limit is 24 years. **(c)** The class width is 5 years. **(d)** There are about 1,500,000 drivers between the ages of 70 and 84. **(e)** The interval 45–49 years has the most drivers. **(f)** The interval 80–84 years has the fewest drivers. **(g)** The distribution is skewed right.

(h)

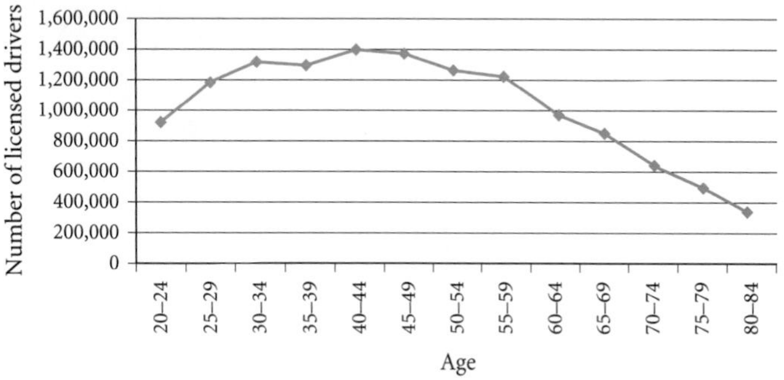

13. **(a)** There are 13 class intervals. **(b)** The lower class limit of the 1st class interval is 20 years; the upper class limit is 24 years. **(c)** The class width is 5 years.

(d)

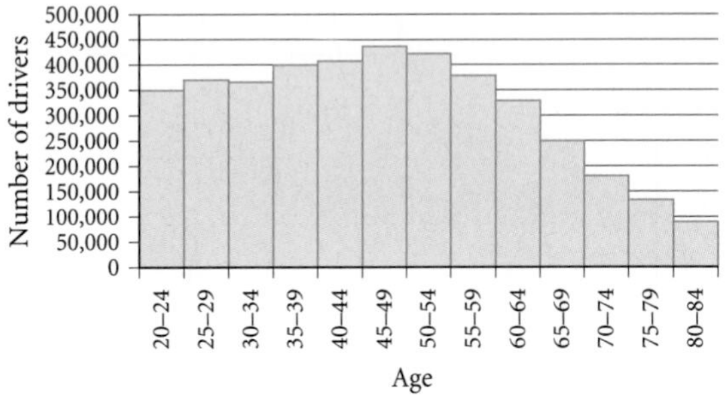

(e)

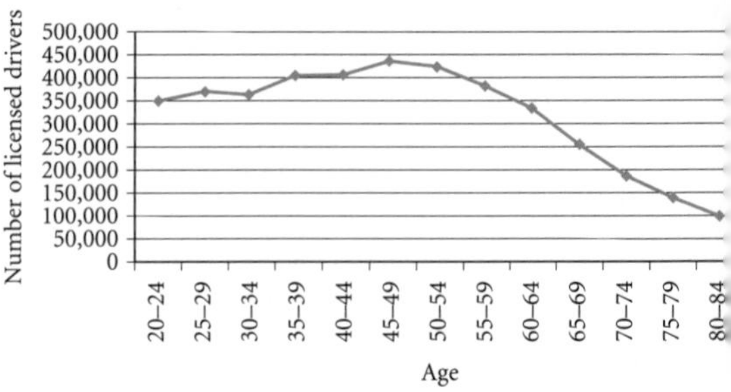

(f) Class interval 45–49 has the most licensed drivers.

(g) Class interval 80–84 has the fewest licensed drivers.

15. **(a)** There are 19 class intervals. **(b)** The lower class limit for the first interval is 0; the upper limit is $1999. **(c)** The class width is $2000.

(d)

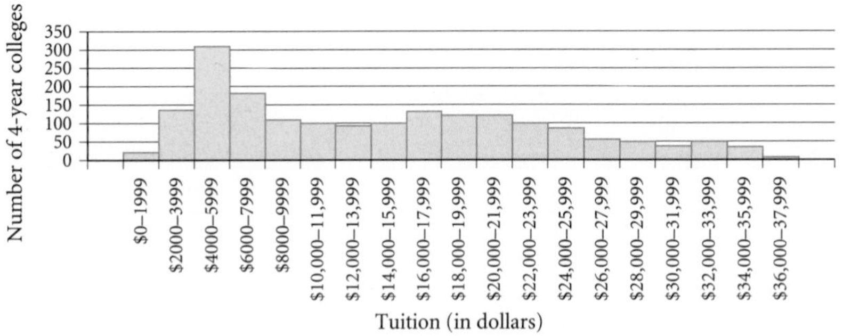

(e)

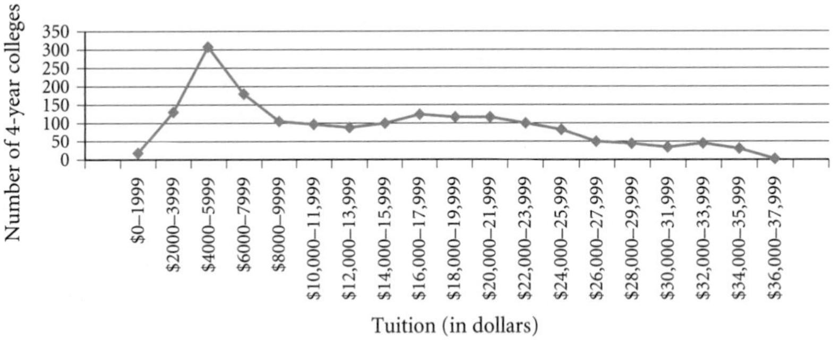

(f) Tuition is most frequently in the $4000–$5999 range.

17. **(a)**

Class Interval	Frequency
11.9–12.4	3
12.5–13.0	1
13.1–13.6	3
13.7–14.2	5
14.3–14.8	1
14.9–15.4	2
15.5–16.0	2
16.1–16.6	3

(b)

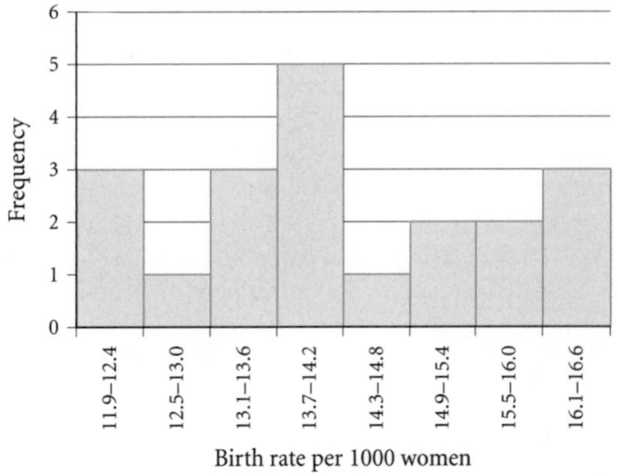

(c)

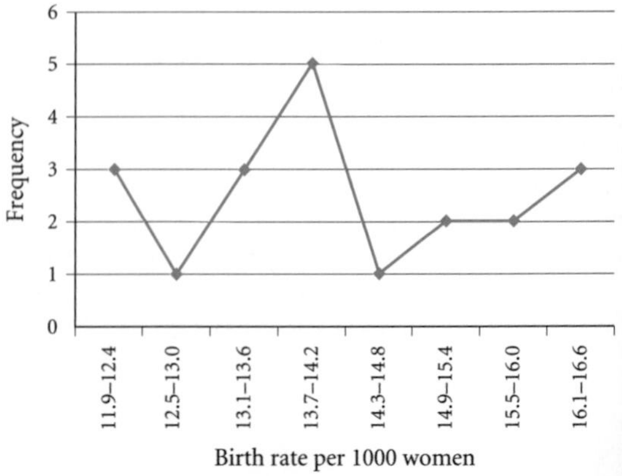

19. (a)

Death Rate	Frequency
0–1.9	7
2–3.9	6
4–5.9	4
6–7.9	2
8–9.9	1

(b)

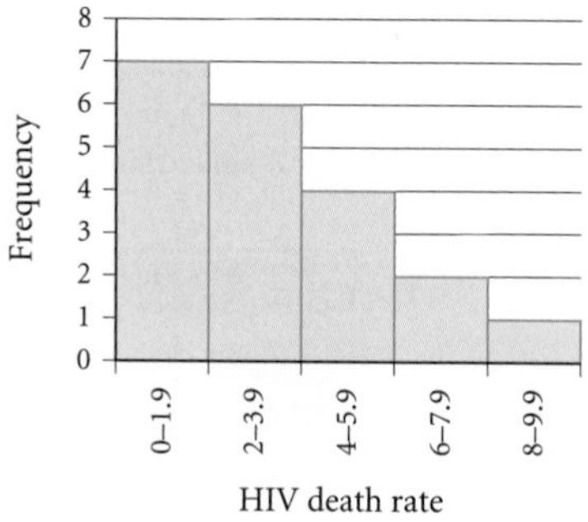

(c)

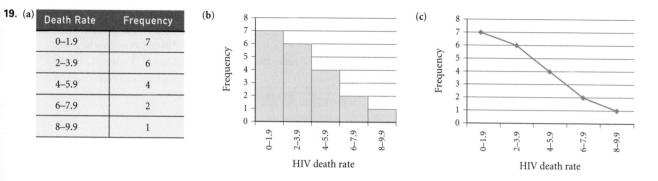

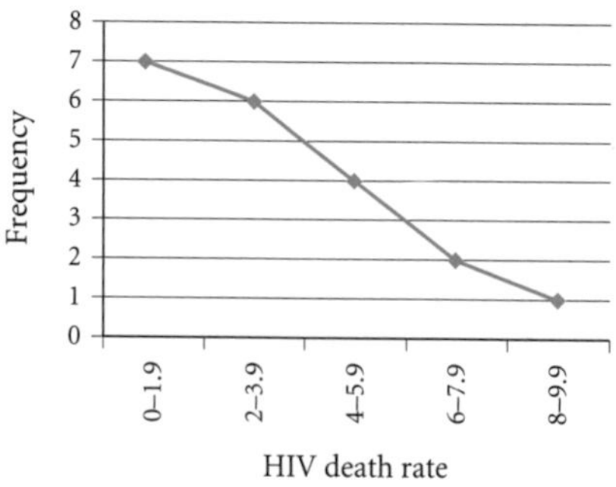

Exercise 9.4 (p. 539)

1. mean, median, mode **2.** True **3.** True **4.** Bimodal **5.** $\mu, \bar{x}$ **6.** False **7.** (a) mean: 31.25 (b) median: 30.5 (c) no mode **9.** (a) mean: 70.4 (b) median: 70 (c) mode: 55 **11.** (a) mean: 78.8 (b) median: 82 (c) mode: 82 **13.** (a) mean: 73.33 (b) median: 77.5 (c) mode: 80 **15.** (a) mean: 28.25 years of age (b) median: 27 years of age (c) mode: 24 and 25 years of age **17.** The mean cost per share is $109.40. **19.** (a) The mean age of a new mother in 2007 was approximately 27.85 years. (b) The median age of a new mother in 2007 was approximately 27.6 years. **21.** (a) The mean age of a licensed driver was approximately 47.49 years. (b) The median age of a licenced driver was approximately 46.9 years. **23.** The mean tuition in 2006–07 was approximately $14,389.94. **25.** (a) mean $41,300; median $36,000 (b) The median describes the salaries better because it is not affected by the extreme value.

Exercise 9.5 (p. 550)

1. dispersion or spread **2.** True **3.** 68 **4.** $n - 1$ **5.** False **6.** False **7.** $s = 7.058$ **9.** $s = 6$ **11.** $s = 13.946$ **13.** mean: $\bar{x} = 32.379$, standard deviation: $s = 7.921$. **15.** mean: 885.333 hours, standard deviation: 69.681 hours. **17.** (a) Range: 17 years (b) $s = 4.86$ years (c) $\sigma = 4.8$ years **19.** (a) Population; we have all of the mothers represented. (b) The standard deviation is 6.28 years. **21.** (a) Population data; all recorded earthquakes below 8.0 are included. (b) The mean magnitude of the earthquakes is 4.03. (c) The standard deviation of the magnitudes of the earthquakes recorded in 2009 is 0.997. **23.** (a) $s = 16.1$ years. (b) $\sigma = 16.1$ years. (c) Answers will vary. **25.** (a) Population; all four-year colleges in the United States are represented. (b) The standard deviation of the tuition is $9083.28. **27.** (a) About 95% of people have IQs between 70 and 130. (b) Approximately 5% of people have IQs either below 70 or above 130. (c) Approximately 2.5% of people have IQs above 130. **29.** (a) About 95% of the kidneys weigh between 265 and 385 grams. (b) About 99.7% of the kidneys weigh between 235 and 415 grams. (c) Approximately 0.3% of the kidneys weigh either fewer than 235 or more than 415 grams. (d) About 81.5% of the kidneys weigh between 295 and 385 grams. **31.** (a) We expect at least 75% of the outcomes to be between 19 and 31. (b) We expect at least 64% of the outcomes to be between 20 and 30. (c) We expect at least 88.89% of the outcomes to be between 16 and 34. (d) We expect at most 25% of the outcomes to be less than 19 or more than 31. (e) We expect at most 11.11% of the outcomes to be less than 16 or greater than 34. **33.** We expect at least 889 boxes to have between 0 and 12 defective watches. **35.** (a) These are population data since all live births in U.S. are included. (b) The mean number of births was 4,108,928. (c) The standard deviation of births was 81,914.5. (d) Exact; the data are not grouped.

Exercise 9.6 (p. 562)

4. mean **5.** Z-score **6.** zero; one **7.** 0.4 **8.** True **9.** $\mu = 8, \sigma = 2$ **11.** $\mu = 18, \sigma = 1$ **13.** (a) $Z = -0.66$ (b) $Z = -0.44$ (c) $Z = -0.01$ (d) $Z = 1.71$ (e) $Z = 2.57$ (f) $Z = 3$ **15.** (a) $A = 0.3133$ (b) $A = 0.3642$ (c) $A = 0.4989$ (d) $A = 0.3888$ (e) $A = 0.4893$ (f) $A = 0.2734$ **17.** $A = 0.3085$ **19.** $A = 0.8181$ **21.** The approximate probability that there are between 285 and 315 successes is 0.75. **23.** The approximate probability of obtaining 300 or more successes is 0.51. **25.** The approximate probability of obtaining 325 or more successes is 0.03. **27.** A−5.48%; B−21.95%; C−34.36%; D−30.13%; F−8.08% **29.** (a) 1365 women are between 62 and 66 inches. (b) 1909 women are between 60 and 68 inches. (c) 1995 women are between 58 and 70 inches. (d) 2 or 3 women are taller than 70 inches. (e) 2 or 3 women are shorter than 58 inches. **31.** (a) Approximately 1 student should weigh at least 142 pounds. (b) We would expect 70% of the students to weigh between 124.61 and 135.39 pounds. **33.** 57.05% of the clothing can be expected to last between 28 and 42 months. **35.** (a) Attendance lower than 10,525 will be in the lowest 70% of the figures. (b) Approximately 77% of the attendance figures are between 8500 and 11,000 persons. (c) Approximately 13% of the attendance figures differ from the mean by at least 1500 persons. **37.** Kathleen had the highest relative standing.

39. (a)

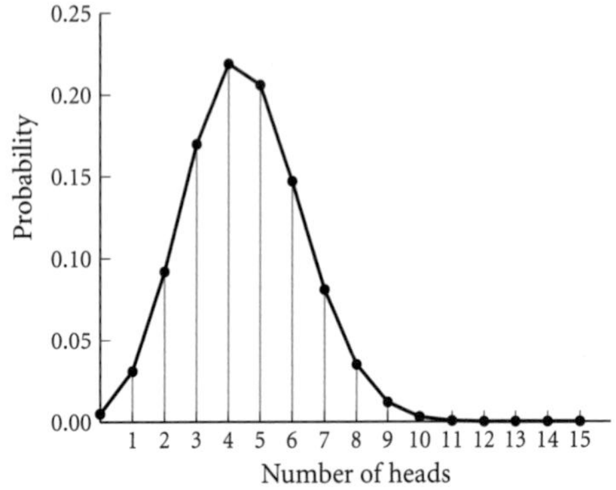

(b) The distribution is skewed right. (c) mean 4.5, standard deviation 1.775 **41.** (a) The approximate probability of having at least 80 but no more than 90 hits is 0.25. (b) The approximate probability of having 85 or more hits is 0.10. **43.** The approximate probability of selecting at least 10 unsealed packages is 0.93.

45.

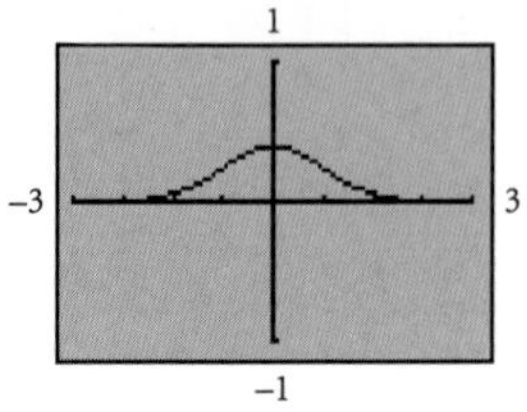

The graph assumes its maximum at $x = 0$.

47. $P[X \geq 10] \approx 0.93$;

Review Exercises (p. 566)

1. circumference, continuous **3.** number of people, discrete **5.** number of defective products, discrete **7.** Answers will vary. All answers should include a method to choose a sample of 100 students from the population in which each student has an equal chance of being chosen. **9.** Answers will vary. All answers should give examples of possible bias.

11. (a)

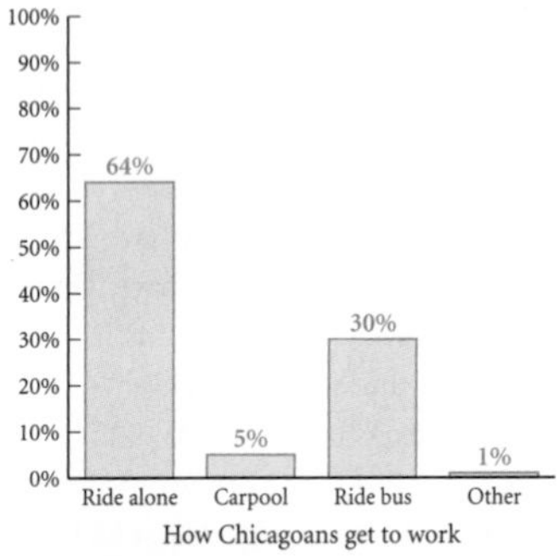

(b)

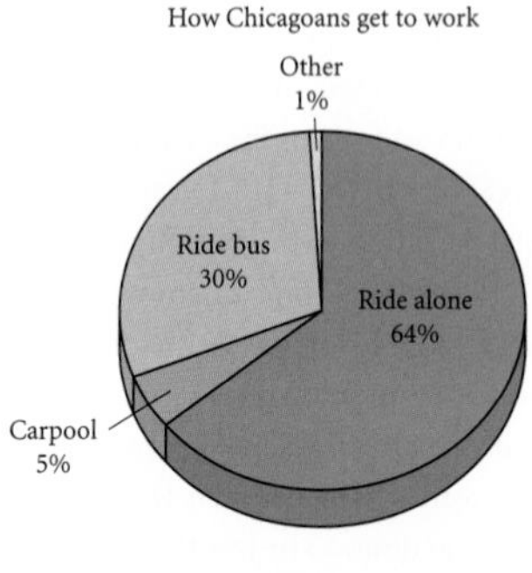

13. (a)

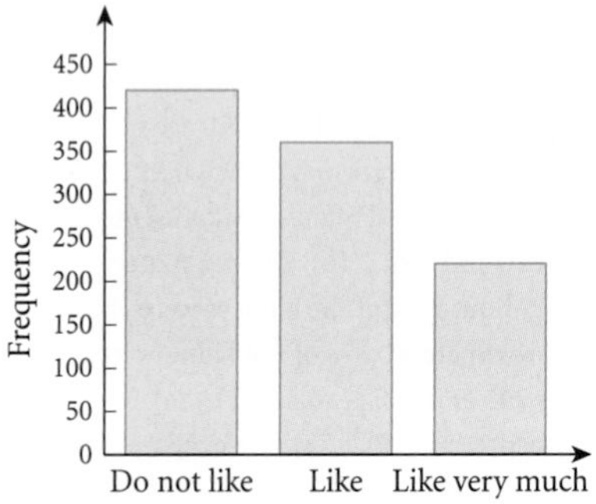

(b)

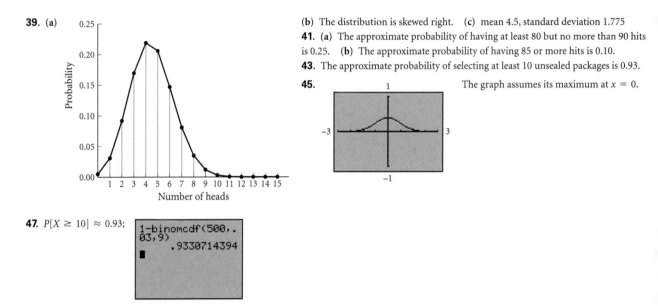

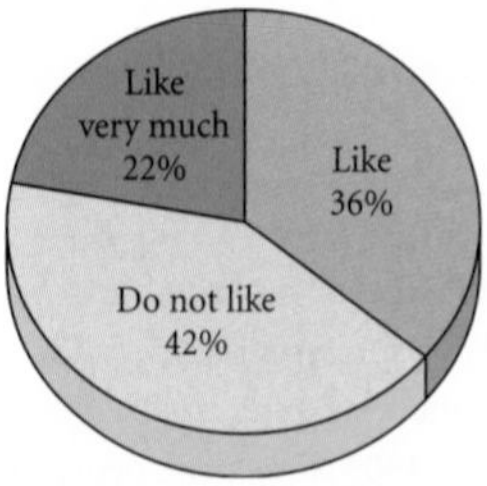

15. (a) American Indians made up the smallest percentage of 4-year college enrollment in 2007. (b) Asian Americans were overrepresented in 4-year colleges in 2007. (c) Approximately 916,000 Hispanic students were enrolled in 4-year colleges in 2007. **17.** (a) High school graduate represents the highest level of educational attainment of most Americans in 2009. (b) Approximately 58,000,000 Americans have at least a bachelor's degree. (c) Approximately 28,000,000 Americans do not have a high school diploma. (d) Approximately 50,000,000 Americans have gone to college but do not have a bachelor's degree.

9. (a)

Score	Frequency	Score	Frequency	Score	Frequency	Score	Frequency
21	2	62	1	74	1	87	2
33	1	63	2	75	1	89	1
41	2	66	2	77	1	90	3
42	1	68	1	78	2	91	1
44	1	69	1	80	4	92	1
48	1	70	2	82	1	95	1
52	2	71	1	83	1	100	2
55	1	72	2	85	2		
60	2	73	2				

The range is 79.

(b)

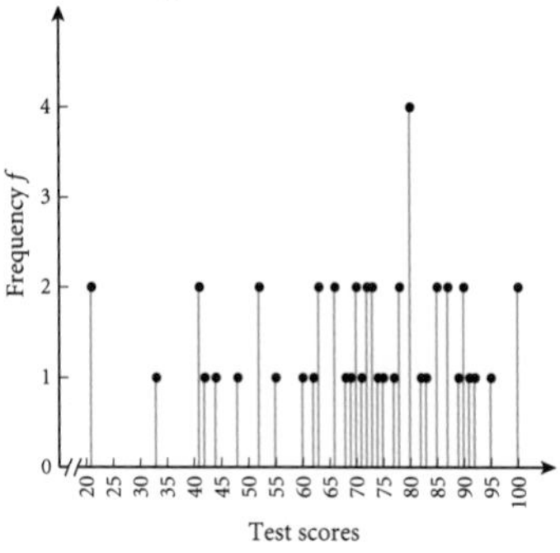

(c)

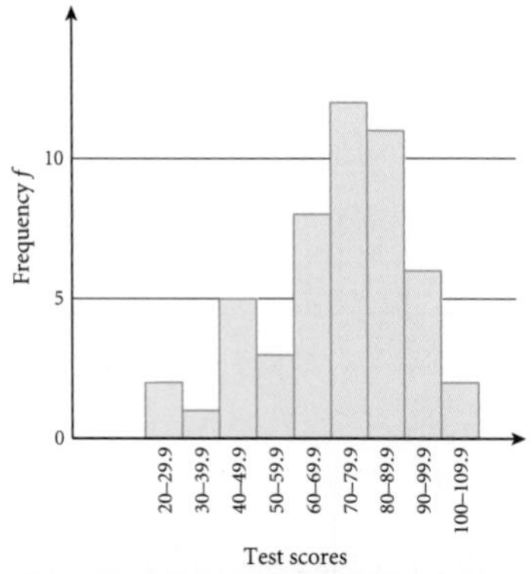

(d)

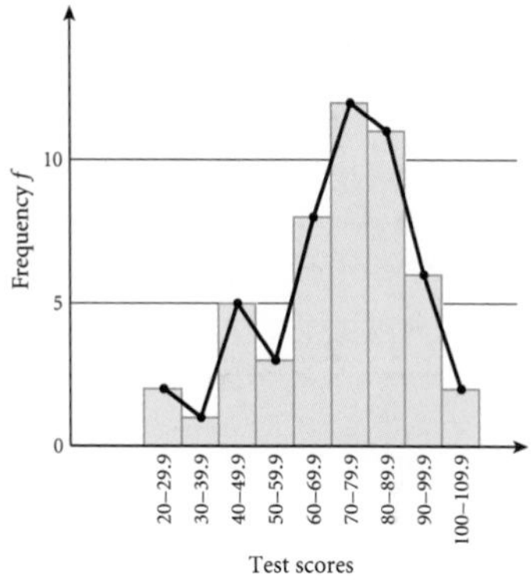

(e) The distribution is skewed left.

(f)

Score	Cumulative Frequency	Score	Cumulative Frequency
21	2	73	26
33	3	74	27
41	5	75	28
42	6	77	29
44	7	78	31
48	8	80	35
52	10	82	36
55	11	83	37
60	12	85	39
62	13	87	41
63	15	89	42
66	17	90	45
68	18	91	46
69	19	92	47
70	21	95	48
71	22	100	50
72	24		

(g)

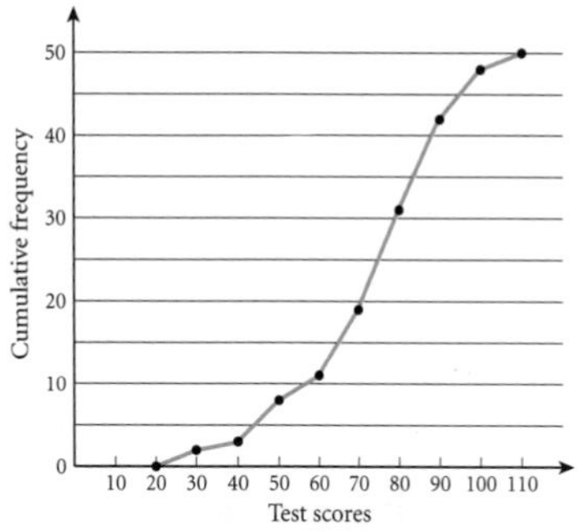

21. (a)

Time	Frequency	Time	Frequency	Time	Frequency	Time	Frequency	Time	Frequency
4′12″	1	4′46″	2	5′08″	1	5′43″	1	6′30″	1
4′15″	1	4′50″	1	5′12″	2	5′48″	1	6′32″	1
4′22″	1	4′52″	1	5′18″	1	5′55″	1	6′40″	1
4′30″	2	4′56″	1	5′20″	3	6′01″	1	7′05″	1
4′36″	1	5′01″	1	5′31″	2	6′02″	1	7′15″	1
4′39″	1	5′02″	1	5′37″	1	6′10″	1		
4′40″	2	5′06″	2	5′40″	2	6′12″	1		

The range is 3 minutes, 3 seconds.

(b)

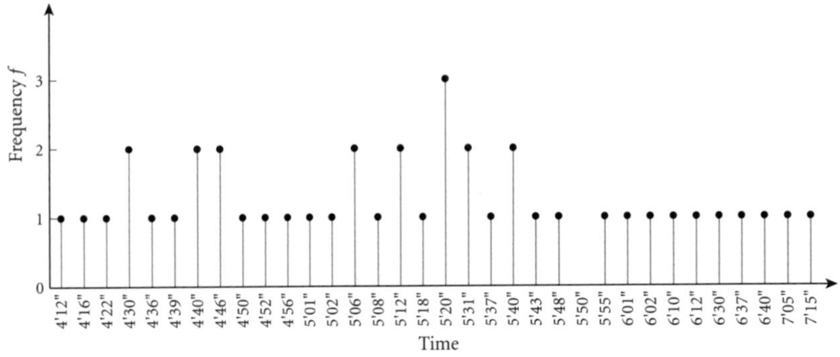

(c)

Class Interval	Frequency f_i
4′00″–4′29″	3
4′30″–4′59″	10
5′00″–5′29″	11
5′30″–5′59″	9
6′00″–6′29″	4
6′30″–6′59″	3
7′00″–7′29″	2

(d)

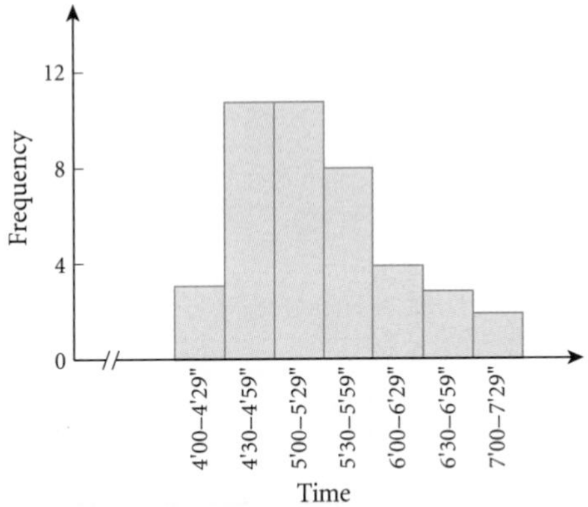

(e)

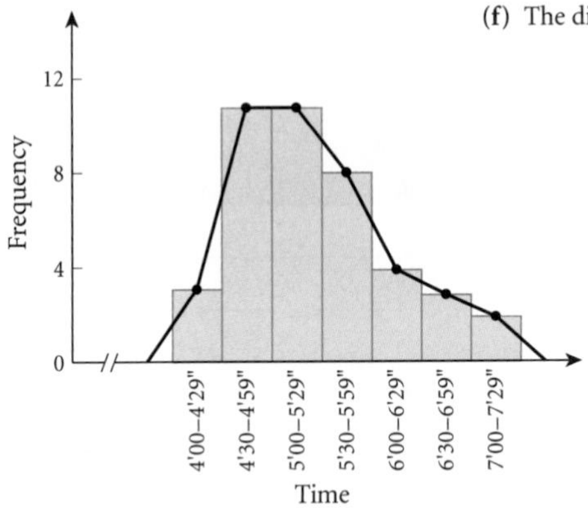

(f) The distribution is skewed right.

(g)

Class Interval	Cummulative Frequency
4′00″–4′29″	3
4′30″–4′59″	14
5′00″–5′29″	25
5′30″–5′59″	33
6′00″–6′29″	37
6′30″–6′59″	40
7′00″–7′29″	42

(h)

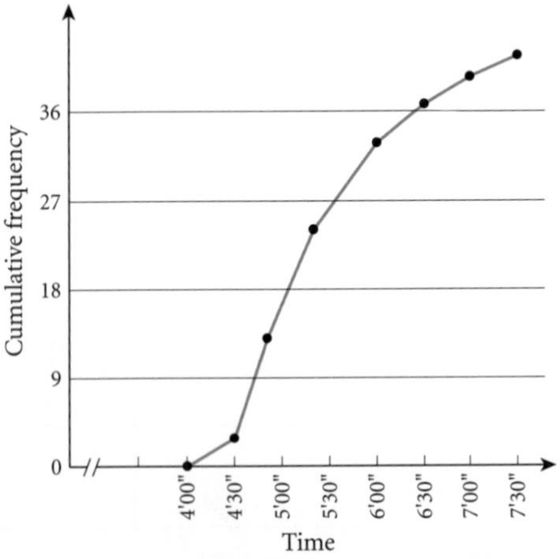

3. (a)

Age	Frequency	Age	Frequency
23	4	32	0
24	6	33	3
25	6	34	1
26	3	35	1
27	5	36	1
28	1	37	1
29	4	38	2
30	1	39	0
31	0	40	1

(b)

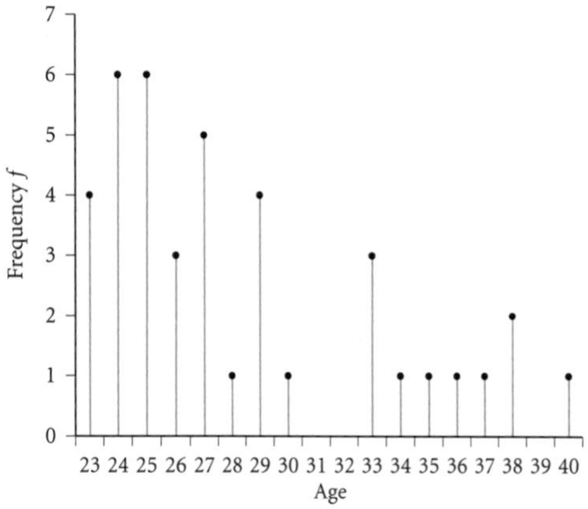

(c) There are 5 class intervals.

Class	Frequency
20.0–24.9	10
25.0–29.9	19
30.0–34.9	5
35.0–39.9	5
40.0–44.9	1

(d)

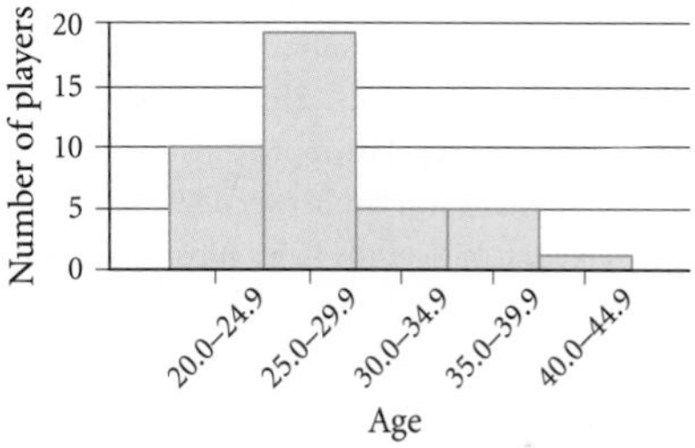

(e)

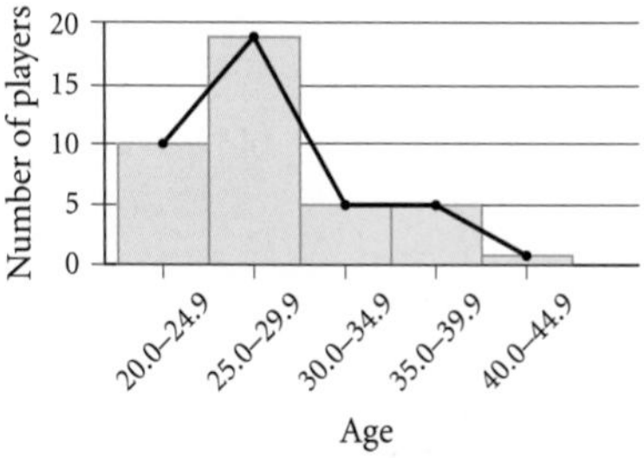

(f) Skewed right

(g)

Class	Frequency	Cumulative Frequency
20.0–24.9	10	10
25.0–29.9	19	29
30.0–34.9	5	34
35.0–39.9	5	39
40.0–44.9	1	40

(h)

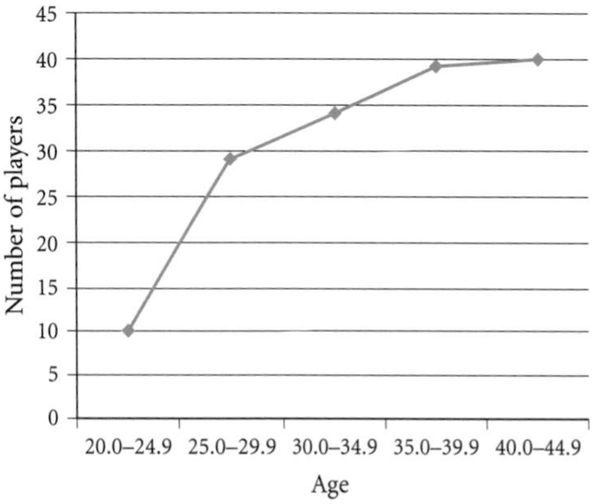

25. (a)

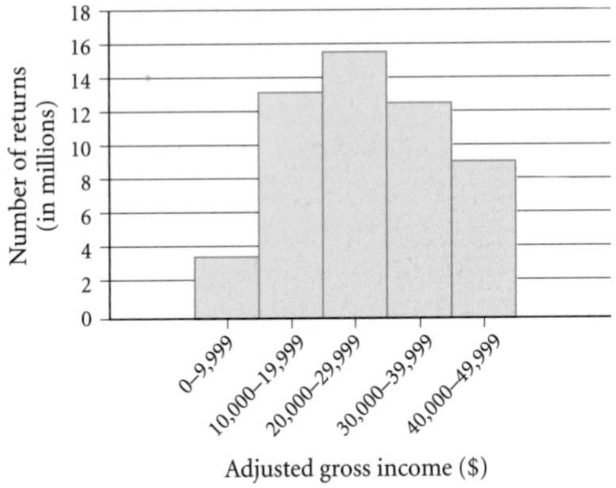

(b)

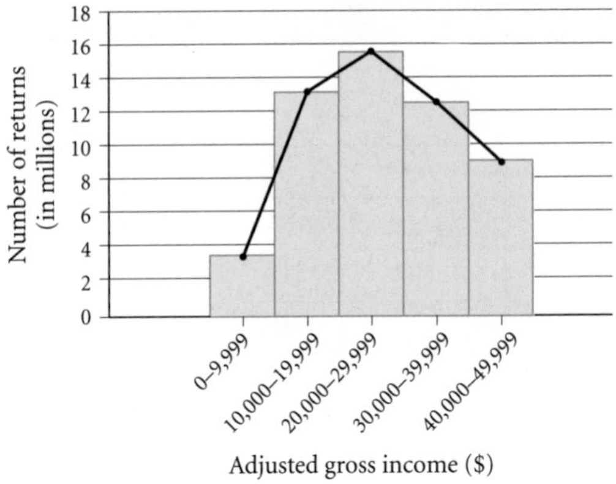

27. (a) Mean: 5.7273 (b) Median: 5 (c) Mode: 0, 4, 8 and 10 (d) Range: 12 (e) Standard deviation: 4.149 **29.** (a) Mean: 16.2 (b) Median: (c) Mode: 7 (d) Range: 98 (e) Standard deviation: 29.5515 **31.** (a) Mean: 7 (b) Median: 7 (c) Mode: 7 (d) Range: 11 (e) Standard deviation: 3.6515 **33.** (a) Answers may vary. We assume they are a sample of Joe's scores calculating parts (b) and (c). (b) Joe's mean score is 75.57. (c) The standard deviation of Joe's scores is 2.99. **35.** (a) The approximate mean age of a female in 2009 was 38.2 years. (b) The approximate median age of a female in 2009 was 38.1 years. (c) The approximate standard deviation of the ages of females in 2009 was 23.3 years. **37.** (a) 441; 759 (b) Approximately 95% of the lightbulbs will last between 494 and 706 hours. (c) About 81.5% of the lightbulbs will last between 547 and 706 hours. (d) The company expects to replace 0.15% of the lightbulbs. **39.** We expect at least 75%, or 750 jars, to have between 11.9 and 12.1 ounces of jam. **41.** The probability a bag weighs less than 9.5 or more than 10.5 pounds is less than or equal to 0.25. **43.** $Z = -0.667$ **45.** $Z = 1.4$ **47.** $Z = 1.66$ **49.** $A = 0.0855$ **51.** $A = 0.7555$ **53.** (a) 68.26% of the scores are between 20 and 30. (b) 2.28% of the scores are above 35. **55** 0.17% of the dogs will die before reaching the age of 10 years, 4 months. **57.** Bob scored equally well on both exams. **59.** There is a probability of 0.95 that this week's production will be between 30 and 50. **61.** The probability of obtaining more than 160 positive results is approximately 0.0008. **63.** The probability is approximately 0.74 that the gate will fail to open between 20 and 30 times in the next 500 attempts.

Mathematical Questions from Professional Exams (p. 574)

1. e **2.** b **3.** c

Exercise 10.1 (p. 584)

5. False   **6.** True   **7.** $1 \times m$ **8.** $v^{(k-1)}; v^{(0)}$ **9.** (a) The entry represents the probability that an object in state 2 will move to state 1.

(b) $v^{(1)} = \begin{bmatrix} \frac{1}{3} & \frac{2}{3} \end{bmatrix}$, $v^{(2)} = \begin{bmatrix} \frac{5}{18} & \frac{13}{18} \end{bmatrix}$ **(c)** $v^{(1)} = \begin{bmatrix} \frac{1}{4} & \frac{3}{4} \end{bmatrix}$, $v^{(2)} = \begin{bmatrix} \frac{13}{48} & \frac{35}{48} \end{bmatrix}$ **11.** $v^{(2)} = \begin{bmatrix} \frac{157}{576} & \frac{419}{576} \end{bmatrix}$ **13.** $v^{(1)} = [0.525 \quad 0.15 \quad 0.325]$

15. $a = 0.4, b = 0.1, c = 1$ **17.** $v^{(5)} = [0.504 \quad 0.496]$ After 5 years, 50.4% of the residents live in the city and 49.6% live in the suburbs.

19. (a) This is a Markov chain because it represents a sequence of experiments each of which results in one of two states and the probability of being in a particular state depends only on the previous state.

(b) $P = \begin{matrix} & R & C \\ R & \\ C & \end{matrix} \begin{bmatrix} 0.90 & 0.10 \\ 0.05 & 0.95 \end{bmatrix}$ **(c)** $P^2 = \begin{bmatrix} 0.815 & 0.185 \\ 0.0925 & 0.9075 \end{bmatrix}$, $P^3 = \begin{bmatrix} 0.74275 & 0.25725 \\ 0.128625 & 0.871375 \end{bmatrix}$

21. (a) This is a Markov chain because it represents a sequence of experiments each of which results in one of nine states and the probability of being in a particular state depends only on the previous state.

23. 57% of wine drinkers will be drinking Pinot Grigio after 2 months.

25. $v^{(10)} = [0.3200 \quad 0.2892 \quad 0.1631 \quad 0.2277]$

27. (a)

$$P = \begin{bmatrix} \frac{1}{2} & 0 & 0 & \frac{1}{2} & 0 & 0 \\ 0 & \frac{1}{2} & 0 & 0 & \frac{1}{2} & 0 \\ 0 & 0 & \frac{1}{2} & 0 & 0 & \frac{1}{2} \\ \frac{1}{2} & 0 & 0 & \frac{1}{2} & 0 & 0 \\ 0 & 0 & 0 & 0 & 0 & 1 \\ 0 & 0 & 0 & 0 & 0 & 1 \end{bmatrix}$$

(b) $v^{(0)} = [0 \quad 1 \quad 0 \quad 0 \quad 0 \quad 0]$

(c) $v^{(10)} = [0 \quad 0.001 \quad 0 \quad 0 \quad 0.001 \quad 0.998]$

(d) The mouse is most likely in room 6.

(b)

$$P = \begin{bmatrix} \frac{1}{2} & 0 & 0 & \frac{1}{2} & 0 & 0 & 0 & 0 & 0 \\ 0 & \frac{1}{2} & 0 & 0 & \frac{1}{2} & 0 & 0 & 0 & 0 \\ 0 & 0 & \frac{1}{2} & 0 & 0 & \frac{1}{2} & 0 & 0 & 0 \\ \frac{1}{3} & 0 & 0 & \frac{1}{3} & 0 & 0 & \frac{1}{3} & 0 & 0 \\ 0 & \frac{1}{3} & 0 & 0 & \frac{1}{3} & 0 & 0 & \frac{1}{3} & 0 \\ 0 & 0 & 0 & 0 & 0 & 1 & 0 & 0 & 0 \\ 0 & 0 & 0 & 0 & 0 & 0 & 1 & 0 & 0 \\ 0 & 0 & 0 & 0 & 0 & 0 & 0 & 0 & 1 \\ 0 & 0 & 0 & 0 & 0 & 0 & 0 & 0 & 1 \end{bmatrix}$$

29. $uA = [u_1 a_{11} + u_2 a_{21} \quad u_1 a_{12} + u_2 a_{22}]$
$u_1 a_{11} + u_2 a_{21} + u_1 a_{12} + u_2 a_{22} = u_1(a_{11} + a_{12}) + u_2(a_{21} + a_{22})$
$= u_1(1) + u_2(1)$
$= u_1 + u_2 = 1$

31. To be a transition matrix, all entries must be between 0 and 1, inclusive, and the sum of the entries in every row must equal 1.

33. If A is a transition matrix, so is A^2 and A^3.

Exercise 10.2 (p. 597)

3. False   **4.** True   **5.** No, when you multiply row 2 by column 1 you will always get a 0. So $p_{21} = 0$ for every power of P.   **7.** No, when you multiply row 1 by column 2 you will always get a 0. So $p_{12} = 0$ for every power of P.

9. Yes, because $P^2 = \begin{bmatrix} \frac{7}{36} & \frac{13}{36} & \frac{4}{9} \\ \frac{1}{8} & \frac{3}{8} & \frac{1}{2} \\ \frac{5}{24} & \frac{1}{3} & \frac{11}{24} \end{bmatrix}$ has all positive entries.   **11.** No, when you multiply row 3 by column 1 you will always get a 0. So $p_{31} = 0$ for every power of P.

13. Yes, because $P^2 = \begin{bmatrix} \frac{1}{3} & \frac{3}{16} & \frac{13}{48} & \frac{5}{24} \\ \frac{1}{3} & \frac{3}{16} & \frac{13}{28} & \frac{5}{24} \\ \frac{5}{18} & \frac{1}{6} & \frac{5}{18} & \frac{5}{18} \\ \frac{1}{3} & \frac{3}{16} & \frac{13}{48} & \frac{5}{24} \end{bmatrix}$ has all positive entries.   **15.** $t = \begin{bmatrix} \frac{3}{7} & \frac{4}{7} \end{bmatrix}$ **17.** $t = \begin{bmatrix} \frac{2}{5} & \frac{3}{5} \end{bmatrix}$ **19.** $t = \begin{bmatrix} \frac{15}{43} & \frac{12}{43} & \frac{16}{43} \end{bmatrix}$

21. (a)
$$P = \begin{array}{c} \\ A \\ B \\ C \end{array}\begin{array}{c} \begin{array}{ccc} A & B & C \end{array} \\ \begin{bmatrix} 0.7 & 0.15 & 0.15 \\ 0.1 & 0.8 & 0.1 \\ 0.2 & 0.2 & 0.6 \end{bmatrix} \end{array}$$
(b) $\mathbf{t} = \begin{bmatrix} \frac{4}{13} & \frac{6}{13} & \frac{3}{13} \end{bmatrix} \approx [0.3077 \quad 0.4615 \quad 0.2308]$. In the long run, the grocers' stock is 30.8% brand A, 46.2% brand B, and 23.1% brand C.

23. (a) The probability the grandson of a Labourite votes Socialist is 0.09. (b) In the long run 55.3% will vote Conservative.

25. (a) The salesperson's movement among the universities can be thought of as a sequence of experiments each of which ends in one of a finite number of states.
$$P = \begin{array}{c} \\ U_1 \\ U_2 \\ U_3 \end{array}\begin{array}{c} \begin{array}{ccc} U_1 & U_2 & U_3 \end{array} \\ \begin{bmatrix} 0 & 1 & 0 \\ \frac{3}{4} & 0 & \frac{1}{4} \\ \frac{3}{4} & \frac{1}{4} & 0 \end{bmatrix} \end{array}$$
(b) After one month, $v^{(1)} = \begin{bmatrix} \frac{1}{2} & \frac{5}{12} & \frac{1}{12} \end{bmatrix}$ (c) In the long run, she sells at U_1 42.9% of the time, at U_2 45.7% of the time, and at U_3 11.4% of the time.

27. $\mathbf{t} = [0.125 \quad 0.875]$ **29.** $\mathbf{t} = \begin{bmatrix} \frac{4}{9} & \frac{2}{9} & \frac{1}{3} \end{bmatrix}$

31. $\mathbf{t} = [0.268 \quad 0.209 \quad 0.206 \quad 0.318]$

Exercise 10.3 (p. 608)

3. True **4.** Four **5.** Yes, state 1 is an absorbing state. **7.** Not absorbing **9.** Yes, states 1 and 3 are absorbing states. **11.** Not absorbing **13.** Not absorbing **15.** Yes, states 2 and 3 are absorbing states.

17. $\left[\begin{array}{cc|c} 1 & 0 & 0 \\ 0 & 1 & 0 \\ \hline \frac{1}{3} & \frac{1}{3} & \frac{1}{3} \end{array}\right]$ **19.** $\left[\begin{array}{cc|cc} 1 & 0 & 0 & 0 \\ 0 & 1 & 0 & 0 \\ \hline \frac{1}{4} & \frac{1}{4} & \frac{1}{4} & \frac{1}{4} \\ 0 & 0 & \frac{1}{2} & \frac{1}{2} \end{array}\right]$ **21.** $\left[\begin{array}{cc|ccc} 1 & 0 & 0 & 0 & 0 \\ 0 & 1 & 0 & 0 & 0 \\ \hline \frac{1}{2} & \frac{1}{4} & 0 & 0 & \frac{1}{4} \\ 0 & 0 & \frac{1}{2} & \frac{1}{2} & 0 \\ 0 & \frac{1}{2} & 0 & 0 & \frac{1}{2} \end{array}\right]$

23. (a) A person starting with \$1.00 is expected to have \$3.00 0.5 time. A person starting with \$2.00 is expected to have \$3.00 one time. (b) A player starting with \$3.00 can expect to play 3 games before absorption. **25.** The probability of accumulating \$3.00 if he starts with \$1.00 is $\frac{4}{19}$. The probability of accumulating \$3.00 if he starts with \$2.00 is $\frac{10}{19}$. **27.** (a) Colleen can expect to place 1.4 wagers before the game ends. (b) The probability Colleen is wiped out is 0.84. (c) The probability Colleen wins the amount needed to buy the car is 0.16. **29.** (a) There are 8 states in the chain, ABC, AB, AC, BC, A, B, C, None. (b) Four of the 8 states are absorbing; they are A, B, C, and None. (c) We would expect about 2.74 rounds of fire. (d) The probability that A survives is 0.192.

31. A decreasing stock should begin to increase in 13.1507 days.

33. (a)
$$\begin{array}{c} \\ \text{R1} \\ \text{R2} \\ \text{R3} \\ \text{R4} \\ \text{R5} \end{array}\begin{array}{c} \begin{array}{ccccc} \text{R1} & \text{R2} & \text{R3} & \text{R4} & \text{R5} \end{array} \\ \begin{bmatrix} 1 & 0 & 0 & 0 & 0 \\ 0.25 & 0.25 & 0.25 & 0 & 0.25 \\ 0.2 & 0.2 & 0.2 & 0.2 & 0.2 \\ 0.25 & 0 & 0.25 & 0.25 & 0.25 \\ 0 & 0 & 0 & 0 & 1 \end{bmatrix} \end{array}$$
(b) Room 1 and Room 5 represent absorbing states for this Markov chain. (c) There is a probability of 0.474 that the mouse has found the cheese in exactly 5 steps.

(d)
$$\begin{array}{c} \\ \text{R1} \\ \text{R5} \\ \text{R2} \\ \text{R3} \\ \text{R4} \end{array}\begin{array}{c} \begin{array}{ccccc} \text{R1} & \text{R5} & \text{R2} & \text{R3} & \text{R4} \end{array} \\ \left[\begin{array}{cc|ccc} 1 & 0 & 0 & 0 & 0 \\ 0 & 1 & 0 & 0 & 0 \\ \hline 0.25 & 0.25 & 0.25 & 0.25 & 0 \\ 0.2 & 0.2 & 0.2 & 0.2 & 0.2 \\ 0.25 & 0.25 & 0 & 0.25 & 0.25 \end{array}\right] \end{array}$$
(e) $I_r = \begin{bmatrix} 1 & 0 \\ 0 & 1 \end{bmatrix}$ $S = \begin{bmatrix} 0.25 & 0.25 \\ 0.2 & 0.2 \\ 0.25 & 0.25 \end{bmatrix}$ $Q = \begin{bmatrix} 0.25 & 0.25 & 0 \\ 0.2 & 0.2 & 0.2 \\ 0 & 0.25 & 0.25 \end{bmatrix}$

(f) $T = \begin{bmatrix} 1.467 & 0.5 & 0.133 \\ 0.4 & 1.5 & 0.4 \\ 0.133 & 0.5 & 1.467 \end{bmatrix}$ (g) $T \cdot S = \begin{bmatrix} 0.5 & 0.5 \\ 0.5 & 0.5 \\ 0.5 & 0.5 \end{bmatrix}$ (h) The mouse can stay out of the trap or away from the cheese for about 2.3 steps, with a 0.5 probability of ending in the trap.

Exercise 10.4 (p. 614)

2. True **3.** Katy's game matrix is

	one finger	two fingers
1 finger	−1	1
2 fingers	1	−1

where the entries are numbers of dimes

5. Katy's game matrix is

	1	4	7
1	−2	5	−8
4	5	−8	11
7	−8	11	−14

where the entries are numbers of dimes

7. The game is strictly determined; the value is −2. **9.** The game is strictly determined; the value is 3. **11.** The game is not strictly determined. **13.** The game is strictly determined; the value is 2. **15.** The game is not strictly determined. **17.** The game is strictly determined if $0 \leq a \leq 3$. **19.** $a \cdot b = 0$ for the game to be strictly determined.

Exercise 10.5 (p. 618)

$E = \$1.42$ **5.** $E = \dfrac{9}{4} = 2.25$ **7.** $E = \dfrac{19}{8} = 2.375$ **9.** $E = \dfrac{17}{9}$ **11.** $E = \dfrac{1}{3}$ **13.** $\begin{array}{c} \\ H \\ T \end{array}\begin{array}{cc} H & T \\ \left[\begin{array}{cc} 1 & -1 \\ -1 & 1 \end{array}\right]\end{array}$ $E = 0$

Exercise 10.6 (p. 625)

1. True

3. The optimal strategy for player I is $P = \begin{bmatrix} \dfrac{3}{4} & \dfrac{1}{4} \end{bmatrix}$. The optimal strategy for player II is $Q = \begin{bmatrix} \dfrac{1}{4} \\ \dfrac{3}{4} \end{bmatrix}$. The expected payoff is $E = \dfrac{7}{4} = 1.75$.

5. The optimal strategy for player I is $P = \begin{bmatrix} \dfrac{1}{6} & \dfrac{5}{6} \end{bmatrix}$. The optimal strategy for player II is $Q = \begin{bmatrix} \dfrac{1}{3} \\ \dfrac{2}{3} \end{bmatrix}$. The expected payoff is $E = \dfrac{1}{3}$.

7. The optimal strategy for player I is $P = \begin{bmatrix} \dfrac{5}{8} & \dfrac{3}{8} \end{bmatrix}$. The optimal strategy for player II is $Q = \begin{bmatrix} \dfrac{5}{8} \\ \dfrac{3}{8} \end{bmatrix}$. The expected payoff is $E = \dfrac{7}{8}$.

9. (a) The optimal strategy for the Democrat is to spend 37.5% of the time on domestic issues and 62.5% on foreign issues. The optimal strategy for the Republican is to spend 50% of the time on domestic issues and 50% of the time on foreign issues. **(b)** The expected payoff is $E = 1.5$, so the Democrat gains 1.5 units by employing the optimal strategy. **11.** The optimal strategy for the spy is to try the deserted exit 8.5% of the time and try the heavily used exit 91.5% of the time. The optimal strategy for the spy's opponent is to wait at the deserted exit 22.5% of the time and wait at the heavily used exit 77.5% of the time. The expected payoff is $E = \dfrac{50}{71} \approx 0.704$, favoring the spy.

Review Exercises (p. 628)

1. Not regular. **3.** Not regular. **5.** Yes, because $P^3 = \begin{bmatrix} \dfrac{5}{12} & \dfrac{77}{288} & \dfrac{91}{288} \\ \dfrac{1}{3} & \dfrac{5}{12} & \dfrac{1}{4} \\ \dfrac{15}{64} & \dfrac{455}{1536} & \dfrac{721}{1536} \end{bmatrix}$ **7.** $t = \begin{bmatrix} \dfrac{4}{7} & \dfrac{3}{7} \end{bmatrix}$ **9.** $t = \begin{bmatrix} \dfrac{3}{8} & \dfrac{1}{4} & \dfrac{3}{8} \end{bmatrix}$

11. $t = \begin{bmatrix} \dfrac{48}{79} & \dfrac{10}{79} & \dfrac{21}{79} \end{bmatrix} \approx \begin{bmatrix} 0.608 & 0.127 & 0.266 \end{bmatrix}$

13. (a) The situation forms a Markov chain because the shifts in market shares can be thought of as a sequence of experiments each of which results in one of a finite number of states.

$$P = \begin{array}{c} A \\ B \\ C \end{array}\begin{array}{ccc} A & B & C \\ \left[\begin{array}{ccc} 0.5 & 0.2 & 0.3 \\ 0.4 & 0.4 & 0.2 \\ 0.5 & 0.25 & 0.25 \end{array}\right]\end{array}$$

(b) After one year, A will have 46.7% of the market, B will have 28.3% of the market, and C will have 25% of the market.
(c) After two years, A will have 47.2% of the market, B will have 26.9% of the market, and C will have 25.9% of the market.
(d) In the long run, A will have 47.3% of the market, B will have 26.6% of the market, and C will have 26.0% of the market.

15. (a) The Markov chain is not absorbing.

17. (a) The Markov chain is absorbing.
(b) The absorbing state is state 2.

(c)
$$P = \begin{array}{c} \\ 2 \\ \text{State } 1 \\ 3 \end{array}\begin{array}{ccc} & \text{State} & \\ 2 & 1 & 3 \\ \left[\begin{array}{c:cc} 1 & 0 & 0 \\ \hdashline \dfrac{1}{3} & 0 & \dfrac{2}{3} \\ \dfrac{1}{4} & \dfrac{3}{8} & \dfrac{3}{8} \end{array}\right]\end{array}$$

19. (a) The Markov chain is not absorbing.

21. **(a)** The Markov chain is absorbing.

(b) The absorbing states are states 1 and 4.

(c)
$$\begin{array}{cc|cc:cc|} & & \multicolumn{4}{c}{\text{State}} \\ & & 1 & 4 & 2 & 3 \\ \hline & 1 & 1 & 0 & 0 & 0 \\ \text{State} & 4 & 0 & 1 & 0 & 0 \\ \hdashline & 2 & 0.3 & 0.1 & 0.5 & 0.1 \\ & 3 & 0.25 & 0.2 & 0.35 & 0.2 \end{array}$$

23. **(a)**
$$P = \begin{array}{c} \\ 0 \\ 1 \\ 2 \\ 3 \\ 4 \\ 5 \end{array}\begin{array}{c} \begin{array}{cccccc} 0 & 1 & 2 & 3 & 4 & 5 \end{array} \\ \begin{bmatrix} 1 & 0 & 0 & 0 & 0 & 0 \\ 0.55 & 0 & 0.45 & 0 & 0 & 0 \\ 0 & 0.55 & 0 & 0.45 & 0 & 0 \\ 0 & 0 & 0.55 & 0 & 0.45 & 0 \\ 0 & 0 & 0 & 0.55 & 0 & 0.45 \\ 0 & 0 & 0 & 0 & 0 & 1 \end{bmatrix} \end{array}$$

(b) Given that the man started with \$2.00, on the average the process will be in state one 1.298 times; in state two 2.361 times in state three 1.412 times and in state four 0.635 time.

(c) The expected length of the game is 5.71 bets.

(d) The probability the man loses all his money is 0.714. The probability he wins \$5 is 0.286.

25. The game is not strictly determined. **27.** The game is strictly determined; the value of the game is 9. **29.** The game is strictly determined. The value of the game is 12. **31.** $E = \frac{1}{3}$ **33.** $E = 1.75$ **35.** $E = \frac{4}{3}$ **37.** The optimal strategy for player I is $P = \begin{bmatrix} \frac{1}{2} & \frac{1}{2} \end{bmatrix}$. The optimal strategy for player II is $Q = \begin{bmatrix} \frac{1}{2} \\ \frac{1}{2} \end{bmatrix}$. **39.** **(a)** The investor should invest in A 41.9% of the time and invest in B 58.1% of the time. **(b)** The percentage gain is 8.37%.

41. The builder should use 60% of the land for the shopping center and 40% of the land for the houses.

CHAPTER 11 Logic and Logic Circuits

Exercise 11.1 (p. 639)

1. Proposition **2.** $p \wedge q$ **3.** False **4.** True **5.** Proposition **7.** Not a proposition **9.** Proposition **11.** Proposition **13.** A fox is not an animal. **15.** I am not buying stocks. **17.** Someone wants to buy my house. **19.** Everybody has a car. **21.** John is an economics major or John is a sociology minor (or both). **23.** John is an economics major and a sociology minor. **25.** John is not an economics major or John is not a sociology minor (or both). **27.** John is not an economics major or John is sociology minor (or both).

Exercise 11.2 (p. 647)

3. True **4.** $p \wedge q \equiv q \wedge p$; $p \vee q \equiv q \vee p$ **5.** $p \wedge p \equiv p$; $p \vee p \equiv p$ **6.** False

7.

p	q	$\sim q$	$p \vee \sim q$
T	T	F	T
T	F	T	T
F	T	F	F
F	F	T	T

9.

p	q	$\sim p$	$\sim q$	$\sim p \wedge \sim q$
T	T	F	F	F
T	F	F	T	F
F	T	T	F	F
F	F	T	T	T

11.

p	q	$\sim p$	$\sim p \wedge q$	$\sim(\sim p \wedge q)$
T	T	F	F	T
T	F	F	F	T
F	T	T	T	F
F	F	T	F	T

13.

p	q	$\sim p$	$\sim q$	$\sim p \vee \sim q$	$\sim(\sim p \vee \sim q)$
T	T	F	F	F	T
T	F	F	T	T	F
F	T	T	F	T	F
F	F	T	T	T	F

15.

p	q	$\sim q$	$p \vee \sim q$	$(p \vee \sim q) \wedge p$
T	T	F	T	T
T	F	T	T	T
F	T	F	F	F
F	F	T	T	F

17.

p	q	$\sim q$	$p \underline{\vee} q$	$p \wedge \sim q$	$(p \underline{\vee} q) \wedge (p \wedge \sim q)$
T	T	F	F	F	F
T	F	T	T	T	T
F	T	F	T	F	F
F	F	T	F	F	F

19.

p	q	$\sim p$	$\sim q$	$p \wedge q$	$\sim p \wedge \sim q$	$(p \wedge q) \vee (\sim p \wedge \sim q)$
T	T	F	F	T	F	T
T	F	F	T	F	F	F
F	T	T	F	F	F	F
F	F	T	T	F	T	T

21.

p	q	r	$\sim q$	$p \wedge \sim q$	$(p \wedge \sim q) \underline{\vee} r$
T	T	T	F	F	T
T	T	F	F	F	F
T	F	T	T	T	F
T	F	F	T	T	T
F	T	T	F	F	T
F	T	F	F	F	F
F	F	T	T	F	T
F	F	F	T	F	F

23.

p	q	$\sim p$	$q \wedge \sim p$	$p \wedge (q \wedge \sim p)$
T	T	F	F	F
T	F	F	F	F
F	T	T	T	F
F	F	T	F	F

25.

p	q	$\sim p$	$\sim q$	$p \wedge q$	$\sim p \wedge \sim q$	$(p \wedge q) \vee (\sim p \wedge \sim q)$	$[(p \wedge q) \vee (\sim p \wedge \sim q)] \wedge p$
T	T	F	F	T	F	T	T
T	F	F	T	F	F	F	F
F	T	T	F	F	F	F	F
F	F	T	T	F	T	T	F

27.

p	$p \wedge p$	$p \vee p$
T	T	T
F	F	F

29.

p	q	r	$p \wedge q$	$(p \wedge q) \wedge r$	$q \wedge r$	$p \wedge (q \wedge r)$	$(p \vee q)$	$(p \vee q) \vee r$	$q \vee r$	$p \vee (q \vee r)$
T	T	T	T	T	T	T	T	T	T	T
T	T	F	T	F	F	F	T	T	T	T
T	F	T	F	F	F	F	T	T	T	T
T	F	F	F	F	F	F	T	T	F	T
F	T	T	F	F	T	F	T	T	T	T
F	T	F	F	F	F	F	T	T	T	T
F	F	T	F	F	F	F	F	T	T	T
F	F	F	F	F	F	F	F	F	F	F

31.

p	q	$p \wedge q$	$p \vee q$	$p \vee (p \wedge q)$	$p \wedge (p \vee q)$
T	T	T	T	T	T
T	F	F	T	T	T
F	T	F	T	F	F
F	F	F	F	F	F

33.

p	q	$\sim q$	$\sim q \vee q$	$p \wedge (\sim q \vee q)$
T	T	F	T	T
T	F	T	T	T
F	T	F	T	F
F	F	T	T	F

35.

p	$\sim p$	$\sim(\sim p)$
T	F	T
F	T	F

37. The compound proposition, "Smith is an ex-convict and Smith is rehabilitated," is equivalent to the compound proposition, "Smith is rehabilitated and Smith is an ex-convict." The compound proposition, "Smith is an ex-convict or Smith is rehabilitated" is equivalent to the compound proposition, "Smith is rehabilitated or Smith is an ex-convict."

39. $(p \vee q) \wedge r \equiv r \wedge (p \vee q)$ (commutative property)

$\equiv (r \wedge p) \vee (r \wedge q)$ (distributive property)

$\equiv (p \wedge r) \vee (q \wedge r)$ (commutative property)

41. Mike cannot hit the ball well or he cannot pitch strikes.

43. The baby is not crying and the baby is not talking all the time.

Exercise 11.3 (p. 654)

1. Hypothesis; conclusion **2.** Tautology **3.** False **4.** True **5.** Converse: $q \Rightarrow \sim p$; contrapositive: $\sim q \Rightarrow p$; inverse: $p \Rightarrow \sim q$ **7.** Converse: $\sim p \Rightarrow \sim q$; contrapositive: $p \Rightarrow q$; inverse: $q \Rightarrow p$ **9.** Converse: If the grass is wet, then it is raining. Contrapositive: If the grass is not wet, then it is not raining. Inverse: If it is not raining, then the grass is not wet. **11.** Converse: If it is not cloudy, then it is not raining. Contrapositive: If it is cloudy, then it is raining. Inverse: If it is raining, then it is cloudy. **13.** Converse: If it is cloudy, then it is raining. Contrapositive: If it is not cloudy, then it is not raining. Inverse: If it is not raining, then it is not cloudy.

15.

p	q	$\sim p$	$p \wedge q$	$\sim p \vee (p \wedge q)$
T	T	F	T	T
T	F	F	F	F
F	T	T	F	T
F	F	T	F	T

17.

p	q	$\sim p$	$\sim p \wedge q$	$p \vee (\sim p \wedge q)$
T	T	F	F	T
T	F	F	F	T
F	T	T	T	T
F	F	T	F	F

19.

p	q	$\sim p$	$\sim p \Rightarrow q$
T	T	F	T
T	F	F	T
F	T	T	T
F	F	T	F

21.

p	$\sim p$	$\sim p \vee p$
T	F	T
F	T	T

23.

p	q	$p \Rightarrow q$	$p \wedge (p \Rightarrow q)$
T	T	T	T
T	F	F	F
F	T	T	F
F	F	T	F

25.

p	q	r	$p \wedge q$	$q \wedge r$	$(p \wedge q) \wedge r$	$p \wedge (q \wedge r)$	$p \wedge (q \wedge r) \Leftrightarrow (p \wedge q) \wedge r$
T	T	T	T	T	T	T	T
T	T	F	T	F	F	F	T
T	F	T	F	F	F	F	T
T	F	F	F	F	F	F	T
F	T	T	F	T	F	F	T
F	T	F	F	F	F	F	T
F	F	T	F	F	F	F	T
F	F	F	F	F	F	F	T

27.

p	q	$p \vee q$	$p \wedge (p \vee q)$	$p \wedge (p \vee q) \Leftrightarrow p$
T	T	T	T	T
T	F	T	T	T
F	T	T	F	T
F	F	F	F	T

29. $p \Rightarrow q$ **31.** $\sim q \Leftrightarrow \sim p$ **33.** $q \Rightarrow p$

35. $p \Rightarrow q \equiv \sim p \vee q$ (Hint)

$p \Rightarrow q \equiv q \vee \sim p$ (Commutative property)

$p \Rightarrow q \equiv \sim q \Rightarrow \sim p$ (Hint)

37. (a)

p	q	r	~q	~r	p ∧ q	p ∧ ~r	(p ∧ q) ⟹ r	(p ∧ ~r) ⟹ ~q	[(p ∧ q) ⟹ r] ⟺ [(p ∧ ~r) ⟹ ~q]
T	T	T	F	F	T	F	T	T	T
T	T	F	F	T	T	T	F	F	T
T	F	T	T	F	F	F	T	T	T
T	F	F	T	T	F	T	T	T	T
F	T	T	F	F	F	F	T	T	T
F	T	F	F	T	F	F	T	T	T
F	F	T	T	F	F	F	T	T	T
F	F	F	T	T	F	F	T	T	T

(b) $(p \wedge q) \Rightarrow r \equiv \sim(p \wedge q) \vee r$

$(p \wedge q) \Rightarrow r \equiv (\sim p \vee \sim q) \vee r$ (De Morgan's property)

$(p \wedge q) \Rightarrow r \equiv \sim p \vee (\sim q \vee r)$ (Associative property)

$(p \wedge q) \Rightarrow r \equiv \sim p \vee (r \vee \sim q)$ (Commutative property)

$(p \wedge q) \Rightarrow r \equiv (\sim p \vee r) \vee \sim q$ (Associative property)

$(p \wedge q) \Rightarrow r \equiv \sim(p \wedge \sim r) \vee \sim q$ (De Morgan's property)

$(p \wedge q) \Rightarrow r \equiv (p \wedge \sim r) \Rightarrow \sim q$

Exercise 11.4 (p. 660)

1. Direct; Indirect or Proof by Contradiction   **2.** True

3. Let p and q be the statements:

p: It rains. q: John goes to school.

Prove: $\sim p$ is true.

Direct Proof:

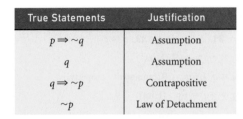

We conclude it is not raining.

Indirect Proof:
Assume $\sim p$ is false.

True Statements	Justification
q	Assumption
$p \Rightarrow \sim q$	Assumption
p	Law of Contradiction
$\sim q^*$	Law of Detachment

The argument resulted in a contradiction, since we are told q is true. So the assumption ~p is false is incorrect, and we have shown ~p to be true. It is not raining.

5. Let p, q, and r be the statements:

> p: Smith is elected president; q: Kuntz is elected secretary;
> r: Brown is elected treasurer.

Prove: $\sim r$ is true.

(a) Direct Proof:

True Statements	Justification
$p \Rightarrow q$	Assumption
$q \Rightarrow \sim r$	Assumption
$p \Rightarrow \sim r$	Law of Syllogism
p	Assumption
$\sim r$	Law of Detachment

Since $\sim r$ is true, Brown is not elected treasurer.

(b) Indirect Proof:

Assume $\sim r$ is false.

True Statements	Justification
r	Law of Contradiction
$p \Rightarrow q$	Assumption
p	Assumption
q	Law of Detachment
$q \Rightarrow \sim r$	Assumption
$\sim r^*$	Law of Detachment

* The argument resulted in a contradiction. So the assumption $\sim r$ is false is incorrect so $\sim r$ is true and we have shown that Brown was not elected treasurer.

7. Invalid. If the hypotheses $p \Rightarrow q$ and $\sim p$ are both true, then p is false. In an implication, if p is false, q can be either true or false so the conclusion, $\sim q$, could be either true or false.   **9.** Valid. Let p: Tami studies, q: Tami fails, and r: Tami plays with dolls too often. We are given $p \Rightarrow \sim q$, $\sim r \Rightarrow p$, and we must show r is true. Using the Law of the Contrapositive we have $q \Rightarrow \sim p$ and $\sim p \Rightarrow r$ are true. Then by the Law of Syllogism, $q \Rightarrow r$. Finally, we are given q. By the Law of Detachment, we conclude r is true.

Exercise 11.5 (p. 665)

1. The output is 1 when (a) both $p = 1$ and $q = 1$ or (b) both $p = 0$ and $q = 0$, or (c) both $p = 0$ and $r = 1$.

3. The output is 1 when p and q are both 1.

5.

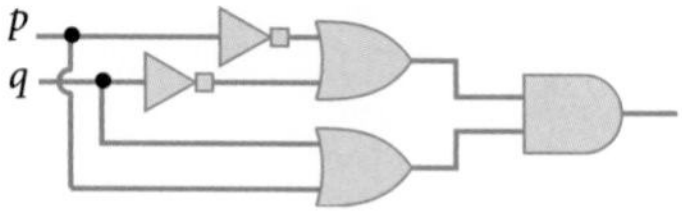

7.

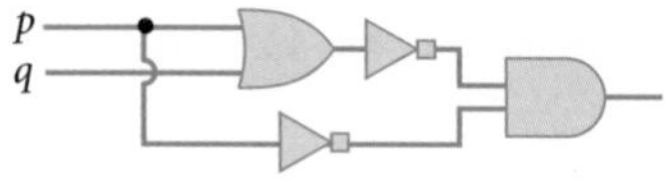

9. (For Problem 1):

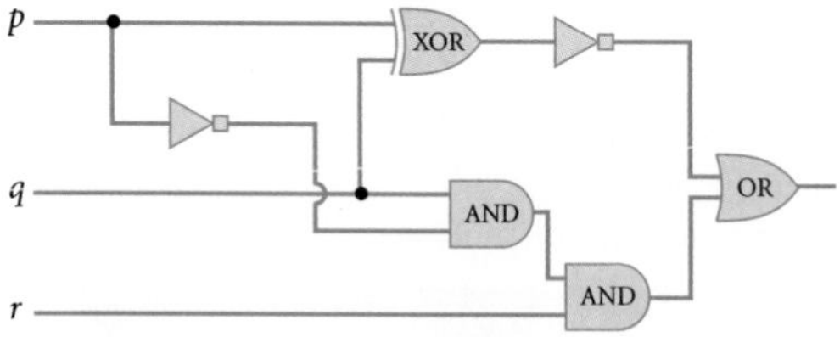

(For Problem 3): $\begin{smallmatrix}p\\q\end{smallmatrix}$ — AND —

(For Problem 5): $\begin{smallmatrix}p\\q\end{smallmatrix}$ — XOR —

(For Problem 7): $\begin{smallmatrix}p\\q\end{smallmatrix}$ — NOR —

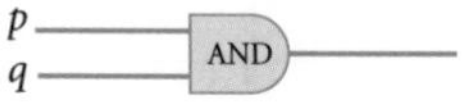

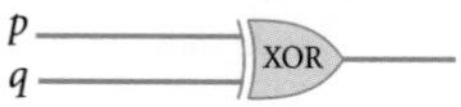

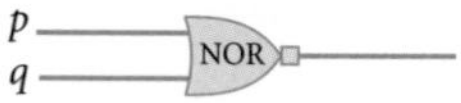

11. The truth table and two possible diagrams for this circuit is either

p	q	$\sim(p \vee q)$
1	1	1
1	0	0
0	1	0
0	0	1

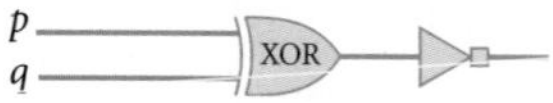

or

p	q	$p \veebar q$
1	1	0
1	0	1
0	1	1
0	0	0

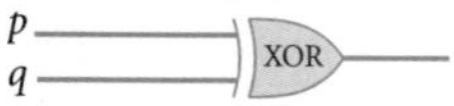

13.

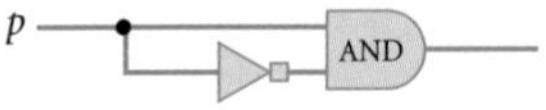

15. $pq \oplus pr \oplus q(\sim r) \equiv pq(r \oplus \sim r) \oplus pr \oplus q(\sim r)$
$\equiv pqr \oplus pq(\sim r) \oplus pr \oplus q(\sim r)$
$\equiv pqr \oplus pr \oplus pq(\sim r) \oplus q(\sim r)$
$\equiv pr(q \oplus 1) \oplus q(\sim r)(p \oplus 1)$
$\equiv pr(1) \oplus q(\sim r)(1)$
$\equiv pr \oplus q(\sim r)$

Review Exercises (p. 666)

1. Proposition **3.** Not a proposition **5.** Proposition **7.** Not a proposition **9.** I go to the math learning center or I complete my math homework. **11.** If I go to the math learning center, then I complete my math homework. **13.** If I don't go to the math learning center, then I don't complete my math homework. **15.** I don't go to the math learning center and I don't complete my math homework. **17.** Nobody is rich. **19.** Either Danny is tall or Mary is not short. **21.**(c) **23.** (a)

25.

p	q	$p \wedge q$	$\sim p$	$(p \wedge q) \vee \sim p$
T	T	T	F	T
T	F	F	F	F
F	T	F	T	T
F	F	F	T	T

27.

p	q	$p \vee q$	$(p \vee q) \wedge p$
T	T	T	T
T	F	T	T
F	T	T	F
F	F	F	F

29. $q \Rightarrow p$ **31.** $p \Leftrightarrow q$ **33.** Define the statements p: The temperature outside is below 30°; q: I wear gloves. **(a)** $p \Rightarrow q$ **(b)** $q \Rightarrow p$; If I wear gloves, then the temperature outside is below 30°. **(c)** $\sim q \Rightarrow \sim p$; If I do not wear gloves, then the temperature outside is not below 30°. **(d)** $\sim p \Rightarrow \sim q$; If the temperature is not below 30°, then I do not wear gloves. **35.** Define the statements p: Stu works on the project; q: Julie helps. **(a)** $q \Rightarrow p$ **(b)** $p \Rightarrow q$; If Stu works on the project, then Julie helps. **(c)** $\sim p \Rightarrow \sim q$; If Stu does not work on the project, then Julie does not help. **(d)** $\sim q \Rightarrow \sim p$; If Julie does not help, then Stu does not work on the project. **37.** Define the statements p: Kurt goes to the club; q: Jessica comes to town. **(a)** $q \Rightarrow p$ **(b)** $p \Rightarrow q$; If Kurt goes to the club, then Jessica comes to town. **(c)** $\sim p \Rightarrow \sim q$; If Kurt does not go to the club, then Jessica does not come to town. **(d)** $\sim q \Rightarrow \sim p$; If Jessica does not come to town, then Kurt does not go to the club. **39.** Define the statements p: Brian comes to the gym; q: Mike works out. **(a)** $q \Rightarrow p$ **(b)** $p \Rightarrow q$; If Brian comes to the gym, then Mike works out. **(c)** $\sim p \Rightarrow \sim q$; If Brian does not come to the gym, then Mike does not work out. **(d)** $\sim q \Rightarrow \sim p$; If Mike does not work out, then Brian does not come to the gym.

41. Define the statements: p: Patrick goes to practice; q: Patrick starts the game. Show that $p \Rightarrow q$ is equivalent to $\sim p \vee q$.

p	q	$\sim p$	$p \Rightarrow q$	$\sim p \vee q$	$p \Rightarrow q \Leftrightarrow (\sim p \vee q)$
T	T	F	T	T	T
T	F	F	F	F	T
F	T	T	T	T	T
F	F	T	T	T	T

43. See the table for Problem 41.

45. Define the statements p: I paint the house, q: I go bowling. Assume the premises $\sim p \Rightarrow q$ and $\sim q$ are true. Show p is true.

Prove: p is true.

(a) Direct Proof:

True Statements	Justification
$\sim p \Rightarrow q$	Assumption
$\sim q \Rightarrow p$	Contrapositive
$\sim q$	Assumption
p	Law of Detachment

So p is true; I paint the house.

(b) Indirect Proof:
Assume p is false.

True Statements	Justification
$\sim q$	Assumption
$\sim p \Rightarrow q$	Assumption
$\sim p$	Law of Contradiction
q*	Law of Detachment

** The proof resulted in a contradiction, so the assumption that p is false is incorrect. We conclude p is true, and I paint the house.*

47. Define the statements p: John is in town, q: Mark gets tickets, and r: We go to the game. Assume the premises $p \Rightarrow q$, $\sim r \Rightarrow \sim q$, and p are true.

Prove: r is true.

(a) Direct Proof:

True Statements	Justification
$p \Rightarrow q$	Assumption
$\sim r \Rightarrow \sim q$	Assumption
$q \Rightarrow r$	Contrapositive
$p \Rightarrow r$	Law of Syllogism
p	Assumption
r	Law of Detachment

So r is true, and we go to the game.

49. Define the statements p: I pay a finance charge, q: My payment is late, r: Colleen sends the mail.

Assume the premises $q \Rightarrow p$, $r \vee q$, and $\sim r$ are true. Prove p is true.

Prove: p is true.

(a) Direct Proof:

True Statements	Justification
$r \vee q$	Assumption
$\sim r$	Assumption
q	A true disjunction has at least one true proposition
$q \Rightarrow p$	Assumption
p	Law of Detachment

So p is true, and I pay a finance charge.

51. Define the statements p: Rob is a bad boy, q: Danny is crying, r: Laura is a good girl.

Assume the premises $p \vee q$, $r \Rightarrow \sim p$, and $\sim q$ are true. We want to prove $\sim r$.

True Statements	Justification
$p \vee q$	Assumption
$\sim q$	Assumption
p	A true disjunction has at least one true proposition
$r \Rightarrow \sim p$	Assumption
$p \Rightarrow \sim r$	Contrapositive
$\sim r$	Law of Detachment

We have shown that $\sim r$ is true. So we conclude: Laura is not a good girl.

(b) Indirect Proof:
Assume r is false.

True Statements	Justification
$\sim r \Rightarrow \sim q$	Assumption
$\sim r$	Law of Contradiction
$\sim q$	Law of Detachment
p	Assumption
$p \Rightarrow q$	Assumption
$\sim q \Rightarrow \sim p$	Contrapositive
$\sim p^*$	Law of Detachment

* The proof resulted in a contradiction, so the assumption that r is false is incorrect. We conclude r is true, and we go to the game.

(b) Indirect Proof:
Assume p is false.

True Statements	Justification
$\sim r$	Assumption
$\sim p$	Law of Contradiction
$q \Rightarrow p$	Assumption
$\sim p \Rightarrow \sim q$	Contrapositive
$\sim q$	Law of Detachment
$r \vee q$	Assumption
q^*	A true disjunction has at least one true proposition

* The proof resulted in a contradiction, so the assumption that p is false is incorrect. We conclude p is true, and I pay a finance charge.

53.

55.

57. $(p \oplus q)[\sim(pq)] = (p \oplus q)(\sim p \oplus \sim q)$

$\quad = p(\sim p) \oplus p(\sim q) \oplus q(\sim p) \oplus q(\sim q)$

$\quad = 0 \oplus p(\sim q) \oplus q(\sim p) \oplus 0$

$\quad = p(\sim q) \oplus (\sim p)q$

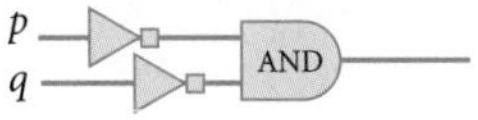

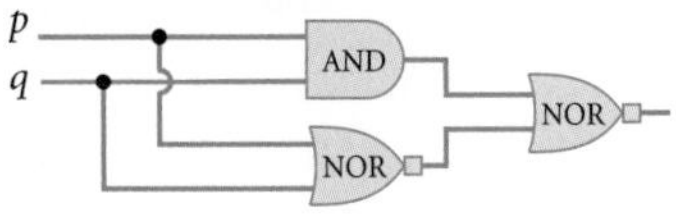

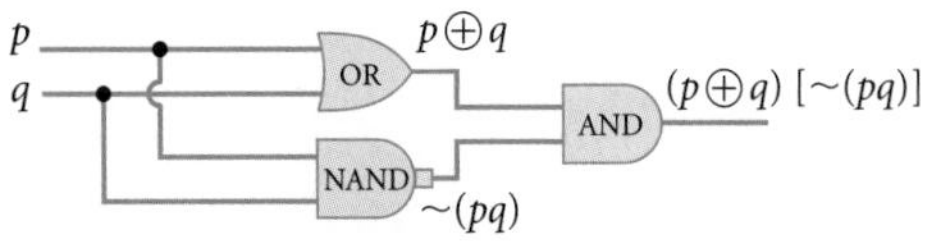

APPENDIX A Review

Exercise A.1 (p. A–14)

1. Rational numbers **2.** 31 **3.** Distributive **4.** $5(x + 3) = 6$ **5.** True **6.** False **7.** False **8.** True **9.** **(a)** 2 and 5 are natural numbers. **(b)** $-6, 2$, and 5 are integers. **(c)** $-6, \frac{1}{2}, 1.333\ldots, 2$, and 5 are rational numbers. **(d)** π is an irrational number. **(e)** All the numbers are real numbers. **11.** **(a)** 1 is a natural number. **(b)** 0 and 1 are integers. **(c)** All the numbers are rational numbers. **(d)** There are no irrational numbers in the set C. **(e)** All the numbers are real numbers. **13.** **(a)** There are no natural numbers in the set E. **(b)** There are no integers in the set E. **(c)** There are no rational numbers in the set E. **(d)** All the numbers are irrational. **(e)** All the numbers are real numbers. **15.** **(a)** 18.953 **(b)** 18.952 **17.** **(a)** 28.653 **(b)** 28.653 **19.** **(a)** 0.063 **(b)** 0.062 **21.** **(a)** 9.999 **(b)** 9.998 **23.** **(a)** 0.429 **(b)** 0.428 **25.** **(a)** 34.733 **(b)** 34.733 **27.** $3 + 2 = 5$ **29.** $x + 2 = 3 \cdot 4$ **31.** $3y = 1 + 2$ **33.** $x - 2 = 6$ **35.** $\frac{x}{2} = 6$ **37.** 7 **39.** 6 **41.** 1 **43.** $\frac{13}{3}$ **45.** -11 **47.** 11 **49.** -4 **51.** 1 **53.** 6 **55.** $\frac{2}{7}$ **57.** $\frac{4}{45}$ **59.** $\frac{23}{20}$ **61.** $\frac{79}{30}$ **63.** $\frac{13}{36}$ **65.** $-\frac{16}{45}$ **67.** $\frac{1}{60}$ **69.** $\frac{15}{22}$ **71.** $6x + 24$ **73.** $x^2 - 4x$ **75.** $x^2 + 6x + 8$ **77.** $x^2 - x - 2$ **79.** $x^2 - 10x + 16$ **81.** $x^2 - 4$ **87.** Subtraction is not commutative. Examples will vary. **89.** Division is not commutative. Examples will vary. **91.** This is true by the symmetric property of real numbers. **93.** All real numbers are either rational or irrational; no real number is both. **95.** $0.9999\ldots = 1$

Exercise A.2 (p. A–25)

1. variable **2.** origin **3.** strict **4.** base; exponent or power **5.** True **6.** True **7.** False **8.** False **9.** $\{4\}$ **10.** False **11.** 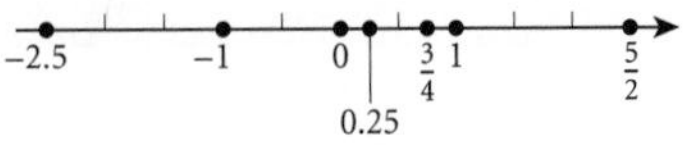

13. $>$ **15.** $>$ **17.** $>$ **19.** $=$ **21.** $<$ **23.** $x > 0$ **25.** $x < 2$ **27.** $x \le 1$ **29.** 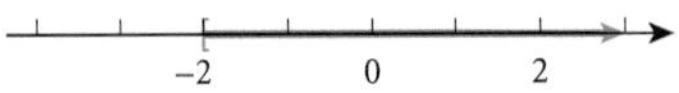

31. 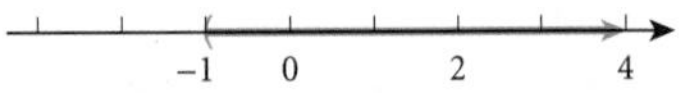

33. 1 **35.** 2 **37.** 6 **39.** 4 **41.** -28 **43.** $\frac{4}{5}$ **45.** 0 **47.** 1 **49.** 5 **51.** 1 **53.** 22 **55.** 2 **57.** (c) $x = 0$ **59.** (a) $x = 3$ **61.** none **63.** (b) $x = 1$, (c) $x = 0$, (d) $x = -1$ **65.** $\{x \mid x \ne 5\}$ **67.** $\{x \mid x \ne -4\}$ **69.** $C = 0°$ **71.** $C = 25°$ **73.** 16 **75.** $\frac{1}{16}$ **77.** $\frac{1}{9}$ **79.** 9 **81.** 5 **83.** 4 **85.** $64x^6$ **87.** $\frac{x^4}{y^2}$ **89.** $\frac{x}{y}$ **91.** -4 **93.** 5 **95.** 4 **97.** 2 **99.** $\sqrt{5}$ **101.** $\frac{1}{2}$ **103.** 81 **105.** 304,006.671 **107.** 0.004 **109.** 481.890 **111.** 0.011 **113.** $\{2\}$ **115.** $\{6\}$ **117.** $\{-1\}$ **119.** $\{-4\}$ **121.** $\{x \mid x \le -3\}$ 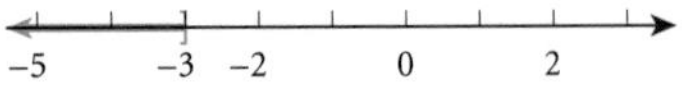

123. $\{x \mid x \ge -1\}$ 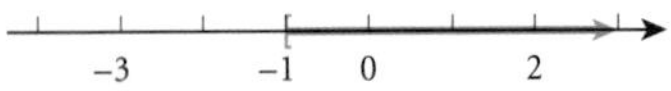

125. $\{x \mid x \ge 1\}$ 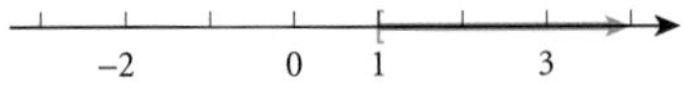

127. $\{x \mid x \le -4\}$ 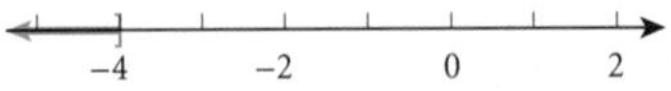

129. $A = l \cdot w$; **131.** $C = \pi \cdot d$; **133.** $A = \frac{\sqrt{3}}{4}x^2$ **135.** $V = \frac{4}{3}\pi r^3$ **137.** $V = x^3$ **139.** **(a)** It costs \$6,000 to produce 1000 watches. **(b)** It costs \$8,000 to produce 2000 watches. **141.** **(a)** $|108 - 110| = |-2| = 2 \le 5$ **(b)** $|104 - 110| = |-6| = 6 > 5$ **143.** **(a)** Yes, $|2.999 - 3| = |-0.001| = 0.001 \le 0.01$. **(b)** No, $|2.89 - 3| = |-0.11| = 0.11 \ge 0.01$. **145.** No, $\frac{1}{3}$ is larger by $0.000333\ldots$. **147.** No.

Exercise A.3 (p. A–33)

3. 3^3 **4.** 2.48 **5.** $\log_{1.8} x = 4$ **6.** 3.238 **7.** 4 **9.** 3 **11.** 2 **13.** 4 **15.** $\frac{1}{64}$ **17.** $\frac{1}{4}$ **19.** **(a)** 11.2116 **(b)** 11.5873 **(c)** 11.6639 **(d)** 11.6648 **21.** 1.4693 **23.** 1.1956 **25.** 0.6587 **27.** 0.9356 **29.** $\log_3 9 = 2$ **31.** $\log_a 1.6 = 2$ **33.** $\log_2 7.2 = x$ **35.** $\log_e 8 = x$ **37.** $2^3 = 8$ **39.** $a^6 = 3$ **41.** $3^x = 2$ **43.** $10^x = 4$ **45.** 0 **47.** 2 **49.** -4 **51.** $\frac{1}{2}$ **53.** 4 **55.** $\frac{1}{2}$ **57.** 0.222 **59.** 13.072 **61.** 81.274 **63.** 23.791 **65.** 55.590 **67.** 1385.002 **69.** 1499.364 **71.** 12,432.323 **73.** 2074.642

Exercise A.4 (p. A–40)

1. 3; 15 **2.** True **3.** 1, 2, 3, 4, 5 **5.** $\frac{1}{3}, \frac{1}{2}, \frac{3}{5}, \frac{2}{3}, \frac{5}{7}$ **7.** $1, -4, 9, -16, 25$ **9.** $\frac{1}{2}, \frac{2}{5}, \frac{2}{7}, \frac{8}{41}, \frac{8}{61}$ **11.** $-\frac{1}{6}, \frac{1}{12}, -\frac{1}{20}, \frac{1}{30}, -\frac{1}{42}$ **13.** $\frac{1}{e}, \frac{2}{e^2}, \frac{3}{e^3}, \frac{4}{e^4}, \frac{5}{e^5}$ **15.** $\frac{n}{n+1}$ **17.** $\frac{1}{2^{n-1}}$ **19.** $(-1)^{n+1}$ **21.** $(-1)^{n+1} \cdot n$ **23.** 1, 3, 5, 7, 9 **25.** $-2, -1, 1, 4, 8$ **27.** 5, 10, 20, 40, 80 **29.** $3, 3, \frac{3}{2}, \frac{1}{2}, \frac{1}{8}$ **31.** 1, 2, 2, 4, 8 **33.** $A, A + d, A + 2d, A + 3d, A + 4d$ **35.** $\sqrt{2}, \sqrt{2 + \sqrt{2}}, \sqrt{2 + \sqrt{2 + \sqrt{2}}}, \sqrt{2 + \sqrt{2 + \sqrt{2 + \sqrt{2}}}}, \sqrt{2 + \sqrt{2 + \sqrt{2 + \sqrt{2 + \sqrt{2}}}}}$

37. (a) $a_1 = 2, r = 2$ (b) $2, 4, 8, 16$ (c) $S_n = 2^{n+1} - 2$ **39.** (a) $a_1 = -\frac{3}{2}, r = \frac{1}{2}$ (b) $-\frac{3}{2}, -\frac{3}{4}, -\frac{3}{8}, -\frac{3}{16}$ (c) $S_n = \frac{3}{2^n} - 3$
41. (a) $a_1 = \frac{1}{4}, r = 2$ (b) $\frac{1}{4}, \frac{1}{2}, 1, 2$ (c) $S_n = 2^{n-2} - \frac{1}{4}$ **43.** (a) $a_1 = 2^{\frac{1}{3}}, r = 2^{\frac{1}{3}}$ (b) $2^{\frac{1}{3}}, 2^{\frac{2}{3}}, 2, 2^{\frac{4}{5}}$ (c) $S_n = 2^{\frac{1}{3}}\left(\frac{1 - 2^{\frac{n}{3}}}{1 - 2^{\frac{1}{3}}}\right)$
45. (a) $a_1 = \frac{1}{2}, r = \frac{3}{2}$ (b) $\frac{1}{2}, \frac{3}{4}, \frac{9}{8}, \frac{27}{16}$ (c) $S_n = -1 + \left(\frac{3}{2}\right)^n$ **47.** After the first payment John owes \$2930.00. **49.** Phil's balance after the first payment is \$18,058.03. **51.** After 7 months there are 21 pairs of mature rabbits. **53.** The sums of the diagonals are 1, 1, 2, 3, 5, 8, 13,. . .. The sums form a Fibonacci sequence.

Section A.5 (p. A–48)

1. 15 **2.** $x^4 + 4x^3y + 6x^2y^2 + 4xy^3 + y^4$ **3.** False **4.** Binomial Theorem **5.** $x^5 + 5x^4y + 10x^3y^2 + 10x^2y^3 + xy^4 + y^5$
7. $x^3 + 9x^2y + 27xy^2 + 27y^3$ **9.** $16x^4 - 32x^3y + 24x^2y^2 - 8xy^3 + y^4$ **11.** The coefficient is 10. **13.** The coefficient is 405. **15.** There are 256 different subsets. **17.** $1.001^5 = 1.00501$ **19.** There are 1023 non-empty subsets. **21.** There are 512 subsets with an odd number of elements.
23. $\binom{10}{7} = \binom{9}{7} + \binom{9}{6} = \left[\binom{8}{7} + \binom{8}{6}\right] + \binom{9}{6} = \left[\binom{7}{7} + \binom{7}{6}\right] + \binom{8}{6} + \binom{9}{6} = \binom{6}{6} + \binom{7}{6} + \binom{8}{6} + \binom{9}{6}$ **25.** $\binom{12}{6}$ **27.** 1

APPENDIX C Graphing Utilities

Exercise C.1 (p. C–2)

1. $(-1, 4)$ quadrant II **3.** $(3, 1)$ quadrant I

5. $X\min = -6$, $X\max = 6$, $X\text{scl} = 2$, $Y\min = -4$, $Y\max = 4$, $Y\text{scl} = 2$

7. $X\min = -6$, $X\max = 6$, $X\text{scl} = 2$, $Y\min = -1$, $Y\max = 3$, $Y\text{scl} = 1$

9. $X\min = 3$, $X\max = 9$, $X\text{scl} = 1$, $Y\min = 2$, $Y\max = 10$, $Y\text{scl} = 2$

11. $X\min = -12$, $X\max = 6$, $X\text{scl} = 1$, $Y\min = -4$, $Y\max = 8$, $Y\text{scl} = 1$

13. $X\min = -30$, $X\max = 50$, $X\text{scl} = 10$, $Y\min = -10$, $Y\max = 100$, $Y\text{scl} = 10$

15. $X\min = -10$, $X\max = 110$, $X\text{scl} = 10$, $Y\min = -20$, $Y\max = 180$, $Y\text{scl} = 20$

Exercise C.2 (p. C–6)

1. (a)
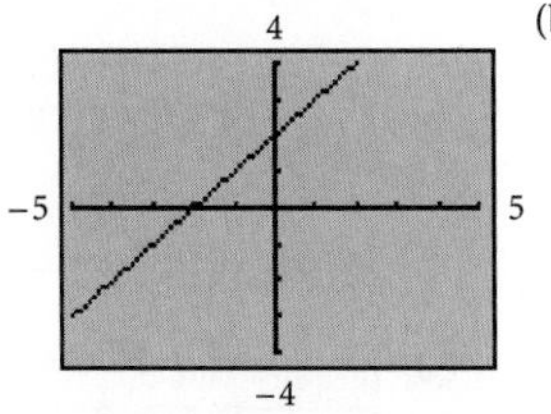

(b)
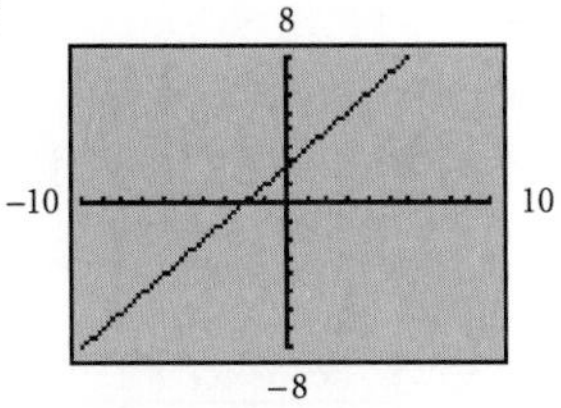

(c)
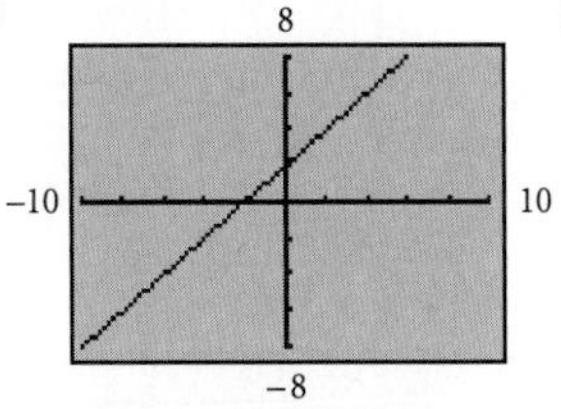

(d)
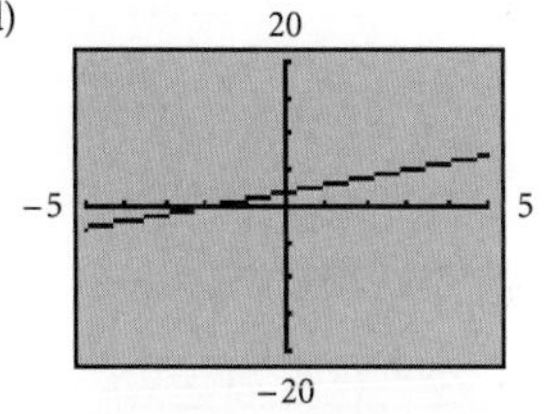

3. (a)
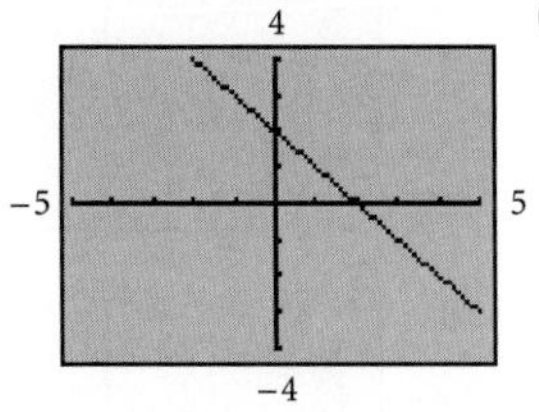

(b)
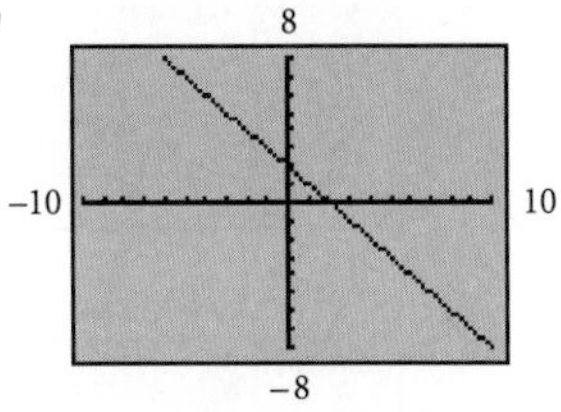

(c)
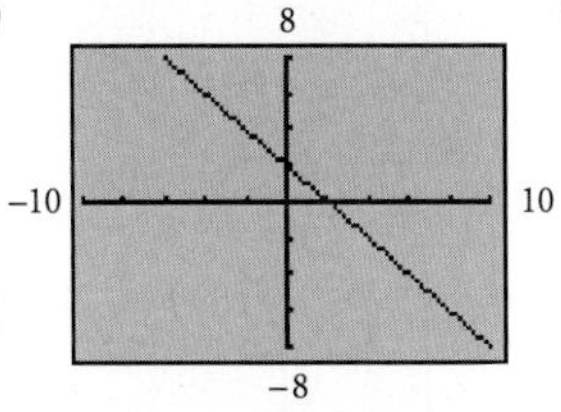

(d)
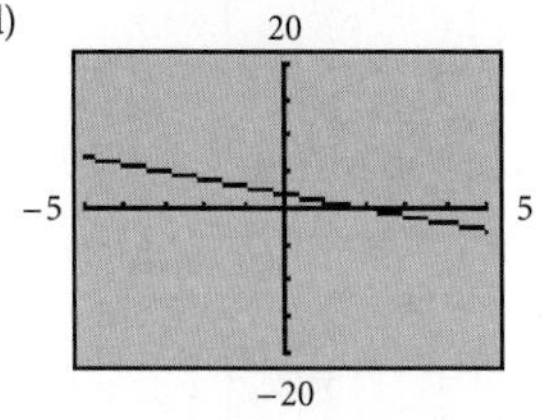

5. (a)
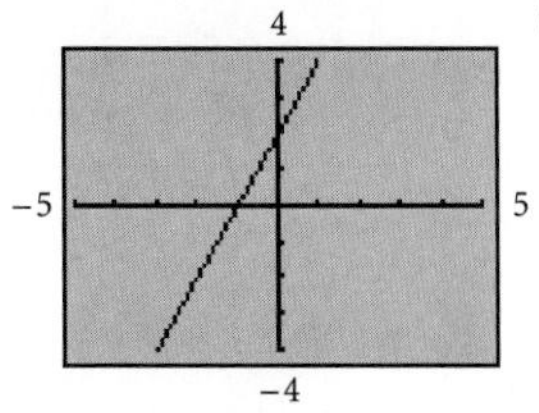

(b)
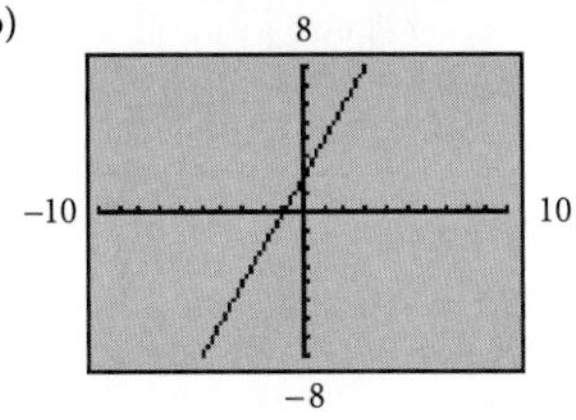

(c)
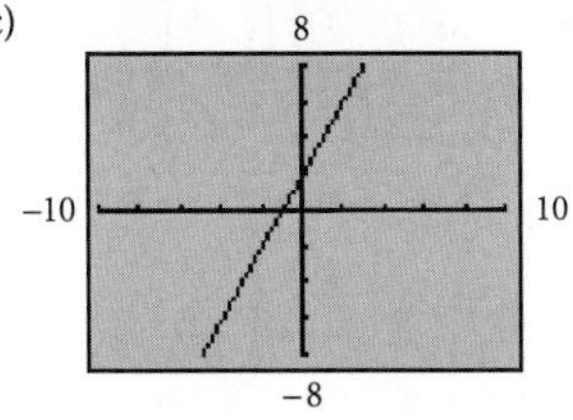

(d)
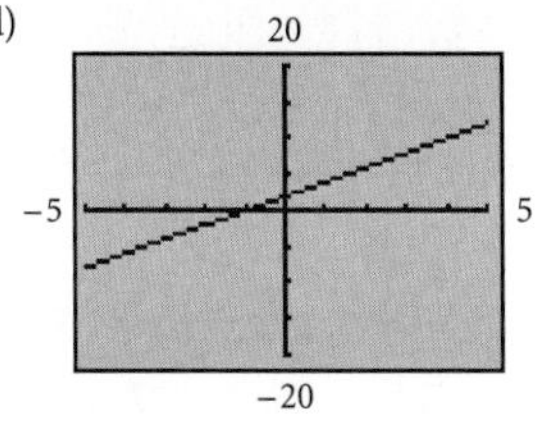

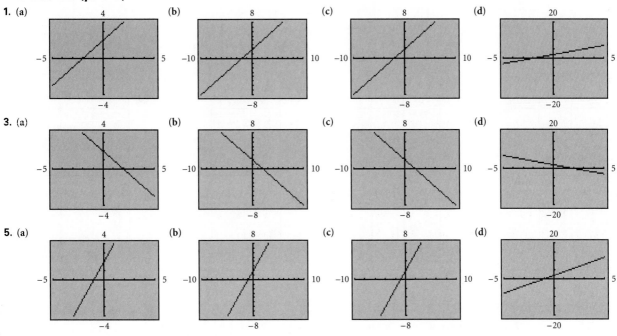

7. (a)
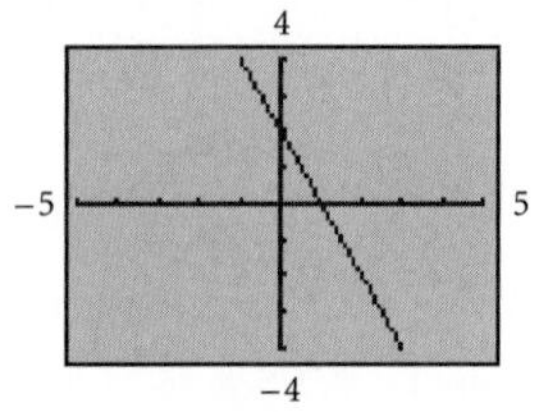

(b)
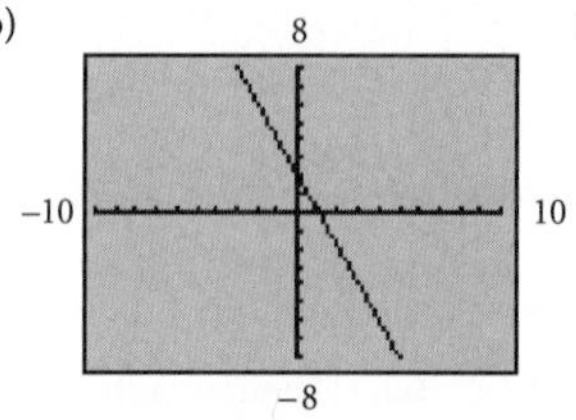

(c)
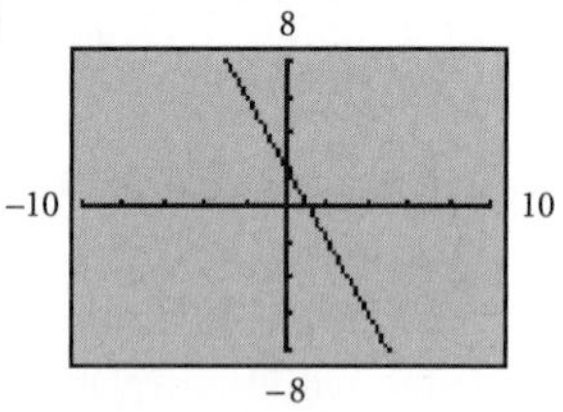

(d)
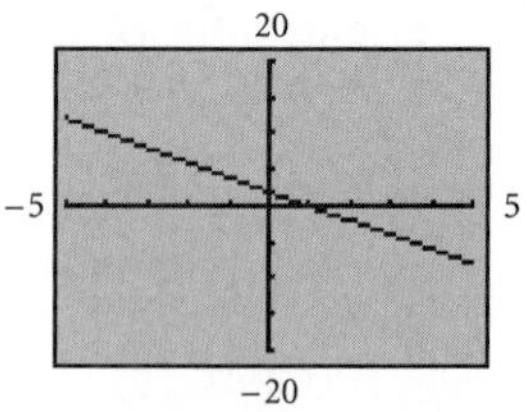

9. (a)
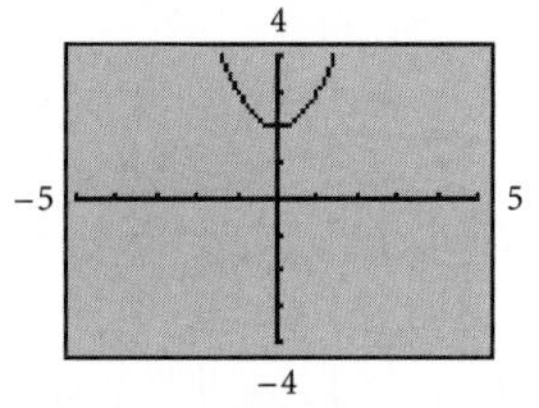

(b)
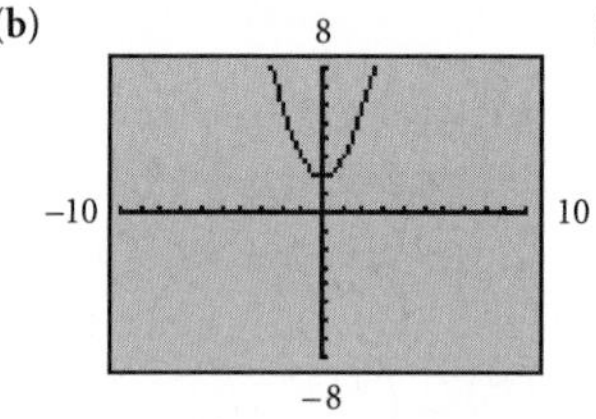

(c)
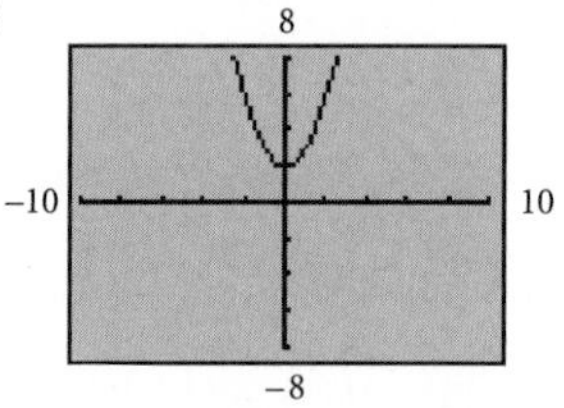

(d)
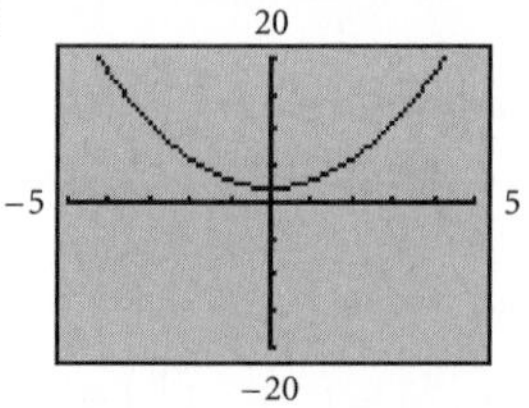

11. (a)
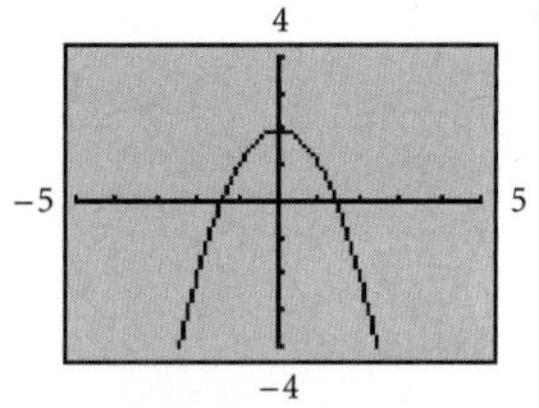

(b)
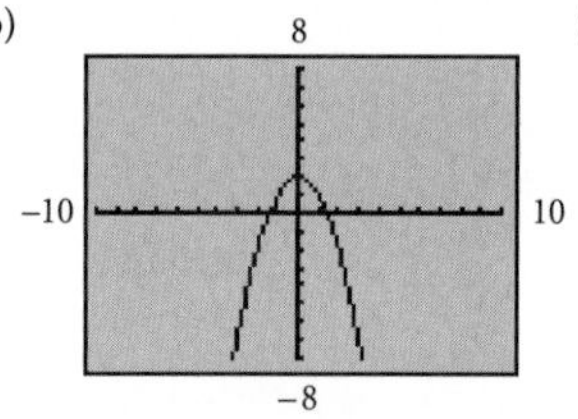

(c)
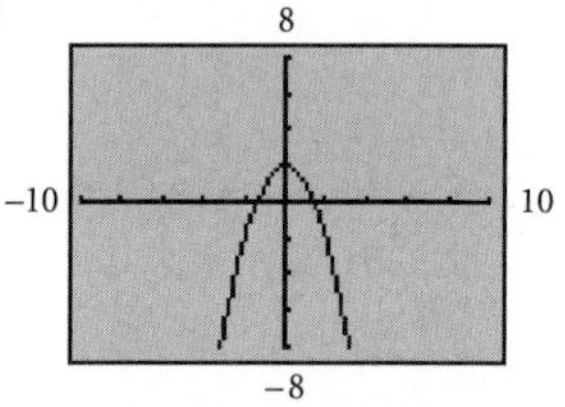

(d)
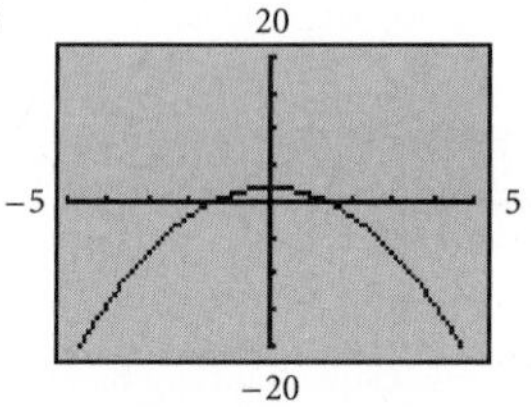

13. (a)
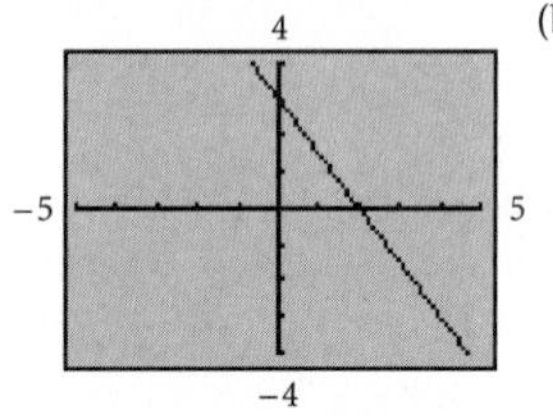

(b)
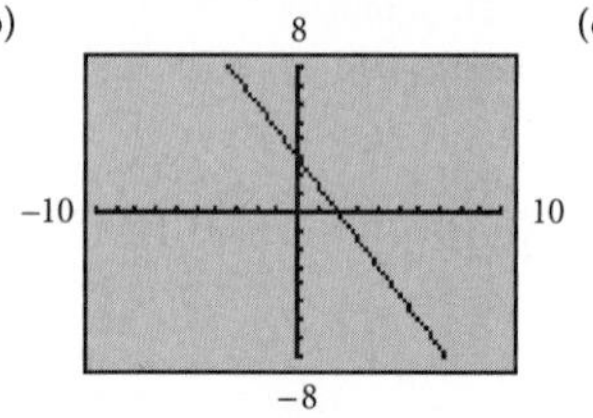

(c)
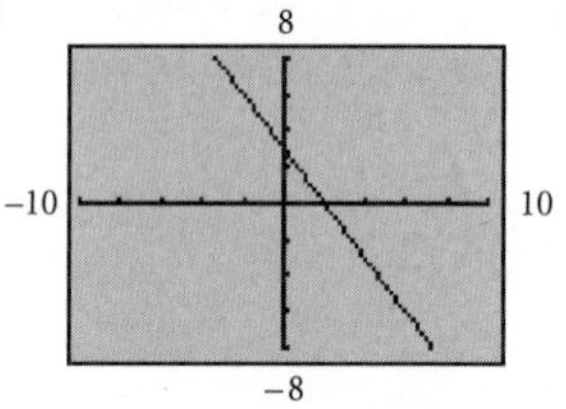

(d)
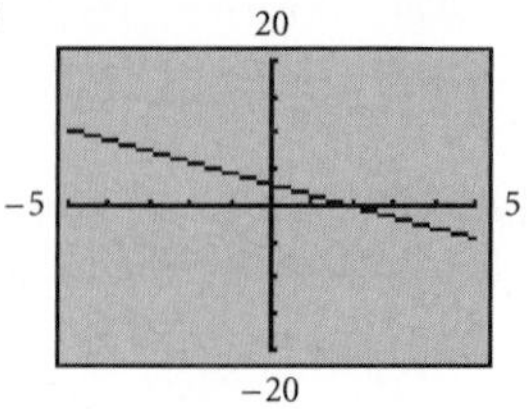

15. (a)
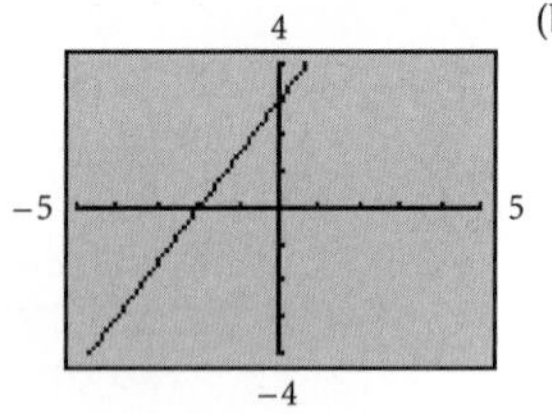

(b)
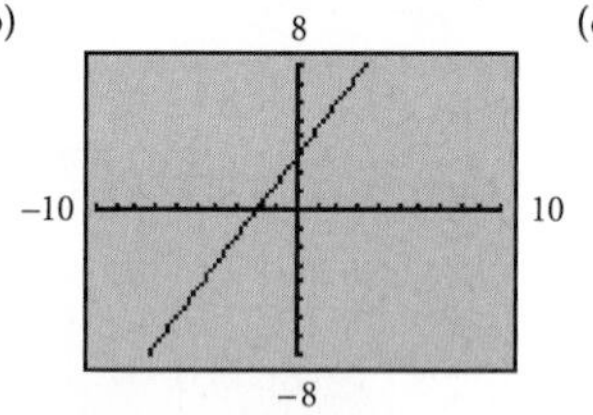

(c)
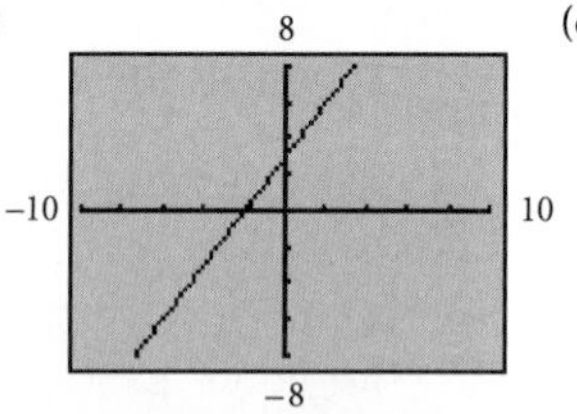

(d)
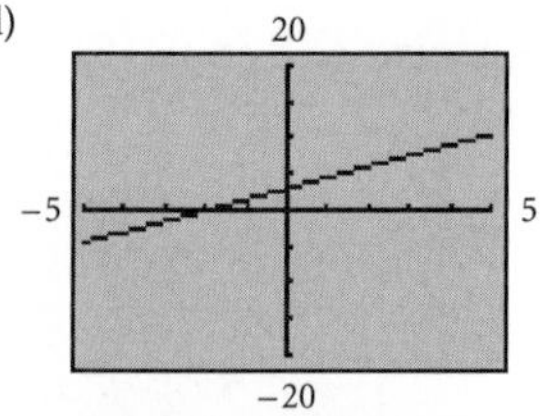

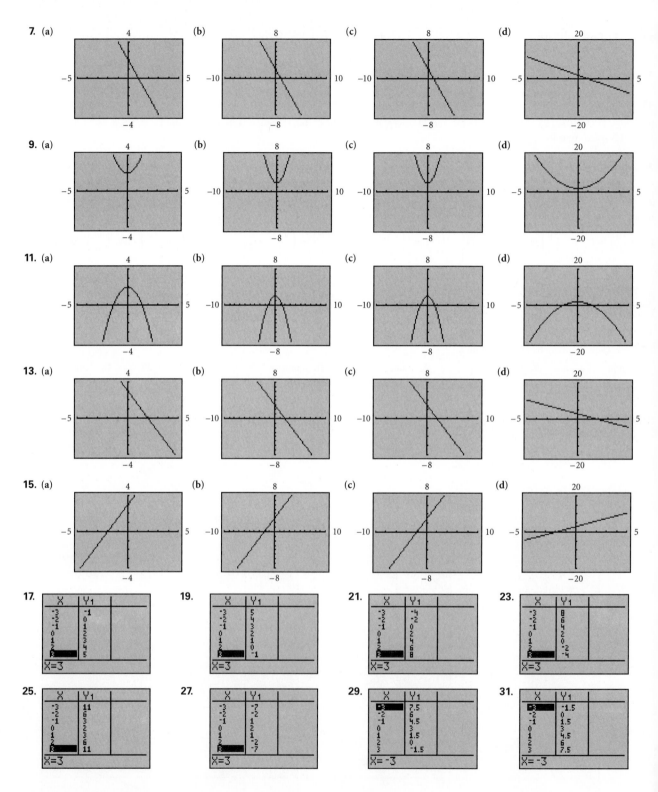

17.

X	Y1
-3	-1
-2	0
-1	1
0	2
1	3
2	4
3	5

X=3

19.

X	Y1
-3	5
-2	4
-1	3
0	2
1	1
2	0
3	-1

X=3

21.

X	Y1
-3	-4
-2	-2
-1	0
0	2
1	4
2	6
3	8

X=3

23.

X	Y1
-3	8
-2	6
-1	4
0	2
1	0
2	-2
3	-4

X=3

25.

X	Y1
-3	11
-2	6
-1	3
0	2
1	3
2	6
3	11

X=3

27.

X	Y1
-3	-7
-2	-2
-1	1
0	2
1	1
2	-2
3	-7

X=3

29.

X	Y1
-3	7.5
-2	6
-1	4.5
0	3
1	1.5
2	0
3	-1.5

X=-3

31.

X	Y1
-3	-1.5
-2	0
-1	1.5
0	3
1	4.5
2	6
3	7.5

X=-3

Exercise Appendix C.3 (p. C–7)

1. Yes **3.** Yes **5.** No **7.** Yes **9.** Answers will vary. One answer is: $Y\min = 1$ $Y\max = 9$ $Y\text{scl} = 1$

Photo Credits

Chapter 1 Page 1, Juice Images/Glow Images; Page 45, Juice Images/Glow Images.

Chapter 2 Page 49, ©Media Bakery; Page 57, Nik Wheeler/Corbis; Page 67, Peter/Pearson/Stone/Getty Images, Inc.; Page 87, ©AP/Wide World Photos; Page 97, John Giustina/Iconica/Getty Images, Inc.; Page 101, ©Media Bakery.

Chapter 3 Page 103, ©Media Bakery; Page 119, Andrew Sacks/Pictures/photolibrary.com; Page 132, ©AP/World Wide Photos; Page 152, Bill Lai/The Image Works; Page 172, ©Media Bakery.

Chapter 4 Page 175, Andrew Zarivny/iStockphoto; Page 184, Day Williams/Photo Researchers, Inc.; Page 203, Allan H. Shoemaker/ Taxi/Getty Images; Page 206, age/fotostock/SUPERSTOCK; Page 213, Andrew Zarivny/ iStockphoto.

Chapter 5 Page 217, ©Media Bakery; Page 235, Chris Thomaidis/Fiser/Getty Images, Inc.; Page 243, Plastock/Photonica 2003/Getty Images; Page 268, Photodisc/Getty Images; Pages 282, Julian Ward/Image Source Limited; Page 289, ©Media Bakery.

Chapter 6 Page 293, Joerg Reirmann/iStockphoto; Page 295, Adam Jones/Getty Images; Page 300 (left), Don Smetzer/Stone/Getty Images; Page 300 (right), Stockbyte/Media Bakery; Page 313, Corbis/Jupiter Images; Page 321, Aurora Creative/Getty Images; Page 328, Banana Stock/photolibrary.com; Page 331, Mark Antmaan/The Image Works; Page 332, Plush Studios/Getty Images; Page 343, ML Harris/Getty Images; Page 352, Joerg Reirmann/iStockphoto.

Chapter 7 Page 355, Stockbyte/Media Bakery; Page 365, Chuck Kennedy/MCTA.andov LLC; Page 366, Mark Lewis/ Stone/Getty Images; Page 371, Jim/Cummins/Taxi/Getty Images; Page 374, ©Media Bakery; Page 376, Photodisc/Getty Images; Page 377, Joe Readie/Getty Images; Page 385, Rob Meeske/iStockphoto; Page 388, ©Media Bakery; Page 397, Photodisc/ Getty Images; Page 402, Ingram Publishing/SUPERSTOCK; Page 407, Digital Vision Ltd./SUPERSTOCK; Page 408, Corbis/Index Stock Imagery; Photolibrary; Page 410, Gray Mortimore/Stone/Getty Images. Inc.; Page 417, Stockbyte/ Media Bakery.

Chapter 8 Page 5, Corbis/Media Bakery; Page 13, David I. Anderson/Plain Dealer/Zuma Press; Page 18, David Frazier/Photo Researchers, Inc.; Page 27, Tom Raymond/Stone/Getty Images, Inc.; Page 32, Photodisc/SUPERSTOCK; Page 34, Heidi Coppock-Beard/ Stone/Getty Images, Inc.; Page 35, Elizabeth Simpson/Taxi/Getty Images, Inc.; Page 36, Blend Images/ Media Bakery; Page 40, Blend Images/Media Bakery; Page 42, Sean Justice/The Image Bank/Getty Images; Page 43, Purestock/Media Bakery; Page 44, Jim Cooper/Stone/Getty Images; Page 48, Photodisc/Punchstock; Page 57, Wiliam Thomas/Cain/Stinger/Getty Images; Page 59, Digital Archive Japan/Punchstock; Page 65, Mike Watson Images/Media Bakery; Page 66, Photodisc/Getty Images, Inc.; Page 67, Michael Melford/The Image Bank/Getty Images, Inc.; Page 73, Elizabeth Simpson; Taxi/Getty Images, Inc.; Page 74, Chase Jarvis/The Image Bank/Getty Images, Inc.; Page 81, Jeff Greenberg/Age Fotostock, Page 421, Jeff Greenberg/Age Fotostock America, Inc.

Chapter 9 Page 505, Daniel Stein/iStockphoto; Page 509, ©Corbis Digital Stock; Page 553, Francois Gohier/Photo Researchers; Page 559, Bob Daemmrich/The Image Works; Page 572, Daniel Stein/iStockphoto.

Chapter 10 Page 575, Heather Nemec/iStockphoto; Page 582, Corbis Digital Stock; Page 594, UPI Photo;Kevin/ Dietsch/News.com; Page 606, Spencer Platt/Getty Images, Inc.; Page 631, Heather Nemec/iStockphoto.

Chapter 11 Page 633, MOSIS Land Group; Page 634, NASA Goddard Space Flight Center; Page 656, Mark Scott/Taxi/Getty Images, Inc.; Page 668, Stollen/Stockphoto.

Subject Index

Lines

Slope

The slope m of the line containing the points $P_1 = (x_1, y_1)$ and $P_2 = (x_2, y_2)$ is

$$m = \frac{y_2 - y_1}{x_2 - x_1} \quad \text{if } x_1 \neq x_2$$

$$m \text{ is undefined if } x_1 = x_2$$

Point-Slope Equation

The equation of the line with slope m containing the point (x_1, y_1) is

$$y - y_1 = m(x - x_1)$$

Slope-Intercept Equation

The equation of the line with slope m and y-intercept $(0, b)$ is

$$y = mx + b$$

General Equation

Any line can be expressed by an equation of the form

$$Ax + By = C$$

where A, B, and C are real numbers and either $A \neq 0$ or $B \neq 0$.

Pairs of Lines

Two Lines are Either

Coincident (identical)

All points on each line are the same.
Coincident lines that are vertical have undefined slope and the same x-intercept.
Coincident lines that are nonvertical have the same slope and the same intercepts.

or

Parallel

The two lines have no points in common.
Parallel lines that are vertical have undefined slope and different x-intercepts.
Parallel lines that are nonvertical have the same slope and different intercepts.

or

Intersecting

The two lines have one point in common.
Intersecting lines have different slopes.

Finance

Simple Interest Formula

If a principal P is borrowed at a simple interest rate of $r\%$ per annum (expressed as a decimal) for a period of t years, the interest I is

$$I = Prt$$

Discounted Loans

If r is the per annum rate of interest, t is the time in years, and L is the amount of the loan, then the proceeds R, the amount received, is

$$R = L - Lrt$$

where Lrt is the discount, the interest deducted from the amount of the loan.

Compound Interest Formulas

The amount A after t years due to a principal P invested at an annual interest rate r compounded n times per year is

$$A = P \cdot \left(1 + \frac{r}{n}\right)^{n \cdot t}$$

The amount A after t years due to a principal P invested at an annual interest rate r compounded continuously is

$$A = Pe^{rt}$$

Amount of an Annuity

Suppose P is the deposit made at each payment period for an annuity paying i percent interest per payment period. The amount A of the annuity after n deposits is

$$A = P\frac{(1 + i)^n - 1}{i}$$

Amortization

The payment P required to pay off a loan of V dollars borrowed for n payment periods at a rate of interest i per payment period is

$$P = V\frac{i}{1 - (1 + i)^{-n}}$$

Counting

Counting Formula

For two sets A and B,

$$n(A \cup B) = n(A) + n(B) - n(A \cap B)$$

Factorials

$0! = 1, 1! = 1, n! = n(n - 1)(n - 2) \ldots . (3)(2)(1)$

Permutations

An ordered arrangement of r objects chosen from n objects.
The number of ordered arrangements of r objects chosen from n objects, in which the n objects are distinct and repetition is allowed, is n^r.
The number of ordered arrangements of r objects chosen from n objects, where $r \leq n$, in which the n objects are distinct and repetition is not allowed, is

$$P(n, r) = \frac{n!}{(n - r)!}$$

The number of permutations of n objects, of which n_1 are of one kind, n_2 are of a second kind, . . . , and n_k are of a kth kind, is

$$\frac{n!}{n_1!\, n_2! \cdots n_k!}$$

where $n_1 + n_2 + \cdots + n_k = n$.

Combinations An arrangement, without regard to order and without repetition, of r objects selected from n distinct objects, where $r \leq n$. The number of such arrangements is

$$C(n, r) = \binom{n}{r} = \frac{n!}{r!(n-r)!}$$

Binomial Theorem

For $n > 1$ a positive integer, $(x + y)^n = \binom{n}{0}x^n + \binom{n}{1}x^{n-1}y + \cdots + \binom{n}{k}x^n y^k + \cdots + \binom{n}{n}y^n$

Probability

Equally Likely Events If the sample space S of an experiment has n equally likely outcomes and the event E in S contains m outcomes, then

$$P(E) = \frac{m}{n}$$

Additive Rule For any two events E and F of a sample space S

$$P(E \cup F) = P(E) + P(F) - P(E \cap F)$$

Complement For any event E in a sample space S,

$$P(E) = 1 - P(\overline{E})$$

Conditional Probability If E and F are two events in a sample space S and if $P(F) \neq 0$,

$$P(E|F) = \frac{P(E \cap F)}{P(F)}$$

Product Rule If E and F are two events in a sample space S,

$$P(E \cap F) = P(F)\, P(E|F)$$

Independent Events Two events E and F of a sample space S are independent if and only if

$$P(E \cap F) = P(E)\, P(F)$$

Bayes' Formula Let S be a sample space partitioned into n events, $A_1, A_2, \ldots, A_n$. If E is an event in S for which $P(E) > 0$, then

$$P(A_j|E) = \frac{P(A_j)\, P(E|A_j)}{P(E)} = \frac{P(A_j)\, P(E|A_j)}{P(A_1)\, P(E|A_1) + P(A_2)\, P(E|A_2) + \cdots + P(A_n)\, P(E|A_n)}$$

for $j = 1, 2, \ldots, n$.

Binomial Probabilities In a Bernoulli trial, the probability of exactly k successes in n trials is

$$b(n, k; p) = \binom{n}{k} p^k q^{n-k} = \frac{n!}{k!(n-k)!} p^k q^{n-k}$$

where p is the probability of success and $q = 1 - p$ is the probability of failure.

Statistics

Sample Data The data used are a sample $x_1, x_2, \ldots, x_n$ taken from the population of N items, $n < N$.

Sample Mean $\bar{x} = \dfrac{x_1 + x_2 + \cdots + x_n}{n}$

Sample Standard Deviation $s = \sqrt{\dfrac{(x_1 - \bar{x})^2 + (x_2 - \bar{x})^2 + \cdots + (x_n - \bar{x})^2}{n - 1}}$

Population Data The data used are from the entire population $x_1, x_2, \ldots, x_N$ of N items,

Population Mean $\mu = \dfrac{x_1 + x_2 + \cdots + x_N}{N}$

Population Standard Deviation $\sigma = \sqrt{\dfrac{(x_1 - \mu)^2 + (x_2 - \mu)^2 + \cdots + (x_N - \mu)^2}{N}}$

Z – score $Z = \dfrac{x - \mu}{\sigma}$

Standard Normal Curve Table

***Z = Z*-Score**

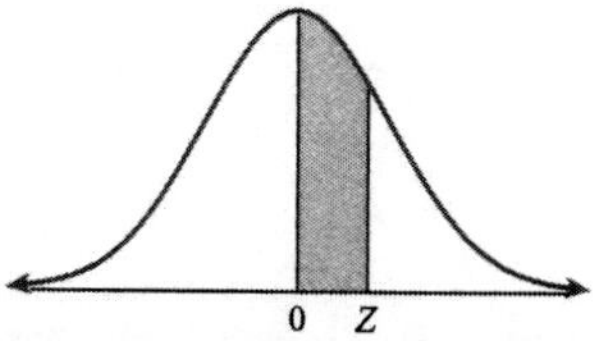

An entry in the table is the area under the curve between $Z = 0$ and a positive value of Z. Areas for negative values of Z are obtained by symmetry.

Z	0.00	0.01	0.02	0.03	0.04	0.05	0.06	0.07	0.08	0.09
0.0	0.0000	0.0040	0.0080	0.0120	0.0160	0.0199	0.0239	0.0279	0.0319	0.0359
0.1	0.0398	0.0438	0.0478	0.0517	0.0557	0.0596	0.0636	0.0675	0.0714	0.0753
0.2	0.0793	0.0832	0.0871	0.0910	0.0948	0.0987	0.1026	0.1064	0.1103	0.1141
0.3	0.1179	0.1217	0.1255	0.1293	0.1331	0.1368	0.1406	0.1433	0.1480	0.1517
0.4	0.1554	0.1591	0.1628	0.1664	0.1700	0.1736	0.1772	0.1808	0.1844	0.1879
0.5	0.1915	0.1950	0.1985	0.2019	0.2054	0.2088	0.2123	0.2157	0.2190	0.2224
0.6	0.2257	0.2291	0.2324	0.2357	0.2389	0.2422	0.2454	0.2486	0.2517	0.2549
0.7	0.2580	0.2611	0.2642	0.2673	0.2703	0.2734	0.2764	0.2794	0.2823	0.2852
0.8	0.2881	0.2910	0.2939	0.2967	0.2995	0.3023	0.3051	0.3078	0.3106	0.3133
0.9	0.3159	0.3186	0.3212	0.3238	0.3264	0.3289	0.3315	0.3340	0.3365	0.3389
1.0	0.3413	0.3438	0.3461	0.3485	0.3508	0.3531	0.3554	0.3577	0.3599	0.3621
1.1	0.3642	0.3665	0.3686	0.3708	0.3729	0.3749	0.3770	0.3790	0.3810	0.3830
1.2	0.3849	0.3869	0.3888	0.3907	0.3925	0.3944	0.3962	0.3980	0.3997	0.4015
1.3	0.4032	0.4049	0.4066	0.4082	0.4099	0.4115	0.4131	0.4147	0.4162	0.4177
1.4	0.4192	0.4207	0.4222	0.4236	0.4251	0.4265	0.4279	0.4292	0.4306	0.4319
1.5	0.4332	0.4345	0.4357	0.4370	0.4382	0.4394	0.4406	0.4418	0.4429	0.4441
1.6	0.4452	0.4463	0.4474	0.4484	0.4495	0.4505	0.4515	0.4525	0.4535	0.4545
1.7	0.4554	0.4564	0.4573	0.4582	0.4591	0.4599	0.4608	0.4616	0.4625	0.4633
1.8	0.4641	0.4649	0.4656	0.4664	0.4671	0.4678	0.4686	0.4693	0.4699	0.4706
1.9	0.4713	0.4719	0.4726	0.4732	0.4738	0.4744	0.4750	0.4756	0.4761	0.4767
2.0	0.4772	0.4778	0.4783	0.4788	0.4793	0.4798	0.4803	0.4808	0.4812	0.4817
2.1	0.4821	0.4826	0.4830	0.4834	0.4838	0.4842	0.4846	0.4850	0.4854	0.4857
2.2	0.4861	0.4864	0.4868	0.4871	0.4875	0.4878	0.4881	0.4884	0.4887	0.4890
2.3	0.4893	0.4896	0.4898	0.4901	0.4904	0.4906	0.4909	0.4911	0.4913	0.4916
2.4	0.4918	0.4920	0.4922	0.4925	0.4927	0.4929	0.4931	0.4932	0.4934	0.4936
2.5	0.4938	0.4940	0.4941	0.4943	0.4945	0.4946	0.4948	0.4949	0.4951	0.4952
2.6	0.4953	0.4955	0.4956	0.4957	0.4959	0.4960	0.4961	0.4962	0.4963	0.4964
2.7	0.4965	0.4966	0.4967	0.4968	0.4969	0.4970	0.4971	0.4972	0.4973	0.4974
2.8	0.4974	0.4975	0.4976	0.4977	0.4977	0.4978	0.4979	0.4979	0.4980	0.4981
2.9	0.4981	0.4982	0.4982	0.4983	0.4984	0.4984	0.4985	0.4985	0.4986	0.4986
3.0	0.4987	0.4987	0.4987	0.4988	0.4988	0.4989	0.4989	0.4989	0.4990	0.4990